DORLING KINDERSLEY
CHILDREN'S ILLUSTRATED ENCYCLOPEDIA

NEW EDITION

DORLING KINDERSLEY
CHILDREN'S
ILLUSTRATED
ENCYCLOPEDIA

DK PUBLISHING, INC.

DK

LONDON, NEW YORK,
MELBOURNE, MUNICH, AND DELHI

FIRST EDITION 1991

Senior Editor Ann Kramer
Senior Art Editor Miranda Kennedy
Editors Christiane Gunzi, Susan McKeever, Richard Platt, Clifford Rosney
Art Editors Muffy Dodson, Debra Lee, Christian Sévigny, Val Wright
Picture Research Anne Lyons
Additional Research Anna Kunst, Deborah Murrell
Picture Manager Kate Fox
Production Manager Teresa Solomon
Editorial Director Sue Unstead

SIXTH EDITION 2006

Editors Jenny Finch, Aekta Jerath
Designers Sheila Collins, Romi Chakraborty
Senior Editor Fran Baines
Managing Editor Linda Esposito
Managing Art Editor Diane Thistlethwaite
Publishing Managers Caroline Buckingham, Andrew Macintyre
Category Publisher Laura Buller
Picture Researcher Bridget Tily
DK Picture Library Martin Copeland
Cartographic Editor Simon Mumford
Cartographer Ed Merritt
Production Controller Erica Rosen
DTP Designers Siu Chan, Harish Aggarwal
DTP Coordinator Pankaj Sharma
Jacket Designer Phil Letsu
Jacket Editor Mariza O'Keeffe
US Editor Alisha Niehaus

First American edition 1991: revised 1993, 1998, 2000
This edition published in the United States in 2006
by DK Publishing Inc.
375 Hudson Street,
New York, New York 10014

06 07 08 09 10 10 9 8 7 6 5 4 3 2 1

A catalog record for this book is
available from the Library of Congress

ISBN-13: 9780756618926
ISBN-10: 0756618924

Reproduced by Colourscan, Singapore.
Printed and bound by Toppan, China.

Discover more at
www.dk.com

CONTENTS

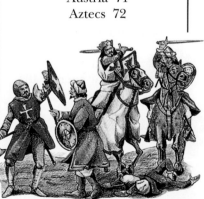

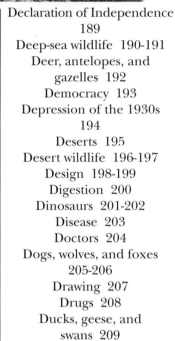

CONTENTS

HOW TO USE THIS BOOK

IT IS EASY TO FIND in-depth information on a wide range of subjects in the *Dorling Kindersley Children's Illustrated Encyclopedia*. The next three pages will show you how. Main entries are in alphabetical order, beginning with Abolitionist Movement and ending with Zoos. Each main entry has either one or more pages to itself. To find your chosen topic, look through the main headings at the top of the pages alphabetically. If you can't find the topic you are looking for, then it is not a main entry and does not have its own page. In that case, turn to the index at the back, which will tell you what page to look at for information about your topic.

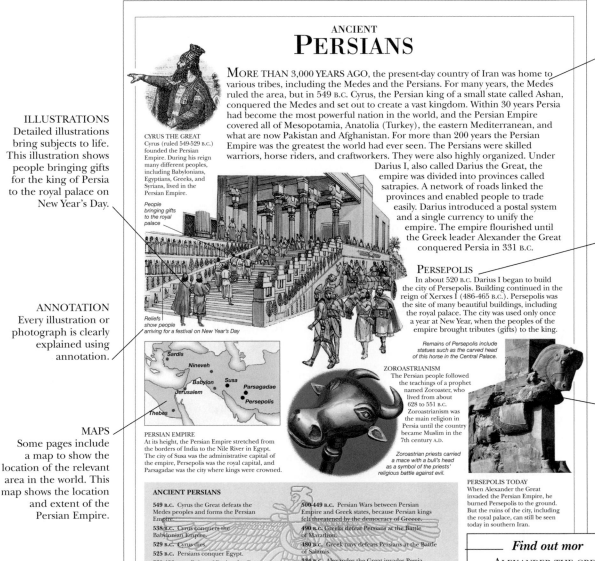

ILLUSTRATIONS
Detailed illustrations bring subjects to life. This illustration shows people bringing gifts for the king of Persia to the royal palace on New Year's Day.

ANNOTATION
Every illustration or photograph is clearly explained using annotation.

MAPS
Some pages include a map to show the location of the relevant area in the world. This map shows the location and extent of the Persian Empire.

TIMELINE
Many historical entry pages include a timeline, which is like a calendar of history on a scroll. Timelines give you all the dates you need, at a glance. This timeline guides you through the rise of the Ancient Persians to the collapse of the Persian Empire.

INTRODUCTION
Each main entry page has an introduction, which provides key facts and general information about a subject. You will be able to gain a basic knowledge of a subject before reading on.

SUB-ENTRIES
Further information on a subject is given in sub-entries, such as this one describing the city of Persepolis, the royal capital of Ancient Persia.

PHOTOGRAPHS
Photographs appear on most pages and show all kinds of subjects. This photograph is of a carved horse's head from the Ancient Persian city of Persepolis.

FIND OUT MORE
The Find Out More box at the lower right-hand corner of the page at the end of every entry directs you to other main entries on related subjects. For example, the Ancient Persians' Find Out More box lists five related entries: Alexander the Great, Assyrians, Babylonians, Ancient Greece, and Middle East. By turning to these you will discover more about the world of the Ancient Persians.

Within the illustration:

ANCIENT
PERSIANS

MORE THAN 3,000 YEARS AGO, the present-day country of Iran was home to various tribes, including the Medes and the Persians. For many years, the Medes ruled the area, but in 549 B.C. Cyrus, the Persian king of a small state called Ashan, conquered the Medes and set out to create a vast kingdom. Within 30 years Persia had become the most powerful nation in the world, and the Persian Empire covered all of Mesopotamia, Anatolia (Turkey), the eastern Mediterranean, and what are now Pakistan and Afghanistan. For more than 200 years the Persian Empire was the greatest the world had ever seen. The Persians were skilled warriors, horse riders, and craftworkers. They were also highly organized. Under Darius I, also called Darius the Great, the empire was divided into provinces called satrapies. A network of roads linked the provinces and enabled people to trade easily. Darius introduced a postal system and a single currency to unify the empire. The empire flourished until the Greek leader Alexander the Great conquered Persia in 331 B.C.

CYRUS THE GREAT
Cyrus (ruled 549-529 B.C.) founded the Persian Empire. During his reign many different peoples, including Babylonians, Egyptians, Greeks, and Syrians, lived in the Persian Empire.

People bringing gifts to the royal palace

Reliefs show people arriving for a festival on New Year's Day

PERSEPOLIS
In about 520 B.C. Darius I began to build the city of Persepolis. Building continued in the reign of Xerxes I (486-465 B.C.). Persepolis was the site of many beautiful buildings, including the royal palace. The city was used only once a year at New Year, when the peoples of the empire brought tributes (gifts) to the king.

Remains of Persepolis include statues such as the carved head of this horse in the Central Palace.

ZOROASTRIANISM
The Persian people followed the teachings of a prophet named Zoroaster, who lived from about 628 to 551 B.C. Zoroastrianism was the main religion in Persia until the country became Muslim in the 7th century A.D.

Zoroastrian priests carried a mace with a bull's head as a symbol of the priests' religious battle against evil.

Map labels: Sardis, Nineveh, Babylon, Susa, Parsagadae, Jerusalem, Persepolis, Thebes

PERSIAN EMPIRE
At its height, the Persian Empire stretched from the borders of India to the Nile River in Egypt. The city of Susa was the administrative capital of the empire, Persepolis was the royal capital, and Parsagadae was the city where kings were crowned.

PERSEPOLIS TODAY
When Alexander the Great invaded the Persian Empire, he burned Persepolis to the ground. But the ruins of the city, including the royal palace, can still be seen today in southern Iran.

ANCIENT PERSIANS

549 B.C. Cyrus the Great defeats the Medes peoples and forms the Persian Empire.

538 B.C. Cyrus conquers the Babylonian Empire.

529 B.C. Cyrus dies.

525 B.C. Persians conquer Egypt.

521-486 B.C. Reign of Darius the Great.

510 B.C. Persians invade southeast Europe and Central Asia.

500-449 B.C. Persian Wars between Persian Empire and Greek states, because Persian kings felt threatened by the democracy of Greece.

490 B.C. Greeks defeat Persians at the Battle of Marathon.

480 B.C. Greek navy defeats Persians at the Battle of Salamis.

334 B.C. Alexander the Great invades Persia.

331 B.C. Alexander defeats Persians at the Battle of Gaugamela. Persian Empire collapses.

Find out more
ALEXANDER THE GREAT
ASSYRIANS
BABYLONIANS
GREECE, ANCIENT
MIDDLE EAST

508

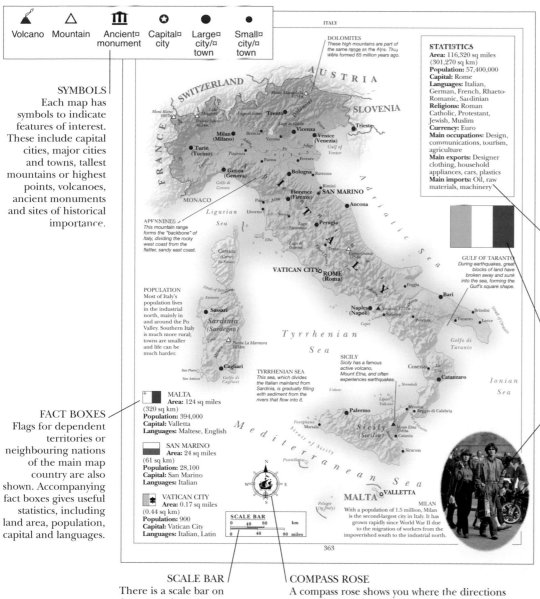

Volcano **Mountain** **Ancient monument** **Capital city** **Large city/town** **Small city/town**

SYMBOLS
Each map has symbols to indicate features of interest. These include capital cities, major cities and towns, tallest mountains or highest points, volcanoes, ancient monuments and sites of historical importance.

DOLOMITES
These high mountains are part of the same range as the Alps. They were formed 65 million years ago.

STATISTICS
Area: 116,320 sq miles (301,270 sq km)
Population: 57,400,000
Capital: Rome
Languages: Italian, German, French, Rhaeto-Romanic, Sardinian
Religions: Roman Catholic, Protestant, Jewish, Muslim
Currency: Euro
Main occupations: Design, communications, tourism, agriculture
Main exports: Designer clothing, household appliances, cars, plastics
Main imports: Oil, raw materials, machinery

APENNINES
This mountain range forms the "backbone" of Italy, dividing the rocky west coast from the flatter, sandy east coast.

POPULATION
Most of Italy's population lives in the industrial north, mainly in and around the Po Valley. Southern Italy is much more rural; towns are smaller and life can be much harder.

GULF OF TARANTO
During earthquakes, great blocks of land have broken away and sunk into the sea, forming the Gulf's square shape.

TYRRHENIAN SEA
This sea, which divides the Italian mainland from Sardinia, is gradually filling with sediment from the rivers that flow into it.

SICILY
Sicily has a famous active volcano, Mount Etna, and often experiences earthquakes.

MALTA
Area: 124 sq miles (320 sq km)
Population: 394,000
Capital: Valletta
Languages: Maltese, English

SAN MARINO
Area: 24 sq miles (61 sq km)
Population: 28,100
Capital: San Marino
Languages: Italian

VATICAN CITY
Area: 0.17 sq miles (0.44 sq km)
Population: 900
Capital: Vatican City
Languages: Italian, Latin

SCALE BAR

FACT BOXES
Flags for dependent territories or neighbouring nations of the main map country are also shown. Accompanying fact boxes gives useful statistics, including land area, population, capital and languages.

MILAN
With a population of 1.5 million, Milan is the second-largest city in Italy. It has grown rapidly since World War II due to the migration of workers from the impoverished south to the industrial north.

363

MAPS
There are maps for all the continents and major countries of the world. Each map shows main regions, physical features, large cities, and some important historical sites. On every map page is a fact box containing flags and information about the region. Photographs show subjects of interest.

STATISTICS BOX
Every map is accompanied by a statistics box giving information on factors such as land area, population, languages, religions, currency, and main occupations.

FLAG
The flag of the major country on the map is always shown. This is the Italian flag.

SUBJECTS OF INTEREST
Photographs show characteristic views of different regions. This one shows a scene in Milan, the fashion centre of Italy.

SCALE BAR
There is a scale bar on each map so that you can work out distances.

COMPASS ROSE
A compass rose shows you where the directions of north, south, east, and west lie on the map.

A biography box gives at-a-glance facts and dates about a person.

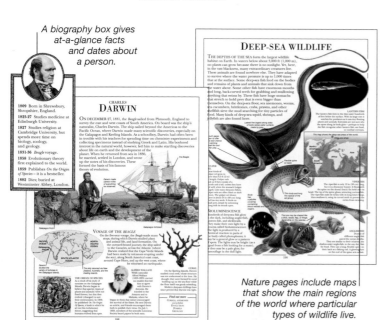

CHARLES DARWIN

1809 Born in Shrewsbury, Shropshire, England.

1825-27 Studies medicine at Edinburgh University.

1827 Studies religion at Cambridge University, but spends more time on biology, zoology, and geology.

1831-36 Beagle voyage.

1858 Evolutionary theory first explained to the world.

1859 Publishes On the Origin of Species – it is a bestseller.

1882 Dies; buried at Westminster Abbey, London.

DEEP-SEA WILDLIFE

Nature pages include maps that show the main regions of the world where particular types of wildlife live.

SWIMMING

BIG BANG

Diagrams explain scientific theories clearly and simply.

Sport pages show the type of equipment used for specific activities.

TYPES OF MAIN ENTRY PAGES
There are main entry pages on a comprehensive range of subject matter, including biography and history, sport, natural history, science, and technology. All main entries appear in alphabetical order to make it easy to find the topic you are looking for.

FACT FINDER

At the back of the encyclopedia is the Fact Finder, which provides an at-a-glance, fact-packed guide to history, geography, nature, science, and world facts. The Fact Finder provides instant information – clearly arranged in tables and charts – that will help you with school projects. It also acts as a reference source to support the subjects in the main entry pages.

A timeline runs across the top of all the history pages so you can compare what happened in each continent on a certain date.

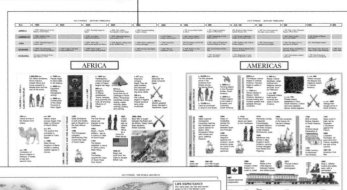

HISTORY TIMELINES
The history timelines summarize the history of the world from prehistory to the present day, with each page concentrating on one continent. Important events are presented in date sequence.

Three-dimensional bar charts give comparative statistics for different countries.

THE WORLD AROUND US
Within this section are three world maps showing different aspects of the current world situation: political boundaries and population growth, energy production and consumption, and the development of global communications. Introduction text describes current trends and how they affect the world we live in. Comparative statistics are shown in accessible charts and graphs.

Charts make complex subjects easy to understand.

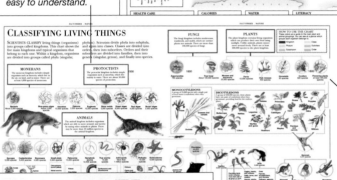

NATURE
This section includes a comprehensive chart classifying plants and animals, a list of endangered species, and many other facts about the natural world.

Many types of plant and animal life are illustrated.

Star maps show the different constellations.

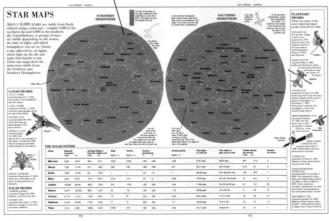

SCIENCE
In the science section you will find star maps, measurement and conversion charts, mathematical formulas, and a periodic table. Useful world facts, such as time zones, weather records, and lists of noteable geographic features, are also included.

SIZE COMPARISONS AND ABBREVIATIONS

SIZE COMPARISONS
Occasionally you will find this girl and boy. They are about 4 ft (1.2 m) tall and are there to give you an idea of the comparative sizes of objects or animals in relation to human beings.

ABBREVIATIONS
Some words are abbreviated, or shortened, in the encyclopedia. The list below explains what the abbreviations stand for:

°C = degrees Celsius
°F = degrees Fahrenheit
mm = millimeter
cm = centimeter
m = meter
km = kilometer
sq km = square kilometer
km/h = kilometers per hour
in = inch
ft = foot
yd = yard
sq mile = square mile
mph = miles per hour
g = gram
kg = kilogram
oz = ounce
lb = pound
l = liter
c. before a date = "about"
B.C. = before Christ
A.D. = anno Domini, which refers to any time after the birth of Christ

INDEX
There is an index at the back of the book in which you can find any subject mentioned in the encyclopedia. The numbers in the index refer to page numbers.
• Numbers in **bold** type refer to main A–Z entries.
• Numbers in *italic* type refer to pages in the Fact Finder, the reference section at the back of the encyclopedia.
• Numbers in normal type refer to general references within the encyclopedia.

*The number **102** tells you that there is a main entry about bridges on page 102.*

The number 762 tells you that there is more information about bridges in the Fact Finder.

The number 648 tells you that brittle stars are mentioned on page 648.

ABOLITIONIST MOVEMENT TO ZOOS

ABOLITIONIST MOVEMENT

THE DECLARATION OF INDEPENDENCE promised equality for all, leading many Americans to question the inequalities of slavery. A movement to abolish slavery and the slave trade took root throughout the Northern states in the late 1780s. Its supporters were known as abolitionists. Although there had been protests against slavery since colonial times, mostly by religious groups, the slave population continued to grow, and tensions between the free states of the North and the slave states of the South escalated. Through newspapers, speeches, and public meetings, abolitionists spread the word about the horrors of slavery, despite strong opposition by Southern slaveholders and their supporters. Others helped support the Underground Rail, a network of houses and people who illegally helped escaping slaves reach safety in the nonslave states. Their crusade spread to England, where abolitionists worked to end the international slave trade.

WOMEN JOIN THE FIGHT
Among several important female campaigners, Sojourner Truth (above) played an active role in the abolitionist movement. Born into slavery in 1797, she was freed in 1827. She traveled the nation with her moving message about the rights of slaves and women.

UNCLE TOM'S CABIN

No other abolitionist writing had the political impact of *Uncle Tom's Cabin*, a novel by Harriet Beecher Stowe. After a trip to a Kentucky plantation, a horrified Stowe decided to write about the evils of slavery. Her novel was simple and melodramatic, but its vivid descriptions of suffering and cruelty turned many people against slavery. Sales were astonishing – 300,000 copies were sold within a year. In the South, Stowe was brutally criticized, but her book proved an effective attack on slavery.

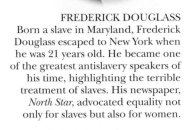

FREDERICK DOUGLASS
Born a slave in Maryland, Frederick Douglass escaped to New York when he was 21 years old. He became one of the greatest antislavery speakers of his time, highlighting the terrible treatment of slaves. His newspaper, *North Star*, advocated equality not only for slaves but also for women.

FIGHTING FOR FREEDOM

Those who opposed slavery joined together to fight for its abolition. Abolitionists traveled throughout the North, spreading their message through rallies, debates, and speeches. One of the most powerful groups was the American Antislavery Society, founded in 1833. Its founder, William Lloyd Garrison, published a newspaper called *The Liberator* to campaign for an end to slavery.

JOHN BROWN
Some abolitionists felt slavery could only be ended by force. In October 1859, abolitionist John Brown and a small band of followers mounted an unsuccessful raid on a government weapons store at Harper's Ferry, Virginia. The local militia killed most of his men, and Brown was captured, tried for treason, and hanged.

An abolitionist rally

Find out more
CIVIL RIGHTS
CIVIL WAR
DECLARATION OF INDEPENDENCE
TUBMAN, HARRIET

ABORIGINAL AUSTRALIANS

THE FIRST INHABITANTS of Australia were nomadic (wandering) people who reached the continent from Southeast Asia about 40,000 years ago. When Europeans settled in Australia at the end of the 18th century, they called these native inhabitants "aboriginals," meaning people who had lived there since the earliest times. Today there are about 410,000 aboriginals in Australia. Most live in cities, but a few thousand still try to follow a traditional way of life. They travel through the bush, hunting with spears and boomerangs (throwing sticks) and searching for food such as plants, grubs, and insects. They have few possessions and make everything they need from natural materials. This way of life does not change or harm the fragile environment of the Australian outback (the interior). The well-being of the land, and its plants and animals, are vital and sacred to the aboriginal people.

ART
Aboriginal art is mostly about Dreamtime and is made as part of the ceremonies celebrating Dreamtime. Paintings of the people, spirits, and animals of Dreamtime cover sacred cliffs and rocks in tribal territories. The pictures are made in red and yellow ocher and white clay, and some are thousands of years old.

Private ceremonies and secret rituals are an important part of aboriginal life. Through dancing, singing, and chanting, young aboriginal people learn about Dreamtime.

Dancers, singers, and musicians paint their bodies with elaborate patterns.

The didjeridu, a wooden wind instrument, is used to play basic rhythms in aboriginal music.

DREAMTIME
Aboriginal Australians believe that they have animal, plant, and human ancestors who created the world and everything in it. This process of creation is called Dreamtime. There are many songs and myths about Dreamtime, which generations of aboriginal people have passed down to their children.

URBAN LIFE
The majority of aboriginal Australians live in cities and towns. Some have benefited from government education and aid programs and have careers as teachers, doctors, and lawyers. Many, though, are poor and isolated from white society. They have lost touch with traditional aboriginal tribal ways, and because they do not fit neatly into white Australian society, they cannot always share its benefits. However, there are now campaigns among urban aboriginal people to revive interest in the tribal culture of their ancestors.

LAND CLAIMS
When British settlers arrived in Australia, they seized sacred sites and other land that belonged to aboriginal people. With the help of aboriginal lawyers, aboriginal Australians campaigned to get the land back. In 1976, the Australian government agreed that aboriginal people have rights to their tribal territories, and some land was returned.

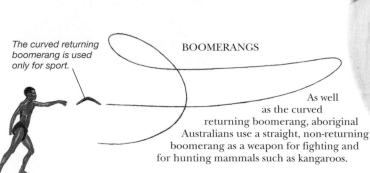

The curved returning boomerang is used only for sport.

BOOMERANGS

As well as the curved returning boomerang, aboriginal Australians use a straight, non-returning boomerang as a weapon for fighting and for hunting mammals such as kangaroos.

Find out more
AUSTRALIA
AUSTRALIA, HISTORY OF
AUSTRALIAN WILDLIFE
FESTIVALS AND FEASTS
MYTHS AND LEGENDS

ADVERTISING

GIANT BILLBOARDS by the side of the road serve the same purpose as tiny classified newspaper advertisements. They tell us what products are available, and try to persuade us to choose one brand instead of another. Today's television commercials reach millions of people, but the first forms of advertising were much more local. Market traders shouted out what they had for sale, and shops displayed large signs to indicate their trade. Modern advertising began about 150 years ago when factories first produced goods in large quantities. Newspapers carried advertisements for everything from hats to patent medicines. Nowadays advertising forms part of the business of marketing, which also includes product design, competitive pricing, packaging, and shop displays. Advertisements appear everywhere, not just on television and radio. They are also broadcast through in-store music, and painted on vehicle sides and in smoke trails in the sky. These advertising messages often amuse us, but not all advertisements are welcome. Strict laws protect the shopper from misleading advertising, and there are restrictions on the advertising of certain harmful products, such as tobacco and alcohol.

COCA-COLA

Successful advertising makes a product so familiar that shoppers ask for it by name. Well-known goods are called brands. Some brands are sold worldwide. Coca-Cola is one of the most famous brand names. It was invented in the United States in 1886. From the beginning, the makers of Coca-Cola advertised the drink widely, using a distinctive symbol, or trademark, of elegantly interlocking red letters. Within 10 years people in every state drank Coca-Cola. Today, the trademark is so well-known that it is recognizable in any alphabet.

© The Coca-Cola Company

LAUNCHING NEW PRODUCTS

Advertising is very expensive, so before launching a new bar, the chocolate company must be sure that it has created an appealing product that people will want to buy.

Market research questionnaire

Sample packaging material   *Storyboard*

STORYBOARDS
Before filming a commercial, a designer must draw the action on paper scene by scene, like a comic strip. A copywriter makes up the script and slogans to go with the pictures.

MARKET RESEARCH
Hundreds of people taste the chocolate bar before it goes on sale, and answer questions about it. This process is called market research. They give their opinions on price, name, and size of the bar, and may look at plans for the wrapper.

CAMPAIGNS
No manufacturer has an unlimited budget, so most advertising is concentrated into campaigns – short, intense bursts of advertising. During the campaign, advertisements appear in very carefully chosen spots. For example, commercials for a chocolate bar might appear during children's television programs, not late at night. Similarly, press ads might appear in magazines aimed at young people.

Press advertisement

Television advertising is very costly, but reaches the biggest audience.

Displays in shops are called point-of-sale advertising.

Catchy tunes feature in much radio advertising.

PROPAGANDA
Government advertisements that inform or advise the public are called propaganda. This poster, for instance, encourages Chinese people to work for a better society. Other campaigns persuade people to stop smoking, or to drive safely.

团结起来, 争取更大的胜利!

Find out more
SHOPS AND SHOPPING
TELEVISION AND VIDEO
TRADE AND INDUSTRY

AFRICA

FEW REGIONS OF THE WORLD are as varied as Africa. On this vast continent there are 53 independent nations and many times this number of peoples and ancient cultures. There are mountains, valleys, plains, and swamps on a scale not seen elsewhere. The northern coast is rich and fertile; below it lies the dry Sahara Desert. South of the Sahara, lush rain forest grows. Most of southern and eastern Africa is savanna, a form of dry plain dotted with trees and bushes. The nations of Africa are generally poor, though some, such as Nigeria, have rich natural resources. Many governments are unstable, and rebellions and civil wars are common. There are few large cities; most are near the coast. The rest of the continent is open countryside where people follow traditional lifestyles.

Africa is roughly triangular in shape. The Atlantic Ocean lies to the west and the Indian Ocean to the east. In the northwest only a few miles of sea separate the African continent from Europe.

SCHOOLS
Schools in African towns and cities are much like schools anywhere in the world. Sometimes, however, pupils must walk many miles from their homes to the schoolhouse.

The Tuareg peoples who inhabit the Sahara are pastoralists.

The Ashanti peoples of West Africa are mainly farmers.

The tall Masai of Kenya herd cattle on the open plains.

PEOPLE
In the African countryside many people live in tribal villages. Some, such as the Kikuyu of East Africa, are descended from tribes that have lived in the same place for many centuries. Others are recent immigrants from other parts of Africa or from other continents.
Borders between countries take little account of these varied cultures. People of one culture may live in two different countries, and in one nation may be found more than a dozen different tribal groupings.

Few pygmies are taller than 5 ft (1.5 m). They live in the dense Congo rain forest.

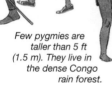

The towers of mosques dominate Cairo's skyline.

The Bushmen roam the deserts of southern Africa and gather wild food from the harsh environment.

CAIRO
Cairo is the capital city of Egypt and the largest city in Africa, with a population of 15 million. It sits on the Nile River near the head of the river's delta. The older part of the city contains narrow, winding streets. The new city has wider streets and many modern office buildings and flats. The people of Cairo are mostly Egyptian, although some come from all over North Africa, as well as from Europe and the Middle East.

KILIMANJARO
The tallest and most beautiful mountain in Africa is Kilimanjaro, in Tanzania. Its highest peak, which rises 19,340 ft (5,895 m), is an extinct volcano. Although the mountain is only a few miles from the equator, the top is always covered in snow. A footpath leads to the top, which can be reached in three days from the nearest road. Many people live on the lower slopes, where they farm tropical fruits.

SAHARA DESERT

The Sahara is the largest desert in the world and covers nearly one-third of Africa. In recent years the desert has spread, destroying farmland and causing famine. In some areas irrigation has stopped the spread of the desert, but long-term irrigation can make the soil salty and infertile. Temperatures have been known to exceed 120°F (50°C) in this inhospitable environment.

MUSIC AND CULTURE

Africa has a rich and varied culture. North Africa shares the Islamic traditions of the Middle East, producing beautiful mosques and palaces. West African music has a strong rhythm, and there are many interesting dances from this region. The area is also home to a flourishing woodcarving industry. Eastern and southern Africa have become famous for beautiful beadwork and colorful festive costumes.

In West Africa, drumming is a highly developed art. People once used drum beats to pass on messages.

MEDICINE AND HEALING

When seeking a cure for sickness, some Africans consult Western-style doctors. Others consult a traditional healer (above). Healers are respected members of a community, with vast knowledge of local herbs and plants and the ways in which they can be used as medicines. To identify the source of an illness, the healer might contact good or evil spirits by going into a trance. Treatment may include animal sacrifice.

WAR AND FAMINE

Civil wars and famines are common in Africa. Many are caused by political disagreements, and some are the result of tribal conflicts. In Chad a civil war lasting many years was fought between the desert Tuaregs, backed by Libya, and the farmers of the wetter areas. In Rwanda and Burundi, fighting between the Tutsi and Hutu tribes has led to thousands of deaths. Other misery is caused by famine. Traditionally, most people grew enough food each year to last until the next harvest. However, African countries increasingly produce export crops and rely on imported food. If food distribution breaks down or drought ruins crops, thousands of people may starve.

RURAL LIFE

Although African cities have been growing fast, most Africans still live in the countryside. They grow their own food and only rarely have a surplus to sell or exchange for other goods. Most tribes have farmed the same land for generations, living in villages with all of their relatives. Sometimes the young men go to live in cities for a few years to earn money in mines or factories. Then they return to the village to marry and settle down. The types of crops grown vary widely. Yams, cassava, and bananas are produced in the lush tropical regions; farmers in drier areas concentrate on cattle and grain.

Road building in Nigeria

DEVELOPMENT

Poor infrastructure, including unreliable roads, railroads, and electricity supplies, holds back the economic growth of many African nations. Most countries rely on loans from Western governments and international banks to pay for their development programs.

Find out more

AFRICA, HISTORY OF
CENTRAL AFRICA
EAST AFRICA
SOUTH AFRICA
WEST AFRICA

POLITICAL AFRICA

Independent African states, with few exceptions, are territorially identical to the colonies they replaced. Until the 1960s, most of Africa was controlled by European countries as part of their overseas empires. By the late 1980s, nearly every country had gained its independence. In many cases, hasty attempts were made to set up European-style governments. Leaders often became dictators, or the army seized power. However, in recent years, there has been a shift toward multiparty democracy.

ALGERIA
Area: 919,590 sq miles (2,381,740 sq km)
Population: 31,800,000
Capital: Algiers

ANGOLA
Area: 481,551 sq miles (1,246,700 sq km)
Population: 13,600,000
Capital: Luanda

BENIN
Area: 43,480 sq miles (112,620 sq km)
Population: 6,700,000
Capital: Porto-Novo

BOTSWANA
Area: 224,600 sq miles (581,730 sq km)
Population: 1,800,000
Capital: Gaborone

BURKINA
Area: 105,870 sq miles (274,200 sq km)
Population: 13,000,000
Capital: Ouagadougou

BURUNDI
Area: 10,750 sq miles (27,830 sq km)
Population: 6,800,000
Capital: Bujumbura

CAMEROON
Area: 183,570 sq miles (475,440 sq km)
Population: 16,000,000
Capital: Yaoundé

CAPE VERDE
Area: 1,556 sq miles (4,030 sq km)
Population: 463,000
Capital: Praia

CENTRAL AFRICAN REPUBLIC
Area: 240,530 sq miles (622,980 sq km)
Population: 3,900,000
Capital: Bangui

CHAD
Area: 495,752 sq miles (1,284,000 sq km)
Population: 8,600,000
Capital: N'Djamena

COMOROS
Area: 861 sq miles (2,230 sq km)
Population: 768,000
Capital: Moroni

CONGO
Area: 132,040 sq miles (342,000 sq km)
Population: 3,700,000
Capital: Brazzaville

DEMOCRATIC REPUBLIC OF CONGO
Area: 905,563 sq miles (2,345,410 sq km)
Population: 52,800,000
Capital: Kinshasa

DJIBOUTI
Area: 8,958 sq miles (23,200 sq km)
Population: 703,000
Capital: Djibouti

EGYPT
Area: 386,660 sq miles (1,001,450 sq km)
Population: 71,900,000
Capital: Cairo

EQUATORIAL GUINEA
Area: 10,830 sq miles (28,050 sq km)
Population: 494,000
Capital: Malabo

ERITREA
Area: 36,170 sq miles (93,680 sq km)
Population: 4,100,000
Capital: Asmara

ETHIOPIA
Area: 435,605 sq miles (1,128,221 sq km)
Population: 70,700,000
Capital: Addis Ababa

GABON
Area: 103,347 sq miles (267,670 sq km)
Population: 1,300,000
Capital: Libreville

GAMBIA
Area: 4,363 sq miles (11,300 sq km)
Population: 1,400,000
Capital: Banjul

GHANA
Area: 92,100 sq miles (238,540 sq km)
POPULATION: 20,900,000
Capital: Accra

GUINEA
Area: 94,926 sq miles (245,860 sq km)
Population: 8,500,000
Capital: Conakry

GUINEA-BISSAU
Area: 13,940 sq miles (36,120 sq km)
Population: 1,500,000
Capital: Bissau

IVORY COAST
Area: 124,503 sq miles (322,463 sq km)
Population: 16,600,000
Capital: Yamoussoukro

KENYA
Area: 224,081 sq miles (580,370 sq km)
Population: 32,000,000
Capital: Nairobi

LESOTHO
Area: 11,718 sq miles (30,350 sq km)
Population: 1,800,000
Capital: Maseru

LIBERIA
Area: 43,000 sq miles (111,370 sq km)
Population: 3,400,000
Capital: Monrovia

LIBYA
Area: 679,358 sq miles (1,759,540 sq km)
Population: 5,600,000
Capital: Tripoli

MADAGASCAR
Area: 226,660 sq miles (587,040 sq km)
Population: 17,400,000
Capital: Antananarivo

MALAWI
Area: 45,745 sq miles (118,480 sq km)
Population: 12,100,000
Capital: Lilongwe

MALI
Area: 478,837 sq miles (1,240,190 sq km)
Population: 13,000,000
Capital: Bamako

MAURITANIA
Area: 395,953 sq miles (1,025,520 sq km)
Population: 2,900,000
Capital: Nouakchott

MAURITIUS
Area: 718 sq miles (1,860 sq km)
Population: 1,200,000
Capital: Port Louis

MOROCCO
Area: 269,757 sq miles (698,670 sq km)
Population: 30,600,000
Capital: Rabat

MOZAMBIQUE
Area: 309,493 sq miles (801,590 sq km)
Population: 18,900,000
Capital: Maputo

NAMIBIA
Area: 318,260 sq miles (824,290 sq km)
Population: 2,000,000
Capital: Windhoek

NIGER
Area: 489,188 sq miles (1,267,000 sq km)
Population: 12,000,000
Capital: Niamey

NIGERIA
Area: 356,668 sq miles (923,770 sq km)
Population: 124,000,000
Capital: Abuja

RWANDA
Area: 10,170 sq miles (26,340 sq km)
Population: 8,400,000
Capital: Kigali

SAO TOME AND PRINCIPE
Area: 372 sq miles (964 sq km)
Population: 175,900
Capital: São Tomé

SENEGAL
Area: 75,950 sq miles (196,720 sq km)
Population: 10,100,000
Capital: Dakar

SEYCHELLES
Area: 108 sq miles (280 sq km)
Population: 80,500
Capital: Victoria

SIERRA LEONE
Area: 27,699 sq miles (71,740 sq km)
Population: 5,000,000
Capital: Freetown

SOMALIA
Area: 246,200 sq miles (637,660 sq km)
Population: 9,900,000
Capital: Mogadishu

SOUTH AFRICA
Area: 471,443 sq miles (1,221,040 sq km)
Population: 45,000,000
Capital: Pretoria

SUDAN
Area: 967,493 sq miles (2,505,815 sq km)
Population: 33,600,000
Capital: Khartoum

SWAZILAND
Area: 6,703 sq miles (17,360 sq km)
Population: 1,000,000
Capital: Mbabane

TANZANIA
Area: 364,900 sq miles (945,090 sq km)
Population: 37,000,000
Capital: Dodoma

TOGO
Area: 21,927 sq miles (56,790 sq km)
Population: 4,900,000
Capital: Lomé

TUNISIA
Area: 63,170 sq miles (163,610 sq km)
Population: 9,800,000
Capital: Tunis

UGANDA
Area: 91,073 sq miles (235,880 sq km)
Population: 25,800,000
Capital: Kampala

ZAMBIA
Area: 285,992 sq miles (740,720 sq km)
Population: 10,800,000
Capital: Lusaka

ZIMBABWE
Area: 150,800 sq miles (390,580 sq km)
Population: 12,900,000
Capital: Harare

Volcano	Mountain	Ancient¤ monument	Capital¤ city	Large¤ city/¤ town	Small¤ city/¤ town

STATISTICS
Area: 11,690,481 sq miles (30,278,093 sq km)
Population: 849,384,400
Number of independent countries: 53
Highest point: Kilimanjaro (Tanzania) 19,340 ft (5,895 m)
Longest river: Nile, 4,160 miles (6,695 km)
Largest lake: Lake Victoria: 26,828 sq miles (69,484 sq km)
Main occupation: Agriculture

MINING
Africans have been mining and processing minerals, including iron ore, copper, and gold, for more than two thousand years. Gold mined in the forest country of western Africa was carried across the Sahara by African traders and exported to Europe and Asia. During the colonial period mining was intensified. Today, South Africa, Zimbabwe, Zambia, and Democratic Republic of Congo possess heavily industrialized mining areas. These areas have yielded minerals such as gold, diamond, copper, and uranium.

Large-scale drilling equipment (above) is used in the gold-mining industry.

Dogon dancers (right) from Mali perform a funeral dance.

MASKS AND DANCE
Masked dance is performed in many communities in west and central Africa and plays an important part in social events. Once inside the costume, the person takes on the character represented by the mask. Often parts of the body are exaggerated with padding or pieces of wood (left). The dance steps, songs, and sounds complete the costume and energetically represent both the spirit world and the world of humans.

CAPE VERDE
The independent republic of the Cape Verde islands lies 385 miles (620 km) off the coast of Senegal in the Atlantic Ocean. The islands have a population of 463,000, but almost twice this number of Cape Verdeans live abroad.

SAO TOME AND PRINCIPE
The volcanic islands of São Tomé and Príncipe form a republic with a population of 175,900. São Tomé, the larger island, lies just north of the equator.

HORN OF AFRICA
Because of its shape, the easternmost point of the African continent is called the Horn of Africa. It is one of the poorest regions on Earth, with few natural resources. Recent droughts and civil wars have killed thousands of people and made many more homeless.

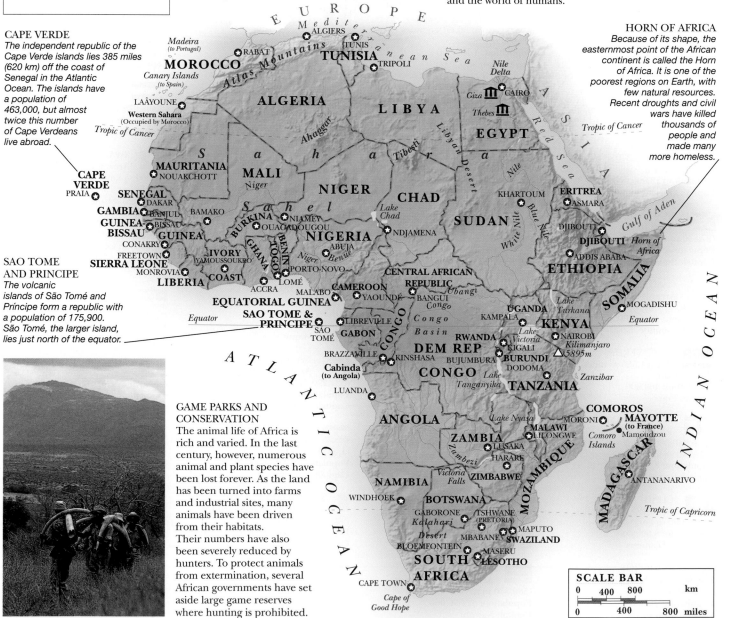

GAME PARKS AND CONSERVATION
The animal life of Africa is rich and varied. In the last century, however, numerous animal and plant species have been lost forever. As the land has been turned into farms and industrial sites, many animals have been driven from their habitats. Their numbers have also been severely reduced by hunters. To protect animals from extermination, several African governments have set aside large game reserves where hunting is prohibited.

SCALE BAR

0	400	800	km
0		400	800 miles

HISTORY OF
AFRICA

FOR MUCH OF ITS HISTORY, Africa has been hidden from outsiders' eyes. The Sahara Desert cuts off communication from north to south for all but the hardiest traveler. The peoples of Africa have therefore developed largely by themselves. By about 1200 B.C., rich and powerful empires such as ancient Egypt had arisen. The empires have disappeared, but they left behind buildings and other clues to their existence. Other African peoples left records of their history in songs that have been passed down from parent to child through countless generations. Europeans remained ignorant of this rich history until, during the 1400s, they explored the west coast. Soon they were shipping thousands of Africans to Europe and the Americas as slaves, a "trade" that destroyed many traditional societies. During the late 1800s, Europeans penetrated the interior of Africa and, within 20 years, had carved up the continent between them. Almost all of Africa remained under European control until the 1950s, when the colonies began to gain their independence. Today, the peoples of Africa are free of foreign control.

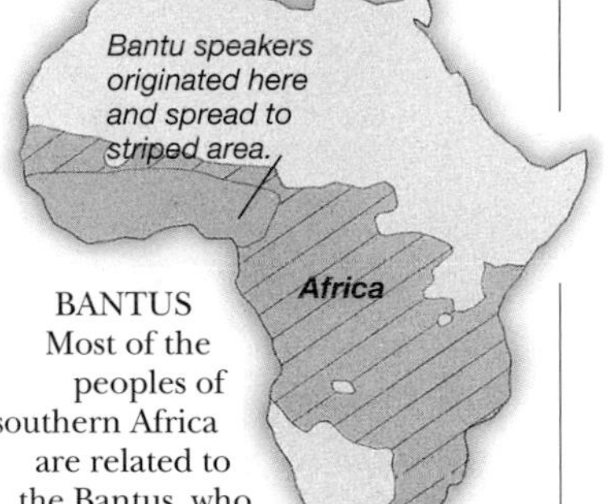

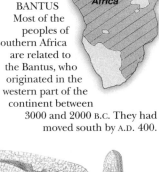

BANTUS
Most of the peoples of southern Africa are related to the Bantus, who originated in the western part of the continent between 3000 and 2000 B.C. They had moved south by A.D. 400.

Bantu speakers originated here and spread to striped area.

Africa

Ivory traders

GREAT ZIMBABWE
The stone city of Great Zimbabwe was a major religious, political, and trading center in southern Africa during the 14th century. It grew rich on the proceeds of herding cattle and mining gold, copper, and iron. The peoples of Great Zimbabwe exported their produce to the coastal port of Sofala in what is now Mozambique, and then up the coast of Africa to Arabia.

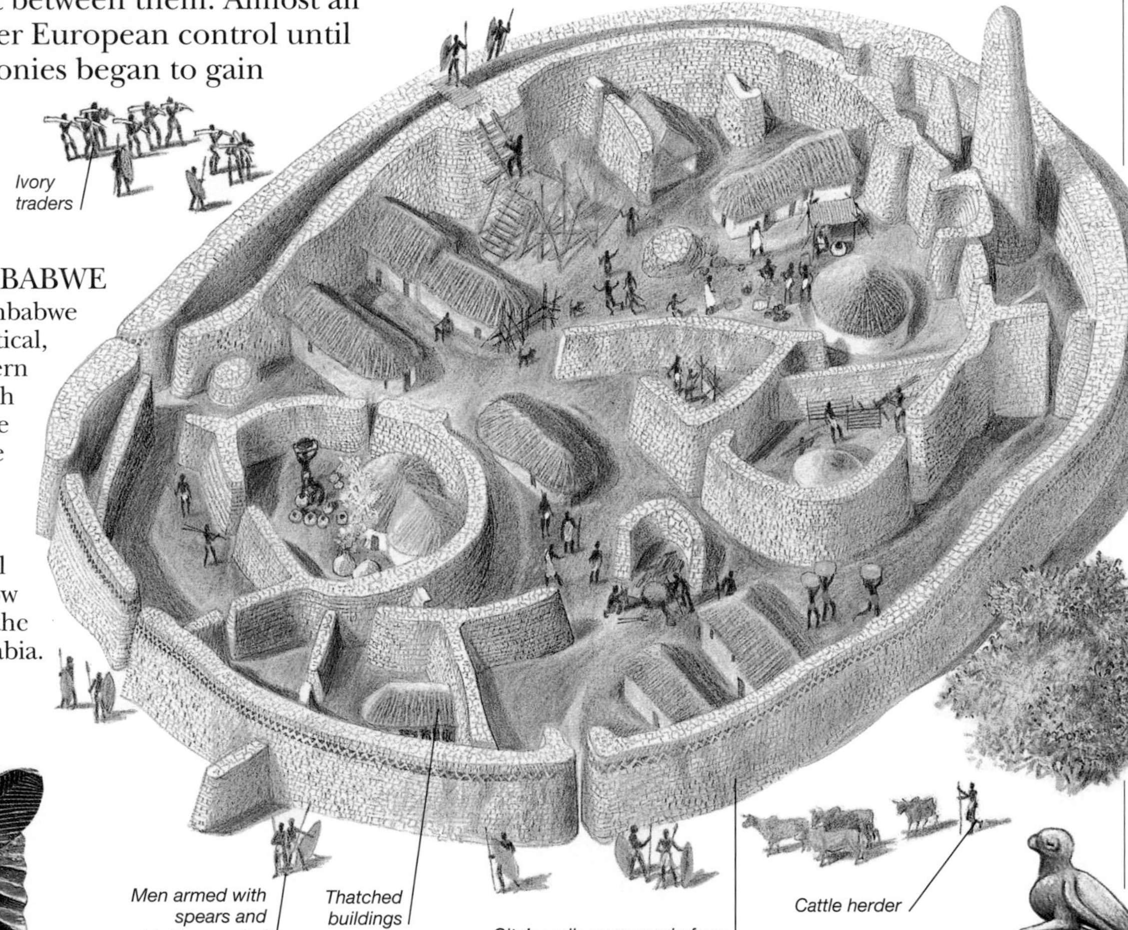

Men armed with spears and shields guarded the city's walls.

Thatched buildings

City's walls were made from huge granite slabs.

Cattle herder

Great enclosure at Great Zimbabwe

BENIN
The West African kingdom of Benin reached the height of its power between the 14th and 17th centuries. Its people traded ivory, pepper, palm oil, and slaves with the Portuguese. They also excelled in casting realistic figures in bronze. On the left is a Benin bronze mask.

SOAPSTONE BIRDS
Soapstone carvings of local birds on columns stood in an enclosure outside Great Zimbabwe. One of these birds has been the national symbol of Zimbabwe since the country gained its independence in 1980.

SCRAMBLE FOR AFRICA

Until the 1880s, European conquest in Africa was restricted to the coastal regions and the main river valleys. But European powers wanted overseas colonies (settlements). Throughout the 1880s and 1890s, European nations competed for land in Africa. By 1900, almost all of Africa was in European hands. The only independent states left were the ancient kingdom of Ethiopia in the east, and the free slave state of Liberia in the west. The cartoon (left) shows Germany as a bird "swooping" onto Africa.

ON THE SWOOP!

ZULU WARS
Some African peoples managed to resist the Europeans for a time. After 1838, the Zulus of southern Africa fought first the Boers (Dutch settlers) and then the British. In 1879, however, Britain finally defeated the Zulus. In 1887, Zululand became a British colony. Above is a picture of the British trying to break through Zulu lines.

INDEPENDENCE
The coming of independence to much of Africa after 1956 did not always bring peace or prosperity to the new nations. Many were weakened by famines and droughts or torn apart by civil wars. Few have managed to maintain civilian governments without periods of military dictatorships. In 1964 Malawi (formerly Nyasaland) became Africa's 35th independent state. Above is the celebration scene.

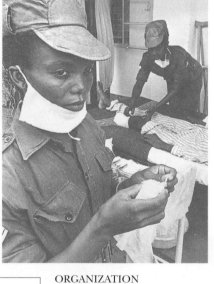

ORGANIZATION OF AFRICAN UNITY
Despite the many political differences that exist between individual African states, they all share problems of poverty, poor health, and lack of schools. In 1963, the Organization of African Unity (OAU) was founded to promote unity in the continent and to coordinate economic, health, and other policies among its 51 member nations. Above are two members of the OAU medical unit treating civil war victims.

NELSON MANDELA
In 1994, Nelson Mandela (left), a leader of the ANC, became the president of South Africa.

APARTHEID

In 1948, the National Party came to power in South Africa. Years of segregation, known as apartheid, followed. This policy gave white people power but denied black people many rights, including the vote. In 1990 the African National Congress (ANC), a banned black nationalist movement led by Nelson Mandela, was legalized, and the apartheid laws began to be dismantled. In 1994, the first-ever free elections were held.

AFRICA

700-1200 Kingdom of Ghana in West Africa grows rich on cross-Saharan trade with the Arabs.

c. 800-1800 Kanem-Bornu kingdom.

1200s Trading cities flourish on east coast.

1235-1500 Kingdom of Mali.

1300-1600 Kingdom of Benin.

1300s Great Zimbabwe flourishes.

1350-1591 Kingdom of Songhai.

1500-1800s Europeans take Africans as slaves to America.

1838-79 Zulus fight against Boers and British.

1880s Europeans take almost total control of Africa.

1957-75 Most of Africa independent.

1990 Namibia independent.

Find out more

AFRICA
BENIN EMPIRE
EGYPT, ANCIENT
PREHISTORIC PEOPLES
SLAVERY

AFRICAN AMERICANS

THE HISTORY OF AFRICAN-AMERICAN PEOPLE has been dominated by the struggle for freedom and equality. From the 1600s to the Civil War, most African Americans worked as slaves, contributing to America's vast agricultural wealth but entitled to none of the benefits or freedoms. Once slavery was abolished, African Americans made some progress toward equal treatment under the law, but widespread segregation hindered their fight. The civil rights movement of the 1950s and 1960s removed racist laws, although racism itself has proved harder to erase. Despite this, there has been a resurgence of interest in African-American culture, and African Americans have continued to flourish in politics, education, and the arts.

CIVIL RIGHTS MOVEMENT
During the 1950s and 1960s, many African Americans joined together to fight for equality and justice. These civil rights activists used mainly peaceful means, such as marches (above), to end racist laws.

THE AFRICAN-AMERICAN PEOPLE

About 30 million African Americans live in the United States. They are the largest minority group in the nation, representing 12 percent of the population. About half of all African Americans live in the southern states. In many major cities, such as Washington, D.C., Atlanta, Detroit, and Newark, African Americans are the majority.

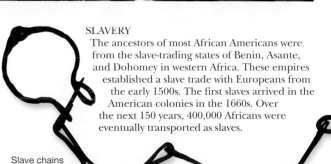

In 1993, Toni Morrison became the first African American to win the Nobel Prize for Literature.

SLAVERY
The ancestors of most African Americans were from the slave-trading states of Benin, Asante, and Dohomey in western Africa. These empires established a slave trade with Europeans from the early 1500s. The first slaves arrived in the American colonies in the 1660s. Over the next 150 years, 400,000 Africans were eventually transported as slaves.

Slave chains

DISCRIMINATION
The Civil War ended slavery, but most newly freed slaves had no homes, and few could read and write. The government built housing and established 4,000 schools (above). However, many states passed laws to limit the civil rights of African Americans, and segregate (separate) them from whites.

BREAKING BARRIERS
Many African Americans have broken barriers in politics, sports, and the arts. In 1983, Guion Bluford became the first African-American astronaut, while in 2005, Condoleezza Rice became the first female African-American Secretary of State.

HARLEM RENAISSANCE
In the 1920s an explosion of literature, art, and music, centered in New York City's Harlem, celebrated African-American culture. Jazz greats Louis Armstrong and Duke Ellington led the movement, often playing in Harlem's Cotton Club (right).

Find out more

ABOLITIONIST MOVEMENT
AFRICA, HISTORY OF
CIVIL RIGHTS
SLAVERY

AFRICAN WILDLIFE

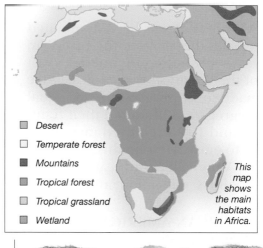

Desert
Temperate forest
Mountains
Tropical forest
Tropical grassland
Wetland

This map shows the main habitats in Africa.

AFRICA HAS AN INCREDIBLE variety of wildlife. The cheetah, the world's fastest animal, lives in Africa, sprinting after its prey in the scrubland and grassland. The huge Nile crocodile lurks in the Nile River. Vast herds of wildebeest, zebra, and buffalo wander the grassy plains, together with the biggest land animal, the elephant, and the largest bird, the ostrich. In Africa's central rain forests are gorillas and chimpanzees. In the Kalahari and Namib deserts, which are among the driest areas on Earth, sand skinks shelter in the shade of giant euphorbia plants, watching out for the poisonous Namibian sidewinder snake. Although humans have turned many regions into farmland, there are still plenty of wild places in Africa.

NATIONAL PARKS
Many wild places in Africa are being destroyed for timber, firewood, and farmland. The Korup National Park in Cameroon is one of Africa's least spoiled rain forest areas. It is now protected as a national reserve.

GIRAFFE
The giraffe is the tallest animal on Earth. A large male can measure 17 ft (5 m) to its horn tips. Its long legs and long neck enable it to reach higher into the trees to feed than any other hoofed mammal. The giraffe's long tail, with its coarse hairs, is an effective fly swatter to flick away flies and other insects.

SAVANNA
The grassy African plains are called savannas. They are home to many spectacular large mammals, including elephants, rhinoceroses, zebras, and lions. The African savannas cover almost a quarter of Africa, mainly in the east and south.

Egyptian vulture has a bald head and neck. It feeds on carrion (remains of dead animals).

The secretary bird is a snake killer found in grassland areas.

HYENA
This hunter-scavenger hunts at night and consumes whatever it can, including goats and other mammals, birds, snakes, fruit, but mainly the remains of other animals' prey. Despite its doglike shape, the hyena is more closely related to the mongoose family.

AFRICAN WETLANDS
The African wetlands consist of swamps and lakes and are inhabited by a great number of herons, pelicans, flamingos, and other water birds, as well as lungfishes and huge schools of cichlids and other fish. In the Kalahari Desert, crocodiles and hippopotamuses live in the water among vast beds of papyrus stems in the Okovango Basin – the largest oasis on Earth.

MEERKAT
The meerkat is a kind of mongoose. It forages for insects, lizards, and other small creatures, moving around a fixed area to look for food. Meerkats live in groups and dig burrows for shelter and for raising young.

Two male hippos fighting each other for their territory

HIPPOPOTAMUS
An adult hippopotamus can weigh more than 2.7 tonnes (2.7 tons), making it one of the heaviest animals on land. During the day, hippopotamuses wallow in mud or bathe in rivers and lakes, almost submerged, with only their ears, eyes, and nostrils showing. At night they come onto land to feed on grass near the riverbank.

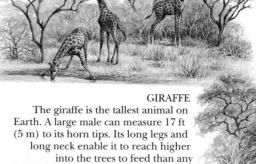

Meerkats sit upright near the burrow entrances to watch for predators.

PANGOLIN
There are seven kinds of pangolins in Africa and in Asia. They live in savanna and forest areas, where they lick up ants and termites with their long, sticky tongues. A pangolin can roll itself into a ball for defense; its overlapping scales help protect it against predators.

Countless beetles and other creatures scavenge and recycle nutrients in the soil.

Find out more
ELEPHANTS
LIONS, TIGERS, and other big cats
MARSH AND SWAMP WILDLIFE

AIR

A MIXTURE OF GASES makes up the air that all plants and animals need for life. We give the name wind to moving air. When air moves, it presses against everything in its path, rustling leaves and lifting kites high above the treetops. Still air presses, too. There is a blanket of air roughly 400 miles (650 km) deep that surrounds the Earth. Although air is light, this layer of air is so thick that it presses down on everything it engulfs. At ground level its force is equal to 34 ft (10.4 m) of water. We do not notice the weight of air pressing down on us, because it presses equally from all sides and because the liquids in our body press outward against the pressure of the air. Atmospheric pressure is lower at high altitudes; in an airplane at a height of about 52,000 ft (16,000 m) above the ground, air pressure is only one-tenth the pressure on the ground.

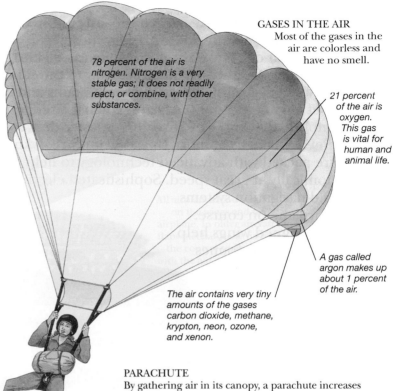

78 percent of the air is nitrogen. Nitrogen is a very stable gas; it does not readily react, or combine, with other substances.

GASES IN THE AIR
Most of the gases in the air are colorless and have no smell.

21 percent of the air is oxygen. This gas is vital for human and animal life.

A gas called argon makes up about 1 percent of the air.

The air contains very tiny amounts of the gases carbon dioxide, methane, krypton, neon, ozone, and xenon.

PARACHUTE
By gathering air in its canopy, a parachute increases air resistance so that the parachutist falls slowly and safely to the ground. Skydivers also use air resistance to control their speed before opening the parachute. They spread their arms and legs to slow the fall.

AIR RESISTANCE
Like any other substance, air occupies space. So when a car moves along, it has to push the air out of the way. This produces a force called air resistance, or drag, which slows down the car. Modern vehicles are designed with sleek, streamlined shapes that make way for the air to move out smoothly. New designs are tested in wind tunnels that blow air at high speed over a model of the car.

AIR PRESSURE

Air pressure can help with everyday tasks. For example, a siphon uses the push of atmospheric pressure to empty a fish tank that is too heavy to lift when full. Many machines work using air pressure. Pumping air under pressure into car tires keeps them solid yet flexible, cushioning passengers from bumps in the road. Many tools, such as pneumatic screwdrivers and drills, are powered by air at high pressure that is produced by mechanical pumps.

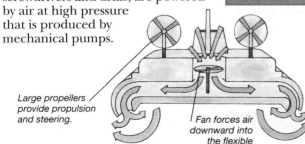

Large propellers provide propulsion and steering.

Fan forces air downward into the flexible rubber skirt.

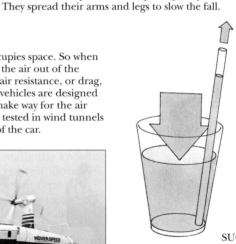

HOVERCRAFT
A layer of pressurized air keeps a hovercraft, or air-cushion vehicle, floating a little distance off the ground and distributes the vehicle's weight evenly. This means the hovercraft can travel over swamps, deep snow, or water without sinking in. A large fan creates the cushion of air that lifts the craft off the ground.

SUCTION
Differences in air pressure provide a useful way of moving liquids and solid objects. For example, when you suck on a drinking straw, you use your lungs as a pump to reduce the air pressure above the liquid in the straw. The higher pressure of the air outside the straw pushes the drink up the straw and into your mouth.

Find out more
ATMOSPHERE
EARTH
OXYGEN
POLLUTION
WEATHER

AIR FORCES

FIRST AIR FORCES
Before the invention of airplanes, armies used balloons and kites to watch and attack their enemies. The first air force pilots flew in aircraft made of wood, canvas, and wire. They fought with machine guns and dropped small bombs out of the cockpit by hand.

HELICOPTERS, JET FIGHTERS, AND BOMBERS play a vital role in modern warfare. As part of an air force, these aircraft support and defend armies and navies. They can also attack targets that are impossible to approach by land or sea. Armies first used airplanes in battle during World War I (1914-18), and by World War II (1939-45) modern air forces had been established. People serving in the air force perform a variety of jobs. The crew of an aircraft includes a pilot, a navigator, and a gunner to operate the weapons. Many more people work on the ground. Radar crews find out where enemy and friendly aircraft are flying. Surface-to-air missile crews try to shoot down enemy aircraft. Rescue crews go to the aid of pilots whose aircraft have crashed in the sea or on land.

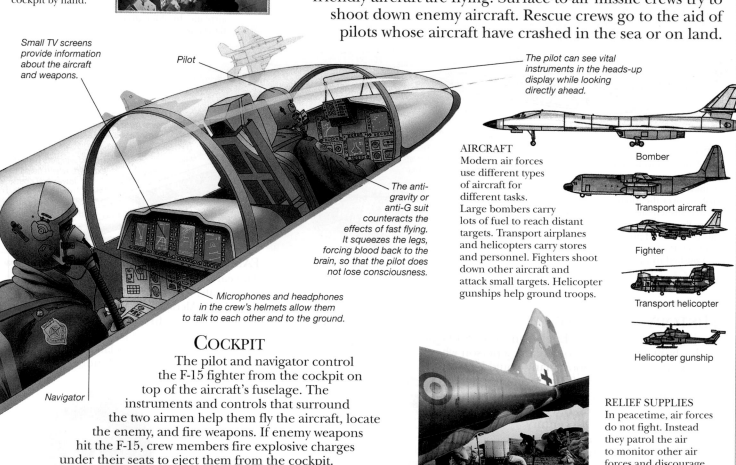

Small TV screens provide information about the aircraft and weapons.

Pilot

The pilot can see vital instruments in the heads-up display while looking directly ahead.

The anti-gravity or anti-G suit counteracts the effects of fast flying. It squeezes the legs, forcing blood back to the brain, so that the pilot does not lose consciousness.

Microphones and headphones in the crew's helmets allow them to talk to each other and to the ground.

Navigator

COCKPIT
The pilot and navigator control the F-15 fighter from the cockpit on top of the aircraft's fuselage. The instruments and controls that surround the two airmen help them fly the aircraft, locate the enemy, and fire weapons. If enemy weapons hit the F-15, crew members fire explosive charges under their seats to eject them from the cockpit. They land by parachute.

AIRCRAFT
Modern air forces use different types of aircraft for different tasks. Large bombers carry lots of fuel to reach distant targets. Transport airplanes and helicopters carry stores and personnel. Fighters shoot down other aircraft and attack small targets. Helicopter gunships help ground troops.

Bomber

Transport aircraft

Fighter

Transport helicopter

Helicopter gunship

RELIEF SUPPLIES
In peacetime, air forces do not fight. Instead they patrol the air to monitor other air forces and discourage them from attacking. During emergencies such as famines and earthquakes, transport planes carry food and supplies to the victims.

AIRCREW
Personnel who fly in aircraft are called the aircrew. They include pilots, navigators, who tell the pilot which course to fly, and loaders, who work in transport planes.

GROUND CREW
People who work on the ground are called the ground crew. They maintain and repair the aircraft. Armorers ensure that fighter planes always have enough ammunition and bombs on board.

Pilots carry flight plans in pads on their knees.

Women aircrew do not usually fly aircraft in battle.

Ground crew use hand signals to show pilots where to park their aircraft.

Engineers check aircraft carefully after every flight.

Find out more
AIRCRAFT
BALLOONS AND AIRSHIPS
HELICOPTERS
NAVIGATION
RADAR
WORLD WAR I
WORLD WAR II

AIRPORTS

EVERY YEAR MORE THAN 100 MILLION PEOPLE pass through the world's airports. Freight terminals handle the millions of tons of cargo carried by aircraft. Whenever people or goods travel by air, they must pass through an airport. Some airports are extremely large. At John F. Kennedy International Airport in New York City nearly 1,000 airplanes take off every day. Some huge international aircraft fly thousands of miles to other continents. Smaller planes make internal flights, taking passengers to other parts of the country. They may land at tiny airports that serve towns or islands. All airports have runways for aircraft to pick up speed and take off. They also have facilities for refueling and making repairs. In larger airports there are restaurants and lounges where passengers can wait to board their flights.

PASSPORTS
International travelers use passports to prove their identity. Officials at the airport often stamp the passport to show that the traveler entered the country legally. The use of passports began in the 16th century but has only become widespread in the last 50 years.

The whole airport can be seen from the control tower.

Ground crew refuel the aircraft from tankers or hydrants.

Catering staff supplies food and drink to the galleys, or kitchens.

Cleaners vacuum the cabin and remove trash.

Engineers make careful checks on all the airplane's functions.

Firefighters stand by while the aircraft refuels.

Ramp for boarding

PASSENGER TERMINAL

A large modern airport employs thousands of people. As soon as an aircraft lands, air traffic controllers direct it toward a disembarkation point, where it stops. Passengers leave the aircraft by means of a ramp or steps from the aircraft to the ground. Baggage handlers remove the suitcases from the aircraft and take them to the terminal for collection. When passengers have their luggage, they go through customs, then take connecting flights or travel onward by bus, car, or train.

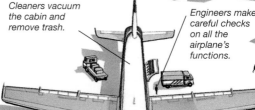

Smugglers hide drugs in hollow ornaments and other objects.

CUSTOMS
Passengers on incoming flights pass through customs. Officials there search baggage and clothing for drugs and other illegal substances, and check for goods on which travelers should pay import or export tax. Smugglers try to trick customs officers by hiding illegal or taxable goods.

SECURITY
Airport authorities carry out security checks to protect aircraft from bombs and armed terrorists. X-ray machines scan hand luggage for bombs and guns. Passengers walk through an arch that detects metal; a heavy lump of metal such as a gun triggers an alarm.

AIR TRAFFIC CONTROL
At a busy airport, as many as 50 aircraft take off and land every hour. Air traffic controllers in the control tower decide when each plane can take off. They also radio instructions to the aircraft that are circling in the sky above, waiting to land.

Find out more
AIRCRAFT
AIR FORCES
TRANSPORTATION, HISTORY OF
X-RAYS

ALEXANDER THE GREAT

By 323 B.C. ONE MAN HAD CONQUERED most of the known world and set up an empire that extended from Asia Minor (now Turkey) to India. The name of the general was Alexander, today known as Alexander the Great. He was the son of King Philip II, ruler of Macedonia, a small but powerful Greek kingdom. In 336 B.C. Philip was murdered and Alexander became king, although he was only 20 years old. Alexander was an ambitious and brilliant general. In 334 he invaded the great Persian Empire ruled by Darius III. After a series of remarkable victories, Alexander then went on to conquer a vast empire running from Egypt in the west to India in the east. When Alexander died, aged only 33, he had led his armies at least 12,000 miles (19,000 km) and had encouraged the spread of Greek culture throughout the known world. After he died, his empire was divided. But he is still considered one of the greatest generals who ever lived.

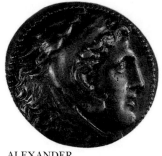

ALEXANDER
As a young man Alexander (356-323 B.C.) was brave and intelligent. He was taught by the Greek philosopher Aristotle, from whom he developed a lifelong interest in philosophy.

PHALANX
The army that Alexander led into Persia (Iran) consisted mostly of infantry, or foot soldiers armed with long spears. The infantry fought in a formation called a phalanx. The men were packed closely together with their spears pointing toward the enemy.

BUCEPHALUS
Alexander rode into battle on a beautiful horse called Bucephalus. According to legend, Bucephalus was completely wild and responded only to Alexander. When Bucephalus died, Alexander built a monument and town, called Bucephala, in honor of him. The city still exists in India today.

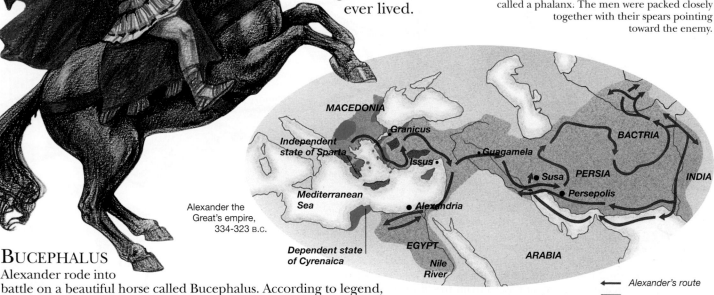

Alexander the Great's empire, 334-323 B.C.

MACEDONIA
Granicus
Independent state of Sparta
Issus
Guagamela
BACTRIA
Susa
PERSIA
INDIA
Persepolis
Mediterranean Sea
Alexandria
Dependent state of Cyrenaica
EGYPT
ARABIA
Nile River

← Alexander's route
Independent region
Dependent region
Alexander's empire

ALEXANDRIA
In 332 B.C. Alexander founded the city of Alexandria (named after himself) on the Mediterranean coast. It soon became a great port and a center of Greek culture and learning, attracting poets and scientists from all over the world. Today, Alexandria is the second-largest city in Egypt.

After Alexander's death, Ptolemy Soter, commander of Egypt, created a huge library at Alexandria. It was said to have contained more than 500,000 books; today only ruins remain.

BATTLES
Alexander fought many battles. Usually he had fewer men than his enemy, but he won because his men were well trained and equipped. At the Battle of Issus in 333 B.C. Alexander, with 36,000 men, defeated Darius and his 110,000 troops. Two years later, with a force of 45,000 men, Alexander again overwhelmed Darius and his 100,000 soldiers at the Battle of Guagamela.

Find out more
ARMIES
GREECE, ANCIENT

ALPHABETS

WHEN PEOPLE FIRST BEGAN TO WRITE, they did not use an alphabet. Instead, they drew small pictures to represent the objects they were writing about. This is called picture writing, and it was very slow because there was a different picture for every word. An alphabet does not contain pictures. Instead, it is a collection of letters or symbols that represent sounds. Each sound is just part of one word. Joining the letters together forms a whole word. The human voice can make about 35 different sounds in speech. So alphabets need at most 35 letters to write any word, and most alphabets manage with fewer. The Phoenicians, who lived about 3,000 years ago in the Middle Eastern country now called Syria, developed the first modern alphabet. The ancient Greeks adapted the Phoenician alphabet, and later the Romans improved it. The Roman alphabet is now used widely throughout the world.

The ancient Romans used the letters of the alphabet for numbers. For example, C is 100.

abcdefghi
jklmnopqr
stuvwxyz

CAPITAL AND SMALL LETTERS
The first Roman alphabet had only capital letters. Small letters started to appear after the 8th century. In English, capital letters are used at the beginning of a sentence, and for the first letter of a name. Capital letters are also used when words are abbreviated, or shortened, to their first letters, such as UN for United Nations.

.,;?!éäêç

SYMBOLS AND ACCENTS
In addition to letters, writers use punctuation marks such as a period to show where a sentence ends. Some languages, such as French, also use accents – marks that show how to pronounce the word. The sloping acute accent over the *e* in *café* makes it sound like the *a* in *day*.

ROMAN ALPHABET
The alphabet used in English and other European languages is based on the Roman alphabet, which had 23 letters. This alphabet is also used in some Southeast Asian languages, such as Vietnamese and Indonesian.

АБВГДЕЁЖЗИЙКЛМНОПРСТУФХЦЧШЩЪЫЬЭЮЯ
Cyrillic (Russian)

ΑΒΓΔΕΖΗΘΙΚΛΜΝΞΟΠΡΣΤΥΦΧΨΩ
Greek

अ आ इ ई उ ऊ ए ऐ ओ औ ऋ क ख ग घ ङ च छ ज झ ञ ट ठ ड ढ ण त थ
द ध न प फ ब भ म य र ल व श ष स ह क्ष त्र ज्ञ श्र
Hindi (India)

MODERN ALPHABETS
The Roman alphabet is only one of the world's alphabets. Many other languages use different symbols to represent similar sounds, and the words may be written and read quite differently from the Roman alphabet. Japanese readers start on the right side of the page and read to the left, or start at the top and read down the page.

In every alphabet, letters have a special order that does not change. Dictionaries, phone books, and many other books are arranged in alphabetical order so that it is easy to find a word or a name.

In traditional printing, raised lead letters are used to print the words on paper.

The Romans did not have the letter W. For J they used I, and for U they used V.

ROSETTA STONE
The ancient Egyptians used a system of picture writing called hieroglyphics. The meaning of this writing was forgotten 1,600 years ago, so nobody was able to read Egyptian documents until 1799 when some French soldiers made a remarkable discovery. Near Alexandria, Egypt, they found a stone with an inscription on it. The words were carved in hieroglyphics and in Greek. Using their knowledge of Greek, scholars were able to discover what the hieroglyphics meant.

CUNEIFORM
About 5,000 years ago in Mesopotamia (now part of Iraq), a form of writing called cuneiform developed. It started off as picture writing, but later letters began to represent sounds. The Mesopotamians did not have paper; instead they wrote on damp clay using wedge-shaped pens. Cuneiform means "wedge-shaped."

CHINESE PICTOGRAMS
In traditional Chinese writing, symbols called pictograms are used to represent ideas. There is a different character for every word.

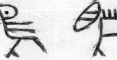
Bird

Horse

Tree

Sun

AMERICAN REVOLUTION

THE UNITED STATES OF AMERICA was born amidst the upheaval of the American Revolution. From the first shots fired in 1775 to the final surrender in 1781, the war was a fierce and brutal struggle between the undisputed superpower of the day, Great Britain, and the people of Britain's 13 North American colonies. The colonists, who were not represented in the British Parliament, resented the taxes imposed on them, and established their own Continental Congress to negotiate with Britain. Skirmishes led to war, with famous battles in New York, Philadelphia, and Boston. As in the Civil War, the conflict divided communities, as many colonists chose to remain loyal to the crown rather than defy the mother country. The American Revolution inspired people all over the world, and led them to fight for their own political freedom.

PAUL REVERE'S RIDE
On the night of April 18, 1775, Boston silversmith Paul Revere took his famous ride through nearby Concord, Massachusetts, to warn the people that the British were coming.

BATTLE OF LEXINGTON

The British army set out from Boston on April 19, 1775, on a secret mission to capture arms and gunpowder stored at Concord. But patriot minutemen, already warned about the British advance by Paul Revere, met the redcoats at Lexington. A shot rang out – poet Ralph Waldo Emerson later described it as the "shot heard round the world" – and the fighting that followed was the first battle of the American Revolution.

BOSTON TEA PARTY

The British government refused to withdraw its tax on tea, a constant reminder to colonists that they were subject to British taxation. On the night of December 16, 1773, some patriots dressed as Mohawk warriors boarded tea ships in Boston harbor and threw the tea overboard as a protest.

This cartoon depicts the repeal of the Stamp Act in 1766.

STAMP ACT
To raise money to pay for stationing troops in the colonies, the British parliament passed the Stamp Act in 1765. A stamp, or seal, had to appear on newspapers, bills of sale, wills – even dice and playing cards. Merchants had to stamp all goods before selling them. This tax enraged the colonists.

LAFAYETTE AND THE FRENCH
From the early days of the war, France gave the colonists money and arms. Benjamin Franklin helped persuade the French to increase aid, and in 1778 the colonists signed a treaty of alliance with the French government. The Marquis de Lafayette, the 21-year-old son of a French aristocrat, served as a general alongside Washington and fought bravely for the rebels.

Mary Hays

MOLLY PITCHERS
Many women served on the battlefield, carrying pitchers of water to cool the cannons. They were known as "Molly Pitchers." One, Mary Hays, took her dead husband's place behind the cannon.

TURTLE
Just over 7 ft (2 m) long and made of wood, the American *Turtle* (right) launched the world's first submarine attack on September 7, 1776. Its designer, David Bushnell, hoped his invention could steal up alongside a British warship and attach a cask of gunpowder to its hull, slipping away before a timer made the cask explode. However, the *Turtle's* attack on HMS *Eagle* in New York Harbor failed.

A patriot rings the Liberty Bell, symbol of American independence.

Thayendanega was a Mohawk leader loyal to the British.

LOYALISTS
As many as one-third of the people living in the colonies wanted to remain British subjects. Some had relatives in England whom they did not want to endanger; others were afraid of the British soldiers. Many of these loyalists joined the British army. The army also recruited Native Americans, who did not like the colonists for taking their land, and slaves, who were given their freedom in return for serving in the army.

PATRIOTS
In the early days of the Revolution, most patriots simply sought a voice in the British parliament. But others saw the opportunity for a united, self-governing nation. Patriots boycotted British goods, including tea, and rallied to the stirring speeches of rebels such as Patrick Henry and Sam Adams.

SURRENDER AT YORKTOWN
Great Britain fought a massive campaign on land and sea to crush the colonial army. Early battles were fought in the northern colonies, but after France entered the war, the British army moved its attention to the South. It captured key southern ports, but the patriots rallied. With the French navy blocking escape by sea, the British army was trapped. In October 1781, a large British force surrendered to George Washington at Yorktown, Virginia.

Commander-in-chief George Washington

Major General Lord Cornwallis, the British commander

AMERICAN REVOLUTION
1767 Britain imposes high taxes on the 13 colonies

1773 Boston Tea Party protests against taxation

1774-75 Continental Congress meets to protest against taxation and prepare the 13 colonies for war

1775 Battle of Lexington marks start of Revolution

1775 British win the Battle of Bunker Hill, MA, the bloodiest conflict of the entire war

1776 Declaration of Independence

1777 Colonists win key battle at Saratoga, NY

1778 France signs alliance with the colonies

1781 General Cornwallis surrenders at Yorktown, VA, in the last major battle of the war

1783 Britain recognizes American independence in the Peace of Paris

Find out more
COLONIES
and colonial America
CONSTITUTION
DECLARATION OF INDEPENDENCE
FRANKLIN, BENJAMIN
WASHINGTON, GEORGE

ANIMALS

THE ANIMAL KINGDOM is one of the largest groups of living things; scientists believe that there are up to 30 million species. Animals range from tiny, simple creatures that look like blobs of jelly to gigantic blue whales. The huge animal kingdom is divided into many groups. A hedgehog, for example, belongs to the order of insectivores because it eats insects. It also belongs to the class of placental mammals. All mammals are vertebrates (animals with backbones) and belong to a group called chordates. An animal is a living creature that feeds, moves, and breeds. During its life cycle, an animal is born, grows, matures, reproduces, and eventually dies. It ingests (takes in) food to build and develop its body. Food provides the animal with the energy to move around. Some animals do not move at all; the adult sponge, for example, spends its life anchored to a rock. All kinds of animals from dinosaurs to dodos have become extinct; many others, including elephants and tigers, may soon disappear, if their habitats are destroyed and if they continue to be killed recklessly for their hides and bones.

FROG
Like all animals, the common green frog is aware of its surroundings and able to move, feed, and reproduce. Frogs belong to the class of animals called amphibians. All amphibians spend part of their lives in or near water.

INTERNAL SKELETONS
The animal world can be divided into vertebrate animals and invertebrate animals. Vertebrates have an internal skeleton with a vertebral column or backbone. In most cases, this is made of bone. Some sea-dwelling vertebrates, such as sharks, have a backbone made of tough, rubbery gristle called cartilage.

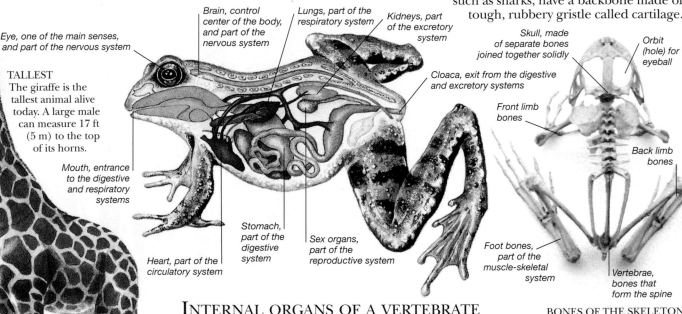

TALLEST
The giraffe is the tallest animal alive today. A large male can measure 17 ft (5 m) to the top of its horns.

Eye, one of the main senses, and part of the nervous system

Mouth, entrance to the digestive and respiratory systems

Brain, control center of the body, and part of the nervous system

Lungs, part of the respiratory system

Kidneys, part of the excretory system

Cloaca, exit from the digestive and excretory systems

Heart, part of the circulatory system

Stomach, part of the digestive system

Sex organs, part of the reproductive system

Skull, made of separate bones joined together solidly

Orbit (hole) for eyeball

Front limb bones

Back limb bones

Foot bones, part of the muscle-skeletal system

Vertebrae, bones that form the spine

INTERNAL ORGANS OF A VERTEBRATE
Inside an animal such as the frog above are many different parts called organs. Organs are all shapes and sizes. Each one has a job to do. Several organs are grouped together to form a body system, such as the digestive system, the circulatory system, and the reproductive system. The nervous system and the hormonal system control and coordinate all the internal systems.

SMALLEST
The smallest organisms are single-celled creatures called protozoa – so tiny they can hardly be seen by the human eye. The tiniest mammals are the bumblebee bat and Savi's pygmy shrew. This pygmy shrew measures only 2.3 in (6 cm) including its tail.

BONES OF THE SKELETON
The skeletons of vertebrate animals are similar in design, but each differs in certain details through adaptation to the way the animal lives. A frog, for example, has long, strong back legs for leaping. All vertebrates have a skull that contains the brain and the main sense organs. Vertebrates also have two pairs of limbs. Some bones, such as the skull bones, are fixed firmly together; others are linked by flexible joints, as in the limbs.

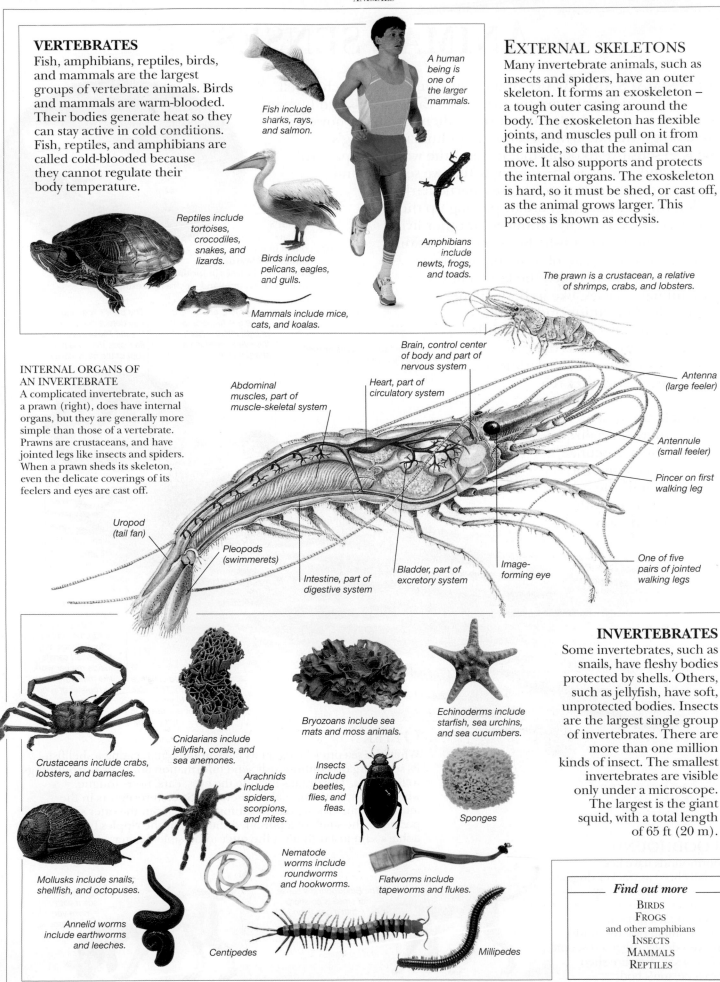

VERTEBRATES

Fish, amphibians, reptiles, birds, and mammals are the largest groups of vertebrate animals. Birds and mammals are warm-blooded. Their bodies generate heat so they can stay active in cold conditions. Fish, reptiles, and amphibians are called cold-blooded because they cannot regulate their body temperature.

Fish include sharks, rays, and salmon.

A human being is one of the larger mammals.

Reptiles include tortoises, crocodiles, snakes, and lizards.

Birds include pelicans, eagles, and gulls.

Amphibians include newts, frogs, and toads.

Mammals include mice, cats, and koalas.

EXTERNAL SKELETONS

Many invertebrate animals, such as insects and spiders, have an outer skeleton. It forms an exoskeleton – a tough outer casing around the body. The exoskeleton has flexible joints, and muscles pull on it from the inside, so that the animal can move. It also supports and protects the internal organs. The exoskeleton is hard, so it must be shed, or cast off, as the animal grows larger. This process is known as ecdysis.

The prawn is a crustacean, a relative of shrimps, crabs, and lobsters.

INTERNAL ORGANS OF AN INVERTEBRATE

A complicated invertebrate, such as a prawn (right), does have internal organs, but they are generally more simple than those of a vertebrate. Prawns are crustaceans, and have jointed legs like insects and spiders. When a prawn sheds its skeleton, even the delicate coverings of its feelers and eyes are cast off.

Brain, control center of body and part of nervous system

Abdominal muscles, part of muscle-skeletal system

Heart, part of circulatory system

Antenna (large feeler)

Antennule (small feeler)

Pincer on first walking leg

Uropod (tail fan)

Pleopods (swimmerets)

Intestine, part of digestive system

Bladder, part of excretory system

Image-forming eye

One of five pairs of jointed walking legs

Crustaceans include crabs, lobsters, and barnacles.

Cnidarians include jellyfish, corals, and sea anemones.

Bryozoans include sea mats and moss animals.

Echinoderms include starfish, sea urchins, and sea cucumbers.

Arachnids include spiders, scorpions, and mites.

Insects include beetles, flies, and fleas.

Sponges

Mollusks include snails, shellfish, and octopuses.

Nematode worms include roundworms and hookworms.

Flatworms include tapeworms and flukes.

Annelid worms include earthworms and leeches.

Centipedes

Millipedes

INVERTEBRATES

Some invertebrates, such as snails, have fleshy bodies protected by shells. Others, such as jellyfish, have soft, unprotected bodies. Insects are the largest single group of invertebrates. There are more than one million kinds of insect. The smallest invertebrates are visible only under a microscope. The largest is the giant squid, with a total length of 65 ft (20 m).

Find out more

BIRDS
FROGS
and other amphibians
INSECTS
MAMMALS
REPTILES

ANIMAL SENSES

ALL ANIMALS ARE AWARE of their surroundings. Touch, smell, taste, sight, and hearing are the five senses that animals and humans use to detect what is happening around them. Animals, however, have a very different array of senses than humans. A dog's nose is so sensitive to odors that it "sees" the world as a pattern of scents and smells, in the same way that we see light and color with our eyes. Many creatures, particularly fish, can determine where they are by picking up the tiny amounts of bioelectricity produced by other living things around them. A fish also detects vibrations in the water using a row of sense organs down each side of its body, called the lateral line.

An animal's senses, like its body shape, are a result of evolution and suit the animal's needs. Eyes would be of little use to a creature such as the cave fish, which lives in endless darkness. Instead, these creatures rely on other senses such as smell and touch. Some senses are extremely specialized. Long, feathery antennae enable a male emperor moth to "smell" the odor of a female moth 3 miles (5 km) away.

HUNTING SENSES
A shark can smell blood in the water hundreds of yards away. As this shark closes in for the attack, it makes use of its keen eyesight and electricity-sensing organs.

A clear lens at the front of the eye focuses rays of light into the back of the eye to produce a sharp image.

The otter's scenting organs can detect many scents in the air. These special organs lie inside the nose in the roof of the nasal cavity.

Lips detect sharp pieces of shell in food, then spit them out.

Sensitive forepaws manipulate food. The otter also uses its paws to crack open shellfish.

The skin and hair roots bear sensors that detect vibrations, light touch, heavy pressure, and heat and cold.

The otter hears by sensing vibrations when they strike its eardrums. To help the otter balance, tiny fluid-filled canals inside the ear work like miniature levels to register gravity.

Whiskers are sensitive to touch. They also respond to vibrations, so they are useful in murky water.

Claws and soles of feet are sensitive to touch.

OTTER
While the sea otter floats on its back in the water, eating a shellfish, its sense organs continuously send information about its surroundings to the brain. The organs include the eyes, ears, nose, tongue, whiskers, fur, skin, and balance sensors. Stretch receptors in the joints and muscles also convey information about the otter's body position. The smell of a poisoned shellfish or the ripples from a shark's fin instantly alert the otter to possible danger.

BLOODHOUND
Bloodhounds have been specially bred as tracker dogs. Their sense of smell may be as much as one million times sharper than a human's sense of smell. Bloodhounds can even detect the microscopic pieces of skin that are shed from a person's body.

The Bloodhound's sense of smell is so sharp that it can even pick up scent that is several days old.

Dog follows scent with nose very close to ground.

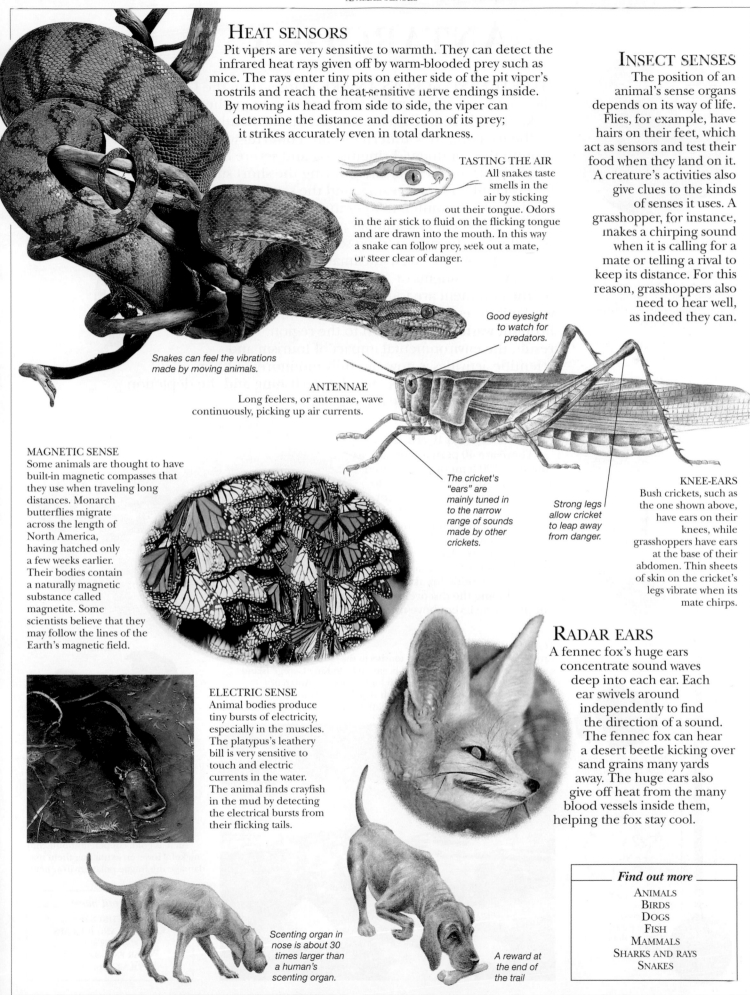

HEAT SENSORS

Pit vipers are very sensitive to warmth. They can detect the infrared heat rays given off by warm-blooded prey such as mice. The rays enter tiny pits on either side of the pit viper's nostrils and reach the heat-sensitive nerve endings inside. By moving its head from side to side, the viper can determine the distance and direction of its prey; it strikes accurately even in total darkness.

TASTING THE AIR
All snakes taste smells in the air by sticking out their tongue. Odors in the air stick to fluid on the flicking tongue and are drawn into the mouth. In this way a snake can follow prey, seek out a mate, or steer clear of danger.

Snakes can feel the vibrations made by moving animals.

INSECT SENSES
The position of an animal's sense organs depends on its way of life. Flies, for example, have hairs on their feet, which act as sensors and test their food when they land on it. A creature's activities also give clues to the kinds of senses it uses. A grasshopper, for instance, makes a chirping sound when it is calling for a mate or telling a rival to keep its distance. For this reason, grasshoppers also need to hear well, as indeed they can.

Good eyesight to watch for predators.

ANTENNAE
Long feelers, or antennae, wave continuously, picking up air currents.

The cricket's "ears" are mainly tuned in to the narrow range of sounds made by other crickets.

Strong legs allow cricket to leap away from danger.

KNEE-EARS
Bush crickets, such as the one shown above, have ears on their knees, while grasshoppers have ears at the base of their abdomen. Thin sheets of skin on the cricket's legs vibrate when its mate chirps.

MAGNETIC SENSE
Some animals are thought to have built-in magnetic compasses that they use when traveling long distances. Monarch butterflies migrate across the length of North America, having hatched only a few weeks earlier. Their bodies contain a naturally magnetic substance called magnetite. Some scientists believe that they may follow the lines of the Earth's magnetic field.

ELECTRIC SENSE
Animal bodies produce tiny bursts of electricity, especially in the muscles. The platypus's leathery bill is very sensitive to touch and electric currents in the water. The animal finds crayfish in the mud by detecting the electrical bursts from their flicking tails.

RADAR EARS
A fennec fox's huge ears concentrate sound waves deep into each ear. Each ear swivels around independently to find the direction of a sound. The fennec fox can hear a desert beetle kicking over sand grains many yards away. The huge ears also give off heat from the many blood vessels inside them, helping the fox stay cool.

Scenting organ in nose is about 30 times larger than a human's scenting organ.

A reward at the end of the trail

Find out more
ANIMALS
BIRDS
DOGS
FISH
MAMMALS
SHARKS AND RAYS
SNAKES

ANTARCTICA

STRETCHING ACROSS AN AREA larger than the United States, the continent of Antarctica sits beneath a huge sheet of ice up to 1.2 miles (2 km) thick. Antarctica is centered on the South Pole and is surrounded by the ice-covered Southern Ocean. Powerful winds create a storm belt around the continent, bringing fog and severe blizzards. It is the coldest and windiest place on earth. Even during the short summers the temperature barely climbs above freezing, and the sea ice only partly melts. In winter, temperatures can plummet to -112°F (-80°C). Few animals and plants can survive on land, but the surrounding seas teem with fish and mammals. Due to its harsh climate, there are no permanent residents of Antarctica. The only people on the continent are tourists, and scientists and staff working in research stations. These few people have brought waste and pollution to the region. As a result, the environmental impact of tourism and scientific activities is now carefully monitored. Other environmental concerns include overfishing and the depletion of the ozone layer above the region.

Situated at the southernmost point of the world, Antarctica covers an area of about 5.5 million sq miles (14 million sq km). The nearest land masses are South America, and New Zealand. The highest point is Vinson Massif, which rises to 16,067 ft (4,897 m).

Radio transmitters allow scientists to track the movements of penguins.

ANTARCTIC TEMPERATURES

28°F (2°C) Seawater freezes. On the Antarctic coast, summer temperatures are only a degree or so warmer than this.

-13°F (-25°C) Steel crystallizes and becomes brittle.

-40°F (-40°C) Synthetic rubber becomes brittle, and exposed flesh freezes rapidly.

-128.2°F (-89°C) Lowest temperature ever recorded, at Vostok Research Station, Antarctica, 1983.

SCIENTIFIC RESEARCH

There are 40 permanent, and as many as 100 temporary, research stations in Antarctica devoted to scientific projects for 15 different nations. Teams of scientists study the wildlife and monitor the ice for changes in the Earth's atmosphere. Antarctic-based research has resulted in a number of scientific breakthroughs, including the discovery of a hole in the ozone layer above the continent.

TOURISM

Cruise liners have been bringing tourists to the Antarctic region since the 1950s. In 1983, Chileans began to fly to King George Island where an 80-bed hotel has been built for vacationers. Antarctica receives several thousand tourists each year. Visitors come to see the dramatic landscape and unique wildlife, such as King penguins.

Platinum

Iron

Gold

MINERAL WEALTH

Antarctica has deposits of minerals, such as gold, copper, uranium, and nickel. However, extracting them may damage the fragile polar environment.

Find out more

CONTINENTS
GLACIERS AND ICE CAPS
INUITS
POLAR EXPLORATION
POLAR WILDLIFE

Legend

Symbol	Meaning
Volcano	Mountain	Ancient monument	Capital city	Large city/town	Small city/town	Research Station

STATISTICS

Area: 5,366,790 sq miles (13,900,000 sq km)
Population: No permanent residents
Capital: None
Languages: English, Spanish, French, Norwegian, Chinese, Polish, Russian, German, Japanese
Religions: Not applicable
Currency: None
Main occupation: Scientific research
Main exports: None
Main imports: None

WHALE PROTECTION

Large-scale whale hunting in Antarctic seas began in the 20th century. The whale population soon fell and in 1948 the International Whaling Commission was set up to monitor the diminishing numbers. Following an international agreement in 1994, a whale sanctuary was created to protect whale feeding grounds from overfishing.

FOREIGN TERRITORIES

Various nations, including Australia, France, New Zealand, Norway, Argentina, Chile, and the UK claimed territory in Antarctica when it was first discovered in the 19th century. However, these claims have been suspended under the 1959 Antarctic Treaty which came into force in 1961. Under the treaty, the continent can be used only for peaceful purposes. Stations may be set up for scientific research but military bases are forbidden.

FROZEN SEAS
During the cold winter months, the seas surrounding Antarctica freeze, almost doubling the size of the continent.

ANTARCTIC ICE
Icebergs barricade more than 90 percent of the Antarctic coastline. The continent contains over 80 percent of the world's freshwater in the form of ice.

LAMBERT GLACIER
The Lambert Glacier is the world's largest series of glaciers. It is 50 miles (80 km) wide at the coast and reaches more than 186 miles (300 km) inland.

PETER I ISLAND
(to Norway)

TRANSANTARCTIC MOUNTAINS
The Transantarctic Mountains run across the continent, splitting it into Greater and Lesser Antarctica.

ROSS ICE SHELF
Ice shelves are permanent floating ice sheets that are attached to land and are constantly fed by glaciers. The Ross Ice Shelf is 600–3,000 ft (183–914m) thick and about 600 miles (966km) long.

Map labels

SOUTHERN OCEAN
Drake Passage
Scotia Sea
South Orkney Islands
South Shetland Islands
King George Island
Weddell Sea
Antarctic Peninsula
Palmer Land
Alexander Island
Bellingshausen Sea
Ellsworth Land
Lesser Antarctica
Marie Byrd Land
Mount Sidley 4181m
Amundsen Sea
Ross Sea
Limit of summer pack ice (December)
Limit of winter pack ice (June)
Coats Land
Berkner Island
Ronne Ice Shelf
Vinson Massif 4897m
Transantarctic Mountains
South Pole+
Roosevelt Island
Ross Ice Shelf
Mount Erebus 3794m
Cape Adare
Oates Land
Queen Maud Land
Enderby Land
Kemp Land
Lambert Glacier
Greater ANTARCTICA
Amundsen-Scott (to US)
South Geomagnetic + Pole
Vostok (to Russian Federation)
Victoria Land
George V Land
Wilkes Land
Cape Darnley
Mackenzie Bay
Prydz Bay
Princess Elizabeth Land
Davis Sea
Shackleton Ice Shelf
Cape Poinsett

SCALE BAR

| 0 | 500 | 1000 | km |
| 0 | 500 | 1000 | miles |

ANTS AND TERMITES

IMAGINE HOW MANY millions of ants and termites live on this planet. There are at least 9,000 different kinds of ants and 2,750 kinds of termites. These tiny creatures are among the most fascinating animals on Earth. Both ants and termites are social insects, living in large groups called colonies where each individual has a specific job to do. The queen (the main female) mates with a male, then spends her life laying eggs. The hordes of workers do such jobs as gathering food and rearing the young. Soldiers and guards protect the nest and the foraging workers. Ants eat a variety of food, including caterpillars, leaves, and fungi. Termites feed mostly on plant matter, and they are among nature's most valuable recyclers.

ANT HEAD
The Asian tree-living ant has simple jaws for feeding on soft insects. Other ants and termites have strong jaws for chewing wood and hard plant stems.

TERMITE MOUND
Many termites make small nests in dead trees or underground. A few kinds of termites build a mound that contains a termite city – a home for many millions of termites. In hot areas the mounds have tunnels and ventilation holes, and may be more than 20 ft (6 m) high. The mounds are often occupied for more than 50 years, and the thick walls help to keep out anteaters and other predators. The queen and king termites live in a royal chamber deep inside the mound.

Front leg

Jaws

Eye

Antenna can bend like an elbow joint.

Middle leg

Thorax

Head

Rear leg

Claw

Ant squirts formic acid from rear of body in self-defense.

Abdomen

Worker ant

Cooling chimney lets air in and out of the termite mound.

Termite mound

Termite mound has many tunnels.

ANT HILL
Most of the passages of an ant hill are underground. Eggs, larvae (grubs), and pupae are kept in separate parts of the nest. Large-jawed sentries guard the entrances. A large ant nest may contain 100,000 ants.

Courtier workers

Queen termite

Soldier termite

Fungus grows on the termites' dung (waste matter) inside the termite mound. These areas are called fungus gardens. Termites feed on the fungus.

Nursery for termite larvae

Queen lays 20,000 or more eggs daily in royal chamber.

King termite

Young female termite

Workers regurgitate (spit out) food for queen, king, and soldier termites. Courtier workers feed and clean queen and king.

WORKER ANT
All worker ants are female. Their long, claw-tipped legs allow them to run fast and climb well. Workers collect food, regurgitate it to feed the other ants, look after eggs and larvae, and clean the nest. They do not have wings, unlike the queen and male ants.

ARMY ANTS
A few ants, such as these army ants of South America, do not make permanent nests and are always on the move. As the colony marches through the forests, they forage for insects, and sometimes even eat large animals alive.

LEAF-CUTTING ANTS
Ants can lift objects that weigh more than they do. Leaf-cutting ants bite off pieces of leaves and carry them back to a huge underground nest. Here they chew the leaves and mix them with saliva to make a kind of compost. Fungus – the leaf-cutting ant's only food – grows on this compost.

TERMITES
The queen and male termites have wings. They take flight and mate, then the queen returns to the nest. The queen does not leave the nest again, and is cared for by the courtier workers. The main male, or king, is larger than the workers and remains with the queen.

Find out more
AFRICAN WILDLIFE
ANIMALS
ECOLOGY AND FOOD WEBS
INSECTS

ARCHAEOLOGY

FOR AN ARCHAEOLOGIST, brushing away the soil that hides a broken pot is like brushing away time. Every tiny fragment helps create a more complete picture of the past. Archaeology is the study of the remains of past human societies, but it is not the same as history. Historians use written records as their starting point, while archaeologists use objects. They excavate, or dig, in the ground or under water for bones, pots, and anything else created by our ancestors. They also look for seeds, field boundaries, and other signs of how long-dead people made use of the landscape. But archaeology is not just concerned with dead people and buried objects. It also helps us understand what may happen to our own society in the future. Archaeology has shown that human actions and changes in the climate or environment can destroy whole communities.

HEINRICH SCHLIEMANN
In 1870 the pioneer German archaeologist Heinrich Schliemann (1822-90) discovered the site of Troy in Turkey. He also set out basic rules for excavation, such as careful recordkeeping. He did not always follow his own rules. His impatient hunt for treasure sometimes destroyed the objects he was seeking.

A grid pattern divides the site into squares so that archaeologists can quickly record the exact location of each find.

In photographs of the site, the stripes painted on poles make it easy to judge the size of objects.

By sketching objects, archaeologists can sometimes record more detail than a camera can.

ANALYSIS
The position and location of the objects uncovered in a dig can provide important information. For this reason archaeologists measure, examine, record, and analyze everything they find, and preserve it if possible. Scientific methods such as radioactive dating enable archaeologists to find out the exact age of objects made thousands of years ago.

Small trowels allow archaeologists to remove soil carefully.

Archaeologists sieve the soil they remove to check for objects they may have overlooked.

A soft brush removes dry soil without damaging the object.

EXCAVATION
Archaeologists gather much of their information about the past by carrying out excavations, or digs. They decide where to dig by looking at aerial photographs, old pictures, maps, documents, or marks on the ground. Then they carefully remove layers of soil, often using trowels and other small tools. The archaeologists keep digging until they reach undisturbed soil with no trace of human occupation.

BRONZE-AGE TOOLS
Archaeologists often find tools from ancient times. The axe and arrowhead shown above date from the Bronze Age and are estimated to have been used by humans between 3,000 and 8,000 years ago.

19th-century drain

17th-century floor

Brick-lined well, c. 1800

16th-century chalk floor

14th-century chalk-lined cesspit

Roman tiled floor

STRATIFICATION
Archaeologists on a dig determine the relative age of each object they find from where it is buried, using the principle of stratification. This principle says that older objects are usually buried deeper in the ground than newer objects.

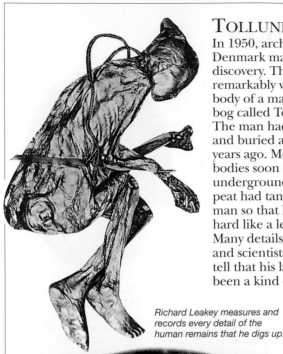

TOLLUND MAN

In 1950, archaeologists in Denmark made a dramatic discovery. They found the remarkably well preserved body of a man in a peat bog called Tollund Mose. The man had been hanged and buried about 2,000 years ago. Most dead bodies soon rot underground, but the peat had tanned Tollund man so that his flesh was hard like a leather shoe. Many details remained, and scientists could even tell that his last meal had been a kind of porridge.

AERIAL PHOTOGRAPHY

Photography of the ground from airplanes began in the 1920s. It made archaeology easier because the high viewpoint reveals traces of buildings, roads, and fields that are invisible from the ground.

THE LEAKEYS

The Leakey family has made major discoveries about the origins of human beings. Louis and his wife, Mary, began to work in the Olduvai Gorge in Tanzania (Africa) in the 1930s. There they showed that human life existed 1,750,000 years ago. They found that human evolution began in Africa, not – as people once thought – in Asia. Since the 1960s their son Richard has continued their research, and now believes that the human race may be more than two million years old.

Richard Leakey measures and records every detail of the human remains that he digs up.

Among the objects found in the tomb of Tutankhamun was a pectoral, or brooch, in the shape of a scarab beetle.

Archaeologists excavating the wreck of the Slava Rossi found Russian icons (religious paintings).

TUTANKHAMUN
The discovery of the tomb of Tutankhamun was one of the most sensational events in the history of archaeology. Tutankhamun was a boy-king who ruled in Egypt 3,500 years ago. In 1922, the British archaeologist Howard Carter (1873-1939) found Tutankhamun's fabulously rich burial place in the Valley of the Kings. Near the boy-king's remains lay gold treasure and beautiful furniture.

Howard Carter (left) found the sarcophagus, or coffin, of Tutankhamun. It was remarkably well preserved.

SHIPWRECKS

The development of lightweight diving equipment over the last 50 years has enabled archaeologists to excavate sites under water. They use many of the same methods that are used on land. Most underwater archaeologists look for shipwrecks, but they sometimes discover landscapes, buildings, and even towns of ancient civilizations.

Find out more

BRONZE AGE
EGYPT, ANCIENT
EVOLUTION
FOSSILS
GEOLOGY
IRON AGE
PREHISTORIC PEOPLES

ARCHITECTURE

EVERY BUILDING YOU SEE – home, school, airport terminal – has been planned by an architect. The word *architect* is Greek for "builder" or "craftworker," and architects aim to design and construct buildings that are attractive, functional, and comfortable. Architecture means designing a building; it also refers to the building style. Styles of architecture have changed over the centuries and differ from culture to culture, so architecture can tell us a lot about people. The Ancient Greeks, for example, produced simple, balanced buildings that showed their disciplined approach to life. Architects are artists who create buildings. But unlike other artists, they must sell their ideas before they are able to produce their buildings.

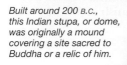

Built around 200 B.C., this Indian stupa, or dome, was originally a mound covering a site sacred to Buddha or a relic of him.

In 447 B.C., the Greek architects Ictinus and Callicrates designed the Parthenon, a temple to the goddess Athena, in Athens, Greece. With its graceful columns, it is a perfect example of classical architecture.

CLASSICAL ARCHITECTURE

The Ancient Greeks and Romans developed a style that we call classical architecture. Most Greek buildings consisted of columns supporting a triangular roof. The types of columns varied according to the particular classical "order" (style) that was used. Everything was simple and perfectly even. The Romans, who came after the Greeks, developed the arch, dome, and vault.

Elegantly curving skyward in several tiers, pagodas were built as shrines to Buddha. On the right is the pagoda of Yakushi-ji Temple, Japan. Each element in the building's design originally had a religious meaning.

Milan Cathedral in Italy (right) is an example of late Gothic architecture.

GOTHIC ARCHITECTURE

With their multitudes of pointed arches, finely carved stonework, and intricate windows, Gothic buildings are the opposite of simple classical ones. The Gothic style of architecture began in western Europe in the 12th century. It was used mainly in building cathedrals and churches. Although most Gothic buildings were huge, their thin walls, pointed arches, and large areas of stained-glass windows made them seem light and delicate.

Following the client's brief, the architect presents a drawing (below) to the client to show how the finished building will look.

FRANK LLOYD WRIGHT

American architect Frank Lloyd Wright (1869-1959) influenced many other architects. He tried to blend buildings into their natural surroundings and create a feeling of space, with few walls, so that rooms could "flow" into one another. At Bear Run, Pennsylvania, he built Falling Water, a house over a waterfall.

ARCHITECTS

If you wanted to build a house, you would approach an architect, giving clear and precise details of what you required (a brief). An architect must know from a client what the building is to be used for, how many people will use it, and how much money is available. A good architect will make sure that the new design fits in with existing buildings around it, and is built from suitable material. The architect then presents drawings and plans to the client. When the plans are approved, work on the building can begin.

     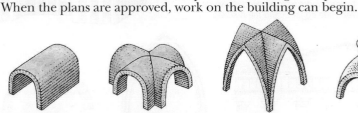 

| Doric column | Ionic column | Corinthian column | Barrel vault | Groin vault | Rib vault | Dome |

EXTRAORDINARY ARCHITECTURE

Some architects design weird and wonderful buildings which really stand out from the rest. A new town was built outside Paris, France, called Marne-la-Vallée. It has many extraordinary buildings, designed by various adventurous architects. The apartment complex, left, is like a monument that people can live in. Two circular buildings face each other across a central courtyard. It was designed by a Spanish architect named Manolo Nunez-Yanowsky.

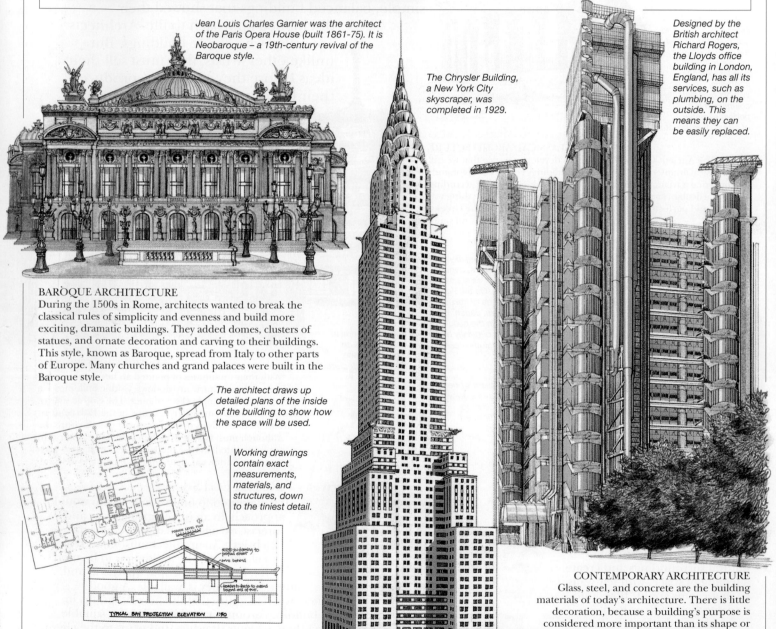

Jean Louis Charles Garnier was the architect of the Paris Opera House (built 1861-75). It is Neobaroque – a 19th-century revival of the Baroque style.

The Chrysler Building, a New York City skyscraper, was completed in 1929.

Designed by the British architect Richard Rogers, the Lloyds office building in London, England, has all its services, such as plumbing, on the outside. This means they can be easily replaced.

BAROQUE ARCHITECTURE

During the 1500s in Rome, architects wanted to break the classical rules of simplicity and evenness and build more exciting, dramatic buildings. They added domes, clusters of statues, and ornate decoration and carving to their buildings. This style, known as Baroque, spread from Italy to other parts of Europe. Many churches and grand palaces were built in the Baroque style.

The architect draws up detailed plans of the inside of the building to show how the space will be used.

Working drawings contain exact measurements, materials, and structures, down to the tiniest detail.

TYPICAL BAY PROJECTION ELEVATION 1:50

The builder works from working drawings (above) when constructing the building.

CONTEMPORARY ARCHITECTURE

Glass, steel, and concrete are the building materials of today's architecture. There is little decoration, because a building's purpose is considered more important than its shape or form. The "international" style – glass and concrete suspended on a steel framework – is seen almost everywhere in the world.

Pediment   Gothic arch   Romanesque arch   Cornice

Find out more

BUILDING
CHURCHES AND CATHEDRALS
CITIES
HOUSES
SCULPTURE

ARCTIC

THE SMALLEST OF THE world's oceans, the Arctic centers on the North Pole. Between the months of December and May, most of the Arctic Ocean is covered by polar sea ice, up to 98 ft (30 m) thick. The ocean is surrounded by the Arctic regions, where much of the ground is permanently frozen to depths of 1,500–2,000 ft (460–600 m). During the long, cold winters in the far north, much of the land is subject to periods of total darkness. This is because of the low angle of the Sun in relation to the ground. Beneath the rocks of the Arctic regions lie rich reserves of iron, nickel, copper, zinc, and oil. Severe weather conditions and very limited transportation mean that these reserves are still underexploited. Yet people such as the Inuit of Canada and Greenland have been known to live in these harsh conditions for at least 3,000 years.

The Arctic Ocean centers on the North Pole, the northern extremity of the Earth's axis. Three of the world's largest rivers, the Ob, Yenisey, and Lena, flow into the frozen waters of the Arctic Ocean. The Arctic regions consist of Alaska, Canada, Greenland, and northern Siberia.

Teams of hardy husky dogs were traditionally used to pull sleds across the frozen ground.

ICEBREAKING

Although half of the Arctic Ocean is covered by ice in winter, special ships called icebreakers can still sail through the ice. During particularly harsh winters, ice can become so dense in harbors and ports that it freezes right down to the seabed, marooning ships for months at a time. Icebreakers are designed to crush the ice with their steel hulls, opening up a lane that other ships can pass through. The Russian atomic-powered *Arcticka* is the world's most powerful icebreaker. It can cut through ice that is 7 ft (2.1 m) thick at 7 mph (11 km/h).

ARCTIC SETTLERS

The Arctic is one of the world's most sparsely populated regions. Today, some 120,000 Inuit (Eskimo) people live in Greenland, Alaska, and Canada. Over the past 3,000 years they have adapted to their icebound conditions, hunting with kayaks (canoes) and harpoons, and existing on a diet of caribou, seal, whale meat, and fish. They lived in houses made of frozen snow (igloos) or semi-underground stone pit-houses. Today, snowmobiles (above) have replaced sleds, and rifles are used for hunting.

COAL MINING
The Norwegian island of Spitsbergen, in the Arctic Ocean, has very extensive coal deposits. Its coal-mining towns are isolated and are desolate places. The sea route to mainland Norway, some 620 miles (1,000 km) away, is frozen for four months of the year. Many Inuit have moved to towns such as these to work in the coal mines.

POLAR BEARS
Between 25,000 and 40,000 polar bears roam the Arctic. Their white coats provide perfect camouflage, and a 4-in (10-cm) layer of body fat keeps them warm. Bears gorge on seals from April to July – they can survive for eight months without food. They can swim as far as 93 miles (150 km) in search of prey.

Find out more

GLACIERS AND ICE CAPS
INUITS
OCEANS AND SEAS
POLAR EXPLORATION
POLAR WILDLIFE

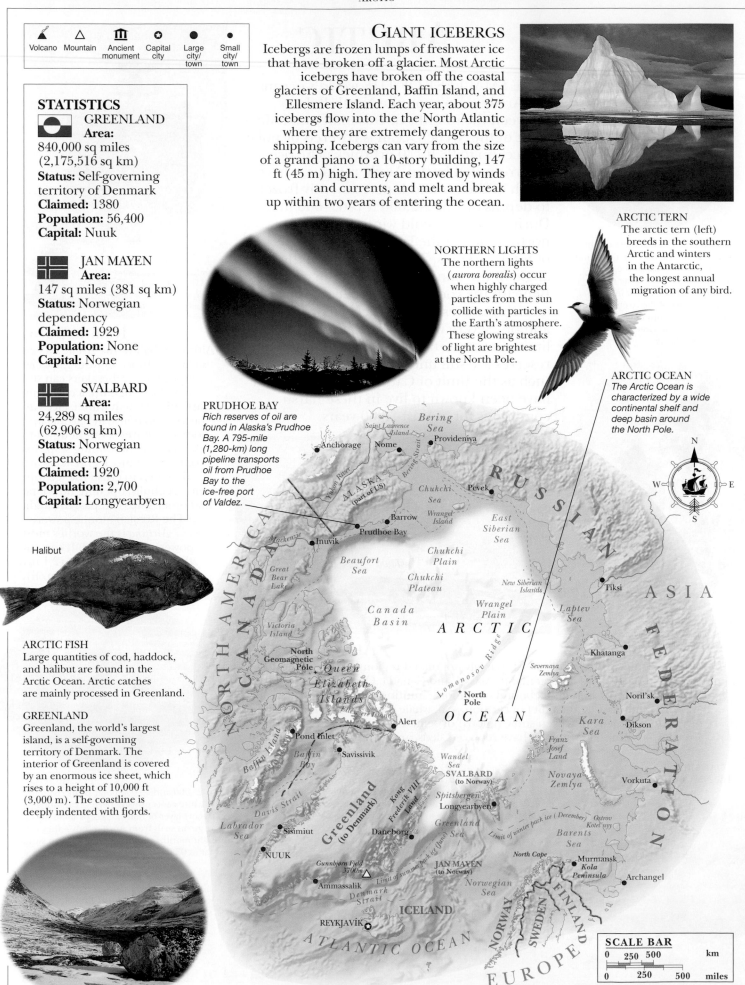

| Volcano | Mountain | Ancient monument | Capital city | Large city/ town | Small city/ town |

STATISTICS

GREENLAND
Area:
840,000 sq miles
(2,175,516 sq km)
Status: Self-governing
territory of Denmark
Claimed: 1380
Population: 56,400
Capital: Nuuk

JAN MAYEN
Area:
147 sq miles (381 sq km)
Status: Norwegian
dependency
Claimed: 1929
Population: None
Capital: None

SVALBARD
Area:
24,289 sq miles
(62,906 sq km)
Status: Norwegian
dependency
Claimed: 1920
Population: 2,700
Capital: Longyearbyen

Halibut

ARCTIC FISH
Large quantities of cod, haddock,
and halibut are found in the
Arctic Ocean. Arctic catches
are mainly processed in Greenland.

GREENLAND
Greenland, the world's largest
island, is a self-governing
territory of Denmark. The
interior of Greenland is covered
by an enormous ice sheet, which
rises to a height of 10,000 ft
(3,000 m). The coastline is
deeply indented with fjords.

GIANT ICEBERGS
Icebergs are frozen lumps of freshwater ice
that have broken off a glacier. Most Arctic
icebergs have broken off the coastal
glaciers of Greenland, Baffin Island, and
Ellesmere Island. Each year, about 375
icebergs flow into the the North Atlantic
where they are extremely dangerous to
shipping. Icebergs can vary from the size
of a grand piano to a 10-story building, 147
ft (45 m) high. They are moved by winds
and currents, and melt and break
up within two years of entering the ocean.

NORTHERN LIGHTS
The northern lights
(*aurora borealis*) occur
when highly charged
particles from the sun
collide with particles in
the Earth's atmosphere.
These glowing streaks
of light are brightest
at the North Pole.

ARCTIC TERN
The arctic tern (left)
breeds in the southern
Arctic and winters
in the Antarctic,
the longest annual
migration of any bird.

ARCTIC OCEAN
*The Arctic Ocean is
characterized by a wide
continental shelf and
deep basin around
the North Pole.*

PRUDHOE BAY
*Rich reserves of oil are
found in Alaska's Prudhoe
Bay. A 795-mile
(1,280-km) long
pipeline transports
oil from Prudhoe
Bay to the
ice-free port
of Valdez.*

ARGENTINA

ARGENTINA CONSISTS OF THREE MAIN REGIONS. In the north lies the hot, humid lands of the Gran Chaco. In the center, the temperate grasslands of the Pampas provide some of the world's best farming country. Argentina is a world leader in beef exports, and a major producer of wheat, corn, fruit, and vegetables. In the far south, the barren semidesert of Patagonia is rich in reserves of coal, petroleum, and natural gas. Argentina was settled by the Spanish in 1543. New European diseases, as well as conflict between the Spanish and Native Americans, considerably reduced Argentina's original population. In the 19th century, many immigrants from southern Europe, especially Spain and Italy, came to Argentina to work on farms and cattle ranches. Although Spanish is the official language today, many other languages are spoken, ranging from Welsh to Basque, reflecting the varied origins of Argentina's many settlers.

Argentina stretches for 2,150 miles (3,460 km) down the southeastern coast of South America. Its border in the west is defined by the Andes. To the south it straddles the Strait of Magellan.

GAUCHOS

These nomadic cowboys of the Argentine Pampas first appeared in the 18th century when they were hired to hunt escaped horses and cattle. Their standard equipment included a lasso, knife, and *bolas* (iron balls on leather straps, thrown at the legs of the escaping animals). In the 19th century, they were hired by ranch owners as skilled cattle herders. Today, Argentine cowboys keep their culture alive. They still wear the gaucho costume of a poncho (a woollen cape), high leather boots, and long, pleated trousers.

ARGENTINIAN WINE
European vines were introduced to Argentina by Spanish missionaries, and thrived in the temperate climate and fertile soils of the central regions. Argentina is the fourth-largest wine-producing country in the world – though much of the wine is for sale in Argentina only.

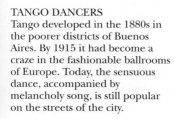

BUENOS AIRES

Argentina's capital, Buenos Aires, is one of the largest cities in South America. Situated on the Plate river estuary, it is also a major port and thriving industrial center. It was founded by Spanish settlers in 1580, and some historic buildings survive. The city expanded in the 19th century when European immigrants flooded to Argentina. Its museums, library, opera house, and cafés all give the city a European flavor.

A street performance (below) of a tango in Buenos Aires. The South American version of the tango developed from a blend of rhythms brought to South America by African slaves, and rhythms from Spain.

TANGO DANCERS
Tango developed in the 1880s in the poorer districts of Buenos Aires. By 1915 it had become a craze in the fashionable ballrooms of Europe. Today, the sensuous dance, accompanied by melancholy song, is still popular on the streets of the city.

ANDES

This wall of mountains forms a natural border between Argentina and its western neighbor, Chile. In 1881, the two countries signed a treaty defining this boundary. In western Argentina, the extinct volcano, Cerra Aconcagua, reaches a height of 22,816 ft (6,959 m). It is the highest peak in the South American Andes.

Find out more

COAL
DANCE
SOUTH AMERICA

BOLIVIA
PARAGUAY
BRAZIL
URUGUAY
ARGENTINA

| Volcano | Mountain | Ancient monument | Capital city | Large city/town | Small city/town |

STATISTICS
Area: 1,068,296 sq miles (2,766,890 sq km)
Population: 38,400,000
Capital: Buenos Aires
Languages: Spanish, Italian, Amerindian languages
Religions: Roman Catholic, Jewish, Protestant
Currency: Argentine peso
Main occupation: Agriculture
Main exports: Beef, wheat, fruit, wine
Main imports: Designer clothing

TIERRA DEL FUEGO
This string of islands is separated from the South American mainland by the Strait of Magellan. They are divided between Argentina and Chile. The landscape, with its mountains, frozen lakes, and glaciers, is bleak and windswept. It is also barren – only stunted trees and mosses grow there. Herds of sheep graze the land. Oil has been discovered in this remote area.

FALKLAND ISLANDS
Discovered by the British in 1592, the Falkland Islands are a self-governing British colony, some 300 miles (480 km) off the coast of Argentina. The cool, windy islands are only suitable for grazing sheep, and meat and wool are their main resource. In 1982, Argentina, claimed the Falklands as their territory. They surrendered after 10 weeks, but British troops still protect the islands.

FALKLAND ISLANDS (to UK)
West Falkland
East Falkland

Atacama Desert
Tropic of Capricorn
Gran Chaco
Pilcomayo
Bermejo
San Salvador de Jujuy
Salta
San Miguel de Tucumán
Formosa
Santiago del Estero
Resistencia
Paraná
Corrientes
Posadas
Cerro Ojos del Salado 6880m
La Rioja
Salado
Laguna Mar Chiquita
San Juan
Santa Fe
Córdoba
Paraná
Concordia
Mendoza
Rosario
Cerro Aconcagua 6959m
Godoy Cruz
Río Cuarto
Gualeguaychú
Salado
San Rafael
Junín
BUENOS AIRES
Pampas
La Plata
River Plate
Santa Rosa
Olavarría
Azul
Dolores
ARGENTINA
Tres Arroyos
Mar del Plata
Zapala
Colorado
Bahía Blanca
Necochea
Neuquén
Bahía Blanca
San Antonio Oeste
Río Negro
Viedma
Lago Nahuel Huapi
Gulf of San Matías
San Carlos de Bariloche
Península Valdés
Esquel
Chubut
Rawson
Chico
Sarmiento
Comodoro Rivadavia
Perito Moreno
Gulf of San Jorge
Caleta Olivia
Deseado
Golfo de Penas
Puerto Deseado
Patagonia
Chico
Santa Cruz
El Calafate
Bahía Grande
Río Gallegos
Strait of Magellan
Río Grande
Tierra del Fuego
Isla de los Estados
Cape Horn
Drake Passage

PACIFIC OCEAN
ATLANTIC OCEAN
Andes
Chile

SCALE BAR
0   200   400   km
0   200   400   miles

ARMIES

EVER SINCE THE ASSYRIAN armies swept across the ancient region of Mesopotamia more than 3,000 years ago, the purpose of armies has been the same: to conquer enemy territory and to defend their country. In Europe, there were no modern-style armies until the 16th century; instead, sections of the population were called to arms whenever the country was at war. Today, however, most nations have a full-time army consisting of highly trained soldiers. Armies vary in size, but most modern armies contain not only personnel but also the latest technology, including helicopters, guided missiles, and tanks. Technology has changed the role of the army. Previously soldiers engaged in hand-to-hand combat; today most armies rely on long-range weaponry.

Pouches on webbing, or harness, hold small equipment.

Mask protects against gas attack.

RECRUITMENT
In 1917, Uncle Sam, symbol of the United States, called on young men to enlist, or volunteer for fighting, in World War I. Some countries recruit volunteers during peacetime but have conscription – compulsory military service – during wartime.

Helmet with protective padding

Mess kit for cooking and eating

TRAINING
Soldiers, such as these Israeli women, are fighters trained for combat on land. In the army men and women learn the techniques of fighting and how to care for their weapons, and they exercise to become fit. They also learn confidence, discipline, and the importance of obeying orders so that they will fight well.

Uniform fabric is colored to look like foliage, so that soldiers are hard to see in battle.

Heavy boots for marching

UNIFORM
A soldier's fighting uniform must be practical. Strong, heavy clothes and boots provide protection against weather. Uniforms are also designed to provide camouflage so that the soldier can hide from the enemy.

Australia

China

United Kingdom

United States

UNIFORMS OF THE WORLD
Soldiers of each country wear identifying uniforms which may be different for war and peace times. Badges or stripes show the rank of the soldier and the unit he or she belongs to.

Find out more
GUNS
NAPOLEONIC WARS
ROCKETS AND MISSILES
VIETNAM WAR
WEAPONS
WORLD WAR I
WORLD WAR II

GUERRILLA ARMIES
In 1808, France invaded and defeated Spain. But Spanish farmers did not give in. They formed small groups and continued the war. They made surprise attacks on French patrols and supply depots. The Spanish called the campaign *guerrilla*, meaning "little war"; this term is still used today to describe similar methods of fighting wars.

Modern guerrillas, such as these in Africa, usually belong to a group of people fighting for religious, national, or political beliefs.

ARMOR

ANCIENT WARRIORS quickly realized that they would survive in battle if they could protect themselves against their enemies. So they made armor – special clothing that was tough enough to stop weapons from injuring the wearer. Prehistoric armor was simple. It was made of leather but was strong enough to provide protection against crude spears and swords. As weapons became sharper, armor too had to improve. A thousand years ago the Roman Empire employed many armorers who made excellent metal armor. But after the fall of Rome in the 5th century, blacksmiths began to make armor and its quality fell. In the 14th century, specially trained armorers invented plate armor to withstand lances, arrows, and swords. But even the thickest armor cannot stop a bullet, so armor became less useful when guns were invented. Today no one uses traditional armor, but people in combat still wear protective clothing made out of modern plastics and tough metals.

ANIMAL ARMOR
Soldiers have used animals in warfare, such as dogs for attack and horses for riding into battle. Armor protected these animals when they fought. The most elaborate animal armor was the elephant armor of 17th-century India.

Arrows bounced off the curves of the helmet. Knights often wore mail or padding beneath the helmet.

The breastplate was flared so that enemy sword strokes bounced off.

The vambrace was a cylindrical piece to protect the upper arm.

The cowter protected the elbow, but allowed it to move freely.

The gauntlet was made up of many small pieces so that the hand could move freely.

The cuisse protected only the front of the leg.

Poleyns had to bend easily when the knight rode a horse.

Greaves were among the earliest pieces of body armor to be made of sheet metal.

HELMETS
A single heavy blow to the head can kill a person, so helmets, or armored hats, were among the first pieces of armor to be made. They are still widely used today. Different shapes gave protection against different types of weapon.

Bronze Age helmets protected against swords more than 3,000 years ago.

Pikemen of the 16th century

Twelfth-century helm

Modern helmets give protection against shrapnel (metal fragments from bombs).

BULLETPROOF VEST
Modern police and security forces sometimes wear bulletproof vests to protect themselves from attack by criminals and terrorists. The vests are made of many layers of tough materials such as nylon and are capable of stopping a bullet.

CHAIN MAIL
Chain mail was easier and cheaper for a blacksmith to make than a complicated suit of plate armor. Mail was very common between the 6th and 13th centuries. It was made of a large number of interlocking rings of steel. It allowed the wearer to move easily, but did not give good protection against heavy swords and axes.

SUIT OF ARMOR
Late 15th-century armor provided a knight with a protective metal shell. The armor was very strong, and cleverly jointed so that the knight could move easily. However, the metal suit weighed up to 70 lb (30 kg), so that running, for example, was virtually impossible.

Find out more
JAPAN, HISTORY OF
KNIGHTS AND HERALDRY
MEDIEVAL EUROPE
ROMAN EMPIRE
WEAPONS

ASIA

THE LARGEST OF THE SEVEN CONTINENTS, Asia occupies one-third of the world's total land area. Much of the continent is uninhabited. The inhospitable north is a cold land of tundra. Parched deserts and towering mountains take up large areas of the central region. Yet Asia is the home of well over half of the world's population, most of whom live around the outer rim. China alone has more than 1.3 billion people, and India has more than one billion. Altogether, Asia contains 48 nations, and many times this number of peoples, languages, and cultures. It has five main zones. In the north is the Russian Federation. Part of this is in Europe, but the vast eastern region, from the Ural Mountains to the Pacific Ocean, is in Asia. The Pacific coast, which includes China, Korea, and Japan, is known as East Asia. To the south of this lie the warmer, more humid countries of Southeast Asia. India and Pakistan are the principal countries of the Indian Subcontinent in south Asia. One of the world's first civilizations began here, in the Indus Valley.

The Ural Mountains form the border between the continents of Asia and Europe. Asia is separated from Africa by the Red Sea. The Bering Strait, only 55 miles (88 km) wide, marks the gap between Asia and North America. Australia lies to the southeast.

Bordered by the Mediterranean and Arabian seas, the Middle East lies to the west where Europe, Asia, and Africa meet.

MIDDLE EAST

The hot, dry lands of the Middle East occupy the southwestern corner of Asia. Almost the entire Arabian Peninsula, between the Red Sea and the Persian Gulf, is desert. To the north, in Iraq and Syria, lie the fertile valleys of the Tigris and Euphrates rivers. Most of the people of the Middle East are Arabs, and speak Arabic.

The Arabs of the Middle East drank coffee long before it reached other countries.

Siberian scientists looking for minerals in North Asia have to work in subzero temperatures, and the cold can freeze their breath.

SIBERIA

The northern coast of Asia is fringed by the Arctic Ocean. The sea here is frozen for most of the year. A layer of the land, called permafrost, is also always frozen. This area is part of the vast region of the Russian Federation called Siberia. Despite the cold, Russian people live and work in Siberia because the region is rich in timber, coal, oil, and natural gas.

TRADE ROUTES

As long as 2,000 years ago, there was trade between East Asia and Europe. Traders carried silk, spices, gems, and pottery. They followed overland routes across India and Pakistan, past the Karakoram Mountains (above). These trade routes were known as the Silk Road; they are still used today.

TROPICAL RAIN FORESTS

The warm, damp climate of much of Southeast Asia provides the perfect conditions for tropical rain forests, which thrive in countries such as Myanmar (Burma) and Malaysia. The forests are the habitat for a huge variety of wildlife, and are home to tribes of people whose way of life has not changed for centuries. But because many of the forest trees are beautiful hardwoods, the logging industry is now cutting down the forests at an alarming rate to harvest the valuable timber.

Sunlight breaks through the dense foliage of the rain forest only where rivers have cut trails through the trees.

PROSPERITY

Some Asian countries, such as Japan and Singapore, are among the world's most prosperous nations. The discovery of oil in a number of other countries, such as Saudi Arabia in the Middle East and Brunei in Southeast Asia, has made them very wealthy.

Brunei's vast oil wealth has enabled the sultan (ruler) to build a magnificent new palace. It is called Istana Nurul Iman, and is only open to the public at the end of the Islamic fasting month of Ramadan.

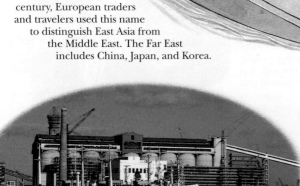

"Floating markets" are a common sight on the busy waterways of East Asia.

Vanilla vines grow well in the warm climate of Indonesia, and women harvest the pods by hand.

FAR EAST

East Asia is often called the Far East. In the 19th century, European traders and travelers used this name to distinguish East Asia from the Middle East. The Far East includes China, Japan, and Korea.

KOREA

The Korean peninsula juts out from northern China towards Japan. The two Korean nations were at war between 1950 and 1953. They have lived in constant mistrust of each other since the war ended, but are now trying to mend the divisions between them. South Korea has a booming economy and is heavily supported by the United States. North Korea is Communist and poorer. The climate favors rice growing, with warm summers and icy winters.

Construction work is a common sight in South Korea, as new offices and factories are built for the country's expanding industries.

SOUTHEAST ASIA

Many different people live in the warm, tropical southeastern corner of Asia. There are ten independent countries in the region. Some of them – Myanmar (Burma), Laos, Thailand, Cambodia (Kampuchea), and Vietnam – are on the mainland attached to the rest of Asia. Further south lie Brunei, Malaysia, and the tiny island nation of Singapore. Indonesia stretches across the foot of the region. It is a scattered nation of more than 13,500 islands. The islands of the Philippines are to the east. Although some of these countries are very poor, Southeast Asia as a whole has one of the most rapidly developing economies in the world.

Hundreds of different languages are spoken in the Indian subcontinent, but Indian schools teach pupils to read and write Hindi, which is the country's official language.

INDIAN SUBCONTINENT

The triangular landmass of south Asia extends south from the Himalaya Mountains to the warm waters of the Indian Ocean. This region is also known as the Indian Subcontinent. It includes not only India but also Pakistan, Nepal, Bangladesh, and Bhutan. At the very southern tip of India lies the island nation of Sri Lanka.

The port of Shanghai lies at the mouth of the Yangtze river.

YANGTZE RIVER

The Yangtze (or Chang Jiang), the world's third-longest river, flows 3,964 miles (6,380 km) through the middle of China, from its source in Tibet to the sea at Shanghai. In 1997, the first stage was completed on the Three Gorges Dam, China's largest construction project since the building of the Great Wall.

Find out more

CHINA
INDIA
JAPAN
RELIGIONS
RUSSIAN FEDERATION
SOUTHEAST ASIA

ASIA

Asia is the world's largest continent. It is a region of contrasts in its landscape, and peoples. The break up of the Soviet Union produced five new central Asian republics. The countries in the south are mainly Muslim, but are divided by religious differences and conflicts.

 AFGHANISTAN
Area: 251,770 sq miles (652,090 sq km)
Population: 23,900,000
Capital: Kãbul

 ARMENIA
Area: 11 506 sq miles (29,800 sq km)
Population: 3,100,000
Capital: Yerevan

 AZERBAIJAN
Area: 33,436 sq miles (86,600 sq km)
Population: 8,400,000
Capital: Baku

 BAHRAIN
Area: 263 sq miles (680 sq km)
Population: 724,000
Capital: Manama

 BANGLADESH
Area: 55,598 sq miles (143,998 sq km)
Population: 147,000,000
Capital: Dhaka

 BHUTAN
Area: 18,147 sq miles (47,000 sq km)
Population: 2,300,000
Capital: Thimphu

 BRUNEI
Area: 2,228 sq miles (5,770 sq km)
Population: 358,000
Capital: Bandar Seri Begawan

 BURMA
Area: 261,200 sq miles (676,550 sq km)
Population: 49,500,000
Capital: Rangoon

 CAMBODIA
Area: 69,000 sq miles (181,040 sq km)
Population: 14,100,000
Capital: Phnom Penh

 CHINA
Area: 3,628,166 sq miles (9,396,960 sq km)
Population: 1,300,000,000
Capital: Beijing

 CYPRUS
Area: 3,572 sq miles (9,251 sq km)
Population: 802,000
Capital: Nicosia

 EAST TIMOR
Area: 5,794 sq miles (15,007 sq km)
Population: 778,000
Capital: Dili

 GEORGIA
Area: 26,911 sq miles (69,700 sq km)
Population: 5,100,000
Capital: Tbilisi

 INDIA
Area: 1,269,338 sq miles (3,287,590 sq km)
Population: 1,070,000,000
Capital: New Delhi

 INDONESIA
Area: 735,555 sq miles (1,904,570 sq km)
Population: 220,000,000
Capital: Jakarta

 IRAN
Area: 636,293 sq miles (1,648,000 sq km)
Population: 68,900,000
Capital: Tehran

 IRAQ
Area: 169,235 sq miles (438,320 sq km)
Population: 25,200,000
Capital: Baghdad

 ISRAEL
Area: 7,992 sq miles (20,700 sq km)
Population: 6,400,000
Capital: Jerusalem

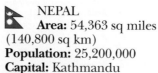 **JAPAN**
Area: 145,869 sq miles (377,800 sq km)
Population: 128,000,000
Capital: Tokyo

 JORDAN
Area: 34,440 sq miles (89,210 sq km)
Population: 5,500,000
Capital: Amman

 KAZAKHSTAN
Area: 1,049,150 sq miles (2,717,300 sq km)
Population: 15,400,000
Capital: Astana

 NORTH KOREA
Area: 46,540 sq miles (120,540 sq km)
Population: 22,700,000
Capital: Pyongyang

 SOUTH KOREA
Area: 38,232 sq miles (99,020 sq km)
Population: 47,700,000
Capital: Seoul

 KUWAIT
Area: 6,880 sq miles (17,820 sq km)
Population: 2,500,000
Capital: Kuwait City

 KYRGYZSTAN
Area: 76,640 sq miles (198,500 sq km)
Population: 5,100,000
Capital: Bishkek

 LAOS
Area: 91,428 sq miles (236,800 sq km)
Population: 5,700,000
Capital: Vientiane

 LEBANON
Area: 4,015 sq miles (10,400 sq km)
Population: 3,700,000
Capital: Beirut

 MALAYSIA
Area: 127,317 sq miles (329,750 sq km)
Population: 24,400,000
Capital: Kuala Lumpur

MALDIVES
Area: 116 sq miles (300 sq km)
Population: 318,000
Capital: Male'

MONGOLIA
Area: 604,247 sq miles (1,565,000 sq km)
Population: 2,600,000
Capital: Ulan Bator

NEPAL
Area: 54,363 sq miles (140,800 sq km)
Population: 25,200,000
Capital: Kathmandu

OMAN
Area: 82,030 sq miles (212,460 sq km)
Population: 2,900,000
Capital: Muscat

PAKISTAN
Area: 307,374 sq miles (796,100 sq km)
Population: 154,000,000
Capital: Islamabad

PHILIPPINES
Area: 115,831 sq miles (300,000 sq km)
Population: 80,000,000
Capital: Manila

QATAR
Area: 4,247 sq miles (11,000 sq km)
Population: 610,000
Capital: Doha

RUSSIAN FED.
Area: 6,592,800 sq miles (17,075,400 sq km)
Population: 143,000,000
Capital: Moscow

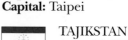 **SINGAPORE**
Area: 239 sq miles (620 sq km)
Population: 4,300,000
Capital: Singapore City

 **SRI LANKA**
Area: 25,332 sq miles (65,610 sq km)
Population: 19,100,000
Capital: Colombo

SYRIA
Area: 71,500 sq miles (185,180 sq km)
Population: 17,800,000
Capital: Damascus

TAIWAN
Area: 13,969 sq miles (36,179 sq km)
Population: 22,600,000
Capital: Taipei

TAJIKSTAN
Area: 55,251 sq miles (143,100 sq km)
Population: 6,200,000
Capital: Dushanbe

THAILAND
Area: 198,116 sq miles (513,120 sq km)
Population: 62,800,000
Capital: Bangkok

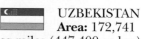 **TURKEY**
Area: 300,950 sq miles (779,450 sq km)
Population: 71,300,000
Capital: Ankara

TURKMENISTAN
Area: 188,455 sq miles (488,100 sq km)
Population: 4,900,000
Capital: Ashgabat

U. A. E.
Area: 32,278 sq miles (83,600 sq km)
Population: 3,000,000
Capital: Abu Dhabi

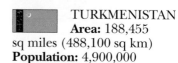 **UZBEKISTAN**
Area: 172,741 sq miles (447,400 sq km)
Population: 26,100,000
Capital: Tashkent

VIETNAM
Area: 127,243 sq miles (329,560 sq km)
Population: 81,400,000
Capital: Hanoi

YEMEN
Area: 203,849 sq miles (527,970 sq km)
Population: 20,000,000
Capital: Sana

Volcano Mountain Ancient monument Capital city Large city/town Small city/town

STATISTICS
Area: 17,940,146 sq miles (46,366,908 sq km)
Population: 3,954,612,000
Highest point: Mount Everest (Nepal) 29,029 ft (8,848 m)
Longest river: Yangtze (China) 3,964 miles (6,380 km)
Largest lake: Caspian Sea 143,205 sq miles (371,000 sq km)

SCALE BAR

0   500   1000   km

0   500   1000   miles

MOUNT EVEREST
The Himalayan mountain range runs along the China-Nepal border southeast from the Pamir mountains. It is a group of rugged peaks and valleys, sometimes described as the "roof of the world." The highest point in the Himalayas is Mount Everest (right) – the world's highest mountain.

URAL MOUNTAINS
The Ural Mountains form a natural border between Asia and Europe.

KURILE ISLANDS
The Kurile Islands are part of the Russian Federation, but Japan claims the southernmost islands in this chain as part of its own territory.

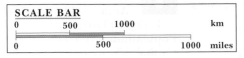

Map labels

ARCTIC OCEAN
PACIFIC OCEAN
INDIAN OCEAN
EUROPE
AFRICA
AUSTRALIA

Bering Sea
East Siberian Sea
Laptev Sea
Kara Sea
Central Siberian Plateau
Lena
Kolyma Range
Kamchatka
Sea of Okhotsk
Kurile Islands
Sakhalin
West Siberian Plain
Ob'
Irtysh
Angara
Lake Baikal
Amur
RUSSIAN FEDERATION
Mediterranean Sea
Black Sea
Lchashen
ANKARA
TURKEY
GEORGIA
TBILISI
ARMENIA
YEREVAN
AZERB.
BAKU
ASTANA
KAZAKHSTAN
Syr Darya
Aral Sea
Lake Balkhash
Altai Mountains
MONGOLIA
Gobi
ULAN BATOR
Inner Mongolia
Sea of Japan (East Sea)
JAPAN
TOKYO
NORTH KOREA
PYONGYANG
SOUTH KOREA
SEOUL
BEIJING
Yellow Sea
Honshu
CYPRUS
NICOSIA
LEBANON
BEIRUT
SYRIA
DAMASCUS
ISRAEL
JERUSALEM
AMMAN
JORDAN
IRAQ
BAGHDAD
Ur
KUWAIT
UZBEKISTAN
TASHKENT
BISHKEK
KYRGYZSTAN
TURKMENISTAN
ASGABAT
Amu Darya
DUSHANBE
TAJIKISTAN
Tarim He
Tien Shan
Tarim He
Tarim
Tianshan Mountains
Yellow River
Huang He
Anyang
CHINA
TAIPEI
TAIWAN
East China Sea
Ryukyu Islands
Caspian Sea
TEHRAN
IRAN
Elburz Mountains
Persian Gulf
AFGHANISTAN
KABUL
ISLAMABAD
Plateau of Tibet
Kunlun Mountains
Mekong
Salween
Xi Jiang
Yangtze
SAUDI ARABIA
RIYADH
MANAMA
BAHRAIN
DOHA
QATAR
ABU DHABI
U.A.E.
PAKISTAN
NEW DELHI
NEPAL
THIMPHU
KATHMANDU
Mount Everest 8850m
BHUTAN
Himalayas
Brahmaputra
DHAKA
BANGLADESH
MYANMAR
Irrawaddy
Salween
HANOI
Hainan Dao
Luzon
MANILA
Gulf of Oman
MUSCAT
OMAN
Arabian Peninsula
JEDDA
Red Sea
SANA
YEMEN
Gulf of Aden
Socotra (to Yemen)
Arabian Sea
Narmada
Godavari
Krishna
INDIA
Bay of Bengal
Andaman Islands (to India)
Nicobar Islands (to India)
SRI LANKA
COLOMBO
Ganges
RANGOON
LAOS
VIENTIANE
VIETNAM
THAILAND
BANGKOK
CAMBODIA
PHNOM PENH
Andaman Sea
Gulf of Thailand
South China Sea
PHILIPPINES
Mindanao
Philippine Sea
BANDAR SERI BEGAWAN
BRUNEI
MALAYSIA
KUALA LUMPUR
PUTRAJAYA
SINGAPORE
Sumatra
Borneo
Celebes
Moluccas
New Guinea
Papua (Irian Jaya)
INDONESIA
Equator
Java Sea
JAKARTA
Java
Flores Sea
Flores
EAST TIMOR
DILI
Timor
Timor Sea
Tropic of Cancer
Tropic of Cancer
Equator

N
W E
S

SEOUL
Modern office buildings crowd together in Seoul, the capital city of South Korea, but a few ancient buildings still survive. The South Gate (below) was built at the end of the 14th century as part of a wall that once surrounded the city. Today, Seoul is spreading far beyond its original boundaries as rapid industrial growth creates a need for more offices, factories, and homes.

EAST TIMOR
In 1975 Indonesia invaded the Portuguese colony of East Timor, the eastern part of the island of Timor. The following year the region was made a province of Indonesia. In a UN-monitored referendum in 1999, voters rejected Indonesian rule and in 2002 East Timor became an independent state.

JAVA
Rice terraces (right) provide the staple food for Indonesia. These fields are on the island of Java, which has only seven percent of Indonesia's land area but is the home of some 60 per cent of the country's people.

HISTORY OF
ASIA

THE VAST CONTINENT OF ASIA is home to the oldest civilizations and religions in the world. Because Asia contains many virtually impassable deserts and mountain ranges, individual countries developed separately from each other. However, links between these countries sprang up as merchants traveled along the Silk Road, Indian kings invaded neighboring countries, Buddhist monks crossed the Himalayas, and Arab traders sailed across the Indian Ocean. As a result, the great Hindu, Buddhist, and Islamic religions spread across the continent. For much of the last 500 years, Europe controlled large parts of Asia, but since 1945 Asian countries have gained their independence. Many of them are now world-class economies.

EARLY CIVILIZATIONS

Asia's extreme land forms, such as the towering peaks of the Himalayas which separate India from China, meant that early Asian cultures had little contact with each other, or with the rest of the world. As a result, the first great Asian civilizations, such as the Indus Valley Civilization in the Indian subcontinent and the Shang Dynasty in China, developed very different and distinct cultures.

Bactrian (two-humped) camel pottery made in China.

HINDUISM

Hinduism began in the ancient civilizations of the Indus Valley, in India, around 2500 B.C. Over the centuries, the religion spread across India to Sri Lanka and the islands of Southeast Asia. Hinduism is the oldest religion in the world still practiced today, and provides a thread linking together all of India's history.

ARAB TRADERS

Arab merchants were great travelers and adventurers, crossing deserts and oceans in search of new markets in which to buy and sell their goods. On their journeys, they converted local people to their Islamic religion, founded by Muhammad in Arabia in the early 600s. As a result, Islam spread across Asia as far as the southeastern islands.

SILK ROAD

The Silk Road was an important trading route that stretched across Asia from Loyang, China's capital, in the east to the Mediterranean Sea in the west. It was called the Silk Road because of the Chinese silk that was traded along its length. The road was not continuous, but was made up of a series of well-marked routes connecting major towns. Here merchants bought and sold their goods, creating a link between Asia and Europe.

Buddhist monks shave their heads and wear saffron-colored robes.

BUDDHIST MONKS

Siddhartha Gautama, the founder of Buddhism, was born in India c. 563 B.C. By his death c. 483 B.C., his teaching had spread throughout India. From about A.D. 100, Buddhist monks took Buddhism across the Himalayas to China, and along the Silk Road into Central Asia. Today, most of the world's Buddhists live in Asia.

MONGOLS

The Mongols were fierce warriors who lived as nomads on the steppes, or grasslands, of Central Asia. In the 1200s they created an empire that stretched from China into eastern Europe. Their power declined in the 1300s, but in 1369 one of their leaders, Tamerlane the Great, became ruler of Central Asia. He built many fine mosques in his capital, Samarkand.

EUROPEAN DOMINATION

In 1498, Portuguese explorer Vasco da Gama sailed to India around the southern tip of Africa. He was the first European to reach Asia by sea. Other Europeans followed, and over the next 400 years, Europeans dominated much of Asia, first as traders and merchants, then as conquerors and colonizers. Only Persia (present-day Iran), Afghanistan, Thailand, and Japan remained free from European control.

Portuguese colonial house in Macau

WORLD WAR II

During World War II (1939-45), the Japanese invaded China and much of Southeast Asia in order to create an empire. Some welcomed the Japanese invaders, because the Japanese threw out the European colonial masters and sometimes gave the people a greater degree of independence. After Japan's defeat in 1945, Britain, France, the Netherlands, and the US returned to take control of their former colonies.

COMMUNIST ASIA

In 1949, the Communist Party finally gained power in China after years of civil war. Communists also took control in North Korea, Mongolia, North Vietnam, Cambodia, and Laos. The Communist governments hoped to improve people's living standards, but failed to match the economic success of Japan and other Asian countries.

The Red Guard, followers of Chinese Communist leader Mao Zedong

Chinese students bearing a portrait of Mao Zedong (1893-1976)

Chinese demonstrate their revolutionary fervor in 1967

ASIA

c. 2,500 B.C. Hinduism is founded in India.

c. 563-c. 483 B.C. Life of Buddha.

500s B.C. The Silk Road is established.

250 B.C. Buddhism spreads to Sri Lanka and Southeast Asia.

A.D. 100 Monks take Buddhism to China and into Central Asia.

850-1200 Chola kings of India take Hinduism to Sri Lanka and into Southeast Asia.

1279 Mongol Empire under Kublai Khan reaches greatest extent.

1369 Tamerlane the Great creates a new Mongol Empire in the city of Samarkand.

1498 Vasco da Gama sails to India.

1600 British merchants establish an East India Company in order to trade with India.

1619 Dutch begin to control the East Indies.

1757 British take over Bengal and expand their rule in India.

1850s French begin to control Southeast Asia.

1937 Japanese troops invade China.

1941-45 World War II rages in eastern Asia and the Pacific.

1947-48 British rule in India comes to an end.

1949 Indonesia becomes independent.

1999 Portuguese hand Macau back to China.

INDEPENDENCE

Following World War II, the European countries began to grant their Asian colonies independence. India became independent from Britain in 1947-48, and Indonesia gained its independence from the Netherlands in 1949. The last colony – the Portuguese territory of Macau – was handed back to China in 1999.

TIGER ECONOMIES

Japan and other countries began rebuilding their economies after World War II. They concentrated on heavy industries such as car manufacturing and shipbuilding, and on hi-tech industries such as computers and electronics. Today Japan is the world's second-biggest economy, while Taiwan, South Korea, Singapore, and others have become industrial powerhouses.

Find out more

CHINA, HISTORY OF
INDIA, HISTORY OF
JAPAN, HISTORY OF
SOUTHEAST ASIA, history of
WORLD WAR II

ASSYRIANS

ABOUT 3,000 YEARS AGO, a mighty empire rose to power in the Middle East where Iraq is today. This was the Assyrian Empire. It lasted for more than 300 years and spread all over the surrounding area from the Nile River to Mesopotamia. Under King Shalmaneser I (1273-44 B.C.) the Assyrians conquered Babylon and many other independent states, and eventually united the region into one empire. With an enormous army, armored horses, fast two-wheeled chariots, and huge battering rams, the Assyrians were highly skilled, successful fighters, ruthless in battle. The Assyrian Empire grew quickly with a series of warlike kings, including Ashurbanipal II and Sennacherib. Great wealth and excellent trading links enabled the Assyrians to rebuild the cities of Nimrud and Nineveh (which became the capital), and to create a new city at Khorsabad. Assyria was a rich, well-organized society, but by the 7th century B.C. the empire had grown too large to protect itself well. Around 612 B.C., the Babylonian and Mede peoples destroyed Nineveh, and the Assyrian Empire collapsed.

WARRIORS
The Assyrians were famed and feared for their strength in battle and for torturing their victims. They developed the chariot and fought with swords, shields, slings, and bows.

Men armed with spears and swords accompanied the king on lion hunts.

ASSYRIAN EMPIRE
In the 7th century B.C., the Assyrian Empire reached its greatest extent. It stretched down to the Persian Gulf in the south and the Mediterranean coast in the west, and included Babylon.

LION HUNT
Hunting and killing lions was a favorite pastime of the Assyrian kings. Lions represented the wild strength of nature. It was considered a noble challenge to seek them out and kill them, although captive lions were also hunted. Only the king was allowed to kill a lion.

ROYAL LIFE
Stone reliefs tell us much about the lives of the Assyrian royalty. This relief sculpture shows King Ashurbanipal II (668-33 B.C.) drinking wine in his garden with his queen. It looks like a quiet, domestic scene; but on another section of this sculpture there is a head hanging from a tree. It is the head of Teumann, the king of the Elamites, whose defeat the king and queen are celebrating.

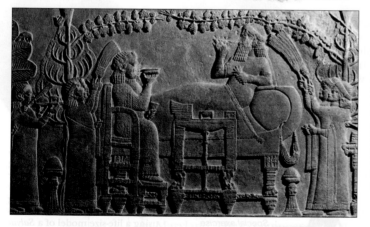

WINGED BULLS
Massive stone sculptures (right) of winged bulls were placed on each side of important doors and gateways.

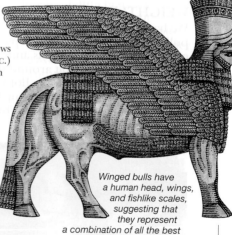

Winged bulls have a human head, wings, and fishlike scales, suggesting that they represent a combination of all the best qualities of animals and people.

Assyrian slaves had to drag the massive sculptures to the palace.

Find out more
BABYLONIANS
MIDDLE EAST

EXPLORING THE UNIVERSE

Stars and other objects in the universe produce streams of tiny particles and many kinds of waves, such as radio waves. Except for light, these waves and particles are all invisible, but astronomers can study them to provide information about the universe. The atmosphere blocks many of the rays, so detectors are mounted on satellites that orbit above the Earth's atmosphere.

INFRARED RAYS

Objects in space can also send out infrared (heat) rays. Satellites and ground-based telescopes pick up these rays. They can reveal the centers of galaxies, and gas clouds called nebulae (right), where stars are forming.

X RAYS

Special satellites carry detectors that pick up X rays. These satellites have discovered black holes, which give out X rays as they suck in gases from nearby stars. This is an X ray image of a supernova, which is an exploding star.

ULTRAVIOLET RAYS

Astronomers can learn about the substances in stars by analyzing ultraviolet (short wavelength) rays that come from them. A computer-generated picture produced by detecting ultraviolet rays (left) gives the composition and speed of gases that circle around in the outer atmosphere of a star.

GAMMA RAYS

Some satellites detect gamma rays, which are waves of very high energy. Gamma rays come from many objects, including pulsars, which are the remains of exploded stars. This is a gamma ray map of our own galaxy.

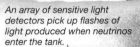

VISIBLE LIGHT

Telescopes on the ground and on satellites detect the light rays that come from planets, comets, stars, and galaxies. Earth's atmosphere distorts light rays, making pictures slightly fuzzy. However, new computer-controlled telescopes are able to reduce this distortion.

Radio image of a quasar. A quasar is a kind of powerful galaxy with a very bright center.

A supernova remnant as seen through an optical telescope.

RADAR SIGNALS

Astronomers produce radar maps of planets and moons by bouncing radio waves off their surfaces. The radar map of Venus (left) was recorded by the *Pioneer Venus* spacecraft of the United States. The map is color-coded to represent plains and mountains on the planet's surface.

RADIO WAVES

Many bodies produce their own radio waves, which are picked up by the large dishes of radio telescopes. Objects called pulsars, quasars, and radio galaxies were discovered in this way.

SKYWATCHERS OF THE PAST

In the third century B.C., the Greek scientist Aristarchus suggested that the Earth and planets move around the Sun. The telescope, first used to observe the heavens by Italian scientist Galileo, proved this to be true and led to many other discoveries. In the 1920s, the astronomer Edwin Hubble found that stars exist in huge groups called galaxies and that the universe is expanding in size.

The ancient observatory at Jaipur, India, contains stone structures that astronomers built to measure the positions of the Sun, Moon, planets, and stars.

An array of sensitive light detectors pick up flashes of light produced when neutrinos enter the tank.

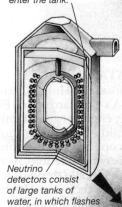

Neutrino detectors consist of large tanks of water, in which flashes of light occur as the neutrinos pass through.

NEUTRINOS

Tiny particles called neutrinos come from stars. Most neutrinos pass right through the Earth, but special detectors lying deep underground can detect a few of them. By studying neutrinos, astronomers can find out about the Sun and exploding stars.

Find out more

BLACK HOLES
MOON
PLANETS
SATELLITES
SPACE FLIGHT
STARS
SUN
TELESCOPES
UNIVERSE

ATLANTIC OCEAN

THE UNDERWATER LANDSCAPE of the Atlantic is dominated by the mid-Atlantic Ridge, the world's longest mountain chain. Some of the ridge's peaks rise above sea level as volcanic islands, such as Iceland and the Azores. The deepest part of the Atlantic, the Puerto Rico Trench, plunges to 30,185 ft (9,200 m) below sea level. The Atlantic Ocean is rich in oil and natural gas. In recent years, offshore oil reserves have been exploited in the Gulf of Mexico, the Niger River Delta, and the North Sea. Sand, gravel, and shell deposits are also mined by the US and UK for use in the construction industry. The Atlantic is the most productive and heavily utilized fishing ground in the world, providing millions of tons a year. The Atlantic Ocean has been crossed by shipping routes for many centuries. It is still heavily used for seaborne trade, especially the bulk transportation of raw materials, such as oil, grain, and iron, to industrial centers.

The Atlantic Ocean is bounded by the Americas in the west, and by Europe and Africa in the east. Along the mid-Atlantic ridge, a long submarine mountain chain, high volcanic peaks pierce the water's surface as islands.

SUBTROPICAL SCILLIES

The Gulf Stream is a warm ocean current that flows up the east coast of North America, and then across to western Europe, driven by north-easterly trade winds. These winds carry moisture and warmth from the ocean to the land. In England's Scilly Islands, subtropical plants flourish in winter because of the impact of the current.

ATLANTIC TOURISM

The volcanic islands which have emerged along the ocean's mid-Atlantic ridge, especially the Canaries, Azores, and Madeira, are major tourist attractions. The fertile black soil of the Canaries is ideal for the cultivation of bananas, tomatoes, sugarcane, and tobacco. The mild subtropical climate attracts winter visitors from Europe.

A trawler braves the rough seas of the Atlantic. Its crew are fishing for lobster.

SUBMARINE ACTIVITY

During the Cold War, from the 1950s to the 1980s, the Atlantic Ocean was patrolled by both the US and Russian navies. Since the 1990s, US and Russian scientists are sharing advances in submarine technology – developed for defense purposes – to survey, map, and analyze the unexplored world beneath the Atlantic.

ATLANTIC FISHING

The Atlantic Ocean, a productive fishing ground for centuries, contains over half the world's total stock of fish. In the North Atlantic, cod, haddock, mackerel, and lobster are the main catch, while the South Atlantic catch is dominated by hake and tuna. Freezer trawlers that can catch and process a ton or more of fish in just an hour are in danger of overfishing the Atlantic. Countries claim exclusive rights to zones extending 200 nautical miles (370 km) from their coastlines to conserve fish stocks.

NAVIGATION
Compasses are vital in crossocean navigation. The compass needle points to magnetic north, in the Canadian Arctic.

ICELANDIC HEATING

Iceland was formed by volcanic action along a fault line in the Earth's crust, 65 million years ago. Iceland still has over 100 volcanoes, many still active. The vast natural heat reserves beneath Iceland's icy surface are being harnessed to provide hot water and heating for much of the population.

Plumes of steam rise from a geothermal power station (left). Iceland has the most silfataras (volcanic vents) and hot springs in the world. The intense heat deep underground creates bubbling hot springs and mud pools.

Find out more

OCEANS AND SEAS
SHIPS AND BOATS
SUBMARINES
VOLCANOES
WIND

OVERSEAS TERRITORIES AND DEPENDENCIES

 ASCENSION
Area: 34 sq miles
(88 sq km)
Status: British dependent
territory of St. Helena
Claimed: 1673
Population: 1,200
Capital: Jamestown
(St. Helena)

 BERMUDA
Area: 20.5 sq miles
(53 sq km)
Status: British Crown colony
Claimed: 1612
Population: 64,400
Capital: Hamilton

 BOUVET ISLAND
Area: 22 sq miles
(58 sq km)
Status: Norwegian
dependency
Claimed: 1928
Population: None
Capital: None

 FAEROE ISLANDS
Area: 540 sq miles
(1,399 sq km)
Status: Self-governing
territory of Denmark
Claimed: 1380
Population: 46,300
Capital: Tórshavn

 FALKLAND ISLANDS
Area: 4,699 sq miles
(12,173 sq km)
Status: British
dependent colony
Claimed: 1832
Population: 3,000
Capital: Stanley

 SAINT HELENA
Area: 47 sq miles
(122 sq km)
Status: British
dependent territory
Claimed: 1673
Population: 7,400
Capital: Jamestown

 TRISTAN DA CUNHA
Area: 38 sq miles
(98 sq km)
Status: British dependent
territory of St. Helena
Claimed: 1612
Population: 300
Capital: Jamestown
(St. Helena)

 SOUTH GEORGIA & THE SOUTH SANDWICH ISLANDS
Area: 1,387 sq miles
(3,592 sq km)
Status: British dependent
territory
Claimed: 1775
Population: No permanent
residents
Capital: None

ATLANTIC YACHT RACING
Crossocean racing began in 1866,
with a race from Connecticut to
Cowes – on the Isle of Wight – which
took 13 days. Single-handed ocean
races became popular in the 1960s.

BERMUDA TRIANGLE
The Bermuda Triangle lies between
Bermuda, Florida, and Puerto Rico.
Many ships, submarines, and airplanes
are said to have disappeared in
its waters. In 1872, a deserted
sailing ship, the *Mary Celeste*,
was found drifting across
the Atlantic – its ten
crew members were
never located.

INDEPENDENT STATES

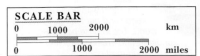 **CAPE VERDE**
Area: 1,556 sq miles
(4,030 sq km)
Population: 463,000
Capital: Praia

 ICELAND
Area: 39,770 sq miles
(103,000 sq km)
Population: 290,000
Capital: Reykjavík

SCALE BAR
0   1000   2000   km
0   1000   2000 miles

ATMOSPHERE

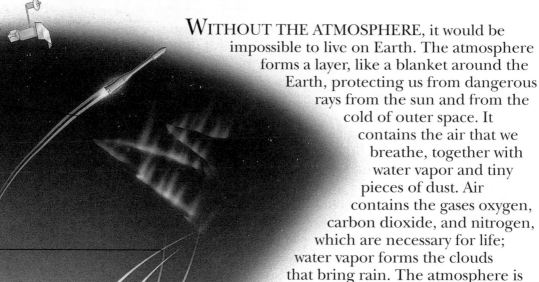

There is no definite upper limit to the atmosphere. The final layer before outer space is called the exosphere; it contains hardly any air at all.

A layer of very thin air called the thermosphere extends from about 50 to 300 miles (80 to 480 km) above the ground. It contains the ionosphere – layers of electrically charged particles, from which radio waves can be bounced around the world.

The mesosphere extends from 30 to 50 miles (50 to 80 km) above the Earth. If meteors fall into this layer, they burn up, causing shooting stars.

Under the mesosphere lies the stratosphere. It extends from 7 to 30 miles (11 to 50 km) up. The stratosphere is a calm region. Airliners fly here to avoid the winds and weather lower down.

Although it is the narrowest layer, the troposphere contains most of the gas in the atmosphere. It reaches about 7 miles (11 km) above the ground, but this varies around the globe and from season to season. Most weather occurs in the troposphere.

WITHOUT THE ATMOSPHERE, it would be impossible to live on Earth. The atmosphere forms a layer, like a blanket around the Earth, protecting us from dangerous rays from the sun and from the cold of outer space. It contains the air that we breathe, together with water vapor and tiny pieces of dust. Air contains the gases oxygen, carbon dioxide, and nitrogen, which are necessary for life; water vapor forms the clouds that bring rain. The atmosphere is held by the pull of the Earth's gravity and spreads out to about 1,250 miles (2,000 km) above the Earth. Three quarters of the air in the atmosphere lies beneath 35,000 ft (10,700 m) because the air gets thinner higher up. The air at the top of Mount Everest is only one-third as thick as it is at sea level. That is why mountain climbers carry an air supply and why high-flying aircraft are sealed and have air pumped into them.

LAYERS OF THE ATMOSPHERE

The Earth's atmosphere is divided into several layers. The main layers, from the bottom upward, are called the troposphere, the stratosphere, the mesosphere, the thermosphere, and the exosphere.

OZONE LAYER

Within the stratosphere, there is a thin layer of the gas ozone. Ozone is a form of oxygen that absorbs ultraviolet rays from the sun. Without the ozone layer, these rays would reach the ground and kill all living creatures. Pollution and the use of certain chemicals are destroying the ozone layer.

Compared to the size of the Earth, the atmosphere forms a very narrow band – approximately equivalent to the skin around an orange.

SKY AND SUNSET

When rays of light travel through the atmosphere, they hit pollen, dust, and other tiny particles. This causes the rays to scatter, or bounce off in all directions. Some colors of light are scattered more than others.

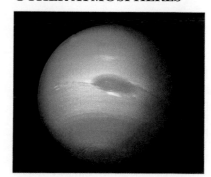

OTHER ATMOSPHERES

Other planets' atmospheres are very different from Earth's. On Neptune (above), the atmosphere is mainly methane gas. Jupiter and Saturn have thick, cloudy atmospheres of hydrogen. None of these planets can support life.

BLUE SKY
The atmosphere scatters mainly blue light; this is why the sky looks blue. The other colors of light are scattered much less than blue so that they come to Earth directly. This causes the area of sky around the sun to look yellow.

SUNSET AND SUNRISE
At sunset and sunrise, when the sun is below the horizon, the light travels through much more of the atmosphere before we see it. The blue light is scattered so much that it is absorbed, or soaked up, by the atmosphere. Only red light reaches us, so the sky looks red.

Find out more
AIR
CLIMATES
OXYGEN
PLANETS
WEATHER

ATOMS AND MOLECULES

A drop of water contains about 3,000 million billion molecules.

LOOK AROUND YOU. There are countless millions of different substances, from metals and plastics to people and plants. All of these are made from about 100 different kinds of "building blocks" joined together in different ways. These building blocks are tiny particles called atoms. Atoms are so small that even the tiniest speck of dust contains more than one million million atoms. Some substances, such as iron, are made of just one kind of atom; other substances, such as water, contain molecules – atoms joined together in groups. Such molecules may be very simple or very complex. Each water molecule contains two hydrogen atoms and one oxygen atom; plastics are made of molecules which often contain millions of atoms. An atom itelf is made up of a dense center called a nucleus. Particles that carry electricity, called electrons, move around the nucleus. Scientists have discovered how to split the nucleus, releasing enormous energy which is used in nuclear power stations and nuclear bombs.

A molecule of water contains three atoms – two hydrogen atoms and one oxygen atom.

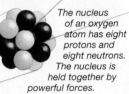

Protons and neutrons are made up of quarks.

Electrons whiz around the nucleus. An atom of oxygen has eight electrons.

There is a lot of empty space in an atom. If the nucleus were the size of a tennis ball, the nearest electron would be about half a mile (1 km) away.

The nucleus of an oxygen atom has eight protons and eight neutrons. The nucleus is held together by powerful forces.

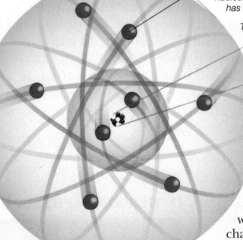

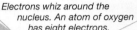

PROTONS AND NEUTRONS
The nucleus of an atom contains particles called protons and neutrons. These contain even smaller particles called quarks. Protons carry electricity. However, they carry a different kind of electricity from electrons. They have a "positive charge," whereas electrons have a "negative charge." Neutrons have no electric charge.

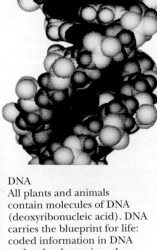

DNA
All plants and animals contain molecules of DNA (deoxyribonucleic acid). DNA carries the blueprint for life: coded information in DNA molecules determines the characteristics of each living thing and its offspring. A DNA molecule consists of millions of atoms arranged in a twisted spiral shape.

DISCOVERING THE ATOM
About 2,400 years ago, the Greek philosopher Democritus believed that everything was made up of tiny particles. It was not until 1808 that English scientist John Dalton proved that atoms exist. Around 1909, New Zealand scientist Ernest Rutherford (below) discovered the nucleus.

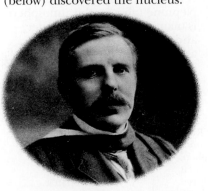

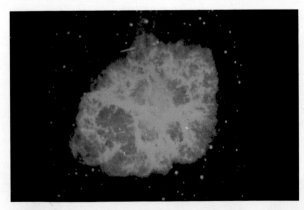

IMMORTAL ATOMS
The particles that make up atoms never disappear but are constantly journeying through the universe as part of different substances. All these particles originated with the formation of the universe around 15,000 million years ago. The atoms that make everything on Earth were formed from the particles in stars, which then exploded like the crab nebula (above).

Find out more
CHEMISTRY
OXYGEN
PHYSICS
PLASTICS
REPRODUCTION

AUSTRALIA

LOCATED BETWEEN THE INDIAN AND PACIFIC OCEANS, Australia is an island continent, and the sixth largest country in the world. It is a land of varied landscapes, including tropical rain forests, vast deserts, snow-capped mountains, rolling tracts of pastoral land, and magnificent beaches. The country boasts a great number of natural features, the most famous of which are the Great Barrier Reef and Uluru (Ayers Rock). Australians have an outdoor lifestyle and enjoy a high standard of living. Almost 90 percent of the country's 19.7 million people live in the fertile strip of land on the east and southeast coast. Many of them live in Melbourne and Sydney, Australia's two largest cities, and in the nation's capital, Canberra. Today, few people live in the dry Australian interior known as the outback. The original inhabitants of Australia, the Aborigines, learned to survive in the harsh conditions there. However, only a small number of the 410,000 Aboriginal population live a traditional life in the outback today. Other Australians are descendants of settlers from Britain, continental Europe, and Southeast Asia.

Australia lies southeast of Asia, with the Pacific Ocean to the east and the Indian Ocean to the west. It is the only country that is also a continent. Together with several nearby islands, Australia covers a total area of 2.94 million sq miles (7.61 million sq km).

SURFING

Surfing is a favorite Australian sport. Surfing carnivals are held regularly in many towns. Polynesian people invented the sport hundreds of years ago; recently it has expanded to include windsurfing, trick surfing, and long-distance surfing. Surfers often travel vast distances to reach a beach with the best waves of the day.

At a surfing carnival lifeguards give demonstrations of lifesaving. Surfing competitions are hotly contested and often draw many spectators.

BEACH CULTURE

The majority of Australians live in towns and cities along the coast. Therefore the beach is the most popular venue for leisure pursuits. Australia's climate is ideal for beach activities such as surfing, swimming, sailing, and beach volleyball. Mild winter temperatures mean that these sports can be enjoyed all year round.

During the celebrations of Australia's 200th anniversary, oceangoing sailing ships gathered in Sydney's famous harbor.

SYDNEY

The city of Sydney is the oldest and largest in Australia. Sydney was founded in 1788 as a British prison colony with about 1,000 prisoners and their guards; today it is home to more than 4 million people. The city stands around Port Jackson, a huge natural bay spanned by Sydney Harbour Bridge. Sydney is a busy industrial center and tourist resort.

Australia's currency is the Australian dollar. On one side the coins feature a portrait of the Queen of England, who is the head of state.

FILMMAKING

The Australian film industry produces a number of important films each year. Some, such as *Picnic at Hanging Rock* (1975), which tells of the mysterious disappearance of a group of Australian schoolgirls, have received international acclaim.

TASMANIA

The island of Tasmania lies off the southeastern coast of Australia, and is a state in itself with a population of nearly half a million. The island has a cooler, damper climate than the rest of the country and is famous for its fruit, vegetables, and sheep. Tin, silver, and other products are mined. Much of western Tasmania is unpopulated and covered in dense forest where native wildlife, such as the Tasmanian devil, below, survives in large numbers.

GREAT DIVIDING RANGE

Running along the eastern coast of the continent from Cape York to Ballarat is a 2,300 mile (3,700 km) mountain chain called the Great Dividing Range. The tallest mountain is Kosciuszko, at 7,310 ft (2,228 m). Other peaks are much lower. The mountains divide the fertile coastal plains from the dry interior. The steep hills were once a major barrier to travel; even today only a few roads and railroads cross from east to west.

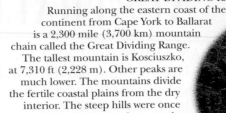

The Three Sisters formation in New South Wales belongs to the Great Dividing Range.

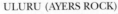

Outback ranchers ride motorcycles or horses to round up cattle and sheep.

OUTBACK

Very few people live in Australia's interior, called the outback. However, sheep and cattle are farmed on the dry land. Some ranches, called stations, cover hundreds of square miles. Because of the great distances, outback Australians live isolated lives and communicate by radio.

Ancient rock and bark paintings show that Aboriginal culture flourished nearly 40,000 years before European settlers arrived.

ULURU (AYERS ROCK)

One of the most impressive natural sights in Australia is Uluru (formerly known as Ayers Rock). This huge mass of sandstone stands in the middle of a wide, flat desert and is 1,142 ft (335 m) high. Although it lies hundreds of miles from the nearest town, Uluru is a major tourist attraction with its own hotel. The rock is particularly beautiful at sunset, when it seems to change color.

STRIP MINING

Australia has huge mineral wealth, and mining is an important industry. The country produces one third of the world's uranium, which is essential for nuclear power. In recent years, iron ore has been excavated in large strip mines where giant digging machines remove entire hills.

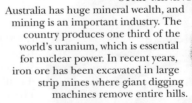

PERTH

Founded in 1829, Perth (below) is the state capital of Western Australia and its financial and commercial heart. Most Australian people live in cities, and the population of Perth reflects the European ancestry of a large percentage of today's Australians.

CANBERRA

Canberra, the capital city of Australia, is situated in the Australian Capital Territory (A.C.T.), an area of 911 sq miles (2,360 sq km) completely surrounded by the state of New South Wales. The capital was designed as a city of parks and gardens by American landscape architect, Walter Burley Griffin. Construction of the city began in 1913. Canberra is a political and educational center rather than a commercial or industrial town.

Hay Street mall (left) is a pedestrian shopping precinct located in Perth's central business district.

ADELAIDE

Adelaide (right) is the capital and chief port of South Australia. A well-planned city, it was designed in a grid pattern by Colonel William Light, the first surveyor-general of South Australia. The city is bordered by 2.7 sq miles (6.9 sq km) of parkland, and was named for Queen Adelaide, wife of King William IV of England.

MELBOURNE

The capital city of Victoria and the second largest city in Australia, Melbourne (below) displays a dramatic mixture of old and new. Melbourne was founded in 1835 by an Australian farmer, John Batman. Nearly 20 years later, gold was discovered in Victoria and Melbourne's population climbed sharply. Today, Melbourne is a leading seaport, and the commercial and industrial center of Victoria.

BRISBANE

The state capital of Queensland and its largest city, Brisbane (right) is a bustling seaport lying above the mouth of the Brisbane River at Moreton Bay. In this way, it is similar to Australia's other state capitals, all of which were founded near rivers close to ocean harbors. Like other state capitals, Brisbane too is the commercial center of its state, with its main business district situated near the waterfront.

St. Paul's Cathedral stands proudly amid modern architecture in Melbourne. The building was designed by William Butterfield in the 1880s in a Gothic style.

Find out more

ABORIGINAL AUSTRALIANS
ARCHITECTURE
AUSTRALIA, HISTORY OF
AUSTRALIAN WILDLIFE
CITIES

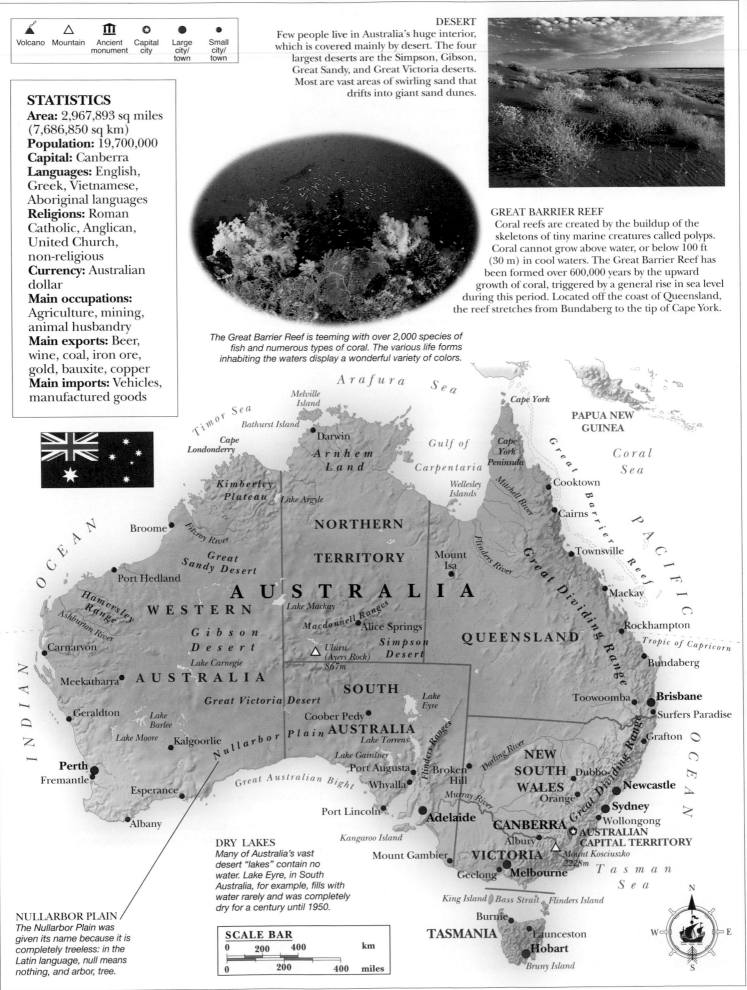

Legend
Volcano | Mountain | Ancient monument | Capital city | Large city/town | Small city/town

STATISTICS
Area: 2,967,893 sq miles
(7,686,850 sq km)
Population: 19,700,000
Capital: Canberra
Languages: English,
Greek, Vietnamese,
Aboriginal languages
Religions: Roman
Catholic, Anglican,
United Church,
non-religious
Currency: Australian
dollar
Main occupations:
Agriculture, mining,
animal husbandry
Main exports: Beer,
wine, coal, iron ore,
gold, bauxite, copper
Main imports: Vehicles,
manufactured goods

DESERT
Few people live in Australia's huge interior,
which is covered mainly by desert. The four
largest deserts are the Simpson, Gibson,
Great Sandy, and Great Victoria deserts.
Most are vast areas of swirling sand that
drifts into giant sand dunes.

GREAT BARRIER REEF
Coral reefs are created by the buildup of the
skeletons of tiny marine creatures called polyps.
Coral cannot grow above water, or below 100 ft
(30 m) in cool waters. The Great Barrier Reef has
been formed over 600,000 years by the upward
growth of coral, triggered by a general rise in sea level
during this period. Located off the coast of Queensland,
the reef stretches from Bundaberg to the tip of Cape York.

*The Great Barrier Reef is teeming with over 2,000 species of
fish and numerous types of coral. The various life forms
inhabiting the waters display a wonderful variety of colors.*

DRY LAKES
*Many of Australia's vast
desert "lakes" contain no
water. Lake Eyre, in South
Australia, for example, fills with
water rarely and was completely
dry for a century until 1950.*

NULLARBOR PLAIN
*The Nullarbor Plain was
given its name because it is
completely treeless: in the
Latin language, null means
nothing, and arbor, tree.*

SCALE BAR
0   200   400   km
0   200   400   miles

HISTORY OF
AUSTRALIA

c. 40,000 B.C. First Aborigines arrive in Australia from Asia.

1770 Captain Cook sails into Botany Bay and claims Australia for Britain.

1788 British convicts arrive.

1901 Australia becomes an independent dominion within the British Empire.

1915 Australian troops fight at Gallipoli in World War I.

1945-65 Government pays fares for poor Europeans to settle in Australia.

AS RECENTLY AS 1600, the only people who knew about Australia were the aboriginal peoples who had lived there for more than 40,000 years. The rest of the world had no idea that the continent existed. In 1606, the Dutch explorer William Jansz landed in northern Australia. Although he did not know it, he was the first European to see the country. Further exploration of the coastline by Dutch and British explorers revealed that Australia was an island. In 1770, the British captain James Cook claimed the east coast of Australia for Britain and named it New South Wales. The British sent convicts to their new colony, forming the basis of Sydney, today the country's largest city. Throughout the 19th century, the population of Australia grew as more convicts arrived, followed by immigrants. For many of them life was tough, but the British colony grew richer when gold was discovered in 1851. Farming also became established. In 1901, Australia became an independent commonwealth, although it remained close to Britain for many years and Australian troops fought in both world wars on the side of Britain. More recently, Australia has set up links with other countries.

ABORIGINES
The first aboriginal peoples probably arrived in Australia from the islands of Southeast Asia about 40,000 years ago. In 1770, there were about 300,000 Aborigines in Australia.

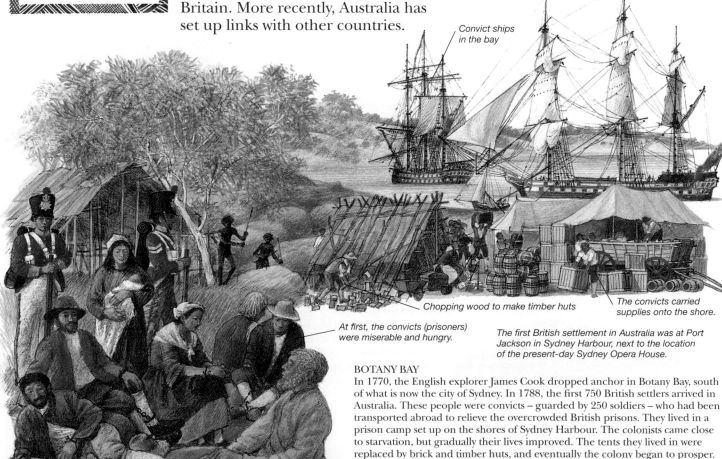

Convict ships in the bay

Chopping wood to make timber huts

The convicts carried supplies onto the shore.

At first, the convicts (prisoners) were miserable and hungry.

The first British settlement in Australia was at Port Jackson in Sydney Harbour, next to the location of the present-day Sydney Opera House.

BOTANY BAY
In 1770, the English explorer James Cook dropped anchor in Botany Bay, south of what is now the city of Sydney. In 1788, the first 750 British settlers arrived in Australia. These people were convicts – guarded by 250 soldiers – who had been transported abroad to relieve the overcrowded British prisons. They lived in a prison camp set up on the shores of Sydney Harbour. The colonists came close to starvation, but gradually their lives improved. The tents they lived in were replaced by brick and timber huts, and eventually the colony began to prosper. In 1868, the transportation of convicts ended, leaving more than 160,000 convicts living in Australia.

EXPLORATION

The first explorers of Australia mapped out the coastline but left the interior largely untouched. In 1606, the Dutch navigator William Jansz briefly visited northeastern Australia. Between 1829 and 1830, the English explorer Charles Sturt explored the rivers in the south but failed to find the inland sea that many people assumed existed in the center of Australia. In 1840, Edward Eyre, from England, discovered the vast, dry salt lakes in South Australia before walking along its southern coast. In 1860 and 1861, the Irishman Robert O'Hara Burke and Englishman William Wills became the first people to cross Australia from south to north. It was not until the 1930s that Australia was completely surveyed.

■ Burke and Wills
□ Sturt
■ Eyre
■ Cook
■ Jansz

Map showing the routes of the different explorers of Australia.

BURKE AND WILLS

In 1860 and 1861, Burke and Wills succeeded in crossing Australia from south to north. However, they both died of starvation on the return journey south.

GOLD RUSH

Gold was discovered in 1851 in New South Wales and Victoria. Thousands of prospectors rushed from all over the world, including China, to make their fortunes in Australia. The national population rose from 400,000 in 1850 to 1,100,000 by 1860. Conditions were tough for the gold miners, and in 1854 a group of miners at Eureka Stockade in Ballarat, near Melbourne, refused to pay the license fee required to mine for gold. The government sent in troops; 24 miners and six soldiers were killed in the battle that followed.

The Aborigines were amazed to see the crowds of white people landing in their territory.

OVERCOMING ABORIGINES

During the 19th century, the European settlers disrupted the aboriginal way of life. Many aboriginal languages and customs died out as their land was taken. Children were taken away from their parents to be educated in the European way. As a result, the Aborigine population fell from 300,000 in 1770 to about 60,000 by 1900.

IMMIGRATION

In 1880, there were only two million people on the vast Australian continent. A century later, almost 15 million people lived there. Most had come to Australia from Britain, Italy, and Greece. In a deliberate attempt to boost the population after 1945, the Australian government offered to pay part of the passage for poor Europeans. About two million people took advantage of the program, which ended in 1965, with one million coming from Britain alone. Asians and other nonwhite peoples were denied entry until the 1960s. Many children traveled on their own. This group of immigrants (left) are on their way to a farm school in Western Australia from Waterloo Station, London, England.

URANIUM MINING

Australia is rich in minerals, like uranium, the raw material used to fuel nuclear power stations and produce nuclear bombs. Although uranium mining increased dramatically during the 1970s, many Australians opposed it because of the dangers of radiation from uranium. In addition, many of the uranium deposits lie within aboriginal tribal lands. Protests have therefore regularly occurred to prevent the exploitation of this dangerous mineral.

Find out more

ABORIGINAL AUSTRALIANS
AUSTRALIA
COOK, JAMES
IMMIGRATION
NUCLEAR AGE

AUSTRALIAN WILDLIFE

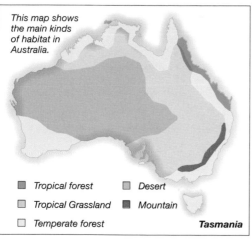

This map shows the main kinds of habitat in Australia.

- ■ Tropical forest
- ☐ Tropical Grassland
- ☐ Temperate forest
- ☐ Desert
- ■ Mountain

Tasmania

OF ALL THE CONTINENTS, Australia has the most unusual assortment of animals and plants. Almost half of the world's 314 kinds of marsupials (pouched mammals) are found only in Australia. Marsupials include kangaroos, koalas, opossums, and bandicoots. The platypus and echidna – the only mammals that lay eggs – also live in Australia. The Australian landscape is very varied. In the northeast are steamy tropical rain forests and swamps, which are home to crocodiles and wading birds. In the central part of Australia there are vast hot deserts made up of sand and rocks. Australia has more desert than any other continent, and there is sometimes no rainfall in these areas for several years. In the south, where the climate is milder, eucalyptus trees grow on rolling grasslands and shrubby bushland.

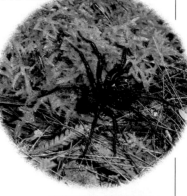

FUNNEL-WEB SPIDER
The large, hairy funnel-web spider is so named because it builds a funnel-shaped web to catch its prey. These spiders are feared by humans because their bite is extremely poisonous.

EUCALYPTUS
There are about 500 different kinds of eucalyptus trees in the world. Almost all of them came originally from Australia. The koala depends mainly on the leaves of a few species of eucalyptus tree for food.

KOALA
The koala is found only in the eucalyptus forests of Australia. It spends most of its life in the trees, feeding at night and sleeping for up to 18 hours each day.

Kangaroos are herbivores (plant eaters); they feed mostly on grasses and leaves.

Strong back legs are well adapted for jumping. A kangaroo can bound along at about 43 mph (70 km/h).

GRASSLAND
Kangaroos live in grassland areas. These areas consist mainly of kangaroo grass, which grows in clumps about 20 in (50 cm) high. Tough, spiky, spinifex plants grow in the drier areas. Many of the grasslands are now used to grow crops and graze farm animals

KANGAROO
There are about 50 different kinds of kangaroo in Australia, including the red kangaroo shown here. Kangaroos have huge back legs and strong tails. The red kangaroo is one of the largest – a male can grow to more than 6 ft (2 m) in height.

RED-NECKED WALLABY
Wallabies are smaller members of the kangaroo family. The red-necked wallaby shown here is nicknamed "the brusher" because it prefers brush and scrubland areas rather than open countryside. It is also called the red wallaby, Eastern brush wallaby, and Bennett's wallaby.

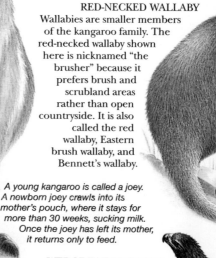

WOMBAT
Wombats live in grassland areas, dry woodlands, and shrublands. They dig a complicated tunnel system with their strong legs and large claws, and come out of their burrow at night to eat plants such as spear grass.

A young kangaroo is called a joey. A newborn joey crawls into its mother's pouch, where it stays for more than 30 weeks, sucking milk. Once the joey has left its mother, it returns only to feed.

WEDGE-TAILED EAGLE
With a wingspan of 8 ft (2.5 m), the wedge-tailed eagle is one of the world's largest eagles. It soars over bush and desert areas of Australia searching for rabbits and similar prey.

Shield bugs are so named because they have a shield-shaped plate on the body. They feed on the sap inside plants and are also known as sap suckers.

RAIN FOREST

Tropical rain forests grow along a strip of Australia's northeastern and northern coast, together with luxurious palms, bunya-bunya pines, tree ferns, and colorful orchids. There are many other forests, including subtropical rain forests of kauri pine and scrub box near the mid-eastern coast of Australia, and cooler temperate rain forests of Antarctic beech in parts of the southeast and on the island of Tasmania.

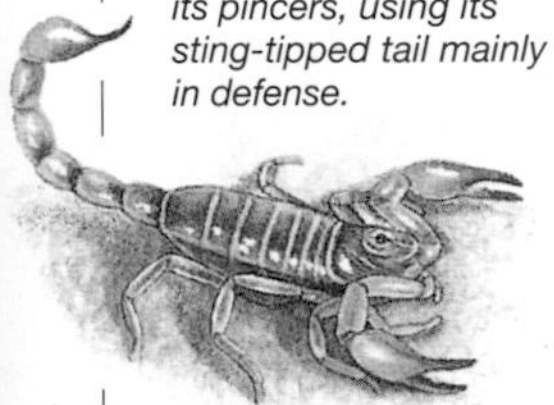

The desert scorpion catches its food of insects and worms with its pincers, using its sting-tipped tail mainly in defense.

LORIKEET

There are seven different kinds of lorikeet in Australia; the one shown here is the rainbow lorikeet. Lorikeets are colorful, noisy relatives of parrots, and gather together in large flocks. They have brush-like tongues for sipping nectar from orchids and other flowers.

BOWERBIRD

In the warmer forests, male bowerbirds build small structures called bowers to attract a female. They use twigs, leaves, stems, and petals to make the bower. Each kind of bowerbird makes its own kind of bower, sometimes using bottle caps and other shiny pieces of rubbish.

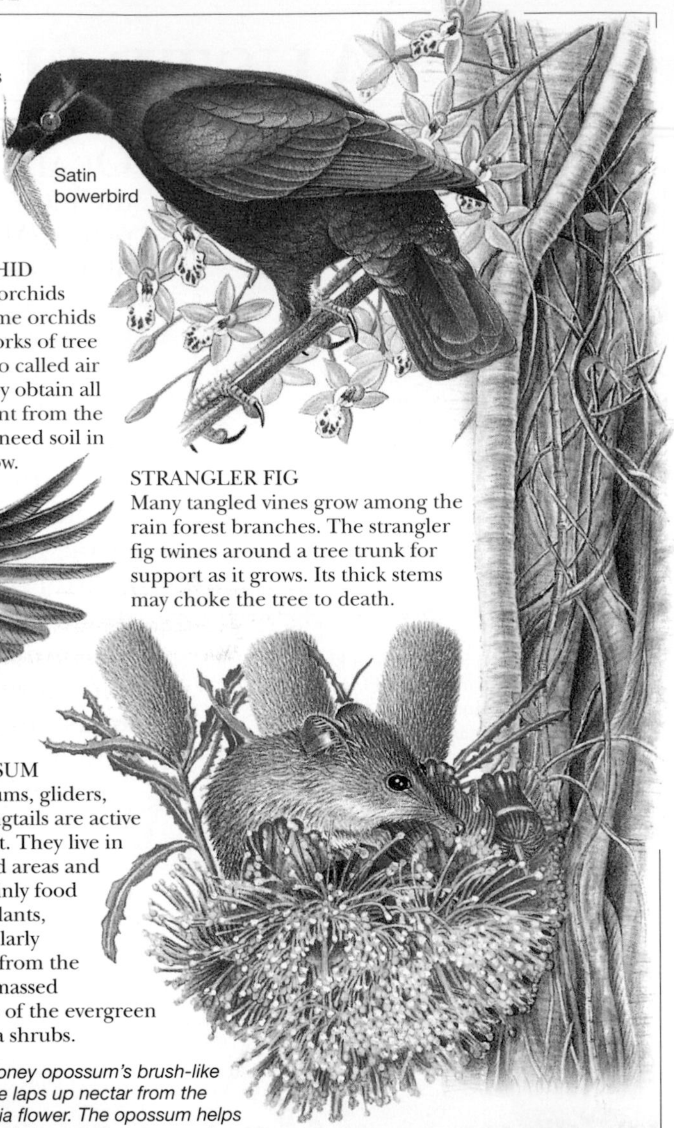

Satin bowerbird

ORCHID

More than 600 kinds of orchids grow in Australia. Some orchids grow high in the forks of tree branches and are also called air plants because they obtain all their nourishment from the air and do not need soil in order to grow.

STRANGLER FIG

Many tangled vines grow among the rain forest branches. The strangler fig twines around a tree trunk for support as it grows. Its thick stems may choke the tree to death.

DESERT

Australia has many poisonous animals, including snakes, spiders, and scorpions. Many poisonous animals live in the vast deserts in the center of the country. Dry scrubland and desert cover more than half of Australia. One of the most common trees is the mulga, a shrublike acacia that provides some food and shelter in the burning heat.

OPOSSUM

Opossums, gliders, and ringtails are active at night. They live in wooded areas and eat mainly food from plants, particularly nectar from the large, massed flowers of the evergreen banksia shrubs.

The honey opossum's brush-like tongue laps up nectar from the banksia flower. The opossum helps the banksia reproduce by carrying its pollen to the next plant.

Australia is home to many kinds of snakes, including the Diamond Python.

NATIONAL PARKS

Australia has more than 2,000 national parks and wildlife reserves, which cover 197 million acres (80 million hectares). These parks include Seal Rock in New South Wales and Lamington National Park, shown left.

DESERT PEA

The Sturt's desert pea is named after the British explorer Charles Sturt (1795-1869). It grows in sandy deserts and blooms only after rainfall. Its seeds may lie in the soil for many years, waiting until the next rainstorm before they can develop.

Barking spiders make a noise by rubbing their mouthparts together. They catch frogs, insects, and small reptiles.

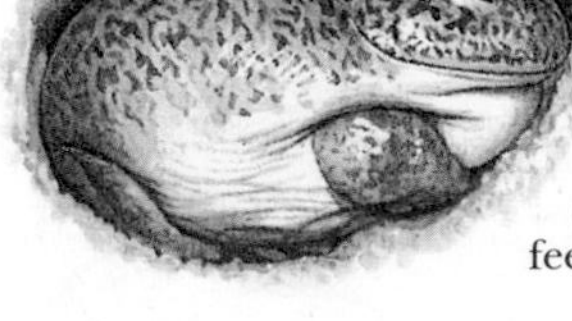

DINGO

Australia's wild dog – the dingo – probably first came to Australia about 40,000 years ago with the aboriginal settlers. Dingoes eat a variety of food, including rabbits, birds, reptiles, and wallabies. They also kill sheep, which makes them unpopular with farmers.

WATER-HOLDING FROG

During the dry season this Australian frog burrows about 20 in (50 cm) below the surface of the soil and forms a bubblelike layer of skin around its body. Only its nostrils are uncovered. After it rains the frog wakes, rubs off the cocoon, and digs its way out. It lays its eggs in the puddles, absorbs water through its skin, feeds, then burrows again.

Find out more

AUSTRALIA
AUSTRALIA, HISTORY OF
FOREST WILDLIFE
MAMMALS
NATIONAL PARKS
SPIDERS AND SCORPIONS

AUSTRIA

Austria is a landlocked country, located at the heart of Europe. To the west it is alpine. The northeast is the fertile valley of the Danube.

AUSTRIA OCCUPIES a strategic position at the heart of Europe. Both the Danube River and the Alpine passes in the west have been vital trade routes for many centuries, linking southern and eastern Europe with the north and west. Until 1918, Austria was part of the Habsburg Empire, which dominated much of Central Europe. Today, it is a wealthy, industrialized nation. In the northeast, the fertile plains that surround the Danube provide rich farming country, and potatoes, beets, and cereals are grown there. In the west, the magnificent mountain scenery of the Alps attracts millions of visitors. Austria is rich in mineral resources, especially iron. It uses hydroelectric power, generated by fast mountain streams, to provide power for its steel and manufacturing industries.

STATISTICS
Area: 32,375 sq miles (83,850 sq km)
Population: 8,100,000
Capital: Vienna
Languages: German, Croat, Slovene
Religions: Roman Catholic, Protestant, Muslim, Jewish
Currency: Euro

AUSTRIAN COFFEE
Coffee was introduced to Vienna by the Turks in the 17th century. Coffee, accompanied by pastries or chocolate cakes, is a famous Viennese speciality.

This miniature features Mozart and his sister Maria-Anna (1751-1829).

MOZART
The composer Wolfgang Amadeus Mozart (1756–91) was born in Salzburg and spent his childhood there. His remarkable early talent and the continuing popularity of his music draws many visitors to the city. This miniature comes from the Mozart Museum in Salzburg.

The Schönbrunn Palace, the summer residence of the Habsburgs

VIENNA
The Habsburg family ruled Austria for several centuries, and Vienna was the capital of their empire. Vienna stands on the Danube River, and is a gateway between eastern and western Europe. The city is most famous for its magnificent 17th-century architecture. Today, it is a major center of trade and industry.

THE TIROL
The alpine district of western Austria is known as the Tirol. The region has a very strong identity and folk culture, and historically it was an important link between Germany and Italy. Salt, copper mining, and dairy farming are important to the economy of the Tirol. Tourists are attracted by its spectacular beauty, especially in winter when skiing is a major attraction.

SCALE BAR

Find out more
COMPOSERS
EUROPE
EUROPE, HISTORY OF

AZTECS

MORE THAN SEVEN HUNDRED YEARS AGO a civilization was born in what is now Mexico. The Aztecs, founders of this civilization, were the last Native American rulers of Mexico. They were a wandering tribe who arrived in the Mexican Valley during the 13th century. The Toltec and Olmec peoples had already established civilizations in this area, and influenced the Aztecs. Over the next 200 years the Aztecs set up a mighty empire of some 12 million people. The Aztecs believed that the world would come to an end unless they sacrificed people to their sun god, Huitzilopochtli. They built pyramids and temples where they sacrificed prisoners from the cities they had conquered. In 1519 Spanish conquistadors (adventurers) arrived in Mexico and defeated the Aztecs. Montezuma II, last of the Aztec emperors, was killed by his own people, and the Aztec empire collapsed.

Victim being sacrificed on top of the temple.

Preaching priest

Aztec pyramid with temple at top

The bodies of sacrificed victims were thrown to the ground.

Causeway

Temple precinct at Tenochtitlán

TENOCHTITLÁN

The Aztec capital, called Tenochtitlán, was a "floating city," built in Lake Texcoco, on one natural and many artificial islands. To reach the mainland, the Aztecs built causeways (raised roads) and canals between the islands. Today Mexico City stands on the site.

AZTEC ARTISTS

The Aztecs made beautiful jewelry using gold, turquoise, pearls, shells, and feathers. They also used other valuable stones, such as obsidian and jade.

HUMAN SACRIFICES

Aztec priests used knives with stone blades to kill up to 1,000 people each week, offering the hearts to their sun god, Huitzilopochtli.

TRIBUTES

The Aztecs became very rich by collecting tributes (payments) from conquered tribes. Cloth, corn, pottery, and luxury goods were brought to Tenochtitlán from the conquered cities by porters, and exchanged in four huge markets. Officials made lists of all the tributes in picture writing. The Aztecs declared war on any tribe that refused to pay tribute.

Ceremonial jade mask

Find out more

CONQUISTADORS
SOUTH AMERICA,
history of

BABYLONIANS

ONE OF THE FIRST CIVILIZATIONS developed about 6,000 years ago in the Middle East, between the Tigris and Euphrates rivers. This region was known as Mesopotamia, meaning "land between rivers." The land was fertile, and farming methods were highly refined. The people were among the first to develop a system of writing, use the wheel, and build cities. One of these cities was Babylon, founded about 2000 B.C. It became the capital city of Babylonia (now part of Iraq). Babylon was an important trading center. It was also a religious center and the site of many splendid temples. Its people were strong and prosperous under the great king Hammurabi, who united the different areas into one empire. Babylon became even more magnificent later, under King Nebuchadnezzar II. In 538 B.C., the Persian king Cyrus the Great conquered Babylon; Alexander the Great of Greece conquered it again in 331 B.C. When the Romans eventually captured Babylon, the capital city lost its importance, fell into ruins, and became part of the Roman Empire.

CYLINDER SEAL
The Babylonians wrote using cylinder seals. These seals were often made of semiprecious stone and were very delicately carved. To sign or stamp a document, a person rolled a cylinder seal over damp clay. This seal clearly shows the god Shamash, the goddess Ishtar (with wings), and the god Ea.

Ziggurat

Ishtar Gate was named after the goddess Ishtar. The gate has been reconstructed, and today it stands in the Berlin Museum, Germany.

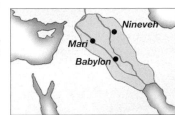

BABYLONIAN EMPIRE
Babylon was one of several important cities in Mesopotamia. For about 2,000 years, its fortunes rose and fell. At its height, under King Hammurabi, and later King Nebuchadnezzar II, the Babylonian empire controlled the entire southern area of Mesopotamia.

BABYLON
The city of Babylon was rebuilt many times before its final destruction. It reached the height of its glory around 600 B.C. It was an impressive city, with massive walls and elaborate religious buildings, including a pyramidlike ziggurat. Babylon also had a fabulous hanging garden – one of the Seven Wonders of the Ancient World.

RUINS OF BABYLON
About 55 miles (90 km) south of Baghdad, Iraq, lie the ruins of ancient Babylon. Although the ruins are sparse, it is still possible to see where the palaces and ziggurat once stood. During the 19th century, archaeologists excavated the site. Today, various parts of the ancient city wall have been rebuilt, as shown above.

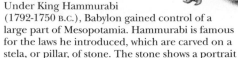

HAMMURABI
Under King Hammurabi (1792-1750 B.C.), Babylon gained control of a large part of Mesopotamia. Hammurabi is famous for the laws he introduced, which are carved on a stela, or pillar, of stone. The stone shows a portrait of Hammurabi standing before Shamash, the god of justice. Beneath this are the laws of Babylon, carved in cuneiform (wedge-shaped) writing. They deal with all aspects of life and show that Babylon was a sophisticated civilization.

NEBUCHADNEZZAR
Nebuchadnezzar II (605-562 B.C.) was one of the most famous kings of Babylonia. Among other conquests, he captured Jerusalem and forced thousands of its people into exile in Babylonian territory. This story is told in the Bible, in the Book of Daniel. Nebuchadnezzar is said to have gone crazy at the end of his reign, as shown in this picture of Nebuchadnezzar by the English artist William Blake (1757-1827).

Find out more
ALPHABETS
ASSYRIANS
PHOENICIANS
WONDERS
of the ancient world

BADGERS AND SKUNKS

Muscular body

Tough, wiry fur

Small ears

Small eyes and poor eyesight

Short, thick legs

Keen sense of smell

Long, strong claws

SETTS

Eurasian badgers live in family groups in a system of tunnels called a sett, which they often build on a bank, or among tree roots. Over the years the badgers extend the sett. A large sett may be 100 years old and have more than 20 entrances; it may house up to 15 badgers. The badgers regularly bring fresh bedding of grass, leaves, and moss to their rest chambers, dragging out the old lining and leaving it near the entrance.

DAWN AND DUSK are the favorite hunting times for badgers and skunks, which prowl at night in search of food. Badgers and skunks are members of the weasel family, found in Europe, North America, Asia, and Africa. Badgers are heavy, sturdy animals, with broad, muscular bodies. They use their strong claws for digging underground homes called setts, where they rest by day. Their thick fur is black, white, and brown. Like badgers, skunks have black and white markings, but their tails are large and bushy. Skunks live in open woodland areas of North and South America. There are three kinds – striped, spotted, and hog-nosed. Striped and hog-nosed skunks live in underground burrows. The spotted skunk also lives underground but can climb trees. Badgers and skunks have an effective way of fending off enemies. They have scent glands on their bodies that produce a very unpleasant smell when the animal is threatened.

HONEY BADGER
The African ratel feeds on honey and is also called the honey badger. The badger relies on a bird called the honey guide bird to lead it to bee and wasp nests, which the badger then breaks into with its strong claws. The thick fur and loose skin of the honey badger seem to shrug off any stings from the bees and wasps.

Badgers are easily recognized by the vivid black and white markings, or "badges," on their faces.

Boar (male badger)

Sow (female badger)

Cubs (young)

Chinese ferret badger

American badger

SKUNK

The striking black-and-white pattern on the striped or common skunk warns other animals to keep away. The skunk is famous for spraying enemies with a stinking substance from glands near its anus. If the spray touches the eyes of another animal, it can cause temporary blindness. There are 10 different kinds of skunk. They eat small animals, insects, birds' eggs, and fruit.

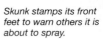

Skunk stamps its front feet to warn others it is about to spray.

STRIPES
Many badgers and skunks have stripes on their faces or along the sides of their bodies. These stripes provide camouflage by helping to break up the animal's outline in twilight. No two faces are exactly the same, so the stripes may also enable the animals to recognize one another.

BADGER CUBS
Two or three cubs are born in late winter or early spring. They play outside the sett entrances during the summer months.

Find out more
ANIMALS
MAMMALS
NESTS AND BURROWS

BALLET

The tips of female dancers' toe shoes are stiffened to allow them to dance on tiptoe without hurting their feet.

MUSIC, DANCE, and mime combine in ballet to tell a story. Ballet began as entertainment for the royal families of Europe more than 300 years ago, and classical ballet style has developed gradually since then. The original French names for steps and jumps are still used. In the 19th century, "romantic" ballet became popular. Dancers in floating white dresses performed *La Sylphide* and *Giselle*. In the early 20th century, the Russian Sergei Diaghilev founded the Ballets Russes, one of the greatest of all ballet companies, which performed all over the world. In ballet, each step and movement is planned in advance. This is called choreography. Great choreographers such as the Russian Fokine (1880-1942) arranged dances for the Ballets Russes. Most ballet dancers begin training at an early age. Ballet dancing is hard work and requires hours of practice.

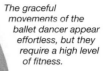

The graceful movements of the ballet dancer appear effortless, but they require a high level of fitness.

MODERN BALLET

In the early 20th century some dancers broke away from classical ballet and moved toward a freer sort of dance. Dancer Isadora Duncan was a pioneer of this more natural style in which performers express ideas in strong movements. Later, choreographer Martha Graham established a modern dance technique. Today, dancers often study the discipline of classical ballet before adopting modern styles.

FONTEYN AND NUREYEV

Toward the end of her career, British ballerina Margot Fonteyn began dancing with a young Russian, Rudolf Nureyev. This famous partnership, shown here in *Romeo and Juliet,* inspired them both and delighted their audiences.

ANNA PAVLOVA

The Russian ballerina Anna Pavlova (1881-1931) was one of the greatest dancers of all time. She worked from the age of 10 to perfect her dancing. Her most famous solo was *Dying Swan,* which was created for her by Fokine.

First Second Third Fourth Fifth

THE FIVE POSITIONS
All ballet movements begin and end with one of the five positions; they were created in the 18th century to provide balance and to make the feet look elegant.

Find out more

COMPOSERS
DANCE
MUSIC
ROCK AND POP
THEATER

BALL GAMES

IN MANY SPORTS AND GAMES, players kick, bowl, or throw a ball around a playing area. They sometimes use bats, rackets, cues, and clubs – as well as their hands, feet, and heads – to roll or drive the ball. The balls vary in shape and size. Most are round, either solid and hard as in billiards and baseball, or hollow as in tennis. Soccer players use a round ball made of leather. In badminton the "ball," called a shuttlecock or bird, has feathers.

Ball games began in prehistoric times. At first they were part of religious ceremonies. People believed ball games would prolong the summer or direct the winds. The Ancient Greeks were among the first to play a ball game for pleasure. Ball games were a vital part of life for the Mayas and Aztecs of Central America. Today, popular ball games range from racket sports such as tennis and squash, to team games such as soccer and baseball.

JAI ALAI
Jai alai, a Spanish game, is also called pelota. Players use a curved scoop called a cesta to hurl a ball (the pelota) at the front wall of the court.

Pool balls are numbered from 1 to 15.

The leather cover of an English soccer ball protects an inflated rubber inner lining.

Three fingerholes enable players to grip a bowling ball.

In table tennis, the "racket" is a solid paddle.

TEAM GAMES

Most of the world's major team sports are ball games, including baseball, basketball, and football. Team games move very fast. Team members need individual skills, such as the ability to run fast; but team skills such as passing the ball are equally important. Team games encourage friendship, discipline, and the ability to work with others.

RACKET GAMES
In racket games such as squash, players use a racket to propel the ball over a net or against a wall. The racket is usually a mesh of strings stretched on a frame. Players compete individually (singles) or in pairs (doubles). Some of these sports do not need a racket: handball players use their hand as the racket.

GOLF
Golfers use clubs to aim the small ball at a hole in the ground. Other ball games require careful aim too. In bowling, the object is to knock down ten or five pins with one ball. Lawn bowlers aim their balls close to a target ball, or jack. In pool and billiards, players aim balls at pockets around a table.

TENNIS
Tennis evolved from a curious game called real, or royal, tennis, which is still played today in a few countries. Real tennis began in France nearly a thousand years ago; its court has open windows, doors, and sloping roofs. Modern tennis is called lawn tennis. It is sometimes played on a grass lawn but usually on a hard surface, such as clay. The top international tennis competitions are held in England, the United States, Australia, and France. Leading tennis players earn huge sums from prize money and equipment sponsorship.

BASEBALL AND CRICKET
Baseball is the national sport of the United States. Winners of the National and American league pennants (championships) compete in the World Series each year. A gentler version, softball, is a popular amateur sport. Cricket players use a wooden bat and a hard ball. Cricket is popular in England, Australia, the West Indies, Pakistan, and India.

Find out more
BASEBALL
FOOTBALL
SOCCER
SPORTS

BALLOONS AND AIRSHIPS

HAVE YOU EVER WATCHED BUBBLES RISE as water boils? That is how balloons and airships fly. They do not need wings to lift them into the air; instead they use a huge, bubble-like bag that floats up because it contains a gas that is lighter than the air around it. In the early days, the gas was usually hydrogen, which was explosive and dangerous. Today, most balloons use hot air, and airships use helium gas. The main difference between balloons and airships is that balloons go where the wind takes them; airships have engines and can fly wherever the pilot chooses. People flew in balloons and airships long before airplanes were invented. But in the 1930s, airplane design improved, and airships and balloons were gradually forgotten. In recent years, however, ballooning has become popular again, and new airships are being built.

MONTGOLFIER BROTHERS
The French brothers Joseph and Jacques Montgolfier built the first balloon that carried people into the air. It made its first free flight in Paris, France, on November 21, 1783, 120 years before the Wright brothers built the first airplane.

HINDENBURG DISASTER
The airships of the 1930s were huge, and the German *Hindenburg* was the largest, with a length of more than 800 ft (244 m). The *Hindenburg* was filled with flammable hydrogen; in 1937 it burst into flame and was destroyed.

Envelope is not rigidly constructed, but is held in shape by the pressure of the gas inside it.

In order to save helium, some airships have special air bags, called ballonets, inside the envelope (the large gasbag). Air is let out instead of helium as the ship goes up, then sucked back in as the airship goes down.

Air let out from ballonet

Propeller fans allow the airship to take off and land vertically and maneuver in the air with great precision.

The gondola carries water ballast (weight to stabilize the craft), which can be let out to help gain height quickly.

Gondola made of Kevlar, a light, extremely strong plastic

Air let out from ballonet

AIRSHIP
Airship engines can propel the craft in any direction. This airship has swiveling propeller fans that drive it up, down, or forward. It can fly at a speed of more than 55 mph (90 km/h).

HOT-AIR BALLOONS
Hot-air balloons consist of a wicker basket and a bright, colorful envelope made of nylon. The envelope can be made in almost any shape, from a camel to a castle. Filling the envelope takes a lot of hot air. The heat from burning propane gas produces the hot air. The propane gas is stored as a liquid in metal cylinders carried in the basket.

Before each balloon flight, the envelope is laid on the ground and held open, and the propane burner is lit to inflate the envelope with hot air.

As the balloon fills up with hot air, it gradually rises. When there is enough hot air to lift the basket, the flight can begin.

GONDOLA
Crew and passengers ride in a cabin called a gondola. This makes an ideal observation platform, because an airship flies slowly and steadily and can stay in the air for hours. The pilot controls the airship with a joystick similar to that in an airplane.

Balloons sometimes carry sand as ballast, which can be thrown out of the basket in order to gain height rapidly.

Once in flight, an occasional blast of hot air from the propane burner is enough to keep the balloon at a steady height.

Find out more
AIR
AIRCRAFT
GAS
PLASTICS
TRANSPORTATION, HISTORY OF

BALTIC STATES
AND BELARUS

THE THREE BALTIC STATES – Lithuania, Latvia, and Estonia – were once Soviet republics. They were the first republics to declare their independence from the Soviet Union in 1991. Traditionally all three countries, with their fertile land and high rainfall, depended on agriculture and rearing dairy cattle. The Soviets, however, encouraged the growth of heavy industry and manufacturing, turning these small republics into industrial nations. When the republics became independent, they had to deal with price rises, food shortages, and pollution. Despite these problems they are beginning to forge links with eastern and western Europe, and new industries are being developed. Tourists are beginning to come to the historic cities of Tallinn and Riga, and the peoples of these countries are rediscovering their history and culture, long suppressed by the Russians.

The Baltic Republics occupy a small stretch of Baltic coast, flanked to the east by Russia, and to the west by Poland and the Russian enclave of Kaliningrad. Belarus lies along the southern border. The Baltic Sea provides an outlet to the North Sea.

ESTONIAN NATIONALITY
During the Soviet era, many Russians settled in the Baltic States. This led to tensions with the Baltic peoples, who tried hard to maintain their own national identity. In Estonia, two-thirds of the population is Estonian. Their language is Finno-Ugric, related to both Finnish and Hungarian.

RIGA
The capital of Latvia lies on the west of the Dvina River, 9 miles (15 km) upstream from the Baltic Sea. The city was founded in 1201, and became an important Baltic trading center. Surviving medieval buildings, such as the castle and cathedral, reflect its prosperity. However, much of this historic legacy was destroyed during the German occupation in World War II (1941-44). It is now a major industrial center and port, although it is icebound between December and April.

THE BALTIC COAST
All the Baltic states face the Baltic Sea. In winter, the Baltic Sea is frozen but in summer Baltic resorts attract tourists. Industrial pollution is damaging this coastline.

BELARUS
Area: 80,154 sq miles (207,600 sq km)
Population: 9,900,000
Capital: Minsk
Languages: Belorussian, Russian

ESTONIA
Area: 17,423 sq miles (45,125 sq km)
Population: 1,300,000
Capital: Tallinn
Languages: Estonian, Russian

LATVIA
Area: 24,938 sq miles (64,589 sq km)
Population: 2,300,000
Capital: Riga
Languages: Latvian, Russian

LITHUANIA
Area: 25,174 sq miles (65,200 sq km)
Population: 3,400,000
Capital: Vilnius
Languages: Lithuanian, Russian

Gulf of Finland
Naissaar — **TALLINN** — Jõhvi — Narva
Paldiski — Rakvere
Vormsi — Haapsalu — Paide
Kärdla — Lake Peipus
Hiiumaa
ESTONIA
Saaremaa — Pärnu — Viljandi — **Tartu**
Kuressaare — Lake Pskov
Gulf — Valga — Võru
Kolka — of — Valmiera
Riga
Talsi — Cēsis
Ventspils — Venta — Madona
Kuldīga — **RĪGA** — Jēkabpils
Saldus — Dobele — Jelgava — Western Dvina
Liepāja — Ludza
Mažeikiai — Joniškis
Kretinga — Plungė — Šiauliai — **Daugavpils**
Klaipėda — Kelmė — **Panevėžys** — Krāslava
Courland — Neman — Kėdainiai — Ukmergė — **Navapolatsk**
Lagoon — Sovetsk — Jurbarkas — Neris — Hlybokaye — **Polatsk** — **Vitsyebsk**
Kaliningrad — Gusev — **Kaunas** — **VILNIUS** — Western Dvina
Chernyakhovsk — Marijampolė — Smarhon' — Lyepyel' — **Orsha**
KALININGRAD — Alytus — Maladzyechna — **Barysaw**
(part of Russ. Fed.) — Druskininkai — Zhodzina — Dnieper — **Mahilyow**
Hrodna — Lida — **MINSK** — Bykhaw
Neman — **BELARUS** — Krychaw
Baranavichy — Slutsk — **Babruysk**
Slonim — Salihorsk — Zhlobin
Svyetlahorsk
Pruzhany — Byaroza — Ptsich — Rechytsa — **Homyel'**
Kobryn — Luninyets — Kalinkavichy
Brest — Pripet
Pinsk — **Mazyr** — Dnieper

Baltic Sea
Gulf of Riga

RUSSIAN FEDERATION

POLAND

UKRAINE

SCALE BAR
0   50   100   km
0   50   100   miles

| Volcano | Mountain | Ancient monument | Capital city | Large city/town | Small city/town |

Find out more
EUROPE, HISTORY OF
OCEANS AND SEAS
SOVIET UNION, HISTORY OF

BARBARIANS

BY THE FOURTH CENTURY A.D., the once great Roman Empire was in decline. A great threat came from tribal groups living outside the boundaries of the empire. The Romans despised these tribes. They thought they were uncivilized because they did not live in cities. Today we often call these tribes barbarians. But in fact they were superb metalworkers, farmers, and great warriors, with well-organized laws and customs. Around A.D. 370 hordes of one particular tribe, the Huns, moved from Central Asia and pushed other tribes further westward and through the frontiers of the Roman Empire. Some of the tribes nearest the empire asked the Romans for shelter. But in 406 hordes of Alans and Vandals swept into Gaul (modern France); in 410 the Visigoths, under Alaric, attacked and captured Rome, and barbarians flooded the Roman Empire. In 1452 the Huns, led by Attila, attacked northern Italy. The Empire was constantly under attack by many Barbarian tribes. Each tribe ruled the area it conquered in its own way.

ATTILA THE HUN
The nomadic Huns were jointly ruled by Attila (434-453) and his brother Bleda. In 452, after killing Bleda, Attila invaded Italy.

SACK OF ROME
In 410 Alaric, king of the Visigoths, captured and looted the great city of Rome, which had been unconquered for 800 years. The sacking of Rome shocked the civilized world, but the empire itself did not collapse until 476.

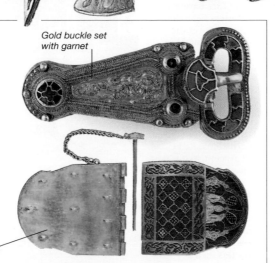

Anglo-Saxons
Alans
Huns
Visigoths
ROME
ROMAN EMPIRE
Vandals

BARBARIAN INVASIONS
By A.D. 500, barbarian tribes had overrun the Western Roman Empire. They divided their territory into separate kingdoms. With time, the invaders adopted some Roman ways, laws, and some Latin words. This map shows the routes of the barbarian invasions in the fifth century.

CRAFTWORK
Each barbarian tribe had its own culture, laws, and customs. Even before A.D. 500 many barbarians had lived inside the Roman Empire, and many eventually became Christians. The barbarians were not just warriors. Their metalwork and jewelry were particularly beautiful.

Gold buckle set with garnet

This gold and enameled fibula was used to fasten a barbarian man's cloak.

Find out more
CHARLEMAGNE
EUROPE, HISTORY OF
ROMAN EMPIRE
VIKINGS

CLARA
BARTON

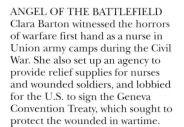

ANGEL OF THE BATTLEFIELD
Clara Barton witnessed the horrors of warfare first hand as a nurse in Union army camps during the Civil War. She also set up an agency to provide relief supplies for nurses and wounded soldiers, and lobbied for the U.S. to sign the Geneva Convention Treaty, which sought to protect the wounded in wartime.

THE RED CROSS FLAG has been a reassuring symbol of humanitarian aid in war and disaster zones since the late 19th century. The American Red Cross was founded in 1881 by Clara Barton. A remarkable and compassionate woman, Barton was a teacher and a clerk who dedicated herself at age 40 to voluntary work. As a nurse in the Civil War (1861-1865), she earned the nickname "Angel of the Battlefield" as she tended the wounded in the line of fire. After the war she traveled to Europe, where she observed the newly formed International Red Cross. Back in the United States, she set up the American Red Cross, serving as president until 1904. Under her leadership, the organization flourished. Today, there are more than 1.3 million American Red Cross volunteers.

THE RED CROSS
The International Red Cross was founded in 1864, largely by Swiss businessman Henri Dunant. This voluntary organization aimed to care for the sick and wounded in wartime, no matter what side they fought on. In 1870, Clara Barton observed the Red Cross in France during the Franco-Prussian War (1870-71). She was so impressed with their work that in 1881 she set up a similar organization in the United States. The American Red Cross concentrated on helping the victims of natural disasters. In 1889, Barton and her coworkers provided food and shelter to thousands of flood victims in Johnstown, Pennsylvania (right).

EARLY LIFE
Barton began teaching when she was 17. She set up one of the first free public schools in New Jersey. Later, she became the first woman to work in the US Patent Office, where she took a job as a clerk.

CLARA BARTON

1821 Born in Oxford, Massachusetts.

1854 Becomes first woman to work in US Patent Office.

1861-65 Obtains and distributes relief supplies on battlefields during Civil War.

1870-71 Volunteers as independent relief worker, Franco-Prussian War.

1881 Founds the American Red Cross and becomes its president.

1912 Dies in Glen Echo, Maryland.

TIRELESS CAMPAIGNER
The American Red Cross grew rapidly under Clara Barton's leadership. Posters (left) drew volunteers from all over the United States and brought in donations to fund the organization's work. Barton worked for the Red Cross well into her eighties. She also campaigned for women's rights and prison reform.

RED CROSS TODAY
The International Red Cross and Red Crescent, as it is now known, provides welfare services in times of both war and peace. These include ambulances, blood banks, first-aid training, and food, medicine, and shelter for refugees and victims of disasters such as floods and famines.

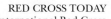

YOUR RED CROSS NEEDS YOU!

RED CROSS IN WARTIME
When World War I broke out in 1914, many thousands of people volunteered to staff Red Cross hospitals (left) and to drive ambulances to carry wounded soldiers from the battlefields. The Red Cross also supplied food parcels to prisoners of war and forwarded letters between the prisoners and their families.

Find out more

CIVIL WAR
FIRST AID
HOSPITALS
LINCOLN, ABRAHAM
WOMEN'S RIGHTS

BASEBALL

BASEBALL IS THE TOP SPORT in the United States and is played in more than 100 countries around the world. This ball game is thought to have originated from the English game of rounders, which was brought to America in the early 1600s by the first English settlers. In 1845, a US sportsman, Alexander Cartwright, wrote a set of rules that form the basis of modern baseball. In 1869, the first professional baseball team, the Cincinnati Red Stockings, was founded. Over the years, baseball stars such as the legendary Babe Ruth have emerged from the field, and today teams such as the New York Yankees inspire fans all over the globe. On the field, two teams of nine take turns to bat and field. The pitcher throws the ball and the batter attempts to hit it and score runs by progressing around four bases without being tagged or forced out by a fielder. The game has nine innings. An inning is over when six batters – three from each side – are out.

FIRST ORGANIZED GAME
The first organized baseball game to be played under the Cartwright rules was held in 1846 at the Elysian Fields in New Jersey. The Knickerbockers beat the New York Nine by 23-1, and Alexander Cartwright, the writer of the rules, umpired at the game.

Baseball cap

Colored jersey

Baseball mitt

Baseball pants, half-way down calf

Pants

The center fielder is one of three outfielders who defend the outfield.

The foul line must extend at least 250 ft (76 m) from the home plate.

Outfield

The pitcher stands on the pitcher's mound.

Infield

An infielder prepares to cover first base.

Foul territory

Cleat

Colored stirrup

BASEBALL FIELD
A baseball field is made up of the infield and the outfield. Two foul lines run from the home plate through first and third bases to create a 90° arc. The area inside the lines is fair territory; the area outside is foul territory.

The batting team waits at the bench or dugout.

The batter stands in the batter's box.

The catcher is behind home plate.

Face mask

Chest protector

PLAYERS
Baseball is a hard-ball game, and protective equipment is required for the catcher, the batter, and base runners. In league baseball, each team has its own equipment, and players wear identical uniforms.

Shin guards protect shins, and are hinged for movement.

Catcher's mitt

EQUIPMENT
In order to play well and to enjoy the game, a baseball player needs to have the proper safety equipment in addition to the basic requirement of a bat, a baseball, and a glove. Players wear protective helmets, masks, mitts, body padding, and buckled shin guards. Cleats are shoes that help the players to get a grip on the ground. A baseball uniform includes a cap, a jersey, pants, and stirrups – all in matching colors.

Bat

Fielder's glove

Catcher's mitt

GLOVES
Catchers and fielders wear padded leather gloves to protect their hands from the high-speed impact of traveling balls. Batters wear gloves to get a really firm grip on the bat.

Ball

Batter's glove

HELMETS
All catchers and batters must wear helmets to protect them from swinging bats and balls that travel at great speed. These plastic helmets have soft foam inserts.

Batter's helmet

**Find out more**
BALL GAMES
SPORTS

BASKETBALL

THE ONLY MAJOR SPORT that is completely American in origin, basketball was invented in Springfield, Massachusetts, in 1891. Perhaps because the game is so simple – you only need a ball, a net, and a few friends to play – its popularity grew quickly. Within a decade, there were both men's and women's college teams and a professional circuit. Today, basketball is the most popular spectator sport in America. There are five players on each team, who try to put the ball into the opposing team's basket and score points. Each basket is worth one, two, or three points, depending on from where the player takes the shot. A referee and an umpire enforce the rules. Under National Basketball Association (NBA) rules, each game is divided into four quarters of 12 minutes, with rest periods.

HISTORY OF BASKETBALL
Basketball was invented by physical education teacher Dr. James Naismith (above). He nailed two fruit baskets high on balconies at each end of a gymnasium, found a soccer ball and two teams, and the first game of basketball began.

MOVING THE BALL
The player with the ball must pass it to another player or shoot before taking two steps, or dribble it by bouncing it along the ground. Defenders try to block passes and shots, or steal the ball away.

PLAYERS
Basketball teams have five players: a center, two forwards, and two guards. Although players change positions throughout the game, the center usually operates close to the basket, the forwards play on the flanks, and the guards play in defense.

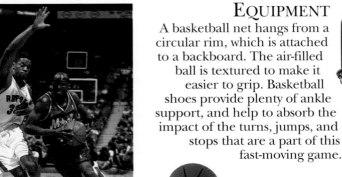

EQUIPMENT
A basketball net hangs from a circular rim, which is attached to a backboard. The air-filled ball is textured to make it easier to grip. Basketball shoes provide plenty of ankle support, and help to absorb the impact of the turns, jumps, and stops that are a part of this fast-moving game.

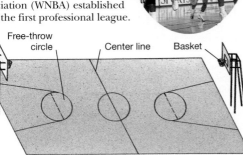

Net and backboard

WOMEN'S BASKETBALL
Women have played basketball for almost as long as men, with collegiate basketball teams competing as early as 1896. Women's basketball became an Olympic sport at the 1976 Summer Games in Montreal, and in 1997 the Women's National Basketball Association (WNBA) established the first professional league.

A basketball is made of eight shaped panels.

High-topped shoe supports the ankle

A player within range of the basket can make a jump shot, releasing the ball at the top of a high jump.

Free-throw circle   Center line   Basket

BASKETBALL COURT
A basketball court is a rectangle split in half by a center line. The two long sides are called sidelines and the two short sides are known as baselines. Above the baseline is a goal, or basket, suspended 10 ft (3 m) above the floor. The free-throw line and circle make a keyhole shape beneath each goal.

Find out more

BALL GAMES
FOOTBALL
SPORTS

BATS

WHEN MOST OTHER CREATURES return to their homes for the night, bats take to the air. Bats are the only mammals capable of flight. They are nighttime creatures with leather-like wings that enable them to swoop and glide through the darkness catching moths and other airborne insects. Although most bats are insectivores (insect eaters), some feed on fruit, nectar, pollen, fish, small mammals, and reptiles. Bats usually give birth to one or two young each year. The young are left in a nursery roost, clustered together for warmth, while the mothers fly off to feed. There are about 1,000 different kinds of bats, including red bats, brown bats, and dog-faced bats. They make up one-quarter of all mammal species, yet few people have ever seen one. Today, many kinds of bats are becoming rare as their roosts are destroyed and their feeding areas are taken over for farming and building.

VAMPIRE BAT
The vampire bat of South America bites mammals and birds to feed on their blood, but it does not usually attack humans.

Bats sleep upside down in a nesting place called a roost.

Bats' wings are supported during flight by long, thin arm and finger bones. When resting, the bat hangs in its roost by its clawed back feet.

FISHING BAT
The South American fishing bat has long legs and sharp claws for catching fish. It uses echolocation to detect ripples on the water's surface, then flies low with its feet dangling in the water. When the bat hooks a fish, its legs pull the slippery prey up to its mouth, where sharp teeth hold the fish securely.

At the top of each wing is a claw, which the bat uses to cling onto rocks as it clambers about in the caves where it lives.

HORSESHOE BAT
There are more than 145 different kinds of horseshoe bats. Their name comes from the fleshy, curved flaps on their noses, which help with echolocation. The greater European horseshoe bat has a wingspan of more than 12 in (30 cm).

FRUIT BAT

The fruit bat is the largest bat; some measure almost 7 ft (2 m) from one wing tip to the other. It is also called the flying fox because it has a fox-like face. Fruit bats roost in trees or caves and fly out at dawn and dusk to feed on fruit, flowers, and leaves. Fruit bats are found in Africa, southern Asia, and Australia. In areas where they live in large numbers, fruit bats cause great damage by eating farm crops.

ECHOLOCATION

Bats find their way in the dark by making squeaks and clicks, which are so high-pitched that most humans cannot hear them. This is called echolocation. The sounds made by the bat bounce off a nearby object such as a tree or a moth. The bat can detect the returning echoes with its large, forward-pointing ears, and in a split second it has worked out the size, distance, and direction of the object.

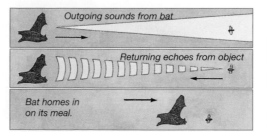

Outgoing sounds from bat

Returning echoes from object

Bat homes in on its meal.

Find out more
ANIMALS
ANIMAL SENSES
FLIGHT, ANIMAL
MAMMALS
WHALES AND DOLPHINS

BEARS AND PANDAS

Small ears

Large head

Small eyes with poor eyesight

Short muzzle

Keen sense of smell

Huge, powerful paws

ALTHOUGH BEARS are often portrayed as cuddly, they are among the most dangerous of all creatures. There are seven kinds of bears. The largest is the polar bear. It stands nearly 10 ft (3 m) tall and weighs more than half a ton. The smallest bear is the sun bear from Southeast Asia, which measures about 4 ft (1.2 m) from head to tail. Other bears include the grizzly and the sloth bear. Bears are heavily built mammals, which eat both flesh and plants. Giant pandas, which eat mostly bamboo shoots, are related to bears. The giant panda is a large black and white creature that weighs about 300 lb (135 kg). Today they are very rare. The red panda, which is much smaller, is more closely related to the raccoon. All bears and the giant panda have poor eyesight, so they find their food mainly by smell.

DANCING BEAR
Bears have sometimes been taken from their natural habitats and trained to entertain people, but this cruel practice is now banned in most countries.

BLACK BEAR

There are two kinds of black bear – one from North America and the other from Southeast Asia. Not all American black bears are completely black. Some are dark brown or reddish brown. Black bears are skillful tree climbers and run fast – up to 25 mph (40 km/h). American black bears inhabit the forests of North America, and many live in national parks.

PAWS
A bear's paws are large, broad, and powerful, with tough, thick claws. Pandas have unusual paws. A modified wristbone acts like a thumb, allowing the panda to grasp bamboo shoots (above).

GIANT PANDA

The giant panda is also called the panda bear. Giant pandas live in central and western China and eat mostly bamboo shoots. There are only a few hundred giant pandas left in the wild, and they have become a worldwide symbol of conservation.

GRIZZLY BEAR

The huge grizzly bear has no enemies apart from humans. Grizzly bears live in North America, Europe, and Asia. The grizzly is also called the brown bear. A female grizzly bear gives birth to two or three cubs in a winter den. Grizzly bears eat almost anything, including spring shoots, fall fruits, animal flesh, and honey taken from bees' nests.

RACCOON
There are 18 kinds of raccoon; all are found in the Americas. They are fast, agile creatures related to bears. Raccoons in populated areas are active mainly at night, when they feed on garbage and farm crops.

In the fall, grizzly bears scoop up salmon that have swum upriver to spawn (lay their eggs).

Find out more
ANIMALS
CONSERVATION
and endangered species
MAMMALS
NORTH AMERICAN WILDLIFE
POLAR WILDLIFE

BEAVERS

THERE ARE TWO KINDS of beavers – the European and the North American. Both are rodents – a group of animals that includes rats, mice, and squirrels. Beavers have long, sharp front teeth for gnawing at plants and trees. These teeth are open-rooted and continue to grow throughout life. Beavers are excellent builders. They use their teeth like chisels to bite through branches, which they drag away to build dams and lodges in rivers and streams. Although beavers go on land to find food, they are aquatic animals and spend most of their time in or near water. They are good swimmers, using their webbed back feet for speed. A beaver can dive and hold its breath underwater for several minutes. The beaver has a flat, scaly tail that it uses for steering and for extra speed, thrusting the tail up and down in the water like a powerful paddle. Beavers also use their tails to warn others of danger by slapping the tail on the surface of the water. During the 18th and 19th centuries, beavers were hunted for their thick fur, which was used to make coats and hats. In some parts of North America, beavers almost died out completely. Today, however, trapping beavers for their fur is controlled and these animals are no longer in danger of extinction.

TEETH
The beaver's huge front incisor teeth can cut through bark and wood to fell small trees for food and for dam building.

DAMS
Using sticks, stones, and mud, beavers build a dam at a suitable place across a stream. The water around the dam spreads out to form a lake, which is where the beavers build their lodge.

Beaver can hold and manipulate small items, such as twigs and stones for the dam, with its front paws.

Beaver uses its flat tail as a rudder when it is swimming underwater.

WOOD FOR DAMS
As wood becomes scarce, beavers may have to travel greater distances to find more. They float tree branches along canals and add them to the dam.

Some lodges are more than 10 ft (3 m) high.

Adult beaver brings leafy twigs home to food store.

FEEDING
Beavers are herbivores (plant eaters). Their food varies according to the season. In fall and winter, beavers feed on bark and soft wood, particularly aspen and willow. They store twigs and branches underwater in the lake or river where they live. Even when the surface of the water is frozen hard in winter, beavers can swim from the underwater entrance of their home to bring back stored food. In spring and summer, beavers feed on grass, leaves, and water plants.

BREEDING
Young beavers are called kits. They are born in spring and can swim a day or two after birth.

Underwater entrances help keep kits safe from predators.

UNDERWATER ENTRANCE
The lodge has several underwater entrances. Inside the lodge the beavers are safe from predators such as wolves, which cannot dig through the strong walls or swim down through the entrances.

LODGE
A beaver family lives in a structure called a lodge, built from tree branches and mud. Inside the lodge, the beavers hollow out a dry chamber above the water level. This is where they rest and sleep. In the fall, the adults coat the outside of the lodge with a layer of mud. The mud freezes in winter and gives protection against predators.

Find out more
ANIMALS
CONSERVATION
and endangered species
MAMMALS
MICE, RATS, AND SQUIRRELS

BRAIN AND NERVES

EVERY THOUGHT AND MOVEMENT that we make is controlled by the brain. The brain is more complex than any computer ever invented. It enables us to think, speak, hear, see, feel, and move. It works non-stop, day and night. The brain consists of billions of living units called neurons or nerve cells. Neurons carry millions of messages to the brain along the spinal cord, which runs down the back and links the brain to the rest of the body. When these messages, or nerve signals, reach the brain, it sorts them out and sends instructions to the rest of the body along the nerves. Nerves are like wires, made of bundles of nerve cells. Sensory nerves take signals from the eyes, ears, and skin to the brain; motor nerves take signals from the brain to the muscles, telling them when to move the body. The average adult human brain weighs about 1.4 kg (3 lb) and has a texture like jelly. It is protected inside the head by the skull.

SLEEP
When we sleep, the body rests but the brain is still working, controlling our breathing and heartbeat. We remember some of our night thoughts as dreams.

CEREBRAL HEMISPHERES
The largest parts of the brain are the two folded cerebral hemispheres. Our thoughts are based in these hemispheres. The outer layer of the brain is called the grey matter. It is rich in nerve cells. The inner layer is called the white matter. It consists mainly of nerve fibres. If the two hemispheres were spread out, they would cover an area the size of a pillowcase.

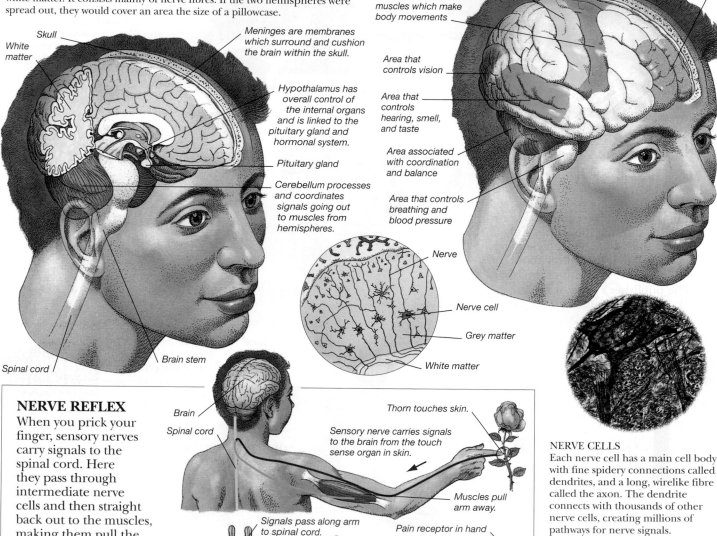

White matter

Skull

Meninges are membranes which surround and cushion the brain within the skull.

Hypothalamus has overall control of the internal organs and is linked to the pituitary gland and hormonal system.

Pituitary gland

Cerebellum processes and coordinates signals going out to muscles from hemispheres.

Spinal cord

Brain stem

Area associated with touch

Area involved with consciousness, creativity, and personality

Area that controls the muscles which make body movements

Area that controls vision

Area that controls hearing, smell, and taste

Area associated with coordination and balance

Area that controls breathing and blood pressure

Nerve

Nerve cell

Grey matter

White matter

NERVE REFLEX
When you prick your finger, sensory nerves carry signals to the spinal cord. Here they pass through intermediate nerve cells and then straight back out to the muscles, making them pull the finger away. This is called a reflex – an automatic reaction that we make without thinking.

Brain

Spinal cord

Thorn touches skin.

Sensory nerve carries signals to the brain from the touch sense organ in skin.

Muscles pull arm away.

Signals pass along arm to spinal cord.

Pain receptor in hand

Nerve cell

Motor nerve carries signals to muscles in arm.

NERVE CELLS
Each nerve cell has a main cell body with fine spidery connections called dendrites, and a long, wirelike fibre called the axon. The dendrite connects with thousands of other nerve cells, creating millions of pathways for nerve signals.

Find out more
HEART AND BLOOD
HUMAN BODY
MUSCLES AND MOVEMENT

BRAZIL

BRAZIL, THE LARGEST COUNTRY in South America, is a land of contrasts. To the south, it is dominated by the rolling grasslands of the Brazilian highlands, while arid deserts lie to the northeast. Three-fifths of Brazil's total land area is covered by the world's largest rain forest, which forms the drainage basin of the Amazon, the world's second-longest river. Increasingly, the rain forest is being cleared for agriculture, cattle ranching, mining, and the timber industry as Brazil's rapidly growing population places more pressure on the land. Rural poverty drives many people to overcrowded cities. São Paulo, the fastest growing city on the continent, is a major industrial center. Brazil was colonized in the 16th century by the Portuguese, who imported African slaves to work on sugar plantations. Today, Brazil is the largest Roman Catholic nation in the world, and has a vibrant mix of Indian, Portuguese, and African cultures.

Brazil borders every country in South America, except Chile and Ecuador. Its Atlantic border is 4,600 miles (7,400 km) long.

SHANTYTOWNS

For many people living in rural poverty, cities seem to offer a chance of employment and a better life. Yet a severe lack of housing in Brazil's major cities has led to the growth of *favelas*. These shanty-towns, built of wood and corrugated iron, sprawl over land which is unfit for other development.

RIO CARNIVAL

Every year, just before Lent, Rio de Janeiro is transformed by a five-day carnival. Huge parades snake their way through the city. Brightly dressed singers, musicians, and dancers fill the streets with color, spectacle, and the sound of *samba* music.

About 22 per cent of the world's coffee comes from Brazil. It is grown in the warm fertile soils of central and southern Brazil.

RIO DE JANEIRO

Rio de Janeiro is located on the Atlantic coast, and sprawls across bays, islands, and the foothills of the coastal mountains. It is dominated by the distinctive shape of Sugarloaf Mountain and the monumental statue of Christ the Redeemer. Founded by the Portuguese in 1565, it was capital of Brazil from 1763 to 1960. Today, this rapidly growing city is a major international port, and a commercial, manufacturing and cultural center. It is also famous for its beaches, annual carnival, and exciting nightlife.

GOLD RUSH

Brazil's mineral wealth ranges from iron and tin to gold and precious stones, such as diamonds and topaz. Since the 1980s, thousands of miners have flooded to the Serra Pelada region, burrowing into the hillside with their bare hands in search of gold.

Swarms of gold prospectors, known as garimpeiros, cover this Brazilian hillside. They chip away rock with pick axes, hoping they might find their fortune in gold.

Carnival party-goers compete with each other for the prize for the most outrageous costume and best-decorated float.

AMAZONIAN RAIN FOREST

The largest surviving area of rain forest in the world is in the Amazon River basin. It is the most biologically diverse habitat in the world and supports millions of species of plants and animals. Scientists estimate that more than 2,000 species can live in just one rain forest tree. The annual average temperature is 79°F (26°C), while annual rainfall can be as high as 80 in (2,000 mm). Rain forest soils are easily washed away when trees and plants are removed. As more and more land is cleared for farming and timber, the rain forest is lost forever.

When rain forests are cleared in equatorial regions, heavy rainfall erodes the soil, leaving a green desert. Crops cannot grow in these conditions and many animals lose their natural habitat.

Brazil nuts

Tropical hardwoods are a valued resource and large logging companies are responsible for much of the loss of rain forest habitat.

FOREST RESOURCES

The Amazonian rain forest is rich in many resources, from plants with medicinal properties and rubber trees which produce latex, to brazil nuts. Brazil nuts (left) can be eaten or crushed to make oil. They are exported worldwide.

In Manaus (right) during the dry season, trucks reverse down to the edge of the Amazon to receive cargo.

AMAZONIAN INDIANS

It is estimated that some 220,000 native Brazilians still live in the rain forest. These peoples, also known as the Amazonian Indians, live a traditional way of life. They survive by hunting, fishing, and clearing small patches of forest for farming corn and manioc. Many Indian groups have been wiped out by disease or by land-hungry miners, settlers, and loggers. Today, most live in protected areas.

WATER HIGHWAY

The mighty Amazon river has the greatest volume of water of any river in the world. It is navigable along its entire 4,000-mile (6,400-km) length. It is a major transport artery, carrying 10 per cent of all Brazilian cargo. The river teems with barges, passenger ships, and patrol boats. River ports, such as Manaus and Belém, are important commercial centres.

MANAUS

Manaus was a rich city in the 19th century, its wealth based on the rubber industry. Today, it is a centre for the cattle ranching, mining, and timber industries of Amazonia. It is also an important cultural centre in this remote region, and is famous for its domed opera house. With a population of one million, Manaus is a magnet for the rural poor who continue to settle there.

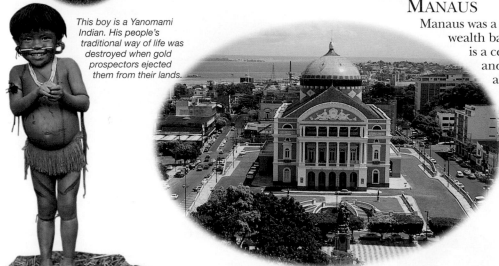

This boy is a Yanomami Indian. His people's traditional way of life was destroyed when gold prospectors ejected them from their lands.

Find out more
FESTIVALS AND FEASTS
FOREST WILDLIFE
RIVERS
SOCCER
SOUTH AMERICA

STATISTICS
Area: 3,286,472 sq miles
(8,511,970 sq km)
Population: 179,000,000
Capital: Brasília
Languages: Portuguese,
German, Italian, Spanish,
Polish, Japanese,
Amerindian languages
Religions: Roman Catholic,
Protestant, Afro-American
Spiritist
Currency: Real
Main occupations: Saw
milling, manufacturing,
coffee and sugar farming
Main exports: Coffee,
soybeans, sugar, orange
juice, steel, cars, computers
Main imports: Gasoline

Volcano · Mountain · Ancient monument · Capital city · Large city/town · Small city/town

IGUACU FALLS
These horseshoe-shaped falls lie on the
Argentine-Brazilian border, where the
Iguaçu River plunges and divides into
some 275 waterfalls, ranging in height
from 200–269 ft (60–82 m). Many of the
individual falls are broken by protruding
rocks, deflecting water and spray to
create a wall of rainbows. At the bottom
of the falls, a curtain of mist rises 500 ft
(150 m) into the air.
This spectacular
region is protected
by the Iguaçu
National Park.

SOCCER
Soccer is a
popular sport in
Brazil. It is followed by
many people, and is even
played on the streets.

*Brazilian soccer
star, Rivaldo.*

MIGRATION
*Northeastern Brazil is
dominated by vast cattle
ranches. Prolonged drought
has driven millions
of farmers
to the cities
of the south.*

BRASILIA
In 1960, the Brazilian
capital began to move to the
purpose-built city of Brasília. It was
thought that this move would kickstart
the development of the sparsely-inhabited interior.
Built to a cross-shaped plan, Brasília's wide boulevards
and large, open plazas are lined with striking federal and
civic buildings, and modern sculptures.

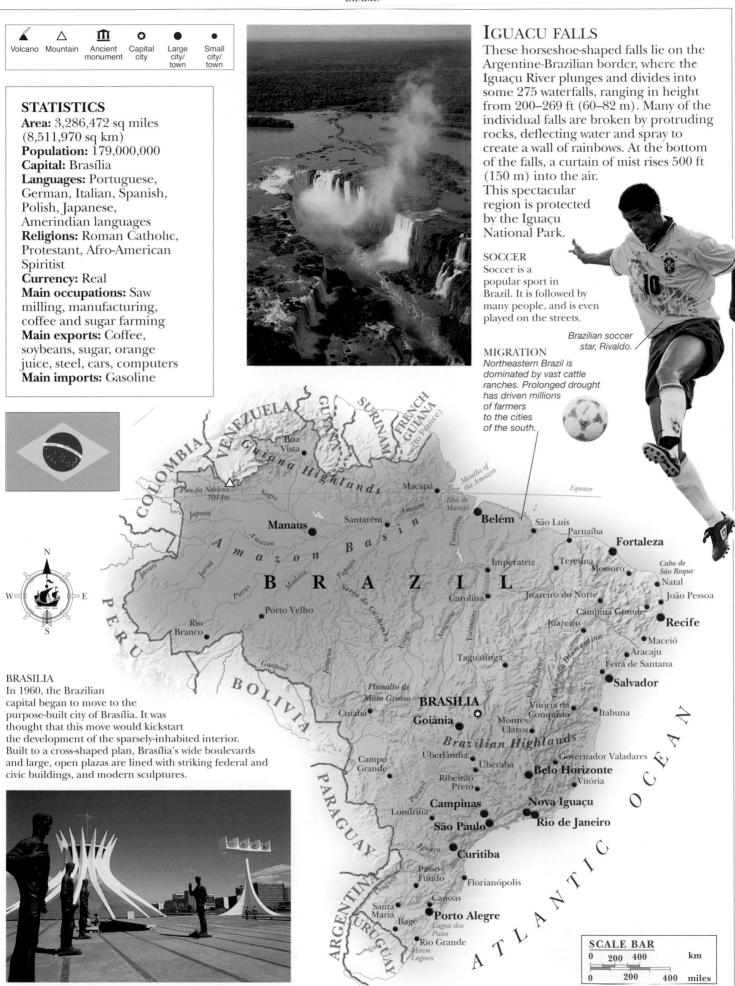

SCALE BAR

0   200   400   km

0   200   400   miles

BRIDGES

TRAVEL ON LAND is easier, safer, and more direct with bridges. Motor vehicles and trains can speed over lakes, rivers, and deep valleys. Bridges raise busy roads over others so that the roads do not meet. Major roads and railroads enter cities on long bridges sometimes called viaducts. Footbridges allow people to cross roads, rivers, and railroads safely.

The first bridges were made by placing tree trunks across rivers, and laying flat stones on rocks in shallow streams. Later, people made rope bridges by weaving plants together, and built stone bridges with strong arches. Similar kinds of bridges are built today with concrete and other strong, modern materials instead of natural materials. Steel beams and cables are used as supports. The world's longest bridge crosses Lake Pontchartrain in the United States. It is almost 24 miles (39 km) long. Land cannot be seen from its centre.

SUSPENSION BRIDGE
A pair of long steel cables fixed to high towers suspends the roadway. Suspension bridges can span the longest distances because they are lightweight.

ARCH BRIDGE
A curved arch firmly fixed to the banks supports the bridge. Arches are very strong structures.

CANTILEVER BRIDGE
Each half of the bridge is balanced on a support in the river. Where the two halves meet, there may be a short central span.

CABLE-STAYED BRIDGE
Sets of straight steel cables attached to towers hold up the bridge from above.

BASCULE BRIDGE
Sections of the bridge tilt like a drawbridge, allowing ships into port.

BEAM BRIDGE
Several columns in the riverbed or the ground support the bridge from beneath. Sometimes the bridge is made of a hollow girder through which cars and trains can run.

BUILDING A BRIDGE
The supports and ends of the bridge are built first, firmly fixed in the ground or the riverbed and banks. The deck of the bridge carrying the road or railroad is then built out from the ends and supports, or lifted onto them.

SUSPENDING THE CABLES
The towers of a suspension bridge are built first. Steel ropes are then placed over the towers. A machine moves along the ropes, spinning long lengths of wire into strong steel cables.

RAISING THE DECK
Long lengths of cable, called hangers, are fixed to the suspending cables. The deck of the bridge is made in sections elsewhere. The sections are taken to the bridge, lifted into position, and attached to the hangers.

KINDS OF BRIDGES
There are various ways of building bridges to span rivers and other barriers. Most bridges rest on solid supports. Pontoon bridges, which are found on some lakes, float on the surface of the water.

THE LONGEST SPANS
The Akashi-Kaikyo Bridge in Japan, has the longest single span of any bridge. The central span is 6,530 ft (1,990 m) long. The bridge was completed in 1997. The Humber Bridge, England, (left) has the fourth longest single span, at 4,626 ft (1,410 m).

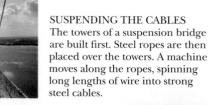

TACOMA BRIDGE DISASTER
The Tacoma Narrows Bridge in Washington, United States, failed in 1940. The wind made the bridge twist back and forth until the deck gave way. Nobody was hurt.

AQUEDUCTS
Bridges that carry water are called aqueducts. The aqueduct may be part of a canal, or it may bring a water supply to a town or city. The Romans built many aqueducts with high stone arches, several of which survive today.

Find out more

ARCHITECTURE
BUILDING

BROADCASTING

TO MEDIEVAL FARMERS, THE WORD broadcast meant to scatter seeds across a wide area of ploughed earth, to make sure that as many of them as possible took root. When the radio was invented at the beginning of the 20th century, the same word was used to describe how sound programs could be sent out far and wide across the world. When television appeared 40 years later, it became possible to broadcast pictures as well as sound. Broadcasting companies were first set up in the 1920s to transmit (send out) radio programs that included news, weather reports, government information, music, and drama. Today there are thousands of radio and TV companies. Radio and TV also let us enjoy sport, concerts, plays, and films in our own homes, and learn new skills from educational programs.

TOWN CRIER
Before radio, TV, and newspapers, news was read out loud on the streets by special "newsreaders" called town criers.

NEWS STUDIO

One of the main functions of broadcasting is to give regular news reports, usually from a studio. Technicians make sure the sound system works and that signals are sent out correctly. Journalists research and write the news stories. Newsreaders present the news. Reports, or bulletins, may include live information from outside broadcasts, and interviews with people in the news.

The studio manager organizes the running order of news stories and brings in outside broadcasts and interviews.

Students try their skills as newsreaders in a mock-up news studio.

BROADCASTING COMPANIES
Nearly every country has its own national broadcasting company, such as the BBC in Britain. These may be paid for by public funds or a license fee. There are also large commercial broadcasters, paid for by advertising or sponsorship. Smaller stations serve local communities.

Broadcasting House, London, home of the BBC

FREE ACCESS
The clockwork radio was invented and developed in the 1990s. Now, most people on the planet can access radio, even without a power supply, and keep up with local and international news.

Live 8 Concert in London, 2005

REACHING THE PEOPLE
Major news items are broadcast almost instantly even to the remotest communities. Huge numbers of people all over the world can join in events such as the first moon landing or the Live 8 concerts, as these events actually happen.

NEWS GATHERING
Journalists work round the clock to collect the most up-to-date news information. Teams of reporters, photographers, and sound engineers are sent to the scenes of major events. Some reporters, such as those reporting on the traffic or covering dramatic events, use helicopters.

Find out more
INFORMATION TECHNOLOGY
NEWSPAPERS
RADIO
TELEVISION AND VIDEO

BRONZE AGE

THE BRONZE AGE refers to a period of time during which the predominant metal employed by a culture was bronze. It usually succeeds the Stone Age and the Copper Age and is followed by the Iron Age. The Bronze Age spans c. 3500 to 1000 B.C. but its onset occurred at different times in different parts of the world. During this period, civilizations sprang up in Egypt, Mesopotamia, the Hwang Ho Valley in China, on the Aegean Islands of the Mediterranean, and in the Indus Valley. People learnt to grow crops and domesticate animals, so they no longer needed to move to find food. This allowed communities more time to learn how to use metals. Bronze was formed by melting copper and tin together and was found to be harder and longer lasting than other metals. It was used to make weapons and ornaments, sometimes by pouring hot molten bronze into molds, for example to make metal pins, or by being heated and beaten into shape. Metalworkers also used gold and copper for luxury items such as jewellery.

MESOPOTAMIA
One of the earliest Bronze Age civilisations began in Mesopotamia, a plain lying between the Tigris and Euphrates rivers. Its fertile land was farmed by the Sumerians, Assyrians, and Akkadians.

AEGEAN CIVILIZATIONS

The rise of the Aegean civilizations coincided with the start of bronzeworking in the region. Several important cultures arose during the Aegean Bronze Age (c. 3000 to 1100 B.C.): chiefly the Cycladic, Minoan, Mycenaean, and Trojan cultures. People became highly skilled in architecture, painting, and other crafts. Metalworkers used bronze to make weapons, such as this Mycenaean dagger blade (right) and tools for everyday use such as axes, adzes, and tweezers. People were often buried with a variety of valuable bronze weapons, household utensils, or ornaments. The Aegean people produced bronze objects in great quantity.

THE MYCENAEANS
The city of Mycenae was ruled by the legendary king Agamemnon, whose remains were found wearing the gold funeral mask shown right. Mycenae was famous for its grand palace, walled fortress, and the beehive-shaped tombs where kings were buried. The Mycenaeans were wealthy and powerful, and dominated the Aegean region from 1450 B.C. onwards.

SHANG DYNASTY
The Bronze Age coincided with the rise of the Shang dynasty (c. 1650 to 1027 B.C.), which was located in the Hwang Ho Valley in China. Its Bronze Age lasted from 1500 to 1000 B.C.. Shang techniques for metalworking and writing spread throughout the area. Most bronze vessels (such as the ritual water vessel shown below) were made for use in religious ceremonies. Bronze was also used to make weapons and chariot fittings for soldiers of the great Shang armies.

WRITING AND THE WHEEL

The earliest form of writing, called cuneiform, emerged during the Bronze Age. It was invented by the Sumerians, who also made the first wheels. Wheels were used on wagons and war chariots, and to make pottery. The chariot shown left is from the city of Ur and is being pulled into battle by wild asses.

Find out more

ASSYRIANS
BABYLONIANS
CELTS
GREECE, ANCIENT
PREHISTORIC PEOPLES
SUMERIANS

BUDDHISM

ONE OF THE WORLD'S great religions, Buddhism, began in India about 2,500 years ago. It grew and spread, and today there are more than 350 million Buddhists worldwide, mainly in Asia. All Buddhists follow the teachings of Buddha, a name which means "Enlightened One". Buddha himself was born in about 563 B.C. He was originally called Siddhartha, and was a wealthy prince who became horrified at the suffering in the world. He left his wealth and family, assumed the name Gautama and began to meditate (think deeply). After three years he achieved enlightenment – complete understanding – became a monk, and traveled extensively to pass his ideas on to others.

Buddhists believe that everyone is reborn after their old body has died. The quality of their new life depends on their karma. Karma is the total of all the good and bad deeds they did in the life they have just left. Buddhists aim to achieve absolute peace – a state they call nirvana. Buddha taught that nirvana could be achieved by following the Eightfold Path: rightness of views, intention, speech, action, livelihood, concentration, mindfulness, and effort.

GOLDEN PAGODA
Buddhist temples usually contain relics of Buddha, such as robes or a sandal. Some, such as the Golden Pavilion in Kyoto, Japan, are magnificent buildings inlaid with gold and decorated with diamonds.

BUDDHAS
Although they vary greatly in size, images of the Buddha all look similar. They represent Buddha sitting on a lotus flower. In the home a small Buddha forms part of a shrine. The image reminds followers of the goodness of Buddha and helps them meditate and pray.

Buddhists burn incense at the shrine and leave offerings of flowers.

FESTIVALS
Bodhi Day – the day Gautama became the Buddha.

Parinirvana – passing of the Buddha into nirvana.

Wesak or Vesakha Puja – a three-day festival to celebrate the main events of Buddha's life.

Dharmachakra Day – when Buddha gave his first sermon.

MONKS
Buddhist monks give up most possessions. They keep only their saffron yellow robes, a needle, a razor, a water strainer, and a large piece of cloth to receive alms (gifts). Monks spend their time praying, teaching, and meditating. Each day they go out to collect food. In some Buddhist countries, boys spend a short time at a monastery as part of their schooling.

WHEEL OF LIFE
Buddhists share with Hindus a belief in the Wheel of Life, also called the Wheel of the Law. This is the continuous cycle of birth and rebirth that traps people who have not yet achieved nirvana. The spokes of the wheel remind the Buddhist of the Eightfold Path.

Find out more
ASIA
CHINA
HINDUISM
JAPAN
RELIGIONS

BUILDING

CRANE
The crane extends as the building rises. It may also be fixed on top of the building.

The frame is constructed of beams made of steel or concrete.

A hoist fixed to the side of the building carries workers to the top.

SKYSCRAPERS TOWER above the streets in many cities. The tallest freestanding building, the CN Tower in Toronto, Canada, reaches 1,815 ft (553 m) into the sky. The highest office building is Taipei 101 in Taiwan, at 1,666 ft (508 m). How are such enormous buildings constructed so that they stay up?

A house has walls built of wood, stone, or brick. They hold up the house, supporting themselves as well as the floors and roof. A skyscraper built like this would fall down. The walls could not support the heavy weight of such a high building. So hidden inside a skyscraper is a frame made of steel or concrete. The frame supports the floors and walls, which are often made of glass. Also hidden are the foundations beneath the skyscraper, which support the weight of the building.

REINFORCED CONCRETE
Liquid concrete is pumped into molds crossed with steel rods. It sets hard, producing a very strong material called reinforced concrete.

MOBILE MIXER
A truck with a revolving drum brings concrete to the site. As the drum turns, it keeps mixing the concrete so that it does not set.

A powerful pump pushes the liquid concrete through the pipe from the ground to the upper floors of the building.

PILES
Beams of steel or concrete, called piles, support the building's base. A huge mechanical hammer, called a pile driver, forces the piles into the ground.

BUILDING SITE
Workers on a building site always wear hard hats to protect their heads. They use many machines to construct a tall building such as a skyscraper. Parts of the building, such as steel beams and concrete slabs, are made elsewhere and brought to the site. Cranes lift the parts into position, and workers fit them together.

Excavators dig out a huge pit to make the foundation of the building.

BULLDOZER
The site is leveled with powerful bulldozers. The curved blade clears vegetation and piles up the soil.

SCAFFOLDING
Builders erect scaffolding made of steel tubes so that they can get to any part of a building. In the Far East, strong scaffolding is often made from lengths of bamboo tied together.

EXCAVATOR
Trenches and holes are dug with excavators. The bucket digs out soil and dumps it into waiting trucks.

FOUNDATIONS
Every building is supported by a foundation. This usually consists of a huge pit that contains a base made of reinforced concrete. The frame is built on top of the base, which supports the huge weight of the building.

BUILDING MATERIALS
Since early times, people have built with wood and stone. Bricks are made from clay. Stone blocks and bricks are laid in rows and joined together with sand and cement. Wood is cut into parts and assembled into structures. Concrete, made by mixing sand, stones, cement, and water, can be moulded to form any structure.

Find out more
ARCHITECTURE
ESCALATORS AND ELEVATORS
HOUSES

BUSES

THE WORD BUS comes from the Latin word omnibus, which means "for all." This is an apt description, for buses were the first kind of public transport, and are still usually the cheapest. The first buses date from the early 19th century when cities grew tremendously during the Industrial Revolution, and working people had to travel further to get to work. Before this time, only people who owned horses and carriages were able to travel long distances. Today, there are buses in cities and villages throughout the world. In most big cities, buses usually run regularly on an organized network of routes, and pick up people at special bus stops. In more remote places, the bus may be just a truck that passes through once in a while and stops wherever there are passengers.

CITY BUS
In busy English cities, where the streets are crowded and there are plenty of passengers, some buses, such as this London bus, have two decks.

ROAD BUS
Away from cities, buses can be longer to provide space for both passengers and luggage. Some road buses, such as this one from Iraq, may be articulated (hinged) to manoeuvre around hairpin bends on mountain roads.

SCHOOL BUS
Many children's first bus ride is on a school bus which takes them to school in the morning and brings them home safely in the afternoon. In comparison to other road vehicles, buses have a very good safety record.

INTERCITY BUS
Long-distance buses and coaches, such as those that travel across the United States, have comfortable reclining seats, toilets, coffee machines, and videos.

COUNTRY BUS
In less industrialized parts of the world, there are often no railroads and most people cannot afford a car, so the bus is the only way to travel. Buses bounce along dusty roads, packed inside and out with people and all their luggage, including chickens, dogs, and other animals.

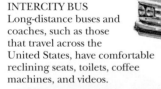

TRAMS AND TROLLEY BUSES

In some cities, such as Amsterdam in the Netherlands, you can catch a tram or a trolley bus instead of a bus. Trams glide along rails laid in the road and run on electric power picked up from overhead cables through rods on the roof. Trolley buses are powered in the same way, but they run on ordinary wheels rather than a track.

BUSES

In the richer countries of the world, buses are becoming increasingly sophisticated. Many city buses have electronic ticket machines and doors that open and shut automatically, and some buses have computers to guide them along the route. In poorer countries, people frequently crowd into battered vans and pickup trucks, all of which serve the same function as buses.

Find out more
CARS
TRANSPORT, HISTORY OF
TRUCKS AND LORRIES

BUTTERFLIES AND MOTHS

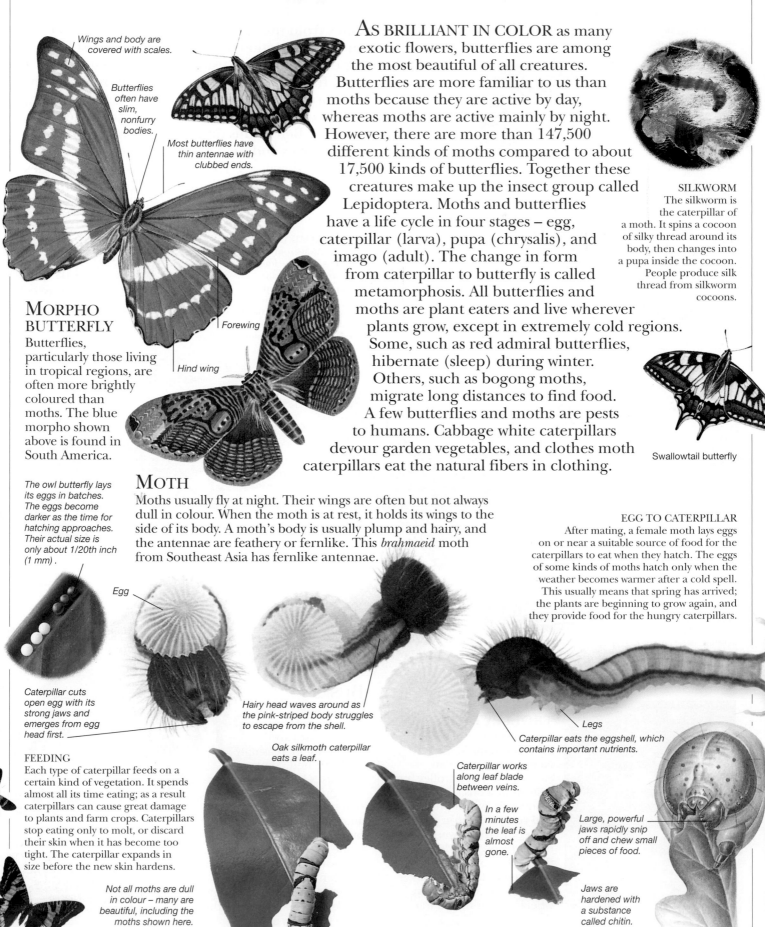

As BRILLIANT IN COLOR as many exotic flowers, butterflies are among the most beautiful of all creatures. Butterflies are more familiar to us than moths because they are active by day, whereas moths are active mainly by night. However, there are more than 147,500 different kinds of moths compared to about 17,500 kinds of butterflies. Together these creatures make up the insect group called Lepidoptera. Moths and butterflies have a life cycle in four stages – egg, caterpillar (larva), pupa (chrysalis), and imago (adult). The change in form from caterpillar to butterfly is called metamorphosis. All butterflies and moths are plant eaters and live wherever plants grow, except in extremely cold regions. Some, such as red admiral butterflies, hibernate (sleep) during winter. Others, such as bogong moths, migrate long distances to find food. A few butterflies and moths are pests to humans. Cabbage white caterpillars devour garden vegetables, and clothes moth caterpillars eat the natural fibers in clothing.

Wings and body are covered with scales.

Butterflies often have slim, nonfurry bodies.

Most butterflies have thin antennae with clubbed ends.

MORPHO BUTTERFLY

Butterflies, particularly those living in tropical regions, are often more brightly coloured than moths. The blue morpho shown above is found in South America.

Forewing

Hind wing

SILKWORM
The silkworm is the caterpillar of a moth. It spins a cocoon of silky thread around its body, then changes into a pupa inside the cocoon. People produce silk thread from silkworm cocoons.

Swallowtail butterfly

The owl butterfly lays its eggs in batches. The eggs become darker as the time for hatching approaches. Their actual size is only about 1/20th inch (1 mm).

MOTH

Moths usually fly at night. Their wings are often but not always dull in colour. When the moth is at rest, it holds its wings to the side of its body. A moth's body is usually plump and hairy, and the antennae are feathery or fernlike. This *brahmaeid* moth from Southeast Asia has fernlike antennae.

EGG TO CATERPILLAR
After mating, a female moth lays eggs on or near a suitable source of food for the caterpillars to eat when they hatch. The eggs of some kinds of moths hatch only when the weather becomes warmer after a cold spell. This usually means that spring has arrived; the plants are beginning to grow again, and they provide food for the hungry caterpillars.

Egg

Caterpillar cuts open egg with its strong jaws and emerges from egg head first.

Hairy head waves around as the pink-striped body struggles to escape from the shell.

Legs

Caterpillar eats the eggshell, which contains important nutrients.

FEEDING
Each type of caterpillar feeds on a certain kind of vegetation. It spends almost all its time eating; as a result caterpillars can cause great damage to plants and farm crops. Caterpillars stop eating only to molt, or discard their skin when it has become too tight. The caterpillar expands in size before the new skin hardens.

Oak silkmoth caterpillar eats a leaf.

Caterpillar works along leaf blade between veins.

In a few minutes the leaf is almost gone.

Large, powerful jaws rapidly snip off and chew small pieces of food.

Not all moths are dull in colour – many are beautiful, including the moths shown here.

Jaws are hardened with a substance called chitin.

Caterpillar is attached to twig by silken thread.

Caterpillar spins silk girdle around its body, then skin of caterpillar begins to split.

Caterpillar of the citrus swallowtail butterfly attaches its body to a twig and prepares to change into a pupa (chrysalis).

Spinnerets produce silken thread.

Silk girdle is finished. The pupa is starting to form inside.

New skin of pupa

Empty skin and legs of caterpillar

CATERPILLAR TO CHRYSALIS

Before its final molt, a caterpillar stops feeding and may change color. It finds a safe place to pupate (change into a pupa, or chrysalis). It anchors itself to a stem with silk thread from spinnerets at its rear end. Many moth caterpillars spin a silken cocoon around themselves for protection. Leafroller caterpillars curl leaves around their bodies and, using their mandibles (mouthparts), stitch them together with silk.

PUPA TO BUTTERFLY

The pupa stage is often called the resting stage. But inside its hard skin the creature is undergoing an amazing transformation, controlled by its chemical hormones. After several weeks, the skin of the pupa splits and the adult butterfly or moth emerges. Its damp, crumpled wings soon spread and dry.

SCALES

Tiny overlapping scales cover the wings of moths and butterflies. The colors and arrangement of the scales create the beautiful pattern of the whole wing.

With folded wings, the Indian leaf butterfly looks just like a dead leaf.

Adult blue morpho butterfly with wings closed

CAMOUFLAGE

Seen alone, a butterfly or moth may look so colorful that it would easily be noticed. But in many species the wing colors and patterns are designed to blend in with the natural surroundings. The shape of the wing may also closely resemble a natural object such as a leaf or a fruit.

Resting pupa of blue morpho butterfly disguised as a leaf

Butterfly begins to emerge.

Blood pumps into wing veins to expand them. Wings gradually dry and harden.

Indian leaf butterfly with wings open

CONSERVATION

Hundreds of species of moths and butterflies are in danger of extinction. They are threatened because the areas where they live are cleared for farms and homes. Butterflies and moths are also killed and sold to collectors because of their great beauty.

The Taenaris macrops butterfly from New Guinea feeds on ripe bananas.

When the wings are open, the eyespots flash like the eyes of a predator.

Queen Alexandra's birdwing butterfly is in danger because the forests where it lives are being cut down.

Spanish moon moth is now a protected species.

Large blue butterflies were extinct in Britain, but have now been reintroduced.

EYESPOTS

The eyespots on a butterfly's wings look like the eyes of a predator such as the owl above.

Find out more

ANIMALS
CAMOUFLAGE, ANIMAL
FLIGHT, ANIMAL
INSECTS

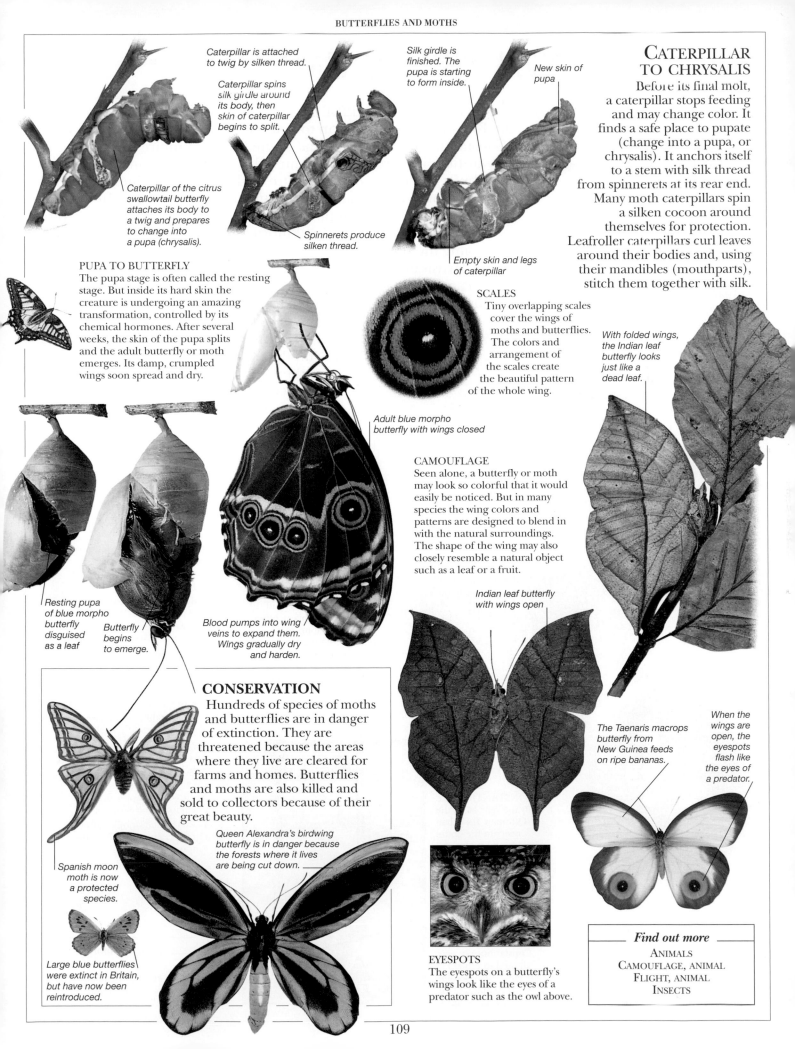

BYZANTINE EMPIRE

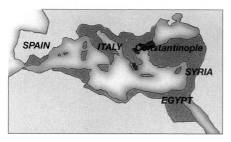

BYZANTINE EMPIRE
In A.D. 565, the Byzantine Empire stretched from Spain in the west to Syria in the east. By 1350, the empire had shrunk to a fragment of its former area.

AS THE ROMAN EMPIRE began to decline in the 3rd century A.D., the Byzantine Empire began to emerge. In 330, the Roman Emperor Constantine moved the capital of the Roman Empire from Rome to Byzantium in Turkey. He renamed the capital Constantinople (now Istanbul), and it became the centre of the new Byzantine Empire. At first the empire, named after Byzantium, consisted only of the eastern part of the Roman Empire. But after the Western Roman Empire collapsed, the Byzantine Empire began to expand. Christianity became the state religion, and Constantinople became a Christian center. Artists and scholars from all over Europe and the Middle East came there to study. Under Emperor Justinian I, the Byzantine Empire regained much of the territory of the old Roman Empire. Trade, art, and architecture thrived. But the empire suffered many attacks. By 642 Muslim Arabs had overrun Byzantine territories in North Africa and the Middle East. Gradually the empire lost its lands in Asia Minor (Turkey) and Southeast Europe. In 1453 the Ottomans captured Constantinople, and the Byzantine Empire ended.

Central dome measures 100 ft (31 m) across.

HAGIA SOPHIA
Justinian I (483-565) built the Hagia Sophia (Church of Holy Wisdom) in the centre of Constantinople. It was the largest Christian church in the Eastern world and was intended to provide a spiritual centre for the Byzantine Empire. After 1453, the church became a mosque (Muslim house of worship). Today the Hagia Sophia is a museum.

Marble floors

BYZANTINE EMPIRE

395 Roman Empire splits into East and West, with Constantinople as the capital of the Eastern Empire.

476 The Western Roman Empire collapses; the Byzantine or Eastern Empire takes over the whole Roman Empire.

527-65 During the reign of Justinian I, the Byzantine Empire reconquers much of the old Roman Empire.

635-42 Byzantine Empire loses control of the Middle East and North Africa to the Arabs.

1071 Byzantine Empire loses Asia Minor to the Turks. Calls in help from Europe.

1333 Ottoman Turks gain a foothold in Europe and begin to encircle Constantinople.

1453 Constantinople falls to the Ottoman Turks; the Byzantine Empire comes to an end.

CONSTANTINE THE GREAT
In 314, Constantine the Great (288-337) became Roman emperor. At that time Christianity was forbidden, but in about 312, Constantine himself had been converted, some say by the sight of a cross in the sky. Christianity became the official religion of the Byzantine Empire and is now known as the Eastern Orthodox Church.

SIEGE OF CONSTANTINOPLE
By the year 1453, the Ottoman Turks had overrun the entire Byzantine Empire and reached the gates of Constantinople. Under the leadership of Sultan Muhammad II, the Ottomans besieged the city and captured it after two months. The Christian inhabitants of Constantinople were allowed to remain in the city, which became the capital of the Muslim empire.

Find out more
CHRISTIANITY
OTTOMAN EMPIRE
ROMAN EMPIRE

JULIUS CAESAR

IN 49 B.C., A BRILLIANT MILITARY COMMANDER and politician named Julius Caesar became head of the Roman Republic. Caesar made himself popular with people by paying for magnificent public games in Rome. After holding various public offices, including that of consul, he was given command of an army and extended the boundaries of the Roman Republic by conquering Gaul (modern France, Belgium, and Switzerland). He also invaded Britain twice. The senate, a group of elected representatives who ruled Rome, feared he might make himself king, so they ordered Caesar to surrender his army, but instead he marched toward Rome. Pompey the Great, Caesar's son-in-law, headed the senate's troops. In 48 B.C. Pompey was murdered, and in 45 B.C. Caesar was elected dictator. But a year later he was violently assassinated.

100 B.C. Born in Rome.
65 B.C. Elected public games organizer.
62 B.C. Elected praetor, a law official.
60 B.C. Forms First Triumvirate.
59 B.C. Elected consul.
58 B.C. Begins Gaul campaign.
55 B.C. Invades Britain.
49 B.C. Fights civil war. Becomes dictator.
48 B.C. Defeats Pompey.
46 B.C. Defeats Pompey's supporters.
45 B.C. Made dictator for life.
44 B.C. Assassinated.

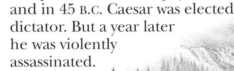

As Caesar wondered whether to cross the Rubicon River, legend has it that a vision of a larger-than-life man appeared, playing a trumpet, luring him across the river. Caesar took it to be a sign from the gods, and gave the order for his troops to proceed.

Each army unit, or legion, carried its own standard, shaped like an eagle.

TRIUMVIRATE

In 60 B.C., Caesar, wanting to be elected consul, allied his fortunes with Pompey (above) and Crassus, another leading politician, to form a three-man group (a triumvirate), that was the most powerful political group in Rome.

CROSSING THE RUBICON

Caesar's victories in Gaul made him very popular with many Romans. However, others feared and distrusted him. In 49 B.C. the senate ordered him to give up his army. Caesar refused and crossed the Rubicon River to invade Italy and begin the civil war.

CAESAR'S DEATH
Many politicians in Rome thought that Caesar had too much power. Led by Marcus Brutus and Gaius Cassius, a number of Pompey's supporters plotted against Caesar and decided to kill him. On March 15, (the Ides of March), 44 B.C., the plotters attacked Caesar in the senate and stabbed him to death. Civil war raged after his death; finally, his adopted son Octavian emerged as victor, and the Roman Empire was born.

LAUREL CROWN
Victorious Roman military commanders often wore laurel wreaths to symbolize their power. Later, emperors would wear a crown of gold olive leaves after a great victory.

Find out more
ITALY, HISTORY OF
ROMAN EMPIRE

CAMELS AND LLAMAS

A CAMEL IS MORE SUITED TO life in the desert than almost any other beast. With a hump full of fat on its back as a permanent store of fluids, the camel is able to travel great distances without eating or drinking. Then, when food is plentiful, the camel's enormous stomach can hold huge amounts of grass and water. There are two kinds of camels – the dromedary and the Bactrian. The guanaco of South America is closely related to the camel, but it has no hump; other members of the camel family include the alpaca, llama, and vicuna, also from South America. Both camels and llamas have long, sturdy legs and are good runners. They have long necks, and their eyes, ears, and nostrils are set high on the head so they can detect danger from a distance. Camels, llamas, and alpacas have been used as beasts of burden for thousands of years. Most dromedary camels are domesticated and kept for meat and other products; Bactrian camels still live wild in the Gobi Desert, in northern Asia.

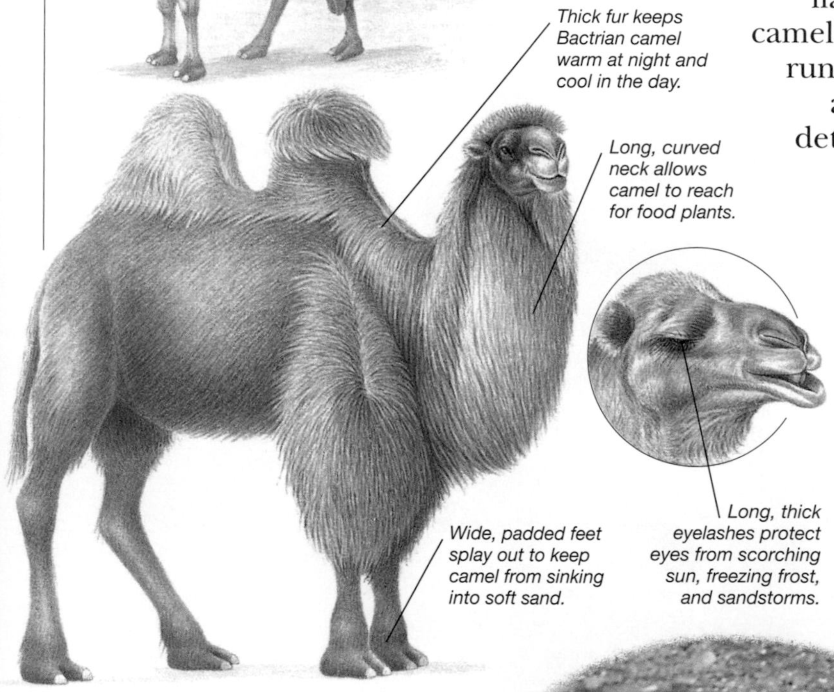

Thick fur keeps Bactrian camel warm at night and cool in the day.

Long, curved neck allows camel to reach for food plants.

Wide, padded feet splay out to keep camel from sinking into soft sand.

Long, thick eyelashes protect eyes from scorching sun, freezing frost, and sandstorms.

SURVIVING A SANDSTORM
In a sandstorm, the camel kneels down on its thick kneepads, presses its ears flat, shuts its long-lashed eyes, seals its mouth, and closes its nostrils almost completely. In this way the camel avoids breathing in too much of the sand and dust whipped up by the storm.

LLAMA
Weighing about 300 lb (140 kg), an average llama is almost 4 ft (1.2 m) tall at the shoulder. Llamas were first domesticated by people more than 4,000 years ago. Cars, trucks, and trains have largely replaced them, but llamas are still used in South America for transportation. Both llamas and alpacas are killed for meat and for their hides. These llamas are carrying goods in Peru.

SHIP OF THE DESERT
Famous for carrying people across the hot lands of North Africa and the Middle East, the camel is often called "the ship of the desert." Camels provide people with milk and meat, and their hair and hides are used to make tents, rugs, and clothes. Camels have tough lips that can grip thorny plant food. They seldom need to drink, but when water is plentiful they can drink about 25 gallons (100 liters) at one time.

GUANACO
The graceful guanaco shown here lives wild in the foothills of the Andes Mountains, in South America. Vicunas live wild too, higher up on the Andean mountain pastures. The vicuna is an officially protected species, but both vicunas and guanacos are still hunted for their meat, hides, and wool.

Almost all the 14 million camels in the world are dromedaries.

The Bactrian, or Asian camel, has long, shaggy fur and two humps.

CAMEL HUMPS
The dromedary or Arabian camel has one hump; the Bactrian or Asian camel has two. An average adult camel is about 7 ft (2.1 m) tall at the hump and weighs approximately 1,100 lb (500 kg).

Find out more
AFRICA
ANIMALS
DESERT WILDLIFE

CAMERAS

ALTHOUGH THE FIRST PHOTOGRAPH was taken only about 180 years ago, cameras are much, much older. Hundreds of years ago, the Chinese found that light entering a dark room through a pinhole would project a fuzzy image of the world outside onto the opposite wall. Many years later, in 1500 in Europe, a room like this was called a camera obscura, which is Latin for "darkened room." In the 17th century some artists drew sketches with the aid of a camera obscura which had a lens instead of a pinhole to make the image sharper and brighter. The discovery of chemicals that darkened when exposed to light finally made it possible to fix the image permanently – on paper, on glass plates, or on film. Today, digital cameras use light-sensitive electronic sensors instead of film. Sophisticated electronic technology in most cameras ensures that each picture gets the right amount of light (autoexposure) and is perfectly sharp (autofocus). But all cameras still work on the same basic principle as the camera obscura of old.

Grip sensors shut down LCD displays to conserve power when camera is not being held

Pop-up flash unit

Sensors read metal strips on the film cassette to detect which type of film is being used

Autofocus zoom lens

Light enters camera

Motordrives advance film and reset shutter after each shot

SINGLE-LENS REFLEX CAMERA
The single-lens reflex (SLR) camera (above) may use either film or a digital sensor. It is popular with photographers for its versatility, and because the viewfinder shows exactly the same view that the camera will record. The lens can be interchanged with others to give a wide view or to magnify the subject.

KINDS OF CAMERAS

There are many different types of cameras, including film, digital, compact, single-lens reflex, disposable, instant-picture, and large-format cameras. Most film cameras use 1.4 in (35 mm) film. Large-format cameras take huge sheets of film up to 10 in (255 mm) wide. Today, tiny digital cameras are also built into most cell phone handsets.

DIGITAL CAMERA
A digital camera captures images electronically rather than on standard film and stores them on removable memory cards. Images can then be transferred to a computer and printed out or sent over the Internet.

Photos stored on the camera's memory card can be viewed on the LCD (liquid crystal display).

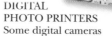

DIGITAL PHOTO PRINTERS
Some digital cameras can be connected directly to printers in order to print out photos, and many printers have slots for memory cards to be inserted. This makes transferring images to a computer unnecessary.

POLAROID CAMERA
The Polaroid "instant-picture" camera uses slim envelopes of plastic instead of a roll of film. Inside is a sheet of film and a pod of chemicals that bursts to process the picture in just 90 seconds.

MOVIE CAMERAS
The movement we see in the movies is an illusion. A movie film is really a series of still pictures projected on to the screen in such quick succession that they seem to merge into one another. If the subject is in a slightly different place in each picture it looks as if it is moving. Most movie cameras take 24 pictures, or frames, every second, on a very long strip of film wound steadily through the camera. The film stops while each picture is taken, then advances quickly, ready for the next picture.

LARGE-FORMAT CAMERA
In early cameras, the lens was focused by moving a bellows – an accordion-like cloth tunnel – in and out. Many photographers still use large-format bellows cameras for high-quality studio work.

Find out more
LIGHT
MOVIES
PHOTOGRAPHY
TELESCOPE
TELEVISION AND VIDEO

ANIMAL
CAMOUFLAGE

A BUTTERFLY that looks like a flower, a bird that resembles a log, a fish that seems as lifeless as a stone – many animals and plants survive by blending in with their surroundings. This is called camouflage. Camouflage includes color, shape, and patterning. For example, it is difficult to spy a newborn deer among the trees because of its pale brown color and speckled coat. A dead-leaf mantis is also difficult to see because of its leaf shape, and a chameleon can change its color to match the color of its surroundings. Camouflage helps animals hide from predators. It also helps predators such as tigers and leopards ambush their prey without being seen. Some animals such as rabbits camouflage themselves by staying absolutely still when in danger so their movements do not give them away.

Chameleon quickly changes color to brown when it moves onto a leafless branch.

Chameleon matches the green coloring of its leafy branch.

ARCTIC HARE

The Arctic hare is brown in summer to match its surroundings of soil and shrubs. In the fall it sheds its fur and grows a new white coat, for camouflage in the winter snow. The Arctic fox preys on the Arctic hare. In winter the Arctic fox also has a white coat for camouflage.

CHAMELEON

The chameleon is famous for changing its color and pattern to match its surroundings. Its color alters when cells in the skin change size, moving their grains of color nearer the surface or deeper into the skin. When the Jackson's chameleon shown here was taken off its branch, its color changed from green and yellow to mottled brown. But it took the chameleon about five minutes to do so.

STICK INSECT
The spindly stick insect is very difficult to recognize among twigs and branches because of its shape and color. It can fold its thin legs alongside its body and look even more like a twig. When danger threatens, it stays absolutely still – like a stick.

TIGER STRIPES
The tiger is camouflaged by its stripes, which match the light and dark patterns of sunlit grasses. The tiger hunts mainly by ambush, creeping stealthily toward its prey in the undergrowth, then charging over the last few yards.

Find out more
ANIMALS
BIRDS
FISH
INSECTS
LIONS, TIGERS,
and other big cats
RABBITS AND HARES

CANADA

THE SECOND LARGEST COUNTRY in the world is also one of the emptiest. Much of Canada is virtually uninhabited. The northern part of the country is a hostile wasteland of snow and ice for much of the year. Few people live among the high Rocky Mountains of the west. Even in the huge wheat-growing plains of the center there are few people. The majority of Canada's 31.5 million inhabitants live in the southeast, close to the border with the United States. Most Canadians speak English, but for some, particularly those in the province of Quebec, French is the first language. This is because they are descendants of the French who settled in Canada during the 16th century. The languages of the native North American and Inuit inhabitants are rarely heard today. Much of Canada's trade is with its neighbor, the United States. However, Canada has close links with many European, Asian, and African nations.

Canada occupies the northern half of North America, stretching from the Pacific to the Atlantic oceans. Part of the country lies within the Arctic Circle. At 3,987 miles (6,416 km) the Canadian-US border is the world's longest continuous frontier between two nations.

TORONTO

More than four million people live in the city of Toronto. It is Canada's business center and capital of the province of Ontario. Toronto has many skyscrapers, including the 1,815 ft (553 m) high Canadian National Tower.

Maple syrup is obtained by cutting into the maple tree and directing the flow of its sap into a collecting vessel.

SPORTS AND LEISURE
Winter sports such as skiing, skating, and ice hockey are popular in Canada because winters are long and there is plenty of snow and ice. Modern ice hockey was invented in Canada in the 1870s and is now played nearly everywhere in the world. During the summer, sailing, canoeing, and field hockey are also popular.

Ice hockey is the Canadian national sport. The country produces some of the best players in the world.

ROCKY MOUNTAINS
Western Canada is dominated by the Rocky Mountains, which stretch from the United States border in the south to Alaska in the north. The mountains are covered in trees and are a haven for bears and other wildlife.

LAW AND ORDER
The nickname of the Royal Canadian Mounted Police – the national police force – is the Mounties. They boast that they "always get their man."

NATURAL RESOURCES

Canada is rich in minerals such as zinc and iron ore and has huge reserves of oil, coal, and natural gas. Just off Canada's east coast lies the Grand Banks, one of the world's richest fishing areas. Waters within 200 miles (320 km) of Canada's coastline are reserved for Canadian fishermen only. The vast forests that grow across the country are a major source of timber. The country's exports are mainly sent south to the United States; the two countries have formed a free-trade zone, which means that exports or imports between them are not taxed.

PROVINCES showing date of joining the Confederation of Canada

 ALBERTA 1905
Area: 255,286 sq miles (661,190 sq km)
Population: 3,223,400
Capital: Edmonton

 BRITISH COLUMBIA 1871
Area: 365,946 sq miles (947,800 sq km)
Population: 4,220,000
Capital: Victoria

 MANITOBA 1870
Area: 250,946 sq miles (649,950 sq km)
Population: 1,174,000
Capital: Winnipeg

 NEW BRUNSWICK 1867
Area: 28,355 sq miles (73,440 sq km)
Population: 751,300
Capital: Fredericton

NEWFOUNDLAND AND LABRADOR 1949
Area: 156,649 sq miles (404,720 sq km)
Population: 517,000
Capital: St. John's

 NOVA SCOTIA 1867
Area: 21,425 sq miles (55,490 sq km)
Population: 937,500
Capital: Halifax

 ONTARIO 1867
Area: 412,298 sq miles (1,068,630 sq km)
Population: 12,449,500
Capital: Toronto

 **PRINCE EDWARD ISLAND** 1873
Area: 2,185 sq miles (5,660 sq km)
Population: 137,700
Capital: Charlottetown

 QUEBEC 1867
Area: 594,857 sq miles (1,540,680 sq km)
Population: 7,568,600
Capital: Quebec

SASKATCHEWAN 1905
Area: 251,865 sq miles (652,330 sq km)
Population: 995,300
Capital: Regina

TERRITORIES showing date of joining the Confederation of Canada

 NORTHWEST TERRITORIES 1870
Area: 519,734 sq miles (1,346,106 sq km)
Population: 42,900
Capital: Yellowknife

 NUNAVUT 1999
Area: 808,185 sq miles (2,093,190 sq km)
Population: 29,700
Capital: Iqaluit

 YUKON TERRITORY 1898
Area: 186,660 sq miles (483,450 sq km)
Population: 31,200
Capital: Whitehorse

In Quebec City, winding streets connect the Lower Town sector on the waterfront and Upper Town on Cape Diamond, a bluff rising 300 ft (91 m) above the St. Lawrence.

This observation deck has a 360-degree view of Vancouver. It is perched on top of Harbour Centre Tower.

VANCOUVER
Vancouver is Canada's leading Pacific port. Situated in southwestern British Columbia, Vancouver overlooks the Strait of Georgia and is surrounded by mountains. The city's many landmarks date from the 1880s and span architectural styles from Renaissance and Art Deco to Modern and Postmodern.

QUEBEC

The city of Quebec (above) is the oldest city in Canada and the capital of the province of Quebec. The French style of its buildings reminds the visitor that many of Quebec's first colonists came from France. Quebec city was founded in 1608 by the French explorer Samuel de Champlain, and Quebec itself remained a French colony until the British took it over in 1759. Today Quebec is the center of French Canadian culture. French is still the official language, and most of the population is Roman Catholic. The Quebecois, the people of Quebec, see themselves as different from other Canadians, and over the years many of them have campaigned for independence.

YUKON TERRITORY

Few people live in the Yukon Territory in northwestern Canada, but the region is rich in silver, zinc, lead, and gold. During the 1890s it was the site of the Klondike gold rush. Prospectors and adventurers who came to the Yukon hoping to strike gold founded Whitehorse, which became the territorial capital in 1952. Winters in the Yukon are long and cold, but in summer the weather becomes warm, with temperatures reaching 60°F (16°C). This allows the growth of many kinds of vegetation which take on a rich variety of colors in the autumn. Moose, caribou, beavers, and bears are common in the Yukon.

Find out more

CANADA, HISTORY OF
INUIT
MOUNTAINS
NATIVE AMERICANS
SPORTS

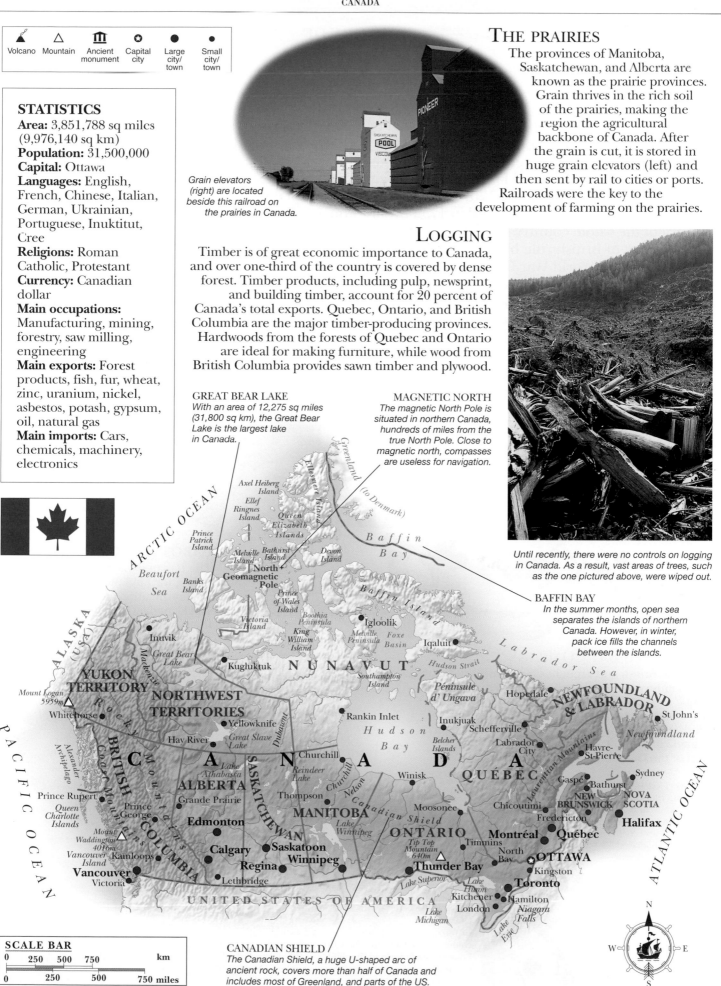

HISTORY OF CANADA

Canada's most popular emblem is the leaf of the local tree, the red maple.

ABOUT TWENTY-FIVE THOUSAND YEARS AGO Canada's first people walked across the land that then existed between Siberia and Alaska. Fishing people from Europe began to explore the rich coast of Canada about 1,000 years ago, and the original Native American inhabitants of the country lost control when British and French settlers began to establish trading posts for fur during the 17th century. Britain and France fought each other for the land, and in 1759 Britain won control of the whole country. A century later, Canada became independent of British rule but remained a British dominion (territory). After World War II, Canada became very prosperous and developed a close business relationship with the United States. During the 1970s French Canadians demanded more power and threatened to make the province of Quebec independent. However, Canada is still united.

Native Americans were the first inhabitants of Canada.

Snowshoes

Log cabin

European traders exchanged goods with Native Americans who trapped wild animals for their valuable furs.

Traders traveled by canoe to trading posts. Transport by canoe also opened the way to missionaries and explorers in Canada.

HUDSON'S BAY COMPANY

Both the British and French set up companies in the 17th century to trade in valuable Canadian furs. These companies grew wealthy and powerful and acted like independent governments. The British Hudson's Bay Company ruled much of northern Canada until 1869 when its lands were made part of the Dominion of Canada.

PIERRE TRUDEAU

Since the 1960s Canada has become increasingly independent of Britain. A new flag was adopted in 1965 and two years later a world fair – Expo '67 – was held to show off Canadian skills in the centenary year of independence. In 1968 Pierre Trudeau (right) was elected as prime minister. A great intellectual, he was a strong supporter of a unified Canada.

DOMINION

In 1867, the four British colonies of Nova Scotia, New Brunswick, and Upper and Lower Canada formed the self-governing Dominion of Canada. Six more colonies joined after 1867. Newfoundland joined in 1949 and Nunavut was created in 1999.

Yukon Territory
Northwest Territories
Nunavut
British Columbia
Alberta
Saskatchewan
Manitoba
Ontario (formerly Upper Canada)
CANADA IN 1867
Newfoundland and Labrador
Prince Edward I.
Nova Scotia
New Brunswick
Quebec (formerly Lower Canada)

CABOT AND CARTIER

The Italian explorer John Cabot, sailing for England, was the first European, after the Vikings, to visit Canada when he sailed along the coast of Newfoundland in 1497. The French explorer Jacques Cartier sailed up the mouth of the St. Lawrence River in 1534. Following these two voyages, both Britain and France laid claim to Canada.

John Cabot

Find out more

CANADA
COOK, JAMES
INUITS
NATIVE AMERICANS
VIKINGS

CARIBBEAN

EXTENDING LIKE a string of pearls, there is a long row of tropical islands curving for more than 2,000 miles (3,200 km) between Mexico and Venezuela. Together they are usually called the Caribbean islands, or sometimes the West Indies. Some are tiny, uninhabited rocks or coral reefs; others are much larger islands with thriving populations. On Martinique for instance, 432,900 people live around the wooded slopes of several volcanoes which tower hundreds of feet above the sea. There are 13 countries and 12 other territories in the Caribbean. Cuba, with a population of 11.3 million people, is the biggest nation. Although each country has its own distinctive culture, many have connections with other countries. These links are left over from the 18th and 19th centuries, when the whole region was colonized by European kingdoms. The ruling nations brought African slaves to the Caribbean to harvest sugarcane. Today, descendants of these slaves make up a large proportion of the population.

The Caribbean Sea covers about 750,193 sq miles (1,943,000 sq km) in area. It is enclosed on three sides by Central America, South America, and the Caribbean islands.

TOURISM
The Caribbean islands are very beautiful, with lush trees, colorful birds, long sandy beaches, and months of sunshine. The region attracts tourists from all over the world. This has created many new jobs, particularly in the towns. Tourism is now the main source of income for several islands.

CRICKET
Cricket is a reminder of the Caribbean's colonial past. It is played, and passionately supported, in many of the former British colonies. For international test matches, the Caribbean islands join forces and compete as the West Indies. The West Indies were victorious in the cricket World Cup in 1975 and 1979.

Brian Lara (right) plays cricket for the West Indies. With 400 runs, he holds the world record for the highest test match score.

AGRICULTURE
More than half the people of the Caribbean earn a living from agriculture. Many work for a landowner, producing crops such as sugar and coffee. They may also rent or own a small plot of land. On this land they grow food to feed their families or to sell in local markets.

BASTILLE DAY
The islands of Guadeloupe and Martinique are part of France, and the people have strong links with this country. They speak the French language, use the French franc for money, fly the French flag, and celebrate French holidays such as Bastille Day. Other Caribbean islands have close political and financial links with Britain, the Netherlands, or the United States.

ARCHITECTURE
Brilliant colors enhance the traditional shapes of Caribbean architecture. Similarly, Caribbean music, literature, art, and food are a unique mixture of European and African culture.

Find out more
CENTRAL AMERICA
COLUMBUS, CHRISTOPHER
SLAVERY

Volcano · Mountain · Ancient monument · Capital city · Large city/town · Small city/town

ANGUILLA
Area: 35 sq miles (91 sq km)
Status: British dependent territory
Claimed: 1650
Population: 12,700
Capital: The Valley

ANTIGUA AND BARBUDA
Area: 170 sq miles (440 sq km)
Population: 67,900
Capital: St. John's

ARUBA
Area: 75 sq miles (193 sq km)
Status: Dutch autonomous region
Claimed: 1643
Population: 70,800
Capital: Oranjestad

BAHAMAS
Area: 5,380 sq miles (13,935 sq km)
Population: 314,000
Capital: Nassau

BARBADOS
Area: 166 sq miles (431 sq km)
Population: 270,000
Capital: Bridgetown

CAYMAN ISLANDS
Area: 100 sq miles (259 sq km)
Status: British dependent territory
Claimed: 1670
Population: 41,900
Capital: George Town

CUBA
Area: 44,218 sq miles (114,524 sq km)
Population: 11,300,000
Capital: Havana

DOMINICA
Area: 290 sq miles (751 sq km)
Population: 69,700
Capital: Roseau

DOMINICAN REPUBLIC
Area: 18,704 sq miles (48,442 sq km)
Population: 8,700,000
Capital: Santo Domingo

GRENADA
Area: 133 sq miles (344 sq km)
Population: 89,300
Capital: Saint George's

GUADELOUPE
Area: 687 sq miles (1,779 sq km)
Status: French overseas department
Claimed: 1635
Population: 440,000
Capital: Basse-Terre

HAITI
Area: 10,714 sq miles (27,750 sq km)
Population: 8,300,000
Capital: Port-au-Prince

JAMAICA
Area: 4,244 sq miles (10,991 sq km)
Population: 2,700,000
Capital: Kingston

MARTINIQUE
Area: 425 sq miles (1,101 sq km)
Status: French overseas department
Claimed: 1635
Population: 393,000
Capital: Fort-de-France

MONTSERRAT
Area: 38 sq miles (101 sq km)
Status: British dependent territory
Claimed: 1632
Population: 9,000
Capital: Plymouth

NETHERLANDS ANTILLES
Area: 385 sq miles (992 sq km)
Status: Dutch autonomous region
Claimed: 1816
Population: 221,000
Capital: Willemstad

PUERTO RICO
Area: 3,435 sq miles (8,897 sq km)
Status: US commonwealth territory
Claimed: 1898
Population: 3,890,000
Capital: San Juan

ST. KITTS AND NEVIS
Area: 104 sq miles (269 sq km)
Population: 38,800
Capital: Basseterre

ST. LUCIA
Area: 238 sq miles (616 sq km)
Population: 162,000
Capital: Castries

ST. VINCENT AND THE GRENADINES
Area: 150 sq miles (388 sq km)
Population: 116,000
Capital: Kingstown

TRINIDAD AND TOBAGO
Area: 1,980 sq miles (5,128 sq km)
Population: 1,300,000
Capital: Port-of-Spain

TURKS AND CAICOS ISLANDS
Area: 193 sq miles (500 sq km)
Status: British dependent territory
Claimed: 1766
Population: 19,400
Capital: Cockburn Town

VIRGIN ISLANDS
Area: 136 sq miles (352 sq km)
Status: US unincorporated territory
Claimed: 1917
Population: 124,800
Capital: Charlotte Amalie

VIRGIN ISLANDS, BRITISH
Area: 59 sq miles (153 sq km)
Status: British dependent territory
Claimed: 1672
Population: 21,700
Capital: Road Town

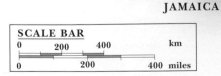

SCALE BAR
0 200 400 km
0 200 400 miles

ISLAND GROUPS

The larger islands of the Caribbean between Cuba and Puerto Rico are often called the Greater Antilles, to distinguish them from the Lesser Antilles to the east. The small islands from the Virgin Islands to Dominica are sometimes called the Leeward Islands; and the islands to the south (Martinique to Grenada), the Windward Islands.

UNITED STATES OF AMERICA

Gulf of Mexico

Grand Bahama Island
Freeport
Great Abaco
Berry Islands
Eleuthera Island
Andros Island
NASSAU
Andros Town
Cat Island

ATLANTIC OCEAN

Tropic of Cancer

B A H A M A S

Tropic of Cancer

HAVANA (LA HABANA)
Matanzas
Pinar del Río
Straits of Florida
Santa Clara
Cienfuegos
CUBA
Long Island
Great Exuma Island
Crooked Island
Acklins Island
Mayaguana
TURKS & CAICOS ISLANDS (to UK)
Cockburn Town

Yucatan Channel
Nueva Gerona
Camagüey
Las Tunas
Matthew Town
Great Inagua
Bayamo
Holguín
Guantánamo
Hispaniola

GEORGE TOWN
CAYMAN ISLANDS (to UK)
Little Cayman
Grand Cayman
Santiago de Cuba
Cap-Haïtien
Gonaïves
Santiago
La Romana
VIRGIN ISLANDS (to US)
BRITISH VIRGIN ISLANDS (to UK)
Road Town
ANGUILLA (to UK)
The Valley

Greater Antilles

NAVASSA ISLAND (to US)
HAITI
PORT-AU-PRINCE
SANTO DOMINGO
PUERTO RICO (to US)
San Juan
Ponce
Charlotte Amalie
ANTIGUA & BARBUDA

Montego Bay
Jamaica Channel
Cayes
Jacmel
DOMINICAN REPUBLIC
BASSETERRE
SAINT KITTS & NEVIS
ST JOHN'S

JAMAICA
KINGSTON

Caribbean Sea

Lesser Antilles

MONTSERRAT (to UK)
Basse-terre
GUADELOUPE (to France)
Windward Islands

DOMINICA
ROSEAU
MARTINIQUE (to France)
Fort-de-france
ST LUCIA
CASTRIES
SAINT VINCENT & THE GRENADINES
KINGSTOWN
Saint Vincent
The Grenadines
BARBADOS
BRIDGETOWN

Leeward Islands

ARUBA (to Netherlands)
Oranjestad
Curaçao
Bonaire
NETHERLANDS ANTILLES (to Netherlands)
Willemstad
GRENADA
ST GEORGE'S
Tobago
TRINIDAD & TOBAGO
PORT-OF-SPAIN
Trinidad
San Fernando

Gulf of Venezuela
Isla de Margarita

COLOMBIA

V E N E Z U E L A

N W E S

HISTORY OF THE
CARIBBEAN

FOR CENTURIES THE BEAUTIFUL Caribbean islands were home to Arawak and Carib peoples, who may have originated in South America. Skillful navigators, they established settlements and lived by farming and fishing. In 1492, the European explorer Christopher Columbus arrived in the Caribbean. Others followed, leading to 500 years of European domination, as first the Spanish, and then the British, French, and Dutch fought for control of the islands. The Europeans enslaved, or killed the native populations, and brought Africans in slave ships to work on sugar plantations. During the 20th century, many islands won their independence from Europe. Today, many of the Caribbean islands depend on a single crop, such as sugar or bananas.

THE FIRST INHABITANTS
The first settlers were the Arawaks, who lived on islands in the north and west, and the Caribs, who settled on the smaller eastern islands. The Arawaks were famous for wood and stone carvings.

Sugarcane

Many thousands of Africans were imported into the Caribbean as slaves.

SLAVERY
When the Spanish conquered the Caribbean in the early 1500s, they enslaved the local people, and forced them to work on sugar, fruit, spice, and coffee plantations. As these slaves died, more were shipped over from Africa. Britain was the main slave-trading nation. British ships took slaves across the Atlantic, and carried sugar and other crops back to Europe.

RASTAFARIANISM
Many people on Jamaica and other Caribbean islands are Rastafarians. They believe black people will eventually return to Africa to achieve their freedom. Rastafarians take their name from Prince Ras Tafari, better known as Haile Selassie. The emperor of Ethiopia from 1930-74, he was the only African ruler to keep his country independent of European control.

THE CARIBBEAN

1492 Christopher Columbus lands in the Bahamas.

1500s Spain takes control of the Caribbean.

1700s British, French, Dutch, and Danes take over many of the islands.

1804 Haiti becomes the first independent black nation in the Caribbean.

1834 Slaves freed as slavery abolished in British Empire.

1898 Cuba wins independence from Spain.

1962 Jamaica and Trinidad and Tobago gain independence from Britain.

1983 US overthrows left-wing regime in Grenada.

1994 US-led invasion overthrows dictatorship in Haiti.

INDEPENDENCE
In 1962, both Jamaica and Trinidad and Tobago gained independence from Britain. Over the next 20 years, eight more British colonies became independent. However, some of the Caribbean still remains under American, Dutch, or French rule.

There was much cause for celebration when Jamaica finally won independence.

CUBA
In 1959, Fidel Castro (b. 1927) overthrew Cuba's corrupt government, and set up a Communist regime. He reformed the country, providing free education and health care for all, but nearly caused a nuclear war in 1962 when the US objected to the placing of Russian missiles on the island.

Find out more

AFRICA, HISTORY OF
CARIBBEAN
COLUMBUS, CHRISTOPHER
IMMIGRATION
SLAVERY

CARS

IF YOU COULD line up all of the world's cars end to end, they would form a traffic jam stretching all the way to the moon; and the line is getting longer, because a new car is made every second. Most cars are family cars, used for trips to school, work, stores, to see friends, and to take vacations. But there are also a number of special-purpose cars, including taxis, sports cars, police patrol cars, and ambulances. Gas or diesel engines power modern cars, just as they did the first cars of the 19th century. But the cars of today are very different from cars even 30 years ago. The latest cars have low, sleek shapes that are attractive and also reduce drag, or air resistance. Other features include powerful brakes for stopping quickly, and electronic engine control systems that allow cars to travel faster and use less fuel.

HOW A CAR WORKS

In most cars, the engine is in the front and drives the back or front wheels (or all four wheels) through a series of shafts and gears. There are usually four or five different gears; they alter the speed at which the engine turns the wheels. In low gear, the wheels turn slowly and produce extra force for starting and climbing hills. In high gear, the wheels turn fast for traveling at higher speeds.

A car radiator is full of water. A pump keeps water flowing around the engine to keep it cool. As the car moves forward, cold air rushes through the radiator, cooling the water before its next circuit around the engine.

The steering wheel turns the steering gear via a long shaft.

Tread, or grooves on the tires, improve traction (grip) in the rain.

This car has a manual gearbox, which means the driver uses the gear lever to change gears. In some cars, gear changes are automatic.

Turning the steering wheel inside the car turns the front wheels toward the left or right.

Suspension springs and shock absorbers soften a bumpy ride for the passengers and keep the wheels firmly on the ground as the car travels over uneven surfaces.

Pressing on the brake pedal pushes a special liquid down tubes, which in turn push on pistons at each wheel. These pistons squeeze the brake pads against steel discs or drums attached to the wheels, slowing down the wheels and stopping the car.

ANTI-POLLUTION DEVICE
Waste gases from the engine of a car are highly toxic (poisonous). To keep them under control some cars have special filters, called catalytic converters, attached to the exhaust system. These filters remove poisonous gases.

TYPES OF CARS

Cars have numerous uses, and there are many different kinds of cars available to suit almost any task. Most family cars combine a large interior with speed and fuel economy. However, for other, more specialized vehicles, safety, luxury, or power may be the most important design feature.

SPORTS CAR
With its large engine, sleek design, and seating for only two people, a sports car is designed purely for speed. Some can travel at about 200 mph (300 km/h).

CRASH PROTECTION
Driver and passengers are cocooned in a strong steel cage to protect them in a crash. But the rest of the car is designed to crumple easily and absorb some of the impact. Wearing seat belts can protect car passengers from injury in a crash.

LUXURY CAR
Large, carefully crafted cars such as the world-famous Rolls-Royce are among the most beautiful and expensive automobiles in the world.

OFF-ROAD VEHICLE
Rugged vehicles built specially for driving across country have powerful engines, four-wheel drive, and heavy ridged tires for extra grip.

HISTORY OF THE CAR

People laughed at the first rickety "horseless carriages" of the 1880s. But rapid technical progress soon made it clear that cars were here to stay. In 1903, cars could already reach speeds of more than 70 mph (110 km/h). But they were expensive and often broke down. Since then cars have become steadily cheaper and more reliable. Now they are everyday transport for millions of people throughout the world.

NICOLAS CUGNOT

The first road vehicles were powered by steam. In 1769, Nicolas Cugnot, a French soldier, built a steam carriage for dragging cannon. It traveled about 3 mph (5 km/h) and had to stop every 10 minutes to build up steam.

DAIMLER AND BENZ

In the 1880s, German engineers Karl Benz and Gottlieb Daimler worked independently to produce the first gasoline engine. In 1885, Karl Benz built his flimsy motorized tricycle (left); the first gas-powered car.

PANHARD AND LEVASSOR

In the 1890s, two Frenchmen, René Panhard and Emile Levassor, built the first car with the engine in the front, the arrangement found in most cars to this day.

The production line for the Ford Model T

FORD MODEL T

Early cars were handmade and cost so much money that only the rich could afford them. In 1908, Henry Ford opened a factory to produce large numbers of the Model T (above). This was the first car cheap enough to be purchased by more people.

Rear airfoil

Wide tires, called slicks, are smooth to minimize rolling resistance, but wide to give a good grip on the track.

Powerful disc brakes can slow the car from 200 mph to 40 mph (300 km/h to 65 km/h) in less than three seconds.

The light aluminum body is carefully shaped to keep drag to a minimum.

The frame is made from ultra-light carbon-fiber composites.

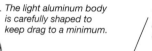

NEW DESIGNS

Prototypes (test models) of new cars are packed with electronics and computers that can do anything from parking the car automatically to finding the best route through town. Many parts of these cars are made from plastics and other new materials; some new engine designs contain ceramic components instead of metal ones.

Enormously powerful engine with 8 or 10 cylinders drives the car along at speeds up to about 250 mph (400 km/h).

A computer continually adjusts the suspension to make sure the wheels do not bounce up from the track.

RACING CAR

Grand Prix racing cars are designed for speed alone, so they are built very differently from road cars. They have big, powerful engines and are made of special light materials. Their ultra-low shape allows them to slice through the air easily so they can travel as fast as possible. Indeed, the driver has to lie almost flat to fit in.

Air foils at the front and back work like upside-down aeroplane wings. Air rushing over them pushes the car firmly onto the track, which improves traction.

Find out more

BUSES
ENGINES
POLLUTION
ROADS AND HIGHWAYS
TRANSPORTATION, HISTORY OF
TRUCKS
WHEELS

CARTOONS

TUMBLING AND SPINNING on the TV screen, cartoon characters make impossible feats look easy. But the process of creating a cartoon is slow and requires great patience. An artist must make 12 drawings of the figure to produce just one second of movement. This kind of movie, called an animated cartoon, first appeared on the screen about 100 years ago. But it was the American Walt Disney who made cartoons famous. In 1937, he produced his first feature-length movie, *Snow White and the Seven Dwarfs*. Today, animated films can be created using computers as well as by traditional methods. An animated movie is just one example of a cartoon. Originally, the word meant the paper pattern an artist made for a painting; today a cartoon usually means a funny drawing. Political cartoons comment on politicians and other public figures, and the imaginary characters in comic strip cartoons help us laugh at ourselves when life gets us down.

The background picture stays the same throughout the movement.

The cels are put in order onto a peg bar.

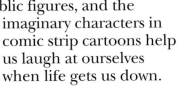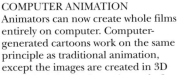

Registration holes at the bottom of each cel keep the image straight.

Each picture is colored in on the back of the cel.

CARTOON FILM
Nine separate drawings follow each other rapidly to create a smooth-flowing sequence of a boy pulling his sweater over his head.

ANIMATION
To make an animated film, artists draw each stage of every movement on clear plastic pages called cels. The background is painted on a separate cel, and shows through the clear cels. Photographing the cels in the correct sequence makes the figures move. Artists may produce a million drawings for one feature-length film.

COMPUTER ANIMATION
Animators can now create whole films entirely on computer. Computer-generated cartoons work on the same principle as traditional animation, except the images are created in 3D using computer software instead of being drawn on cels. Advances in technology mean that computer animation can be very lifelike. *The Incredibles* (2004) won an Oscar for its animation.

EUROPE

HISTORICAL CARTOONS
Cartoons can help politicians attack their opponents. Daumier, a 19th-century French artist, was a harsh critic of the French government. In this cartoon, Daumier balanced a figure representing Europe on the tip of a bayonet, to show how unstable European politics had become.

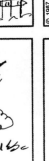

COMIC STRIP
The comic strip tells a story in a series of pictures. Sometimes the meaning is clear from the pictures alone; sometimes speech balloons put words in the characters' mouths. Characters such as Snoopy (above) and Superman have amused generations of children, and many adults follow their adventures.

Find out more
DRAWING
MOVIES
MAGAZINES
NEWSPAPERS

CASTLES

THE MASSIVE WALLS AND TOWERS of a castle were designed to make it impossible for enemy soldiers to destroy it. Inside was a whole world in miniature – lords and ladies, government officials, soldiers, servants, animals, gardens, treasure stores, and dungeons where prisoners could be tortured. The best site for a castle was on a hill surrounded by water. If there were no natural features, the builders made an artificial hill or dug a deep ditch and filled it with water to make a moat. A well-built castle with a good military commander in charge could withstand an enemy siege for many months. Most castles were built between the 9th century and the 16th century, when many countries were almost constantly at war. Early castles were small and made of wood; the later stone buildings housed town-sized populations, many are still standing today. The invention of gunpowder at the end of the 13th century made castles hard to defend. As times grew more peaceful, kings and lords moved into comfortable country houses.

LOOPHOLES
Archers fired through loopholes – narrow slits in the walls which were wider on the inside to make aiming easier. The inner walls were often higher than the outer walls, so archers could fire at the attackers over the heads of their own soldiers.

Siege engines had to be tall enough for attackers to fire down on castle defenders.

Castle by night

Sandbags protected the attacking archers.

Towers which stuck out from the walls gave archers a clear view of the attackers trying to climb the walls.

Even if the attackers built a bridge across a moat, they could be stopped by boiling water or hot sand dropped on them from above.

DEFENDING A CASTLE
During a siege, attackers tried to climb over the walls, smash them down with siege engines, or starve out the inhabitants. The defenders used archers with bows and arrows to keep attackers away from the walls. If the archers failed, soldiers pushed the attackers' scaling ladders away with poles and poured tubs full of boiling water or hot sand onto the enemy below. Deep moats or solid rock foundations stopped the attackers from digging under the walls. In peacetime, the knights and soldiers of the castle trained for war by jousting and playing war games in elaborate tournaments.

Attackers used a battering ram to break down drawbridge.

Deep moats surrounded castle walls.

HOW CASTLES DEVELOPED

International wars, especially the Crusades in the Middle East, led to bigger armies, more powerful weapons, and stronger, more sophisticated defenses. These wars speeded up castle building.

Motte

Bailey

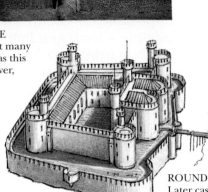

NORMAN CASTLE
The Normans built many stone castles such as this one (above) at Dover, England, between the 11th and 13th centuries.

MOTTE AND BAILEY
Early castles were built as a motte (hill) and bailey (court). They were made of wood and burned easily.

"Fairy tale" turret

SPANISH CASTLE
Some castles, such as the Alcázar in Segovia, Spain, became magnificent royal palaces.

ROUND TOWERS
Later castles had round towers. Rocks bounced off the curved surface and did less damage.

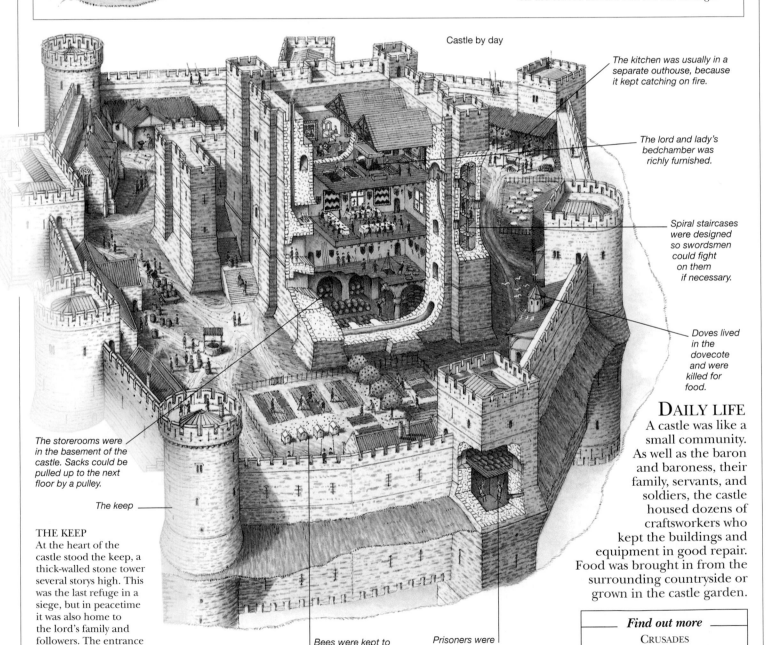

Castle by day

The kitchen was usually in a separate outhouse, because it kept catching on fire.

The lord and lady's bedchamber was richly furnished.

Spiral staircases were designed so swordsmen could fight on them if necessary.

Doves lived in the dovecote and were killed for food.

The storerooms were in the basement of the castle. Sacks could be pulled up to the next floor by a pulley.

The keep

THE KEEP

At the heart of the castle stood the keep, a thick-walled stone tower several storys high. This was the last refuge in a siege, but in peacetime it was also home to the lord's family and followers. The entrance to the keep was always on the first floor, through the guardroom. Above this was a great hall for feasting, and sometimes sleeping. The lord's own rooms were on the top floor.

Bees were kept to provide honey, and herbs were grown for medicinal purposes.

Prisoners were kept in chains in the dungeons.

DAILY LIFE

A castle was like a small community. As well as the baron and baroness, their family, servants, and soldiers, the castle housed dozens of craftsworkers who kept the buildings and equipment in good repair. Food was brought in from the surrounding countryside or grown in the castle garden.

Find out more
CRUSADES
KNIGHTS AND HERALDRY
MEDIEVAL EUROPE
NORMANS

CATS

WHEN YOU WATCH a cat stalking a bird, it is easy to see how cats are related to lions and tigers. All cats are excellent hunters. They have acute senses and sharp teeth and claws, and they are strong and agile. Cats do most of their hunting at night, and have evolved excellent eyesight in dim conditions. Even a domestic cat, or house cat, could survive in the wild by catching mice, small birds, insects, and other creatures. Many exotic pedigree (purebred) cats, however, might not be able to live for long in the wild, since most are used to a pampered lifestyle indoors.

The ancestor of our domestic cats is a wild tabby-coloured cat that has existed for about one million years – the African wild cat. This small wild cat spread through Africa, Asia, and Europe, until it was gradually tamed by people in Africa, where it helped protect food stores from rats and mice. Since then, domestic cats have been bred by people into many different types, from striped tabbies and Persian longhairs to the tailless Manx cat. Three thousand years ago, domestic cats were a common sight in Egypt, where they were held in great esteem. Today there are more than 500 million domestic cats around the world.

WILD CATS
The wild cat looks similar to the domestic tabby cat, but it has a heavier build and a larger head. Wild cats have black stripes on their legs and tail.

AGILITY
Cats have exceptional balance and often climb trees, walls, and fences when they are hunting or exploring. Cats also have extremely quick reflexes in case of a fall. As a cat drops, the balance organs inside its ears tell it at once which way is up. The cat rights its head, followed by its body, then lands safely on all four paws.

Cat suddenly falls.

Head twists around first.

Body follows head around.

Legs stretch out for landing.

BLACK CATS
For thousands of years, black cats have been associated with magic and witchcraft. They are still believed by some people to bring both good and bad luck.

Long flexible tail helps cat balance on narrow ledges.

Large ears can pick up faint sounds.

Touch-sensitive whiskers for feeling in the dark

Claws retracted in sheaths to keep them sharp

Pupils open wide in dim light to let in more light.

Pupils are narrow in bright light to let in less light.

EYES
In dim conditions, a cat's pupils open wide to let the maximum amount of light into the eye. The tapetum lucidum, a mirror-like layer inside the eye, reflects the light at the back of the eye. This is why a cat's eyes shine in the dark.

DOMESTIC CAT

There are more than 100 official breeds of domestic cat, and many more unofficial breeds. Cat experts are continually creating new varieties by selective breeding. The Bombay cat (left) is a new breed which was developed in the United States in the 1970s. It was bred by mating a Burmese with an American Black Shorthair. Although the Bombay has very short, dense hair, it still shows all the main features of a typical cat.

KITTENS

Young cats are called kittens. They spend hours chasing their tails, springing on each other, and having mock fights. Their play has a serious purpose. It helps them develop hunting skills, quick reactions, and strength and suppleness for those times when they have to fend for themselves.

GROOMING
Cats are famous for their cleanliness. Every day they spend at least an hour washing their fur with saliva and licking it with their rough-surfaced tongues. This makes the fur smooth and glossy. It also helps keep body heat in, removes pests, and stimulates the skin's blood flow.

SLEEPING
The average cat sleeps 16 hours each day, usually in short intervals called cat naps. A cat's body is designed for quick bursts of action, with much rest between.

BEHAVIOR

Domestic cats resemble their wild ancestors in several ways. Although most domestic cats do not have to catch their own food, they show many signs of hunting behavior such as being particularly active at dawn and dusk, and stalking and pouncing on pretend prey. Much of this behavior is instinctive, or inborn, and does not have to be learned. A cat that is brought up away from all other cats still behaves in this way.

HUNTING
A cat's sensitive nose easily picks up the scent of a mouse. As the cat nears its victim, its eyes and ears also come into use. After stalking up silently and slowly, the cat leaps forward with bared claws and grabs the prey, often biting it on the back of the head to break its neck.

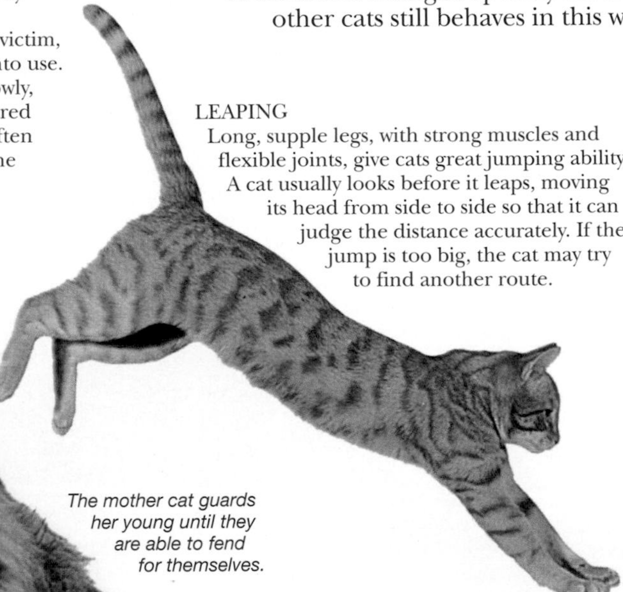

LEAPING
Long, supple legs, with strong muscles and flexible joints, give cats great jumping ability. A cat usually looks before it leaps, moving its head from side to side so that it can judge the distance accurately. If the jump is too big, the cat may try to find another route.

During lactation (milk-feeding), the kittens suck milk from teats on their mother's abdomen.

The mother cat guards her young until they are able to fend for themselves.

HAIRLESS CAT
The sphynx breed of cat was developed in the 1960s from a kitten that was born without fur. The sphynx has bare skin except for a few fine, dark, downy hairs on its face, paws, and tail tip. It is unlikely that a hairless cat such as this one could survive in the wild for long.

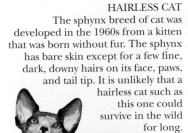

BREEDING

Female cats, or queens, are pregnant for about nine weeks. They give birth to between one and 10 kittens, but two to five kittens is average. A family of young kittens is called a litter. Newborn kittens are helpless. Their eyes are closed for the first week or more, and they do not begin to crawl for about two weeks. They feed on their mother's milk at first. After about eight weeks they gradually stop taking milk and begin to eat solid foods. This process is called weaning. About four weeks later, the mother cat is ready to mate again.

Ancient Egyptians kept domestic cats to guard grain stores. Cats became so celebrated that some were worshiped as gods, and statues such as the one shown here were made.

Find out more
ANIMAL SENSES
ANIMALS
EGYPT, ANCIENT
LIONS, TIGERS, and other big cats
MAMMALS

CAUCASUS REPUBLICS

THESE RUGGED AND MOUNTAINOUS republics lie between the flat steppelands of the Russian Federation and the high plateaus of Southwest Asia. All three countries were once part of the Soviet Union, and gained their independence in 1991. The region is rich in natural resources, with many contrasting climates and landscapes. Georgia's western borders on the Black Sea coast are lush and green with a warm, humid climate, while much of Armenia is semidesert and high plateau. Farming is important for all three countries; crops include apricots, peaches, cereals, citrus fruits, grapes, and tea. The mountains are rich in mineral resources, such as iron, copper, and lead, while the Caspian Sea has plentiful oil. There are over 50 ethnic groups living in the Caucasus, each retaining their own language and culture. Since independence, there have been growing ethnic and religious tensions.

Georgia, Azerbaijan, and Armenia are sandwiched between the high mountains of the Greater and Lesser Caucasus. The Black Sea borders the west of the region, while the landlocked Caspian lies to the east. Beyond the Caucasus Mountains to the north lies the Russian Federation.

CAUCASUS
The Caucasus in the north of the region form a high mountain barrier isolating it from the Russian Federation. Many peaks in the Caucasus rise to more than 15,000 ft (4,600 m).

OIL RIGS
In 1900, Azerbaijan was one of the world's main oil producers, supplying the entire Soviet Union. Caspian Sea oil resources are still being exploited, although lack of investment in rigs has reduced the potential output. Oil is piped from Baku, the center of the industry, to Iran, Russia, Kazakhstan, and Turkmenistan.

BLACK SEA
The Black Sea is an inland sea between Asia and Europe. It is connected to the Mediterranean Sea by the Bosporus, the Sea of Marmara, and the Dardanelles.

YEREVAN
Yerevan, the capital of Armenia, is located on the Razdan river, 14 miles (23 km) from the Turkish frontier. The city has long been a commercial center, and today its markets are packed with traders selling fruits, vegetables, and rugs woven locally from silk and wool. During the Soviet era the city expanded rapidly, its growth encouraged by the building of hydroelectric plants on the Razdan, which powered chemicals and engineering industries.

SCALE BAR
0   50   km
0   50   miles

Volcano Mountain Ancient monument Capital city Large city/town Small city/town

ARMENIA
Area: 11,505 sq miles (29,000 sq km)
Population: 3,100,000
Capital: Yerevan

AZERBAIJAN
Area: 33,436 sq miles (86,600 sq km)
Population: 8,400,000
Capital: Baku

GEORGIA
Area: 26,911 sq miles (69,700 sq km)
Population: 5,100,000
Capital: Tblisi

Find out more
ASIA
ASIA, HISTORY OF
MOUNTAINS
OIL
SOVIET UNION, HISTORY OF

CAVES

BENEATH THE SURFACE of the Earth lies a secret world. Caves run through the rock, opening out into huge chambers decorated with slender stone columns. Underground rivers wind through deep passages, and waterfalls crash down on hidden lakes. Caves such as these are many thousands of years old; they were formed as water slowly dissolved limestone rocks. But not all caves are underground. Sea cliffs contain caves that have been eroded by the waves. Caves also develop inside glaciers and within the solidified lava around volcanoes.

Caves are damp, dark places. Some are only large enough to contain one person; others, such as the network of caves in Mammoth Cave National Park, in Kentucky, stretch for hundreds of miles. One of the world's deepest caves, in France, lies almost 1 mile (1.5 km) below the ground. Prehistoric peoples used caves for shelter. Caves at Lascaux, France, contain wall paintings and ancient tools that are perhaps 20,000 years old. A few cave dwellers still live today in parts of Africa and Asia.

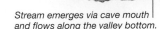

Stalactites and stalagmites take thousands of years to grow.

STALACTITES

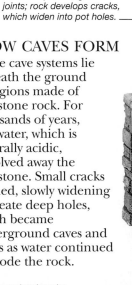

Slender stalactites often hang from a cave roof. Drops of water seeping down from above dissolve a white mineral called calcite from the rock. As the water dries, small amounts of calcite are left behind. These build up to form stalactites. This process is usually very slow; stalactites grow only about 1 in (2.5 cm) in 500 years.

Water drop falls from tip of stalactite.

STALAGMITES

Water dripping from the roof or from a stalactite falls to the cave floor, leaving layers of calcite on the floor. In this way a pillar called a stalagmite slowly builds upward.

A stalactite and stalagmite may grow and meet to form a column from floor to roof.

HOW CAVES FORM

Large cave systems lie beneath the ground in regions made of limestone rock. For thousands of years, rainwater, which is naturally acidic, dissolved away the limestone. Small cracks formed, slowly widening to create deep holes, which became underground caves and rivers as water continued to erode the rock.

Ridges and grooves in the limestone surface

Water seeps through rock joints; rock develops cracks, which widen into pot holes.

Steplike rock formations

Stream emerges over waterfall.

Craggy limestone cliffs

Sinkhole – point at which a stream plunges underground

Sparse vegetation

Groundwater fills a previously dry cavern to the level of the water table, which can rise and fall over time.

Steep channel carved by stream.

Underground lake

Later passage eroded by stream.

Stream emerges via cave mouth and flows along the valley bottom.

Spelunkers marvel at the fascinating rock formations around an underground lake at the mouth of a cave in France.

SPELUNKING

The sport of exploring caves is called potholing or spelunking. Clambering around in caves is a dirty and often wet pastime, so spelunkers wear tough clothing. Other important equipment includes nylon ropes, a helmet with a light, and ladders made of steel cables. Spelunkers work in teams and may stay in a cave for several days. Spelunking can be dangerous; rain can cause flooding, and spelunkers can be trapped by sudden rockfalls.

Find out more

BATS
GEOLOGY
PREHISTORIC PEOPLES
ROCKS AND MINERALS
VOLCANOES

CELTS

TWO THOUSAND YEARS AGO, much of western Europe was inhabited by a fierce, proud, artistic people known as the Celts. They were skilled warriors, farmers, and metalworkers. For several hundred years their art and culture dominated northwestern Europe. All Celts shared a similar way of life, but they were not a single group of people. They included many different tribes, such as the Atrebates of southern Britain and the Parisii of northern France. Most Celts lived in villages or hill forts, some of which developed into small towns. But the Celts never formed a unified nation. Between 3000 B.C. and A.D. 100 they were absorbed into the Roman Empire. Today, Celtic-speaking people can still be found in parts of Britain, Ireland, and France.

BOUDICEA
In A.D. 61, Boudicea (or Boadicea), queen of the Iceni, a Celtic tribe in Britain, led a massive revolt against Roman oppression. The Britons, however, were no match for the well-organized Romans, and the revolt was suppressed.

Livestock was kept for food and dairy produce.

Huts were covered in clay and thatch to protect them from bad weather.

Woven wooden frame of hut

The Celts wove their own cloth on looms.

THE HOME
Celtic families lived together in one large hut. Some huts were made of stone; others of wattle and daub – wood-framed huts covered in clay to make a hard wall. Thatch was often used to keep the rain out. An iron cauldron hung over a fire for cooking meat or boiling water. Bread was cooked in a domed clay oven. Members of the family wove cloth, worked as farmers, or made pots.

DRUIDS
Druids, a very important group in Celtic society, were priests who led religious ceremonies, acted as judges and advisers, and were responsible for teaching the sons of chiefs. Druidism involved the worship of many gods. Oak trees and mistletoe were also sacred to Druids.

METALWORKING
The Celts worked with many different metals including iron, bronze, copper, gold, and silver. Farm tools, weapons, shields, chariots, and helmets were made from metal, and many were beautifully decorated with distinctive plants and animals, as shown on the border around this page.

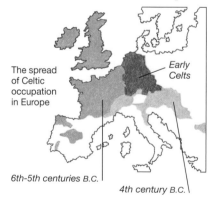

The spread of Celtic occupation in Europe

Early Celts

6th-5th centuries B.C.

4th century B.C.

CELTIC LANDS
The earliest Celts lived in central Europe, in what is now southern Germany. By about 500 B.C., Celts had spread out to cover much of Europe, from Ireland to the Black Sea.

Find out more
IRON AGE

CENTIPEDES
AND MILLIPEDES

WITH MORE LEGS than most other creatures, the centipede is a speedy predator. This active hunter runs swiftly after insects and other small prey, and sometimes chases millipedes, too. Centipedes and their slower-moving relatives, the millipedes, belong to the larger animal group called arthropods, which means "jointed feet." They may have as many as 180 pairs of legs – centipedes have one pair on each body segment; millipedes have two pairs on each segment. There are about 3,000 kinds of centipedes and 10,000 kinds of millipedes. Both kinds of creatures are found in dark, moist woodland areas, in soil, in leaf litter, and in rotten wood. Most centipedes lay their eggs in the soil, leaving the young to hatch and fend for themselves. Millipedes lay eggs in batches of between 30 and 100. Some millipedes leave the eggs in the soil; others make a nest from hardened excrement or spin a silk cocoon for protection. Millipedes are mainly plant eaters. They are important recyclers of dead leaves and wood, chewing them up and returning the nutrients to the soil in their droppings.

VELVET WORM
The wormlike peripatus, or velvet worm, has many legs and is similar in shape to centipedes and millipedes. This picture shows a peripatus attacking a forest millipede by covering it with sticky threads.

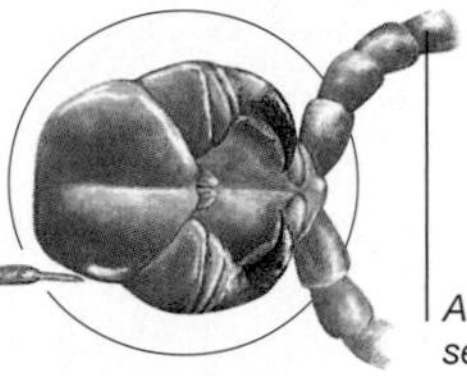

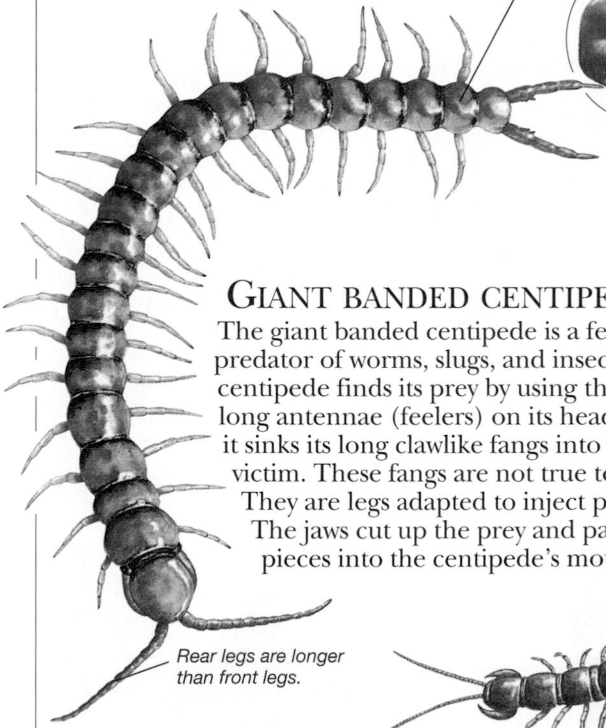

Flat body allows centipede to creep easily into cracks.

Antennae (feelers) sense the movement and scent of prey.

GIANT BANDED CENTIPEDE
The giant banded centipede is a fearsome predator of worms, slugs, and insects. A centipede finds its prey by using the two long antennae (feelers) on its head. Then it sinks its long clawlike fangs into the victim. These fangs are not true teeth. They are legs adapted to inject poison. The jaws cut up the prey and pass the pieces into the centipede's mouth.

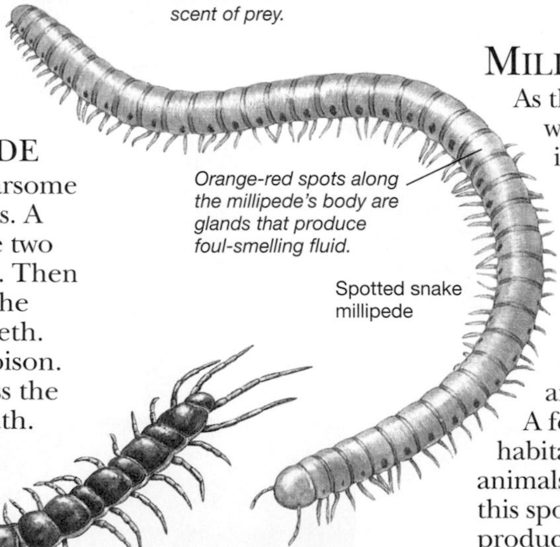

Orange-red spots along the millipede's body are glands that produce foul-smelling fluid.

Spotted snake millipede

MILLIPEDE
As the millipede pushes its way slowly through the soil, its legs move in waves, 10 to 20 legs at a time. The millipede's mouthparts are specialized for scraping and chewing plant material. Most millipedes feed on decomposing plant matter; others eat plant roots and are pests on farm crops. A few millipedes live in rocky habitats and caves and prey on animals. Most millipedes, including this spotted snake millipede, produce a foul-smelling substance to deter predators.

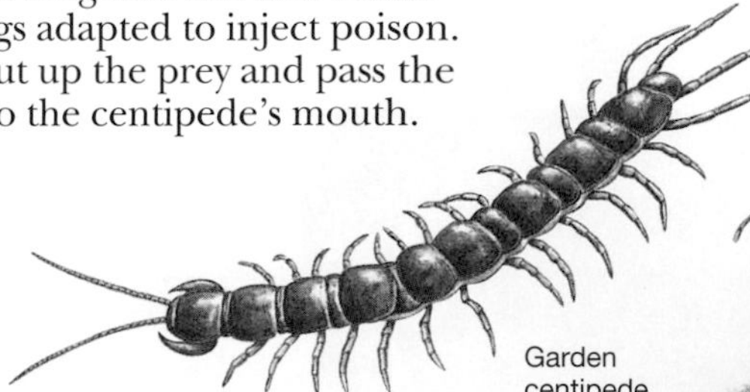

Rear legs are longer than front legs.

GARDEN CENTIPEDE
The common garden centipede attacks any animal of its own size, including other centipedes. Garden centipedes have 15 pairs of legs and are found mainly in damp places under logs, stones, bark, and leaves.

Garden centipede

POISONOUS CENTIPEDE
Some centipedes are huge, such as the long scolopendra centipedes of Africa, Asia, and the Americas. They grow to about 12 in (30 cm) long. These giant centipedes sometimes wander into houses, where they feed on household pests. Their poisonous bite can be dangerous, so these centipedes are best avoided.

The hard exoskeleton, or outer casing, on a millipede's body is divided into many segments. These segments overlap and allow the millipede to curl its body up in self-defense when threatened.

These creatures are well named – centipede means "a hundred legs," and millipede means "a thousand legs."

Millipede's legs move together in waves when it is walking.

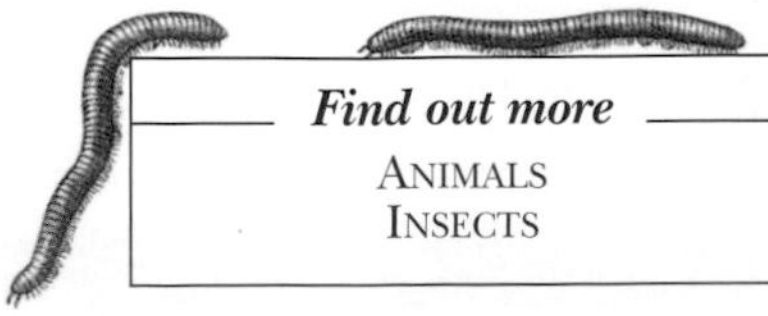

Find out more
ANIMALS
INSECTS

CENTRAL AFRICA

The Equator runs through the countries of Central Africa, exercising a strong influence on both climate and vegetation. The extreme north of the region borders the arid Sahara Desert. The south is dominated by the Congo River basin and equatorial rain forest.

MUCH OF CENTRAL AFRICA is covered by dense rain forest drained by the Congo River, which flows in a sweeping arc for 2,900 miles (4,666 km). Most of the countries in this region were once French colonies. Their fortunes have varied since independence in the 1960s. The Democratic Republic of Congo has rich mineral deposits and fertile land, but civil wars and conflict with Rwanda (1996-97) have kept it poor. Chad has also suffered from civil wars while the Central African Republic is one of the world's poorest countries, the victim of an unstable government. To the west, Gabon, Cameroon, and Congo have profited from oil and timber, and are comparatively stable. Everywhere, most people support themselves by farming. In the humid tropical lowlands, diseases such as malaria are widespread, and infant mortality is high.

FULANI
The Fulani are nomads who spread across West Africa and into Chad, Guinea, and Cameroon during the 11th century. From the 14th century, they converted to Islam, spreading the faith through persuasion and conquest. Some Fulani are still cattle-herding pastoralists, while others have adopted settled agriculture or live in towns.

TIMBER INDUSTRY
The equatorial rain forests of Central Africa are a major source of hardwoods such as mahogany, ebony, and teak. Timber is an important export for several countries, especially Gabon and Cameroon. However, the timber industry poses a severe threat to the rain forests, which take many years to recover. In addition, most timber companies are foreign-owned, and take profits out of the countries.

Controlled fires, as pictured above, "burn off" rain forest in Cameroon, clearing land for agriculture and industry.

Established in 1925, Virunga National Park (right) is Africa's oldest national park. It is also a World Heritage site.

OIL WEALTH
The Congo, Gabon, and Cameroon have all discovered extensive offshore oil reserves in the Atlantic Ocean. Exports of oil are vital economically, as they can earn these countries foreign currency. In the Congo, oil accounts for 85 per cent of the country's exports. This overdependence on oil can be disastrous when world oil prices fluctuate. Oil is also Gabon's main export, and profits from oil have been plowed back into its health service, one of the best in Africa.

VIRUNGA NATIONAL PARK
Virunga National Park is located in the northeast corner of the Democratic Republic of Congo, and was created in 1925. It is dominated by the Virunga Mountains, a range of both dormant and active volcanoes which extend into Rwanda and Uganda. The mountains are cloaked with cloud forests, and are a famous refuge for gorillas, an endangered species. Lake Edward occupies much of the center of the park, and the open countryside surrounding it is populated by herds of elephants and okapi.

LIBREVILLE
Gabon's capital, Libreville ("free town"), was founded by freed slaves in 1849. It lies on a string of hills which enclose a port. The modern European-style center is ringed by traditional African villages.

> ### *Find out more*
> AFRICA
> AFRICA, HISTORY OF
> AFRICAN WILDLIFE
> SLAVERY

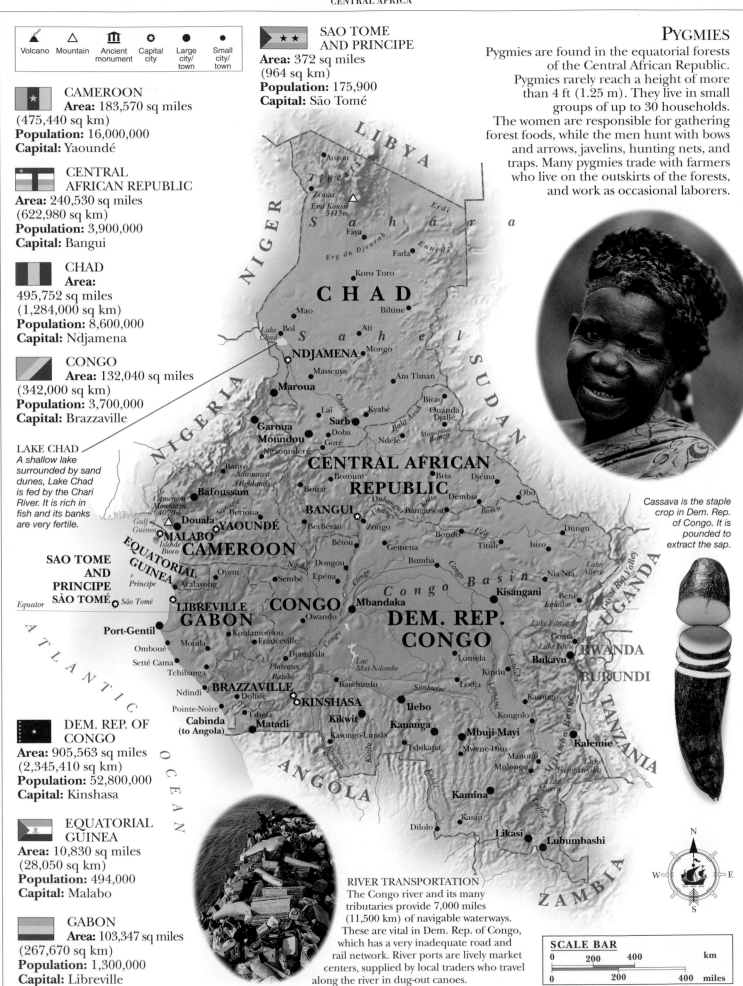

| Volcano | Mountain | Ancient monument | Capital city | Large city/town | Small city/town |

CAMEROON
Area: 183,570 sq miles (475,440 sq km)
Population: 16,000,000
Capital: Yaoundé

CENTRAL AFRICAN REPUBLIC
Area: 240,530 sq miles (622,980 sq km)
Population: 3,900,000
Capital: Bangui

CHAD
Area: 495,752 sq miles (1,284,000 sq km)
Population: 8,600,000
Capital: Ndjamena

CONGO
Area: 132,040 sq miles (342,000 sq km)
Population: 3,700,000
Capital: Brazzaville

LAKE CHAD
A shallow lake surrounded by sand dunes, Lake Chad is fed by the Chari River. It is rich in fish and its banks are very fertile.

SAO TOME AND PRINCIPE
Area: 372 sq miles (964 sq km)
Population: 175,900
Capital: São Tomé

DEM. REP. OF CONGO
Area: 905,563 sq miles (2,345,410 sq km)
Population: 52,800,000
Capital: Kinshasa

EQUATORIAL GUINEA
Area: 10,830 sq miles (28,050 sq km)
Population: 494,000
Capital: Malabo

GABON
Area: 103,347 sq miles (267,670 sq km)
Population: 1,300,000
Capital: Libreville

PYGMIES

Pygmies are found in the equatorial forests of the Central African Republic. Pygmies rarely reach a height of more than 4 ft (1.25 m). They live in small groups of up to 30 households. The women are responsible for gathering forest foods, while the men hunt with bows and arrows, javelins, hunting nets, and traps. Many pygmies trade with farmers who live on the outskirts of the forests, and work as occasional laborers.

Cassava is the staple crop in Dem. Rep. of Congo. It is pounded to extract the sap.

RIVER TRANSPORTATION

The Congo river and its many tributaries provide 7,000 miles (11,500 km) of navigable waterways. These are vital in Dem. Rep. of Congo, which has a very inadequate road and rail network. River ports are lively market centers, supplied by local traders who travel along the river in dug-out canoes.

SCALE BAR
0   200   400   km
0   200   400   miles

CENTRAL AMERICA

LIKE LINKS IN A CHAIN, the seven Central American countries seem to tie together the continents of North and South America. The climate is hot and steamy; trees, plants, and jungle animals thrive around the marshy coasts and in the high mountains. More than 2,500 years ago Native Americans made Central America their home. Some of the people who live there today are direct descendants of these early inhabitants. Many are *mestizos:* people with both Native American and European ancestors. European people first came to Central America around 1500, and the Spanish empire ruled the area for more than three centuries. By 1823, many of the countries had gained independence, but this did not bring peace and prosperity to their people. Most Central Americans are still very poor and have no land. There are too few jobs and not enough food. Governments in the region have been unable to solve these problems, and wars and revolutions are common.

Central America forms an isthmus, or narrow land bridge, from Mexico in the north, to Colombia in the south.

There are many active volcanoes in Central America. The largest is Tajumulco in Guatemala.

The soil in the valleys is very fertile.

Jungle covers the eastern coastal plain and many mountains.

MAYA

Between A.D. 250 and 900 Native American people called the Maya lived in Central America, where they created a vast empire. They built great cities at Palenque and Tikal (in present-day Mexico and Guatemala) and constructed huge stone temples and palaces in the shape of pyramids. To feed the people in the cities, the Maya became skilled at cultivating food. They used ingenious farming methods to grow plentiful crops on the small areas of suitable land.

PEOPLE
More than 38 million people live in Central America, mostly in the countryside and in small towns. The biggest city is Guatemala City, which has a population of over 2 million. Most people speak either Spanish or one of the local Native American languages. In Belize, many people speak English. Many Central Americans are Christians, and the Roman Catholic Church is an important influence in everyday life and culture.

EDUCATION
Civil wars and other armed conflicts have disrupted normal life in Central America. One result is that many people are illiterate. However, in Nicaragua there is a major campaign to teach people to read.

Bananas grown in Honduras are eaten all over the world.

Nicaragua was an important cotton producer until civil war disrupted farming.

In Panama sugar is extracted from sugarcane, which grows rapidly in the hot, humid climate.

Belize processes grapefruit and exports juice.

Coffee is Guatemala's most important export.

INDUSTRY
Agriculture is the major industry in Central America; many of the countries depend on one main crop for their income. Both Belize and El Salvador also make textiles and light industrial products. Guatemala produces oil for export.

Find out more

AZTECS
CARIBBEAN
CONQUISTADORS
MEXICO

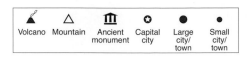

| Volcano | Mountain | Ancient monument | Capital city | Large city/town | Small city/town |

STATISTICS
Area: 201,993 sq miles (523,160 sq km)
Population: 38,756,000
Number of independent countries: 7

PANAMA CANAL
The Panama Canal is a great international waterway connecting the Atlantic and Pacific oceans. It is more than 50 miles (80 km) long and up to 500 ft (150 m) wide, with a minimum depth of 39 ft (12 m). Over 13,000 ships from all over the world pass through the canal's locks each year. Most of their cargo travels to and from the United States.

PACIFIC COASTAL STRIP
Half the population of Central America lives on the western slopes, which are higher and drier than the lowlands that border the Caribbean coast. Most people in the west work as farmers, producing coffee, bananas, sugarcane, and cotton.

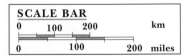

SCALE BAR

BELIZE
Area: 8,865 sq miles (22,960 sq km)
Population: 256,000
Capital: Belmopan
Currency: Belizean dollar

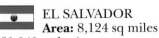

COSTA RICA
Area: 19,730 sq miles (51,100 sq km)
Population: 4,200,000
Capital: San José
Currency: Colón

HONDURAS
Area: 43,278 sq miles (112,090 sq km)
Population: 6,900,000
Capital: Tegucigalpa
Currency: Lempira

EL SALVADOR
Area: 8,124 sq miles (21,040 sq km)
Population: 6,500,000
Capital: San Salvador
Currency: Colón

NICARAGUA
Area: 50,193 sq miles (130,000 sq km)
Population: 5,500,000
Capital: Managua
Currency: Córdoba

GUATEMALA
Area: 42,043 sq miles (108,890 sq km)
Population: 12,300,000
Capital: Guatemala City
Currency: Quetzal

PANAMA
Area: 29,761 sq miles (77,080 sq km)
Population: 3,100,000
Capital: Panama City
Currency: Balboa

COSTA RICA
More than half of Costa Rica's people live on a broad, fertile plateau surrounded by volcanic ranges (above). Small farms dot the area; coffee, corn, rice, and sugar are grown on the hillsides. Unlike other Central American countries, Costa Rica enjoys political stability.

CENTRAL ASIA

A LANDSCAPE OF HIGH MOUNTAINS, fertile valleys, and extensive deserts, Central Asia was once peopled by nomads who roamed the land with their animal herds, searching for new pastures. The Silk Road, a trade route from China to Europe, once passed through the region, and a number of towns were founded along it. From 1922 to 1991 most of the region was part of the Soviet Union. During this period traditional ways of life began to disappear, and new technology made the land more productive. Today, the independent states of the region use mountain streams to generate electricity, and divert water to irrigate the arid land. A large range of crops – vegetables, wheat, fruits, and tobacco – are grown. Cotton is a major crop, and is exported by Uzbekistan. Afghanistan, to the south, has been plagued by warfare. Its economy is in a state of collapse due to the conflict.

In the east and south, the Central Asian mountains form a barrier between Central Asia and China and Pakistan. To the west lies Iran and the eastern shores of the Caspian Sea. To the north lie the flat steppelands of Kazakhstan.

SAMARQAND
One of the oldest cities in Central Asia, Samarqand was situated on the ancient Silk Road from China to Europe. Some of its finest buildings date to the 13th and 14th centuries, when Samarqand was the center of an Islamic empire.

The monuments of the Registan Square (below) are decorated with mosaics, marble, and gold.

Samarqand is still a major trading center, exporting silk and cotton, fruits, vegetables, and tobacco.

Animal breeding is important to the Kyrgyz because they have so little land to farm. The Kyrgyz are known for their skilled horsemanship.

KYRGYZ NOMADS
Mainly from Kyrgyzstan, the Kyrgyz are a nomadic people, who traditionally live on the high plateaus by herding sheep, goats, yaks, horses, and camels. They lived in *yurts* – felt-covered frame tents. During the Soviet era many Kyrgyz were forced to settle on large collective farms.

CARPETS
Woolen carpets from Turkmenistan and Uzbekistan have distinctive geometrical designs. They are made by hand-knotting the wool. They are used as saddle cloths, wall hangings, and prayer mats.

ARAL SEA
In Uzbekistan, cotton farmers are diverting the flow of the Amu Darya to water their fields. The inland Aral Sea, also fed by the river, is drying up. More than half the sea's water has been lost since 1960 and its salt content has increased fourfold. The sea is too salty for fish, and fishing ports are now surrounded by grounded ships and barren land. Fertilizers have poisoned drinking water, leading to health problems.

COTTON HARVEST
Uzbekistan is one of the world's largest cotton-cultivators. Cotton is also grown elsewhere in Central Asia, which is the northernmost of the great cotton regions of the world. Uzbekistan makes and exports machinery used to harvest and process the cotton. The gathering of the white, fluffy cotton is highly mechanized.

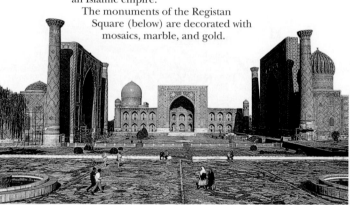

Find out more
ASIA
DAMS
ISLAM
OCEANS AND SEAS
SOVIET UNION, HISTORY OF

Volcano	Mountain	Ancient monument	Capital city	Large city/town	Small city/town

AFGHANISTAN
Area: 251,770 sq miles (652,090 sq km)
Population: 23,900,000
Capital: Kabul
Languages: Persian, Pashtu, Dari, Uzbek, Turkmen
Religions: Sunni Muslim, Shi'ite Muslim
Currency: Afghani

KYRGYZSTAN
Area: 76,640 sq miles (198,500 sq km)
Population: 5,100,000
Capital: Bishkek
Languages: Kyrgyz, Russian
Religions: Muslim, Russian Orthodox
Currency: Som

TAJIKISTAN
Area: 55,251 sq miles (143,100 sq km)
Population: 6,200,000
Capital: Dushanbe
Languages: Tajik, Russian
Religions: Sunni Muslim, Shi'ite Muslim
Currency: Tajik ruble

TURKMENISTAN
Area: 188,455 sq miles (488,100 sq km)
Population: 4,900,000
Capital: Ashgabat
Languages: Turkmen, Uzbek, Russian
Religions: Sunni Muslim, Eastern Orthodox
Currency: Manat

UZBEKISTAN
Area: 172,741 sq miles (447,400 sq km)
Population: 26,100,000
Capital: Tashkent
Languages: Uzbek, Russian
Religions: Sunni Muslim, Eastern Orthodox
Currency: Som

KHYBER PASS
The Khyber Pass is the gateway from the mountains of Afghanistan to the densely populated plains of the Indian subcontinent. A narrow road, built during the late 19th century, winds its way between sheer cliffs, and at one point the pass is only 15 ft (5 m) wide. During the Second Afghan War (1879-80) the pass was the scene of many battles between British troops and local tribesmen.

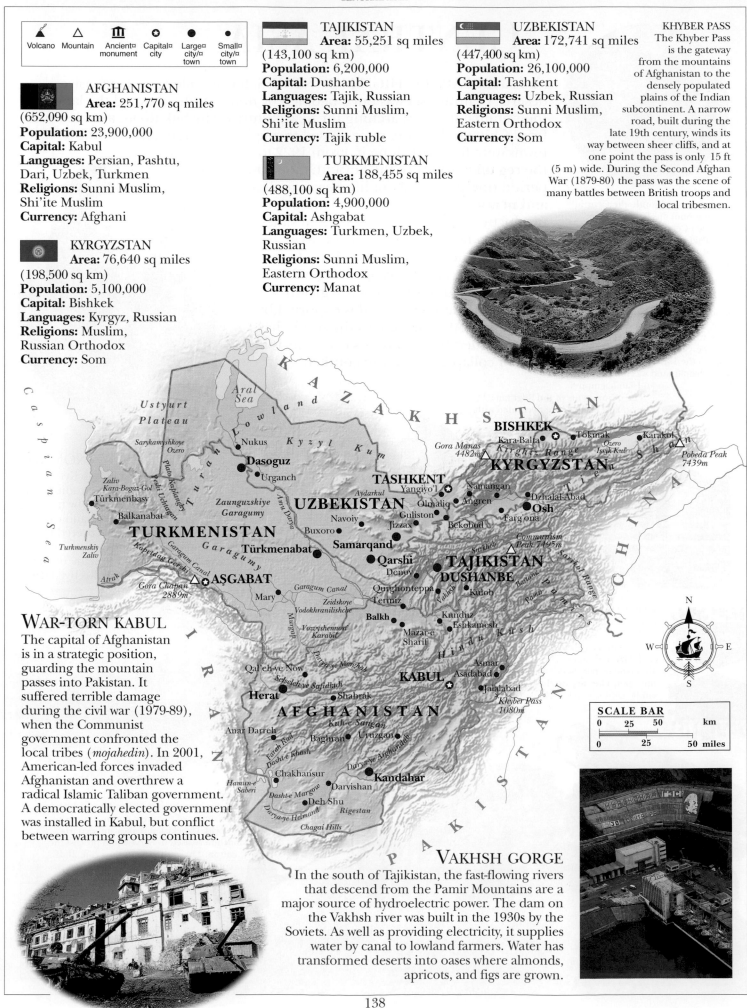

WAR-TORN KABUL
The capital of Afghanistan is in a strategic position, guarding the mountain passes into Pakistan. It suffered terrible damage during the civil war (1979-89), when the Communist government confronted the local tribes (*mojahedin*). In 2001, American-led forces invaded Afghanistan and overthrew a radical Islamic Taliban government. A democratically elected government was installed in Kabul, but conflict between warring groups continues.

VAKHSH GORGE
In the south of Tajikistan, the fast-flowing rivers that descend from the Pamir Mountains are a major source of hydroelectric power. The dam on the Vakhsh river was built in the 1930s by the Soviets. As well as providing electricity, it supplies water by canal to lowland farmers. Water has transformed deserts into oases where almonds, apricots, and figs are grown.

SCALE BAR

CHARLEMAGNE

TWELVE CENTURIES AGO, one man ruled most of western Europe. Charlemagne could hardly read or write, yet he built up a vast empire. Charlemagne was a Frank – one of the peoples who had invaded the Roman Empire when it collapsed in the 5th century – and who then settled in northern France. When he became king in A.D. 768, his territory was small, and threatened by its French neighbors. Charlemagne soon overcame them all and then invaded northern Italy. He was a great warrior. He fought the people of Hungary, and the Saxons in Germany. He also invaded Spain and stopped the Muslims living there from threatening the rest of Europe. Charlemagne's aim was not just to rule more countries; he wanted to convert the inhabitants to Christianity. To achieve this goal, he became ruthless with those who opposed him. However, he was not an especially cruel ruler. He reformed the countries he conquered, and, perhaps because he was not an educated man, he encouraged learning and set up many schools. The Pope, who was head of the Catholic Church, rewarded Charlemagne by crowning him Emperor of the Romans in 800, for Charlemagne's European empire was the first to be formed since the fall of Rome. When he died 14 years later, Charlemagne was the most powerful ruler in Europe.

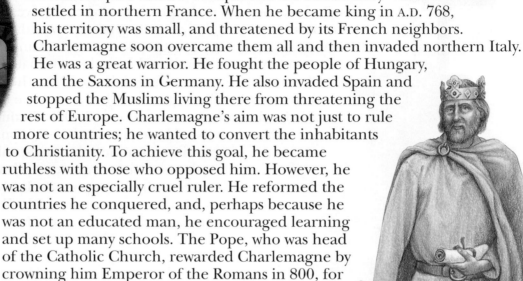

THRONE
Charlemagne was a very powerful ruler, but his marble throne was plain and undecorated. The throne was a copy of the one described in the Bible, from which King Solomon ruled his Kingdom of Israel. Charlemagne built a chapel in his palace to house his throne. The chapel survives today as part of Aachen Cathedral, in Germany.

CORONATION
Pope Leo III crowned Charlemagne Emperor of the Romans on Christmas Day in 800, at St. Peter's Basilica in Rome. Charlemagne became the first Roman emperor for more than three centuries. Although he accepted the title, he believed that it had little value.

WHAT HE LOOKED LIKE
There are few known portraits of Charlemagne, but those that remain show a tall, bearded, blond-haired man.

This coin dates from Charlemagne's period of rule.

HOLY ROMAN EMPIRE
Charlemagne's domain (colored pink here) covered most of Europe. Though his empire was split up after his death, what remained later became known as the Holy Roman Empire (colored green). The last emperor, Francis II, resigned the title in 1806. Some say he abolished the empire to stop Napoleon Bonaparte, emperor of France, from taking the title. Others say Napoleon ended it because he didn't want a rival emperor in Europe.

Holy Roman Empire

Charlemagne's empire

Part of both empires

ROYAL TOMB
Scenes from Charlemagne's life cover his tomb in Aachen Cathedral. One panel shows his armies besieging the town of Pamplona in Spain. The tomb is richly decorated with gold, and set with precious stones.

Find out more
BARBARIANS
MEDIEVAL EUROPE
NAPOLEON BONAPARTE

CHEMISTRY

HAVE YOU EVER WONDERED why cooking changes raw, tough food into a tasty meal? Cooking is just one example of a chemical reaction that converts raw materials into new substances. Chemists use chemical reactions to make plastics, medicines, dyes, and many other materials that are important in everyday life. They also study what substances are made of and how they can be combined to make new materials. Chemicals are the raw materials used by a chemist. More than 4 million different chemicals have been made by chemists; there are about 35,000 chemicals in common use. These chemicals can be made by combining simple substances, called elements, into more complicated substances called compounds. Early chemists considered four elements – fire, water, air, and earth. Today, we know there are 92 that occur in nature, and a few others that can be made in laboratories. The most common element in the universe is hydrogen, which is the main component of stars.

APPARATUS
Chemists use special flasks and jars to mix chemicals, together with equipment that is electronic and automated.

CHEMICAL REACTIONS

When different substances combine to form new materials, a chemical reaction occurs. Some reactions need heat to start them off; others produce heat as the reaction proceeds.

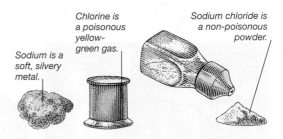

Sodium is a soft, silvery metal.

Chlorine is a poisonous yellow-green gas.

Sodium chloride is a non-poisonous powder.

H₂O

Chemists use a shorthand to describe chemicals. H_2O is the symbol for water, and shows that each water molecule contains two hydrogen atoms (H) and one oxygen atom (O).

ELEMENTS AND COMPOUNDS
Elements are substances that are made of a single kind of atom. When different elements combine, their atoms join to produce molecules of a new substance, which is called a compound. For example, common salt is a compound called sodium chloride. It is made by combining the element sodium and the element chlorine. When the two elements combine, they form a compound that is entirely different from either of the elements used to produce it.

HISTORY OF CHEMISTRY
The Egyptians were the first chemists. The word chemistry comes from *Chem*, the name for Ancient Egypt. Modern chemistry began around 1790 when a Frenchman, Antoine Lavoisier, explained how chemical reactions work. In 1808, an English scientist, John Dalton, showed that substances were made from atoms. By 1871, a Russian teacher, Dimitri Mendeleyev, had produced the periodic table, which classifies elements according to their properties and is the cornerstone of chemistry.

ALCHEMY
Early chemistry, called alchemy, was a mixture of magic and guesswork. From about A.D. 300, alchemists tried to make gold from lead, mercury, and other cheap metals. They also tried to find an elixir, or preparation, to prolong life. Although the alchemists did not succeed in these aims, they found ways of separating substances and making them pure. They also discovered many new substances.

Find out more

ATOMS AND MOLECULES
EGYPT, ANCIENT
HEAT
PHYSICS
SCIENCE, HISTORY OF

CHINA

To DESCRIBE CHINA you need to use enormous numbers. The country is vast, covering more than 3.6 million sq miles (9.3 million sq km). China's written history stretches back 3,500 years – longer than any other nation's. 1,300 million people live there, and one-fifth of the world's population is Chinese. In such a large country, there are many variations, including four major language families. The land, too, is tremendously varied. The east and southeast, where most people live, is green and fertile. Other parts of the country are barren deserts of sand and rock. Organizing and feeding the huge and varied Chinese population is a mammoth task. Since 1949, China has been ruled by a Communist government which has tried to provide adequate food, education, and health care to every part of the nation. During the late 1970s, Communist party moderates embraced economic reforms that lifted government controls and encouraged private enterprise. Consequently, China became the world's third-largest economy in the mid 1990s. China's human rights record, however, is still criticized because of political oppression at home and in Tibet.

China is the fourth-largest country in the world. It is situated in eastern Asia. The Russian Federation and Mongolia lie to its north, and Southeast Asia and the Indian subcontinent to its south and west. The East China Sea is to its east.

TRANSPORTATION
Private cars are almost unknown in China. The bicycle is the main method of transportation for people and luggage.

Tiananmen Square, Beijing

Chinese farmers make use of every suitable piece of land, carving steps, or terraces, in the hillsides to grow rice and other crops.

Rice is grown in flooded fields called paddies.

BEIJING
The capital city of China is Beijing (formerly Peking). Modern Beijing spreads out around the older central area. To the north and west are houses and Beijing University. The industrial area is to the east of the center. At the heart lies Tiananmen (Gate of Heavenly Peace) Square. Here parades and celebrations take place on national holidays. In 1989, the government forcibly disbanded a pro-democracy student demonstration here, killing thousands.

AGRICULTURE AND LAND USE
Most Chinese people are crowded together in just 15 percent of the total land area, mainly in river valleys in the east. Three in ten live in huge cities; the rest live in the countryside. There they grow rice and wheat and raise pigs and other livestock. Much of the rest of the country is mountainous and wild. The Takla Makan Desert in the west is dry and cold, and few people live there.

NEW YEAR
China's most important festival is the celebration of New Year. Each year is named after an animal and people celebrate with colorful processions. Tangerines with leaves are the lucky fruits of the New Year. Odd numbers are unlucky, so people always give presents of tangerines in pairs.

FAMILY LIFE
The family is the most important institution in Chinese life. Children respect their parents and look after them in their old age. China's population is growing, and the government now rewards parents who limit their families to just one child. This policy works well in the cities, but in farming communities, people need large families to labor in the fields.

HAN CHINESE

China has a large number of ethnic groups. The Han Chinese people make up about 90 percent of the total population. Their ancestors may have come east from Turkestan, which is now partly in western China, Central Asia, and Afghanistan. However, it is possible that Han Chinese people descended from Mongolian tribes who moved south.

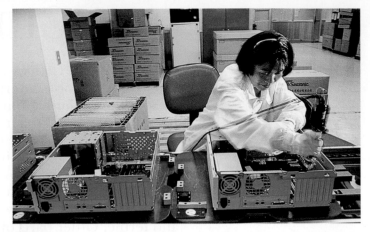

PANDAS

The giant panda lives only in the mountainous forests of southwestern China. It feeds almost exclusively off bamboo. The woody grass is low in nutrients, so pandas must eat about 84 lb (38kg) of it every day to survive. The panda is classified as an endangered species, and fewer than 1,600 remain in the wild today. They live in areas of forest set aside as nature preserves by the Chinese government.

INDUSTRIAL TAIWAN

Boasting a highly educated and ambitious workforce, Taiwan is one of Asia's wealthiest economies. The country produces about 10 percent of the world's computers, and is the world's leading television producer. It also specializes in shoe manufacturing. Taiwan's mineral industry is not significant because mineral resources are relatively modest.

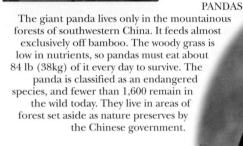

LHASA

Monasteries in Lhasa, capital of Tibet, are reminders that the city was once the center of Lamaism (Tibetan Buddhism). The religion is an important part of Tibetan life, and at one time one-sixth of all Tibetan men were monks. The head of the religion, the Dalai Lama, was also the ruler of the country. However, in 1950 Communist China invaded Tibet, and has ruled the region ever since.

SHANGHAI

The largest city in China, Shanghai (right) is one of the world's biggest seaports. For centuries China was closed to the west, but in 1842 the Treaty of Nanking, between China and Britain, opened the port to western trade. Since then Shanghai has been the leading commercial and industrial center in China. Today, about half of China's foreign business passes through the city.

The spectacular Potala Palace (left) in Lhasa was built in the 17th century.

To Western eyes in the Middle Ages, the Chinese junk (left) seemed an ungainly figure. However, the junk is still widely used today.

JUNK

The junk is an oceangoing sailing vessel of ancient unknown origin. By the Middle Ages, Chinese junks had sailed to the waters of Indonesia and India. The junk carries up to five sails consisting of panels of linen or matting flattened by bamboo strips. Each sail can be spread or closed with a pull, like a venetian blind. A massive rudder, which steers the boat, replaces a keel or a centerboard, and keeps the boat from tipping over or drifting with the wind. The hull is partitioned by solid bulkheads, which adds greatly to the boat's strength.

Most Chinese people work in agriculture. However, over 25 percent of China's 750 million strong workforce is employed in industries such as textiles (left) and electronics.

MEDICINE

Medicine in China is a mixture of East and West. Modern surgical and drug techniques are borrowed from Europe and the United States. However, doctors still use traditional cures which have been popular for thousands of years, including herbs and other natural remedies. To relieve pain, Chinese doctors sometimes use acupuncture, a technique in which fine needles are inserted into specially-chosen parts of the body. "Barefoot doctors," or locally-trained healers, keep people healthy in the countryside.

Acupuncture charts show the positions of meridians, or lines of energy, where the acupuncturist inserts needles.

A Chinese apothecary (pharmacist) makes use of a wide range of natural plant and animal cures.

INDUSTRY

Chinese factories have been modernized since 1949, but in comparison with the factories of Japan or the United States some are still old-fashioned. However, China is the world's leading manufacturer of television sets, and produces other electrical goods, farm machinery, machine tools, toys, and textiles. With such a huge population, there is no shortage of workers.

FOOD

Rice is one of the main ingredients of Chinese food, as are noodles and many vegetables. Dried foods, soybeans, fish, and meat are also used in Chinese cooking, which varies considerably in the different regions of China.

The Chinese eat with chopsticks. They hold both sticks in one hand, and pinch the tips together to pick up food.

Buddhist monks in Tibet spend much time studying and writing.

HONG KONG AND MACAO

At midnight on July 29-30, 1997, Hong Kong (above) returned to Chinese sovereignty. The city had been a British colony for 157 years. Two years later, Hong Kong's neighbor, Macao, ceased to be a Portuguese colony. It officially came under Chinese rule at midnight on December 19-20, 1999.

The Beijing Opera performs traditional and new works, mainly with political themes.

CHINESE LANGUAGE

Mandarin, the main language of China, is spoken in all but the southeast coastal areas. Within each language there are many dialects, or regional variations. Although each vocabulary is different, all the variations are written in the same script.

Chinese writing consists of thousands of symbols, each one representing a different word or idea.

兒童百科全書

CULTURE

China has a rich and ancient culture: paintings found in some Chinese tombs are more than 6,000 years old. Today, artistic traditions continue in the form of folkdancing and music; movies, opera, and theater are all very popular. Artists are encouraged to produce works that depict the achievements of the Chinese people.

Find out more

ASIA
CHINA, HISTORY OF
COMMUNISM
MAO ZEDONG
MONGOL EMPIRE

The dragon is a sign of good luck in China.

Clouds represent the sky.

Water, topped by foam and waves, represents the sea.

Mountain represents the Earth.

DRAGON ROBE

Only an emperor or a member of the imperial family could wear the yellow silk dragon robe. The robe on the left was woven about 100 years ago. The design of the swirling sea, waves, mountains, clouds, and dragons shows that its wearer was the ruler of the universe.

CHINA

500,000 years ago China's best-known fossil human, Peking man, makes tools.

c. 5000 B.C. First villages established.

c. 3500 B.C. First Chinese city built.

c. 1523-1027 B.C. Shang dynasty rules northern China. Writing and the calendar are developed; cities are built.

551-479 B.C. Life of Confucius.

221-206 B.C. Ch'in dynasty unites China. Great Wall built.

206 B.C-A.D. 220 Han dynasty. Buddhist religion arrives. Paper and ink invented.

A.D. 618-906 T'ang dynasty. Gunpowder and printing invented.

868 Earliest known book printed.

960-1279 Sung dynasty. Compass invented.

1279-1368 Mongols invade and rule China.

1368-1644 Ming dynasty. European traders and missionaries arrive.

1644-1911 Manchu (Quing) dynasty. Foreign domination increases.

1911 Emperor gives up throne.

1912 China becomes a republic.

1921 Chinese Communist Party founded.

1931 Japan invades Manchuria.

1937-45 Japan invades rest of China.

1945-49 Communists gain control of the country; set up People's Republic of China, led by Mao Zedong.

1966-76 Cultural Revolution creates upheaval in society

1989 Tiananmen Square massacre of pro-democracy students.

SUN YAT-SEN

In 1911, a rebellion broke out against the corrupt and inefficient Manchu dynasty, and in 1912 a republic was declared. The first president of China was Sun Yat-sen (1866-1925; right). He founded the Kuomintang (Chinese National Party). He tried to modernize the country, but his authority was disputed and he soon resigned. However, Sun continued to dominate Chinese politics until his death.

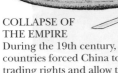

COLLAPSE OF THE EMPIRE

During the 19th century, many foreign countries forced China to grant them trading rights and allow their citizens to ignore Chinese law. The cartoon above shows Britain, Germany, Russia, Italy, and Japan sharing the Chinese "cake" among them. But the Chinese resented this interference in their affairs and rebelled against the hated foreigners.

MAO ZEDONG

Mao Zedong (1893-1976) was the leader of the Chinese Communist party, founded in 1921. He fought a civil war with Chiang Kai-shek, leader of the Kuomintang Party, which took power in 1928. In 1949, the Communists expelled Chiang Kai-shek and took power. Mao was leader of China until his death.

Find out more

CHINA
COMMUNISM
JAPAN, HISTORY OF
MAO ZEDONG
MONGOL EMPIRE

CHRISTIANITY

Church windows tell Bible stories in pictures made from stained glass.

FROM VERY HUMBLE ORIGINS, Christianity has grown to be the largest of all world religions. Christians are the followers of Jesus Christ, a Jew who lived almost 2,000 years ago in the land that is now Israel. Jesus was a teacher and a prophet, but Christians believe that He was also the Son of God and that He came into the world to save people from sin, or doing wrong. Jesus was killed by His enemies, but His disciples (group of followers) taught that He rose from the dead and rejoined His father in heaven, a basic Christian belief called the Resurrection. After Jesus' death, His followers began to spread His teaching. Christianity grew, but it was against the law in most lands, and many early Christians died for their beliefs. Today, more than 1.6 billion people throughout the world practice Christianity. There are different divisions within Christianity; the three most prominent are Protestantism, the Roman Catholic Church, and the Eastern Orthodox Church. Each has its own way of worshiping. But despite their differences, all Christian groups share a belief in the teachings of Jesus Christ. Most Christians worship by meeting in groups called congregations. They pray together and sing hymns (sacred songs).

In New Testament stories, Jesus compares God to a good shepherd, caring for his "flock" of believers.

BIBLE

The Bible is sacred to both Christians and Jews, who believe it contains the word of God. It consists of two parts – the Old and New Testaments. Both Jews and Christians accept the Old Testament, but only Christians accept the New Testament. The New Testament includes the gospels, or teachings of Christ, as told by His followers – Matthew, Mark, Luke, and John. Christians try to follow the central message of the New Testament, which is to love God and their fellow humans and to forgive their enemies.

COMMUNION

Before He died, Jesus shared a simple meal of bread and wine with His closest followers. He asked them to remember Him in this special way. Today, the ceremony of Holy Communion, in which worshipers receive bread and wine, is a reminder of Christ's Last Supper and helps Christians feel closer to God. Roman Catholic and Eastern Orthodox churches celebrate communion in the form of Mass.

FEASTS AND HOLY DAYS

Advent Preparation for Christmas.

Christmas December 25; birth of Jesus.

Palm Sunday Jesus enters Jerusalem, Sunday before Easter.

Good Friday Jesus' death, the Friday before Easter Sunday.

Easter Sunday late March or April; celebrates Jesus' Resurrection (return to life).

The birth of Jesus is remembered at Christmas. This feast is popular with many non-Christians as well, who enjoy the atmosphere of festive goodwill.

Easter is the most important feast in the Christian calendar. It celebrates the rising of Jesus from the dead three days after his crucifixion.

SIR WINSTON
CHURCHILL

1874 Born at Blenheim Palace, Oxfordshire, England.

1893 Enters the Royal Military College at Sandhurst.

1899 Taken prisoner during Boer War in South Africa, but escapes.

1900 Elected Member of Parliament.

1906-15 Holds cabinet posts.

1919 Appointed secretary of state for war.

1940-45 As prime minister, leads Britain in World War II.

1951-55 Prime minister again.

1965 Dies.

I**N 1940, BRITAIN** badly needed a strong leader. The country was at war with Germany and faced the danger of invasion. Winston Churchill's appointment as prime minister provided the leadership that the British people wanted. He went on to guide the country through the worst war the world had ever experienced. In his underground headquarters he formed the plans that helped to win the war. Churchill's wartime glory came at a surprising time. He was 66 and had held no important government post for many years. He had been almost alone in urging a strong army and navy to oppose the German threat. Working people remembered how he helped crush the general strike of 1926 and cut their wages. But when victory came in World War II, all of this was forgotten, and everyone cheered Churchill as one of the greatest politicians of the age.

YOUNG WINSTON
As a young soldier and newspaper reporter in India and Africa, Churchill had many adventures. He became world famous when he escaped from a Boer prison in 1899.

WARTIME PRIME MINISTER
As wartime leader, Churchill traveled the country visiting bombed cities and raising people's spirits. His simple "V for Victory" sign seemed to sum up British determination to win the war. His most important work took place behind the scenes, where he directed the British war effort. He met the leaders of the then Soviet Union and the United States to draw up plans for fighting the war and for the postwar peace settlement. Above, he is seen giving the "V" sign to American sailors.

HOLDING THE LINE!

BRITISH BULLDOG
Churchill's famous British determination was often portrayed in cartoons and posters. This 1942 American poster shows him as a bulldog.

PAINTING
Churchill was an enthusiastic amateur painter. He also wrote many books about history. These hobbies kept him busy after 1945 when he lost his post as prime minister in a disastrous election. He did not return to power until 1951.

BROADCASTS
During World War II, Churchill made many radio broadcasts, which inspired the nation. Churchill always explained the situation clearly and listed the dreadful problems that lay ahead, yet he left no doubt that the enemy would eventually be defeated.

Find out more
UNITED KINGDOM, HISTORY OF
WORLD WAR I
WORLD WAR II

CIRCUSES

EARLY CIRCUS ACTS such as tumbling and bull-leaping go back to very ancient times. But the circus that we know today was not developed until 1768, when the Englishman Philip Astley started a trick-riding show in London. He soon added other acts such as tightrope walkers and strong men, and in 1793 John Ricketts set up similar circuses in the United States. These early circuses took place indoors in special buildings; later, traveling tented circuses such as Barnum and Bailey were developed. They moved from town to town, taking the show and its spectacular acts to the audience. Today, the circus combines tightrope acts, juggling, clowns, bareback riders, and animal acts and is one of the most popular forms of family entertainment. Circus work is highly skilled. Venice, Florida, is home to the world's only clown college.

FLYING TRAPEZE
Trapeze artistes rely on split-second timing as they perform their midair somersaults. This daring act was invented by the Frenchman Jules Léotard in 1859.

CIRCUS RING
Philip Astley discovered that the perfect area for bareback riding was a circle measuring 42 ft (12.8 m) in diameter. This has become the standard circus ring size.

Joseph Grimaldi

Clowns' painted egg heads

BIG TOP
Some circuses take place in a huge tent called the big top. The big top must be very strong to resist high winds and to support lighting and rigging for aerial acts. The performers and circus animals live in caravans and trailers.

RINGMASTER
At the beginning of each performance, the ringmaster strides into the ring, carrying a whip to show that he is in charge. The ringmaster has many responsibilities. Before introducing each act, he makes sure that the clothes and equipment are ready. He keeps the mischievous clowns in order and makes sure the show runs smoothly.

CLOWNS

Every clown is unique. With their funny clothes and makeup, clowns are a special part of every circus. Making people laugh is a serious business, and clowns learn many skills. They may be musicians or acrobats, mimes or comedians. The first real clown, Joseph Grimaldi, was a stage clown in the 19th century; and circus clowns take their nickname, Joey, and their white faces from him. British clowns "register" their makeup by drawing the design on an egg.

Unicyclist

CIRCUS PARADE

Marching through the street, the parade lets everyone know the circus is in town. Highly-trained horses are part of circus tradition, but many people now think that it is cruel to tame wild animals such as lions and tigers in the ring.

Drummer

Many circus acts rely on balance. The unicyclist's outstretched arms help keep him upright.

Flame eater

Clown

Find out more

THEATER

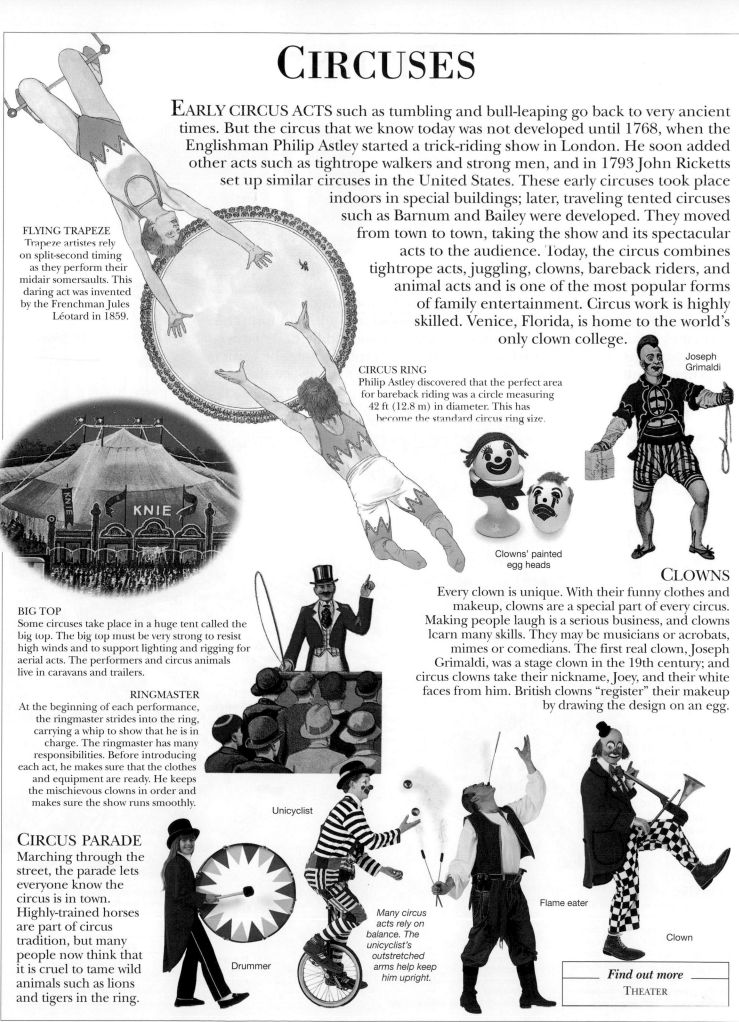

CITIES

ONE THIRD OF ALL the world's people live in cities. The world's largest city, Tokyo, Japan, has a population of more than 20 million. But not all cities are vast, because the word city can mean different things. In many places, a city is any large town. In Europe, it is usually a town with a cathedral. And in some places, like the United States, "city" is the name given to an urban area with definite boundaries.

City people need many services: water, power, sanitation, transport, schools, and shops are all essential. Providing these services requires a lot of organization. Badly run cities are unpleasant and unhealthy, with problems such as poor housing, traffic congestion, and pollution. The first cities developed as trading centers in Asia and the Middle East about 7,000 years ago. Rich cities, such as Alexandria in Egypt, became the centers of government and power. Like today's cities, they had markets, banks, hotels, factories, and places of entertainment.

CAPITAL CITIES
The most important town of any country is called the capital. It is usually the place where the government is based, but it may not be the biggest city in the country. Some capital cities, such as Brasilia, have been specially built in modern times.

Brasilia was built to replace Rio de Janeiro as the capital of Brazil.

Factories require a lot of space, so they are built in the outer parts of cities. They need easy access to roads and railroads so they can send their goods to other parts of the country.

The city center usually contains the most stylish shops. Shopping districts are built close to residential areas on the outskirts of town.

Land is expensive in the city center, so office developments grow upward rather than outward.

MODERN CITY
The oldest part of the city often forms the center. Farther out are the industrial zones and the areas where people live, all connected by a network of roads.

Cities must have a good public transportation system, with flyovers or underground railroads, to avoid traffic jams.

Quiet parks and other recreation areas provide a restful break from the busy city streets.

Some families live in homes close to the city center. More live a few miles from the center in less crowded areas called suburbs.

PLANNING
Many cities grow up around their historical centers with no overall plan. However, some cities, such as Washington, D.C., have been carefully planned from the start. Streets and squares, transportation, sewers, business centers, and sports facilities are all carefully mapped out before any building starts.

Swiss-French architect Le Corbusier (1887-1965) planned this city for three million people.

The city streets follow a grid pattern.

Find out more
ARCHITECTURE
INDUSTRIAL REVOLUTION
ROADS AND HIGHWAYS

CIVIL RIGHTS

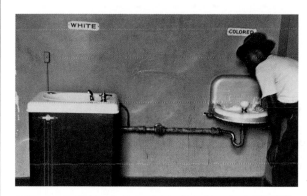

EVERY PERSON IS ENTITLED to freedoms and rights, protected by the laws of the nation. However, for decades African Americans were denied their civil rights. As slaves, they had none. After the Civil War they were granted some important rights. But the law stood in the way of equality, allowing states to segregate (separate by race) whites and African Americans by offering "separate but equal" public facilities. During the 1950s and 1960s, African-American leaders such as Martin Luther King, Jr., used marches and demonstrations, nonviolent resistance, the courts, and the press to help erase racist laws and win equality for all. These efforts were known as the civil rights movement.

SEPARATE BUT NOT EQUAL

From the 1880s to the 1960s, many states enforced segregation through "Jim Crow" laws. Businesses and institutions were ordered to provide separate facilities for whites and for African Americans, including everything from schools and buses to drinking fountains. The facilities were certainly separate, but they were rarely equal.

Martin Luther King, Jr.

FREEDOM RIDES

In 1957, the courts gave African Americans the right to sit wherever they liked on a bus, but the law was rarely enforced. In May 1961, civil rights activists staged Freedom Rides – interracial bus journeys from Washington, DC through the South – to persuade them to uphold the law.

National guardsmen protect civil rights activists on a Freedom Ride through Alabama.

THE STRUGGLE FOR EQUALITY

1896 Supreme Court upholds "separate but equal" laws.

1942 Congress of Racial Equality (CORE) founded.

1954 Brown v. Board of Education rules segregation unconstitutional.

1957 First Civil Rights Act protects voting rights of African Americans.

1963 Martin Luther King, Jr. leads march on Washington.

1965 Voting Rights Act outlaws discrimination against voters.

MARCHING FOR FREEDOM

For five days in 1965, civil rights activists marched the 54 miles of the Alabama highway from Selma to Montgomery. Led by Martin Luther King, Jr., the march focused national attention on discrimination. The marchers were met with protests and violence, but their efforts put pressure on Congress. The Voting Rights Act, protecting African-American voter registration, was signed.

THE NAACP

Founded in 1909, the National Association for the Advancement of Colored People (NAACP) led the fight against segregation, relying on peaceful but powerful ways of protest such as petitions, boycotts, and lawsuits.

ROSA PARKS

Rosa Parks (1913-2005) took a bus ride into history on December 1, 1955, when she refused to give up her seat for a white man in Montgomery, Alabama. Parks became a symbol of the civil rights movement, and founded an organization to help young African Americans find careers.

Find out more

ABOLITIONIST MOVEMENT
AFRICAN AMERICANS
CONSTITUTION
HUMAN RIGHTS
KING, MARTIN LUTHER, JR.

CIVIL WAR

ONLY 80 YEARS after the states of America had united to win their independence, the Civil War (1861-65) bitterly divided the nation and threatened to destroy the Union. The war was fought between the Northern states, who supported Abraham Lincoln's federal government and hoped to bring an end to slavery, and the Southern states, who withdrew from the Union and formed their own government under Jefferson Davis, in the hope of preserving slavery and their agricultural way of life. The brutal four-year conflict killed more Americans than any other war, and devastated much of the South. The Confederacy was defeated in 1865, and slavery was abolished the same year.

Free states   Slave states   Territories

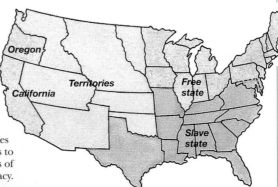

A DIVIDED NATION

The fight over slavery was a key cause of the war, but other crucial differences divided the North and the South. Their economies were quite separate. The South's economy was based on agriculture, especially cotton (above), with slaves supplying the labor. The North's economy depended on trade and manufacturing, and had most of the nation's banks, factories, and transportion.

CONFEDERACY

In 1861, there were 19 free states, in which slavery was banned, and 15 slave states, in which slavery was allowed. The federal government had outlawed slavery, and many Southerners feared that if more free states joined the Union from the Territories, they would be outnumbered. Eleven slave states eventually split from the free states to form the Confederate States of America, or the Confederacy.

AFRICAN-AMERICAN SOLDIERS

At the start of the Civil War, many African Americans worked behind the lines to support the Union. However, after Lincoln issued the Emancipation Proclamation in 1863, African-American troops were allowed to join the army. About 200,000 men served in the army and the navy, most of them Southerners who had fled to the North. The most famous African-American unit, the 54th Massachusetts Regiment, included the sons of abolitionist Frederick Douglass.

SPIES AND SCOUNDRELS

Some of the most daring actions of the war took place far from the frontlines. Both armies used spies to gather information about their enemies. Virginian spy Belle Boyd (right) rode her horse across enemy lines to carry secrets to the South. Sarah Thompson, a Union spy, provided information that led to the capture of a Confederate general.

GETTYSBURG

Fought in July 1863, the Battle of Gettysburg, Pennsylvania, proved to be the turning point of the war. The Union army took a strong defensive line and managed to hold back Confederate attacks for three days. The ferocious fighting led to heavy casualties on both sides. However, the Confederates lost nearly a third of their fighting force. Their battered army retreated to the South, and never again recovered the strength to launch a major attack.

THE END OF THE WAR

On April 9, 1865, with his army surrounded and his troops exhausted and hungry, Confederate general Robert E. Lee surrendered to Union general Ulysses S. Grant at Appomatox Courthouse, Virginia. More than 600,000 Americans died during the war, and many more were injured. The economic cost to both sides was enormous. The destruction was particularly bad in the South, where Union General Sherman's march through Georgia devastated the region. President Lincoln made a speech urging the two sides to reconcile, but only six days after the surrender he was assassinated.

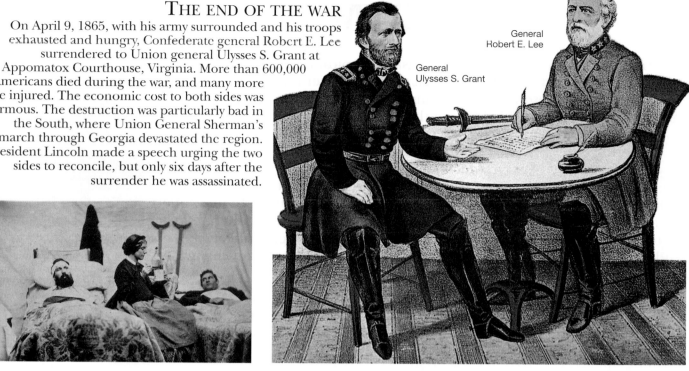

General
Ulysses S. Grant

General
Robert E. Lee

CASUALTIES OF WAR
More than half a million Americans died in the Civil War, and many times that number were wounded. The sick and wounded were treated at hospitals set up near the battlefield (above) or on hospital ships. More than twice as many Civil War soldiers died of disease as were killed on the battlefield. Dysentery, malaria, and typhoid spread quickly, and medical staff struggled with unsanitary conditions and shortages of food, medicine, and sterile medical equipment.

COVERING THE WAR
The Civil War was the first war to be widely photographed and reported in the media. Newspapers sent journalists to the field and received their on-the-scene reports by telegraph. Artists drew war sketches for magazines, and photographers such as Matthew Brady captured the faces – and the horrors – of the war.

A POPULAR WAR
No other war in American history has captured more interest than the Civil War. It is the subject of numerous books, movies, television programs, and websites, and its battlefields and monuments are popular tourist sites. Many people participate in full battle reenactments, complete with replica uniforms and weapons.

A reenactment society performs a salute in front of the state capitol building in Little Rock, Arkansas.

Union soldier

Confederate soldier

YANKS AND REBS
Three million people fought in the Civil War, most as infantrymen. Southern soldiers were nicknamed "Johnny Reb," after rebel; Northern soldiers were called "Billy Yank."

CIVIL WAR HISTORY

1860 Abraham Lincoln is elected president.

1860-61 Eleven Southern states leave the Union to form the Confederacy.

1861 Confederates attack Fort Sumter, SC; Civil War begins.

1862 Confederate victory at Fredericksburg, VA.

1862 Naval battle between the battleships *Monitor* and *Merrimack*.

1862 Battle of Shiloh, TN.

1863 Lincoln issues Emancipation Proclamation.

1863 Confederate victory at Chancellorsville, VA.

1863 Confederate defeat at Gettysburg marks turning point.

1863 Union victories at Vicksburg, NS and Chattanooga, TN.

1864 Union General Sherman captures Atlanta, GA, and begins "march to the sea."

1864 Confederate General Lee surrenders to Union General Grant; Civil War ends.

1865 Slavery abolished.

Find out more

ABOLITIONIST MOVEMENT
AFRICAN AMERICANS
SLAVERY

CLOTHES

FROM ELEGANT SILKS to practical working outfits, the clothes people wear reflect how they live. The first clothes were animal skins that kept out the cold and rain. Clothes still give protection against the weather, but society also dictates their shape – a business suit looks out of place on a beach, and nobody goes to the office in a bathing suit. Clothing fashions change from year to year and garments go "out of fashion" quickly. Fashion started as a way to display wealth. When clothes were expensive, only rich people could afford to be fashionable. Through the centuries fashion has evolved as lifestyles changed. For instance, when women had few rights, fashionable dresses restricted movement, just as society limited what women could do. But as women gained more freedom, trousers became popular, and women could move around more easily.

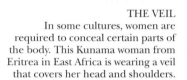

Hat, scarf, and gloves made from wool help to keep out the winter cold.

COLD CLIMATE
Traditionally, clothes for a cold climate are made from animal skins. The fur, worn inside, traps a layer of air that resists the flow of heat from the body. Modern jackets and trousers are made of closely woven nylon and are wind and waterproof. Down padding traps air between the feathers to keep heat in.

Veil for modesty

THE VEIL
In some cultures, women are required to conceal certain parts of the body. This Kunama woman from Eritrea in East Africa is wearing a veil that covers her head and shoulders.

FUNCTIONAL CLOTHES
Sometimes the function of clothes – the job they have to do – is the most important influence on their design. For example, the function of bad-weather clothes is to keep out cold, wind, and rain; style or color is not so important. Functional garments are also worn for religious reasons, for different types of work, and for sports. So, religious garments may need to cover the body, factory clothes must be made from durable fabrics, and sports wear should be lightweight.

BUSINESS SUIT
Dress codes vary at modern workplaces. Some organizations encourage casual wear while others, such as some corporate firms, prefer their staff to come to work in formal suits.

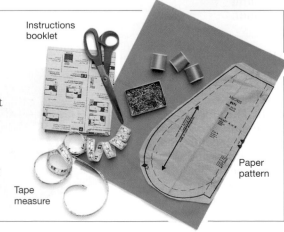

Multi-layered clothing to keep out heat

MAKING CLOTHES
Today, most people in Europe and North America buy mass-produced clothes in shops. But homemade clothes are still popular among people who want original clothes in the fabric of their choice, or who cannot afford clothes sold in shops. Paper patterns show how to cut each piece of fabric. Pinning the cut pieces of fabric holds them together to make sewing easier.

Instructions booklet

Tape measure

Paper pattern

WARM CLIMATE
People who live in desert climates wear long, loose, cotton robes. The robes have a double function: they protect the skin from the harmful rays of the sun and keep the body cool by trapping layers of air between the folds of cloth. Traditional Arab costume includes a long tunic, a cloak, and a head cloth.

BUSTLE

Past fashions can look strange or ridiculous today. In the late 19th century the bustle was popular. It made a dress stick out at the back.

DRESSES

Clothing has changed through the ages. Ancient Greek dresses were pieces of cloth draped around the body. In 14th-century Europe, dresses were tailored to fit. In the 16th century, women's vests were stiffened with whalebone. Tight corsets were used until the end of the 19th century. Fashions changed, and a simple, loose-fitting slip replaced the awkward bustle under women's dresses. The 1920s saw an even greater change: more practical shifts were worn and skirts were short for the first time.

MINI DRESSES

Clothing gradually grew simpler and less restrictive. In the1960s, young people had more independence than ever before. Women expressed their freedom by wearing very short skirts.

The bustle was a cushion or wire framework tied around the waist under a dress.

It took a mass of cloth, lace, whalebone, and steel to complete this elegant-looking 19th-century dress.

Fashionable boots accompanied a variety of outfits in the 1960s.

FASHION HOUSES

The most fashionable clothes come from *haute couture* (high fashion) designers. Their companies are called fashion houses. Models show off the designers' new creations at fashion shows called collections. Designer Coco Chanel (1883-1971) revolutionized women's clothing when she created simple and comfortable dresses, suits, and sweaters from jersey, a knitted fabric that stretches as the wearer moves.

Coco Chanel's clothes were the first fashionable garments that were uncluttered and easy to wear.

Early Levi's advertisements stressed the strength of the clothes.

BLUE JEANS

Inexpensive, easily washed, and durable, blue jeans first appeared in the United States in 1850. A miner digging for gold in the California gold rush asked tailor Levi Strauss to make him a sturdy pair of trousers, because ordinary fabric wore out so quickly. Jeans are made of denim, a tough cotton fabric colored with the natural blue indigo dye.

UNIFORMS

People who belong to the same group or organization often wear similar garments so that they can be easily identified. These standard clothes are called uniforms. Uniforms promote a sense of team spirit and companionship, so many people are proud of their uniforms. Some, such as nurses' uniforms, are very functional and protect the wearer while at work.

Students

Nurse

Soccer player   Police officer

PROTECTIVE CLOTHING

Workers such as fire fighters and nuclear power workers need clothes that protect them while they are at work. This fire fighter (above) is wearing a fire-resistant suit that also shields him from high temperatures. An oxygen mask prevents him from suffocating in smoke-filled areas.

Find out more

DESIGN
TEXTILES

COAL

PEOPLE HAVE used coal for cooking and heating for thousands of years. During the 19th century, coal was the world's most important fuel. It powered the steam engines that made the Industrial Revolution possible. Today, coal is still used in vast amounts. Most coal is burned at power stations to produce electricity, and burning coal meets much of the world's energy needs. Coal is also an essential raw material for making many products, the most important of which are iron and steel. Coal is often called a fossil fuel because it is formed from the fossilized remains of plants that are millions of years old. Sometimes a piece of coal bears the imprint of a prehistoric plant or insect. The Earth contains reserves of coal which, with careful use, may last for hundreds of years. But many people are concerned that coal burning adds to global pollution.

A lump of anthracite, a type of hard black coal

FORMATION OF COAL

1 PREHISTORIC SWAMP
Coal began to form in swamps as long ago as 300 million years. Dying trees and other plants fell into the water, and their remains became covered in mud.

2 PEAT
The plant remains slowly dried out under the mud, forming layers of peat, a fuel that can be dug from the ground.

3 LIGNITE
Layers of peat became buried. Heat and pressure turned the peat into lignite, or brown coal. Lignite is dug from shallow pits called strip mines.

4 BLACK COAL
Intense heat and pressure turned deeper layers of peat into a soft black coal called bituminous coal, and anthracite.

COAL MINERS

For centuries, miners had to cut coal by hand. Now there are drills and computer-controlled cutting machines to help them.

MINING

Mine shafts are dug down to seams (layers) of coal far below the surface. Miners dig a network of tunnels to remove coal from the seams. In addition to coal, many other useful minerals, such as copper, are mined. The deepest mine is a gold mine in South Africa nearly 2.5 miles (4 km) deep.

Pumps circulate fresh air through the mine.

Skip (shuttle car) lifts coal to surface.

Air shaft

Railroad takes miners to the coal faces.

Miners' cage carries miners up and down mine.

Miners use cutting machine to dig out coal at coal face.

Miners have lamps on their helmets which light up everything in front of them in the dark depths of a mine.

USES OF COAL

A few steam-powered trains still burn coal, and some homes have open fires or coal-fired heating systems. The main use for coal is in the production of electricity. Heating coal without air produces coke, which is used to make steel, and coal gas, which may be burned as a fuel. Another product is coal-tar pitch, which is used in making roads. Coal is also treated to make chemicals which are used to produce drugs, plastics, dyes, and many other products.

A large coal-fired power station in Berlin, Germany

Conveyor belts take coal to shaft.

Supports hold roof and sides of tunnels in place.

Find out more

ELECTRICITY
FIRE
INDUSTRIAL REVOLUTION
IRON AND STEEL
PREHISTORIC LIFE
TRAINS

COLD WAR

IN THE AFTERMATH OF WORLD WAR II, the United States and the Soviet Union emerged as the world's most powerful countries, or "superpowers." Over the next 40 years, the two superpowers and their allies were locked in conflict and competition in what became known as the Cold War. Each tried to extend its influence by stockpiling weapons, making alliances with other countries, and developing the technology to launch people – and weapons – into space. The rival blocks expressed hostility by backing different sides in conflicts such as the Korean War and the Vietnam War. Cold War tensions continued until 1989, when a wave of political change exploded across the Soviet Union and Eastern Europe, bringing the Cold War to a close.

IRON CURTAIN DESCENDS
After World War II, the Soviets seized control of Eastern Europe. In a famous speech in 1946, British leader Winston Churchill said that, "an iron curtain has descended across the continent."

COLD WARRIORS

In 1945, British Prime Minister Winston Churchill, US President Harry Truman, and Soviet premier Joseph Stalin met at Potsdam in Germany (left). The three leaders hoped to decide the future of postwar Europe. Stalin promised that the Eastern European countries occupied by the Soviets would be free to elect their own governments, and that the people would keep their civil liberties. Instead, politicians loyal to the Soviet Union – and backed by the Russian military – gained power, and the secret police rounded up and jailed opponents of Stalin. The battle between two new world powers had begun.

Winston Churchill, Prime Minister of Britain from 1940-45

Harry Truman, President of the United States from 1945-53

Joseph Stalin, leader of the Soviet Union from 1922-53

KGB emblem   CIA emblem

SECRET SERVICES
The Cold War was also fought in the shadows, as thousands of spies risked their lives to gather and pass on the secrets of the superpowers. The CIA (Central Intelligence Agency) led espionage (spying) and counterespionage for the United States. Soviet espionage was conducted by the KGB (Committee of State Security).

BERLIN AIRLIFT
In 1945, Britain, France, USA, and the Soviet Union occupied Germany and divided Berlin among them. During a confrontation in 1948, Stalin blocked roads from Soviet-occupied East Germany to allied-occupied West Berlin, cutting off food supplies. However, the Western allies forced Stalin to end his blockade when they flew in supplies.

SPIES IN THE SKY
The Americans flew U-2 planes over the Iron Curtain to spy on the Soviets. These planes could fly at high altitudes while photographing military and strategic sites on the ground. On May 1, 1960, a U-2 reconnaissance plane was shot down over the Soviet Union. The pilot, Gary Powers, was captured and jailed, reviving Cold War tensions between the superpowers.

U.S. AIR FORCE   66708

NATO
In 1949, the United States and its European allies formed the North Atlantic Treaty Organization (NATO). A military alliance, its aim was to prevent a Soviet invasion of Europe. In response, the Soviets formed an alliance of communist states called the Warsaw Pact.

NATO logo

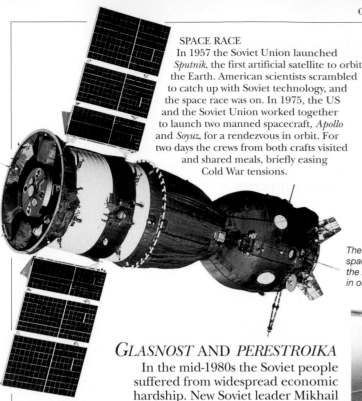

SPACE RACE
In 1957 the Soviet Union launched *Sputnik*, the first artificial satellite to orbit the Earth. American scientists scrambled to catch up with Soviet technology, and the space race was on. In 1975, the US and the Soviet Union worked together to launch two manned spacecraft, *Apollo* and *Soyuz*, for a rendezvous in orbit. For two days the crews from both crafts visited and shared meals, briefly easing Cold War tensions.

The Soviet Soyuz spacecraft docked with the American Apollo while in orbit above the Earth.

THE ATOMIC AGE
After the first atomic bombs were dropped in 1945, the United States and the Soviet Union began a nuclear arms race. Both superpowers built and stockpiled an arsenal of nuclear weapons great enough to destroy every living thing on earth. The fear of nuclear war dominated American and Soviet relations for decades, as both sides struggled to prevent an all-out conflict while maintaining a strong defense. The superpowers began to disarm in the late 1980s.

Mikhail Gorbachev was president of the Soviet Union from 1985 to 1991.

GLASNOST AND PERESTROIKA
In the mid-1980s the Soviet people suffered from widespread economic hardship. New Soviet leader Mikhail Gorbachev introduced a group of reforms known as *perestroika* (economic reform) and *glasnost* (openness) to revitalize the economy. Gorbachev's policies greatly improved Soviet relations with the West, and inadvertently created the conditions that led to the collapse of Communism in the Soviet Union and throughout Eastern Europe.

George Bush (left), President of the United States, and President Boris Yeltsin of the Russian Federation agree on arms reductions at the START treaty talks in 1991.

NUCLEAR DISARMAMENT
In December 1987, American President Ronald Reagan and Soviet leader Mikhail Gorbachev signed the Intermediate-range Nuclear Forces (INF) treaty to eliminate an entire class of weapons delivery systems. The START (Strategic Arms Reduction Talks) treaty of 1989 and 1991 (with the newly created Russian Federation) further reduced the superpowers' arsenals.

IRON CURTAIN IS RAISED
Gorbachev's pledge to end Soviet political domination of Eastern Europe triggered the rapid collapse of communist regimes across the region. In November 1989, one of the most vivid symbols of the Cold War, the Berlin Wall, was opened, and the people from both sides of Berlin united to tear it down. Germany was reunited in 1990, bringing a close to the Cold War. By the end of 1991, the Soviet Union itself ceased to exist, breaking apart into independent republics.

COLD WAR CONFRONTATION
1945 World leaders meet in Potsdam, Germany, but fail to reach an agreement.

1946 Iron curtain falls across Eastern Europe.

1948 Berlin airlift ignites Cold War tensions.

1950 Korean War begins.

1953 Stalin dies; Korean War ends.

1957 Soviets launch *Sputnik*.

1961 Construction of the Berlin Wall begins.

1962 Cuban Missile Crisis threatens nuclear war.

1965 American intervention in Vietnam begins.

1985 Gorbachev comes to power in the USSR.

1987 INF Treaty cuts number of nuclear weapons.

1989 Berlin Wall falls.

1991 Soviet Union collapses; Warsaw Pact disbands.

Find out more
ASTRONAUTS AND SPACE TRAVEL
COMMUNISM
KOREAN WAR
RUSSIAN FEDERATION
SOVIET UNION, HISTORY OF
WORLD WAR II

COLOMBIA

Volcano	Mountain	Ancient monument	Capital city	Large city/ town	Small city/ town

COLOMBIA IS DOMINATED by the Andes in the west, and the upper reaches of the mighty Amazon in the east. Much of the land is sparsely populated and not suitable for agriculture. The rain forests of the east are rich in wildlife, containing over 1,500 species of birds, numerous monkeys, and endangered felines such as jaguars and ocelots. In the lowlands to the west of the Andes, the subtropical climate provides ideal conditions for growing both coffee, Colombia's main crop, and coca, the basis of Colombia's illegal drugs trade. Originally populated by many native tribes, Colombia was settled by the Spanish in 1525. Colombia became independent in 1819, but has had a history of civil wars and conflict, most recently as a result of the drugs trade.

STATISTICS

Area:
439,733 sq miles
(1,138,910 sq km)
Population: 44,200,000
Capital: Bogotá
Languages: Spanish, Amerindian languages, English Creole
Religions:
Roman Catholic
Currency:
Colombian peso
Main occupations:
Agriculture, mining, drug trafficking
Main exports: Coffee, coal, cocaine, gold, platinum, silver, emeralds

Colombia lies at the far north of the South American continent, and borders both the Caribbean Sea and the Pacific Ocean.

EMERALDS
Most of the world's emeralds are found in Colombia, and some of the finest examples are found near the capital, Bogotá.

Guambiano Indians

AMERINDIANS

The original Native American population of Colombia intermarried with Spanish colonists. Today, half of Colombia's population is *mestizo*, which means of mixed European and native descent. Yet some 400 native tribes survive, speaking more than 180 languages. These Guambiano people live on reservations, where they make a living from growing corn, wheat, and potatoes, and selling their craft goods to tourists.

Caribbean Sea
Riohacha
Santa Marta
Barranquilla
Cartagena
Gulf of Darien
Sincelejo
Montería
Cúcuta
PANAMA
Barrancabermeja
Bucaramanga
Bello
Medellín
Sogamoso
Itagüí
Manizales
Tunja
Armenia
BOGOTÁ
Tuluá
Villavicencio
Buenaventura
Guaviare
Cali
COLOMBIA
Popayán
San José del Guaviare
Florencia
Pasto
Vaupés
Mitú
PACIFIC OCEAN
Magdalena
Llanos
Meta
VENEZUELA
Equator
Equator
ECUADOR
Caquetá
BRAZIL
Putumayo
PERU

N
W — E
S

SCALE BAR			
0	400	800	km
0	400	800	miles

COFFEE
Colombia's main export is coffee, grown on tropical evergreen shrubs which require both high temperatures and high rainfall. Its berrylike fruits are processed to extract the seeds, which are then dried in the sunlight. Further processing frees the seeds from their coverings, and the beans are ready for export. Drying the beans by hand is very hard work, and increasingly machines are being used.

Find out more

GEMS AND JEWELRY
SOUTH AMERICA
SPAIN, HISTORY OF

Maine
(to Massachusetts)

New Hampshire

New York

Massachusetts

Pennsylvania

Rhode Island

Connecticut

New Jersey

Virginia

Delaware

Maryland

North Carolina

South Carolina

Georgia

COLONIES AND
COLONIAL AMERICA

IN THE 100 YEARS FOLLOWING THE VOYAGES of Christopher Columbus, many other Europeans sailed to America, leaving the Old World behind for a new life in a new land. Spanish settlers founded the first European colony in what is now the United States at Saint Augustine, Florida, in 1565. The English built their first colony in 1585. By 1700, over 250,000 colonists populated the area between Maine in the north and the Carolinas to the south. America's first cities developed into thriving trade centers, with their own schools, churches, books, and money. Many colonists began to think of themselves not as Europeans, but as Americans.

THE AMERICAN FRONTIER
Many Europeans explored the American frontier, seeking new territories for trade. French adventurers, including Father Jacques Marquette (left), explored the Mississippi and established a thriving fur trade in the Great Lakes region. They exchanged guns with native peoples for the beaver pelts that were so valuable in Europe.

The first Pilgrims sailed from England aboard the Mayflower, a ship similar to this model.

THIRTEEN COLONIES
Although Spain founded the first settlement, it was mainly English people who first colonized the United States. England's first colonies were in North Carolina, but these failed. In 1607, English settlers built Jamestown, Virginia, their first successful colony. England later founded or took over 11 other colonies, including the Dutch colony of New York and the Swedish colony of Delaware. These 13 early colonies later became the 13 original states of the United States of America.

THE FIRST AMERICANS
As many as 500,000 native peoples representing many tribes and speaking numerous languages lived in the area that became the 13 colonies. These people, mistakenly called Indians by the Europeans, had hunted and planted the lands and fished the rivers long before the first European ships appeared. As the colonists increased in numbers, the native peoples were forced westward.

THE LOST COLONY
In 1587, the English founded a colony on the North Carolina coast. That summer Virginia Dare was born – the first English child born in America. But when supply ships returned to the colony in 1590, its residents had mysteriously vanished without a trace.

Slave ships were brutally overloaded with their human cargo.

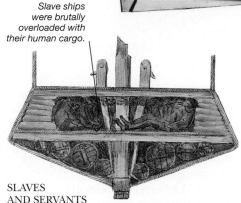

SLAVES
AND SERVANTS
Some people came to the colonies against their will. The first slaves were brought to Virginia from West Africa in 1619. Eventually there were slaves in all 13 colonies. Indentured servants from Europe were given passage to America in return for years of unpaid labor.

THE PILGRIMS
In 1620 the *Mayflower* landed at Plymouth, Massachusetts, carrying 102 English settlers known as Pilgrims. They had fled England to find the freedom to practice their Puritan faith. The Pilgrims faced terrible hardships, but they were lucky enough to settle near a friendly tribe of native peoples, the Patuxets, who taught them how to plant corn, fish with nets, and hunt deer – skills essential to the survival of their colony.

Find out more

AMERICAN REVOLUTION
CONSTITUTION
NATIVE AMERICANS
PILGRIMS
SLAVERY
UNITED STATES, HISTORY OF

COLOR

A WORLD WITHOUT COLOR would be a dull place. It would also be difficult to live in. Imagine how hard it would be to tell if traffic lights meant stop or go if there were no red or green. Nature has color signals too: the bright colors of a tree frog warn other animals that it is poisonous, and the beautiful colors of a flower attract bees to its nectar. Not every creature sees colors in the same way; some animals, such as guinea pigs and squirrels, are color-blind and cannot distinguish between different colors at all. Color is really the way our eyes interpret different kinds of light. Light is made up of tiny, invisible waves, and each wave has a particular size or wavelength. Each colored light is composed of different wavelengths, which our eyes are able to detect. White light, such as light from the Sun, is actually a combination of light of all the colors of the rainbow.

Indigo

Violet

Blue

Green

Yellow

Orange

Red

PRISM
A triangular chunk of glass, called a prism, separates all the colors in white light. When light goes through a prism, it is refracted, or bent, because glass slows it down. But every color goes through at a different speed, and is bent to a different degree, so the colors spread out when they leave the prism.

SPECTRUM
When a prism splits white light into colors, they always come out in the same order, with red at one end and violet at the other. This is called the spectrum. When sunlight is refracted by raindrops, a rainbow is produced which contains all the colors of the spectrum.

Mixing any two primary colors produces secondary colors.

PAINT PRIMARIES
Red, yellow, and blue are the primary colors of paints. Mixing them together in the correct amounts gives black.

MIXING COLORS
Red, green, and blue are called the primary colors of light. This is because you can mix red, green, and blue light in different proportions to make any color in the spectrum. In printing there is a different set of primary colors: cyan (green-blue), magenta (blue-red), and yellow. These too can be mixed to give any color except white.

LIGHT PRIMARIES
When the three primary colors of light are mixed together in the correct proportions they make white. During rock concerts and theater performances, lighting technicians produce a wide range of colors on the stage by mixing differently colored spotlights.

COLORED OBJECTS
Objects look colored because of the way they reflect the light that hits them. When white light falls on any surface, some colors are absorbed, or taken in, and some bounce off. When we look at the surface, we see only the colors that bounce off. It is this colored light that produces the color we perceive the object to be.

RED SHOES
When daylight hits a pair of red shoes, they look red because they reflect only red light and absorb all the other colors.

BLACK SHOES?
In blue light, red shoes look black because all the blue light is absorbed, and no light is reflected.

Find out more
CAMOUFLAGE, ANIMAL
EYES
LIGHT
PRINTING
RAIN AND SNOW

CHRISTOPHER
COLUMBUS

IN 1492 THREE SMALL SAILING SHIPS named the *Niña,* the *Pinta,* and the *Santa Maria* left Spain on a daring voyage. Their aim was to find a new sea route to Asia in search of spices and gold. In command was Christopher Columbus, an Italian sailor from Genoa. Unlike other explorers of the time, who were sailing east, Columbus believed that if he sailed west he would reach India and its luxuries within a few months. The Spanish were eager to profit from trade with India and the rest of Asia, and Columbus persuaded Queen Isabella of Spain to pay for his expedition. He set sail in August and two months later sighted land which he believed was Asia. In fact, Columbus had arrived in the Caribbean Islands. He did not realize what he had found, but his journey paved the way for later European settlement in the Americas.

North America

South America

Landed on San Salvador October 12, 1492.

Cuba

Hispaniola

Began homeward voyage January 16, 1493.

THE FIRST VOYAGE
Columbus's voyage to the Caribbean lasted four months. He made three more voyages, reaching Central America on his final voyage.

PTOLEMY'S WORLD MAP
The map used by Columbus had been produced by the ancient Greek mapmaker Ptolemy in the 2nd century. The world it showed did not include the continents of North and South America, Australia, or the Pacific.

EXPLORING THE CARIBBEAN
When Columbus arrived in the Caribbean he was welcomed by the Carib and Arawak people. Native Americans became known as Indians because the early explorers thought they were in India.

Captain's cabin held navigation equipment and a chest to store treasure captured on the voyage.

Food and other supplies were stored here.

Bowsprit was a spar, or horizontal mast, supporting triangular sails.

THE CREW
The *Santa Maria* carried a crew of 40. The main risk of a long voyage was running out of food and fresh water.

THE *SANTA MARIA*
Columbus's flagship was a slow, clumsy, wooden cargo ship, no larger than a modern fishing trawler. The ship relied on wind power, and conditions on board were cramped and difficult.

Spare canvas for mending sails.

Off-duty sailors slept wherever there was space.

Find out more
CARIBBEAN
CONQUISTADORS
EXPLORERS

COMETS AND METEORS

ON A CLEAR NIGHT you may see several shooting stars in the space of an hour. A shooting star, or meteor, looks like a point of light that suddenly darts across the sky and disappears. A meteor occurs when a piece of dust from space, called a meteoroid, burns up as it enters the Earth's atmosphere. As the meteor plummets to Earth at a speed of about 150,000 mph (240,000 km/h), friction with the air produces intense heat, which leaves a bright glow in the sky. Meteors usually burn up about 56 miles (90 km) from the Earth's surface.

Many meteoroids are fragments from comets that orbit the Sun. A comet appears as a faint, fuzzy point of light that moves across the night sky for weeks or months. As it nears the Sun, the comet grows a "tail." Then it swings past the Sun and travels away, becoming smaller and fainter. Comets often reappear at regular intervals (every few years) as they travel past Earth on their orbits.

COMET TAIL
As a comet approaches Earth, the heat of the Sun turns the ice into gas. The gas escapes, along with dust, and forms one or more tails (the gas and dust form separate tails). The tails always point away from the Sun. They get shorter as the comet moves away from the Sun.

Dust tail can be up to about 600,000 miles (1 million km) long. It shines white because the particles of dust reflect sunlight.

Gas tail can be up to 62 million miles (100 million km) long. The gas tail has a bluish glow. This is because the heat of the Sun makes the gas molecules emit blue-colored light.

The size of a comet's nucleus can range from a few hundred yards across to more than about 6 miles (10 kms) across.

The solar wind – a blast of charged particles that stream from the Sun – blows the comet's gas tail away from the Sun. When the comet approaches the Sun, its tails follow. The tails lead when the comet moves away from the Sun.

COMETS
A comet consists of a central core, or nucleus, of dust and ice; a cloud of gas and dust around the nucleus, called the coma; and one or more tails. Astronomers have observed hundreds of comets and believe that about one billion other comets orbit the Sun unseen, far beyond the most distant planet.

In 2004, the Stardust spacecraft flew past comet Wild 2, sending back many pictures, including this enhanced, composite image.

Chinese astronomers probably observed Halley's Comet more than 2,200 years ago. The comet also appears in the 11th-century Bayeux tapestry, which shows the Norman Conquest of England.

HALLEY'S COMET
The English astronomer Edmund Halley (1656-1742) was the first to realize that some comets appear regularly. In 1705 he showed that the comet now called Halley's Comet returns past the Earth every 75 or 76 years.

METEORS
There are two ways in which meteors occur: individually and in showers. This spectacular meteor shower (left) occurred in 1833. Similar impressive displays occur every 33 years during November. At this time the Earth passes through a swarm of meteors, called the Leonids, that spread out along the orbit of a comet.

METEORITES
Huge lumps of rock called meteorites pass through the Earth's atmosphere without burning up completely. About 25,000 years ago, a meteorite that weighed about 900,000 tons caused a crater in Arizona (above), 4,000 ft (1,200 m) across. Some scientists believe that the impact of a huge meteorite about 65 million years ago may have destroyed many animal species.

Find out more
ASTRONOMY
BLACK HOLES
EARTH
PLANETS
ROCKS AND MINERALS
STARS
SUN

COMMUNISM

AFTER 1917, A NEW WORD came into popular use – Communism. It was then that Russia set up the world's first Communist government. By 1950, nearly one-third of the world's population lived under Communist rule. The word communism comes from the Latin word *communis,* meaning "belonging to all." More than 2,000 years ago, the Greek writer, Plato, put forward the earliest ideas about Communism in his book *The Republic.* Much later, Vladimir Lenin, the Russian revolutionary, developed modern Communism from the writings of the German philosopher Karl Marx. Unlike Capitalists, who believe in private ownership, Communists believe that the state should own a country's wealth and industry, and wealth should be shared according to need. In Communist countries, the Communist party controls every aspect of daily life. During the 20th century, Communism was a major political force. People in Communist countries, however, resented economic hardship and their lack of personal freedom. From the late 1980s, various countries, including the former Soviet Union, rejected Communist rule.

CHAINS AROUND THE WORLD
"The workers have nothing to lose . . . but their chains. They have a world to gain," wrote Marx in his *Communist Manifesto.* On this magazine cover, a worker strikes down "chains" that bind the world.

KARL MARX
Communism is based on the ideas of Karl Marx (1818-83). His major work, *Das Kapital,* became the Communist "bible." He believed that all history is a struggle between the rich rulers and the poor workers, and that the workers will eventually overthrow their rulers in a revolution. Marx died in exile in London, England.

SPREAD OF COMMUNISM
After 1917, Communism spread from Russia to many other countries elsewhere in the world (shown in red above). In Eastern Europe and North Korea, Communist governments were installed after occupation by the Soviet army. In China and Southeast Asia, local armed Communist groups took power after fighting long wars.

CAPITALISM	COMMUNISM
Owner Worker	Worker Worker
Under Capitalism, companies own all the factories. Workers are paid wages but do not always share the profits.	Under Communism, the factories are owned by the state. The state sets wage levels for workers, and uses profits for other investments.

CHINA
In 1949, China became a Communist state under Mao Zedong (1893-1976). China has the largest Communist party in the world, with 63 million members. Since the 1970s, China's rulers have gradually abandoned Communist economic policies, encouraging private enterprise to create economic growth. However, the party has kept a tight grip on power. It encourages people to take part in group sports, such as tai chi (left).

FIDEL CASTRO
In 1959, Fidel Castro (left), a Cuban lawyer, led a revolution against Cuba's dictator, President Batista. Castro became head of government, and Cuba became a Communist state. Castro seized all American property and promised freedom to the Cuban people. In the 1960s Castro encouraged and supported Communist movements throughout Central and South America.

___

Find out more
CHINA, HISTORY OF
COLD WAR
MAO ZEDONG
RUSSIAN REVOLUTION
SOUTH AMERICA, HISTORY OF
SOVIET UNION, HISTORY OF

COMPOSERS

AN AUTHOR CREATING A STORY has a choice of more than a hundred thousand words made up from the 26 letters of the alphabet. With only the 12 notes of the chromatic scale – the notes on the piano from any C to the next C above – a composer can make an infinite variety of music of many different styles. These can include jazz, folk, pop, or what is known as classical music.

Composers learn their craft through writing exercises in harmony and counterpoint. Harmony is placing the main tune on the top line with chords (three or more notes sounding together) in support; counterpoint is placing the principal theme in any position with other tunes weaving around it. Composers also discover what instruments can or cannot do, what they sound like, and how to explore their capabilities. The best way to learn all this is to study the music of many composers. Great composers move audiences to tears of joy or sadness with their talent for expressing emotion through music.

In the 15th century beautiful colored pictures decorated the margins of composers' works.

PURCELL
English composer Henry Purcell (1659-95) sang in the King's Chapel in London (above) when he was a boy. At the age of 20 he became the organist at Westminster Abbey, London. He composed beautiful chamber music and dramatic operas such as *Dido and Aeneas*.

Each member of the orchestra uses a line of the score showing only the music for his or her individual instrument.

HOW COMPOSERS WORK
Most composers begin by either inventing themes or melodies that are developed for one or more instruments, or by setting words for one or more voices. Sometimes, as with operas and choral works, both voices and instruments are used. Blending them together so that all are heard clearly is a skilled job. The music is written out in a score. A symphony can last up to an hour, or an opera up to three hours, so composing can be hard work.

Composers of orchestral music write a complete score, which includes the instrumental parts played by every section of the orchestra.

Many composers like to write music sitting at the piano, so that they can play the tunes as they work on them.

BAROQUE MUSIC
The music of the 17th and early 18th centuries was called Baroque, after the elaborate architectural styles popular in the same period. It is complex music in which the instruments weave their melodies in and out like threads in a rich, colorful tapestry.

BACH
The greatest of the Baroque composers was Johann Sebastian Bach (1685-1750) of Germany. The *Brandenburg Concertos*, which he completed in 1721, are among his best-known works.

HANDEL
George Frideric Handel (1685-1759) was born in Germany and moved to England in 1712. He composed music for the English royal family and wrote many famous choral works.

Handel wrote one of his most famous pieces of music to accompany a royal fireworks display in 1749.

CLASSICAL ERA

Serious music is often called classical to distinguish it from popular music. However, to musicians, classical music is the music composed in the late 18th and early 19th centuries. Classical composers extended the harmony and forms of the Baroque era. The symphony developed in this period. Joseph Haydn (1732-1809) composed 104 symphonies.

MOZART

Wolfgang Amadeus Mozart (1756-91) of Austria was a talented composer and performer by the age of five. He went on to write chamber music, symphonies, and concertos, as well as great operas such as *The Magic Flute*.

Mozart performed all over Europe when he was only six.

BEETHOVEN

The German composer Ludwig van Beethoven (1770-1827; above) was completely deaf for the last 10 years of his life but continued to compose some of the greatest music in the world. His late works moved music toward the Romantic movement.

ROMANTIC MOVEMENT

From about 1820 composers began to experiment with new harmonies and forms, achieving a much wider emotional range. For composers such as Tchaikovsky, formal rules were less important than creating drama, painting pictures in sound, or telling stories.

TCHAIKOVSKY

The Russian composer Peter Ilyich Tchaikovsky (1840-93) was unhappy in his personal life, which brought great emotional depth to his music. He wrote many well-known ballets and symphonies, including the famous *1812 Overture*.

Stravinsky's ballet The Firebird *caused a sensation at its first performance in Paris in 1910.*

Playing a tune on an electric piano adds the notes to the score on the screen.

COMPUTER COMPOSITION

Computers can help composers to write music. The composer can use an electronic instrument to enter the melodies into the computer, where they can be stored, altered, and printed out.

MODERN MUSIC

In the 20th century there were great changes in serious music. Russian-born composer Igor Stravinsky (1882-1971) experimented with new harmonies, creating sounds that his audiences sometimes found difficult to understand. Composers such as the German Karlheinz Stockhausen (b. 1928) challenged listeners' ideas about music. In *Zyklus*, for example, Stockhausen tells the percussionist to start on any page of the score and play to the end before starting again at the beginning.

COMPOSERS

800s Composers begin to write down their music for the first time. At the same time, monks develop a form of chant, called plainsong, for singing church services.

1300-1600 Composers of the late Medieval and Renaissance period start to develop harmony by combining different voices together, producing a richer sound called polyphony.

1597 Jacopo Peri (1561-1633) of Italy composes *Dafne*, the first opera.

1600s Baroque music begins, and composers gradually make their music more complicated and elaborate.

1750-1820 The rise of classical music introduces simpler, popular tunes that more people could enjoy.

1817-23 Beethoven composes the *Choral symphony*, the first symphony to use a choir.

1820s The romantic era begins, and composers start to look for new ways to make their music appeal to the listeners' emotions.

1850s Composers in eastern and northern Europe begin to write nationalistic music, based on traditional songs and stories from their countries.

1865 Richard Wagner's (1813-83) opera *Tristan and Isolde* points the way toward modern music.

1888 Russian nationalist composer Nikolai Rimsky-Korsakov composes his *Scheherazade*, based on the *Thousand and One Nights*.

1900s The modern era in music begins. Composers of the impressionist movement write music that creates atmosphere, movement, and color in sound.

1905 French impressionist composer Claude Debussy (1862-1918) writes *La Mer* (*The Sea*).

1924 George Gershwin composes *Rhapsody in Blue* for jazz orchestra and piano.

1959 German composer Karlheinz Stockhausen (born 1928) writes *Zyklus* for one percussion player.

Find out more

MUSIC
MUSICAL INSTRUMENTS
OPERA AND SINGING
ORCHESTRAS
RENAISSANCE

COMPUTERS

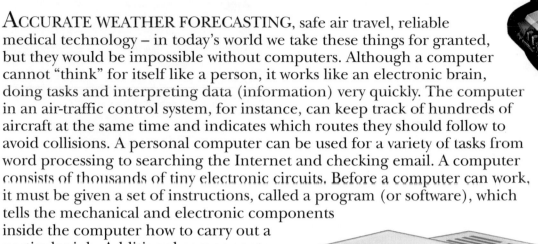

ACCURATE WEATHER FORECASTING, safe air travel, reliable medical technology – in today's world we take these things for granted, but they would be impossible without computers. Although a computer cannot "think" for itself like a person, it works like an electronic brain, doing tasks and interpreting data (information) very quickly. The computer in an air-traffic control system, for instance, can keep track of hundreds of aircraft at the same time and indicates which routes they should follow to avoid collisions. A personal computer can be used for a variety of tasks from word processing to searching the Internet and checking email. A computer consists of thousands of tiny electronic circuits. Before a computer can work, it must be given a set of instructions, called a program (or software), which tells the mechanical and electronic components inside the computer how to carry out a particular job. Additional components, such as a memory card or an internal modem, can be slotted into the computer as required.

HIDDEN COMPUTERS
People usually think of computers as having a screen and a keyboard, but this is not always the case. Many devices, such as washing machines, cars, and cameras, contain tiny computers that are specially programmed to control their function.

MEMORY
A computer memory consists of two types of microchips: ROM (Read-Only Memory) contains permanent instructions; RAM (Random Access Memory) holds programs and information as they are needed. The microchips store information in the form of electric charges.

PERSONAL COMPUTERS

Many homes, schools, and offices use personal computers – small computers designed for use by one person. A personal computer consists of four basic units: a keyboard, to type in information; a memory, to store information and programs; a processing unit, to carry out the instructions contained in the program; and a monitor, for displaying the results of the computer's work.

Monitor displays data

The CPU (central processing unit), or microprocessor, is a microchip which does calculations and other similar tasks.

A hard disk consists of several magnetic disks. An electromagnet "writes" information onto them and "reads" data from them.

ROM memory chip

The keyboard has keys similar to those of a typewriter. Pressing the keys feeds information into the computer. Letters or numbers appear on screen, or the computer performs a function.

RAM memory chip

Power supply

TYPES OF DISK
Information can be stored for long periods on magnetic disks. There are many types of disks, including hard disks, which store vast quantities of data, and floppy disks, which store less information but are removable and can be used to carry data from one computer to another. CD-ROMS (Compact Disc-Read-Only Memory), which hold 650 times as much information as a floppy disk, are the most popular format for multimedia programs.

Floppy disk

CD-ROM

MOUSE
A device called a mouse moves an arrow on the screen. The mouse ball is connected to two slotted wheels. As each wheel turns, it interrupts a beam of light. From the changes in the light beam, the computer detects where the mouse has moved.

Mouse

How computers work

A computer converts everything it handles, such as letters of the alphabet, into numbers. The numbers are stored in the computer in the form of electronic signals in which "on" stands for 1 and "off" stands for 0. All numbers, letters, and pictures are represented by sequences of 1s and 0s. This is called binary code. The computer does all its different tasks, such as inserting a word into a sentence, by doing rapid calculations with these numbers. Once it has finished its job, the computer changes the numbers into words and pictures that we can understand.

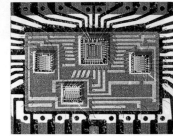

All computers contain a set of microchips (left). Inside a microchip are millions of tiny electronic parts that store and process electronic signals.

SOFTWARE

The programs that make a computer perform different tasks are called software. A computer can perform many different jobs simply by using different software programs, from computer games and word processing packages to painting programs and scientific applications that do complex calculations.

HARDWARE

Computer machinery is called hardware. There are many different kinds of hardware: personal computers, small portable computers, and large mainframe computers on which many people can work simultaneously. Hardware also includes components such as monitors, printers, and other computer equipment (below).

Monitor displays information.

Hard drive is stored inside tower unit.

Speaker

CD-ROM drive

Zip disk drive

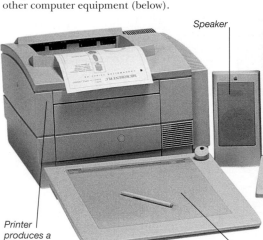

Keyboard

Printer produces a paper copy of the material shown on the screen.

Graphics tablet allows images to be drawn onto the screen with a special pen.

Mouse pad

Mouse

Scanner copies an image from a photograph or book and transfers it into the computer.

HISTORY OF COMPUTERS

In 1834, English inventor Charles Babbage designed the first programmable mechanical computer. However, he could not make the machine as it was too complex for the technology of his day. The first electronic computer, ENIAC, was built in the US in 1946. During the 1980s, transistors and microchips enabled computers to become smaller and more powerful. Easy-to-use software programs such as those developed by Microsoft (below) encouraged the spread of computers in people's homes. In the 1990s, web browsers opened the Internet to private individuals.

In 1975, American Bill Gates (1955-) founded the Microsoft company. By the late 1990s, Microsoft was supplying more than half the world's software.

Bluetooth

Wi-Fi

Router connected to Internet or local network

Mobile phone

NEW TECHNOLOGY

Computers are becoming increasingly portable and versatile. Wireless or "Wi-Fi" technology means they can connect to the Internet via radio signals, and the similar "Bluetooth" enables them to communicate without cables over short distances with pocket computers, cell phones, and even printers, keyboards, and mice.

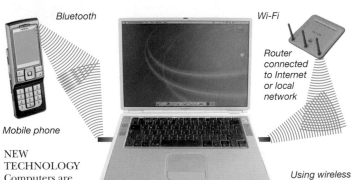

Using wireless connections, a laptop computer can be used to send e-mails or surf the Internet from almost anywhere.

Handheld or "pocket" computers can send and receive e-mails, be used as cell phones, and let you work on files from your desktop computer.

Find out more

ELECTRONICS
MACHINES
MATHEMATICS
ROBOTS
TECHNOLOGY

CONGRESS

A cast-iron dome tops the the Capitol building.

THE POWER TO MAKE LAWS in the United States rests with Congress, the legislative branch of the federal government. Established by the Constitution in 1787, Congress is split into two houses, the Senate and the House of Representatives, with about equal powers. The Senate consists of 100 members, two from each of the 50 states. The House has 435 members; the number of members is based on each state's population. Although lawmaking is the chief duty of Congress, its members also control government taxing and spending, regulate interstate and international trade, maintain the armed forces, and even declare war. The two largest political parties, the Democrats and the Republicans, control Congress. The party with the most members is the majority party; the other is the minority party. The majority party takes charge of all the congressional committees, where most of the daily work of government is done.

THE CAPITOL
For two centuries, the Senate and the House have met inside the Capitol, in Washington, D.C. Each group meets separately, except for special joint sessions held in the larger House chambers.

SENATE

Edward Kennedy, a Massachusetts senator since 1962, campaigns for office.

Each of the 50 states, regardless of its size and population, has two senators. Senators are elected for six-year terms of office. The vice president is the presiding officer of the Senate. The Constitution gives the Senate the power to approve or reject presidential appointments to important government jobs. Senators must also approve treaties by a two-thirds majority.

THE NATION'S LAWMAKERS

The Constitution established the framework of Congress and gave it the power to make laws. Its bicameral (two-house) system was created as a compromise between the leaders of small states, who wanted equal representation, and those of large states, who argued for representation based on population. A new Congress meets every two years, after voters have elected all of the representatives and one-third of the senators.

President Roosevelt signs a bill.

HOW A BILL BECOMES LAW

Any citizen can propose a law, but all bills must be formally introduced by members of Congress. Each bill is sent to a committee that deals with the business of the bill. If the committee decides to go ahead, a public hearing is held to debate each bill. The sponsors and supporters of a bill often lobby other members to gain their support. Through bargaining and compromise, a bill might eventually reach the floor for a vote. Once the House and Senate have both voted to pass the bill, the president has ten days to either make it a law or return the bill to Congress.

Rebecca Felton was the first female senator in 1922.

Kentucky congressman Henry Clay was Speaker of the House from 1811-25.

THE NATION'S VOICE
Each member of Congress represents many citizens, but Congress has not always reflected the diversity of the people. The first woman senator, Rebecca Felton, was appointed in 1922; ten years later, Hattie Caraway became the first woman elected to the office. Today, many women and members of minority groups hold key congressional seats.

HOUSE OF REPRESENTATIVES
Each state is divided into congressional districts of about equal population. The members of the House are elected from these districts, for two-year terms. The head of the House, the Speaker, is one of the most powerful people in Congress. The Speaker assigns bills to committees, and gives members the right to speak during debates.

Find out more

CONSTITUTION
POLITICAL PARTIES
PRESIDENCY

CONQUISTADORS

AT THE BEGINNING OF THE 16TH CENTURY the first Spanish adventurers followed Christopher Columbus to the Caribbean and South and Central America. These conquistadors (the Spanish word for conquerors) were soldiers hungry for gold, silver, and land. They took priests with them, sent by the Catholic Church to convert the Native Americans. The two most famous conquistadors were Hernando Cortés (1485-1547), who conquered the Aztecs of Mexico, and Francisco Pizarro (1470-1541), who conquered the Incas of Peru. Although the conquistadors took only small numbers of soldiers along, they were successful partly because they had brought guns, horses, and steel weapons. But what also came with the conquistadors were European diseases such as smallpox and measles, against which the Native Americans had no resistance. These diseases wiped out more than 70 million Native Americans and destroyed their civilizations. By seizing the land, the conquistadors prepared the way for a huge Spanish empire in the Americas that was to last until the 19th century.

EL DORADO
The first conquistadors heard legends of a golden kingdom ruled by "El Dorado," the golden man. They kept searching for this amazing place but never found it. Most of the beautiful goldwork they took to Europe was melted down and reused.

Hernando Cortés

Montezuma

HERNANDO CORTES
In 1519, Cortés set out from Cuba to conquer Mexico, against the governor Velázquez's wishes. Velázquez believed that Cortés was too ambitious. From an early age Cortés had sought adventure and wealth. Eventually his wish was fulfilled and he controlled the whole of Mexico.

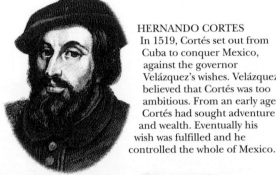

NEW SPAIN
The Spanish quickly settled in the conquered areas and created the empire of New Spain. The wealth from its silver mines and ranches became the envy of Europe.

■ Aztecs
■ Incas

MONTEZUMA MEETS CORTES
When the Aztec emperor Montezuma met Cortés in Tenochtitlán, he believed that Cortés was the pale-skinned, bearded god Quetzalcoatl, who was prophesied to return from the east. He welcomed Cortés with gifts and a ceremony. But Cortés captured him and took over the Aztec empire.

NATIVE AMERICANS
After conquest, the Native Americans were treated cruelly and forced to work for the Spanish. Many slaved in the gold mines. It was not long before their old way of life disappeared forever.

FRANCISCO PIZARRO
In 1532, Pizarro marched into Peru with 200 soldiers. He seized the Inca emperor, Atahualpa, ransomed him for a roomful of gold, and then had him killed. The leaderless Inca empire crumbled.

Find out more
AZTECS
COLUMBUS, CHRISTOPHER
EXPLORERS
INCAS
MAYA
SOUTH AMERICA, HISTORY OF

CONSERVATION
AND ENDANGERED SPECIES

ANIMALS AND PLANTS ARE DYING OUT at a greater rate today than ever before. Living things have become extinct throughout the Earth's history – often due to dramatic changes in the climate – but, humans are now posing a greater threat. Thousands of animals and plants are endangered (in danger of extinction) because we cut down forests and drain wetlands to farm or build on the land where they live. We change the environment so much that animals and plants cannot survive. This is called habitat loss. Another great threat is hunting. People hunt animals for their fur, hide, horns, and meat, and sometimes simply because they consider animals a nuisance. Pollution is yet another serious threat, damaging many oceans, rivers, and forests. Conservation is the management and protection of wildlife and its habitats. It includes sheltering and trying to save wild animals and plants from destruction by humans. People are more aware of these threats to wildlife than ever before, and there are conservation organizations in many parts of the world. They work to protect endangered creatures by setting aside areas in the wild where animals and plants can live in safety.

GREENPEACE
International organizations such as Greenpeace work in various ways to save endangered polar wildlife, particularly whales and seals. Here, a Greenpeace worker is spraying a seal pup with harmless red dye so that seal hunters will not want to kill the pup for its beautiful fur.

CACTUS
The Mexican neogomesia cactus and dozens of other cacti are very rare because plant collectors have taken them from the wild.

Neogomesia cactus

PYGMY HOG
There may be only about 100 pygmy hogs left on Earth following the destruction of their grassland home in the Himalayan foothills of Assam, India.

SIAMESE CROCODILE
Many crocodiles and alligators have been killed for their skins, to be made into leather bags, shoes, and belts. Today, about 20 members of the crocodile family are in danger of extinction, including the Siamese crocodile and the Orinoco crocodile.

Siamese crocodile

GALAPAGOS TORTOISE
This huge reptile has suffered from the rats, dogs, and other animals that people have taken to the Galapagos Islands, in the East Pacific Ocean. It is now a protected species.

CONSERVING NATURE
Conservation involves studying wild places, identifying the animals and plants that live there, and observing what happens to them. The International Union for the Conservation of Nature and Natural Resources (IUCN) collects scientific data and works on conservation in many countries, together with organizations such as the United Nations Environment Program (UNEP).

SLIPPER ORCHID
Many orchids are in danger because collectors bring them away from the wild. Drury's slipper orchid has almost disappeared from its natural region in India, and may soon be extinct.

GIANT WETA CRICKET
New Zealand has many kinds of weta crickets. Fossils have been found that are more than 180 million years old. Today, several species of weta cricket are in danger of extinction, including the giant weta cricket shown here.

RED-KNEED TARANTULA
The red-kneed tarantula from Mexico (left) is rare because many people keep exotic spiders as pets. This tarantula is not a true tarantula but a member of the bird-eating spider group.

GRAY BAT
Many kinds of bats are threatened because of the loss of their forest homes to farmland, and because of the increasing use of insecticides on the food they eat. The American gray bat, shown at right, is endangered.

JAPANESE GIANT SALAMANDER
The Japanese giant salamander, shown at left, is the world's largest amphibian, growing to more than 5 ft (1.5 m) long. Today it is rare. Sometimes people catch it for its meat.

AFRICAN VIOLET
The African violet is a well-known houseplant, but it has almost disappeared from its natural habitat – tropical mountain forests in Tanzania, Africa.

SPADEFOOT TOAD
There are many kinds of spadefoot toad. The Italian spadefoot toad shown here is particularly endangered.

MONK SEAL
Nature reserves have been set up for the Mediterranean monk seal so that it will not be disturbed by tourists on the coasts where it breeds.

GOLDEN LION TAMARIN
Clearing forests for timber and farmland endangers the lives of many monkeys. Many tamarins and marmosets have been killed in South America because people mistakenly believed that they spread the diseases malaria and yellow fever.

DODO
The dodo was a flightless bird that lived on islands in the Indian Ocean. All dodos were extinct by about 1800.

VICTORIA'S BIRDWING BUTTERFLY
The Victoria's birdwing butterfly was first collected by scientists in 1855, when they shot it with guns. Today this butterfly and many other kinds of butterflies are endangered because collectors kill them.

JACKASS PENGUIN
This flightless seabird is also called the black-footed penguin. Its numbers have decreased in South Africa because of water pollution and because fishing boats catch the fish the penguin eats.

SUMATRAN RHINOCEROS
Rhinoceroses are in great danger of extinction, but poachers (illegal hunters) still kill them and sell their horns. The horns are carved into dagger handles or powdered into traditional Chinese medicine. There are only a few hundred Sumatran rhinoceroses left in Sumatra and mainland Southeast Asia.

CAPTIVE BREEDING
One way to help an endangered species recover its numbers is by breeding it in captivity. Experts capture a few animals from the wild, raise them carefully, and encourage them to breed in captivity. Later, they release, or reintroduce, the offspring into a suitable area. The notornis is a flightless bird that scientists believed to be extinct until it was rediscovered in 1948. Eggs from its nests are hatched in an incubator, and the chicks are kept warm with tiny electric blankets. They are fed by someone wearing a puppetlike glove that resembles the parent bird.

Notornis

HABITAT LOSS
Tropical rain forests are being destroyed at an alarming rate. Trees are burned or sold for timber, and the land is farmed or used for roads and buildings. Scientists believe that many rain forests contain kinds of animals and plants that we have never seen. For every plant or creature that is threatened or extinct, there may be 100 that we do not know about.

CONTROLLING TRADE
Some animals and plants are taken from the wild for their skins and other products. Elephants are killed for their ivory tusks. Colorful flowers are made into pulp to make dyes. The Convention on International Trade in Endangered Species (CITES) has lists of hundreds of species, or kinds, of plants and animals. Selling or exporting these animals or their products without a special license is illegal. All whales, dolphins, and porpoises are on this list; so are all monkeys, apes, and lemurs.

SNAKE SKIN
The brightly colored objects shown above were once the skins of snakes and lizards. The skins are dyed different colors, then made into all sorts of leather goods, including bags and shoes.

SNOW LEOPARD
The snow leopard lives high in the mountains of the Himalayas and Central Asia. In winter its fur becomes thicker to keep out the bitter cold. In the past, the snow leopard's winter coat was much prized by fur traders. Today, the snow leopard and many other big cats are protected by the CITES agreement, but they are still hunted illegally in some remote areas.

Find out more
ANIMALS
ECOLOGY AND FOOD WEBS
FOREST WILDLIFE
NATIONAL PARKS
PLANTS
POLLUTION

CONSTITUTION

JAMES MADISON
Virginian James Madison was a strong negotiator who was called the "Father of the Constitution" because of his important work on the document.

IN THE AMERICAN REVOLUTIONARY WAR (1775-81), the 13 American states worked together to win independence from British rule. However, after the war, each state made its own laws, printed its own money, and collected its own taxes. In May 1787, a convention met in Philadelphia to draw up a document to create a single strong nation from 13 very different states. The delegates worked to find a compromise between state and federal powers, and to guarantee individual freedom under a strong national government. This new plan, the Constitution of the United States, established the basic laws of the country. It set forth the framework of the federal government, and spelled out the rights of the people. Perhaps most importantly, the Constitution allowed room for improvement, by amendment.

UNITING THE STATES

The Constitution established the federal government and divided its powers among three branches: the executive branch (represented by the president), the legislative branch (Senate and House of Representatives), and the judicial branch (Supreme Court and federal courts). A system of "checks and balances" was written into the Constitution, giving each branch the opportunity to overrule the others. The Supreme Court has the final say in interpreting the Constitution.

Benjamin Franklin, James Madison, George Washington, and other delegates sign the Constitution in 1787.

Suffragettes use the right to protest in 1913.

AMENDMENTS

At first, several states refused to sign the Constitution. They feared that the newly strengthened federal government would take power from the states and the people. As a compromise, the Constitution was amended in 1791. The first ten amendments are called the Bill of Rights, and guarantee personal freedoms.

THE FRAMERS OF THE CONSTITUTION

Known as the framers of the Constitution, the 55 delegates to the Constitutional Convention represented 12 of the 13 states. Famously described as well-bred, well-read, well-fed, and well-wed, about half were lawyers, half college graduates, and many owned slaves. The oldest and most famous delegate, 81-year-old Pennsylvania statesman Benjamin Franklin (right), was so frail he had to be carried to the meetings in a sedan chair, but his wealth of experience proved vital to the creation of the new government.

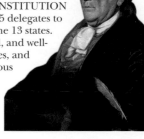

BILL OF RIGHTS

First Guarantees freedom of worship, freedom of the press, and the right to protest.

Second Right to bear arms.

Third Soldiers cannot be housed in private homes.

Fourth Right to be free from unreasonable seizure.

Fifth Protection from testifying against oneself.

Sixth Guarantees the right to a speedy public trial.

Seventh Trial by jury.

Eighth Prohibits cruel and excessive punishment.

Ninth Rights not defined may still be protected.

Tenth Powers not given to the federal government rest with the states and people.

WE THE PEOPLE?

The first Constitution was written for the people, by the people – except women, slaves, Native Americans, and those too poor to own land. Slaves, such as poet Phillis Wheatley (left), were denied rights and protection. But its provision for amendments allowed the Constitution to be improved.

Find out more

AMERICAN REVOLUTION
CIVIL RIGHTS
FRANKLIN, BENJAMIN

CONTINENTS

ALMOST A THIRD OF THE SURFACE of the Earth is land. There are seven vast pieces of land, called continents, which make up most of this area. The rest consists of islands, which are much smaller landmasses completely surrounded by water. The seven continents are crowded into almost one half of the globe; the huge Pacific Ocean occupies most of the other half. The largest continent is Asia, which has an area of more than 17 million sq miles (44 million sq km).

Most scientists now agree that, about 200 million years ago, the continents were joined together in one huge landmass. Over millions of years they drifted around and changed shape, and they are still moving today. The continents lie on vast pieces of solid rock, called plates, that collide and move against one another. These movements cause volcanoes and earthquakes, push up mountains, and create huge trenches in the Earth's crust.

3 THE WORLD TODAY
The Americas have moved away from the other continents and joined together, and India has joined Asia. Australia and Antarctica have drifted apart.

Europe
Asia
North America
Africa
South America
Australia
Antarctica

The continents are made of many smaller pieces of land that have been pushed together.

1 PANGAEA
The continents were joined in one supercontinent, called Pangaea, which began to break apart about 200 million years ago.

Asia
North America
Laurasia
Africa
Europe
India
South America
Gondwanaland
Australia
Antarctica

2 BREAKUP
About 135 million years ago, Pangaea split up into two areas – Gondwanaland and Laurasia.

North America
Asia
Europe
India
Australia
PANGAEA
South America
Africa
Antarctica

CONTINENTAL DRIFT

A glance at the globe shows that the eastern sides of North and South America and the western sides of Europe and Africa follow a similar line. In 1912, Alfred Wegener, a German meteorologist, suggested that the continents once fitted together like pieces of a jigsaw puzzle. This huge piece of land then broke up, and the continents drifted apart.

PLATE TECTONICS

The continents and oceans lie on top of several huge plates of rock about 60 miles (100 km) deep. These plates float on the hot, molten rock in the mantle underneath. Heat from the Earth's interior makes the plates move, carrying the continents with them. Mountains and undersea ridges, deep trenches, and huge valleys form at the edges of the plates as they move and collide.

Pacific Ocean
Trench
South America
Atlantic Ocean
Mountains and volcanoes
American plate
Undersea ridge
Africa
Nazca plate
Molten rock from Nazca plate forces its way up, forming volcanoes along edge of continent.
Indian Ocean
Nazca plate moves under American plate, forming trench in ocean floor.
Hot rock rises from below, pushing the American and African plates apart and forming an undersea ridge.
Mantle
African plate
Indian plate

MOVING PLATES

The plates move about 1 in (2.5 cm) every year – about as fast as your fingernails grow. The Atlantic Ocean is widening at this speed as the Americas drift apart from Europe and Africa.

SAN ANDREAS FAULT
The San Andreas fault in California is at the border between two plates. They slide against one another, causing severe earthquakes.

Find out more
EARTH
EARTHQUAKES
GEOLOGY
MOUNTAINS
OCEANS AND SEAS
VOLCANOES

JAMES COOK

1728 Born in Yorkshire, England.

1741 Signs on as ship's boy on the coal ship *Freelove*.

1759 Charts St. Lawrence River in Canada.

1772-75 Voyage to discover "southern continent," a land that scientists thought must exist. Circles Antarctica.

1775 Promoted to captain.

1776-79 Voyage to discover a northwest passage around North America.

1779 Killed in Sandwich Islands (Hawaii).

IN THE LATE SUMMER OF 1768, a small sailing ship left Plymouth, England, on an expedition to the Pacific Ocean. In charge of the ship was Lieutenant James Cook, who was to become one of the greatest explorers the world has ever known. Cook was an outstanding navigator. He was also a fine captain. He insisted that his sailors eat sauerkraut (pickled cabbage) and fresh fruit, and so became the first captain to save his crew from scurvy, a disease caused by lack of vitamin C. The voyage lasted three years. On his return to England, Cook was sent on two more voyages: one to the Antarctic, the other to the Arctic. On these voyages he became the first European to visit a number of Pacific islands, sailed farther south than any other European, and added many lands, including Australia and New Zealand, to the British Empire.

ENDEAVOUR

Cook's ship, the *Endeavour*, was originally a coal ship. Cook chose this ship because it was sturdy, spacious, and easy to handle. On the *Endeavour* voyage, Cook added many new territories to the British Empire.

The Endeavour *was 98 ft (30 m) long, weighed 360 tons, and carried 112 sailors and five scientists.*

Cook stocked up with fresh fruit at every landing.

Cook purified the air in the ship once a week by burning vinegar and gunpowder.

KEEPING RECORDS

Cook made many maps, took regular measurements, and recorded every event of the voyages in minute detail. The scientists onboard collected botanical specimens from the lands they visited. In an age before cameras, artists on board made drawings of all the people, plants, and wildlife they saw to show to people at home. They collected so many specimens in one bay in Australia that they named it Botany Bay. It later became a dreaded prison colony.

Sydney Parkinson was the ship's artist on board the Endeavour. *He drew this plant,* Banksia serrata, 1, *around 1760.*

FIRST VOYAGE

The British Royal Navy sent Cook on his first voyage to observe the planet Venus passing between the Earth and the sun. He also had secret orders from the government to sail into uncharted regions to prove the existence of a southern continent, which they wanted to add to their empire. He did not succeed, but in the attempt he became the first European to visit New Zealand and the eastern coast of Australia.

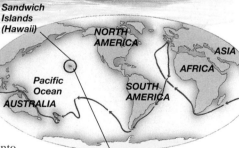

Sandwich Islands (Hawaii)

NORTH AMERICA

ASIA

AFRICA

Pacific Ocean

SOUTH AMERICA

AUSTRALIA

Islanders killed Captain Cook here on February 14, 1779.

Find out more

AUSTRALIA, HISTORY OF
EXPLORERS
NEW ZEALAND, HISTORY OF

CORALS,
ANEMONES, AND JELLYFISH

Tentacles trail more than 50 ft (15 m) from a man-of-war's body.

Sea wasp

IN THE WARM, TROPICAL SEAS surrounding coral islands live some of the most fascinating sea creatures. Despite being so different in appearance, corals, jellyfish, and anemones belong to the same family. The fabulous corals that make up coral reefs are created by little animals called polyps, which look like miniature sea anemones. Every polyp builds a cup-shaped skeleton around itself, and as the polyps grow and die, their skeletons mass together to create a coral reef. Unlike coral-building polyps, jellyfish can move around freely, trailing their long tentacles below their soft bodies as they swim. Some jellyfish float on the surface and are pushed along with the current. Anemones anchor themselves to rocks, where they wait for fish to swim through their tentacles.

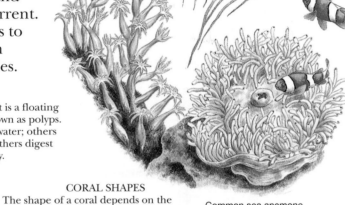
Carijoa coral

JELLYFISH
The sea wasp jellyfish uses its tentacles to sting fish. Tentacles contain venom which is painful to humans and can cause death.

Clown fish

CLOWN FISH
These fish live in harmony with sea anemones. The thick, slimy mucus on their bodies keeps them safe from the stinging cells. Clown fish keep anemones clean by feeding on particles of food among their waving tentacles.

MAN-OF-WAR
The Portuguese man-of-war is not one jellyfish. It is a floating colony of hundreds of jellyfish-like creatures known as polyps. Some polyps form the float, which drifts on the water; others bear stinging tentacles for paralyzing prey; still others digest the prey and pass the nutrients through the body.

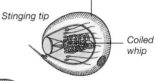
Stinging cell body
Stinging tip
Coiled whip
Whip thrown out

CORAL SHAPES
The shape of a coral depends on the arrangement and growing pattern of the tiny polyps that build it. Corals can be dazzling in color and extraordinary in shape, resembling all kinds of objects. This Carijoa coral looks like a branching tree.

Common sea anemone

Anemone slowly engulfs a trapped fish.

STINGING CELLS
Each jellyfish tentacle is armed with deadly weapons. If a fish touches a tentacle, stinging cells containing tiny coiled-up threads are triggered into action. They shoot out a hollow whip like a harpoon, injecting paralyzing poison into the prey.

ANEMONE
As a fish stops struggling, the anemone's tentacles shorten and pull it into the mouth, through to the stomach chamber in the "body" of the anemone. Any undigested remains pass out later.

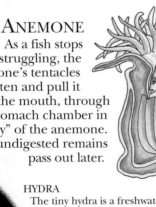

HYDRA
The tiny hydra is a freshwater polyp that lives in ponds. It may be green, brown, or gray in color. Hydras feed on other tiny water creatures which they catch with their tentacles. Each tentacle has stinging cells that contain poison to paralyze the prey. Hydras reproduce by growing "buds" on their "stalk." The buds break off to form new hydras. This is a form of asexual reproduction.

HOW CORAL REEFS ARE FORMED

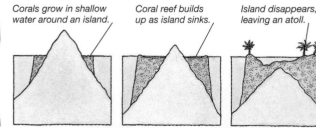
Corals grow in shallow water around an island.
Coral reef builds up as island sinks.
Island disappears, leaving an atoll.

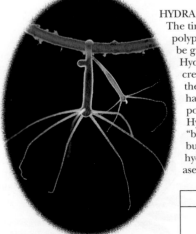

Corals live in shallow water around an island where bright sunlight makes them grow. As movements in the Earth's surface make the island sink, corals form a reef. Finally the island disappears, leaving a ring of reefs called an atoll.

Find out more
ANIMALS
DEEP-SEA WILDLIFE
OCEAN WILDLIFE

COWS,
CATTLE, AND BUFFALOES

EVERY TIME WE EAT ice cream or drink milk, we should thank the dairy cow. Each year, cows, or dairy cattle, provide us with millions of gallons of milk to make many different dairy products. The dairy cow is just one member of the much larger family of animals called cattle. Humans first domesticated cattle about 5,000 years ago. Today, cattle are bred on every continent for their meat, milk, and hides. There are many different kinds of cattle – all have horns, distinctive split (two-toed) hooves, and live in herds. As a group they are often described as ruminants or cud chewers because of the way in which they digest food. Wild cattle include the water buffalo of Central and Southeast Asia and the rare anoa, found in the rain forest of Celebes, in Indonesia.

SACRED COW
Because they provide sustenance, cows are regarded as sacred in parts of Asia. Here the Hindu goddess Parvati is shown seated on a cow.

Horns can be used in defense, but they are sometimes removed by cattle breeders.

Ears can swivel to locate the direction from which a sound comes.

Milk comes from cow's udder.

Tail is used as a fly swatter.

Split (two-toed) hoof

Jersey cow and calf

CHEWING THE CUD
Cattle have large, four-chambered stomachs. They eat grass and other plants, which they swallow and partly digest in the rumen (the first chamber of the stomach). Later, the cow regurgitates, or brings up the coarse, fibrous parts of the food as small masses called cud. The cow chews the cud then swallows it again, and it goes into the reticulum (the second chamber). The food then passes into the omasum and finally into the abomasum, where digestion takes place. This complex method means that the cow can extract all the nutrients from the food.

Small intestine

Rumen

Reticulum

Omasum

Abomasum

Large intestine

Food takes more than three days to pass through the entire digestive system.

North American bison

CATTLE
There are about 12 billion domestic or farm cattle around the world. Their ancestors were wild cattle called aurochs; the last aurochs died out in 1627. Over many years, breeders have developed various types of domestic cattle. Each is suited to a particular climate and produces mainly meat, milk, or hides for leather. Jersey, Guernsey, Ayrshire, and Holstein are dairy (milk-giving) breeds; Hereford, Angus, Charolais, and Brahman are beef (meat-giving) breeds.

BISON
Herds of bison, sometimes mistakenly called buffalo, once roamed the North American plains by the millions. A century ago, however, so many had been killed by settlers that only 500 were left alive. Today, there are about 50,000 bison in America, living in protected wildlife parks. The smaller European bison has also been saved from extinction by being bred in captivity, then released into the wild.

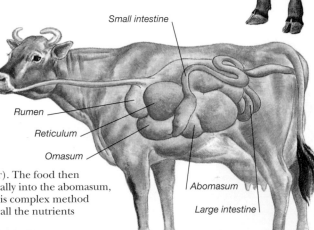

BUFFALO
There are about 130 million domestic water buffaloes in Asia, Europe, North Africa, and South America. They pull farm equipment and provide meat and milk. With their wide hooves and thickset legs, water buffalo can walk easily in mud along riverbanks and lakesides. They are often used to farm flooded rice paddies.

> ### Find out more
> ANIMALS
> FARM ANIMALS
> FARMING
> MAMMALS
> NORTH AMERICAN WILDLIFE

CRABS
AND OTHER CRUSTACEANS

THOUSANDS OF DIFFERENT kinds of crabs scuttle over our sandy shores and skulk in rock pools. They range from tiny parasitic crabs living inside mussels to the giant Japanese spider crab, whose legs can be more than 10 ft (3 m) long. Crabs breathe underwater using gills, but some can also survive out of water for a long time. All crabs are protected by strong, hard shells like a suit of armor on the outside of their bodies. Crabs, along with lobsters and crayfish, belong to the animal group called crustaceans. Their bodies are divided into sections, with jointed limbs and two pairs of antennae on the head. A crab begins life as an egg, which develops into a larva, then into an adult crab. Each time the crab reaches another growing stage, it sheds the outer layer of its shell, revealing a new layer beneath.

HERMIT CRAB
The hermit crab often makes its home in the empty shell of a whelk, which protects it from predators such as gulls.

EDIBLE CRAB
The so-called edible crab is only one of many kinds of crustaceans that are caught, cooked, and eaten by people around the world.

Three sets of mouthparts for sorting food

Fiddler crab

Eye on stalk

Antenna

Huge claw for defense

Carapace (shell)

Eight walking legs

LOBSTER
The lobster scavenges on the seabed for dead fish and other animal remains. One claw has blunt knobs for crushing; the other has sharp "teeth" for cutting. The biggest lobsters are 2 ft (60 cm) long and can live as long as humans – up to 70 years.

Antenna

Crushing claw

Carapace over front part of body

Four pairs of walking limbs

Eye on stalk

Telson (tailpiece)

Six segments on abdomen

SHRIMPS AND PRAWNS
These little sea creatures are good scavengers. During the day they dig into the sand and hide. At night they emerge to hunt for food using their long feelers. When in danger, prawns and shrimps escape by scooting backward with a flick of their tail fan.

Long antenna (feeler)

Shrimp

Tail fan

Feeding claw

Tail fan

Prawn

Feeding claw

Long antenna (feeler)

BARNACLES
These sea crustaceans have no heads. Their long, feathery legs beat the water, collecting tiny food particles. Acorn barnacles live in volcano-shaped shells cemented onto rocks. Goose barnacles attach themselves to driftwood by their stalks.

Goose barnacles

Acorn barnacles

WHERE CRUSTACEANS LIVE
Some crustaceans such as the yabby (a freshwater shrimp) and the water flea live in rivers and lakes. A few crustaceans live on land. The woodlouse, for example, can be found under dead leaves and in damp woodland areas.

Woodlouse

Water flea

Yabby

Find out more
ANIMALS
OCEAN WILDLIFE
SEASHORE WILDLIFE

CROCODILES AND ALLIGATORS

LOOKING LIKE AN OLD LOG, lying low in the water but ready to snap up almost any animal, the crocodile seems like a survivor from a prehistoric age – and it is. One hundred million years ago, crocodiles prowled through the swamps with the dinosaurs. Crocodiles and alligators belong to the reptile group called crocodilians. This group includes 14 kinds of crocodiles, seven kinds of alligators (five of which are commonly called caimans), and one kind of gavial. Crocodilians are carnivorous (meat-eating) reptiles; they lurk in rivers, lakes, and swamps, grabbing whatever prey they can. Crocodiles and alligators eat fish and frogs whole. They drag larger prey such as deer under the water, where they grip the animal in their jaws and spin rapidly, tearing off chunks of flesh. Crocodiles and alligators occasionally eat humans.

Nile crocodiles measure up to 20 ft (6 m) long and weigh more than 1 ton.

Female carries the young in her mouth.

CROCODILE
The fourth tooth on each side of the crocodile's lower jaw is visible when the mouth is closed.

ALLIGATOR
Unlike crocodiles, no lower teeth are visible when the alligator's mouth is closed.

CAIMAN
The caiman has a broad mouth for eating a variety of prey.

GAVIAL
The gavial has a long, slender mouth with sharp teeth for catching fish.

NILE CROCODILE
The Nile crocodile is found in many watery parts of Africa. Like most reptiles, the female lays eggs, which she looks after until they hatch. The newly hatched young listen for their mother's footsteps and call to her. She gently gathers them into her mouth in batches and carries them to the safety of the water.

YOUNG
After about three months, the young crocodiles hatch out of the eggs. The mother guards them closely because they are in danger of becoming food for large lizards and foxes.

CROCODILE SMILE
Crocodiles often bask in the sun with their mouths wide open. Blood vessels inside the mouth absorb the sun's warmth. This raises the animal's body temperature and gives the crocodile the energy to hunt for its prey in the evening.

ALLIGATOR
There are two kinds of true alligators – the Chinese and the American alligators. Today, the Chinese alligator is in great danger of extinction – only a few hundred survive. The American alligator lives in rivers and swamps across the southeastern United States, where it eats fish, water birds, and anything else it can catch. In more populated areas, the American alligator also grabs unwary farm animals.

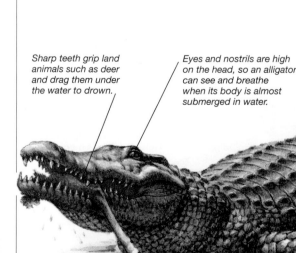

Sharp teeth grip land animals such as deer and drag them under the water to drown.

Eyes and nostrils are high on the head, so an alligator can see and breathe when its body is almost submerged in water.

Long tail swishes back and forth for rapid swimming.

American alligator

Legs fold along body when alligator is swimming.

| *Find out more* |
| ANIMALS |
| LIZARDS |
| PREHISTORIC LIFE |

CROWS, JAYS, AND RAVENS

THE MEMBERS OF THE CROW FAMILY are among the best known of all birds because of their large size, bold habits, and noisy "crowing" calls. There are 117 kinds of crows. They include carrion crows, jays, magpies, ravens, and rooks. Many crows in Europe, North America, Africa, and Australia live in open countryside and are pests to farmers because they eat seeds and grains. In Asia and South America, however, some jays and magpies live in dense forests and are seldom seen. Crows have varied diets. Apart from seeds, they eat fruit, insects, small mammals, and dead animals, as well as birds' eggs and nestlings. They are good mimics and can imitate the sounds of other birds, animals, and human speech. In bird intelligence tests, members of the crow family, particularly jackdaws and ravens, score higher than any other birds.

ROOKERIES
Rooks breed in colonies high in the treetops. They build big nests of sticks and twigs early in spring.

COMMON CROW
Crows can be a nuisance to farmers because they spoil their crops. These clever birds are rarely fooled for long by a scarecrow standing in the field.

Crows often feed on newly planted seeds.

MAGPIE
The magpie is famous as a bird thief. It is attracted by bright objects it spots on the ground. It is known to make off with coins, jewelry, and other shiny objects, which it then hides or buries. Magpies live in Europe, North America, North Africa, and Asia.

JAY
The brightly colored European jay lives mainly in woodlands, where it feeds on acorns, beechnuts, fruit, and berries. The blue jay is beautifully patterned in blue and black, and lives among the trees in parks and gardens of central and eastern North America. There are also colorful jays in Asia.

RAVEN
The raven is the largest of the crow family, with a wingspan of 6 ft (2 m). Ravens were once thought to bring bad luck, probably because they fed on the dead bodies of criminals left hanging on the gallows.

Leg feathers puffed out

Head feathers fluffed out

CROW COURTSHIP
Many crows perform elaborate dances and displays in the breeding season, when the male courts the female. Here a male raven puffs out his feathers and bows to his partner while making *kaaa*-ing sounds.

JACKDAW
Tree holes and chimney tops provide nesting places for the European jackdaw. It builds a nest of twigs lined with grass, hair, fur, and wool plucked from the backs of sheep. Like magpies, jackdaws are attracted to shiny objects.

Male raven performing bowing ceremony

Find out more
BIRDS
FLIGHT, ANIMAL

CRUSADES

NINE CENTURIES AGO, the Pope appealed to Christians to recapture the holy city of Jerusalem from the Turkish Muslims who had seized it. Thousands of European Christians – knights, princes, pilgrims, and peasants – responded to the call and set out on a long warring pilgrimage, called a crusade, from western Europe to Palestine (now Israel). Four years later, after battles, starvation, and disease, the surviving crusaders captured the city of Jerusalem. The crusaders set up a Christian kingdom on the shores of Palestine that lasted nearly a century. But in 1187, Saladin recaptured Jerusalem. At least seven more crusades set out. None were successful, but links between Europe and the Middle East were established that still continue today.

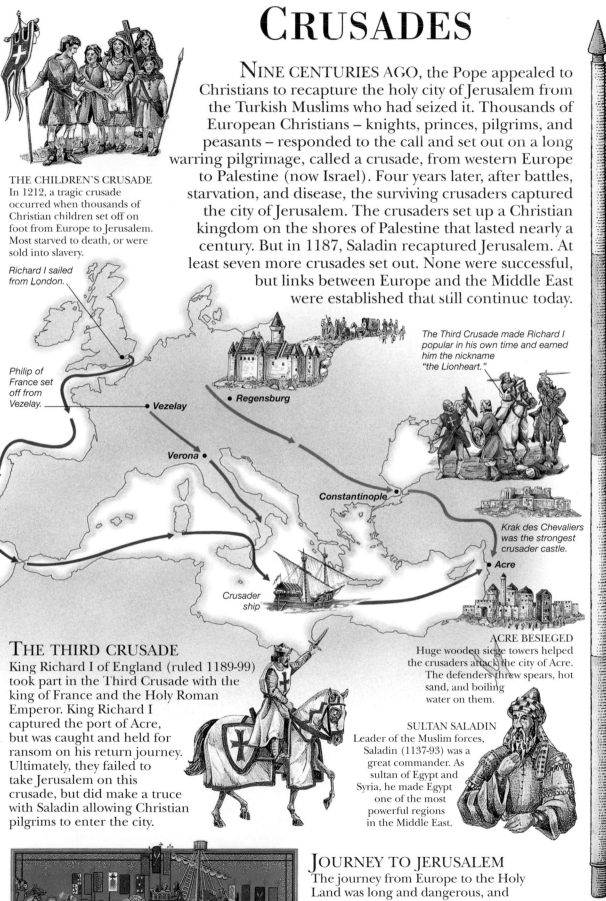

THE CHILDREN'S CRUSADE
In 1212, a tragic crusade occurred when thousands of Christian children set off on foot from Europe to Jerusalem. Most starved to death, or were sold into slavery.

Richard I sailed from London.

Philip of France set off from Vezelay.

• **Vezelay**

• **Regensburg**

Verona •

The Third Crusade made Richard I popular in his own time and earned him the nickname "the Lionheart."

Constantinople

Krak des Chevaliers was the strongest crusader castle.

• **Acre**

Crusader ship

ACRE BESIEGED
Huge wooden siege towers helped the crusaders attack the city of Acre. The defenders threw spears, hot sand, and boiling water on them.

THE THIRD CRUSADE
King Richard I of England (ruled 1189-99) took part in the Third Crusade with the king of France and the Holy Roman Emperor. King Richard I captured the port of Acre, but was caught and held for ransom on his return journey. Ultimately, they failed to take Jerusalem on this crusade, but did make a truce with Saladin allowing Christian pilgrims to enter the city.

SULTAN SALADIN
Leader of the Muslim forces, Saladin (1137-93) was a great commander. As sultan of Egypt and Syria, he made Egypt one of the most powerful regions in the Middle East.

JOURNEY TO JERUSALEM
The journey from Europe to the Holy Land was long and dangerous, and many of the crusaders died on the way. Those who went back to Europe from Palestine took silks and spices with them, as well as Islamic learning such as mathematics and astronomy.

___ *Find out more* ___
CASTLES
WEAPONS

THE CRUSADES

1096 First Crusade (also known as the People's Crusade) sets off. Many peasants die on the way, though knights survive.

1097 Crusaders arrive in Constantinople (now Istanbul).

1098 French and Norman armies capture Antioch.

1099 Crusaders capture Jerusalem. Divide coastal land into four kingdoms.

1147-49 Second Crusade attacks Muslims in Spain, Portugal, and Asia Minor.

1187 Saladin conquers Jerusalem and most of Palestine.

1189 Third Crusade sets off led by the kings of England and France and Frederick I, the Holy Roman Emperor. Frederick dies on the way.

1191-92 Crusaders capture Acre but return to Europe.

1202-04 Fourth Crusade sets off. Crusaders capture Constantinople and steal treasure.

1217 Fifth Crusade sets off. Crusaders capture Damietta, Egypt, but return it and make a truce.

1228-29 Sixth Crusade. Emperor Frederick II makes a 10-year truce.

1248-50 Seventh Crusade. Louis IX of France captures Damietta but is forced to return it.

1270 Eighth Crusade. Louis IX dies. This final crusade returns to Europe.

DAMS

EVERY DAY, FACTORIES and homes use up huge amounts of water. For example, an oil refinery uses 10 times as much water as the gasoline it makes. Dams help to provide us with much of the water we need by trapping water from flowing rivers. Building a dam across a river creates a huge lake, called a reservoir, behind the dam. Reservoirs also provide water to irrigate large areas of farmland. A reservoir can store the water that falls in rainy seasons so that there is water during dry periods. By storing water in this way, dams also prevent floods. Flood barriers are dams that can stop the sea from surging up a river and bursting its banks. Some dams provide electricity as well as water. They contain hydroelectric power stations powered by water from their reservoirs.

Lake Mead

Lift shaft inside dam goes down to hydroelectric power station.

Water from the reservoir enters the intake towers.

Roadway along top of dam

Arched, concrete dam wall

Water flows down pipes to hydroelectric power station.

Pipes carry excess water to the Colorado River so that the dam does not break or overflow.

Hoover dam

Tunnel that was excavated to divert river while dam was built.

Dam shown with water removed from one side.

CONCRETE DAMS
There are two main types of concrete dam: arch dams and gravity dams. Arch dams (either single-arch or multiple-arch) are tall, curved shells of concrete as little as 10 ft (3 m) thick. Because their arched shape makes them very strong, they do not burst. Large gravity dams are also made of concrete. Their vast weight keeps them from giving way.

Water flows down to Colorado River.

Hydroelectric power station

Overflow water

HOOVER DAM
The Hoover Dam in the United States, one of the world's highest concrete dams, is 726 ft (221 m) high. It is an arch dam that spans the Colorado River, supplying water for irrigation and electricity to California, Arizona, and Nevada. Lake Mead, the reservoir formed by the dam, is 115 miles (185 km) long.

EMBANKMENT DAMS
The biggest dams are embankment dams, made by piling up a huge barrier of earth and rock. A core of clay or concrete in the center keeps water from seeping through the dam. The side is covered with stones to protect it from the water. The world's highest dam is the Rogunsky Dam in Tajikistan, an embankment dam 1,066 ft (325 m) high.

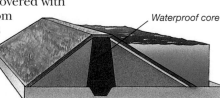

Waterproof core

FLOOD BARRIERS
Movable dams called flood barriers are built on rivers to control flooding. Built in 1982, this barrier across the Thames River in England protects London from flooding by North Sea gales. Large, curved gates rise if the river gets too high.

THE EFFECTS OF DAMS
The reservoir that forms in the valley behind a dam floods the land, often damaging the environment. For example, the Aswan High Dam in Egypt was built to control the flooding of the Nile River, but changing the river's flow has destroyed the fertility of the surrounding land.

A dam prevents fish, such as salmon, from swimming up and down a river. Some dams have a fish ladder, a pipe, or pools through which fish can swim past the dam.

Find out more
ELECTRICITY
FARMING
LAKES
RIVERS
WATER

DANCE

WHEN PEOPLE HEAR MUSIC, they often tap their feet and clap their hands. Dancing is a natural activity, and there are many different styles, ranging from the hectic breakdance to the graceful, elegant waltz. However, all forms of dance share the same rhythmic movements that people have enjoyed since time began. Prehistoric cave paintings show people moving in a lively way. They kept time by clapping and stamping. Later, dancers began to move in patterns with more formal steps, and dancing in couples or in groups at balls or dances became a part of social life. In many countries special costumes are part of folk-dancing traditions.

RITUAL DANCE
In religious rituals, dance is a way of thanking the gods or asking for their help. These Native Americans are performing a fertility dance. It is important that the steps are always danced in the same order.

Square dancers often dress up in cowboy or cowgirl style.

This modern jazz dancer combines the grace and elegance of traditional ballet with soft, fluid poses that more closely express personal feelings. The swirling movements of her dress complement and enhance her performance.

SQUARE DANCING
Square dancing is very sociable. Four couples form a square and change partners in a sequence of moves. A caller shouts out instructions such as "Swing your partner to the right." This traditional North American dance has many variations.

MODERN DANCE
Most traditional dances have a prearranged series of steps and movements, but modern dance forms encourage dancers to move more freely. Contemporary dance emerged at the beginning of the 20th century. U.S. dancer Isadora Duncan was one of the first performers to move away from orthodox ballet and develop her own style. Jazz dance emerged in the 1920s and has been central to modern dance.

Love – putting on a ring

Marriage – tying the love knot around the bride's neck

MIME
Mime mixes dance and acting to create a language without words that can be understood by people from many cultures. The dancer shown here is from India, but mime is also part of other Eastern and Western dance styles.

Modern dancers often devise their own steps and perform barefoot.

There are six styles of Indian classical dance. These styles usually involve miming out stories from ancient mythology.

ROCK 'N' ROLL
The emergence of rock 'n' roll music in the 1950s led to the first mass form of modern dance. The music had a strong beat and lyrics that young people could relate to. Rock 'n' roll steps were wild and daring, and were very different to conservative social dancing.

DANCE AND WORSHIP
In India, almost all performing arts are linked to religion. *Bharatanatyam* is a classical dance style from Tamil Nadu, southern India. It is linked to ancient temple dances. Performers paint their hands and feet with red dye. In ancient times, the dancers came from special families and were known as *devadasis*.

Find out more
BALLET
INDIA
MOVIES

CHARLES
DARWIN

ON DECEMBER 27, 1831, the *Beagle* sailed from Plymouth, England to survey the east and west coasts of South America. On board was the ship's naturalist, Charles Darwin. The ship sailed beyond the Americas to the Pacific Ocean, where Darwin made many scientific discoveries, especially on the Galapagos and Keeling Islands. As a schoolboy, Darwin had often been in trouble with his teachers for spending time on chemistry experiments and collecting specimens instead of studying Greek and Latin. His boyhood interest in the natural world, however, led him to make startling discoveries about life on Earth and the development of the planet. When he returned from sea in 1836, he married, settled in London, and wrote up the notes of his discoveries. These formed the basis of his famous theory of evolution.

1809 Born in Shrewsbury, Shropshire, England.

1825-27 Studies medicine at Edinburgh University.

1827 Studies religion at Cambridge University, but spends more time on biology, zoology, and geology.

1831-36 *Beagle* voyage.

1858 Evolutionary theory first explained to the world.

1859 Publishes *On the Origin of Species* – it is a bestseller.

1882 Dies; buried at Westminster Abbey, London.

The *Beagle*

Darwin made careful notes of everything he observed.

Galapagos finch

Galapagos tortoise

VOYAGE OF THE *BEAGLE*

On the five-year voyage, the *Beagle* made many stops, during which Darwin studied plant and animal life, and land formation. On the outward-bound journey, the ship sailed to the Canaries, across the Atlantic (where Darwin realized that the Cape Verde Islands had been made by volcanoes erupting under the sea), along South America's east coast, around Cape Horn, and up the west coast, where he witnessed an earthquake.

PACIFIC OCEAN

Galapagos Islands

NORTH PACIFIC OCEAN

SOUTH ATLANTIC OCEAN

Darwin studied the wildlife in the isolated Galapagos Islands.

The ship returned via New Zealand, Australia, and the Keeling Islands.

THE ORIGIN OF SPECIES
As a result of his study of wildlife on the Galapagos Islands, Darwin began to believe that species (types of plants and animals) were not fixed forever, but that they evolved (changed) to suit their environment. In 1859, he published *On the Origin of Species,* a book in which he set out his evolutionary theory, suggesting that humans evolved from apes.

ALFRED WALLACE
Welsh naturalist Alfred Wallace (1823-1923) carried out studies that led him to agree with Darwin's theories. He traveled to the Amazon and to Malaysia, where he began to think that nature encouraged the survival of the fittest. He sent Darwin an article, and friends encouraged them both to publish their views. On July 1, 1858, members of the scientific Linnaean Society heard papers by both men.

CORAL
On the Keeling Islands, Darwin studied coral reefs, whose structure was not understood at the time. He thought they were formed by coral building up on the sea floor while the floor itself was gently subsiding. Modern deep-sea drillings have since proved that Darwin was right.

Find out more

CORALS, ANEMONES
and jellyfish
EVOLUTION
FOSSILS
GEOLOGY

DECLARATION OF INDEPENDENCE

WITH ITS BOLD PROCLAMATION that the people have a right to a government of their own choice, the Declaration of Independence announced the separation of the 13 North American colonies from Great Britain in 1776. When armed conflict began between Britain and its colonies in 1775, few American colonists wanted separation from British rule. Instead, they sought to gain a voice in the British government. However, as Britain clamped down on its rebels, sending large armies to the colonies, support grew for the colonists to secure their freedom outside the Empire. In the summer of 1776, the Continental Congress met in Philadelphia to draft a document – the Declaration of Independence – explaining why the colonists should be free to govern themselves.

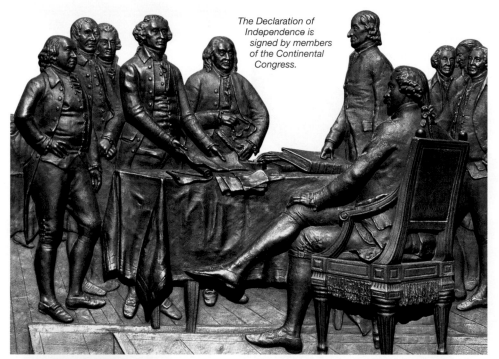

The Declaration of Independence is signed by members of the Continental Congress.

THOMAS JEFFERSON
Thomas Jefferson (1743-1826), a wealthy Virginian landowner and lawyer, drew on his knowledge of political philosophy to craft the Declaration. Jefferson died on July 4, 1826, on the fiftieth anniversary of the Declaration.

THE FOUNDERS

The language of the Declaration summed up years of colonial frustration with British rule, asserting that "all men are created equal" and are thus entitled to "life, liberty, and the pursuit of happiness." Among the five men who served on the committee to draft the Declaration were two future presidents – John Adams and Thomas Jefferson – and Benjamin Franklin, a writer, scientist, and diplomat who was, in his lifetime, one of the most famous men in the world. These men are often called America's "founding fathers."

FOURTH OF JULY

The Declaration of Independence was adopted on July 4, 1776. To mark this great event, the Fourth of July, or Independence Day, is celebrated as a great national holiday. Philadelphia's citizens marked the first anniversary of freedom with a spontaneous celebration, and in 1873 Pennsylvania became the first state to declare Independence Day a holiday. Now, Americans mark the day with barbecues, picnics, family gatherings, and fireworks.

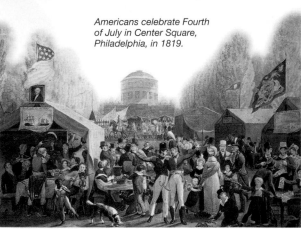

Americans celebrate Fourth of July in Center Square, Philadelphia, in 1819.

LIBERTY BELL
This famous symbol of American independence was rung every Fourth of July until a crack silenced it in 1948. The bell is displayed in Philadelphia at the Independence National Historical Park.

SIGNATORIES
After its adoption, the Declaration was copied onto parchment and signed by 56 members of the Continental Congress. One signature, by John Hancock, is much larger than the others. Today, Americans often ask for your "John Hancock" when they want your signature.

Find out more

AMERICAN REVOLUTION
COLONIES
and colonial America
FRANKLIN, BENJAMIN
JEFFERSON, THOMAS

DEEP-SEA WILDLIFE

THE DEPTHS OF THE SEA form the largest wildlife habitat on Earth. In waters below about 3,000 ft (1,000 m), no plants can grow because there is no sunlight. Yet, here, in the vast blackness, many extraordinary creatures live. These animals are found nowhere else. They have adapted to survive where the water pressure is up to 1,000 times that at the surface. Some deep-sea fish feed on the bodies and remains of plants and animals that sink down from the water above. Some other fish have enormous mouths and long, back-curved teeth for grabbing and swallowing anything that swims by. These fish have huge stomachs that stretch to hold prey that is even bigger than themselves. On the deep-sea floor, sea anemones, worms, sea cucumbers, brittlestars, crabs, prawns, and other shellfish sieve the mud searching for tiny particles of food. Many kinds of deep-sea squid, shrimps, and jellyfish are also found here.

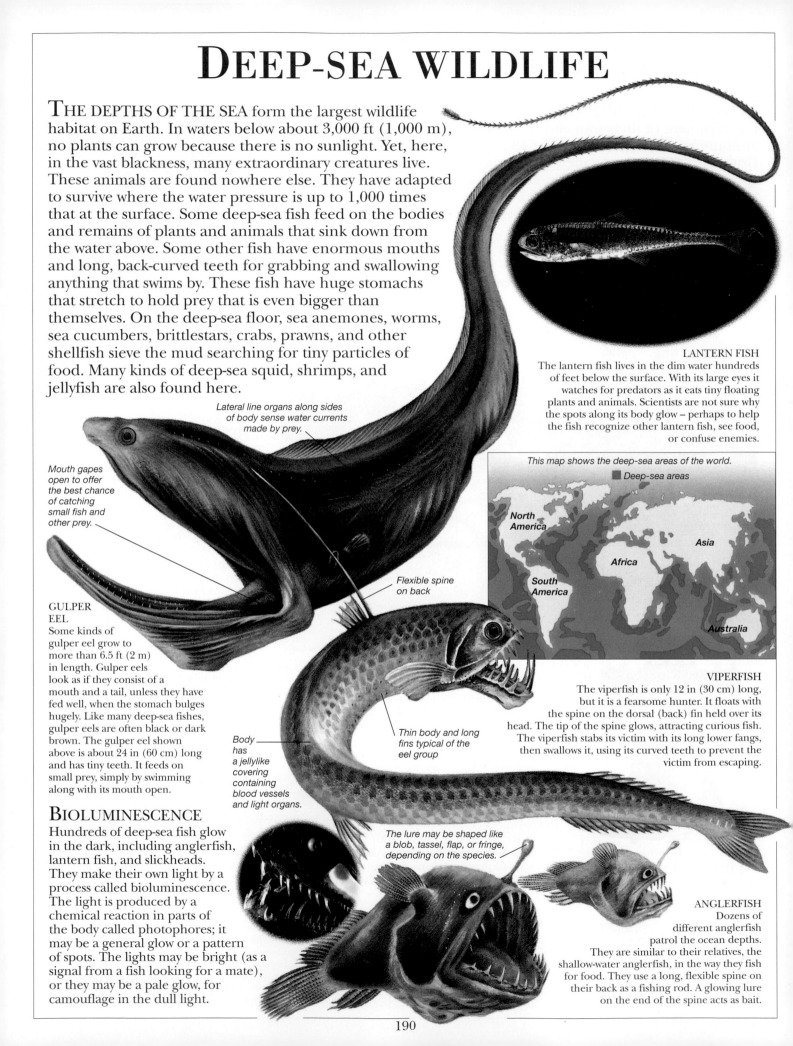

LANTERN FISH
The lantern fish lives in the dim water hundreds of feet below the surface. With its large eyes it watches for predators as it eats tiny floating plants and animals. Scientists are not sure why the spots along its body glow – perhaps to help the fish recognize other lantern fish, see food, or confuse enemies.

Lateral line organs along sides of body sense water currents made by prey.

Mouth gapes open to offer the best chance of catching small fish and other prey.

This map shows the deep-sea areas of the world.
■ *Deep-sea areas*

North America
South America
Africa
Asia
Australia

Flexible spine on back

GULPER EEL
Some kinds of gulper eel grow to more than 6.5 ft (2 m) in length. Gulper eels look as if they consist of a mouth and a tail, unless they have fed well, when the stomach bulges hugely. Like many deep-sea fishes, gulper eels are often black or dark brown. The gulper eel shown above is about 24 in (60 cm) long and has tiny teeth. It feeds on small prey, simply by swimming along with its mouth open.

Body has a jellylike covering containing blood vessels and light organs.

Thin body and long fins typical of the eel group

VIPERFISH
The viperfish is only 12 in (30 cm) long, but it is a fearsome hunter. It floats with the spine on the dorsal (back) fin held over its head. The tip of the spine glows, attracting curious fish. The viperfish stabs its victim with its long lower fangs, then swallows it, using its curved teeth to prevent the victim from escaping.

BIOLUMINESCENCE
Hundreds of deep-sea fish glow in the dark, including anglerfish, lantern fish, and slickheads. They make their own light by a process called bioluminescence. The light is produced by a chemical reaction in parts of the body called photophores; it may be a general glow or a pattern of spots. The lights may be bright (as a signal from a fish looking for a mate), or they may be a pale glow, for camouflage in the dull light.

The lure may be shaped like a blob, tassel, flap, or fringe, depending on the species.

ANGLERFISH
Dozens of different anglerfish patrol the ocean depths. They are similar to their relatives, the shallow-water anglerfish, in the way they fish for food. They use a long, flexible spine on their back as a fishing rod. A glowing lure on the end of the spine acts as bait.

CONSERVATION

Unlike other wildlife areas, such as the rain forests, the deep sea is not in great danger from habitat loss or pollution. However, harmful polluting chemicals have been found at great depths. Fishing boats have also overfished many shallow seas and are now fishing in deeper waters. Deep-sea fish such as these orange roughy fish (right) may soon be in danger because of overfishing.

Fang tooth has a lure on head to attract small fish.

Needlelike teeth give the fang tooth fish its name.

Thin body shape and light organs along underside may reduce the risk of being seen from below by a predator.

Hatchetfish

Eyes have large yellow lenses to spy prey, especially small glowing fish and shellfish.

SULFUR VENTS

At some places on the sea floor, hot water and gases bubble up through the rocks. These places are called sulfur vents. They emit (give out) energy-rich chemicals that are used by bacteria for growth. Other animals feed on the bacteria. Blind crabs and giant worms 10 ft (3 m) long live around the vents. They are thc only creatures that do not depend on the sun for energy.

SEA LILY
This animal is an upside-down version of its relative, the starfish. It is attached to the seabed by a stalk. Its branched tentacles gather and trap food, then sweep it to the mouth in a stream of mucus (spit).

DEEP-SEA SQUID
Squid swim among the sea lilies, hunting for fish and other prey. The giant squid also swims near the sea bottom.

SEA CUCUMBER
The cylindrical-shaped sea cucumber is an animal, and a relative of the starfish. It has a frill of tentacles at one end, around the mouth. These tentacles sweep up bits of food from the muddy floor as the sea cucumber moves along on its many tubed feet.

Sea cucumber

Sea lily

HATCHETFISH
The deep-sea hatchetfish has a tall, thin body, shaped like an ax-head. It looks like its relative, the freshwater hatchetfish. The deep-sea hatchetfish stays about 1,700 ft (500 m) below the surface by day and swims up at night to eat tiny shellfish and other floating food.

LIFE ON THE SEABED

Many kinds of animals filter, sieve, and sift the water and muddy sludge on the sea floor for tiny pieces of food. In places where ocean currents bring abundant food, these creatures cover the seabed. Most of them are blind and slow-moving. When some deep-sea fish are brought to the surface, the decrease in water pressure makes them swell and burst. Scientists study them with special remote-control led submersibles, which can carry cameras as deep as 20,000 ft (6,000 m).

Find out more

ATMOSPHERE
FISH
OCEAN WILDLIFE
OCTOPUSES AND SQUID
STARFISH AND SEA URCHINS
UNDERWATER EXPLORATION

DEER, ANTELOPES, AND GAZELLES

The pronghorn antelope of North America is one of the fastest animals on land. It sprints at almost 55 mph (90 km/h) – as fast as a car.

MAJESTIC ANTLERS and graceful movements give deer an impressive appearance. Deer and their relatives, antelopes and gazelles, are well-equipped to flee from danger. Their brown or gray coloring acts as camouflage, and their excellent hearing, sight, and smell help them to detect predators and leap away with great speed. There are 47 kinds of deer. They are mainly woodland creatures, but some, such as reindeer (caribou), live in the frozen Arctic. Antelopes and gazelles are found mostly in deserts and open grasslands. Other members of this group include the wildebeest, or gnu, and the dik-dik.

REINDEER
Reindeer, or caribou, live in Scandinavia, North America, and Siberia, in the Russian Federation. Both male and female caribou have antlers. Only the males of other kinds of deer have antlers.

Male red deer is called a stag or buck.

Female deer is called a hind or doe.

Reindeer stags rutting

Deer, antelopes, and gazelles graze on plants in the same way as cows and sheep.

Male fallow deer's antlers are palmate (flattened).

This antelope's horns have a ridged pattern.

Points (tips of topmost antler branches)

Soft layer of velvety fur covers growing antler.

Tines (tips of lower antler branches)

Layers of bone inside antler

Bony connection to skull

HORNS AND ANTLERS
Antelopes, cattle, and gazelles have horns on their heads which grow throughout life. Horns are made of a bone core covered with keratin, and some are twisted like corkscrews. Male deer have antlers on their heads, made of bone. The deer sheds and grows a new set of antlers each year.

Young red deer is called a fawn.

Eland measures up to 6 ft (2 m) high at the shoulder and 11 ft (3.5 m) in length.

Royal antelope measures 10 in (25 cm) at the shoulder.

A 10-year-old child measures about 4 ft (1.2 m).

ANTELOPES
There are about 100 different kinds of antelope. These hoofed mammals are closely related to cattle and goats. The eland is the largest antelope. It is found in grassland areas of eastern and southern Africa. Elands do not need to drink often because they absorb enough water from the plants they eat. Elands live for about 15 years. The royal antelope, from western Africa, is the smallest antelope.

HERDS
Most deer, antelopes, and gazelles live in groups called herds. During the fall, male deer battle with each other to gain a harem – a group of females – and sometimes for territory. Red deer males roar at each other, lock antlers, and try to push their opponent to the ground. This behavior is called rutting. Usually, the largest, strongest males win. These large males then defend their group and its territory against other herds.

FAWN
The red deer calf, or fawn, is born in late spring and stays hidden in the undergrowth. Its spotted coat provides good camouflage in the dappled shade. The spots soon fade and the coat changes to rusty reddish brown.

Find out more

AFRICAN WILDLIFE
FOREST WILDLIFE
NORTH AMERICAN WILDLIFE

DEMOCRACY

THE WORD "DEMOCRACY" COMES FROM the ancient Greek words *demos,* which means "people," and *kratia,* which means "power." Democracy means "rule by the people." Within a democracy, all persons have the right to play a part in the government of their country. In most democracies, all persons over the age of 18 can elect a member of parliament to represent them in the national government; and a councillor – their representative in local government. Occasionally they vote about an issue in a referendum. Twenty-five hundred years ago the people of Athens, Greece, practised a form of democracy. Men met in one place to decide on laws for their community. Today, most democracy is representative. Because there are usually too many people in a country to be involved in making every decision, the people elect representatives to make decisions on their behalf.

A poster showing political parties campaigning for votes in the United States, 1908.

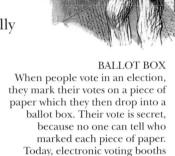

BALLOT BOX
When people vote in an election, they mark their votes on a piece of paper which they then drop into a ballot box. Their vote is secret, because no one can tell who marked each piece of paper. Today, electronic voting booths are replacing ballot boxes.

REPRESENTATIVE DEMOCRACY
Representative democracy means that citizens vote for certain people to represent them. People form political parties and citizens vote for their favored party in elections. The different parties compete with each other for votes in election campaigns. Getting the right to vote (suffrage) has been a dedicated struggle for both men and women. Today, adult men and women in most countries can vote.

Indians queue to cast their vote at polling booths around the country.

MAJORITY RULE
Democracy means government by the people, but one group of people might want to do one thing and another group something completely different. In that case, the view of the majority (the larger group of people) rules. This could lead to the views of the minority being ignored, so many democratic countries and organizations have a constitution (a set of rules) that safeguards the rights of individuals and minorities. A few countries still do not have a democracy and are ruled by just one person, usually called a "dictator."

Pro-democracy demonstrators in former Czechoslovakia light candles at a vigil.

Minority vote

Majority vote

VOTING
India is the biggest representative democracy in the world: more than 600 million people are able to vote. In the general election of 2004, close to 400 million people went to the polling stations to vote for their representatives in the national parliament. When so many people vote, it can take several days for all the votes to be counted.

EASTERN EUROPE
From 1989, people in Communist Eastern Europe demanded democratic governments. They felt they did not have enough say in how their countries were run. In 1990, what was then Czechoslovakia became the first of many Eastern European Communist countries to declare themselves a real democracy.

Find out more
COMMUNISM
GOVERNMENT AND POLITICS
GREECE, ANCIENT
LAW

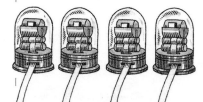

DEPRESSION
OF THE 1930s

IN OCTOBER 1929, prices on the New York Stock Exchange crashed and investors lost vast amounts of money. This was the beginning of an economic depression, or slump, which was to affect the whole world throughout the following decade. The crash caused untold panic and the near-collapse of the American economy. Banks stopped lending money, factories closed, and trade declined. The result was mass unemployment: by 1932, as many as 13.7 million US workers were unemployed. The depression quickly spread across the world and hit almost every nation. Many countries had relied on loans from the United States to help them recover from World War I (1914-18). Now these loans stopped.

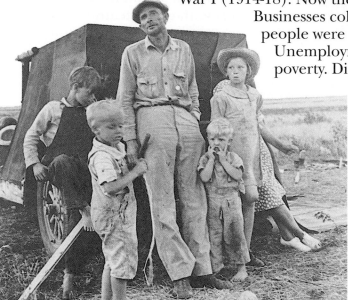

Businesses collapsed, and millions of people were thrown out of work. Unemployment caused misery and poverty. Disillusioned and frightened people turned to extreme right-wing political parties, such as the National Socialist German Workers' (Nazi) Party in Germany. The buildup to World War II ended the Depression, because increased production of arms created jobs.

DUST BOWL

During the 1930s, a terrible drought turned the soil of the American plains into dust. High winds blew clouds of dust over fields and farms, which hid the sunlight. The region became known as the Dust Bowl. Many ruined farmers were forced to trek across the country to find work in the orchards and farms of California.

TENNESSEE VALLEY AUTHORITY
When Franklin D. Roosevelt became US president in 1932, he set up many programs to improve the economy. The Tennessee Valley Authority was given money to employ people to build massive dams and hydroelectric power stations in southeastern United States.

Amount of sales on the New York Stock Exchange 1929-32.

WALL STREET CRASH
On October 24, 1929, known as "Black Thursday," the boom years that had followed World War I came to an end. To get richer, people had been investing a lot of money in the New York Stock Exchange. When it crashed, people wildly tried to sell their shares. In two months, stock values had declined by one-third. Many people lost all their savings, and thousands of companies collapsed.

JARROW MARCH
In Britain, mass unemployment led to "hunger marches." In 1936, some 200 out-of-work and hungry men marched 300 miles (480 km) from Jarrow, in the northeast of England, to the capital, London, in order to draw people's attention to their plight.

Find out more
GERMANY, HISTORY OF
ROOSEVELT, FRANKLIN DELANO
WORLD WAR I
WORLD WAR II

DESERTS

ONE FIFTH OF THE EARTH'S LAND consists of dry, hostile regions called deserts, empty of all but a few plants, the hardiest of animals, and some wandering tribes. Life for desert dwellers, such as the Bedouin nomads who roam the Middle East, is a constant fight for survival, because food and water are scarce.

Little rain falls in deserts because the air is warm and no clouds can form. The clear skies make most deserts scorch with the sun's heat by day; but with no clouds to trap heat, the temperature may drop below freezing at night. Not all deserts are blazing hot and covered with vast stretches of sand; many are strewn with rocks, and deserts in some parts of Asia are often cold because they lie at high altitudes. New deserts can form in regions where droughts often occur and where people cut down all the trees, or allow their animals to eat all the plants, a process called overgrazing. During the 1970s, drought and overgrazing turned the Sahel region of Central Africa into desert, and the problem still exists today.

MONUMENT VALLEY
Fantastic columns of rock adorn Monument Valley, Utah. Sand carried by the wind wears away the rock to form pillars with extraordinary shapes.

SAND

Desert temperatures soar by day and plunge by night. Rock continually expands and contracts as it warms and cools, and its surface breaks up into fragments. These fragments are blown by the wind and grind down other rocks. Eventually, millions of tiny pieces of rock cover the desert as sand. But the wind may also blow away the sand and leave bare rock or stony ground.

SAND DUNES
Many deserts contain huge mounds of sand called dunes. The wind heaps up sand to form the dunes, which slowly advance over the desert as the wind blows. The dunes are like waves of sand and can be 100 ft (33 m) high or more.

SANDSTORMS
Strong winds blow sand and dust, which sweep over the desert in swirling clouds. High winds can blow fine particles of dust across entire continents.

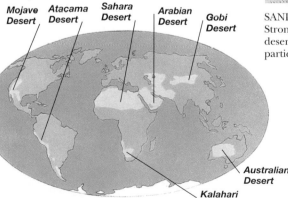

Mojave Desert
Atacama Desert
Sahara Desert
Arabian Desert
Gobi Desert
Australian Desert
Kalahari Desert

DESERTS OF THE WORLD
Two great belts of desert climate encircle the world on either side of the equator. Deserts also form in regions sheltered from rain by high mountains. The largest desert in the world is the Sahara in North Africa, covering an area of more than 3.5 million sq miles (9 million sq km). Some cold deserts lie in the hearts of continents where the winds are dry.

OASES
Desert travelers often seek an oasis, pockets of water in the desert. The water comes from a great distance and flows under the desert, reaching the surface in springs. This oasis is in the Tamerza Desert, Tunisia.

IRRIGATION
Irrigation can change desert regions into green and fertile land. The water may come from dams across nearby rivers, or it may be pumped up from wells in the ground.

Find out more
CAMELS AND LLAMAS
CLIMATES
DESERT WILDLIFE

DESERT WILDLIFE

THE VAST, DRY EXPANSE OF A DESERT may look uninhabited, but all kinds of plants and animals survive in these sandy regions – including insects, reptiles, mammals, and fish. Deserts are the driest places on Earth; some have less than 4 in (10 cm) of rainfall each year. Desert animals have adapted to the lack of water in various ways. Camels, for example, can survive for a long time without drinking. Other animals find enough water in the plants and insects they eat, so they never have to drink at all. Plants such as baobab trees have deep-growing roots to search for water underground.

Other problems for desert wildlife are the extremes of temperature and the lack of shelter. Some deserts are scorching hot; others are freezing cold. Desert mammals have thick fur to keep out heat as well as cold. Many find shelter from the sun and icy winds by digging burrows. In hot deserts, animals stay in their burrows by day and hunt at night when the temperature is lower.

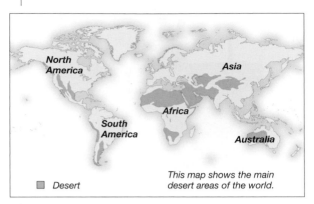

Desert

This map shows the main desert areas of the world.

MONGOOSE
These adaptable mammals hunt by day for all kinds of small animals, including bees, spiders, scorpions, mice, and snakes. A mongoose has extremely quick reactions, so it can easily dodge an enemy such as a snake. The mongoose then leaps onto the snake and kills it with one bite.

TAWNY EAGLE
The tawny eagle survives well in desert conditions. Its incredible eyesight enables it to spot a rabbit or lizard thousands of feet away. When it sees prey, the tawny eagle dives at great speed and grabs the victim in its powerful talons.

COBRA
The hooded cobra kills small mammals, frogs, and lizards by biting them with its deadly fangs full of venom (poison). When this snake is in danger, it rears up its head and spreads out the ribs in the loose skin of its neck to form a hood. The hood makes the cobra look bigger and more threatening.

COLD DESERTS
It is often bitterly cold at night and during the winter in deserts such as the Gobi Desert in Asia. This is partly because the Gobi is very high – about 3,500 ft (1,000 m) above sea level. Day temperatures rise as high as 122°F (50°C), then fall to -40°F (-40°C). For some creatures, a burrow is the only place that provides warmth. Some animals, such as the mongoose, dig their own burrow; others, such as snakes, take over an empty burrow or kill and eat the occupier.

LONG-EARED HEDGEHOG
The long-eared hedgehog shown here has large ears that give off excess warmth to keep the animal cool. Prickly spines protect it from predators. During the day, the long-eared hedgehog stays in its burrow; at night it hunts for insects and worms.

Long-eared hedgehog

Many lizards prowl across the dry sand, flicking their tongues in and out to taste the air. This monitor lizard eats eggs belonging to birds and other reptiles.

JERBOA
Many small mammals live in the desert, including various kinds of mice, gerbils, and jerboas. With its long back legs, the northern jerboa shown here can leap away from danger, keeping its large toes spread out to prevent it from sinking in the soft sand. Jerboas feed on seeds and other plant matter.

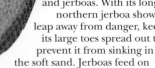

Northern jerboa

CONSERVATION

Most desert wildlife is not in urgent need of conservation measures because deserts are not seriously threatened by habitat destruction. However, some deserts are being turned into farmland for growing cereals, fruit, and other crops, and this destroys the unique desert plant life.

DORCAS GAZELLE

Dorcas gazelles are found across northern Africa, the Middle East, and India. They are an endangered species because they are being forced out of their natural habitat by farm animals and crops.

DATE PALM

The date palm tree has many different uses. The nourishing date fruit is food for people and animals, the stringy bark and wood are made into matting and ropes, and the leaves are fashioned into roofs and sunshades.

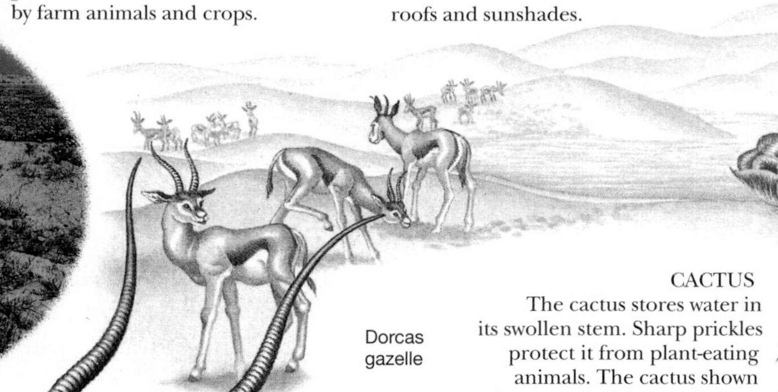

Dorcas gazelle

CACTUS

The cactus stores water in its swollen stem. Sharp prickles protect it from plant-eating animals. The cactus shown here is called the prickly pear cactus. The fruit is edible.

HOT DESERTS

The Sahara in Africa is the world's largest and hottest desert. At midday in the Sahara, the scorching sand is so hot that it can burn through skin in seconds. The temperature in the shade soars to more than 130°F (55°C). Few animals are active. Yet as the sun sets and the air and sand cool, many creatures emerge from under rocks and out of burrows. Dew falls at night, providing the plants and animals with much-needed moisture.

ROADRUNNER

The roadrunner can fly, but it usually races along the ground and runs into the undergrowth if it is disturbed. Roadrunners live in deserts and dry, open country in North America, feeding on all kinds of small animals, including grasshoppers and snakes, and eggs, and certain fruits.

ADDAX

This large grazing antelope from the Sahara never drinks – it obtains enough water from its food. Like other sandy desert dwellers, the addax's feet splay out widely to spread the animal's weight and keep it from sinking in the sand. The addax's horns have spiral ridges. The horns are used for defense and in contests for control of the herd.

SIDEWINDER

A row of S-shaped marks in the sand at daybreak is a sign that a sidewinder snake passed during the night, probably on the trail of a mouse or a rat. This snake's wavelike way of moving means that only two small parts of its body touch the ground at any time, giving a better grip on the shifting sand.

NAKED MOLE RAT

This hairless rat is virtually blind and lives in underground tunnels in groups called colonies. The colonies are organized in a similar way to an ant's nest, with one queen who gives birth to all the young. Naked mole rats feed only on tubers that they find in the soil.

YUCCA MOTH AND YUCCA PLANT

The yucca is a desert lily. It has pale, scented flowers that attract the tiny female yucca moth. The moth climbs into the flower and gathers pollen, then flies to another yucca. Here the yucca moth lays its egg in the flower's ovary (egg-bearing part), and transfers pollen. As the yucca's fruit ripens, the moth caterpillar feeds on it. The yucca moth and the yucca flower could not exist without each other.

PINK FAIRY ARMADILLO

Measuring only 6 in (15 cm) long, the pink fairy armadillo lives in the deserts of South America. It leaves its tunnel at nightfall to dig up ants, worms, and other food.

Find out more

BUTTERFLIES AND MOTHS
DEER, ANTELOPES, and gazelles
DESERTS
NORTH AMERICAN WILDLIFE
REPTILES
SNAKES

DESIGN

THE OBJECTS AROUND US HAVE BEEN CAREFULLY shaped to do their jobs as well as possible. But before they are made, they have to be designed. Design is the process of planning and deciding the best way to make and style an object. Good design means that an object fits its purpose. For instance, a chair that is stable and comfortable is well designed. A lamp that can be easily moved so light is cast all over a work surface is also good design. If the object is also attractive, inexpensive, and safe, its design is even better. To meet these needs, designers – people who work in design – have to understand the properties of the materials they work with. There are various different types of design, including garden, industrial, fashion, and graphic design. Today, computers are playing a greater role in design.

Desk lamp is designed so light can be angled.

Designer working at drawing board

INDUSTRIAL DESIGN

The area of design that is concerned with developing practical products, such as cars, computers, office furniture, and lighting, is known as industrial design. Industrial designers may also be involved in planning the layouts of buildings, or designing packaging or company logos.

24PK

Designed in the 1960s by Alec Issigonis, the Mini car looked good, was cheap to run, and easy to park.

DESIGN METHODS
Traditionally, designers worked at a drawing board, using paper and pens to produce two-dimensional plans. Today, most designers use computers to create three-dimensional models, or plans that can be rotated on screen, and looked at from every angle.

Designer can create three-dimensional model on screen.

DESIGN PROCESS

Initial sketch

The design process has a number of stages. Design also means to sketch, and a designer usually begins his or her work by doing a sketch of the object to be produced—for example, a vacuum cleaner. Working from the sketch, the designer then produces a prototype, or rough model. This is usually tested to make sure it works properly, and is safe. Finally, the object is made in a factory.

Prototype or rough model

The finished product

A Bauhaus tea set designed by Walter Gropius.

BAUHAUS
In Germany in 1919, architect Walter Gropius (1883-1969) founded an important school of design called the Bauhaus. It attracted great artists and architects and revolutionized design by combining art and crafts to produce goods that were beautiful and useful. Its striking designs were famous worldwide.

1970s fabric designed in the style of the Bauhaus.

In the late 19th century, fashionable outdoor wear for both sexes included a long cloak. Gentlemen wore shiny top hats and leaned elegantly on canes; ladies peered from beneath large decorative bonnets.

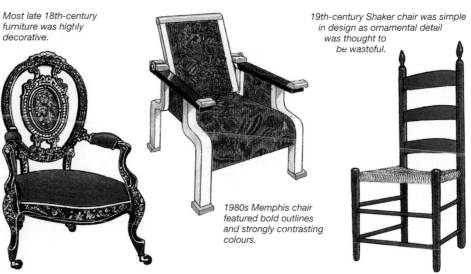

Most late 18th-century furniture was highly decorative.

1980s Memphis chair featured bold outlines and strongly contrasting colours.

19th-century Shaker chair was simple in design as ornamental detail was thought to be wasteful.

FASHION DESIGN

Nothing changes faster than the design of clothes. Each year designers create new garments that will appeal to the fashion-conscious public. Designers use new fabrics that are easy to care for and which keep out rain, wind, and cold. Some clothes are specially designed to suit the needs of mountaineers, sailors, athletes, and other people who work or play outdoors. Some are designed for comfort and durability. Even babies' diapers are designed for easy fitting and maximum absorption. But many clothes are made just to look colorful, appealing, or outrageous.

CHANGING DESIGNS

Design evolves to suit changing tastes and the availability of new materials. Much of the furniture made in the 19th century was highly decorative, except for the simple items designed by the deeply religious Shaker sect. The Thonet chair of 1850 used wood that was shaped in a new way and cut manufacturing costs. The outline of a Bauhaus chair stressed its purpose of supporting the sitter's weight. Rethinking exactly how people sit produced the kneeling chair during the 1970s. Modern designers are again introducing ornamentation, as on the Memphis chair (above).

1970s kneeling chair helped office workers sit correctly.

1850s Thonet bentwood chair was mass-produced using new manufacturing techniques.

The severe lines of a 1920s Bauhaus reclining chair emphasized the shape of the human body.

INTERIOR DESIGN

Interior designers create the feel of a room through choice of color and furnishings, making the best of the space available. For this bedroom, the designer has selected attractive items that are comfortable, safe, and easy to use. The bedroom features washable wallpaper and nontoxic toys, flameproof fabrics, and safety-tested lights. The storage areas have adjustable shelving.

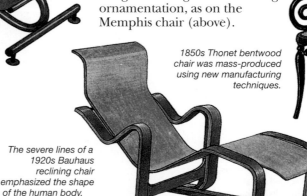

Container holds coffee grounds for easy cleaning.

Secure, lipped lid

Insulated handle

High, drip-free spout

Wide, stable base

Air vents keep base cool.

PRODUCT DESIGN

Product design should be functional and stylish: for example, a coffeepot must hold hot coffee but also look good on the table. The designer considers all sorts of factors – the shape, the materials to suit its purpose, its safety and durability, cost of manufacture, and the retail price to the customer.

Find out more
ADVERTISING
ARCHITECTURE
CLOTHES
FURNITURE

DIGESTION

HUMANS MUST EAT TO LIVE. The body needs food to work properly and to grow and repair itself. Food contains water and five vital nutrients – proteins, carbohydrates, fats, vitamins, and minerals. For food to be useful, the body has to break it down, or digest it, and combine it with oxygen. The digestive system consists of a long tube called the alimentary canal, which runs from the mouth to the anus. Each part does a particular job. The stomach is like a bag, in which chewed food is mixed with acids and digestive juices. The small intestine pushes the food along by a squeezing action called peristalsis. The tiny particles of digested food pass easily through the walls of the small intestine and into the bloodstream, to be used by the body. The large intestine absorbs water from the food and turns the waste products into semi-solid lumps called feces.

DIGESTION
Digestion begins in the mouth, as teeth crush the food. Watery saliva moistens the food and makes it easy to chew and swallow. The muscular walls of the stomach churn the food into a soup-like liquid and mix it with powerful digestive juices. The broken-down nutrients are small enough to seep through the lining of the small intestine and into the blood vessels in its wall.

Teeth chew, crunch, and grind food into a pulp.

Tongue tastes different flavors.

Salivary glands produce a watery liquid to mix with food and help with swallowing.

Esophagus pushes swallowed food down through the chest, behind the windpipe and heart, into the stomach.

Liver

Stomach is where muscles crush food into a pulp and mix it with digestive juices.

Small intestine absorbs digested food into the body.

Large intestine absorbs water from undigested pieces of food.

Rectum is the last part of the large intestine.

EATING FOOD
When you swallow food, it enters your throat. A flap called the epiglottis folds over the entrance to the windpipe so that food goes into the esophagus and not into the lungs, where it could cause choking.

LIVER
The liver is the body's "chemical factory." It receives digested nutrients from the intestines and converts them into more easily used forms, such as glucose (blood sugar) for muscle fuel.

SMALL INTESTINE
The small intestine is coiled into the lower part of the body. It is very long, measuring about 20 ft (6 m) in length. Its lining has many folds and ridges, so that it can absorb as many nutrients as possible.

Pancreas produces digestive juices.

LARGE INTESTINE
The large intestine is much shorter than the small intestine, but three times as wide, measuring up to 2.5 in (7 cm) in width.

Anus is where waste products leave the body as feces.

STOMACH
This bag is lined with a thick layer of slimy mucus. Tiny glands in the lining produce strong digestive juices, which contain substances such as enzymes and acids.

Bitter

Sour

Salty

Sweet

TONGUE
The tongue is a flexible muscle. On its surface are tiny nodules called taste buds that sense different flavors. The tip of the tongue can taste sweet flavors, the part behind the tip tastes salty flavors, the sides taste sour flavors, and the back tastes bitter flavors.

VILLI
Each fold of the lining of the small intestine has thousands of microscopic finger-shaped projections called villi. The villi allow the small intestine to absorb more nutrients.

ENZYMES
Digestive juices contain proteins called enzymes that dissolve the food into tiny particles the body can absorb.

Find out more
FOOD AND FOOD TECHNOLOGY
HEALTH AND FITNESS
HUMAN BODY
MUSCLES AND MOVEMENT

DINOSAURS

WE HAVE KNOWN ABOUT DINOSAURS for only 150 years or so, but these great creatures roamed the Earth for 160 million years – long before humans appeared. Scientists first learned about dinosaurs in the 1820s, when they discovered the fossilized bones of unknown creatures. Today, these fossils show us where dinosaurs lived, what they looked like, and what they ate. Dinosaurs were reptiles and lived on land. Their name means "terrible lizard," and, like lizards, many of them had tough, scaly skin. There were hundreds of different kinds of dinosaurs, divided into two main groups. The Ornithischians (bird-hipped dinosaurs), such as *Protoceratops*, had hipbones similar to birds; the Saurischians (lizard-hipped dinosaurs), such as *Diplodocus*, had hipbones similar to lizards. Not all dinosaurs were giants – *Compsognathus* was the size of a chicken and *Heterodontosaurus* was the size of a large dog. Some dinosaurs, such as *Tyrannosaurus rex*, were carnivores (meat-eaters); others, such as *Stegosaurus*, were herbivores (plant-eaters). About 65 million years ago, dinosaurs and the swimming and flying reptiles that lived at the same time died out. The reason for this is still a mystery.

REPTILES
Dinosaurs were reptiles, like crocodiles, alligators, and the lizard shown above. Like other reptiles, dinosaurs had scaly skin and laid eggs. Unlike lizards and other reptiles, dinosaurs had long legs, so they could move faster on land.

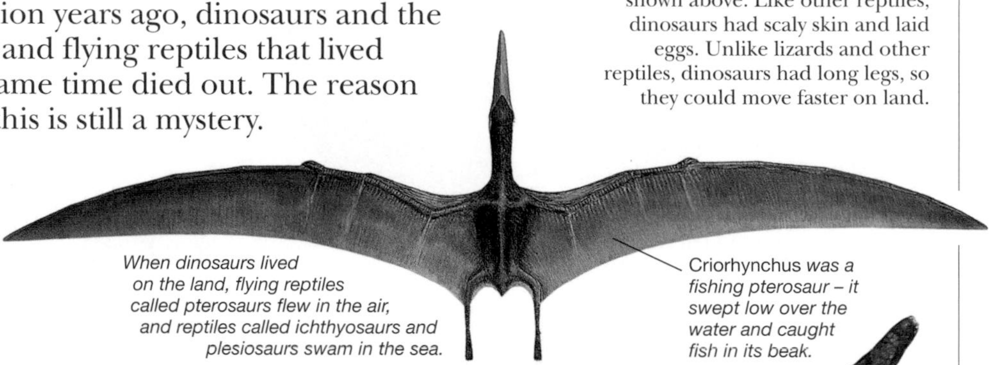

When dinosaurs lived on the land, flying reptiles called pterosaurs flew in the air, and reptiles called ichthyosaurs and plesiosaurs swam in the sea.

Criorhynchus was a fishing pterosaur – it swept low over the water and caught fish in its beak.

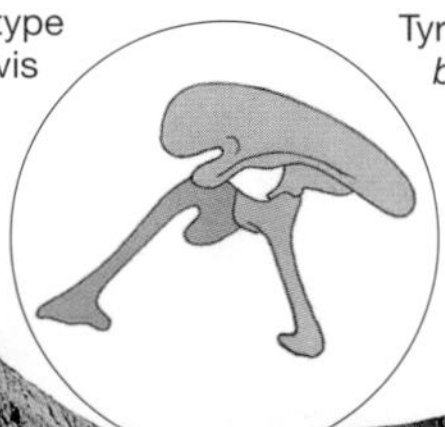

A lizard-type pelvis

Tyrannosaurus rex belonged to the group of lizard-hipped dinosaurs called Saurischians.

Tyrannosaurus had tiny hands that did not reach its mouth. We do not know what the hands were used for.

Carnivorous dinosaurs often had large, strong claws for grabbing their prey. The claw shown here belonged to Baryonyx, which is nicknamed "Claws."

TYRANNOSAURUS REX
The gigantic *Tyrannosaurus* was the largest carnivorous dinosaur. It was also the largest known meat-eating land animal of all time. Scientists first discovered its fossils in North America. *Tyrannosaurus* measured 46 ft (14 m) in length and stood almost 20 ft (6 m) high. Its massive teeth were more than 6 in (15 cm) long. *Tyrannosaurus* weighed almost 7 tons, so it was probably too heavy to run and hunt other dinosaurs. *Tyrannosaurus* fed on small creatures and dead dinosaurs.

GORGOSAURUS
Carnivorous dinosaurs, such as the *Gorgosaurus*, had huge teeth and powerful jaw muscles for a strong bite. Not all dinosaur teeth were this large, though; some were as small as human teeth.

Jaw bone of a *Gorgosaurus*

DIPLODOCUS

The largest dinosaurs, including *Diplodocus*, belonged to the group of plant-eaters called sauropods. At 88 ft (27 m) in length, *Diplodocus* was one of the longest dinosaurs. Its long, thin tail made up most of its length. With its slim body, it probably weighed only about 9 tons.

Protoceratops *was about 6 ft (2 m) long. It probably snipped at plants with its beak-like mouth.*

Diplodocus *was a herbivore; all its teeth were at the front of its mouth for nibbling at tough leaves.*

PROTOCERATOPS

Scientists discovered fossils of *Protoceratops* in the Gobi Desert, Mongolia, in the 1920s. The bones of adults and young were found, together with fossilized eggs. About 80 million years ago, this area was a nesting site for many families of *Protoceratops*.

BREEDING

The fossils of *Protoceratops* show that the female scooped out a shallow hole in the sand and laid the eggs in a circular pattern. Scientists found many nests near each other, which shows that these dinosaurs bred in colonies, or groups, in the same way as some birds do today.

TYPES OF DINOSAURS

Dinosaurs varied greatly in size and shape, and they did not all live at the same time. Some lived 200 million years ago; others lived 70 million years ago. This chart gives the sizes of some dinosaurs in comparison to the size of a 10-year-old child.

| Coelophysis | Diplodocus | Iguanodon | Ornithosuchus | Triceratops |
| 210 MYA | 140 MYA | 120 MYA | 210 MYA | 65 MYA |

| Protoceratops | Comp-sognathus | Baryonyx | Euplocephalus | Tyrannosaurus |
| 80 MYA | 140 MYA | 120 MYA | 75 MYA | 70 MYA |

Scientists have been able to reconstruct some dinosaur species, such as the Tuojiangosaurus.

THE END OF THE DINOSAURS

There are many ideas about the end of the dinosaurs. Some people believe they died out because a giant meteorite crashed into the Earth, throwing up a dust cloud and blotting out the sun. Without sunlight, the plants and the dinosaurs that fed on them could not survive.

BARYONYX

In 1983, the fossilized claw and bones of a dinosaur were found in Surrey, England. This dinosaur is named *Baryonyx*. Fossilized scales of fish were found in this dinosaur's stomach, so it was probably a fish-eater and may have used its claws to catch fish.

IGUANODON

Iguanodon was a herbivore. As an adult, it was about 33 ft (10 m) long, with small hooves on its hands and feet. Some scientists believe that *Iguanodon* lived in herds because, in some areas of Europe, they have found many fossilized skeletons of *Iguanodon* together in one place.

Iguanodon *had versatile hands – the three middle fingers acted like hooves, the little finger could grasp food, and the spiked thumb was a fearsome weapon.*

Iguanodon *belonged to the bird-hipped group of dinosaurs called Ornithischians.*

Heavy tail balanced the rest of Iguanodon's body.

Bird-type pelvis

Find out more

EVOLUTION
FOSSILS
PREHISTORIC LIFE
PREHISTORIC PEOPLES

DISEASE

AT SOME POINT IN YOUR LIFE you may have a disease. It may be relatively harmless or it may be quite serious. Disease is a sickness of the body or mind. There are thousands of diseases that can strike almost any part of the body. They range from measles and the common cold to heart disease and emotional disorders such as depression. Some diseases are chronic (lasting for a long time); arthritis is a chronic disease that makes the joints swell painfully. Other diseases, which are called acute, occur in short, sharp attacks and include flu (influenza). There are many different causes of disease. Harmful microorganisms (microscopic plants or animals) can invade the body and cause infectious diseases. Poor living conditions can also cause disease. Some diseases occur at birth; others may be passed from parent to child. The reasons for some diseases such as cancer are unclear. Scientists are constantly working to understand the causes of diseases and find possible cures.

ENVIRONMENTAL DISEASE
Living conditions affect people's health. Nuclear radiation in the atmosphere can cause cancer; pollution of the air from chemicals such as lead can affect health, particularly that of children; and swimming in water that is polluted with sewage can cause serious infections such as hepatitis, typhoid, and cholera.

Covering a sneeze can help prevent the flu virus from spreading.

There are several different types of bacteria (below). Each consists of a single living cell. Some bacteria cause disease in humans and animals, but most are harmless.

Causes boils

Causes typhoid

Causes sore throat

Viruses are smaller than a living cell. Viruses cause disease when they enter healthy cells in order to reproduce. The flu virus (above) is spread from person to person by coughing and sneezing.

BACTERIA AND VIRUSES
Infectious diseases are the only diseases that can spread from person to person. Most are caused by microscopic organisms called bacteria and viruses that invade the body. Typhoid and cholera are examples of diseases caused by bacteria; chicken pox and measles are caused by viruses.

Heart disease is often caused by blockage of blood vessels in the heart. It has been linked to a rich, fatty diet and smoking.

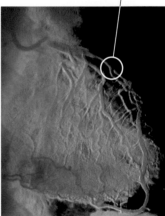

AIDS
Our bodies have natural defenses that help us fight disease. One is the immune system, which attacks diseases that invade our bodies. In the 1980s, a new disease began to spread. Known as acquired immunodeficiency syndrome (AIDS), it stops the immune system from working correctly and can result in death.

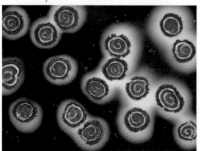

AIDS virus particles under a microscope.

HEREDITARY AND CONGENITAL DISEASES
Parents can pass on certain diseases, called hereditary diseases, to their children. Sickle cell anaemia is a hereditary blood disease. Hereditary diseases do not usually affect all the children in a family, and may appear late in life. Diseases that appear at birth such as spina bifida, a defect of the spinal cord and nervous system, are called congenital diseases.

Hereditary diseases are passed from parents to children in their genes.

NUTRITIONAL DISEASES
In parts of the world, particularly Africa and Asia, many people do not have enough to eat. Lack of food can cause many disorders, including anemia, rickets, and scurvy. In places such as Europe and North America, many people eat too much. Overeating can also cause disorders, including obesity (fatness), diabetes, and heart disease.

EPIDEMICS
When a disease affects many people at the same time, it is called an epidemic. Epidemics of AIDS and of malaria, a disease carried by mosquitoes, affect many parts of Africa. AIDS epidemics are also affecting industrialized countries. In Western countries, too, so many people suffer from heart disease and cancer that these diseases are sometimes described as epidemic.

Find out more
DOCTORS
DRUGS
GENETICS
HEALTH AND FITNESS
HOSPITALS
MEDICINE
MEDICINE, HISTORY OF

DOCTORS

IF YOU ARE ILL, you may need to see a doctor. A doctor is someone who is trained to recognize what is wrong with sick people and know what will make them well. A general practitioner is usually the first doctor you see. These doctors, who are also called physicians, have a knowledge of many different types of illness. They also perform checkups and give vaccinations. Depending on your illness, the doctor may send you to a surgeon or some other specialist. Surgeons are doctors who carry out surgery or operations. They cut open the patient's body and take out or repair the sick organ. Other specialists include pediatricians, who specialize in treating children. To be licensed as a doctor takes five years of study at a medical school, and one year of internship (practical training) at a hospital.

HIPPOCRATIC OATH
Doctors have existed since ancient times. Hippocrates was a famous Greek doctor who lived 2,500 years ago. He swore an oath to preserve life and to work for the benefit of everyone. Today, doctors still swear the same oath when they complete their training.

The stethoscope enables the doctor to hear lung sounds and the flow of the blood.

DOCTOR'S TOOLS
Physicians use X rays and a variety of special instruments to help them find out what is wrong with their patients.

X-ray photographs reveal broken bones and some diseases, such as lung cancer.

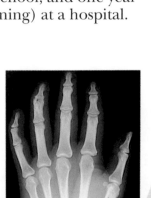

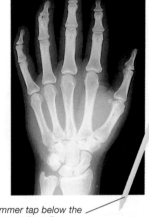

The inflatable cuff of the sphygmomanometer temporarily stops the flow of blood, so that the doctor can measure its pressure.

With an otoscope the doctor can get a clear view inside the ears.

Doctors use an ophthalmoscope to examine the eyes.

A hammer tap below the knee tests the reflexes: a healthy patient's knee jerks.

DOCTOR'S OFFICE
A family doctor sometimes visits sick patients in their homes; patients who are well enough visit the doctor in his or her office. There the doctor asks questions and examines the patient, then makes a diagnosis (decides what is wrong). Before giving any treatment, the doctor may also need to take X rays or do blood tests.

MICROSURGERY
With the aid of microscopes, surgeons can see and operate on minute parts of the body. This technique, called microsurgery, makes it possible to repair or cut out damaged organs that are too small to work on without magnification. Microsurgeons can operate on delicate structures in the eye and the ear, and try to reconnect nerves and blood vessels of fingers or toes that have been cut off.

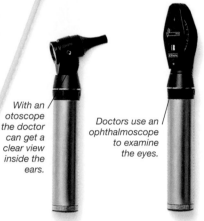

TRAVELING DOCTORS
In remote parts of the world, doctors travel from village to village to treat health problems. If there are not enough doctors, health workers can learn to treat common health problems. In Australia and Canada "flying doctors" reach isolated areas by airplane.

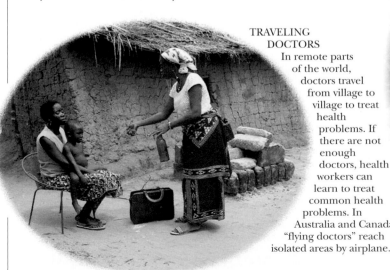

Find out more
DISEASE
HEALTH AND FITNESS
HOSPITALS

DOGS,
WOLVES, AND FOXES

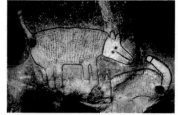

EARLY DOGS
The domestic dog is one of the 35 species of the dog family. As this early cave painting shows, it existed as long ago as the Stone Age.

Extremely sensitive nose for tracking animals and people

Reasonable eyesight in daylight; night vision weak.

WHEN A PET DOG BARKS at a stranger or walks around in a circle before settling down to sleep, it is behaving in the same way that its wild wolf cousins did thousands of years ago. The dog family is made up of about 35 different species, one of which is the domestic dog. There are many different breeds of domestic dog, from Labradors to terriers. Other types of dog include the Asian dhole, the African wild dog, many kinds of foxes, and three species of jackals. These fast-running hunters are built for chasing prey; their elongated skulls are thought to be adaptations for seizing prey on the run. Many wild dogs, such as wolves and dingos, live in extended family groups called packs. Each pack has a leader, to whom all the other animals in the pack submit. A domestic dog sees its owner as a pack leader and is willing to obey that person's commands.

GRAY WOLF
This wolf is believed to be the ancestor of our domestic dogs. It is the largest member of the dog family, measuring at least 6 ft (2 m) in length, including its tail. Where food is readily available, wolves may form a pack consisting of up to 20 members. When food is difficult to find, a large pack of wolves splits up into smaller groups of about seven animals.

Good hearing, with ears that turn to locate the source of a sound

Dogs have four claws on each paw. The tough toe pads help them grip when they run.

Long, strong legs for fast, sustained running

GERMAN SHEPHERD
This dog has a long muzzle and large ears, and still resembles its wolf ancestors. It is a strong, agile, extremely intelligent breed of dog – popular both as a working dog and as a pet.

Tail is used to give social signals, such as wagging when happy.

Fur coat keeps animal warm and dry.

Meat-eating teeth, with large, pointed canines for seizing and tearing at prey

DOMESTIC DOGS
Dogs have lived in harmony with humans for more than 10,000 years. It is probable that over thousands of years, early humans caught and tamed several members of the dog family, at first to help with hunting, herding, and guarding, and, much later, to keep as pets. Today, 203 breeds of domestic dogs are recognized in Britain, and more than 150 in the United States.

WORKING DOGS
Dogs are trained to do many jobs for humans. Some tasks, such as herding sheep or guarding property, involve the dog's natural instincts. Other jobs include guiding the blind, pulling sleds, and racing. Many dogs are trained by the police and the military to find people who are trapped or in hiding.

RED FOX

Few animals are as adaptable as the red fox, which lives in almost every country north of the equator. Red foxes eat almost anything, including insects and fish. The fox springs up and pounces on its prey like a cat. This creature's legendary cunning helps it survive in suburban yards and city dumps. In towns and cities, it feeds on scraps from garbage cans.

Mongrels are domestic dogs that are not pedigree – such as the three dogs shown here.

A female coyote usually has one litter of puppies each year.

COYOTE

The North American coyote is closely related to wolves, jackals, and domestic dogs. Like most dogs, the female is pregnant for nine weeks before giving birth to about five puppies. The puppies feed on their mother's milk for up to seven weeks. After the first four weeks they also eat food regurgitated, or brought up, by their parents. Coyotes were thought to live alone, but we now know that some form small packs.

PANTING
When a dog becomes hot, it cannot lose heat from its skin because it does not have sweat glands on its body. Instead, the dog opens its mouth and pants to give off heat from its mouth and tongue.

YORKSHIRE TERRIER
This small dog measures only 7 in (18 cm) in height. It is an agile runner, originally bred for catching rats.

MANED WOLF
The maned wolf is being bred in zoos and parks in an attempt to save it from extinction.

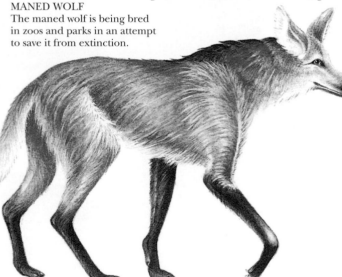

CRAB-EATING FOX
The crab-eating fox, also called the common zorro, is from South America. It eats many kinds of food, including crabs, as it forages along the coast. Other common zorros live far inland in woods and grassland and never even see a crab.

TOY DOGS

Dog breeders have created dogs of all sizes and shapes by mating dogs with unusual features, such as short legs or small ears. The smallest breeds, known as toy dogs, have become quite different from their distant ancestors, the wolves. A chihuahua, one of the smallest recognized breeds, can weigh less than 2 lbs (1 kg).

CONSERVATION

The long-legged, maned wolf from South America is one of many members of the dog family that are officially listed as in danger of extinction. Many wolves and foxes, including the gray wolf, have been hunted not only for their beautiful fur, but also because they sometimes attack farm animals. One of the greatest threats to the dog family is the loss of the natural areas where they live, which are now used for farmland, houses, and factories.

PUPPIES
Young dogs, such as the Labrador puppy shown here, spend much of their time in play – tumbling, jumping, and biting and shaking things. These games help the young dog develop hunting skills for adult life.

Find out more

AFRICAN WILDLIFE
ANIMALS
ANIMAL SENSES
AUSTRALIAN WILDLIFE
CONSERVATION
and endangered species
MAMMALS
POLAR EXPLORATION

DRAWING

EARLY PEOPLE MAY HAVE begun to draw by scratching images in the dirt with sticks or their fingers, possibly outlines copied from shadows. They then learned to use natural earth pigments and charcoal to draw on other surfaces. They may have started to draw in order to communicate ideas. Points of soft lead, tin, copper, and other metals were used from ancient times up to the 18th century. Today, people draw with chalk, charcoal, crayon, pastel, pencil, or pen and ink. Paper is the most practical medium for drawing on. Creative drawings are often done as preparations for paintings or sculptures; a painter may sketch out an idea in a drawing before starting to paint a picture. But many drawings are seen as finished works of art. Drawing has practical as well as artistic uses. An architect has to draw up detailed, accurate plans in order for a building to be constructed properly. Courtroom artists draw pictures of scenes during a trial where photographers are not allowed. And before photography was invented, artists drew battles and other events for newspapers.

ALBRECHT DÜRER
The German artist Albrecht Dürer (1471-1528) made many drawings of people, landscapes, and animals. His brush drawing *Praying Hands* (above) was a study for part of an altarpiece for a German church. Dürer also produced a variety of paintings, engravings, and woodcuts.

PENS AND PENCILS
The "lead" pencil we use today is a mixture of graphite and clay fired at a high temperature and mixed with wax. This kind of pencil was not developed until the end of the 18th century. To get the best results, good-quality paper is necessary. Paper sometimes has a textured surface that adds to the character of the drawing.

Pencils range from 7H, which gives a hard, fine line, to 8B, which gives a soft, dark line.

Charcoal sticks were used by early peoples to sketch on the walls of caves.

Pastels are powdered pigments bound together with gum or resin.

Drawing ink is generally water resistant.

Conté crayons are made by mixing chalk and pigment with fatty materials such as wax.

Colored pencils

Metal nib pen

TECHNICAL DRAWING
Architects, engineers, and designers make technical drawings of their designs with the aid of instruments such as T squares and compasses. Technical drawings show exactly how to construct things, from bridges to airplanes, so they must be very accurate. A technical artist needs to have a steady hand and pay great attention to detail. A mistake in the drawing could be disastrous.

SKETCH
Artists often make sketches – quick drawings – to record things that they see or to prepare for a finished work. The Italian artist Leonardo da Vinci (1452-1519) made thousands of sketches to record his observations. He filled notebooks with drawings of human anatomy, machines, plants, and plans of cities. Above is one of his sketches: a study for the *Head of Leda*.

Find out more
ARCHITECTURE
CARTOONS
PAINTING

DRUGS

IF YOU ARE ILL, the doctor might give you a drug. Drugs, or medicines, are substances used in the treatment of illnesses. They can relieve the symptoms (effects) of a disease, ease pain, and prevent or cure illnesses. Drugs are also used to treat a wide range of emotional disorders such as depression. There are thousands of different kinds of drugs in use today. Each drug has a specific function and often acts on a single part of the body, such as the stomach. There are many sources of drugs. They may be natural or synthetic (artificial). Medicinal plants and herbs yield natural drugs that have been in use for thousands of years. Scientists constantly search for new drugs and often make them from chemicals. In many cases, the discovery of a drug has eased suffering and saved many lives. Antibiotics, such as penicillin for example, cure infections that would have been fatal 50 years ago.

Drugs can be dangerous. Today, many containers are made with specially designed caps that are difficult for children to remove.

Some drugs, such as antihistamines for treating allergies (sensitivity to certain substances), work more quickly if they are injected directly into the bloodstream through a needle and syringe.

The body can absorb creams and ointments through the skin. Medicinal creams are often used to treat skin disorders.

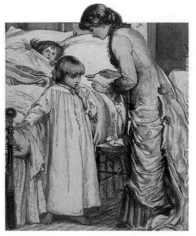

ORAL MEDICINES
Many drugs are taken orally (by mouth). The drug passes through the digestive system and into the bloodstream, which carries the drug to the relevant part of the body.

Some drugs, particularly those for small children, are dissolved in a sweet-tasting syrup. Special spoons that hold a fixed amount of liquid ensure that the patient receives the correct dose. Medicines can also be given by oral syringe.

Tablets containing drugs are made with a smooth shape so that they are easy to swallow.

Some powdered drugs dissolve in water, which helps them enter the bloodstream more rapidly than if they are taken as pills.

TYPES OF DRUG
Different drugs have different uses. They range from antibiotics (for treating infections) to painkillers, such as aspirin. Anesthetics are used to put patients to sleep before surgery. There are different ways of taking drugs. They can be swallowed, injected, put on the skin, used in a spray, or inhaled.

Tablets and capsules contain carefully measured amounts of drugs. When they are swallowed, the drugs slowly filter into the bloodstream via the digestive system. Some tablets have a coating that dissolves slowly, releasing the drug at a controlled rate.

DRUG ADDICTION
Many drugs, including some of those recommended by doctors, are addictive. This means that the user becomes dependent on them. Drug addiction can lead to illness and death. The use of many dangerous drugs such as heroin, crack, and cocaine is illegal. However, other addictive drugs, such as alcohol and nicotine (in cigarettes), are not prohibited by law.

SOURCES OF DRUGS
In the past, all drugs used in treating illnesses came from natural sources, particularly herbs and plants. Today, most drugs are made from chemicals, and some are made by genetic engineering, a method in which the cells in bacteria or yeasts are altered to produce drugs.

Some drugs such as insulin (for treating diabetes) can be obtained from pigs and cattle.

The heart drug digitalis originally came from a flower called the foxglove.

Aspirin is made from chemicals originally found in willowtree bark.

The antibiotic penicillin first came from a mold called penicillium.

Find out more

DISEASE
DOCTORS
FLOWERS AND HERBS
HEALTH AND FITNESS
MEDICINE
MEDICINE, HISTORY OF

DUCKS, GEESE, AND SWANS

A swan weighs about 28 lb (13 kg).

To reach takeoff speed, it has to run over the water.

The swan has to flap its wings very hard.

Large, powerful wings lift the swan into the air.

During flight, the feet tuck under the body.

WATERFOWL IS THE NAME given to the ducks, geese, and swans that live on the lakes and rivers of the world. Many waterfowl have long, flexible necks that allow them to reach down into the water for food. They spend much of their time preening and spreading oils over their feathers with their beaks. The oils are made in special glands; they keep the plumage waterproof and help keep the bird warm. Most waterfowl live in flocks except in the breeding season; some, such as barnacle and brent geese, migrate long distances to their nesting grounds. Many waterfowl are kept by people for their eggs, meat, and feathers. Eiderdown, often used to stuff quilts, is the soft, downy under-feathers of the eider duck.

Canada

United States

SWAN
The female black-necked swan carries her fluffy cygnets (young swans) on her back when she is swimming, to keep them warm and safe from predators. Cygnets can fly about three months after hatching.

Canada geese fly north in pairs to breed.

Legs are at the back of body, for efficient swimming.

DIVING DUCKS AND DABBLING DUCKS
The two main groups of ducks are divers and dabblers. Dabblers, such as mallard ducks, pintail, widgeons, and teals, feed at the surface or stick their tails in the air and dabble just below the surface. They sweep their bills from side to side, sieving out seeds, flies, and other bits of food. Diving ducks, such as pochards and tufted ducks, swim down below the surface to peck at water plants, worms, shellfish, and other small water creatures.

CANADA GEESE
Each spring, Canada geese fly from Mexico and the southern United States to breeding grounds in Canada. They fly in V-shaped formations and often change position so the leader of the flock does not get too tired. Canada geese nest in grass-lined hollows on islands and marshes. Like most geese and swans, Canada geese stay with their partners for many years. Both geese bring up the young goslings (baby geese), and the family stays together until the next breeding season.

WEBBED FEET
Most waterfowl have short legs and webbed feet that work well as paddles but make it difficult to walk on land.

Webbed foot has claws on the toes for scratching in the earth.

TUFTED DUCK
Tufted ducks eat zebra mussels, a type of freshwater shellfish, as well as small fish, tadpoles, and water insects.

MALLARD
Most male dabbling ducks are more colorful than the females, with bright patches on both wings.

Find out more
BIRDS
FLIGHT, ANIMAL
LAKE AND RIVER WILDLIFE
MIGRATION, ANIMAL

EAGLES
AND OTHER BIRDS OF PREY

IN THE SAME WAY that sharks are hunters in the sea and lions are hunters on land, eagles are powerful hunters in the sky. Birds of prey, such as eagles, falcons, hawks, and vultures, are also called raptors. There are about 300 different kinds, and they all have extremely sharp eyesight. They can spy their prey on the ground from a great height. Raptors have long, strong legs with sharp claws, called talons, for grasping their victims, and a sharp, hooked beak for tearing flesh. One of the largest, most majestic eagles is the Australian wedge-tailed eagle, with a wingspan of 8 ft (2.5 m). The Eurasian kestrel is a common bird of prey, often seen hovering alongside roads watching for prey in the grass. Many birds of prey are rare because the countryside where they live has been turned into farmland, and pesticides poison their food.

FISH EAGLE
The African fish eagle has long feathers on the tips of its wings to help it control its gliding. Its sharp eyes are always on the lookout for fish as it patrols the lakes, swamps, and rivers of Africa south of the Sahara Desert.

HAWK
The sparrow hawk (above) is a nimble woodland hunter of smaller birds. It can swoop down on its prey with a surprise dive, or chase it with twists and turns among the trees.

FALCONRY
For hundreds of years, falcons, hawks, and other birds of prey have been trained to hunt from a gloved hand. Birds such as this Eurasian kestrel are hooded before the hunt, to keep them calm. Falconry is especially popular in the Middle East.

Huge, powerful wings for soaring and diving

Excellent eyesight for spying fish

Large, strong beak for tearing flesh

Long, sharp talons on toes for grasping prey

BALD EAGLE
Because of their size and strength, eagles are popular symbols and emblems. The American bald eagle (left), a type of fish eagle, is the national emblem of the United States. It is not really bald but looks that way because the white feathers on its head contrast with the dark body.

CONDOR
Condors are among the largest flying birds. Their huge wings measure 10 ft (3 m) from tip to tip. The South American Andean condor can glide for hours and hours high above remote mountains.

SCAVENGERS
Vultures and condors feed mainly on dead and dying animals, known as carrion. They circle in the sky watching for food. When one vulture sees some carrion, it drops quickly, followed by nearby vultures. Soon there may be 50 or more vultures pecking over the dead body.

KING VULTURE
Like all vultures, the colorful South American king vulture has a bald head and neck. This vulture lives in rain forests, and soars over the treetops, marshes, and grasslands in search of dead animals to scavenge. The king vulture also hunts small reptiles and mammals.

King vulture watches for prey.

A brilliant orange head and a gray feather collar make the king vulture look "dressed to kill."

> **Find out more**
> ANIMALS
> BIRDS
> FLIGHT, ANIMAL
> OWLS

EARS

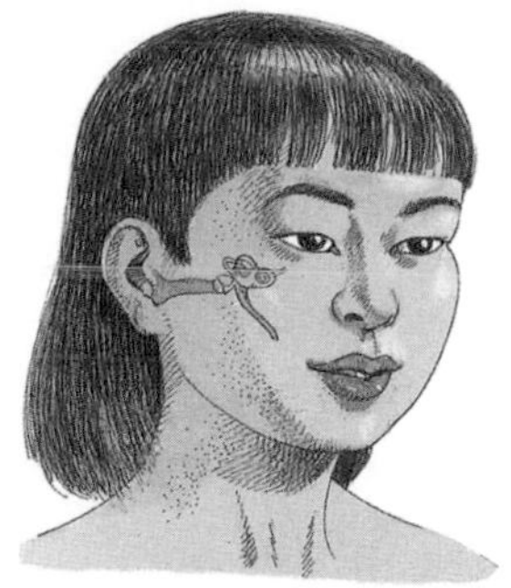

Ultrasonic sound is above the human range of hearing.

THE EARS ARE THE ORGANS of hearing and balance. They collect sound vibrations from the air and turn them into messages called nerve signals that are passed to the brain. Each ear has three main parts – the outer ear, the middle ear, and the inner ear. The outer ear includes the part you can see. It consists of the ear flap, or auricle, and the ear canal. The middle ear consists of the eardrum and three tiny bones called the ossicles. These three bones send sounds from the eardrum to the inner ear. The main part of the inner ear is the snail-shaped cochlea, which is full of fluid. The cochlea changes vibrations into nerve signals. The inner ear also makes sure that the body keeps its balance. Although we can hear many different sounds, we cannot hear as wide a range as most animals. Also, unlike rabbits and horses, we cannot swivel our ears toward the direction of a sound – we have to turn our heads.

INSIDE THE EAR
The ear canal is slightly curved. It measures about 1 in (2.5 cm) in length. The delicate parts of the middle and inner ear lie well protected deep inside the skull bone, just behind and below the level of the eye.

Human   Dog   Dolphin   Bat

RANGE OF HEARING
Humans can hear sounds that vary from a low growl to a piercing scream. Many animals, including dogs, can hear sounds that are far too high-pitched for us to detect. A human's range of hearing is 30-20,000 hertz (vibrations per second); a bat's range of hearing is up to 100,000 hertz.

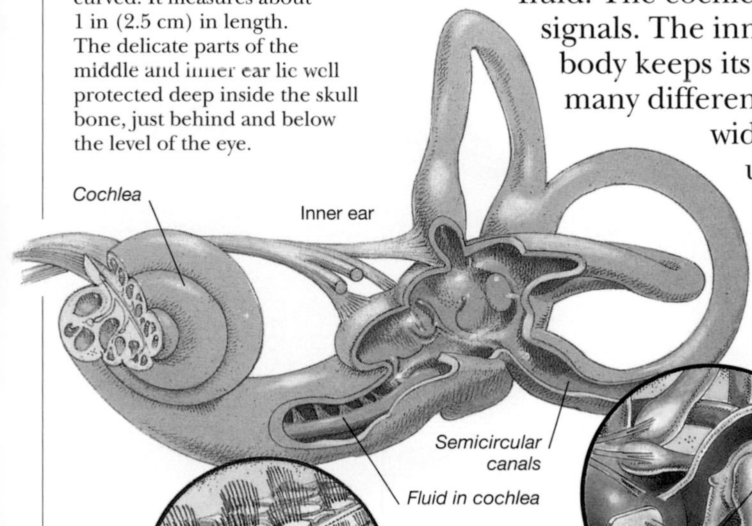

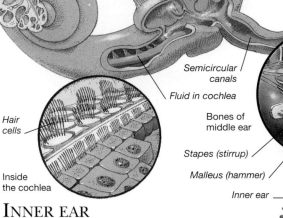

Cochlea

Inner ear

Hair cells

Inside the cochlea

Semicircular canals

Fluid in cochlea

Bones of middle ear

Stapes (stirrup)

Malleus (hammer)

Inner ear

MIDDLE EAR BONES
The middle ear bones (ossicles) are called the malleus (hammer), incus (anvil), and the stapes (stirrup).

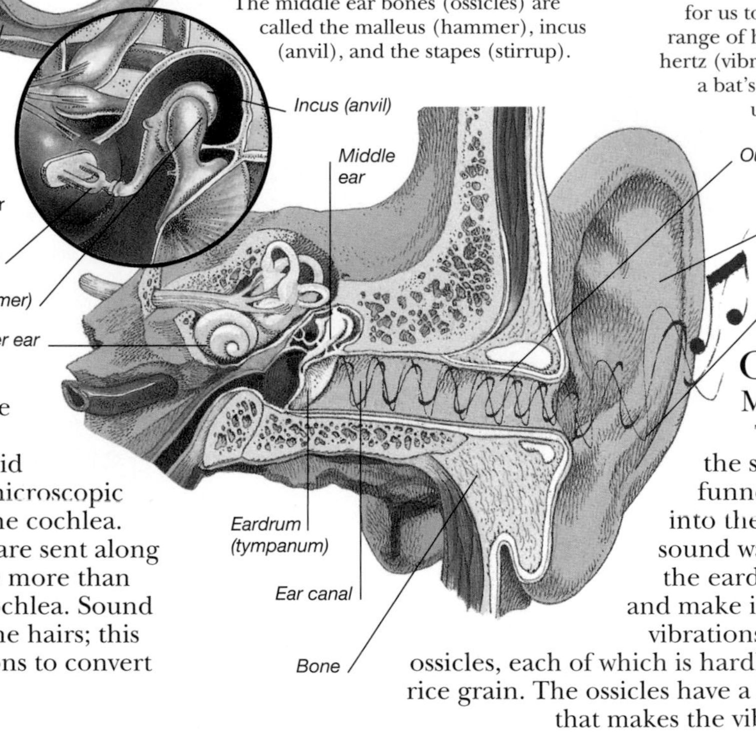

Incus (anvil)

Middle ear

Outer ear canal

Ear flap (auricle)

Soundwaves

INNER EAR
The stirrup bone presses on a thin, flexible part of the cochlea's wall, called the oval window, and passes its vibrations to the fluid inside the cochlea. The vibrations shake microscopic hairs on cells along a thin membrane in the cochlea. This movement creates nerve signals that are sent along the cochlear nerve to the brain. There are more than 20,000 microscopic hair cells inside the cochlea. Sound vibrations make cochlear fluid flow over the hairs; this is how the hair cells receive sound vibrations to convert into nerve signals that travel to the brain.

Eardrum (tympanum)

Ear canal

Bone

OUTER AND MIDDLE EAR
The ear flap on the side of the head funnels sound waves into the ear canal. The sound waves bounce off the eardrum at the end and make it vibrate. These vibrations pass along the ossicles, each of which is hardly bigger than a rice grain. The ossicles have a leverlike action that makes the vibrations louder.

ANIMAL HEARING
Creatures such as fish and squid have sense organs to detect vibrations in the water. Fish have a lateral line – a narrow groove along each side of the body. Hair cells in the lateral line can sense the sound or movement of nearby animals. The catfish shown here also has whiskers called barbels that can sense vibrations.

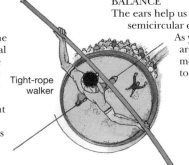

Tight-rope walker

BALANCE
The ears help us keep our balance. The three semicircular canals inside the ear contain fluid. As you move your head, the fluid flows around. Tiny hair cells sense this movement and produce nerve signals to tell the brain which way "up" you are.

> ### *Find out more*
> HUMAN BODY
> SKELETONS
> SOUND

EARTH

A LARGE BALL OF ROCK spinning through space is our home in the universe. This is the Earth, one of the nine planets that circle around the Sun. The Earth is the only place we know of that supports life. It has oxygen in its atmosphere and water in its oceans, both of which are essential for life. And of all the planets in the solar system, the Earth is at just the right distance from the Sun to be neither too hot nor too cold. Land makes up less than one-third of the surface of the Earth; more than two-thirds is the water in the oceans. The Earth's interior consists of layers of rock that surround a core made of iron and nickel.

The processes that support life on Earth are in a natural balance. However, many people are worried that pollution, human overpopulation, and misuse of resources may destroy this balance and make the Earth unsafe for plants and animals.

EARTH IN SPACE
When astronauts first saw the Earth from space, they were enthralled by the beauty of our blue planet. This picture shows the Earth rising over the Moon's horizon.

ATMOSPHERE
A layer of air called the atmosphere surrounds the Earth. It is roughly 1,250 miles (2,000 km) deep and contains mainly the gases nitrogen and oxygen. The atmosphere shields the Earth from harmful ultraviolet rays coming from the Sun and prevents the Earth from becoming too hot or too cold.

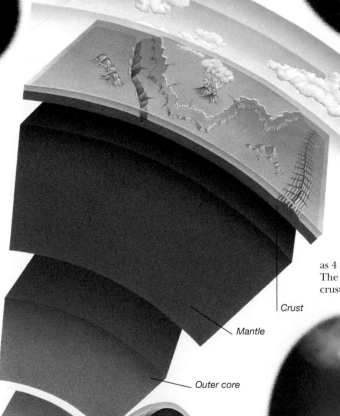

Clouds containing tiny drops of water float low in the atmosphere, carrying water from the seas and land that falls as rain.

Atmosphere

OCEANS
The oceans are large water-filled hollows in the Earth's crust. Their average depth is 2.2 miles (3.5 km).

MANTLE
Under the crust is the mantle, a layer of rock about 1,800 miles (2,900 km) thick. The temperature rises to 6,700°F (3,700°C) at the base of the mantle, but high pressure there keeps the rock solid.

CRUST
The top layer of rock at the surface of the Earth is called the crust. It is up to 44 miles (70 km) deep beneath the continents, but as little as 4 miles (6 km) deep under the oceans. The temperature at the bottom of the crust is about 1,900°F (1,050°C).

Crust

Mantle

OUTER CORE
The core of the Earth consists of two layers – the outer core and the inner core. The outer core is about 1,240 miles (2,000 km) thick and is made of liquid iron. Its temperature is approximately 4,000°F (2,200°C).

Outer core

LIQUID ROCK
The interior of the Earth is very hot, heated by radioactive decay of the rocks inside the Earth. The temperature is so high that some rock inside the Earth is molten. This liquid rock rises to the surface at volcanoes, where it is called lava.

INNER CORE
A ball of solid iron and nickel about 1,712 miles (2,740 km) across lies at the center of the Earth. The temperature at the center is about 8,100°F (4,500°C).

The Earth is made of layers of air, water, iron, nickel, and rock around a core of iron and nickel.

Inner core

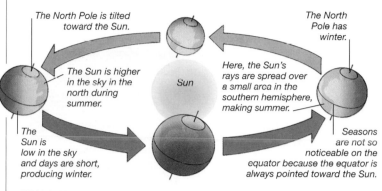

The North Pole is tilted toward the Sun.

The North Pole has winter.

The Sun is higher in the sky in the north during summer.

Sun

Here, the Sun's rays are spread over a small area in the southern hemisphere, making summer.

The Sun is low in the sky and days are short, producing winter.

Seasons are not so noticeable on the equator because the equator is always pointed toward the Sun.

SEASONS
Seasons change as the Earth moves around the Sun. The Earth's axis is tilted at an angle of 23.5° to its orbit, which makes the poles point toward or away from the Sun at different times of the year.

EARTH FACTS

Diameter at equator	7,926 miles (12,756 km)
Diameter at poles	7,900 miles (12,714 km)
Circumference at equator	24,901 miles (40,075 km)
Land area	29.2% of Earth's surface
Ocean area	70.8% of Earth's surface
Mass	5,900 billion billion tons (6,000 billion billion tonnes)
Time for one spin	23 hours 56 minutes 4 seconds
Time to orbit Sun	365 days 6 hours 9 minutes 9 seconds
Distance from Sun	93 million miles (150 million km)

The Earth spins around its axis, which passes through the North and South poles. It also orbits the Sun at the same time.

1 A cloud of gas and dust contracted (shrank) to form the Sun about 4.6 billion years ago. The rest of the cloud then contracted further and broke up into large clumps of particles of ice and rock. After a short time, the particles stuck to each other and began to form the planets.

2 The Earth may have taken about 100 million years to grow into a ball of rock. The new planet became hot as the rock particles crashed into one another. The surface was molten, and the young Earth glowed red-hot.

FORMATION OF THE EARTH
Scientists have calculated that the Earth is nearly 4.6 billion years old. Some Moon rocks and meteorites (pieces of rock that fall to Earth from space) are the same age, which suggests that the whole solar system formed at the same time. The Sun, Earth, and the other planets were formed from a huge cloud of gas and dust in space.

3 Radioactivity in the rocks caused more heat, and the whole planet melted. Molten iron then sank to the center of the Earth to form its core. Lighter rocks floated above the iron, and about 4.6 billion years ago the surface cooled to form the crust. Volcanoes erupted and poured out gases, which formed the atmosphere, and water vapor condensed (changed into liquid) to fill the world's oceans.

GEOTHERMAL ENERGY
The heat from the interior of the Earth provides a source of safe, clean energy, called geothermal energy. Hot rocks lie close to the surface in Iceland, Italy, and other parts of the world. The rocks heat underground water and often make it boil into steam. Wells dug down to these rocks bring up the steam and hot water, which are used to generate electricity and heat buildings.

THEORIES OF THE EARTH
People once believed that the Earth was flat. About 2,500 years ago, the Greeks found out that the Earth is round. Aristarchus, a Greek scientist, suggested in 260 B.C. that the Earth moves around the Sun. It was not until 1543 that Polish astronomer Nicolaus Copernicus (1473-1543; right) reasserted this idea. New theories are still evolving. For instance, one idea called the Gaia theory suggests that the whole planet behaves as a living organism.

4 Tiny living things began to grow at least 3.5 billion years ago. Some produced oxygen, which began to build up in the atmosphere about 2.5 billion years ago. The continents broke up and slowly moved into their present-day positions. They are still moving slowly today – a process called continental drift.

Water that filled the oceans may have also come from comets that collided with the young Earth.

Find out more
ATMOSPHERE
CLIMATES
CONTINENTS
GEOLOGY
OCEANS AND SEAS
RADIOACTIVITY
ROCKS AND MINERALS
UNIVERSE

EARTHQUAKES

ONCE EVERY 30 SECONDS, somewhere in the world, the Earth shakes slightly. These earth tremors are strong enough to be felt, but cause no damage. However, every few months a major earthquake occurs. The land shakes so violently that roads break up, forming huge cracks, and buildings and bridges collapse, causing many deaths. Earthquakes are caused by the movements of huge plates of rock in the Earth's crust. They occur in places that lie on the boundaries where these plates meet, such as the San Andreas fault, which runs 270 miles (435 km) through central California. In some cases, scientists can tell in advance that an earthquake is likely to occur. In 1974, for example, scientists predicted an earthquake in China, saving thousands of lives. But earthquake prediction is not always accurate. In 1989, a major earthquake struck San Francisco without warning, killing 67 people.

INSTANT CHAOS
Destruction can be so swift and sudden that people have no time to escape. Falling masonry crushes cars and blocks roads.

CAUSES OF EARTHQUAKES

The Earth's crust consists of several vast plates of solid rock. These plates move very slowly and sometimes slide past each other. Most severe earthquakes occur where the plates meet. Sometimes the edges of the plates grip each other and cannot move, so pressure builds up. Suddenly the plates slip and lurch past each other, making the land shake violently.

The rocks suddenly slip along the fault: a movement of a few feet is enough to cause a severe earthquake.

The place within the Earth where an earthquake occurs is the focus.

FAULT
A deep crack, or fault, marks the boundary of two plates.

The earthquake is usually strongest at the epicenter, the point on the Earth's surface directly above the focus.

Rocks grip along the fault.

RICHTER SCALE
The severity of an earthquake is measured on the Richter scale, which runs from 0 to 9. An earthquake reaching 8 on the scale can flatten a city. The Richter scale measures the movement of the ground, rather than the damage an earthquake causes, which varies from place to place.

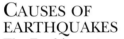

An earthquake in the Indian Ocean on December 26, 2004, caused tsunamis that devastated the coasts of parts of South East Asia, India, and Africa. It was one of the worst natural disasters of recent times.

SEISMOLOGY

Sensitive equipment can pick up vibrations far from an earthquake. This is because the sudden slip of rocks produces shock waves that move through the Earth. The study of earthquakes and the shock waves they cause is called seismology.

TSUNAMIS
Earthquakes that occur on the ocean floor, can produce a wave called a tsunami that races toward the shore. The wave is not very high in mid-ocean. But it begins to rise as it nears the coast, sometimes growing to about 250 ft (75 m) high. The tsunami smashes onto the shore, destroying buildings and carrying boats far inland. Tsunamis, which are often wrongly called tidal waves, are also caused by volcanic eruptions.

EARTHQUAKE BELTS
Earthquakes occur only in certain parts of the world. This map shows the world's earthquake belts, which also extend through the oceans. Most severe earthquakes happen near boundaries between plates in the Earth's crust, so the belts follow the edges of the plates.

Find out more
CONTINENTS
EARTH
GEOLOGY
VOLCANOES

EAST AFRICA

EAST AFRICA IS A REGION of physical contrasts, ranging from the semidesert of the north to the fertile highlands of Ethiopia and Kenya, and from the coastal lowlands to the forest-covered mountains of the west. Most people live off the land. Coffee, tea, and tobacco are grown as cash crops, while nomadic groups herd cattle in the savanna grassland which dominates much of the region. Four of the world's poorest countries – Ethiopia, Eritrea, Somalia, and Djibouti – lie along the Horn of Africa. Their traditional livelihoods of farming, herding, and fishing have been disrupted by drought, famine, and civil war between ethnic groups. Kenya, with its fertile land and warm, moist climate is by contrast, stable and prosperous, its income boosted by wildlife tourists. Ethnic conflict has brought chaos to Sudan, Rwanda, and Burundi, while Uganda is slowly recovering from civil war.

East Africa straddles the Horn of Africa, and is bordered by both the Red Sea and the Indian Ocean. It is dominated by the Great Rift Valley and, in the north, the upper reaches of the Nile river. Desert in the north gives way to savanna grasslands in much of the region.

DINKA

The Dinka (above) are a nomadic people who live in the highlands of Sudan. They move their herds of cattle around according to the seasons, taking them to graze the savanna grasslands in spring, when the rivers flood and the land is fertile. Cattle are of supreme importance to the Dinka. They form part of a bride's wealth, and are offered as compensation, or payment, for marriage. Young men are presented with a special ox, and their adult name is inspired by the shape and color of the animal.

TEA CULTIVATION
The highlands of Ethiopia and Kenya are major tea-producing areas. The flavor of tea grown slowly in cool air at altitudes of 3,000-7,000 ft (1,000-2,000 m) is considered the finest. The leaves are dried, rolled, and blown with hot air, which ferments them, producing a rich black color and strong flavor.

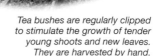

Tea bushes are regularly clipped to stimulate the growth of tender young shoots and new leaves. They are harvested by hand.

The various styles of architecture in Mogadishu (right) reflect the city's history.

MOGADISHU
The capital of Somalia was one of the earliest Arab trading settlements in eastern Africa, dating to the 10th century. The city is dominated by a major port, and is a mixture of historic Islamic buildings and modern architecture. Civil war in the 1980s and 1990s has, however, destroyed much of the city.

LALIBELA
The kings of Ethiopia converted to Christianity in the 4th century, but it was not until the 12th century that Christianity held sway over most of the population. King Lalibela built 11 remarkable churches, which were carved out of rock below ground level. They are still major pilgrimage centers for Ethiopian Christians today.

KAMPALA
Since 1962, Kampala has been the capital of independent Uganda. It is located in the southern part of the country, on the hills overlooking Lake Victoria. It is an export center for coffee, cotton, tea, sugar, and tobacco. Locally produced foods, such as cassava, millet, and sweet potatoes, are sold at lively street markets. Kampala has rainfall on nearly every day of the year, and violent thunderstorms 242 days a year.

THE GREAT RIFT VALLEY

Stretching from Syria to Mozambique, the Rift Valley is a huge gash in the Earth's surface, formed where Africa and the Arabian peninsula are gradually moving apart. The Great Rift Valley, which was formed some 30 million years ago, is 4,000 miles (6,400 km) long, and up to 40 miles (64 km) wide. In Kenya and Tanzania, the valley is marked by deep fjordlike lakes. Elsewhere, volcanic peaks have erupted and wide plateaus, such as the Athi Plains in Kenya, have formed where lava has seeped through the Earth's surface.

MASAI

The Masai people herd cattle in the grasslands of Kenya and Tanzania. The young men paint their bodies with ocher and have elaborate plaited hairstyles. Masai warriors wear beaded jewelry. They are famed for their toughness and endurance. Each man may take several wives, and is responsible for his own herd of cattle, which are driven to pasture far from the village during the dry season. Mothers pass on cattle to their sons. The staple diet of the Masai is cow's milk, supplemented by corn.

The Masai keep their cattle for milk. They also drink blood drawn from the veins of living cows.

WILDLIFE

The Great Plains of East Africa contain some of the world's most spectacular wildlife. In Kenya, ten percent of all the land has been absorbed into more than 40 national parks. Tourists go on wildlife safaris to Kenya (below) to see herds of lions, antelopes, leopards, and elephants. Poaching animals, especially elephants for ivory, remains a major problem, and national parks are closely guarded by game wardens.

Diseases such as cholera thrive in crowded refugee camps like the one pictured here.

A herd of elephants wander the savannah in Kenya in search of water. A number of lions watch the elephants, waiting to kill any weak animal.

GORILLAS

The forested mountains of Rwanda and Uganda are the last remaining refuge for gorillas, the world's rarest ape. Gorillas have long been targeted by poachers, hunters, and collectors. The Albert National Park was established in 1925 for their protection, but civil war in the 1960s disrupted the gorilla population. Much of their forest habitat was also cleared for agriculture, further reducing numbers.

Since the 1980s, national parks have been carefully guarded, and limited educational and tourist programs put in place. Gorilla numbers in Rwanda have risen, but recent conflict once again threatens their survival.

REFUGEE CAMP

Many of the boundaries in central East Africa date back to colonial times and cut across ethnic borders. In Rwanda, the majority Hutus rebelled against the ruling Tutsis with terrible consequences. The country descended into violent chaos, and many people were forced to flee to refugee camps in Tanzania. There has also been conflict between Hutus and Tutsis in neighboring Burundi.

Find out more

AFRICA
AFRICAN WILDLIFE
ELEPHANTS
GRASSLAND WILDLIFE
LIONS

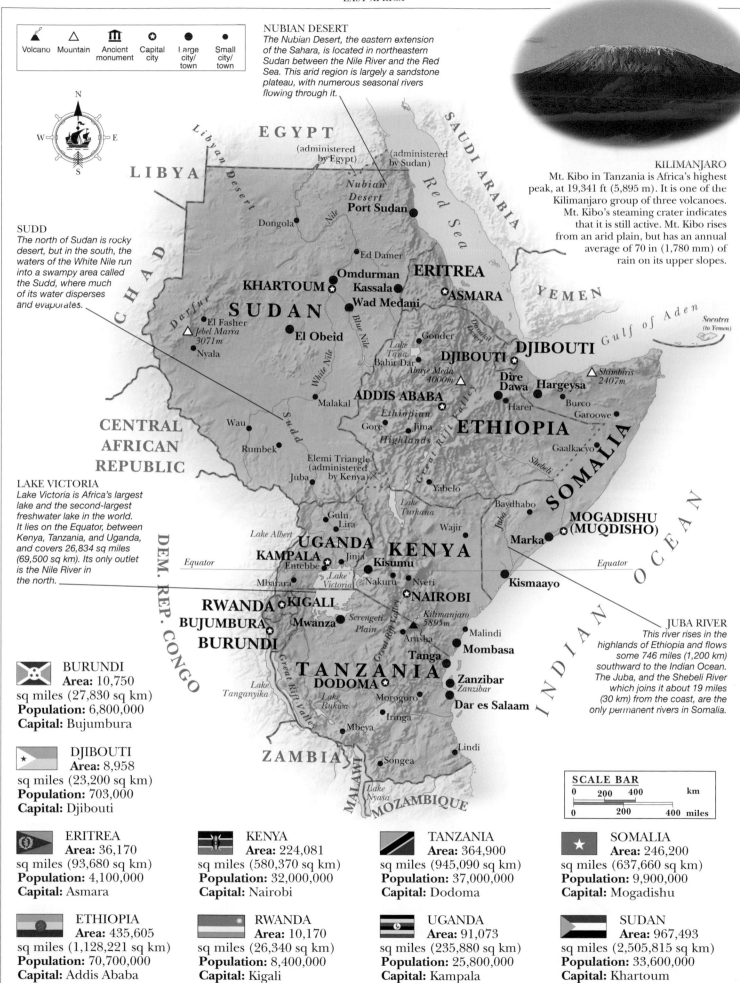

Volcano **Mountain** **Ancient monument** **Capital city** **Large city/town** **Small city/town**

NUBIAN DESERT
The Nubian Desert, the eastern extension of the Sahara, is located in northeastern Sudan between the Nile River and the Red Sea. This arid region is largely a sandstone plateau, with numerous seasonal rivers flowing through it.

KILIMANJARO
Mt. Kibo in Tanzania is Africa's highest peak, at 19,341 ft (5,895 m). It is one of the Kilimanjaro group of three volcanoes. Mt. Kibo's steaming crater indicates that it is still active. Mt. Kibo rises from an arid plain, but has an annual average of 70 in (1,780 mm) of rain on its upper slopes.

SUDD
The north of Sudan is rocky desert, but in the south, the waters of the White Nile run into a swampy area called the Sudd, where much of its water disperses and evaporates.

LAKE VICTORIA
Lake Victoria is Africa's largest lake and the second-largest freshwater lake in the world. It lies on the Equator, between Kenya, Tanzania, and Uganda, and covers 26,834 sq miles (69,500 sq km). Its only outlet is the Nile River in the north.

JUBA RIVER
This river rises in the highlands of Ethiopia and flows some 746 miles (1,200 km) southward to the Indian Ocean. The Juba, and the Shebeli River which joins it about 19 miles (30 km) from the coast, are the only permanent rivers in Somalia.

SCALE BAR
0   200   400   km
0   200   400   miles

BURUNDI
Area: 10,750 sq miles (27,830 sq km)
Population: 6,800,000
Capital: Bujumbura

DJIBOUTI
Area: 8,958 sq miles (23,200 sq km)
Population: 703,000
Capital: Djibouti

ERITREA
Area: 36,170 sq miles (93,680 sq km)
Population: 4,100,000
Capital: Asmara

KENYA
Area: 224,081 sq miles (580,370 sq km)
Population: 32,000,000
Capital: Nairobi

TANZANIA
Area: 364,900 sq miles (945,090 sq km)
Population: 37,000,000
Capital: Dodoma

SOMALIA
Area: 246,200 sq miles (637,660 sq km)
Population: 9,900,000
Capital: Mogadishu

ETHIOPIA
Area: 435,605 sq miles (1,128,221 sq km)
Population: 70,700,000
Capital: Addis Ababa

RWANDA
Area: 10,170 sq miles (26,340 sq km)
Population: 8,400,000
Capital: Kigali

UGANDA
Area: 91,073 sq miles (235,880 sq km)
Population: 25,800,000
Capital: Kampala

SUDAN
Area: 967,493 sq miles (2,505,815 sq km)
Population: 33,600,000
Capital: Khartoum

ECOLOGY AND FOOD WEBS

WE CAN LOOK AT NATURE in the same way that we look at a complicated machine, to see how all the parts fit together. Every living thing has its place in nature, and ecology is the study of how things live in relation to their surroundings. It is a relatively new science and is of great importance today. It helps us understand how plants and animals depend on each other and their surroundings in order to survive. Ecology also helps us work toward saving animals and plants from extinction and solving the problems caused by pollution. Plants and animals can be divided into different groups, depending on their ecological function. Plants capture the Sun's light energy and use it to produce new growth, so they are called producers; animals consume (eat) plants and other animals, so they are called consumers. All of the plants and animals that live in one area and feed off each other make up a community. The relationships between the plants and animals in a community is called a food web; energy passes through the community via these food webs.

ECOSYSTEM

A community and its surroundings, including the soil, air, climate, and the other communities around it, make up an ecosystem. The Earth can be seen as one giant ecosystem spinning through space. It recycles its raw materials, such as leaves and other plant matter, and is powered by energy from the Sun.

The European kingfisher has little to fear. Its brightly colored plumage warns predators that it is foul-tasting. The kingfisher is well named – it is extremely skillful at fishing.

FOOD CHAINS AND FOOD WEBS

A plant uses the Sun's energy to grow. An herbivore (plant-eater) eats the plant. A carnivore (meat-eater) or an omnivore (plant-and meat-eater) then eats the herbivore. This series of events is called a food chain.

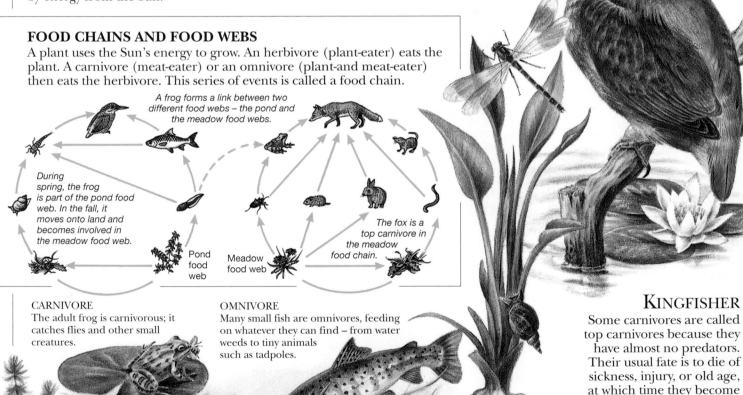

A frog forms a link between two different food webs – the pond and the meadow food webs.

During spring, the frog is part of the pond food web. In the fall, it moves onto land and becomes involved in the meadow food web.

The fox is a top carnivore in the meadow food chain.

Pond food web

Meadow food web

Plants form the beginning of the food chain in a pond, as they do on land.

CARNIVORE
The adult frog is carnivorous; it catches flies and other small creatures.

OMNIVORE
Many small fish are omnivores, feeding on whatever they can find – from water weeds to tiny animals such as tadpoles.

DETRITIVORE
Certain types of worms and snails are called detritivores because they eat detritus, or rotting matter, at the bottom of a pond or river. They help recycle the materials and energy in dead and dying plants and animals.

HERBIVORE
As a young tadpole, the frog is an herbivore, eating water weeds.

KINGFISHER
Some carnivores are called top carnivores because they have almost no predators. Their usual fate is to die of sickness, injury, or old age, at which time they become food for scavengers. The European kingfisher shown here eats a wide variety of food, including small fish such as minnows and sticklebacks, water snails and beetles, dragonfly larvae, tadpoles, and small frogs. The kingfisher is therefore at the top of a complex food web.

HABITAT

A habitat is a place where a certain animal or plant usually lives. There are several characteristic habitats, such as oak forests, mangrove swamps, and chalk cliffs. A habitat often has one or a few main plants, such as the pampas grass, which grows in the grassland habitats of South America. Certain characteristic animals feed on these plants. Some animals live in only one or two habitats; the desman, for example, is a type of muskrat found only in fast-running mountain streams. Other animals, such as red foxes and brown rats, are able to survive in many different habitats. The coral reef shown here is one of the Earth's richest habitats. Its warm, shallow water is full of nutrients, and the sunlight encourages many different forms of life.

BIOME

A biome is a huge habitat, such as a tropical rain forest or a desert. The deserts of Africa, Central Asia, and North America each have distinct kinds of plants and animals, but their ecology is similar. Each of these large habitats, or biomes, has a big cat as a top predator – the caracal (a kind of lynx) in Africa, the bobcat in North America, and Pallas's cat in central Asia. The major types of plants that grow in a biome are determined by its climate. Areas near the equator with very high rainfall become tropical rain forests, and in cold regions near the Arctic and Antarctic, only tundra plants can survive.

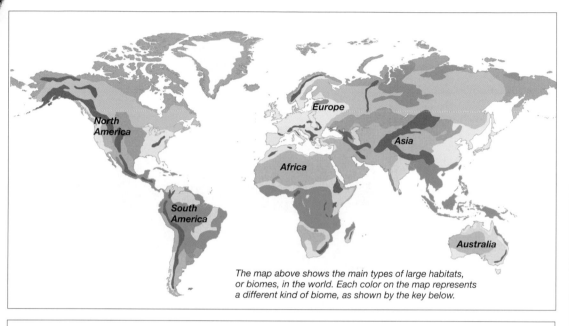

North America
Europe
Asia
Africa
South America
Australia

The map above shows the main types of large habitats, or biomes, in the world. Each color on the map represents a different kind of biome, as shown by the key below.

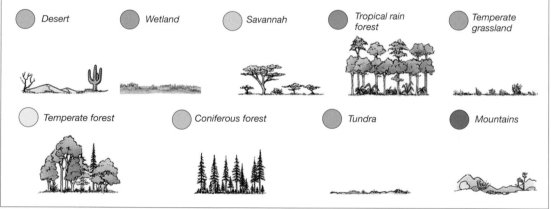

Desert   Wetland   Savannah   Tropical rain forest   Temperate grassland

Temperate forest   Coniferous forest   Tundra   Mountains

PESTICIDES

Farmers and gardeners use pesticides to kill insects that are pests on vegetable and cereal crops. In 1972, the insecticide called DDT was banned in the United States because it caused great damage to wildlife. When DDT is sprayed on crops, some of it is eaten by herbivores such as mice and squirrels. The insecticide builds up inside the animal's body. A bird of prey such as a hawk eats the animal, and the DDT becomes concentrated (builds up) in the bird's body. The DDT causes the bird to make very thin or deformed eggshells, which break and kill the developing chicks inside. Since DDT was banned, the number of falcons has slowly risen.

Today, falcons and other birds of prey are rare. Many have died as a result of the pesticides used by farmers to kill insects on farm crops.

Find out more

ANIMALS
CONSERVATION
and endangered species
EAGLES
and other birds of prey
LAKE AND RIVER WILDLIFE
PLANTS
POLLUTION

THOMAS EDISON

THE MOST IMPORTANT INVENTOR in American history, Thomas Alva Edison held 1,093 patents (legal rights) for inventions – the most ever issued to one person. His most famous inventions included electric lighting, the phonograph, and key improvements to the telegraph, telephone, and moving pictures. Edison said that genius is 2 percent inspiration and 98 percent perspiration; this kind of persistence led to his greatest work. Edison surrounded himself with a team of talented engineers, mechanics, and craftsmen, creating one of the first research laboratories. He was also a legendary businessman, and raised money to develop his products.

1847 Born in Milan, Ohio.

1869 Awarded his first patent, for a voting machine.

1877 Invents the phonograph.

1879 Perfected electric light bulb.

1882 His power station is the world's first.

1889 Forms General Electric Company.

1900 Invents alkaline storage battery.

1909 First commercially successful phonograph.

1912 Edison produces first movies.

1931 Dies in New Jersey.

EDISON'S ELECTRIC LIGHT
In 1878, Edison began research on electric lighting. By the following year, he had created an incandescent lamp bulb (above), which produced light by passing electricity through a filament (wire) to make it glow. Once he had perfected the bulb, he worked to develop electric power plants to provide electricity to homes. The first plant opened in 1882; by the 1890s Edison's power stations lit hundreds of cities.

Black Maria, Edison's movie studio

EDISON'S LABORATORY
Edison was one of the first inventors to establish a research laboratory. He used a team of experts and technicians to develop ideas, which he would then improve upon. Many large corporations later established research laboratories like Edison's.

MOVING PICTURES
In 1889, Edison helped found the motion picture industry with the invention of the kinetoscope, the first practical motion-picture device that used a roll of film. Viewers looked through a peephole to see a series of images shown in rapid succession, giving the impression of continuous action. In 1893, Edison built a film studio called Black Maria, the first building designed for making movies.

WIZARD OF MENLO PARK
Edison opened a laboratory at Menlo Park, New Jersey, in 1876, where he worked full-time on his inventions. His favorite invention was the phonograph, which Edison called a "talking machine." Its crank turned a sharp point around a cylinder. The user turned the crank while speaking to cut a pattern of grooves into the foil. When a needle was moved back over the cylinder, the machine replayed the voice.

Earpiece

Mouthpiece

This wall-mounted telephone was invented by Thomas Edison in 1879.

EDISON AND THE TELEPHONE
Although Alexander Graham Bell patented the telephone, Edison made crucial improvements to his friend's design by adding a carbon transmitter that made a speaker's voice louder and clearer, and a separate receiver to cut out static.

Edison (left) displays his phonograph.

Find out more
ELECTRICITY
MOVIES
TELEPHONES

EDUCATION

LEARNING DOES NOT ONLY take place at school. Education – the process of acquiring knowledge – begins when we are born and continues throughout life. Learning to speak, for instance, is a basic skill we acquire at an early age by imitating and repeating the sounds produced by our family and others around us. As we grow older, traveling, reading, and other activities also increase our knowledge. Formal education begins when we have learned certain basic skills, such as speech, and can benefit from going to school. Through kindergarten, grade school, and high school, we learn vital skills and valuable knowledge. After graduating from high school, many students go on to college where they widen their general knowledge and study one or more subjects in depth. School and college can also help us recognize and develop the individual talents and skills that each of us possesses, and show us how we can use this potential in a career and to benefit society as a whole. Universities, technical schools, internships, and work-study programs provide education to match an individual's chosen career.

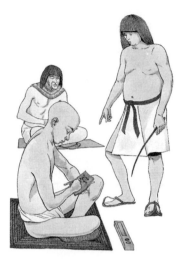

SCRIBE SCHOOLS
In Ancient Egypt only educated scribes could read and write. Boys who trained to be scribes laboriously wrote and copied each day. At first they wrote on useless objects such as broken pottery; when their work improved, they were allowed to write on papyrus, a precious kind of paper. Girls were educated at home, learning domestic skills from their mothers.

CHOICES IN EDUCATION
No two people are the same. For this reason education offers students a wide choice. From the arts, or humanities, students may choose subjects such as fine arts (painting and sculpture), languages, and law. From science subjects there is the choice of pure science, such as physics; applied science, such as engineering; and medicine.

PHRENOLOGY BY L.N. FOWLER.

Scientists in the 19th century believed that portions of the human brain were reserved for specific kinds of knowledge. Modern medicine has proved it wrong.

UNIVERSITY
Many students continue their education at a college or university. The basic college degree, the bachelor's degree, usually takes four years to earn. Some then go on to earn a master's degree and doctorate (Ph.D).

EDUCATION FOR THE FEW
Free education for all has become available only during the last 100 years. Before then only the very wealthy could afford education. During the Middle Ages, Latin was the language of learning in Europe; it was essential for those who wanted to work in the Church, in medicine, or in law.

GREEK EDUCATION
The Ancient Greek philosopher Aristotle held strong views about education. He believed that from the age of seven, children should learn gymnastics, music, reading, writing, and drawing. Later studies would include physics, philosophy, and politics. Aristotle's ideal was an active and enquiring mind in a healthy body.

PRACTICAL LEARNING
Education is designed to meet a society's needs. The children of tribes who live in tropical rain forests learn survival skills, such as building boats and hunting. In developing societies, however, the educational system must produce the scientists and engineers the country needs in order to industrialize.

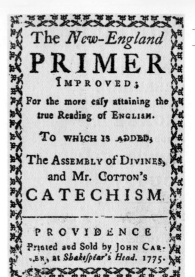

LEARNING BY THE BOOK

Colonial students were taught from Latin texts, the Bible, and hornbooks. The first standard American textbook, *The New England Primer* (right), was printed in 1690 and used for over a hundred years. It taught the two R's common to early American education – reading and religion. Noah Webster's *American Spelling Book* of 1783 standardized American spelling and started the craze for spelling bees. In 1836, McGuffey's *Readers* first appeared. These books used stories, traditional tales, and poems to teach reading as well as moral lessons to children.

The paper or parchment lesson on a hornbook was covered with a thin layer of protective horn.

AMERICAN SCHOOLING

Young American students of the 1800s probably sat quietly at desks that were bolted to the floor in rows. A single schoolroom would be shared among students of different ages. Pupils learned the three R's – reading, writing, and 'rithmetic (mathematics) as well as religion – by memorization. The teacher stood by with a hornbook, a paddle-shaped board holding the day's lesson, and disciplinary ruler at the ready. Today's students still learn the basics, but they participate more by asking questions, discussing ideas in groups, and working independently.

HIGHER EDUCATION IN AMERICA

The nation's oldest college, Harvard University, was founded in 1636 in Cambridge, Massachusetts, primarily to train men for the clergy. Colleges later expanded their courses to teach the "liberal arts" – natural sciences, social sciences, and humanities. In 1833, Oberlin College in Ohio became the first to offer education to both men and women. Vassar, the first women's college, was founded in 1861. There are more than 2,000 colleges and universities in the United States today, many offering two- and four-year degree programs as well as graduate degrees.

Students in the library at Vassar College, 1945

HORACE MANN
One of the first people to champion state-supported, public education in the United States was lawyer Horace Mann (above). He was chosen as the first state secretary of education in 1837. Mann also worked to improve conditions for teachers, and established the first teacher training colleges in the United States.

Computers are an integral part of education today.

ADULT EDUCATION

The first night schools were established in New York City in the 1830s, to give newly-arrived immigrants who worked during the day the opportunity to learn English. Today, adults from all walks of life return to school to learn new job skills, study new technologies, continue their academic education, and explore new interests and hobbies.

DISTANCE EDUCATION
Most schools teach computer skills as part of the curriculum. Many colleges offer classes online via the Internet; a student can now complete a course without ever stepping into a classroom.

Find out more

BOOKS
INTERNET
SCHOOLS
UNITED STATES, HISTORY OF

ANCIENT
EGYPT

THE RICH, FERTILE SOIL of the Nile Valley gave birth to Egypt, a civilization that began over 5,000 years ago and lasted more than 3,000 years. The Nile River made the black soil around it productive, and the civilization of Egypt grew wealthy. For much of its history Egypt was stable. Its pharaohs ruled with the help of officials called viziers who collected taxes and acted as judges. The Egyptians worshiped many gods and believed that when they died they went to the Next World. Pharaohs built elaborate tombs for themselves; the best known are the magnificent pyramids. The Egyptians also made great advances in medicine. Gradually, however, the civilization broke down, leaving it open to foreign invasion. In 30 B.C. the Romans finally conquered the empire.

PHARAOHS

The rulers of Ancient Egypt were called pharaohs, meaning "Great House." They were thought to be divine and had absolute power: all the land in Egypt belonged to them. People believed the pharaohs were the sons of Ra, the Sun god. Above is a famous pharaoh, Tutankhamun, who died when he was only 18.

The internal layout of the Great Pyramid

Grand Gallery

King's Chamber

Entrance

Escape shaft

Queen's Chamber

PYRAMIDS

The Egyptians believed in an eternal life after death in a "perfect" version of Egypt. After their bodies had been preserved by embalming, pharaohs were buried in pyramid tombs. The earliest pyramids had steps. People believed the dead king's spirit climbed the steps to join the Sun god at the top. Later, the pyramids were built with smooth slanted sides. However, people could rob the pyramid tombs easily, so later pharaohs were buried in unmarked tombs in the Valley of the Kings and guarded day and night.

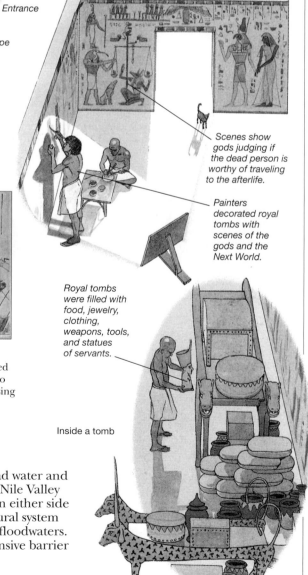

Scenes show gods judging if the dead person is worthy of traveling to the afterlife.

Painters decorated royal tombs with scenes of the gods and the Next World.

Royal tombs were filled with food, jewelry, clothing, weapons, tools, and statues of servants.

Inside a tomb

Painting of the time shows cattle being transported across the Nile River in special wide boats.

TRANSPORT AND TRADE

The quickest way to travel in Egypt was by water. Barges carried goods along the Nile, and Egyptian traders traveled in ships to ports around the eastern Mediterranean and the Red Sea. Using a system called bartering, they exchanged gold, grain, and papyrus sheets for silver, iron, horses, cedar wood, and ivory.

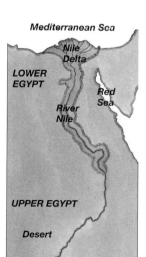

Mediterranean Sea

Nile Delta

LOWER EGYPT

Red Sea

River Nile

UPPER EGYPT

Desert

NILE RIVER

Each year, the Nile River burst its banks and spread water and fertile silt over the land. This "inundation" of the Nile Valley made the land fertile for about 6 miles (10 km) on either side of the river. The Egyptians planned their agricultural system around this area, farming the land by storing the floodwaters. The desert on either side provided a natural defensive barrier and a rich source of minerals and stone.

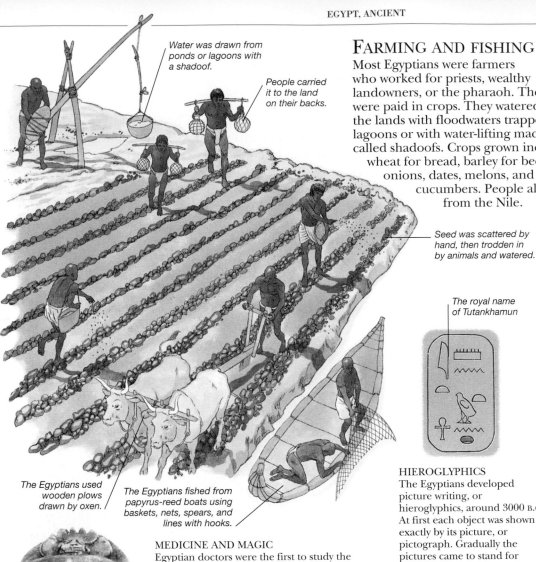

Water was drawn from ponds or lagoons with a shadoof.

People carried it to the land on their backs.

Seed was scattered by hand, then trodden in by animals and watered.

The Egyptians used wooden plows drawn by oxen.

The Egyptians fished from papyrus-reed boats using baskets, nets, spears, and lines with hooks.

FARMING AND FISHING

Most Egyptians were farmers who worked for priests, wealthy landowners, or the pharaoh. They were paid in crops. They watered the lands with floodwaters trapped in lagoons or with water-lifting machines called shadoofs. Crops grown included wheat for bread, barley for beer, beans, onions, dates, melons, and cucumbers. People also fished from the Nile.

The royal name of Tutankhamun

HIEROGLYPHICS

The Egyptians developed picture writing, or hieroglyphics, around 3000 B.C. At first each object was shown exactly by its picture, or pictograph. Gradually the pictures came to stand for sounds. Groups of "sound hieroglyphs," or phonograms, were used to spell words.

NEFERTITI

Nefertiti was the wife of the pharaoh Ikhnaton, who ruled from 1367 to 1355 B.C. She had great influence over her husband's policies. Usually, however, the only women who held important titles were priestesses.

MEDICINE AND MAGIC

Egyptian doctors were the first to study the body scientifically. They also carried out some effective dentistry. However, many "cures" were based on magic.

Scarab beetles were sacred to the Egyptians, who used them as charms to ward off illness.

Headrest amulet

Relief of the time showing Ancient Egyptian medical tools.

ANCIENT EGYPT

c. 10,000-5000 B.C. First villages on the banks of the Nile. Slow growth of the two kingdoms of Upper and Lower Egypt.

c. 2630 B.C. First step pyramid built at Saqqara.

c. 2575 B.C. During Old Kingdom period, bronze replaces copper. Pyramids built at Giza. Dead bodies are embalmed.

c. 2134 B.C. Old Kingdom ends with power struggles.

c. 2040 B.C. Middle Kingdom begins. Nobles from Thebes reunite the country. Nubia conquered.

c. 1640 B.C. Middle Kingdom ends.

1550 B.C. New Kingdom begins. Permanent army.

1400 B.C. Egypt reaches height of its power.

1070 B.C. Egyptian power begins to decline.

332 B.C. Alexander the Great conquers Egypt.

51 B.C. Cleopatra rules.

30 B.C. Egypt becomes a Roman province.

MUMMIES

The Egyptians thought that if they preserved their bodies after death, they would "live" forever. So they made "mummies" – corpses that did not decay. Embalmers removed the liver, lungs, and brain from the dead body, leaving the heart inside. They then coated the body with saltlike natron crystals to preserve it, and finally wrapped the whole package in bandages.

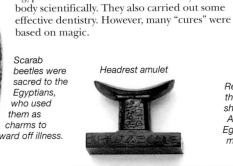

An idealized portrait of the dead person was painted on the coffin.

The internal organs were wrapped in linen and placed in canopic jars.

Linen protected the body.

Coffin was richly decorated with hieroglyphs of spells to help the dead person in the afterlife.

Find out more
AFRICA, HISTORY OF
ALPHABETS
ARCHAEOLOGY
CATS

ALBERT
EINSTEIN

PHYSICIST ALBERT EINSTEIN was one of the greatest scientific thinkers of all time. His theories, or ideas, on matter, space, and time revolutionized our understanding of the universe, and have formed the basis of all modern physics. He is probably best known for his work on relativity, first published in 1905, which astounded the scientific community. In this, Einstein showed that for everything slower than light, speed and time are relative. The faster anything travels, the slower time seems to pass. Later, his work on relativity led to other revolutionary ideas on energy and mass, and in 1921 he was awarded the Nobel Prize. From 1933 he lived in the United States. A scientific genius, he was also a pacifist, and deeply religious.

1879 Born in Ulm, Germany.

1900 Graduates with degrees in math and physics, Switzerland.

1902-09 Works in patent office, Switzerland.

1905 Publishes Special Theory of Relativity.

1916 Publishes General Theory of Relativity.

1921 Awarded Nobel Prize for Physics.

1933 Emigrates to US.

1955 Dies Princeton, New Jersey.

THE YOUNG EINSTEIN
Einstein was born in Germany, and, as a small boy, was very curious about things around him. When he was 15, the family moved to Switzerland, where Einstein was educated. By the time he graduated, he was already pondering the nature of light. He worked in a patent office and at the age of 26 wrote his first paper on relativity.

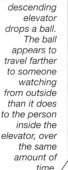

Someone in a descending elevator drops a ball. The ball appears to travel farther to someone watching from outside than it does to the person inside the elevator, over the same amount of time.

A visual puzzle helps to demonstrate the theory of relativity.

Albert Einstein working in his study in Princeton.

Einstein was famous for his untidiness.

Different relative viewpoints can alter our perceptions.

RELATIVITY
The concept of relativity is very difficult to grasp. One of the central ideas is "time dilation," time seeming to slow down when things are moving in relation to an observer who is still. This effect increases at very high speeds approaching the speed of light. This increase is not easy to show, because we cannot notice it at the slow speeds we experience. Nothing can travel faster than light, so the speed of light is constant.

ATOMIC ENERGY
Einstein produced the famous equation $E = mc^2$, where energy (E) = mass (m) multiplied by the square of the speed of light (c). It showed that an immense amount of energy could be released by splitting the nucleus of an atom. This contributed to the development of the atom bomb. From 1946, Einstein was opposed to atomic weapons.

SCIENTIST
Einstein developed his revolutionary theories by devising what he called "thought experiments." For example, he wondered what the world would look like if he rode on a beam of light. Such simple questions often had surprising answers, which Einstein confirmed with complex mathematics. At the time, many people did not believe Einstein's theories, but later research has proved him correct.

Find out more
ATOMS AND MOLECULES
SCIENCE, HISTORY OF
TIME

ELECTRICITY

A FLASH OF LIGHTNING leaping through the sky during a thunderstorm is one of the most visible signs of electricity. At almost all other times, electricity is invisible, but hard at work for us. Electricity is a form of energy. It consists of electrons – tiny particles that come from atoms. Each electron carries a tiny electric charge, which is an amount of electricity. When you switch on a light, about one million billion electrons move through the bulb every second. Cables hidden in walls and ceilings carry electricity around houses and factories, providing energy at the flick of a switch. Electricity also provides portable power. Batteries produce electricity from chemicals, and solar cells provide electricity from the energy in sunlight. Lamps, motors, and dozens of other machines use electricity as their source of power. Electricity also provides signals which make telephones, radios, televisions, and computers work.

CURRENT ELECTRICITY

Electricity comes in two forms: electricity that flows, and static electricity, which does not move. Flowing electricity is called current electricity. Billions of electrons flow along a wire to give an electric current. The electricity moves from a source such as a battery or power station to a machine. It then returns to the source along another wire. The flow of electric current is measured in amperes (A).

Electricity flows into homes through cables that run either underground or above street level on poles.

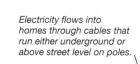

Some power stations generate electricity by burning coal and oil. Other stations are powered by nuclear energy.

A transformer boosts the voltage (force) of the electricity to many thousands of volts.

Tall pylons support long cables that carry the electricity safely above the ground to all parts of an area.

Another transformer reduces the voltage of the electricity to levels suitable for domestic appliances.

CONDUCTORS AND INSULATORS

Electricity flows only through materials called conductors. These include copper and many other metals. Conductors can carry electricity because their own electrons are free to move. Other substances, called insulators, do not allow electricity to flow through them. This is because their electrons are held tightly inside their atoms.

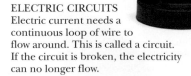

Electrons flow through copper conductor.

Most plastics are insulators.

Batteries produce direct current, which flows one way around a circuit.

Battery pushes electric current around the circuit.

Power stations produce alternating current, which flows first in one direction and then the other.

Wires connect battery and bulb to form a circuit.

Bulb in bulb holder

ELECTRIC CIRCUITS

Electric current needs a continuous loop of wire to flow around. This is called a circuit. If the circuit is broken, the electricity can no longer flow.

SUPERCONDUCTORS

Ordinarily conductors, while letting most electricity flow through them, also resist it to some extent. So a certain amount of electricity is lost. However, some materials lose their resistance when very cold. They become superconductors.

A superconductor can produce a strong magnetic field which makes a small magnet hover above it.

STATIC ELECTRICITY

There are two types of electric charge, positive (+) and negative (–). Objects usually contain equal numbers of both charges so they cancel each other out. Rubbing amber (fossilized resin from trees) against wool or fur makes it pick up extra electrons, which carry a negative charge. This charge is called static electricity. It produces an electric force which makes light objects, such as hair and feathers, cling to the amber.

GENERATOR

Generators produce electricity from the energy of movement. A coil of wire moves between the poles of a magnet. This produces an electric current in the coil. Small, simple generators that power bicycle lamps are called dynamos. Large generators in power stations produce huge amounts of electricity for homes and factories.

Basic generator

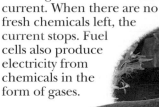

Coil of wire

Magnetic field produced by magnet.

A simple generator (above) contains a coil of wire that spins between the poles of a magnet. A current flows in the coil when it moves through the magnetic field.

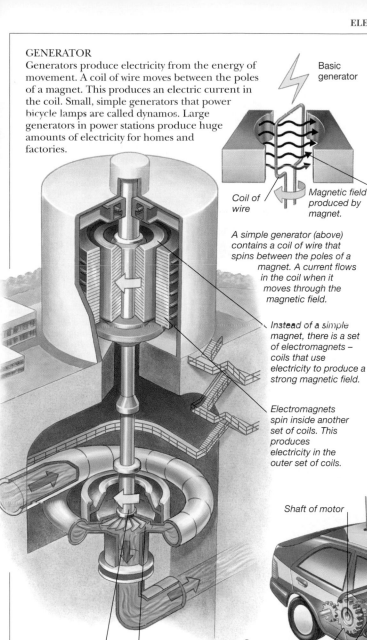

Instead of a simple magnet, there is a set of electromagnets – coils that use electricity to produce a strong magnetic field.

Electromagnets spin inside another set of coils. This produces electricity in the outer set of coils.

A shaft connected to the turbine (a set of vanes) drives the generator.

In a hydroelectric power station, water falling from a dam spins a turbine.

Shaft of motor

Gears connect motor to wheels of car.

Coil of wire

Magnet produces magnetic field.

Electric current flows from battery into coil, producing a magnetic field.

The magnetic force pushes on the coil and makes it spin around.

ELECTRICITY FROM CHEMICALS

Chemical energy from food changes into movement in your muscles. Chemical energy can also change into electrical energy. This is how a battery works. Chemicals react together inside a battery and produce an electric current. When there are no fresh chemicals left, the current stops. Fuel cells also produce electricity from chemicals in the form of gases.

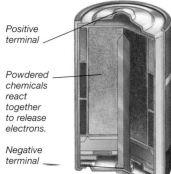

ELECTRIC EEL

The rivers of South America are the home of the electric eel. This eel has special organs in its long body that work like batteries to produce electricity. With a powerful electric shock, the electric eel can stun its prey.

Positive terminal

Powdered chemicals react together to release electrons.

Negative terminal

BATTERY

Connecting a battery in a circuit makes the chemicals inside react to produce an electric current. The battery provides a force that pushes electrons around the circuit. The energy provided by this force is measured in units called volts.

Inside the battery, the electrons flow from the positive terminal and back to the negative terminal.

ELECTRIC MOTOR

Many machines are powered by an electric motor, which contains a coil of wire placed between the poles of a magnet. The electric current fed to the motor flows through the coil, producing a magnetic field. The magnet pushes on the coil and makes it spin around and drive the shaft of the motor.

ELECTRIC SHOCKS

Living things make use of electricity. Weak electric signals pass along the nerves to and from the brain. These signals operate the muscles, maintain the heartbeat, and control the way in which the body works. A strong electric current can give an electric shock that damages the human body and may even cause death. *Never* play with an electricity supply because of the danger of electric shock.

DISCOVERY

About 2,500 years ago, the Ancient Greeks found that rubbing amber (fossilized resin) produces a charge of static electricity. The Greek for amber is *elektron*, which is how electricity got its name. Around 1750, American scientist Benjamin Franklin (left) discovered that lightning is electricity and explained what electric charges are. At the end of the 18th century, Italian scientists Luigi Galvani and Alessandro Volta produced the first electric battery.

Benjamin Franklin (1706-90) studied the electrical nature of lightning by flying a kite during a thunderstorm.

A bird sitting on an electric cable does not get an electric shock. The electricity does not pass into its body because the bird is touching only one wire and does not complete an electric circuit.

Find out more

ATOMS AND MOLECULES
ELECTRONICS
ENERGY
FISH
MAGNETISM

ELECTRONICS

The semiconductor silicon comes from sand, which is a compound of silicon and oxygen.

A diode is made from the junction between pieces of n- and p-type semiconductors.

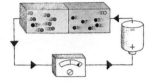

ELECTRICITY is a source of power that drives machines and provides heat and light. Electricity is also used to produce signals that carry information and control devices. Using electricity in this way is called electronics. We are surrounded by thousands of electronic machines, including computers, CD players, telephones, and televisions. All these machines contain circuits through which electric currents flow. Tiny electronic components in the circuits control the flow of the current to produce signals. For instance, a varying current may represent sound in a telephone line, or a number in a computer. The most important electronic component is the transistor. A small radio receiver may contain a dozen transistors; a computer contains thousands of miniaturized transistors inside microchips.

A diode allows current to flow through it in only one direction. The current is carried by the flow of holes and electrons.

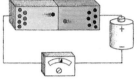

If a battery is connected the other way around, holes and electrons cannot cross the junctions so current cannot flow.

SEMICONDUCTORS
Most electronic components are made of materials such as silicon, which are called semiconductors. Semiconductors control the flow of current because they contain a variable number of charge carriers (particles that carry electricity). In n-type semiconductors, the charge carriers are negatively charged electrons; in p-type semiconductors, the charge carriers are positively charged "holes" – regions where electrons are absent.

Capacitor stores electric charge. In a radio circuit, capacitors help tune the circuit so that it picks up different radio frequencies.

CIRCUIT BOARD
An electronic device such as a telephone contains an electronic circuit consisting of several components joined together on a circuit board. Every circuit is designed for a particular task. The circuit in a radio, for instance, picks up and amplifies (boosts) radio waves so they can be converted into sound.

Diode allows current to pass in only one direction.

Resistor reduces the amount of current flowing in the circuit.

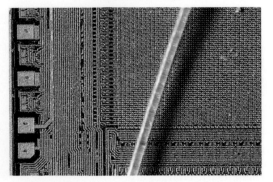

Transistor boosts the strength of electrical signals.

Variable resistor allows the flow of current to be varied.

Wires are used to connect some components.

Microchip in plastic casing

Metal tracks on the underside of the board connect components.

CONTROLLING CURRENT
Electronic circuits do several basic jobs. They may amplify current; they may produce an oscillating current – one that rapidly changes direction, essential for generating radio waves; or they may switch current on and off.

Oscillation: Some circuits convert a steady one-way current (direct current, or DC) into a varying alternating current (AC).

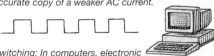

Amplification: An amplifier circuit generates a strong AC current that is an accurate copy of a weaker AC current.

Switching: In computers, electronic circuits rapidly switch current on and off in a code that represents data.

MICROCHIPS
Microchips, or silicon chips, contain circuits consisting of hundreds of thousands of microscopic components. These circuits are squeezed onto the surface of a semiconductor less than 1 in (25 mm) square.

TRANSISTOR
Transistors lie at the heart of most electronic machines. They boost current and voltage in amplifier circuits, store information in computers, and perform many other tasks. Physicists William Shockley, John Bardeen, and Walter Brattain invented the transistor in 1947.

Find out more

COMPUTERS
ELECTRICITY
RADIO
SOUND RECORDING
TECHNOLOGY

ELEPHANTS

GREAT TUSKS, huge ears, and a strong trunk make the elephant one of the most magnificent creatures on Earth. Elephants are the largest living land mammals and among the most ancient. They are extremely strong and highly intelligent, and have been trained to work with humans for thousands of years. There are three kinds of elephants – African Savannah, Forest, and Asian (Indian). African elephants are slightly bigger than Asian elephants, with much larger ears. A large male measures more than 10 ft (3 m) high at the shoulder and weighs more than 5.3 tons. The elephant's trunk reaches to the ground and high into the trees to find food. The trunk is also used for drinking, smelling, greeting other members of the herd, and as a snorkel in deep water.

WOOLLY MAMMOTH
The prehistoric mammoth became extinct about 10,000 years ago. Frozen remains of mammoths have been found in Alaska and Siberia.

TRUNK
The trunk is formed from the nose and the long upper lip. It is extremely sensitive to touch and smell. The elephant uses its trunk to grasp leaves, fruits, and shoots, and place them in its mouth. In order to drink, the elephant must squirt water into its mouth because it cannot drink through its trunk.

Head and jaws are huge, with wide, ridged teeth for chewing plant matter

Huge ears help to cool elephant by allowing heat to escape.

Ears are used to threaten other animals.

Two nostrils at tip of the trunk

When bathing, the elephant sucks water into its trunk, then squirts it over the body.

Tusks are massive upper incisor teeth, made of ivory. They can split bark from trees and gouge roots from the ground.

Wide, flat, soft-soled feet leave hardly any tracks.

ASIAN ELEPHANT
There are probably fewer than 50,000 Asian elephants left in the wild in remote forests of India, China, and Southeast Asia. Female or cow elephants are quite easy to tame between the ages of about 10 and 20 years. They are caught and kept in captivity, and used for clearing forests and towing logs. Asian elephants are also dressed and decorated for ceremonies and processions.

BREEDING
A newborn elephant calf weighs 220-260 lb (100-120 kg) at birth. It sucks milk from the teats between its mother's front legs until it is about four years old. A young elephant stays with its mother for the first 10 years of its life. By the age of six it weighs about one ton, and at about 15 years of age it is ready to breed.

AFRICAN ELEPHANTS
In the late 1970s there were about 1.3 million elephants in Africa. Today there are half that number. Poachers kill them for their ivory, and farms are built on the land where they live. In reserves, however, where elephants are protected, their numbers have increased. Here, they are culled (killed in a controlled way) to prevent them from damaging the countryside. Today elephants are on the official list of endangered species, and the trade in elephants and ivory is controlled by international agreement.

A six-year-old male African elephant

**Find out more**
AFRICAN WILDLIFE
ANIMALS
CONSERVATION
and endangered species
MAMMALS

ELIZABETH I

MORE THAN 400 YEARS AGO, one woman brought 45 years of peace and prosperity to England through her determination and wisdom. Queen Elizabeth I began her life as a neglected princess whose mother had been executed by her father. She was ignored and imprisoned as a girl; but upon the death of her half sister, Queen Mary, Elizabeth became a strong and popular queen. She tried to end years of religious conflict between Catholics and Protestants by insisting that the Church of England should be moderately Protestant so that it included as many people as possible. Elizabeth avoided expensive foreign wars for many years. Her most dangerous conflict was with Philip II, king of Spain, who sent the Armada (fleet of ships) against England. The queen's court was a center for poets, musicians, and writers. Her reign is often called England's Golden Age.

1533 Born, the daughter of Henry VIII and Anne Boleyn.

1536 Mother is executed for treason.

1554 Imprisoned in the Tower of London.

1558 Crowned queen.

1559 Establishes Protestant Church of England by the Act of Supremacy.

1587 Orders execution of Mary, Queen of Scots.

1588 Faces the Armada.

1603 Dies.

SIR WALTER RALEIGH
One of Elizabeth's favorite courtiers was Sir Walter Raleigh (1552-1618). In 1584 she knighted him, and later made Raleigh her Captain of the Guard. He made several voyages across the Atlantic, set up an English colony in Virginia, and brought tobacco and potatoes from the Americas to Europe.

ELIZABETHAN AGE
Elizabeth was the first monarch to give her name to an age. During her reign the arts of music, poetry, and drama flourished. Despite foreign threats and religious unrest at home, she won the loyalty and admiration of her subjects.

SPANISH ARMADA
In July 1588 Philip II, king of Spain, launched his Armada of nearly 150 ships to invade England and restore the Catholic religion. Sir Francis Drake (1540-96) sailed in command of a large group of warships to oppose the Armada. Aided by stormy weather, the English defeated the great fleet.

MARY, QUEEN OF SCOTS
Mary was Elizabeth's Catholic cousin and heir. Forced to abdicate her own throne in Scotland, she fled to England to seek Elizabeth's protection. Mary became involved in Catholic plots against Elizabeth, who reluctantly ordered her execution.

Find out more

THEATER
UNITED KINGDOM, HISTORY OF

ENERGY

THE MOVEMENT OF A CAR, the sound of a trumpet, the light from a candle – all these things occur because of energy. Energy is the ability to make things happen. For example, when you throw a stone, you give it energy of movement which shows itself when the stone hits the ground. All life on Earth depends on energy, almost all of which comes from the Sun. The Sun's energy makes plants grow, which provides the food that animals eat; the energy from food is stored in an animal's muscles, ready to be converted into movement. Although energy is not an object that you can see or touch, you can think of it as something that either flows from place to place, or is stored. For instance, energy is stored by water high at the top of a waterfall. As soon as the water starts to fall, the stored energy changes into moving energy which flows to the bottom of the waterfall.

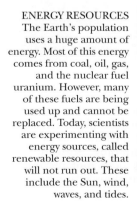

WORK, ENERGY, AND POWER
When a force moves an object, energy is transferred, or passed, to the object or its surroundings. This transfer of energy is called work. The amount of work done depends on the size of the force and how far it moves. For instance, this weightlifter does a lot of work lifting a heavy weight through a large distance. Power is the rate of doing work. The weightlifter produces more power the faster he lifts the weight.

POTENTIAL ENERGY
Energy can be stored as potential energy until it turns into another form such as movement. Examples include water in a raised reservoir waiting to flow through turbines, chemical energy in a battery waiting to drive an electric current, and a coiled spring waiting to be released.

KINETIC ENERGY
An object such as an airplane needs energy to make it move. Moving energy is called kinetic energy. When the plane stops, it loses kinetic energy. This often appears as heat – for instance, in the plane's brakes.

TYPES OF ENERGY

Energy takes many forms, and it can change from one form into another. For example, power stations turn the chemical energy stored in coal or oil into heat energy which boils water. Turbines change the heat energy of the steam into electrical energy which flows to homes and factories.

Heat energy, such as the warmth of the Sun, is carried by invisible waves called infrared or heat radiation.

Light is one form of energy that travels in waves. Others include X rays and radio waves.

Sound waves are vibrations of the air, so they carry kinetic energy.

Some power stations produce electricity from nuclear energy, which comes from the nuclei (centers) of atoms.

Electrical devices turn the energy of electric currents into many other forms of energy, including heat, light, and movement.

A battery runs out when all its stored energy has been converted into heat in the wires, and heat and light in the bulb.

Oil and coal contain stored chemical energy which changes into heat and light when these fuels are burned.

ENERGY CYCLE
Energy cannot be created or destroyed; it can only change from one form into another. The only exception might seem to be when matter changes into energy in a nuclear reactor. However, the rule still applies because matter and energy are really the same and one can be converted into the other.

ENERGY RESOURCES
The Earth's population uses a huge amount of energy. Most of this energy comes from coal, oil, gas, and the nuclear fuel uranium. However, many of these fuels are being used up and cannot be replaced. Today, scientists are experimenting with energy sources, called renewable resources, that will not run out. These include the Sun, wind, waves, and tides.

Rows of solar panels for producing electricity

Find out more

ELECTRICITY
HEAT
LIGHT
NUCLEAR ENERGY
SOUND
SUN
WATER
WIND

ENGINES

FOUR-STROKE ENGINE
Most car engines are four-stroke engines, which means that each piston makes a set of four movements.

Piston 2 rises and compresses (squeezes) fuel-air mixture.

Piston 4 rises and pushes waste gases out through exhaust valve.

Piston 3 is pushed down by expanding gases when the mixture explodes.

Spark plug produces electrical spark that ignites fuel-air mixture.

Valves open and close to admit and expel the fuel-air mixture.

Piston 1 moves down and sucks fuel-air mixture in through inlet valve.

The piston moves up and down inside the cylinder.

Most engines have between four and eight cylinders. These work in sequence to produce continuous movement.

Crankshaft changes the up-and-down movement of the pistons into a circular movement that drives the wheels.

WHEN PREHISTORIC PEOPLE discovered fire, they found a way of obtaining energy, because burning releases heat and light. About one million years later, the steam engine was invented, and for the first time people could harness that energy and turn it into movement. Today, there are many different kinds of engines that drive the world's transportation and industry. All engines serve one function – to use the energy stored in a fuel such as oil or coal, and change it into motion to drive machines. Before engines were invented, tasks such as building and lifting depended on the strength of people and their animals. Today, engines can produce enough power to lift the heaviest weights and drive the largest machines. The most powerful engine is the rocket engine; it can blast a spacecraft away from the pull of the Earth's gravity and out into space.

INTERNAL-COMBUSTION ENGINE
The engine that powers almost all of the world's cars is the internal-combustion engine. It uses the power of gases created by exploding fuel to produce movement. A mixture of air and tiny droplets of gasoline enters the engine's cylinders, each of which contains a piston. An electrical spark ignites (sets alight) the fuel mixture, producing gases that thrust each piston down.

ELECTRIC MOTORS
Gas and diesel engines produce waste gases that pollute the air and contribute to the greenhouse effect (which causes the Earth's temperature to rise). Electric motors are clean, quiet, and produce no pollution. Several car manufacturers are developing cars powered by electric motors. Hybrid cars such as the Toyota Prius (below) use a combination of electric and gas power to provide good performance with low pollution.

DIESEL ENGINE
Many trains and trucks have powerful diesel engines, which are internal-combustion engines that burn diesel fuel instead of gasoline. The engine works in the same way as a gas-fueled engine, but does not have spark plugs. Instead, each cylinder has an injector that squirts diesel fuel into the cylinder. The piston compresses the air, making it very hot. The hot air is all it needs to make the diesel fuel explode.

JET ENGINE

The jet, or gas turbine, engine now powers most high-speed aircraft. The engine blasts a jet of hot, fast-moving air backward out of its exhaust; this pushes the engine forward. Fans at the front of the engine spin and suck air into it, and squeeze it at high pressure into several combustion chambers. There, flames of burning kerosene heat the air, which expands and rushes toward the exhaust. As the air streams out, it spins a turbine, which drives the fans at the front of the engine.

FRANK WHITTLE
In 1928, English pilot and engineer Frank Whittle (born 1907) suggested the idea of the jet engine. Whittle's engine powered an experimental aircraft for the first time in 1941. However, the first jet-powered flight was made during the 1930s in Germany, where engineer Hans von Ohain had developed his own jet engine.

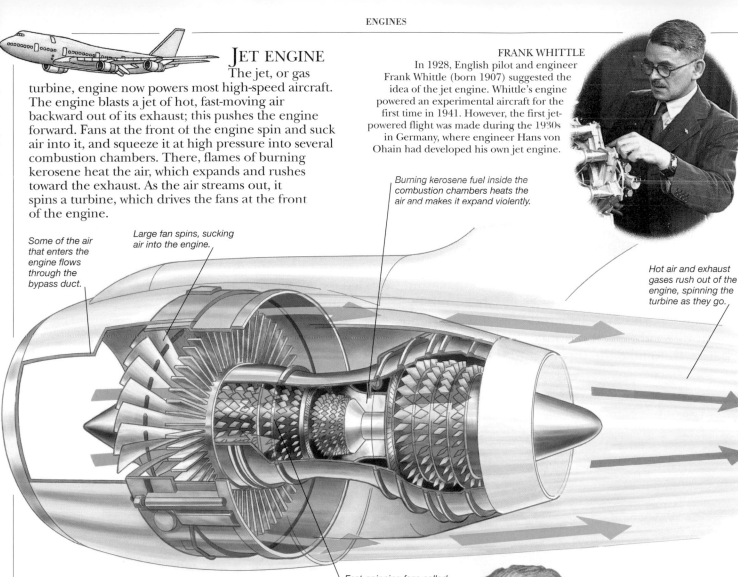

Some of the air that enters the engine flows through the bypass duct.

Large fan spins, sucking air into the engine.

Burning kerosene fuel inside the combustion chambers heats the air and makes it expand violently.

Hot air and exhaust gases rush out of the engine, spinning the turbine as they go.

Fast-spinning fans called compressors increase the pressure of the air and push it into the combustion chambers.

TURBOFAN ENGINE

A turbofan engine is a very efficient kind of gas turbine engine. Some of the air flows through a bypass duct around the main part of the engine. This increases the amount of air flowing through the engine, giving it more thrust. The duct also helps make the engine quieter.

STEAM ENGINE
The steam engine was developed during the 18th century and greatly changed people's lives. It led to the development of industry and transportation. People left the land to work in the new factories that contained steam-powered machines, and steam railroads allowed people to travel farther and faster than ever before.

JAMES WATT
The first engine was a simple steam engine invented by the Greek scientist Hero in the 1st century A.D., but it was little more than a toy. In 1712, the British engineer Thomas Newcomen built the first real engine. It was a huge steam engine used to pump water out of mines. In 1769, another British engineer, James Watt (left), greatly improved the steam engine. The unit of power, the watt, is named after him.

Boiler burns wood or coal, producing heat.

Hot air and smoke pass through pipes that run through the water tank. The heat turns the water into steam.

Steam and smoke escape through a valve and pour out of the smokestack.

Steam passes through a pipe to a cylinder. The steam pushes a piston back and forth inside the cylinder.

The movement of the piston drives the wheels of the train.

Find out more
AIRCRAFT
CARS
ELECTRICITY
ROCKETS AND MISSILES
TRAINS
TRANSPORTATION, HISTORY OF

ENGLISH CIVIL WAR

IN 1649, CHARLES I, king of England, was put on trial for treason and executed. His death marked the climax of the English Civil War, also called the English Revolution, a fierce struggle between king and Parliament (the law-making assembly) over the issue of who should govern England. The struggle had begun many years before. Charles I believed that kings were appointed by God and should rule alone; Parliament believed that it should have greater power. When the king called upon Parliament for funds to fight the Scots, it refused to cooperate, and in 1642 civil war broke out. England was divided into two factions – the Royalists (also called Cavaliers), who supported Charles, and the Roundheads, who supported Parliament. Charles was a poor leader, and the Roundheads had the support of the navy and were led by two great generals – Lord Fairfax and Oliver Cromwell. By 1649 Cromwell had defeated Charles and declared England a republic. Despite various reforms, Cromwell's rule was unpopular. In 1660, the army asked Charles's son, Charles II, to take the throne and the monarchy was restored.

CHARLES I
King Charles I (reigned 1625-49) was the only English monarch to be executed. He ignored the Parliament, and ruled alone from 1629 to 1640. After a disagreement with the Parliament in 1642, Charles raised an army and began the civil war that ended his reign. The picture above depicts the scene of his execution.

Parliamentary (New Model) army

Royalist cavalry

Royalist officers wore wide-brimmed hats.

Pikeman

BATTLE OF NASEBY
At the Battle of Naseby in 1645, the heavily armed and well-organized pikemen and musketeers of Cromwell's "New Model Army" crushed the Royalists.

OLIVER CROMWELL
The English Republic (1649-60) was organized and ruled mainly by Lord Protector Oliver Cromwell (1599-1658). Cromwell was an honest, moderate man and a brilliant army leader. But his attempts to enforce extreme purity upon England made him unpopular with many.

RUMP PARLIAMENT
At the end of the English Civil War, all that was left of King Charles's Parliament was a "rump" Parliament, whose members refused to leave. In 1653, Cromwell, determined to get rid of any remnant of the king, dismissed Parliament. He pointed at the mace, the speaker's symbol of office, and laughingly called it a bauble (left).

DIGGERS
During these turbulent years, new political groups emerged. Some, such as the Diggers, were very radical. They believed that ordinary people should have a say in government and wanted to end private property.

Find out more

CIVIL WAR
UNITED KINGDOM,
history of

ESCALATORS AND ELEVATORS

WORKING, SHOPPING, and traveling in a city would be difficult without escalators and elevators. People would have to walk up and down stairs in skyscrapers, big department stores, tall apartment buildings, and deep subway stations. An elevator travels up and down between the floors of a building. People and goods ride inside the elevator. An escalator is a staircase in which the steps move up or down. Some elevators and escalators travel up and down the outside of a building, giving a bird's-eye view of the surroundings.

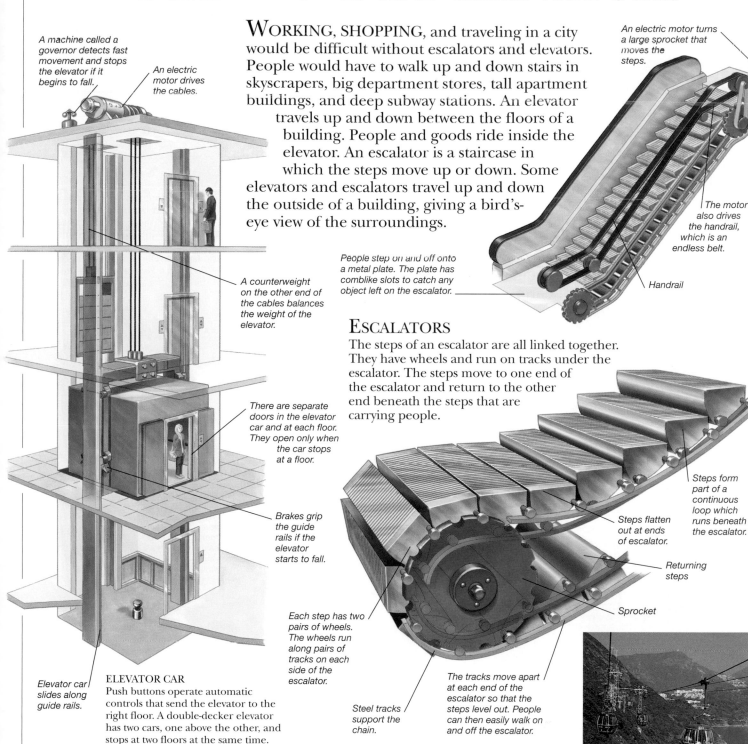

A machine called a governor detects fast movement and stops the elevator if it begins to fall.

An electric motor drives the cables.

An electric motor turns a large sprocket that moves the steps.

A counterweight on the other end of the cables balances the weight of the elevator.

The motor also drives the handrail, which is an endless belt.

People step on and off onto a metal plate. The plate has comblike slots to catch any object left on the escalator.

Handrail

ESCALATORS
The steps of an escalator are all linked together. They have wheels and run on tracks under the escalator. The steps move to one end of the escalator and return to the other end beneath the steps that are carrying people.

There are separate doors in the elevator car and at each floor. They open only when the car stops at a floor.

Brakes grip the guide rails if the elevator starts to fall.

Steps form part of a continuous loop which runs beneath the escalator.

Steps flatten out at ends of escalator.

Returning steps

Sprocket

Each step has two pairs of wheels. The wheels run along pairs of tracks on each side of the escalator.

The tracks move apart at each end of the escalator so that the steps level out. People can then easily walk on and off the escalator.

Steel tracks support the chain.

Elevator car slides along guide rails.

ELEVATOR CAR
Push buttons operate automatic controls that send the elevator to the right floor. A double-decker elevator has two cars, one above the other, and stops at two floors at the same time.

ELEVATORS
Most elevators have strong steel cables that support the car, which travels along guide rails up and down a shaft. Some elevators are pushed up from below by a long steel tube. The world's fastest elevators can rise about 56 ft (17 m) in a second.

THE OTIS SAFETY ELEVATOR
In 1854, an American engineer called Elisha Otis demonstrated his safety elevator. While standing on the elevator, he ordered the rope to be cut. A safety mechanism automatically gripped the guide rails and kept the elevator from falling. Otis's invention made the building of skyscrapers possible. All elevators now have safety mechanisms of this kind.

CABLE CARS
A moving cable pulls cable cars and ski elevators up mountain slopes and steep hills. These cable cars are in Hong Kong.

Find out more
ARCHITECTURE
BUILDING
MACHINES

EUROPE

COMPARED TO ITS mighty eastern neighbor, Asia, Europe is a tiny continent. But the culture of Europe has extended far beyond its boundaries. Europe has a long history of wealth, industry, trading, and empire building. Much of its prosperity comes from its green and fertile land, which is watered by numerous rivers and plenty of rain. Yet the climate varies considerably across the continent. The countries of southern Europe border the Mediterranean Sea. Vacationers visit the coast of this enclosed sea to enjoy its long, hot summers. The far north, in contrast, reaches up into the icy Arctic Circle. There are also a number of high mountain ranges within Europe, including the Alps and the Pyrenees. The ethnic composition of Europe's 725 million people is as varied as the landscape. The continent is culturally diverse with a rich history. The Nordic people of the north have blond hair, fair skin, and blue eyes, while many Europeans in the south have darker skin and dark, curly hair.

Europe lies to the north of the Mediterranean Sea and overlooks the northern part of the Atlantic Ocean. It includes the surrounding islands, such as the British Isles and Iceland. The Ural Mountains in the Russian Federation mark the long eastern border with Asia.

EURO
The European Union made a major move toward monetary union when the Euro was introduced as a single European currency. Eleven EU countries, including Germany and France, formally adopted the currency in 1999, and the Euro replaced the national currencies of 12 countries at the start of 2002 (Greece joining in with the original 11). Other EU countries, such as Britain and Denmark, kept their national currencies.

Old European buildings may look picturesque, but the architecture is more than decorative. The mellow brick and stone provide essential protection against the cool, damp weather.

To meet increasing competition from abroad, particularly from Japan, European companies have modernized their factories.

INDUSTRY
Large-scale industry began in Europe. Labor-saving inventions of the 18th and 19th centuries enabled workers in European factories to manufacture goods cheaply and in large numbers. The Industrial Revolution soon spread to other parts of the world, including the United States, India, and Japan. Manufacturing industries still play a vital role in most European countries.

Austrian composer Johann Strauss, Jr. (1825-99) named his famous waltz tune The Blue Danube after the river.

DANUBE RIVER
Europe's second-longest river is the Danube. The Danube flows from the Black Forest in Germany to the Black Sea and passes through nine European countries: Germany, Austria, Slovakia, Hungary, Croatia, Serbia, Romania, Bulgaria, and Ukraine.

CITIES
Most European cities predate those in Australia and America. Many are of ancient origin and have grown gradually over several centuries. As a result, they differ enormously in design and layout to their modern counterparts abroad. Originally designed to cope with small volumes of traffic, Europe's cities are composed of an irregular mixture of narrow, winding streets and wider boulevards. Modern cities, designed with current modes of transportation in mind, are carefully planned and tend to follow a more uniform grid pattern.

TRADE

Europeans have always been great traders. Between the 15th and 18th centuries, the countries of Europe were the most powerful in the world. They took their trade to all corners of the globe, and their settlers ruled parts of the Americas, Africa, India, Southeast Asia, and Australia. Almost all of these regions are now independent, but many still retain traces of European culture.

European trade and money formed the basis of the world's banking system.

The people paint the houses white to reflect the heat of the sun.

SCANDINAVIA

A great hook-shaped peninsula encloses most of the Baltic Sea in northern Europe and extends into the Arctic Ocean. Sweden and Norway occupy this peninsula. Together with Denmark to the south, they make up Scandinavia. Finland, to the east of the Baltic, and the large island of Iceland in the North Atlantic are often also included in the group.

In the warm climate of the Mediterranean region olives, oranges, lemons, sunflowers, melons, tomatoes, and eggplants grow well.

Goats and sheep are more common than cattle, which require richer pasture.

MEDITERRANEAN

Ten European countries border the Mediterranean Sea: Spain, France, Monaco, Italy, Slovenia, Croatia, Bosnia and Herzegovina, Serbia, Albania, and Greece. A small part of Turkey is also in Europe. The Mediterranean people have traditionally lived by farming (above), but many of these countries now have thriving industries. Though the climate around the Mediterranean is much warmer than that of northern Europe, winters can still be chilly.

ART AND CULTURE

Europe has its own traditions of art and culture which are quite distinct from those of other parts of the world. Oil painting, classical music, and ballet had their origins in Europe. The traditions of European theater, music, literature, painting, and sculpture all began in ancient times.

Tallinn (left), Estonia's capital city, is a major Baltic port.

BALTIC STATES

Lithuania, Latvia, and Estonia, low-lying agricultural countries on the eastern coast of the Baltic Sea, are together called the Baltic States. They were formed in 1918 and remained independent until 1940 when they were occupied by the Soviet Union. In 1991, Lithuania became one of the first of the former Soviet republics to achieve independence, followed a few months later by Estonia and Latvia.

Find out more

FRANCE
GERMANY
ITALY
RUSSIAN FEDERATION
SCANDINAVIA
SPAIN
UNITED KINGDOM

STATISTICS

Area: 4,053,309 sq miles (10,498,000 sq km)
Population: 725,200,000
Highest point: El' brus, Caucasus Mountains (European Russia) 18,511 ft (5,642 m)
Longest river: Volga (European Russia) 2,290 miles (3,688 m)
Largest lake: Ladoga (European Russia) 7,100 sq miles (18,300 sq km)
Main occupations: Agriculture, manufacturing, industry
Main exports: Machinery and transportation equipment
Main imports: Oil and other raw materials

EUROPEAN UNION

In 1957, five European countries agreed to form the European Economic Community (EEC). They believed that economic and political cooperation would reduce the likelihood of wars between the member countries and would bring prosperity to the peoples of Europe. In December 1991, the Maastricht Treaty created the European Union (EU) and committed its member states to the introduction of a single currency. The EU flag (below) has 12 yellow stars on a blue background. The Union now has 25 members.

 **ALBANIA**
Area: 11,100 sq miles (28,750 sq km)
Population: 3,200,000
Capital: Tirana

ANDORRA
Area: 181 sq miles (468 sq km)
Population: 69,000
Capital: Andorra la Vella

AUSTRIA
Area: 32,375 sq miles (83,850 sq km)
Population: 8,100,000
Capital: Vienna

BELGIUM
Area: 12,780 sq miles (33,100 sq km)
Population: 10,300,000
Capital: Brussels

 BELARUS
Area: 80,154 sq miles (207,600 sq km)
Population: 9,900,000
Capital: Minsk

 BOSNIA AND HERZEGOVINA
Area: 19,741 sq miles (51,130 sq km)
Population: 4,200,000
Capital: Sarajevo

BULGARIA
Area: 42,822 sq miles (110,910 sq km)
Population: 7,900,000
Capital: Sofia

 CROATIA
Area: 21,830 sq miles (56,540 sq km)
Population: 4,400,000
Capital: Zagreb

CZECH REPUBLIC
Area: 30,260 sq miles (78,370 sq km)
Population: 10,200,000
Capital: Prague

DENMARK
Area: 16,629 sq miles (43,069 sq km)
Population: 5,400,000
Capital: Copenhagen

ESTONIA
Area: 17,423 sq miles (45,125 sq km)
Population: 1,300,000
Capital: Tallinn

FINLAND
Area: 130,552 sq miles (338,130 sq km)
Population: 5,200,000
Capital: Helsinki

FRANCE
Area: 212,930 sq miles (551,500 sq km)
Population: 60,100,000
Capital: Paris

GERMANY
Area: 137,800 sq miles (356,910 sq km)
Population: 82,500,000
Capital: Berlin

GREECE
Area: 50,521 sq miles (131,990 sq km)
Population: 11,000,000
Capital: Athens

HUNGARY
Area: 35,919 sq miles (93,030 sq km)
Population: 9,900,000
Capital: Budapest

 ICELAND
Area: 39,770 sq miles (103,000 sq km)
Population: 290,000
Capital: Reykjavik

 IRELAND
Area: 27,155 sq miles (70,280 sq km)
Population: 4,000,000
Capital: Dublin

ITALY
Area: 116,320 sq miles (301,270 sq km)
Population: 57,400,000
Capital: Rome

 LATVIA
Area: 24,938 sq miles (64,589 sq km)
Population: 2,300,000
Capital: Riga

LIECHTENSTEIN
Area: 62 sq miles (160 sq km)
Population: 33,100
Capital: Vaduz

 LITHUANIA
Area: 25,174 sq miles (65,200 sq km)
Population: 3,400,000
Capital: Vilnius

 LUXEMBOURG
Area: 998 sq miles (2,586 sq km)
Population: 453,000
Capital: Luxembourg

 MACEDONIA
Area: 9,929 sq miles (25,715 sq km)
Population: 2,020,000
Capital: Skopje

MALTA
Area: 124 sq miles (320 sq km)
Population: 394,000
Capital: Valletta

 MOLDOVA
Area: 13,000 sq miles (33,700 sq km)
Population: 4,300,000
Capital: Chisinau

 MONACO
Area: 0.75 sq miles (1.95 sq km)
Population: 32,100
Capital: Monaco

NETHERLANDS
Area: 14,410 sq miles (37,330 sq km)
Population: 16,100,000
Capital: Amsterdam, The Hague

 NORWAY
Area: 125,060 sq miles (323,900 sq km)
Population: 4,500,000
Capital: Oslo

 POLAND
Area: 120,720 sq miles (312,680 sq km)
Population: 38,600,000
Capital: Warsaw

PORTUGAL
Area: 35,670 sq miles (92,390 sq km)
Population: 10,100,000
Capital: Lisbon

ROMANIA
Area: 88,934 sq miles (237,500 sq km)
Population: 22,300,000
Capital: Bucharest

RUSSIAN FED.
Area: 5,592,800 sq miles (17,075,400 sq km)
Population: 143,000,000
Capital: Moscow

SAN MARINO
Area: 24 sq miles (61 sq km)
Population: 28,100
Capital: San Marino

 **SERBIA AND MONTENEGRO**
Area: 39,449 sq miles (102,173 sq km)
Population: 10,500,000
Capital: Belgrade

SLOVAKIA
Area: 19,100 sq miles (49,500 sq km)
Population: 5,400,000
Capital: Bratislava

SLOVENIA
Area: 7,820 sq miles (20,250 sq km)
Population: 2,000,000
Capital: Ljubljana

SPAIN
Area: 194,900 sq miles (504,780 sq km)
Population: 41,100,000
Capital: Madrid

SWEDEN
Area: 173,730 sq miles (449,960 sq km)
Population: 8,900,000
Capital: Stockholm

SWITZERLAND
Area: 15,940 sq miles (41,290 sq km)
Population: 7,200,000
Capital: Bern

UKRAINE
Area: 223,090 sq miles (603,700 sq km)
Population: 47,700,000
Capital: Kiev

UNITED KINGDOM
Area: 94,550 sq miles (244,880 sq km)
Population: 59,800,000
Capital: London

VATICAN CITY
Area: 0.17 sq miles (0.44 sq km)
Population: 900
Capital: Vatican City

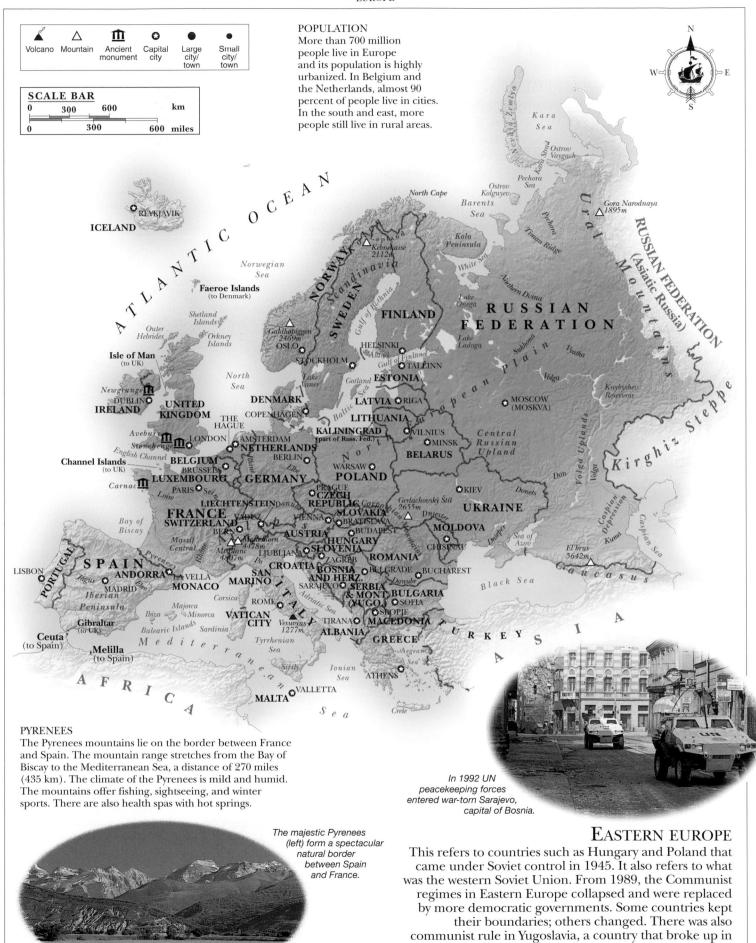

POPULATION
More than 700 million people live in Europe and its population is highly urbanized. In Belgium and the Netherlands, almost 90 percent of people live in cities. In the south and east, more people still live in rural areas.

Volcano	Mountain	Ancient monument	Capital city	Large city/town	Small city/town

SCALE BAR

0   300   600   km

0   300   600   miles

N
W   E
S

ATLANTIC OCEAN

ICELAND
REYKJAVIK

Nógaja Zemlya

Kara Sea

Ostrov Vaygach

Pechora Sea

Ostrov Kolguyev

North Cape

Barents Sea

Kola Peninsula

Timan Ridge

Gora Narodnaya 1895m

Ural Mountains

RUSSIAN FEDERATION (Asiatic Russia)

Norwegian Sea

Faeroe Islands (to Denmark)

Shetland Islands

Outer Hebrides

Orkney Islands

NORWAY

SWEDEN

Scandinavia

Kebnekaise 2112m

Lapland

Gulf of Bothnia

FINLAND

White Sea

Northern Dvina

Lake Onega

RUSSIAN FEDERATION

European Plain

Lake Ladoga

Sukhona

Vyatka

Kuybyshev Reservoir

Galdhøpiggen 2469m
OSLO

HELSINKI

Åland

Lake Vänern

STOCKHOLM

Gotland

Gulf of Finland

TALLINN

ESTONIA

RIGA

Volga

Moscow (MOSKVA)

Central Russian Upland

Isle of Man (to UK)

North Sea

DENMARK
COPENHAGEN

Baltic Sea

LATVIA

LITHUANIA

VILNIUS

MINSK

BELARUS

Volga Uplands

Kirghiz Steppe

Newgrange
DUBLIN
IRELAND

UNITED KINGDOM

THE HAGUE
AMSTERDAM
NETHERLANDS
BERLIN

KALININGRAD (part of Russ. Fed.)

WARSAW

North European Plain

POLAND

KIEV

Don

Donets

Avebury
Stonehenge
LONDON

English Channel

Channel Islands (to UK)

BELGIUM
BRUSSELS

Elbe

GERMANY

PRAGUE
CZECH REPUBLIC

Danube

VIENNA

Gerlachovský Štít 2655m

UKRAINE

Dniester

Caspian Depression

Carnac
LUXEMBOURG
PARIS
Seine

Loire

LIECHTENSTEIN
VADUZ

SLOVAKIA
BRATISLAVA

BUDAPEST

Dnieper

CHISINAU
MOLDOVA

Sea of Azov

Kuma

Caspian Sea

FRANCE
SWITZERLAND
BERN

AUSTRIA

HUNGARY

Carpathian Mountains

Bay of Biscay

Massif Central

Mt Blanc 4807m
Matterhorn 4478m

Po

SLOVENIA
LJUBLJANA

ZAGREB

ROMANIA

BELGRADE

BUCHAREST

El'brus 5642m

Caucasus

Rhône

CROATIA

BOSNIA AND HERZ.

Danube

PORTUGAL

SPAIN

Pyrenees

ANDORRA
LA VELLA

SAN MARINO

SARAJEVO

SERBIA & MONT. (YUGO.)

BULGARIA
SOFIA

Black Sea

LISBON

MADRID

MONACO

Corsica

ROME

ITALY

Adriatic Sea

SKOPJE

MACEDONIA

Tagus

Iberian Peninsula

Ebro

Majorca

VATICAN CITY

TIRANA

ALBANIA

GREECE

TURKEY

ASIA

Gibraltar (to UK)

Ibiza

Minorca

Balearic Islands

Sardinia

Vesuvius 1277m

Aegean Sea

Ceuta (to Spain)

Melilla (to Spain)

Mediterranean

Tyrrhenian Sea

Sicily

Ionian Sea

ATHENS

AFRICA

MALTA
VALLETTA

Sea

Crete

PYRENEES
The Pyrenees mountains lie on the border between France and Spain. The mountain range stretches from the Bay of Biscay to the Mediterranean Sea, a distance of 270 miles (435 km). The climate of the Pyrenees is mild and humid. The mountains offer fishing, sightseeing, and winter sports. There are also health spas with hot springs.

The majestic Pyrenees (left) form a spectacular natural border between Spain and France.

In 1992 UN peacekeeping forces entered war-torn Sarajevo, capital of Bosnia.

EASTERN EUROPE
This refers to countries such as Hungary and Poland that came under Soviet control in 1945. It also refers to what was the western Soviet Union. From 1989, the Communist regimes in Eastern Europe collapsed and were replaced by more democratic governments. Some countries kept their boundaries; others changed. There was also communist rule in Yugoslavia, a country that broke up in the early 1990s. After much bitter fighting, the separate states of Serbia, Croatia, Slovenia, Macedonia, and Bosnia and Herzegovina were formed.

EUROPEAN UNION

IN THE 75 YEARS BETWEEN 1870-1945, France and Germany fought each other three times. After the end of World War II in 1945, the two nations decided to live together as friends, not enemies, by combining their industrial strength. Four other countries joined them, and by 1951 the European Steel and Coal Community was created. Seven years later, the six countries signed the Treaty of Rome to set up the European Economic Community. Since then, the Community has grown into a European Union (EU) of 25 countries, including Britain and Ireland. The EU has a huge impact on daily life in Europe, from the price of food to the color of passports. Many Europeans, however, resist the idea of the EU becoming a "superstate" with its own army and constitution.

JEAN MONNET
French economist Jean Monnet (1888-1979) helped to set up the European Coal and Steel Community, and was its first president. He told the French government that this would prevent another war with Germany.

THE FLAG
The flag of the European Union was first used in 1955 and consists of 12 five-pointed stars on a blue background.

Countries of Europe which do not form part of the EU.

A meeting of the European Parliament in Strasbourg.

MEPs sit in a semicircle.

EU MEMBERSHIP
The six original members of the EU were France, West Germany, Netherlands, Belgium, Luxembourg, and Italy. Britain, Ireland, and Denmark joined in 1973, Spain and Portugal in 1981, Greece in 1986, East Germany in 1990, and Finland, Sweden, and Austria in 1995. Cyprus, Czech Republic, Estonia, Hungary, Latvia, Lithuania, Malta, Poland, Slovakia, and Slovenia joined in 2004.

■ *Original members*

■ *Current members*

EUROPEAN PARLIAMENT

Every five years, the voters of Europe elect 626 Members of the European Parliament (MEPs) to represent them in Strasbourg, France. MEPs have the power to approve or throw out the Commission (the EU government), reject the annual budget, and question the Commission on its policies. The European Parliament is not as powerful as a national parliament, but it plays an important part in deciding how the European Union will develop.

Common passport allows holder to travel freely in the EU.

WHAT THE EU DOES
The EU looks after farming, fishing, economic, industrial, and cultural affairs. It helps the poorer parts of Europe by building roads, and paying for education and training projects. Everybody in the EU holds a common European passport.

PASSPORT

The EU helps farmers to produce and sell food.

Euro coins

EUROPEAN MONETARY UNION
EU countries first linked their currencies together in 1979, and began to move towards full monetary and economic union. In 1999, 11 member countries joined the euro, or single currency. Euro bank notes and coins came into use in those countries in 2002, replacing national currencies such as the French franc and German mark.

EUROPEAN UNION

1951 France, Germany, Italy, and the Benelux countries set up European Coal and Steel Community.

1957 ECSC members sign Treaty of Rome to set up European Economic Community (EEC) and Euratom, the atomic energy authority.

1967 ECSC, EEC, and Euratom merge to form the European Community.

1979 European Monetary System begins operation.

1993 Moves toward closer union result in the European Union (EU).

2002 The Euro becomes the currency of 12 EU countries.

2004 Ten more countries join the EU.

Find out more

EUROPE
EUROPE, HISTORY OF
TRADE AND INDUSTRY

HISTORY OF
EUROPE

EUROPE IS THE SECOND-SMALLEST continent, but it has played an important part in world history. The Ancient Greek and Roman empires stretched into North Africa and the Middle East, and their art, thinking, and science are still influential today. More than a thousand years later, Portuguese and Spanish explorers sailed to new continents, and even around the world. This marked the start of a period of European dominance of world affairs that lasted 400 years. Throughout its long history, however, Europe's countries have rarely been at peace, and in the 20th century, quarrels between European nations led to two world wars. Since 1945, with the rise of the United States as a world superpower, Europe's global political influence is less, but it remains culturally important.

PREHISTORIC EUROPE
The first Europeans were primitive hunters who moved around in search of food and shelter. By about 5000 B.C., Europeans were growing crops and domesticating animals. They settled in villages, and in northern Europe they built large burial mounds for their dead.

GREECE AND ROME
In about 900 B.C., the Greeks set up powerful city-states, such as Athens and Sparta. Their merchants traded around the coast of the Mediterranean Sea, founding colonies from Spain to the Black Sea. The Roman Empire began in 753 B.C. and by A.D.117 controlled most of Europe, northern Africa, and the Middle East.

Roman aquaduct at Nîmes, southern France

Rose window, Chartres Cathedral

CHRISTIANITY
In the 300s, Christianity became the official religion of the Roman Empire. Gradually, over the next 700 years, it spread throughout Europe. Headed by the Pope in Rome, the Roman Catholic Church was very powerful. It unified the continent, and dominated all aspects of daily life, including education.

MEDIEVAL TRADE
Trade prospered in medieval Europe. In the 13th century, a group of towns around the Baltic and North Sea formed the Hanseatic League, trading from ports such as Lübeck and Bruges, and monopolizing trade until the 1600s. Cloth, spices, and gold were sold at great trade fairs.

Portuguese caravel

EUROPEAN DOMINATION
In mid-1400s, the Portuguese set out to explore the coast of Africa in a new, fast ship – the caravel. They set up trading stations, and were followed by other European explorers and traders, who moved outward from Europe to all parts of the globe. Europeans soon came to dominate world trade, setting up colonies in the Americas, Asia, and Africa, and building vast empires.

THE ENLIGHTENMENT

In the 18th century, European thinkers began to reject old beliefs based on religion and superstition and to develop new ideas based on reason and science. An intellectual revolution, called the Enlightenment, broke out across Europe. New ideas about government led to the French and American revolutions. Religious toleration increased, and economics, philosophy, and science prospered.

WORLD WARS

In the 1900s, conflicts between European powers caused two devastating world wars. World War I (1914-18) weakened Europe, but war broke out again in 1939. At its end in 1945, cities were in ruins, thousands were homeless, and two new "superpowers" – the USA and the Soviet Union – had emerged.

Kemal Ataturk (1881–1939), "Father of the Turks"

Russian tanks in the streets of Budapest, Hungary, in 1956.

Intellectuals gather to discuss new ideas in science.

BREAK-UP OF EMPIRES

After World War I, the multinational empires of Germany, Austro-Hungary, Ottoman Turkey, and Russia broke up as the different nationalities within them created independent countries, such as Czechoslovakia and Poland. Kemal Ataturk abolished the old Islamic government of the Ottoman Empire, and created the non-religious country of Turkey.

COMMUNIST EUROPE

By 1945, Europe was effectively divided into Communist countries dominated by the former Soviet Union, and non-Communist nations influenced by the United States. Germany was split into two nations. Life was often harsh in Communist countries, and civil liberties were restricted. Revolts broke out in East Germany (1953), Hungary (1956), and Czechoslovakia (1968), but Russian troops put them down.

THE COLLAPSE OF COMMUNISM

By the late 1980s, Communism was losing its hold, and the Soviet Union (USSR) withdrew its support from Eastern Europe. In 1989, East Germans demonstrated for union with West Germany and pulled down the wall that divided their capital city, Berlin. Germany was reunited the following year. Popular protests then overthrew Communist governments throughout Eastern Europe.

HISTORY OF EUROPE

5000 B.C. Stone Age peoples begin to settle in villages.

900 Greek city-states founded.

753 Rome founded.

A.D. 117 Roman Empire at its height.

313 Christianity is tolerated throughout Roman Empire.

1000s Christianity spreads throughout Europe.

c. 1241 Hanseatic League established between Hamburg and Lübeck merchants.

1492 Columbus crosses Atlantic; leads to European dominance in the Americas.

1498 European explorers reach India.

1517 Reformation leads to emergence of Protestantism.

1700s Age of Enlightenment.

1800s European empires control most of Africa and Asia.

1914-18 World War I devastates Europe.

1939-45 World War II leads to division of European into Communist and non-Communist sectors.

1957 Treaty of Rome sets up European Economic Community (EEC).

1989 Fall of Berlin Wall leads to end of Communism in Eastern Europe.

1991 USSR divided into 15 separate countries.

1991-99 Wars in the Balkans as Yugoslavia breaks up.

YUGOSLAVIA

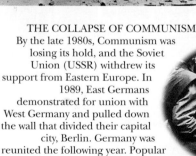

In the 1990s, Yugoslavia fell apart as Serbia, its largest and most powerful province, tried to take control. Slovenia, Croatia, and Bosnia and Herzegovina all declared independence, leading to terrible atrocities on all sides. Serbia pursued "ethnic cleansing" – killing or expelling all non-Serbs, notably in Bosnia and Kosovo. War between Serbia and NATO – a military alliance of Western Europe and the USA – led to an uneasy peace in 1999.

Find out more

EUROPEAN UNION
MEDIEVAL EUROPE
WORLD WAR I
WORLD WAR II

EVOLUTION

AROUND 150 YEARS AGO, an English naturalist named Charles Darwin shocked the world when he wrote a book suggesting that humans were related to apes. Today Darwin's idea still forms the basis of what we call the theory of evolution. The word evolution means "unfolding," and it is used to describe the way that all living things evolve, or change with time. There are three main parts to the theory. The first is called variation. All living things vary in size, shape, color, and strength. No two animals or plants are exactly the same. The second part of the theory is that these variations affect whether a living thing can survive and breed. Certain features, such as color, may mean that one animal or plant has a better chance of surviving than another. Some animals and plants have features that suit their surroundings. In other words, they are better adapted, and these useful features are called adaptations. The third part of the theory is inheritance. The adaptations that help a living thing to survive, such as its color or shape, may be passed on to its offspring. If the offspring inherit the adaptations, they too will have a better chance of survival. Gradually, over many generations, the better-adapted plants and animals flourish, and those that are less well adapted die out. Many people believe that this process of evolution has led to the millions of different species that inhabit the Earth today.

NATURAL SELECTION
Charles Darwin wrote a book called *On the Origin of Species*, published in 1859, which explained his theory of evolution. Many people laughed at Darwin's idea that humans were related to animals. Above is a cartoon of the time, picturing Darwin as a monkey.

African elephant of today

Evolution of the elephant

Moenitherium lived about 38 million years ago.

Woolly mammoth lived about two million years ago.

Platybelodon lived from 12 to 7 million years ago.

Trilophodon lived from 26 to three million years ago.

EVIDENCE FROM THE PAST
Fossils – the remains of animals and plants preserved in rocks – provide evidence for evolution. They show how animals and plants have gradually changed through time. For example, each of the elephants shown above lived for a certain amount of time, as we know by the age of their fossilized bones. Scientists cannot be certain that the first type of elephant gradually evolved into the next, but it is unlikely that each elephant appeared completely separate from the others. It is far more likely that these elephants were related. As we find more fossils, the relationships between various kinds of animals and plants become clearer.

EVIDENCE FROM THE PRESENT
Animals and plants alive today also provide evidence for evolution. In Hawaii, there are several kinds of honeycreepers that look similar. It is unlikely that this is by chance. More likely, these different honeycreeper birds all evolved from one kind of honeycreeper. This first honeycreeper flew to the islands five million years ago. Since that time, natural selection has produced several similar, but separate, species.

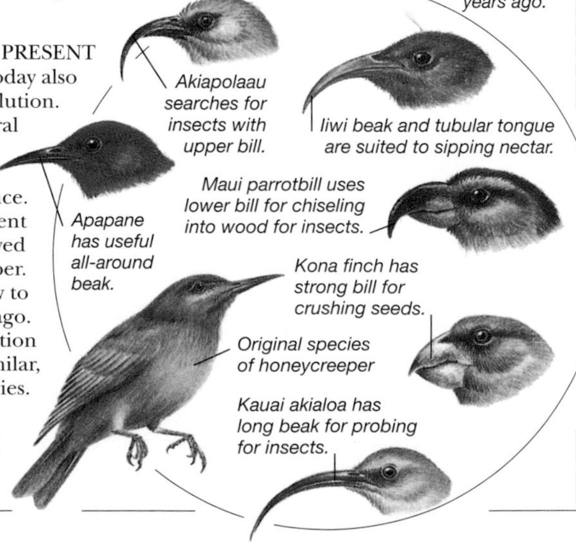

There are 28 species of honeycreepers on the Hawaiian Islands. Scientists believe they evolved from one species of bird.

Akiapolaau searches for insects with upper bill.

Iiwi beak and tubular tongue are suited to sipping nectar.

Apapane has useful all-around beak.

Maui parrotbill uses lower bill for chiseling into wood for insects.

Kona finch has strong bill for crushing seeds.

Original species of honeycreeper

Kauai akialoa has long beak for probing for insects.

HOW EVOLUTION OCCURS

Imagine some green frogs, living and breeding in green surroundings. Most of the young inherit the green coloring of their parents. They are well camouflaged and predators do not notice them in the grass. Their green color is an adaptation which helps them to survive. A few of the young have different colors, because of variation. Predators can see them in the grass, and these frogs are soon eaten – this is natural selection at work. Then the environment slowly changes to yellow as the grass dies. Now the green frogs show up on the sand, and predators eat them. Gradually, the following generations of frogs change from mainly green to mainly yellow. A new species has evolved.

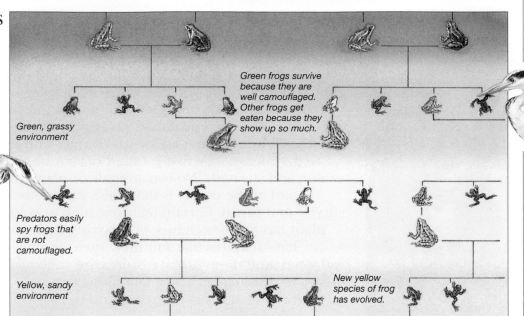

Green, grassy environment

Green frogs survive because they are well camouflaged. Other frogs get eaten because they show up so much.

Predators easily spy frogs that are not camouflaged.

Yellow, sandy environment

New yellow species of frog has evolved.

CHANGING ENVIRONMENTS

As the environment changes, living things evolve. About 200 years ago in Britain, peppered moths had mostly light-colored wings that matched the light-colored tree trunks where they rested, so birds of prey could not see them easily. During the Industrial Revolution, smoke from factory chimneys made the tree trunks darker in some areas. Light-colored moths became easier to see. Gradually, more dark-colored moths evolved, which were better camouflaged on the dark tree trunks.

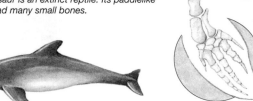

The ichthyosaur is an extinct reptile. Its paddlelike front limb had many small bones.

The dolphin is a mammal. Its paddle has the typical bones of the mammal arm and hand.

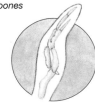

The penguin is a bird that cannot fly. It has the typical bird's wing bones in its paddle.

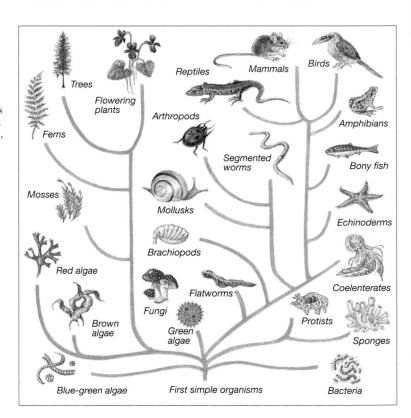

Trees

Flowering plants

Reptiles

Mammals

Birds

Arthropods

Ferns

Amphibians

Segmented worms

Bony fish

Mosses

Mollusks

Echinoderms

Red algae

Brachiopods

Flatworms

Coelenterates

Brown algae

Fungi

Green algae

Protists

Sponges

Blue-green algae

First simple organisms

Bacteria

EVOLUTIONARY TREE

Scientists believe that all living things are related and that they have evolved from the same ancestors over millions of years. This chart is called an evolutionary tree. It has lines between the main groups of animals and plants alive today, showing which ones are most closely related.

CONVERGENT EVOLUTION

Evolution sometimes makes different animals and plants look similar. This is called convergent evolution. It means that different animals or plants that live in the same environment, such as the sea, gradually take on the same adaptations, such as body shape. All the animals shown above have evolved, or developed, the same streamlined body form, because this is the best shape for moving speedily through water.

Find out more

ANIMALS
DARWIN, CHARLES
DINOSAURS
FOSSILS
GEOLOGY
PREHISTORIC LIFE
PREHISTORIC PEOPLES

EXPLORERS

TODAY, PEOPLE ARE AWARE of the remotest corners of the world. But hundreds of years ago, many did not know that countries other than their own even existed. In the 6th century, an Irish saint, Brendan, is said to have sailed across the Atlantic in search of a new land. But it was not until the early 15th century that strong seaworthy ships were developed and Europeans such as Christopher Columbus were able to explore in earnest. Turkish Muslims had controlled the overland trade route between Europe and the Indies (East Asia) since the 11th century. They charged such high prices for Asian goods that European merchants became eager to find a direct sea route to Asia which would bypass the Turks. The sailors who searched for these routes found the Americas and other lands previously unknown to Europeans. Of course, people already lived in most of these "newly discovered" lands, and the results of these explorations were often disastrous for their inhabitants. All too often, the new arrivals exploited and enslaved the native peoples, destroying their cultures.

VIKINGS
The Vikings came from Norway, Sweden, and Denmark. Looking for new lands in which to settle, they sailed to Iceland, Greenland, and North America in their long ships, navigating by the sun and the stars.

PACIFIC ISLANDS
Europeans exploring the Pacific Ocean in the 1500s were amazed to find that prehistoric peoples had found the Pacific Islands before them. In about 30,000 B.C., the original Polynesians moved from southeast Asia to the islands in the western Pacific, sailing in fragile canoes. By A.D. 1000, they had settled on hundreds of other islands.

Maori ancestors leaving for New Zealand

EARLY IDEAS
The first explorers had few maps. Early ideas about the shape of the world were hopelessly inaccurate. Many people thought the world was flat and that those who went too far might fall off the edge. Some believed that the world was supported by a tortoise (above).

PERILS OF THE SEA
Early sailors faced many natural dangers such as storms, reefs, icebergs, and fog. The sea was an alien territory, and rumors and legends spoke of huge sea monsters which swam in unknown waters. These stories were probably based on sightings of whales and other marine creatures. They were exaggerated by returning sailors telling tall tales of their adventures. Writers and artists added more gruesome details to these descriptions, and so the myths grew.

DISCOVERIES
Explorers took gold, treasure, and exciting new vegetables from the Americas to Europe; they also carried silks, jewels, and spices from Asia. People in Europe were eager to obtain these goods and wanted more. This led to a great increase in trade between East and West.

Silk from China

Potatoes from North America

Tomatoes and chiles from the Americas

Spices from South Asia

Chocolate was made from cacao beans from the Americas.

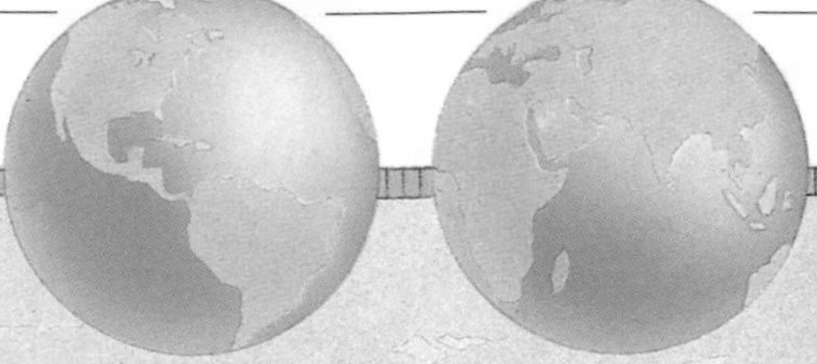

INQUISITIVE EUROPEANS

Once Europeans had an idea of the correct shape of the world, they set out to explore it more thoroughly. Some were driven by curiosity, some by greed, and some by a desire to convert the peoples who lived in faraway places to Christianity. All faced hardships and dangers.

SIR HENRY MORTON STANLEY (1841-1904)
Welsh-born Henry Stanley worked for a New York newspaper. He led an expedition into Africa to find the missing Scottish explorer David Livingstone. When he found him, he uttered the famous words "Dr. Livingstone, I presume?" Stanley later explored much of Central Africa around Lake Victoria.

MARY KINGSLEY (1862-1900)
A fearless and determined Englishwoman, Mary Kingsley traveled in West Africa, trading and making scientific studies. On her travels, she was entertained by cannibals. She was one of the first to demand fair treatment for the people of Africa by their colonial rulers.

AMERIGO VESPUCCI (1451-1512)
The first European to explore the Brazilian coast, Italian-born Amerigo Vespucci gave his name to America. He was in charge of a school of navigation in Seville, Spain. Vespucci believed in a southwestern route to the Indies around South America.

FERDINAND MAGELLAN (1480-1521)
Leader of the first European expedition to sail around the world, Portuguese explorer Magellan proved that there was a southwestern route to the Indies through the Pacific.

VASCO DA GAMA (1469-1524)
Despite bad weather and hardships on the voyage, Portuguese-born Vasco da Gama reached the East African coast and proved that there was a southeastern route to India. He was the first European to sail around the southern tip of Africa.

Marco Polo leaving Venice

WONDERS OF CHINA
On his travels, Marco Polo became a favorite of Kublai Khan, the Mongol ruler. Marco later published a detailed account of his journey and the wonders he had seen. Few believed the account and it was years before Europeans realized that he had experienced a great civilization – the empire of China.

Marco Polo's journey from Italy to China lasted more than 24 years.

Siberia

EUROPE

Venice

ASIA

China

Arabia

Journey to China

India

Journey home

MARCO POLO
Marco Polo (1254-1324) was an Italian explorer. His father and uncle were merchants from Venice, Europe's greatest trading city. They took the 17-year-old Marco with them on a journey from Italy to China.

Find out more
COLUMBUS, CHRISTOPHER
CONQUISTADORS
COOK, JAMES
POLAR EXPLORATION

EYES

AS YOU READ THIS PAGE, you are using the two organs of sight – the eyes. Our eyes enable us to learn a great deal about the world around us. Each eyeball measures about 1 in (25 mm) across and sits in the front of the skull in the eye socket, or orbit. The eyes can swivel around in their sockets so that you can see things above, below, and to the side. Each eye has an adjustable lens and sees a slightly different view of the same scene. The eyes work together, controlled by the brain. This is called binocular vision. The lens of each eye allows rays of light to enter from the outside and project a picture onto the retina – the inner lining of the eye. The retina converts the light into nerve signals which travel along optic nerves to the brain, where images are formed.

EAGLE SIGHT
A golden eagle has the sharpest eyesight in the world. It can see rabbits and other prey from a distance of more than half a mile (1 km).

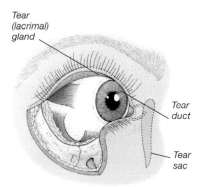

EYE SOCKETS
The eyelid and eyelashes protect the front of the eye. When you blink, the eyelids sweep moisture over the eyeball, keeping it clean. The moisture is produced in the tear glands above the eyes. These glands also produce tears when you cry. Tiny holes called tear ducts drain the fluid into the tear sac, to the inside of the nose.

Tear (lacrimal) gland
Tear duct
Tear sac

OUTER EYE
Light rays enter the curved front of the eye called the cornea, where they are partly focused. They pass through the pupil, which enlarges in dim conditions to let in more light and shrinks in bright conditions to protect the inside of the eye from too much light. The rays are then focused onto the retina by the lens.

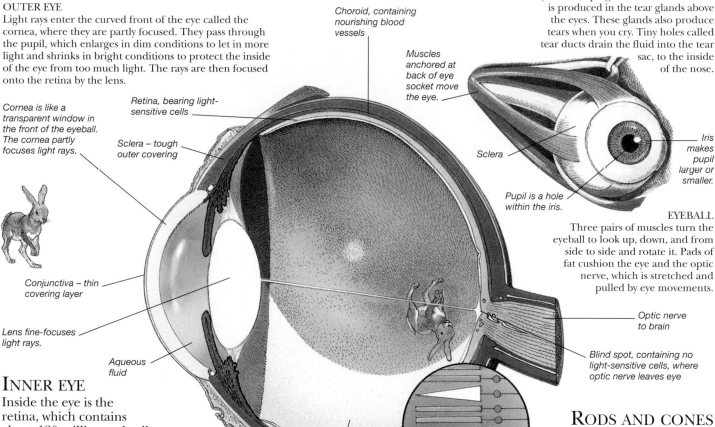

Choroid, containing nourishing blood vessels

Muscles anchored at back of eye socket move the eye.

Cornea is like a transparent window in the front of the eyeball. The cornea partly focuses light rays.

Retina, bearing light-sensitive cells

Sclera – tough outer covering

Sclera

Pupil is a hole within the iris.

Iris makes pupil larger or smaller.

Conjunctiva – thin covering layer

Lens fine-focuses light rays.

Aqueous fluid

Eye muscles

Vitreous fluid

Optic nerve to brain

Blind spot, containing no light-sensitive cells, where optic nerve leaves eye

EYEBALL
Three pairs of muscles turn the eyeball to look up, down, and from side to side and rotate it. Pads of fat cushion the eye and the optic nerve, which is stretched and pulled by eye movements.

INNER EYE
Inside the eye is the retina, which contains about 120 million rod cells, mainly around the sides, and seven million cone cells, mainly at the back. When an image lands on the retina it is upside down, but nerve signals reaching the brain turn the image right side up.

RODS AND CONES
The retina contains millions of light-sensitive cells called rods and cones. The rods are sensitive to black and white, and the cones are sensitive to different colors. Rods and cones produce nerve signals when light falls on them.

CLEAR AND DEFECTIVE VISION
Clear vision depends on the lens bending light rays to the correct angle so that the rays form a sharp picture on the retina. In farsighted people, either the lens is too weak or the eyeball is too small for its focusing power. In the shortsighted, the lens is too strong, or the eyeball is too big. Glasses and artificial lenses, such as contact lenses, help the eye's own lens to focus the rays correctly, thus correcting defective vision.

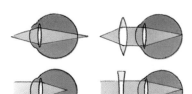

FARSIGHTEDNESS
Rays are focused behind the retina. A convex lens corrects the focus.

SHORTSIGHTEDNESS
Rays are focused in front of retina. A concave lens corrects the focus.

Find out more
CAMERAS
COLOR
EARS
HUMAN BODY
LIGHT

FACTORIES

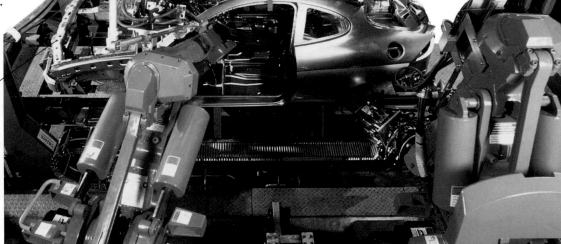

The car body travels down the assembly line between rows of robots, which weld it together.

Arm extends to car

MILLIONS OF PEOPLE AROUND THE WORLD work in factories, making goods of all kinds from T-shirts to jumbo jets. Factories are buildings in which people work together on machines manufacturing, or producing, items for sale. The factory system began in Britain during the Industrial Revolution, when huge numbers of people moved from the country to towns to work in factories. Skilled craftworkers, who had produced handmade items in small workshops, were replaced by factory production lines of semiskilled or unskilled workers, each performing a set task. One machine could do the work of many individuals, which greatly increased the number of goods that could be produced. Known as mass-production, this is the basis of modern manufacturing. Today, robots replace many factory workers.

HENRY FORD
US industrialist Henry Ford (1863-1947) pioneered assembly line mass-production. In 1913 he introduced assembly-line methods to make his new car, the Model T. The cars were pulled through the factory on trolleys. Workers stayed in the same place on the line, performing set tasks as the vehicles moved past them.

VICTORIAN FACTORY
The first factories were noisy, unclean, and dangerous. Early factory workers included women and small children.

ROBOT ASSEMBLY LINE
In many car factories, computer-controlled machines, or robots, have replaced most of the workers on the assembly line. The machines can be programmed to perform a wide variety of tasks from painting to welding. They are expensive to buy, but, unlike human workers, can be set to work day and night with perfect accuracy.

FACTORY SHIP
Factory ships move to where the raw materials for their product – fish – can be found. Instead of having to come back to harbor to process the fish, they stay at sea for months at a time. Below decks, workers prepare and freeze the catch, which is then stored in the hold. Factory ships follow fish around the world's oceans.

CLEAN CHIP MANUFACTURE
While some factories are dirty and noisy, others need to be as clean as the operating room of a hospital. Computer chips are very delicate and are made in the cleanest conditions possible, to prevent them from being damaged. Workers in computer chip factories wear protective clothes, and the building is sealed to prevent dust from getting in.

CHILD LABOR
In the 1800s, politicians in Britain passed laws to protect women and children from exploitation by factory owners. Today, most indusrial nations have laws governing child labor. However, in some parts of the world, children still work in factories. They are employed because they provide very cheap labor.

Find out more

FISHING INDUSTRY
INDUSTRIAL REVOLUTION
TRADE AND INDUSTRY

FARM ANIMALS

Female sheep are called ewes, males are called rams, and the young are called lambs.

Merino sheep have the best quality wool. The ancestor of today's Merino sheep is the Spanish Merino – a breed of sheep that is about 1,000 years old.

The Suffolk is an English breed that was first developed about 100 years ago.

Meat from adult sheep is called mutton.

Female chickens are called hens. Males, like the one shown here, are usually more colorful. They are called roosters.

HAMBURGERS, sausages, butter, and cheese are produced from animals that we keep on farms. Many other foods, including eggs, bacon, and yogurt, also come from farm animals. Farm animals include pigs, cows, sheep, rabbits, goats, and chickens. People keep these animals for their meat, milk, fur, and skins. We use the skins, or hides, of cows, pigs, and sheep to make shoes, and the wool of sheep, goats, and rabbits to make clothes. People have been keeping animals on farms for at least 9,000 years. Many are kept in small enclosed areas called pens, others in fields, and still others in cages. The first farm animals were wild creatures that people captured and domesticated, or tamed. Today's chickens are descended from tropical forest birds of southeast Asia. Throughout the ages, farmers have bred (mated) the healthiest, most docile animals with the best milk, meat, or wool production, to produce the breeds that we know today.

The female pig is called a gilt before she has any young, and a sow once she has young. Male pigs are called boars.

AMERICAN HAMPSHIRE PIG
The American Hampshire pig has little fat on its body, so the pork and bacon from this pig are lean (that is, they have little fat).

The Rhode Island red is named after the state of Rhode Island. It is a good egg layer and is well-known for its meat.

Chicks are sold for meat when they are about eight weeks old and weigh about 4.5 lb (2 kg).

POULTRY
Many people keep chickens as a source of meat and eggs. These chickens scratch around in farmyards and fields, eating seeds, worms, insects, and scraps. They lay their eggs in a small chicken coop or any other secluded place. This is called free-range rearing – the chickens are able to wander freely. Most chickens are raised indoors, under controlled conditions.

PLYMOUTH ROCK
There are about 7,000 million chickens around the world, and about 500 breeds. The Leghorn is the most common egg-laying hen. The Plymouth rock shown here is a fast-growing chicken that produces tasty meat in a short time.

SHEEP
Wool comes from sheep, goats, rabbits, camels, alpacas, and vicunas. Young sheep, or lambs, produce the softest, finest wool. The largest flocks of sheep are in Australia, where there are about 140 million sheep. The sheep we farm for wool are sheared for their fleeces (coats) once a year. An expert shearer with electric clippers can shear one sheep every 40 seconds. The wool is washed and combed, then stretched and twisted into yarn for woollen fabric. Here, a woman in Nepal is spinning wool by hand to make into carpets and rugs.

INTENSIVE REARING

Some farm animals, such as pigs and chickens, are kept under controlled conditions in huge hangarlike buildings. Chickens are raised by the thousands in this way, for their meat or their eggs. These chickens sit in wire cages and cannot run around freely or scratch for their food. The food, temperature, and light in the building are controlled so that each chicken lays up to 300 eggs each year. Pigs are kept in pig units like the one shown here. They are fed an exact mixture of nutrients that makes them put on the most weight in the least time. Some kinds of pigs gain more than 1.5 lb (0.7 kg) in weight each day. A pig may be sold for pork when it is only three months old.

PIG

There are about 800 million pigs scattered around the world. Some are allowed to roam freely to feed on roots, worms, and household scraps; others are kept inside buildings (see above). There are more than 80 breeds of pigs, and some of the largest weigh more than 450 lb (200 kg). Almost every part of a pig can be eaten, including the trotters, or feet. Pork is the name for fresh pig meat; cured or preserved pig meat is called bacon or ham.

ZEBU

Cattle are the most numerous of farm animals, with a worldwide population of about 1 billion. They were first used to pull carts. Today some cattle are bred for their meat (beef breeds), others for their milk (dairy breeds), and some for both (dual-purpose breeds). There are about 200 breeds of cattle. The zebu cattle shown here have a hump at the shoulders and a long, narrow face. They were originally from India and are suited to hot climates. Zebu are also used to pull plows.

TURKEY

Today's most common breed of turkey is the White Holland, which was developed from the bronze turkey, shown here. Turkeys came originally from North America. When Europeans first traveled to North America in the 16th century, they domesticated (tamed) turkeys and took some back to Europe.

Male turkeys, or toms, are often twice the weight of the female hens. Young turkeys are called poults.

In many parts of the world, people keep goats for their milk, which is made into cheese and yogurt.

Every November, millions of turkeys are eaten in celebration of Thanksgiving.

DUCKS AND GEESE

Waterfowl such as ducks and geese are kept mainly for their meat, especially in Southeast Asia. They also provide fluffy down (underfeathers) for stuffing mattresses, quilts, and clothing. Geese are good guards in the farmyard, beacause they hiss at strangers. The most common egg-laying waterfowl are Indian runner ducks, khaki campbell ducks, and Emden and Chinese geese.

The Toulouse goose, from France, looks like its wild ancestor, the greylag goose. Adult birds weigh more than 28 lb (13 kg).

The Indian runner duck is kept in large flocks and can move swiftly on its long legs.

GOAT

The goat was one of the first animals to be domesticated. Goats feed on thorny bushes, spiky grasses, and woody stems, and they can leap up easily into the branches of small trees to eat the leaves. Almost 500 million goats are kept worldwide, often in dry and mountainous regions. They are used for their milk, meat, skins, and wool. The main dairy breed is the Anglo-Nubian, which produces up to 1,200 pints (660 liters) of milk each year.

Find out more

COWS, CATTLE,
and buffaloes
DUCKS, GEESE, AND SWANS
FARMING
FARMING, HISTORY OF
HORSES, ZEBRAS, AND ASSES
MOUNTAIN WILDLIFE

FARMING

TO STOCK THE FOOD SHELVES of supermarkets in Europe and the Americas, farmers make nature and technology work in harmony. They use machinery to plow and reap great fields of wheat; they fertilize and irrigate greenhouses full of vegetables and orchards of fruit; and they rear animals indoors to fatten them quickly. Through this intensive agriculture, Western farmers feed up to ten people from land that once fed one. However, not all the world's farmers can be so productive. Those who have plots on hilly land cannot use machines. Instead they graze a few animals or cultivate the land with inefficient hand tools. Farmers in dry climates must be content with lower yields or choose less productive crops that will tolerate dry soil. And farmers who cannot afford machines and fertilizers are forced to use slower farming methods that have not changed for centuries.

SUBSISTENCE FARMING
In some developing countries, most farming families grow only sufficient food for themselves. This is called subsistence farming. In a good year it provides enough food for all. But a drought or an increase in the population may lead to famine and starvation.

CROPS
Almost all crops that are grown today are the descendants of wild plants. However, special breeding has created varieties that give high harvests. Grain crops such as wheat have especially benefited. Modern varieties have much larger grains than traditional species. However, this new "superwheat" is not as resistant to disease as other varieties and must be grown carefully.

Superwheat

Ordinary wheat

Plowing

Harvesting

Planting seeds

Spraying

FARM MACHINERY
Modern grain farming requires special machinery at different times of the year. In spring a plow breaks the soil into furrows for planting. A seed drill puts a measured amount of seed into the prepared soil and covers the seed so that birds do not eat it. A sprayer covers crops with pesticides to kill harmful diseases and pests. Finally, a combine harvester cuts the crop and prepares it for storage.

A baler rolls up the straw – the cut stalks of wheat left after the grain has been harvested – and ties it into tight round bundles called bales.

ORGANIC FARMING
Some farmers in Western countries prefer to grow crops and raise animals in a natural, or organic, way. They do not use artificial pesticides or fertilizers. Organic food is more expensive, but it may be healthier to eat.

Organic farmers use natural fertilizers, such as seaweed or animal dung, to make the soil more productive.

In intensive chicken houses, conveyor belts carry food to the hens in the crowded cages, and take away the eggs.

INTENSIVE FARMING
The purpose of intensive farming is to increase the production of crops and animals, and to cut food prices. Food animals such as chickens and pigs are kept indoors in tiny, overcrowded pens. Many people feel this is unnatural and cruel, and prefer to eat only "free-range" animals – animals that have been allowed to move freely in the farmyard.

Find out more
FARM ANIMALS
FARMING, HISTORY OF

HISTORY OF
FARMING

EARLY FARMING

The first farmers domesticated (tamed) wild animals and kept them in herds to provide meat, milk, hides, and wool. Some people became nomadic herders rather than farmers; they moved their animals continuously in search of new pasture. The picture shown here was painted in a cave in the Sahara Desert in Africa about 8,000 years ago, at a time when the desert was grassland.

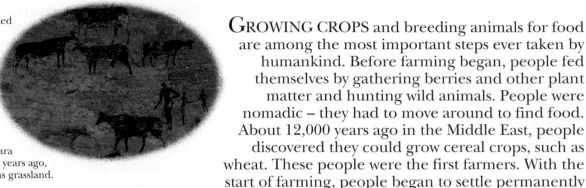

GROWING CROPS and breeding animals for food are among the most important steps ever taken by humankind. Before farming began, people fed themselves by gathering berries and other plant matter and hunting wild animals. People were nomadic – they had to move around to find food. About 12,000 years ago in the Middle East, people discovered they could grow cereal crops, such as wheat. These people were the first farmers. With the start of farming, people began to settle permanently in one place. Villages grew into towns and cities. Farmers produced enough food to support the population, so some people were free to do other jobs such as weaving, and making pottery and tools. Since everyone depended on farming for their food, however, many people died of starvation when the crops failed because of bad weather. Over the centuries people have tried many different ways of producing better crops. In the agricultural revolution of the 1700s, new scientific methods helped overcome the problem of crop failure. Today, farming is a huge international industry.

CROP GROWING

In about 10,000 B.C., farmers in the Middle East began to plant crops to provide food. Cereals, such as wheat, barley, and millet were the main crops. In the Far East, people first grew rice in about 5,000 B.C.

The huge Berkshire pig was first bred for meat in the 18th century.

IRRIGATION

Farmers need a good supply of water for their crops. In China and other Far Eastern countries, where rice is the main crop, water flows along channels on the terraced hillsides to make the paddies for growing rice.

MEDIEVAL FARMING

In the 11th century the hard horse collar came to Europe from China. It allowed horses, rather than oxen, to pull plows. By the 13th century, European farms consisted of open fields and each peasant farmer had a piece of land. Later, much of the land was enclosed with ditches or hedges.

MECHANIZATION

During the 19th century, the development of steam power and, in the 20th century, the combustion engine changed agriculture forever. Tractors replaced horses as the main source of power, and railroads and refrigerated ships meant that food could be transported all over the world.

Steam
tractor

Seed drill

AGRICULTURAL REVOLUTION

During the 18th century, new methods of agricultural production were developed and breeds of livestock were improved, such as the huge Berkshire pig (above). The invention of new machines, such as the seed drill, allowed farmers to produce more crops.

Find out more
ENGINES
FARM ANIMALS
FARMING

FESTIVALS AND FEASTS

ALL OVER THE WORLD people set aside special times during the year for festivals and feasts. Most of these celebrations are linked to a society's religious or traditional beliefs. Festivals also celebrate the changing seasons and special events in a country's history. Rituals, such as singing or exchanging gifts, often form part of annual festivals, and in many societies certain actions, pictures, and objects take on a special meaning at festival time. For instance, at Chinese New Year, golden fish become symbols of wealth. Very different cultures sometimes share the same symbols in their festivals: Christians light candles at Christmas, and Hindus do the same at their festival of Diwali. Dressing up in elaborate costumes and sharing meals are festive activities common to many parts of the world.

MAYPOLE
In Britain, young people once celebrated the coming of spring by dancing around a maypole. This was usually a hawthorn or may tree decorated with blossoms and ribbons for the May Day festival.

CHINESE NEW YEAR
New Year in the Chinese calendar falls in late January or early February. Chinese people living in the rest of the world remember the customs of their homeland by holding processions led by huge dragons, and by exploding firecrackers.

The procession is lit by lanterns.

People set off crackling fireworks.

CARNIVALS
Carnivals began in Roman Catholic countries such as Mexico as a way of using up foods that were forbidden during the fast of Lent, which precedes Easter. At the famous Mardi Gras in New Orleans, Louisiana, the streets are filled with music, dancing, and long processions of people wearing colorful costumes.

THANKSGIVING
In 1621, the Pilgrim settlers of Plymouth, Massachusetts, celebrated their first harvest by inviting local Native Americans to join them in a Thanksgiving feast. The local people had helped the settlers to survive by teaching them how to grow native crops, such as corn. Today, families gather together on Thanksgiving Day, a national holiday celebrated in November, to share the traditional dinner of turkey and pumpkin pie.

JACK-O'-LANTERN
Lighting candles inside frightening pumpkin faces scares away evil spirits on Halloween, October 31.

Find out more

BUDDHISM
CHRISTIANITY
HINDUISM
ISLAM
JUDAISM
RELIGIONS

FIRE

A BOLT OF LIGHTNING hitting a tree or the red-hot lava from a volcano can start a fire in seconds. It was probably from natural events such as these that prehistoric people discovered fire about one million years ago. Later they learned how to make fire for themselves by rubbing sticks together or by striking certain stones, such as flint. Today, fire works for us in many ways. The heat from fire cooks food, warms homes, and provides energy in engines and power stations. Fire is the heat and light that are produced when something burns. Burning occurs when a substance rapidly combines with oxygen gas, which makes up about one-fifth of the air around us. Each material has a certain temperature, called its ignition temperature, above which it will burst into flame. Once it is burning, it produces so much heat of its own that it continues to burn. When fire gets out of control, it can be very dangerous. Every year, fires kill and injure thousands of people and cause great damage to property.

A cage raised on a long motorized boom carries firefighters high in the air to rescue people and spray water or foam over the flames.

MATCHES
Fire requires three things: fuel, heat, and oxygen. To produce fire we rub the match against the box to produce heat. The heat makes chemicals in the head of the match burst into flame as they combine with oxygen from the air.

When people are trapped by fire, firefighters use tools such as hatchets to break open windows and doors. Firefighters wear strong fireproof and waterproof clothing and breathe with the aid of oxygen tanks so they can work in smoke or fumes.

Fire produces smoke, ash, and dangerous gases that can make people collapse or die.

FIRE ENGINE
There are several kinds of fire engine. All contain powerful pumps that force water through hoses at high pressure.

Fire engines carry ladders, oxygen tanks, lamps, crowbars, and many other items of equipment that the fire crew may need as they fight a fire.

Water tank contains a limited supply of water for the hoses.

FIRE HYDRANT
Fire hydrants, like large faucets on the street, provide unlimited water from the city supply for fighting fires.

HOW FIRES SPREAD
Fires are often the result of carelessness: a smoldering match or cigarette left on the ground has caused many huge forest fires. Once started, a fire can spread in three ways. Currents of hot air can carry burning fragments that start new fires. Heat radiation from the flames can set nearby objects alight. And metal objects can conduct the heat of a fire to another place, starting a new fire.

In 1988, huge forest fires occurred in Yellowstone National Park.

FIRE DEPARTMENT
Firefighters are specially trained to put out fires quickly and safely. They race to the scene of a fire as soon as the alarm is raised. The firefighters' first task is to rescue people who are trapped in a burning building. Then they pump water or foam over the flames to put out the fire.

Squeezing the handle punctures a cylinder of compressed carbon dioxide gas. The gas expands and forces the water out of the nozzle.

Water should never be used on electrical fires because water conducts electricity.

FIRE EXTINGUISHER
There are different kinds of fire extinguisher for tackling different kinds of fires. A water extinguisher puts out wood and paper fires because it removes heat from the flames. Other types, such as foam extinguishers, kill fire by smothering it and depriving it of oxygen.

Firefighters may give oxygen to people who have breathed in too much smoke.

Find out more
HEAT
OXYGEN
PREHISTORIC PEOPLES

FIRST AID

IN AN EMERGENCY, quick, calm help is vital. For example, someone who chokes on food cannot wait for a doctor. Instead, nonmedical people close by must remove the obstruction immediately so that the choking person can breathe. This sort of rapid treatment is called first aid, and it varies depending on the injury. For slight injuries such as cuts, a doctor may not be needed. Instead, first aid consists of cleaning the wound and applying a bandage. Some accidents result in broken bones. Then first aid involves keeping the injured person calm and still, and getting him or her to a hospital. And in a major emergency, such as a traffic accident or a heart attack, first aid may involve restarting the injured person's heart while waiting for an ambulance. Unskilled first aid can do more harm than good, but training is easy. A course lasting half a day is enough to learn skills that could help you save lives.

AIRWAYS
The first step is to check that the victim's airways, or breathing passages, are clear of obstructions.

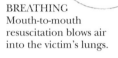

BREATHING
Mouth-to-mouth resuscitation blows air into the victim's lungs.

CIRCULATION
Checking circulation means making sure that the heart is pumping blood and that there is no bleeding. Cardiac massage (left) can help to restart the heart.

FIRST-AID TECHNIQUES
Skilled first aid means learning basic skills and staying calm in an emergency. Important techniques involve helping an unconscious person whose heart or breathing has stopped, and preventing severe loss of blood. When treating someone who has lost consciousness, trained first aiders follow the ABC code, as shown above.

PARAMEDICS
At the scene of an accident, paramedics give emergency treatment to the injured. Paramedics are highly trained first-aid professionals. Their emergency ambulances contain lifesaving equipment such as defibrillator machines, which are used to restart the hearts of heart attack victims. Paramedics save many lives because treatment begins immediately, even before the patient reaches the hospital.

RED CROSS
The sign of a red cross is recognized everywhere. The Red Cross organization began in Europe in the 19th century. Today, members of the Red Cross teach first aid, collect blood for transfusions, and carry out disaster relief.

FIRST-AID KIT
Every home and car should have a first-aid kit containing items needed for emergency treatment. Keep the box clean and dry and clearly labeled. Replace items as soon as you use them or if the protective seal is accidentally broken.

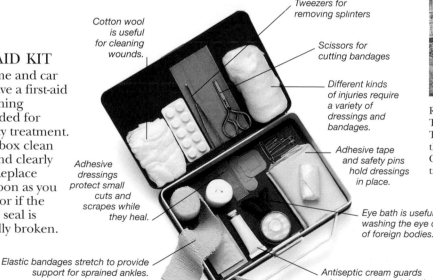

Cotton wool is useful for cleaning wounds.

Tweezers for removing splinters

Scissors for cutting bandages

Different kinds of injuries require a variety of dressings and bandages.

Adhesive tape and safety pins hold dressings in place.

Adhesive dressings protect small cuts and scrapes while they heal.

Eye bath is useful for washing the eye clean of foreign bodies.

Elastic bandages stretch to provide support for sprained ankles.

Antiseptic cream guards minor cuts against infection.

Find out more
DISEASE
HEALTH AND FITNESS
HOSPITALS
MEDICINE

FISH

FEATURES OF A FISH

The cod has all the features of a typical fish – a streamlined body for speed, a powerful tail, and fins for balance and steering. The lateral line along the body is a row of sense organs. These organs detect movements made by other creatures in the water.

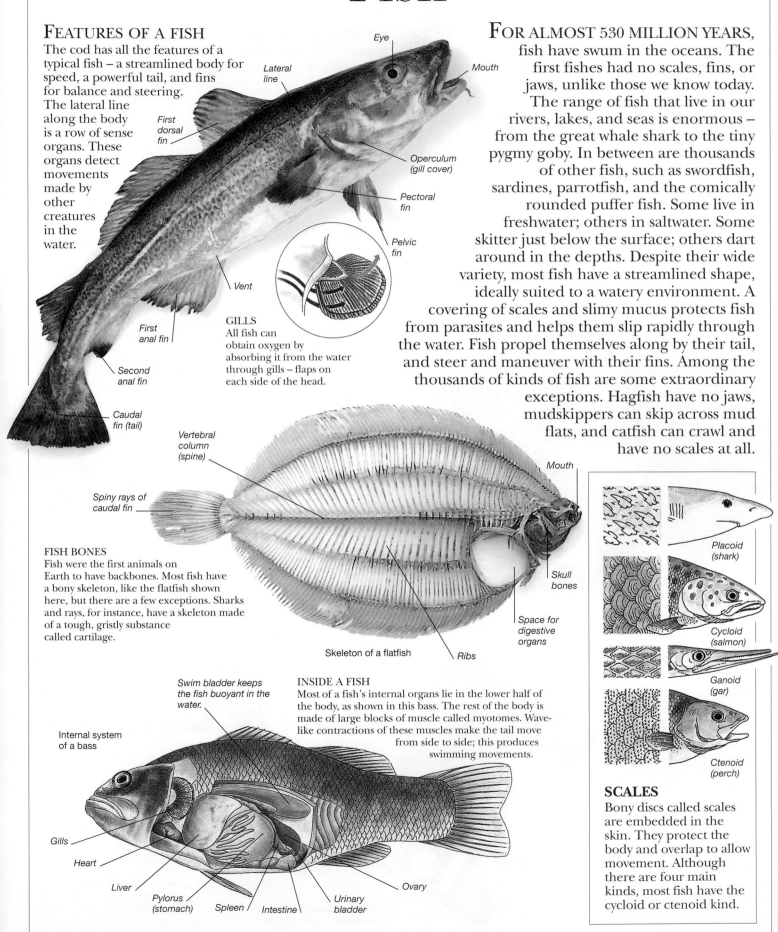

Eye

Lateral line

Mouth

First dorsal fin

Operculum (gill cover)

Pectoral fin

Pelvic fin

Vent

First anal fin

Second anal fin

Caudal fin (tail)

GILLS

All fish can obtain oxygen by absorbing it from the water through gills – flaps on each side of the head.

FOR ALMOST 530 MILLION YEARS, fish have swum in the oceans. The first fishes had no scales, fins, or jaws, unlike those we know today. The range of fish that live in our rivers, lakes, and seas is enormous – from the great whale shark to the tiny pygmy goby. In between are thousands of other fish, such as swordfish, sardines, parrotfish, and the comically rounded puffer fish. Some live in freshwater; others in saltwater. Some skitter just below the surface; others dart around in the depths. Despite their wide variety, most fish have a streamlined shape, ideally suited to a watery environment. A covering of scales and slimy mucus protects fish from parasites and helps them slip rapidly through the water. Fish propel themselves along by their tail, and steer and maneuver with their fins. Among the thousands of kinds of fish are some extraordinary exceptions. Hagfish have no jaws, mudskippers can skip across mud flats, and catfish can crawl and have no scales at all.

Vertebral column (spine)

Spiny rays of caudal fin

FISH BONES

Fish were the first animals on Earth to have backbones. Most fish have a bony skeleton, like the flatfish shown here, but there are a few exceptions. Sharks and rays, for instance, have a skeleton made of a tough, gristly substance called cartilage.

Mouth

Skull bones

Space for digestive organs

Skeleton of a flatfish

Ribs

Placoid (shark)

Cycloid (salmon)

Ganoid (gar)

Ctenoid (perch)

SCALES

Bony discs called scales are embedded in the skin. They protect the body and overlap to allow movement. Although there are four main kinds, most fish have the cycloid or ctenoid kind.

Swim bladder keeps the fish buoyant in the water.

Internal system of a bass

INSIDE A FISH

Most of a fish's internal organs lie in the lower half of the body, as shown in this bass. The rest of the body is made of large blocks of muscle called myotomes. Wave-like contractions of these muscles make the tail move from side to side; this produces swimming movements.

Gills

Heart

Liver

Pylorus (stomach)

Spleen

Intestine

Urinary bladder

Ovary

STRANGELY SHAPED FISH

Each kind of fish is suited to its own way of life. The butterfly fish uses its long nose to pick food from crevices in rocks. Flying fish use their enlarged fins as "wings" for gliding as they leap out of the water. The bright colors on a lionfish warn other creatures of the deadly poison in its fin spines.

Lionfish

Flying fish

Long-nosed
butterfly fish

SCHOOL OF FISH

Small fish often live in large groups called schools, twisting and turning together as they search for food. A predator is sometimes so confused by their numbers and quick, darting movements that it cannot single out a fish to attack.

School of sea goldfish
on a Red Sea coral reef

FEEDING

Fast predatory fish, such as barracudas, have long, slim, streamlined bodies and sharp teeth. Slower swimmers usually have more rounded bodies. Despite its shape, the parrotfish is an agile swimmer. It slips through cracks in the rock in search of food.

*Parrotfish
eating algae
on a coral reef.*

Sea horses

SEA HORSE

Sea horse eggs are deposited by the female into the male's front pouch, where they develop for about four weeks. When the eggs hatch, the young sea horses emerge from the pouch.

*Sea horses use their
tails to cling to seaweed.*

BREEDING

Most fish reproduce by depositing their eggs and sperm in the water, then leaving the fertilized eggs to develop into fish. Some fish, such as sticklebacks and bowfins, look after the eggs and the young (called fry) once they have hatched. Other fish, such as some types of sharks, give birth to fully formed young fish after the eggs have developed in the mother's body.

MOUTHBREEDERS

The cichlid fish, found in African lakes, keeps its eggs safe inside its mouth. When the young hatch they swim out, then return to the parent's mouth for safety.

Cichlid fish
and young

EUROPEAN EELS

Adult eels lay eggs in the Sargasso Sea. The eggs hatch into larvae, which swim north for the next three years. Upon reaching reach Europe they change into elvers and swim up river. There, they grow into yellow eels, then adults.

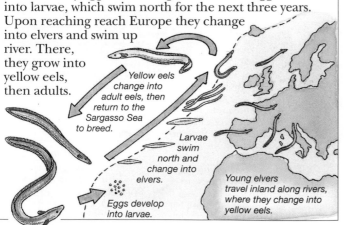

*Yellow eels
change into
adult eels, then
return to the
Sargasso Sea
to breed.*

*Larvae
swim
north and
change into
elvers.*

*Young elvers
travel inland along rivers,
where they change into
yellow eels.*

*Eggs develop
into larvae.*

Royal
gramma
fish

TROPICAL OCEAN FISH

Fish, especially those from tropical waters, are among the brightest of all animals. Their dazzling colors and lively patterns have many different purposes. They help fish hide from predators among the coral, warn neighboring fish to keep out of their territory, show other creatures that they are poisonous, or advertise for a mate.

Find out more
ANIMALS
DEEP-SEA WILDLIFE
MIGRATION
OCEAN WILDLIFE
SEASHORE WILDLIFE

FISHING INDUSTRY

THE WORLD'S RIVERS, seas, and oceans provide one of the most important of all foods. Fish are a rich source of protein and other vital nutrients. It is possible to catch a few fish using just a hook on the end of a piece of string. But to feed large numbers of people, a huge industry exists to catch millions of fish. Japanese fishing boats, for instance, catch more than 35,000 tons of fish each day. Fishing fleets use different methods to catch these vast numbers of fish, such as nets, traps, and hooks. Some nets are several miles long and can catch more than 100 million fish in one haul. Baskets, boxes, and other traps are left in the sea for shellfish, such as crabs, lobsters, and crayfish. Hooks are arranged in a longline – a single line carrying hundreds of hooks – that is attached to a fishing boat and can trap huge numbers of fish at one time.

WHALING
For two centuries whaling has been a major industry and has made some species of whale almost extinct. As whales come to the surface to breathe, whale hunters shoot them with harpoons – huge explosive arrows fired from guns.

Drift nets are up to 60 miles (100 km) long. They catch fish very effectively, but may also harm other marine life.

FISHING GROUNDS
Fishing boats catch most fish near the coast in the seas above the continental shelf (shown in the dark blue on the map). This shelf is an extension of the continents covered by shallow sea water. Deep-water currents rich in nutrients rise onto the shelf and create good feeding grounds for fish.

At night lights attract fish into the dip nets.

SEA FISHING
Seines are nets that float down from the surface. Drawing the net into a circle around a school, or group, of fish forms a huge bag which encloses the catch. Gill nets are long curtains of net which trap fish by the gills. Some gill nets float on the surface as drift nets; others are fixed to the sea bottom with anchors. A trawl is a large net bag towed behind a boat. Dip nets are hung over the side of the fishing boat on a frame. Lifting the frame catches the fish.

Weights keep the mouth of the trawl net open.

The purse seiner tows its net in a huge circle to enclose the fish.

FREEZING FISH
Once a fish is dead, its flesh quickly rots. Freezing, canning, drying, smoking, and pickling all slow the decay and preserve the fish. Freezing is the best method. Large fishing boats have freezing plants on board to preserve the catch – the harvest of fish – before returning to port.

FISH FARMS
Not all fish are caught in the wild. Some fish, such as carp, salmon, trout, and shellfish, can be bred in controlled conditions on fish farms. In the United States, fish farmers raise catfish for food. Fish farmers build pens in lakes, ponds, or estuaries (river mouths). They hatch fish from eggs, then keep the fish until they are big enough to sell.

Find out more
FARMING
FISH
FOOD AND FOOD TECHNOLOGY
OCEAN WILDLIFE

FLAGS

BRIGHTLY COLORED FLAGS flying in the wind have special meanings. They are used to send messages, greet the winner of a race, or encourage people to fight for their country. Every nation now has its own flag, which is a symbol of that country. Most organizations, such as the International Red Cross, also have their own flags. A flag is a piece of cloth with an easily recognized design. One edge is fixed to a pole, and the rest flaps freely. Flags have always been important in battles. The leader of each warring army carried a flag. In the confusion of war, soldiers looked for their flag to see where their leader was. Capturing the enemy's flag often meant winning the battle. Before telephones or radio were invented, flags were a quick way to send messages. Today, signal flags are rarely used, but some flag codes have kept their meaning. Waving a white flag in war means that you want to surrender. And flying a flag halfway up the mast is a sign of respect for someone who has died.

The cap provides a neat, decorative top to the flagpole.

The edge of the flag is the part most exposed to the wind, so it will be the first to show wear and tear.

Flags can be any shape, but most national flags are rectangular.

The sleeve or heading is made of tough material into which the hoist rope is sewn.

The halyard is the long rope used to raise the flag.

NATIONAL FLAGS

The flags of many nations have symbols to represent the qualities or traditions of the country and its people. The Australian flag has a Union Jack – the British flag – to show the country's historic connection with Great Britain. The small stars on the flag are in the shape of the constellation *Crux Australis* (Southern Cross), which is visible only in the Southern Hemisphere.

CHECKERED FLAG

Waving a black-and-white checkered flag at the end of an auto race shows that the winner has crossed the finish line. Other flags are used as signals to drivers in car racing. A black flag indicates that the driver must make a pit stop. A yellow-and-red-striped flag warns drivers that there is oil on the track. A red flag tells drivers to stop at once.

FLYING FLAGS

Flags make impressive decorations when they fly in a group in front of a building. Important buildings belonging to international organizations, such as the United Nations, may fly the flags of all their different members. Similar rows of flags brighten up hotels, supermarkets, and factories.

SIGNAL FLAGS

One of the earliest uses of flags was to send signals at sea. There was a flag for each letter of the alphabet and each number. Signalers spelled out words or used special combinations of flags to represent whole words. In the message above, for instance, "have" or "they have" is spelled with the flags for A, E, and L.

End of message flag

N
D
Q

Sharks

A
E
L

Have

F
L
G

Eaten

R
K
D

My

C
T
W

Captain

SEMAPHORE

With just two flags a signaler can spell out messages. Each flag position represents a different letter of the alphabet or a number. This system is called semaphore. Using large, plain, but colorful flags, messages can be sent over long distances, as far as the eye can see.

 C

 E

 **X**

Find out more
KNIGHTS AND HERALDRY
NAVIES
SHIPS AND BOATS

FLIES AND MOSQUITOES

SOME OF THE SMALLEST creatures in the world are the most dangerous to humans. Flies and mosquitoes carry some of the world's most serious diseases. With their habit of sucking blood and scavenging on garbage, many of these insects spread cholera, malaria, and yellow fever. There are about 120,000 kinds of fly, including bluebottles, horseflies, fruit flies, tiny gnats, and almost invisible midges. We call many small, winged insects flies, but the only true flies are those with two functional wings; they belong to the insect group *Diptera*. All flies lay eggs. The eggs hatch into larvae called grubs or maggots. The maggots feed and grow into pupae or chrysalises, from which the adult flies finally emerge. Despite their unpopularity with humans, flies play a vital role in nature. They pollinate flowers and recycle nutrients as they scavenge, and they are a source of food for many larger animals.

Housefly can walk upside down.

Housefly has excellent eyesight and spongelike mouthparts.

Eggs

Larva (maggot)

The bluebottle, or blowfly, lays thousands of eggs in dustbins and on meat. Within just a few weeks these eggs produce thousands more flies.

Housefly feeding on rotting meat

Compound eye

Antenna

Tiny hairs and hooks on feet enable fly to walk on the ceiling.

Wing

MOSQUITO

The mosquito has needle-shaped mouthparts that pierce the skin to suck the blood of humans, horses, and other animals. If a female *Anopheles* mosquito bites a person with malaria, it takes in blood infected with the microscopic organisms that cause this disease. When the mosquito goes on to bite another victim, the organisms pass into that person's blood, and so the disease spreads. The map below shows those parts of the world where malaria is most severe.

FLIES AND DISEASE

Houseflies, bluebottles, and similar flies feed on and lay their eggs in rotting matter, including garbage and excrement. Their mouthparts and feet pick up bacteria, or germs, which rub off when they settle on our food, dishes, and kitchen equipment. The illnesses which spread in this way range from minor stomach upsets to deadly infections such as typhoid.

North America

Asia

Africa

South America

Australia

Areas where malaria occurs

Malaria is one of the most serious and widespread diseases. It kills about one million people each year.

Hoverfly's wingtips make a figure-eight pattern with each wing beat.

HOVERFLY
The hoverfly is one of the most expert fliers. It can hover perfectly still, even in a wind, then dart straight up, down, sideways, or backward. Tiny ball-and-stick structures behind the wings, called halteres, rotate rapidly and act as stabilizers during flight.

LIFE CYCLE OF A DRONE FLY
The drone fly is a kind of hoverfly. It resembles a bee in appearance and makes a low droning sound in flight. After mating, the female lays her eggs near a puddle, a polluted pond, or other stagnant (nonmoving) water. The larvae, known as rat-tailed maggots, live in the water, breathing through the long tail which acts like a snorkel. The rat-tailed maggots wriggle onto drier soil before pupating. When the adults emerge from the pupal cases, they fly off to feed on pollen and nectar from flowers.

Female drone fly lays eggs near water in a drain.

Adult fly emerges 4-6 weeks after eggs are laid.

Rat-tailed maggots (larvae) feed on rotting and decaying plant and animal matter in the drain.

Maggots (larvae) crawl out of water and change into pupae (pupate).

> *Find out more*
> ANIMALS
> DISEASE
> FLIGHT, ANIMAL
> INSECTS

ANIMAL
FLIGHT

BIRDS, BATS, AND INSECTS are the only animals that truly fly. Other animals, such as flying squirrels, flying fish, and flying lizards, swoop or glide, but cannot climb upward into the air under their own power. Life in the air has several advantages for flying animals – some birds, such as hawks, can hunt their prey in midair; other birds can quickly escape from their predators. Birds are also able to migrate very long distances to find more suitable feeding areas in a cold season – the Arctic tern, for example, migrates about 11,000 miles (18,000 km) from the North Pole to the South Pole every year. Another bird, the swift, spends much of its life in the air, landing only to nest. A swift eats and drinks on the move for nine months of the year. Birds, bats, and insects are also able to find food on land quickly and efficiently – a hummingbird hovers to gather nectar, a fruit bat flies into a tree to feed on fruit, and a dragonfly swoops over a pond to catch small flies. All flying animals from bees to buzzards need plenty of food to provide them with the energy to take to the air. Animals first began to fly about 300 million years ago, when Earth's prehistoric coal swamps were becoming overcrowded with all kinds of creatures. Through evolution, special features began to develop, such as a flap of skin on the body for gliding. In order to fly, an animal needs a lightweight body and strong muscles with which to flap its wings. Birds have hollow bones to save weight when they are in flight, so that a huge bird such as the golden eagle weighs less than 9 lb (4 kg).

ARCHAEOPTERYX
One of the first birds known to have existed is called *Archaeopteryx*. Fossil remains date back 150 million years. *Archaeopteryx* could glide and fly through the air.

Elastic fibers allow the wings to shrink so the bat can fold them neatly.

SOOTY TERN
The sooty tern lives on the move for up to 10 years. It returns to the ground only to breed.

WINGS
The wings of a flying animal are light so that they can be flapped easily. They are broad and flat, to push the air downward and give lift. Wings must also be flexible for control in the air. An insect's wings are made of a thin membrane stiffened by tubelike veins. A bird's wings have bones and muscles at the front; feathers form the rest of the surface. A bat's wings consist of a thin layer of muscles and tough fibers sandwiched between two layers of skin that are supported by bones.

Main bones in the wing

Wings stretch between the forearm and finger bones.

Powerful wing-flapping pectoral muscles are in the bat's chest.

Bat

Feathers near the wing root shape the wing smoothly into the body.

Flight feathers are light and stiff, with strong shafts and large, smooth vanes.

Covert feathers are at the front of the wing. They are small and packed closely together, to give a smooth edge.

Wing of a kestrel

Primary flight feathers help to reduce turbulence.

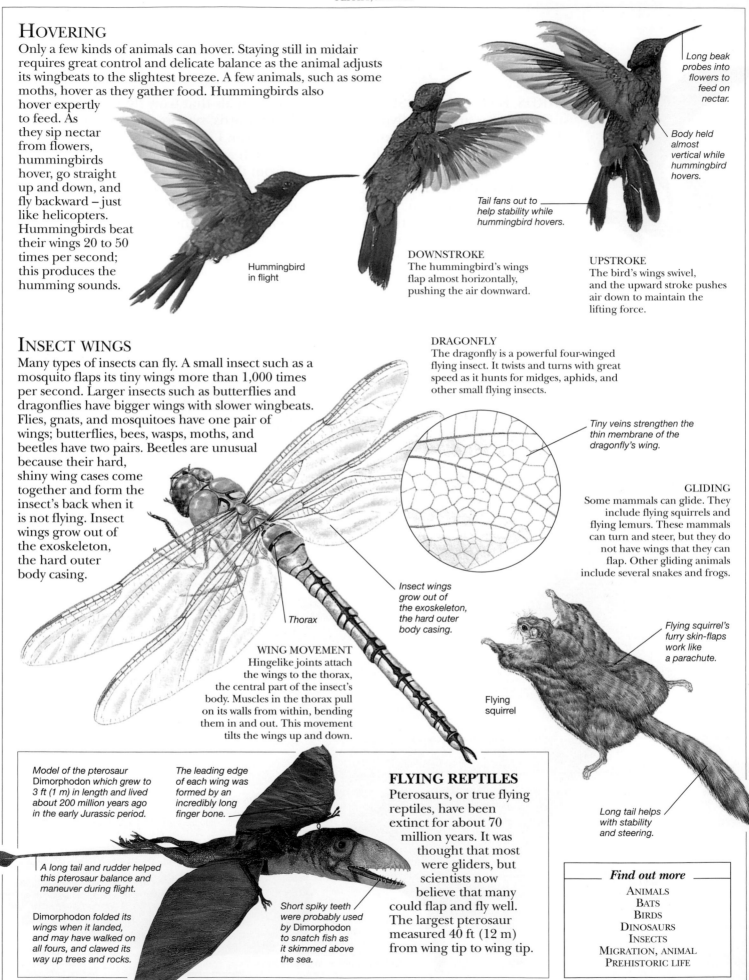

HOVERING

Only a few kinds of animals can hover. Staying still in midair requires great control and delicate balance as the animal adjusts its wingbeats to the slightest breeze. A few animals, such as some moths, hover as they gather food. Hummingbirds also hover expertly to feed. As they sip nectar from flowers, hummingbirds hover, go straight up and down, and fly backward – just like helicopters. Hummingbirds beat their wings 20 to 50 times per second; this produces the humming sounds.

Hummingbird in flight

Long beak probes into flowers to feed on nectar.

Body held almost vertical while hummingbird hovers.

Tail fans out to help stability while hummingbird hovers.

DOWNSTROKE
The hummingbird's wings flap almost horizontally, pushing the air downward.

UPSTROKE
The bird's wings swivel, and the upward stroke pushes air down to maintain the lifting force.

INSECT WINGS

Many types of insects can fly. A small insect such as a mosquito flaps its tiny wings more than 1,000 times per second. Larger insects such as butterflies and dragonflies have bigger wings with slower wingbeats. Flies, gnats, and mosquitoes have one pair of wings; butterflies, bees, wasps, moths, and beetles have two pairs. Beetles are unusual because their hard, shiny wing cases come together and form the insect's back when it is not flying. Insect wings grow out of the exoskeleton, the hard outer body casing.

DRAGONFLY
The dragonfly is a powerful four-winged flying insect. It twists and turns with great speed as it hunts for midges, aphids, and other small flying insects.

Tiny veins strengthen the thin membrane of the dragonfly's wing.

Insect wings grow out of the exoskeleton, the hard outer body casing.

Thorax

WING MOVEMENT
Hingelike joints attach the wings to the thorax, the central part of the insect's body. Muscles in the thorax pull on its walls from within, bending them in and out. This movement tilts the wings up and down.

GLIDING
Some mammals can glide. They include flying squirrels and flying lemurs. These mammals can turn and steer, but they do not have wings that they can flap. Other gliding animals include several snakes and frogs.

Flying squirrel's furry skin-flaps work like a parachute.

Flying squirrel

Long tail helps with stability and steering.

Model of the pterosaur *Dimorphodon* which grew to 3 ft (1 m) in length and lived about 200 million years ago in the early Jurassic period.

The leading edge of each wing was formed by an incredibly long finger bone.

A long tail and rudder helped this pterosaur balance and maneuver during flight.

Dimorphodon folded its wings when it landed, and may have walked on all fours, and clawed its way up trees and rocks.

Short spiky teeth were probably used by *Dimorphodon* to snatch fish as it skimmed above the sea.

FLYING REPTILES

Pterosaurs, or true flying reptiles, have been extinct for about 70 million years. It was thought that most were gliders, but scientists now believe that many could flap and fly well. The largest pterosaur measured 40 ft (12 m) from wing tip to wing tip.

Find out more
ANIMALS
BATS
BIRDS
DINOSAURS
INSECTS
MIGRATION, ANIMAL
PREHISTORIC LIFE

FLOWERS AND HERBS

THE EXQUISITE BEAUTY, color, and scent of flowers have inspired artists and poets for centuries. Flowers are among the most brightly colored of all living things. They include sun-loving desert marigolds, hardy poppies in the snowy Arctic, tropical orchids, and cultivated garden roses, as well as some tiny inconspicuous flowers. Without the thousands of different flowers and herbs that grow on the Earth, bees could not make honey, butterflies and hummingbirds would have no food, we would have no flowerbeds, and perfume would have no fragrance. For most of us, the word "flower" describes any flowering plant that is particularly colorful or pretty. To the botanist who studies plants, however, a flower refers strictly to the reproductive part of a plant – its bloom or blossom. The word "herb" is an everyday name we give to smaller, less colorful flowering plants whose leaves and blossoms have a strong, pleasant scent and taste.

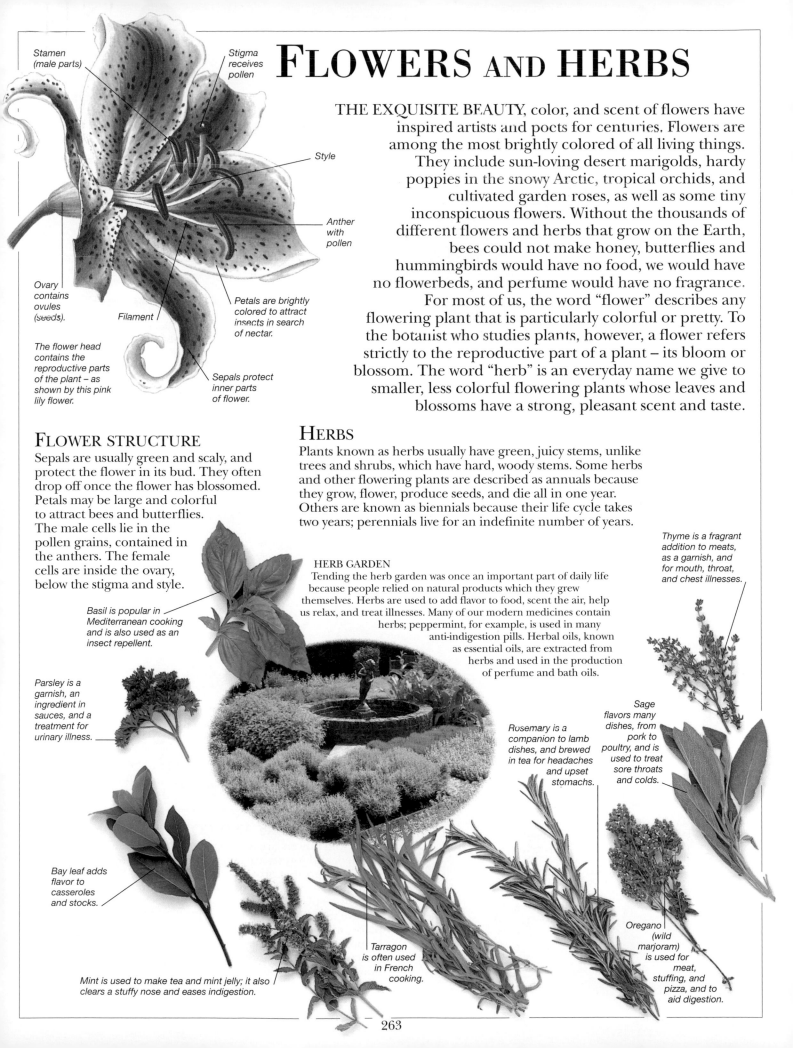

Stamen (male parts)

Stigma receives pollen

Style

Anther with pollen

Ovary contains ovules (seeds).

Filament

Petals are brightly colored to attract insects in search of nectar.

The flower head contains the reproductive parts of the plant – as shown by this pink lily flower.

Sepals protect inner parts of flower.

FLOWER STRUCTURE

Sepals are usually green and scaly, and protect the flower in its bud. They often drop off once the flower has blossomed. Petals may be large and colorful to attract bees and butterflies. The male cells lie in the pollen grains, contained in the anthers. The female cells are inside the ovary, below the stigma and style.

HERBS

Plants known as herbs usually have green, juicy stems, unlike trees and shrubs, which have hard, woody stems. Some herbs and other flowering plants are described as annuals because they grow, flower, produce seeds, and die all in one year. Others are known as biennials because their life cycle takes two years; perennials live for an indefinite number of years.

Basil is popular in Mediterranean cooking and is also used as an insect repellent.

Parsley is a garnish, an ingredient in sauces, and a treatment for urinary illness.

HERB GARDEN
Tending the herb garden was once an important part of daily life because people relied on natural products which they grew themselves. Herbs are used to add flavor to food, scent the air, help us relax, and treat illnesses. Many of our modern medicines contain herbs; peppermint, for example, is used in many anti-indigestion pills. Herbal oils, known as essential oils, are extracted from herbs and used in the production of perfume and bath oils.

Thyme is a fragrant addition to meats, as a garnish, and for mouth, throat, and chest illnesses.

Rosemary is a companion to lamb dishes, and brewed in tea for headaches and upset stomachs.

Sage flavors many dishes, from pork to poultry, and is used to treat sore throats and colds.

Bay leaf adds flavor to casseroles and stocks.

Oregano (wild marjoram) is used for meat, stuffing, and pizza, and to aid digestion.

Mint is used to make tea and mint jelly; it also clears a stuffy nose and eases indigestion.

Tarragon is often used in French cooking.

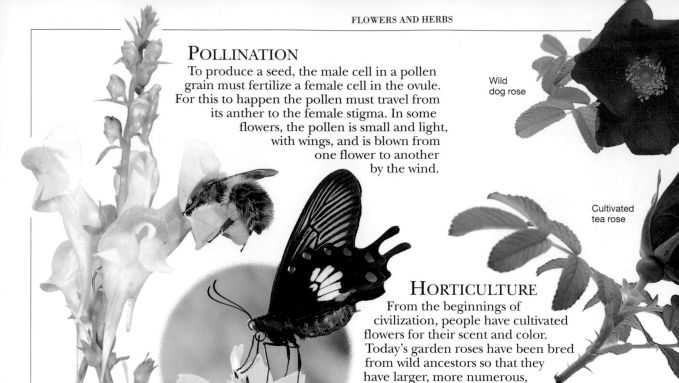

Wild
dog rose

Cultivated
tea rose

POLLINATION

To produce a seed, the male cell in a pollen grain must fertilize a female cell in the ovule. For this to happen the pollen must travel from its anther to the female stigma. In some flowers, the pollen is small and light, with wings, and is blown from one flower to another by the wind.

HORTICULTURE

From the beginnings of civilization, people have cultivated flowers for their scent and color. Today's garden roses have been bred from wild ancestors so that they have larger, more numerous, and more colorful petals, sweeter scents, and a longer flowering time. The art of gardening is called horticulture.

BEES AND FLOWERS

Bees help pollination. As a bee feeds on nectar and pollen, more pollen inside the flower sticks to the bee's legs and body and is carried by the bee to the next flower, where it pollinates the female parts.

NECTAR

Butterflies, moths, bats, and birds feed on the sweet, energy-rich nectar inside each flower. Bees convert nectar into honey in the beehive.

BIRD-OF-PARADISE FLOWER

The bird-of-paradise plant comes originally from riverbanks in southern Africa and is now grown in many parks and gardens. Each plant has brilliant orange flowers which form a shape that looks like the head and beak of a bird of paradise. The bird-of-paradise flowers rise one after the other from a long, stiff, green-pink casing.

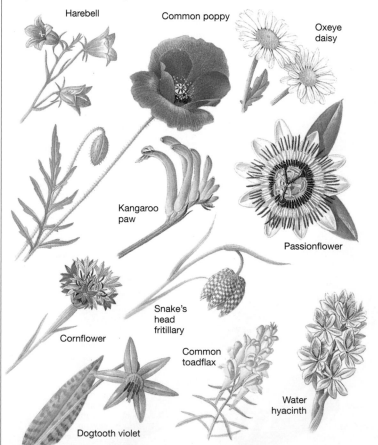

Harebell

Common poppy

Oxeye daisy

Kangaroo paw

Passionflower

Cornflower

Snake's head fritillary

Common toadflax

Dogtooth violet

Water hyacinth

PERFUME

A flower's smell attracts butterflies, bees, and people, too. Lily of the valley and rose are used in the manufacture of perfumes and soaps.

Lily of the valley flowers have a sweet scent. Their leaves are scented too.

WILD FLOWERS AND CONSERVATION

Many wild flowers are in danger of extinction. Marshes are drained, and forests are felled for farmland and buildings, so the flowers that grow there are destroyed. Rare and beautiful blooms are at risk because they are dug up illegally by plant collectors. To save rare flowers, the places where they grow must be protected. As forests are cut down, thousands of flowers are disappearing even before they are known to science.

Find out more

BEES AND WASPS
CONSERVATION
and endangered species
FRUITS AND SEEDS
PLANTS

FOOD AND FOOD TECHNOLOGY

FOOD PRESERVATION
Food goes bad because of bacteria (harmful organisms) that can grow in it. Bacteria cannot thrive in salted, smoked, frozen, high-acid, or high-sugar foods. Tinned food has all the air drawn out and is heat-treated to stop decay from within. Irradiating foods with gamma rays to kill bacteria is the most modern method of preservation, but some doubt its safety.

ALL LIVING THINGS need food; it is the basic fuel of life. It keeps us warm, gives us energy, and helps us grow. Our daily pattern of eating and drinking is called our diet. Diets vary across the world according to the availability of food. Humans can digest a wide range of foods from both plant and animal sources, but some people, called vegetarians, choose not to eat meat for health, religious, or other reasons. Lack of the right kinds of food can lead to disease, inadequate growth, and eventually starvation. Eating too much of the wrong kinds of food can cause heart disease and other illnesses.

Fruit and vegetable market

NUTRITION
A balanced diet is one that provides everything the body needs for health and growth. Energy-giving foods contain carbohydrates and fats, which are burned up slowly by the body. Energy in food is measured in calories. A 10-year-old needs about 2,000 calories a day. Body-building food is called protein and comes mainly from meat, fish, milk, eggs, nuts, and cereals. Vitamins are necessary to keep skin and eyes healthy and blood vessels strong. Water helps dissolve and digest food. Small quantities of minerals are needed for growth: calcium helps keep teeth strong, and iron is necessary for healthy blood. Fiber in food cannot be digested, but it enables our intestines to grip the food as it passes through.

FAMINE AND PLENTY
The world's farms produce enough to feed everyone, but food does not reach the hungry. Western nations have mountains of grain that is surplus for them. However, in various parts of the world, more than 40 million people starve. Many even die of hunger.

Pasta and rice are basic or "staple" foods and provide bulk, energy, and protein. Grains, cereals, and legumes such as peas and beans are also staple foods. Their use varies from country to country.

Poultry and meat provide protein for body building and fat for energy.

Seaweed

Nuts are a good source of protein and fat.

Fungi provide small amounts of fiber and minerals.

Fruits and vegetables provide vitamins, fiber, and natural sugar. Some vegetables, such as potatoes, provide carbohydrates for energy.

REGIONAL FOOD
Food varies across the world according to climate, local customs, and religious beliefs. In France, cooks use local seaweed found around coastlines and snails in their recipes. The diet of some Aboriginal Australians and Africans includes insects and grubs.

Eggs and milk products provide a great deal of fat. They are also high in protein, vitamins, and minerals.

Fish and shellfish are rich in body-building protein, minerals, and vitamins.

Snail

The closed cooking range, with an oven in which heat levels could be regulated, was invented by Benjamin Thompson in 1795.

TRADITIONAL COOKING

The oldest method of cooking is roasting over an open wood fire. Stewing or boiling, using a pot hanging over an open fire, came later. The first "modern" closed range, with top burners and an oven fueled by wood or coal, was introduced in the 18th century. In the 1850s, gas became the new fuel, followed in the early 20th century by electricity.

Modern stoves may run on gas or electricity or a mixture of both.

MICROWAVE OVEN

A microwave oven cooks with high-frequency electromagnetic waves (microwaves) instead of radiated heat. Microwaves cause the water molecules in food to vibrate, which makes them become hot. The heat cooks the solid parts of the food. Metal blocks microwaves, which is why metal dishes cannot be used in a microwave oven.

For safety, the door cannot open when the oven is on.

FOOD PREPARATION

Many foods have to be cooked before we eat them to make them easier to digest and taste better. Boiling or steaming cooks food with water, frying or grilling uses fast heat, usually on top of the stove, and stewing, roasting, and baking need the slow heat of an oven. Uncooked foods, such as salad, also need to be prepared, by washing, chopping, and mixing.

FOOD PROCESSOR

The electric food processor, or blender, has made it possible to do laborious jobs extremely quickly. Using different tools and attachments, processors can mix raw ingredients for cakes, make pastry dough, chop, slice, and grate raw vegetables, make breadcrumbs, blend pâtés, and turn cooked fruit and vegetables into a purée or soup. They can whip cream and beat eggs, too.

Mixing bowl

Wear a clean apron and keep hands and utensils clean.

Wooden spoon

Metal saucepan

Freshly ground pepper adds flavor to savoury foods.

KITCHEN SAFETY

Oven mitt

Preparing and cooking food is fun, but it must be done carefully to avoid accidents and prevent germs from spreading. Wash your hands before you start and whenever you move on to different ingredients. Use oven mitts to move hot dishes in and out of the oven and protect yourself from splashes with a clean apron.

Apron

Rolling pin for dough

Measuring cup

EQUIPMENT

Most cooking pans are made of metal that can conduct heat to the food inside them without melting. Wooden spoons are used to stir hot food in a saucepan; because wood does not conduct heat, so your hands are protected as you work. Glass is used for measuring cups so you can easily see the amount inside. Bowls can also be made of glass.

Find out more

DIGESTION
FRUITS AND SEEDS
HEALTH AND FITNESS

FOOTBALL

Football legend Jim Thorpe played with the Canton, Ohio Bulldogs.

THE GAME OF FOOTBALL is a strategic battle between two teams as they try to move a ball, by running with it or passing it, across the other team's goal line for a touchdown. The team with the ball plays offense; the team trying to stop them by tackling or blocking the player with the ball plays defense. At the start of the game, the offense begins an attack on the goal. If the offense is not able to move the ball 10 yd (9 m) forwards after four plays, the ball is given to the other team. Possession of the ball shifts many times during a game. Before each play begins, the teams face each other at the scrimmage line. The ball is passed to the quarterback, who may hand the ball off to a teammate or make a longer throw to another player. A typical game is divided into four 15-minute quarters, with many time-outs.

HISTORY OF FOOTBALL

Football probably originated from the English game, rugby. Soccerlike games were popular at US colleges from the 1860s. After a visiting Canadian team brought rugby to Harvard University, players began to run and tackle as well as kick the ball. In 1879, Yale University coach Walter Camp proposed new rules that led to the development of the modern game.

A scrimmage line

PLAYERS

Each team consists of 11 players. In professional football, players specialize in offensive or defensive positions. Players on the offensive team include the quarterback, running backs, wide receivers, offensive linemen, and tight end. Defensive positions include defensive backs, defensive linemen, and linebackers. Other players specialize in kicking the ball.

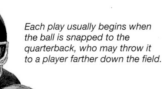
Each play usually begins when the ball is snapped to the quarterback, who may throw it to a player farther down the field.

Football

Helmet

Body padding

EQUIPMENT

The oval-shaped football is usually made of leather. Its textured surface and lacing along one seam help players to grip the ball.

Football is a contact sport and the players need to be protected from injury. Plastic helmets with face masks protect the head, while the body is protected with special padding – shoulder pads, hip pads, thigh pads, and knee pads – all worn under the uniform.

SUPER BOWL

The National Football League (NFL) stages a spectacular championship game between the winners of its two conferences. This game, called the Super Bowl, decides the NFL title and attracts a huge television audience around the world.

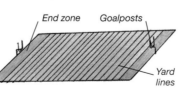
End zone   Goalposts

Yard lines

DOWNS AND TOUCHDOWNS

The offensive team has four plays to move the ball forward 10 yd (9 m), for a first down. Each first down gives it another four chances to move the ball forward. If a team fails to make a first down, it loses possession. A player who carries the ball into the opposing team's end zone makes a touchdown, worth six points.

FOOTBALL FIELD

A football field is a rectangle 100 yd (91 m) long and 53 ⅓ yd (49 m) wide, with yard lines marked across its width every 5 yd (4.5 m). A 10-yard (9-m) end zone extends beyond the goal lines. Goalposts rise above each end zone, through which the ball is kicked for a goal.

Find out more

BALL GAMES
SOCCER
SPORTS

FORCE AND MOTION

WHAT IS IT THAT MAKES OBJECTS MOVE? Why does a boat float? How does a magnet work? Left to itself, any object would remain still, but when it is pushed or pulled, it begins to move. Something that pushes or pulls is called a force. Forces often produce motion, or movement. For example, an engine produces a force that pushes a car forward. There are several different kinds of forces. A magnet produces a magnetic force which pulls pieces of iron toward it, and a rubber band produces an elastic force when you stretch it. Liquids produce forces, too. A boat floats because of the force of water pushing upward on the hull. And a drop of water holds together because of a force called surface tension, which makes all liquids seem as though they have an elastic skin around them. From the smallest particle inside an atom to the largest galaxy, the whole universe is held together by powerful forces. One of these forces is gravity, which holds us onto the surface of the Earth.

CHANGING DIRECTION
When you move in a circle, on a fairground ride for example, a constant force is needed to change the direction of your motion. This force acts towards the center of the circle. On the ride shown above, the force comes from the tension in the ropes that support the seats.

ACCELERATION
The action of a force produces motion, making an object accelerate (speed up). For example, the force produced by the engine makes a ship accelerate. The stronger the force, the greater the acceleration.

INERTIA
It takes a strong force to start a heavy object moving. In the same way, a strong force is needed to make it slow down and stop. This reluctance to start or stop moving is called inertia. The heavier the object, the greater its inertia.

Water and air resist motion, producing a force called drag. A small boat accelerates easily and soon reaches its cruising speed. But drag increases as speed increases. When drag force balances the driving force of the engines, speed stays constant.

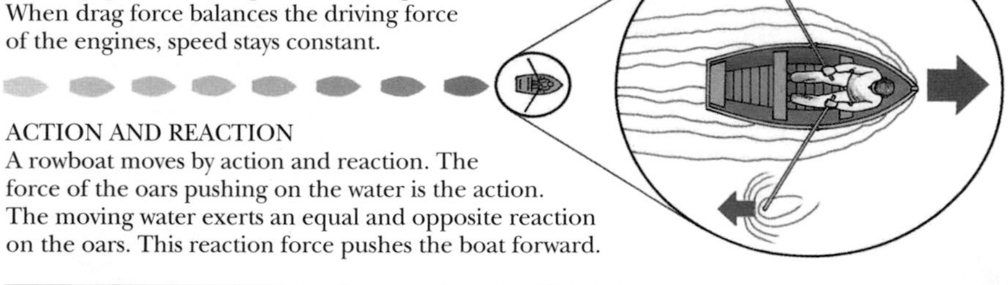

ACTION AND REACTION
A rowboat moves by action and reaction. The force of the oars pushing on the water is the action. The moving water exerts an equal and opposite reaction on the oars. This reaction force pushes the boat forward.

NEWTON'S LAWS OF MOTION
In 1687, the English scientist Isaac Newton (1642-1727) published his three laws of motion. The first law explains that an object stays at rest or moves at a constant speed unless a force pushes or pulls it. The second law explains how force overcomes inertia and causes acceleration. The third law explains that when a force (or action) pushes one way, an equal force (or reaction) always pushes in the opposite direction.

In an arch bridge, the piers (ends of the bridge) support the weight of the arch.

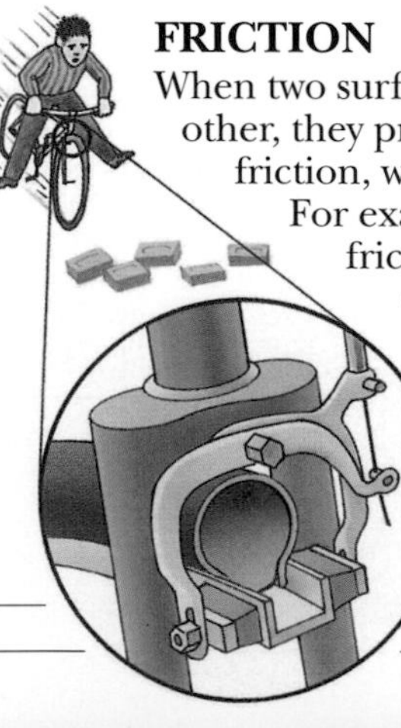

FRICTION
When two surfaces rub against each other, they produce a force called friction, which opposes motion. For example, brakes use friction to slow a wheel down. Friction produces heat and wastes energy. Putting a layer of oil between the moving parts of a machine reduces friction and improves efficiency.

STATIC FORCES
When two teams in tug-of-war pull equally hard on the rope, neither team moves. This is because the forces produced by the teams balance exactly. Forces that balance and produce no movement are called static forces. A bridge stays up because of the balance of static forces. Its weight pushing down is balanced by parts of the structure pushing up.

Find out more

ATOMS AND MOLECULES
BRIDGES
GRAVITY
MAGNETISM
PHYSICS

FOREST WILDLIFE

This map shows the main forest areas of the world.

North America

Asia

Africa

South America

Australia

☐ Temperate forest
☐ Coniferous forest
■ Tropical forest

TREES ARE THE MOST IMPORTANT plants in a forest. They provide all kinds of animals, including monkeys, squirrels, and parrots, with food, homes, and escape routes from predators. The most common tree in any kind of forest often gives the forest its name, from the pine forests in the cold north to the steamy teak forests in the tropical regions.

A forest consists of different layers of vegetation. The forest floor is covered with leaf litter. Here, parts of trees and other plants rot into the soil, helped by the millipedes, worms, and other small creatures that feed on them. The next layer of the forest is called the herb layer. It consists of small flowers and ferns that grow wherever enough sunlight filters through the trees. Bushes, shrubs, and young trees make up the under-storey of the forest. Next is a layer of tall tree trunks, laced with trailing vines and creepers. The uppermost part of the forest is called the canopy. Leaves grow in the sunlight; insects, birds, and bats pollinate the flowers; and fruit ripens to feed a host of creatures.

LONG-EARED OWL
The long-eared owl swoops silently among the trees at twilight and during the night. These owls roost by day in a tree, and their mottled brown plumage provides good camouflage. The tufts on the feathers of this owl's head look like long ears – hence the name.

WOLVERINE
The wolverine of northern forests is an exceptionally strong animal for its size. It tackles animal prey much larger than itself and also eats carrion (dead animals), fruit, and berries. The wolverine is nicknamed the "glutton" because of its large appetite.

CONIFEROUS FORESTS
Pines and firs make up coniferous forests. These trees are evergreen – they keep their leaves all year, providing shelter for animals. The leaves are very tough, and only a few animals can eat and digest them. A few types of conifer, such as the larches, lose their leaves in the fall.

BROAD-LEAVED FORESTS
The trees in a broad-leaved forest are called deciduous trees because their leaves drop off in the fall, to be replaced by new leaves the next year. These trees blossom in the spring, which is the main animal breeding time. The new shoots provide food for animals. In the fall, animals feed on the fruit, nuts, and berries of these trees, so they can survive the winter.

Ferns, such as bracken, grow quickly and rapidly cover clearings. Bracken is common on every continent except Antarctica. It spreads by sending out branching underground stems.

Bluebells are one of the spring woodland flowers. Some bluebells have pink flowers; others have white ones.

Wood anemone

ROE DEER
The roe deer's reddish brown coat blends in well with the bracken where it lives. It lives alone for most of the year, feeding at twilight on the buds, shoots, and leaves of trees and shrubs.

Several heavy-bodied, strong-legged birds live in the forest, including pheasants such as the blue peacock shown here. These birds can fly but they often avoid danger by running into the dense forest undergrowth.

CONSERVATION

As the forests are cut down or burned, animals lose their homes. Tree-living creatures such as this American uakari monkey are most at risk. These monkeys depend on the flowers and fruit from the large old trees in rain forests. Worldwide conservation organizations are trying to stop the destruction of the rain forests in order to save monkeys and thousands of other creatures.

TANAGER

The paradise tanager is a noisy, active bird that lives high up in the rain forest canopy. Paradise tanagers keep their bright plumage all year and flutter from tree to tree in search of insects and ripe fruit.

TROPICAL FORESTS

In tropical forests, the climate is much the same all year round. High temperatures and heavy rainfall make tropical rain forests some of the richest places for wildlife. There are many more species of trees than in any other kind of forest, and thousands more kinds of animals.

SLOTH

Few animals move more slowly than the sloths of Central and South America. They hang from branches with their curved claws, eat leaves, and move so slowly that tiny green simple plants called algae grow on their coats. The algae help camouflage the sloths among the trees.

PARROT

The male and female eclectus parrots shown here are so differently colored that for many years people believed they were two different species of birds. These parrots live in the forests of New Guinea and Australia. Like all parrots, they have huge bills for cracking seeds.

TOUCANET

With its large, light bill, the toucanet is an excellent berry picker. Its bright colors help it advertise for a mate in the breeding season. There are 42 kinds of toucanets, and they are all found in tropical South America. Toucanets nest in tree holes and eat birds' eggs and nestlings, fruit, insects, frogs, and lizards.

Several kinds of frogs, lizards, snakes, and squirrels have evolved, or developed, ways of gliding through the air from a high branch to escape from predators or to reach food. The gliding snake flattens its ribs as it leaps, to make a streamlined ribbon shape.

Atlas moth resting on a bromeliad flower

POISON ARROW FROG

It is so damp in rain forests that frogs spend their lives in the trees and do not need to find water elsewhere. Frogs lay their eggs, or spawn, in pools of rain which collect on leaves, fungi, and in flowers such as bromeliads, which grow on trees. Poison arrow frogs live in the rain forests of South America. Their bright colors warn predators of the deadly poison in their skin.

ATLAS MOTH

The atlas moth is one of the largest moths in the world, with a wingspan of 12 in (30 cm). Today, atlas moths are rare. In the past, people killed thousands of them simply for their butterfly collections.

LEMUR

There are 20 different kinds of lemur. These mammals are related to monkeys, and they live in trees in Madagascar, an island off the east coast of Africa. Mouse lemurs weigh only 2 oz (60 gm).

Ground ginger is a spice made from the root of the ginger plant, which came originally from the forests of Asia.

Leaf roller ants curl up leaves on the forest floor and join the edges into a tube to make a nesting site.

Find out more

BIRDS
BUTTERFLIES AND MOTHS
CONSERVATION
and endangered species
FROGS AND OTHER AMPHIBIANS
OWLS

FOSSILS

THE FIRST PLANTS, the earliest animals, the beginnings of human life – we know about prehistoric times because of fossils. Fossils are the remains of dead animals and plants that have been preserved for thousands or millions of years. A fossil might be the tooth of a dinosaur embedded in rock, or the outline of a leaf on a stone. By studying fossils, we can learn what ancient creatures and plants looked like and how they lived. Most fossils are of plants and animals that lived in water. When the living plant or animal died, its soft parts rotted away, leaving the hard pieces such as bones or leaf veins. Gradually, layers of mud piled up and squeezed the remains of the plant or animal at great pressure. Slowly the mud, bones, and other remains fossilized, or turned to rock, in the place where they lay underground. Over many thousands of years, the movements of the Earth twisted and buckled the rocks, lifting the fossils closer to the surface of the soil. Sun, rain, and wind wore away the rocks and exposed the fossil.

Fossil collecting is a hobby that anyone can enjoy. You can find fossils in rocks, on beaches, and in quarries.

AMMONITE
Some of the most common fossils are the shells of sea creatures called ammonites. Ammonites were related to squid and octopuses. They were very widespread about 250 million years ago. The smallest ammonites measured less than 1 in (2 cm) across; the largest measured about 8 ft (2.5 m) across. Ammonites died out with the dinosaurs about 65 million years ago.

Fossil of a fish called Sparnodus – an ancestor of the sea bream

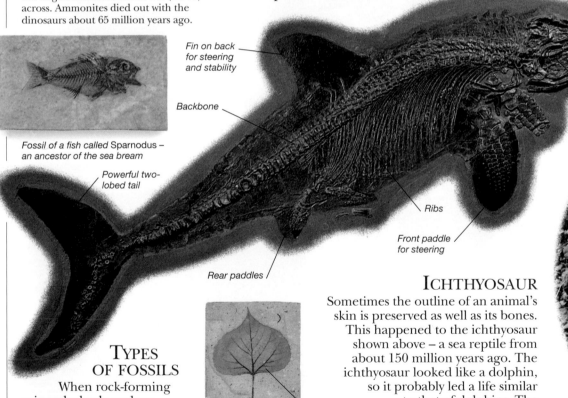

Fin on back for steering and stability

Backbone

Powerful two-lobed tail

Rear paddles

Ribs

Front paddle for steering

Long jaws and short, sharp teeth

Large eye socket

TYPES OF FOSSILS
When rock-forming minerals slowly replace the original parts of a dead creature or plant, they make a mineralized fossil. Sometimes the parts of a creature or plant rot away after being buried, leaving a hole in the rock; this is called a mold fossil. If the hole fills up with rock minerals, it becomes a cast fossil. The fossilized signs of animals, such as footprints, droppings, and tracks, are called trace fossils.

Mineralized fossil of a poplar leaf, 25 million years old

Cast fossil of a creature called a trilobite, which lived in the sea

ICHTHYOSAUR
Sometimes the outline of an animal's skin is preserved as well as its bones. This happened to the ichthyosaur shown above – a sea reptile from about 150 million years ago. The ichthyosaur looked like a dolphin, so it probably led a life similar to that of dolphins. The outline of this fossil shows a fin on the back and a two-lobed tail. The dozens of sharp teeth in the long jaws tell us that this animal grabbed fish and other slippery prey.

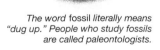

The word fossil literally means "dug up." People who study fossils are called paleontologists.

Find out more
DINOSAURS
EVOLUTION
PREHISTORIC LIFE
ROCKS AND MINERALS

FRANCE

THE LARGEST COUNTRY in western Europe is France – a land of green, open spaces dotted with picturesque towns and small cities. Its many fine old country palaces, or châteaux, are reminders of France's long history. But it is a modern nation, too, with flourishing industries. France is also one of the leading countries in the European Union (EU), the organization that promotes political and economic union between the member states. Northern France has cool, wet weather. The south, with its Mediterranean coast, is drier and warmer. Rolling hills rise from the coasts and valleys, providing good farmland. The rugged hills of the Massif Central occupy the middle of the country. The mountains of the Pyrenees and the Alps line the southwest and eastern borders. France also includes the Mediterranean island of Corsica, and some islands thousands of miles away in the Pacific Ocean and the Caribbean Sea. A democratically elected government and president rule France from Paris.

France shares its long eastern border with Italy, Switzerland, Germany, Luxembourg, and Belgium. Spain is to the south. The south of France lies on the Mediterranean Sea coast, and the Atlantic Ocean is to the west.

Workers on small, family-run estates may still pick grapes by hand. Many people spend their vacations picking grapes, but it is hard work.

Even the smaller winemakers now use some modern equipment, such as stainless-steel fermentation vats.

WINEMAKING

France produces about a fifth of the world's wine. Many famous wines are named after French regions, such as Champagne and Bordeaux. Most French wine comes from cooperatives – local groups of farms that share wine-producing and bottling facilities. Some wine, however, is still made on the small estates attached to the old châteaux. The grapes are picked in the early autumn. Pressing the grapes extracts the juice, which then ferments (reacts with yeast) in large vats to produce the alcohol and the distinctive taste of the wine. Only when this process is complete can the wine be bottled.

The Louvre in Paris is one of the world's most famous art galleries. The glass pyramid was added in 1989.

MARSEILLES

France's biggest seaport is Marseilles, on the Mediterranean coast. The warm climate of southern France makes possible the lively, outdoor lifestyle of the city. There is a long history of trade with the rest of the Mediterranean. Marseilles has a large Arab population, mainly from North Africa.

PARIS

People have lived along the Seine River where Paris now stands since ancient times. Paris is the capital of France. France has a population of more than 60 million; one-fifth live in and around Paris. It is one of Europe's greatest cities, with wide, tree-lined streets called boulevards, and many famous monuments and museums. The city of today was largely replanned and rebuilt during the 19th century.

EIFFEL TOWER

Built to impress visitors to the Paris Exhibition of 1889, the Eiffel Tower was originally meant to be a temporary structure. It was designed by the French engineer Alexandre-Gustave Eiffel. Eiffel was internationally famous for his bridge and aqueduct designs. The tower is built of steel girders weighing 7,700 tons (7,000 tonnes), and 2.5 million rivets hold it together. It reaches a height of 1,050 ft (322 m) and up until the construction of the Empire State Building in New York City in 1931, it was the tallest building in the world. Visitors can reach its various levels by elevator or by climbing hundreds of steps.

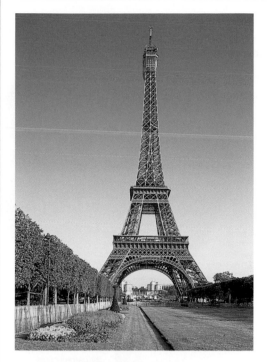

When it was first built in the 19th century, the Eiffel Tower was fiercely criticized. It has now become the symbol of Paris and a much-loved feature of the city.

MONACO

A tiny country on the Côte d'Azur, Monaco lies in southeastern France. The heart of the country is the sophisticated city of Monte Carlo, famous for its casinos and auto-racing Grand Prix. Monaco is an independent principality, ruled for much of its history by the Grimaldi family (above). Only a small part of the population is originally from Monaco; more than half the people are citizens of France. They are drawn by the lenient tax laws and high standard of living, and earn more per capita than any other country in the world.

Normandy is a region of gentle hills and farmland, and is especially known for its hedgerows.

NORMANDY

The region of Normandy lies between Paris and the English Channel. Normandy is a farming area, known throughout France for its dairy products and its apples. By grazing their cattle in the orchards, many local farmers get double use from the land. They sell the apples as dessert fruits, or turn them into cider and an apple brandy called calvados. Cream from the Normandy cattle makes some of France's most famous cheeses, including Brie and Camembert.

LOIRE RIVER

The valley of the Loire River is famous for its beautiful castles, called châteaux, such as this one at Gien. Kings, nobles, or wealthy landowners built the châteaux as their country homes. They often chose a site on high ground and surrounded the château with a moat, which made it easy to defend the château from attackers. The Loire Valley is also an important wine-producing area.

TGV design has evolved over the years. This train has a sharp aerodynamic nose to increase its speed.

TRANSPORTATION

The French are not only pioneers of aviation – they co-built the Concorde – they also lead the world in high-speed train technology. With speeds of up to 185 mph (300 km/h) the French TGV (Trains à Grande Vitesse) is the world's fastest train. The first TGV line, from Paris to Lyon, was opened in 1983. TGV lines have since been built to Belgium, Italy, and Spain. The Channel Tunnel links France to the UK.

FRENCH CUISINE

French cooks are considered among the best in the world. There are numerous good restaurants, even in very small towns, and the quality of ordinary daily food is very high. Food specialists who take great pride in their work produce outstanding cooked meats, pastries, and bread, including the famous stick-shaped baguette. French cheeses, such as Camembert, are eaten all over the world.

A patisserie specializes in sweet, delicious pastries, and produces a wide range for its customers every day.

TOUR DE FRANCE

Cycling is an enormously popular pastime in France. The world's most famous cycling race is the Tour de France (Tour of France), which takes place every summer. The route follows public roads covering about 2,200 miles (3,500 km), primarily in France and Belgium, but briefly in four other countries. The race takes place over 26 days, and the world's best cyclists take part.

The town square is the traditional spot for games such as boules or petanque, French versions of lawn bowling.

In fine weather, café owners put tables and chairs out on the sidewalks so their customers can eat and drink in the open air.

The extract of scented flowers, such as lavender, is a major ingredient in perfume.

COUNTRY TOWNS

Much of France consists of open country where most working people earn a living from farming. One in every five French people lives and works in the countryside. The farming communities spread out around small market towns, which provide markets, banks, restaurants, shops, and supermarkets. Each town contains a *mairie* – the offices of the local government administration. The *mairie* often overlooks the central square, where people meet to talk and perhaps enjoy a game of *boules*.

PERFUME AND FASHION

Two of France's best-known industries are the manufacture of perfume and *haute couture*, or high fashion. Many of the most famous and most expensive brands of perfume are French. French designers dominated fashion for most of the 20th century. The Paris collections, shown in the spring of each year, are the most important of the international fashion shows and are attended by designers from all over the world. They set the trends which the rest of the world will follow.

The 176 luminous stained-glass windows of Chartres Cathedral (right) attest to the talents of Chartres craftsworkers.

CHARTRES

France is a mainly Roman Catholic country. There are churches in every village, and cathedrals in the cities. The cathedral of Chartres, in northern France, was completed in 1260. It is famous not only for its fine architecture, but also for its magnificent stained-glass windows. There are 176 windows, covering a total area of 28,000 sq ft (2,600 sq m), the equivalent of 10 tennis courts.

Find out more

CHURCHES AND CATHEDRALS
EUROPE
FRANCE, HISTORY OF
FRENCH REVOLUTION
NORMANS

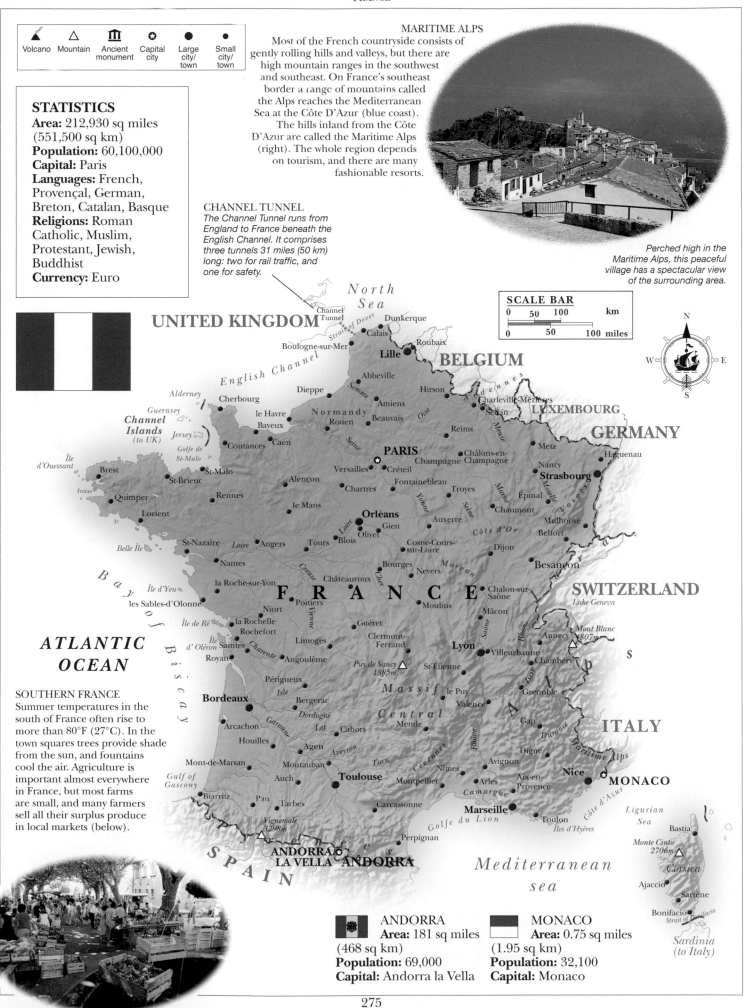

Volcano   **Mountain**   **Ancient monument**   **Capital city**   **Large city/town**   **Small city/town**

STATISTICS
Area: 212,930 sq miles
(551,500 sq km)
Population: 60,100,000
Capital: Paris
Languages: French,
Provençal, German,
Breton, Catalan, Basque
Religions: Roman
Catholic, Muslim,
Protestant, Jewish,
Buddhist
Currency: Euro

MARITIME ALPS
Most of the French countryside consists of gently rolling hills and valleys, but there are high mountain ranges in the southwest and southeast. On France's southeast border a range of mountains called the Alps reaches the Mediterranean Sea at the Côte D'Azur (blue coast). The hills inland from the Côte D'Azur are called the Maritime Alps (right). The whole region depends on tourism, and there are many fashionable resorts.

Perched high in the Maritime Alps, this peaceful village has a spectacular view of the surrounding area.

CHANNEL TUNNEL
The Channel Tunnel runs from England to France beneath the English Channel. It comprises three tunnels 31 miles (50 km) long: two for rail traffic, and one for safety.

SCALE BAR
0   50   100   km
0   50   100 miles

SOUTHERN FRANCE
Summer temperatures in the south of France often rise to more than 80°F (27°C). In the town squares trees provide shade from the sun, and fountains cool the air. Agriculture is important almost everywhere in France, but most farms are small, and many farmers sell all their surplus produce in local markets (below).

UNITED KINGDOM

North Sea

Channel Tunnel   Dunkerque
Strait of Dover   Calais   Roubaix
Boulogne-sur-Mer   **Lille**

BELGIUM

Abbeville   Hirson   *Ardennes*
English Channel   Dieppe   Amiens   Charleville-Mézières

LUXEMBOURG

Alderney   Cherbourg   le Havre   *Normandy*   Beauvais   Sedan
Guernsey   Bayeux   Rouen   *Oise*   Reims   Metz   Haguenau

GERMANY

Channel Islands (to UK)   Coutances   Caen   *Seine*   Châlons-en-Champagne   Nancy
Golfe de St-Malo   **PARIS**   Champagne

Île d'Ouessant   Brest   St-Malo   Versailles   Créteil   Troyes   Épinal   **Strasbourg**
St-Brieuc   Alençon   Fontainebleau   *Moselle*
Iroise   Quimper   Rennes   Chartres   *Yonne*   Chaumont   Mulhouse
le Mans   Auxerre   *Vosges*   Belfort
Lorient   **Orléans**   *Seine*
Belle Île   Angers   Tours   Gien   *Côte d'Or*   Dijon
St-Nazaire   *Loire*   Blois   Olivet   Cosne-Cours-sur-Loire   Besançon
Nantes   *Cruse*   Châteauroux   Bourges   Nevers   *Morvan*
Île d'Yeu   la Roche-sur-Yon   **F R A N C E**   *Cher*   Moulins   Chalon-sur-Saône   **SWITZERLAND**

Bay of Biscay   Niort   Poitiers   *Lake Geneva*   Mâcon
Île de Ré   la Rochelle   *Vienne*   Guéret
Île d'Oléron   Rochefort   Limoges   Clermont-Ferrand   Mont Blanc 4807m   Annecy

ATLANTIC OCEAN

Saintes   Royan   *Charente*   Angoulême   St-Étienne   Villeurbanne   **Lyon**   Chambéry
Périgueux   *Puy de Sancy 1885m*   *Massif*   le Puy   Grenoble
Bordeaux   Bergerac   *Isle*   *Central*   Valence   *Alps*
Dordogne   Mende   Gap   **ITALY**
Arcachon   *Lot*   Cahors   *Durance*
Houilles   *Garonne*   Agen   *Aveyron*   *Cévennes*   Digne   *Maritime Alps*
Mont-de-Marsan   Montauban   *Tarn*   Nîmes   Avignon   **Nice**
Gulf of Gascony   Auch   **Toulouse**   Montpellier   Arles   Aix-en-Provence   **MONACO**
Biarritz   Pau   Tarbes   Carcassonne   *Camargue*   *Côte d'Azur*
Vignemale 3298m   **Marseille**   Toulon   *Ligurian Sea*
Pyrenees   Perpignan   *Golfe du Lion*   *Îles d'Hyères*   Bastia
ANDORRA LA VELLA   **ANDORRA**   *Monte Cinto 2706m*
S P A I N   *Mediterranean sea*   *Corsica*
Ajaccio   Sartene
Bonifacio   *Strait of Bonifacio*
Sardinia (to Italy)

ANDORRA
Area: 181 sq miles
(468 sq km)
Population: 69,000
Capital: Andorra la Vella

MONACO
Area: 0.75 sq miles
(1.95 sq km)
Population: 32,100
Capital: Monaco

HISTORY OF
FRANCE

THE AREA OF EUROPE that we call France takes its name from a tribe of warriors who conquered the region more than 1,000 years ago. The Franks ruled much of Europe for more than four centuries and were the first people to dominate all of France after the Roman Empire collapsed in A.D. 476. Frankish power was strongest under Charlemagne at the start of the ninth century, but ended in 895 when Vikings from Scandinavia settled in northern France. These Northmen, or Normans, as they became known, invaded England in 1066, establishing a link between these lands that was to last for 500 years. The English at one time dominated France, but by 1453 were driven out of everywhere except Calais. Over the next 300 years, the French kings gained immense power and set a pattern for other European royal families of the time. However, the monarchy became increasingly unpopular with the common people, and in 1789 King Louis XVI was overthrown in a revolution that shocked and inspired people all over the world. The French people abolished royal rule and instead chose to govern themselves. They set up the first of a series of republics that have made France one of the most powerful countries in the western Europe.

CARNAC
The ancient Stone Age inhabitants of France were capable builders. More than 7,500 years ago they built many long straight rows of standing stones at Carnac in Brittany. These stones were probably used in religious ceremonies.

ROMAN ENGINEERING
The Romans occupied Gaul from 58 B.C. to A.D. 486. They constructed many roads and towns, which they supplied with running water from canals. To carry the canals across valleys they built aqueducts, such as this one crossing the Gard River.

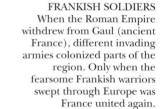

FRANKISH SOLDIERS
When the Roman Empire withdrew from Gaul (ancient France), different invading armies colonized parts of the region. Only when the fearsome Frankish warriors swept through Europe was France united again.

FEUDAL FRANCE
For almost 1,000 years, French peasants labored under the feudal system. They had no land of their own and had to work for the local landowners. The system was finally abolished by the French Revolution.

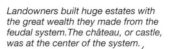

Landowners built huge estates with the great wealth they made from the feudal system. The château, or castle, was at the center of the system.

Peasants worked hard on the owner's land, and in return were allowed to grow their own food.

The peasants worked the land with plows drawn by oxen.

FIELD OF THE CLOTH OF GOLD
By the 16th century, France was a major power in Europe. In 1520, the French king Francis I met Henry VIII of England at a lavish ceremony to sign a peace treaty between the two countries. The place where they met was later called the Field of the Cloth of Gold.

VERSAILLES
Under King Louis XIV and his successors in the 18th century, the arts and crafts in France were among the finest in Europe. Louis built a magnificent palace at Versailles, outside Paris. Ornate sculptures and fountains filled the grounds.

HISTORY OF FRANCE

5700 B.C. Carnac constructed.

58 B.C.-A.D. 486 Roman occupation.

500 Franks settle in country.

768-814 Charlemagne rules Frankish empire.

895 Vikings begin to raid France.

1337-1453 Hundred Years' War against England.

1431 Joan of Arc is burned to death by the English.

1515-47 Reign of Francis I.

1562-98 Wars of Religion between Catholics and Protestants.

1643-1715 Reign of Louis XIV.

1789 Outbreak of French Revolution.

1792 France becomes a republic.

1799 Napoleon seizes power.

1815 Defeat of Napoleon at Waterloo; king restored.

1830 July Revolution throws out king.

1848 Second Republic set up.

1852 Napoleon III sets up Second Empire.

1870-71 Prussia defeats France in Franco-Prussian War. Leads to Third Republic.

1914-18 World War I. France at war with Germany.

1940 Germany invades France.

1944 France liberated from Germany.

1954-62 War with Algeria.

1957 France and other western European nations set up the European Community.

1958-69 Charles De Gaulle is president.

1981 France elects its first socialist president, François Mitterand; he served until 1995.

JEAN JACQUES ROUSSEAU
A philosopher and a writer, Rousseau (1712-78) greatly influenced 18th-century French thinking. He criticized society, thinking that it made people evil. His ideas directly influenced the development of the 1789 French Revolution.

PARIS
The French capital has always been at the center of the country's politics. In 1871 the city rebelled against the terms the government had accepted to end a war against Prussia. The Parisians barricaded the streets and set up a commune to run the city. The government savagely crushed the rebellion, killing 17,000 people. After the commune the architect Baron Haussmann (1809-91) made the streets of Paris wider to make it impossible to set up barricades.

REVOLUTIONS
France has a strong tradition of revolution by the people against absolute domination by a king. In the July revolution of 1830, the people rose up against Charles X, who tried to rule with the total power of Louis XIV. This uprising is shown in a patriotic painting by Eugene Delacroix (above).

The engineer Alexandre Gustave Eiffel (1832-1923) built his famous Eiffel Tower to celebrate the 100th anniversary of the French Revolution.

Wide streets to avoid barricading

ALGERIA
France had colonies in North Africa, including Algeria. During the 1950s many colonies gained independence, but France wanted to keep Algeria, home to almost a million French settlers. Discontent and bad living conditions led the Algerians to revolt, and a war followed. French troops occupied Algeria (above). In 1962, after much fighting, France finally granted Algeria independence.

CHARLES DE GAULLE
During World War II, De Gaulle (1890-1970) was leader of the Free French. He became president of France in 1958. As president he led France through difficult times during which Algeria became independent. De Gaulle retired in 1969.

Find out more
FRANCE
FRENCH REVOLUTION
JOAN OF ARC
LOUIS XIV
NAPOLEON BONAPARTE

BENJAMIN FRANKLIN

A HIGHLY ACCOMPLISHED statesman, inventor, and writer, Benjamin Franklin was one of the most remarkable Americans of his time. Born to a poor Boston candlemaker, Franklin worked in his brother's print shop. At 17, he ran away to Philadelphia to open a shop of his own. Franklin became Philadelphia's most famous citizen, with an endless list of achievements. He founded a public library, organized a hospital, and founded a school that later became the University of Pennsylvania. Franklin's experiments with electricity brought him acclaim throughout Europe. He used his fame to promote the interests of the American colonies, helping to persuade the British to repeal the Stamp Act and convincing the French to help the colonists fight the British in the American Revolution.

1706 Born in Boston, Massachusetts.

1718 Apprenticed to his brother James, a printer.

1723 Runs away to Philadelphia to start his own printing press.

1732 First edition of *Poor Richard's Almanac* was published.

1752 Publishes reports on his experiments with electricity.

1776 Helps draft the Declaration of Independence.

1776 Travels to France as special US envoy.

1787 Framer of the US Constitution.

1790 Dies in Philadelphia.

Benjamin Franklin wearing bifocals, his own invention.

A COLONIAL STATESMAN

During his long career as a politician, Franklin spoke for the interests of the colonies, secured the political and financial support of the French government, and played a crucial role in shaping both the Declaration of Independence and the Constitution. He spent his later years negotiating treaties in France; in 1783, his work on the Peace of Paris treaty marked the end of the Revolutionary War.

Benjamin Franklin accompanies George Washington and John Paul Jones into the Constitutional Convention in 1787.

FRANKLIN'S INVENTIONS

Science and invention were two of Franklin's lifelong passions. Franklin's experiments with electricity – most famously his kite experiment, which proved that lightning is a form of electricity – amazed scientists and led to his invention of the lightning rod, which diverts lightning bolts away from buildings. His other inventions included the fuel-efficient Franklin stove, the bifocal lens (a single lens with two different strengths), and the odometer, a machine that measures distances traveled when attached to a wheel.

CITY OF BROTHERLY LOVE

With a population of more than 300,000, Franklin's home, Philadelphia (from the Greek for "brotherly love"), was the largest city in the colonies. Quaker William Penn founded this Pennsylvanian settlement in 1682, which developed into a bustling port with a thriving textile and shipbuilding trade. Franklin's gifts to the city include its public library – where his statue stands above a doorway (right) – which was the first circulating library in America.

POOR RICHARD'S ALMANAC

For more than 25 years, Franklin wrote this popular yearly calendar. It had jokes, proverbs, and advice on how to get on in the world from Franklin's humble, hard-working character Poor Richard.

Find out more

AMERICAN REVOLUTION
COLONIES
and colonial America
CONSTITUTION
DECLARATION OF INDEPENDENCE

FRENCH REVOLUTION

THE EXECUTION OF LOUIS XVI
"Because the country must live, Louis must die."
With those words, the king of France was killed
on the guillotine on January 21, 1793.

"LIBERTY! EQUALITY! FRATERNITY!"
This slogan echoed throughout France in
1789 as the hungry French people united
to overthrow the rich noblemen who
ruled the country. The revolution put
ordinary people in control of France and
gave hope to oppressed people all over
the world. The revolution started when the
bankrupt king Louis XVI summoned the
French parliament for the first time since
1614. Instead of helping him raise taxes,
they seized power. In Paris, a crowd stormed the Bastille prison, the symbol of
royal authority. The king had to support the revolution, but in 1792 France
became a republic, and Louis was executed. Counterrevolution broke out in
parts of France in 1793, which led to a Reign of Terror that undid many of the
benefits of the revolution. In 1799 a military takeover put Napoleon
Bonaparte in power and ended the revolution.

THE REVOLUTION

May 1789 Estates General (parliament) meets at Versailles.

July 1789 Paris crowd storms Bastille prison.

Aug 1789 Declaration of the Rights of Man.

June 1790 Nobility is abolished.

June 1791 Louis XVI tries to flee from Paris.

Aug 1792 King Louis imprisoned.

Sept 1792 Monarchy abolished and France becomes a republic.

Mar 1793 Counter-revolution in Vendée region.

Sept 1793 Start of Reign of Terror.

July 1794 Terror ends when Robespierre is overthrown.

Nov 1795 A new republic, the Directory, takes power.

Nov 1799 Napoleon Bonaparte overthrows Directory and assumes power.

MAXIMILIEN ROBESPIERRE
When 35-year-old lawyer
Robespierre came to power in
1793, he took severe measures
to safeguard the revolution.
He presided over the Reign
of Terror but was himself
executed in 1794.

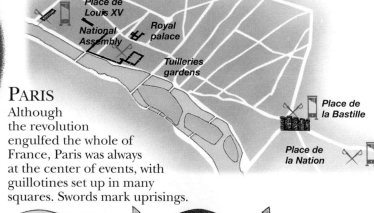

Place de Louis XV

National Assembly

Royal palace

Tuilleries gardens

Place de la Bastille

Place de la Nation

PARIS
Although
the revolution
engulfed the whole of
France, Paris was always
at the center of events, with
guillotines set up in many
squares. Swords mark uprisings.

The red bonnet worn by the revolutionaries, and the republican tricolor flag

MARIANNE
The new revolutionary
calendar started from
the day the king was
overthrown. Marianne
– a symbolic but
imaginary revolutionary
woman shown here on
a stamp – illustrated the
first month.

SANS-CULOTTES
The well-dressed aristocrats sneered
at the revolutionaries and called them
sans-culottes because they wore plain
trousers instead of fancy stockings. The
revolutionaries adopted this name as their
own. Their clothes came to symbolize the
new way of life in revolutionary France.

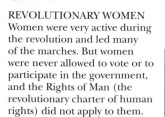

REVOLUTIONARY WOMEN
Women were very active during
the revolution and led many
of the marches. But women
were never allowed to vote or to
participate in the government,
and the Rights of Man (the
revolutionary charter of human
rights) did not apply to them.

Find out more
FRANCE, HISTORY OF
NAPOLEON BONAPARTE
NAPOLEONIC WARS

FROGS AND OTHER AMPHIBIANS

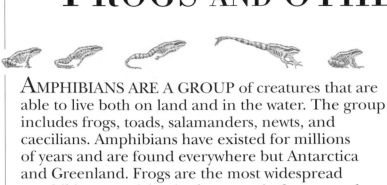

AMPHIBIANS ARE A GROUP of creatures that are able to live both on land and in the water. The group includes frogs, toads, salamanders, newts, and caecilians. Amphibians have existed for millions of years and are found everywhere but Antarctica and Greenland. Frogs are the most widespread amphibians, surviving in deserts, rain forests, and mountainous regions. The limbless caecilian is found only in tropical areas. Caecilians burrow in the earth and swim by wriggling like eels. Frogs, in contrast, can swim, hop, and climb trees using their long back legs. Most amphibians breed in water, where they lay eggs that develop into larvae (tadpoles). During the larval stage, amphibians breathe through gills; as adults they develop lungs for breathing on land. Several kinds of frogs and salamanders are brightly colored, and some have glands in the skin that produce toxins (poisons) to ward off predators.

Frogs rely on their eyes to watch for prey. They also use their eyes to judge distances when they are leaping.

Front legs act as shock absorbers when the frog lands.

AMPHIBIANS

Some amphibians lay spawn (eggs) in water; others lay eggs out of water, on leaves, or in holes underground. The frogspawn you see in a pond hatches into limbless tadpoles. As the tadpoles grow in the water, they develop limbs. They gradually change into frogs and climb onto the land. This process is called metamorphosis.

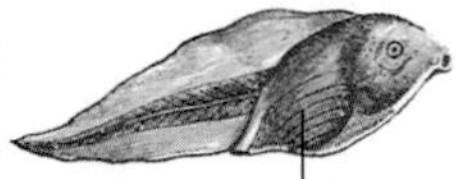

After hatching from its egg, the tadpole starts to swim, breathing through gills.

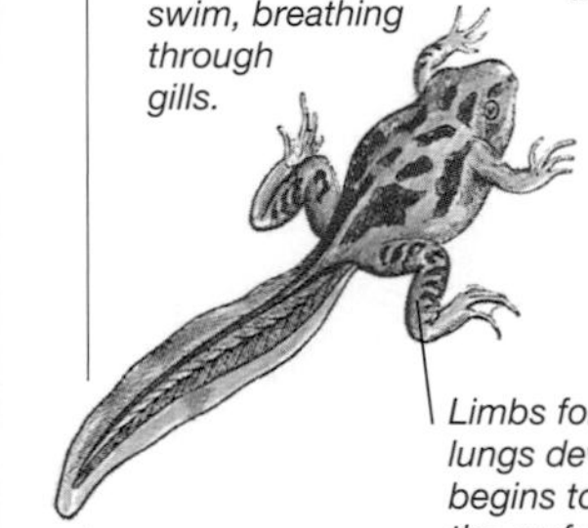

About 16 weeks after hatching, the young frog leaves the water.

Tail becomes smaller and eventually disappears.

Limbs form, and internal lungs develop. Tadpole begins to gulp air from the surface of the water.

Frog's toes are sticky.

RED-EYED TREE FROG

Tree frogs often have longer, leaner bodies than frogs that live mainly in water. A frog's long back legs can kick powerfully for swimming and leaping away from predators. The red-eyed tree frog shown above has sticky disks on its toes that give a good grip on leaves and bark. Today, red-eyed tree frogs are in danger of extinction.

SALAMANDER

After the tadpole stage, the fire salamander crawls up onto land and lives among leaves in moist woodland areas. The females return to the water to give birth to 10 to 15 live young. The fire salamander is so named because it hides in logs, and is sometimes seen emerging from a log fire.

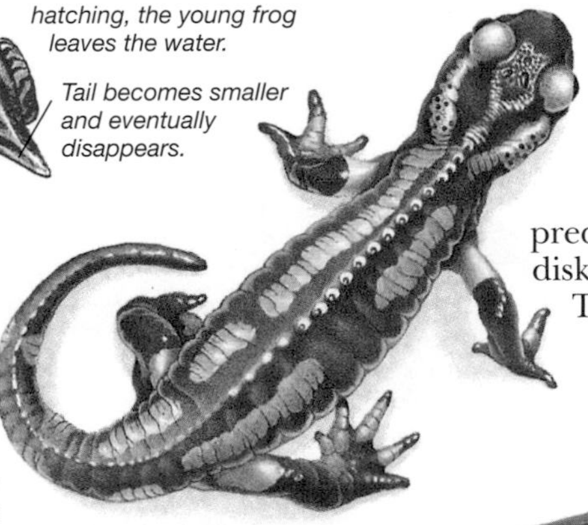

Fire salamander

Mandarin newt

NEWT

Salamanders and their relatives, the newts, resemble lizards in shape. In the breeding season newts often become brighter in color, and may be red, yellow, or orange, such as the mandarin newt shown here. These colors warn predators that the glands in the skin produce horrible-tasting or poisonous fluids.

Asian leaf frog

CANE TOAD

The cane or marine toad shown here originated in Central and South America. During the 1930s it was brought to Australia to eat the beetles that were pests in sugar cane plantations. Today the cane toad itself is regarded as a pest.

Cane toad grows up to 9 in (23 cm) in body length.

Tomato frog

> ### Find out more
> ANIMALS
> AUSTRALIAN WILDLIFE
> CONSERVATION
> and endangered species

FRUITS AND SEEDS

ALL FLOWERING PLANTS, from tiny weeds to mighty oaks, develop from seeds. Each seed contains an embryo (a young plant) plus a store of food for the embryo's growth. A fruit is the seed container; it protects the developing seeds until they are dispersed by animals, the wind, water, or the plant itself. Fruits include lemons, melons, cherries, and tomatoes. The hard little stones, or pips, inside are the seeds. Many fruits, such as oranges and blackcurrants, are an important source of food. They contain large amounts of vitamin C, necessary for good health. People have cultivated fruits for centuries; today, fruit growers produce millions of tons of fruit every year. Strangely enough, some foods that we call vegetables, such as cucumber, are in fact fruits, bursting with tiny seeds. So, too, are spices such as whole chiles and peppercorns. Yet rhubarb, which is often cooked as a fruit, is really the pink stem of a leaf.

Seeds (pips)

Core

There are more than 1,000 varieties of cultivated apples.

APPLE
The apple's flesh, which is what we eat, grows from the receptacle of the flower, so it is a false fruit. The apple core is formed from the ovary, and the pips inside are the seeds. Pears, quinces, and hawthorn berries are formed in the same way; they are also known as pomes.

TRUE AND FALSE FRUITS
Fruits have different names, depending on which part of the flower develops into the main part of the fruit. Fruits are usually described as either true or false fruits. A true fruit develops from the female parts of the flower. A false fruit is one that includes some other part of the flower, such as the receptacle, or flower base.

The bright red fruits of the mountain ash (rowan) develop from clusters of white flowers.

GRAPE
Berries are juicy, succulent true fruits with pips inside. They include grapevine berries, which we call grapes. About 5,000 kinds of grapes are used to make wine, or are dried into currants and raisins for cakes and cookies. Other berries include gooseberries, tomatoes, and bananas. Citrus fruits, such as oranges, lemons, and grapefruits, are also berries.

PLUM DRUPE
Drupes are juicy, succulent true fruits like berries. Unlike berries, however, drupes do not have pips. Instead, they have a hard stone which contains the seed. Plums, cherries, and apricots are all drupes. A blackberry is a collection of drupes.

Cherry

Plum

Runner bean pod

PEA LEGUME
Legumes are dry, non-juicy fruits. Their seeds are contained in a long outer casing called a pod. Pods are found on pea and bean plants, as well as sweet peas and laburnums. We eat the fruits of pea and bean plants.

Pea

Pea pod

POPPY CAPSULE
Capsules are hard, dry fruits found on poppies, violets, snapdragons, and the horse chestnut tree. The poppy capsule is like a saltshaker. The tiny seeds fall through holes at the top when the wind blows.

Walnut fruit (drupe)

NUT
A nut is a dry, hard-cased fruit such as an acorn or hazelnut, with only one seed inside. Most hard, woody fruits or seeds are called nuts, but the fruit of the walnut is actually a drupe, and the Brazil nut is really a seed.

Walnut "nut" is the seed.

Outer shell of Brazil nut

Hard casing

Brazil "nuts" are the seeds of a South American tree. The seeds grow in melon-sized fruit pods.

Brazil nut (seed) that we eat

Sunflower seeds are used in margarine, animal food, and as a snack.

Seed cases

Seed head

Seeds

SUNFLOWER
The sunflower grows about 8 ft (2.5 m) high. After fertilization, the large flower ripens to form a plate-sized seed head. Sunflower seeds contain large amounts of vitamins and edible oil.

GERMINATION

Seeds need warmth, moisture, and air in order to germinate (grow). The seeds of certain tropical plants start to germinate within a few days; the seeds of most other plants remain dormant, or asleep, until conditions are right. Many tree and shrub seeds must pass through a cold winter before they can begin to grow.

Dormant seed

Radicle (young root)

First leaves

Young shoot

Root hairs begin to grow.

WHEAT

The seeds of cereals such as wheat and other grasses have only one seed leaf. These seeds are called monocotyledons.

RUNNER BEAN

A runner bean has a food store in the form of two seed leaves that are called cotyledons.

First true leaves

Plumule (young shoot)

Testa (seed case) containing seed leaves

Radicle (young root) begins to grow.

First true leaves open.

Shoot lengthens.

Plumule grows upward.

Roots develop branches.

Roots lengthen.

Sycamore fruit has wings to carry it through the air.

Seed is contained inside fruit.

HOW SEEDS ARE SPREAD

Plants have several ways of spreading their seeds. Some seeds have wings or parachutes that are blown by the wind. The coconut plant has seeds that float and are carried on water. The sweet pea has a pod that snaps open and flings the seeds out. Animals also disperse seeds. Birds eat berries and other fruits, then drop the seeds as they feed or pass them out after digestion.

BIRDS

Birds and monkeys are the main seed spreaders for many fruits. Seeds stick to the bird's bill to be wiped off later on the ground.

ACORN

A large oak tree bears thousands of ripe fruits called acorns. Animals cannot eat them all; a few survive to grow into new oak trees.

BURIERS

Squirrels bury nuts to eat during the winter. Sometimes squirrels forget where they have buried these nuts, and the forgotten seeds may sprout the following spring.

WIND

The light, winged, helicopter-shaped fruits of sycamore trees twirl in the wind, far away from the parent tree. Pines also have winged seeds. Many plants, such as cotton and dandelions, have seeds with fine silky plumes or parachutes that catch the breeze.

WATER

Aquatic plants such as water lilies and lotus flowers produce fruits that float away downriver on water currents. The fruits often grow into new plants far away from the parent plant.

Lotus flower lives in water. Its seeds float away downstream to grow elsewhere.

HOOKS AND BURRS

Numerous kinds of fruits and seeds have hooks and burrs on their outer casings. These hooks catch onto the fur or feathers of a passing mammal or bird and sometimes onto our shoes, socks, and clothing, to fall off later. Well-known hooked fruits are burdock, cleavers, agrimony, and South African grapple fruit.

In the fall, the badger picks up many seeds on its fur as it pushes through undergrowth. The seeds eventually drop off and grow into new plants.

EXPLOSIVE PODS

Fruits such as those of the lupin are still soft and fleshy when they shed their seeds. When they are fully ripe, the casing suddenly splits open, and the seeds pop out with explosive force.

DANDELION

Each time you blow on the head of a dandelion you spread the seeds on their feathery parachutes.

Find out more

FLOWERS AND HERBS
GRASSES AND CEREALS
PLANTS
TREES

FURNITURE

WHEN WE SIT DOWN to work or eat, when we lie down to sleep, furniture supports our bodies comfortably. When we carry out tasks in the office, school, or kitchen, furniture has surfaces at just the right height so that we do not bend or stretch. And furniture organizes all our belongings close at hand yet out of sight. We take for granted our chairs, beds, tables, and cabinets because we use them every day. But until the 19th century, furniture was handmade, and few families could afford very much. Most homes had a table but only simple stools or benches to sit on. People stored their few clothes and possessions in a chest and slept on mattresses on the floor. Today most furniture is made in factories. Much of it is very practical, with easy-to-clean surfaces at convenient heights. But there are other styles, too, to fit in with any interior. Reproduction furniture, for example, imitates the styles of the past, with rich upholstery and carved wood.

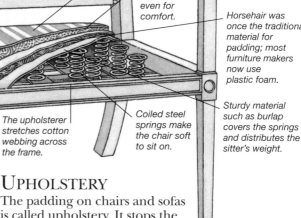

A bed from the Ancient Roman town of Pompeii

EARLY FURNITURE
More than 2,000 years ago wealthy Roman citizens used bronze tables in the town of Pompeii, Italy. In Egypt the tomb of Tutankhamun contained exquisite furniture that was buried with the boy king 3,500 years ago.

ANTIQUES
When carpenters such as Englishman Thomas Chippendale (1718-79) were making furniture by hand, many of the objects they crafted were both beautiful and easy to use. Today these items of furniture are called antiques. Some are valuable and highly prized.

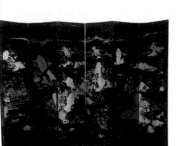

Antique screen from Japan

MOVABLE FURNITURE
European and North American families do not move into new homes often, so their furniture is made to stay in one place. But nomadic people carry their homes with them, so big chairs and tables are not practical. For example, the Bedouin of the Middle East furnish their desert tents with easy-to-pack rugs, cushions, and bedrolls.

South American Indians invented the hammock as a bed they could carry easily.

The woven rush back holds the sitter upright.

The covering material is attractive and hardwearing.

The chair frame of jointed wood supports the upholstery.

Padding is thick and even for comfort.

Horsehair was once the traditional material for padding; most furniture makers now use plastic foam.

The upholsterer stretches cotton webbing across the frame.

Coiled steel springs make the chair soft to sit on.

Sturdy material such as burlap covers the springs and distributes the sitter's weight.

UPHOLSTERY
The padding on chairs and sofas is called upholstery. It stops the hard frame of the furniture from digging into your body. Many different materials are needed to make a comfortable seat, because upholstery must be firm in some places to provide support and prevent backache, but soft and yielding elsewhere for comfort.

TYPES OF FURNITURE
Furniture designs have evolved to suit their role. For example, kitchen cabinets have solid doors to hide pots and pans, but the doors of china cabinets are glass to display attractive crockery.

Drawers in the cabinet store cutlery and keep it clean. The upper part shows off the best china.

A well-designed desk is a miniature office. The locking drawers hide precious documents, and compartments keep stationery clean.

The cotton-filled futon is a sofa which folds out to make a bed. It originated in Japan as a way to save space in small homes.

Glassmakers first made mirrors in the 16th century. The three hinged panels enable the user to see his or her face from the side.

Find out more

DESIGN
EGYPT, ANCIENT
HOUSES

GAMES

SKIPPING in the schoolyard and playing world-championship chess have one thing in common – they are both games. Some games are similar to organized sports and, like sports, games provide pleasure, relaxation, excitement, and challenge. There are thousands of different games. Some, such as chess, have the same rules everywhere. But others vary from place to place; for example, there are many variations on the rules of the card game poker. Many games share the same playing equipment: dice are similar all over the world, but players use dice in a huge range of games. Not all games require special equipment: you can make the playing pieces for some games in a few minutes from string, toothpicks, sticks, or stones. Some games make you think, others call for physical skills, and some require both. You can play some games by yourself, some need two to play, while others are fun only when played in a group.

DICE
Throwing dice, usually in pairs, adds chance to a game. In many board games, such as Monopoly®, the number of spots facing up when the dice come to rest determines the number of squares or sections players may move along. Standard dice have spots from one to six. Variations include poker dice, which have faces similar to playing cards.

COMPUTER GAMES
To operate computer games, players use buttons, a keyboard, or levers called joysticks. People play against the computer or against each other.

SKIPPING
Players usually chant traditional songs when skipping. With a long enough rope, several players can skip together.

HOPSCOTCH
Most hopscotch games have 9 to 12 numbered squares. Hopscotch calls for good balance when hopping between squares.

TAG
In tag, the player chosen to be "it" tries to catch the other players.

PIGGY IN THE MIDDLE
Two players throw a ball to each other. The "piggy" in the middle tries to intercept or catch it.

PLAYGROUND GAMES
Around any playground you will see a variety of games taking place. Some, such as skipping, occupy a small corner and people wait their turn. Others, such as tag, need more space.

SUITS
A pack of playing cards has four suits or groups, each with thirteen similar cards. The four suits are, from left to right, hearts, spades, diamonds, and clubs.

Some card games, such as the old English game of Happy Families, require a deck of special cards.

Cards in suits are numbered from one, or ace, to ten, and there are three "royal" cards: jack, queen, and king.

BOARD GAMES
People first marked out boards to play games 4,000 years ago. Board games such as chess and checkers originally represented the field of battle, in which the players captured enemy soldiers. In backgammon, players take their pieces through enemy territory. Many modern board games imitate common aspects of life, such as buying and selling property, as in Monopoly.

CARD GAMES
A standard set of cards is called a pack or deck. With its 52 cards you can play countless games of skill or chance. The game of bridge requires good concentration and an excellent memory. But you can learn to play snap in a few seconds, and all you need are quick reflexes.

PACHISI
A variation of backgammon, pachisi is an ancient royal game of India. Two or four players throw dice and try to get their counters to the inner center of the board.

Find out more
PUZZLES
SPORTS
TOYS

GAS

The natural gas we use
today is millions of years
old. It was formed from
the remains of prehistoric
plants that lived
on land and in
the sea. New gas
deposits are still
being created.

BURNING GAS TO MAKE HEAT is a quick and easy way to warm
the home and to cook. Gas is also used in industry, both for heat
and as a raw material. Most of the gas we use for fuel is natural
gas. It is extracted from deposits buried deep underground
or under the seabed. Gas for burning can also be made by
processing coal to produce coal gas. These fuel gases
are not the only kinds of gas: there are many
others with different uses. For instance,
the air we breathe is made up of
several gases mixed together.

1 In the sea, tiny plants sink and
a layer of dead plants builds up
on the seabed. The sea plants
are buried in mud.

GAS DELIVERY
Natural gas is piped
to homes for use
in stoves and
heaters. Gas stored
in metal bottles
supplies homes that
are not connected
to the pipeline.

2 On land, too,
mud covers
dead plants and trees.
Slowly the mud hardens
into rock. More layers of
rock form above and press
down on the plants, burying
them deeper and heating them up.

3 The pressure and heat slowly
change the sea plants into oil and then
into gas. Land plants turn first to coal before
becoming oil and gas. A layer of rock now traps the
gas in a deep deposit. Earth movements may have
raised the rocks containing the gas above sea level,
so that the gas now lies under the land.

*Huge drills on a production
platform sink wells to reach
gas deposits,
which lie as deep
as 4 miles (6 km)
below the seabed.*

6 Gas flows from terminals to large tanks,
where it may be frozen and stored as a
liquid. The gas can also be stored in huge
underground caverns. Pumps push gas
along pipes to the places where it
is needed.

4 Gas flows up the well to
the production platform,
and a pipeline takes it to a
terminal on land. Gas from
inland wells flows straight to
the terminal.

GAS FOR INDUSTRY
Not all gas is used in the
home. Many power stations
burn gas to generate
electricity. In dry places,
such as deserts, the heat from burning gas is used
to process seawater in order to produce salt-free
drinking water. Gas is also used as a fuel in factories
producing all kinds of things, from roasted peanuts
to cars. Chemicals made from gas are vital
ingredients in the manufacture of plastics, fertilizers,
paints, synthetic fiber, and many other products.

5 Raw gas has to
be cleaned and
dried before it can
be used. The gas
terminal removes
impurities
and water.

*Gas
storage
tank*

Gas deposit

Oil deposit

*A gas layer
often forms
above a layer
of oil.*

*The pressure of the
gas helps force the
oil up wells to the
production platform.*

USEFUL GASES
Gas wells produce several different kinds of gas. Methane is the
main component, but other fuel gases, called propane and
butane, also come from gas deposits. The gas terminal stores
these gases in metal cylinders for use in houses
where there is no gas connection. Gas deposits
are also a source of helium. Helium is used to fill
balloons because it is very light and does not burn. Air
is another source of useful gases. Carbon dioxide, the gas
that makes the bubbles in carbonated drinks, comes
from air. Air also contains a little neon gas. Some
advertising signs are glass tubes filled with neon.
The gas glows when electricity passes through it.

*Neon
sign*

*Helium gas
balloons*

Find out more
AIR
COAL
HEAT
OIL
OXYGEN

GEMS AND JEWELRY

A RING MOUNTED with beautiful gems, such as diamonds, seems to flash with fire as it catches the light. Yet the gems were once dull stones buried in rock. Their beauty is the work of gem cutters who shape the gems, and jewelers who mount them in settings of gold, silver, and other precious metals. Sometimes people wear gems such as sapphires and diamonds for good luck. Gems are stones used to make jewelry. They are either precious stones, such as rubies and emeralds, or semiprecious stones, such as opal and jade.

Gems also have industrial uses: rubies are used in lasers, and diamond-tipped drills dig through rock in the search for oil. Most gems are hard; diamond, for instance, is the hardest material in the world.

Polished blue sapphire

Jade is a hard gem made up of many tiny crystals.

CROWN JEWELS
Priceless gems line the British crown jewels. The Royal Scepter (above) contains the world's largest cut diamond, the 3.7 oz (106 g) Star of Africa.

This ruby crystal, called the Edwardes Ruby, is famous for its size and quality.

Cut ruby

PRECIOUS STONES

Gems such as diamonds come from transparent minerals found in rocks. In their pure form, these minerals are colorless. But metals and other impurities in the minerals produce color. The metal chromium turns the colorless mineral beryl green, producing emerald, a precious stone. Gemstones are often found in riverbeds. They are long-lasting and remain in the bed after running water has worn away the surrounding rock.

SAPPHIRE AND RUBY
The crystals of colored minerals make valuable gems. Sapphires and rubies are varieties of a mineral called corundum. The presence of iron and titanium turns corundum blue, to produce sapphires; chromium produces red rubies.

OPAL
Beautiful patterns of rainbowlike colors glisten inside opals. These gems consist mainly of silica, the same mineral found in sand. Opals do not need facets; instead, tiny spheres of silica within opal reflect and scatter light, producing colors from milky white to black, the most highly prized opal.

The sheen and colors of titanium metal make it ideal for jewelry.

Vein of opal embedded in sedimentary rock

Polished white opal

Setting made of gold

Tiger's-eye consisting mainly of quartz

Imitation diamond brooch made from cut glass

Pearls form inside the shells of oysters.

Coral forms from the remains of tiny sea creatures.

Lapis lazuli jewelry has been known of for more than 6,000 years.

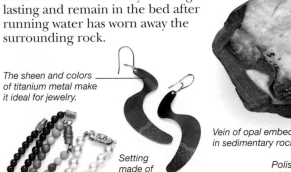
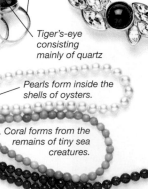

CUTTING GEMS
A gem sparkles because it has many-angled sides, or facets, that reflect light striking and entering the gem. Gem cutters split gemstones and then carve and polish the pieces to form the facets. There are several different kinds of cuts, some with complex patterns of facets.

Table cut   *Cabochon*   *Rose cut*

Step cut   *Pear brilliant*   *Round brilliant*

JEWELRY

Rings, brooches, bracelets, earrings, and necklaces are worn as jewelry by both men and women. Fine pieces are made from gold, diamonds, and other precious materials. But semiprecious stones and organic materials such as pearls and amber also make lovely jewelry. So do inexpensive materials such as shells, coral, wood, and plastic. Some jewelry contains imitation gems made of inexpensive materials, such as glass, instead of precious stones.

Find out more
CORALS, anemones, and jellyfish
METALS
ROCKS AND MINERALS
SHELLS AND SHELLFISH

GENETICS

THE SCIENCE OF GENETICS has officially existed ever since the word "gene" was coined in 1909 by the Danish botanist Wilhelm Johannsen (1857-1927). He invented the term to describe the "particles" of inheritance that pass characteristics from one generation of plant or animal to the next. The field of genetics developed over the course of the 20th century, and produced important discoveries about how genes work. Scientists showed that genes are made up of lengths of deoxyribonucleic acid (DNA), which are connected together to make chromosomes. Genes contain the instructions by which plant and animal cells are built. Genes are passed from both parents to their children through sexual reproduction. By this process, called heredity, inheritable characteristics are passed from one generation to the next.

Each "rung" is a pair of chemicals called bases.

DNA
Deoxyribonucleic acid is the full name of DNA. It is the molecule that holds the genetic code within genes. Its structure is a double helix, with chemical bonds that attach one side of the helix to the other, rather like the rungs of a ladder. Each "rung" is made up of a pair of chemicals selected from a choice of four chemicals, so the way in which genetic information is coded is actually very simple.

The sides of the "ladder" are made up of phosphate and sugar molecules.

The DNA molecule looks something like a twisted ladder in this model. In real life it is a chain of tens of thousands of atoms.

HEREDITY
When a plant or animal is created, it inherits a combination of genetic information from both of its parents. Heredity is the passing of characteristics from parents to children. It means that a baby shares characteristics from each of its parents, but it also ensures that each baby is usually different from its brothers and sisters.

Blue eye

Some of the traits controlled by genes can be easily seen. The genes in this girl's cells make her eyes blue, her hair straight, and her skin fair.

Albino hamster has white fur and red eyes.

Hamster with normal coloring

Wavy hair

MUTATION
When new DNA is being created, sometimes a mistake can occur during the copying process. These mistakes are called mutations, and they may appear as a defect or a new characteristic. If a mutation turns out to be useful, it may become common in future generations.

Children resemble their parents but are not identical to them.

GENES
Chromosomes become extremely long when they are untangled. This is because a chromosome consists of a tightly coiled, long string of segments. A single segment is called a gene. A gene is a part of a chromosome that is responsible for a particular trait, such as eye colour. Genes vary in length depending on how much code they need to contain the information required for a trait.

The genes in this boy's cells make his eyes brown, his hair wavy, and his skin dark.

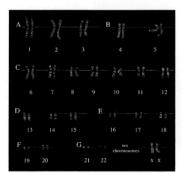

The sex chromosomes determine whether a cell is male or female. Males contain an XY pair, while females contain an XX pair.

CHROMOSOMES
The nucleus of a living cell contains a number of pairs of chromosomes. They are rather like filing cabinets that store all of the genetic information of the plant or animal. Chromosomes are arranged in pairs that separate in the course of reproduction and in the creation of new cells.

X chromosome

MENDEL

Gregor Mendel (1822-84), Austrian scientist, discovered the laws of heredity through experiments with pea plants. In 1866, he showed that features in a plant, such as the production of a smooth or a wrinkled pea, are determined by the genetic information given to the plant by its parents. He called this information "particles," some 43 years before the word "gene" was invented by the Danish scientist Wilhelm Johannsen (1857-1927).

Gregor Mendel was an ordained priest and combined religion with his work as a scientist.

PATTERNS OF INHERITANCE

Different forms of the same gene are called alleles, and they can be dominant or recessive. Dominant alleles always show up, even if the information they carry comes from only one parent. Recessive means that a certain feature might not be seen in a plant or animal even though it is carrying the right alleles. Recessiveness is sometimes linked to gender.

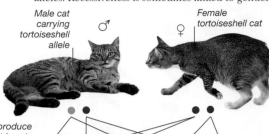

Male cat carrying tortoiseshell allele ♂

Female tortoiseshell cat ♀

The cats produce male and female kittens. Only females can be tortoiseshell.

♂   ♂   ♀   ♀

The second kitten, who carries two tortoiseshell alleles, does not have a tortoiseshell coat because he is male.

Only one kitten is tortoiseshell like her mother, because she carries two alleles and is female.

TWINS

If a fertilized human embryo splits in two it will develop into identical twins. Each twin shares the same genetic information. In fact, they are not entirely identical, because each fetus develops in a slightly different way after the original split. Therefore, identical twins can appear to be remarkably similar yet have quite different personalities. Non-identical twins develop from two separate embryos.

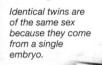

Identical twins are of the same sex because they come from a single embryo.

The world's media took a great interest in Dolly, the first large mammal to be cloned.

CLONING DOLLY

Clones are one or more identical organisms that share identical genes but unlike twins are not produced by natural reproduction. For many years, scientists have been interested in cloning identical copies of animals and plants. In 1997, scientists successfully cloned a sheep, known as Dolly. The experiment led to a worldwide debate about the ethics of cloning.

GM FOODS

The plants and animals that produce GM (genetically modified) foods have had their genes changed by scientists. In theory, genetic modification is just a way of speeding up the process of selection by breeding, which is already done in the natural way. There is much to be learned before we can be sure that genetic modification is a safe thing to do.

GENETICS

1858 Darwin publishes his theory of evolution.

1866 Mendel discovers laws of heredity.

1905 X and Y sex chromosomes discovered.

1918 Forty-eight chromosomes discovered in all human cells.

1927 Genetic mutation in fruit flies created using x-rays.

1950 DNA and RNA discovered.

1953 Watson, Crick, and Wilkins discover the double helix of DNA.

1967 DNA synthesized.

1976 Artificial gene created.

1981 First gene transplant at Ohio University.

1984 Embryonic clone produced.

1985 Genetic fingerprinting introduced.

1997 Dolly the sheep cloned.

Find out more

ATOMS AND MOLECULES
RADIOACTIVITY
REPRODUCTION

GEOLOGY

OUR EARTH CHANGES all the time. Mountains rise and wear away. Continents move, causing oceans to widen and narrow. These changes are slow. It would take a million years to notice much difference. Other changes, such as when an earthquake shakes the land or a volcano erupts, are sudden. Geology is the study of how the Earth changes, how it was formed, and the rocks that it is made of.

Clues to the Earth's history are hidden in its rocks. Geologists survey (map out) the land and dig down to the rocks in the Earth's crust. The age and nature of the rocks and fossils (remains of prehistoric plants and animals) help geologists understand the workings of the Earth. Geologists also help discover valuable deposits of coal, oil, and other useful minerals. They study the land before a large structure such as a dam is built, to make sure that the land can support the great weight. Geologists also warn people about possible disasters. Using special instruments, they detect the movement of rocks and try to predict volcanic eruptions and earthquakes.

GEOLOGISTS AT WORK
Rocks at the Earth's surface reveal their past to the expert eyes of geologists. For example, huge cracks in layers of rock show that powerful forces once squeezed the rocks.

SATELLITE MAPPING
Satellites circle the Earth and send back photographs of the surface from space. The pictures show features of the land in great detail and help geologists identify the rocks. Satellites have also measured the size and shape of the Earth.

Studying the rocks in the ocean floor can reveal the slow movements of the Earth's crust.

AERIAL SURVEYS
Airplanes carry special cameras that produce three-dimensional views of the land below, and instruments that measure the strength of the Earth's magnetism and gravity.

SEISMIC TESTS
Special trucks strike the ground with huge hammers, producing shock waves, called seismic waves, which bounce off the layers of rock below. Computers use these waves to draw pictures of the layers of rock within the Earth.

DRILLING
Rigs bore shafts as deep as 10,000 ft (3,000 m) below the ground and bring up samples of the rock layers beneath.

RADIOACTIVE DATING
Rocks contain substances which decay over millions of years, giving off tiny amounts of nuclear radiation. By a process called radioactive dating, which measures this radioactivity, geologists can find out how old the rocks are.

SANDSTONE
The top and youngest layer of rock is sandstone. It sometimes forms from desert sands. The criss-cross pattern shows how the wind blew sand to form the rock.

SHALE
A layer of shale rock shows that the land must have been beneath shallow water. Mud from a nearby river built up and compacted, forming shale.

BASALT
Lava from a volcano formed this layer of basalt. The land rose from the sea, and a volcano erupted nearby to cover the rock below with lava.

LIMESTONE
The lowest and oldest layer contains fossils of tiny creatures, showing that 100 million years ago, during the time of the dinosaurs, the region was under the sea.

ROCK SAMPLE
The layers of rock in this sample (above) come from deep underground.

THE HISTORY OF GEOLOGY

The ancient Greeks and Hindus were the first peoples to study and date the rocks of the Earth. During the late 18th century, the Scottish scientist James Hutton became the first European geologist to realize that the Earth is millions of years old and that it changes constantly. But his ideas were not accepted until after his death. In 1912, Alfred Wegener, a German meteorologist, proposed that the continents move. But it was more than 50 years before his idea was found to be true.

In 1795 James Hutton founded the modern science of geology with his book The Theory of the Earth.

EXAMINING THE EARTH
The Earth's crust is made of layer upon layer of different kinds of rock which have been laid down over millions of years. The topmost layers usually formed most recently and the lowest layers are the oldest. By uncovering these layers of rock, geologists can trace back the history of the Earth.

Find out more
COAL
CONTINENTS
EARTH
EARTHQUAKES
FOSSILS
GAS
OIL
ROCKS AND MINERALS

GEOMETRY

Circular American quarter

THE STUDY OF SHAPES, POINTS, LINES, curves, surfaces, and angles is called geometry. It takes its name from two Greek words meaning "Earth," and "to measure." The world around us is full of geometrical shapes. Liquids have flat surfaces, and raindrops are perfect spheres. Objects fall in straight lines and spin in circles. Crystals grow into prisms with square, triangular, or hexagonal sections. A knowledge of geometry helps us to understand these shapes. Geometry also has many practical everyday uses. Architects use geometry to construct buildings that will not fall down. Engineers need geometry to build safe roads and bridges. Pilots and sailors use geometrical principles when plotting routes. The principles of geometry were first discovered and written down by Ancient Greek scholars, but we still use them today.

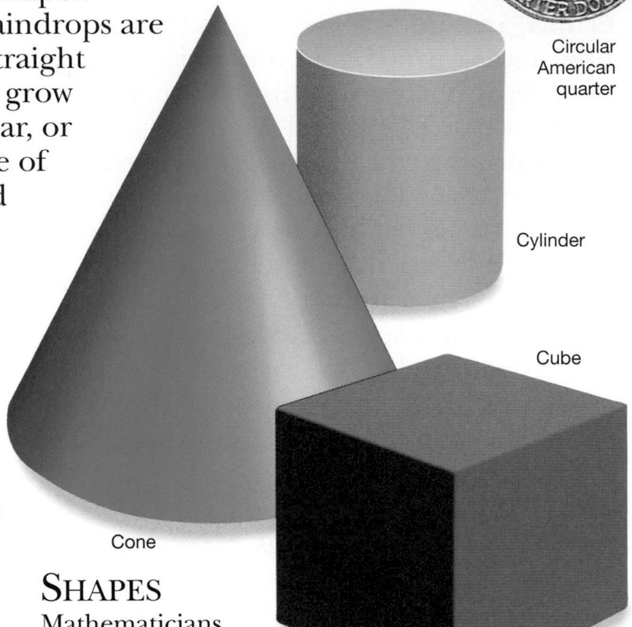

THALES
The Ancient Greek philosopher and scientist Thales (c. 624-c. 547 B.C.) visited Egypt and Babylon, where he studied local methods of astronomy and landsurveying. He developed the first theories about geometry based on his studies. He is also said to have predicted the solar eclipse of 585 B.C.

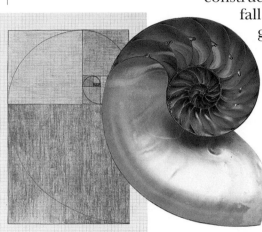

Cone

Cylinder

Cube

SHAPES
Mathematicians use geometry to describe the mathematical properties of shapes. They use terms such as lengths, angles, areas, and volumes to describe the relationships between sides, corners, and surfaces. Shapes may be two-dimensional, such as circles, triangles, rectangles, and polygons. Or they may be three-dimensional, such as cones, cylinders, and cubes.

The diagram above shows that the shell uses a sequence of curves within squares. These decrease in size by a particular percentage each time, so creating the shell's spiral.

NATURAL GEOMETRY
Many things in nature possess geometric properties. An Italian mathematician, Leonardo Fibonacci (c. 1170-c. 1250), noticed that objects such as snail shells have shapes that use geometric sequences of measurements to form complicated curves such as spirals.

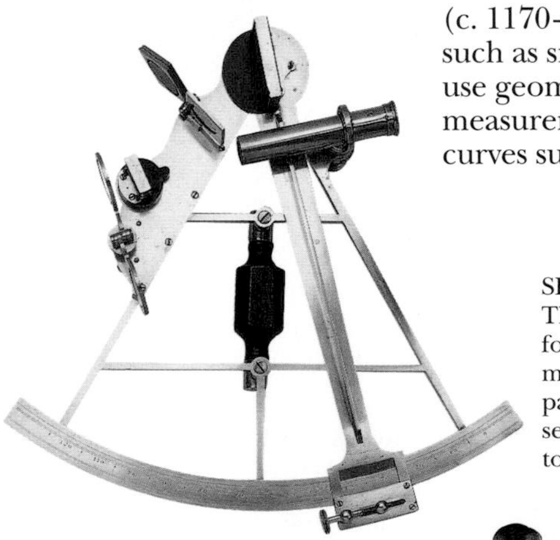

SEXTANT
The sextant was invented in the 1730s for navigating on board ship. By measuring the angle between a particular star and the horizon, the sextant uses the geometry of triangles to calculate the ship's position.

GEOMETRY IN USE
Many everyday activities make use of geometry, including architecture and engineering. For example, the famous glass pyramid at the Louvre in Paris, France, is triangular, and is made up from hundreds of smaller triangles. The entire structure is a combination of two- and three-dimensional geometric shapes.

ANGLES
Geometry is concerned with angles, or the amount by which a line or object turns. Angles are formed by lines meeting at points, and are measured in degrees (°). A right angle is at 90° to a straight line. An obtuse angle is greater than 90°, and an acute angle is less than 90°.

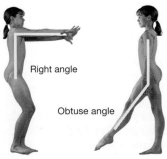

Right angle

Obtuse angle

Acute angle

Find out more

ARCHITECTURE
GREECE, ANCIENT
MATHEMATICS
NAVIGATION

GERMANY

THE NATION OF GERMANY occupies a central position in northern Europe. The 82.5 million German people also play a central role in the economy, way of life, and traditions of Europe. Germany is an old country, and its borders have changed often over the centuries. For much of the second half of the 20th century, Germany consisted of two separate nations: West Germany (the Federal Republic of Germany) and East Germany (the German Democratic Republic). In 1990 they again became one nation. Germany is a rich and fertile land, and its farms are among the world's most productive. The landscape rises gently from the sandy coasts and islands on the North Sea and Baltic Sea. Flat plains dominate the northern part of the country, and in the south there are forests and the soaring Alps. The region's cool, rainy weather helps agriculture. Farms produce livestock and dairy products, cereals, potatoes, sugar beets, fruits, and vegetables. Most people, however, live in and around the towns where Germany's energetic industries are based.

Germany lies at the heart of Europe. Its landscape varies greatly from the flat plains of the north to the peaks of the Bavarian Alps in the south.

Sausage sellers specialize in various kinds of wurst and often sell their wares from tiny stalls or vans.

Beer gardens attached to bars and cafés are popular in warm weather.

The Brandenburg Gate stands on the line that once divided East and West Berlin.

WURST AND BEER

Germany produces some excellent wine and is also famous for its beer. Germans often drink beer with the traditional snack of a sausage (wurst) and a bread roll, accompanied by a large dollop of mild mustard. There are numerous kinds of wurst, and every region has its speciality. Frankfurters, a type of wurst, originally came from Frankfurt.

BERLIN

Reinstated as the capital of Germany in 1990, Berlin grew up on the banks of the Spree River. Canals also link Berlin to the Elbe and Oder rivers. Berlin was devastated in World War II. In 1949 the city was split between the two states of East and West Germany. For many years a wall separated the people in the eastern and western sectors, and the two parts of the city still look very different. New buildings have made western Berlin look like any other modern European city. Eastern Berlin still suffers poor infrastructure and buildings.

Leitz camera factory

INDUSTRY

There is a wide range of industries in Germany, producing electrical goods, computers, tools, textiles, and medicines. Coal mines in the central Ruhr region produce large quantities of brown coal, or lignite, to fuel the factories. Western Germany is famous for high-quality precision goods, such as BMW cars and Leitz cameras.

BAVARIA

Covering the entire southeastern part of the country, Bavaria is the largest state in Germany. Most of the region is cloaked by forests and farms. In the south, the Bavarian Alps form a natural border with Austria. Bavaria is a magnet to tourists, who come to see its fairy-tale palaces (left) and spectacular scenery. The region's traditional costume is *Lederhosen* (leather shorts), suspenders, and a cap for men, and *Dirndlkleider* (a full-length dress with puffed sleeves) for women.

The enchanting, gray granite Schloss Neuschwanstein *is hidden away in the Bavarian Alps.*

DÜRER

Born in Nuremberg, Albrecht Dürer (1471-1528), is famous for his paintings and engravings. He produced his first self-portrait at the age of 13, and painted himself at intervals throughout his life thereafter. He produced this self-portrait (above) when he was 26. At the age of 15, Dürer was apprenticed to Michael Wolgemut, Nuremberg's chief painter and book illustrator. He was inspired by the painters of the Italian Renaissance and resolved to depict people and things in realistic detail. In 1512, Dürer became court painter to the Emperor Maximilian, and gained international fame.

SEMPER OPERA HOUSE

The architect Gottfried Semper (1803-79) built his first opera house, the Royal Theater, on Theaterplatz Square in Dresden, in the years 1838-1841. Almost 30 years later it burned to the ground and the opera was forced to move to temporary premises. Public pressure persuaded Semper to create a second opera house between 1871 and 1878. The new building (right) followed the style of the Italian High Renaissance. Following its destruction during an air raid in World War II, it was rebuilt in its original form between 1977 and 1985. Its exquisite acoustics and opulent interior decoration make it a model for opera houses throughout the world.

DRESDEN

The city of Dresden in eastern Germany was once the capital of a historic German state called Saxony. Although there are still some beautiful buildings in Dresden, including the former royal palace (below), most of the city's fine architecture was destroyed by Allied bombing in World War II (1939-45). Dresden has now been completely rebuilt, and many of the buildings restored.

BROTHERS GRIMM

Jakob (1785-1863) and Wilhelm (1786-1859) Grimm were born in Hanau, near Frankfurt. Devoted to each other, the brothers went to the same school and university, and lived together until Wilhelm's death. The Grimm brothers are famous for their collections of German folktales, which include the well-known tales of *Cinderella, Hansel and Gretel, Rapunzel, Snow White and the Seven Dwarfs, Sleeping Beauty,* and *Little Red Riding Hood.* The brothers did not create these stories themselves, but gathered them together from the accounts of country folk, and old books. Most of the stories date back hundreds of years.

Dresden was once admired as the "Florence on the Elbe."

Snow White and the Seven Dwarfs

RHINE RIVER

The Rhine is the longest river in Germany. It begins in Switzerland and later forms the German border with France. Finally it cuts through the western part of Germany toward the Netherlands and the sea. Large river barges can sail up the Rhine as far as Basel, Switzerland. Vineyards on the steep banks of the southern part of the river produce much of Germany's famous white wine.

The buildings in parts of Bonn have a modern architectural style.

BONN

Between 1949 and 1990, Bonn was the capital of West Germany. Bonn, an ancient city, stands on the Rhine River on the site of a Roman camp. It is a university town with many beautiful buildings in traditional German style. Bonn was the birthplace of composer Ludwig van Beethoven (1770-1827).

SPORTING ACHIEVEMENT

Germany has produced some excellent athletes over the past few decades. Sports stars include Boris Becker, Steffi Graf, and Michael Stich in tennis, Michael Schumacher in auto racing, and Katja Seizinger in skiing. The German government encourages sports, mainly because it promotes good health. Prizewinning athletes also bring great honor to their country.

The joining of East and West Germany brought together some of the world's finest athletes. When the two countries were rivals, East German competitors were aided by excellent sports facilities, and special privileges gave them time to train. They won many more events than their West German counterparts.

RUHR VALLEY

Much of Germany's heavy industry is concentrated in the valley of the Ruhr River. Huge coal seams provide the valley with a rich source of power, and factories in the region produce iron, steel, and chemicals. The Ruhr Valley is Germany's most densely populated area.

Wild boar still roam in the larger forests and are hunted for their meat.

FORESTS

Great forests cover many of the hills and mountains of the central and southern regions of Germany. These forests are prized for their beauty and for their valuable timber, which is used widely in industry. The most famous forests include the Thüringer Wald, the forests of the Harz Mountains in Central Germany, and the Schwarzwald, or Black Forest, in southwestern Germany.

OBERAMMERGAU

Once every 10 years an extraordinary event takes place in this small town in the Bavarian Alps of southern Germany. The inhabitants of Oberammergau get together to perform a passion play, which tells the story of Christ's crucifixion. The villagers first performed the play in 1634 in an effort to stop the plague. They have maintained the custom ever since. It is now a major tourist attraction, attended by thousands of visitors from Germany and abroad.

Find out more

EUROPE
GERMANY, HISTORY OF

STATISTICS
Area: 137,800 sq miles
(356,910 sq km)
Population: 82,500,000
Capital: Berlin
Languages: German
Religions: Protestant,
Roman Catholic, Muslim
Currency: Euro
Main occupations:
Engineering,
manufacturing
Main exports: Cars, heavy
engineering, electronics,
chemicals
Main imports: Energy
sources, raw materials

Volcano **Mountain** **Ancient monument** **Capital city** **Large city/ town** **Small city/ town**

CARS
Germany is
Europe's largest
vehicle producer,
specializing in
high-quality cars.
American and Japanese
car companies are based
here, attracted by the
skilled workforce.

HAMBURG
Located on the Elbe River, Hamburg is
the second-largest city in Germany and
its economic center. The city is also the
country's busiest port.

RHINE RIVER
The Rhine is Germany's
main waterway. It is
an important
transportation route to
and from northern ports.
It meanders across
820 miles (1,320 km),
from its source in
Switzerland to the
North Sea.

GERMAN BORDERS
Germany is positioned
in the very center of
Europe, and has land
borders with no less than
nine countries. It is not
surprising, then, that it is
Europe's biggest trading
nation. All kinds of raw
materials flow into
Germany across its
borders, for the
nation has few natural resources.
Manufactured goods cross
Germany's borders in the opposite
direction. Of all Germany's borders,
that with France is the busiest: more
than ten percent of all German trade
is with France.

SCALE BAR
0   50   100   km
0   50   100   miles

DENMARK

North Sea

North Frisian Islands

Helgoland

East Frisian Islands

Baltic Sea

Rügen

Pomeranian Bay

Oderhaff

Fehmarn

Kiel

Lübeck

Rostock

Schwerin

Neubrandenburg

Hamburg

Bremerhaven

Müritz

Oder

Bremen

Oldenburg

Ems

Wever

Aller

Elbe

Eberswalde-Finow

Osnabrück

Münster

Hanover
(Hannover)

Wolfsburg

Havel

Potsdam

BERLIN

Frankfurt
an der Oder

Magdeburg

Elbe

Spree

Leine

Saale

Halle

Leipzig

Cottbus

NETHERLANDS

Essen

Dortmund

Ruhr

Kassel

Duisburg

Düsseldorf

Cologne
(Köln)

Aachen

Bonn

Rheinisches Schiefergebirge

Mosel

Koblenz

Rhine
(Rhein)

Harz

Dresden

GERMANY

Erfurt

Jena

Chemnitz

Thüringer Wald

Werra

Fulda

Erzgebirge

Fichtelberg
1214m

BELGIUM

LUXEMBOURG

FRANCE

Mainz

Frankfurt am Main

Heidelberg

Main

Würzburg

Nuremberg
(Nürnberg)

CZECH
REPUBLIC

Bohemian Forest

Grosser Arber
1456m

Neckar

Heilbronn

Regensburg

Danube
(Donau)

Stuttgart

Schwäbische Alb

Black Forest

Danube
(Donau)

Ulm

Augsburg

Lech

Inn

Munich
(München)

Freiburg im Breisgau

Konstanz

Lake
Constance

Oberammergau

Bavarian Alps

Zugspitze 2962m

SWITZERLAND

LIECHTENSTEIN

AUSTRIA

POLAND

N
W E
S

HISTORY OF
GERMANY

FOR MOST OF ITS HISTORY, the land of Germany has consisted of many small independent states, each with its own ruler and set of laws. Over the years there have been many attempts to unite these states into one country. In the 800s Charlemagne, emperor of the Franks, ruled most of Germany and what is now France. His successors tried to maintain this union by setting up the Holy Roman Empire. This empire consisted of Germany and surrounding areas, but Germany was united only in name, for the different states fiercely protected their independence. During the 1500s the Reformation, a movement to reform the Roman Catholic Church, divided Germany into Protestant and Catholic states. Prussia emerged as the strongest state, challenging the dominance of the Austrian Hapsburg family. In 1871, the various states of Germany became one country under Prussian rule. But after Germany was defeated in World War II (1939-45), the country was divided again into two separate states – Communist East Germany (German Democratic Republic) and non-Communist West Germany (Federal Republic of Germany). In 1990, East and West Germany were once again united into one country.

FRANKISH KINGDOM
During the 3rd century the Franks, one of many warlike tribes in Germany, settled along the Rhine River. By the 800s the West Franks ruled what is now France, and the East Franks governed Germany. The Franks were skilled metalworkers, as shown by the bronze buckle and belt fitting above.

PEASANTS' WAR

In 1524, the German peasants rose against their lords. They demanded better social and economic conditions, including the right to elect their clergy and to hunt and fish. They were encouraged by the teachings of Martin Luther (1483-1546), who wanted to reform the Church. But Luther supported the lords, who crushed the revolt without mercy a year after it had begun.

Prussian territories 1740

Baltic Sea

North Sea

East Prussia

West Prussia

Brandenburg

Poland

Tecklenburg

Ravensburg

Cleves

Mark

PRUSSIA
Following the Thirty Years' religious war, which nearly destroyed Germany, there was no central power, until Prussia began its rise to power. Prussia was originally a small state in what is now northern Poland. It slowly grew in size until, under the leadership of King Frederick the Great (reigned 1740-86), it became the most powerful state in Germany.

FRANKFURT PARLIAMENT
In 1815, a German Confederation was set up to protect the independence of the 39 separate states that existed in Germany at the time. But Germany was less advanced and prosperous than other European countries. Many people were dissatisfied and wanted unity. In 1848, a group of politicians set up a parliament (law-making group) to meet in Frankfurt to prepare for German unity. The plan failed in 1849 when the Prussian king, Frederick William IV, refused to be emperor. Soon the German Confederation was reestablished.

OTTO VON BISMARCK

In 1871, statesman Otto von Bismarck (1815-98), chancellor of Prussia, united Germany under Prussian leadership. Bismarck built the new republic of Germany into a great power. He was famous for his political skill.

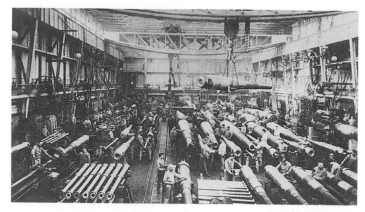

KRUPPS FACTORY

Arms manufacturers, such as Krupps (above), founded in 1811, helped create a powerful German military for the new united Germany.

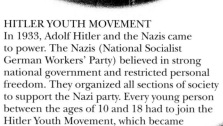

HITLER YOUTH MOVEMENT

In 1933, Adolf Hitler and the Nazis came to power. The Nazis (National Socialist German Workers' Party) believed in strong national government and restricted personal freedom. They organized all sections of society to support the Nazi party. Every young person between the ages of 10 and 18 had to join the Hitler Youth Movement, which became the only youth group allowed to exist under German law.

DEPRESSION

The German economy was hit badly by the peace settlement after World War I (1914-18). By 1931, the country, like the rest of the world, was in an economic slump. Thousands of people were out of work and had to line up for food. In desperation, many supported extreme political parties, such as the Nazis, which they hoped would help them out of their poverty.

UNITED GERMANY

In 1961 the Communists built a big wall of concrete and barbed wire in Berlin, the former German capital, dividing it into East and West Berlin. This was to block the escape route into West Germany, where living and working conditions were much better. In 1989, the people of Berlin demolished the wall, and the following year East and West Germany were united.

DIVIDED GERMANY

After losing World War II, Germany was divided into two: the Federal Republic of Germany (non-Communist) in the West, and the German Democratic Republic (Communist) in the East.

GERMANY

200s Franks settle along the Rhine River.

c. 800 Charlemagne creates a huge Frankish kingdom in western Europe, uniting Germany for the first time.

843 East Franks form the first all-German kingdom.

962 King Otto I is crowned the first Holy Roman Emperor; the empire consists of a loose grouping of German states.

1300s Austrian Hapsburg family begins to dominate Germany.

1517 Martin Luther begins Reformation in Wittenberg.

1524-25 Peasants' War

1555 Religious conflict following the Reformation ends at the Peace of Augsburg.

1740-86 Prussia emerges as the most powerful German state.

1815 German Confederation is established.

1848-49 Frankfurt Parliament attempts to unify Germany.

1862 Otto von Bismarck becomes chancellor of Prussia.

1871 Germany united as a single state under Prussian leadership.

1914-18 Germany and Austria fight Russia, France, and Britain in World War I.

1919 Treaty of Versailles imposes harsh peace terms on Germany, which becomes a republic.

1933 Nazi party takes power.

1939-45 Germany invades rest of Europe during World War II.

1945 Russian, American, and British troops defeat Germany.

1949 Germany is divided into Communist East Germany and non-Communist West Germany.

1961 Berlin Wall divides city.

1989 Berlin Wall demolished.

1990 East and West Germany unite to form one state.

Find out more

CHARLEMAGNE
GERMANY
HOLOCAUST
REFORMATION
WORLD WAR II

GLACIERS
AND ICE CAPS

SNOW FALLING on the world's tallest mountain peaks never melts. The temperature rarely rises above freezing, and fresh falls of snow press down on those below, turning them to ice. A thick cover of ice, called an ice cap or ice sheet, builds up, or snow collects in hollows. Ice flows down from the hollows in rivers of ice called glaciers. They move very slowly, usually less than 3 ft (1 m) a day, down toward the lower slopes. There it is usually warmer, and the glaciers melt. However, in the Arctic and the Antarctic, glaciers do not melt. Instead they flow down to the sea and break up into icebergs or form a floating ice shelf. A huge ice cap covered much of North America and Europe a million years ago during the last Ice Age. When the weather became warmer, about 10,000 years ago, some ice melted, and the ice sheet shrank. Today, ice sheets can only be found in Greenland and Antarctica.

GLACIERS
Glaciers often join together, just as small rivers meet to form bigger rivers. The ice may be more than 0.5 mile (1 km) deep.

ICE CAP
Ice caps cover vast areas. When the thickness of the ice reaches about 200 ft (60 m) its enormous weight sets it moving.

VALLEY GLACIER
The ice fills a valley, moving faster at the center than at the sides of the glacier. Cracks called crevasses open in the surface.

MORAINE
The glacier acts like a huge conveyor belt, carrying broken rocks, called moraines, down from the mountaintop. The moving ice also plucks stones and boulders from the base and sides of the valley. This material is carried along within the glacier, and is called englacial moraine.

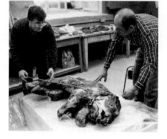

FROZEN MAMMOTHS
In the Russian Federation, ice and frozen soil have preserved huge hairy elephants, called mammoths, just as if they were in a deep freeze. The last mammoths lived in North America, Europe, and Asia during the Ice Age.

CIRQUES
The hollow where the ice collects to start the glacier is called a cirque or corrie.

A river flows down the center of the valley.

Streams of water form as the glacier melts.

Rocks in the melting ice build up a wall called a terminal moraine.

SHAPING THE LANDSCAPE
Glaciers slowly grind away even the hardest rock and reveal a changed landscape when they retreat. Deep valleys and lakes, together with rivers and waterfalls, now exist where there were none before.

Waterfall

Deep U-shaped valley carved out by the glacier

Lake formed behind moraines

ICEBERGS
Huge pieces of floating ice are called icebergs. Nine-tenths of the ice floats below the water, so icebergs are a danger to ships. In 1912 the ocean liner *Titanic* sank after colliding with an iceberg.

ICE AGE
A deep ice sheet covered about a third of the world's land during the last Ice Age. Ice extended as far south as St. Louis, Missouri, and London, England. There had been ice ages before the last one, and there could be more in the future.

FJORDS
The sea rose at the end of the Ice Age, drowning valleys formed by glaciers. These deep, steep-sided inlets are called fjords. The coast of Norway has many fjords.

Find out more
ANTARCTICA
ARCTIC
MOUNTAINS
POLAR WILDLIFE
RAIN AND SNOW

GLASS AND CERAMICS

STICKY CLAY AND DRY SAND are more familiar on the end of a shovel than on the dinner table. Yet these are the basic ingredients in the manufacture of the plates we eat from, and the jars and bottles in which we buy preserved food and drink. Glass and ceramic materials share some useful qualities: they resist the flow of heat and electricity, and they have a hard, nonreactive surface. But they are different in other ways: light passes through glass but not ceramics, and ceramics stay strong when they are heated. In their most basic forms glass and ceramic objects are brittle, but special additives and manufacturing methods make both materials much tougher. Glass and ceramics are ancient materials. The Egyptians made decorative glass beads more than 5,000 years ago, and pottery is even older.

Spark plug for car engine

CERAMICS
Damp clay is easy to mold into pottery and tiles; heat sets the shape permanently. Ceramics resist heat and electricity, so they are ideal for insulating objects that get hot, such as spark plugs.

STAINED GLASS
Strips of lead hold together the many pieces of colored glass in the stained glass windows that decorate homes, churches, and temples.

GLASS
Containers of clear glass both protect their contents and display them. Lenses are specially shaped pieces of glass that bend and concentrate light. But not all glass is functional; some glassware is simply decorative.

Glass bottle for holding medicines

Glass bottle for holding ink

Ornate glassware jug made in the 1930s

Pottery mug

Ceramic tile

ENAMEL
Enamel is a glasslike layer on metal and other objects that protects them from damage and corrosion. Colored enamel gives ornaments a beautiful appearance.

Magnifying glass which is a large convex lens.

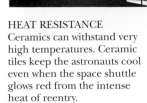
HEAT RESISTANCE
Ceramics can withstand very high temperatures. Ceramic tiles keep the astronauts cool even when the space shuttle glows red from the intense heat of reentry.

MAKING GLASS

Sand   Limestone   Soda ash   Recycled glass

Heating sand, limestone, and soda ash in a furnace together with recycled glass produces molten glass.

The molten glass is poured onto a pool of molten tin, which makes the glass spread into a flat sheet suitable for windows.

The glass sets and hardens on the cooler tin.

FIBERGLASS
Strengthening plastic with fibers of glass produces a material called fiberglass or glass-reinforced plastic, which is tough enough to be used for car bodies.

A lump of hot, soft glass is placed in a bottle-shaped mold.

Blowing air into the mold makes the glass inflate into a bubble, which expands to form the bottle.

The glass then cools and sets hard.

GLASSBLOWING
The breath of the glassblower inflates soft glass on the end of a tube into a bubble. Skillful shaping makes the bubble into fine glassware as it cools.

___ *Find out more* ___
CHURCHES AND CATHEDRALS
LIGHT
PLASTICS
POTTERY

GOVERNMENT AND POLITICS

THE ADMINISTRATION OF A COUNTRY'S affairs is undertaken by a government whose policies direct decision making. Governments have many roles: they decide how money raised through taxes will be divided among the different public services, such as health, education, welfare, and defence. They also maintain the police for the safety of society, and the armed forces for the defence of the nation. As a result of differing cultural and political traditions, government and policies vary from country to country. There are, however, three main types of government: republican, monarchical, and dictatorial. Most countries are republics, with people voting in an election to choose their government and head of state. In a monarchy, the head of the royal family is the head of state. Countries in which a single ruler has seized absolute power – often through a military take-over – are known as dictatorships.

PLATO
More than 2,000 years ago the Greek philosopher Plato wrote the first book about governments and how they rule people – what today we call politics. His book, *The Republic,* set out ideas for democracy, a Greek word meaning "government by the people".

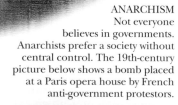

MONARCHY
In a monarchy a king or queen rules the country. Today only a few monarchs, such as the king of Saudi Arabia, have political power; but four centuries ago, in Europe, monarchs made the laws and collected taxes.

SEATS OF POWER

Every government has a meeting place where members discuss policies and pass laws. The seat of power also houses the administrators who assist the government. The U.S. government has its seat of power in Washington, D.C., where a political history is evident in buildings such as the Jefferson Memorial (right), which commemorates the early 19th century president, Thomas Jefferson. In the U.S. government there are two groups of elected representatives, the Senate and the House of Representatives, known as Congress.

The Jefferson Memorial, Washington, D.C.

Thabo Mvuyelwa Mbeki is sworn in as president of the Republic of South Africa in 1999.

ANARCHISM
Not everyone believes in governments. Anarchists prefer a society without central control. The 19th-century picture below shows a bomb placed at a Paris opera house by French anti-government protestors.

PRESIDENCY
In a republic, such as South Africa, the people vote for their head of state. In this case, the president holds real political power, and is responsible for the administration of the country and for its foreign policy. In France, power is divided between the president and the prime minister. In some countries, such as India, the president is more of a symbolic figurehead, who takes on a ceremonial role, rather like that of some monarchs.

Presidential seal

LOCAL GOVERNMENT

Cities, towns, and counties are served by local governments, usually headquartered in a city hall (right). Many cities elect a mayor, who works with local officials in the city council to run the city government. The local government ensures safety for city residents through fire departments and police forces, and maintains local parks and roads. It is also responsible for hospitals. One of the most important, and costliest, jobs of local government is administering the public school system.

SHARED POWERS
The government of the United States is a federal system, in which powers are shared between the national government and state and local governments. The federal government, headed by the president, works for all Americans. Under its umbrella are state governments, which in turn share their powers with the local governments of cities, towns, and villages.

EMERGENCY SERVICES
Local governments are responsible for providing emergency services for their communities. Firefighters provide safety for the people who work and live in the area. Many fire departments also provide medical care in other, nonfire emergencies, giving immediate assistance to a victim before he or she goes to a hospital.

GOVERNMENT SERVICES
More than 20 million people in the United States are employed by the government, making it the nation's largest employer. The government employs people in all sorts of occupations, from astronaut to zoologist, policeman to nurse. One government worker familiar to all Americans is the mail carrier.

GOVERNOR
The chief executive of a state is called the governor. Most governors have the power to appoint state officials, direct the state's budget, veto bills from the state legislature, command the state militia, and grant pardons. A governor is elected by popular vote to a two- or four-year term.

Jennifer Granholm, governor of Michigan since 2002

State capital of Vermont in Montpelier

STATE GOVERNMENT

State governments are organized in the same way as the federal government, with an executive branch headed by the governor, a legislative branch (state congress), and a judicial branch (state courts). Each state has its own constitution, but state laws must not conflict with the Constitution of the United States. State governments are responsible for education policy, public works (such as road repairs), welfare, and public safety.

UNCLE SAM

The character of "Uncle Sam" has come to symbolize the United States government. Legend has it that the real Uncle Sam was a New York meatpacker named Samuel Wilson. During the War of 1812, Wilson supplied rations to the Army with the initials "US" (for US Army) marked on each barrel. When a visitor to Wilson's plant asked what the initials stood for, an employee humorously replied it must be his boss, Uncle Sam. Soon, everyone was using this nickname to represent the federal government. Uncle Sam's stars-and-stripes costume appeared in cartoons from the 1830s. Uncle Sam has been used to promote everything from war bonds to ice cream.

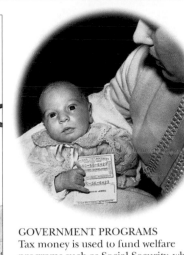

GOVERNMENT PROGRAMS
Tax money is used to fund welfare programs such as Social Security, which includes unemployment insurance, pensions, and family aid. Each citizen is issued a Social Security card (above).

MONEY AND TAXES
The Constitution gives the federal government the power to coin money. The US Mint is responsible for making coins, and for safeguarding the gold and silver reserves stored at Fort Knox, Kentucky. The Bureau of Engraving and Printing makes paper money. However, the money used to fund government programs, such as national defense, postal services, firefighting services, and Social Security, is not simply printed or minted – it comes from taxes.

FEDERAL GOVERNMENT
The workings of the federal government affect everyone, no matter what state or city they live in. The Constitution established the structure of the federal government, and outlined its powers. Some responsibilities entrusted to the federal government include national defense, regulating trade between states, collecting taxes, printing money, and providing for the welfare of all citizens. The federal government also liaises with the governments of other nations.

DEFENSE
One of the most important functions of the federal government is to provide for the nation's defense. The United States government spends many billions of dollars each year to maintain its armed forces. The federal government is entrusted with the power to declare war, and the president is the commander-in-chief of the armed forces. The Department of Defense is headquartered in the Pentagon, in Arlington, Virginia (above).

The Capitol building, Washington, D.C.

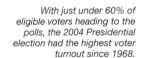

With just under 60% of eligible voters heading to the polls, the 2004 Presidential election had the highest voter turnout since 1968.

ELECTION DAY
People vote to elect a government to represent their wishes. Voter turnout is on the decline, and less than half of all those qualified usually vote. To encourage greater participation, a number of states have made laws to make voter registration simpler.

Find out more

CONGRESS
LAW
POLITICAL PARTIES
PRESIDENCY

GRASSES AND CEREALS

THERE ARE MORE THAN 10,000 different kinds of grasses throughout the world. They include lawns, fields of barley, towering bamboos, and the African grasslands, where huge ostriches graze. Grasses are slender, flowering plants, with stiff stems and long narrow leaves called blades. Their many small roots are matted together. The flowers are feathery tufts without petals at the top of the stem. Grasses are pollinated by the wind, and seeds develop from the flowers in the same way as other flowering plants. Inside each seed is a grain, a rich food store for the plant, and also for us. Grasses are the major source of food for humans. We eat cereal grains in the form of bread, cookies, and cakes, and also feed them to animals. Wheat and barley were two of the first plants cultivated (grown) by humans, about 10,000 years ago. Today wheat, rice, and corn are among the world's most important food crops.

Harvesting cereal grain by hand is slow, hard work. A modern combine harvester can do the work of up to 100 farm hands.

CEREALS

The ripe seeds of cereals such as oats, wheat, barley, rye, and corn are farmed to make breakfast cereals and other kinds of food. The stems are woven into baskets and turned into straw for animal bedding and thatching on houses. The leaves and stalks are put into a tower or a pit called a silo, where they are kept soft and damp. In time they turn into silage, or animal fodder.

MILLET
Millet seeds are made into flat breads and porridges. Millet is also common in birdseed and animal fodder.

BARLEY
Most barley is made into animal food. It is also brewed into beer.

Barley

Millet

Oats

Wheat

Single rye grass flower

Stamen (male part)

Rye

BAMBOO
Bamboo is a grass that grows up to 90 ft (27 m) tall. Its hollow, woody stems are used for making houses and furniture; it also makes very strong scaffolding.

SUGARCANE
Sugarcane plants grow up to 15 ft (4.5 m) high. At harvest time, the cane is cut off close to the ground and stripped of its leaves, then brought to a sugar mill. In the sugar mill the cane is shredded and then squeezed, and the syrup is turned into sugar for cooking and making candy.

WHEAT
There are more than 30 kinds of wheat. Durum wheat is used to make spaghetti, macaroni, and other pastas. Bread wheat is ground into flour to make bread and other baked foods.

RYE
Rye is used to make bread. It is also fed to farm animals and made into straw.

Rice

RICE
Rice belongs to the grass family. It is an important source of food in many parts of the world. Rice is also made into breakfast cereals.

THATCH
Dried grasses are used for thatching the roofs of houses.

Find out more
FRUITS AND SEEDS
GRASSLAND WILDLIFE
PLANTS
SOIL

GRASSHOPPERS AND CRICKETS

THE CHIRPING OF A GRASSHOPPER or a cricket is one of nature's most recognizable sounds. The sound is made by a male to attract a female or to warn off rival males. The insect produces the sound by rubbing together the ridged veins on the front wings, or by rubbing part of the back leg against the wing vein. Grasshoppers and crickets belong to the insect group called Orthoptera – a group that also includes katydids and locusts. There are more than 20,000 kinds of grasshoppers and crickets, living in all but the coldest regions. Grasshoppers are herbivores (plant eaters), feeding on leaves and stems, and crickets are omnivores (plant and meat eaters). A few of these creatures live underground and eat roots or digest nutrients in the soil. Most crickets and katydids have long antennae, sometimes longer than their bodies. Grasshoppers and locusts have much shorter antennae. All these insects have long back legs adapted for leaping. A large grasshopper can jump over a yard in one leap.

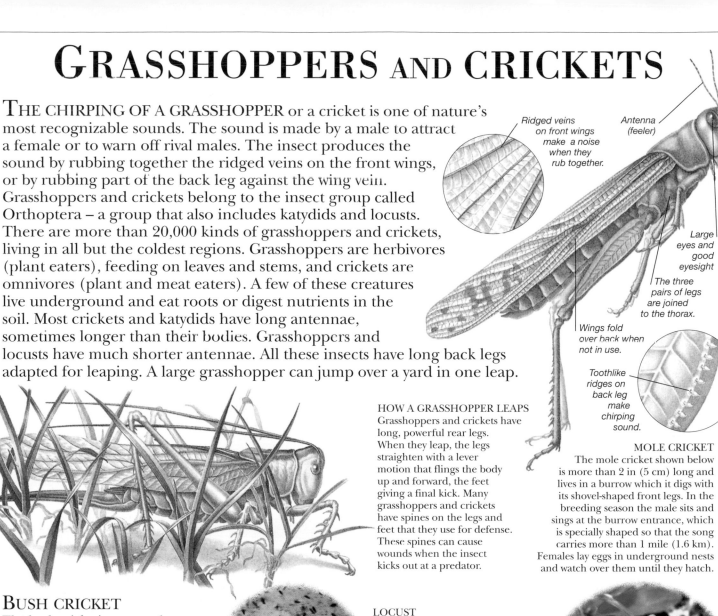

Ridged veins on front wings make a noise when they rub together.

Antenna (feeler)

Large eyes and good eyesight

The three pairs of legs are joined to the thorax.

Wings fold over back when not in use.

Toothlike ridges on back leg make chirping sound.

HOW A GRASSHOPPER LEAPS
Grasshoppers and crickets have long, powerful rear legs. When they leap, the legs straighten with a lever motion that flings the body up and forward, the feet giving a final kick. Many grasshoppers and crickets have spines on the legs and feet that they use for defense. These spines can cause wounds when the insect kicks out at a predator.

MOLE CRICKET
The mole cricket shown below is more than 2 in (5 cm) long and lives in a burrow which it digs with its shovel-shaped front legs. In the breeding season the male sits and sings at the burrow entrance, which is specially shaped so that the song carries more than 1 mile (1.6 km). Females lay eggs in underground nests and watch over them until they hatch.

BUSH CRICKET
The bush cricket's green color provides good camouflage in hedges and bushes. The wings of the male are longer than its body. The female has a long flattened egg-laying tube, called the ovipositor, at the rear end of the body. Bush crickets eat leaves and small insects.

LOCUST
Desert and migratory locusts breed quickly when weather and vegetation conditions are suitable. They form vast swarms of more than 50 billion locusts. These swarms devastate farm crops, causing famine and starvation.

Many grasshoppers and crickets are active fliers. They have two pairs of wings. The front pair are leathery and protect the delicate fanlike wings at the back. As the insect leaps, the wings open.

Back legs kick out as grasshopper leaps forward.

BREEDING
After mating, the female grasshopper or cricket lays eggs through the ovipositor, usually in soil or in plant matter. Special muscles stretch the abdomen and force the eggs between particles of soil. The eggs hatch into larvae called nymphs, or hoppers. The hoppers look like smaller versions of their parents but are wingless. They feed hungrily and molt (shed) their skin, becoming larger and more like the adults each time. Several weeks or months later, after about five molts, the hoppers shed their skin again and become full-sized winged adults.

Ovipositor

Katydid lays its eggs in the soil.

Wings close as grasshopper lands.

Find out more
ANIMAL SENSES
ANIMALS
INSECTS

GRASSLAND WILDLIFE

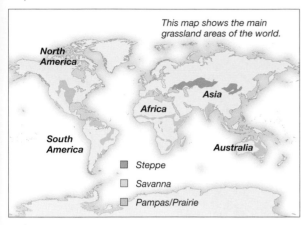

This map shows the main grassland areas of the world.

North America

Asia

Africa

South America

Australia

☐ Steppe
☐ Savanna
☐ Pampas/Prairie

GRASSLAND AREAS
The main grassland areas in the world are the Asian steppes, African savannas and grasslands, North American prairies, and South American pampas, which blend into tropical Amazonian savanna. There are also tropical grasslands in parts of India and across Australia.

VAST AREAS OF AFRICA, the Americas, Asia, and Australia consist of grasslands – areas too dry for forests, but not too dry for grasses. Grasses themselves are flowering plants that can grow again quickly after animals eat them. Grasses also recover quickly if fire sweeps across the plains in the hot, dry season. The fire burns only the upper parts of the grass, so the roots and stems are not damaged. Grasslands provide a home for many different animals. Each survives by feeding on a different part of the grass plants. Zebras, for example, eat the coarse, older grass while wildebeest (gnu) graze on new shoots. Thomson's gazelles nibble close to the ground. Grasshoppers, ants, and termites shelter among the grass stems and roots; these insects, in turn, are food for larger animals such as anteaters and armadillos. The lack of trees in grassland areas means that small animals and certain birds have to dig burrows for shelter and for breeding. Each type of grassland has burrowing rodents; prairie dogs and pocket gophers live in North America, susliks in Asia, ground squirrels in Africa, and vizcachas and tuco-tucos in South America.

Thistles grow in grassy areas throughout the world. Their prickles protect them against grazing animals. The flowers are often purple, and form fluffy white seed heads.

SOUTH AMERICAN PAMPAS
The largest mammals on the South American pampas are the pampas deer, guanaco, and rodents such as the viscacha, which burrows for shelter and safety. A fast-running bird called the rhea also lives on the South American pampas, feeding on grasses and other plants.

VISCACHA
The viscacha is related to the guinea pig. A male viscacha weighs about 17 lb (8 kg), almost twice the size of the female. Viscachas dig a system of burrows with their front feet and pile up sticks and stones near the various entrances. They eat mainly plant leaves and stems.

GIANT ANTEATER
With large claws on its second and third fingers, the giant anteater can easily rip a hole in an ant's nest or a termite mound as it searches for food. The giant anteater uses its long, sticky tongue to lick up the ants and termites. Its tongue measures about 24 in (60 cm) in length.

BURROWING OWL
The burrowing owl lives on the South American pampas. It often makes its nest in an empty burrow taken over from a viscacha. Burrowing owls eat grasshoppers, insects, small mammals, birds, lizards, and snakes.

PAMPAS GRASS
The white, fluffy seed heads of pampas grass are a familiar sight in parks and gardens. Wild pampas grass covers huge areas of Argentina, in South America. Pampas leaves have tiny teeth, like miniature saws, that easily cut human skin.

Tail protects anteater's body as it sleeps in a shallow hole, listening for predators such as pumas.

JACKAL
Golden jackals eat whatever they can find on the African savanna, including fruits, small mammals, eggs, birds, and the carcasses (dead bodies) of larger animals such as zebras.

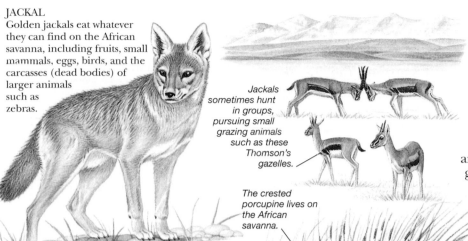

Jackals sometimes hunt in groups, pursuing small grazing animals such as these Thomson's gazelles.

The crested porcupine lives on the African savanna.

THOMSON'S GAZELLE
These swift-moving mammals live on the grassy plains of Africa in herds of up to 30 animals. They all have horns, but those of the male are larger than those of the female. Thomson's gazelles are often the prey of other grassland animals, such as the cheetah and the jackal.

SAVANNA
The huge grassland areas of eastern and southern Africa are called savannas. These areas are home to the world's largest herds of grazing animals, including zebra, wildebeest, and hartebeest. Many large grazers wander from one area to the next, following the rains to find fresh pastures. Acacia and baobab trees dot the landscape, providing shade for resting lions, ambush cover for leopards, and sleeping places for baboons.

CONSERVATION
Many grassland areas are now used as farmland, and the natural wildlife is being squeezed into smaller areas. As a result, these areas become overgrazed and barren. Grassland animals are also threatened by human hunters. In the past the Asian saiga antelope was killed for its horns. Today it is protected by law, but it is still seriously endangered, with only 50,000 left in the wild.

A newborn saiga antelope is fluffy and has no horns.

CRESTED PORCUPINE
The crested porcupine has sharp spines on its back for protection. It warns enemies to stay away by rattling the hollow quills on its tail. If an intruder ignores these warnings, the porcupine runs backward into the enemy, and the quills come away and stick into the intruder's flesh.

Wild peonies are found in many grassy habitats around the world. Many garden peony plants came originally from the hardy wild peonies that grow in grassland areas.

STEPPE
The vast plains of Asia are called steppes. In the western part of Asia the rainfall is more than 10 in (25 cm) each year, and grasses and other plants grow well. Toward the eastern part of Asia there is less than 2.5 in (6 cm) of rainfall yearly, and the grasses fade away into the harsh Gobi Desert. Saiga antelopes, red deer, and roe deer graze on the rolling plains.

GRASS SNAKE
The grass snake lives on riverbanks and in marshes, mainly in Europe and Asia. Grass snakes are good swimmers.

PALLAS'S CAT
This long-furred cat lives in mountains, high steppes, and open country across Central Asia. At night it hunts for hares, birds, and mice.

Head-body length of about 24 in (60 cm)

Strong, agile, stout body with short legs

Soft, thick fur to keep out the cold winds

BROOK'S GECKO
Sharp claws and sticky toe pads enable the gecko to climb over smooth rocks, along crevices, and in cracks. The Brook's gecko is active at night catching insects, and hides by day under rocks or in an empty termite or ant nest.

PALLAS'S SANDGROUSE
The mottled plumage (feathers) of Pallas's sandgrouse gives it excellent camouflage among the brownish grasses and stones of the Asian steppe. It needs little water and can survive on dry, tough seeds and other plant parts.

Find out more
AFRICAN WILDLIFE
HORSES, ASSES, AND ZEBRAS
LIONS, TIGERS,
and other big cats
LIZARDS

GRAVITY

FALLING

Earth's gravity makes falling objects accelerate (speed up). Their speed does not depend on how heavy they are: a light object falls as fast as a heavy object unless air slows it down. The Italian scientist Galileo Galilei (1564-1642) noticed this about 400 years ago.

A heavy rock weighs much more than an egg of the same size. However, both objects fall at the same rate and hit the ground at the same time.

THE EARTH MOVES around the sun, traveling about 50 times faster than a rifle bullet. A strong force holds the Earth in this orbit. This is the force of gravity; without it, the Earth would shoot off into space like a stone from a catapult. Everything possesses gravity; it is a force that attracts all objects to each other. However, the strength of the force depends on how much mass is in an object, so gravity is only strong in huge objects such as planets. Although you cannot feel it, the force of gravity is also pulling on you. The Earth's gravity holds you to the surface of the Earth, no matter where you are. This is because gravity always pulls toward the center of the Earth. Sometimes you can see or feel the effects of gravity. For example, the effort you feel when you climb up a flight of stairs is because you are fighting against the force of gravity.

When you drop a ball, it falls because gravity is pulling it toward the center of the Earth.

Gravity pulls all objects down toward the center of the Earth.

MASS AND WEIGHT

An object's mass is the amount of material it contains. Mass stays the same wherever the object is in the universe. The weight of an object is the force of gravity pulling on it. Weight can change. Because the moon is smaller than the Earth, its gravity is weaker, about one sixth as strong as Earth's. Therefore, an astronaut on the moon weighs only one sixth of her weight on Earth, but her mass remains the same.

MOON AND EARTH

Gravity keeps the moon moving in its orbit around the Earth. The moon's gravity has effects on the Earth, too. When the moon is directly over the sea, its gravity pulls the seawater toward it, which produces a high tide; low tide follows when the Earth rotates away again.

Objects fall in the opposite direction on the other side of the Earth.

The force of gravity gets weaker as you go further from the center of the Earth. On top of a high mountain, gravity is slightly weaker than at sea level; so objects weigh fractionally less.

EARTH'S GRAVITY

People on the opposite side of the Earth are upside down in relation to you. But they do not fall off into space. They are held on to the surface of the Earth just as you are. This is because the force of gravity pulls everything toward the center of the Earth. Down is always the direction of the Earth's center.

ISAAC NEWTON

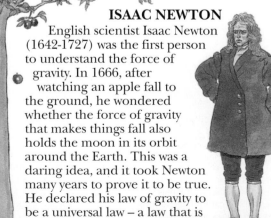

English scientist Isaac Newton (1642-1727) was the first person to understand the force of gravity. In 1666, after watching an apple fall to the ground, he wondered whether the force of gravity that makes things fall also holds the moon in its orbit around the Earth. This was a daring idea, and it took Newton many years to prove it to be true. He declared his law of gravity to be a universal law – a law that is true throughout the universe.

CENTER OF GRAVITY

It is best to carry a large, unwieldy object such as a ladder by holding it above its center. The weight of the ladder balances at the center, which is called its center of gravity or center of mass. An object with a large or heavy base has a low center of gravity. This stops it from falling over easily.

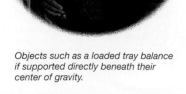

Objects such as a loaded tray balance if supported directly beneath their center of gravity.

Find out more

ASTRONAUTS
and space travel
PHYSICS
SCIENCE, HISTORY OF
UNIVERSE
WEIGHTS AND MEASURES

GREECE

| Volcano | Mountain | Ancient monument | Capital city | Large city/town | Small city/town |

GREECE IS A LAND of wild mountains, remote valleys, and scattered islands. Most people make their living by farming; olives grow on the dry hillsides, while hardy sheep and goats thrive in the rugged landscape. Greece is the world's third-largest producer of olive oil, and also exports citrus fruits, grapes, and tomatoes. With one of the largest merchant fleets in the world, Greece is a seafaring nation – people and goods travel by boat. In recent years, tourism has transformed the Greek economy. Millions of visitors are attracted to Greece by its landscape, and by its rich history as the birthplace of democracy in the 5th century B.C.

Lying at the eastern end of the Mediterranean, Greece is surrounded by the Mediterranean, Aegean, and Ionian seas. It consists of a mainland, the Peloponnese Peninsula, and over 2,000 islands.

STATISTICS
Area: 50,961 sq miles (131,990 sq km)
Population: 11,000,000
Capital: Athens
Languages: Greek, Turkish, Macedonian, Albanian
Religions: Greek Orthodox, Muslim
Currency: Euro

THE GREEK ISLANDS
The Greek mainland is surrounded by many islands. Ships and ferries unite these scattered communities. In summer, the islands, with their warm climate, fishing villages, and beautiful beaches, are major tourist centers, attracting over nine million visitors. In winter, the small islands are deserted by summer residents, who return to the mainland.

ORTHODOX PRIESTS

The Eastern Orthodox Church was founded in Constantinople (Istanbul) in the 4th century A.D. The Greek Orthodox Church became independent in 1850 and is the official religion of Greece, with more than 10 million members. Distinctively dressed priests are a common sight.

OCTOPUS
Octopuses are a Greek delicacy, but are becoming scarce due to overfishing in the Mediterranean.

ATHENS
The ancient city of Athens, the cultural center of Greece in the 5th century B.C., is generally considered to be the birthplace of western civilization. The fortified acropolis (above) rises 328 ft (100 m) above the city. It is crowned by the Parthenon temple, dedicated to the city's patron goddess Athena, and built in 432 B.C. Today, this busy modern city is a major commercial, shipping, and tourist center, and seat of the Greek government.

SCALE BAR
0   50   100   km
0   50   100   miles

Find out more
ARCHAEOLOGY
CHRISTIANITY
DEMOCRACY
GREECE, ANCIENT

ANCIENT GREECE

MANY WESTERN WORDS, ideas, and sources of entertainment have their roots in the world of Ancient Greece. About 2,500 years ago, the Greeks set up a society that became the most influential in the world. Greek architects designed a style of building that is copied to this day. Greek thinkers asked searching questions about life that are still discussed. Modern theater is founded on the ancient Greek plays that were performed under the skies thousands of years ago. And the Greeks set up the world's first democracy (government by the people) in Athens. However, only free men born in Athens were actually allowed to have a say in government. Ancient Greek society went through many phases, with a "golden age" between around 600 and 300 B.C. Arts and culture flourished at that time. The Macedonians, under Philip of Macedon, finally conquered the civilization, but it continued under Philip's son Alexander, who spread Greek culture and thinking throughout the Middle East and North Africa.

TEMPLE OF HERA
The Greeks built temples to worship their many gods. This temple at Paestum, Italy, was built to honor the goddess Hera, who was the protector of women and marriage.

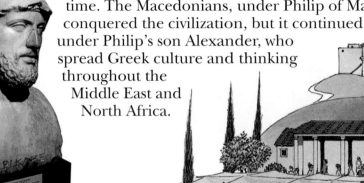

PERICLES
As leader of Athens, Pericles (c.490-429 B.C.) carried out a program to beautify the city. This included the building of the Parthenon, a temple to the goddess Athena.

There were many busy markets in Athens, where people came to buy and sell their goods.

ATHENS
During the golden age, the Greek world consisted of independent, self-governing cities, known as city-states. With its own superb port at Piraeus, Athens was the most important city-state. It became the center of Greek civilization and culture, attracting many famous playwrights and thinkers, such as Socrates. Athens practiced the system of *demokratia* (democracy). People gathered together in the agora (marketplace) to shop and talk. The acropolis (high city) towered above Athens.

SPARTA

Spartan hoplites

The second major city-state of Greece, Sparta, revolved around warfare. Spartans led tough, disciplined lives. Each male Spartan began military training at the age of seven and remained a soldier until 60. Women kept very fit by running and wrestling. The fierce Spartan hoplites (foot soldiers) were feared throughout the Greek world.

Athens (in Attica) and dependent states (shown in pink), c. 450 B.C.

GREEK WORLD
The Greek world consisted of many city-states and their colonies, spread throughout the Mediterranean region.

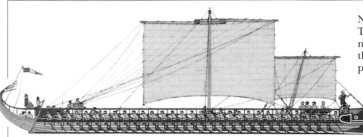

NAVY
The Athenians possessed a powerful navy, consisting of a fleet of more than 200 triremes – warships powered by a square sail and rowed by 170 men seated in three ranks. The battle tactic involved rowing furiously and ramming the enemy's ship. In 480 B.C., during wars against the Persians, the Athenian navy crushed the Persian fleet at the sea battle of Salamis.

Modern reconstruction of a Greek trireme

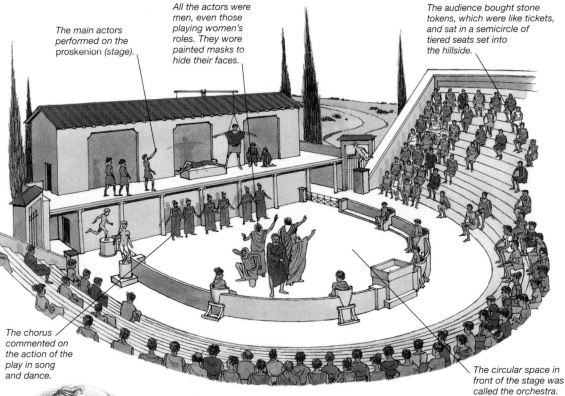

The main actors performed on the proskenion (stage).

All the actors were men, even those playing women's roles. They wore painted masks to hide their faces.

The audience bought stone tokens, which were like tickets, and sat in a semicircle of tiered seats set into the hillside.

The chorus commented on the action of the play in song and dance.

The circular space in front of the stage was called the orchestra.

GREEK THEATER

Drama was born in Athens. It began as singing and acting as part of a religious festival to honor the god Dionysus. The audience watched a series of plays; at the end of the festival, prizes were given for the best play and best actor. From these beginnings, playwrights such as Sophocles and Aristophanes started to write tragedies and comedies. Tragedies involved dreadful suffering; comedies featured slapstick humor and rude jokes.

THINKERS
Great thinkers from Athens dominated Greek learning and culture during the 5th and 4th centuries B.C. Socrates (469-399 B.C.; above) was one of the most famous. He discussed the meaning and conduct of life. He also questioned people cleverly, often proving that their ideas were wrong. Socrates wrote no books himself, but one of his followers, Plato (427-347 B.C.), made him the subject of many of his books.

VASE PAINTING
Painted scenes on Greek pottery give us clear clues about daily life in Ancient Greece. The paintings often show a touching scene, such as a warrior bidding his family farewell as he goes off to war. They also show the many gods that the Greeks worshiped.

Amphora (vase) from Attica shows Zeus, king of the gods, at the birth of Athena, his daughter.

ANCIENT GREECE

1500 B.C. Minoan civilization (on island of Crete) at its height.

c. 1400 Mycenaean civilization, centered in great palaces on the Greek mainland, dominates Greece.

c. 1250 Probable date of the Trojan Wars between Mycenaeans and the city of Troy.

c. 1000 Greek-speaking peoples arrive in Greece and establish the first city-states.

776 First Olympic Games held at Olympia, Greece.

750s First Greek colonies founded.

c. 505 Democracy is established in Athens.

400s Golden age of Greek theater.

490-479 Persian Wars; Greek states unite to defeat Persians.

490 Greeks defeat Persians at Marathon.

480 Greeks destroy the Persian fleet at the Battle of Salamis.

479 Final defeat of Persians at Plataea.

461-429 Pericles rules in Athens; Parthenon built.

431-404 Peloponnesian War between Athens and Sparta leads to Spartan domination of Greece.

359 Philip becomes king of Macedonia.

338 Philip of Macedonia conquers Greece.

336-323 Alexander the Great, son of Philip, sets up Greek empire in Middle East.

Find out more
ALEXANDER THE GREAT
ARCHITECTURE
DEMOCRACY
MINOANS
SCULPTURE
THEATER

GUNS

THE FIRST GUNS appeared during the early 14th century. They consisted of a thick metal tube that was closed at one end and was packed with gunpowder. Lighting the fuse caused the gunpowder to explode, blasting a stone or iron ball out of the end of the tube. In the 16th century, pistols were invented to be used as concealed weapons and for personal protection. However, they were useless at a range of more than 30 ft (9 m), and once fired had to be laboriously reloaded. Modern guns range from large, powerful artillery weapons to small, light pistols. Sophisticated engineering has given guns great accuracy and power, and many guns can be fired several times without reloading. However, even the most modern guns work on the same basic principle as the early cannon.

Eighteenth-century highwaymen, armed with early pistols, attacking a stagecoach.

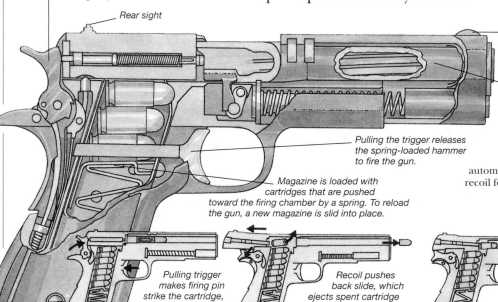

Hammer drives firing pin into the back of the cartridge, making the charge explode.

Rear sight

To aim the pistol, the front and rear sights are lined up.

When the gun is fired, bullet shoots through barrel.

Pulling the trigger releases the spring-loaded hammer to fire the gun.

Magazine is loaded with cartridges that are pushed toward the firing chamber by a spring. To reload the gun, a new magazine is slid into place.

AUTOMATIC PISTOL
The pistol is loaded with cartridges, each of which contains a lead bullet and a small charge of explosive. When the hammer of the gun strikes the charge, it explodes, producing gases that expand violently. The force of the expanding gases pushes the bullet along the barrel. The gun recoils, or jerks backward, when it is fired. In automatic or self-loading weapons such as machine guns, recoil forces another cartridge into place, ready for firing.

Pulling trigger makes firing pin strike the cartridge, detonating its explosive charge.

Recoil pushes back slide, which ejects spent cartridge case; the next cartridge springs into firing chamber.

The slide snaps back, pushing new cartridge into place, ready for firing.

BULLETS
When a bullet is fired, its casing remains behind. The force of the explosion ejects the spent cartridge case through a slot in the barrel.

ARTILLERY
Heavy guns, or artillery, are used to bombard enemy positions. They fire shells – hollow bullet-shaped cylinders packed with high explosive – over distances of more than 20 miles (32 km). The latest artillery weapons are guided by computers and laser rangefinders, and their shells are equipped with special homing devices so that they can hit their targets with great accuracy.

Pakistani soldiers aiming a light artillery piece high up in the Himalayas.

KINDS OF GUN
There are four main types of hand-held gun: pistols, for personal protection; rifles, for accurate firing over long distances; submachine guns, which produce a spray of bullets; and shotguns, which fire a mass of lead fragments for sport shooting.

SUBMACHINE GUN
With one squeeze of the trigger, a submachine gun can fire many bullets in quick succession. It is small and light so that a soldier can carry it easily into battle.

MACHINE GUN
A machine gun is often mounted onto a vehicle because it is too heavy to hold. It is fed with bullets attached to a long belt and can fire about 600 rounds per minute.

REVOLVER
Revolvers have a rotating cylinder with six chambers, allowing six shots to be fired without reloading.

RIFLE
A rifle is a long-barreled gun that is fired from the shoulder. Inside the barrel is a spiral of grooves that make the bullet spin as it is fired. The flight of a spinning bullet is very stable, which makes the rifle a very accurate weapon. A rifle bullet can travel at about 2,200 mph (3,500 km/h).

Find out more
ARMIES
TANKS
WEAPONS

GYMNASTICS

To SUCCEED, GYMNASTS must be strong, flexible, brave, and graceful. Most people, however, can do some gymnastics. Children, for example, learn to do handstands and cartwheels at school, and these simple activities are the basis for all gymnastic moves. Gymnastics, as a form of acrobatic exercise, dates back to Ancient Greece. Today, it is an increasingly popular spectator sport. There are two main types: rhythmic gymnastics and artistic gymnastics, performed on apparatus such as the horse or vault. There are eight competitive events. Both men and women do floor exercises, and the vault. Men compete on bars, horse, and rings. Women compete on the beam and asymmetric bars. Judges award points out of ten. Many champions arc teenagers.

RHYTHMIC GYMNASTICS
A fairly new branch of the sport is rhythmic gymnastics, which is practised by women and girls. Competitors use hoops, ribbons, or balls in their display. The focus is on grace and beauty. Gymnasts combine elements of ballet with traditional gymnastic moves. The result is a floor routine which judges mark on artistic as well as sporting merits.

Gymnast rotates her body forward, keeping her legs together.

Gymnast keeps legs straight.

Rotation in the air

Hands push off

Head up, facing forward

SCORING POINTS
To gain high scores, gymnasts must perform the moves correctly according to set rules and hold their bodies in the right position at the same time. The vaulter, for example, must keep his toes pointed and his legs split during the entire movement.

Toes pointed

Controlled landing

The finish

VAULTING
The shortest and most explosive discipline in gymnastics is the vault. The gymnast sprints down a runway, pushes off from a springboard to provide power, and twists off the vaulting horse. The gymnast aims to keep the right shape throughout the vault, and then land, feet together, without losing balance.

Feet together at landing

HIGH BAR
Events on the high bar are for men only. The gymnast performs while swinging around the bar, holding on with both hands, or only one hand. The most difficult moves involve letting go of the bar, and catching it again. Women compete on asymmetric bars, which consist of one high and one lower bar.

Hands firmly on floor, fingers outstretched for balance

BALANCE
Gymnasts need good balance for floor exercises, and for working on the beam, which is very narrow.

> **Find out more**
> MUSCLES AND MOVEMENT
> OLYMPIC GAMES
> SPORTS

HAPSBURGS

DURING THE 900s a family named Hapsburg owned some land in France and Switzerland. From this position they rose to dominate European history for more than 1,000 years. The name Hapsburg comes from one of the family's first castles, the Habichtsburg, in Switzerland. Through a series of wars, inheritances, and careful marriages, the family acquired more and more land. By the 1500s it owned most of southern and central Europe and much land in the Americas. The Hapsburg possessions became so big that, in 1556, the Hapsburg emperor, Charles V, split the land between members of his family. Philip II governed one half from Madrid, Spain, while Ferdinand of Austria governed the other half from Vienna, Austria. The Spanish Hapsburgs died out in 1700, but the Austrian Hapsburgs continued to expand their empire. In the 19th century, however, their power began to weaken because the empire contained so many different peoples. When it collapsed after World War I (1914-18), four new nations emerged: Austria, Czechoslovakia, Hungary, and Yugoslavia.

CHARLES V
Under Charles V, who reigned as Holy Roman Emperor from 1519 to 1556, the Hapsburgs reached the height of their power. Charles V ruled a vast empire shown in pink on the map above.

Joseph II

JOSEPH II
From the time of Rudolf I onward, the Hapsburg family extended its power throughout Europe. Joseph II, son of Maria Theresa, was appalled by the living conditions of his poorer subjects. He began reforms that included freeing serfs and abolishing privileges.

MARIA THERESA
In 1740, Maria Theresa came to the Austrian throne. She was only 23 and her empire was bankrupt. Over the next 40 years, she pulled Austria back from poverty and restored Hapsburg power in Europe.

AUSTRIA
Under Maria Theresa, Austria became the leading artistic center of Europe. Austria was home to the composers Franz Joseph Haydn and Wolfgang Amadeus Mozart. Artists and architects came from all over Europe to work on great palaces such as the Schönbrunn in Vienna (above).

HAPSBURGS
1273 Rudolf I becomes the Holy Roman Emperor.

1282 Albert I becomes first Hapsburg ruler of Austria.

1438 Albert II becomes Holy Roman Emperor.

1519 Charles V becomes Holy Roman Emperor.

1526 Ferdinand, brother of Charles, acquires Bohemia.

1556 Charles V splits Hapsburg lands in half.

1700 Charles II, last Spanish Hapsburg monarch, dies.

1740-1780 Maria Theresa increases Hapsburg power in Europe.

1781 Joseph II, son of Maria Theresa, introduces major reforms and frees serfs.

1867 Austrian empire is split between two monarchs: Austrian and Hungarian.

1918 Charles I, last Hapsburg emperor, gives up throne.

Find out more
AUSTRIA
CHARLEMAGNE
EUROPE, HISTORY OF
GERMANY, HISTORY OF
SPAIN, HISTORY OF

HEALTH AND FITNESS

Regular, vigorous exercise helps prevent heart disease.

Better hygiene and a more balanced diet could eliminate much ill health in developed nations.

ARE YOU HEALTHY? Before answering, think about what you understand by "health." It doesn't just mean freedom from disease. Health is a measure of how sound and vigorous both your body and mind are. A truly healthy person has a sense of physical and mental well-being. Our health is precious and easily damaged. But there is much we can do to maintain it. Eating well, exercising, and getting enough sleep all help keep us healthy. Standards of health and health hazards are different from place to place. In some parts of the world, many people have serious health problems because they are poor, hungry, and without clean drinking water. In other places, stress at work, lack of exercise, and too much food bring their own health problems, such as heart disease. People also damage their health through the use of alcohol, tobacco, and dangerous drugs.

KEEPING HEALTHY

Food plays a large part in health. A healthy diet includes fresh fruit and vegetables, meat, fish, bread, eggs, and milk, but not too many fatty, salty, or sugary foods. Exercise keeps the heart strong and prevents us from gaining too much weight.

IMMUNIZATION

Good health includes preventing disease. Immunization, sometimes called inoculation or vaccination, involves injecting the body with a vaccine. This is a tiny dose of the infecting agent of the disease, which has been specially treated to render it safe. The vaccination provides immunity, or protection, against the disease. It is now possible to immunize against diphtheria, polio, tetanus, measles, mumps, rubella, tuberculosis, meningitis, and lots of others. Immunization has completely eliminated one disease – smallpox.

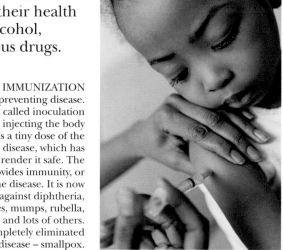

A doctor or nurse usually gives immunizations by injection.

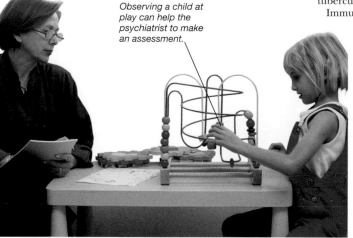

Observing a child at play can help the psychiatrist to make an assessment.

MENTAL HEALTH

A healthy mind is just as important as a healthy body. Stress, drug abuse, physical disease, and family problems such as divorce can all damage mental health. Specialist doctors who treat mental health problems are called psychiatrists. Other sources of help include drug therapy, counseling, and self-help groups.

HEALTH CHECKUPS

Through routine medical checkups, doctors can detect health problems such as cancer at the early stages, when treatment is most effective. Checkups can also reveal hereditary health problems – diseases that pass from parents to children.

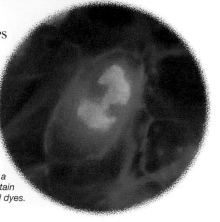

To reveal cancer cells on a microscope slide, technicians stain the tissue sample with colored dyes.

PUBLIC HEALTH

Dirt and lack of hygiene damage health. If not controlled, they can extend to whole cities and affect large populations. The Great Plague of London in 1665 is a good example. During the 1840s, pioneers of public health in Europe worked to introduce clean water supplies and good sewage systems. Now, international agencies like the World Health Organization, have been set up to monitor public health.

EXERCISE ROUTINES

Regular exercise improves blood circulation, makes the heart and lungs work well, keeps muscles strong and toned, and keeps joints supple. It is good for the brain as well as the body, and makes us feel happy and alert. With all exercise routines, you need to do a warm-up sequence before you start and a cool-down sequence at the end to prevent strain on muscles.

CYCLING

Cycling is an enjoyable way to exercise as it takes place in the fresh air and can easily be fitted into your daily routine—if you cycle to school, for example. Cycling can be as vigorous or as gentle as you like, builds stamina, strengthens leg muscles, and improves the oxygen flow to heart and brain. As it is not a weight-bearing activity, it can be done safely by all age groups.

Always wear a safety helmet.

Keep your bicycle oiled and serviced.

Use the ball of the foot on the pedals.

HEALTHY EATING

Food is the fuel that gives us energy day after day. It also provides us with all the materials our bodies need for growing and for repairing themselves, and the vitamins we need to maintain strong and healthy immune systems that fight off illness. One-third of our daily diet should be fresh fruit and vegetables.

Globe artichokes are good for the liver.

Fennel helps the kidneys to function well.

Zucchini are rich in folic acid and potassium.

Avocados contain the vitamins E and B6, and the mineral potassium.

Garlic improves blood circulation.

Red peppers are an excellent source of vitamin A.

Onions help lower fat levels in blood.

Stretching exercises keep you supple.

POSTURE

Good posture is part of being fit and well. Standing up straight, but relaxed, with your weight balanced on both feet encourages good circulation and prevents back strain. Sitting in a slumped position strains your back, shoulders, neck, and chest, and inhibits your breathing.

Strain on neck and back.

Pressure on the chest prevents proper breathing.

FITNESS AND FUN

Make sure you choose an exercise that you enjoy doing. The more fun you have, the more you will exercise and the healthier you will feel. There are many types of exercise to choose from that are both fun and can improve strength, stamina, and mobility. Trampolining, football, tennis, badminton, all types of dancing, gymnastics, swimming, or running are all good choices.

Keep knees slightly bent.

MENTAL FITNESS

It is important to keep your brain fit as well as your body. A healthy diet, regular sleep, and plenty of exercise to make sure that the blood delivers nutrients and oxygen to the brain will keep your brain in good physical condition. Doing crosswords and puzzles that make you think, such as chess, are enjoyable ways to make sure you stay mentally alert.

Stand comfortably straight, not rigidly.

Find out more

DIGESTION
HEART AND BLOOD
SPORTS

HEART AND BLOOD

OUR BODIES CONTAIN about 8 pints (4.5 liters) of blood. The heart, an organ in the chest, pumps blood continuously to every part of the body. The heart is such a powerful pump that it takes only about a minute for each blood cell to travel all the way around the body and back to the heart. Traveling along tubes called blood vessels, blood carries oxygen and nourishment from digested food to every part of the body. Blood also carries away harmful waste products such as carbon dioxide. Blood consists of red and white blood cells, platelets, and a watery liquid called plasma. A drop of blood the size of a pinhead contains about five million cells. About once every second the muscular walls of the heart contract, squeezing blood out of the heart and into blood vessels called arteries. The arteries divide many times until they form a network of tiny blood vessels called capillaries. The capillaries gradually join up again to form veins, which carry the blood back to the heart, where it is sent to the lungs for fresh oxygen.

INSIDE THE HEART

The heart has four chambers – two on each side. The upper chamber is called the atrium. Blood from the veins flows into the right atrium, and then into the lower chamber, called the ventricle. The thick, muscular walls of the left ventricle force the blood out into the arteries. The heart consists of two pumps, working side by side. The left pump sends blood full of oxygen (oxygenated) around the body. As the blood passes its oxygen to various parts of the body, it becomes stale (deoxygenated) and returns to the heart through the right pump. The right pump sends it to the lungs for fresh oxygen, then back through the left pump again to be sent around the body once more.

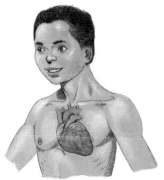

HUMAN HEART
The heart is protected by the rib cage. An adult's heart is the size of a clenched fist and weighs about 9 oz (300 g).

ARTERIES
Blood reaches the heart muscle through coronary arteries. The two main coronary arteries are about as wide as drinking straws. Arteries have thick walls in three layers – a tough outer layer, a muscular middle layer, and a smooth lining.

CAPILLARIES
The tiny blood vessels that carry blood between the smallest arteries (arterioles) and the smallest veins (venules) are called capillaries. Capillaries allow oxygen and nutrients to pass through their walls to all the body cells.

VEINS
Veins carry deoxygenated blood (blue-colored blood that contains little oxygen) back to the heart from other parts of the body. The largest veins in the body are the two venae cavas, which carry the deoxygenated blood to the right side of the heart, to be pumped to the lungs for oxygen. Veins are thinner, less elastic, and less muscular than arteries.

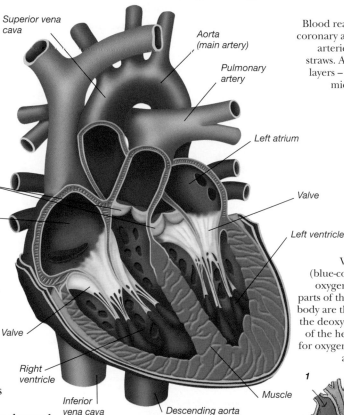

Superior vena cava

Aorta (main artery)

Pulmonary artery

Left atrium

Valves

Right atrium

Valve

Left ventricle

Valve

Right ventricle

Inferior vena cava

Descending aorta

Muscle

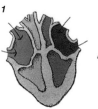 
Blood enters atria (upper chambers). *Blood flows through to ventricles (lower chambers).*

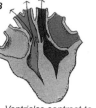 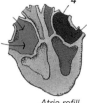
Ventricles contract to pump blood into arteries. *Atria refill with blood.*

BLOOD CELLS
There are three types of blood cells. Red blood cells carry oxygen from the lungs to the rest of the body. White blood cells protect the body against illness and fight infection. Platelets, which are the smallest type of blood cell, help the blood to clot. All blood cells are produced in the bone marrow inside the bones.

White cell

Red cell   Platelets

HOW BLOOD CLOTS
When you cut yourself and blood flows out of the wound, platelets in the blood stick together and a fine meshwork of fibers forms. This meshwork traps more blood cells and forms a clot to seal the wound.

HEART BEAT
On average, an adult's heart beats 60 to 70 times each minute, and this rises to more than 150 beats after strenuous activity. Each heartbeat has two main phases. The phase when the heart muscle is fully contracted, squeezing out blood, is called systole. The phase when the heart relaxes and refills with blood is called diastole.

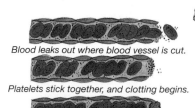
Blood leaks out where blood vessel is cut.

Platelets stick together, and clotting begins.

Tiny meshwork of platelets begins to form.

Blood clot forms, sealing the cut.

Find out more
BRAIN AND NERVES
HUMAN BODY
LUNGS AND BREATHING
MUSCLES AND MOVEMENT

HEAT

STAND IN THE SUNSHINE: you feel warm. Go for a fast run: you will get hot. The warmth of sunshine comes from heat generated in the center of the sun. Your body also produces heat all the time, and this heat keeps you alive. Heat is important to us in many ways. The sun's heat causes the weather, making winds blow and rain fall. The Earth's interior contains great heat, which causes volcanoes to erupt and earthquakes to shake the ground. Engines in cars, aircraft, and other forms of transportation use the heat from burning fuel to produce movement. Power stations change heat into electricity that comes to our homes. Heat is a form of energy.

White-hot steel

Everything, even the coldest object, contains heat – a cold object simply has less heat than a hot object. All things are made of tiny particles called molecules. Heat energy comes from the vibrating movement of molecules. Hot objects have fast-moving molecules; molecules in colder objects move more slowly.

A solid, such as the ice on this window pane, has rows of molecules that vibrate back and forth. The molecules are locked together, so solids are often hard and cannot be squashed.

SOLIDS, LIQUIDS, AND GASES
A substance can be a solid, a liquid, or a gas, depending on how hot it is. Changing the temperature can change the substance from one state to another. For instance, liquid water becomes a solid – ice – when it is cold and a gas – steam – when it is hot.

A gas, such as steam, has molecules that move around freely so that the gas spreads out to fill its container.

A liquid, such as water, has molecules that are close together. The molecules can move around more easily than in a solid, so a liquid can flow.

A process called convection spreads heat through gases and liquids. For example, hot air above a heater rises. Cold air flows in to take its place, becomes hot, and rises. In this way, a circular current of air moves around a room, carrying heat with it.

Warm rising air

Convection heater

BOILING POINT
At a temperature called the boiling point, a liquid changes into a gas. Below the boiling point the gas changes back to a liquid again. The boiling point of water is 212°F (100°C).

MELTING POINT
Heating a solid makes it melt into liquid. This happens only at a certain temperature, which is called the melting point. Below this temperature, the liquid freezes to a solid again. The melting point of ice is 32°F (0°C).

Cool incoming air

All objects give out heat rays that travel through air and space. The heating element of an oven cooks food with heat rays. The transmission (movement) of heat by heat rays is called radiation. It is not the same as nuclear radiation.

Heat travels through solid objects by a process called conduction. Metal conducts heat well. For instance, a metal spoon in a cup of coffee gets hot quickly. Other substances, such as wood and plastic, do not conduct heat well. They are called insulators and are used to make items such as saucepan handles.

A liquid slowly changes into a gas at a temperature lower than its boiling point. This is called evaporation. The steam from this hot cup of coffee is evaporated water.

HEAT ENERGY
Heat is just one of many forms of energy. Sources of heat change one type of energy into heat energy. A burning fire, for example, changes chemical energy in its fuel into heat energy. Electric heaters change electrical energy into heat.

The digestive system of an animal or a person changes chemical energy from food into heat energy inside the body.

INFRARED RAYS
Heat rays are also called infrared rays. They are invisible rays very similar to red light rays, which is why the rays are called infrared. All objects give out these rays, and hot objects produce stronger infrared rays than cold objects. Some electric heaters have curved reflectors that send heat rays forward just as a mirror reflects light rays.

This is a thermogram (heat picture) of a person's face. It was taken by a special camera that uses infrared rays instead of light rays. The hottest parts are yellow in the picture.

TEMPERATURE

Temperature is a measure of how hot an object is. A hot object has a higher temperature than a cold object. When objects are extremely cold, they have negative temperatures: a minus sign indicates how many degrees the temperature is below zero on the temperature scale.

Center of the Sun, about 27 million°F (15 million°C)

Center of the Earth, about 8,100°F (4,500°C)

Aluminum melts, 1,220°F (660°C)

Water boils, 212°F (100°C)

Normal body temperature, 98.6°F (37°C)

Water freezes, 32°F (0°C)

Oxygen becomes liquid, -360°F (-218°C)

Absolute zero, -460°F (-273°C)

FAHRENHEIT
Temperatures marked with an "F" are recorded using the Fahrenheit scale of temperature. In the Fahrenheit scale, water freezes at 32°F and boils at 212°F. A few countries, including the United States, use the Fahrenheit scale.

Level of column indicates temperature against scale.

Digital display accurately records temperature within one tenth of a degree.

Column of colored alcohol

ABSOLUTE ZERO
The lowest temperature of all is called absolute zero. At absolute zero, -460°F (-273°C), molecules stop moving. Scientists have cooled substances almost to absolute zero, but the exact temperature can never be reached.

CELSIUS
Temperatures marked with a "C" are recorded in the Celsius (also called Centigrade) scale of temperature. In this scale, water freezes at 0°C and boils at 100°C. Scientists and most countries of the world use the Celsius scale.

EXPANSION AND CONTRACTION

Most things expand (get slightly larger) when they get hot. They contract (shrink) again when they cool. This happens because the molecules inside an object make larger, more rapid vibrations as the object heats up. The molecules therefore take up more space, causing the object to expand. The Golden Gate bridge in San Francisco expands by up to 3 feet (0.9 m) in the summer months because of the hotter weather.

THERMOMETER

A thermometer is an instrument that measures temperature. A digital thermometer has a display that shows the temperature in numbers. Glass thermometers contain a thin column of mercury (a liquid metal) or colored alcohol that expands and rises in the thermometer as the temperature increases.

When vapor condenses back into a liquid, it gives out heat to the air around the condenser.

Liquid changes to vapor in evaporator by taking heat from inside the refrigerator and cooling it.

Surrounding cool air outside the refrigerator removes heat.

Vapor changes back to liquid in condenser, and continues its cycle around the refrigerator.

Electric pump forces liquid around pipes inside refrigerator.

Heat is taken from air inside the refrigerator.

REFRIGERATOR
When liquids evaporate (change into a gas), they take heat from their surroundings. In a refrigerator, a liquid circulates, going through a cycle of evaporation and condensation (changing back into a liquid again). As the liquid evaporates, it takes heat from the food in the refrigerator.

SWEATING AND SHIVERING

Your body usually has a steady temperature of 98.6°F (37°C). It automatically keeps you from getting too hot or too cold. Sweating cools you down if you get too hot. Shivering helps to warm you up when you get too cold. Hairs on your skin stand up when your body gets cold and help to trap a layer of air around the skin, which stops heat loss.

Shivering makes muscles move and produce heat.

Drops of sweat evaporate, which cools the skin.

Find out more

ATOMS AND MOLECULES
EARTH
ENGINES
FIRE
STARS
SUN
VOLCANOES

HELICOPTERS

OF ALL FLYING machines, the helicopter is the most versatile. It can fly forward, backward, or sideways. It can go straight up and down, and even hover in the air without moving. Because helicopters can take off vertically, they do not need to use airport runways and can fly almost anywhere. They can rescue people from mountains, fly to oil rigs out at sea, and even land on the roofs of skyscrapers. Helicopters come in many shapes and sizes. Some are designed to carry only one person; others are powerful enough to lift a truck. All helicopters have one or two large rotors. The rotor blades are shaped like long, thin wings. When they spin around, they lift the helicopter up and drive it through the air.

Gas turbine engine (one of three)

Rotor blades, made of ultra-strong plastic

Cockpit with automatic flight control system

ALL-PURPOSE HELICOPTER

The EH101 can transport 30 passengers or troops, carry 16 stretcher patients as an air ambulance, or lift a load of more than 6 tons. It flies at 170 mph (280 km/h).

Radar dome contains radar antenna.

Mission control console, equipped with radar screens and computers

Helicopter body, made of light metal alloys and strong plastics

Tail plane and fins keep the helicopter stable as it flies.

Tail rotor steers the helicopter and keeps it from spinning around.

Wheels fold into pods on sides of helicopter.

Rescue Man lowered down to life raft

Life raft contains survivors from shipwreck.

TAKING OFF

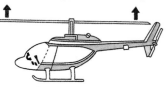

The rotor blades produce a lifting force that supports the helicopter.

The collective-pitch stick adjusts the rotors so the helicopter can go up, hover, or go down.

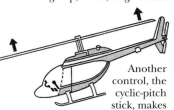

Another control, the cyclic-pitch stick, makes the main rotor tilt so that it can pull the helicopter in any direction – backward, forward, or sideways.

The tail rotor keeps the helicopter from spinning around. Pedals control the tail rotor so the helicopter can be turned to face any direction.

DEVELOPMENT

The Italian artist and scientist Leonardo da Vinci sketched a simple helicopter about 500 years ago, but it was never built. It was not until 1907 that a helicopter carried a person. It was built by a French mechanic named Paul Cornu.

Russian-born Igor Sikorsky built the VS-300 in the US in 1939. It was the first single-rotor helicopter, and it set the style for machines to come.

TWIN-ROTOR HELICOPTER

Large helicopters, such as this Boeing Chinook, may be twin-rotor machines. They have two main rotors that spin in opposite directions, and no tail rotor. The largest helicopter in the world is the Russian Mil Mi 12. It has twin rotors and is powered by four gas turbine engines.

Main rotor

Main rotor

Find out more

AIRCRAFT
ARMIES
MILITARY AIRCRAFT
PLASTICS

HIBERNATION

Senses such as hearing and sight are inactive during hibernation.

MANY WARM-BLOODED ANIMALS need extra energy in order to stay warm in the cold winter months, but the source of that energy – food – is scarce in winter. Some animals survive winter by migrating to a warmer place; others, such as bats and hedgehogs, hibernate in a safe and unexposed place such as a nest, burrow, or cave. In true hibernation, the body processes slow down almost to a standstill – the heartbeat occurs only every now and then, and the animal takes only a few breaths per minute. The body temperature falls to only a few degrees above the outside temperature – as low as 32°F (0°C) in a hamster. If the outside temperature drops below zero, chemical reactions in the animal's body switch on to keep it from freezing to death. A hibernating animal feasts on extra food in the fall so it can build up reserves of fat in its body and survive the winter months without food.

Dormouse curls up into a ball shape to reduce heat loss from its body.

Dormouse builds nest on or near ground, using stems, moss, and leaves.

Furry tail wraps around face for protection and insulation.

Up to half of body weight is lost during hibernation.

DORMOUSE

One of the best-known hibernators is the dormouse. In fall it feeds eagerly to build up stores of body fat, then settles into a winter nest among tree roots or in dense undergrowth. Its heart slows to only one beat every few minutes, and its breathing slows down. Its body temperature also drops to a few degrees above the surroundings.

BLACK BEAR

The winter sleep of bears, skunks, and chipmunks is not as deep as the true hibernation of bats and mice. The American black bear's heartbeat slows but the body temperature drops by only a few degrees. This means that the bear can stir itself from its winter sleep quite rapidly during a spell of slightly warmer weather. Although it wakes up, the bear does not eat and continues to live off its body fat until the spring. Some female bears give birth during the winter months.

TORPOR

To save energy, some small, warm-blooded animals such as bats and hummingbirds allow their bodies to cool and their heartbeat and breathing to slow down for part of the day or night. This is called torpor. Large animals such as bears do not become torpid because they would need too much energy to warm up again afterward. Bats often huddle together as they hang upside down to prevent too much heat loss. When the cold season comes, bats fly to a special cave or tree called a hibernaculum, where they begin true hibernation.

AESTIVATION

Many desert animals sleep during the hot, dry season to survive the intense heat. This is called aestivation – the opposite of hibernation. Desert creatures which aestivate include lizards, frogs, insects, and snails. Before aestivation begins, snails seal their shell openings with a film of mucus that hardens in the heat.

Snails cluster on grass stems to aestivate, away from predators on the ground.

Find out more
BATS
BEARS AND PANDAS
MICE, RATS, AND SQUIRRELS
MIGRATION
SNAILS AND SLUGS

HINDUISM

HINDUISM, ONE OF THE OLDEST RELIGIONS, began in India more than 5,000 years ago. Hinduism has no single founder, but grew gradually from early beliefs. Today there are many different Hindu groups or sects. They may worship the same Hindu gods, but they do not all share the same religious beliefs. Nevertheless, most Hindus believe that people have a soul that does not die with them. Instead, the soul leaves the dying body and enters a new one being born. People who live good lives are reincarnated, or born again, in a higher state. Bad deeds can lead to rebirth as an animal or an insect. It is possible to escape from the cycle of death and rebirth through Karma, that is, good deeds that bring an individual to the state of Moksha (liberation). Hindus are born into castes, or groups, which give them their rank in society. Rules restrict how people of different castes may mix and marry. Today, there are about 900 million Hindus in the world. They live mainly in India and East Africa.

GODS

There are three primary gods – Vishnu, Brahma, and Shiva – created by the energy of the universe. For the purpose of worship, however, a Hindu may choose any one of the gods as his deity. Vishnu, the preserver, appears in 10 different incarnations (forms). Two of the most popular are Rama and Krishna. Stories of the gods and their battles against evil are told in ancient Indian scriptures (writings) such as the *Mahabharata*.

More gentle than the fierce Shiva, Vishnu comes to restore order and peace to the world.

The four heads of Brahma, the creator, looking in all four directions, show that he has knowledge of all things.

Shiva, the destroyer, rules over the death and life of everything in the world. It is thought that when Shiva dances, he destroys all life.

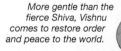

MARRIAGE

Family life and marriage are very important to Hindus. Parents are often involved in their children's choice of partner. Women are required to be dutiful and obedient to their fathers and husbands. A wedding ceremony is accompanied by music and feasting. The bride and groom exchange colorful garlands of flowers and make solemn promises to each other before a priest.

TEMPLES

In southern and central India, there are large temples that contain ornate carvings and statues of the many Hindu gods. Priests look after the temples. They bathe the idols every day, and decorate them with ornaments. Visitors come to pray and bring offerings of flowers and food. After the food has been blessed, it is shared by the worshipers or given to the poor.

Find out more

FESTIVALS AND FEASTS
INDIA
RELIGIONS

HISPANIC AMERICANS

Many Hispanic-American children are bilingual (speak two languages).

AMERICANS OF SPANISH-SPEAKING DESCENT are known as Hispanic Americans. Hispanic people established colonies in the area that became the United States long before British settlers arrived, especially in America's Southwest, where Hispanic culture thrived for centuries. Hispanic Americans descend from several countries and cultures, including the original Spanish colonists, and later immigrants from other parts of Latin America. Although Hispanic Americans come from different backgrounds, most are united by important traditions: the Spanish language, and the Roman Catholic Church.

THE HISPANIC PEOPLE

With more than 22 million people, Hispanics are the second largest minority group in America. Some trace their roots to the Spanish-speaking people who colonized the American Southwest, while others emigrated from Mexico, Puerto Rico, Cuba, and other parts of Central and South America. Mexican Americans are the largest Hispanic group.

In the 1960s, many Cubans emigrated by boat to America.

CELEBRATIONS
Many Hispanic Americans observe the holidays of their homelands. Mexican-American festivals such as the Day of the Dead (right), a traditional feast to honor dead ancestors, and *Las posadas*, a Christmas festival of lights, are celebrated in cities with Hispanic populations.

San Xavier mission, near Tucson, Arizona, was established in 1700.

AMERICA'S SECOND LANGUAGE
In response to the growth of the Spanish language, some states have passed laws making English the official language, putting educational programs for new immigrants at risk.

HISPANIC IMMIGRATION
The Mexican Revolution of 1910 brought chaos, and many Mexicans fled to the United States. However, immigration restrictions and discrimination reduced their numbers until the US relaxed the laws to meet labor shortages after World War II. In the mid-1900s, large numbers of Puerto Ricans and Cubans came to the United States. More recently, others have fled to escape conflicts in Central America.

LATIN MUSIC
The distinctive rhythms of Latin music have long been popular in the United States, from the heyday of Cuban dances such as the mambo and the salsa to Mexican mariachi bands. Modern artists, such as Gloria Estefan and Carlos Santana, have introduced new audiences to Latin music.

SPANISH MISSIONS
From the 16th century onward, Spanish settlers in the American Southwest built missions. They hoped to spread Catholicism, the Spanish language, and European culture to the native peoples.

Find out more

CARIBBEAN
CENTRAL AMERICA
IMMIGRATION
MEXICO
SPAIN, HISTORY OF

HOCKEY

THE GAME OF ICE HOCKEY is one of the fastest of all team sports. Its players swarm across the rink on ice skates, swinging their sticks to knock a hard rubber puck into the other team's goal. A goalkeeper, who is protected with heavy padding, defends the goal. If the puck completely crosses the goal line, a point is scored. Hockey players are constantly on the move – the game does not stop even when players are substituted. The speed of play results in plenty of rough-and-tumble action, with players slamming into walls, the ice, and sometimes each other. Three officials enforce penalties when the action gets too rough, and make sure the rules are followed. A hockey game is divided into three periods, each lasting 20 minutes, with an overtime period if the game is tied.

STANLEY CUP
The National Hockey League's (NHL) greatest prize is the Stanley Cup. The original cup was donated by Lord Stanley of Preston, the Governor General of Canada, in 1893. As a result of past mishaps, the original cup is kept safely in a bank vault and a new trophy is awarded to the champion team each year.

GOALKEEPER
The goalkeeper, or goalie, defends the goal in a rectangle called the crease. The goalie must block incoming shots, either by using the stick, stopping a shot with the body, or catching the puck in a glove.

Hockey skates

HOCKEY RINK
A rectangle of ice with rounded corners, the hockey rink is enclosed with wooden and glass walls. The goals are at opposite ends of the rink. The rink is marked with a red center line, two blue zone lines, and five face-off spots. These are used to start or restart the game, by dropping the puck between two opposing players.

Goal posts

Face-off circle

Hockey helmet

A puck is 3 in (7.5 cm) in diameter and 1 in (2.5 cm) thick.

EQUIPMENT
Players move and strike the puck with a hockey stick that has a thick blade at the end. The puck is a tough, black rubber disk that can shoot across the ice at speeds of up to 110 miles (177 km) an hour. Pucks are frozen before being used to make them less bouncy. Skates are padded to protect the ankle, toe, and instep, and a helmet protects the head.

Goalie's hockey stick is slightly thicker

PLAYERS
Each team has six players on the ice during a hockey game, with substitutes for all positions waiting on the benches. The goalkeeper defends the goal area. Two defenders play on either side of the goalkeeper, to assist with blocking shots and tackling opposing attackers. Three forwards, called the left, center, and right wings, try to move the puck up the ice and score in the opposing team's goal. Ice hockey players wear padding on the chest, shoulders, arms, and shins, as well as thick leather gauntlets, to protect them from being hurt by either the ice or the puck.

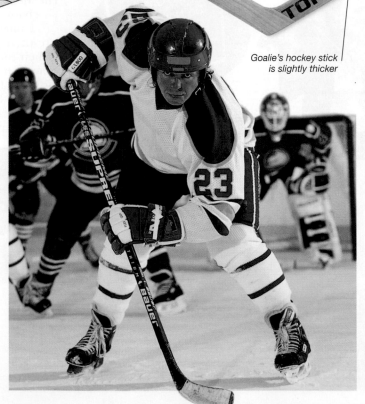

HISTORY OF HOCKEY
As early as the 1830s, freezing winters inspired Canadians to develop a simple game similar to field hockey, but played on ice. By the 1880s, the first professional teams had been formed in Canada.

Find out more

BALL GAMES
CANADA, HISTORY OF
SPORTS

HOLIDAYS

SPECIAL DAYS SET ASIDE FOR CELEBRATION and fun are called holidays. The word comes from the Anglo-Saxon for "holy day," because the first holidays honored sacred events or holy people. Today, there are holidays to mark important historical events, honor special people, give thanks, or celebrate a new season or a new year. Other holidays – Valentine's Day, April Fools' Day, and Halloween – have their own special traditions that are celebrated just for fun. Many countries have national holidays, established by tradition or law and observed every year on the same day. In the United States, the president and Congress have declared ten public holidays, but it is up to each state to decide the legal holidays within its borders.

HONORING HISTORY
Most countries celebrate the anniversaries of important historical events with public holidays. Government employees and many other workers are given the day off, and schools may close so that most people can celebrate the day. In North America, public holidays marking a nation's independence are celebrated in Canada on July 1, and in Mexico on September 15 and 16. In the United States, Independence Day is marked on July 4 – huge fireworks displays light up the sky and people celebrate with picnics and parties.

CELEBRATING SPECIAL LIVES
Some holidays remember America's heroes. The first president George Washington, explorer Christopher Columbus, and civil rights leader Martin Luther King, Jr., are all honored with public holidays. America remembers its war dead on Memorial Day, and celebrates the lives of those who served in the armed forces on Veterans' Day. Labor Day is a holiday to honor working people.

Korean War memorial

Valentines made from lace were popular in Victorian times.

NATIONAL HOLIDAYS

New Year's Day January 1

Martin Luther King, Jr.'s Birthday Third Monday in January

Washington's Birthday Third Monday in February

Memorial Day Last Monday in May

Independence Day July 4

Labor Day First Monday in September

Columbus Day Second Monday in October

Veterans' Day November 11

Thanksgiving Day Fourth Thursday in November

Christmas Day December 25

TRADITIONAL HOLIDAYS
Some holidays are celebrated just for fun. On Valentine's Day, people exchange special cards with their loved ones. Mother's Day and Father's Day are set aside to remember parents. On Halloween, children dress up in costumes and go from house to house collecting treats.

Hispanic Americans hold an Easter parade in New York.

RELIGIOUS HOLIDAYS
Each religion has its own holidays. Christians celebrate the birth of Jesus Christ at Christmas, and Christ's resurrection at Easter. For Jewish people, Rosh Hashanah, the new year, and Yom Kippur, a day of reflection and hope, are special holidays. Ramadan is a sacred Muslim holiday, a time for fasting and reflection. Buddhists celebrate events in the life of the Buddha.

New Year revelers celebrate in New York's Times Square.

NEW YEAR
The passing of one year and the start of another is celebrated throughout the world. In Western countries, New Year's Eve is observed on December 31. People celebrate the stroke of midnight with toasts and parties, and many cities hold huge street celebrations. On New Year's Day (January 1), many people draw up lists of resolutions – their wishes and promises for the upcoming year.

Find out more
DECLARATION OF INDEPENDENCE
FESTIVALS AND FEASTS
KING, MARTIN LUTHER, JR.
RELIGIONS
WASHINGTON, GEORGE

HOLOCAUST

IN 1933, ADOLF HITLER'S NAZI PARTY came to power in Germany. The Nazis were deeply anti-Semitic (prejudiced against Jews) and began to attack German Jews. At first they rounded up Jews and sent them to labor or concentration camps, together with other people the Nazis did not like, such as gypsies, homosexuals, and Communists. Jews in German-occupied Europe were forced into ghettos (closed-off areas of a city) or shot. In 1942, the Nazis decided to kill all European Jews in an act of genocide (the deliberate extermination of an entire people). Noone knows how many were murdered in death camps such as Auschwitz and Treblinka, but more than six million Jews lost their lives before the end of World War II. This terrible event in human history is called the Holocaust.

YELLOW STAR
After 1941, Jews over the age of six in German-occupied Europe were required to sew a yellow star onto their clothes. This made it easy to identify them. Jews were also made to wear yellow stars in the camps.

GHETTOS
In Warsaw and other East European cities occupied by the Germans after 1939, Jews were herded into ghettos. These ghettos were isolated from the rest of the city and their inhabitants denied proper food or medical care. In 1943, the Germans attacked the Warsaw ghetto in order to kill everyone inside. The Jews fought back, but by 1945 only about 100 of the original 500,000 inhabitants were still alive.

Oscar Schindler

RESISTANCE
Many Jews resisted the Nazis, by attacking German forces and supplies. Both the Hungarian and Italian governments, although German allies, at first refused to hand over their Jews, while the Swedish diplomat Raoul Wallenberg helped many Jews escape to Sweden in 1944. Most famously, German businessman Oscar Schindler saved about 1,200 Jews from death, by giving them essential war work in his munitions factory.

THE "FINAL SOLUTION"
After the invasion of Poland in 1939 and Russia in 1941, the number of Jews under German rule increased. At a conference at Wannsee, Berlin, in 1942, the Nazis decided on what they called the "Final Solution": to kill all Jews in specially-built extermination camps. These included Auschwitz and Treblinka in Poland, and Belsen, Dachau, and Buchenwald in Germany.

Gates to Auschwitz

COMMEMORATION
After the war, the United Nations tried to repay the Jews for their suffering by creating a Jewish homeland – Israel – in Palestine in 1948. Holocaust museums have been opened in Berlin and elsewhere. Many countries have an official Holocaust commemoration day on January 27 – the anniversary of the liberation of Auschwitz, the first camp to be freed.

Jewish Museum, Berlin

THE HOLOCAUST
1933 Hitler's Nazi Party takes power in Germany.

1935 Nuremberg Laws forbid marriage between Jews and non-Jews.

1937 Jewish businesses confiscated.

1938 The Night of Broken Glass (9-10 November); synagogues, shops, and homes destroyed.

1942 "Final Solution" begins.

1943 Jews in the Warsaw ghetto wiped out.

1945 Concentration camps liberated.

1948 Israel founded.

ANNE FRANK
In order to escape the Nazis, many European Jews went into hiding. Thirteen-year-old Anne Frank and her family hid for two years in the back attic of a house in Amsterdam, Holland. In 1944, they were betrayed and sent to a concentration camp, where Anne died of typhus in 1945, aged 16. While in hiding, Anne kept a diary of daily events and her hopes for the future. Published in 1947, her diary was translated into more than 50 languages.

Find out more
ISRAEL
JUDAISM
WORLD WAR II

HORSEBACK RIDING

HORSES AND HUMANS HAVE TEAMED up for more than 2,000 years, and horses were an essential means of transportation for many centuries. Riding for sport and leisure developed in the 17th century and is still enjoyed today. Horseback riding is a wonderful pastime, particularly for young people, and there are many competitive events. These range from polo through cross-country competitions. Riding is fun, but it also takes skill, practice, and even some courage, especially for jumping. Riders sit on a saddle and put their feet in stirrups, which hang from the saddle. They hold reins attached to a bit in the horse's delicate mouth. The rider controls the horse, urging it into a walk, trot, canter, or turn by using gentle pressure from legs, hands, and body. Riders wear special clothing, including helmets to protect their heads.

STIRRUPS
Around 300 B.C., tribes in Central Asia developed a stirrup to hold a rider's feet. Stirrups made it easier to fight in the saddle. Modern stirrups are usually made of steel.

Rider presses with inside leg to encourage pony to turn.

PONY CLUBS
Many young riders who want to compete in horse events join pony clubs. These organize sporting events and games, which improve riding skills. Pony clubs also teach young riders how to look after their horse and its tack (saddle, bridle, and other equipment), and organize riding camps.

POLO
In this fast and exciting game, two teams, each consisting of four riders, compete against each other on a large field. Players use a mallet to hit a wooden ball through the goal. The team that scores the most goals wins. Polo ponies have to be very agile, and players use their legs to guide them. The game is fast and ponies become tired quickly. Players may change ponies several times during a game.

Pommel

SADDLES
The saddle is an important piece of riding equipment. It provides a comfortable seat for the rider, and helps to protect the horse's spine. A strap, called a girth, runs under the horse's body to keep the saddle in place. The Western saddle has a horn-shaped pommel and wide stirrups.

Western saddle

Walking

Trotting

Cantering

WALKING, TROTTING, AND CANTERING
Horses have three main leg movements, or gaits: walking, trotting, and cantering. A walking horse moves each leg in turn. When trotting, the horse moves its legs in diagonal pairs, and the rhythm is rather jerky. Cantering is much smoother. A rider encourages the horse to move from one pace to another by altering the length of the reins, or giving specific aids, such as applying leg pressure. Riders sit down for all movements, except trotting, when they can either sit or rise to the trot. Horses can also gallop, but only for short distances.

EVENTING
Eventing can last for one, two, or three days, and tests a horse's and rider's agility and endurance. Activities include dressage, which tests obedience, and a gruelling cross-country race. Showjumping over high fences and tricky water jumps is the final event.

Find out more
HORSES,
zebras, and asses
OLYMPIC GAMES
SPORTS

HORSES
ZEBRAS, AND ASSES

FOR THREE THOUSAND YEARS before trains and cars were invented, horses were a fast, efficient method of transportation. These swift, graceful creatures are easy for humans to train. Today there are more than 75 million domestic (tame) horses, divided into more than 100 different breeds. Horses, asses, and zebras belong to the equid family, a group that also includes donkeys and mules. Equids are long-legged mammals with hoofed feet, flowing tails, and a mane on the upper part of the neck. They can run or gallop with great speed. A keen sense of smell, good eyesight, and sharp hearing mean that they are always alert and ready to flee from danger. Horses, asses, and zebras are grazing animals which feed almost entirely on grasses, which they crop with their sharp front teeth.

TEETH
Experts can tell the age of a horse by the number, angle, and size of its teeth, and the way the teeth have worn down with use. Most adult horses have between 40 and 42 teeth.

UNICORN
The unicorn is an imaginary horselike creature. It often appears in legends and folktales as a symbol of purity.

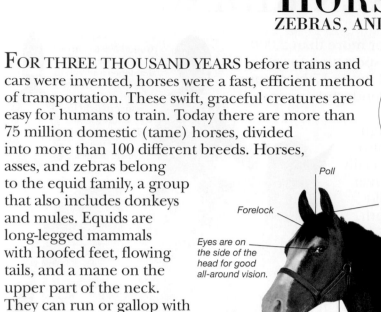

Poll

Forelock

Large ears can swivel to detect which direction a sound comes from.

Eyes are on the side of the head for good all-around vision.

Mane covers upper neck.

Withers

Back

Flank

Croup

Dock

Muzzle

Long jaws and strong cheek muscles for chewing grass

Neck

Chest

Horse uses long, coarse hairs of tail as a fly-swatter and as a social signal.

Elbow

Knee

Heel

Frog

Sole

Horseshoe

Cannon

Bones

Fetlock

Pastern

Hoof

Today's domestic horse

Hyracotherium

HOOVES
Horses walk on the tips of their toes. On each foot is a strong, hard hoof made of bone. There is a pad on the sole of the hoof called the frog. The frog acts like a shock absorber when the horse runs. People also put metal horseshoes on a horse's hooves to protect them on hard roads and rough ground.

THE FIRST HORSES
Hyracotherium, one of the first horses, lived in woodland areas more than 50 million years ago. It was only 2 ft (60 cm) high. Through evolution, horses gradually became larger and began to live in more open grassland areas.

ADULTS AND YOUNG
An adult male horse is called a stallion; an adult female is a mare. Young males are called colts; young females are fillies.

HORSES AND HUMANS
Domestic horses have been trained to do many jobs, from pulling carts to carrying soldiers into battle. Many sports and leisure activities involve horses, such as show jumping, polo, rodeo, flat racing, and steeplechasing. Champion horses are worth millions of dollars, and the first prize at a famous horse race may be thousands of dollars.

In some countries horses and mules are still used instead of cars. They are also used on farms to plow fields, fertilize crops, and pull produce to market.

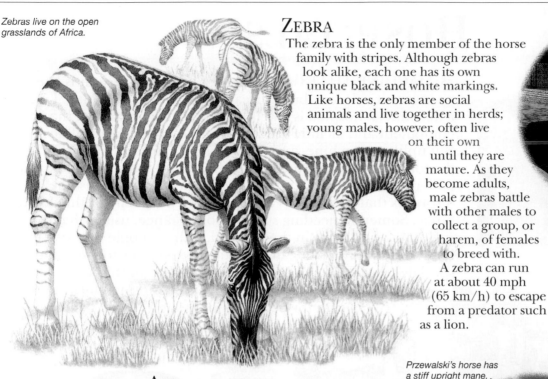

Zebras live on the open grasslands of Africa.

ZEBRA

The zebra is the only member of the horse family with stripes. Although zebras look alike, each one has its own unique black and white markings. Like horses, zebras are social animals and live together in herds; young males, however, often live on their own until they are mature. As they become adults, male zebras battle with other males to collect a group, or harem, of females to breed with. A zebra can run at about 40 mph (65 km/h) to escape from a predator such as a lion.

DONKEY
A donkey is a domesticated ass. Donkeys, together with horses and asses, have been hauling loads for people for thousands of years. They are often called beasts of burden. Another beast of burden, the mule, is the offspring of a female horse and a male donkey.

ASS

There are two kinds of wild ass – the African ass and the Asian ass. The African ass lives in dry, rocky areas of North Africa; the Asian ass is found in Asia. Asses need very little water and survive in the wild by eating tough, spiky grasses. Like other members of the horse family, the female ass has one young at a time, called a foal. The foal can walk a few minutes after birth.

A wild ass and a smaller domesticated ass

Przewalski's horse has a stiff upright mane.

PRZEWALSKI'S HORSE
Also called the Asian horse or "wild horse," Przewalski's horse is closely related to the domestic horse. Herds of these horses once lived on the high plains of Mongolia, in northern Asia. Today there are only a few hundred left in zoos and wildlife parks around the world, although there have been attempts to introduce them back into the wild in Mongolia.

GALLOPING
Horses move at a walk, trot, canter, or gallop, in increasing order of speed. When a horse gallops, all its hooves are off the ground for a split second during each stride. The fastest race horses can gallop at more than 40 mph (65 km/h) over a short distance.

All four hooves lift off the ground in mid-gallop.

Light horses are best equipped for racing.

TYPES OF HORSES
There are three main kinds of horses – draft horses such as Shires; light horses such as Arabian horses; and ponies such as Shetland ponies. Draft horses pull plows, and light horses take part in races.

HOW WE MEASURE HORSES
Horses are measured in hands from the ground to the withers (the highest point of the shoulder). One hand equals 4 in (10 cm). Shire horses are the largest horses. Shetland ponies are among the smallest.

Shire horse may be more than 6 ft (18 hands, 180 cm) at the shoulders and weigh more than 2,500 lb (1,135 kg).

Appaloosa is about 5 ft (15 hands, 150 cm) high.

Shetland pony is 4 ft (12 hands, 120 cm) high.

Find out more
ANIMALS
HORSEBACK RIDING
MAMMALS
TRANSPORTATION, HISTORY OF

HOSPITALS

A MACHINE THAT CAN make sick people well sounds like an inventor's dream, but it already exists – it is a hospital. Like a machine, a hospital is a well-run unit that contains all the equipment and facilities needed to treat every kind of illness. But unlike a machine, a hospital is a human place staffed by doctors, nurses, and operating staff, all of them trained to make patients well. Hospitals are needed because there are some disorders that physicians cannot treat in the home or the doctor's office. Someone needing surgery, for instance, usually has to spend a day or more in the hospital. Other people may visit the hospital for a short time during the day, perhaps to see a skin specialist, or for medical tests such as X rays. In this way, hospitals also provide facilities for diagnosing illness, and care for people who, though not ill, need medical attention, such as women giving birth.

EARLY HOSPITALS
Until the 19th century, hospitals were unhealthy, crowded places where the poor were treated. People with dangerous infectious diseases were also taken to hospitals to prevent them from infecting others.

GENERAL HOSPITALS

Some hospitals treat only certain patients, such as those with mental illnesses; but general hospitals treat patients suffering from all kinds of problems. Most towns and cities have a general hospital. General hospitals contain medical wards, surgical wards for people having operations, maternity wards for women having babies, and children's wards. They also have intensive care units, emergency rooms, and operating rooms.

ACCIDENTS AND EMERGENCIES
People who are injured or suddenly become very ill may be rushed by ambulance to the emergency rooms.

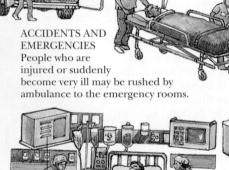

In the intensive care unit the staff uses electronic monitoring devices to keep constant track of the condition of seriously ill patients.

A powerful lamp lights the area where the surgeon operates.

OPERATING ROOM
Surgeons carry out operations in specially equipped rooms where everything is kept very clean to prevent infection.

Nurses carefully monitor the medication that each patient receives.

WARDS
Some patients stay in a ward – a room with several beds. Hospital departments, such as surgery, are also called wards.

NURSING
A nurse is a man or a woman who is trained to care for the ill and injured. Nurses check the condition of their patients, give them medication, and keep them as comfortable as possible.

CHILDREN'S HOSPITALS
Some cities have special hospitals that are only for children. Nurses and doctors who work in children's hospitals are specially trained to care for babies and children. Parents can usually stay with their children throughout the day and, if necessary, can sleep in the hospital at night.

Find out more

DOCTORS
MEDICINE
MEDICINE, HISTORY OF
X RAYS

HOUSES

LEARNING THE ART OF BUILDING enabled our ancestors to escape from the dark caves in which they sheltered from the weather and from predators. Building houses as they went, these first settlers moved to parts of the world where there was no natural shelter. Even in the icy wastes of the Arctic, the Eskimo people learned to use ice to build domed igloos. Most houses, though, consist of walls and a roof, built in a huge variety of styles. Local materials dictate the kind of house that rises in a particular place, but climate is important too. For instance, houses in the mountains of the Alps have steep roofs to shed the heavy layers of snow that fall in the winter. Modern houses are often complex structures, hiding in their walls networks of pipes and cables that supply water and energy and carry away waste. But in central Turkey, some people live in caves like those that provided the first shelter in prehistoric times.

MOBILE HOMES
The horse-drawn wagon which took fairground workers from place to place was the forerunner of today's mobile home.

Mud was one of the first materials to be used for building houses.

HOUSEBOATS
A floating house solves the problem of finding a place to live in an overcrowded city where there is no more room to build. The houseboats are usually permanently moored.

MUD HOUSES
The people of New Mexico traditionally use dried mud to build houses. Because there is little rain, the mud stays hard, and building and repairs are quick and easy. Thick walls and small windows keep out the sun's fierce heat and retain warmth at night.

WOODEN HOUSES
American pioneers built their houses with wood, the best building material on hand. Wooden houses are well suited to cold, forested regions, not only because wood is plentiful but also because it is a good insulator and keeps out the cold.

This kind of houseboat is found in Hong Kong.

The earliest wooden houses were crude log cabins. The walls and roof of this house are made of sawed timber.

APARTMENTS
City and town apartments house hundreds of families on small plots of land, where there is room for just a few low-rise homes. The tallest buildings are made of strong materials such as steel and concrete.

HOUSE OF THE FUTURE
The newest building techniques aim to conserve energy. In the future, people may live in better-insulated homes that need little fuel. The wind will generate electricity, the sun's rays will heat water, and computers will control the windows and heating system.

SHANTYTOWN
Many cities are ringed with shantytowns because people crowd in to the city to seek work but can find nowhere affordable to live. Some build their own homes with any materials they can find. Others remain homeless, sleeping on the streets.

Find out more
ARCHITECTURE
BUILDING
FURNITURE
INUITS

HUMAN BODY

FROM THE MOMENT we are born to the moment we die, our bodies do not stop working for a second. The human body is a complex collection of more than 50 billion living units called cells. There are about 200 different types of cells, including nerve cells, called neurons, and specialized cells called gland cells. Glands produce substances such as hormones and enzymes, which they release into the body for different purposes. Each type of cell in the body does a particular job. Cells that do similar jobs are grouped together to form tissues, such as muscle tissue and nerve tissue. Tissues, in turn, are grouped together to form organs, which are the main separate parts of the body. The lungs, heart, liver, and kidneys are some of the main organs. The organs work together as systems, and each system carries out one major function. For example, the heart, blood vessels, and blood form the circulatory system, which carries oxygen and nutrients around the body and carries away waste products. All the different systems work together, controlled by the brain. The entire body is a living marvel of design.

THE BODY'S ABILITIES
The human body is capable of amazing feats of balance and coordination. Many animals can run faster or jump higher, but our bodies are very adaptable. An extremely complex brain controls the body and gives us the intelligence to use our physical abilities to the best advantage.

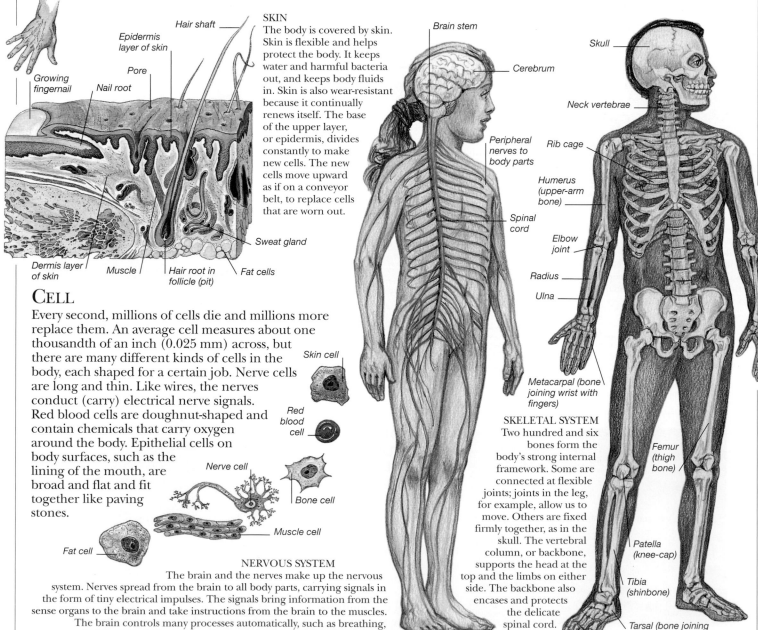

SKIN
The body is covered by skin. Skin is flexible and helps protect the body. It keeps water and harmful bacteria out, and keeps body fluids in. Skin is also wear-resistant because it continually renews itself. The base of the upper layer, or epidermis, divides constantly to make new cells. The new cells move upward as if on a conveyor belt, to replace cells that are worn out.

Hair shaft
Epidermis layer of skin
Pore
Growing fingernail
Nail root
Dermis layer of skin
Muscle
Hair root in follicle (pit)
Fat cells
Sweat gland

CELL

Every second, millions of cells die and millions more replace them. An average cell measures about one thousandth of an inch (0.025 mm) across, but there are many different kinds of cells in the body, each shaped for a certain job. Nerve cells are long and thin. Like wires, the nerves conduct (carry) electrical nerve signals. Red blood cells are doughnut-shaped and contain chemicals that carry oxygen around the body. Epithelial cells on body surfaces, such as the lining of the mouth, are broad and flat and fit together like paving stones.

Skin cell
Red blood cell
Nerve cell
Bone cell
Muscle cell
Fat cell

Brain stem
Cerebrum
Peripheral nerves to body parts
Spinal cord

Skull
Neck vertebrae
Rib cage
Humerus (upper-arm bone)
Elbow joint
Radius
Ulna
Metacarpal (bone joining wrist with fingers)

SKELETAL SYSTEM
Two hundred and six bones form the body's strong internal framework. Some are connected at flexible joints; joints in the leg, for example, allow us to move. Others are fixed firmly together, as in the skull. The vertebral column, or backbone, supports the head at the top and the limbs on either side. The backbone also encases and protects the delicate spinal cord.

Femur (thigh bone)
Patella (knee-cap)
Tibia (shinbone)
Tarsal (bone joining leg and foot)

NERVOUS SYSTEM
The brain and the nerves make up the nervous system. Nerves spread from the brain to all body parts, carrying signals in the form of tiny electrical impulses. The signals bring information from the sense organs to the brain and take instructions from the brain to the muscles. The brain controls many processes automatically, such as breathing, heartbeat, and digestion, without our having to think about them.

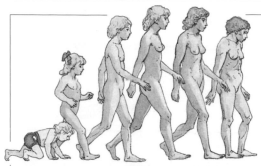

There are several stages of development in everyone's lifetime – from birth through childhood, adolescence, and adulthood, to old age.

GROWTH AND DEVELOPMENT

As the human body grows, it develops many skills. Babies learn to smile, sit up, crawl, walk, and talk. Learning continues at school. On average, the peak of physical abilities is reached between 18 and 25 years of age. Later, more changes occur with age. The skin becomes wrinkled and less elastic, the joints are less flexible, bones become more brittle, muscles are less powerful, and there is some loss of height and graying of hair.

In many older people, decrease in physical strength is offset by the wisdom and knowledge gained from a lifetime of experience.

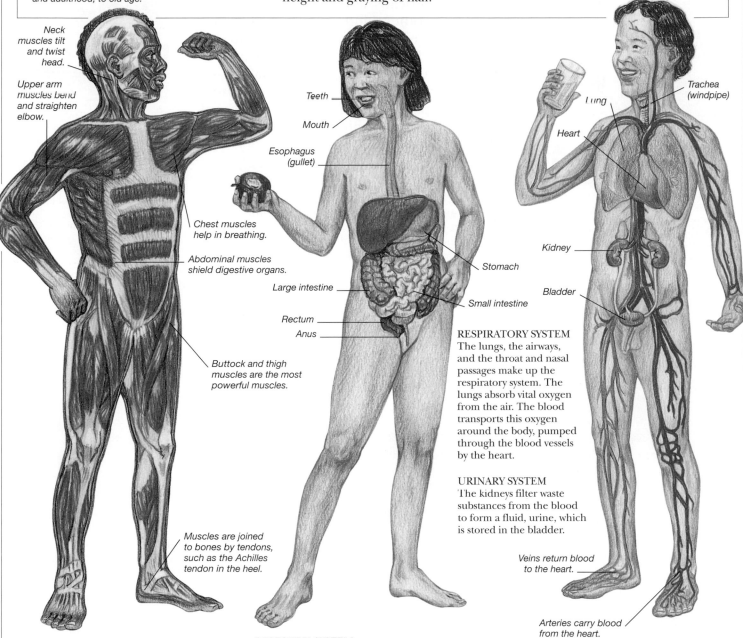

Neck muscles tilt and twist head.

Upper arm muscles bend and straighten elbow.

Chest muscles help in breathing.

Abdominal muscles shield digestive organs.

Buttock and thigh muscles are the most powerful muscles.

Muscles are joined to bones by tendons, such as the Achilles tendon in the heel.

Teeth

Mouth

Esophagus (gullet)

Stomach

Large intestine

Small intestine

Rectum

Anus

Trachea (windpipe)

Lung

Heart

Kidney

Bladder

Veins return blood to the heart.

Arteries carry blood from the heart.

RESPIRATORY SYSTEM
The lungs, the airways, and the throat and nasal passages make up the respiratory system. The lungs absorb vital oxygen from the air. The blood transports this oxygen around the body, pumped through the blood vessels by the heart.

URINARY SYSTEM
The kidneys filter waste substances from the blood to form a fluid, urine, which is stored in the bladder.

MUSCULAR SYSTEM
There are about 650 muscles in the body. Some, such as the arm muscles, can be controlled at will, to pull on the bones of the skeleton and move the body. Others, such as the muscles of the heart and intestine, work automatically.

DIGESTIVE SYSTEM
The mouth, esophagus, stomach, and intestines are part of the digestive system. These organs work together to break down food into particles that are small enough to pass through the lining of the intestine and into the blood. The mouth and teeth chop and chew food, and the stomach churns it with powerful digestive chemicals. The liver is the main organ for converting absorbed nutrients into forms more suitable for use by the various organs. The large intestine deals with wastes and leftover food.

Find out more

BRAIN AND NERVES
EARS
EYES
HEART AND BLOOD
LUNGS AND BREATHING
REPRODUCTION
SKELETONS
TEETH

HUMAN RIGHTS

MOST OF US BELIEVE that we have the right to be treated fairly and equally within society, regardless of our race, sex, religion, or social group. This equal treatment includes the right to vote, to work, and to be educated. When these rights are protected by law, they are called legal or civic rights. In some countries, they are spelled out in a constitution. However, throughout history, many groups, including African-Americans, black South Africans, Native Americans, and women, have not been considered equal to others, and have had few, if any, civil or human rights. This kind of targeted mistreatment is called discrimination. In the 20th century, many different groups, including blacks, homosexuals, women, and people with disabilities, fought long and sometimes bitter campaigns to achieve their rights and obtain equal treatment within society, and these struggles continue today.

MOHANDAS GANDHI
Human rights activists – those who fight for civil rights – use peaceful methods. They unite and mobilize people. In 1915, Mohandas Gandhi (1869-1948) began to lead the struggle against British rule in India. Using nonviolent civil disobedience, Gandhi's fasts and marches led to India's independence from British rule in 1947.

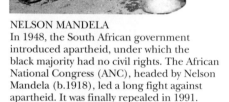

NELSON MANDELA
In 1948, the South African government introduced apartheid, under which the black majority had no civil rights. The African National Congress (ANC), headed by Nelson Mandela (b.1918), led a long fight against apartheid. It was finally repealed in 1991.

AFRICAN-AMERICAN RIGHTS

Under the US Constitution, African-Americans are guaranteed full citizenship, including the right to vote. But in the 1890s, laws passed in the southern states removed these rights, reducing African-Americans to second-class citizens, and introducing racial segregation (separation). Under the leadership of Martin Luther King, Jr. (1929-68), a civil rights movement emerged. It used nonviolent methods, such as sit-ins (see left), where African-Americans peacefully occupied segregated public places. Finally, Congress passed the Civil Rights Act in 1964 and the Voting Rights Act in 1965. These laws outlawed discrimination on the grounds of race, color, or religion in schooling, voting, and employment.

AMNESTY INTERNATIONAL

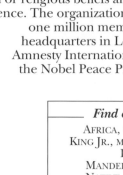

A worldwide human rights organization, Amnesty International was founded in 1961 following a legal appeal by a British lawyer, Peter Benenson, after he read about two Portuguese students who were imprisoned for raising their glasses in a toast to freedom. Amnesty works to obtain prompt and fair trials for all prisoners, to end torture and executions, and to secure the release of people imprisoned solely for their political or religious beliefs and who have not used or advocated violence. The organization has more than one million members and has its headquarters in London. In 1977, Amnesty International was awarded the Nobel Peace Prize for its work.

AMERICAN INDIAN MOVEMENT
Since the 1960s, Native Americans have become more forceful in demanding equal rights. In 1968, the American Indian Movement (AIM) formed to fight for civil rights and improved conditions on reservations. A militant organization, AIM conducted a number of high-profile protests. In 1973, they occupied Wounded Knee in South Dakota, the site of a massacre of Sioux people in 1890. Federal marshals surrounded the protestors, and a siege began in which two AIM members were killed. Since then, some Native Americans have won land rights, but discrimination still continues today.

IMMIGRATION

FROM THE ARRIVAL OF THE FIRST COLONISTS in the 1600s, the United States has been a nation of immigrants. People from all over the world have come to the US, contributing to its rich ethnic heritage. Some hoped to escape poverty, war, or discrimination in their native lands, while others came to find adventure, a fresh start, and new opportunities. At first, the United States encouraged immigration – there were roads and railroads to be built, factories to run, and jobs to fill as the nation flourished. As the numbers of immigrants began to rise dramatically, however, pressure grew to limit the flow of newcomers and the first immigration laws were enacted.

Reenacting a Pilgrim harvest at Plymouth Rock, MA

THE GREAT WAVE

From the early 1900s to the Great Depression of the 1930s, a huge wave of immigrants – more than 30 million people – poured into the United States from every part of the world. Many came from Europe, where economic troubles, political changes, and restrictive religious laws drove them to seek new homes and new lives elsewhere.

THE FIRST IMMIGRANTS

Most of the early colonists who settled in what became the United States came from England in the 17th and 18th centuries. Some of these early immigrants could not afford the travel costs and came as indentured servants. These people agreed to work for a fixed number of years to pay for their passage.

CHINESE IMMIGRATION

In the mid-1800s, many Chinese people crossed the Pacific to California in search of gold. They were met with violent anti-Chinese protests, unfair taxes, and laws to stop further immigration. However, labor shortages on the railroads led American companies to hire Chinese workers, who helped build the country's first transcontinental railroad line in 1869.

Chinese immigrants work on the railroad in California.

Eastern European immigrants seek a new life in the United States, 1900.

FLEEING FAMINE AND POVERTY

More than seven million people entered the US from 1820 to 1870, mostly from northern and western Europe. About a third were Irish, seeking escape from a famine brought on by potato crop failures in the 1840s. Another third were from Germany, where political unrest forced thousands to flee. While most new immigrants settled on the East Coast, many Germans traveled to the rich farmlands in the middle of the country.

RELIGIOUS FREEDOM

Many people came to America seeking the freedom to practice their chosen religion, a right guaranteed by the first amendment to the Constitution. In colonial times, religious groups such as the Quakers and the Puritans fled from harsh treatment in England and founded settlements in the New World. More than two and a half million Jews from Eastern Europe emigrated to the United States between 1880 and 1920, to escape ethnic and religious persecution.

An immigrant family arrives in New York in 1910.

ELLIS ISLAND

Most immigrants who came to the United States during the mass migration of the early 1900s entered the country via New York City, the most popular destination for steamship companies. Ellis Island, just off the southern tip of Manhattan, near the Statue of Liberty, was the chief immigration station for the US from 1892 to 1954. More than 12 million immigrants passed through its doors. Today, Ellis Island is a museum celebrating the United States' immigrant heritage.

IMMIGRATION LIMITS
By 1910, most immigrants had come from Southern and Eastern Europe. Their large numbers threatened some native-born Americans. Consequently, Congress passed the first quota laws limiting the number of people allowed into the country.

PRESERVING HERITAGE
Many immigrants choose to settle in communities made up of people from their native lands. Most American cities contain ethnic neighborhoods, where residents continue to speak their native language as well as English. These neighborhoods have ethnic shops, places of worship, and businesses. They are also the site of many traditional festivals.

El Salvadorian girls celebrate Central American Pride Day in Chicago.

ILLEGAL IMMIGRANTS
In 1924, the Border Patrol was established to prevent people from crossing into the country without permission. Agents keep watch on the 8,000-mile (13,000 km) long US border. The 1996 Immigration Act doubled the number of Border Patrol agents and denied social services to illegal immigrants. People still risk their lives to enter the country, especially through Mexico (above). Millions of illegal aliens, or noncitizens, live in the US today.

NEW IMMIGRANTS
The United States government limits the number of new immigrants allowed each year. In 1990, immigration laws were revised to favor relatives of American citizens, workers with skills needed in the United States, and refugees from war zones. A lottery was established for permanent resident visas, also known as green cards. The largest groups of immigrants to the US today are from Latin America and Asia.

BECOMING A CITIZEN
Although the Constitution gives rights to noncitizens, only citizens are able to vote in elections and hold US passports. An immigrant who wants to become a citizen of the United States must successfully pass a test on American history, answer written questions in English, and take an oath of allegiance to the United States.

Find out more

HISPANIC AMERICANS
STATUE OF LIBERTY
UNITED STATES, HISTORY OF

INCAS

IN THE 12TH CENTURY, a tribe of Native Americans moved down from the Andes Mountains of South America to settle in the fertile Cuzco Valley. By the end of the 15th century they had conquered a huge territory of 440,000 sq miles (1,140,000 sq km) containing more than 10 million people. The Incas won this land with their powerful army and then controlled it with a remarkable system of communications. Inca engineers built a network of paved roads that crisscrossed the empire. Relays of imperial messengers ran along these roads (there were no horses or wheeled vehicles), traveling 150 miles (250 km) a day as they took messages to and from the capital city of Cuzco. At the head of the empire was the chief Inca, who was worshiped as a god and who held absolute power over all his subjects. But in 1525 the chief Inca, Huayna Capac, died, and civil war broke out between two rivals for his throne. In 1532 a small force of Spanish soldiers arrived in the country and found it in disarray. They quickly overwhelmed the Incan army, and by 1533 the Inca empire was completely under Spanish rule.

South America

Inca empire

INCA EMPIRE
In 1525, at its height, the Inca empire stretched for more than 2,000 miles (3,200 km) along the Pacific coast of South America, including ruling over much of present-day Ecuador, Peru, Bolivia, and Chile.

MACHU PICCHU
Covering an area of 5 sq miles (13 sq km), the fortress city of Machu Picchu was built on a series of terraces carved into the side of a mountain more than 7,500 ft (2,280 m) above sea level.

Llamas have been used as pack animals for 4,000 years.

An Inca woman weaving an elaborately designed piece of cloth.

QUIPU
The Incas did not have a written language. Instead, they used quipus – lengths of knotted string – to record every aspect of their daily life. Historic events, laws, gold reserves, population statistics, and other items of information were all stored accurately in this way.

The Incas were expert goldsmiths and often placed gold figurines (right) in their graves. Much of the Incan gold was melted down by Spanish invaders.

Color of string, number of knots, and length of string indicated what was recorded on the quipu.

WEAVING
The Incas wove lengths of beautiful, colorful cloth with elaborate patterns. The wool they used came from the mountain animals – llamas, alpacas, and vicunas – that the Incas kept on their farms. Many of their designs depicted jaguars and pumas.

TERRACE FARMING
The Incas were expert at farming every available piece of fertile land in their mountainous empire. They built terraces along the steep hillsides and watered them with mountain streams so that crops could be grown and animals kept to feed all the people who lived in the cities.

Find out more
CAMELS AND LLAMAS
CONQUISTADORS
SOUTH AMERICA, HISTORY OF

INDIA
AND SUBCONTINENT

A TRAVELER IN INDIA would need to speak more than 1,000 languages to understand conversations in every part of the country. Hindi and English are the two official languages, and 14 other languages are spoken nationwide. Many people, however, speak a local language as well. The majority of Indians are Hindu in religion, but there are many Muslims, Sikhs, Christians, and Buddhists. Geographically, the country is very varied, too. The north is mountainous, and in the center the Ganges river waters a rich plain of productive farmland. In the south a hot and fertile coastal region surrounds a dry inland plateau. With a population of more than one billion, India is the second most populated country in the world (China is the first). About 70 percent of the people live in small, often very poor villages, and work on the land. The rest live in big cities, where some work in modern factories and offices. Recent advances in farming have made the land more productive, and after many years of famine, India can now feed itself.

India, Pakistan, Nepal, Bhutan, Bangladesh, and Sri Lanka occupy the Indian subcontinent. China is to the north, and to the east lie the jungles of Southeast Asia. The Indian Ocean washes the southern shores; the mountains and deserts of Iran and Afghanistan enclose the subcontinent on the west.

PRINTING BLOCKS
Traditional wooden printing blocks are still used in the production of colorful textiles.

TEA
In 1824, tea plants were discovered in the hills along the frontier between Burma and the Indian state of Assam. The British first introduced tea culture to India in 1836 and Sri Lanka in 1867, and today most of the world's tea comes from the Indian Subcontinent. The low tea bushes grow well on the sheltered, well-drained foothills of the Himalayas. Only the leaves near the tip of the plant are picked; they are then dried, rolled, and heated to produce the final product. Tea also grows in southern India and Sri Lanka.

Picking tea is laborious and often painful work. Most tea pickers are women. They spend long days picking the crop by hand.

TEXTILES
The production of textiles, carpets, and clothing is one of the major industries in India. Millions of people work at spinning, weaving, and finishing a wide range of cotton and other goods, often printed with designs that have been in use for centuries. Many of these products are exported. There are large factories, but some people also work in their own homes.

MODERN INDIA
India is one of the most industrialized countries in Asia, with a wide range of engineering, electronic, and manufacturing industries. Its railroad system is one of the world's biggest. Traditional costumes and ways of life, however, coexist with modern industries.

KARAKORAM MOUNTAINS
A high mountain range separates the Indian Subcontinent from China to the north. Most of the range is part of the Himalayas. At its western end, the Himalayas continue as the Karakoram range, which forms Pakistan's northern border. Few people have their homes in these mountainous regions. Nevertheless, the mountains have a great influence on people living thousands of miles away. Most of the rivers that irrigate the fertile plains of the Indian Subcontinent begin in the Himalayas.

PAKISTAN

Pakistan was formed in 1947, when the end of British rule in India led to the creation of two separate states; the predominantly Hindu India, and the predominantly Muslim Pakistan. Pakistan originally included what is now Bangladesh, then known as East Pakistan. Bangladesh became independent in 1971 after a revolt against rule from West Pakistan (present-day Pakistan). India and Pakistan are in bitter conflict over the area at Pakistan's northeastern border known as Kashmir; both India and Pakistan consider the region to be a part of their country. Pakistan's other major concern at present is overpopulation; the country's resources are relatively small in comparison to the size of its population.

Expansion of Mumbai is confined by its island location, so the city has one of the highest population densities in the world.

SHERPAS

The Sherpa people (right) of Nepal are famed for their mountaineering skills. They often act as guides for climbers and hikers on expeditions in the Nepalese Himalayas.

MUMBAI

One of India's largest cities is Mumbai, which has a population of more than eight million. The city is the capital of the western state of Maharashtra, and is a major port for western commerce. Mumbai is built on an island, and has a superb natural harbor to the east. Cotton is grown nearby, and Mumbai is the largest cotton textile center in the country. One half of the people living in Mumbai work in the textile industry.

KERALA

The state of Kerala in southwest India borders the Arabian Sea. The eastern part of the state is hilly, but much of the land area is a flat plain. Kerala is one of the most densely populated states in India. Fishing is important for the local economy. Near the coast, the people of Kerala grow crops of cashew nuts, coconuts, and rice, and there are tea, rubber, coffee, and pepper plantations to the east. Although the government has encouraged modern farming techniques, traditional methods of agriculture and transportation are common, such as the canoe in the picture (left). Forestry is also important in Kerala. In the mountains there are forests of teak, ebony, and rosewood, as well as a wide variety of wildlife.

BHUTAN

Most people in Bhutan are descendants of Tibetans who migrated to the area centuries ago. Like their neighbors, they are predominantly Buddhist, and look on the Dalai Lama as their spiritual leader. The dense forests and high mountains that cover the country are home to many animals native to the Indian Subcontinent, such as tigers (left), monkeys, and elephants. In an effort to protect Bhutan's culture and natural environment the government of Bhutan does not allow many tourists to enter the country.

INDIAN PEOPLE

India has one of the most diverse populations in the world. Throughout history, one race after another has settled in India, each bringing its own culture, customs, and languages. The races often intermarried, but not all aspects of society became mixed and diluted: many groups clung to their traditions. For instance, there is no one Indian language, and people in different parts of the country often have their own unique local language.

BOLLYWOOD

The Indian film industry produces even more films than Hollywood. About 800 full-length feature films are shot each year, mainly in Mumbai, nicknamed "Bollywood." Chennai (Madras) is also a center of the film industry.

A still from a film by Indian film director, Satyajit Ray. His work is shown and admired worldwide.

MUSIC

Traditional Indian music is very complex, with a wide range of rhythms. Melodies are based on ragas – a fixed series of notes the performer must play as a basis for improvising (making up the tune). Bhangra – a new music combining traditional Indian music from Punjab with western rock music – has become popular among young people in recent years.

SACRED WATERS

From its source in the Himalayas, the Ganges river (below) flows eastward across India, then turns south. The river's 1,560-mile (2,510-km) course takes it through Bangladesh to reach the sea in the Bay of Bengal. Hindus consider the river to be sacred. They believe that bathing in its waters washes away sins and cures illness. Indians rely on the waters of the Ganges for the irrigation of agricultural land.

Cows are sacred to Hindus in India and must not be harmed.

DANCE

Traditional Indian dances have a variety of forms and rhythms. They differ according to region, occupation, and caste.

DELHI

The ancient city of Delhi lies on the hot plains of northern India. In 1638 it became the capital city of the Indian Mogul empire. When the British took control of India in the 1800s, they moved the capital to Kolkata (Calcutta), in the east of the country. In 1912, the British began to build a new city in the outskirts of Delhi from where they could govern their vast Indian empire. New Delhi has been the nation's capital since India gained independence in 1947.

The Taj Mahal is built of the finest white marble and is a supreme example of Islamic architecture.

TAJ MAHAL

The Taj Mahal (left), at Agra in northern India, was built in 1631 by Shah Jahan, the Mogul emperor of India. It was constructed as a tomb and memorial for his beloved wife, Mumtaz Mahal. She was the mother of 14 children. The Taj Mahal is built of white marble and inlaid with semiprecious stones.

Find out more

ASIA
BUDDHISM
HINDUISM
INDIA, HISTORY OF
SOUTHEAST ASIA
SOUTHEAST ASIA, HISTORY OF

Volcano | Mountain | Ancient monument | Capital city | Large city/town | Small city/town

STATISTICS
Area: 1,269,338 sq miles (3,287,590 sq km)
Population: 1,070,000,000
Capital: New Delhi
Languages: Hindi, Urdu, Bengali, Marathi, Telugu, Tamil, Bihari, Gujarata, Kanarese
Religions: Hindu, Muslim, Christian, Sikh, Buddhist
Currency: Rupee
Main occupations: Agriculture, industry
Main exports: Rice, iron ore, cut diamonds, coal
Main imports: Petroleum, coal, steel

AMRITSAR
The city of Amritsar is in Punjab in northwest India. It is the most important religious center for the Sikhs, who live mainly in northern India. The town surrounds a sacred pool, and on a small island in the pool stands the Golden Temple (above). In 1984 Sikhs fighting for an independent Sikh state in the area occupied the temple, and the government sent in troops to remove them.

SCALE BAR
0 — 250 — 500 km
0 — 250 — 500 miles

NATURAL BORDER
A massive, towering wall of snow-capped mountains stretches in an arc between the Indian Subcontinent and the rest of continental Asia.

BANGLADESH
Bangladesh lies on the Ganges delta, where the Ganges, Brahmaputra, and Meghna rivers split up into dozens of smaller rivers before flowing into the Bay of Bengal. The area is prone to monsoons, which are a type of tropical storm, and floods are very common throughout most of the country. Most people live in wooden houses raised on stilts above the flood level, to keep their homes from being washed away in severe monsoons.

BANGLADESH
Area: 55,598 sq miles (143,998 sq km)
Population: 147,000,000
Capital: Dhaka

BHUTAN
Area: 18,147 sq miles (47,000 sq km)
Population: 2,300,000
Capital: Thimphu

NEPAL
Area: 54,363 sq miles (140,800 sq km)
Population: 25,200,000
Capital: Kathmandu

PAKISTAN
Area: 307,374 sq miles (796,100 sq km)
Population: 154,800,000
Capital: Islamabad

SRI LANKA
Area: 25,332 sq miles (65,610 sq km)
Population: 19,100,000
Capital: Colombo

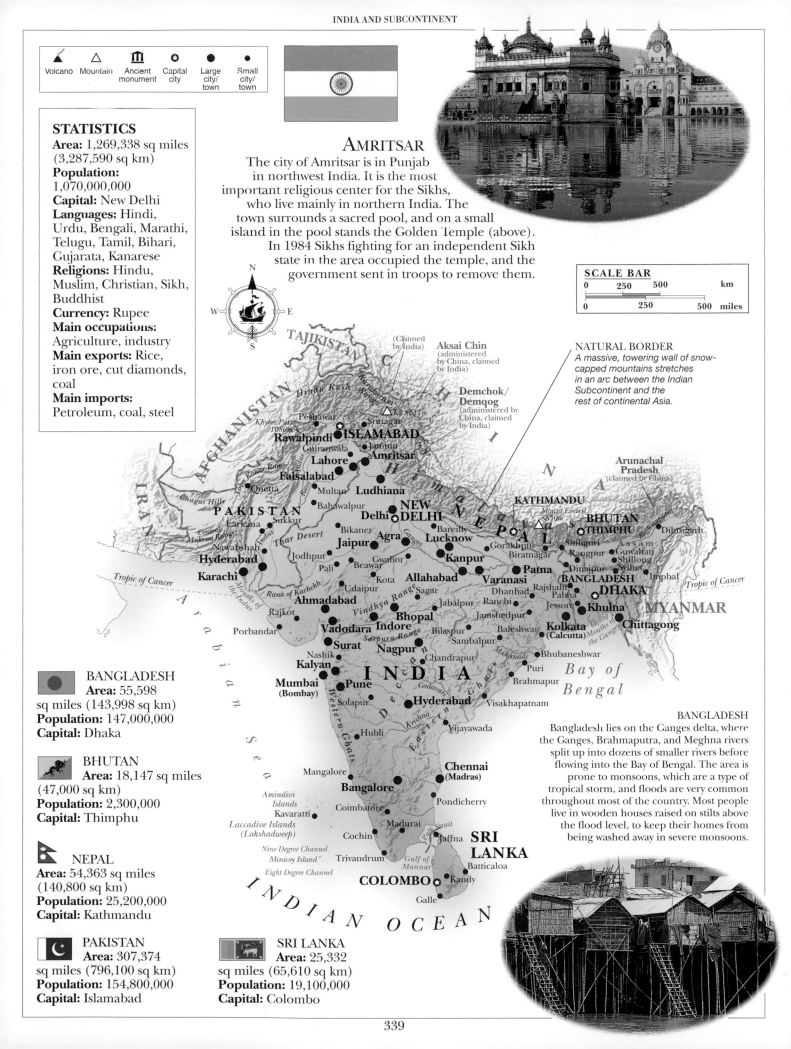

HISTORY OF
INDIA

INDUS VALLEY CIVILIZATION
The peoples of the Indus Valley used the water from the Indus River to enrich their soil. They built Mohenjo-Daro and Harappa, the world's first cities. Craftsworkers created elegant and beautiful figures of people, animals, and gods, such as this seal in the form of a bull.

NEARLY 5,000 YEARS AGO, a civilization grew up around the Indus River in southern Asia. The peoples of this region built the world's first cities. Since that time India has been the birthplace of two great religions, Hinduism and Buddhism. Over the centuries, India has had many rulers and has been invaded many times. The first invaders were the Aryans, from the northwest. At the time, India consisted of several city-states, often in conflict. The Maurya dynasty, or ruling family, finally emerged around 322 B.C., and under one of its emperors, Asoka, India entered a period of peace. The Gupta dynasty came next, followed by the Moguls, who created a splendid civilization. But differences between various religious groups of Muslims, Sikhs, and Hindus weakened India. Between the 17th and 18th centuries, the British East India Company took control of much of the country; a century later the British government took over India. Many Indian people wanted independence. In 1947 India gained freedom from Britain, but was plunged into conflict between Muslims and Hindus. British and Indian leaders divided the country into two nations: India and Pakistan.

GUPTA EMPIRE
A family of wealthy land owners, the Guptas, founded their empire in A.D. 320, under Chandra Gupta I. Within a century the empire covered much of northern and eastern India. A golden age of cultural life began. The Guptas devised the decimal system of counting and writing numbers that we still use today. The empire collapsed in the seventh century after tribes invaded from Central Asia.

EAST INDIA COMPANY
In 1600, the British founded the East India Company to trade with India. By 1765, the company was governing parts of India itself, but in 1858 the British government took over. The company ceased to exist in 1873. The drawing on the right shows an Englishman traveling by Indian elephant.

MOGUL EMPIRE
In 1526, Babur, the Mogul ruler arrived from central Asia and established his rule on an administratively weak India. The Moguls were Muslims, and they built some of the most magnificent mosques (Muslim places of worship) and palaces in the world. In 1858, the Mogul empire collapsed and the British took control of almost all the landmass.

BRITISH RAJ

From the early 16th century, Portugal, France, Britain, and the Netherlands all tried to take control of India. The British were the most successful. By the mid-1800s, they ruled the entire Indian subcontinent. In 1876 the British queen, Victoria, became empress of India. The government of India was called the British Raj (from an Indian word meaning "rule"). The Raj employed a civil service to administer the country from the capital city of New Delhi, which was completed in 1931.

MOHANDAS GANDHI

The leader of the movement for Indian independence from British rule was Mohandas Gandhi (1869-1948). Called the Mahatma, meaning "great soul," Gandhi attempted to unite all of India's different religions and peoples. He stressed the importance of *satyagraha*, or non-violent resistance to British rule.

NEHRU FAMILY

The first prime minister of India was Jawaharlal Nehru (1889-1964; above). Two years after his death, his daughter, Indira Gandhi (right), became prime minister. She remained India's leader almost continuously until she was assassinated in 1984, when her son Rajiv succeeded her. In 1989, he lost majority in the Parliament; in 1991 he too was assassinated.

PAKISTAN AND BANGLADESH

When the British ruled the country most Indians were Hindus, but there were Muslims also. There was much conflict between Hindus and Muslims. In 1947, when India achieved independence, the British partitioned (divided) India.

A train from Pakistan carries terrified Hindu refugees.

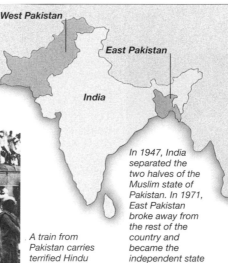

West Pakistan

East Pakistan

India

In 1947, India separated the two halves of the Muslim state of Pakistan. In 1971, East Pakistan broke away from the rest of the country and became the independent state of Bangladesh.

Find out more

BUDDHISM
HINDUISM
INDIA
INDUS VALLEY CIVILIZATION
SOUTHEAST ASIA, HISTORY OF

INDIAN OCEAN

MORE THAN ONE BILLION PEOPLE live in the countries that fringe the Indian Ocean and on some of the 5,000 islands that are scattered across its surface. The world's third-largest ocean provides a major link between Europe and Asia. The monsoon winds, which bring heavy rainfall to many of the countries surrounding the ocean, also have an impact on the currents, which reverse direction completely between March and August. Early navigators used the winds and currents to carry them from Arabia to southern India and Indonesia, bringing the Islamic religion and culture with them. Malays and Indonesians took the journey westward, settling in Madagascar. Most of the islands of the Indian Ocean are small and uninhabited. However, many tourists are drawn to their beautiful palm-fringed beaches, and in some places tourism is beginning to supplement traditional ways of life based on fishing and farming.

The Indian Ocean is bounded by Africa to the west, India and Australia to the east, and Asia to the north. In the south, it merges with the Antarctic Ocean. In the north, the Suez Canal gives access, via the Red Sea, to the Mediterranean.

MONSOON
The lands around the Indian Ocean are dependent on monsoon rainfall. Monsoons are seasonal winds, blowing from the southwest in summer and northeast in winter, that bring torrential downpours. Very heavy monsoon rains swell rivers, causing disastrous flooding often accompanied by diseases such as cholera. The Bay of Bengal is especially vulnerable to flooding.

SEYCHELLES
The island republic of the Seychelles consists of 40 scattered mountainous islands. These are surrounded by over 70 coral islands, which are low-lying and sparsely populated. The main islands are outstandingly beautiful; their hillsides are blanketed with tropical vegetation, fringed by silvery-white beaches. Temperatures are constant throughout the year, reaching a daytime high of 86° F (30° C). The Seychelles attract year-round visitors from the northern hemisphere.

STILT FISHERMEN
There are fewer areas of shallow water, where fish breed, in the Indian Ocean than in the Pacific or the Atlantic. For this reason large-scale fishing, using trawlers and factory ships, has not developed in the region. Most fishing takes place on a local basis, near island coastlines. Tuna is the most valuable catch. In Sri Lanka, fishermen – precariously perched on stilts – use poles and lines to catch their fish.

MADAGASCAN VILLAGE
Most Madagascans are descendants of Malays and Indonesians who crossed the Indian Ocean in the 7th century A.D. These villagers come from the southeastern coast. The east coast is densely populated and poor. Most of Madagascar's ruling class come from the central plateau.

MADAGASCAR
The world's fourth-largest island lies off Africa's eastern coast. Most of the population is concentrated in the narrow strip of fertile land along the east coast, which has a humid, tropical climate. Farming dominates the economy. Rice and cassava are the main crops, while coffee and vanilla are grown for export. Poultry, sheep, pigs, and goats are all kept on a small scale. The government's attempts to modernize livestock farming have not been successful.

Find out more
AFRICA
ASIA
CORALS
OCEANS AND SEAS
SOUTHEAST ASIA

CHRISTMAS ISLAND
Area: 52 sq miles (134.6 sq km)
Status: Australian external territory
Claimed: 1958
Population: 1,300
Capital: Flying Fish Cove

 COMOROS
Area: 861 sq miles (2,230 sq km)
Population: 768,000
Capital: Moroni
Languages: Arabic, Comoran, French
Religions: Muslim, Roman Catholic
Currency: Comoros franc

 MADAGASCAR
Area: 226,660 sq miles (587,040 sq km)
Population: 17,400,000
Capital: Antananarivo
Languages: Malagasy, French
Religions: Traditional beliefs, Christian, Muslim
Currency: Malagasy franc

 MALDIVES
Area: 116 sq miles (300 sq km)
Population: 318,000
Capital: Male'
Languages: Dhivehi (Maldivian)
Religions: Sunni Muslim
Currency: Rufiyaa

 MAURITIUS
Area: 927 sq miles (2,400 sq km)
Population: 1,200,000
Capital: Port Louis
Languages: English, French, French Creole
Religions: Hindu, Roman Catholic
Currency: Mauritian rupee

RÉUNION
Area: 972 sq miles (2,517 sq km)
Status: French overseas department
Claimed: 1649
Population: 777,000
Capital: Saint-Denis

 SEYCHELLES
Area: 176 sq miles (455 sq km)
Population: 80,500
Capital: Victoria
Languages: English, French, French Creole
Religions: Roman Catholic
Currency: Seychelles rupee

Volcano Mountain Ancient monument Capital city Large city/town Small city/town

SCALE BAR
0 · 1000 · 2000 · km
0 · 1000 · 2000 · miles

ARAB DHOW
Dhows are Arab trading boats made of teak or coconut planks sewn together with twine. They are lateen-rigged, which means that they have one, or sometimes two, triangular sails. Dhows are fast and maneuverable. They were a vital tool in the Arab exploration of the Indian Ocean from the 8th century A.D. Using the monsoon winds, Arab merchants soon gained control of Indian Ocean trade and spread Islam as far as Indonesia.

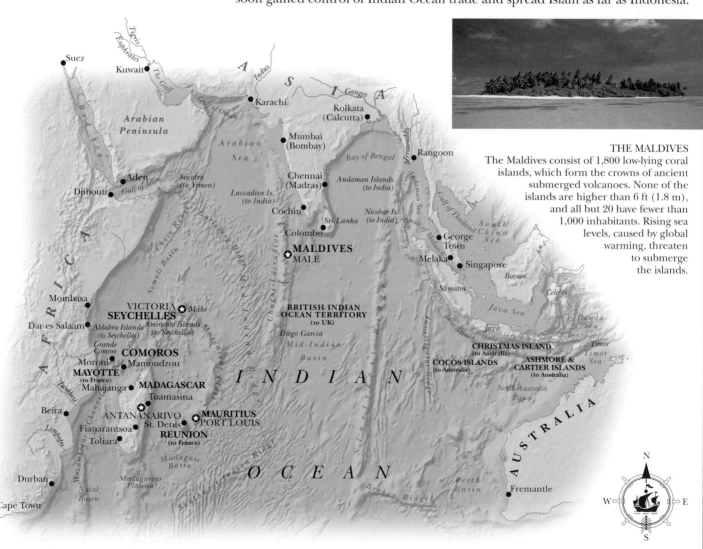

THE MALDIVES
The Maldives consist of 1,800 low-lying coral islands, which form the crowns of ancient submerged volcanoes. None of the islands are higher than 6 ft (1.8 m), and all but 20 have fewer than 1,000 inhabitants. Rising sea levels, caused by global warming, threaten to submerge the islands.

INDUSTRIAL REVOLUTION

THE WORLD WE LIVE IN TODAY, with its factories and huge cities, began less than 300 years ago in Britain, then spread to Europe and the United States. Beginning in about 1760, great changes took place that altered people's lives and methods of work forever, changes that are known today as the Industrial Revolution. Machines powered by water and, later, steam were invented to produce cloth and other goods more quickly. It took many workers to run these big machines, so poor people moved from the country into the new industrial towns to be near the factories. There were more jobs and higher wages in the cities, but life was often miserable. Although the Factory Act in 1833 banned young children in Britain from working in factories, there were no laws to control how long people worked each day, or to make sure the machines were safe.

FACTORY OWNERS
Robert Owen (1771-1858) was a generous British factory owner who tried to improve working conditions. Many other owners grew rich by demanding long hours of work for low wages.

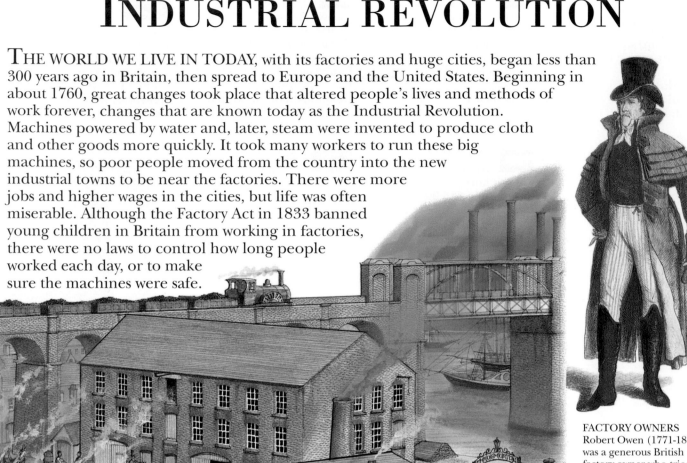

Factory workers lived in overcrowded houses, which often became slums.

Barges on new canals carried factory goods from one town to another.

Chimneys from the new factories created a lot of smoke. This made the towns dirty and polluted.

NEW TOWNS
Factory towns were built as fast and as cheaply as possible. Large families were crowded into tiny houses, and the water supply was often polluted. Diseases spread rapidly, and many people died young.

NEW TECHNOLOGY
Stronger metals were needed to make machines, so cast iron and steel were developed. Steam to drive the new engines was made by burning coal to boil water. Coal mines were driven deep into the ground. Cotton cloth was the first product to be made completely by machine. The new goods were produced in large numbers so they were cheap to buy.

Cotton replaced wool as the main material for making clothes.

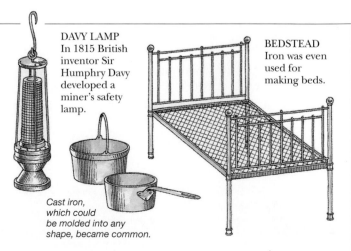

DAVY LAMP
In 1815 British inventor Sir Humphry Davy developed a miner's safety lamp.

Cast iron, which could be molded into any shape, became common.

BEDSTEAD
Iron was even used for making beds.

INDUSTRIAL REVOLUTION

1708 Englishman Abraham Darby invents coke smelting of iron.

1733 John Kay, of England, develops "flying shuttle," which mechanizes weaving.

1760 Start of Industrial Revolution, Britain.

1765 James Hargreaves, of England, invents "spinning jenny." It increases output of spun cotton. Scotsman James Watt develops steam engine, which is used to drive machinery in cotton industry.

1769 Richard Arkwright's water frame used to spin strong thread. Speeds up production; early beginning of Factory Age in England.

1779 English weaver Samuel Crompton develops spinning "mule," which spins many threads at once.

1784 Henry Cort, England, develops puddling furnace and rolling mill. Produces high quality iron.

1789 First steam-powered spinning loom, England. Speeds up textile production.

1793 Eli Whitney's cotton gin mechanizes cotton production in the US.

1804 Englishman Richard Trevithick builds first railroad locomotive.

1825 First public railroad from Stockton to Darlington, England.

1828 Development of hot-blast smelting furnace in England.

1842 Mines Act in Britain bans women and children from working underground.

1851 Great Exhibition in London displays new industrial products and techniques.

1856 Bessemer converter developed in England. Changes pig iron into steel.

1870 Industrialization established in Britain, Germany, and United States.

MILLS

The first factories were water-driven cotton mills which produced cloth. They were noisy, dangerous places to work in. Mill owners employed many women and children because they could pay them lower wages than men.

STEAM HAMMER

Unlike humans, steam-powered machines could work tirelessly, turning out vast quantities of goods. This steam hammer, invented in 1839, could hammer iron forgings with tremendous power and great accuracy.

The Clifton suspension bridge, Avon

BRUNEL

Isambard Kingdom Brunel (1806-59) was probably the greatest engineer of the Industrial Revolution. His most famous bridge was the Clifton suspension bridge across the Avon Gorge. He also designed and built the Great Western Railway and the *Great Britain*, which was the first large steamship with an iron hull and a screw propeller.

CO-OPS AND UNIONS

Working people fought to improve their conditions. Some set up labor unions to fight for shorter hours and better pay. Others created co-op stores to provide wholesome food at reasonable prices. These stores later grew into a cooperative movement.

Find out more

FACTORIES
FARMING
SCIENCE, HISTORY OF
TEXTILES
TRADE AND INDUSTRY

INDUS VALLEY CIVILIZATION

ABOUT 4,500 YEARS AGO, one of the greatest ancient civilizations developed along the banks of the Indus River in the western Punjab. The Indus Valley people occupied a huge area, bigger than Ancient Egypt and Sumer together. Many of them lived in villages, farming the valley's fertile soil. But the civilization centered on the two large cities, Harappa and Mohenjo-daro. These cities were carefully planned, with streets running in straight lines, similar to a modern American town. With their courtyard houses and walled citadels, they were the most impressive cities of their time. But floods often damaged the walls, and the buildings needed repairing regularly. It was probably a combination of water damage and poor harvests that led to the decline of the civilization. After 1800 B.C. the Indus Valley civilization came to an end.

INDUS VALLEY
The Indus River flows through eastern Pakistan. The Indus people lived in a broad strip of land on either side of the river.

SEAL
Indus merchants carried small seals such as this, which they probably used as stamps to sign documents or mark goods. Each seal has a picture of an animal, together with a few characters in the Indus Valley's unique script. No scholar has been able to decipher this writing.

Citadel area contained large buildings, such as the great bath and granary, protected by a strong wall.

Most houses had two stories and a central courtyard.

Straight main streets show that city was carefully planned.

MOHENJO-DARO
Flat-roofed, mud-brick houses lined the straight streets of Mohenjo-daro. Each house had several rooms, with small windows to keep out the hot sun. A courtyard provided a shaded space for working. Most houses also had a bathroom, with a toilet that drained out into sewers beneath the streets. The city also contained a great bathhouse, which may have been used for religious purposes. Historians think that Mohenjo-daro and Harappa each had about 40,000 inhabitants.

INDUS GODS
Many houses in Mohenjo-daro and Harappa contained small pottery statues of a female figure with a head-dress and jewelry. She was probably a mother goddess. Indus Valley people may have worshiped her at home, hoping that she would bring them good harvests and a plentiful food supply.

WHEELED TOYS
The children of the Indus Valley played with pottery toys such as this wheeled oxcart. It is probably a model of similar, full-size carts that were used to take corn to the city's great granary. Archaeologists have also found dice, marbles, and small wheeled animals.

Find out more
CITIES
INDIA, HISTORY OF
RELIGIONS
WHEELS

INFORMATION TECHNOLOGY

THE TERM "INFORMATION TECHNOLOGY," or IT for short, is used to describe technologies that handle, store, process, and transmit, or pass on, information. When people talk about IT, they usually mean the use of computers to store and pass on information, but radio, television, telephones, fax machines, and DVD players are also examples of information technology. Information technology in some form has existed since humans developed pictures and writing, while later inventions such as printing made information more widely available. Modern information technology is based on electronics; vast amounts of information, including pictures and sounds, can be stored as electric signals and transmitted anywhere in the world. Information technology is used in every part of our lives from schools and hospitals to shopping. Its impact has been enormous, making the world truly a "global village."

An early rotary-dial telephone

Camera

EARLY IT
The telephone and the camera were the information technology tools of the 19th century. They had a great impact on society. With the telephone, people could talk to each other all around the world. Using the camera, they could make a record of their lives and families.

USING INFORMATION TECHNOLOGY
To use information technology, you need access to hardware and software. Hardware means the actual machinery, namely computers. Software refers to the programs or applications inside the computer, which actually run it. Programs range from word processing to multimedia and games. They are constantly being updated.

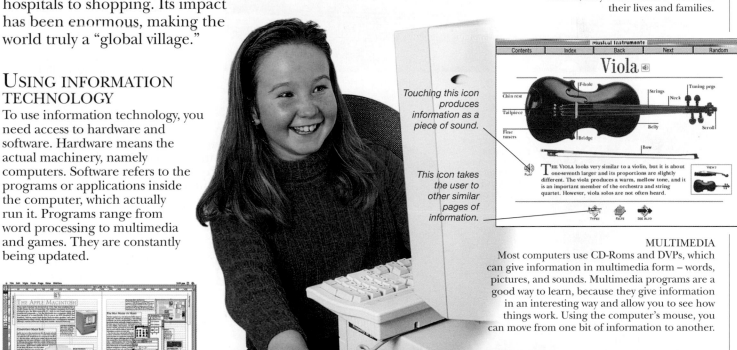

Touching this icon produces information as a piece of sound.

This icon takes the user to other similar pages of information.

MULTIMEDIA
Most computers use CD-Roms and DVPs, which can give information in multimedia form – words, pictures, and sounds. Multimedia programs are a good way to learn, because they give information in an interesting way and allow you to see how things work. Using the computer's mouse, you can move from one bit of information to another.

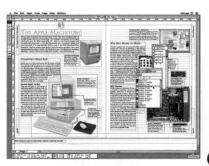

DESKTOP PUBLISHING
Software known as desktop publishing programs (DTP) enable words and pictures to be moved around on screen. DTP is used in publishing, but it also means people can write and design fan magazines, posters, and newsletters in their own homes.

SPREADSHEETS
Some computers contain software programs called spreadsheets. A spreadsheet program stores figures or other information that needs to be shown in the form of tables or charts. The program can do calcuations, such as adding up, or determining percentages. Spreadsheets have many uses, including working out accounts or progress charts.

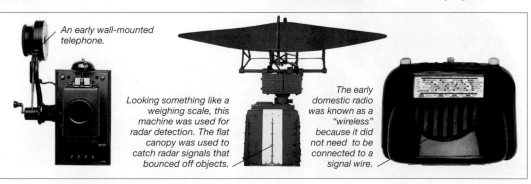

EARLY ELECTRONICS
The use of electronics in information technology has a long history. Materials and designs used for early technology may look dated, but the the early inventions served the same purpose as today's modern examples.

An early wall-mounted telephone.

Looking something like a weighing scale, this machine was used for radar detection. The flat canopy was used to catch radar signals that bounced off objects.

The early domestic radio was known as a "wireless" because it did not need to be connected to a signal wire.

OFFICE COMMUNICATION

In the early 20th century, a new kind of workplace came into being – the office. Early offices contained manual typewriters and telephones. These were followed by machines powered by electricity, such as electric typewriters and photocopiers. Today, the modern office is computerized and relies completely on the latest information technology, from computers and email to fax machines and scanners.

TRANSPORTATION

Information technology is important in transportation, and is used to control airplanes, large ships, and some cars. The cockpit of an aircraft, in particular, has become very sophisticated. The information supplied by the technology to the pilots is so accurate that pilots do not need to look out of the aircraft to fly safely, but can rely on the technology to "fly by wire."

HOSPITALS

Information technology is very useful in hospitals, and medicine in general, and it is now possible to diagnose and treat many illnesses without physically looking inside the body. Scanning devices enable a doctor to monitor the development of an unborn baby on screen, checking on progress and identifying any problems at an early stage.

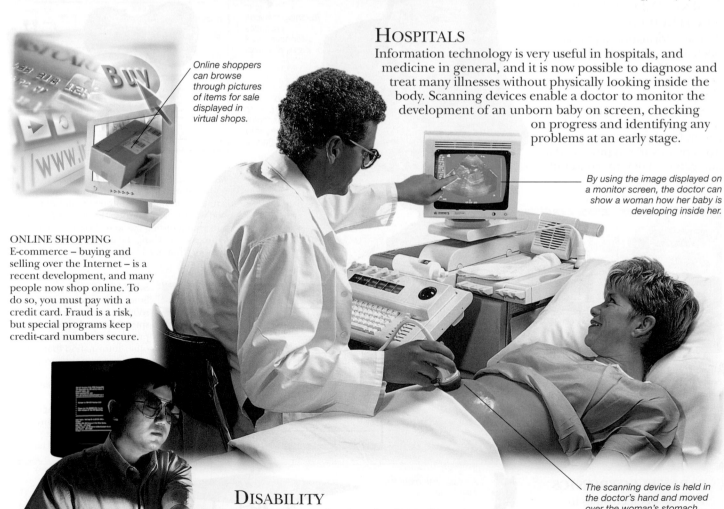

Online shoppers can browse through pictures of items for sale displayed in virtual shops.

ONLINE SHOPPING

E-commerce – buying and selling over the Internet – is a recent development, and many people now shop online. To do so, you must pay with a credit card. Fraud is a risk, but special programs keep credit-card numbers secure.

By using the image displayed on a monitor screen, the doctor can show a woman how her baby is developing inside her.

The scanning device is held in the doctor's hand and moved over the woman's stomach, where it collects information that is shown on screen.

DISABILITY

Information technology has brought major advantages for people with disabilities. This is because the technology can be designed to make the most of each person's physical abilities. For example, word-activated processors are available for blind people, who can both receive and send sound messages. People with physical disabilities can communicate via email, or access information through the Internet, without leaving home.

Find out more
COMPUTERS
ELECTRONICS
INTERNET
TECHNOLOGY

INSECTS

THE EARTH IS CRAWLING with insects; in fact, they make up the largest group of animals. There are at least one million different species, including beetles, butterflies, ants, and bees. Insects first appeared on Earth more than 500 million years ago and are found in almost every kind of habitat, from cold mountains to tropical rain forests. Although all insects have six legs and a body covered by a hard exoskeleton (outer skeleton), they vary enormously in size and shape. The goliath beetle weighs more than 3.5 oz (100 gm); the tiny fairyfly is almost invisible to the human eye. Some insects cause problems for humans. Flies spread disease, and weevils and locusts eat farm crops. Parasites such as ticks and lice live and feed on farm animals and sometimes on humans, too. But insects are a vital part of nature. They pollinate flowers and are an important source of food for many birds, bats, and reptiles. Certain insects are also very useful to humans – without bees, for example, there would be no honey.

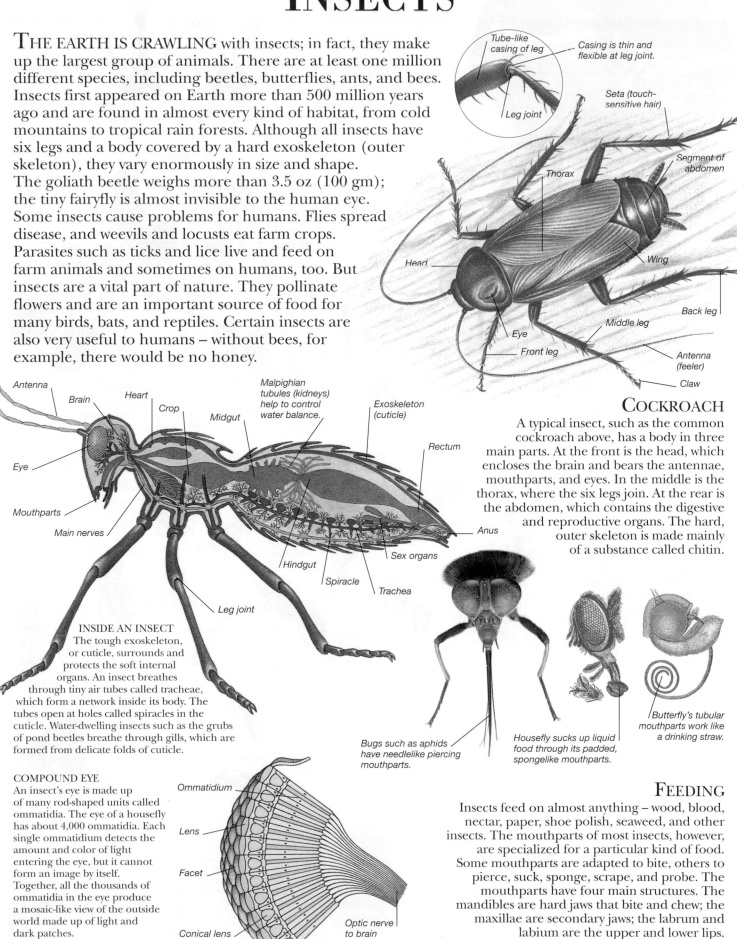

Tube-like casing of leg

Casing is thin and flexible at leg joint.

Leg joint

Seta (touch-sensitive hair)

Thorax

Segment of abdomen

Head

Wing

Eye

Middle leg

Back leg

Front leg

Antenna (feeler)

Claw

COCKROACH

A typical insect, such as the common cockroach above, has a body in three main parts. At the front is the head, which encloses the brain and bears the antennae, mouthparts, and eyes. In the middle is the thorax, where the six legs join. At the rear is the abdomen, which contains the digestive and reproductive organs. The hard, outer skeleton is made mainly of a substance called chitin.

Antenna

Brain

Heart

Crop

Midgut

Malpighian tubules (kidneys) help to control water balance.

Exoskeleton (cuticle)

Rectum

Eye

Mouthparts

Main nerves

Anus

Hindgut

Sex organs

Spiracle

Trachea

Leg joint

INSIDE AN INSECT

The tough exoskeleton, or cuticle, surrounds and protects the soft internal organs. An insect breathes through tiny air tubes called tracheae, which form a network inside its body. The tubes open at holes called spiracles in the cuticle. Water-dwelling insects such as the grubs of pond beetles breathe through gills, which are formed from delicate folds of cuticle.

COMPOUND EYE

An insect's eye is made up of many rod-shaped units called ommatidia. The eye of a housefly has about 4,000 ommatidia. Each single ommatidium detects the amount and color of light entering the eye, but it cannot form an image by itself. Together, all the thousands of ommatidia in the eye produce a mosaic-like view of the outside world made up of light and dark patches.

Ommatidium

Lens

Facet

Conical lens

Optic nerve to brain

Bugs such as aphids have needlelike piercing mouthparts.

Housefly sucks up liquid food through its padded, spongelike mouthparts.

Butterfly's tubular mouthparts work like a drinking straw.

FEEDING

Insects feed on almost anything – wood, blood, nectar, paper, shoe polish, seaweed, and other insects. The mouthparts of most insects, however, are specialized for a particular kind of food. Some mouthparts are adapted to bite, others to pierce, suck, sponge, scrape, and probe. The mouthparts have four main structures. The mandibles are hard jaws that bite and chew; the maxillae are secondary jaws; the labrum and labium are the upper and lower lips.

COURTSHIP

Some insects, such as the praying mantises shown here, have complicated courtship behavior. After mating, the female mantis often grasps and eats the male mantis; the nutrients in the body of the male help the eggs to develop.

ANTENNAE

Sense organs called antennae detect smells and vibrations in the air and in solid objects. Often, the male has larger, more branched antennae than the female. These help detect the scent that she releases into the air at mating time. Near the antennae there are often several tiny single-lens eyes called ocelli.

Indian beetle has antlerlike antennae.

Weevil has elbow-jointed antennae.

The praying mantis is the only insect that can turn its head to look directly behind.

METAMORPHOSIS

Most insects hatch from eggs. Some insects, such as the butterfly, hatch into a larva or caterpillar, which feeds voraciously and moults (sheds its skin) several times. It then forms a chrysalis and pupates, finally emerging as a mature adult butterfly. These great changes in form are known as complete metamorphosis. Other insects, such as grasshoppers, hatch into nymphs, which look like small versions of the parent, but without proper wings. They moult in order to grow and finally become adult after the final moult when they have wings. This is called incomplete metamorphosis.

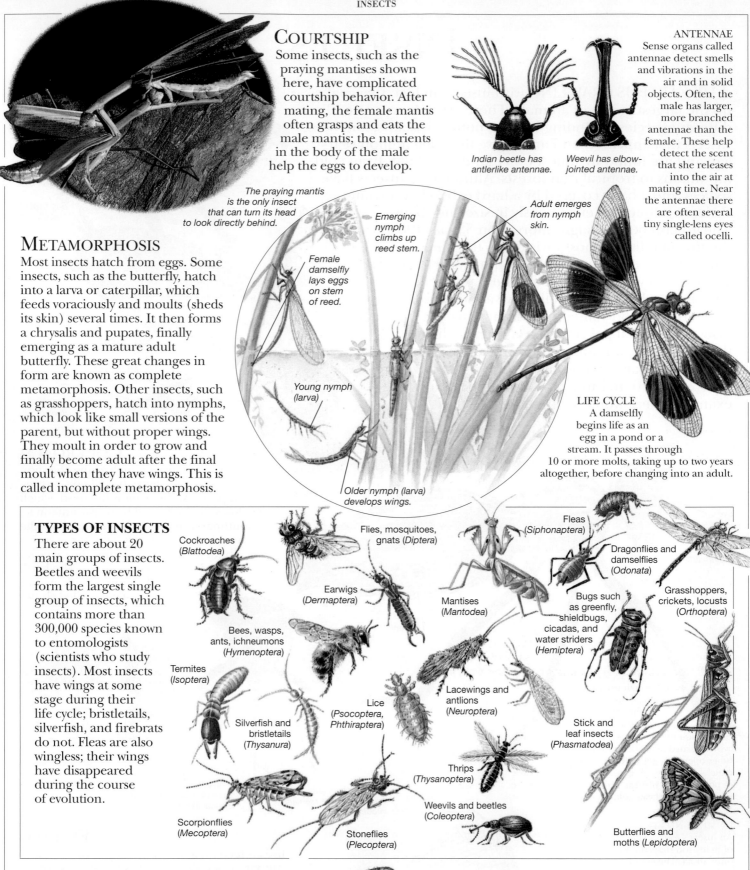

Female damselfly lays eggs on stem of reed.

Emerging nymph climbs up reed stem.

Adult emerges from nymph skin.

Young nymph (larva)

Older nymph (larva) develops wings.

LIFE CYCLE

A damselfly begins life as an egg in a pond or a stream. It passes through 10 or more molts, taking up to two years altogether, before changing into an adult.

TYPES OF INSECTS

There are about 20 main groups of insects. Beetles and weevils form the largest single group of insects, which contains more than 300,000 species known to entomologists (scientists who study insects). Most insects have wings at some stage during their life cycle; bristletails, silverfish, and firebrats do not. Fleas are also wingless; their wings have disappeared during the course of evolution.

Cockroaches (*Blattodea*)

Flies, mosquitoes, gnats (*Diptera*)

Fleas (*Siphonaptera*)

Dragonflies and damselflies (*Odonata*)

Earwigs (*Dermaptera*)

Mantises (*Mantodea*)

Bugs such as greenfly, shieldbugs, cicadas, and water striders (*Hemiptera*)

Grasshoppers, crickets, locusts (*Orthoptera*)

Bees, wasps, ants, ichneumons (*Hymenoptera*)

Termites (*Isoptera*)

Silverfish and bristletails (*Thysanura*)

Lice (*Psocoptera, Phthiraptera*)

Lacewings and antlions (*Neuroptera*)

Stick and leaf insects (*Phasmatodea*)

Thrips (*Thysanoptera*)

Weevils and beetles (*Coleoptera*)

Scorpionflies (*Mecoptera*)

Stoneflies (*Plecoptera*)

Butterflies and moths (*Lepidoptera*)

FLEA

A flea can leap more than 12 in (30 cm) into the air, which is similar to a person jumping 800 ft (245 m), or a 70-story building, like St. Paul's Cathedral in London, England.

Legs kick down for extra acceleration.

Like other insects, fleas have powerful muscles, and the elastic springiness of the cuticle helps the legs to rebound quickly during movement.

St. Paul's Cathedral

Find out more
ANTS AND TERMITES
BEETLES
BUTTERFLIES AND MOTHS
FLIES AND MOSQUITOES
GRASSHOPPERS
and crickets

INTERNET

FOR CENTURIES THE MOST IMPORTANT way of passing on knowledge was through books, but when the Internet (short for international network) was established, it gave people a way of sending and receiving information through personal computers. Words, pictures, music, videos, and any other type of data that can be turned into digital form are all sent from computer to computer, as electronic signals traveling over telephone, radio, or satellite. The Internet was first set up in 1969 by the US Defense Department, but in 1994 it became open to everybody. We now use the Internet to search for information, send and receive e-mail messages, share photos, buy and sell goods, play games, listen to music, and watch movies and TV.

INFORMATION
The Internet is like a vast library of electronic books. No one knows exactly how many pages there are. Search engines cover nearly 10 billion – but the number grows by millions more every day.

A page from the Dorling Kindersley website: web pages are regularly updated.

Electronic mail can send a letter halfway round the world in seconds.

The Internet uses the telephone system to link computers with each other.

Information can be sent all over the world via global satellite links.

WORLD WIDE WEB
Most information on the Internet is given in the form of web pages. These are electronically linked to form websites stored on the World Wide Web (WWW). Website information is released through web servers (very large computers). To link up with the web, you send a request from your computer to a web server.

SURFING THE NET
Looking for information on the Internet is called "surfing". Using a search engine (a kind of electronic catalog), you type in one or more keywords describing what you are looking for. The search engine will match your keywords against its huge index of the web and produce a list of sites likely to contain what you want. Usually, the most popular and most relevant sites are listed first.

List of web sites

Search engine

Thumbnail images

Site categories

E-MAIL
Any Internet user can send a message directly to another by electronic mail or e-mail. You need your own e-mail address and a computer with a modem so it can connect to the Internet. A modem translates messages into electronic data that can be sent from one computer to another and displayed on screen.

You can use the Internet to send an e-mail message around the world as easily as making a local telephone call.

Find out more
COMPUTERS
INFORMATION TECHNOLOGY
TELEPHONES
SATELLITES

INUITS

THE FROZEN ARCTIC was one of the last regions of the world to be inhabited by humans. The Inuit (Eskimo) people, who originally came from Asia, settled in the Arctic about 4,000 years ago. A Native American tribe named them *Eskimo*, which means "eaters of raw meat;" but the newcomers called themselves *Inuit*, which simply means "real men." Inuits were nomadic. They moved around in family groups, hunting animals such as seals and caribou. Inuit families survived the bitter cold of winter by digging shelters into the ground. They made roofs for the shelters from driftwood or whalebone, with a covering of turf. For clothes, they used double layers of caribou or polar bear fur. Today most Inuits live in small settlements or towns, but they are proud of their culture. They preserve it in language, art, and song, and hunting is still an essential part of Inuit life.

North Alaskan Inuits

Polar Inuits

West Greenland Inuits

GREENLAND

ALASKA

CANADA

Pacific Inuits

Caribou Inuits

INUIT COMMUNITIES
Inuits live in Siberia in the Russian Federation, in Alaska, Canada, and Greenland. There are many different groups, each named after the area in which they live. The Polar Inuits of Greenland live the furthest north of all the world's peoples.

Today Inuits hunt on snowmobiles instead of sleds.

A hunting trip takes many days, and supplies are carried by snowmobile.

To catch a seal, the Inuit cuts a hole in the sea ice. When the seal comes up to the hole to breathe, the Inuit shoots it.

HUNTING
Inuits hunt for food to eat and furs to sell. They do not hunt animals for sport. They respect foxes, caribou, seal, walrus, and other Arctic wildlife, and their hunting does not threaten the long-term survival of these animal species. Hunting takes patience and skill, and some Inuits travel 3,000 miles (5,000 km) a year on hunting trips. When they are hunting away from home in winter, they build temporary shelters, called igloos, from blocks of snow.

Inuits eat raw and cooked seal meat.

INUIT ART
During the long winter months there is little daylight in the Arctic, so the hours of hunting are limited. In the past, skilled Inuit carvers used the time to work wood, bone, soapstone (soft rock), and walrus tusks. They created beautiful statues of animals, people, and especially favored hunting scenes. Today, museums and collectors eagerly seek good Inuit carvings.

Inuit artists use their skills to decorate everyday tools, such as this arrow straightener.

INUIT LIFE
There are about 25,000 Inuits in North America. Most live in wooden houses equipped like a typical North American home. Some Inuits are still full-time hunters; most others work in many different businesses and industries.

A team of 10 to 15 husky dogs pull the traditional Inuit sled. With an expert driver at the reins, a dog team can travel 50 miles (80 km) in a day.

Find out more
ANTARCTICA
ARCTIC
CANADA
POLAR EXPLORATION
POLAR WILDLIFE

IRAN

Iran lies at the heart of Asia, bordered by the Caspian Sea in the north, and the Persian Gulf and Gulf of Oman to the south. The Elburz Mountains and Zagros Mountains enclose the central plateau, a land of barren, rocky deserts.

A LAND OF RUGGED MOUNTAINS and harsh deserts, Iran was ruled for many centuries by the shah, or king. In the 1979 revolution, the shah was overthrown and Iran became an Islamic republic, ruled according to strict religious laws. Between 1980 and 1988, border disputes led to a devastating war between Iran and its western neighbor, Iraq. The cost of the prolonged war has strained the economy. Although Iran has very substantial oil reserves, it has very few other industries. Eggs from sturgeon caught in the Caspian Sea are used to make caviar, an expensive delicacy, which is exported. Fine, handmade carpets are also an important source of income for villagers, who grow wheat, barley, and rice, and herd sheep. Iran's strict Islamic laws have discouraged tourists, although the country has a great wealth of historic buildings and magnificent mosques.

STATISTICS
Area: 636,293 sq miles (1,648,000 sq km)
Population: 68,900,000
Capital: Tehran
Languages: Farsi (Persian), Azerbaijani, Gilaki, Mazenderani, Kurdish, Baluchi, Arabic, Turkmen
Religions: Shi'ite Muslim, Sunni Muslim
Currency: Iranian rial

THE KURDS

The Kurds are an ethnically and linguistically distinctive group who live in Iran, Iraq, and Turkey. They were once sheep- and goat-herding nomads in the Iranian highlands, although in recent years they have turned to farming and village life. There are about 25 million Kurds, the largest group of stateless people in the world. In Iran, they are pressured to become part of mainstream society, and they are severely discriminated against in Turkey.

CARPET WEAVERS

Iran's famous carpets are made by hand-knotting the wool, which is colored with a range of vegetable dyes. Many of the patterns used are hundreds of years old, and were created for the opulent carpets used in royal palaces and mosques. Each region prides itself on its carpets, specializing in unique designs and color combinations.

CASPIAN SEA
The Caspian Sea is a salt lake that lies between Europe and Asia. It sits 28 m (92 ft) below sea level.

MASHHAD

Most Iranians belong to the minority Shi'ah branch of Islam, and Mashhad is their main shrine, the place where the Shi'ah leader Riza (770–819) was martyred. Iran has a religious government that imposes severe restrictions on the people. Women must wear the chador, a dress covering all but the face and hands, and public behavior is closely monitored.

SCALE BAR
0 100 200 300 km
0   100   200   300 miles

Find out more
ASIA
EARTHQUAKES
ISLAM
PERSIANS, ANCIENT

IRELAND

OFF THE NORTHWEST COAST of Europe lies one of the most beautiful islands in the world. For centuries, writers and singers have praised the lush countryside and wild mountains of Ireland. Despite its beauty, Ireland is not a rich country and has few natural resources. It has no coal, no iron ore, or reserves of oil. Nevertheless, Ireland's influence has been far-reaching, for the country is rich in its people and their distinctive Gaelic culture. Few corners of the world lack an Irish community whose members keep alive the memory and customs of their homeland. In 1973, Ireland (Eire) joined the European Economic Community (now the European Union). Until then, its powerful neighbor and former ruler, the United Kingdom, had always dominated the country's economy. As a member of the Union, Eire is slowly becoming more prosperous and economically independent of the United Kingdom. New high-tech industries are replacing traditional agriculture and textiles as the main sources of employment.

Ireland is the smaller of the two main British Isles. The other – Britain – is to the east, and the Atlantic Ocean is to the west. Ireland is divided into Ireland (Eire), which is independent, and the province of Northern Ireland, which is part of the United Kingdom.

Blocks of peat – carbon-rich soil consisting of decomposed plant life – are dug up from the marshy countryside and left to dry before being used as fuel.

DUBLIN

The capital city of Ireland is Dublin. It lies on the Liffey River not far from the Irish Sea. The Vikings founded Dublin in the 9th century, and the city has many historic buildings and beautiful town squares.

COUNTRYSIDE

Wet west winds blow across Ireland from the Atlantic Ocean, soaking parts of the country with more than 80 in (200 cm) of rain each year. This makes the farmland very productive; about 16 percent of the people work in farming and food processing industries.

GEOGRAPHY

Mountains to the south, west, and north surround Ireland's large central plain. The plain is marshy in places, and there are many lakes, called loughs. Lough Neagh (right) in Northern Ireland, the biggest lake in the British Isles, is famous for its wildfowl and salmon.

The Ha'penny Bridge, which spans the Liffey River, is accepted as the symbol of Dublin. Opened in 1816, its name comes from the fee once charged to use it.

MUSIC

Ireland has a strong musical tradition. Irish rock and classical artists are well known internationally. The Corrs, U2, and Boyzone are all very successful Irish bands. Traditional Irish music and dancing is also very important to Ireland's cultural heritage.

Pipes, fiddles, and banjos are all used in traditional Irish music.

INDUSTRY

Once renowned for its traditional industries of glass, lace, and linen, Ireland now also produces medicine, electronics, and other modern goods. Many people work in the tourism industry.

Find out more

CELTS
EUROPE
IRELAND, HISTORY OF
UNITED KINGDOM
UNITED KINGDOM, HISTORY OF
VIKINGS

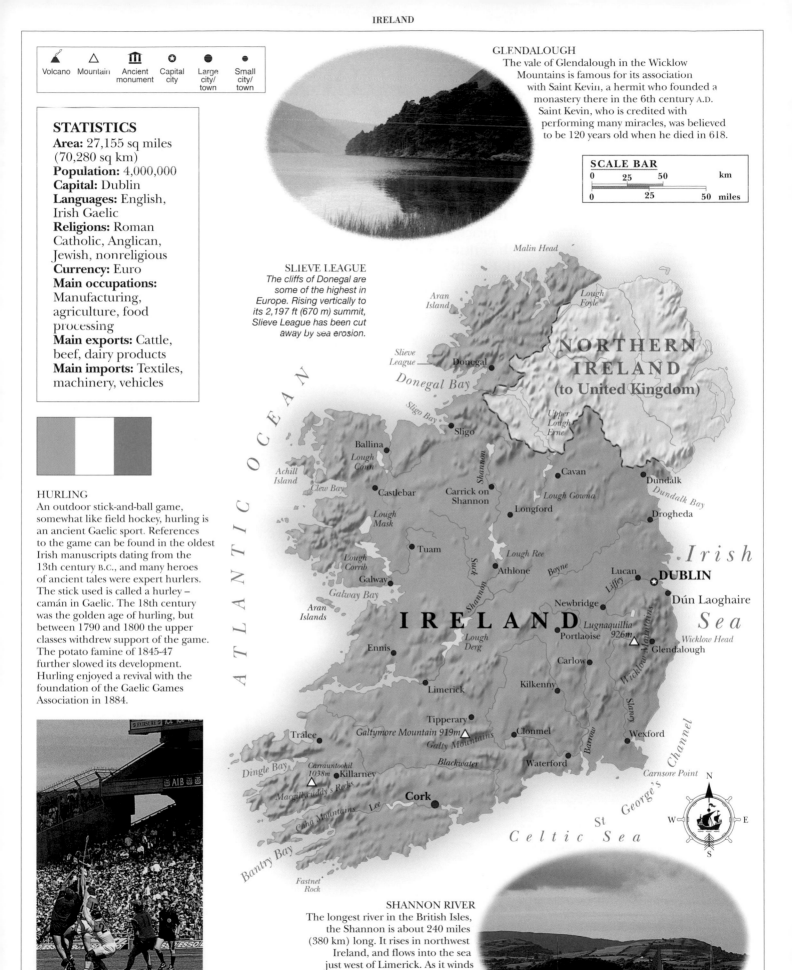

Volcano △ **Mountain** 🏛 **Ancient monument** ✴ **Capital city** ● **Large city/town** ● **Small city/town**

STATISTICS
Area: 27,155 sq miles (70,280 sq km)
Population: 4,000,000
Capital: Dublin
Languages: English, Irish Gaelic
Religions: Roman Catholic, Anglican, Jewish, nonreligious
Currency: Euro
Main occupations: Manufacturing, agriculture, food processing
Main exports: Cattle, beef, dairy products
Main imports: Textiles, machinery, vehicles

HURLING
An outdoor stick-and-ball game, somewhat like field hockey, hurling is an ancient Gaelic sport. References to the game can be found in the oldest Irish manuscripts dating from the 13th century B.C., and many heroes of ancient tales were expert hurlers. The stick used is called a hurley – camán in Gaelic. The 18th century was the golden age of hurling, but between 1790 and 1800 the upper classes withdrew support of the game. The potato famine of 1845-47 further slowed its development. Hurling enjoyed a revival with the foundation of the Gaelic Games Association in 1884.

GLENDALOUGH
The vale of Glendalough in the Wicklow Mountains is famous for its association with Saint Kevin, a hermit who founded a monastery there in the 6th century A.D. Saint Kevin, who is credited with performing many miracles, was believed to be 120 years old when he died in 618.

SCALE BAR
0   25   50   km
0   25   50   miles

SLIEVE LEAGUE
The cliffs of Donegal are some of the highest in Europe. Rising vertically to its 2,197 ft (670 m) summit, Slieve League has been cut away by sea erosion.

SHANNON RIVER
The longest river in the British Isles, the Shannon is about 240 miles (380 km) long. It rises in northwest Ireland, and flows into the sea just west of Limerick. As it winds its way down the country, the river passes through numerous lakes, the largest of which is Lough Derg.

HISTORY OF
IRELAND

THE FIRST STONE AGE hunters arrived in Ireland from Europe. The Celts followed and divided Ireland into small kingdoms. The Celtic age produced fantastic legends and wonderful stories of gods, battles, and heroes. In A.D. 432, St. Patrick brought Christianity to the land, and became Ireland's patron saint. A golden age followed during which Irish Christians studied, painted, and wrote literature. Ireland became the cultural center of Europe. In 795, Viking raiders shattered this peace. They built settlements, including Dublin, the capital. During the 12th century the Normans gained control of most of Ireland. Monarchs Henry VIII, Elizabeth I, and James VI all used the planting of Protestant English and Scottish people on lands seized from the Irish as a way of increasing the number of subjects loyal to the British crown. This worked especially well in areas of Ulster, which accounts for much of today's conflicts in Northern Ireland.

ARDAGH CHALICE
During its golden age, Irish craftsworkers made many magnificent treasures. The silver Ardagh chalice, one of the most famous, is decorated with bronze and gold.

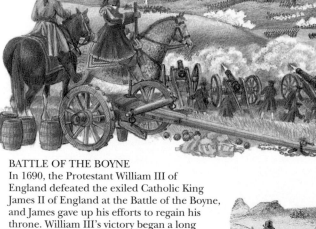

BATTLE OF THE BOYNE
In 1690, the Protestant William III of England defeated the exiled Catholic King James II of England at the Battle of the Boyne, and James gave up his efforts to regain his throne. William III's victory began a long period of harsh English rule over the Irish Catholics. This was called the Penal Law.

POTATO FAMINE
In the 1800s, most Irish people lived on small holdings and were very poor. They ate mainly potatoes. The crop failed many times, but 1845 and 1848 were the worst years. More than 750,000 people starved and thousands emigrated.

EASTER REBELLION
On Easter Monday in 1916, Irish Republicans, impatient with the delay in implementing self-government, rose up in armed revolt. The British army crushed the rebellion and executed 15 of the rebels. The dead rebels became heroes, and support for the Republican cause grew.

THE TROUBLES
In 1922, the Irish Free State (South) was created. In Northern Ireland the Protestant majority ran the government. In 1968 Catholic marches for civil rights were suppressed, and years of mistrust sparked off new violence. The British army was called in to keep peace but conflict developed with their arrival. People from all sides of the community still seek a peaceful solution.

IRELAND

C. 600 B.C. Celts invade Ireland.

A.D. 795 Vikings raid Ireland.

1014 King Brian Boru defeats the Vikings at Clontarf.

1170 Normans land in Ireland.

1641 Rebellion by the Irish against English government.

1690 Battle of the Boyne followed by Protestant domination.

1798 United Irishmen rebellion is defeated.

1845-49 Potato famine. Population falls by three million.

1916 Easter Rebellion.

1919-23 War of Independence. Six counties of Ulster remain with the UK. Anglo-Irish treaty causes civil war in the south.

1973 Ireland joins the EC.

1997 Belfast-born Mary McAleese succeeds Mary Robinson as Ireland's president.

Find out more
ENGLISH CIVIL WAR
IMMIGRATION
IRELAND
UNITED KINGDOM, HISTORY OF

IRON AGE

IN SEVERAL EARLY LANGUAGES the word for iron meant "metal from the sky." This was probably because the first iron used to make tools and weapons came from meteorites that fell to Earth from space. Ironworking probably began in the Middle East some 6,000 years ago. At first, people hammered iron while it was cold. Later they learned how to smelt iron – heat the iron ore so they could extract the iron and work with it properly. Unlike bronze, which early people also used, iron did not melt. Instead it was reduced to a spongy mass that people hammered and reheated until it was the right shape. Special furnaces were needed to reach the right temperature. The Hittites, who lived in what is now Turkey, were the first people we know of who traded in iron. But it was not until around 1000 B.C. that knowledge of smelting spread and the Iron Age truly began. In western Europe, the Celts were one of the first peoples to make and use iron.

This razor is around 2,500 years old and would have been as sharp as a modern razor.

IRON AGE

4000 B.C. First iron objects, made from meteoric iron, appear in the Middle East.

c. 1500 B.C. People in the Middle East find out how to extract (smelt) iron from iron ore and how to work it by heating and hammering (wrought iron). The Hittites dominate the trade.

1000 B.C. Iron Age begins in the Middle East and Greece. Iron-working also develops in India.

c. 800 B.C. Use of iron spreads across Europe. Celts become expert workers in iron.

c. 400 B.C. Chinese discover how to make cast-iron objects by melting iron ore and pouring it into molds.

A.D. 1760 Industrial revolution leads to a renewed use of iron. Also leads to great advances in ironworking techniques.

HILL FORT
The Celts fortified hill-tops with ditches and ramparts. These forts were places of refuge in wartime; they were also administrative and trading centers, and enclosures for livestock.

IRONWORKING
Early furnaces were shallow stone hearths that people filled with iron ore and charcoal. Bellows helped raise the temperature to about 2,192°F (1,200°C), hot enough to make the iron workable. The Celts used deeper furnaces in which the iron collected at the bottom and impurities, called slag, gathered at the top.

Iron horseshoe

Hammering the iron into shape

Heating iron ore in a furnace

Iron pin

Spring

Brooch made of glass discs

TOOLS
People made useful tools from iron such as a saw with a serrated edge (far left) and tongs (left); the tongs were used to hold metal while beating it into shape.

WEAPONS
Iron weapons were greatly superior to bronze ones. They had much sharper edges and, thus, were more effective. This dagger has a handle shaped like a human figure.

CLOTHING
The Celts loved decoration. Celtic clothes were woollen, often with checked patterns. Richer men and women wore heavy twisted neckbands called torcs in gold or bronze, and cloaks fastened with ornate brooches.

Find out more
BRONZE AGE
CELTS
INDUSTRIAL REVOLUTION
IRON AND STEEL

IRON AND STEEL

HUGE STRUCTURES like oil tankers and bridges and tiny objects like nuts and bolts are all made from steel. The world produces about 787 million tons of steel every year; it is the most widely used of all metals. Steel is made from iron, one of the most common metals in the Earth's crust, and carbon, which comes from coal. Iron has many uses, including making car engine parts and magnets. Our bodies also need iron to work properly. A healthy diet must include foods such as green vegetables, which contain iron. Pieces of iron fall to Earth in meteorites from space. Most iron, however, comes from iron ore in rock. Heating the ore with coke (from coal) produces iron. The Hittites of Turkey perfected iron smelting about 1500 B.C. This was the beginning of the Iron Age, during which iron gained widespread use for making weapons and tools.

Iron and steel were once used to make weapons and armor, such as this 16th-century helmet.

Limestone
Iron ore
Coke
Blast furnace
Sinter

Slag floats above the molten iron.

Molten iron is drained from the furnace into large ladles.

Oxygen is blown through pipe onto surface of pig iron.

After blowing with oxygen, the converter tilts to discharge molten steel.

Molten steel from converter

Continuous casting

The molten steel may be cast into large blocks called ingots.

RAW MATERIALS
Ironmaking starts with iron ore, coke (a form of carbon from coal), and limestone. They are mixed and treated to make lumps called sinter.

BLAST FURNACE
The ingredients enter the top of the blast furnace and move down inside. A blast of very hot air flows up the furnace. The heat produces molten iron from the ore and coke. Limestone removes impurities, which form a layer called slag.

MAKING IRON AND STEEL
Making metals by heating their ores is called smelting. Huge factories smelt iron ore by heating it with coke to produce iron, which is rich in carbon. Removing most of the carbon produces steel. Steels of different quality are made by adding metals, such as nickel.

STEEL CONVERTER
Molten iron from the blast furnace is poured into a steel converter where hot air or oxygen is blown over it. The heat burns up most of the carbon from the iron, leaving molten steel. Steel from old cars and other waste can be recycled by adding it to the converter.

Casting uses molten steel from the converter.

Forging

Rolling

CONTINUOUS CASTING
Molten steel from the converter sets as it cools and is held in shape by rollers. The long slab is then cut up into lengths and rolled into steel products.

RUST
Iron and steel objects get rusty when they are left outside in damp conditions. Moist air causes rust. It changes iron into iron oxide, a red-brown compound of iron and oxygen. Rusting weakens the metal so that it crumbles away.

SHAPING STEEL
Passing a hot slab between rollers presses the soft steel into plates or sheets. A forge presses the steel into more complex shapes. Casting uses a mold, in which molten steel cools and sets into shape.

USES OF STEEL
Different kinds of steel are made by varying the amount of carbon and other metals in it. Low-carbon steel goes into car bodies; stronger medium-carbon steel is used for making ships and steel beams that support structures. High-carbon steel is very strong but difficult to shape, and is used for springs and rails that get much wear. Steel containing tungsten metal resists heat and is used in jet engines.

STAINLESS STEEL
Adding the metals chromium and nickel produces stainless steel, which does not rust. Cutlery and cookware are often made of stainless steel. This metal is also used to make equipment that must be kept very clean in places such as hospitals and dairies.

Find out more
COAL
INDUSTRIAL REVOLUTION
IRON AGE
METALS

ISLAM

IN THE 7TH CENTURY, the prophet Muhammad founded a religion in Arabia that was to become a powerful force in the world. The religion came to be known as Islam, and its followers are called Muslims (or Moslems). Muslims believe that many prophets or teachers have been sent by God, including Moses and Jesus Christ, but Muhammad was the last of them. Like Christians and Jews, Muslims believe in one God, Allah. Islam means "submission to the will of God," and Muslims commit themselves to absolute obedience to Allah. Islamic life is based on a set of rules called the five pillars of Islam. Muslims believe that by following these rules, they will reach heaven. There is also a strict code of social behavior, and alcohol and gambling are forbidden. Some Muslim women wear clothes that cover their bodies completely. Today there are around 1.3 billion Muslims living mainly in the Middle East, Asia, and Africa. Islam is a rapidly growing faith. Its popularity has been increased by Islamic fundamentalists – extremely religious people who call for a return to strict, traditional Islamic values.

KORAN
The sacred book of Islam is the Koran. Muslims believe the Koran is the direct word of God as revealed to his messenger, Muhammad.

ISLAMIC FESTIVALS
Day of Hijrah First day of Islamic year.

Ramadan Month-long fast.

Eid ul-Fitr Feast to mark the end of Ramadan.

Lailat ul-Qadr Revelation of Koran to Muhammad.

Meelad ul-Nabi Muhammad's birthday.

Lailut ul-Isra Death of Muhammad.

MOSQUES
The Muslim place of worship is the mosque. Before entering, Muslims remove their shoes and wash. The faithful kneel to pray, with their heads touching the floor. At prayer time Muslims face the mihrab, an empty recess which faces the direction of Mecca. Although they must attend the mosque on Fridays, at other times Muslims pray wherever they are.

BLUE MOSQUE
The first mosques were very simple, but some later buildings such as the Blue Mosque at Istanbul, Turkey (right), are magnificent examples of Islamic art. Islam forbids realistic images of humans or other living things, so the tiled walls are decorated with intricate designs and beautiful calligraphy.

MINARETS
Five times a day, muezzins, or criers, stand at the top of tall towers called minarets to call fellow Muslims to prayer.

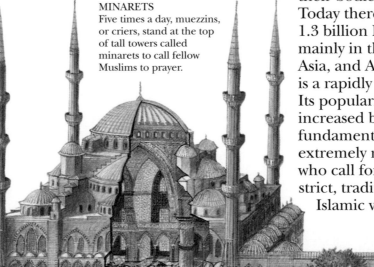

Before kneeling in prayer in the mosque, Muslims wash their faces, hands, and feet.

MUHAMMAD
The shahada is the Islamic declaration of faith. "None is to be worshiped save Allah: Muhammad is his prophet."

MECCA
The birthplace of Muhammad is Mecca, Saudi Arabia, and every Muslim tries to visit the holy city at least once in a lifetime. The Kaaba, the sacred shrine, is the central point of this pilgrimage. Inside the Kaaba is a black stone which dates from ancient times.

Muslim pilgrims must walk seven times around the Kaaba.

Find out more
CRUSADES
FESTIVALS AND FEASTS
MUHAMMAD
RELIGIONS

ISRAEL

Volcano	Mountain	Ancient monument	Capital city	Large city/ town	Small city/ town

Israel lies at the eastern end of the Mediterranean Sea. Lebanon lies to the north, Syria and Jordan to the east, and Egypt to the southwest.

THE MODERN STATE OF ISRAEL has existed only since 1948. It was created on the sites where there had been Jewish settlements in earlier times. Jews from all over the world flocked to the new state, especially the survivors of Nazi anti-semitism. They revived the ancient language of Hebrew as the national language of Israel. But there have been many problems. The region had previously been the land of Palestine, and many Arab Palestinians left when the country became Israel. However, others have remained, and today they make up about 15 percent of Israel's 6.4 million population. Israel has also fought several wars with neighboring Arab countries to secure its borders. It still occupies some territory gained in these wars, causing continual Palestinian unrest. Israel is now a wealthy country; the Israelis have developed many modern industries and converted large areas of desert into farmland.

STATISTICS
Area: 7,992 sq miles (20,700 sq km)
Population: 6,400,000
Capital: Jerusalem
Languages: Hebrew, Arabic, Yiddish, German, Russian, Polish, Romanian, Persian
Religions: Jewish, Muslim, Christian, Druze
Currency: New Israeli shekel
Main occupations: Agriculture, manufacturing, finance
Main exports: Potash, bromine, salt, wine, citrus fruits
Main imports: Water

WAILING WALL
Israel occupies much of the Holy Land described in the Bible. The land is sacred not only to Jews, but also to Christians and Muslims. The Wailing Wall in Jerusalem is the most sacred Jewish monument. It is all that remains of a temple built by King Herod 2,000 years ago. Visitors gave the wall its name when they heard the sad sound of devout Jews mourning the destruction of the temple.

TEL AVIV-YAFO

The main commercial and industrial centre of Israel is Tel Aviv-Yafo, the country's second largest city. It was once two separate towns, but Tel Aviv grew rapidly and absorbed its neighbor, the ancient port of Yafo.

DEAD SEA
The world's saltiest sea, the Dead Sea, is also the lowest area of water on Earth: it is 1,312 ft (400 m) below the level of the Mediterranean Sea. The Jordan river flows into this hot, barren place. The water evaporates in the heat of the sun, but the salt in the water is left behind. Over the centuries the salt has become very concentrated.

Map labels:
LEBANON · SYRIA · Mediterranean Sea · Nahariyya · 'Akko · Zefat · Golan Heights · Haifa (Hefa) · Sea of Galilee (Lake Tiberias) · Teverya · Nazareth · Jenin · Netanya · West · Tel Aviv-Yafo · Nablus · Petah Tiqwa · Holon · Bank · Rehovot · Ramla · Jericho · Ashdod · JERUSALEM · Ashqelon · Bethlehem · Dead Sea · Gaza Strip · Gaza · Hebron · -392 m · Rafah · 'Arad · Be'er Sheva' · Telalim · New Zohar · ISRAEL · Negev · Sappir · Mizpe Ramon · Be'er Menuha · Jordan · JORDAN · Wadi at 'Arabah · EGYPT · Elat · Gulf of Aqaba

Visitors to Dead Sea resorts bathe in mud because they believe it is good for their skin.

Tel Aviv's city center symbolizes the modern, prosperous face of Israel.

SCALE BAR			
0	25	50	km
0	25		50 miles

Find out more
CHRISTIANITY
CRUSADES
ISLAM
JUDAISM
MIDDLE EAST

ITALY

Many Italian farmhouses are old and picturesque; the machinery is usually modern.

Italy is in southern Europe and forms part of the northern coast of the Mediterranean Sea. It shares borders with France, Switzerland, Austria, and Slovenia.

SHAPED LIKE A BOOT, complete with heel and toe, Italy juts out far into the Mediterranean Sea from southern Europe. Between the country's east and west coasts rise the Apennine Mountains, which divide Italy into two along its length. Northern Italy is green and fertile, stretching from the snowcapped Alps to the middle of the country. It includes farmlands in the great flat valley of the Po River, and large industrial towns such as Turin and Milan. Factories in the north produce cars, textiles, clothes, and electrical goods. These products have helped make Italy one of the most prosperous countries in Europe. Southern Italy, by contrast, is dry and rocky. There is less farming and industry, and the people are poorer. Sicily and Sardinia, the two largest islands of the Mediterranean, are also part of Italy. Rome, the capital, lies at the center of the nation. It is the home of Italy's democratic government and also the Vatican, the headquarters of the Roman Catholic Church.

AGRICULTURE
Italian farmers grow almost enough to feed Italy's population of 57.4 million. They also export fresh and processed food. Italy is famous for its olives and olive oil, tomatoes, wine, pasta, cheese, fruit, and meat products, such as salami and ham. Italy also grows large quantities of grain, particularly wheat, as well as rice, potatoes, and sunflowers, which are used to make cooking oil. Almost one-third of Italians live in rural areas.

ROME
A walk through Rome is like a walk through history. Since the city was first built more than 2,500 years ago, each new generation has added something. Today, modern city life goes on around ancient Roman arenas, 15th-century churches, and 17th-century palaces. Like many of Italy's historic towns, Rome attracts thousands of tourists every year.

Ferrari makes one of the leading Grand Prix racing cars.

PASTA
There are at least 200 shapes of pasta, including ravioli, spaghetti, and macaroni. Pasta is a type of dough made from durum wheat flour, which is rich in gluten, a kind of protein. Served with a tasty sauce, it is Italy's favorite dish. Marco Polo is said to have brought the recipe for pasta from China to Italy.

CARS
The Italian auto industry produces some of Europe's finest cars. Manufacturers such as Alfa Romeo, Ferrari, and Lamborghini have always had a reputation for speed and stylish design.

VENICE
Venice is one of the world's oldest cultural and tourist cities. From the late medieval period, it became Europe's greatest seaport, serving as the continent's commercial and cultural link to Asia. Like many other Italian towns, Venice boasts magnificent buildings from the past. Its ornate marbled and frescoed palaces, towers, and domes attract thousands of tourists every year. The city was built on about 120 small islands, in a lagoon which remains permanently flooded. A causeway over 2.5 miles (4 km) long connects Venice with mainland Italy. Cars are not allowed in the old city, and people travel by boat on more than 170 canals. The traditional boat, called a gondola (above), is still a common form of transportation.

The fairy-tale fortress of Rocca Tower, perched high on a rocky outcrop, overlooks San Marino.

The Doric Temple (right) in the Valley of the Temples, Sicily, was built during the period 460-450 B.C.

SAN MARINO

San Marino is the third-smallest independent state in Europe, after Monaco and the Vatican City. It is about 9 miles (14 km) long and 5 miles (8 km) wide, and is situated mostly on the slopes of Monte Titano on the Adriatic coast. Tourism provides a great source of income to the country, as do the frequent issues of its own postage stamps. The Sammarinese, as the inhabitants of San Marino are called, are ruled by two capitani reggenti ("captains regent") who are elected every six months. San Marino has had a treaty of friendship with Italy since 1862.

SICILY

Sicily is the largest island in the Mediterranean Sea. It belongs to Italy, from which it is separated by the Strait of Messina. The island's highest point is Mount Etna, an active volcano which reaches a height of 10,930 ft (3,332 m). Farming and tourism are the primary sources of income. Increasing numbers of tourists are attracted by the island's beautiful beaches and ancient ruins.

ROMAN CATHOLICS

More than half of all Christians are Roman Catholics. They follow the leadership of the Pope in the Vatican and, together with other Christians, believe in three beings in one God: the Creator and Father; Jesus Christ as God become man; and the Holy Spirit. More than 80 percent of Italians are Roman Catholic.

St. Peter's Basilica, Vatican City, Rome, is the world's largest Christian church. Shaped like a cross, it is nearly 700 ft (210 m) long and extends to about 450 ft (137 m) at its widest point.

Mary, the virgin mother of Christ, is regarded by Roman Catholics as the highest of all human beings.

VATICAN CITY

Vatican City is a walled city in Rome, and the headquarters of the Roman Catholic Church. It is the official residence of the Pope, and the smallest independent state in the world, with an area of 0.17 sq miles (0.44 sq km). The Vatican has its own flag, national anthem, stamps, and coins, as well as a newspaper and radio station. St. Peter's Basilica, which overlooks a grand piazza (left), dominates the city.

SARDINIA

Sardinia is an island 109 miles (175 km) off mainland Italy, in the Mediterranean Sea. It is a self-governing political region of Italy with its own president and elected regional assembly. The central Italian government, however, controls education, justice, communications such as railroads and postal services, defense, and national taxation.

This is the southernmost reach of the Gennargentu Mountains, Sardinia.

MALTA

Malta is a small country in the Mediterranean Sea just south of Sicily. Since ancient times, it has been a vital naval base because of its position on trade routes to the East. Romans, Arabs, French, Turks, Spanish, and British have all colonized or fought over the island. Malta finally gained independence from Britain in 1964, joining the EU in 2004. Tourism is a major source of the country's income.

Find out more

EUROPE
ITALY, HISTORY OF
RENAISSANCE
ROMAN EMPIRE

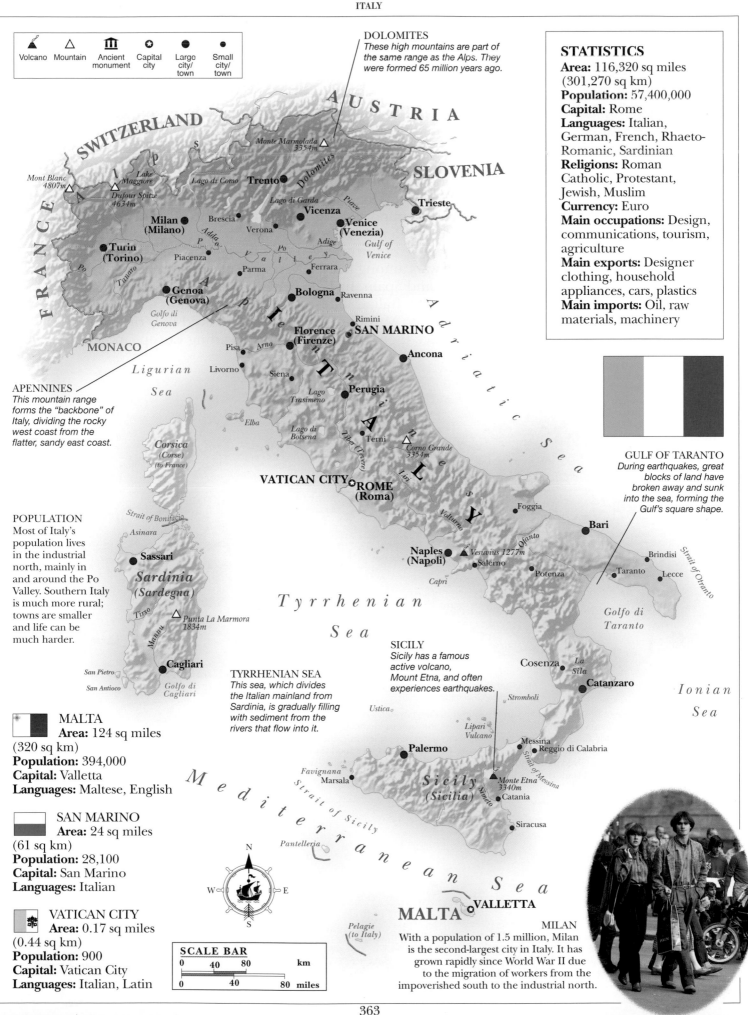

Volcano · **Mountain** · **Ancient monument** · **Capital city** · **Large city/town** · **Small city/town**

DOLOMITES
These high mountains are part of the same range as the Alps. They were formed 65 million years ago.

STATISTICS
Area: 116,320 sq miles (301,270 sq km)
Population: 57,400,000
Capital: Rome
Languages: Italian, German, French, Rhaeto-Romanic, Sardinian
Religions: Roman Catholic, Protestant, Jewish, Muslim
Currency: Euro
Main occupations: Design, communications, tourism, agriculture
Main exports: Designer clothing, household appliances, cars, plastics
Main imports: Oil, raw materials, machinery

SWITZERLAND
AUSTRIA
SLOVENIA
FRANCE
MONACO

Mont Blanc 4807m
Dufour Spitze 4634m
Lake Maggiore
Lago di Como
Monte Marmolada 3354m
Trento
Dolomites
Trieste
Milan (Milano)
Brescia
Vicenza
Verona
Venice (Venezia)
Gulf of Venice
Turin (Torino)
Adda
Piacenza
Po
Parma
Ferrara
Adige
Piave
Tanaro
Po Valley
Genoa (Genova)
Golfo di Genova
Bologna
Ravenna
Rimini
Florence (Firenze)
SAN MARINO
Pisa
Arno
Ancona
Livorno
Siena
Perugia
Lago Trasimeno
Elba
Lago di Bolsena
Terni
Corno Grande 3354m
VATICAN CITY
ROME (Roma)
Liri
Tiber (Tevere)
Foggia
Volturno
Ofanto
Bari
Brindisi
Naples (Napoli)
Vesuvius 1277m
Salerno
Capri
Potenza
Taranto
Lecce
Golfo di Taranto
Strait of Otranto

APENNINES
This mountain range forms the "backbone" of Italy, dividing the rocky west coast from the flatter, sandy east coast.

Ligurian Sea
Corsica (Corse) (to France)

POPULATION
Most of Italy's population lives in the industrial north, mainly in and around the Po Valley. Southern Italy is much more rural; towns are smaller and life can be much harder.

Strait of Bonifacio
Asinara
Sassari
Sardinia (Sardegna)
Tirso
Punta La Marmora 1834m
Mannu
Temo
San Pietro
San Antioco
Cagliari
Golfo di Cagliari

Tyrrhenian Sea

TYRRHENIAN SEA
This sea, which divides the Italian mainland from Sardinia, is gradually filling with sediment from the rivers that flow into it.

Ustica

SICILY
Sicily has a famous active volcano, Mount Etna, and often experiences earthquakes.

Cosenza
La Sila
Catanzaro
Ionian Sea
Stromboli
Lipari Vulcano
Messina
Reggio di Calabria
Strait of Messina
Palermo
Favignana
Marsala
Sicily (Sicilia)
Monte Etna 3340m
Simeto
Catania
Siracusa

GULF OF TARANTO
During earthquakes, great blocks of land have broken away and sunk into the sea, forming the Gulf's square shape.

Adriatic Sea

MALTA
Area: 124 sq miles (320 sq km)
Population: 394,000
Capital: Valletta
Languages: Maltese, English

SAN MARINO
Area: 24 sq miles (61 sq km)
Population: 28,100
Capital: San Marino
Languages: Italian

VATICAN CITY
Area: 0.17 sq miles (0.44 sq km)
Population: 900
Capital: Vatican City
Languages: Italian, Latin

Mediterranean Sea
Pantelleria
Pelagie (to Italy)
MALTA
VALLETTA

N W E S

SCALE BAR
0   40   80   km
0   40   80   miles

MILAN
With a population of 1.5 million, Milan is the second-largest city in Italy. It has grown rapidly since World War II due to the migration of workers from the impoverished south to the industrial north.

HISTORY OF
ITALy

FOR 500 YEARS Italy was at the center of the powerful Roman Empire. In 476 the empire fell. Various tribes conquered Italy and divided it among them. Because Rome was the center of the Catholic Church, Italian popes grew powerful during the Middle Ages. During the 1300s, independent city-states developed from communities that had grown rich through industry, trade, and banking. These city-states became very powerful, and their wealthy rulers supported arts during the 14th and 15th centuries – a period known as the Renaissance. For a time, Italian ideas and styles dominated the whole of Europe. But the city-states, weakened by constant squabbling and wars among themselves, were taken over by the Hapsburg family of Austria and Spain. In 1796 Napoleon invaded Italy, and a movement for unification of the Italian states grew. This unification was achieved in 1861. Dictator Benito Mussolini (1883-1945) involved Italy disastrously in World War II. Since then, Italy has become a leading European nation.

ETRUSCANS
The Etruscans lived in an area of western Italy called Etruria in about 800 B.C. They were great traders, farmers, artists, and engineers and built a civilization of small city-states. The Romans eventually conquered the Etruscans but adopted many of their customs, including gladiatorial fights and chariot racing. Above, in an Etruscan sculpture, a chariot runs over a fallen man.

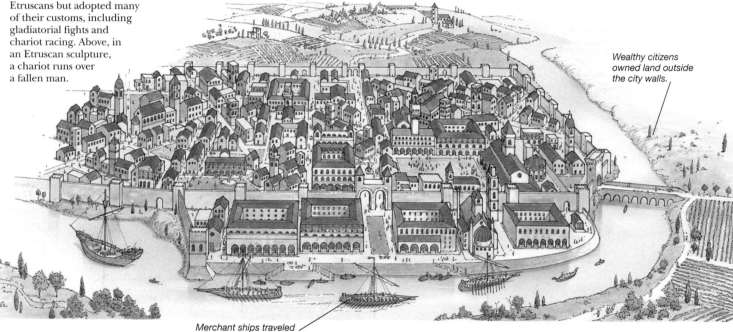

Wealthy citizens owned land outside the city walls.

Merchant ships traveled in search of trade.

CITY-STATES
During the Renaissance (a flourishing of arts and learning), Italian city-states such as Venice and Florence were important centers of learning. In Florence, the famous Medici family came to power in 1434 and ruled for almost 300 years. Many other city-states were ruled by princes elected by rich citizens who owned huge estates outside the city walls. The estates produced food for the craftworkers and scholars who lived in the city. Most city-states were near the sea, making it easy for Italian merchants to travel to distant countries in search of trade.

DOGE'S BARGE
Venice, the most powerful Italian city-state, was built on a lagoon and crisscrossed by canals. Its huge fleet of ships enabled it to set up a rich empire in the eastern Mediterranean. Each year the ruler of Venice, called the doge, went to sea in his magnificent barge and gave thanks for this wealth by "marrying" the sea with a golden ring. The doge lived in the palace shown at right.

SAVOY
Milan
Venice
REPUBLIC OF VENICE
Genoa
REPUBLIC OF GENOA
Florence
PAPAL STATES
Siena
Corsica
Rome
Naples
KINGDOM OF NAPLES

RENAISSANCE ITALY
At the end of the Renaissance, rivalry and constant fighting weakened the city-states. Italy became easy prey and an attractive prize for invaders from Spain, Austria, and France, who laid claims to the land.

GARIBALDI

In 1860, Giuseppe Garibaldi (1807-82) became an Italian hero. He led a small army of 1,000 volunteer soldiers, called Red Shirts, to free Sicily from the rule of the king of Naples, so that the island of Sicily could become part of a new united Italy.

CAVOUR

Camillo di Cavour (1810-61), prime minister of Piedmont, was a brilliant statesman who dreamed of a united Italy. He led the movement to unite all the Italian states into one country.

MUSSOLINI

In 1922, Benito Mussolini (below) became dictator of Italy. Mussolini introduced a form of government called fascism, under which the government controlled everything in the country. Mussolini's vast building projects created jobs, but his secret police silenced his opponents. Mussolini, who was also called Il Duce (the leader), wanted to make Italy great, but he became unpopular when his armies were defeated in World War II.

Benito Mussolini making a speech

NAPOLEON

Napoleon Bonaparte (above, on horseback) invaded Italy and defeated the Austrian Hapsburgs, who ruled it at the time. He destroyed the old system of many different governments and introduced a single system with the same laws. For the first time since the days of Ancient Rome, Italians from different regions were ruled in the same way. Many began to dream of a united Italy, free from foreign rulers.

PALIO

Each summer a colorful festival takes place in the ancient Etruscan city of Siena, northern Italy. This pageant, called the Palio, celebrates the power of the city-state, and comes to a climax with a horse race staged in the main square of the city. The race is fast and dangerous. Each *contrada* (city district) is represented by a colorful flag and symbol, and competes fiercely for the honor of winning.

ITALY

509 B.C. Romans drive out Etruscans and establish the Roman republic.

A.D. 476 German barbarians overthrow last Roman emperor, Romulus Augustulus. Invading German tribes break up empire.

c. 1300 Renaissance begins in Italy.

1796 Napoleon Bonaparte invades and seizes Italy.

1815 Napoleon defeated at Waterloo. Representatives from Austria, Great Britain, Prussia, and Russia (the victorious nations) meet at the Congress of Vienna. Most of Italy is returned to its old rulers.

1858 Cavour, prime minister of the Kingdom of Piedmont, makes a treaty with Napoleon III of France to defend the kingdom from the Austrians.

1859 Combined French and Piedmontese army defeats Austrians.

1861 All of Italy, except Venice, San Marino, and the city of Rome, join to become the Kingdom of Italy. Victor Emmanuel II, king of Piedmont, becomes King of Italy.

1871 Rome becomes capital of Italy, but the Pope's territory of Vatican City remains an independent state.

1915 Italy joins World War I, fighting with the Allies (Britain, France, and Russia).

1922 Benito Mussolini becomes ruler of Italy.

1940 Italy joins World War II, fighting with the Germans.

1943 Italy surrenders to Allies.

1945 Italian resistance fighters kill Mussolini.

1946 Italy becomes a republic.

1949 Italy joins North Atlantic Treaty Organization (NATO) with 11 other Western countries, to protect against Soviet expansion.

1957 Italy joins the EEC (European Economic Community).

Find out more

ITALY
NAPOLEON BONAPARTE
NAPOLEONIC WARS
RENAISSANCE
ROMAN EMPIRE

JAPAN

THE TOPS OF A SUBMERGED mountain chain form the islands of Japan. About three-quarters of the country is too steep to farm or build on. Japan has a population of 128 million, most of whom live in valleys and on the narrow coastal plain. Japan is a leading industrial nation, but its success is fairly recent: until 1853 the country was closed to foreigners, and the government refused to import modern machines. More recently, Japanese companies have been very successful in exporting their own goods, so Japan sells more than it buys and has become very wealthy. Western influence is strong, but the Japanese are very proud of their traditional culture and religion. They continue to practice old customs while developing modern technology. Most people follow both the Buddhist and Shinto religions. The head of state is an emperor, but the government is democratic. In the past the country was ruled by noblemen and samurai, professional soldiers who had a strict code of honor. Although the samurai have long been disbanded, their code still influences everyday life.

BONSAI
Japanese bonsai trees are pruned so that they do not grow more than a few inches high.

Japan is located in the Pacific Ocean, off the east coast of Asia. North and South Korea are to the west, and the Russian Federation to the north. There are four main islands, covering almost 144 sq miles (370,000 sq km).

TOKYO
The largest city in Japan is the capital, Tokyo. More than 20 million people live in the city and suburbs, and the whole area is extremely overcrowded. Fumes from cars and industry are a major problem, but effective measures are being taken to reduce pollution.

INDUSTRY
Although Japan has few raw materials such as metal ores or coal, Japanese industry is among the most successful in the world. The country's main resource is its workforce. Japanese workers are very loyal to their companies, and many workers take their vacations together, exercise together, and sing the company song daily. Managers are equally devoted to the company and pride themselves on their cooperation with the workers. New technology and techniques are introduced quickly and help boost prosperity.

SUSHI
Traditional Japanese food consists mainly of fish and rice. Often the fish is eaten raw or lightly cooked in dishes called sushi.

SUMO WRESTLING
The national sport of Japan is sumo wrestling. It attracts large crowds and is shown on television. The two contestants try to push each other out of a small ring. Success depends on strength and weight, so sumo wrestlers go to schools where they train and follow a special diet. Successful wrestlers may become extremely rich and famous. The sport is traditional and follows an elaborate pattern controlled by officials in decorative costume.

BULLET TRAIN
Japan has more than 16,000 miles (25,000 km) of railroads. The most famous train is the Shinkansen, or bullet train, which runs from Tokyo to Fukuoka. The train covers the 731 miles (1,176 km) in less than six hours at an average speed of 122 mph (195 km/h) per hour.

Mount Fuji, a 12,388 ft (3,776 m) tall volcano, is sacred to the Japanese.

Japanese people travel more by train than travelers in any other country.

RICE CAKES
Rice cakes called *chimaki* are traditionally eaten throughout Japan. The rice cakes are cone-shaped and wrapped in a bamboo leaf. A similar snack, called *sasadango*, is also eaten in some areas of northern Japan.

VEHICLE INDUSTRY
Japanese vehicle manufacturers became world leaders in the 1980s thanks to their stylish designs, new technology, and efficient production methods. Today, automobiles are the country's biggest export. Japanese vehicle manufacturers have also opened a number of factories in Europe and the US.

This Kawasaki ZZ-R1100 has a top speed of 175 mph (282 km/h).

KYUSHU
The southernmost island of Japan, Kyushu, is mountainous; the highest point is a volcano, Mount Aso. Kyushu is the most densely populated of the Japanese islands, and is linked to Honshu island by a railroad tunnel under the Shimonoseki Strait.

SAKE
Sake is a Japanese alcoholic beverage made from fermented rice. It is the national beverage, and is served with special ceremony. Before being served, it is warmed in a small earthenware or porcelain bottle called a *tokkuri* (right).

ZEN GARDEN
Rock gardens, designed to represent the universe in miniature, are found in Zen Buddhist monasteries in Japan. These gardens are not literal representations of a landscape, but they give the impression of water and land. Sand or gravel symbolizes water, while rocks represent land. The Zen garden has no plants, trees, or water, only raked gravel or sand, and rock groupings. These "dry gardens" were introduced by Buddhist monks in the 1300s.

KITES
Carp kites are flown on the fifth day of May to celebrate *Kodomono-hi*, or children's day. The carp is a strong robust fish, renowned for its energy and determination, because it must swim upstream against the current, often jumping high out of the water. The carp is thought to provide a good example to Japanese boys in particular, who must overcome obstacles and be successful. A group of carp kites represent a family and the largest kite symbolizes the father.

Zen Buddhists believe that performing simple tasks such as raking pebbles in a Zen garden can bring enlightenment to the mind.

OSAKA
Japan's third-largest city is Osaka, on the south coast of the island of Honshu. Osaka is a major industrial center, with steel, chemical, and electrical industries. It is also one of the oldest cities in Japan, and has many Buddhist and Shinto temples. Osaka is the site of an impressive castle built in the 16th century by the shogun (warlord) Toyomoti Hideyoshi, who once ruled Japan. In 1970 Osaka was the host city for the World's Fair.

Find out more
ASIA
DEMOCRACY
EARTHQUAKES
JAPAN, HISTORY OF
WEAPONS

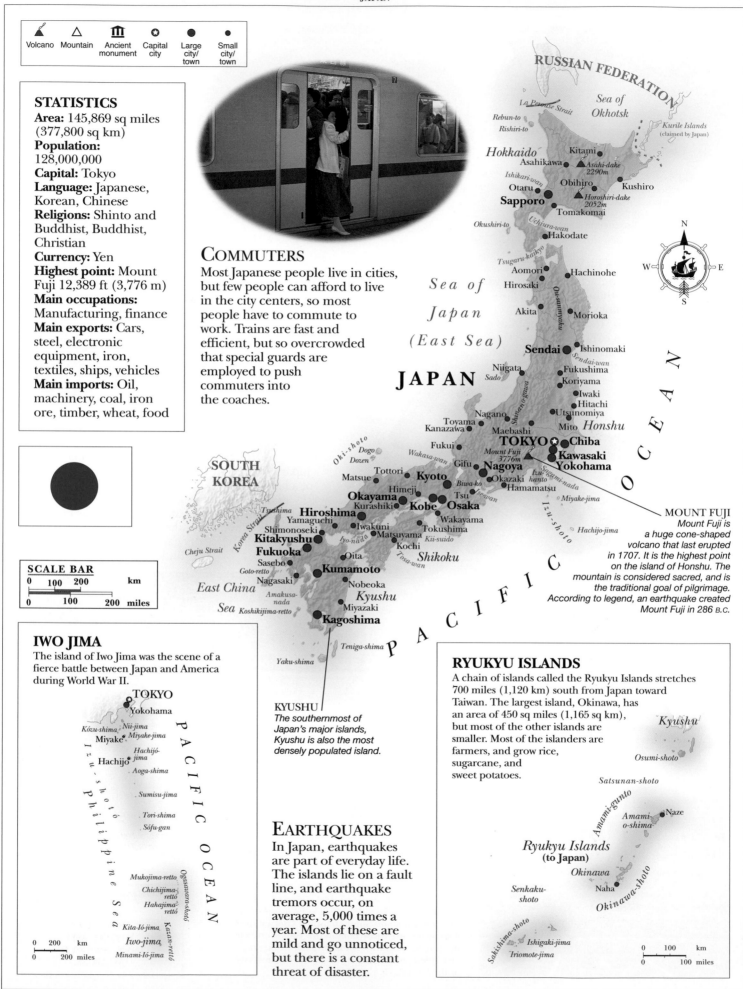

Volcano   **Mountain**   **Ancient monument**   **Capital city**   **Large city/town**   **Small city/town**

STATISTICS

Area: 145,869 sq miles (377,800 sq km)
Population: 128,000,000
Capital: Tokyo
Language: Japanese, Korean, Chinese
Religions: Shinto and Buddhist, Buddhist, Christian
Currency: Yen
Highest point: Mount Fuji 12,389 ft (3,776 m)
Main occupations: Manufacturing, finance
Main exports: Cars, steel, electronic equipment, iron, textiles, ships, vehicles
Main imports: Oil, machinery, coal, iron ore, timber, wheat, food

COMMUTERS

Most Japanese people live in cities, but few people can afford to live in the city centers, so most people have to commute to work. Trains are fast and efficient, but so overcrowded that special guards are employed to push commuters into the coaches.

SCALE BAR

0   100   200   km
0   100   200   miles

IWO JIMA

The island of Iwo Jima was the scene of a fierce battle between Japan and America during World War II.

EARTHQUAKES

In Japan, earthquakes are part of everyday life. The islands lie on a fault line, and earthquake tremors occur, on average, 5,000 times a year. Most of these are mild and go unnoticed, but there is a constant threat of disaster.

MOUNT FUJI

Mount Fuji is a huge cone-shaped volcano that last erupted in 1707. It is the highest point on the island of Honshu. The mountain is considered sacred, and is the traditional goal of pilgrimage. According to legend, an earthquake created Mount Fuji in 286 B.C.

KYUSHU

The southernmost of Japan's major islands, Kyushu is also the most densely populated island.

RYUKYU ISLANDS

A chain of islands called the Ryukyu Islands stretches 700 miles (1,120 km) south from Japan toward Taiwan. The largest island, Okinawa, has an area of 450 sq miles (1,165 sq km), but most of the other islands are smaller. Most of the islanders are farmers, and grow rice, sugarcane, and sweet potatoes.

Map labels

RUSSIAN FEDERATION
Sea of Okhotsk
Kurile Islands (claimed by Japan)
La Perouse Strait
Rebun-to
Rishiri-to
Hokkaido
Kitami
Asahikawa
Asahi-dake 2290m
Ishikari-wan
Obihiro
Kushiro
Otaru
Horoshiri-dake 2052m
Sapporo
Tomakomai
Okushiri-to
Uchiura-wan
Hakodate
Tsugaru-kaikyo
Sea of Japan (East Sea)
Aomori
Hachinohe
Hirosaki
Oku-sanmyaku
Akita
Morioka
JAPAN
Sendai
Ishinomaki
Sendai-wan
Niigata
Fukushima
Sado
Koriyama
Shinano-gawa
Iwaki
Nagano
Hitachi
Toyama
Utsunomiya
Honshu
Kanazawa
Maebashi
Mito
Fukui
TOKYO
Chiba
Mount Fuji 3776m
Kawasaki
Oki-shoto
Gifu
Yokohama
Dogo
Nagoya
Dozen
Izu-hanto
Wakasa-wan
Okazaki
Tottori
Hamamatsu
Sagami-nada
Matsue
Kyoto
Biwa-ko
Tsu
Miyake-jima
Himeji
Ise-wan
Okayama
Kobe
Osaka
Kurashiki
Wakayama
Izu-shoto
Hiroshima
Iwakuni
Matsuyama
Tokushima
Hachijo-jima
Yamaguchi
Iyo-nada
Kochi
Kii-suido
Shimonoseki
Shikoku
Kitakyushu
Kii-suido
Fukuoka
Oita
Tosa-wan
Sasebo
Kumamoto
Nagasaki
Nobeoka
Goto-retto
Kyushu
Amakusa-nada
Miyazaki
Koshikijima-retto
Kagoshima
Teniga-shima
Yaku-shima
East China Sea
SOUTH KOREA
Tsushima
Korea Strait
Cheju Strait

Iwo Jima map
TOKYO
Yokohama
Kozu-shima
Nii-jima
Miyake
Miyake-jima
Hachijo-jima
Hachijo
Aoga-shima
Sumisu-jima
Tori-shima
Sofu-gan
Mukojima-retto
Chichijima-retto
Hahajima-retto
Ogasawara-shoto
Kita-Io-jima
Iwo-jima
Kazan-retto
Minami-Io-jima
PACIFIC OCEAN
Izu-shoto
Philippine Sea
0   200   km
0   200   miles

Ryukyu Islands map
Kyushu
Osumi-shoto
Satsunan-shoto
Amami-gunto
Naze
Amami-o-shima
Ryukyu Islands (to Japan)
Okinawa
Naha
Senkaku-shoto
Okinawa-shoto
Sakishima-shoto
Ishigaki-jima
Iriomote-jima
0   100   km
0   100   miles

PACIFIC OCEAN

HISTORY OF
JAPAN

THE GROUP OF ISLANDS THAT FORM JAPAN remained isolated from the rest of the world until quite recently. During the 6th century A.D., Japan absorbed ideas from its neighbor, China. It also adopted China's Buddhist religion and the Chinese system of imperial rule. But 200 years later, Chinese influence declined, and the imperial system broke down. Until the 1860s, powerful families, and then shoguns (military generals), ruled Japan in the name of the emperor. People rarely invaded Japan successfully. The Mongols tried and failed in the 13th century. During the 16th century, European traders were also unsuccessful. But in 1868, Japan began to look toward the West. Within 50 years it had built up a strong, modern economy and a large empire. All this was destroyed during World War II (1939-45). However, Japan has recovered and is once again rich.

NARA
Nara, the first capital city of Japan, was the political and religious center of the country. It was the site of the Buddhist Horyuji Temple (above).

TEA CEREMONY
After the 14th century, the ritual ceremony of drinking tea became very popular in Japan. The ceremony was based on the Zen Buddhist principles of self-discipline and meditation, and was very popular among the warlike shoguns and samurai.

Curved samurai sword

Special suit of armor which a samurai could get into quickly from the side or from below

SHOGUNATE
The shogunate was a hereditary military dictatorship. During shogun rule, an aristocratic class of knights called the samurai gained considerable power. These warriors protected the lands of the daimyo (local lords) and followed a code of honor known as the Bushido – "the way of the warrior." Samurai warriors committed hara kiri (suicide) if they lost their honor.

THE TALE OF GENJI
In the early 11th century a Japanese woman named Murasaki Shikibu wrote one of the world's first novels. More than 600,000 words long, *The Tale of Genji* describes the adventures of a young prince and his travels in search of love and education. The novel was written in Japanese at a time when the official language of the country was Chinese: only commoners and women were allowed to speak Japanese.

A.D. 400s Yamato clan unites Japan.

794 Capital city of Kyoto founded.

1192 Minamoto Yoritomo becomes first shogun.

1281 "Divine wind" saves Japan from Mongols.

1338-1573 Civil wars.

1542 Portuguese sailors visit Japan.

1549 St. Francis Xavier introduces Christianity to Japan.

1592, 1597 Japan invades Korea.

1639 Almost all Europeans leave.

1853 US Navy forces Japan to trade with the West.

1868 Meiji restoration returns power to emperor.

1868 Tokyo becomes national capital.

1889 Constitutional government.

1904-5 Russo-Japanese War.

1910 Japan takes control of Korea.

1914-18 Japan fights Germany in World War I.

1937-45 Japan invades China, Southeast Asia; bombs Pearl Harbor in 1941, bringing United States into World War II.

1945 US drops first atomic bombs on Hiroshima and Nagasaki; Japanese surrender.

1989 Hirohito dies.

TOKUGAWA DYNASTY

In 1603, Ieyasu of the Tokugawa family became shogun. His dynasty (family) ruled Japan until the shogunate was overthrown in 1868. Ieyasu put down the Christian movement which had been brought in by Saint Francis Xavier. Foreigners were expelled, and contact with the outside world was forbidden.

Samurai warriors

Tea ceremony

WESTERNIZATION

In 1853, Commodore Matthew Perry of the US Navy sailed into Tokyo Bay and demanded that Japan end its isolation and begin trading with the outside world. Dramatic changes followed. The shogunate ended, and the young emperor Meiji took power. Within 50 years, Japan became one of the world's leading industrial and economic powers. Factories and railroads were built, a national education system was set up, and students were sent abroad to learn about Western life.

SINO-JAPANESE WAR

Japan went to war with China in 1894-95 over the control of Korea, and then with Russia in 1904-5 in order to gain colonies in Taiwan, Korea, and China. Both wars revealed the new Westernized Japan to be a powerful force in world affairs.

KAMIKAZE

In the 13th century, a storm destroyed the Mongol fleet and saved Japan from invasion. Japanese called the storm kamikaze, meaning "divine wind." During World War II, the Japanese used kamikaze pilots, who crashed their bomb-laden planes onto American warships. These "suicide pilots" believed that they, like the storm, were saving Japan, and were blessed by the emperor, whom they believed to be divine.

HIROHITO

According to tradition, the first emperor of Japan was descended from the sun goddess and took power around 660 B.C. An unbroken line of descent then stretched to Hirohito, who in 1926 became the 124th emperor. In 1946, after the Japanese defeat in World War II, Hirohito publicly rejected the divinity of the emperor. He died in 1989. His son Akihito became emperor in 1990.

Find out more

CHINA, HISTORY OF
JAPAN
NUCLEAR AGE
WORLD WAR I
WORLD WAR II

THOMAS JEFFERSON

THE AUTHOR OF THE DECLARATION OF INDEPENDENCE and the third president of the United States, Thomas Jefferson helped to shape the American spirit. Born in Virginia, Jefferson began his career as a lawyer. At 25 he joined the Virginia legislature, where he became a leading voice for colonial self-rule. In 1776, Jefferson wrote the Declaration of Independence; its adoption led to the American Revolution. He took up a diplomatic post in Paris in 1784. In 1801, Jefferson was elected to the first of two terms as president. Jefferson's policies were shaped by his belief in the right of people to govern themselves.

1743 Born in Shadwell, VA.

1767 Begins law practice.

1776 Writes the Declaration of Independence.

1785 Serves as minister to France.

1789 Appointed US secretary of state.

1796 Elected vice president.

1801 Begins first of two terms as president.

1819 Founds the University of Virginia.

1826 Dies at Monticello.

Benjamin Franklin (left), John Adams (center), and Thomas Jefferson (right) study the Declaration of Independence.

PRESIDENT

Thomas Jefferson served as secretary of state under George Washington and vice president under John Adams. In 1800 he was nominated for president, but the result was a tie. After a vote in Congress, Jefferson was named president the following year. In his first term, he worked to reduce the government's national role. He tried to make the presidency less formal, asking guests to shake his hand instead of bowing. He was elected to a second term in 1804, and managed to maintain the United States' neutrality while the Napoleonic wars raged in Europe.

PATRIOT

Jefferson joined the Virginia legislature in 1769, and soon became one of those patriots leading the fight for fair representation in Britain. In 1775 and 1776, he was chosen as delegate to the Continental Congress. Because of his knowledge of the law and his clear writing skills, he was asked to draft the Declaration of Independence.

Before the Louisiana purchase, the United States stretched from the Atlantic coast to the Mississippi River.

LOUISIANA PURCHASE

One of the most important achievements of Jefferson's presidency was the purchase of the Louisiana Territory from France in 1803, which doubled the size of the United States. Jefferson had always encouraged westward expansion. He sent Meriwether Lewis and William Clark on their famous expedition (1804-08) from the Missouri River across the Rockies to the Pacific.

Jefferson holds the Declaration of Independence.

MONTICELLO

Jefferson was a self-taught architect and he built his home, Monticello (above), on a hilltop near Charlottesville, VA. Inside were several of Jefferson's own inventions, including a swivel chair, and an indoor weather vane connected to the roof.

Find out more

AMERICAN REVOLUTION
DECLARATION OF INDEPENDENCE
UNITED STATES, HISTORY OF

JESUS CHRIST

ONE OF THE WORLD'S MAJOR RELIGIONS – Christianity – was inspired by a man named Jesus Christ. We know about Jesus from the New Testament gospels, which were written by Matthew, Mark, Luke, and John, men who knew Him. The gospels declare that Jesus was a Jew born in Bethlehem, in the Roman province of Judea, and was believed by many to be the Son of God. At the age of 30 He began to travel around Palestine (then under Roman rule) preaching a new message. He told stories called parables to explain His ideas. The gospels also describe miracles – amazing things He did such as raising the dead. However, some people thought His ideas might cause rebellion against Roman rule. He was arrested, tried, and sentenced to death. When Jesus appeared to his disciples (closest followers) after His death, they were convinced that God had raised Him from the dead. The Christian church was founded on the belief, and Christianity eventually swept across the Roman Empire.

NATIVITY
The birth of Jesus, which took place in a stable in Bethlehem, is called the Nativity. Every year, on December 25, Christians celebrate Jesus' birthday.

WHERE JESUS LIVED
Jesus spent His childhood in Nazareth. He preached mainly in Judea and Galilee.

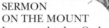

Jesus' travels around Palestine

Sidon
Tyre
Galilee
Nazareth
Tiberias
Caesarea
Samaria
Jericho
Judea
Jerusalem
Bethlehem
Dead Sea
Gaza

SERMON ON THE MOUNT
Jesus taught that God was a kind, loving father, and that people should not fight back when attacked, but should "turn the other cheek." He stressed the importance of love. His Sermon on the Mount contained new ideas describing how ordinary people who were humble, gentle, and poor would go to heaven. He also taught His followers a special prayer – the Lord's Prayer.

RESURRECTION
On Sunday morning, three days after Jesus' death, the tomb in which His body had been placed was found empty. The gospels of Matthew, Mark, Luke and John tell how He appeared to his disciples and, after 40 days of teaching them, rose to heaven.

LAST SUPPER
Near the end of His life Jesus shared a last supper with his 12 disciples. Using bread and wine as symbols of His body and blood, Jesus told them to remember Him by this feast. To this day, the last supper is reenacted during Communion, when Christians share wine and bread as part of church services.

CRUCIFIXION
Jesus was accused of treason against Rome and condemned to death by the Roman governor, Pontius Pilate. He was sentenced to be crucified – nailed to a cross on a hill called Calvary, outside Jerusalem. After His death, His body was sealed in a tomb.

Find out more
CHRISTIANITY
RELIGIONS

JOAN of ARC

IN THE EARLY 15TH CENTURY the French finally defeated the English, who had ruled much of their country. The warrior who led them into battle was a woman who has since become one of the best-loved heroines of French history. Joan of Arc was born into a farming family in 1412. She could not read or write, but she was inspired and stubborn, and could debate with educated people. As a young girl, Joan heard "voices" of saints and angels. The voices told her that she must restore the rightful king to the throne of France. Joan convinced the heir to the throne (the Dauphin) – who later became King Charles VII – to support her. In 1429, when only 17, she led the French army to victory at Orléans. Joan led her country's troops in other successful battles, but in 1430 she was caught by a powerful group of French people from Burgundy. They sold her to the English, who imprisoned her and put her on trial as a heretic – a person who does not believe in the official teachings of the Church. Joan was found guilty, and on May 30, 1431, she was executed in Rouen by being burned at the stake. After her death the English were driven out of France, and Joan's reputation as a heroine flourished. Legends about Joan became widespread, and in 1920 she was made a saint.

The banner flown by Joan in battle

MEETING THE DAUPHIN
This contemporary tapestry shows Joan's arrival at the Château of Chinon in February 1429, in the company of six armed men. She is greeted by the Dauphin Charles, who wears a golden crown – a token of his claim to the disputed French throne.

THE MAID OF ORLEANS

Joan of Arc was a brave fighter who wore a suit of armor like a man. She was deeply religious, and prayed for guidance before going into battle. She was known as the "Maid of Orléans" because she led the French army to victory at Orléans.

JOAN'S HELMET
Joan may have worn this helmet in battle against the English. There is a hole in the side made by an arrow or a crossbow bolt.

THE FEARLESS LEADER

Joan demonstrated that previous French defeat had resulted from military error and that, with better tactics, victories were possible. At first the troops were reluctant to follow Joan, but they soon realized that they won when obeying her commands. Joan's first victory was the lifting of the English siege of Orléans in 1429, which swelled the troops' confidence in their young leader. The Orléans victory was followed by similar success at Jargeau, Meung, Beaugency, and Patay. Her thrilling run came to an end when she was captured at Compiègne on May 24, 1430.

Joan leads the French troops into battle at Orléans.

CROSS OF LORRAINE
During World War II (1939-45), France was occupied by Germany, partly under German military control and partly under a pro-German French government. The fighters of the French Resistance movement adopted the cross of Lorraine, originally Joan of Arc's symbol, because they shared her aim – to rid their country of foreign domination.

Find out more
FRANCE, HISTORY OF
MEDIEVAL EUROPE

JUDAISM

THE HISTORY OF THE JEWISH PEOPLE and of their religion, Judaism, are closely linked. All Jews believe in one God who, more than 4,000 years ago, made a special agreement with their ancestor, Abraham. They were to become God's chosen people. In return they promised to obey his laws and to spread his message to others. Jews believe that a Messiah, God's messenger, will one day come to transform the world into a better place and to restore the ancient Jewish kingdom that was destroyed in the 6th century B.C. Judaism aims for a just and peaceful life for all people on earth. Jewish scriptures explain that to achieve this aim, correct behavior is very important. Orthodox Jews – those who interpret the scriptures very strictly – obey many rules about their day-to-day activities, including how to dress and what to eat. For example, they do not eat pork or shellfish. Many Jews, however, are not orthodox and apply the rules less strictly. For all Jews, Hebrew is the language of worship. It is also the national language of Israel, the Jewish homeland. However, Jews live and work all over the world, speaking many different languages. Their strong family life and the laws that guide them unite them wherever they live.

JEWISH FESTIVALS

Yom Kippur (Day of Atonement) Tenth day of New Year; holiest of festivals, with 24 hours of fasting.

Purim (Feast of Lots) Early spring festival.

Passover (Pesach) Eight-day spring festival.

Shavuot (Feast of Weeks) Harvest festival in early summer.

Rosh Hashanah (New Year) Early fall.

Sukkoth (Feast of Tabernacles) Nine-day fall festival.

Hanukkah (Festival of Lights) Eight-day winter festival.

Jews light candles in a menorah, or branched candlestick, during Hanukkah.

Jewish men wear a skull cap called a yarmulke or kipa.

TALMUD

Jewish religious leaders are called rabbis. They are responsible for teaching and explaining the laws of Judaism. They study two holy books: the Talmud (right) and the Torah which is kept as a scroll. The Talmud contains instructions for following a Jewish way of life and understanding Jewish laws.

During prayers Jewish men wear a tallith, or prayer shawl, over their shoulders.

The Talmud contains instructions for following the Jewish way of life.

TORAH

The first five books of the Hebrew Bible – the Torah (left) – contain the laws of Judaism and the early history of the Jewish people. Other sections of the Hebrew Bible contain the psalms, the words of the prophets, and other holy writings. For Jews, the Torah is the most important of books.

SYNAGOGUE

Jews worship in the synagogue. Prayer, study, and special family occasions such as weddings and bar and bat mitzvahs (the celebrations of children becoming adult Jews) take place here. A *minyan* (quorum of 10 males) is required to formally recite Kaddish (memorial prayers) and read from the Torah.

Find out more

FESTIVALS AND FEASTS
ISRAEL
RELIGIONS

JOHN F. KENNEDY

AN ASSASSIN'S BULLET abruptly ended the promise that John Fitzgerald Kennedy brought to the American presidency. His family name meant politics in their hometown of Boston. Kennedy graduated from Harvard University, then served in the US Navy. After the war, Kennedy launched his political career, serving first in the House of Representatives, then in the Senate. In 1956, he began a long campaign for the presidency, which ended with his winning by a small margin in 1960. He brought youth and vigor to the White House, and his wife Jackie became a fashion icon.

1917 Born in Brookline, Massachusetts.

1940 Graduates from Harvard University.

1941-45 Serves in US Navy during World War II.

1945 Wins election to US House of Representatives.

1952 Elected to US Senate.

1953 Marries Jacqueline Bouvier.

1960 Elected 35th President of the US.

1961 Berlin Wall divides East and West Berlin.

1962 Presides over the Cuban missile crisis.

1963 Assassinated in Dallas, Texas.

THE KENNEDY DYNASTY

Kennedy was born into America's most glamorous and famous political dynasty. His grandfather was a state senator in Massachusetts, and his father served as ambassador to Great Britain. His mother's father was mayor of Boston and a US congressman. Three of the nine Kennedy children developed political careers: John; Robert, who became attorney general during his brother's presidency, then served as a US senator for New York until his own assassination in 1968; and Edward (known as Ted), who has represented Massachusetts in the Senate since 1962.

In his time, President Kennedy was the youngest president of the United States, and the first Roman Catholic to hold the office.

Cartoon of Cuban leader Fidel Castro

CUBAN MISSILE CRISIS

When satellites revealed Soviet missiles in Cuba within striking distance of several US cities, Kennedy ordered a naval blockade. For 13 days, the world was on the brink of war, until the missiles were withdrawn.

KENNEDY'S ASSASSINATION

In 1963, Kennedy and his wife, campaigning in Texas, rode an open-top car through Dallas. Shots rang out and Kennedy slumped down. He died half an hour later. Police arrested Lee Harvey Oswald, who denied the shooting. Two days later, as Oswald was taken to prison, he was killed by a lone gunman in front of a nationwide television audience.

WARTIME HERO

Kennedy served in the US Navy during World War II. After saving his crew in an encounter with a Japanese destroyer near the Solomon Islands, he was awarded a medal for bravery.

John Kennedy was also awarded the Purple Heart, a medal given to those wounded in action.

A NEW BEGINNING

Kennedy campaigned for president with the promise of a new frontier for Americans. Although many voters worried about his lack of experience, Kennedy defeated Richard Nixon. In his inaugural address, Kennedy urged Americans to, "Ask not what your country can do for you – ask what you can do for your country." During Kennedy's short time in office, the US had its first manned space flights, the civil rights movement brought equality closer for African Americans, and the testing of atomic bombs was outlawed.

Find out more

COLD WAR
PRESIDENCY
WORLD WAR II

MARTIN LUTHER
KING, JR.

IN 1963 A BAPTIST MINISTER from Alabama led 250,000 people in a march on Washington, D.C., and delivered a moving and powerful speech. He was Martin Luther King, Jr., and his mission in life was to achieve equality and freedom for black Americans through peaceful means. Under his leadership the civil rights movement won many victories against segregation laws; laws that prevented blacks from voting, separated blacks from whites in schools and other places, and gave white people better opportunities and more freedom. Martin Luther King, Jr. encouraged people to practice nonviolent protest: demonstrations, "sit-ins," and peaceful disobedience of the segregation laws. King went to jail several times and faced constant threats of violence and death, but he continued to work for civil rights. Some white people hated him because he was black, and some black people disliked him because he refused to use more extreme and violent methods. King was assassinated in 1968, but his dream of a country without racial discrimination lives on today. In 1986, the United States began to observe a national holiday in his name.

1929 Born, Atlanta, Georgia.

1954 Baptist minister.

1955 Earns PhD in Philosophy.

1955-56 Leads Montgomery bus boycott.

1957 Southern Christian Leadership Conference.

1963 March on Washington, D.C.

1964 Nobel Peace Prize.

1965 Selma-Montgomery march.

1968 Assassinated.

1986 Holiday established.

PUBLIC SPEAKER

Martin Luther King, Jr.'s words inspired millions of Americans, black and white. At the August 1963 march on Washington, King made a speech that has since become famous. He said: "I have a dream that one day this nation will rise up and live out the true meaning of its creed: We hold these truths to be self-evident; that all men are created equal."

CIVIL RIGHTS MOVEMENT

Black Americans remained second-class citizens throughout the southern states until very recently. They were not allowed to vote, and restrictions were placed on where they could sit in buses and restaurants. During the late 1950s, a movement arose which demanded equal rights for all Americans. Martin Luther King, Jr. and others organized nonviolent protests designed to force changes in the law. In 1964-65, racial discrimination was finally outlawed throughout the United States.

BUS BOYCOTT

In December 1955, Rosa Parks, a black seamstress who worked in an Alabama department store, was arrested for refusing to give up a bus seat reserved for white people. For one year, Martin Luther King, Jr. and his friends persuaded people to boycott (refuse to use) every bus in Montgomery, Alabama, until the segregation of the bus seats was declared illegal.

Find out more

CIVIL RIGHTS
HUMAN RIGHTS
SLAVERY
UNITED STATES, HISTORY OF

KITES AND GLIDERS

CHINESE KITES
Flowing, painted tails in the shape of dragons, birds, and butterflies are typical of traditional Chinese kites. This centipedelike kite is made from 15 round paper and bamboo kites strung together.

Without a line to hold it at the correct angle to the wind, a kite would not be able to fly.

NO FLYING machine is as old as the kite. People in China were flying silk kites more than 3,000 years ago; and legends tell how in 202 B.C. General Huan Theng terrified his enemies with kites whose taut strings wailed eerily in the breeze. Fifteen hundred years later, Marco Polo, the great Italian traveler, came back from China with tales of vast kites that hoisted prisoners into the air to test the wind. In Europe, children have played with toy kites for more than 1,000 years. Gliders owe their origins to kites, and they too are old. In about 1800, the English inventor George Cayley found that a kite with arched wings and a tail could glide through the air without a breeze to lift it or a string to guide it. Later, Cayley built a glider large enough to carry a person. This rough prototype (test model) was the forerunner not only of the streamlined gliders of today but of all winged aircraft.

FLAT KITES
The oldest and simplest kites are diamond-shaped and have flat frames. They can also be strung together to make spectacular writhing serpents.

DELTA KITES
Triangular "delta" kites are simple to build and fly well in light winds. Hang gliders are based on the delta kite.

BOX KITE
Elaborate box kites have a frame that may be a combination of squares, triangles, and rectangles. Box kites are the most stable fliers of all.

HANG GLIDERS
The hang glider is the cheapest and simplest form of aircraft, and hang gliding is becoming an increasingly popular sport. When a hang glider takes to the air, the fabric of the wings arches up to give an aerofoil shape, like an ordinary aircraft wing. Without this, the craft would plummet, not glide, through the air.

The wing is made from lightweight dacron fabric stretched over a long aluminum tube. On some hang gliders, curved spars help give the wing its aerofoil shape.

The pilot hangs under the wing and steers by shifting body weight to one side or the other.

Straps hold the pilot safely in position.

Gliders have long, thin wings which give a lot of lift (upward force) but keep air resistance to a minimum.

Eventually the glider loses height and lands.

The pilot looks for isolated clouds, which often indicate a thermal.

GLIDERS

Because a glider has no engine, it ultimately can fly only downward. Modern gliders are streamlined and made of light fiberglass so that they lose height very slowly. However, a glider needs help to fly far. To take off, an airplane or a truck tows the glider into the air. Then the pilot looks for pockets of rising warm air, called thermals, to keep the glider flying high in the sky.

As the truck moves off, the glider rises into the air.

Once the glider is high enough, the pilot releases the winch line, and the glider flies free.

Warm air rising over a city or a sun-warmed field carries the glider upward in a spiral.

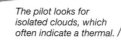

Find out more
AIRCRAFT
CHINA, HISTORY OF
PLASTICS

KNIGHTS AND HERALDRY

Argent a
mullet azure

Vert a lily or

Ermine a cross
crosslet gules

Azure a
dolphin argent

Sable a
bee or

A THOUSAND YEARS AGO men who fought in battle on horseback were called knights. At first they were just powerful warriors who terrified the enemy's foot soldiers. But by the 13th century the knights of western Europe had an important role in society. They fought in the armies of the king or queen in return for land. Knights also protected the peasants who lived and worked on the land, and in exchange the peasants gave the knights their service and produce. Heraldry developed as a way of identifying knights in battle. Armor completely covered the knights' faces and bodies, and they all looked alike. Thus, each knight chose "arms" – a unique colored pattern or picture which everyone could recognize. He displayed his arms on a linen tunic worn over his armor. This was his "coat of arms." The chosen pattern remained in the knight's family and was passed on from father to son.

The knight's symbol, or device, was painted or sewn onto all his equipment.

A fall from horseback meant defeat, and often injured the knight.

Gules a lion
rampant or

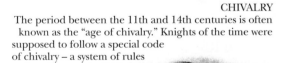

Or a chief
indented purpure

TOURNAMENTS AND JOUSTING

Tournaments began in France in the middle of the 11th century as peacetime training exercises for knights. They soon developed into major events with elaborate rules. Teams of knights fought fierce mock battles over great areas of land, and the losing side paid a ransom or handed over valuable possessions. During the 13th century, tournaments became better organized and took place in a single field. Only two knights jousted at a time, or fought with blunt weapons. Later, tilting replaced jousting and the knights used lances to knock their rivals to the ground.

CHIVALRY

The period between the 11th and 14th centuries is often known as the "age of chivalry." Knights of the time were supposed to follow a special code of chivalry – a system of rules about honor, obedience to God and the king, and protecting the weak. In reality, many knights forgot the code. They honored only people of noble birth and stole from the poor and weak.

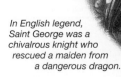

In English legend, Saint George was a chivalrous knight who rescued a maiden from a dangerous dragon.

Argent a talbot
statant sable

Azure a fess
erminois

Gules a
lymphad argent

Azure an owl
argent

Vair a chevron
sable

KNIGHTHOOD

The training to become a knight started at seven years of age. Girls were not allowed to become knights, but boys began as pages in the household of their father's lord. Pages learned the rules of knightly service and how to use weapons. At the age of 15 or 16, a page became a squire. The squire was the personal servant to his master and learned the skills needed for fighting on horseback. After five years the squire could become a knight. At first this was an honor that any knight could bestow on a squire. Today, only English kings and queens can grant knighthoods, but the title is a formal one given to people who deserve national recognition and has lost most of its original meaning.

Dubbing a squire, or tapping him on the shoulders with a sword, made him into a knight.

Once he became a knight, the squire had to supply his own equipment.

THE KNIGHTS OF THE ROUND TABLE

King Arthur and his knights are said to have held their court at a round table in the ancient capital of Camelot. If it really did exist, Camelot was probably built in the west of Britain some fifteen centuries ago. According to legend, Arthur led his band of Celtic knights in battle against Saxon invaders. The knights of Camelot became heroes and had many adventures.

Caerleon Castle, Wales, possible site of Camelot

SHIELDS

Each knight displayed his arms on a shield. The shield had two parts: the field, or surface, painted in a plain color or a pattern; and the charge, which displayed a symbol, such as an animal or bird. The arms appeared everywhere on the knight's equipment. Sometimes the area above the shield design might show an image of a helmet with a crest, silk wreath, and mantling (a cloth for protection from the sun). The knight's motto, or slogan, could also be added below the shield. The full combination of designs was called a heraldic achievement (a herald was an expert in arms).

Gules a barrel palewise or

Argent a rose gules

Vert a garb or

Sable a boar's head erased or

KNIGHTS HOSPITALLERS

Knights from northwest Europe fought in the Crusades – a series of religious wars between Christians and Muslims that took place in the Middle East from the 11th through the 13th centuries. The warriors formed powerful alliances, one of which was the Knights Hospitallers. This group set up hospitals along the Crusaders' routes to war.

NAMING SHIELDS

The blazon, or description, below each shield names the field and charge and gives their colors and other details in a language based on medieval French.

The charge is a dragon vert (green). He is sitting "sejant" – with forepaws on the ground.

KEY TO BLAZONS	
Argent	Silver
Azure	Blue
Gules	Red
Or	Gold
Purpure	Purple
Sable	Black
Vert	Green

The field on this shield is or (gold).

Or a dragon sejant vert

Argent a thistle proper

Or a lion passant gules

Gyronny argent and gules

Argent an eagle displayed sable

Sable a cross engrailed or

Gules a rod of Aesculapius or

Azure a harpy or

Vert a unicorn rampant argent

Find out more

ARMOR
CASTLES
CRUSADES
MEDIEVAL EUROPE
WEAPONS

KOREA

THE KOREAN PENINSULA has a long history of invasion and occupation by its two powerful neighbors, China and Japan. In 1948, it was divided into Communist North and democratic South, and the invasion of the South by the North led to the Korean War (1950-53). The war devastated both countries, but their subsequent histories have been very different. South Korea, once a rural society, became a major industrial power, and one of the world's leading ship-builders and car manufacturers. It also became a center of high technology and electronics. The economy of the North, an isolated and repressive Communist regime, is a marked contrast. Heavy industry has created severe pollution and nationwide electricity blackouts are common. In 1995 and 1996, floods wrecked harvests, and many people suffered terrible hardship.

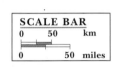

The Korean peninsula is bordered by China and, in the far northeast, Russia. On the west it is bordered by the Yellow Sea and, in the east, by the Sea of Japan. The peninsula is divided, along the 38th parallel, into North and South Korea.

NORTH KOREA

Area: 46,540 sq miles (120,540 sq km)
Population: 22,700,000
Capital: Pyongyang
Languages: Korean, Chinese
Religions: Nonreligious, traditional beliefs, Ch'ondogyo, Buddhist
Currency: North Korean Won

NORTH KOREA

The Communist republic of North Korea invaded the South in 1950, leading to the Korean War (1950-53). The border that now divides the two countries is the most militarized in the world. North Korea now has one of the world's largest military organizations, a huge army, and an advanced arms industry. Its military might is regularly displayed at regimented parades.

GINSENG
Korea is a major exporter of the valuable ginseng root, believed to improve health, and promote long life and vigor.

SOUTH KOREA

Area: 38,232 sq miles (99,020 sq km)
Population: 47,700,000
Capital: Seoul
Languages: Korean, Chinese
Religions: Mahayana Buddhist, Protestant, Roman Catholic, Confucianism
Currency: Won

SEOUL
Seoul was the capital of Korea from 1394 to 1948, when it became capital of South Korea. It is a fast-expanding city of over 10 million people. The orderly, rectangular street patterns of the city center give way to sprawling suburbs on the low surrounding hills. Seoul is a major commercial and manufacturing center, with many small-scale textile factories. It is congested with traffic, and pollution is becoming a major problem.

Map labels

SCALE BAR
0   50   km
0   50   miles

RUSS. FED.

CHINA

Paektu-san 2750m

Najin

Ch'ongjin

Hyesan

Kanggye

Ch'osan

Kimch'aek

Huich'on

Sinp'o

Hamhung

Sinuiju

Chongju

Yalu

Taedong-gang

Nangnim-sanmaek

Hamgyong-sanmaek

Tumen

NORTH KOREA

East Korea Bay

Sea of Japan (East Sea)

Sinmi-do

Sunch'on

Wonsan

Kosong

(North and South Korea have been divided by a ceasefire agreement since 1953)

Korea Bay

PYONGYANG

Namp'o

Sariwon

Changyon

Haeju

Ch'unch'on

Sokch'o

Kangnung

Ongjin

Taebaek-sanmaek

Tonghae

Paengnyong-do

SEOUL (SÔUL)

Inch'on

Suwon

Yellow Sea

Ch'ungju

Ch'onan

Sangju

Andong

Taejon

Kimch'on

P'ohang

SOUTH KOREA

Kunsan

Taegu

Namwon

Ulsan

Masan

Pusan

Kwangju

Koje-do

Sunch'on

Mokp'o

Namhae-do

Tsushima

Ko-saki

JAPAN

Kogum-do

Korea Strait

Chin-do

Cheju Strait

Cheju

East China Sea

Cheju-do

N W E S

Find out more
ARMIES
ASIA
ASIA, HISTORY OF
COMMUNISM
JAPAN, HISTORY OF

CHINA

SOVIET UNION

NORTH KOREA

• Pyongyang

Armistice line, 1953

38th parallel

Inchon • Seoul

SOUTH KOREA

Pusan •

JAPAN

KOREAN WAR

IN THE MIDST OF THE COLD WAR, a "hot war" in Korea brought world superpowers head-to-head in a bloody conflict. On June 25, 1950, 90,000 North Korean troops, trained and armed by the Soviet Union, poured over the border into South Korea. The United Nations (UN) demanded a withdrawal, but the fighting continued. In its first military role, the UN sent troops from 16 of its member nations, commanded and led by the United States, to fight alongside the South Korean Army. China soon entered the war on the North Korean side. Three years of brutal fighting ended with an armistice agreement in 1953, but despite the huge loss of life, little had changed.

United Nations troops pose for a photo at the 38th parallel.

NORTH AND SOUTH KOREA
Communist-ruled North Korea and US-supported South Korea were divided at the 38th parallel of latitude after World War II. Both North and South Korea claimed possession of the entire country, and their troops often clashed at the border in the years leading up to North Korea's invasion. No peace agreement was negotiated after the war, and tensions between the two nations continue to this day.

United Nations helmets

UNITED NATIONS
The United Nations had only been in existence for five years when the Korean War began. The organization chose to play a military role for the first time in its history, presenting a major challenge to its member nations.

WAR ON LAND
In the early stages of the war, the North Korean army easily advanced to the South Korean port of Pusan, in the southeast of the country. But UN forces surprised the North Koreans with an amphibious landing at Inchon in 1950. UN troops advanced far into North Korea, but after China entered the war, they retreated south.

GENERAL MACARTHUR
President Truman named General Douglas MacArthur as commander-in-chief of the UN forces. However, MacArthur wanted to expand the war and attack targets in China, so Truman removed him from command in 1951.

THE HUMAN COST
The Korean War devastated the entire country. More than a million South Korean civilians were killed and several million more were made homeless. The North Koreans lost an estimated 1,600,000 troops, while 57,000 UN soldiers were killed. Despite these losses, Korea remained a divided country, with few political changes.

Korean civilians flee the fighting.

KOREAN WAR HISTORY

1950 North Korean troops invade South Korea.

1950 UN enters the war.

1950 UN forces stop the deepest North Korean advance.

1950 Allied troops land behind enemy lines at Inchon.

1950 China enters the war in support of North Korea.

1951 Seoul is captured by North Korean forces, then reoccupied by UN forces; truce talks begin.

1952 UN plan rejected; truce talks broken off.

1953 North Korea accepts UN plan; armistice agreement ends the fighting.

Find out more

COMMUNISM
COLD WAR
KOREA
UNITED NATIONS

LABOR MOVEMENT

MUCH OF WHAT WORKERS take for granted today – fixed working hours, a minimum wage, paid vacations, a safe workplace, and the power to negotiate – was gained after years of bitter struggle by working people. During the Industrial Revolution, there were few laws to govern how companies treated their workers; as a result, hours were long, pay was low, and working conditions poor. From the 1830s, workers joined together to form the first unions. By the 1880s, national unions had successfully won better working conditions, while meeting opposition from employers. Public opinion turned in favor of workers' rights, and legislation in the 1930s brought about the first national labor policy.

STRIKE

The struggle for workers' rights turned violent in the years following the Civil War. Many workers, from shoemakers to newspaper carriers, and railroad workers to coal miners, felt they had no recourse but to strike, or refuse to work. In an effort to stop strikes, owners hired their own security forces (above) and pressured the police to fight back. Many striking workers lost their jobs, and some met with violence and even death.

Samuel Gompers

WORKERS UNITE

As more people started to accept the need for organized labor, the first powerful national unions emerged. The American Federation of Labor (AFL), a group of skilled craft unions headed by cigarmaker Samuel Gompers, was founded in 1886. Under his leadership, the AFL won eight-hour days, shorter working weeks, safer working conditions, and the right of the union to negotiate directly with the employer. The AFL grew quickly – by 1901, there were over a million members.

WORKERS' RIGHTS

1834 First national labor union, the National Trade Union, is founded.

1860 Shoe workers in Lynn, MA, strike and win better wages.

1869 Noble Order of the Knights of Labor unites nearly 750,000 workers.

1886 Skilled workers form the AFL (American Federation of Labor).

1935 Committee for Industrial Organization (CIO) unites unskilled and semiskilled workers.

1935 Congress passes the National Labor Relations Act.

1938 Congress passes the Fair Labor Standards Act.

1955 AFL and CIO merge.

WOMEN LABOR LEADERS

As the Industrial Revolution exploded, the need for cheap labor sent women – and children – into factories, especially in the garment and textile industries. Many women workers joined unions to highlight exploitation and seek better working conditions and pay.

Elizabeth Flynn successfully led a waiters' strike in New York in 1919.

President Roosevelt's New Deal legislation helped strengthen unions.

LABOR LEGISLATION

Prior to the 1930s there were few national labor laws, and employers used the courts to halt union activity. As part of his New Deal program, President Franklin D. Roosevelt introduced new and sweeping laws regulating labor unions. In 1932, a new law limited the use of courts in labor disputes, and made it illegal for employers to ask job seekers to pledge not to join unions. The Labor Relations Act of 1935 gave workers the right to form unions without interference from their employers.

STRIKE! APRIL 26 SMC

AFL–CIO

The Congress of Industrial Organizations (CIO) was established in 1938 to organize factory workers. In 1955, the AFL and CIO combined their strength. The opportunity for massive strikes gave the unions greater political influence.

Find out more

CIVIL RIGHTS
CONGRESS
INDUSTRIAL REVOLUTION

LAKE AND RIVER WILDLIFE

THE WATER IN LAKES and rivers is teeming with all kinds of life. Grasses, reeds, and other plants grow along the water's edge, providing food and shelter for insects, nesting birds, and mammals such as water voles and muskrats. In rivers, the fast-flowing water sweeps away plants, but in lakes, tiny floating plants are food for small creatures such as water fleas and shrimps, which are in turn eaten by bigger fish. Larger floating waterweeds provide shade for basking fish. Fallen leaves, animal droppings, and rotting plant matter form a rich mud at the bottom of rivers and lakes, where worms, snails, and other small organisms live. Today, many lakes and rivers are suffering from serious pollution. Industrial chemicals, farm fertilizers, untreated sewage, and a host of other damaging substances discharged into lakes and rivers have upset or destroyed the natural wildlife balance.

FRESHWATER
The water in lakes and rivers is called freshwater. Although it makes up only about 0.03 percent (that is, 1 part in 3000) of all the water on Earth, freshwater is home to thousands of different plants and animals.

Pickerell weed grows at the water's edge of lakes and rivers.

MUSKRAT
The muskrat is a rodent that usually eats water plants but also feeds on small animals such as fish, frogs, and freshwater shellfish.

Muskrat swims powerfully with its webbed back feet and uses its long, hairless tail as a rudder for steering.

GIANT OTTER
The largest member of the otter family lives in South America. The giant otter grows to more than 5 ft (1.5 m) long including its tail. It hunts catfish, piranha, and other fish. Unlike other otters, the giant otter prefers to stay in streams and pools and is not often seen on land. Today, this otter is very rare and is on the official list of endangered species.

RUDDY DUCK
The ruddy duck is found in open waters in many parts of Europe. It has a stiff, upward-pointing tail and dives in search of plants, small water insects, larvae, and worms.

PIKE
The northern pike is a large, fearsome predator with a huge mouth and sharp teeth for seizing many kinds of fish, as well as frogs, water birds, and small mammals. Pike live in lakes and slow-moving rivers; the biggest pike grow to more than 3 ft (1 m) long.

FALSE MAP TURTLE
One of the many water creatures that suffer from pollution of rivers and lakes is the false map turtle from North America, shown here. The harmful chemical waste that we pour into the water has also reduced this turtle's food of snails and shellfish.

RIVER PLANTS
The speed of the water in a river has a great effect on the wildlife. In a fast river, the water sweeps the river bed clean of sand and mud, leaving only pebbles. Nothing can grow in the middle of a river, and the riverbank consists mainly of plants, such as willows, that hang over the water. In a slow river, sand and mud can settle, and plants such as irises take root more easily.

Pond weed is food for many different lake and river fish.

CRAYFISH
The crayfish, found in rivers, is a freshwater relative of saltwater lobsters. It is active mainly at night and walks along the river bed on its four pairs of legs, eating a wide range of food, from plant matter to worms, shellfish, and small fish.

Cattail grows to 8 ft (2.5 m) high.

LAKE WILDLIFE

Trees such as willows and alders line the edge of many lakes; rushes, tussock sedges, reeds, and other marshy plants grow closer to the water. Plants such as water lilies and water horsetails grow in the shallow water and stick up above the surface. Each type of plant is food for a different assortment of animals.

WILLOW
The willow tree thrives in the damp soil of riverbanks, and the shores of lakes. Its long, penetrating roots help strengthen the bank.

HERON

Many kinds of herons visit lakes and rivers all over the world. Herons wade slowly in shallow water, at times standing perfectly still for several minutes, then suddenly striking at a frog or a fish with their long, spear-shaped bills.

MOORHEN
During the breeding season the male and female moorhen build a nest among the vegetation at the water's edge, and the female lays up to 11 eggs. The moorhen's long, splayed toes enable it to walk on floating leaves on rivers, lakes, and marshes. These birds eat pond weeds, fruit, and sometimes insects.

Dragonflies are a familiar sight around lakes and rivers during the summer months.

WATER LILIES
There are about 200 kinds of water lilies. Their leaves and flowers float on the surface of the water, and their long stems stretch down about 6 ft (2 m) to the roots embedded in the mud below.

WATER BOATMAN
This aquatic insect uses its paddle-like legs to row across the surface of the water. The back swimmer, a similar creature, swims upside down, often near the surface.

WATER SNAKE
Many snakes can swim; the water snake is an expert swimmer. It glides across the lake with hardly a ripple. Water snakes prey on small mammals, frogs, fish, and small water birds and their eggs and nestlings.

Diving beetles breathe by trapping air under the hard wing cases that cover the body.

MIRROR CARP
Carp are fish that live in slow-flowing rivers and weed-filled lakes. Mirror carp are so named because their bodies are covered with large, shiny, mirrorlike scales. Mirror carp search the river bottom for small plants, shellfish, and worms.

Insect larvae, fish fry (young), and other small creatures shelter among the plants along the water's edge.

DIVING BEETLE
The diving beetle is a fierce predator. It hunts tadpoles, small fish, water worms, and insects.

CONSERVATION
The axolotl shown here is a kind of Mexican salamander. It cannot survive on land and is found only in lakes such as Lake Xochimilco, Mexico. Like many other lake and river creatures, the axolotl is threatened by pollution. Thousands of lakes in the world are now lifeless because of the damaging substances that flow into them. Today, many lakes and rivers are being turned into nature reserves in order to protect the birds, fish, mammals, and other wildlife they contain.

Axolotl means "water beast."

Find out more
ANIMAL SENSES
DUCKS, GEESE, AND SWANS
FISH
FROGS AND OTHER AMPHIBIANS
SNAKES

LAKES

WATER FROM RIVERS, MOUNTAIN SPRINGS, and rain fills hollows in the ground and forms lakes, which are areas of water surrounded by land. Lakes also form in depressions dug out of the ground by glaciers, or in holes in limestone rocks. Some lakes are artificial: reservoirs are lakes made by building dams across rivers. Several landlocked seas, such as the Caspian Sea and the Dead Sea, are really lakes. The Caspian Sea, which lies between Europe and Asia, is the world's biggest lake. Its surface covers an area almost as large as Japan.

Lakes sustain a wealth of plant and animal life and are often surrounded by fertile land. Freshwater lakes provide water for towns and cities, and recreation areas for swimming, sailing, and waterskiing. Large lakes, such as the Great Lakes in North America, are used to transport goods in ships. However, lakes do not last forever. Silt and plants can fill up a lake over a period of years and turn it into a swamp.

SALTY LAKES
Salt collects in lakes that have no outlet, such as the Dead Sea between Israel and Jordan. The water is so salty that people can float in it without swimming.

VOLCANIC LAKES
Rainwater fills the volcanic crater at the summit of Mount Mazama, Oregon, to form Crater Lake. It is 1,932 ft (589 m) deep, making it the deepest lake in the United States.

KINDS OF LAKES
Lakes form in hollows dug by glaciers during the Ice Age, and in places where glaciers have left barriers of rock across valleys. Water dissolves huge holes in limestone regions, which often fill with rainwater to create lakes. Lakes can also form in volcanic craters.

FRESHWATER LAKES
The water in freshwater lakes is not salty like the sea, because the lakes are constantly fed and drained by rivers. The largest group of freshwater lakes are the Great Lakes in the United States and Canada. Lake Superior (left) is the largest of the Great Lakes.

The great lakes are all linked to each other, and also to the Atlantic Ocean by the St Lawrence seaway.

Plants grow on the damp, fertile soil.

3 DYING LAKE The soil layers extend into the lake. Plants grow and the layers become land. This continues until the lake vanishes.

Soil and mud build up at sides and bottom of lake.

THE LIFE OF A LAKE
Lakes are not permanent features of the landscape. They may come and go as their water supply rises and falls. Lakes can slowly fill with soil and stones washed down from the land above the lake. The outlet river may deepen and drain the lake.

River flows into lake.

River drains lake.

2 SHRINKING LAKE
The river carries soil, which falls to the bottom as it enters the lake. A layer of soil builds up along the edge of the lake.

SWAMPS AND MARSHES
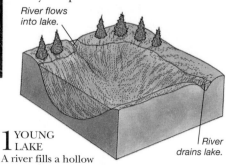
The Everglades is a large region of swamps in Florida. Swamps, or marshes, can form at the edge of a lake where the ground is soaked with water or covered with shallow water. They also form on land where water cannot drain away.

1 YOUNG LAKE
A river fills a hollow in the ground to create the lake. The water flows through the lake, running out into another river.

> ### Find out more
> DAMS
> GLACIERS AND ICECAPS
> LAKE AND RIVER WILDLIFE
> MARSH AND SWAMP LIFE
> RIVERS
> WATER

LANGUAGES

THE ABILITY TO TALK is one of the skills that makes humans different from the rest of the animal world. Some mammals and birds have simple "languages" of just a few noises, but human speech is much more highly developed. In English, for example, most people use a vocabulary (a list of words) of about 5,000 words in talking, and 10,000 in writing. A language is a way of organizing spoken sounds to express ideas. Human language developed over thousands of years, and people in different countries use different languages. Some languages share words with the languages of nearby countries. For instance, book is *libro* in both Italian and Spanish, and *livre* in French; in English we get the word library from the same source. There are now some 5,000 different languages and many dialects – local versions of major languages.

TOWER OF BABEL
At the beginning of this Bible story, everyone spoke the same language. But when people tried to build a tower to reach heaven, God became angry. He made many languages so that people could not understand and help one another.

English is spoken by 330 million people as a first language, and by about 600 million as a second or third language.

About two-thirds of China's population, 850 million people, speak Mandarin Chinese.

France once ruled many countries in West Africa, and people there still speak French as well as their local languages.

There are at least 845 languages in India. Hindi and English are the official languages.

Some people have no difficulty in learning foreign languages and can speak several fluently; the record is about 28.

There are about 700 languages in Papua New Guinea.

LATIN
For many centuries, educated people of many nationalities spoke Latin as well as their native, or first, language. Throughout Europe, scholars, governments, and the Church used Latin.

COMMON LANGUAGES
A map of national languages shows how European nations have explored the world: for example, English settlers took their language to the United States, Canada, Australia, and New Zealand. Spain conquered much of South America, and Spanish is still spoken there. But many people using these languages also have their own local language, which is part of their native culture.

- Mandarin Chinese
- English
- Russian
- Spanish
- French
- Portuguese
- Arabic
- Other

SIGN LANGUAGE
Human speech and hearing make language possible. People who have difficulty speaking or hearing cannot use a spoken language. Instead, they communicate using hand signals. There are signs and gestures for all the common words, and signs for individual letters.

S P E A K

Find out more
ALPHABETS
EDUCATION
SIGNS AND SYMBOLS

LASERS

IF SOMEONE ASKED YOU what is the brightest, most intense light of all, you might say sunlight. You would be wrong. The light from lasers is even brighter; in fact, it is the brightest light known. A laser produces a pencil-thin beam of colored light that can be so intense that it will burn a hole through steel, or so straight and narrow that it can be aimed precisely at a tiny mirror on the moon, more than 238,000 miles (384,000 km) away.

A scientist named Theodore Maiman built the first laser in 1960. Maiman created the beam by flashing ordinary light into a special rod of synthetic ruby. Today's lasers work with many other materials besides ruby. Gas lasers, for instance, use gases such as argon, which gives a low-power beam ideal for delicate surgery. In contrast, powerful solid-state lasers produce a beam using solid rods of crystals such as emerald.

LASER SHOW
Multicolored lasers produce spectacular light shows for rock concerts and public celebrations.

In ordinary light, such as that from a flashlight, light waves are jumbled up together and spill out in all directions.

Laser light bounces back and forth between the mirrors at either end of the tube. Some light gets through the half-silvered mirror at the front.

Gas atoms in laser tube produce laser light.

Tube contains mixture of gases, such as helium and neon.

Electric discharge excites the gas atoms into firing off photons.

LASER

An electric spark gives energy to atoms in the laser tube. This extra energy makes some atoms fire off photons – tiny bursts of light. These photons hit other atoms, making them fire off photons, too. Mirrors reflect the photons back and forth along the tube, making them bump into more atoms as they go. Some of the photons surge through a "partial" mirror at the front of the laser to form the beam.

Lasers produce a straight, narrow beam, and laser light itself is "coherent," which means that all the light waves travel in step.

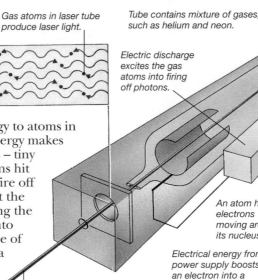

Gas laser

An atom has electrons moving around its nucleus.

Electrical energy from power supply boosts an electron into a different energy state.

When the electron returns to its original state, it gives out a photon of laser light.

Laser light hits other atoms, which in turn produce laser light.

This laser sends out a continuous beam of light. "Pulsed" lasers emit the beam in regular rapid bursts.

HOLOGRAMS

A hologram is a photograph made with laser light. When you look at a hologram, you see a three-dimensional view of the object, just as with the real thing. Holograms are made by splitting a laser beam into two. One beam, the reference beam, goes straight to the photographic film; the other hits the object of the hologram first, breaking up its neat pattern of light waves. The film records the way the disturbed "object" beam upsets the undisturbed reference beam, producing a three-dimensional image.

USES OF LASERS
Lasers are used in industry to drill steel and engrave microchips with speed and precision; by engineers to line up bridges and skyscrapers with pinpoint accuracy; in phone networks to carry calls swiftly and clearly through optical fibers; and by doctors to treat cancer and perform delicate eye operations.

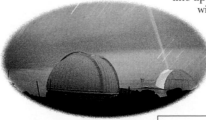

Laser beams are bounced off satellites in space to help scientists track the movement of the Earth's continents.

LAW

NO SOCIETY COULD EXIST WITHOUT RULES that define a person's rights and obligations. Law is the set of rules by which a society is governed. Every country has its own legal system. The American legal system has its roots in the common law practices of England, so called because the law applied to everybody. Common law systems are based upon legal precedents, or earlier court rulings on similar cases. There are two separate levels of courts in the United States – state and federal – to try cases involving either state or federal laws. There are also two types of law – civil and public. Civil laws govern disputes between two parties, while public law relates to a person's obligations as a citizen. Known as the "law of laws," the Constitution is the ultimate law in America – it has force over all other national and state laws, and contains conditions that all laws must meet.

ROMAN LAW
The Romans developed the most complete system of laws in the ancient world. By the 6th century A.D., Roman emperor Justinian I (shown on the coin above) had collected the laws of the Empire together into a comprehensive code that is still influential today.

CIVIL LAW
Civil law cases concern people's rights and responsibilities in their relations with other people. Some of the matters dealt with by civil law include property ownership, marriage and divorce, adoption and child support, contracts and other business agreements, and wills and inheritance. If a person feels their civil-law rights have been violated in some way, they may file a civil suit, or lawsuit, in court (left). The court will decide whether any amends should be made. Typical civil law cases involve landlord and tenant disagreements, child custody disputes, insurance claims, traffic accidents, and medical malpractice.

The police enforce criminal law, which is a part of public law. This officer is issuing a speeding ticket.

JUSTICE FOR ALL
Statues representing justice wear a blindfold to show that all people are entitled to equal treatment under the law, regardless of their social status, class, or race. The scales show that justice – through the law – weighs opposing evidence like a balance weighs goods. The sword represents swift punishment for the guilty. However, sometimes not all law is fair, as governments can make laws that remove freedoms, as well as safeguard them.

A figure representing justice holds the scales.

HISTORY OF AMERICAN LAW
Colonial American lawyers used English law books and English court rules. After independence, American law rapidly outgrew its English roots, especially property and business law. Common law remained at the core of the US legal system, and was followed in every state except Louisiana. Louisiana was originally colonized by the French, which meant that French law codes were practiced there for many years.

The courthouse and jail in Marietta, Ohio, were built in 1798.

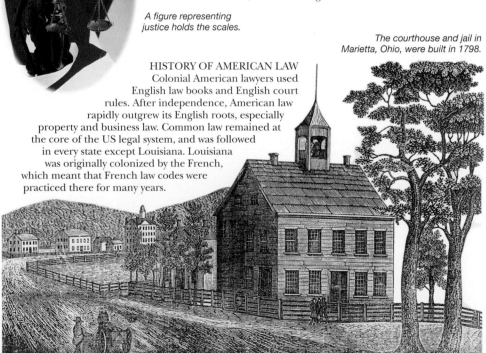

PUBLIC LAW
A person's rights and duties as a member of a community, and as a citizen, are established by public law. Its branches include: criminal law, which defines crimes and rules for arrest, trial, and punishment; constitutional law, which relates to the rights and responsibilities set forth by the Constitution; administrative law, which deals with the day-to-day workings of the government; and international law, which concerns agreements between countries. In a public law court, the government tries a person who has committed a specific crime.

A 1950s jury hears a murder case.

Scott Peterson was tried in a famous televised case.

TRIAL BY JURY

A jury is a group of people chosen to decide the truth from the evidence given in a court of law. Although each state has its own qualifications for jury service, the 12 people chosen to hear the case must be unbiased. In a trial, the evidence is presented to the jury by lawyers for the prosecution and for the defence. The jury then reviews the evidence. Lawyers may call witnesses to testify and answer questions about the facts of the case. The judge makes a charge to the jury – a statement of the rules of law that apply to the particular case. The jury leaves the courtroom to discuss the charge until they reach an agreement on the verdict.

TRIAL BY TELEVISION

Many states allow television to film court cases. Recently, television coverage of sensational, high-profile trials – such as those of Michael Jackson and Scott Peterson – has drawn huge audiences. Some people believe that the cameras undermine justice, because the publicity draws attention away from the facts of the case and influences the jury. Others argue that allowing trials to be televised safeguards the public's right to be informed.

CHALLENGING THE LAW

The courts in America have the power of judicial review, which means they can throw out any laws that do not agree with the United States Constitution, or individual state constitutions. This power was established in a famous Supreme Court case of 1803, Marbury v. Madison. In this decision, Chief Justice John Marshall (left) ruled for the first time that an act of Congress was unconstitutional. This case set a precedent that allowed other acts of Congress to be challenged.

Judge Zobel sums up for a jury.

INTERNATIONAL LAW

Even though all nations do not share the same legal systems, they cooperate under the rules of international law. These laws are made with the consent of two or more countries. International law deals with crimes like hijacking and terrorist acts, such as the Oklahoma City bombing (left). Many countries share extradition treaties so that accused people can be returned to the country where they committed a crime if they are captured elsewhere.

The Attorney General (here, Alberto Gonzales) is the nation's chief lawyer.

JUDGES

A public official called a judge presides over all trials. Judges have to be lawyers because they apply the rules of law to court cases. The judge is responsible for ensuring a fair trial, and decides the punishment if the accused is found guilty.

LAWYERS

A lawyer is licensed to represent people in court or give them advice in matters of law. Learning to become a lawyer takes several years, and most states require people to pass a special test called a bar exam before they are allowed to practice.

Find out more

CONSTITUTION
GOVERNMENT AND POLITICS
POLICE
SUPREME COURT

LEONARDO DA VINCI

A HIGHLY TALENTED ARTIST and scientist, Leonardo da Vinci was years ahead of his time. He was one of the greatest figures in the movement called the Renaissance, the revival of art and learning that began in Italy in the 15th century. Today, many people remember Leonardo for painting some of the most famous pictures of his time, but he achieved a great deal more than this. He designed castles and weaponry, invented machines, studied physics and mathematics, and made accurate scientific drawings of plants, animals, and the human body. He was probably one of the world's greatest all-around geniuses.

1452 Born near the village of Vinci, in Italy.

1466 Moves to Florence; works in studio of the artist Verrochio.

1482 Works as architect, engineer, and painter in Milan, in northern Italy.

1503 Begins *Mona Lisa*.

1503 Designs famous flying machine.

1513 Makes pioneering study of lenses and optics.

1515 Studies anatomy.

1516 Dies in France.

MONA LISA
Leonardo's best-known portrait is of Mona Lisa, the wife of a rich Florentine. The painting is famous for Mona Lisa's haunting smile, and for the softly blended colors, an effect known as *sfumato*. The painting is in the Louvre Gallery in Paris.

MACHINERY
Leonardo's notebooks are crammed with designs for ingenious machines. Some of these devices, such as a pump, an armored car, and a machine for grinding lenses, could actually have been built and used. Others, like his famous "ornithopter" flying machine with its flapping wings, would never have worked, but they were still ahead of their time.

RENAISSANCE MAN
In Leonardo's time, people believed it was possible for a person to become highly skilled in all branches of learning – such a person is called a "Renaissance man." Leonardo produced new ideas in practically every area he studied. He wrote down many of these ideas in a series of beautifully illustrated notebooks.

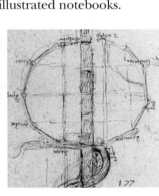

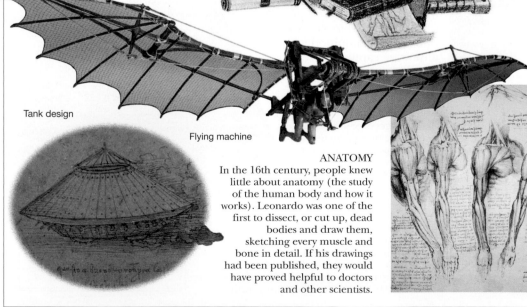

Tank design

Flying machine

ANATOMY
In the 16th century, people knew little about anatomy (the study of the human body and how it works). Leonardo was one of the first to dissect, or cut up, dead bodies and draw them, sketching every muscle and bone in detail. If his drawings had been published, they would have proved helpful to doctors and other scientists.

ARCHITECTURE
Buildings and town planning fascinated Leonardo. He designed an "ideal city" which was never built. The streets of the city were arranged in a grid pattern, like a modern American town. He also designed bathhouses, together with drainage networks and systems for garbage collecting, which were unknown at the time.

Find out more
DRAWING
HELICOPTERS
RENAISSANCE

LEWIS AND CLARK

IN 1804, PRESIDENT THOMAS JEFFERSON sent Meriwether Lewis and William Clark to lead an expedition to explore the wild and largely unknown lands west of Missouri to the Pacific Ocean. Their instructions were to explore and chart the region, to make contact with Native Americans, and to find out if there was a water link between the Atlantic and Pacific oceans. Lewis and Clark were not experienced explorers, but they successfully led a band of about 40 men, traveling by boat, horse, and foot, some hazardous 8,000 miles (13,000 km) to the Pacific and back. They returned home as heroes with important and exciting new information about the region, which later encouraged US expansion westward.

WILLIAM CLARK
Clark (1770-1838) was a lieutenant in the army. He resigned in 1796 but rejoined the army in 1804 to go westward with Lewis. Although untrained, he mapped accurate routes for the expedition and assembled records of the journey for publication.

MERIWETHER LEWIS
Lewis (1774-1809) was private secretary to President Jefferson. Co-leader of the expedition, he served as the party's naturalist, collecting animal and plant specimens.

SACAJAWEA
Lewis and Clark encountered many Native Americans on their journey. None was as important as Sacajawea (1786-1812), also known as "Bird Woman." She joined the expedition in 1805 and guided the explorers over mountain trails. Her presence encouraged friendly relations with the Native Americans.

ROUTE OF THE EXPEDITION
The expedition left St. Louis on May 14, 1804, traveling along the Missouri River by boat. In November, the explorers reached what is now North Dakota, where they spent the winter with native Mandans. In April 1805, they continued up the Missouri. Leaving the river, they struggled on a perilous journey over the Rocky Mountains, then paddled up the Columbia River, finally reaching the Pacific in November. They spent the winter on the Pacific coast, before retracing their steps, arriving back in St. Louis on September 23, 1806.

BOATS
The expedition set sail for the Pacific Ocean in a flat-bottomed keelboat and two smaller "pirogues," or dug-out canoes similar to those used by Native Americans. In rough water, the travelers were forced to tow the boats from land or carry them around rapids.

WILDLIFE
The expedition returned with valuable samples of animals, plants, rocks, and minerals. Lewis became particularly interested in grizzly bears, one of which tried to attack him. He reported a large number of grizzlies, which pleased President Jefferson, who was eager to develop the fur trade in the United States.

Grizzly bear

Early settlers traveled across North America in a covered wagon.

WESTWARD EXPANSION
Lewis and Clark's expedition proved there was no direct water link between the Atlantic and Pacific oceans. However, Lewis and Clark's information about the diversity and richness of the lands attracted hundreds of traders and settlers to the West. From the 1840s, increasing numbers made their way on the long journey westward in covered wagons, or "prairie schooners."

Find out more
BEARS AND PANDAS
NATIVE AMERICANS
NORTH AMERICAN WILDLIFE
UNITED STATES OF AMERICA
UNITED STATES, HISTORY OF

LIGHT

WITHOUT LIGHT, life on Earth would be impossible. Sunlight provides the energy to make plants grow and keep all living things alive. Light itself is a form of energy that travels as tiny packets of electromagnetic energy called photons. When photons enter our eyes they stimulate special light-sensitive cells so that we can see. Other forms of energy that travel as electromagnetic waves include radio waves, X rays, and microwaves in microwave ovens. Just as there is a spectrum of colors in light, there is also an electromagnetic spectrum. In fact, light waves are also a type of electromagnetic wave, and the colors in light form a small part of the electromagnetic spectrum. Light waves and all other electromagnetic waves travel at 186,000 miles (300,000 km) per second, which is so fast that they could circle the world almost eight times in a second. Nothing in the universe can travel faster than light.

LIGHTBULB

In the middle of every electric lightbulb is a tiny spiral of tungsten wire called the filament. When an electric current is sent through the filament, it warms up so much that it glows white hot. It is the brightly glowing filament that produces light.

Filament made of tungsten metal

Bulb is filled with an inert gas such as argon to keep the filament from catching fire and burning out, as it would do in air.

Filament and electric terminals are sealed into an airtight glass bulb.

Electrical contact is made when the bulb terminal is screwed into the socket.

The explosion of gunpowder inside a firework produces a burst of colored light.

Nuclear reactions inside the center of the Sun produce intense heat and light. All stars produce light from nuclear reactions.

Searchlights give out very intense light, often produced by an electric spark between two pieces of carbon.

BRIGHTNESS OF LIGHT

The farther you are from a light, the less bright it will seem. This is because light spreads out in all directions from its source. So when you are far away, the light is spread over a wide area. Many stars, for instance, are much brighter than our Sun, but their light is spread out over so vast an area that by the time it reaches us, the stars seem no brighter than a candle.

Some deep-sea fish have luminescent stripes and spots along their bodies that give out light.

Shine a flashlight on a wall and watch the pool of light grow larger and dimmer as you move the flashlight farther away.

A candle is a wide source of light, so it produces a fuzzy shadow.

Candles and lanterns give out light.

When things burn they give out light as well as heat.

SOURCES OF LIGHT

Many different objects give off light. The Sun, electric lightbulbs, and fireworks are incandescent, which means they glow because they are hot. But not all lights are hot. Chemicals, not heat, produce the glowing spots on the bodies of some deep-sea fish. All cool lights, including fluorescent lights, are called luminescent.

LIGHT AND SHADOW

Light travels in straight lines, so, in most cases, it cannot go around obstacles in its path. When light rays hit a solid object, some bounce back and some are absorbed by the object, warming it up a little. The area behind receives no light rays and is left in shadow.

FLUORESCENT LIGHT

A lot of energy in an electric lightbulb is wasted as heat. Fluorescent tubes are cooler and more economical. When an electric current is passed through the gas in the tube, gas atoms emit invisible, ultraviolet light. The ultraviolet light strikes phosphors – chemicals in the tube's lining – and makes them glow with a brilliant white light.

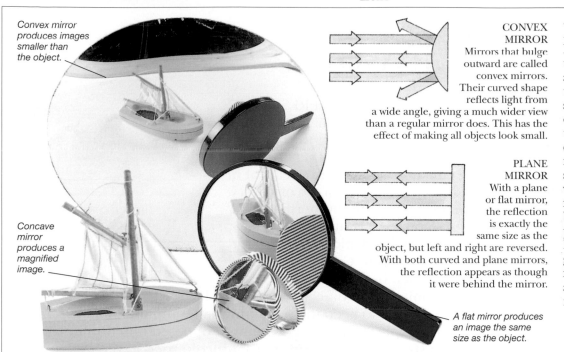

Convex mirror produces images smaller than the object.

Concave mirror produces a magnified image.

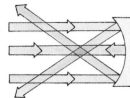

CONVEX MIRROR

Mirrors that bulge outward are called convex mirrors. Their curved shape reflects light from a wide angle, giving a much wider view than a regular mirror does. This has the effect of making all objects look small.

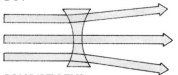

PLANE MIRROR

With a plane or flat mirror, the reflection is exactly the same size as the object, but left and right are reversed. With both curved and plane mirrors, the reflection appears as though it were behind the mirror.

A flat mirror produces an image the same size as the object.

MIRRORS

Light passes easily through transparent substances such as glass and water, but not through opaque objects such as paper. Most opaque objects have a rough surface that scatters light in all directions. However, a mirror has a smooth surface, so it reflects light in a regular way. When you look at your face in a mirror, the light bounces straight back, producing a sharp image. Most mirrors are made of glass; your face is reflected from a shiny metal coating at the back of the mirror, not from the glass.

CONCAVE MIRROR

A concave mirror, which is curved inward, forms two kinds of image. If the object is close to the mirror, the reflection is larger than the real thing. If the object is far away, the image formed is small and upside down.

Rays travel in straight lines in cool air

Upside-down image forms

Rays are bent as they pass through layer of warm air

MIRAGE

In the hot desert, weary travelers are often fooled by the sight of an oasis. The oasis appears on the horizon, only to vanish as the travelers hurry toward it. What they have seen is an illusion called a mirage. In the example above, light rays traveling from the palm tree are bent upwards by the warm air. The observer's eyes interpret the light as having traveled in a straight line, so he sees a watery reflection of the tree on the ground.

FIBER OPTICS

Fiber optic cables are channels that carry light. They are flexible so they can carry light around corners. The fibers are long, thin filaments of glass; the light bounces back and forth along the inner surface of the glass. Fiber optics are valuable for seeing into awkward places. Doctors can use fiber-optic endoscopes to see inside a patient's body without opening the body up.

LENSES AND REFRACTION

Glasses, cameras, telescopes, and microscopes use lenses to create particular kinds of images. The lenses in a telescope, for example, produce a magnified view of a distant object. All lenses work on the principle that although light always travels in straight lines, it travels slower through glass than through air. If a light ray strikes glass at an angle, one side of the ray will hit the glass just before the other and will slow down earlier. The effect is to bend the light ray slightly, just as a car pulls to one side if it has a flat. This bending of light is called refraction.

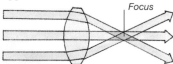

CONCAVE LENS

A concave lens is thicker at the edges than in the center, so it spreads light rays out. If you look through a concave lens, everything appears smaller.

Focus

CONVEX LENS

Convex lenses bring light rays together. At the focus, where light rays from a distant object meet, they form an image of the object that can be seen on a screen.

Magnifying glasses are convex lenses.

Light refracts when it passes through water, because the water slows it down. This makes objects look as though they are bent.

Find out more
CAMERAS
COLOR
EYES
LASERS
PHOTOGRAPHY
PLANTS
SUN

ABRAHAM
LINCOLN

ONE OF THE MOST FAMOUS PRESIDENTS in US history is Abraham Lincoln. But when he was elected in 1860, less than half the country supported him, and he remained very unpopular with many people for the entire five years of his presidency. Lincoln did not approve of slavery, and many landowners in the southern United States still kept slaves. As a result of his election, 11 southern states left the Union and declared themselves an independent Confederacy, or alliance. Civil war then broke out between the Union and the Confederacy. Lincoln was a capable war leader. He struggled to keep the remaining states united under his leadership. Many people in his own government opposed him. But in 1865 he led the Union states to victory. Afterward, Lincoln tried to repair the damage done by the war and bring together the two opposing sides.

1809 Born in Kentucky.

1831 Moves to New Salem, Illinois, where he works as a storekeeper, surveyor, and postmaster while studying law.

1834 Elected to state legislature.

1836 Qualifies as a lawyer.

1842 Marries Mary Todd.

1846 Elected to Congress.

1855, 1859 Runs unsuccessfully for Senate.

1860 Elected president.

1861 Mobilizes 75,000 volunteers to put down the southern rebellion.

1863 Issues Emancipation Proclamation.

1864 Re-elected president.

1865 Assassinated.

LINCOLN'S BIRTHPLACE
This log cabin in Kentucky is a replica of the birthplace of Abraham Lincoln. The poverty of Lincoln's childhood influenced his political ideas.

GETTYSBURG ADDRESS
Abraham Lincoln was famous for his speeches. In 1863, he attended the dedication of a national cemetery on the site of the Civil War battlefield in Gettysburg, Pennsylvania. He made a speech known as the Gettysburg Address. He hoped that "these dead shall not have died in vain."

THE DEATH OF LINCOLN
On April 14, 1865, Abraham Lincoln was watching a play at Ford's Theatre in Washington, D.C. John Wilkes Booth, an actor who supported the southern states in the Civil War, crept quietly into the president's box and shot him. The president died from his wounds the next day.

MOUNT RUSHMORE
The faces of four American presidents – George Washington, Thomas Jefferson, Theodore Roosevelt, and Abraham Lincoln – are carved out of rock on the side of Mount Rushmore in the Black Hills of South Dakota.

ABOLITION
The move to abolish slavery in the United States grew under Lincoln. Led by white middle-class northerners, many freed slaves joined the abolition movement. Some, such as Andrew Scott (right), fought in the Union army during the Civil War. Slaves fled from South to North (and freedom) via the Underground Railroad – a secret escape route. Harriet Tubman, a famous pioneer of the railroad, helped 300 slaves to escape in this way.

> ### Find out more
> ABOLITIONIST MOVEMENT
> CIVIL WAR
> SLAVERY
> TUBMAN, HARRIET
> UNITED STATES, HISTORY OF

LIONS
TIGERS, AND OTHER BIG CATS

FEW CREATURES ARE HELD in such awe as lions, tigers, cheetahs, and leopards, which we often call the big cats. These agile predators have strong, razor-sharp teeth and claws, muscular bodies, and excellent senses. Their beautiful striped and spotted fur breaks up their outline and camouflages them, allowing them to ambush unwary zebras, giraffes, and other prey. There are seven kinds of big cats. The tiger is the largest. A fully grown tiger may measure more than 10 ft (3 m) from nose to tail; a fully grown lion is almost as big.

The first large cats lived 45 million years ago. Many, including the lion, cheetah, and leopard, still inhabit parts of Africa. Snow leopards and lions dwell in the mountains and forests of Asia. Jaguars are the largest of the big cats in North and South America. They are equally at home swimming in lakes or climbing trees.

CUBS
Like all young big cats, tiger cubs have pale markings when they are born. After a few months, the pale stripes change to black and orange.

HUNTING PREY
Lions live mainly on savannas (grassy plains) and scrubland, and the females do most of the hunting. This picture shows two adult lionesses charging at a young gazelle, separating it from the rest of the herd.

LION PRIDE
Lions are the only big cats that live in groups, called prides, which may be up to 30 strong. The pride roams over an area of 40 sq miles (100 sq km) or more, depending on the abundance of prey in the area. The large male lions protect the pride's territory against other prides. The lions also defend the females against other males.

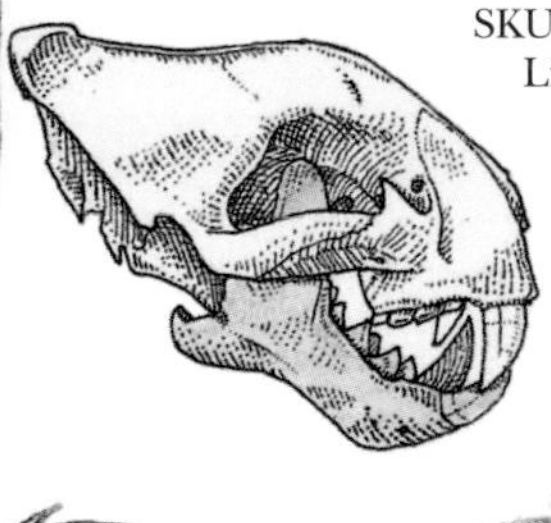

SKULL AND TEETH
Lions and other big cats have short, strong skulls with powerful jaws. Their spearlike canine teeth are used to grab hold of the victim. The large molar teeth tear flesh and gristle as the jaw opens and closes.

Lion has a thick, shaggy mane.

Large, strong canine teeth for tearing prey

The dominant male is the strongest member of the pride. It can measure 8 ft (2.5 m) in length, and 3 ft (1 m) high at the shoulder.

Large feet and sharp claws

CARNIVORES
Lions, tigers, and other big cats are true carnivores (flesh-eaters). Lions usually eat large prey such as antelopes and zebras. One giraffe is often enough to feed a whole pride of lions.

CLAWS OUT

When a cat pounces on a victim or climbs up into a tree, it unsheathes its sharp claws. Muscles in the feet pull the claws out and draw back the sheaths.

CLAWS IN

Most of the time, a cat's claws are protected in muscular sheaths. This keeps the claws sharp and less likely to break. The claws are extended when the cat cleans its feet.

LEOPARD

The leopard weighs about 130 lb (60 kg), and its body measures about 5 ft (1.5 m). Leopards are adaptable creatures. They can survive in hot tropical forests or on cold mountainsides. They may also live close to towns and villages.

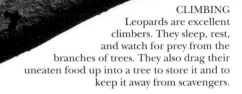

CLIMBING

Leopards are excellent climbers. They sleep, rest, and watch for prey from the branches of trees. They also drag their uneaten food up into a tree to store it and to keep it away from scavengers.

PANTHER

The black panther (right) is a leopard with dark coloring. In daylight, its spots show black in its dark gray-brown fur.

JAGUAR

The jaguar (below) stalks its prey in the same way as the tiger. Jaguars eat a variety of other creatures, including tapirs, fish, frogs, rodents, sloths, and small caimans (South American crocodiles).

ROARING

Only the big cats can roar, and they do so loudly, although the jaguar and snow leopard roar only rarely. The roar is a way of expressing anger, and warns other creatures to keep away.

TIGER

Unlike most cats, the tiger does not mind water. A tiger sometimes pulls its dead prey near the water's edge, because it needs to take frequent drinks during a meal. Tigers stalk their prey through dense undergrowth, then bound over the last 50 ft (15 m) or so, taking their victim by surprise. On average, a tiger consumes about 40 lb (18 kg) of meat a day.

CHEETAH

No animal can outrun a cheetah over a short distance. Cheetahs can speed along at about 60 mph (100 km/h) – as fast as a car. Unlike other cats, the cheetah's claws are always extended, because it has no sheaths to withdraw them into. This gives the cheetah extra grip as it starts its run. If a stalking cheetah is detected before it gets within about 600 ft (180 m) of its prey, it does not make the final dash.

☐ Lions

☐ Tigers

■ Cheetahs

☐ Leopards

CONSERVATION

Leopards and other big cats have been overhunted for their fur and because they attack livestock and, very rarely, people. The trade in big cats and fur products is now banned by an international agreement. The maps show the main areas of the world where these big cats still live.

Cheetah

Find out more

AFRICAN WILDLIFE
ANIMALS
CAMOUFLAGE, ANIMAL
CATS
CONSERVATION
and endangered species
MAMMALS
ZOOS

LITERATURE

LITERATURE INCLUDES PLAYS, poems, novels, and short stories. It is writing that carries strong and lasting value through offering the reader important insights into the nature of human emotions. For example, the English playwright William Shakespeare (1564-1616) often based his plays on old or well-known stories, and because Shakespeare was a very skilled writer and had a great understanding of human nature, his plays still excite audiences of all nationalities hundreds of years after they were written. Literature can be powerful, as it can express the writer's thoughts, ideals, and beliefs. Authors, or writers, have often used literature to protest injustice in the world, make a social criticism, and influence the opinions of peoples or governments. For instance, in *The Grapes of Wrath*, American novelist John Steinbeck (1902-68) drew public attention to the suffering of homeless farmers fleeing from Oklahoma to California during the Great Depression of the 1930s.

GULLIVER'S TRAVELS
English author Jonathan Swift (1667-1745) wrote *Gulliver's Travels* in 1726. Although he did not write the book for children, the first two parts have long been popular with young people.

When the people of Lilliput find Gulliver sleeping in their land, they tie him down on the ground so that he cannot move.

The arrogant and petty-minded Lilliputians represent the ruling class of 18th-century England.

PLOT
The collection of events that occur in a work of literature is called the plot. *Gulliver's Travels* tells the story of Lemuel Gulliver, a ship's surgeon. In the first part, Gulliver is shipwrecked in an imaginary land called Lilliput, where the people are only a few inches tall. In the second tale, he meets the giants of Brobdingnag. In the third story, Gulliver visits various strange lands. Finally he is marooned among the Houyhnhnms – a race of horses that are wiser and more intelligent than their repulsive human servants, the Yahoos. Rejected by the Houyhnhnms, Gulliver returns to England, where he is no longer able to tolerate the company of other humans.

The Lilliputian politicians discuss new wars against their enemies.

THEME
Writers use their plots and characters to explore key themes such as love, death, morality, and social or political issues. *Gulliver's Travels* seems just an adventure story, but the underlying theme is 18th-century England, where the Lilliputians and other nationalities represent different types of people with their good and bad qualities.

CHARACTERS
An essential part of most literature is the writer's description of the characters – the people who take part in the plot. A writer portrays a character's personality by describing how they react to events in the story. For example, Swift shows that Gulliver was a kindhearted man by describing how he entertained the tiny Lilliputian people: "I would sometimes lie down, and let five or six of them dance on my Hand. And at last the Boys and Girls would venture to come and play at Hide and Seek in my Hair."

ORAL LITERATURE
Long before writing was invented, storytelling, or oral literature, was used to pass on myths and history. The heroine of a traditional Arabic story called *The Thousand and One Nights* is a storyteller named Scheherazade (right). Her cruel husband vows to kill her in the morning, but she charms him with a tale and so delays her death. Each night she tells another story and lives for one more day. After many stories her husband changes his mind and spares Scheherazade's life.

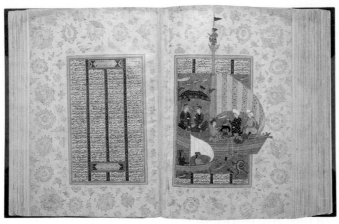

This copy of the Book of Kings *is written in Arabic script.*

EPICS AND SAGAS

Epics and sagas tell of legendary heroes and their deeds. An epic tells the story as a long poem, while a saga is written in prose. The national Persian epic, the *Book of Kings (Shah-nameh)* by Firdausi (c.935-1020), is 1,000 years old, and tells the story of Persian kings and their battles against monsters in mythical times. Other great epics include Homer's *Iliad* and *Odyssey*; Virgil's *Aeneid*; *Beowulf*, a 10th-century epic written in Old English; and John Milton's *Paradise Lost* and *Paradise Regained*.

BIOGRAPHY

A biography is a book that describes a person's life. In an autobiography the author writes of his or her own life. US writer Mark Twain (right) was portrayed in J. Kaplan's biography *Mr. Clemens and Mark Twain* (the title refers to Twain's real name, Samuel Langhorne Clemens).

POETRY

Poetry is different from other forms of literature because it usually has rhythm and rhyme. In a rhythmic poem, such as a song, the accents or beats in each line follow a pattern that is repeated in each verse.

In poems that rhyme, lines end with words that sound similar. One of the world's greatest poets was the American Walt Whitman (1810-92), whose poems express a great love of his country and its people. His collection of poems *Leaves of Grass* (1855) is considered one of his best works.

NOVELS

A novel is a long story about fictional (unreal) characters, which is written in prose. This form of writing only began in the early 17th century, and has had a dramatic rise in popularity because there are novels to suit all tastes. Some offer insights into everyday life, and some tell of fantastic adventures that keep you turning the pages. American author Louisa May Alcott wrote *Little Women* (1868-69), which tells the story of four sisters and their lives. This remains one of the best-loved children's books ever written. Many successful modern authors are now rewarded with high incomes from sales of their books, as well as from movies based on their novels.

Louisa May Alcott

DRAMA

Literature that is written to be performed by actors is called drama. Different countries have their own forms of drama. There is little scenery in Japanese Noh drama (below), which was first performed in the 14th century. The all-male actors use dance, mime, and masks for each performance, which can last for several hours. Noh drama is influenced by the religious beliefs of Buddhism and Shintoism.

Noh actors perform a program of five plays, based on classical literature, romances, or poetry, accompanied by a chorus with an orchestra of drums and flute.

STORIES

Most stories describe a single incident or events that take place over a short period of time. There are children's stories about every subject ranging from adventures to ghosts. One of the best-known story writers was the Danish author Hans Christian Andersen (1805-75), who wrote tales such as *The Emperor's New Clothes* and *The Ugly Duckling*.

A Hans Christian Andersen story, The Princess and the Pea, *tells how a single pea beneath a heap of mattresses keeps a princess awake all night.*

Find out more
BOOKS
POETRY
PRINTING
THEATER
WRITERS AND POETS

Captain John Smith

US LITERATURE

MODERN AMERICAN LITERATURE reflects the great diversity of the American people. Most early literature was based on English styles of the period. Once the colonists had separated from England, however, writers sought to establish American themes in an American style. By the middle of the 19th century, American literature was flourishing. However, the Civil War changed things. Many people were shocked by the brutality of the war, and alarmed at the fragility of American democracy. A new generation of writers emerged, who looked at the world directly and honestly.
Each period of social change that followed, from the World Wars to the Civil Rights movement, inspired American writers to develop a truly American voice.

Moby Dick's huge tail tosses the whalers from their boat.

COLONIAL LITERATURE
American literature began with oral legends of its native people. The first American book was Captain John Smith's *A True Relation of Virginia* (1608), the story of the English settlement at Jamestown.

MOBY DICK
Regarded as one of the greatest American novels, Herman Melville's *Moby Dick* (1851) describes in dramatic fashion Captain Ahab's obsessive pursuit of a huge whale – Moby Dick – and the tragic consequences for his ship and crew.

Nathaniel Hawthorne reads from The Scarlet Letter.

WORDS FROM A NEW NATION
The most successful author after the American Revolution was Washington Irving. Written in 1819, his best-loved tale, *Rip Van Winkle* (above), is the story of a man who awakens after a 20-year sleep.

LITERATURE IN AN ERA OF CHANGE
In the mid-1800s, America was expanding and changing rapidly. Much of its literature romanticized the nation, but other works questioned the effects of American expansion. Novels reached huge audiences, including Nathaniel Hawthorne's *The Scarlet Letter* (1850), a story of hiding a sinful truth in a Puritan village.

AMERICAN POETRY
Like fiction, much of the poetry of the 1800s was sentimental. However, exceptional poets such as Walt Whitman and Emily Dickinson (right) broke new ground, establishing the first truly American poetry. Whitman's fresh style captured the energy of the new nation, while Dickinson's short, thought-provoking poems profoundly influenced modern writers.

Tom Sawyer with his friend Huck Finn

THE ADVENTURES OF HUCKLEBERRY FINN
Mark Twain's pair of novels set near the Mississippi River are favorites of American readers. *The Adventures of Tom Sawyer* (1876) tells of the antics of a mischievous small-town boy and his best friend Huck Finn. *The Adventures of Huckleberry Finn* (1884) continues the story. Huck and a runaway slave named Jim share adventures as they float down the Mississippi on a raft. Huck narrated the story in his own everyday American speech – a first in fiction.

REALISM
At the end of the 1800s, many novelists sought to portray the lives of ordinary people as they were. Among these realists were Theodore Dreiser, Upton Sinclair, and Stephen Crane (above), whose novel *The Red Badge of Courage* (1895) showed the brutal effects of the Civil War.

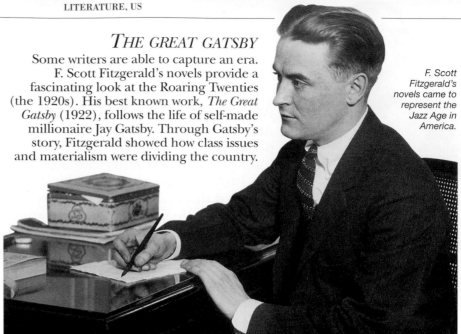

In poems such as The Four Quartets, T.S. Eliot explored new techniques in verse composition.

THE GREAT GATSBY

Some writers are able to capture an era. F. Scott Fitzgerald's novels provide a fascinating look at the Roaring Twenties (the 1920s). His best known work, *The Great Gatsby* (1922), follows the life of self-made millionaire Jay Gatsby. Through Gatsby's story, Fitzgerald showed how class issues and materialism were dividing the country.

F. Scott Fitzgerald's novels came to represent the Jazz Age in America.

TWENTIETH CENTURY POETRY

In the early 20th century, poets such as T.S. Eliot, ee cummings, and Robert Frost broke away from traditional styles, using everyday language to make poetry more expressive. Sylvia Plath famously put herself and her feelings at the center of her poems.

THE GRAPES OF WRATH

John Steinbeck's *The Grapes of Wrath* (1939), published just after the Great Depression, told the moving story of the Joad family, poor Oklahoma farmers who make the difficult trek west in search of a better life. The Joads face hard challenges with each mile they cross, but manage to maintain their dignity. Steinbeck's book exposed to the world the underside of the American dream. He was awarded a Pulitzer Prize for the novel in 1940.

A poster advertising the 1940 movie of The Grapes of Wrath

Arthur Miller's Death of a Salesman *(below) won the Pulitzer Prize for theater.*

MODERN FICTION

Thousands of novels of every type have been published in recent decades as a modern American voice has emerged. Among American authors read around the world are John Cheever and John Updike, who examined and exposed life in the suburbs; Philip Roth and Saul Bellow, who captured the Jewish-American voice; and Flannery O'Connor, who wrote about strong characters of the South. Experimental fiction, by writers such as Thomas Pynchon, Kurt Vonnegut, and Joseph Heller (left), explored new literary forms.

TWENTIETH CENTURY DRAMA

Just as 20th-century novelists were drawn toward realism, playwrights also wrote about more realistic subjects. Eugene O'Neill, widely regarded as America's leading dramatist, wrote plays about people from all walks of life. Tennessee Williams wrote about the conflict between tradition and modernism in the South, while Arthur Miller's famous play, *Death of a Salesman*, portrayed the anguish in the life of an ordinary man.

STRONG VOICES

African-American writers have made an important contribution to American literature. Novelists James Baldwin, Richard Wright, and Ralph Ellison wrote about the difficulties of living in a white-dominated society. Toni Morrison and Alice Walker (right) created characters who rise above terrible circumstances in their novels *Beloved* and *The Color Purple* respectively. Poet Gwendolyn Brooks uses traditional forms to describe modern injustices.

Find out more

BOOKS
POETRY
THEATER
WRITERS AND POETS

LIZARDS

THE LARGEST GROUP of reptiles is the lizard family, with about 4,300 kinds. Lizards live in almost every habitat except the open sea and the far north. The huge Komodo dragon is the largest, and tiny geckos are the smallest – some are less than 1 in (2 cm) long. A typical lizard such as the iguana has a slim body, a long tail, legs that splay out sideways, and five-toed feet. There are many variations, however; skinks are often extremely long, with short legs. They seem to move effortlessly through loose soil with a wriggling motion. Snake-lizards are even more snakelike, with no front legs and small, paddle-shaped back legs. Several kinds of lizards, including the slowworm, have lost their limbs during the course of evolution. Like other reptiles, most female lizards lay eggs, which they bury in the soil or hide under rocks until the young hatch.

Lizards can hear through their ear openings.

Long tail for balance

Green iguana

CRESTED WATER DRAGON

This lizard is found in Asia and lives mainly in trees that grow close to water. Like most lizards, the water dragon is able to swim. Unlike most other lizards, however, which move on all four legs, the crested water dragon runs on two legs if it is threatened, which gives it more speed on land.

Typical scaly skin like other reptiles, such as snakes and crocodiles

Outstretched claws give extra balance.

LIZARD TAILS
In the same way that a starfish regrows its arms, a lizard can regrow its tail. When a predator such as a bird or cat grabs a lizard by its tail, the lizard sheds the tail in order to escape. The vertebrae (backbones) along the tail have cracks in them, so the tail breaks off easily. The broken-off part of the tail often twitches for a few minutes, confusing the enemy while the lizard runs away. The tail grows back to its original length in about eight months.

Loose skin around neck looks like a huge collar.

The more the frilled lizard opens its mouth, the more the frill expands.

Tail waves around to frighten enemy.

Tree skink has lost the end of its tail.

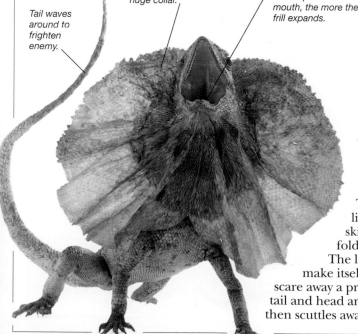

Tail has regrown fully within a few months.

Tokay gecko

FRILLED LIZARD
The Australian frilled lizard has a flap of loose skin around its neck that folds flat along the body. The lizard raises the frill to make itself look bigger in order to scare away a predator. It also waves its tail and head around to alarm its enemy, then scuttles away.

TOKAY GECKO
The pads on the feet of the tokay gecko are covered with about one million microscopic hairlike structures that help the gecko grip onto surfaces. The rubber soles of sneakers and hiking boots look like the soles of the gecko's feet.

TEGU LIZARD
The young tegu lizard shown left is found in tropical areas of South America. It feeds mostly on young birds and mammals, and also eats other lizards. Like most lizards, the tegu has a tough, scaly skin, a forked tongue, five claws on its feet, and movable eyelids.

Five claws on feet

Forked tongue

Male anole lizard inflates its red throat sac.

ANOLE LIZARD

Anole lizards belong to the iguana family of lizards. There are many different kinds, found in tropical areas of Central and South America. Anole lizards are territorial (they guard their territory). The males inflate their red-colored throat sacs, which they display to each other as a sign of aggression. Anole lizards are sometimes called American chameleons.

KOMODO DRAGON

The Komodo dragon is the largest lizard – up to 10 ft (3 m) long. It scavenges on dead animals and also catches deer, pigs, and wild boars. Komodo dragons are found only on a few of the Lesser Sunda Islands, Indonesia.

Komodo dragon lizards feasting on the carcass (dead body) of a deer

GILA MONSTER

Only two lizards have a poisonous bite – the Gila monster and the Mexican beaded lizard, both from southern North America. The Gila monster (right) is found in dry, scrubby areas. It hides in a burrow by day and emerges at night to eat small animals such as mice, and the eggs of birds and other reptiles.

Gila monster feeding on newborn mice

GREEN GECKO
Many lizards are colored to blend in with their surroundings. Tree-climbing lizards such as this green gecko are often bright green to match the leaves; desert-dwelling lizards are sand-colored or brown. Many kinds of chameleons can change their color according to their surroundings.

THORNY DEVIL
The extraordinary looking thorny devil is also called the moloch. Spines protect its body from nose to tail. Thorny lizards live in dry parts of Australia, where they forage for ants. When the young molochs hatch from their eggs, they look like tiny, spiny versions of their parents.

IGUANA
Like all lizards, iguanas depend on heat from the environment to keep their bodies warm and active. They spend much of the day basking in the sun, absorbing its warmth to prepare for activity. At night they become slow and sluggish as their body temperature falls. The Galapagos marine iguanas shown here dive to more than 35 ft (11 m) deep into the sea in search of seaweed.

After each dive, Galapagos marine iguanas sunbathe on the rocks to warm up again.

Slow-worms grow to about 20 in (50 cm) in length.

SLOWWORM
The slowworm is not really a worm, but a lizard. It is not slow either; when disturbed, slowworms can wriggle away rapidly to safety. Slowworms are found in fields and scrubland in Europe, northern Africa, and southwestern Asia. They feed on slugs, spiders, and insects. Unlike most lizards, slowworms give birth to fully formed young.

Find out more
CAMOUFLAGE, ANIMAL
DESERT WILDLIFE
NORTH AMERICAN WILDLIFE
REPTILES

LOUIS XIV

IN 1643, LOUIS XIV became king of France. He ruled for 72 years and made his country the most powerful in Europe at that time. While Louis was still young, his mother and his chief minister, Cardinal Mazarin, ruled on his behalf. During this time the nobility rose up against the throne and tax policies in a rebellion called the Fronde. However, when Louis was 23, he took complete charge of France and ruled as an absolute monarch, making all decisions himself. He moved his court to Versailles, just outside Paris, and appointed Jean Colbert, a French statesman, as his finance minister. Under Colbert's control, trade and industry flourished. Louis XIV fought a series of wars and increased the territory of France. But the many wars cost France a lot of money, and the country became nearly bankrupt. Taxes were raised to pay off debts, causing much hardship among the poor.

VERSAILLES PALACE

The palace at Versailles was magnificent. Its many rooms included a hall of mirrors that was 240 ft (73 m) in length and lavishly decorated. Formal gardens with fountains and sculpted hedges surrounded the palace. Louis spent one-tenth of all France's wealth on its upkeep. Even so, many parts of the palace were overcrowded, dark, and cold. Today, Versailles palace is open to the public.

The hall of mirrors at the palace of Versailles was a place for nobles to congregate.

Detailed embroidery on chair typical of Louis XIV style of furniture

SUN KING

Louis XIV surrounded himself with splendor. His court was a center for the great writers, artists, and musicians of the time. He said of himself *"L'état c'est moi"* – "I am the state." Louis was given the nickname "the Sun King" after the Greek god Apollo, who was also a patron of the arts.

FURNITURE
Louis XIV employed groups of expert craftsworkers to make furniture for his palace at Versailles. The style of the furniture, such as this walnut chair, was elaborate and ornate. It became known as the Louis XIV style.

Find out more

FRANCE, HISTORY OF
FRENCH REVOLUTION

LOW COUNTRIES

SMALL AND DENSELY populated, the Low Countries are highly developed industrial nations with thriving economies. Nearly one-third of the Netherlands lies below sea level. Over the last four centuries, Dutch engineers have reclaimed land by pushing back the North Sea with a network of barriers, or dikes. In northern Belgium, the land is also flat and low-lying, although to the south it rises toward the forested uplands of the Ardennes. Belgium only became independent in the 19th century. It is divided by language; Dutch (Flemish) is spoken in the north, while French is spoken in the south. Farming is important throughout the region. The fertile land and cool, rainy climate is ideally suited to dairy and crop farming. Major industries produce iron and steel, natural gas, clothing, textiles, and electrical goods. The tiny country of Luxembourg has the highest living standards in Europe, and is known as a major banking center.

The Low Countries lie in northwest Europe, with Germany to the east and France to the south. To the west lies the North Sea.

BULB FIELDS
The Dutch have been famous for their flower bulbs since the 16th century, when tulips first arrived in Europe from the Middle East. In spring, fields of spring flowers are a spectacular sight. Fresh-cut flowers are flown all over the world.

AMSTERDAM
A city of 90 islands connected by 1,000 bridges, Amsterdam is linked by canal to the North Sea. The city became important in the Middle Ages, and many of the churches, towers, and gabled merchants' houses of the old city still stand today. In the 17th century, Amsterdam was the financial capital of the world. Since 1945, new suburbs have been built on polders (reclaimed land), tripling the size of the city.

LUXEMBOURG
The capital of Luxembourg stands on a sandstone plateau, cut into deep ravines by the Alzette River. The Old Town centers on the Grand Ducal Palace (1572), the Cathedral, and the Town Hall. Luxembourg is a thriving industrial and banking center.

LAND RECLAMATION
Over the centuries, low-lying land has been reclaimed from the sea. Engineers built dikes to enclose areas of shallow water, which were then drained. From the 14th century, windmills were used to drain water and pump it into canals. On the windswept lowlands, windpower was very effective, although it has now been replaced by steam and electric pumps. However, storms and high tides are still a major threat to the people of the Netherlands.

Porters carry trays of cheese at the famous market in Alkmaar.

CHEESE
Much of the cheese produced in the Netherlands is made from the milk of cows, which graze on areas of reclaimed land. The country's most famous cheeses are Gouda, and Edam, which has a red wax rind.

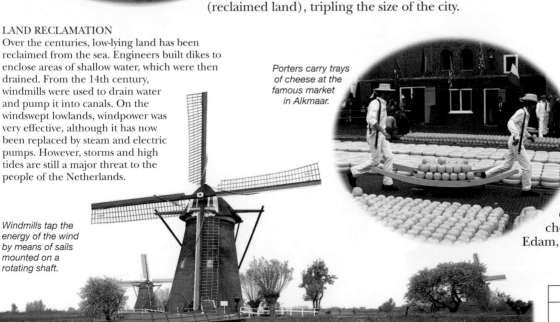

Windmills tap the energy of the wind by means of sails mounted on a rotating shaft.

Find out more
EUROPE
EUROPEAN UNION
FLOWERS AND HERBS
PORTS AND WATERWAYS
WORLD WAR I

Volcano	Mountain	Ancient monument	Capital city	Large city/town	Small city/town

BELGIUM
Area: 17,780 sq miles (33,100 sq km)
Population: 10,300,000
Capital: Brussels
Languages: Flemish, French, German, Dutch
Religions: Roman Catholic, Muslim
Currency: Euro

LUXEMBOURG
Area: 998 sq miles (2,586 sq km)
Population: 453,000
Capital: Luxembourg
Languages: Letzeburgish, German, French
Religions: Roman Catholic, Protestant, Greek Orthodox, Jewish
Currency: Euro

NETHERLANDS
Area: 14,410 sq miles (37,330 sq km)
Population: 16,100,000
Capital: Amsterdam, The Hague ('s-Gravenhage)
Languages: Dutch, Frisian
Religions: Roman Catholic, Protestant, Muslim
Currency: Euro

EU HEADQUARTERS
In 1957, all three low countries were founding members of the European Economic Community (EEC). Brussels is now the administrative headquarters of the European Union (EU), while Luxembourg is the headquarters of the European Investment Bank and the Court of Justice.

BELGIAN BEER
Belgium is famous for its beer, which is produced in many local breweries and exported worldwide. Another important export is fine Belgian chocolate; Belgium is the world's third-largest exporter.

SCALE BAR

km
0   50   100

miles
0   50   100

BRUSSELS
Brussels, the capital of Belgium, is an international economic and financial center. The city expanded rapidly in the 19th century, and became the center of Belgium's growing steel, chemical, and textile industries. The Grand Place (above) is the heart of the Old Town. Brussels is now a major financial center, with its own stock exchange.

WAR CEMETERY
The Flanders region of southwest Belgium is imprinted with memories of World War I. One of the costliest battles of the four-year war was Passchendaele, in 1917, in which an estimated 800,000 Allied and German troops were killed. Vast war cemeteries, such as Tyne Cot, near Ieper (left), attract many visitors.

Map labels:

West Frisian Islands — Terschelling, Schiermonnikoog, Ameland, Vlieland, Texel, Waddenzee

NETHERLANDS

Leeuwarden, Groningen, Assen, Klazienaveen, Den Helder, Alkmaar, IJsselmeer, Lelystad, Zwolle, Almelo, Zaanstad, Haarlem, AMSTERDAM, Apeldoorn, Enschede, Leiden, Amersfoort, THE HAGUE ('S-GRAVENHAGE), Utrecht, Neder Rijn, Arnhem, Rotterdam, Lek, IJssel, Dordrecht, Waal, Nijmegen, Goeree, Overflakkee, Bergse Maas, Schouwen, Zierikzee, Breda, 's-Hertogenbosch, Noord-Beveland, Tholen, Roosendaal, Tilburg, Helmond, Middelburg, Zuid-Beveland, Venlo, Terneuzen, Eindhoven, Ostend, Bruges (Brugge), Antwerp, Maas, Roeselare, Ghent (Gent), Rupel, Ijzer, Scheldt, Leie, Mechelen, Hasselt, Genk, Kerkrade, Ieper, Aalst, Leuven, Dender, Maastricht, Kortrijk, BRUSSELS, Tournai, BELGIUM, Charleroi, Liège, Mons, Namur, Meuse, Botrange 694m, Hautes Fagnes, Sambre, Fagne, Famenne, Weiswampach, Ourthe, Bastogne, Sûre, Diekirch, Recogne, Ardenne, Neufchâteau, LUXEMBOURG, Semois, Grevenmacher, Arlon, Virton, Alzette, LUXEMBOURG, Esch-sur-Alzette, Moselle

North Sea, FRANCE, GERMANY

N W E S

HISTORY OF THE
LOW COUNTRIES

Charles of Burgundy

THE NETHERLANDS, BELGIUM, AND LUXEMBOURG were once thought of as a single region called the Low Countries. From the 1100s to the 17th century, the area was ruled by Europe's major powers—Germany, France, and Spain. In 1568, the northern region (what is now the Netherlands) turned to Protestantism and rebelled against Catholic Spain. Spain recognized the Netherlands' independence in 1648, and the country flourished throughout the 1600s. France regained its power over part of the region in the 18th century, ruling until the fall of Napoleon in 1815, when the Netherlands, Belgium, and the Duchy of Luxembourg united as the Kingdom of the Netherlands. Belgium declared its independence in 1830, and Luxembourg in 1890. Today, all three countries thrive as founder members of the European Community.

BURGUNDY AND SPAIN
In 1400s, Burgundy ruled the Low Countries. In 1516, Charles, Duke of Burgundy became king of Spain, bringing the Low Countries under Spanish rule.

THE GOLDEN CENTURY
In the 1600s, the Netherlands grew rich on international trade and exploration, so the period was known as "the Golden Century." Amsterdam was the trading center and money market of the Western world, taking over from Antwerp, Belgium, which was captured by the Spanish in 1576. Rich merchants built large houses along Amsterdam's canals.

Dutch East Indiaman, or oceangoing cargo ship

Merchants checking cargoes of spices, gold, and pottery

Amsterdam

Routes to Africa, Indonesia, and Australasia

At its height, the Dutch Empire covered every continent.

Routes to North and South America

Pacific Ocean

Atlantic Ocean

Indian Ocean

Pacific Ocean

TULIPMANIA
The tulip was brought to Europe from Turkey in the 16th century and soon became fashionable. A craze called "tulipmania" swept through the Netherlands between 1634 and 1637. People invested money in tulips, and the price for rare bulbs went up until they were worth more than gold. When prices fell, many people went bankrupt.

LOW COUNTRY COLONIES
The Dutch East Indies (now Indonesia), set up in the early 17th century, was the largest of the Low Country colonies. In 1634, the Dutch captured the Antilles (Curaçao, Aruba, Bonaire, Saba, St. Eustatius, and St. Martin Island) from Spain. By 1674, they had taken Surinam from Britain.

Dutch architecture in Caribbean colors on the island of Curaçao.

THE GREAT TRADERS
The Netherlands became a leading sea power in the 17th century by finding new trade routes. The Dutch East India Company was founded in 1602 to trade with Indonesia and southern Africa. The Dutch West India Company, founded in 1621, opened routes to America, Australasia, and West Africa.

HOLDING BACK THE SEA
Much of the Low Countries, especially the Netherlands, is below sea level. For centuries, the Dutch have fought to hold back the North Sea, building large earth walls called dikes to prevent flooding. They also set up thousands of windmills across the country to pump water away from the land along canals. Today, electric pumps are used.

NEW AMSTERDAM

In 1624, the Dutch West India Company set up the colony of New Netherland in northern America. They built its capital, New Amsterdam, on the island of Manhattan, which they bought from Native Americans for goods worth 60 Dutch guilders. In 1664, the English took over the colony by force, and renamed it New York.

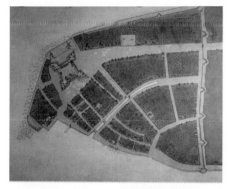

ANGLO-DUTCH WARS

Between 1652 and 1674, the Dutch and the English fought three wars for the control of sea trade routes. The Dutch won, even after France joined in to help England in 1670. England signed a truce with the Dutch in 1674.

CONGRESS OF VIENNA

After Napoleon's defeat at Waterloo in 1815, the other European powers were determined to prevent the French from becoming so powerful again. They met at the Congress of Vienna in 1815, and decided to make the Low Countries stronger to stop France expansion in that direction. The Netherlands and Belgium were joined together as the Kingdom of the Netherlands, ruled by Prince William VI of the Netherlands as King William I and Grand Duke of Luxembourg.

Cartoon of diplomats at the Congress of Vienna

BELGIAN INDEPENDENCE

Belgium remained under Spanish rule when the Netherlands declared its independence in 1568. Mostly Catholic, Belgium revolted against the Protestant Netherlands in 1830 and seized its independence under Charles Rogier. Fighting lasted only a month, then the people elected Prince Leopold of Saxe-Coburg as their first king, Leopold I.

Tank warfare in World War II

THE BATTLEFIELD OF EUROPE

The Low Countries have been the site of many of Europe's battles. Napoleon was defeated at Waterloo, in Belgium. In World War I, the battles of Ypres, Mons, and Namur were fought in Belgium; in World War II, the Battle of the Bulge (1944) was fought all over Belgium and Luxembourg.

LUXEMBOURG

The name Luxembourg comes from a word meaning "little castle". Luxembourg began life as a castle (built in 963) but later it became a duchy (ruled by a duke) until the Netherlands took it over in 1443. In 1815, it was made a Grand Duchy, ruled by the Netherlands. In 1890, Queen Wilhelmina came to the Netherlands' throne, and as Luxembourg's laws did not allow women to rule, the Grand Duchy ended the alliance. Today Luxembourg is a separate, independent country.

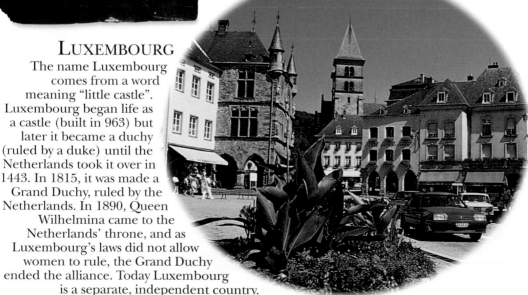

Modern Luxembourg is a very prosperous country.

LOWLAND HISTORY

1300s-1400s Burgundy rules the region.

1516 Charles of Burgundy becomes king of Spain.

1648 Spain recognizes Dutch independence.

1652-74 Anglo-Dutch Wars.

1652 Dutch settlers arrive in South Africa.

1776 Dutch side with America in War of Independence.

1795-1814 France controls the Netherlands.

1815 Belgium and the Netherlands unite.

1830 Belgium declares independence.

1890 Luxembourg declares independence.

1914-18 Belgium fights with Allies in World War I; the Dutch remain neutral.

1948 Benelux – an economic trading association between Belgium, Netherlands and Luxembourg – formed.

1957 Benelux countries sign Treaty of Rome to set up European Economic Community (EEC).

1967 Benelux countries are founder members of EU.

Find out more

EUROPEAN UNION
EUROPE, HISTORY OF
NAPOLEONIC WARS

LUNGS AND BREATHING

WE NEED OXYGEN TO LIVE, and we get oxygen by breathing air. When we breathe in, air is sucked through the nose or mouth, down the windpipe, and into the lungs, two powerful organs in the chest. The lungs absorb as much oxygen from the air as possible. The oxygen travels in the blood from the lungs to every part of the body. Our bodies use oxygen to burn up the food we eat and convert it into energy. Then harmful carbon dioxide is breathed out of the body by the lungs. The whole process is called respiration. The lungs, together with the airways, throat, and nasal passages, form the respiratory system. Each lung is surrounded by a thin covering or membrane called the pleura. The lungs themselves contain air tubes, blood vessels, and millions of tiny air sacs called alveoli. If you spread these air sacs out flat, they would cover the area of a tennis court.

HOW WE MAKE SOUNDS
We use the air flowing in and out of our lungs to make sounds. We speak, shout, laugh, and cry by making air flow over two small leathery flaps called the vocal cords. These are located in the larynx (voice box), in the lower part of the throat. Muscles in the throat stretch the flaps tighter to change from low notes to high notes.

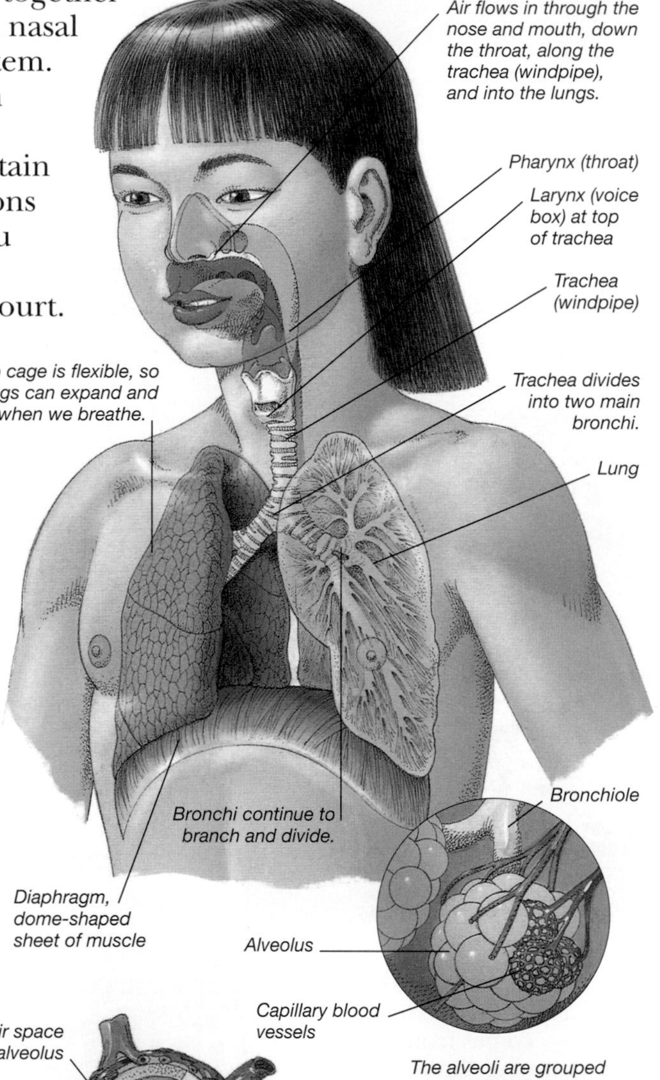

Air flows in through the nose and mouth, down the throat, along the trachea (windpipe), and into the lungs.

Pharynx (throat)

Larynx (voice box) at top of trachea

Trachea (windpipe)

Trachea divides into two main bronchi.

Lung

The rib cage is flexible, so the lungs can expand and shrink when we breathe.

Bronchi continue to branch and divide.

Diaphragm, dome-shaped sheet of muscle

Bronchiole

Alveolus

Capillary blood vessels

The alveoli are grouped together like bunches of grapes. Tiny tubes called bronchioles bring fresh oxygen-containing air to the alveoli.

BREATHING

Lungs empty of air as you breathe out.

Lungs fill with air as you breathe in.

Diaphragm relaxes and rises.

Diaphragm contracts and flattens.

BREATHING OUT
When you breathe out, the diaphragm and chest muscles relax. The lungs are spongy and elastic, so they spring back to their smaller size after they have been stretched. This blows air back out of the lungs.

BREATHING IN
When you breathe in, the diaphragm contracts (becomes flatter) and pulls down the base of the lungs. Muscles between the ribs contract to swing the ribs up and out. These actions stretch and enlarge the lungs, so that air is sucked in.

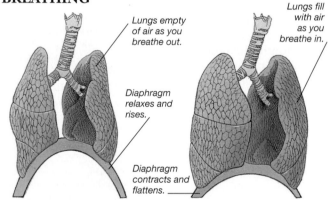

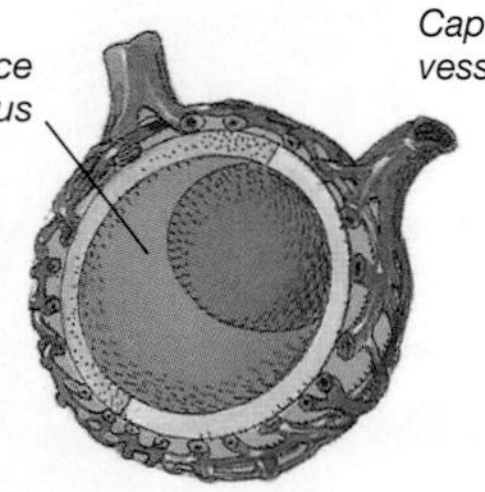

LUNGFISH
Most animals that live on land have lungs. Many water animals, however, including most fish, breathe using feathery flaps called gills. Oxygen in the water passes through the thin gill coverings to the blood inside the fish's body. The lungfish shown here is an unusual animal because it has lungs and gills, so it can breathe in both ways and can survive out of water for a long time.

Air space inside alveolus

ALVEOLUS
Each alveolus is surrounded by a network of very fine blood vessels called capillaries. Oxygen passes from the air space inside the alveolus, through the lining, and into the blood. Carbon dioxide passes in the opposite way.

Find out more
BRAIN AND NERVES
HEART AND BLOOD
HUMAN BODY
MUSCLES AND MOVEMENT
OXYGEN
SKELETONS

MACHINES

INCLINED PLANE

Simple machines reduce the effort needed to move or lift an object, but the object has to travel a greater distance. The simplest machine is the ramp, or inclined plane. You need less force to push an object with a downward load up an inclined plane than you need to lift it straight up. This is because the object moves a greater distance along the plane. The gentler the slope, the further you have to push, but the easier it is.

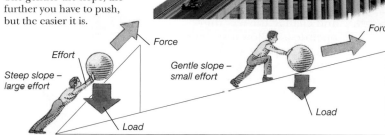

WHAT DO A SAW and a computer have in common? Both are machines. One is simple and the other very complex, but both are tools that do work for us. Machines perform tasks that we would find difficult or even impossible to do. You cannot cut through wood with your bare hands, for example, but it is easy with a saw. Likewise, a computer can do calculations rapidly that would take you an enormous amount of time. All machines need a source of energy. Mechanical machines, such as a corkscrew, use the energy of movement. A motor or a person's muscles drive the machine with a certain amount of force called the effort. The machine then applies this movement but produces a larger force to move a load. For example, your fingers operate a can opener, but the blade of the can opener moves with much more force than that produced by your fingers. Many hand-powered machines help us perform tasks for which we do not have enough strength. They use devices known as simple machines. These include levers, gears, pulleys, and screws.

Effort

Force

Steep slope – large effort

Gentle slope – small effort

Load

Force

Load

SCREW

A screw moves forward a shorter distance than it turns. It therefore moves forward with a much greater force than the effort needed to turn it. The screw bites into the wood with great force and is held strongly.

Archimedes' screw (above) is an ancient device for raising water. As it turns, the screw shifts water along its thread instead of moving itself forward.

The screw makes use of the principle of the inclined plane.

The thread of the screw is like a slope wrapped around a cylinder.

PLOW
The plow has a cutting blade that bites into the soil and a V-shaped blade that turns the soil over.

PERPETUAL MOTION

Many inventors have tried to build a machine that, once started, would never stop. It would run on its own without any source of energy. However, such a perpetual motion machine is impossible. This is because all machines lose some energy as they work. Without a constant source of energy, a machine always slows down and stops.

In this machine, the motion of the balls was supposed to keep the wheel turning.

WEDGE
The wedge is a form of inclined plane. Instead of moving a load along a slope, the wedge is a slope that pushes a load aside or upward as it moves forward. The wedge pushes with greater force than the effort needed to move the wedge. Sharp blades are thin wedges that make cutting an easy task.

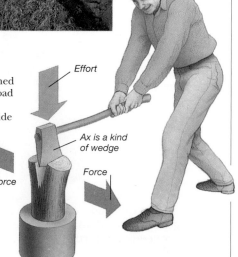

Effort

Ax is a kind of wedge

Force

Force

PULLEYS

Lifting a heavy load is easy with a pulley system. It contains a set of wheels attached to a support. A rope goes around grooves in the wheels. Pulling the rope raises the lower wheel and the load. A pulley system allows you to lift a heavy load with little effort, but you must pull the rope a large distance to raise the load by a small amount.

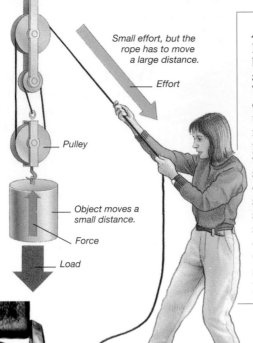

Small effort, but the rope has to move a large distance.

Effort

Pulley

Object moves a small distance.

Force

Load

AUTOMATIC MACHINES

Many machines do not need to be operated by people. These are automatic machines. They contain mechanisms or computers to control themselves. These machines may simply perform a set task whenever it is required; automatic doors, for example, open as people arrive. Other machines are able to check their own work and change the way they operate to follow instructions. One example is an aircraft autopilot, which guides the plane through the skies.

Traffic lights are machines that control traffic automatically.

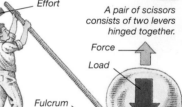

Fulcrum

GEARS

Gears are interlocking toothed wheels. They can increase force or speed depending on the relative size of the wheels and their number of teeth. A gearwheel driven by a smaller wheel turns less quickly than the smaller wheel but with greater force. A wheel driven by a larger wheel turns faster but with less force.

Mechanical clocks and watches contain gears that turn the hands at different speeds.

LEVER

A long stick propped up on a small object (a fulcrum) helps you move a heavy load. The stick is a simple machine called a lever. Pushing down on the end farthest from the fulcrum raises the other end with greater force, helping you move the load. Other kinds of levers can increase either the force applied to, or the distance moved by, a load.

Effort

Fulcrum

A pair of scissors consists of two levers hinged together.

Force

Load

There are three types of lever. A crowbar is called a first-class lever. The fulcrum is between the load and the effort, which is the force that you apply.

Force

Fulcrum

Load

Effort

A wheelbarrow is a second-class lever. The load lies between the fulcrum and the effort.

Fulcrum

Force

Effort

Load

A fishing rod is a third-class lever. The load moves a greater distance than the effort, but with less force. The effort pushes between the load and the fulcrum.

WHEEL AND AXLE

Several machines use the principle of the wheel and axle. One example is the winch, in which a handle (the wheel) turns a shaft (the axle) that raises a load. The handle moves a greater distance than the load rises. The winch therefore lifts the load with a greater force than the effort needed to turn the handle.

Effort

Force

Load

STEERING WHEEL
The steering wheel on a car is an example of the wheel and axle. The shaft turns with greater force than the effort needed to turn the steering wheel.

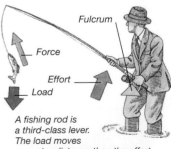

Find out more

ENGINES
FACTORIES
INDUSTRIAL REVOLUTION
ROBOTS
TECHNOLOGY

MAGAZINES

WHATEVER YOUR INTEREST, you'll find a magazine that tells you more about it. Like newspapers, new issues of a magazine go on sale regularly – usually weekly or monthly. But magazines last longer than newspapers. Often, two or three people read the magazine before discarding it. Some magazines, such as scientific journals, are more like reference books. Their buyers keep them to refer to months or even years later. The simplest magazines, such as neighborhood newsletters, are sheets that have been roughly photocopied and stapled together. Other magazines cover topics with a wide appeal. They are printed in color on glossy paper and have many pictures. The editor-in-chief decides what goes into the magazine. Other editors and journalists write the features and articles. The art director is responsible for the style and look of the magazine. Designers choose pictures and lay out the pages.

LIFE MAGAZINE
The first magazines began in Europe in the 17th century. But modern magazines started only when it was possible to print photographs on their pages. One of the greatest picture magazines is *Life*, which first appeared in 1936. *Life* tells stories with a series of pictures and few words.

Popular science magazines explain new discoveries in simple terms.

Pictures in geography magazines show remote corners of the world.

Food magazines contain recipes and restaurant reviews.

Publishers may produce different editions of a fashion magazine for readers in each country.

COMICS
Children and adults read comics. The word comic is short for comic strip, because the first comics were collections of comic strips from newspapers. They were originally called funnies. A new type of comic, containing adventure stories, first appeared in the 1930s and led to the many different comics of today.

Fan clubs produce magazines about popular celebrities.

Superman, one of the world's best-known comic-strip heroes, first appeared in Action Comics in 1938.

© 1982 DC Comics Inc. Used with permission

MAGAZINES FOR EVERYONE
There are magazines for every reader's interest. There are fashion, beauty, and family magazines, as well as magazines on every activity from sailing and fishing to computers and the arts. Magazines such as *Time* and *Newsweek* give the background to current events in more depth than newspapers or television news. Specialized magazines cover subjects such as science or hobbies. Fanzines are magazines about pop stars. Trade magazines are for businesses such as publishing, banking, or engineering.

NEWSSTANDS
At a newsstand you can choose from a wide range of national and foreign magazines on subjects such as politics, fashion, and lifestyle.

JOURNALIST
Magazines are sometimes called journals, so the editors and writers who create them are called journalists. An editor decides what will appear in the magazine and chooses the writer. The writer carries out research or interviews and writes the article. Then the editor corrects errors and makes sure the article fits into the space on the page.

Find out more
ADVERTISING
CARTOONS
NEWSPAPERS

MAGNETISM

ORIGIN OF MAGNETISM

Iron contains millions of tiny magnets called magnetic dipoles. Normally, all of the dipoles point in different directions, so their magnetism cancels out. In a magnet, the dipoles point the same way so that their magnetism combines.

MAGNETIC FIELD

The area around a magnet in which its magnetic force works is called its magnetic field. For instance, a paper clip is pulled toward the magnet (right) when it is placed within the magnetic field of the magnet.

All magnets attract iron and steel objects but not plastic or wooden ones.

THE FORCE of magnetism is invisible, yet you can see its power when a magnet drags a piece of metal toward it. A material that attracts certain metals such as iron is called a magnet. Materials that are attracted by a magnet are called magnetic. Every magnet has two poles – places at which magnetic objects cluster. The Earth itself is a huge magnet; its magnetic poles are close to the geographical North and South poles. One pole of a magnet is attracted to the Earth's northern magnetic pole and is called the magnet's north pole; the other is attracted to the south and is called the magnet's south pole. Materials that retain their magnetism all the time are called permanent magnets. An electric current flowing in a coil of wire produces a magnet called an electromagnet that can be switched on and off. Electromagnets are used in electric motors, loudspeakers, and many other devices.

MAGNETIC POLES

The north pole of one magnet and the south pole of another magnet attract each other.

A magnetic pole, such as a south pole, repels (pushes away) another pole of the same kind.

LODESTONE

Magnetite is an iron ore that often possesses magnetism. It was once commonly called lodestone, which means "guiding stone," because early navigators used it as a compass.

The magnetic north and south poles lie a small distance away from geographical North and South.

GEOMAGNETISM

The Earth produces a magnetic field that makes it seem as though it has a huge "bar" magnet inside it. Electric currents flowing within the Earth's liquid iron core cause the Earth's magnetism, which is called geomagnetism.

The geographical North and South poles lie on the Earth's axis, which is the line around which the Earth spins.

The pattern of lines shows the Earth's magnetic field. The field is strongest where the lines are closest together.

ELECTROMAGNETS

An electromagnet is a coil of wire. An electric current within the coil creates a magnetic field. The field can be made stronger by winding the wire around a piece of iron. Turning off the current switches off the magnetic field. Some cranes use an electromagnet instead of a hook.

COMPASS

The needle inside a magnetic compass is a thin, light magnet, balanced so that it swings freely. The needle's north pole points toward the Earth's magnetic north pole, which is very close to the geographical north. People use magnetic compasses to navigate at sea and on land.

Find out more

EARTH
ELECTRICITY
MAPS
NAVIGATION

MAMMALS

THE ANIMAL GROUP CALLED MAMMALS includes the heaviest, tallest, and fastest animals on land – the elephant, the giraffe, and the cheetah. Mice, whales, rhinoceroses, bats, and humans are also mammals. Like birds, mammals are warm-blooded (endothermic), but three features set them apart from all other creatures. All mammals are covered in fur or hair, all feed their young on milk, and all have a unique type of jaw. The jawbone helps us to identify the fossilized bones of prehistoric mammals that lived on Earth millions of years ago. Mammals are also members of the group known as vertebrates because they all have vertebrae (backbones). Today there are more than 5,000 kinds of mammals, including carnivores (meat-eaters) such as tigers; herbivores (plant-eaters) such as rabbits; and omnivores (meat- and plant- eaters) such as bears. Cattle, sheep, goats, and most other farm animals are mammals, and many pets are mammals, too, including cats, dogs, and guinea pigs. Mammals live nearly everywhere. They are found on land, in the sea, and in the sky, from the coldest Arctic to the most searing heat of the desert.

MARSUPIAL YOUNG
Marsupials are very tiny when they are born. At birth, a kangaroo is less than 1 in (2.5 cm) long. It crawls through its mother's fur into a pocket-like pouch on the abdomen, where it attaches itself to her teat and suckles milk.

A mammal's body is covered in fur.

A kangaroo's large tail is so strong that it can act as a prop for the kangaroo to lean on.

Young male joey

PLACENTAL MAMMALS
Most mammals, including monkeys, cats, and dogs, are called placental mammals because the young develop inside the mother's womb, or uterus, and are fed by means of the placenta. The placenta is a specialized organ embedded in the wall of the womb. It carries nutrients and other essential materials from the mother's blood to the baby's blood. These nutrients help the young to grow and develop. After the young are born, the placenta comes out of the uterus as afterbirth.

POUCHED MAMMALS
Kangaroos, opossums, wallabies, koalas, wombats, and bandicoots are all known as marsupials, or pouched mammals. These animals carry their young in their pouches until the young are able to fend for themselves. Once it has left the pouch, the joey (young kangaroo) returns to the pouch to suck milk. Marsupials are found in Australia and New Guinea, South America, and North America. A few marsupials, such as the shrew opossum of South America, do not have pouches.

MONOTREME MAMMALS
Three kinds of mammals lay eggs. They are called monotreme mammals, and include the platypus and the two types of echidna (spiny ant-eater). All are found in Australasia. After about 10 days, the young hatch out of the eggs, then feed on their mother's milk.

PRIMATES
Monkeys, apes, and humans belong to a group called primates. Primates are able to grasp with their hands. Most primates have thumbs and big toes, with flat fingernails rather than claws. Members of the primate group range in size from the mouse lemur, which weighs only 2 oz (60 g), to the gorilla, which weighs up to 610 lb (275 kg).

SPINY ANTEATER
The short-beaked spiny anteater, or echidna, lays a single egg in a temporary pouch on its abdomen. The young echidna hatches, then sucks milk from mammary glands on its mother's abdomen.

MAMMAL GROUPS

There are about 27 main groups of mammals, some of which are shown below. Rodents make up half of all mammals; bats account for one quarter. There are only three kinds of elephant, and the aardvark is in a group of its own.

Humans

Elephants

Cats, dogs, and other carnivores

Camels, horses, and other hoofed mammals

Aardvarks

Anteaters, armadillos, and other toothless mammals

Bats and flying foxes

Monkeys, apes, and other primates

Sea cows and dugongs

Seals, sea lions, and walruses

Whales, dolphins, and porpoises

Hares, rabbits, and pikas

Hedgehogs, moles, and other insectivores

Squirrels, rats, mice, and other rodents

Tree shrews

Most puppies feed on their mother's milk for two or three months. A mother shrew suckles her young for four weeks; a mother whale feeds her youngster for six months or more.

MAMMAL MILK

Mammals are the only creatures that feed their young with milk. When the female is about to give birth, she starts to produce milk in mammary glands on the chest or abdomen. When the young are born, they suck the milk from the mother's teats. Mother's milk is an ideal food for the young – warm and nourishing, and full of special substances that protect the young from disease. As the babies grow larger and stronger, they take less milk and begin to eat solid foods. This process is called weaning.

Rhinoceros

The gestation usually lasts for 15 months; one young is born.

Rabbit

Gestation usually lasts for 30 days; as many as eight young are born in a litter.

GESTATION

The time between mating and birth, when the young develop in the mother's womb, is called the gestation or pregnancy period. In general, large mammals have longer pregnancies and fewer young than small mammals.

Dirty fur harbors pests and also lets heat escape, so many mammals spend time cleaning or grooming their fur.

HAIR AND FUR

Fur or hair protects the mammal's skin from injury and the sun's rays. It also keeps heat in and moisture out. The colors and patterns of the fur provide camouflage. Water-dwelling mammals such as beavers have special oily, waterproof fur. The porcupine's spines are modified hairs and the rhinoceros's horn is made from strong hairs tightly packed together.

ARMADILLO

Some mammals, such as armadillos and pangolins, have reptile-like scales instead of fur. The scales, or scutes, of an armadillo are made of a type of horn and bone that grows from the skin. Hairs grow between the scutes and also cover the animal's soft-skinned underbelly.

BODY TEMPERATURE

Mammals and birds are called warm-blooded animals because they can maintain a high body temperature even in cold conditions. Mammals do, however, need plenty of food to provide the energy for warmth. The heat to warm a mammal is produced by chemical reactions in the body, particularly in the muscles.

Huskies are able to stay warm in deep snow because of their thick fur.

Find out more

ANIMALS
ANIMAL SENSES
AUSTRALIAN WILDLIFE
FARM ANIMALS
FLIGHT, ANIMAL
HIBERNATION
PREHISTORIC LIFE

NELSON
MANDELA

IN FEBRUARY 1990 the 72-year-old Nelson Mandela walked into freedom after spending more than 27 years in prison. He had spent his life opposing the white-led South African government, which practiced the policy of apartheid, or separation of the races. Within four years Mandela led his party, the African National Congress (ANC), to victory in the general election and became the first-ever black president of a multiracial, democratic South Africa. By the time he retired in 1999 he was one of the most famous and deeply-loved political leaders in the world.

1918 Born in Mvezo, Transkei.

1942 Gained law degree; practices in Johannesburg.

1952 Becomes deputy national president of the ANC.

1962 Imprisoned as a leader of the ANC.

1964 Sentenced to life imprisonment and sent to Robben Island (until 1985).

1990 Released from prison.

1993 Wins Nobel Peace Prize.

1994 Elected first black president of South Africa.

1999 Steps down as president.

AFRICAN NATIONAL CONGRESS

In 1912, the African National Congress was formed to protect the interests of the black population of South Africa. It tried to achieve a multiracial, democratic country through peaceful means, but the South African government thought it was revolutionary, and banned it in 1961. From 1952, Mandela was a senior member of the organization. He became its leader in 1991.

ROBBEN ISLAND
Nelson Mandela spent 21 of his 27 years in prison on Robben Island, a high-security prison off the coast of Cape Town. He broke rocks in the quarry and studied with other ANC prisoners. Now the prison is closed, and people visit Mandela's cell.

TRUTH AND RECONCILIATION
In order to heal the wounds left by apartheid, Mandela set up the Truth and Reconciliation Commission. A Nobel Peace Prize winner, Archbishop Desmond Tutu, ran the commission. It examined the events of the apartheid era, and tried to reconcile (bring together) former enemies.

FREE NELSON MANDELA
People campaigned worldwide to free Mandela from prison. They boycotted (refused to buy) South African goods, such as fruit and wine, and demonstrated against the South African government. In 1988, a huge rock concert was held at London's Wembley Stadium to mark Mandela's 70th birthday.

WINNIE MANDELA
In 1961, Mandela married Winnie Mdikizela (b. 1934). She campaigned for his release, but her political activities were controversial. They divorced in 1996.

PRESIDENT
The first multiracial elections in South Africa were held in 1994. Mandela led the ANC to a huge victory and became president. He worked to obtain peace, and unite all the peoples of his troubled country. When famous people – including the Prince of Wales and the Spice Girls – came to see him, he always wore one of his distinctive shirts.

Find out more
AFRICA, HISTORY OF
HUMAN RIGHTS
SOUTH AFRICA, HISTORY OF

MAO ZEDONG

ONE MAN TRANSFORMED CHINA from a backward peasant society into one of the most powerful nations in the world. That man was Mao Zedong. Mao was born to a peasant family, and as a young man he traveled widely, observing the conditions of the poor. He became interested in communism as a way to improve people's lives and, in 1921, helped set up the Chinese Communist Party. There followed a long period of struggle between the Communists, led by Mao, and the Nationalist Party (who believed in strong national government), led by Chiang Kai-shek. The struggle ended in a civil war. In October 1949, the Communist Party was victorious and took power in China. Mao proclaimed China a people's republic. Under his leadership, the Communists put everything under state control. Mao's face became a familiar sight. Since his death in 1976, many people have criticized Mao for causing the deaths of millions during his rule.

1893 Born in Shaoshan, Hunan province.

1921 Founding member of Chinese Communist Party.

1928 Establishes Chinese Soviet (Communist) Republic in Kiangsi province.

1934-35 Leads The Long March.

1945-49 Leads Communists in fight to overthrow Nationalist government.

1958 Great Leap Forward

1966-69 Cultural Revolution

1976 Dies.

LONG MARCH

In October 1934, Mao led his Communist supporters from their stronghold, Juichin, in Kiangsi province to Yenan, in Shensi province, in northwest China. Kiangsi was under attack from Chiang Kai-shek. More than 100,000 people marched for more than a year, covering 6,000 miles (9,700 km). Only 8,000 marchers survived the ordeal.

Route of the March

The Long March

CULTURAL REVOLUTION

After the failure of the Great Leap Forward, Mao lost influence inside the Communist Party. In 1966, he launched the Cultural Revolution, a campaign to regain power and get rid of foreign influences. For three years, China was in turmoil as every aspect of society was criticized by the Red Guards, followers of Mao. They armed themselves with the *Little Red Book*, which contained Mao's thoughts.

GREAT LEAP FORWARD

In 1958, Mao launched a plan to improve the Chinese economy. The Great Leap Forward, as it was called, set up huge agricultural communes and encouraged the growth of small, labor-intensive industries. However, the policy failed, leading to millions of deaths through famine.

PERSONALITY CULT

Mao Zedong encouraged a cult of his personality to unite the country. His round face, with the familiar mole on the chin, adorned every public building in China. He was praised as the father and leader of his nation, and huge rallies were held at which he addressed his followers.

Find out more

CHINA, HISTORY OF
COMMUNISM

MAPS

EARLY TRAVELERS FOUND THEIR WAY by asking directions from strangers they met. Their guides created the first maps by scratching rough drawings of the route on the ground. Maps still show the positions of different places, but travelers today need many different maps. For local journeys, they use large-scale maps that cover a small area but show lots of detail. For longer journeys, travelers may use a small-scale map that shows a larger area in less detail, or they may use an atlas (a book of maps) of whole countries. There are also special-purpose maps; political maps, for example, show legal boundaries. Utility companies need large-scale maps to show them where to dig for power lines and water pipes. Sailors use a special kind of map, called a chart, which shows coastlines and water depths.

MAPPA MUNDI
An English priest created the Mappa Mundi, or map of the world, between 1280 and 1300. It shows how Christians of that time viewed their world but was of little use to travelers. For religious reasons, Jerusalem is at the center, and east is at the top of the map.

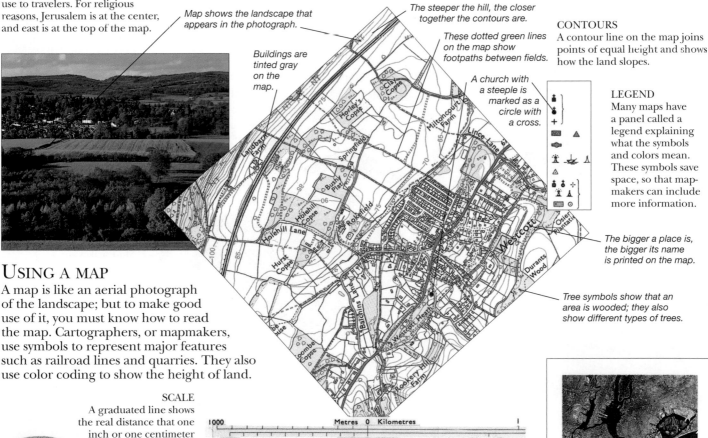

Map shows the landscape that appears in the photograph.

Buildings are tinted gray on the map.

The steeper the hill, the closer together the contours are.

These dotted green lines on the map show footpaths between fields.

A church with a steeple is marked as a circle with a cross.

CONTOURS
A contour line on the map joins points of equal height and shows how the land slopes.

LEGEND
Many maps have a panel called a legend explaining what the symbols and colors mean. These symbols save space, so that mapmakers can include more information.

The bigger a place is, the bigger its name is printed on the map.

Tree symbols show that an area is wooded; they also show different types of trees.

USING A MAP
A map is like an aerial photograph of the landscape; but to make good use of it, you must know how to read the map. Cartographers, or mapmakers, use symbols to represent major features such as railroad lines and quarries. They also use color coding to show the height of land.

SCALE
A graduated line shows the real distance that one inch or one centimeter represents on the map.

| 1000 | | Metres | 0 | Kilometres | | 1 |
| 1000 | | Yards | 0 | Miles | | |

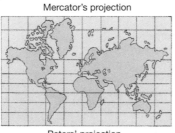

The equator is 0° latitude.

LONGITUDE AND LATITUDE
Lines of longitude, or meridians, run between the North and South poles on a world map showing you how far east or west you are. Longitude is measured in degrees from the meridian that runs through Greenwich, England. Lines of latitude are parallel to the equator and show how many degrees north or south you are.

Mercator's projection

Peters' projection

MERCATOR'S PROJECTION
To represent the round Earth on a flat sheet of paper, mapmakers use a projection. Imagine a glass globe with a light at its center. The light projects shadows of the continents onto a flat screen. All projections distort the world's shape, areas, or distances. The most familiar world map is Gerhard Mercator's projection made in 1569. This shows the correct shapes of the continents but distorts their areas. Arno Peters' projection, published in 1973, distorts the shapes of countries but shows their true areas. It counteracts the focus on Europe encouraged by Mercator, whose map makes Europe look bigger than it really is.

New York area from a satellite

SATELLITE MAP
Satellites can now map every part of the world. Their sensors send video photographs of the Earth's surface to ground stations, which turn them into maps.

Find out more
EXPLORERS
MAGNETISM
NAVIGATION
SATELLITES

MARSH AND SWAMP WILDLIFE

THE SALT AND FRESHWATER HABITATS of swamps and marshland are called wetlands. Marsh and swamp wildlife includes crocodiles, frogs, birds, fish, and countless plants. At different times of the year, the water level of marshes and swamps rises and falls. In summer the land dries up, and in winter it floods. Wetlands are generally unsuitable for large mammals – except the African swamps where hippopotamuses live. Smaller mammals such as muskrats live in North American swamps, and the European marshes are home to many birds. The main plant life consists of reeds, rushes, saw grass, and cattail. Large trees are found only in the tropical mangroves, where the trees form dense thickets. Willows and other waterside trees grow in the higher, drier ground around the marsh.

PROBOSCIS MONKEY
This large-nosed monkey lives among the mangrove trees of river and coastal swamps. The proboscis monkey is a good swimmer. Proboscis monkeys eat leaves, flowers, and fruit.

CONSERVATION
Farming and industry threaten many swamplands, but some animals, such as the marsh harriers shown here, are protected. They live in the Coto Doñana National Park in Spain – one of Europe's most important wetlands.

PELICAN
These fish-eating birds build their nests in remote marshland areas. Some species breed on the ground, some in trees. Others, such as spot-billed and Dalmatian pelicans, are very rare because of destruction of their nesting sites.

Front fins help the mudskipper walk on mud and grip roots.

COTTONMOUTH
Most snakes are good swimmers and climbers, and they can travel through swamps with ease in search of prey. The cottonmouth, also called the water moccasin, is a North American swamp dweller with a very poisonous bite.

SWAMP RABBIT
This large rabbit from North America can swim well and dives to escape from predators. Swamp rabbits eat water plants, grasses, and other vegetation.

Swamp mud is usually so dense and waterlogged that, unlike normal soil, it contains almost no oxygen. The roots of mangrove trees stick up above the mud, to absorb the oxygen they need to grow.

MUDSKIPPER
This unusual fish has a store of water in its large gill chambers, which allows it to live out of water for long periods. From time to time it skitters over the mud to a pool to take in a new supply of water.

MARSHLAND
Marshes are nursery areas for many insects whose larvae live in water, such as dragonflies and mosquitoes. Insect larvae and worms form the main diet of many fish and water birds. Frogs, toads, and tadpoles are also eaten by larger creatures.

MANGROVE SWAMPS
Mangroves are trees that grow in muddy tropical swamps. Some kinds of mangrove trees grow in freshwater; others tolerate salty water and grow on the coast or in river estuaries. Their roots and trunks trap mud, and their seeds begin to grow while they are still attached to the parent tree. When the seeds drop into the mud, they quickly establish roots so they are not washed away.

Archer fish adjusts its aim if it misses, and fires again.

ARCHER FISH
The archer fish spits drops of water at insects on over-hanging twigs. The insects fall off the twigs, into the water, where the fish gulps them down.

The drops of water hit the insect like tiny bullets.

Find out more
BIRDS
FISH
MONKEYS AND APES
RABBITS AND HARES
SEASHORE WILDLIFE
SNAKES

MATERIALS

EVER SINCE EARLY HUMANS started using tools about 2.5 million years ago, materials have played an important part in our lives. This is because everything we use is made from some sort of material. A material is anything that is used to make something; it is not just a woven fabric like the material in your clothes. Buildings, cars, and furniture are all made from materials of one kind or another. Some materials are natural, such as the stone and timber of a house. Others are artificial, like the plastic used to make the keyboard of a computer. Natural materials can also be further divided into categories such as minerals, metals, and organics. Every material has its own properties, making it better suited for some jobs than others, and scientists are always inventing more materials.

METAL
Because they are tough and durable, metals have been used for centuries. Pure metals such as iron are natural elements. Metals can also be mixed to make alloys, which are usually stronger than pure metals.

Racket frame made of plastic containing graphite.

Sports clothes made from synthetic nylon and polyester, and natural cotton.

RUBBER
Some materials, such as rubber, exist in natural and synthetic forms. Natural rubber is the gummy sap of rubber trees. It is expensive to produce, so scientists have found ways to copy its chemical makeup and produce it more cheaply.

Chair made from wood, a tough natural material.

Tennis balls made from rubber with a woollen felt coating.

Sunglasses made from plastic.

Cap made from natural cotton fabric.

Socks made from natural fibers.

Beverage can made from aluminum metal.

GLASS
Some containers are made from glass, a tough material that lets light through and resists heat. Glass is made from sand, which is crushed quartz, a natural mineral that forms glassy crystals. Glassmakers melt sand, then cool it quickly so it solidifies without forming crystals.

Plastic egg box

Flax plants are used to make linen.

Paper made from wood pulp.

Shoes made from canvas, with rubber soles for flexibility.

ORGANICS
Any materials that come from plants or animals are known as organic. They include bone, leather, wool, cotton, silk, and wood. Throughout history, people have continued to use organic materials to make a whole range of objects, from furniture to clothes to musical instruments. Each organic material has its own particular properties. Wool, for instance, is warm, strong, and absorbent.

PLASTICS
There are many kinds of plastic. Some copy natural materials, but others are specially designed for new applications. The word "plastic" actually means "capable of being molded," and it is this property that makes plastics so useful. Some plastics melt when heated and are easily formed into shapes. Others are heated to make them set, so they can be used for objects that become hot, such as kettles.

Find out more
GLASS AND CERAMICS
METALS
PLASTICS
TEXTILES

MATHEMATICS

PROBABILITY THEORY
Probability theory is the analysis of chance. For instance, if you repeatedly roll two dice, you can use probability theory to work out how often you can expect a certain number to come up.

SENDING A SPACECRAFT to a distant planet is like trying to throw a stone at an invisible moving target. Space scientists do not use trial and error; instead they use the science of mathematics to direct the spacecraft precisely to its target. Mathematics is the study of number, shape, and quantity. There are several different branches of mathematics, and they are valuable both in science and in everyday life. For instance, arithmetic consists of addition, subtraction, multiplication, and division of numbers; it helps you figure out the change when you buy something. Geometry is the study of shape and angle; it is useful in carpentry, architecture, and many other fields. Algebra is a kind of mathematical language in which problems can be solved using symbols in place of varying or unknown numbers. Branches of mathematics that relate to practical problems are called applied mathematics. However, some mathematicians study pure mathematics – numerical problems which have no known practical use.

SYMMETRY

A symmetrical object is made up of alike parts. Many symmetrical patterns and shapes occur in nature. A starfish exhibits lateral symmetry, since one of its arms looks the same when reflected in a line drawn along its length. This line is called an axis. The starfish also displays rotational symmetry, as it looks the same when rotated around its central point.

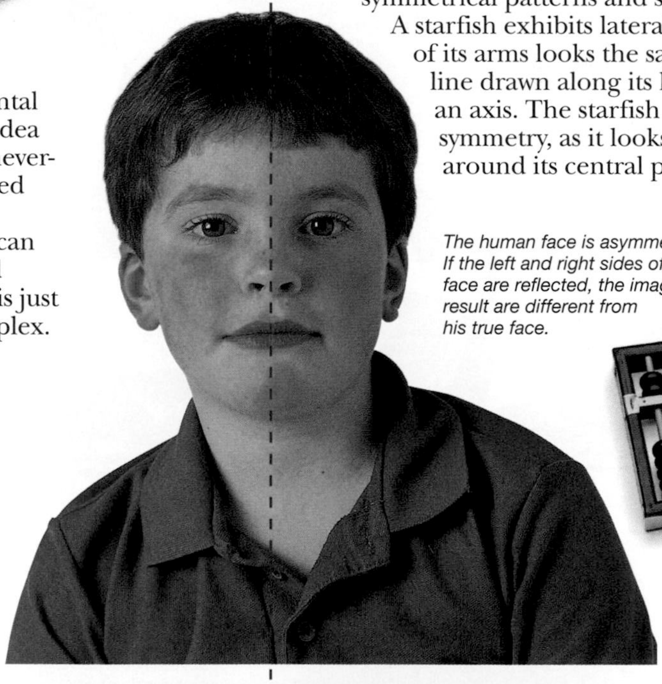

The human face is asymmetrical. If the left and right sides of this boy's face are reflected, the images that result are different from his true face.

INFINITY

Pure mathematicians study the fundamental ideas of numbers and shapes. One such idea is the concept of infinity, which means "never-ending." The pattern shown above is called a fractal. It is produced by a computer according to a strict formula (rule). You can enlarge any part of the pattern again and again, but you will still get a pattern that is just as intricate. The pattern is infinitely complex.

EUCLID

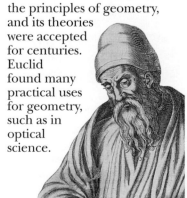

The ancient Greek mathematician Euclid (c. 330-275 B.C.) was the first to formulate theories on the nature of shapes and angles. His book *Elements* outlined the principles of geometry, and its theories were accepted for centuries. Euclid found many practical uses for geometry, such as in optical science.

PARTS OF A CIRCLE

A circle is a shape in which every point on its circumference, or outside margin, is the same distance from the center. The diameter is the line that exactly bisects a circle, passing through the center. The distance from the center to the circumference is the radius. The slice of circle between two radii is a sector, and the part of the circumference that bounds a sector is an arc.

Circumference — Radius — Arc — Sector — Center — Diameter

ABACUS

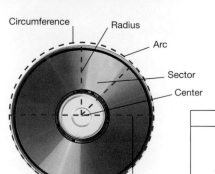

The abacus, or counting frame, is an ancient calculating device which comes from China. It consists of rows of beads that represent units of tens, hundreds, and thousands. The abacus is worked by moving the beads along the rows. People in Asian countries still use the abacus as a rapid tool for adding, subtracting, multiplying, and dividing.

Find out more

COMPUTERS
GEOMETRY
NUMBERS
WEIGHTS AND MEASURES

MAYA

DEEP IN THE TROPICAL FORESTS of Mexico, the Mayan people created one of the most amazing ancient civilizations, which reached its height between A.D. 250 and 900. The Maya built cities with huge stone temples. Each city was the center of a separate kingdom, with a king who was treated like a god. The Maya were great scholars who developed systems of mathematics and astronomy. They even created their own writing system and used it to carve inscriptions about their history on stone plaques that they set up in their cities. Despite their sophistication, the Maya had only the simplest technology. They used stone tools, and did not know about the wheel. By the 1500s the Spanish had conquered the region.

MAYAN CIVILIZATION
The Maya came from the Yucatan Peninsula and the highlands to the south, in what is now eastern Mexico. They also built cities in parts of modern Guatemala and Honduras.

Outer shell of stone concealed earth base and royal tomb.

Temple contains historic inscriptions.

FLINT CARVING
Craftworkers made their tools out of stones such as flint or obsidian (a black, naturally-occurring glass). They could work these materials to make a sharp edge. The Maya became highly skilled at this type of stoneworking, and made intricate carvings in strange shapes to show off their skill. Many were made to place in graves or as offerings to the gods.

Priests used the main staircase.

PALENQUE
The Temple of the Inscriptions at Palenque was a famous Mayan pyramid. Deep inside the base was a secret chamber containing the tomb of a local king, Pacal, who died in about A.D. 684. In the temple on top of the pyramid were stone tablets carved with glyphs that recorded the history of the local kings up to Pacal's reign. Its ruins still exist today.

People taking part in ceremonies could stand on the main stepped levels.

Pot shaped like a jaguar

GLYPHS
Mayan writing was made up of a series of signs which archaeologists call glyphs. Many of the glyphs were simplified pictures of the objects they stood for. Some represented sounds, which were used to build up words. Others were symbols that stood for different numbers. The Maya used glyphs to record their calendar, and to write inscriptions about their history.

Glyph describing a Mayan noblewoman called Lady Xoc

BLOOD SACRIFICE
Some Mayan communities believed that their gods would be pleased if people were killed in their honor. They also saw sacrificial blood as food for the gods. In some places a pot shaped like a jaguar, a beast sacred to the Maya, was used to collect the blood.

Stone ring acted as "goal."

Players used their elbows to hit the ball.

BALL GAME
Many cities had a ball court where people played a game with a rubber ball. Players wore padded clothing, and were only allowed to touch the ball with their hips, arms, or elbows. The aim was to get the ball through a small stone ring at the side of the court. Players who lost were sometimes put to death.

___Find out more___
BRONZE AGE
CENTRAL AMERICA
WHEELS

MEDICINE

TWO HUNDRED AND FIFTY YEARS AGO, most people lived no longer than 35 years. Today, in the industrialized parts of the world, the average lifespan has increased to more than 70 years. Better food and hygiene have helped, but one of the main reasons for this change is the advances made in medicine. Medicine is the branch of science concerned with the prevention, diagnosis (identification), and treatment of disease and damage to the human body. Medical scientists are constantly searching for new ways of treating diseases. Treatments include drugs, radiation therapy, and surgery. Preventive measures, such as vaccinations against infections, are becoming an increasingly important part of modern medicine.

DIAGNOSIS
A doctor's first step with a sick patient is to diagnose the illness. This can be done in various ways – by asking the patient about his or her symptoms (physical feelings), by making a physical examination of the patient, and by carrying out medical tests if necessary.

BRANCHES OF MEDICINE
Medicine is a huge subject and nobody can hope to know it all. Thus, doctors, nurses, and other medical workers often become expert in a single area of medicine, a process that can take years and years of study.

Neurology is concerned with disorders of the brain and nerves.

Ophthalmology is the treatment of disorders of the eyes.

Orthopedics is the care of the spine, bones, joints, and muscles.

Psychiatry is the study of mental health problems.

Cutting into the body to cure illness is called surgery.

Dermatology is concerned with the skin and skin diseases.

Pediatrics is the medical care of children.

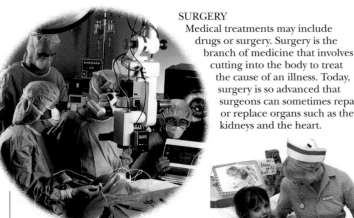

SURGERY
Medical treatments may include drugs or surgery. Surgery is the branch of medicine that involves cutting into the body to treat the cause of an illness. Today, surgery is so advanced that surgeons can sometimes repair or replace organs such as the kidneys and the heart.

RECOVERY
Recovery from an illness or an operation may take only a few hours or as long as several weeks. Much depends on the severity of the illness and the impact the treatment has on the body.

MEDICAL TECHNOLOGY
Modern medicine makes use of a wide range of technology. Latest developments include body scanners which use a strong magnetic field or ultrasound (very high-frequency sound waves) to produce an image of the interior of the human body. Such equipment has revolutionized medicine.

Doctors use brain scanners to check patients for tumors or damage to the brain.

Rue is prescribed for some digestive disorders.

Catmint is a cold cure that was first used by prehistoric people.

Mint is used for settling a stomach upset.

HOLISTIC MEDICINE
The word *holistic* means "of the whole." The principle of holistic medicine is to treat the whole person – body and mind – rather than just the affected part. Holistic therapies (treatments) include acupuncture (stimulating the nerves by inserting needles into the skin) and aromatherapy (treatment using oils containing fragrant plant extracts).

HISTORY OF
MEDICINE

TREPANNING
Ten thousand years ago, healers tried to cure an ill person by cutting a hole in his or her skull. Healers believed that the hole in the head released evil spirits that caused pain. This was known as trepanning.

SINCE THE EARLIEST TIMES, people have looked for ways of curing their illnesses. Early people believed that disease was a punishment from the gods. They also believed that priests and magicians could heal them. In Ancient Greece, people visited temples when they were ill and sacrificed animals to Asclepius, the Greek god of healing. They also drank and bathed in medicinal waters and followed strict diets in the hope of being cured. During the fifth century B.C. the Greek doctor Hippocrates declared that it was nature, not magic, that caused and cured disease. Hippocrates was famed as "the father of medicine," and he and his followers wrote many medical books. The spirit of enquiry, which was part of the Renaissance (a cultural movement beginning in 14th-century Europe), encouraged experiments that put European medicine on a firm scientific basis. Many people began to question the traditional ideas about medicine. Scientists such as Vesalius (1514-1564) began to study the bodies of dead people to learn more about disease and how to treat it. Since then, there have been many more discoveries in medicine, and the battle against disease continues.

HUMORS
The Greek physician Galen (c. A.D. 130-200) introduced the idea that the body contained four fluids called humors – blood, phlegm, yellow bile, and black bile. He believed that a person's mood depended on which of these four fluids ruled the body, and that if the fluids were not balanced, illness would result.

WILLIAM HARVEY
In 1628, an English doctor named William Harvey (1578-1657) discovered that blood constantly circulates around the body. He described how blood is pumped by the heart into the arteries and returns to the heart through the veins. He showed that valves in the veins stop the blood from flowing backward. At first, Harvey was scorned for contradicting old ideas, but later he became physician to Charles I, King of England.

HERBALISM
For thousands of years, people have used herbs and plants in healing. Herbalists wrote lists of herbs and their uses. Monks were also famed for their knowledge of herbs. The first pharmacists, called apothecaries, used herbs to make potions, or medicines. In Europe during the Renaissance, however, many herbalists were accused of being witches. Many people are now turning to herbs as a natural way of treating illnesses.

Harvey drew detailed diagrams to explain his theory of circulation.

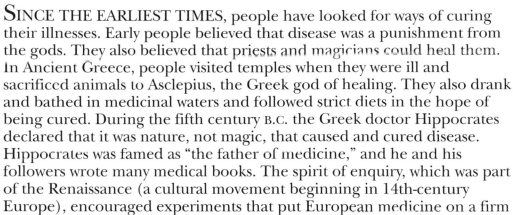

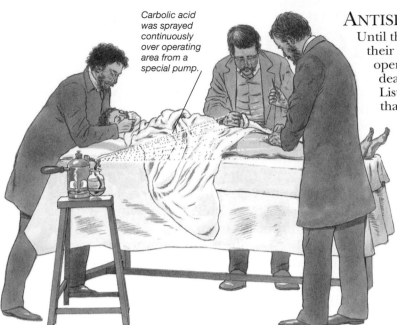

Carbolic acid was sprayed continuously over operating area from a special pump.

ANTISEPTICS

Until the late 19th century, surgeons did not wash their hands or their medical instruments before operating on a patient. Many patients died from deadly infections following an operation. Joseph Lister (1827-1912), an English surgeon, guessed that infection with bacteria might be the cause of these deaths. In 1865, Lister developed an antiseptic spray called carbolic acid. This spray could destroy bacteria in the operating room, so there was a dramatic drop in the number of deaths following operations.

Leeches are parasites that attach themselves to a host. They secrete a substance that stops blood clotting while they feed on it.

BLOOD-LETTING
Doctors once believed that too much blood in the body was the cause of disease. They removed the excess blood by blood-letting. Doctors either cut open a vein to let the blood out, or they applied bloodsucking creatures called leeches to the body. The leech attached itself to the patient with its sucker, made a wound, then sucked out blood. The exact spot for blood-letting depended on what was wrong with the patient.

ALEXANDER FLEMING

Bacteria cause many of the illnesses that affect humans, so for years scientists tried to find a substance that would kill bacteria but would not harm human tissue. The Scottish bacteriologist Alexander Fleming (1881-1955) was the first person to identify an antibacterial substance. Fleming carried out his research in a laboratory at St. Mary's Hospital, London, England. In 1928, Fleming noticed that a mold that had accidentally developed on a dish of bacteria culture caused the bacteria to die. In 1941, the researchers Howard Florey and Ernst Chain purified the mould, *Penicillium*, to produce penicillin, the world's first antibiotic. Penicillin is widely used in the treatment of many diseases, including meningitis and pneumonia. Fleming shared the 1945 Nobel Prize for Medicine with Florey and Chain.

HISTORY OF MEDICINE

c. 8000 B.C. Early healers practice trepanning.

400s B.C. Hippocrates, a Greek, begins scientific medicine.

1543 Vesalius publishes first scientific study of human body.

1615 Santorio, an Italian doctor, designs mouth thermometer.

1683 Anton van Leeuwenhoek, a Dutch scientist, discovers bacteria.

1796 Edward Jenner gives first smallpox vaccination.

1816 Rene Laennec, a French doctor, invents stethoscope.

1842 American surgeon, Horace Long, operates using general anesthetic.

1895 Wilhelm Roentgen, a German physicist, discovers x-rays, which enable doctors to see inside the human body.

1900s Polish-born Marie Curie and her husband, Pierre Curie of France, discover the chemical element radium to treat cancer.

1900s Scottish bacteriologist, Alexander Fleming, discovers penicillin.

MEDICAL PIONEERS

Through the centuries many people have shaped modern medicine. The Flemish doctor Vesalius produced accurate drawings of the human body; Dutchman Anton van Leeuwenhoek (1632-1723) first discovered microbes, now called bacteria; and the English doctor Edward Jenner (1749-1823) discovered vaccinations – a way of preventing certain diseases by injection.

LOUIS PASTEUR
Frenchman Louis Pasteur (1822-1895) showed that bacteria caused disease. He invented pasteurization – the heating of milk and beer to destroy harmful bacteria.

SIGMUND FREUD
The Austrian doctor Sigmund Freud (1856-1939; below) was interested in finding out how the mind works. He treated patients with mental disorders by listening to them talk about their dreams and thoughts. This treatment was called psychoanalysis. In 1900, Freud published *The Interpretation of Dreams*, which explained his method.

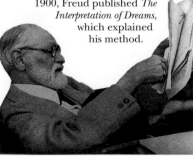

Find out more
DRUGS
EGYPT, ANCIENT
GREECE, ANCIENT
MEDICINE

MEDIEVAL EUROPE

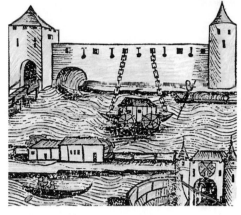

FAIRS
Great fairs were held every year in towns, such as Winchester, England, which were on important trade routes. Merchants traveled from all over Europe to sell their goods at these fairs.

LORDS AND LADIES feasting in castle banquet halls, peasants working on the land, knights in armor – all these are associated with a time in European history known as the medieval period or the Middle Ages. This was a time of great change in Western Europe between the 5th and 15th centuries. During the 5th century, the Roman Empire fell to invading German tribes. Western Europe then broke up into many kingdoms. Trade collapsed, and people had to make their living from the land. Gradually, powerful landowners, or lords, emerged and the feudal system developed. The early medieval period of Europe is sometimes called the Dark Ages because the learning of Ancient Greece and Rome almost disappeared. But the Christian church gave leadership to the people. Trade gradually improved. By about the 13th century, the Middle Ages had reached their height. Feudalism governed society, and monasteries (where monks lived) were the centers of learning. The medieval times came to an end in the 15th century when the Renaissance swept through Europe.

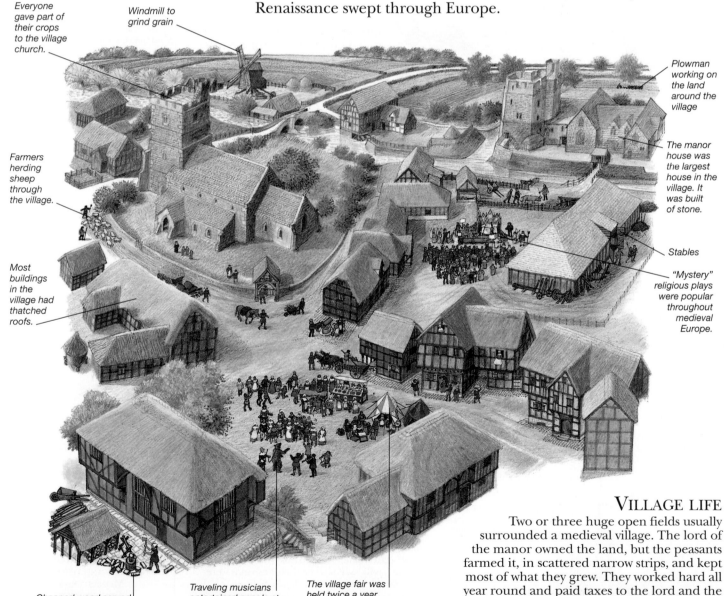

Everyone gave part of their crops to the village church.

Windmill to grind grain

Plowman working on the land around the village

Farmers herding sheep through the village.

The manor house was the largest house in the village. It was built of stone.

Most buildings in the village had thatched roofs.

Stables

"Mystery" religious plays were popular throughout medieval Europe.

Chopped wood served for repairs to the house and to make fire.

Traveling musicians entertained people at the fair. Sometimes there were dancing bears.

The village fair was held twice a year.

VILLAGE LIFE
Two or three huge open fields usually surrounded a medieval village. The lord of the manor owned the land, but the peasants farmed it, in scattered narrow strips, and kept most of what they grew. They worked hard all year round and paid taxes to the lord and the church in the form of work and goods.

Shoemakers

TOWN SCENE

Trade increased in the later medieval period, making merchants wealthy and powerful. Towns became important trading centers with a new class of craftspeople. The craftspeople created organizations called guilds to control the prices and quality of their goods.

People bought fabric to make their own clothing.

The poultry trader sold geese.

FEUDALISM

Kings gave their vassals – powerful nobles – tracts of land called fiefs. In return for this land, the vassals fought for the king when required. The vassals divided their land into manors (estates), which they gave to lesser nobles and knights. In return, the knights and lesser nobles worked for the lord of the manor, and had to fight for him when called on.

14th-century manuscript (right) shows feudal structure, with the king at the top.

Hunting (above) was a popular sport for upper-class medieval women.

A French medieval woman, Christine de Pisan (left), earned her living as a writer.

WOMEN

Peasant women worked very hard all their lives. They brought up their children, spun wool and wove clothing, and helped with all the farmwork. Upper-class women also led busy lives. They often ran the family estates while their husbands were away traveling around their lands, fighting against neighboring lords, or on a Crusade to the Holy Land. Women also nursed the sick and provided education for children in their charge.

Find out more
BLACK DEATH
CHURCHES AND CATHEDRALS
KNIGHTS AND HERALDRY
MONASTERIES
RENAISSANCE
ROMAN EMPIRE

METALS

IMAGINE A WORLD WITHOUT METALS. There would be no cars or airplanes, and skyscrapers would fall down without the metal frames that support them. Metals have countless uses because they possess a unique combination of qualities. They are very strong and easy to shape, so they can be used to make all kinds of objects – from ships to bottle tops. Almost all metals conduct electricity. Some are ideal for wires and electrical equipment. Metals also carry heat, so they make good cooking pots. These qualities can be improved by mixing two or more metals to make alloys. Most metallic objects are made of alloys rather than pure metals. There are more than 80 kinds of pure metals, though some are very rare. Aluminum and iron are the most common metals. A few metals, such as gold, occur in the ground as pure metals; the rest are found as ores in rock. Metals can also be obtained by recycling old cars and cans. This reduces waste and costs less than processing metal ores.

Gold watch

Mercury thermometer

Copper wire

Silver-plated frame

PURE METALS
The rarity and luster of gold and silver have been prized for centuries. Other pure metals have special uses. Electrical wires are made of copper, which conducts electricity well. Mercury, a liquid metal, is used in thermometers.

Airplane fuselage made of aluminum alloys

BOEING 737-400

ALUMINUM
The most common metal in the Earth's crust is aluminum. The metal comes from an ore called bauxite, which contains alumina, a compound of aluminum and oxygen. Aluminum is light, conducts electricity and heat, and resists corrosion. These qualities mean that the metal and its alloys can be used in many things, including aircraft and bicycles, window frames, paints, cookware, and electricity supply cables.

A lump of bauxite

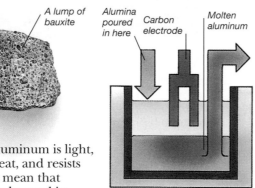

Alumina poured in here

Carbon electrode

Molten aluminum

ELECTROLYSIS
Passing an electric current through alumina separates it into aluminum and oxygen. This process is called electrolysis.

Thin, flexible aluminum foil is useful for cooking and storing food because it is nonreactive and can stand high temperatures.

ALLOYS
Most metal objects are made of steel or other alloys. This is because alloys are often stronger or easier to process than pure metals. Copper and tin are weak and pliable, but when mixed together they make a strong alloy called bronze. Brass is a tough alloy of copper and zinc that resists corrosion. Alloys of aluminum are light and strong and are used to make aircraft.

METAL FATIGUE
Metals sometimes fail even though they may be very tough and strong. Corrosion weakens some metals, as in the case of rusty steel. Repeated bending can cause metal parts to break – an effect called metal fatigue.

Keys may break after considerable use.

METALWORKING
There are many ways of shaping metal. Casting is one method of making objects such as metal statues. Hot, molten metal is poured into a mold where it sets and hardens into the required shape. Metal can also be pressed, hammered, or cut into shape.

WELDING
Metal parts can be joined by welding. Welders apply heat from a gas flame or an electric spark to the edges of two pieces of metal. The heat causes the edges to melt so that they can be joined together.

Find out more
BRONZE AGE
IRON AGE
IRON AND STEEL
ROCKS AND MINERALS
SCULPTURE

MEXICO

THE WEALTH OF MEXICO has traditionally come from the land. Precious metals lie buried in the mountains and rich crops grow in the valleys. Oil flows from wells on the coast. The Mexican people began to exploit these advantages centuries ago. Farming supported most of the people, and from the country's mines came silver to make beautiful jewelry. The mineral wealth of the country attracted invading Europeans early in the 16th century, and Spain ruled Mexico for the next three centuries. A revolt against Spanish rule gave the Mexican people independence in 1821. The discovery of oil early in the 20th century brought new wealth to Mexico. The government invested this wealth in new factories, and in social services to relieve hunger and improve health and education. In 1994, the North American Free Trade Agreement (NAFTA) reduced trade barriers between Mexico, Canada, and the United States, promising long-term economic benefits. However, the border between Mexico and the US has been strengthened as a result of US concern over the estimated 850,000 illegal crossings each year.

Mexico is part of the continent of North America and lies between the United States to its north and Central America to its south.

José Guadalupe Posada (1852–1913) drew humorous illustrations, many of which supported the Mexican Revolution.

POLITICS AND REVOLUTION

Mexico was a Spanish colony from 1521 to 1821, when it became an independent republic. After a long period of political unrest, there was a revolution in 1910, in which half a million people died. From 1929, the Institutional Revolutionary Party (IRP) governed Mexico. However, in 2000 it lost the presidential election for the first time. Mexico is now a functioning democracy.

MEXICO CITY

More than 18 million people live in and around Mexico City, the capital of Mexico, making it one of the most populous cities in the world. The city lies 1 mile (1.6 km) above sea level in a natural basin surrounded by mountains. These mountains trap the pollution from the city's industries. As a result, Mexico City is one of the world's most unhealthy cities, with an inadequate water supply, a lack of housing, and the constant threat of earthquakes adding to its many problems.

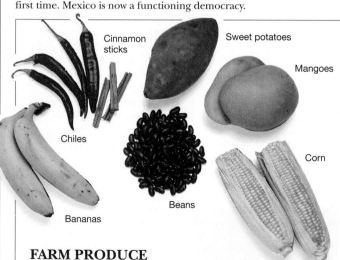

Cinnamon sticks

Sweet potatoes

Mangoes

Chiles

Corn

Beans

Bananas

Mexican artisans are skilled at making fine jewelry from the precious metals found in their country.

FARM PRODUCE

Less than one-quarter of the population of Mexico lives and works on the land, growing staple or food crops. Increasingly, however, farmers are growing coffee, cotton, sugar, and tomatoes for export. These cash crops take vital land away from the crops that the Mexican people themselves need for food. Most of the farmers are members of cooperatives, pooling their limited resources to help one another.

MINERAL WEALTH

Copper, silver, zinc, mercury, and other valuable metals are among the many minerals found in Mexico. Oil is the country's most important resource. In 1974, vast new reserves were discovered in the south of the country.

> **Find out more**
>
> CONQUISTADORS
> NORTH AMERICA
> VOLCANOES

| Volcano | Mountain | Ancient monument | Capital city | Large city/town | Small city/town |

STATISTICS

Area: 756,061 sq miles
(1,958,200 sq km)
Population: 104,000,000
Capital: Mexico City
Languages: Spanish,
Nahuatl, Maya, Zapotec,
Mixtec, Otomi, Totonac,
Tzotzil, Tzeltal
Religions: Roman Catholic,
Protestant
Currency: Mexican peso
Main occupations:
Subsistence farming,
manufacturing, oil
production
Main exports: Oil, cotton,
machinery, coffee
Main imports: Machinery,
vehicles, chemicals

SIERRA MADRE

The main mountain system
of Mexico, the Sierra Madre, runs
1,500 miles (2,400 km) southeast
from the border with the United
States. There are three ranges – in
the east, south, and west – and they
enclose Mexico's central plateau.
Mexico's third-highest mountain,
Volcán Iztaccihuatl (right), is in the
Sierra Madre del Sur, the southern range.
The mountain has three separate summits,
and its name means "White Woman" in the Aztec
language, because the peaks resemble
a woman wearing a hood.

The tallest peak of Volcán Iztaccihuatl rises to 17,274 ft (5,268 m).

POPULATION

Most of northern Mexico is sparsely populated
because of the hot, dry climate and lack of good
farmland. As people have migrated from the
countryside in search of work, the cities have grown
dramatically; almost 75 percent of Mexicans now
live in urban areas. Mexico City is home to almost a
quarter of the population and is one of the world's
largest cities. Rapid, unplanned growth has led to
poor sanitation and water supplies.

GUANAJUATO

Spanish prospectors searching for gold
founded Guanajuato (below) in 1554.
The town is the capital of Guanajuato
state in the mountains of Central Mexico
and rises more than 6,726 ft (2,050 m)
above sea level. It is built in a ravine and
has steep, winding streets.

RIO GRANDE

*The Rio Grande
flows from Colorado
in the United States
and forms much
of Mexico's
northern border.
It crosses
a vast arid region
on its way to the
Gulf of Mexico.*

BAJA CALIFORNIA

*Baja California
is also called
Lower California.
The peninsula is
in Mexico, and is
not part of the US
state with which
it shares a name.*

MEXICAN FABRICS

The Mexican people have
been expert weavers since
ancient times. They are skilled at
producing brightly colored fabrics, with
bold, geometric designs, like the striped skirt
worn by the girl on the left. Today most Mexican
fabrics are mass-produced in large factories.

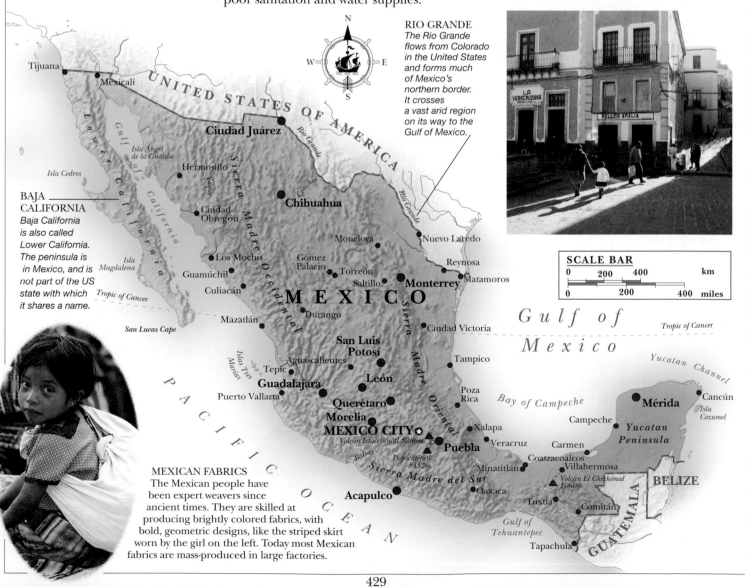

SCALE BAR

| 0 | 200 | 400 | km |
| 0 | 200 | 400 | miles |

MICE,
RATS, AND SQUIRRELS

THE LITTLE HOUSE MOUSE is the second most numerous mammal on Earth after humans. It has beady black eyes, a long thin tail, and large front teeth, and belongs to the mammal group called rodents. This group includes rats and squirrels. All rodents have chisellike incisor teeth for nibbling nuts and berries. The teeth wear down as the animal gnaws, but continue to grow throughout life. There are more than 1,000 kinds of rats and mice, found in every kind of habitat. Mice have small bodies, almost hairless tails, pointed noses, and sensitive whiskers; rats resemble mice but are larger. The most common rats are brown and black rats, which live in large groups. Rats are well known as carriers of the bubonic plague (Black Death). They also damage buildings and electrical wires with their gnawing and tunneling. Most squirrels are similar to rats and mice in shape, but have bushy tails. Tree squirrels such as red, gray, and flying squirrels live in woodland areas, often high up in trees. Ground squirrels such as chipmunks have shorter tails and never climb trees.

House mice and brown rats are often a nuisance to humans, eating stored grain and spoiling crops.

Strong chewing muscles and cheek pouches for carrying food

Big ears and good hearing

Keen sense of smell

Molars (cheek teeth) for chewing

Rodent skull

Chisel-like front incisors for gnawing

HARVEST MOUSE

A typical mouse has round black eyes, large ears, and sharp claws. The harvest mouse is one of the smallest mice. Its body is only 2.5 in (6.5 cm) long and weighs one third of an ounce (10 g). The harvest mouse feeds on corn and wheat stalks. Using grass stems, it weaves a breeding nest the size of a tennis ball in cornfields. Harvest mice also live and nest in the long grass of bushes, shrubs, and woodland clearings.

Large eyes stick out of head for all-around vision.

Tail is used as a counterbalance.

BROWN RAT

The brown rat, also called the common rat or Norway rat, is fast and agile. It swims well, eats almost anything, and can gnaw its way through wood, stonework, and metal plates in order to get at food. It has spread to all parts of the globe, even surviving in sewers. A brown rat grows up to 20 in (50 cm) long from the tip of its nose to the tip of its tail.

LEMMING

These small rodents are related to mice but have a blunt snout, squat body, short tail, and very thick fur. Lemmings live in the most northern parts of the world. They can survive the coldest winters by burrowing under the snow and eating mosses, roots, stems, and bulbs. Contrary to popular belief, lemmings do not deliberately hurl themselves off cliffs to drown in the sea. When they migrate in great numbers to find more food, however, some die of starvation or are drowned as they try to cross deep rivers.

SQUIRREL

With its sharp claws for clinging to bark, and its long, fluffy tail to help with balance, the squirrel is well adapted for life in the trees. Squirrels are great acrobats, able to leap through the treetops with ease. The American gray squirrel was introduced to Europe two centuries ago and is now widespread in forests and parks. The European red squirrel, however, has become rarer in some areas, particularly in Britain. Squirrels rest and sleep in a drey – a ball-shaped nest of twigs and leaves built in a tree. In the breeding season, the female makes an extra-strong drey where she raises two or three young.

Red squirrel

BREEDING

Mice and other small rodents have to breed at a fast rate In order to replace those killed by predators and bad weather. In good conditions, when few die, their numbers soar. One female house mouse can give birth to more than 50 young in one year. After about two weeks, the young are covered in fur, they can see and hear, and they begin to explore away from the nest. Within three weeks, the young have finished feeding on their mother's milk and are ready to leave the nest. After only six weeks, her first litter of mice also starts to breed.

Squirrel sleeps in the drey during the coldest weather but may come out on warmer days to look for food.

Newborn mice are bald, blind, and deaf; they stay warm and hidden in the nest.

GERBIL

Many rodents line their nests with shredded plant material such as stalks, stems, and bark. The Mongolian gerbil shown here is from the dry areas of Central Asia. Gerbils are popular pets.

CHIPMUNK

The chipmunk belongs to the squirrel family and is sometimes known as the ground squirrel. Chipmunks hold pieces of food in their front paws and nibble skillfully, using their incisors as levers to crack a nut or seed at its weakest point. Chipmunks are bold and curious, and they are often seen looking for tidbits in parks and picnic areas of North America. Whatever a chipmunk cannot eat, it carries back to its nest in its bulging cheek pouches.

Like all rodents, voles groom their fur and spread special body oils through it to keep it untangled, free of pests, and water-repellent. If the fur became soggy, the animal would soon die of cold.

VOLE

The vole is a close relative of the lemming and has a similar blunt-nosed, stocky shape. There are almost 100 different kinds of voles living in all sorts of habitats, from the snowy Arctic to subtropical forests. The muskrat of North America is one of the largest voles. Another, the water vole, is often mistaken for a brown rat when it is swimming.

> *Find out more*
>
> ANIMALS
> BLACK DEATH
> MAMMALS
> NESTS AND BURROWS

MICROSCOPES

WITHIN ALL OBJECTS there is a hidden world much too tiny for us to see. With the invention of the microscope in the 16th century, scientists were able to peer into this world and unravel some of the great mysteries of science. They discovered that animals and plants are made of millions of tiny cells, and later were able to identify the minute organisms called bacteria that cause disease. Early microscopes consisted of a single magnifying lens; today's microscopes have several lenses and can be used to see very tiny objects. Electron microscopes are even more powerful. Instead of light, they use a beam of electrons – tiny particles which are normally part of atoms – to magnify objects many millions of times. Scientists use electron microscopes to study the smallest of living cells and to delve into the structure of materials such as plastics and metals.

Observer looks through eyepiece.

Objective lenses of different power can be swung into position when needed.

The objective lens produces an image which the eyepiece magnifies (makes larger).

The object being studied rests on a glass slide.

Condenser lenses concentrate a beam of light onto the object.

A strong beam of light strikes a mirror under the microscope. The beam shines onto the object from below.

Optical microscopes can reveal living cells such as these cells which come from a human cheek. They are magnified more than 200 times.

OPTICAL MICROSCOPE

The optical, or light, microscope has two main lenses: the objective and the eyepiece. High-quality microscopes contain several additional lenses which help to give a clear, bright image. Different objectives can be fitted which give a range of magnification from about 10 times to 1,500 times normal size.

ELECTRON MICROSCOPES
Objects must be cut into thin slices in order to see them with a microscope. However, a scanning electron microscope can magnify a whole object such as this ant (right), which is about 15 times normal size.

With a scanning electron microscope the image appears on a monitor screen.

INVENTING THE MICROSCOPE

Although the Romans used magnifying lenses about 2,000 years ago, the first true microscope appeared around 1590, built by Dutch lensmakers Hans and Zacharias Janssen. In 1663, English scientist Robert Hooke studied insects and plants with a microscope. He found that cork was made up of tiny cells, a discovery of great scientific importance. Microscopes aroused great interest in microscopic life, as this old etching shows.

IMAGING ATOMS
Special electron microscopes can show individual atoms, which are so small that a line of 0.5 million atoms would only span the width of a human hair. This piece of silicon (above) is magnified 45 million times, revealing its atoms.

Find out more
ATOMS AND MOLECULES
BIOLOGY
MICROSCOPIC LIFE

MICROSCOPIC LIFE

ALL AROUND US there are living things that we cannot see because they are too small. They float in the air, they swim in puddles and oceans, and they coat rocks, soil, plants, and animals. Microscopic life includes bacteria and viruses; single-celled animals called protoctists; and single-celled plants called algae. It also includes the microscopic stages in the lives of larger plants and animals, such as the tiny pollen grains of flowers and the spores of mushrooms. From bacteria to algae, all are so small that we can see them only through a microscope. Viruses, which are the smallest and simplest of all living things, must be magnified one million times before we can see them. Microscopic life has a crucial role to play. Plankton consists of millions of algae and protozoa, and is an important food for water creatures. Bacteria in soil help to recycle nutrients. Some microscopic life, such as viruses, can cause disease.

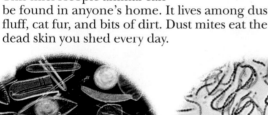

Dust mite

DUST MITE
This microscopic animal can be found in anyone's home. It lives among dust, fluff, cat fur, and bits of dirt. Dust mites eat the dead skin you shed every day.

DIATOM
Microscopic plants called diatoms live in lakes, rivers, and oceans. There are thousands of different kinds of diatoms, providing food for many insects and water creatures. Diatoms live and grow by using sunlight and the nutrients in the water. Around their bodies are strong shell-like walls made of silica – the same material found in sand grains.

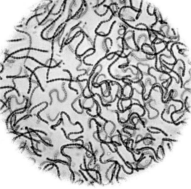

ALGAE
The slimy scum that you see on the surface of a stagnant pond is blue-green algae. These algae are not true plants. They are more closely related to bacteria. Blue-green algae were among the first forms of life to appear on Earth more than 2,000 million years ago.

POLLEN
Microscopic grains of pollen grow on the male part of a plant, called the stamen. Each kind of plant has a different type of pollen grain with its own pattern and shape.

Hollyhock
pollen grain

Passionflower
pollen grain

AMOEBA
The amoeba is a single-celled organism. It lives in ponds and puddles. We need to magnify an amoeba at least one thousand times before we can see it. The amoeba moves by stretching out a part of its body known as a pseudopod, or "false foot." The rest of the body then flows into the pseudopod. Amoebas feed by engulfing prey such as bacteria with their pseudopods; then the whole body flows over the prey.

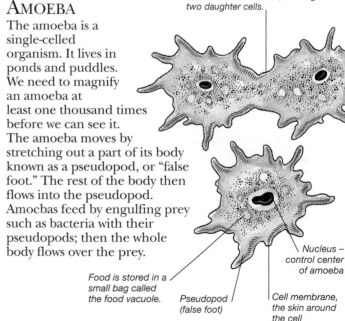

Amoeba divides in half, forming two daughter cells.

Nucleus – control center of amoeba

Food is stored in a small bag called the food vacuole.

Pseudopod (false foot)

Cell membrane, the skin around the cell

HOW AN AMOEBA REPRODUCES
To reproduce, the amoeba divides into two. This is called fission. First the nucleus splits in two, then the rest of the body divides in half to form two separate amoebas. These are called daughter cells.

Find out more
DISEASE
HUMAN BODY
MICROSCOPES
OCEAN WILDLIFE

MIDDLE EAST

LESS THAN 100 YEARS AGO, many of the inhabitants of the Middle East were Bedouins – desert-dwelling nomads who lived in tents and led their animals in search of food. The rest of the population lived in small towns and villages and made a living as farmers or craftsworkers. Almost everyone was poor and uneducated. Today, the lives of their children and grandchildren have been transformed by the discovery of oil. Many people have grown rich from the new industries and services related to oil production and refining. In some countries, notably Kuwait and Bahrain, there is free education and medical care for everyone. Oil transformed the international importance of the Middle East as well. The region had little influence in world affairs. Now it controls one-quarter of the world's oil production, and decisions made in the Middle East affect the economies of Europe, the Americas, and Asia. But despite this massive change, traditional customs have not been completely abandoned, and the religion of Islam continues to dominate daily life throughout the Middle East, as it has done for more than 1,300 years.

The Middle East consists of 15 independent countries. They sit at the crossroads of three great continents – to the northwest lies Europe, to the southwest is Africa, to the north and east are the Caucasus and Central Asian republics, all part of Asia.

WATERWAYS
Rising in the mountains of Turkey, the Tigris and Euphrates rivers irrigate the almost rainless land of the Middle East as they flow in parallel to the Persian Gulf. The fertility of the Euphates-Tigris Delta, known as Mesopotamia in ancient times, gave rise to the world's first cities.

MODERNIZATION
The discovery of oil brought great wealth and rapid industrial and social change to the Middle East. But governments in the region recognize that the oil will eventually run out, so they have spent some of the money they earned from selling oil in encouraging and modernizing local industry and business. Many Middle Eastern countries have also invested in property and businesses in other nations throughout the world.

At a banking school in the Middle East, students learn the skills that will help them modernize business in their country.

The areas bordering the Euphrates and Tigris rivers are swamps and marshlands. Here, small boats replace the camel as the most common means of transportation.

LANDSCAPE AND CLIMATE
Most of the Middle East consists of hot, dry, rocky deserts. A crescent of fertile land stretches west from the Tigris and Euphrates rivers through northern Iraq and Syria and then south into Lebanon and Israel. Turkey and Iran are mountainous, as are the southern parts of the Arabian Peninsula. In the southeast of Saudi Arabia lies the Rub' al Khali, a vast, uninhabited sandy desert known as the Empty Quarter.

Camels are well adapted to the harsh conditions of the Middle East, and are still a popular form of transportation.

SUEZ CANAL

More than 100 miles (160 km) in length, the Suez Canal links the Mediterranean Sea and the Red Sea. The canal took ten years to build, and when completed in 1869, it cut more than 7,000 miles (11,000 km) from the distance that sailing ships traveled to reach the Far East. Today, nearly 50 ships pass through the canal each day. The Suez Canal is an important trade route and has often been at the center of conflict in the Middle East. The waterway has been closed by war and political disagreements several times, most recently by the Arab-Israeli Six Day War of 1967.

The Suez Canal is not wide enough for ships traveling in opposite directions to pass each other. Vessels must travel in convoy (above), passing only at bypasses, where stretches of the canal has been doubled.

Splendid architecture, financed by revenue from oil, can be found in Abu Dhabi (below).

DUBAI

The city-state of Dubai on the Persian Gulf has a modern center, but on the outskirts it merges into the surrounding desert. Rainfall on the Arabian Peninsula where Dubai stands averages less than 4 in (100 mm) a year, and in most places the only natural water comes from underground springs. Desalination plants turn salt water from the Persian Gulf into a supply of drinking water for the city.

Dubai, part of the federation of United Arab Emirates, is generally flat, with large areas covered by dunes and barren rock.

ABU DHABI

The rulers of many Middle East states invested income from sales of oil to improve the living conditions of their people and develop the economies of their nations. In the 1960s the city of Abu Dhabi was just a fishing village on the Persian Gulf. Today it is the capital city of the Abu Dhabi sheikdom in the United Arab Emirates, complete with an international airport and high-rise downtown area. Abu Dhabi's revenues from oil royalties give it one of the world's highest per capita incomes.

Muslim guerrillas fight in the streets of Lebanon.

UNITED ARAB EMIRATES

Like many Middle East nations, the United Arab Emirates has no democratic government. Instead, the country is ruled by a group of wealthy emirs (kings) who have absolute power over their people. Each emir controls his individual emirate, or kingdom, but they meet in the Federal Supreme Council of Rulers to make decisions that affect the whole country. Today, oil provides most of the country's wealth, but shipping has traditionally been important, and there are major ports at Abu Dhabi, Dubai, and Sharjah.

The port at Sharjah is built to accommodate the most modern container ships.

A statue of the former Iraqi dictator Saddam Hussein is toppled in a square in central Baghdad after the 2003 invasion.

MIDDLE EAST WARS

Bitter wars have caused much suffering and death in the Middle East. Israel and its Arab neighbors have fought four wars over the last 60 years. Iran and Iraq were constantly at war throughout the 1980s , and Lebanon was devasted by a civil war. In 1991 UN forces defeated Iraq after the Iraqis had invaded Kuwait. In 2003 American and British forces invaded Iraq and overthrew the dictator Saddam Hussein.

Find out more

DESERTS
IRAN
ISLAM
ISRAEL
OIL

BAHRAIN
Area: 263 sq miles
(680 sq km)
Population: 724,000
Capital: Manama

CYPRUS
Area: 3,572 sq miles
(9,251 sq km)
Population: 802,000
Capital: Nicosia

IRAN
Area: 636,293 sq miles
(1,648,000 sq km)
Population: 68,900,000
Capital: Tehran

IRAQ
Area: 169,235 sq miles
(438,320 sq km)
Population: 25,200,000
Capital: Baghdad

ISRAEL
Area: 7,992 sq miles
(20,700 sq km)
Population: 6,400,000
Capital: Jerusalem

JORDAN
Area: 34,440 sq miles
(89,210 sq km)
Population: 5,500,000
Capital: Amman

KUWAIT
Area: 6,880 sq miles
(17,820 sq km)
Population: 2,500,000
Capital: Kuwait

LEBANON
Area: 4,015 sq miles
(10,400 sq km)
Population: 3,700,000
Capital: Beirut

OMAN
Area: 82,030 sq miles
(212,460 sq km)
Population: 2,900,000
Capital: Muscat

QATAR
Area: 4,247 sq miles
(11,000 sq km)
Population: 610,000
Capital: Doha

SAUDI ARABIA
Area: 829,995 sq miles
(2,149,690 sq km)
Population: 24,200,000
Capital: Riyadh

SYRIA
Area: 185,180 sq km
(185,180 sq kmx)
Population: 17,800,000
Capital: Damascus

TURKEY
Area: 297,154 sq miles
(769,630 sq km)
Population: 71,300,000
Capital: Ankara

Volcano	Mountain	Ancient¤ monument	Capital¤ city	Large¤ city/¤ town	Small¤ city/¤ town

OIL INDUSTRY
Deposits of oil and natural gas were first discovered in the Persian Gulf in the early 1900s. Today, more than half the world's oil reserves are located in the Persian Gulf. The oil industry has made several of the countries very rich, particularly Saudi Arabia, the United Arab Emirates, Bahrain, and Kuwait.

The roofs of buildings in Bahrain extend across sidewalks, providing shade from the scorching sun.

BAHRAIN
The island of Bahrain is little more than 30 miles (50 km) long. Oil wells and refineries provide employment for many people, but tourism is important, too; in 1986 a causeway was opened, linking Bahrain to Saudi Arabia. Since then, many visitors from neighboring Gulf States with strict Islamic laws have visited Bahrain to enjoy its liberal lifestyle.

UNITED ARAB EMIRATES
Area: 32,278 sq miles
(83,600 sq km)
Population: 3,000,000
Capital: Abu Dhabi

YEMEN
Area: 203,849 sq miles
(527,970 sq km)
Population: 20,000,000
Capital: Sana

SCALE BAR
```
0    200   400        km
0         200         400  miles
```

ANIMAL
MIGRATION

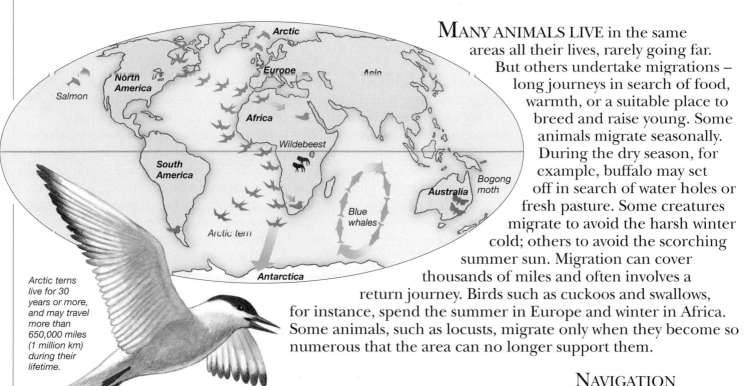

MANY ANIMALS LIVE in the same areas all their lives, rarely going far. But others undertake migrations – long journeys in search of food, warmth, or a suitable place to breed and raise young. Some animals migrate seasonally. During the dry season, for example, buffalo may set off in search of water holes or fresh pasture. Some creatures migrate to avoid the harsh winter cold; others to avoid the scorching summer sun. Migration can cover thousands of miles and often involves a return journey. Birds such as cuckoos and swallows, for instance, spend the summer in Europe and winter in Africa. Some animals, such as locusts, migrate only when they become so numerous that the area can no longer support them.

Arctic terns live for 30 years or more, and may travel more than 650,000 miles (1 million km) during their lifetime.

ARCTIC TERN
The longest migration in the world is made by the Arctic tern. This champion migrator travels from the top of the globe to the bottom each year and back again. Arctic terns spend the summer in the Arctic, where they rear their young and feed on insects, fish, and shellfish. After the short summer, they fly south, and some reach the Antarctic. The direct journey is 9,000 miles (15,000 km), yet many terns go even farther, flying east across the North Atlantic, then west across the South Atlantic. After another summer near the South Pole, they migrate north again.

NAVIGATION
Some animals seem to navigate, or find their way, by following the position of the Sun, Moon, or stars. Others may have a built-in compass that senses the Earth's magnetic field or the electric field of ocean currents. Scientists are not sure how animals know where to migrate, especially young animals that have never made the journey before.

WILDEBEEST
During the dry season in Africa, huge herds of gnus (also called wildebeest) set out in search of fresh grassland and water. Sometimes they travel more than 1,000 miles (1,500 km) before they reach a suitable place.

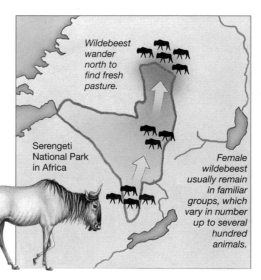

Wildebeest wander north to find fresh pasture.

Serengeti National Park in Africa

Female wildebeest usually remain in familiar groups, which vary in number up to several hundred animals.

SALMON
Salmon hatch from eggs in rivers and streams, then swim to the ocean, where they spend most of their lives. As adults, they migrate thousands of miles back to the river where they were born, to breed. They are so sensitive to the chemicals in the stream where they hatch that they can find their way back to the same spot even after a few years. Salmon are powerful swimmers, and leap out of the water as they fight their way upstream.

BOGONG MOTH
Some animals migrate in summer rather than winter. During the hot, dry summer in southeastern Australia, bogong moths sleep in cool caves and rock crevices high in the mountains. This type of hibernation is called aestivation. In fall, the moths fly down over the lowlands. Some keep flying when they reach the coast, and perish at sea.

Spring: Adult bogong moths migrate to mountain regions above 4,000 ft (1,200 m).

Summer: Adults gather in mountain caves and among rocks to rest during the hot, dry season.

Fall: Adult moths wake and fly down to the lowlands to lay eggs.

Find out more

ANIMALS
BIRDS
BUTTERFLIES AND MOTHS
FISH
HIBERNATION

MILITARY AIRCRAFT

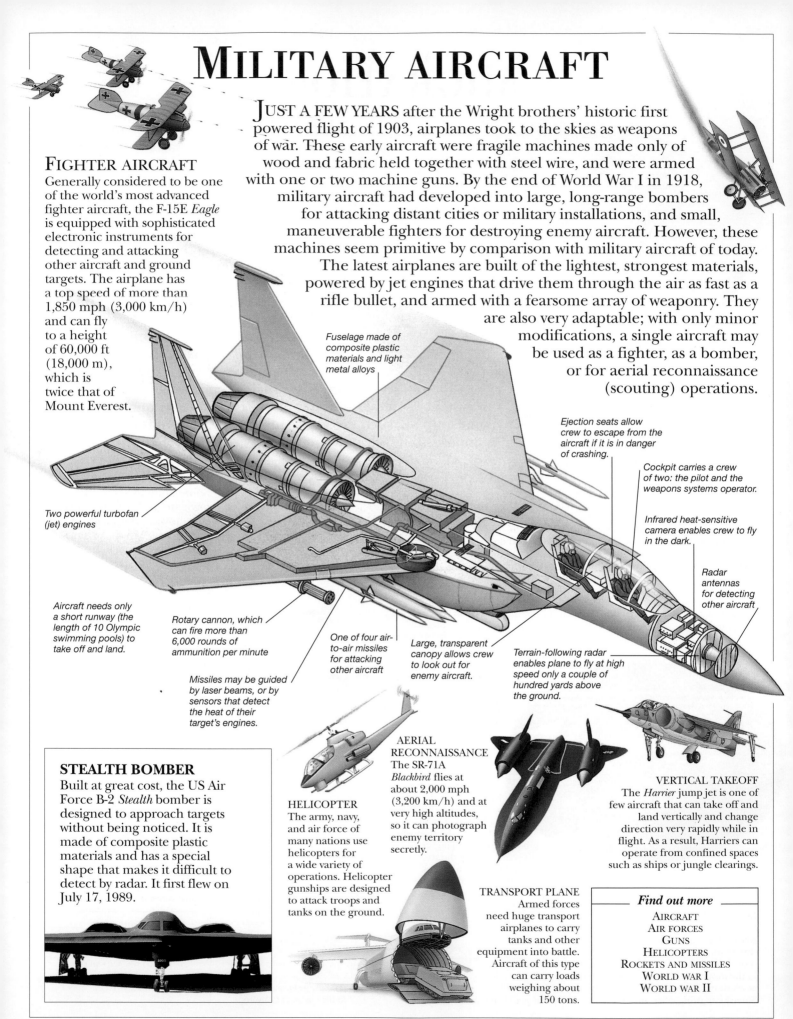

JUST A FEW YEARS after the Wright brothers' historic first powered flight of 1903, airplanes took to the skies as weapons of war. These early aircraft were fragile machines made only of wood and fabric held together with steel wire, and were armed with one or two machine guns. By the end of World War I in 1918, military aircraft had developed into large, long-range bombers for attacking distant cities or military installations, and small, maneuverable fighters for destroying enemy aircraft. However, these machines seem primitive by comparison with military aircraft of today. The latest airplanes are built of the lightest, strongest materials, powered by jet engines that drive them through the air as fast as a rifle bullet, and armed with a fearsome array of weaponry. They are also very adaptable; with only minor modifications, a single aircraft may be used as a fighter, as a bomber, or for aerial reconnaissance (scouting) operations.

FIGHTER AIRCRAFT

Generally considered to be one of the world's most advanced fighter aircraft, the F-15E *Eagle* is equipped with sophisticated electronic instruments for detecting and attacking other aircraft and ground targets. The airplane has a top speed of more than 1,850 mph (3,000 km/h) and can fly to a height of 60,000 ft (18,000 m), which is twice that of Mount Everest.

Fuselage made of composite plastic materials and light metal alloys

Ejection seats allow crew to escape from the aircraft if it is in danger of crashing.

Cockpit carries a crew of two: the pilot and the weapons systems operator.

Infrared heat-sensitive camera enables crew to fly in the dark.

Two powerful turbofan (jet) engines

Radar antennas for detecting other aircraft

Aircraft needs only a short runway (the length of 10 Olympic swimming pools) to take off and land.

Rotary cannon, which can fire more than 6,000 rounds of ammunition per minute

One of four air-to-air missiles for attacking other aircraft

Large, transparent canopy allows crew to look out for enemy aircraft.

Terrain-following radar enables plane to fly at high speed only a couple of hundred yards above the ground.

Missiles may be guided by laser beams, or by sensors that detect the heat of their target's engines.

STEALTH BOMBER

Built at great cost, the US Air Force B-2 *Stealth* bomber is designed to approach targets without being noticed. It is made of composite plastic materials and has a special shape that makes it difficult to detect by radar. It first flew on July 17, 1989.

HELICOPTER

The army, navy, and air force of many nations use helicopters for a wide variety of operations. Helicopter gunships are designed to attack troops and tanks on the ground.

AERIAL RECONNAISSANCE

The SR-71A *Blackbird* flies at about 2,000 mph (3,200 km/h) and at very high altitudes, so it can photograph enemy territory secretly.

TRANSPORT PLANE

Armed forces need huge transport airplanes to carry tanks and other equipment into battle. Aircraft of this type can carry loads weighing about 150 tons.

VERTICAL TAKEOFF

The *Harrier* jump jet is one of few aircraft that can take off and land vertically and change direction very rapidly while in flight. As a result, Harriers can operate from confined spaces such as ships or jungle clearings.

Find out more

AIRCRAFT
AIR FORCES
GUNS
HELICOPTERS
ROCKETS AND MISSILES
WORLD WAR I
WORLD WAR II

MINOANS

FOR NEARLY A THOUSAND YEARS, a glittering civilization dominated the Mediterranean. Its people were known as the Minoans, after their legendary king Minos. In about 6000 B.C., settlers had traveled from mainland Greece to the island of Crete. Blessed with rich soil and a fruitful sea, these people became prosperous and developed a rich culture that reached its height between 2200 B.C. and 1500 B.C. They built huge palaces, such as the palace at Knossos, their main city. The Minoans were great seafarers. They traded throughout the Mediterranean region and with Egypt, carrying passengers, wine, oil, cloth, and bronze in their ships. They grew wheat, vines, and olives, and herded sheep on the mountain slopes. Quite suddenly, a huge volcanic eruption devastated the Minoan civilization. It was not until early 20th century that an archaeologist uncovered the palace at Knossos and amazed the world.

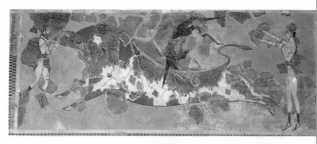

BULL DANCE
Young Minoan men and women performed life-threatening acrobatic feats, probably for religious reasons. They took turns leaping through the horns of a charging bull. After the dance they sacrificed the bull and spread its blood on the land. Few would have survived this type of sport.

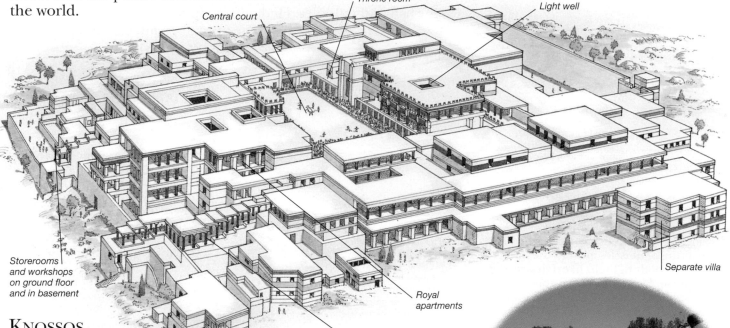

Central court

Throne room

Light well

Storerooms and workshops on ground floor and in basement

Separate villa

Royal apartments

Red-painted pillars supported flat roof.

KNOSSOS

The main Minoan palace at Knossos was five stories high in places and contained more than 1,300 rooms. The walls bore colorful paintings showing scenes from Minoan life. The palace itself contained rooms with religious shrines, workrooms for craftsworkers, storerooms, and living quarters.

Cyclonia

Crete

Knossos

Phaestos

MINOAN EMPIRE
The Minoans built a network of towns on the island of Crete and set up many trading posts around the shores of the eastern Mediterranean. After the volcanic eruption on the nearby island of Thera in about 1550 B.C., peoples from mainland Greece overran Crete. They were called Mycenaeans. The Minoan civilization then went into decline.

Fresco of fisherboy was discovered in a house on the island of Thera. (Fresco is the ancient art of painting on plaster.)

MINOAN POTTERY
The Minoans produced outstanding pottery. They used potter's wheels to make eggshell-thin, finely decorated pots and huge storage jars called pithoi (above). Oil, wine, and grain were kept in the pithoi.

FISHING
Minoan sailors fished the stormy waters around Crete and traded all over the eastern Mediterranean. Fishing was the basis of the Minoan economy.

Find out more
EGYPT, ANCIENT
GREECE, ANCIENT

MOLES, SHREWS,
AND HEDGEHOGS

Despite having short legs, a hedgehog can move surprisingly fast.

NIGHTTIME IS WHEN hedgehogs, moles, and shrews are most active. These small mammals are well adapted to living in the dark. Their eyesight and hearing are poor, but their sense of smell is keen, and their sensitive whiskers enable them to feel their way in the dark. Hedgehogs measure about 9 in (23 cm) in length, with a short tail, a long snout, and stiff needle-like spines covering the top of the body. Most hedgehogs rest in burrows during the day and emerge at night to hunt for insects and earthworms. The common European mole spends most of its life underground. Its soft, velvety fur lies flat and smooth in any direction, which enables the mole to move around easily in the earth. The mole uses its curved front feet and long claws for digging tunnels in search of insects. Shrews are also suited to dark conditions. They look like mice but are smaller, with a longer nose and tiny eyes. Most shrews live on land; the water shrew has adapted to life in rivers and streams, where it hunts for fish and tadpoles. Hedgehogs, moles, and shrews all belong to a large animal group called insectivores (insect-eaters).

When alarmed, the hedgehog rolls itself into a ball. The legs and face are gradually hidden.

The hedgehog usually peeps out to check that the danger has passed, before rolling over onto its front.

HIBERNATION
During winter, hedgehogs roll up into a ball and hibernate until spring arrives.

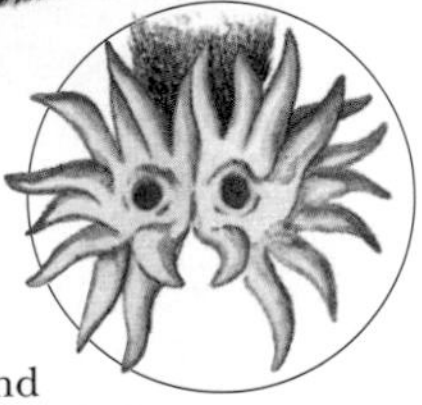

STAR-NOSED MOLE
The star-nosed mole shown here has an unusual nose that is very sensitive to touch and vibrations. The mole's nose helps it find worms and beetles in the darkness.

MOLE
There are about 35 different kinds of moles, found throughout the world. Like other moles, the European mole shown here lives mainly underground, digging new tunnels daily, each about 2 in (5 cm) wide. The mole patrols the tunnels regularly in search of worms and insects that have fallen through the walls.

EUROPEAN HEDGEHOG
When it senses danger, the European hedgehog rolls itself into a ball. It tucks its head and feet into the center of the ball, and a ring of muscles around the lower part of its body tightens like a drawstring on a purse. Hedgehogs have about 5,000 spines; when danger threatens, the spines stick straight out.

SHREW
The smallest shrews measure just 2 to 3 in (5 to 8 cm) in length from nose to tail. Their tiny bodies lose heat so rapidly that in order to survive, shrews have to eat their own weight in food every day.

MOLEHILL
A molehill is made from the excess soil that the mole pushes out of the way as it digs. The large burrow shown here is where the mole rests and raises its young.

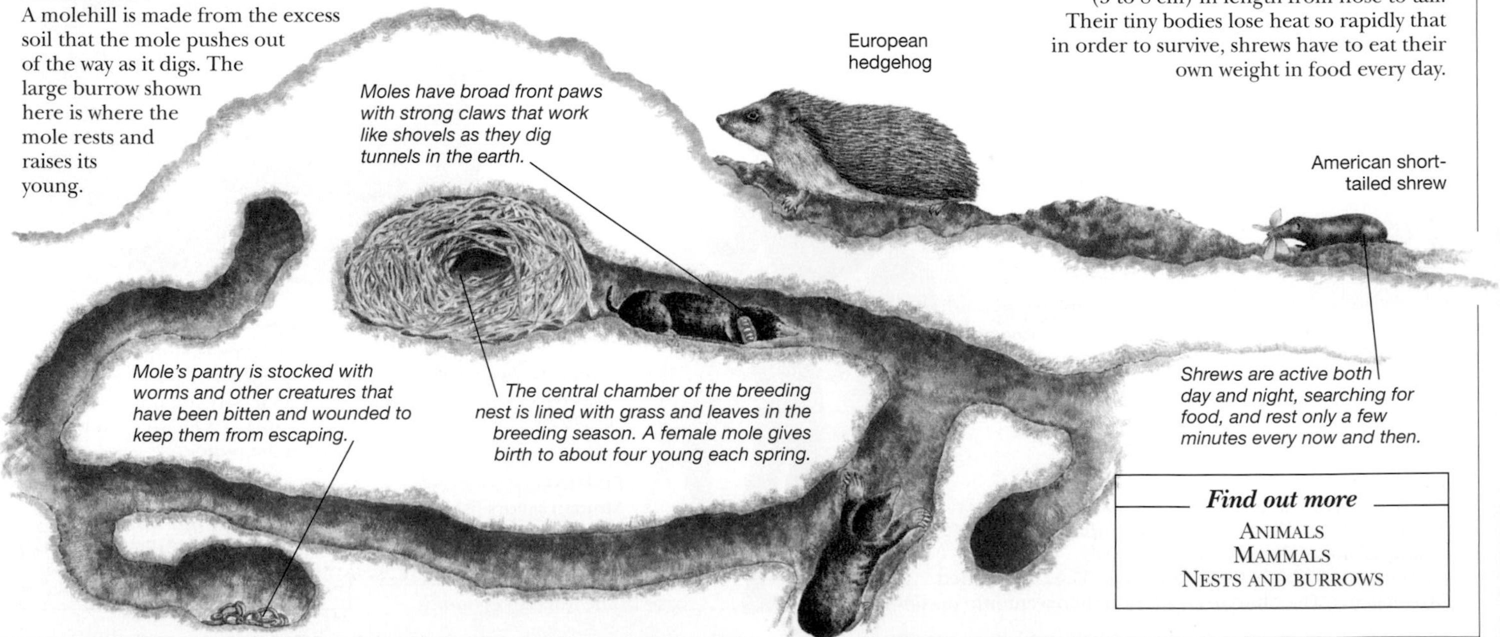

Moles have broad front paws with strong claws that work like shovels as they dig tunnels in the earth.

European hedgehog

American short-tailed shrew

Mole's pantry is stocked with worms and other creatures that have been bitten and wounded to keep them from escaping.

The central chamber of the breeding nest is lined with grass and leaves in the breeding season. A female mole gives birth to about four young each spring.

Shrews are active both day and night, searching for food, and rest only a few minutes every now and then.

Find out more
ANIMALS
MAMMALS
NESTS AND BURROWS

MONASTERIES

DURING THE MIDDLE AGES, men who wanted to devote their lives to the Christian religion often became monks and entered a monastery. They promised to give up all their possessions and never to marry. They followed a hard routine of worship and work. Monks attended up to eight services each day in the abbey church. Regular hours were set aside for working, praying, studying, and recreation. Most monks never left their monastery. They grew their own food, raised their own animals, and made most of the things they needed. Monasteries helped the sick and gave food to the poor. They were also important centers of learning.

LEARNING
Many monasteries had schools and large libraries where trained monks copied and decorated books by hand.

MONASTERIES
The abbey church was the center of monastery life and the largest building. Monks ate in the refectory.

Dormitory where monks slept

11th-century monastery

Cloisters (covered walkways)

Herb garden for medicine and food

Bees kept for honey and wax

Orchard for growing fruit

Refectory

Sick people were cared for in the infirmary, or hospital.

Monasteries had rooms where travelers could stay.

CLOTHING
Monks wore sandals on their feet and coarse robes called habits. The tops of their heads were shaved in a hairstyle called a tonsure; this represented Christ's crown of thorns.

ORDERS OF MONKS
Different types, or orders, of monks organized their lives in different ways. Some orders devoted most of their time to prayer and meditation; others spent more time doing physical work.

NUNS AND NUNNERIES
Religious houses for women were called nunneries or convents. Some nuns entered nunneries for religious reasons; others went to escape from brutal husbands. Nuns taught, prayed, and studied, and followed the same hard routine as monks. Some orders were strict; others were more relaxed. Religions that still have nuns today include Christianity and Buddhism.

Find out more
CHRISTIANITY
CHURCHES AND CATHEDRALS
MEDIEVAL EUROPE
RELIGIONS

MONEY

THE NEXT TIME YOU ARE about to buy something, look at your money. Coins and notes are just discs of metal and sheets of paper, yet the store accepts them as payment for useful, valuable goods. Money is a token that people trade for goods of an agreed value, and strange objects have been used for money throughout the world. Tibetans once used blocks of dried tea! It does not really matter what you use as money, provided that everyone can reach an agreement about what it is worth. Many early coins were made from precious metals, such as gold and silver; but in 11th-century China, paper banknotes, or bills, first appeared. Unlike gold, banknotes had no real value. However, the bank that issued them promised to exchange them for gold. English banknotes still have the same promise printed on them. The United States government stopped exchanging bills for gold in 1971.

Some Native Americans used wampum belts made of clamshell beads for money.

The first Chinese coins were made of bronze in the shape of tools, such as the head of a hoe.

The metal of a modern coin is almost worthless, so the value of the coin is stamped on it.

MINT
A government-controlled factory called a mint produces coins and paper money. Each coin is stamped with a special design, including its value, and often the year of manufacture. This stamping process is known as "minting."

A strip of plastic or metal thread is embedded in the paper.

Specially made paper includes a watermark, which is visible only when the note is held up to the light.

The weight of a coin made of precious metal indicates its value.

COINS
People from ancient Lydia (now Turkey) were the first to make coins, about 2,700 years ago. Their coins were made from electrum, a mixture of gold and silver. Today, coins are used only for small denominations (sums of money). Paper money is used for larger sums, because notes are more difficult to forge than coins.

The loops and whirls are machine-engraved and extremely difficult to copy.

BANKNOTES
Governments issue banknotes and guarantee their value. It is a crime for anyone else to copy and print banknotes. The crime is called forgery, or counterfeiting, and banknotes have complicated designs to make copying difficult. Thomas De La Rue & Company is one of the world's most successful banknote printers. Their specimen note includes various security features that make their notes very difficult to copy.

All credit cards have to be signed by the user and can be used only by that person.

Many credit cards incorporate holograms that are difficult to copy.

BANKS
Most people deposit, or store, their money in a bank. Banks keep this money safe in a vault or lend it to their other customers. The bank has an account, or record, of how much each of its customers has deposited. Banks pay out notes and coins when their customers need money to make purchases. People with bank accounts can also buy things by writing checks – notes that the bank promises to exchange for cash.

The raised letters imprint your name and card number on the receipt.

CREDIT CARDS
A credit card is a piece of plastic that can be used in place of money. When you use it to buy something, you sign a receipt. The credit card company pays for the goods, and you pay the credit card company a month or so later. Credit cards are carefully made to reduce the risk of forgery or misuse.

Find out more

ROCKS AND MINERALS
SHOPS AND SHOPPING
STOCK EXCHANGE
TRADE AND INDUSTRY

MONGOL EMPIRE

IN THE LATE 1100s, a masterful chieftain united a group of wandering tribes into a powerful army. He was called Genghis Khan; the tribes were the Mongols. All were toughened by a harsh life spent herding on the treeless plains of northeastern Asia. Determined to train the best army of his time, Genghis built up a formidable cavalry force. Using new weapons such as smoke bombs and gunpowder, they were invincible. In 1211, the Mongols invaded China, then swept through Asia. They moved at incredible speed, concentrating their forces at critical moments. All their military operations were planned to the smallest detail. Looting and burning as they came, they struck terror into the hearts of their enemies. In 1227, Genghis Khan died, leaving a huge empire to his four sons, who extended it through Asia Minor into Europe. However, the empire broke apart as rival khans (Mongol kings) battled for control.

GENGHIS KHAN
Temüjin (1162-1227) was the son of a tribal chief. His father was murdered when Temüjin was still a child, and when he grew up he defeated his enemies, united all other tribes under his control, and took the title Genghis Khan, "prince of all that lies between the oceans." He aimed to conquer the world.

Khanate of the Golden Horde
Khanate of Jagatai
Empire of Kublai Khan
Khanate of Hulagu

Armor-piercing arrow

MONGOL KHANATES
After Genghis's death, the Mongol Empire divided into four khanates, or states, with different rulers. Kublai, grandson of Genghis, ruled the eastern khanate. The smaller western empires, although briefly united in the 1300s by Tamerlane the Great, gradually disintegrated.

Cavalry controlled horses with their feet to leave their hands free for fighting.

Horses in battle gear

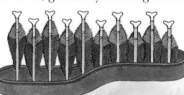

MONGOL EMPIRE

1206 Temüjin unites all the tribes of Mongolia.

1219 Mongols invade Persia.

1223 Mongols invade Russia.

1237 Batu, grandson of Genghis Khan, invades north Russia.

1240 Batu invades Poland and Hungary.

1260 Mamelukes, Egyptian warriors, defeat Mongols.

1279 Kublai Khan defeats China.

1370 Tamerlane the Great conquers the western khanates.

Strung bow

COMPOSITE BOW
Mongols made their deadly bows out of wood, horn, and sinew, which gave the bows incredible power. The Mongols were superb archers, able to string, aim, and fire at full gallop. They developed armor-piercing arrows, whistling arrows for signaling, and even arrows tipped with grenades.

Unstrung bow

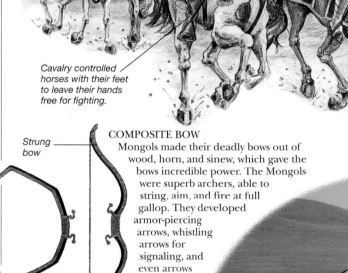

YURTS
Tribes wandered the Mongolian steppes following their herds of sheep, goats, cattle, and horses. They lived in circular tents called yurts, that they took with them when they moved. The women drove wagons which held the yurts; the men hunted, looked after the herds, and traded for grain and metal. Mongols of today still live in yurts.

Find out more
CHINA, HISTORY OF
EXPLORERS
RUSSIA, HISTORY OF

MONKEYS AND APES

AMONG THE MOST INTELLIGENT creatures on Earth are the apes – chimpanzees, gorillas, gibbons, and orangutans. They have large brains, long arms, fingers, and toes, and their bodies are covered in hair. In body shape and intelligence these creatures resemble humans. Both apes and humans belong to the larger group known as Primates. Closely related to apes are monkeys, a larger group of animals that includes baboons, macaques, colubuses, and marmosets. Monkeys and apes have a similar body form, although monkeys tend to be smaller. A pygmy marmoset weighs only 5 oz (150 g), whereas a huge male "silverback" gorilla weighs as much as 400 lb (180 kg). Both monkeys and apes have a rounded face, small ears, and large eyes that face forward. They use their front limbs like arms, and their hands can grasp strongly and manipulate delicately. Most monkeys have tails, which they use as a counterbalance as they swing through trees. In some monkeys, the tail is strong and prehensile (grasping); apes, however, have no tails. Apes and monkeys feed on a variety of foods, including fruit, leaves, insects, and birds' eggs.

ORANGUTAN

The richly colored orangutan is found in the forests of Borneo and Sumatra in southeastern Asia. Orangutans spend most of their time high up in the trees searching for fruit, shoots, leaves, and insects. They live alone, except where there is plenty of food.

Prehensile hand can grasp.

Arms are very long in relation to the body.

Shaggy coat of reddish-brown hair

GORILLA

Measuring up to 6 ft (2 m) in height, gorillas are the largest apes. Gorillas are slow, gentle creatures – unless disturbed – and they spend their time resting and eating leaves, stems, and shoots. Gorillas live in small family groups that travel slowly through the forest, eating some but not all of the food in one area before moving onto another place.

Today, orangutans are in danger of extinction because their forest homes are being cleared for timber and farmland.

BREEDING
A gorilla group contains between five and 10 animals. There is one large male, several females, and their young of various ages. The young are born singly; a female gives birth about every four years.

PRIMATES
All monkeys and apes belong to the mammal group called primates. Other primates include bush babies, pottos, tarsiers, and humans. Today, many primates, including gibbons and the other apes, are on the official list of endangered species.

MACAQUE MONKEY
Monkeys and apes show behavior that we describe as "intelligent." These creatures communicate well, have good memories, and are able to solve problems. A famous example is the Japanese macaque monkeys that discovered that by washing its food in water it could get rid of the dirt and sand on it. Other members of the troop saw what the monkey was doing and copied it.

GIBBON

A gibbon's muscular arms and hands are so long that the knuckles touch the ground even when the gibbon stands upright. Gibbons live in family groups of a male, a female, and two to four young. There are 14 kinds of gibbon; the largest is the siamang, which weighs about 22 lb (10 kg). The siamang is so heavy that it cannot swing out to the tips of thin branches as other gibbons can.

The acrobatic gibbon swings through the trees of southeastern Asia and rarely comes down to the ground.

Gibbons feed mainly on fruit and young leaves.

Young chimpanzees spend much of their time playing with objects and chasing each other. This helps prepare the chimp to find food and fight off enemies in adult life.

Most monkeys and apes depend on trees for shelter and food, particularly in the rain forests.

COMMUNICATION

Many monkeys communicate by sounds. The howler monkey of South America produces extremely loud howling noises using its specialized larynx (voice box). These sounds warn other howler troops to stay out of the group's territory. The leading male howler is usually the main shouter and can be heard nearly 2 miles (3 km) away.

CONSERVATION

The forests where monkeys and apes live are being cut down at a great speed. Newly planted trees are soon removed for timber, so they do not provide homes for the local wildlife. Dozens of different kinds of monkeys are at risk. Among them is the woolly spider monkey of Brazil. Some non-profit organizations have taken up their cause. Their three-point program works through rescue and rehabilitation, conservation education, and research.

BABOON

The African baboon can climb but usually walks or gallops on all fours. Baboons are easy to study because they live in open country, and scientists have learned much about their social life. Baboons live in troops. Each troop is based around senior females and their offspring. Growing males tend to live alone while they are maturing. When a male becomes an adult he joins a troop, but has to battle with other males to establish his rank. The troop protects itself against predators such as lions and against other baboon troops that stray into its territory.

CHIMPANZEE

Chimpanzees are the animals that remind us most of ourselves – because of their facial expressions and the way they play games, make tools, and solve puzzles. Chimpanzees live in groups that sometimes fight with neighboring groups. Their main foods are fruit, leaves, seeds, flowers, insects, and sometimes larger creatures such as monkeys and deer. Chimpanzees live deep in the forests and open grassland of Africa. Pygmy chimps or bonobos are found only in the thick forests of the Democratic Republic of Congo (Zaire).

Find out more

AFRICAN WILDLIFE
ANIMALS
CONSERVATION
and endangered species
FOREST WILDLIFE
MAMMALS

MOON

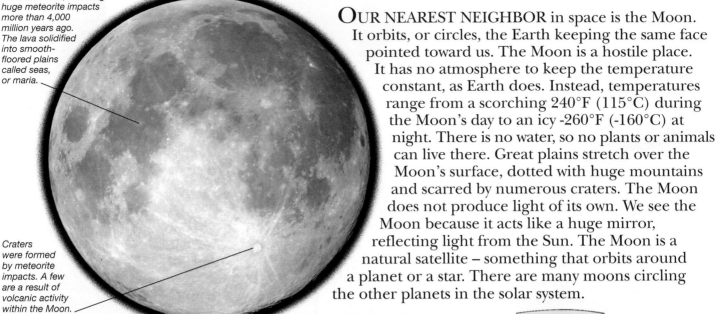

Lava once flowed from the Moon's interior, following huge meteorite impacts more than 4,000 million years ago. The lava solidified into smooth-floored plains called seas, or maria.

Craters were formed by meteorite impacts. A few are a result of volcanic activity within the Moon.

OUR NEAREST NEIGHBOR in space is the Moon. It orbits, or circles, the Earth keeping the same face pointed toward us. The Moon is a hostile place. It has no atmosphere to keep the temperature constant, as Earth does. Instead, temperatures range from a scorching 240°F (115°C) during the Moon's day to an icy -260°F (-160°C) at night. There is no water, so no plants or animals can live there. Great plains stretch over the Moon's surface, dotted with huge mountains and scarred by numerous craters. The Moon does not produce light of its own. We see the Moon because it acts like a huge mirror, reflecting light from the Sun. The Moon is a natural satellite – something that orbits around a planet or a star. There are many moons circling the other planets in the solar system.

BIRTH OF THE MOON
There have been many theories to explain the formation of the Moon. Scientists have suggested that the Moon may be a piece of the Earth that broke away millions of years ago. Today, however, most astronomers believe that the Moon was formed when an asteroid the size of Mars struck the Earth about 4.5 billion years ago.

LUNA 3
Until 1959, the far side of the Moon had never been seen. In October of that year, the Russian space probe *Luna 3* (right) sent back the first photographs of this part of the Moon.

The gravitational attraction of the Moon causes tides to rise and fall in the Earth's oceans.

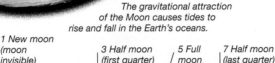

1 New moon (moon invisible)
3 Half moon (first quarter)
5 Full moon
7 Half moon (last quarter)
2 Crescent moon
4 Gibbous moon (waxing)
6 Gibbous moon (waning)
8 Old moon

Moon seen from here

PHASES OF THE MOON
As the Moon orbits the Earth, different shapes, or phases, appear, depending on the amount of the sunlit side of the Moon that is visible from Earth.

OTHER MOONS
Our solar system contains more than 150 known moons. Nearly all circle the giant outer planets and are made of ice mixed with rock. The largest planet, Jupiter, has at least 63 moons, three of them larger than our own Moon. One, Io (seen alongside Jupiter, left), is alive with active volcanoes. Another, Ganymede, is the largest satellite in the solar system. Some of Saturn's moons are very small and orbit in the outer sections of the planet's rings.

Armstrong's crew member, Edwin Aldrin, stands by the lunar module.

LUNAR LANDINGS
In 1966, the Russian *Luna 9* spacecraft made the first controlled landing on the Moon. It was only three years later, in July 1969, that American astronaut Neil Armstrong climbed down from the *Apollo 11* lunar module to become the first person on the Moon.

MOON FACTS	
Distance from Earth	238,855 miles (384,401 km)
Diameter at equator	2,160.5 miles (3,477.8 km)
Time for each orbit	27 days, 7 hours, 43 minutes
Time between full moons	29 days, 12 hours, 43 minutes
Gravity at surface	1/6 of Earth's surface gravity
Brightness	1/425,000 brightness of Sun

Find out more
ASTRONOMY
EARTH
OCEANS AND SEAS
PLANETS
SPACE FLIGHT

MOSSES, LIVERWORTS,
AND FERNS

MISTY TROPICAL RAIN FORESTS and moist, shady woodlands shelter some of the simplest land plants. These are mosses and liverworts, also seen on logs, stone walls, and garden lawns. They are quite different from other plants. They have no true root systems, flowers, or seeds. Instead, mosses and liverworts have tiny rootlets that absorb only a small amount of water from the soil, and short-stemmed leaves that take in moisture from the air. There are 11 different types of non-flowering plants.

Ferns are also flowerless. They are an ancient group of plants that have grown on Earth for more than 300 million years. Unlike mosses and liverworts, ferns do have true roots, with tubes inside their stems that carry water to the leaves. The giant tree ferns are the largest of all ferns. They grow up to 65 ft (20 m) high and look like palm trees. The smallest ferns in tropical rain forests are tiny, with leaflike fronds less than 0.5 in (1 cm) long. Ferns grow in most kinds of soil, but not in hot desert sand.

HORSETAILS
Horsetails are fernlike plants with no flowers. About 300 million years ago, forests of giant horsetails grew up to 150 ft (46 m) high. Their remains have turned into coal.

Carpet of moss covers wet bark on log.

HOW MOSS REPRODUCES
The leafy moss plant has male and female organs. The fertilized spores grow in the brown spore-containing capsules, which are held above the leaves on long stalks.

FERN
A new fern frond gradually unfurls. When it is mature, brown dots called sori appear on the frond. These sori contain spores. The spores grow into tiny heart-shaped plants, which bear male and female organs.

Tip of frond uncurls.

Polypody fern fronds stay green all winter.

Sori are on the underside of fern frond.

Fern

Curled-up frond of polypody fern

MOISTURE-LOVING PLANTS
Mosses and liverworts grow beside streams and rivers because they need the moisture from the water. They do not have roots to absorb water from the soil and pass it to their leaves. Instead, their leaves take in moisture from the air.

Liverwort

BRACKEN
Bracken is found on every continent except Antarctica. It has far-reaching roots and underground stems, and spreads quickly across grassland and woodland. Bracken is a nuisance to many farmers and gardeners because it is very difficult to remove once it has become established.

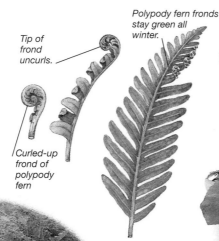
Bracken spreads into a pasture, reducing the grazing area.

LIVERWORT
The liverwort grows close to the ground, from which it soaks up moisture. Some liverworts, mosses, and ferns grow on trees and other plants, which they cling to for support.

Liverworts take their name from their shape, which looks like the human liver.

BOG MOSS
Sphagnum moss is one of the few plants found in wet, marshy areas. It grows very well in swamps, forming wet, spongy hummocks. As the sphagnum dies, it rots slowly, and over many centuries turns into mossy peat below the surface.

Find out more
FOREST WILDLIFE
MARSH
and swamp wildlife
PLANTS
SOIL

MOUNTAINS

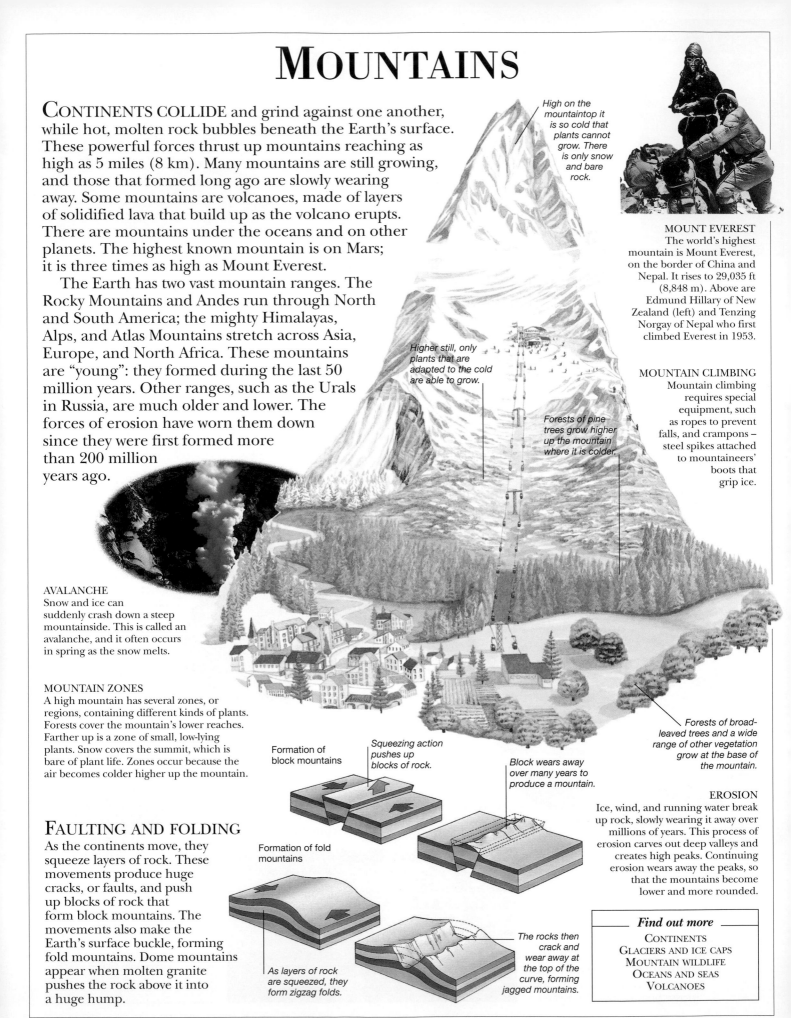

CONTINENTS COLLIDE and grind against one another, while hot, molten rock bubbles beneath the Earth's surface. These powerful forces thrust up mountains reaching as high as 5 miles (8 km). Many mountains are still growing, and those that formed long ago are slowly wearing away. Some mountains are volcanoes, made of layers of solidified lava that build up as the volcano erupts. There are mountains under the oceans and on other planets. The highest known mountain is on Mars; it is three times as high as Mount Everest.

The Earth has two vast mountain ranges. The Rocky Mountains and Andes run through North and South America; the mighty Himalayas, Alps, and Atlas Mountains stretch across Asia, Europe, and North Africa. These mountains are "young": they formed during the last 50 million years. Other ranges, such as the Urals in Russia, are much older and lower. The forces of erosion have worn them down since they were first formed more than 200 million years ago.

High on the mountaintop it is so cold that plants cannot grow. There is only snow and bare rock.

Higher still, only plants that are adapted to the cold are able to grow.

Forests of pine trees grow higher up the mountain where it is colder.

MOUNT EVEREST
The world's highest mountain is Mount Everest, on the border of China and Nepal. It rises to 29,035 ft (8,848 m). Above are Edmund Hillary of New Zealand (left) and Tenzing Norgay of Nepal who first climbed Everest in 1953.

MOUNTAIN CLIMBING
Mountain climbing requires special equipment, such as ropes to prevent falls, and crampons – steel spikes attached to mountaineers' boots that grip ice.

AVALANCHE
Snow and ice can suddenly crash down a steep mountainside. This is called an avalanche, and it often occurs in spring as the snow melts.

MOUNTAIN ZONES
A high mountain has several zones, or regions, containing different kinds of plants. Forests cover the mountain's lower reaches. Farther up is a zone of small, low-lying plants. Snow covers the summit, which is bare of plant life. Zones occur because the air becomes colder higher up the mountain.

Forests of broad-leaved trees and a wide range of other vegetation grow at the base of the mountain.

FAULTING AND FOLDING
As the continents move, they squeeze layers of rock. These movements produce huge cracks, or faults, and push up blocks of rock that form block mountains. The movements also make the Earth's surface buckle, forming fold mountains. Dome mountains appear when molten granite pushes the rock above it into a huge hump.

Formation of block mountains

Squeezing action pushes up blocks of rock.

Block wears away over many years to produce a mountain.

Formation of fold mountains

As layers of rock are squeezed, they form zigzag folds.

The rocks then crack and wear away at the top of the curve, forming jagged mountains.

EROSION
Ice, wind, and running water break up rock, slowly wearing it away over millions of years. This process of erosion carves out deep valleys and creates high peaks. Continuing erosion wears away the peaks, so that the mountains become lower and more rounded.

Find out more
CONTINENTS
GLACIERS AND ICE CAPS
MOUNTAIN WILDLIFE
OCEANS AND SEAS
VOLCANOES

MOUNTAIN WILDLIFE

LAMMERGEIER
The lammergeier is one of the biggest vultures. It has a wingspan of about 10 ft (3 m) and soars over the high mountain peaks of Africa, Asia, and Europe. This bird of prey feeds mostly on carrion (bodies of dead animals).

THE MOUNTAIN RANGES of the world are home to all kinds of wildlife – from tiny beetles to huge bears. Lower slopes are often covered with lush vegetation and are rich in animal life. Higher up the mountain the temperature is lower, and there is less wildlife. Mammals living here have thick fur to survive the cold. In places too steep for most creatures to climb, surefooted goats and chamois leap with ease over the rocks. Near the top of the mountain the wind is so strong that only powerful birds such as condors can fly. In some windy areas, the insects have lost their wings during the course of evolution; wings would be useless to them. Spiders and wingless insects live higher up the mountain than any other creature. As you climb higher, the temperature drops by 6.5°F (3.6°C) for every 1,000 ft (300 m) of height. Above about 8,000 ft (2,400 m) small shrubs grow, bent and twisted by the icy winds. Higher up still, only mosses and lichens grow, and at the very top there is permanent snow and ice.

CONSERVATION
Wildlife parks protect mountain animals such as the bobcat shown here. In the past people hunted the bobcat for its fur; today this cat is an endangered species.

This map shows the main mountain ranges of the world.

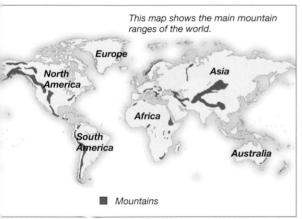

■ Mountains

The mountain goat is a North American relative of the European chamois. Its body is more thickset and sturdy, and it is three times the weight of a chamois. The mountain goat moves slowly and deliberately through deep snow.

CHAMOIS
A rubbery hoof pad allows the chamois to grip stony surfaces with ease as it leaps nimbly among rocks in search of grasses, herbs, and flowers. Chamois live in groups of up to 30 females and young. The males live alone except in the breeding season.

MOUNTAIN PLANTS
High up where trees do not grow, alpine flowers bloom in the short summer. The word *alpine* means above the tree line. The leaves of most alpine flowers grow low and flat so they are protected from the bitter winds. These flowers are pollinated mainly by flies, butterflies, and other insects that have survived the winter as eggs or as adults under the snow.

The trumpet gentian is named for its deep trumpet of petals. It grows in stony places and in damp, short turf at heights of 10,000 ft (3,000 m), in the Alps, Pyrenees, and Apennines of Europe.

Today the edelweiss is a protected plant in many areas.

The alpine longhorn beetle shown here suns itself on mountain flowers and feeds on their pollen.

SPECTACLED BEAR
The only bear in South America is the spectacled bear, so named because of the markings around its eyes. It lives in the Andes Mountains and is found in warm, moist forests and mountains at heights of 11,500 ft (3,500 m). Spectacled bears eat a wide range of foods, including leaves, fruits, insects, eggs, small deer, and other mammals.

ROCK HYRAX
The small, furry, stoutly built hyrax of Africa is the closest living relative of the elephant – the largest animal on land. Rock hyraxes live at heights of up to 13,300 ft (4,000 m) in rocky places such as Mount Kenya.

Hyraxes eat mainly grasses.

Find out more
BEARS AND PANDAS
CONSERVATION
and endangered species
EAGLES
and other birds of prey
LIONS, TIGERS,
and other big cats
MOUNTAINS

MOVIES

IN A PARIS café in December 1895, people sat down to watch the world's first motion picture. It was shown by two French brothers, Louis and Auguste Lumière, and though it consisted only of a few short, simple scenes, movies have been popular ever since. The first movies were silent, with titles on the screen to explain the story. A pianist accompanied the movie with the right type of music – for example, fast and furious music during a chase scene. The United States took the lead in making movies. Soon the public began to select its favorite actors and actresses, and the first movie stars were created, such as Rudolph Valentino. In 1927, the first full-length "talkie" – movie with sound – was shown, and from then on the public would settle for nothing less. Technical improvements continued. In the United States, Metro-Goldwyn-Mayer and a few other powerful studios made 95 percent of the movies. During the 1950s, television captured people's attention and the film industry went into decline. In recent years, movies have become popular again. Russia, Germany, France, and Japan have produced movies that have influenced filmmaking throughout the world, and there are many national film industries.

CHARLIE CHAPLIN
The British actor Charles Chaplin (1889-1977) created a movie character that touched the hearts of millions: a silent little tramp with a funny walk.

HOLLYWOOD
Southern California had the ideal climate and scenery for making films. Between 1907 and 1913 a Los Angeles neighborhood called Hollywood became the center of the American film industry. Not all stars were human: King Kong (above) was an animated model.

The senior electrician on the film set is called the gaffer.

Teams of expert makeup artists and dressers prepare an actress or actor for a day's shoot.

The art director designs the sets and chooses suitable locations for filming away from the studio.

A continuity worker makes sure that scenes shot out of order match each other. He or she notes the details of each shot to ensure that there are no mistakes when the scenes are put in order.

Sound technicians follow the actors with microphones suspended from long poles (booms).

Lighting experts operate huge lamps to ensure that the light looks as natural as possible in a movie. Lighting is needed on location as well as in the studio.

The producer chooses the script, finds financial backing, picks the director and the technical teams, oversees the filming, and organizes publicity.

The director guides the actors' performances, the action, and the camera angles, and gives the film its style and character.

The cinematographer leads a team that also includes the camera operator. Camera assistants help with focusing, load magazines, and operate the clapper board. Workers called grips move the camera down tracks or rails for the camera to run along smoothly.

MOVIE SET
Set builders make movie sets – from city streets to tropical jungles – inside huge buildings like aircraft hangars, or outdoors on studio grounds. Hundreds of people are involved in getting things ready for the first filming of the day. When all is satisfactory, a red warning light goes on, the studio is told to stand by for a take (an attempt at a scene), sound and cameras roll, and the director shouts "Action!"

Acting on the big screen is very different from the theater. In close-ups, every movement can be seen, and actors have to play their part with subtle facial expressions. They must also be able to act the story out of sequence.

Stuntmen and stuntwomen take the place of actors in dangerous action. They risk their lives performing stunts, such as falling from a great height, crashing a car, or leaping from a moving train.

SPECIAL EFFECTS

Special effects have created a vast new fantasy world in films. In a technique known as back projection, first used as early as 1913, the cinematographer projected a previously filmed background onto a screen from behind. Actors or models were then filmed in front of the screen, giving the impression that they were actually at that location. Glass screens painted with realistic backgrounds, studio sets wired up with controlled explosions, special smoke and wind machines, and stop-frame animation of models were all used to help bring make-believe scenes to life. As recently as the 1970s, life-like models were still being filmed in a studio to produce gruesome horror effects, such as the shark in *Jaws*, and convincing space battles, such as those in *Star Wars*. Today, almost all of these effects are created digitally using powerful computers.

The actors are filmed against a background of solid blue or green color.

"BULLET-TIME" SLOW MOTION EFFECT

Each small hole in the scene above conceals a still camera taking a picture of the scene from a different angle. The series of shots is put together in sequence on computer, along with thousands of extra "in-between" frames created in software. The effect is of the camera moving around the action in extreme slow motion.

The actors are superimposed on a new background, and the wires supporting them are erased.

On computer, the colored background is easily removed using a software filter – sometimes called "Chromakey".

SPIELBERG

Directors often become stars in their own right. Director Steven Spielberg was born in 1946. He shot his first movie when he was 12 and won a contract with Universal Studios, Hollywood, after leaving college. He became one of the most successful directors ever, with blockbusters such as *Jaws* (1975), *Jurassic Park* (1993), *War of the Worlds* (2005), and Oscar winners such as *Schindler's List* (1993).

DIGITAL TRICKERY

Digital video editing software allows moviemakers to insert actors into almost any environment imaginable. Actors are filmed in front of a green or blue "matte" background, which is later replaced with a new scene – one either filmed elsewhere or created on computer. Real people can also be combined with computer-generated characters and models, as in *Harry Potter*, and whole armies can be created that have an "artificial life" entirely of their own, as in *Lord of the Rings*.

EDITING

The film editor sees that all the shots are in the right order, and that the movie lasts the right amount of time. But editing is more complex than that. A good editor can improve the movie by cutting out sequences that slow down the action or inserting close-up shots to make a scene more dramatic. Editing is a highly skilled process. In the past it involved physically cutting and taping together pieces of film, though now it is usually done digitally. Directors and film editors work together for hours to get the right combination of shots in each scene.

DUBBING

The sound editor is responsible for assembling the soundtrack for the movie. This consists of dozens of separate tracks, including all the dialog, music, sound effects, and background sound. After editing, these sounds have to be balanced against each other and blended in a process called dubbing. Technicians known as mixers watch the film and operate controls on a sound console to get perfect timing and balance of sounds.

FILMS

1895 First public film show held in Paris.

1905 The first nickelodeon theater opens in the United States.

1907 Hollywood founded.

1927 *The Jazz Singer* is the first full-length movie with sound.

1927 The Academy of Motion Picture Arts and Sciences is set up.

1928 American cartoonist Walt Disney (1901-66) launches his most popular cartoon character, Mickey Mouse, in the movie *Steamboat Willie*.

1929 First Academy Awards.

1935 First full-spectrum Technicolor feature, *Becky Sharp*, is released.

1953 First CinemaScope (wide screen) movie, *The Robe*, released.

1995 *Toy Story*, first completely computer-animated feature movie, released.

Find out more

CAMERAS
CARTOONS
TELEVISION AND VIDEO
THEATER

MUHAMMAD

DURING THE 600s, one man founded what was to become one of the world's great religions. His name was Muhammad, and the religion was Islam. Muhammad came from Mecca in southwestern Arabia (now Saudi Arabia), and was born into one of the city's Arab clans around A.D. 570. Orphaned at an early age, he became a merchant and married Khadija, a wealthy widow, with whom he had three daughters. At the time, the Arab people worshiped many gods and prayed to idols and spirits. Muhammad came to believe that there was only one God, named Allah, and that he had been chosen to be Allah's prophet. Muhammad's family and friends were the first to share his beliefs, but his views angered the people of Mecca and he was forced to flee to Medina, a city north of Mecca. There he proclaimed the principles of Islam and won many converts. After a series of holy wars, Muhammad and his followers conquered Mecca in 630. Missionaries spread the message of Islam far and wide, and by the time of Muhammad's death in 632, Arabia was an Islamic state.

PROPHET OF ISLAM
The Angel Gabriel told Muhammad that he had been chosen by God to be a prophet, in the same way as Moses and Abraham before him.

HEGIRA

People came to Mecca to worship and trade at the Kaaba, a huge shrine that contained hundreds of idols. Muhammad was persecuted when he spoke out against the worship of idols. In 622, he fled with a few of his followers to Medina. Their journey is called the Hegira (meaning "flight" or "migration"). Today, the Kaaba is a holy shrine for Muslims (followers of Islam). It is surrounded by a great mosque (Muslim temple) and visited by thousands of pilgrims each year.

Pilgrims walk seven times around the Kaaba.

MOUNT HIRA
At age 40, Muhammad began to meditate in a cave on Mount Hira, north of Mecca. Here he had a vision in which the Angel Gabriel spoke the words of God to him and told him that he was to preach that people should believe in only one God – Allah. The teachings of Allah were revealed to Muhammad in a series of visions throughout his life.

MUHAMMAD'S TEACHINGS
Muhammad did not claim to be divine. He believed that he was the last of the prophets and that he had received messages from God, which he had to pass onto others. He taught that there is only one God, that people should be obedient to God's will, and that all people were equal. He also preached against the selfishness of the rich, the unjust treatment of women, slaves, and poor people, and cruelty to animals. In 632, knowing that his life was coming to an end, he led a farewell pilgrimage to Mecca. There he delivered a famous sermon on the most important principles of Islam.

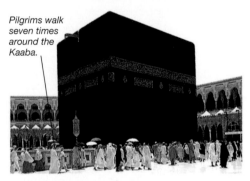

FATIMA AND ALI
Muhammad's daughter Fatima (605-633) traveled with her father to Medina. She later married Muhammad's cousin, Ali. Fatima's children went on to found the city of Kahira (Cairo) in Egypt.

Fatima

Muhammad

Ali

DEATH OF MUHAMMAD
After the farewell pilgrimage, Muhammad went back to Medina, but died within a few days of his return. His tomb lies in the Prophet's Mosque at Medina. After his death, his followers wrote down his teachings in the Qur'an (Koran), the holy book of Islam.

MUHAMMAD

c. A.D. 570 Born in Mecca.

595 Marries Khadija, a wealthy widow.

610 Has a vision of the Angel Gabriel telling him to proclaim a new faith, Islam.

613 Begins preaching to the people of Mecca.

622 Leaves Mecca and travels to Medina.

624 Meccan army defeated at Battle of Badr by much smaller Muslim force.

630 Conquers Mecca.

632 Dies in Medina.

Find out more
ISLAM
RELIGIONS

MUSCLES AND MOVEMENT

EVERY MOVEMENT YOU MAKE is powered by muscles. Muscles are controlled by nerve signals from the brain. There are three main types of muscle – skeletal, smooth, and cardiac. Skeletal muscle is also called striated muscle, and it covers the bones of the skeleton. It is attached to the bones by long cords called tendons. When the muscle contracts, or shortens, it moves the bone. Skeletal muscles are also called voluntary muscles because they can be controlled at will. Smooth muscle is found in the digestive system, bladder, and blood vessels. It is called involuntary muscle because it works automatically, even when you are asleep. Cardiac muscle is found only in the heart. All muscles need energy in order to work properly. Blood carries oxygen and glucose (sugar) to muscles to provide them with fuel. As a muscle works harder, it needs more fuel, so the heart pumps faster to supply it with more blood.

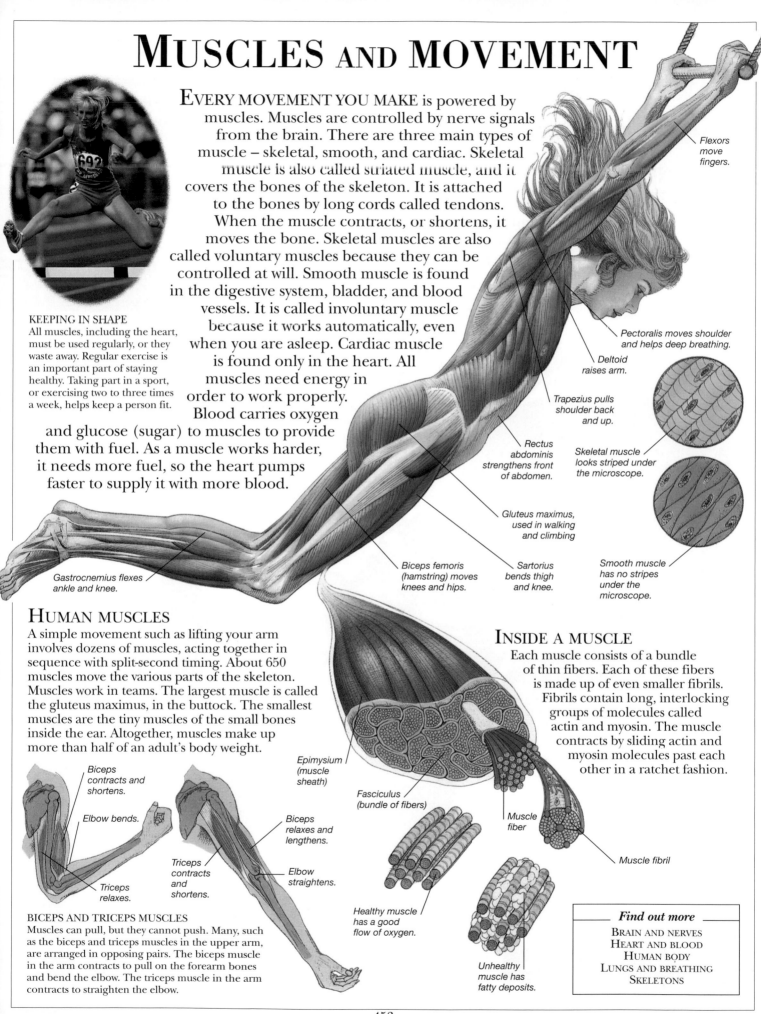

KEEPING IN SHAPE
All muscles, including the heart, must be used regularly, or they waste away. Regular exercise is an important part of staying healthy. Taking part in a sport, or exercising two to three times a week, helps keep a person fit.

Flexors move fingers.

Pectoralis moves shoulder and helps deep breathing.

Deltoid raises arm.

Trapezius pulls shoulder back and up.

Rectus abdominis strengthens front of abdomen.

Skeletal muscle looks striped under the microscope.

Gluteus maximus, used in walking and climbing.

Smooth muscle has no stripes under the microscope.

Gastrocnemius flexes ankle and knee.

Biceps femoris (hamstring) moves knees and hips.

Sartorius bends thigh and knee.

HUMAN MUSCLES
A simple movement such as lifting your arm involves dozens of muscles, acting together in sequence with split-second timing. About 650 muscles move the various parts of the skeleton. Muscles work in teams. The largest muscle is called the gluteus maximus, in the buttock. The smallest muscles are the tiny muscles of the small bones inside the ear. Altogether, muscles make up more than half of an adult's body weight.

Biceps contracts and shortens.

Elbow bends.

Triceps relaxes.

Biceps relaxes and lengthens.

Triceps contracts and shortens.

Elbow straightens.

BICEPS AND TRICEPS MUSCLES
Muscles can pull, but they cannot push. Many, such as the biceps and triceps muscles in the upper arm, are arranged in opposing pairs. The biceps muscle in the arm contracts to pull on the forearm bones and bend the elbow. The triceps muscle in the arm contracts to straighten the elbow.

Epimysium (muscle sheath)

Fasciculus (bundle of fibers)

Healthy muscle has a good flow of oxygen.

Unhealthy muscle has fatty deposits.

INSIDE A MUSCLE
Each muscle consists of a bundle of thin fibers. Each of these fibers is made up of even smaller fibrils. Fibrils contain long, interlocking groups of molecules called actin and myosin. The muscle contracts by sliding actin and myosin molecules past each other in a ratchet fashion.

Muscle fiber

Muscle fibril

Find out more
BRAIN AND NERVES
HEART AND BLOOD
HUMAN BODY
LUNGS AND BREATHING
SKELETONS

MUSEUMS AND LIBRARIES

BUILDINGS THAT ARE USED FOR COLLECTING and displaying works of art or interesting objects are known as museums. Some museums contain general collections; others are more specialized. Museum staff, called curators, acquire and care for exhibits. They also study and keep records of the collection, preserve and restore exhibits, and make sure they are displayed to the public in an informative way. Libraries are collections of books and documents. The librarian's job includes classifying the books by subject, and ensuring that books can be found easily on the shelves. The first museums and libraries date back to ancient times. Today, people can visit museums and libraries in most cities for information on a huge range of topics.

This is how the ISBN appears.

ISBN BOOK CODE
Every book has an ISBN (International Standard Book Number). This number, in the form of a barcode, carries all the information that a library needs to catalog a book correctly.

This working model of a grain pit is hand-driven, enabling visitors to interact with the process.

GRAIN PIT

INTERACTIVE MUSEUM
The first publicaly funded museums were set up in the 19th century. Exhibits were displayed in glass cases and could not be touched. Today, especially in science museums, interactive displays using working models and computer technology encourage a more "hands-on" approach. Audio-visual guides also make a museum visit exciting.

LIBRARIES
The first public library opened in Athens, Greece, in 330 B.C. Until the 18th century, most libraries were reference libraries, where people could read books, but not take them away. Today, lending libraries let people borrow books to read at home.

School group investigating an interactive exhibit at the Science Museum, London.

Curved prow of Viking longboat

Children are allowed to touch and move the museum exhibit.

The Guggenheim Museum building is a work of art in itself.

ART GALLERIES
Museums that specialize in works of art are called art galleries. Major art galleries usually contain a range of different artworks, but some concentrate on one artist, or the art of a particular period. The new Guggenheim Museum in Bilbao, northern Spain, displays 20th-century American and European art.

LOCAL COLLECTIONS
The major national collections and specialized museums are usually found in the capital or big cities of the world, from the National Museum in Phnom Penh, Cambodia, through to the Natural History Museum in England. However, small towns and villages often contain a museum that houses a purely local collection.

SPECIALIZED MUSEUMS
Many museums specialize in one particular area. These include science museums, natural history museums, and those that concentrate on one particular period of history, such as the time of the Vikings. Many smaller museums started life as private collections, specializing in the interests of the original collector.

Find out more

BOOKS
EDUCATION
PAINTERS
REFERENCE BOOKS

MUSHROOMS,
TOADSTOOLS, AND OTHER FUNGI

BRIGHTLY COLORED TOADSTOOLS, delicate mushrooms, and the furry green mold on a rotting piece of bread all belong to a unique group of organisms called fungi. Fungi are neither plants nor animals. They are the great decomposers of the natural world. Fungi feed by releasing chemicals called enzymes that rot away whatever they are feeding on. The dissolved nutrients and minerals are absorbed and recycled by the fungi. Many kinds of fungi grow in damp woodlands and lush, grassy meadows, especially during the fall. There is no scientific difference between mushrooms and toadstools, but toadstools are often more colorful, and some are extremely poisonous.

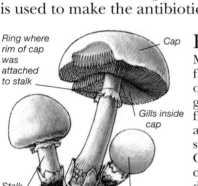

Champignon mushrooms grow in a ring in meadows and in gardens. Many people used to believe these were magic fairy rings.

The part of a mushroom that we eat is called the cap. It contains spores – minute cells that grow into new mushrooms when they are released from the cap. Some harmful fungi cause diseases on plants and ringworm in humans. Yeast is a fungus used to make bread dough rise. Another fungus is used to make the antibiotic drug penicillin.

MOLD
The decaying parts of plants and animals are rotted away by pinmold, which grows on damp bread, and is the blue mold growing on this peach.

Ring where rim of cap was attached to stalk

Cap

Gills inside cap

Stalk

Young cap

Spores are released from between the gills of mature caps.

EDIBLE FUNGI

Many mushrooms and other fungi are edible; some are not only delicious but also are a good source of minerals and fiber. Cultivated mushrooms are farmed in dark, damp sheds on beds of peat. Collecting wild fungi to eat can be very dangerous. Some deadly poisonous fungi look just like edible mushrooms.

OYSTER MUSHROOM
The oyster mushroom is common on beech trees; its cap looks like the shell of an oyster. Oyster mushrooms are tasty and keep well when they are dried.

BEEFSTEAK FUNGUS
This fungus grows on trees. It is called the beefsteak bracket because it looks like a piece of undercooked steak.

FIELD MUSHROOM
During the fall, field mushrooms spring up overnight in damp pastures and meadows.

MOREL
Prized for its flavor, the morel's cap is crisscrossed with patterned ridgework.

CHANTERELLE
The funnel-shaped cap of the chanterelle mushroom is yellow and smells like an apricot. It is found in oak, beech, and birch woods. It grows slowly, preserves well, and is much prized by chefs.

GIANT PUFFBALL
When the giant puffball ripens, its top breaks open, and clouds of tiny spores puff out with the slightest breeze or the smallest splattering of rain.

DUTCH ELM DISEASE
Dead and dying elm trees are a familiar sight in Europe and North America. A deadly fungus carried on the bodies of elm bark beetles, which live on elm trees, has killed millions of trees. The fungus grows through the bark, blocking the water-carrying tubes inside the trunk.

POISONOUS FUNGI

People die every year from eating poisonous fungi. Some of these are brightly colored toadstools that are easily recognized. Others, such as the destroying angel, look harmless, but cause death rapidly if they are eaten.

Death cup

The bright red fly agaric toadstool is poisonous. Small amounts can cause unconsciousness.

The harmless-looking death cup is one of the most poisonous fungi. Less than 1 oz (28 g) can kill a person in only a few hours.

Fly agaric

___ *Find out more* ___
DRUGS
FOOD
FOREST WILDLIFE
PLANTS
SOIL

MUSIC

MUSICIANS MAKE MUSIC by carefully organizing sounds into a regular, pleasing pattern that anyone can appreciate. Notes are the starting point for all music. A note is a regular vibration of the air that musicians create with musical instruments or with their voices. The more rapid the vibration, the higher the pitch of the note – the higher it sounds to a listener. Certain notes sound better together than others. Most music uses these notes, organized into a scale. A scale is a series of notes that increase gradually and regularly in pitch. Musicians usually play or sing notes at fixed time intervals. We call this regular pattern of notes the rhythm or meter of the music. A melody or tune is a combination of the rhythm, the notes the musician plays, and their order. The melody is the overall pattern that we hear and remember – and whistle or hum days or perhaps weeks later.

Ancient musicians of Ur in Sumer (now Iraq) played lutes, flutes, pipes, and percussion instruments.

THE FIRST MUSIC
The chanting of prehistoric people was probably the earliest music. The oldest surviving musical instruments are mammoth bones from northern Eurasia; musicians may have banged them together or blown them to make notes about 35,000 years ago.

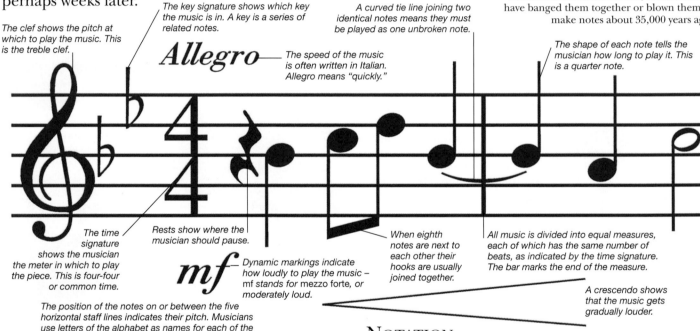

The clef shows the pitch at which to play the music. This is the treble clef.

The key signature shows which key the music is in. A key is a series of related notes.

A curved tie line joining two identical notes means they must be played as one unbroken note.

The speed of the music is often written in Italian. Allegro means "quickly."

The shape of each note tells the musician how long to play it. This is a quarter note.

The time signature shows the musician the meter in which to play the piece. This is four-four or common time.

Rests show where the musician should pause.

mf Dynamic markings indicate how loudly to play the music – mf stands for mezzo forte, or moderately loud.

When eighth notes are next to each other their hooks are usually joined together.

All music is divided into equal measures, each of which has the same number of beats, as indicated by the time signature. The bar marks the end of the measure.

A crescendo shows that the music gets gradually louder.

The position of the notes on or between the five horizontal staff lines indicates their pitch. Musicians use letters of the alphabet as names for each of the eight notes in an octave.

NOTATION

Composers need a way of writing down the music they create. Musical notation is a code of symbols and signs that records every aspect of the music. Monks were the first to use musical notation in the 9th century, to help them remember the tunes of holy songs. The system in use today had developed fully by about A.D. 1200.

JAZZ
The essential ingredient of jazz is improvisation – the musicians make up some or all of the music as they play it. Black musicians created the very first jazz music at the beginning of the 20th century in New Orleans, Louisiana. Jazz is a mixture of blues, religious gospel, and European music.

Charlie "Bird" Parker (1920-55) popularized a new form of jazz, called "bebop," in the 1940s.

CHAMBER MUSIC
Classical – rather than pop – music for small groups of instruments is called chamber music. Chamber music was so called because it began as music for enjoyment in chambers, or rooms, in the home. Composers wrote different types of music for theaters or churches. Today, performances of chamber music often take place in concert halls.

TRADITIONAL MUSIC

In much traditional music, the composer is unknown, and the music itself may not be written down. Performers are often non-professional musicians who learn the tunes "by ear" – by listening to each other play – so they do not need a written score. Musicians sometimes make small changes as they play, so there are often many slightly different versions of the same traditional melody.

Cheerleaders keep time with marching music and encourage spectators to join in songs and chants.

Buddhist monks blow large horns as part of their religious ceremonies.

RELIGIOUS MUSIC

Music has always played an important part in religion. In religious ceremonies, music inspires people to think about their God or gods. It accompanies religious songs and sacred dances. Composers also choose religious themes for music that is not part of worship: *Messiah* by the German composer George Frideric Handel (1685-1759) sets part of the Bible to music.

MILITARY AND MARCHING MUSIC

Music with a strong, steady beat helps soldiers march in step. Today, military bands are not the only ones to play marching music. High schools and football teams often have their own marching bands, which entertain the crowds at halftime and on special occasions.

ROCK MUSIC

During the 1950s, a new form of popular music was heard for the first time. Rock and roll songs had a powerful beat and words that young people could relate to. This form of music began in the United States, where it grew from traditional rhythm and blues played primarily by black musicians. Over the years it has influenced many other musical forms.

Singer Elvis Presley (1935-77) sold millions of rock and roll records and starred in 33 movies.

CLASSICAL MUSIC

Classical music has become increasingly popular in recent years, partly thanks to the efforts of young musicians such as violinist Vanessa Mae. Mae started writing her own music at age nine, and by age 18 had made several records and performed in classical concerts all over the world. She has also mixed classical with modern by combining the sounds of acoustic and electric violins.

Find out more
COMPOSERS
MUSICAL INSTRUMENTS
OPERA AND SINGING
ORCHESTRAS
ROCK AND POP

MUSICAL INSTRUMENTS

THE LOUD TWANG of an electric guitar might seem far removed from the delicate trill of a classical violin, yet these two instruments make their different sounds in a similar way. Both use a stretched string to create the vibrations we hear as music. The guitar and the violin evolved in a similar manner, but they actually belong to different families of musical instruments.

CONCH HORNS
Conch sea shells made fine trumpets in ancient times – as they still do in modern Peru.

String instruments such as the violin make their notes when the musician plucks the strings or draws a stretched bow – a bundle of horsehair – across them. Electric instruments, such as the electric guitar, produce weak vibrations that must be amplified for the audience to hear the music. There are five other instrument groups: woodwind, percussion, brass, keyboard, and electronic. This short list includes a huge variety: some instruments, such as the hollow wooden flute, are very simple; others, such as the synthesizer, are highly complex.

STRING INSTRUMENTS
Vibrating strings stretched across these instruments make the musical note: the finer the string and the shorter its length, the higher the note. The size of the instrument also affects its sound. The small violin, for example, produces higher sounds than the large double bass. Musicians pluck the strings of guitars, harps, and lutes, and usually use a bow to play the violin, viola, cello, and double bass.

Playing the violin

CELLO
The four cello strings make a rich, mellow sound.

VIOLIN
To play the violin the musician holds it under the chin.

WOODWIND INSTRUMENTS
Blowing into a woodwind instrument makes the air inside vibrate; this produces the musical notes. Covering the holes in the tube with fingers or keys changes the length of the vibrating air, producing different notes. The instruments with the shortest tubes, such as the piccolo, make the highest notes. Other woodwind instruments are the bassoon, English horn, saxophone, clarinet, oboe, and flute.

FLUTE
To play a side-blown flute such as this one, you blow across the tube.

Upper joint

Keys

Body joint

Keys

Head joint

Lip plate

Blowhole

Bell joint

Playing the oboe

Reed

OBOE
The mouthpiece of an oboe is a double reed (a piece of thin wood). The instrument makes a clear, sad sound.

A flautist playing a side-blown concert flute

Tip

Reed

OBOE REED
Most professional oboe players make their own reeds by binding two pieces of split cane to a tube called a staple.

Staple

A wood frame pulls horse-hair tight across the bow. Sliding the bow across the strings makes them vibrate.

BRASS

Some of the most exciting sounds in music come from brass instruments. This group includes the French horn, trumpet, bugle, cornet, trombone, and tuba. The instruments are long tubes of brass or other metal curved around for easier handling. Sounds produced by the musician's lips on the mouthpiece vibrate down the tube. Pressing the valves opens more of the tube, making the pitch of the note lower. The trumpet has a long history. When the Egyptians buried King Tutankhamun more than 3,000 years ago, they placed a trumpet in his tomb.

Playing the horn

THE CORNET
Musicians in military and brass bands often play the cornet, which is descended from the horns that were blown to announce the arrival of a mail coach. The cornet is one of the smallest brass instruments, with a tube about 4.5 ft (1.5 m) long.

Cornet player

FRENCH HORN

Uncurled, this horn is 16 ft (5 m) long. It developed from an 18th-century hunting horn and makes a rich, warm sound. The Austrian composer Wolfgang Amadeus Mozart created four pieces of music for the French horn.

PERCUSSION

Bells, gongs, and drums are percussion instruments. There are many more types of percussion instruments, because all over the world people find different objects, such as beads and seeds, that make a noise when beaten or shaken. Some percussion instruments, such as the xylophone and timpani, are tuned to play definite notes.

Bass strings

Treble strings

Tuning pins

Sounding board

SNARE DRUM
The wire spring on the bottom skin of the snare drum vibrates when the player strikes the top skin.

KEYBOARDS
Hammers strike strings in the piano when the pianist presses a key. Pedals keep the note sounding when the key is released. Electronic keyboards also create piano sounds.

Iron frame

Pedals

Keyboard

Dampers

Hammers

TRADITIONAL INSTRUMENTS

Musicians in symphony orchestras play only a few of the world's vast range of musical instruments. Many more are used in the traditional or folk music of individual countries. Some of these instruments developed unique shapes in different parts of the world, as musicians explored the music-making potential of local materials. However, some are remarkably similar: the bagpipes are played in Europe, Asia, and Africa.

A flute player from Thailand

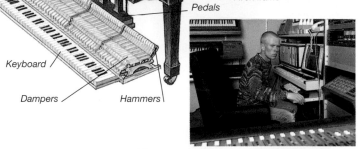

ELECTRONIC INSTRUMENTS

These instruments can produce an exciting array of sounds, by either simulating existing instruments or synthesizing completely new sounds. The musician can feed sounds into the memory of the instrument and then play them back together to simulate a whole orchestra.

Find out more

COMPOSERS
MUSIC
ORCHESTRAS
ROCK AND POP

MYTHS AND LEGENDS

THE TROJAN HORSE LEGEND
Greek soldiers conquered the besieged city of Troy by hiding in a huge wooden horse. When the Trojans took the horse inside the city walls, the Greeks emerged and conquered Troy.

BEFORE THERE WERE ANY BOOKS, storytelling was an important way of passing on knowledge and beliefs from one generation to the next. Often, the stories took the form of myths that explained mysteries of nature, such as the origins of thunder. Ancient peoples told stories about gods and goddesses, and about human heroes with special powers. These myths became part of art and literature. Legends, though, were often based on real people and real-life events. To make a better tale, parents exaggerated the details as they repeated the legends to their children. Every country has its own legends. Paul Bunyan, the hero of stories told by North American lumberjacks, supposedly carved out the Grand Canyon by dragging his pick behind him. Sometimes, legendary monsters were created, such as the werewolf that appears in stories from many cultures.

SUN GODS
The same myths can be found in widely different cultures thousands of miles apart. This is because natural things such as the rain, the sea, and the moon are common to everyone. Many peoples worshiped sun gods: Surya in India and Apollo in Ancient Greece were both believed to ride across the sky in chariots of flame.

The Indian sun god, Surya – as painted on a doorway in Jaipur, India

The Egyptian sun god, Ra

CREATION MYTHS
Most peoples used myths to explain how the world may have begun. This Native American myth was told by members of the Kwakiutl tribe.

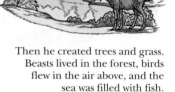

A raven, flying over water, could find nowhere to land. He decided to create the world by dropping small pebbles to make islands.

Then he created trees and grass. Beasts lived in the forest, birds flew in the air above, and the sea was filled with fish.

After many failed attempts, the raven succeeded in making the first man and woman out of clay and wood. At last, his world was complete.

WILLIAM TELL
A famous Swiss legend describes how William Tell insulted his country's hated Austrian rulers. His punishment was to shoot an apple balanced on his son's head. He succeeded, and later led a revolt against Austrian rule.

GODS AND GODDESSES
The ancient Greeks worshiped many gods and goddesses. The goddess Athena took part in battles and loved bravery. Athens, the capital of Greece, is named after her. Quetzalcoatl appears in Mexican mythology as one of the greatest Aztec gods. As god of air, Quetzalcoatl created the winds that blew away the rain.

Athena, the Greek goddess of bravery

Quetzalcoatl, the Mexican god of air

Find out more
GREECE, ANCIENT
LITERATURE
RELIGIONS

NAPOLEON BONAPARTE

IN A LAVISH CEREMONY IN 1804, Napoleon Bonaparte crowned himself Emperor of the French. He was an unlikely figure to lead his country, and spoke French with a thick Corsican accent. Yet he was one of the most brilliant military leaders in history. Napoleon first caught the public eye in 1793, when he commanded an attack against the British fleet occupying the French port of Toulon. In 1795, he crushed a revolt in Paris and soon led the French armies to victory in Italy. By 1799, Napoleon was strong enough to take power with the help of the army. He made himself First Consul and restored the power of the French government after the chaos left by the French Revolution. He introduced many social reforms, laying the foundations of the French legal, educational, and financial systems. Napoleon was a military genius who went on to control Europe from the English Channel to the Russian border. But he suffered a humiliating defeat in Russia, and when the British and Prussians beat him at the Battle of Waterloo in 1815, Napoleon was sent out of France into exile on a British island in the South Atlantic. He died six years later.

August 15 1769 Born on the island of Corsica.

1779-84 Military school

1799 Becomes ruler of France.

1804 Crowned Emperor.

1812 Defeated in Russia.

1814 Exiled to island of Elba in the Mediterranean.

1815 Returns to France; defeated at Waterloo.

May 5 1821 Dies in exile on the island of St. Helena.

NAPOLEONIC EMPIRE

At the height of his power in 1812, Napoleon ruled Europe from the Baltic to the south of Rome, and his relations ruled Spain, Italy, and parts of Germany. The rest of Germany, Switzerland, and Poland were also under French control; and Denmark, Austria, and Prussia were allies. Only Portugal, Britain, Sweden, and Russia were independent.

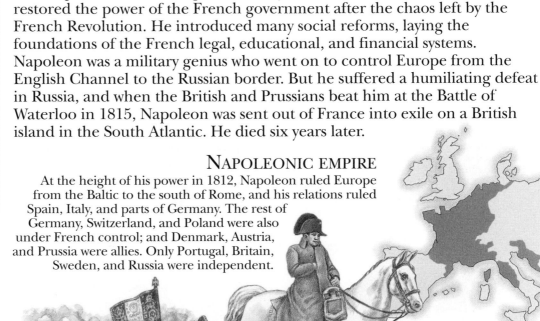

EMPEROR
On December 2, 1804, Napoleon crowned himself Emperor of the French in a ceremony at Notre Dame Cathedral in Paris. He had already changed his Italian-sounding name, Buonaparte, to the French name of Bonaparte. Now he was to be known as Napoleon I.

1812 AND THE RETREAT FROM MOSCOW
Napoleon invaded Russia in June 1812 with a force of more than 500,000 men. The Russians retreated, drawing the French army deeper into the country. Napoleon captured the capital, Moscow, but was forced to retreat because he could not supply his army. The harsh Russian winter killed many troops as they returned to France.

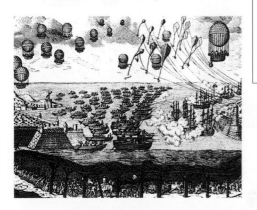

INVASION OF ENGLAND
In 1805, Napoleon assembled an army of 140,000 soldiers by the English Channel and drew up plans to invade England which he called "a nation of shopkeepers." These plans included crossing the Channel by ship and balloon, and digging a tunnel under the sea. The invasion was canceled when the British admiral Nelson defeated the French fleet at the Battle of Trafalgar.

Find out more

FRANCE, HISTORY OF
FRENCH REVOLUTION
NAPOLEONIC WARS

NAPOLEONIC WARS

TWO CENTURIES AGO, a series of bloody wars engulfed Europe, causing hardship to millions of people and disrupting trade. Sparked by the French Revolution, the Napoleonic Wars began in 1792 and continued for nearly a quarter of a century. On one side was revolutionary France, and on the other the old kingdoms of Britain, Austria, Russia, and Prussia. At first the countries encircling France fought the new republic because they wanted to put down the revolution. But after Napoleon became ruler in 1799, the French conquered most of Europe, until only Britain remained free. The French army was the most powerful in Europe, but paying the troops required high taxes. Too few people volunteered to join the army, so the government had to force people to fight. These measures were unpopular in the countries that France occupied, and led to revolts in Spain and elsewhere.

SPANISH CAMPAIGN
Napoleon invaded Spain in 1808 and put his brother on the Spanish throne. The Spanish fought back with what they called a guerrilla or "little war." Many were executed or died in the fighting.

NAPOLEONIC WARS

1792 France declares war on Austria.

1793 France declares war on Britain, Holland, and Spain.

1799 Napoleon takes power.

1803 Britain declares war on France.

1805 Napoleon defeats Russians and Austrians.

1806 Defeats Prussians.

1807 Defeats Russians at Friedland.

1808 France occupies Spain and Portugal.

1812 Napoleon's invasion of Russia ends in disaster.

1813 Austrians, Prussians, and Russians defeat Napoleon at Leipzig.

1814 Napoleon exiled to island of Elba, off Italy.

1815 Napoleon escapes, marches on Paris. Final defeat at Waterloo.

French field gun unit artillery

WAR ON LAND
Napoleon organized his army brilliantly. His genius lay in making the right decisions at the right time and in using his forces in the most effective way. With superior tactics he often beat far larger forces.

BATTLE OF TRAFALGAR
Horatio Nelson was an admiral in the British navy. At the battle of Trafalgar in 1805, Nelson destroyed the French fleet by attacking in a fan formation, rather than by sailing side by side, as the French had expected. He died in the battle.

How Nelson attacked the French fleet

Traditional sea battle

BATTLE OF THE PYRAMIDS
In July 1798, Napoleon conquered Egypt, which was then part of the Ottoman Empire. At the Battle of the Pyramids, he defeated the Mamelukes who ruled the country.

DUKE OF WELLINGTON
"A Wellington Boot, or the Head of the Army." Cartoons made fun of everyone who took part in the wars, including the Duke of Wellington, the British army commander who defeated Napoleon at Waterloo.

Find out more

FRANCE, HISTORY OF
NAPOLEON BONAPARTE
SPAIN, HISTORY OF

NATIONAL PARKS

Bridal Veil Falls, Yosemite National Park, California

FROM THE DEPTHS of the Grand Canyon to the peaks of Denali, every American can share in the country's scenic and historic places through the national park system. The first national park, Yellowstone, was established by an act of Congress in 1872. Today there are more than 370 national park areas in the United States. The spectacular landscapes of the best known parks – Yellowstone, the Grand Canyon, Yosemite, and the Great Smoky Mountains – attract tourists from all over the world.

The park system also helps preserve America's heritage, from seashores and highways to battlefields and monuments.

Surveyors camp in the Yellowstone region, 1871.

PRESERVING THE PARKS

America's national parks attract millions of visitors each year, drawn by the incredible scenery as well as the many opportunities for outdoor recreation. Most Americans live within a day's drive of a park, making it an ideal tourist destination. Overcrowding in some parks led to the founding of the National Parks Association in 1919, to help preserve the park system.

THE FIRST PARK

In 1870, members of an expedition exploring the Yellowstone region in Wyoming came up with the idea of preserving the land by giving it to the nation. The following summer, the government sent a geologist to survey the region. His report, and the enthusiastic support of the public, helped persuade Congress to set aside the area for the enjoyment of all the people. In 1872, President Ulysses S. Grant signed the bill that established Yellowstone as the first national park.

Grand Canyon park ranger

Alcatraz Island, San Francisco

URBAN PARKS

Not all national parks are located in remote areas. The largest and most popular urban park is the Golden Gate National Recreation Area, in San Francisco, California. More than 19 million people visit the park each year. Alcatraz Island, site of a former maximum-security federal prison, is found within the park's boundaries.

HISTORIC PLACES

The park system was expanded in 1906 to include national monuments – landmarks and structures of historic or scientific interest. These include sites such as the ancient cave dwellings in the Bandelier National Monument (left) and the Gila Cliff Dwellings, both in New Mexico, as well as early colonial settlements. In 1933, the park service was given control of military landmarks such as historic battlefields from the Revolutionary and Civil Wars.

OUTDOOR CLASSROOMS

Archaeologists, naturalists, and historians work at most national parks, often leading educational programs that help teach park visitors about their surroundings. Archaeologists can be seen excavating dinosaur bones in parks such as the Dinosaur National Monument, Utah (above).

NATIONAL PARK SERVICE

The National Park Service was established in 1916 to maintain and administer the park areas. Each park has a resident superintendent, assisted by a team of park rangers. Rangers build roads, trails, and campsites, run park museums, and offer tours and talks to visitors.

Find out more

ARCHAEOLOGY
CONSERVATION
and endangered species
NORTH AMERICAN WILDLIFE

NATIVE AMERICANS

THE FIRST PEOPLE to live in North America arrived from Asia more than 20,000 years ago. They wandered over the Bering Strait, which was a land bridge at the time and now separates Asia and North America, following animals they were hunting. Gradually these early people settled into different tribes. Over the centuries the tribes developed organized societies. During the 1500s, Europeans arrived in North America for the first time. They thought they were in the "Indies," or Asia, so they called the Native Americans "Indians," a misleading name. The Europeans wanted land and threatened the existence of native North Americans. The natives fought many wars with the new settlers. During the 1800s, the tribes resisted when the United States government tried to make them leave their homelands. After a bitter struggle, the Native Americans were moved onto reservations – areas of land set aside for them – where many still live today.

Smoke flap open for ventilation

Straight poles are bound together at the top to form a cone shape.

Bison hide was used to make the tepee cover.

WOMEN
Women played an important part in the life of a tribe. They provided the food, made the clothes, and raised the children. The women of the Hopi Indians of the Southwest also owned the houses and organized the village.

Lodge pins made from bone held the hides together.

Paintings that told a story decorated the hides.

Door flap

TEPEES
The Sioux and other tribes on the Great Plains lived in tepees. Tepees were made of bison hides stretched over a wooden frame and were easy to put up. Flaps at the top of the tepee could be opened to allow smoke from the fire to escape.

A fire was lit inside the tepee for cooking and warmth.

GERONIMO
One of the most successful native chiefs in leading resistance to the "white man" was Geronimo (1829-1909), of the Chiricahua Apache Indians. Geronimo led raids across the southwestern states and into Mexico. In 1886, he was captured and exiled to Florida. Later he was released and became a national celebrity.

SIGN LANGUAGE
Each tribe of the natives spoke its own language. But people from different tribes were able to communicate with each other using a special sign language they all understood.

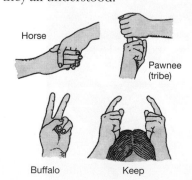

Horse

Pawnee (tribe)

Buffalo

Keep

TRIBES
The native peoples of North America belonged to numerous tribes. Most of them hunted, fished, and farmed. Among the best known tribes are the Cheyenne, Comanche, and Sioux, who lived on the Great Plains; the Apache, Navajo, and Pueblo, who lived in the Southwest; and the Iroquois, Huron, and Cherokee, who lived in the East.

CANOES

Northern tribes who lived by rivers and lakes, such as the Penobscot and Malecite, built canoes from the bark of birch trees. These strong, fast canoes were light enough to be carried overland when they could not be paddled.

Bark hull — *Paddles*

SIOUX

The Sioux lived on the Great Plains. They hunted bison on horseback, using the skins for clothing and tepees, the meat for food, and the bones and horns for tools. The Sioux were noted for their bravery and fighting skills and fought a long series of battles with European settlers and gold miners who took over their territory in the 1880s. In 1876, the Sioux defeated the US cavalry at the now famous Battle of the Little Bighorn in Montana. Eventually the Sioux were driven onto reservations.

WEAPONS

Natives used bows and arrows, knives, and clubs as weapons. Many also carried tomahawks. During the 16th century, they got rifles from European traders.

Bow, made of wood

Quiver, used for holding arrows

Bow case holds the bow when not in use.

Tomahawks were axes with stone or iron heads. It was the Europeans who first made a combined ax blade and tobacco pipe.

PUEBLOS

The Pueblos were a peaceful tribe that lived in the southwest. They farmed vegetables for food and were skilled craftsworkers, weaving brightly-colored cloth from homespun cotton and making pots. Their multistoried houses were built of stone or adobe (sun-dried clay bricks) and were occupied by several families. Today, many Pueblos live on reservations in Arizona and New Mexico.

CRAFTSWORK

Many natives were skilled craftsworkers. They produced beautifully decorated clothes and headdresses. This pair of men's moccasins, from the Blackfeet tribe of western Canada, are made of stitched leather decorated with leather thongs and embroidered with colored beads.

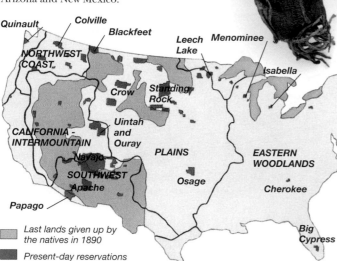

Quinault · *Colville* · *Blackfeet*
NORTHWEST COAST
Leech Lake · *Menominee*
Crow · *Standing Rock* · *Isabella*
CALIFORNIA-INTERMOUNTAIN
Uintah and Ouray
PLAINS
Navajo
SOUTHWEST
Apache · *Osage*
Papago
EASTERN WOODLANDS
Cherokee
Big Cypress

Last lands given up by the natives in 1890

Present-day reservations

TRIBAL LANDS

Before the Europeans arrived, the natives occupied most of what later became the United States. The tribes were roughly grouped into six geographical regions. European settlement gradually forced the natives to the west and southwest, so that by 1890 they were living on a few scattered reservations.

MODERN RESERVATIONS

The 1.5 million natives in the United States live on reservations that they govern themselves. The Navajo reservation, for example, covers over 15 million acres in Arizona, New Mexico, and Utah. Recently, several tribes, such as the Pacific Northwest Coast Indians, have protested successfully and regained lost land.

Find out more
AZTECS
CANADA, HISTORY OF
INCAS
SIGNS AND SYMBOLS
UNITED STATES, HISTORY OF

NAVIES

IN THE DAYS BEFORE cars and aircraft, sea travel was the fastest way to get around the world. However, sea travel was also dangerous: pirates robbed cargo ships, and in wartime opposing countries raided each other's vessels. The Ancient Greeks, Persians, and Romans were among the first to build ships for war at sea. In the 16th century, European nations organized navies as a way of protecting civilian shipping from attack. They used the ships to defend cargo and passenger vessels visiting their new colonies overseas. In wartime, modern navies do their traditional job. They guard merchant ships and sail out in groups, or fleets, to attack the enemy until the sea is secure for trade again. Naval ships also transport soldiers to war zones and supply invasion forces with food and ammunition. In peacetime the oceans are safe for shipping, so navies train for war and are useful in other ways. Sailors help with rescue work after an earthquake or hurricane. Navies also pay goodwill visits to promote friendship between countries.

PRESS GANG
An 18th-century sailor's life was harsh, and few volunteered. The press gang forced or "impressed" men to join the navy. The sailors in the press gang kidnapped those who refused to join.

BATTLE OF TRAFALGAR
The first navies relied on wind power, and sea battles were tests of both fighting and sailing skills. At the Battle of Trafalgar in 1805, the British navy defeated a combined French and Spanish fleet, sinking or capturing more than half the enemy ships.

AIRCRAFT CARRIERS
Fighter planes based on aircraft carriers defend the fleet from enemy air attack. The runway deck is short, so a catapult gives airplanes added power for takeoff. Carriers are huge and have few guns, and other warships must protect them in battles.

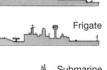

Aircraft carrier

Destroyer

Frigate

Submarine

Patrol craft

NAVAL SHIPS
A navy needs many different ships. Aircraft carriers act as floating airfields. Fast-moving destroyers and frigates attack enemy ships. Nuclear submarines defend the fleet and carry missiles to hit targets on land. Patrol craft are very fast and are used to defend ports and other land sites.

Parking area

Aircraft on the hangar deck are raised on giant elevators for takeoff.

To increase launch speed and give aircraft added lift, the carrier steams into the wind while aircraft takeoff.

Takeoff area is short, so steam catapults give aircraft extra speed.

Aircraft wings fold to save storage space.

Crew's living quarters

USS FORRESTAL
A typical aircraft carrier, such as the USS Forrestal of the United States navy, carries about 90 aircraft. Most are fighters, but one fifth are used as supply planes or for scouting. Most of the interior of the ship is taken up by hangars, repair areas, and ammunition stores.

UNIFORMS
Each nation has its own naval uniform, carrying information about the person wearing it. There are many different tasks on board a ship; jobs also vary from ship to ship. These uniforms therefore vary, too. For example, a gunner on a destroyer wears a helmet, and a deckhand on an aircraft carrier wears goggles and earphones.

United States   United Kingdom   China   Russia

Find out more
NAVIGATION
SHIPS AND BOATS
WARSHIPS
WORLD WAR I
WORLD WAR II

NAVIGATION

EVEN IN A CITY with signs and street names to help you, it is easy to get lost. But imagine if you were out in open country or sailing in a boat without a map. How would you find your way? The earliest sailors faced this problem as they made their voyages of discovery. The answer was to watch the Sun by day and the stars by night. Because the Sun always rises in the east and sets in the west, sailors could work out in which direction they were traveling. The position of stars in the sky also gave them their direction: Polaris, the North Star, for instance, is almost in line with the Earth's North Pole. Navigation is the process of working out where you are and in which direction you are traveling. This can be on land, at sea, or in the air. Today, navigators have many aids to help them find their way. There are detailed maps of almost every part of the world, and electronic systems which use radar and satellites can fix the position of an aircraft or ship to within a few hundred yards. Such advances in navigation make even the longest journey easy and safe.

MAP AND COMPASS
Marks on a map show paths, hills, and other features. A magnetic compass shows which way to point a map so that it represents the landscape. The Chinese first used magnetic compasses about 1,000 years ago; about 2300 B.C. the first map was drawn in Babylon.

NAVIGATION SYSTEMS

Today, ships and aircraft travel around the world without danger of becoming lost. Navigators use a gyrocompass, which gives the direction of travel more precisely than a magnetic compass. Ships and airplanes have electronic navigation systems which guide them automatically. In the Global Positioning System (GPS), computers can calculate the position of an aircraft, ship, or vehicle on the basis of satellite signals.

Radar warns a navigator of nearby objects such as other boats or aircraft. A radar scanner sends out a beam of radio waves as it rotates, and receives the echoes bouncing back from any object within range.

For safety, a boat or aircraft traveling at night carries a red light on the port side (left) and a green light on the starboard side (right). This tells others the direction it is traveling in.

Navigation satellites beam radio signals to Earth. A computer on board a boat or airplane uses these signals to guide the vessel anywhere in the world with great precision.

A radio receiver on board a boat compares the times that signals arrive from land-based radio beacons and uses this information to calculate the boat's position. This system is called radio direction finding.

SEXTANT
For more than 250 years, navigators have used a device called a sextant. A sextant gives a measurement of the angle between two objects in the sky, such as two stars. From this angle, it is possible to calculate the position of a ship or an aircraft.

Buoy with radar reflector

A sonic depth finder measures depth of water, which is important for navigating around coasts. It beams high-pitched sound waves toward the sea bed. The time taken for the echo to return gives the depth.

LIGHTHOUSE
Coastal waters can be dangerous because of rocks and tides. Lighthouses send out a bright beam of light to warn ships. The interval at which the light flashes identifies the lighthouse and so helps navigators find their position.

BUOYS
Floating markers called buoys mark dangers such as hidden rocks. Buoys either mark a safe channel or indicate the dangerous areas themselves. The shape and color of the buoys show on which side a boat should pass.

AUTOPILOT
The autopilot will keep a boat or a plane on a chosen course by adjusting the steering gear automatically. The autopilot of an airliner controls the plane for most of its flight. Some computerized autopilot systems can even guide a plane through takeoff and landing.

Find out more
AIRCRAFT
MAGNETISM
MAPS
RADAR
SATELLITES
SHIPS AND BOATS

NESTS AND BURROWS

MOST ANIMALS need shelter and a place to bring up their young. A nest in a tree or a burrow underground protects an animal against predators and extremes of temperature. Many creatures, including birds and squirrels, build nests. Some creatures weave complicated nests. The harvest mouse makes a ball-shaped nest among cornstalks, where it rests and sleeps. Other animals, including birds, build a nest only during the breeding season, in which they lay eggs or give birth to live young. They line the nest with moss, grass, fur, or feathers to keep it warm and dry. Rabbits and foxes dig burrows, or tunnels, in the ground; a desert tortoise digs a burrow in which to hide from the midday sun. Some burrows are shallow; others, such as rabbit warrens, are deep, with escape routes, dead ends, and a separate burrow for the breeding nest.

Nesting boxes and dovecotes encourage many birds to breed in the same place each year.

Natural building materials from the surrounding area, such as lichens, help camouflage the nest.

Nest has a soft, thick lining of moss, hair, and feathers to keep eggs warm.

Flamingo nests are cone-shaped and made of mud.

Wagtail weaves twigs and stems together to strengthen the nest.

FLAMINGO
Many animals, such as these African flamingos, nest in large groups called colonies. When a predator approaches, flamingos make such a noise that few predators dare to enter the colony. In a flamingo colony there is safety in numbers.

NESTS
Many birds spend weeks making a nest in a sheltered place. Each kind of bird has its favorite materials, such as twigs, grass, or fur. Each also chooses a particular place to make the nest, such as a tree or a spot on the ground. A pied wagtail, for example, often builds its nest around farm buildings and uses twigs, straw, leaves, and moss, with a lining of hair and feathers. A gray wagtail builds its nest beside fast-flowing water and uses grasses and moss, with a lining of hair.

TRAP-DOOR SPIDER
The trap-door spider digs a small burrow in loose soil and hides in it. Using silk that it produces from its body, the spider glues particles of soil together to make a neatly fitting, well-disguised door. As an insect or other prey passes by, the spider flips open the door and grabs the victim.

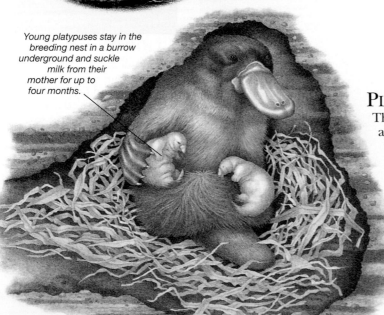

Young platypuses stay in the breeding nest in a burrow underground and suckle milk from their mother for up to four months.

PLATYPUS BURROW
The Australian platypus digs a complex breeding burrow up to 66 ft (20 m) long in the riverbank. Here, the female lays eggs and raises the young when they hatch. Each time the platypus enters or leaves the burrow to feed, it digs its way out and rebuilds the series of doors made of mud along the tunnel to protect its young from intruders.

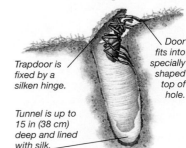

Trapdoor is fixed by a silken hinge.

Door fits into specially shaped top of hole.

Tunnel is up to 15 in (38 cm) deep and lined with silk.

Find out more
ANTS AND TERMITES
BEES AND WASPS
BIRDS
MICE, RATS, AND SQUIRRELS
RABBITS AND HARES

NEWSPAPERS

THE PAGES OF A NEWSPAPER keep everyone in touch with local, national, and world events. Newspapers provide more details about events than television news programs have time for, and stories in the paper cover a wide range of topics. In addition to news, there is information about politics, the arts, sports, fashion, business, technology, and the environment. Newspapers also contain opinions or points of view; some newspapers support a political party, and others try to remain independent. Local newspapers concentrate on events in one city or neighborhood; national newspapers sell countrywide and cover events at home and overseas. A big newspaper has a large staff of editors, reporters, feature writers, cartoonists, photographers, typesetters, printers, and many others who work through the night to deliver the latest news each morning. Many newspapers are also published on the Internet.

THE BROADSIDE
Before the first newspaper was published in 17th-century Germany, people read the news in "broadsides." These were single sheets of printed paper.

ON THE NEWSSTAND
Every country has its own newspapers. Some are published daily, others weekly. Some sell millions of copies a day, others just a few thousand a week. Each newspaper has a unique format – a special type style and general layout that sets it apart from others on the newsstand.

International Herald Tribune

France

Spain

International Arabic paper

NEWSROOM
The heart of a newspaper is the newsroom or editorial room. Here, national news and reports from all over the world come pouring in via the telephone, fax machine, and Internet. Here, too, reporters write their stories, assistant editors check them, and editors make decisions about how important each story is and which to include in the newspaper.

PRINTING PRESS
The thunder of the press shakes the floor as it prints newspapers each night. Huge reels of paper up to 5 miles (8 km) long roar through the press. Some machines can print, fold, cut, and stack more than 1,000 newspapers a minute. Trucks and trains rush them to newsstands so people can buy them first thing in the morning.

Short pieces of text called captions explain what is happening in the pictures.

FRONT PAGE
Big headlines and photographs of important, newsworthy events feature on the front page. In an eventful day the editor may need to change the lead story several times before the last copies of the paper are printed. Front pages carry the news that makes history – the outbreak of war, for example, or a major disaster such as the sinking of the *Titanic*.

> **Find out more**
> ADVERTISING
> CARTOONS
> INFORMATION TECHNOLOGY
> MAGAZINES
> PRINTING

NEW ZEALAND

New Zealand lies in the Pacific Ocean, east of Australia. There are two large islands – the North Island and the South Island – and many smaller ones, making a total area of 103,733 sq miles (268,670 sq km).

THE ISLAND NATION of New Zealand is a fascinating mixture of cultures and peoples. Maori people were the original inhabitants of the country, which they call Aotearoa; and they still live there, together with the descendants of the early British settlers and immigrants from other European and Asian countries. Only 3.9 million people live in New Zealand, and there are few large towns. The people are young – more than half of them are less than 35 years old – and the number of births per 1,000 of population is among the highest of all developed nations. A former British colony, New Zealand became fully independent in 1947. It is a leading Pacific nation and has strong links with many of the small islands in the region, such as Niue. The landscape of New Zealand is varied. There are towering mountains, glaciers, volcanoes, lakes, hot springs, sandy beaches, rolling hills, and plains.

KIWI
New Zealand lies far from other land masses, and as a result its wildlife has developed in an unusual way. The kiwi, which cannot fly, is the most famous of all New Zealand creatures. There are several other species of flightless birds.

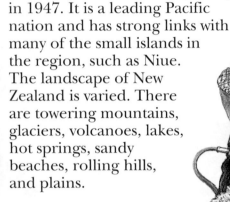

Sheep shearers work very quickly: some can clip a lamb in under a minute.

WELLINGTON

The capital of New Zealand is Wellington, which stands at the southern tip of the North Island. The city lies around a large natural harbor and is a busy port. Older wooden buildings stand close to recent structures built in a more modern style.

MAORI CULTURE
The Maoris, a Polynesian people, arrived in New Zealand around 950 A.D. from islands in the Pacific. Today their descendants keep alive the rich culture of wood carving, weaving, and music and dance, which they brought with them.

FARMING

New Zealand has a warm, moist climate which is ideal for many types of farming. Sheep and cattle ranching are the biggest businesses. There are two cattle and 13 sheep for every human in New Zealand. The country exports more dairy products and lamb than any other nation and is the second largest exporter of wool. Over the past 15 years production of other crops, such as kiwi fruit, oranges, and lemons, has increased. Newly built fishing boats have helped New Zealand's fleet increase its catch, and today the country is a major seafood exporter.

SOUTH ISLAND

Although the South Island is the largest New Zealand island, it has fewer inhabitants than the North Island. The western side of the island is covered by the Southern Alps, a region of mountains and glaciers, parts of which have not been explored. The rest of the island consists of farmland, grazing land for sheep and cattle, and a few ports and coastal cities.

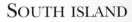

Find out more

COOK, JAMES
MOUNTAINS
NEW ZEALAND, HISTORY OF
OSTRICHES AND EMUS
PACIFIC OCEAN

Volcano   **Mountain**   **Ancient monument**   **Capital city**   **Large city/ town**   **Small city/ town**

STATISTICS

Area: 103,730 sq miles (268,680 sq km)

Population: 3,900,000

Capital: Wellington

Languages: English, Maori

Religions: Anglican, Presbyterian, Roman Catholic, Methodist, non-religious

Currency: New Zealand dollar

Main occupations: Agriculture

Main exports: Butter, wool, lamb, fruit, vegetables, fish, cork, wood, textiles

Main imports: Manufactured goods, iron, steel

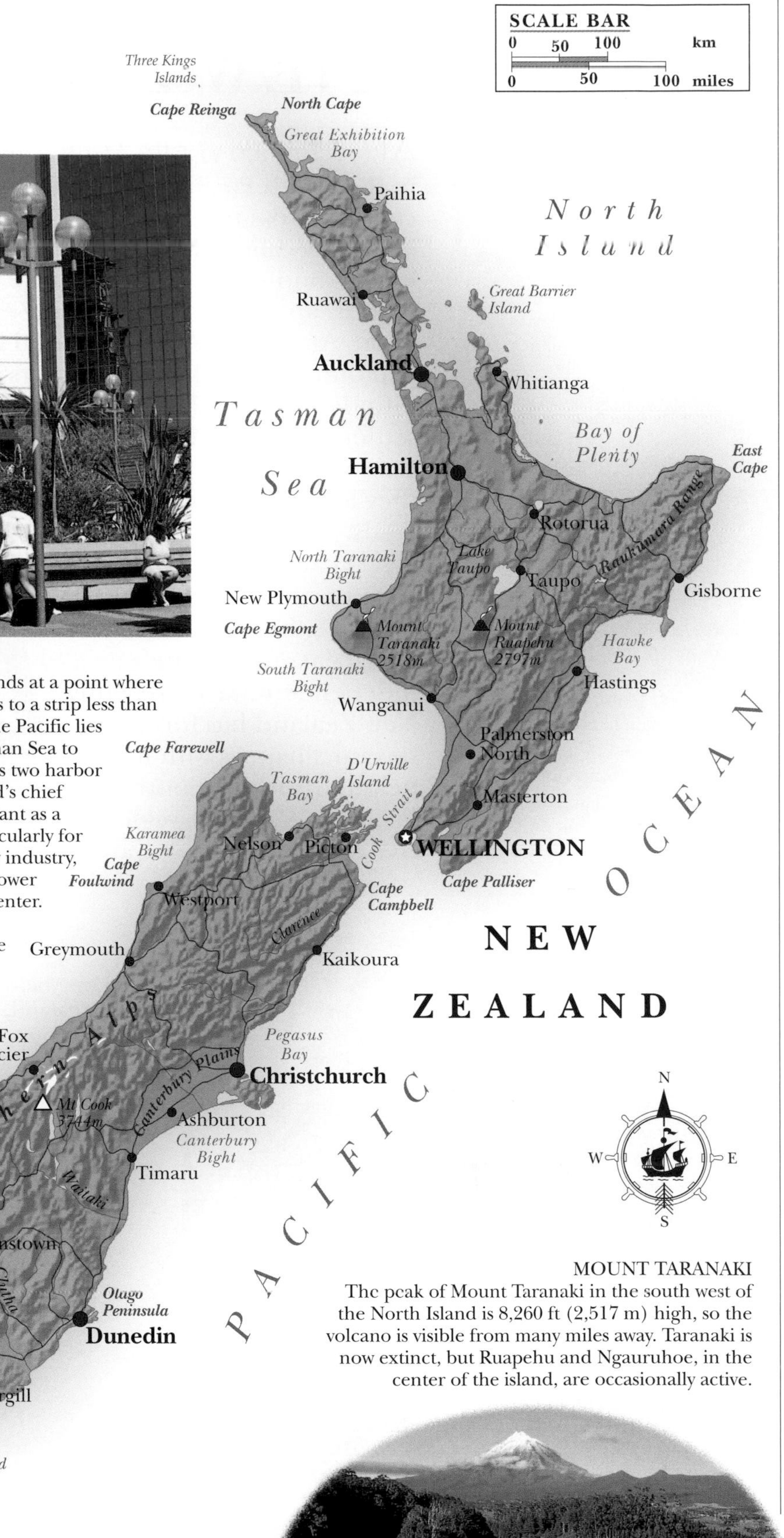

SOUTHERN ALPS

On the west coast of the South Island the Southern Alps nearly reach the shore of the Tasman Sea. The terrain is mountainous and steep, with only a few passes between the east and west coasts.

Sutherland Falls, 1,904 ft (580 m)

Aged 19, Jonah Lomu (right) became the youngest ever All Black team member. He was voted player of the tournament at the 1995 World Cup.

AUCKLAND

The city of Auckland stands at a point where the North Island narrows to a strip less than 1 mile (1.5 km) wide. The Pacific lies to the east, and the Tasman Sea to the west, so Auckland has two harbor areas and is New Zealand's chief port. Auckland is important as a distribution center, particularly for New Zealand's vital dairy industry, and high-rise buildings tower over the city's business center. Auckland has a mixed population: a third of the people who live in the city are Polynesian.

RUGBY

Rugby is New Zealand's favorite sport. The national team, the All Blacks, are world famous. They are named after their black shirt and shorts. The All Blacks perform the *haka*, a Maori dance, before each international game. Rugby was introduced to New Zealand by Charles John Monro, a New Zealander educated in England. The first game was played by Nelson College and Nelson Football Club in 1870.

MOUNT TARANAKI

The peak of Mount Taranaki in the south west of the North Island is 8,260 ft (2,517 m) high, so the volcano is visible from many miles away. Taranaki is now extinct, but Ruapehu and Ngauruhoe, in the center of the island, are occasionally active.

Map labels: Three Kings Islands, Cape Reinga, North Cape, Great Exhibition Bay, Paihia, North Island, Ruawai, Great Barrier Island, Auckland, Whitianga, Tasman Sea, Bay of Plenty, East Cape, Hamilton, Rotorua, Raukumara Range, North Taranaki Bight, Lake Taupo, Taupo, Gisborne, New Plymouth, Mount Taranaki 2518m, Mount Ruapehu 2797m, Hawke Bay, Cape Egmont, South Taranaki Bight, Hastings, Wanganui, Cape Farewell, D'Urville Island, Palmerston North, Tasman Bay, Masterton, Karamea Bight, Nelson, Picton, Cook Strait, WELLINGTON, Cape Foulwind, Cape Campbell, Cape Palliser, Westport, Clarence, NEW ZEALAND, Greymouth, Kaikoura, South Island, Fox Glacier, Southern Alps, Pegasus Bay, Christchurch, Mt Cook 3744m, Canterbury Plains, Ashburton, Waitaki, Canterbury Bight, Milford Sound, Fiordland, Lake Wakatipu, Timaru, Lake Te Anau, Queenstown, Clutha, Te Anau, Otago Peninsula, Dunedin, Waiau, Invercargill, Foveaux Strait, Stewart Island, South West Cape, PACIFIC OCEAN

HISTORY OF
NEW ZEALAND

ABOUT 1,000 YEARS AGO, a group of people landed on a string of islands in the South Pacific. These people were the Maoris, and they had traveled in canoes across the Pacific Ocean from the distant islands of Polynesia to a land they called Aotearoa. For about 700 years, the Maoris lived on the islands undisturbed. In 1642, the Dutch Explorer Abel Tasman visited the islands, and named them New Zealand, after a province in the Netherlands. Soon, American, Australian, and European sealers and whalers were exploiting the rich coastal waters and in 1840, the British founded the first European settlement. The Maoris fought the settlers until 1870, when they lost control of their lands. As a British colony, New Zealand grew wealthy by exporting its agricultural produce. In 1907, New Zealand became independent. More recently, New Zealand has formed several alliances with its neighbors in the South Pacific to keep the region free from nuclear weapons.

MAORIS

Long before the Europeans arrived in New Zealand, the Maoris had established a thriving agricultural community. They grew sweet potatoes and caught fish and fowl. They wore colorful clothes woven from flax. They lived in houses made of rushes and wood. Today, more than 500,000 Maoris still exist, most of whom live on the North Island.

Traditional Maori cloak made out of feathers

Protestors try to interrupt the path of a nuclear submarine.

TREATY OF WAITANGI
In 1840, the Maoris granted sovereignty, or ownership, of their country to Britain. In return, Britain promised protection of their rights and property. New Zealand then became a colony of the British Empire.

INDEPENDENCE
In 1852, Britain granted New Zealand self-government. The country gave pensions to workers and was the first in the world to give women the right to vote. In 1907, New Zealand gained full independence, but ties with Britain remained strong. The British monarch, Queen Elizabeth II, seen here with Prince Philip in a traditional Maori cloak, is the nation's head of state.

NUCLEAR-FREE ZONE
In 1983, antinuclear protesters blockaded the USS *Phoenix* nuclear submarine in Auckland Harbour. In 1985, New Zealand signed the treaty of Rarotonga, which declared the South Pacific region to be a nuclear-free zone. When France continued to carry out nuclear tests in Mururoa Atoll, in the South Pacific Ocean, these were fiercely opposed by other Pacific countries.

Find out more

COOK, JAMES
EXPLORERS
NEW ZEALAND

NORMANS

BAYEUX TAPESTRY
Dating from the 11th century, the Bayeux tapestry was produced to record the Norman Conquest of England. It shows scenes of battle, and can be seen today at Bayeux, in France.

TODAY, SOLID STONE CASTLES in England, Sicily, and France stand as reminders of the Normans, warriors from northern France, who transformed Europe during the 11th and 12th centuries. The Normans were descendants of the Norsemen, or Vikings, and were formidable fighters. They settled in northern France during the early 900s in an area now known as Normandy. The Normans were not only warriors but also skilled administrators. Their dukes created a complex and efficient society by dividing their kingdom into areas called fiefs. A knight controlled each fief. The Normans reached their height of power under William, Duke of Normandy, who led the conquest of England in 1066. They quickly transformed England into a Norman kingdom, building castles to defend their conquests, as well as churches, monasteries, and cathedrals. The Normans continued to rule England until 1154. After this, the Saxons and Normans began to merge into one nation. In 1204 the king of France conquered Normandy and took it over.

WILLIAM THE CONQUEROR
William, Duke of Normandy (c. 1028-87), was a brilliant but ruthless general and administrator. He led the Norman invasion of England and, after defeating the Saxon king, Harold II, was crowned king of England.

DOMESDAY BOOK
In 1085, King William I ordered a complete survey of England. Known as the Domesday Book, it contained thorough details of people, goods, animals, and lands for every single village in the country.

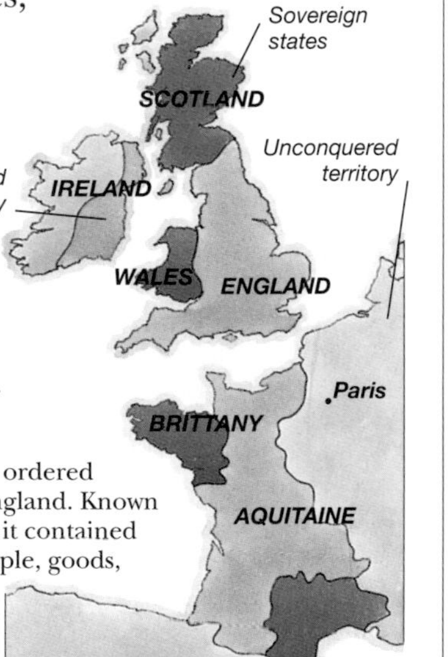

Sovereign states

SCOTLAND

Unconquered territory

Conquered territory

IRELAND

WALES   ENGLAND

.Paris

BRITTANY

AQUITAINE

EMPIRE
At their height of power under Henry II (reigned 1154-89), the Normans had conquered northern France, England, southern Italy, and Sicily. They did not survive as a separate group, but merged with the peoples they had conquered.

ARCHITECTURE
The Normans were skilled architects. They built strong castles to guard their conquests, such as the Tower of London, which stands to this day. They also built churches, cathedrals, and monasteries. Norman churches have intricately carved arches over the doors and windows, and massive walls and pillars.

Find out more
CASTLES
FRANCE, HISTORY OF
UNITED KINGDOM, HISTORY OF
VIKINGS

NORTH AFRICA

THE COUNTRIES OF NORTH AFRICA have suffered many invasions, from the Romans to the French and British. But the conquest by the armies of Islam in the 7th century was to have a major impact on the region, giving it a shared religion, language, and sense of identity. Much of North Africa is dominated by the largest desert on Earth, the Sahara. It is sparsely populated by dwindling numbers of nomads. Most people live along the fertile coastal strip on the banks of the Nile. Cities increasingly attract migrants from the country – Cairo is the fastest-growing city in the Islamic world with a population of over 15 million. In Algeria and Libya, the desert has revealed hidden riches – vast reserves of oil are fueling modernization programs. Many tourists visit Morocco, Tunisia, and Egypt, attracted by ancient ruins, medieval cities, and sunny beaches.

The North African coast occupies the southern shores of the Mediterranean, where the climate is mild and the land fertile. The Atlas Mountains and the rolling hills of Algeria and Tunisia lie between the coast and the sand seas and barren rocks of the Sahara.

KAIROUAN
When Islamic Arabs conquered North Africa in the 7th century, they founded many cities that are still important today. The walled city of Kairouan, in Tunisia, is a sacred shrine for Muslims in Africa. The Great Mosque was built in the 9th century. Its imposing marble courtyard, where the people pray, is surrounded by columns.

People who live in the desert regions of Africa, such as these Berber men (left), wear loose clothes to keep cool, and veils to protect themselves from the wind-blown sands of the desert.

NILE AGRICULTURE

The River Nile floods every summer, carrying rich mud from the highlands of Ethiopia and Sudan to the arid deserts of Egypt. It was this annual miracle that provided the foundations of Ancient Egyptian civilization. Today, nearly 99 percent of the Egyptian population lives along the green and fertile land on the banks of the Nile. Egypt is a leading producer of dates, melons, and cotton. Most Egyptian farmers use centuries-old methods; donkeys and mules are still used to pull heavy loads and carry water.

BERBERS

The Berbers are the original people of northwest Africa. They were converted to Islam in the 8th century. Arab invaders drove them into the Atlas Mountains, where many still live in remote villages. In the Sahara, Berbers live a nomadic life herding camels, sheep, and goats.

LEPTIS MAGNA
The Roman ruins of Leptis Magna (right) are the finest in Africa. The city dates to the 5th century B.C. It became part of the Roman Empire and was abandoned after the Arab conquest in 643 A.D.

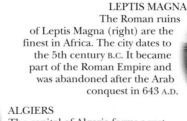

ALGIERS
The capital of Algeria forms a vast amphitheater of dazzling white buildings on the Mediterranean coast. The old Muslim quarter of the city sprawls across the hills, a maze of winding streets and high-walled houses. The French colonial quarter, with its public squares and tree-lined avenues, is found near the harbor. The French captured the city, an unruly center of Mediterranean piracy, in 1830. They left in 1962.

Find out more
AFRICA
AFRICA, HISTORY OF
DESERTS
ISLAM

Volcano	Mountain	Ancient monument	Capital city	Large city/town	Small city/town

ALGERIA
Area: 919,590 sq miles (2,381,740 sq km)
Population: 31,800,000
Capital: Algiers

MOROCCO
Area: 269,757 sq miles (698,670 sq km)
Population: 30,600,000
Capital: Rabat

EGYPT
Area: 386,660 sq miles (1,001,450 sq km)
Population: 71,900,000
Capital: Cairo

TUNISIA
Area: 63,170 sq miles (163,610 sq km)
Population: 9,800,000
Capital: Tunis

LIBYA
Area: 679,358 sq miles (1,759,540 sq km)
Population: 5,600,000
Capital: Tripoli

WESTERN SAHARA
Area: 102,703 sq miles (266,000 sq km)
Population: 273,000
Capital: Laayoune
Status: disputed territory occupied by Morocco

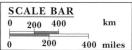

SCALE BAR
0 200 400 km
0 200 400 miles

ATLAS MOUNTAINS

The Atlas Mountains are a group of ranges, running roughly parallel to the Mediterranean coast. They stretch 1,500 miles (2,410 km) from southeast Morocco to northeast Tunisia. The High Atlas Mountains rise to 13,655 ft (4,165 m) at the summit of Jbel Toubkal. Mountain reservoirs provide water for lowland farmers, and many tourists visit the Middle Atlas range for winter sports.

NILE RIVER
The Nile is the world's longest river. It flows 4,158 miles (6,695 km) to the Mediterranean Sea.

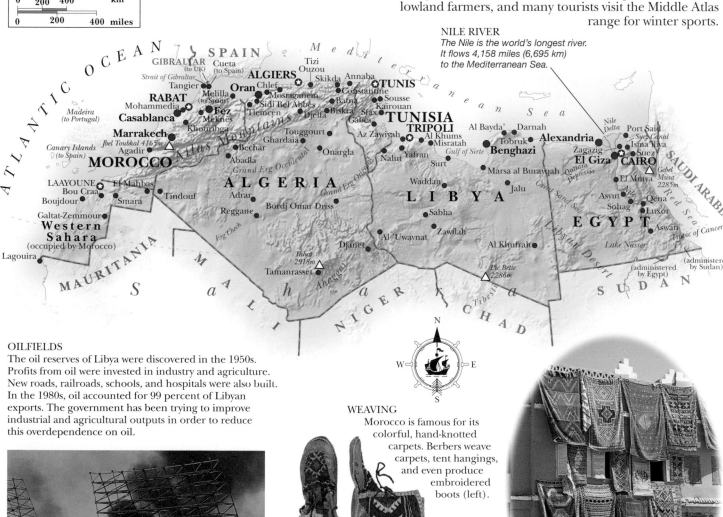

OILFIELDS
The oil reserves of Libya were discovered in the 1950s. Profits from oil were invested in industry and agriculture. New roads, railroads, schools, and hospitals were also built. In the 1980s, oil accounted for 99 percent of Libyan exports. The government has been trying to improve industrial and agricultural outputs in order to reduce this overdependence on oil.

WEAVING
Morocco is famous for its colorful, hand-knotted carpets. Berbers weave carpets, tent hangings, and even produce embroidered boots (left).

SOUK

The souk (market) is the commercial heart of North African towns. Each trade is located in a particular street. Smelly trades, such as tanning leather, are always located as far away from the mosque as possible.

NORTH AMERICA

The North American continent stretches from the Arctic Circle to the tropics and is flanked by the Atlantic, Pacific, and Arctic oceans. The five Great Lakes of North America form the largest area of freshwater in the world.

THE NORTH AMERICAN continent is a region of great contrasts. Impressive mountain chains – the Appalachians and Rockies – run down its east and west coasts, enclosing a vast, and mostly flat, landscape, crisscrossed by mighty rivers such as the Mississippi and Missouri. The north is blanketed with coniferous forests. The central Great Plains are grasslands, once grazed by huge herds of buffalo. In the north the Arctic region is permanently frozen, while in the south arid deserts and rocky canyons bake in year-round sunshine. Tropical forests cover southern Mexico, and in the southeastern US, semitropical wetlands harbor many endangered species. Native Americans are descendants of the peoples who first settled the continent over 25,000 years ago. They were displaced by European colonists who explored and settled on the continent from the 16th century. Successive waves of immigrants, first from Europe, and then from the rest of the world, settled in North America, drawn by its wealth of natural resources, its fertile prairies, and its vibrant cities – home to most of its population.

THE BIG FREEZE
Severe winter weather is common in the center of the continent, especially around the Great Lakes, which often freeze over in winter. Chicago, on Lake Michigan, is prone to severe snowstorms, which can cut off the city. In 1998, a freak icestorm in the Canadian Great Lakes region froze power lines, blacking out the area for several days.

ROCKIES
The Rocky Mountains form the backbone of the American continent, separating the great plains of the east from the high plateaux and basins of the west. Stretching from the Canadian Arctic to New Mexico, they are highest in Colorado, where some 254 mountains are over 13,000 ft (4,000 m). The highest point, Mt. Elbert, is 14,149 ft (4,312 m).

TUNDRA IN ALASKA
Tundra is a Finnish word meaning "treeless heights." It describes the landscape of Alaska (above), where the only vegetation is lichens, mosses, turf, and low-lying shrubs. The average temperature is below freezing, and in winter it can plummet to -89.6°F (-32°C). These low temperatures leave a layer of permanently frozen soil which can reach depths of 5,000 ft (1,525 m).

AUTUMN IN NEW ENGLAND
The climate of North America ranges from the hot rain forests of Yucatán to the frozen Arctic. The eastern coast of the US has four distinct seasons. The colors of autumnal leaves, especially the bright red of the maple, is a famous sight which attracts many tourists.

GRAND CANYON
Canyons are dramatic, deep rock formations created by the eroding flow of a river. The most famous is the Grand Canyon in Arizona, formed by the Colorado River. It is 220 miles (350 km) long, and plunges to depths of 5,970 ft (1,820 m). The processes of erosion started about 5–6 million years ago. Some of the rocks at the base are 2 billion years old – the oldest rocks known in the US.

Limestone, sandstone, shale, and granite are eroded at different speeds, giving the Grand Canyon its distinctive layered colors.

Moose live in the subarctic forests. They have huge antlers, long legs, and fleshy muzzles.

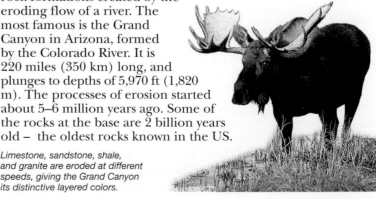

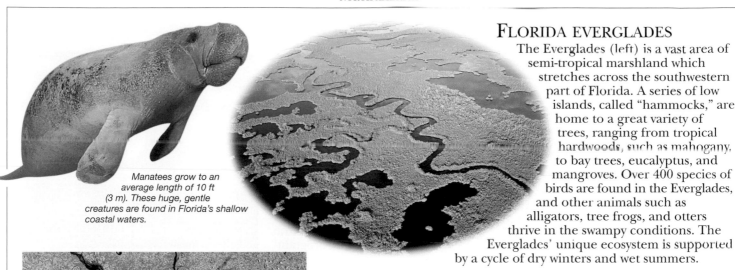

Manatees grow to an average length of 10 ft (3 m). These huge, gentle creatures are found in Florida's shallow coastal waters.

FLORIDA EVERGLADES

The Everglades (left) is a vast area of semi-tropical marshland which stretches across the southwestern part of Florida. A series of low islands, called "hammocks," are home to a great variety of trees, ranging from tropical hardwoods, such as mahogany, to bay trees, eucalyptus, and mangroves. Over 400 species of birds are found in the Everglades, and other animals such as alligators, tree frogs, and otters thrive in the swampy conditions. The Everglades' unique ecosystem is supported by a cycle of dry winters and wet summers.

MISSISSIPPI

At 3,740 miles (6,020 km) long, the Mississippi is the main river artery of the US and one of the busiest commercial waterways in the world. It rises in northern Minnesota, flowing south and receives the waters of the Missouri and Ohio rivers in its middle reaches. It drains into the Gulf of Mexico, where it forms a delta which is moving the shoreline out to sea at a rate of nearly 6 miles (10 km) every 100 years.

Mississippi River

Missouri River

This satellite image (above) shows the Mississippi and Missouri rivers converging near St. Louis during flooding in 1993.

This bison's thick hair and beard accentuate its size.

A barn and yellow canola crop on the Great Plains just east of Washington

GREAT PLAINS

The Great Plains, which stretch across the center of North America, were once areas of grassland (prairie) grazed by huge herds of buffalo (bison). Over-hunting wiped out the buffaloes and, as the frontier of pioneer settlement moved further west throughout the 19th century, the Plains were settled by farmers. Today, this is one of the most intensively farmed regions in the world, a vast producer of both corn and wheat.

BISON

The so-called American buffalo that used to roam the Great Plains of North America is actually a bison. A fully grown bison stands 6.6 ft (2 m) high and weighs more than 1,985 pounds (900 kilograms). Traditionally the bison provided food and clothing for the Native Americans living on the Plains. Up until the 18th century, the bison population flourished as the Native American method of hunting had little effect on numbers. It was not until the "white man" arrived with rifles that the herds were dramatically reduced. During construction of the railroads in the 19th century, whole herds were shot to feed the rail workers. Today, only 40,000-50,000 bison remain. Most live on reserves, protected by American law.

URBAN LIFE

Much of the North American continent, such as the drier south and west, is sparsely populated, but there are great concentrations of population and industry in urban areas – especially in the temperate regions along the coasts and along the shores of the Great Lakes. New York (right) lies at the center of a vast conurbation of cities, which stretches from Boston to Washington D.C. Accessible to both the Atlantic Ocean and the Hudson River, New York developed as a major port. Today, it is the US's main financial, commercial, and cultural center. Toronto is the largest urban area in Canada. It is a key industrial center. The city and its surrounding area produce more than half of Canada's manufactured goods.

BALD EAGLE

The bald eagle, the only eagle native to North America, has been the US national bird since 1782. It has a wingspan of 7 ft (2 m), and is found mainly along the coasts. It is a protected species in the US.

NATIVE AMERICANS

The first people to settle North America crossed into the continent from Asia more than 25,000 years ago. As they settled, they adapted to many different climatic conditions, resources, and terrain. Today, after centuries of conflict with European settlers, many Native Americans now live on government reservations. The Navajo are the largest tribe in the US. Most of them live on a large reservation in the Southwest. The tribe is famous for weaving and silverwork, and many of their hand-made artifacts are sold to tourists.

OIL RIG

The US has an abundance of natural resources, including oil, coal, and minerals. Oil was found along the coast of East Texas in 1901. After Alaska, Texas is the US's main oil-producing state. Oil is transported to refineries on the Gulf Coast by pipeline, tanker, and train. Houston is the capital of the oil business, although it is also the center of high-tech industries and home to the space shuttle program.

NATURAL HAZARDS

A chain of volcanoes stretches from the US-Mexican border to the southern end of South America. Popocatapetl, one of Mexico's many dormant volcanoes, is 17,888 ft (5,452 m) high, with a crater 500 ft (152 m) deep. Central Mexico is also vulnerable to earthquakes, which often hit the country's most heavily populated regions. In 1985, an earthquake in Mexico City killed some 9,500 people.

El Castillo, the temple-pyramid at Chichén-Itzá, is 73ft (22m) high. It stands in the main plaza of the city.

Joshua trees grow in the higher and cooler parts of California's desert.

DESERT

The barren deserts of the Southwest are harsh and arid places, swept by fierce winds and baked by searing heat. Only the hardiest animals, such as snakes, lizards, and reptiles, can survive these conditions. Spiny-leaved Joshua trees thrive in the desert, and can live for up to 1,000 years.

Rugged formations of pink and gray rocks and boulders form a stark desert vista.

CHICHEN-ITZA

The history of Mexico's urban civilizations dates back to c. 1150 B.C., and the elaborate ritual centers of the Olmec. The Maya built monumental cities and temples in the jungles of the Yucatán from c. 200 A.D. They are thought to be the first American civilization to develop a writing system. The Mayan pyramid-temple at Chichén Itzá dates to the 12th century A.D.

Find out more

CANADA
MEXICO
NORTH AMERICAN WILDLIFE
UNITED STATES OF AMERICA

| Volcano | Mountain | Ancient monument | Capital city | Large city/town | Small city/town |

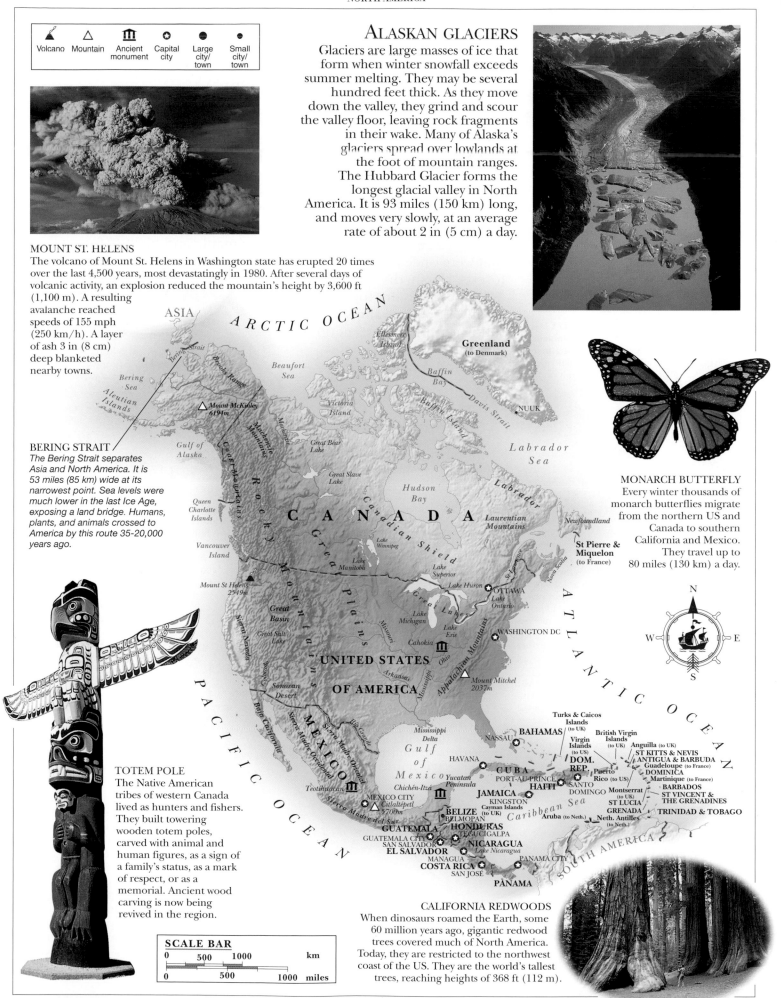

ALASKAN GLACIERS

Glaciers are large masses of ice that form when winter snowfall exceeds summer melting. They may be several hundred feet thick. As they move down the valley, they grind and scour the valley floor, leaving rock fragments in their wake. Many of Alaska's glaciers spread over lowlands at the foot of mountain ranges. The Hubbard Glacier forms the longest glacial valley in North America. It is 93 miles (150 km) long, and moves very slowly, at an average rate of about 2 in (5 cm) a day.

MOUNT ST. HELENS

The volcano of Mount St. Helens in Washington state has erupted 20 times over the last 4,500 years, most devastatingly in 1980. After several days of volcanic activity, an explosion reduced the mountain's height by 3,600 ft (1,100 m). A resulting avalanche reached speeds of 155 mph (250 km/h). A layer of ash 3 in (8 cm) deep blanketed nearby towns.

BERING STRAIT

The Bering Strait separates Asia and North America. It is 53 miles (85 km) wide at its narrowest point. Sea levels were much lower in the last Ice Age, exposing a land bridge. Humans, plants, and animals crossed to America by this route 35-20,000 years ago.

MONARCH BUTTERFLY

Every winter thousands of monarch butterflies migrate from the northern US and Canada to southern California and Mexico. They travel up to 80 miles (130 km) a day.

TOTEM POLE

The Native American tribes of western Canada lived as hunters and fishers. They built towering wooden totem poles, carved with animal and human figures, as a sign of a family's status, as a mark of respect, or as a memorial. Ancient wood carving is now being revived in the region.

CALIFORNIA REDWOODS

When dinosaurs roamed the Earth, some 60 million years ago, gigantic redwood trees covered much of North America. Today, they are restricted to the northwest coast of the US. They are the world's tallest trees, reaching heights of 368 ft (112 m).

SCALE BAR

| 0 | 500 | 1000 | km |
| 0 | 500 | 1000 | miles |

Map labels:

ASIA
ARCTIC OCEAN
Bering Strait
Brooks Range
Beaufort Sea
Ellesmere Island
Greenland (to Denmark)
Baffin Bay
NUUK
Bering Sea
Aleutian Islands
Mount McKinley 6194m
Mackenzie Mountains
Mackenzie
Victoria Island
Great Bear Lake
Buffin Island
Davis Strait
Labrador Sea
Gulf of Alaska
Coast Mountains
Great Slave Lake
Queen Charlotte Islands
Rocky Mountains
Great Bear Lake
Hudson Bay
Labrador
Laurentian Mountains
Newfoundland
Vancouver Island
CANADA
Canadian Shield
St Pierre & Miquelon (to France)
Lake Winnipeg
Lake Manitoba
Lake Superior
Nova Scotia
Mount St Helens 2549m
Sierra Nevada
Great Basin
Great Salt Lake
Lake Michigan
Lake Huron
Great Lakes
OTTAWA
Lake Ontario
Lake Erie
Missouri
Cahokia
Ohio
WASHINGTON DC
Columbia
UNITED STATES OF AMERICA
Arkansas
Mississippi
Appalachian Mountains
Mount Mitchel 2037m
ATLANTIC OCEAN
PACIFIC OCEAN
Sonoran Desert
Baja California
MEXICO
Rio Grande
Sierra Madre Oriental
Mississippi Delta
Gulf of Mexico
Turks & Caicos Islands (to UK)
BAHAMAS
NASSAU
HAVANA
CUBA
British Virgin Islands (to UK)
Virgin Islands (to US)
Anguilla (to UK)
ST KITTS & NEVIS
ANTIGUA & BARBUDA
Guadeloupe (to France)
DOMINICA
Martinique (to France)
BARBADOS
ST VINCENT & THE GRENADINES
GRENADA
TRINIDAD & TOBAGO
Teotihuacan
Sierra Madre Occidental
Yucatan Peninsula
Chichén-Itzá
PORT-AU-PRINCE
HAITI
DOM. REP.
Puerto Rico (to US)
SANTO DOMINGO
Montserrat (to UK)
ST LUCIA
Neth. Antilles (to Neth.)
MEXICO CITY
Citlaltépetl 5700m
JAMAICA
KINGSTON
Cayman Islands (to UK)
Caribbean Sea
Aruba (to Neth.)
BELIZE
BELMOPAN
GUATEMALA
GUATEMALA CITY
SAN SALVADOR
EL SALVADOR
HONDURAS
TEGUCIGALPA
NICARAGUA
Lake Nicaragua
MANAGUA
COSTA RICA
SAN JOSÉ
PANAMA CITY
PANAMA
SOUTH AMERICA
Sierra Madre del Sur

NORTH AMERICAN WILDLIFE

THE CONTINENT OF NORTH AMERICA has a stunning array of wildlife, including golden eagles, bobcats, coyotes, cacti, and giant redwood trees. There are ice-covered Arctic islands across the far north, bordered by cold, treeless tundra where the ground is frozen for many months each year. Reindeer scratch in the tundra snow searching for mosses and lichens. South of the tundra is a vast belt of coniferous forests, with pines, spruces, larches, and firs. Today, large areas of these forests are logged (cut down), but wolves, bears, and lynx still live in the wilderness areas. In the midwest are great grassland prairies; in the east are maple and hickory forests that were once huge; and in the west are mountains and redwood forests. Harsh, dry deserts such as Death Valley are found in the southwest, with swamps in the far southeast, and desert merging into the tropical forests of Central America.

This map shows the main kinds of habitat in North America.

North America

- ☐ Desert
- ☐ Tundra
- ☐ Mountains
- ☐ Temperate forest
- ☐ Temperate grassland
- ☐ Coniferous forest
- ☐ Tropical rainforest

BALD EAGLE
The bald eagle is the national emblem of the United States; it has a wingspan of about 6 ft (2 m). Bald eagles feed mainly on fish.

CACTUS
The giant saguaro cactus is found mainly in Arizona. It is a slow-growing cactus, but it may reach a height of 45 ft (14 m). Its white flowers attract many insects, including swallowtail butterflies.

COTTONTAIL RABBIT
Like many dryland plant-eaters, the desert cottontail rabbit stays near rocks or undergrowth and dashes to safety if it spies an approaching predator. The cottontail is so named because its white bobtail resembles a boll (seed head) of cotton.

DESERTS
The cactus is one of many plants that survive in the North American southwest, despite the dry climate. Cacti have plump stems which store water, and spines to prevent animals from eating them. In Mexico there are hundreds of different kinds of cacti.

GRASSLANDS
Most of the natural prairie that once covered the North American midwest is now farmland. However, many animals are able to survive, particularly small burrowing rodents such as prairie dogs, below. Their tunneling helps break up the soil, improve drainage, and recycle nutrients.

WETLANDS
The lakes, swamps, and marshes of the southeast are called the wetlands. They are home to many plants, fish, and reptiles, including the water hyacinth plant and the American alligator, which can measure about 18 ft (6 m) long. Many other water creatures also live here, including frogs, toads, and red-eared turtles.

ALFALFA
This plant is a member of the pea family, originally from South America. Today, farmers grow it for animal feed; humans also eat alfalfa.

PRAIRIE DOG
These animals are so named because they make a barking sound like a dog. They live in groups called coteries, consisting of a male, a few females, and their young. The coteries are grouped into wards, and the wards are grouped into towns. Towns may cover more than 100 acres (40 hectares).

COLLARED LIZARD
This lizard eats other lizards and insects. Collared lizards measure up to 20 in (50 cm) long.

Ring of soil around burrow entrance keeps out rainwater.

PUMA

The American puma is a member of the cat family. It is also called the cougar or mountain lion. The puma can survive in thick forest or open semidesert. A large male puma may measure nearly 6 ft (1.8 m) long and weigh almost 220 lb (100 kg). Pumas prowl mainly at night, hunting prey that ranges from rats and rabbits to adult deer. In the past, people hunted and killed pumas because they sometimes attack farm animals.

NORTH AMERICAN FORESTS

In the vast conifer forests of the far north, summer is short and winter is long and bitterly cold. In the fall, bears eat almost continuously to build up fat, spruce grouse turn to their tough winter diet of pine needles and twigs, and migratory birds such as warblers fly south. Moose and reindeer shelter among the trees, browsing for food in the snow, and watching out for wolves. In the spring the migratory birds return, insects begin to buzz among the branches, and deer feed on the new growths of leaves and water plants.

SNOWY OWL

In the far north of the continent, the snowy owl swoops by day on voles, mice, lemmings, rabbits, Arctic hares, ducks, and other birds. Male snowy owls are usually white or slightly flecked; females are larger and more striped.

REDHEADED WOODPECKER

Woodpeckers probe under bark and in wood for grubs, beetles, and similar animals. They use their stiff tail as a prop against the trunk as they hammer with their sharp bill.

MOOSE

The moose is the largest of all deer. A large male moose has huge flattened antlers and measures up to 7 ft (2.1 m) at the shoulder. Females are smaller and do not have antlers. In summer, moose wade into the thawed marshes, lakes, and rivers to chew on water plants. In winter, they survive on buds, twigs, and other woody plant matter. Unlike many deer, moose live alone except in the breeding season.

MOUNTAINS

The Rocky Mountains provide many different habitats for wildlife. Above about 4,500 ft (1,400 m) the surrounding grassland changes to sagebrush and juniper trees, then to firs and pines at 6,500 ft (2,000 m). Above 10,500 ft (3,200 m), only mountain grasses and small flowers grow during the short summer. These rugged mountains are a refuge for spectacular animals such as bears, wolverines, and bighorn sheep and Rocky Mountain goats, which are preyed on by the lynx.

The porcupine is a good tree climber.

Moose live in the forest areas of North America and also in Europe, where they are called elks.

Virginia creeper plant

AMERICAN WOODCOCK

This bird lives in forest areas in North America. Woodcocks probe in soft soil with their long bills searching for worms and grubs. They detect their prey partly by smell, and by using the sensitive tip of the bill.

PORCUPINE

The North American porcupine feeds on conifer needles and tree bark. In summer it spends more time on the ground, where it feeds on stems, flowers, seeds, and fruit. Porcupines have long spines on their backs for defense. Although they look like hedgehogs, the two animals are not related.

Find out more

DEER, ANTELOPES, and gazelles
EAGLES and other birds of prey
LIONS, TIGERS, and other big cats
LIZARDS
OWLS
RABBITS AND HARES

NUCLEAR AGE

IN 1945, THE FIRST atomic bombs were dropped on the Japanese cities of Hiroshima and Nagasaki. The years since 1945 have sometimes been called the nuclear age because the knowledge that nuclear bombs can destroy civilization has affected political decisions and attitudes toward war. The term nuclear age also describes the growth of nuclear energy. In 1953, US President Dwight Eisenhower launched the Atoms for Peace program to develop nuclear power for peaceful uses, such as generating electricity. At first nuclear energy was welcomed; but today many people believe that it is dangerous. The nuclear "arms race" between the United States and the Soviet Union, which began in 1945, caused political tension for years. By the 1980s, the United States and the Soviet Union owned enough nuclear weapons to destroy every living thing on Earth. Many people wanted to rid the world of nuclear weapons, and in the mid-1980s both superpowers began to disarm.

NUCLEAR FISSION
In 1939, the German scientists Fritz Strassman (above left) and Otto Hahn discovered that energy could be created by splitting uranium atoms into two. This process, called nuclear fission, was later developed to produce the energy to create electricity and the explosion to make a nuclear bomb.

HIROSHIMA
On August 6, 1945, an American warplane dropped an atomic bomb on the city of Hiroshima in an effort to end World War II. The city was destroyed, and about 130,000 people were killed. The people of Hiroshima commemorate the event every year in "Peace City," a place where the ruins have been left untouched in memory of those killed.

NUCLEAR ENERGY
In 1954, the world's first nuclear power station opened in the Soviet Union. Today there are about 440 nuclear power stations producing 15 percent of the world's energy. Above is a 1950s cooking demonstration: a woman cooks hamburgers using electricity produced by atomic power.

ANTI-NUCLEAR MOVEMENTS
Opposition to nuclear weapons began in the 1950s as people thought about the horrors of a nuclear war. Throughout the world people adopted the peace symbol (left) as they demonstrated against nuclear weapons.

GROWTH OF NUCLEAR WEAPONS
In 1945, there were three nuclear weapons in existence. By 1962, the number had risen to about 2,000. By 1990, the total number had grown to about 25,000. Together, these weapons had one million times more power than the bomb dropped on Hiroshima. The United States and the Soviet Union owned the most nuclear weapons, but six other countries also developed nuclear arms: Britain, France, China, India, Pakistan, and Israel.

1945: only three nuclear weapons exist.

1962: the number of nuclear weapons is in the thousands.

1990: the number of nuclear weapons is over 25,000.

NUCLEAR DISARMAMENT
During the 1980s, the United States and the Soviet Union discussed nuclear disarmament. In 1987, US President Reagan and Soviet Premier Gorbachev agreed to dismantle some intermediate-range nuclear weapons (left). In 1993, US President Bush and Russian President Yeltsin signed a treaty agreeing to reduce their nuclear arsenals by two-thirds within ten years.

Find out more
NUCLEAR ENERGY
SOVIET UNION, HISTORY OF
UNITED STATES OF AMERICA, history of
WORLD WAR II

NUCLEAR ENERGY

THE ATOMS THAT MAKE UP everything in the universe are the source of a huge amount of energy called nuclear energy. Nuclear energy produces the searing heat and light of the Sun, the deadly explosions of nuclear weapons, and vast amounts of electricity in nuclear power stations. Nuclear energy is based on the fact that matter and energy are different forms of the same thing, and one can be converted into the other. In a nuclear reaction, a tiny amount of matter changes into an enormous amount of energy. The nuclear reaction occurs in the nuclei (centers) of atoms. This can happen in two ways: when the nucleus of a heavy atom splits, in a process called fission, and when two lightweight nuclei join together, in a process called fusion. In nuclear weapons, fission or fusion occurs in a split second. In contrast, nuclear power stations produce electricity from fission reactions that work at a controlled rate.

Experimental nuclear fusion reactor near Oxford, England

Hydrogen nucleus

Neutron

Hydrogen nucleus with extra neutrons

Helium nucleus

NUCLEAR FUSION
Scientists are trying to build reactors that use nuclear fusion, a process which produces less dangerous waste than nuclear fission (below). Nuclear fusion occurs when hydrogen atoms smash together and join to form heavier atoms of helium. However, nuclear fusion is extremely difficult to achieve. Hydrogen atoms must be held by a magnetic field and heated to a temperature higher than that in the Sun's center for fusion to occur.

Neutron hits nucleus of uranium atom.

Fission occurs, releasing energy and neutrons.

Reactor core contains pellets of uranium dioxide fuel held in fuel rods. Two thimble-sized pellets would produce enough electricity for one person's domestic supply for one year.

If neutrons travel too rapidly, they bounce off uranium atoms without producing fission. The fuel is surrounded by water, which slows the neutrons down so they produce fission. A material that slows neutrons in a reactor is called a moderator.

Pump for high-pressure water system

Control rods absorb neutrons and slow down the nuclear reaction. In an emergency, the control rods drop into the reactor core and shut off the nuclear reaction.

NUCLEAR FISSION
Nuclear power stations produce energy from the fission of atoms of uranium dioxide. The impact of a particle called a neutron makes an atom of uranium split. This releases heat energy and two or three neutrons. The neutrons strike other uranium atoms and make them divide. Soon, many atoms begin to split, producing a huge amount of energy.

Protective clothing worn when handling nuclear waste

The high-pressure water flows through pipes in a steam generator which transfers its heat to a separate water system. The water in this second system boils to form steam.

Water is pumped around the reactor core at high pressure in a sealed circuit. The nuclear reactions heat the water to more than 570°F (300°C), but the high pressure keeps it from turning into steam.

Pressurized water reactor (PWR)

Steam spins turbines that drive generators, producing electricity.

A third water circuit acts as a coolant, changing the steam back into water which returns to the steam generator once again.

NUCLEAR RADIATION
Some waste from nuclear power stations is radioactive – it produces deadly nuclear radiation consisting of tiny particles or invisible waves that can damage living cells. Some radioactive waste may last for thousands of years, so it is buried underground in sealed containers. Many people are concerned about the dangers of nuclear waste and are demanding an end to nuclear energy production.

NUCLEAR POWER STATION
A fission reaction becomes continuous only if there is a certain amount of fuel present, called the critical mass. In a nuclear reactor, rods contain uranium fuel. The fuel rods are placed close together to provide the critical mass that starts the reaction.

Find out more
ATOMS AND MOLECULES
ENERGY
NUCLEAR AGE
PHYSICS
RADIOACTIVITY
SOVIET UNION, HISTORY OF
WEAPONS

NUMBERS

WHEN WE WANT TO KNOW how many things we have, or measure how large something is, we use numbers. Numbers are symbols that describe an amount. There are only ten number symbols: 0, 1, 2, 3, 4, 5, 6, 7, 8, and 9, but they can be put together in many different ways to make other numbers of any size. Besides counting and measuring, numbers can also be used to work out time and distances, or to put things in order. The skill of working with numbers is called arithmetic. Early humans probably used their fingers and thumbs to count. Because we have ten digits – eight fingers and two thumbs – we developed a system of counting that was based on tens. This is called the decimal system, after the Latin word for ten. Numbers are just as important as words for passing on information. They can be written down, so that other people can read and use them.

FRACTIONS
Sometimes the number 1 has to be divided into portions. Parts of a whole number are called fractions.

COUNTING
When people needed to count higher than ten, they used objects such as pebbles to represent multiples of ten. So, five pebbles and three fingers stood for the number 53. Making calculations with pebbles led to the invention of the abacus, and later the slide rule and calculator.

Calculator

Using fingers

Ruler

Pebbles

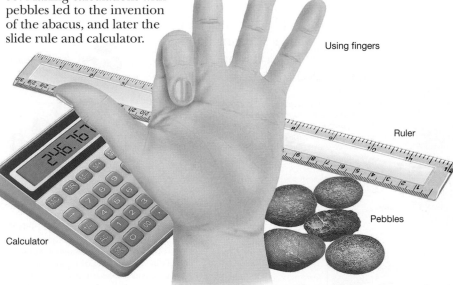

Cardinal numbers

A fraction, two-thirds

A decimal fraction, ten and sixty-five hundredths

NUMBERS IN HISTORY
People have invented many different ways of representing numbers with symbols. The modern decimal system has now been taken up all over the world, but older systems are still used in a few places. Even the Ancient Roman system is used sometimes, especially on clock faces.

The Babylonians invented a number system based on ten about 3,500 years ago, but the symbols took a long time to write down.

I II III IV V VI VII VIII IX X

The Ancient Roman number system goes back to about 500 B.C. It is an awkward system, but it is still sometimes used today.

In about 200 B.C. the Hindus used a number system based on ten. About 1,400 years ago they modified it to include zero.

o 1 2 3 4 5 6 7 8 9 10

By the 15th century, Hindu-Arabic numbers had replaced Roman numerals as the most popular number system.

0 1 2 3 4 5 6 7 8 9 10

Today, most countries use a modern version of the Hindu-Arabic number system, because it makes calculations easy.

Cricket scoreboard

USING NUMBERS
If you look around, you will see how numbers are used in everyday life. For example, scoreboards, speed limits, distances, prices, TV channels, and the time of day are all shown using numbers. Page numbers in the index of this book show where to find the topics that interest you. Money is also divided into units to make it simple to understand.

TYPES OF NUMBER
Whole numbers that stand for quantities, such as 1, 2, or 3, are called cardinal numbers. Numbers that put things in order, such as 1st, 2nd, or 3rd, are known as ordinal numbers. In a fraction, the number below the line shows how many parts the whole is divided into; the number above shows how many of those parts are being described.

Find out more
COMPUTERS
GEOMETRY
MATHEMATICS
STATISTICS

OCEANS AND SEAS

YOUR FEET MAY BE RESTING firmly on the ground, but more than two thirds of our planet is covered with water. Oceans and seas make up 71 percent of the Earth's surface. They influence the climate, supply us with food, power, and valuable minerals, and provide a home for a fascinating range of plant and animal life.

The oceans and seas began millions of years ago when the Earth cooled from its original molten state. Water vapor escaped from inside the Earth in volcanic eruptions, cooled, and fell as rain. It filled vast hollows and basins surrounding rocky land masses. These gradually moved around to form the continents and oceans as they exist today. As rivers formed on the land and flowed into the seas, they dissolved minerals from the rocks, making the oceans and seas salty.

OCEAN HUNTERS
Fishing boats sail the oceans and seas to bring us the fish and other sea creatures that we eat. The best fishing grounds are in shallow seas, where the water teems with fish. But catches must be controlled; otherwise the numbers of fish will fall as the fish fail to breed.

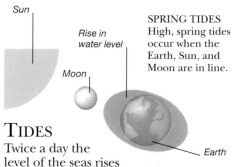

Sun

Rise in water level

SPRING TIDES
High, spring tides occur when the Earth, Sun, and Moon are in line.

Moon

TIDES

Twice a day the level of the seas rises and falls. These changes in level are called tides. They are caused mainly by the pull of the Moon's gravity on the Earth. When the Moon lies directly over the ocean, its gravity pulls the water toward it. Water also rises on the opposite side of the Earth, because the Earth itself is pulled toward the Moon.

Earth

THE WORLD'S OCEANS AND SEAS
Oceans are vast bodies of water, usually separating the continents. The Pacific Ocean, which is the largest and deepest, lies between America and Asia and covers more than a third of the globe. The others, in order of size, are the Atlantic, Indian, and Arctic oceans. The Arctic Ocean lies between the land masses around the North Pole and is largely covered by ice. Seas, bays, and gulfs are smaller bodies of water that lie between arms of land, or between islands and land masses. Some, such as the Caspian and Dead seas, are entirely surrounded by land and are really not seas but large lakes.

Pacific Ocean

Indian Ocean

North Pacific Ocean

South Atlantic Ocean

The Pacific, Atlantic, and Indian oceans surround Antarctica. This area is sometimes called the Antarctic Ocean.

Atlantic Ocean

Indian Ocean

The Arctic Ocean is an ice-covered ocean at the North Pole.

OCEAN CURRENTS

The water in the oceans is constantly moving in great circular streams, or currents, which can flow about as fast as you walk. Winds blow the surface layer of the oceans to form these currents, which carry warm or cold water along the shores of continents, greatly affecting the weather there. Sometimes, currents flow deep below the surface, moving in the opposite direction to surface currents. For example, surface currents carry warm water away from the equator, while currents deep beneath the sea bring cold water back to the equator. Most seas have strong currents. But the waters of the Sargasso Sea, which lies in the North Atlantic Ocean, are almost still, causing the sea to become choked with seaweed.

THE *KON TIKI* EXPEDITION
Early peoples may have used the currents to travel across oceans. In 1947 the *Kon Tiki* expedition, led by Norwegian explorer Thor Heyerdahl, tested this theory by sailing a light wooden raft from Peru to the Polynesian Islands.

GULF STREAM
Water heated by the Sun flows out from the Gulf of Mexico. This warm current crosses the Atlantic Ocean and flows around the shores of western Europe. There the winter weather is mild, while places on the other side of the ocean away from the current are freezing cold.

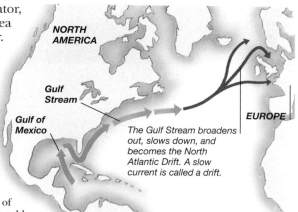

NORTH AMERICA

Gulf Stream

Gulf of Mexico

EUROPE

The Gulf Stream broadens out, slows down, and becomes the North Atlantic Drift. A slow current is called a drift.

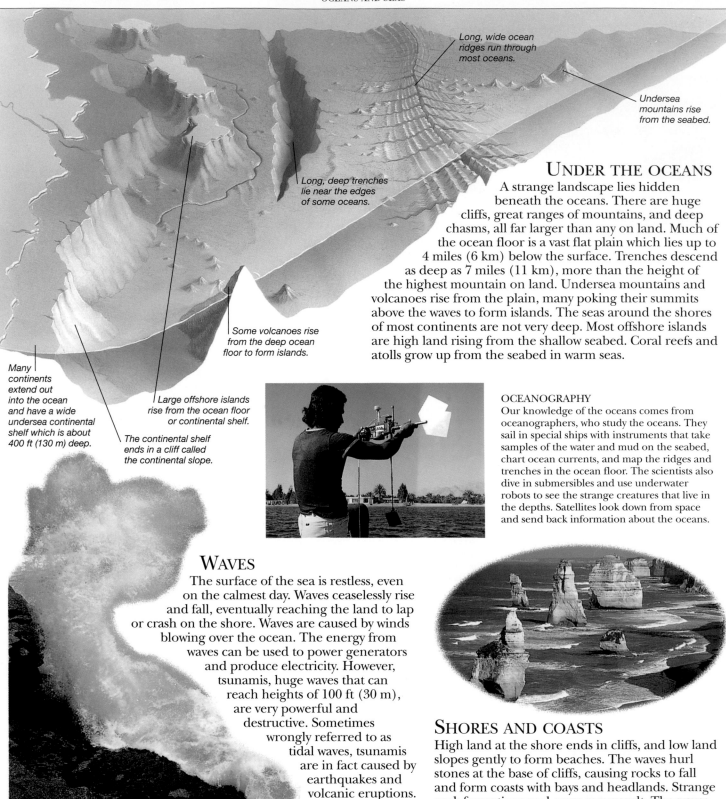

Long, wide ocean ridges run through most oceans.

Undersea mountains rise from the seabed.

Long, deep trenches lie near the edges of some oceans.

Some volcanoes rise from the deep ocean floor to form islands.

Many continents extend out into the ocean and have a wide undersea continental shelf which is about 400 ft (130 m) deep.

Large offshore islands rise from the ocean floor or continental shelf.

The continental shelf ends in a cliff called the continental slope.

UNDER THE OCEANS

A strange landscape lies hidden beneath the oceans. There are huge cliffs, great ranges of mountains, and deep chasms, all far larger than any on land. Much of the ocean floor is a vast flat plain which lies up to 4 miles (6 km) below the surface. Trenches descend as deep as 7 miles (11 km), more than the height of the highest mountain on land. Undersea mountains and volcanoes rise from the plain, many poking their summits above the waves to form islands. The seas around the shores of most continents are not very deep. Most offshore islands are high land rising from the shallow seabed. Coral reefs and atolls grow up from the seabed in warm seas.

OCEANOGRAPHY

Our knowledge of the oceans comes from oceanographers, who study the oceans. They sail in special ships with instruments that take samples of the water and mud on the seabed, chart ocean currents, and map the ridges and trenches in the ocean floor. The scientists also dive in submersibles and use underwater robots to see the strange creatures that live in the depths. Satellites look down from space and send back information about the oceans.

WAVES

The surface of the sea is restless, even on the calmest day. Waves ceaselessly rise and fall, eventually reaching the land to lap or crash on the shore. Waves are caused by winds blowing over the ocean. The energy from waves can be used to power generators and produce electricity. However, tsunamis, huge waves that can reach heights of 100 ft (30 m), are very powerful and destructive. Sometimes wrongly referred to as tidal waves, tsunamis are in fact caused by earthquakes and volcanic eruptions.

SHORES AND COASTS

High land at the shore ends in cliffs, and low land slopes gently to form beaches. The waves hurl stones at the base of cliffs, causing rocks to fall and form coasts with bays and headlands. Strange rock formations and caves may result. The waves batter the rocks and break them up into pebbles and then into sand. Beaches form at the base of cliffs, and the sea also sweeps pebbles and sand along the shore to form beaches elsewhere.

Water reaches base of circle in trough of wave.

Water reaches top of circle in crest of wave.

Crest topples over to break on shore.

HOW WAVES MOVE

The water in a wave does not move forward. It moves in a circle, so the water only goes up and down as a wave passes. The approaching shore holds back the base of the wave, making the top of the wave move faster to break on the shore.

Find out more

CONTINENTS
DEEP-SEA WILDLIFE
EARTHQUAKES
FISHING INDUSTRY
INDIAN OCEAN
OCEAN WILDLIFE
SEASHORE WILDLIFE

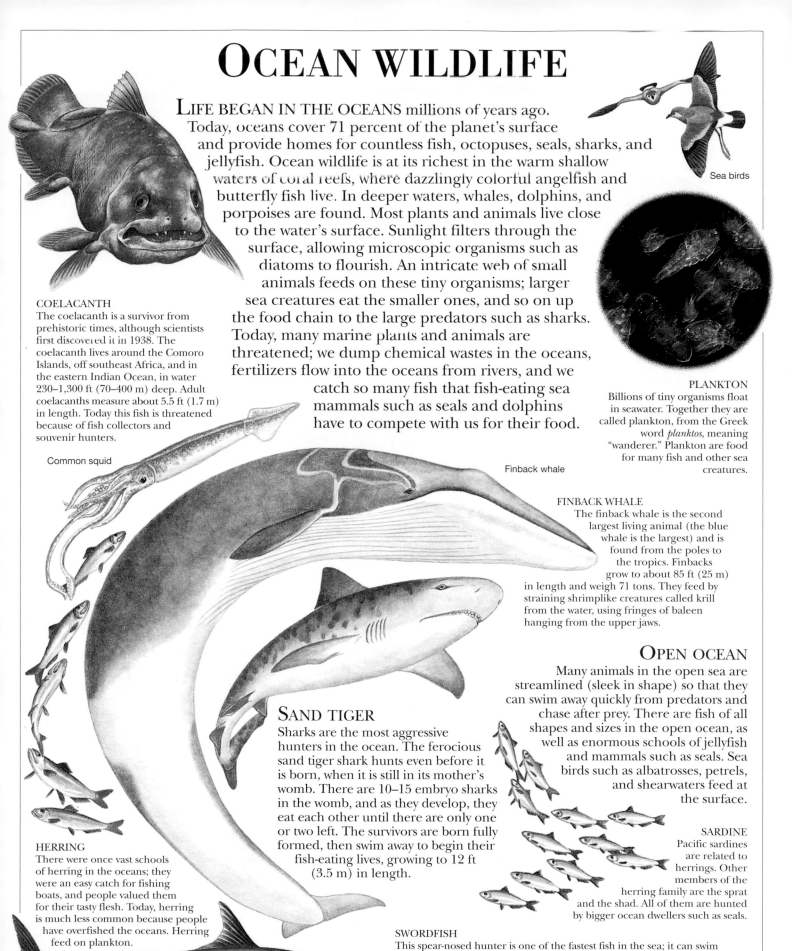

OCEAN WILDLIFE

LIFE BEGAN IN THE OCEANS millions of years ago. Today, oceans cover 71 percent of the planet's surface and provide homes for countless fish, octopuses, seals, sharks, and jellyfish. Ocean wildlife is at its richest in the warm shallow waters of coral reefs, where dazzlingly colorful angelfish and butterfly fish live. In deeper waters, whales, dolphins, and porpoises are found. Most plants and animals live close to the water's surface. Sunlight filters through the surface, allowing microscopic organisms such as diatoms to flourish. An intricate web of small animals feeds on these tiny organisms; larger sea creatures eat the smaller ones, and so on up the food chain to the large predators such as sharks. Today, many marine plants and animals are threatened; we dump chemical wastes in the oceans, fertilizers flow into the oceans from rivers, and we catch so many fish that fish-eating sea mammals such as seals and dolphins have to compete with us for their food.

Sea birds

COELACANTH
The coelacanth is a survivor from prehistoric times, although scientists first discovered it in 1938. The coelacanth lives around the Comoro Islands, off southeast Africa, and in the eastern Indian Ocean, in water 230–1,300 ft (70–400 m) deep. Adult coelacanths measure about 5.5 ft (1.7 m) in length. Today this fish is threatened because of fish collectors and souvenir hunters.

Common squid

Finback whale

PLANKTON
Billions of tiny organisms float in seawater. Together they are called plankton, from the Greek word *planktos*, meaning "wanderer." Plankton are food for many fish and other sea creatures.

FINBACK WHALE
The finback whale is the second largest living animal (the blue whale is the largest) and is found from the poles to the tropics. Finbacks grow to about 85 ft (25 m) in length and weigh 71 tons. They feed by straining shrimplike creatures called krill from the water, using fringes of baleen hanging from the upper jaws.

OPEN OCEAN
Many animals in the open sea are streamlined (sleek in shape) so that they can swim away quickly from predators and chase after prey. There are fish of all shapes and sizes in the open ocean, as well as enormous schools of jellyfish and mammals such as seals. Sea birds such as albatrosses, petrels, and shearwaters feed at the surface.

SAND TIGER
Sharks are the most aggressive hunters in the ocean. The ferocious sand tiger shark hunts even before it is born, when it is still in its mother's womb. There are 10–15 embryo sharks in the womb, and as they develop, they eat each other until there are only one or two left. The survivors are born fully formed, then swim away to begin their fish-eating lives, growing to 12 ft (3.5 m) in length.

HERRING
There were once vast schools of herring in the oceans; they were an easy catch for fishing boats, and people valued them for their tasty flesh. Today, herring is much less common because people have overfished the oceans. Herring feed on plankton.

SARDINE
Pacific sardines are related to herrings. Other members of the herring family are the sprat and the shad. All of them are hunted by bigger ocean dwellers such as seals.

SWORDFISH
This spear-nosed hunter is one of the fastest fish in the sea; it can swim in bursts at speeds of 60 mph (95 km/h). The swordfish resembles the marlin and sailfish, and weighs up to 1,500 lb (675 kg). Swordfish injure their prey with sideways slashes of the sword, and then devour them.

Swordfish

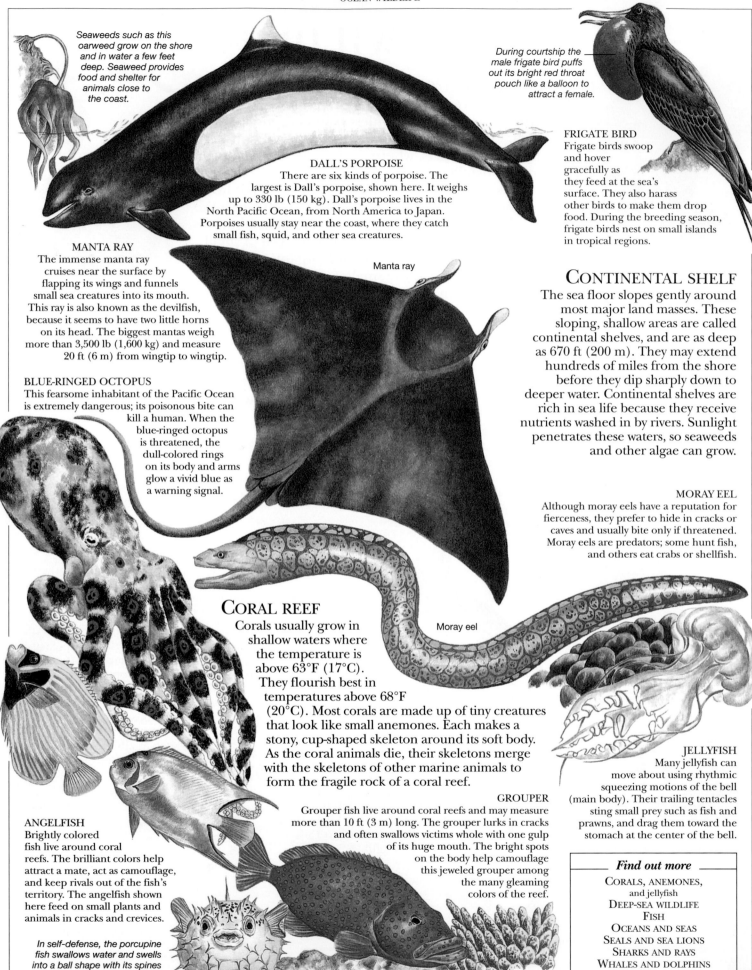

Seaweeds such as this oarweed grow on the shore and in water a few feet deep. Seaweed provides food and shelter for animals close to the coast.

During courtship the male frigate bird puffs out its bright red throat pouch like a balloon to attract a female.

FRIGATE BIRD
Frigate birds swoop and hover gracefully as they feed at the sea's surface. They also harass other birds to make them drop food. During the breeding season, frigate birds nest on small islands in tropical regions.

DALL'S PORPOISE
There are six kinds of porpoise. The largest is Dall's porpoise, shown here. It weighs up to 330 lb (150 kg). Dall's porpoise lives in the North Pacific Ocean, from North America to Japan. Porpoises usually stay near the coast, where they catch small fish, squid, and other sea creatures.

Manta ray

CONTINENTAL SHELF
The sea floor slopes gently around most major land masses. These sloping, shallow areas are called continental shelves, and are as deep as 670 ft (200 m). They may extend hundreds of miles from the shore before they dip sharply down to deeper water. Continental shelves are rich in sea life because they receive nutrients washed in by rivers. Sunlight penetrates these waters, so seaweeds and other algae can grow.

MANTA RAY
The immense manta ray cruises near the surface by flapping its wings and funnels small sea creatures into its mouth. This ray is also known as the devilfish, because it seems to have two little horns on its head. The biggest mantas weigh more than 3,500 lb (1,600 kg) and measure 20 ft (6 m) from wingtip to wingtip.

BLUE-RINGED OCTOPUS
This fearsome inhabitant of the Pacific Ocean is extremely dangerous; its poisonous bite can kill a human. When the blue-ringed octopus is threatened, the dull-colored rings on its body and arms glow a vivid blue as a warning signal.

MORAY EEL
Although moray eels have a reputation for fierceness, they prefer to hide in cracks or caves and usually bite only if threatened. Moray eels are predators; some hunt fish, and others eat crabs or shellfish.

CORAL REEF
Corals usually grow in shallow waters where the temperature is above 63°F (17°C). They flourish best in temperatures above 68°F (20°C). Most corals are made up of tiny creatures that look like small anemones. Each makes a stony, cup-shaped skeleton around its soft body. As the coral animals die, their skeletons merge with the skeletons of other marine animals to form the fragile rock of a coral reef.

Moray eel

JELLYFISH
Many jellyfish can move about using rhythmic squeezing motions of the bell (main body). Their trailing tentacles sting small prey such as fish and prawns, and drag them toward the stomach at the center of the bell.

GROUPER
Grouper fish live around coral reefs and may measure more than 10 ft (3 m) long. The grouper lurks in cracks and often swallows victims whole with one gulp of its huge mouth. The bright spots on the body help camouflage this jeweled grouper among the many gleaming colors of the reef.

ANGELFISH
Brightly colored fish live around coral reefs. The brilliant colors help attract a mate, act as camouflage, and keep rivals out of the fish's territory. The angelfish shown here feed on small plants and animals in cracks and crevices.

In self-defense, the porcupine fish swallows water and swells into a ball shape with its spines poking outward.

Find out more
CORALS, ANEMONES, and jellyfish
DEEP-SEA WILDLIFE
FISH
OCEANS AND SEAS
SEALS AND SEA LIONS
SHARKS AND RAYS
WHALES AND DOLPHINS

OCTOPUSES AND SQUID

SEA CREATURES SUCH AS THE OCTOPUS and squid have always held a strange fascination for humans. With their powerful tentacles and strange shape, they were once thought of as sea monsters. Octopuses and squid are clever, active creatures, the biggest and most intelligent of all the invertebrates (animals without backbones). They have sharp eyesight, a large brain, fast reactions, and the ability to remember. Octopuses, squid, and their relatives, the cuttlefish, are mollusks, related to shelled animals with soft bodies such as snails and clams. Unlike snails and clams, octopuses, squid, and cuttlefish have no outer shells, though squid have a very thin shell called a pen inside the body. The white oval cuttlebones of cuttlefish are often seen washed up on beaches. An octopus has eight "arms" covered with suckers which it uses for moving around. Squid and cuttlefish have eight short "arms" and two long tentacles which curl and uncurl. They use their arms as rudders for swimming and their tentacles for catching prey.

Some large octopuses measure 30 ft (9 m) across with their "arms" spread out. However, stories of giant octopuses that swallow divers whole are untrue.

Water can be squirted out through siphon for jet-propelled movement.

Mouth is on underside; it has a horny "beak" for cutting food, and saliva that contains poison.

COMMON OCTOPUS
The common octopus lurks in caves or crevices during the day. It emerges at night to hunt for crabs, shellfish, and small fish. It has a hard beaklike mouth and a rough tongue.

CUTTLEFISH
Octopuses, squid, and cuttlefish can change color in less than a second. This can provide camouflage so that the creature blends in with the surroundings. It may also indicate a change of mood – a male cuttlefish turns black with rage when it is angry. The dappled red coloring of the cuttlefish shown here is a good disguise among the coral.

Each "arm" has two rows of powerful suckers for moving, feeling, and grabbing prey.

INK CLOUD
Octopuses and squid have an ink gland attached to the digestive system. To confuse an enemy, they squirt ink out of the siphon and cannot be seen behind the dark, watery screen. This ink was once used by artists and is called sepia, which is also the scientific name for cuttlefish.

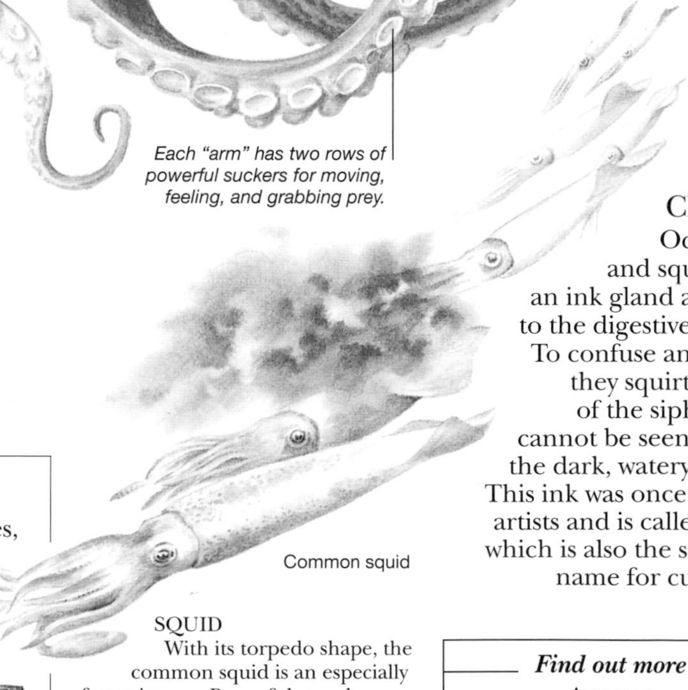

GIANT SQUID
Measuring 60 ft (20 m) in length including its tentacles, the giant squid is the world's largest invertebrate. It is an important source of food for sperm whales.

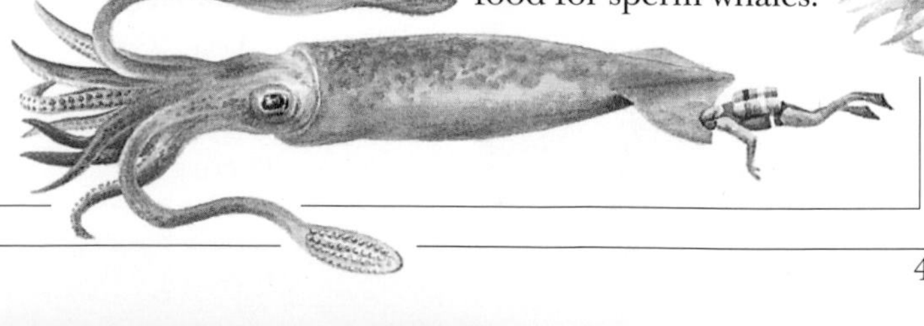

Common squid

SQUID
With its torpedo shape, the common squid is an especially fast swimmer. Powerful muscles inside the body squirt water rapidly through the siphon, pushing the creature along through the water.

Find out more
ANIMALS
DEEP-SEA WILDLIFE
OCEAN WILDLIFE

OIL

WITHOUT OIL, modern life would grind to a halt. Oil is needed to make the fuels that drive cars, trucks, diesel trains, ships, and aircraft. Power stations burn oil to produce much of the world's electricity, and many homes use oil-burning furnaces for heating. Oil is also very important because it is needed to make plastics, textiles, and other useful products. Oil is a dark, thick liquid that lies deep underground and beneath the seabed. Oil wells are bored to obtain oil, which is also called crude oil or petroleum. Crude oil contains a mixture of chemicals and many different types of oil. Lubricating oil is made from crude oil. It helps machine parts slide easily so that the machine works well.

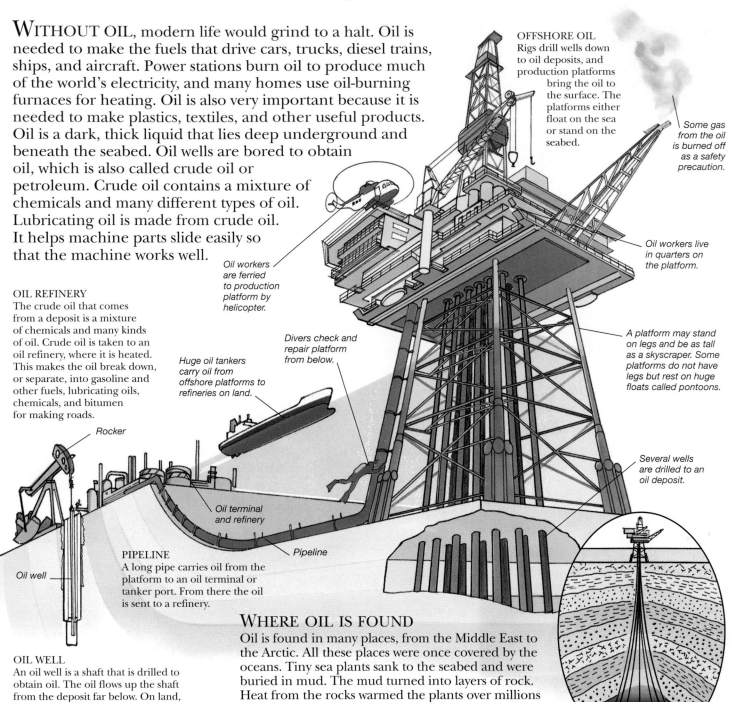

OFFSHORE OIL
Rigs drill wells down to oil deposits, and production platforms bring the oil to the surface. The platforms either float on the sea or stand on the seabed.

Some gas from the oil is burned off as a safety precaution.

Oil workers live in quarters on the platform.

Oil workers are ferried to production platform by helicopter.

A platform may stand on legs and be as tall as a skyscraper. Some platforms do not have legs but rest on huge floats called pontoons.

Divers check and repair platform from below.

Huge oil tankers carry oil from offshore platforms to refineries on land.

Several wells are drilled to an oil deposit.

OIL REFINERY
The crude oil that comes from a deposit is a mixture of chemicals and many kinds of oil. Crude oil is taken to an oil refinery, where it is heated. This makes the oil break down, or separate, into gasoline and other fuels, lubricating oils, chemicals, and bitumen for making roads.

Rocker

Oil terminal and refinery

Oil well

Pipeline

PIPELINE
A long pipe carries oil from the platform to an oil terminal or tanker port. From there the oil is sent to a refinery.

OIL WELL
An oil well is a shaft that is drilled to obtain oil. The oil flows up the shaft from the deposit far below. On land, a machine called a rocker pumps up the oil.

WHERE OIL IS FOUND
Oil is found in many places, from the Middle East to the Arctic. All these places were once covered by the oceans. Tiny sea plants sank to the seabed and were buried in mud. The mud turned into layers of rock. Heat from the rocks warmed the plants over millions of years and changed them into oil and natural gas.

VEGETABLE OILS
Plants and vegetables, such as olives, peanuts, sunflowers, and corn, provide valuable oils. Olive oil is made by crushing ripe olives; sunflower oil comes from sunflower seeds. These oils are used in cooking, and sunflower oil is used to make margarine. Factories treat plant and vegetable oils to make other products, such as soap and paints.

Olive oil

Olives

CHEMICALS FROM OIL
An oil refinery produces many chemicals from crude oil, which are called petro-chemicals. Factories use these chemicals to make plastics, textiles, and other products. Polyethylene, for example, is made from a gas that comes from oil. Chemicals from oil are also used to make drugs, fertilizers, detergents, and dyes and paints in all colors.

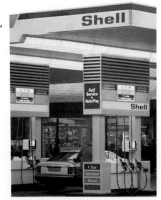

GASOLINE
Gasoline is one of the most important of all oil products. Diesel fuel is another kind of motor fuel made from oil.

Find out more

GAS
GEOLOGY
PLASTICS
ROCKS AND MINERALS
TEXTILES

OLYMPIC GAMES

Five interlocking rings make up the Olympic symbol.

EVERY TWO YEARS, the world's best athletes compete in the Summer or Winter Olympics. About 10,000 athletes from nearly 200 nations take part in the Summer Olympics, in more than 25 sports. The Winter Games are smaller, with 1,800 athletes from nearly 80 countries competing in seven sports.

The inspiration for today's Olympics came from Ancient Greek games of more than 2,000 years ago. The modern Olympics began in Athens, Greece, in 1896. Individual excellence and team achievement are the theme of the Olympic Games, not competition between nations. The International Olympic Committee (IOC) chooses a city, not a country, to host the games. No one country "wins" the games, and there is no prize money. Instead, individuals and teams compete for gold (first place), silver (second), and bronze (third) medals – as well as for the glory of taking part.

The opening ceremony for the Olympics is a spectacular occasion.

OLYMPIC FLAME

The Olympic Games open with a spectacular ceremony. The most important part is the lighting of the Olympic Flame with a burning torch. Teams of runners carry the torch from Olympia, in Greece, site of the ancient games, to the stadium where the games are to be held. This ceremony dates back to 1928, when Baron Pierre de Coubertin, founder of the modern Olympics, urged the athletes to "keep alive the flame of the revived Olympic spirit."

Ski jumping, shown here, is one of the most exciting events in the Winter Olympics.

ANCIENT GAMES

The ancient Olympics began as a religious festival. At first they consisted of just one race, but at their height the games lasted five days and included sports such as wrestling and chariot racing. Only men could compete in or watch the ancient Olympics. Women held their own games in honor of the goddess Hera.

POLITICS AND THE GAMES

The huge international audience for the Olympics ensures that any political protests and terrorist acts that occur gain maximum publicity. In 1968, winning athletes raised clenched fists to show that they supported a campaign to give black people more power. Four years later, an act of terrorism caused the deaths of 11 Israeli athletes at Munich, Germany.

The black power salute

WINTER OLYMPICS

A separate Winter Games takes place every four years, midway between two Summer Olympics. It includes ice and snow sports such as skating and skiing.

The Games include a variety of team and individual sports. New ones are added, and old ones are sometimes dropped.

Running   Cycling   Weightlifting   Gymnastics

Find out more

BALL GAMES
GREECE, ANCIENT
GYMNASTICS
SPORTS
TRACK AND FIELD SPORTS

OPERA AND SINGING

THE HUMAN VOICE is a versatile musical instrument. It has inspired many composers to write beautiful solo songs and works for groups of singers, or choirs, as well. Every voice is unique. Some women have a high soprano voice; others a deep, rich contralto. The male voice can range from a very high countertenor to a low bass. There are also variations in between. In the Middle Ages monks sang as part of their religious life, and wandering troubadours sang poetic songs of bravery and love. In the 17th century a new form of sung drama called opera began in Italy. New musical forms required trained voices, and by the 18th century great professional singers were delighting audiences everywhere. Today, singers perform all kinds of historical music, but constantly explore new ways of using their voices.

SYDNEY OPERA HOUSE
This striking opera house overlooking Sydney Harbor in Australia caused much debate when it opened in 1973. It was designed to match the shape of ships in the harbor. Hanging ceilings beneath the roofs create the right acoustics.

FAMOUS SINGERS

The greatest opera singers are those who can touch the emotions of their audience. Some, like Nellie Melba, moved people with the beauty of their voices. Maria Callas brought characters such as Aida and Tosca to life through superb acting as well as singing. Singers such as Kiri Te Kanawa and Placido Domingo sing popular songs as well as opera.

Maria Callas

GRAND OPERA

In grand opera every word is sung. Most of the main characters have an opportunity to show off their voices by singing arias, or solos. Some arias, such as "One fine day" from Puccini's *Madame Butterfly*, are very well known. Operas composed by Puccini, Verdi, Wagner, and Mozart also include fine music for the chorus, a group of opera singers who are not featured in solos.

MUSICALS

Musical comedies first became popular in the United States at the beginning of this century. Like opera, they have solos and a chorus, but the stories are mostly spoken. Spectacular dance routines are an important ingredient in musicals such as composer and conductor Leonard Bernstein's *West Side Story*. Many successful musicals are later made into films.

The film Fiddler on the Roof *drew on Russian and Hebrew musical traditions.*

FIDDLER ON THE ROOF
Popular musicals can turn performers into stars. Topol (above), found fame in *Fiddler on the Roof*, directed by choreographer Jerome Robbins.

WORK SONGS

In the days before steam was used to power ships, special songs called sea chanties were a popular accompaniment to heavy work. Singing them helped the sailors keep a steady, repetitive rhythm as they hauled on ropes to lift a sail or raise the anchor.

Find out more
COMPOSERS
MUSIC
ORCHESTRAS
THEATER

ORCHESTRAS

THE THRILLING SOUND made by an orchestra is no accident. An orchestra is not just a random collection of instruments brought along by the musicians; it is a carefully planned group of different families or types of instruments. Each family has its own part to play in the performance of a piece of music. The symphony orchestra is the largest group of musicians who perform together. They play four main sections of instruments: strings, woodwinds, brass, and percussion. Orchestras in the past were not so well organized, and for a long time musicians simply played whatever instruments they owned. But in the 18th century, composers wanted to make sure that their music would sound the same whenever it was played. Thus they wrote on the sheet of music which parts of the tune were to be played by which instruments of the orchestra. By the early 20th century the form of the symphony orchestra was established, and many large cities in Russia, the United States, and Europe had their own symphony orchestras.

GAMELAN
Indonesian orchestras are called gamelans. Most of the instruments belong to the percussion family: gongs, metallophones, xylophones, and gong chimes. Flutes, two-string fiddles, and zithers complete the gamelan, which has about 30 players.

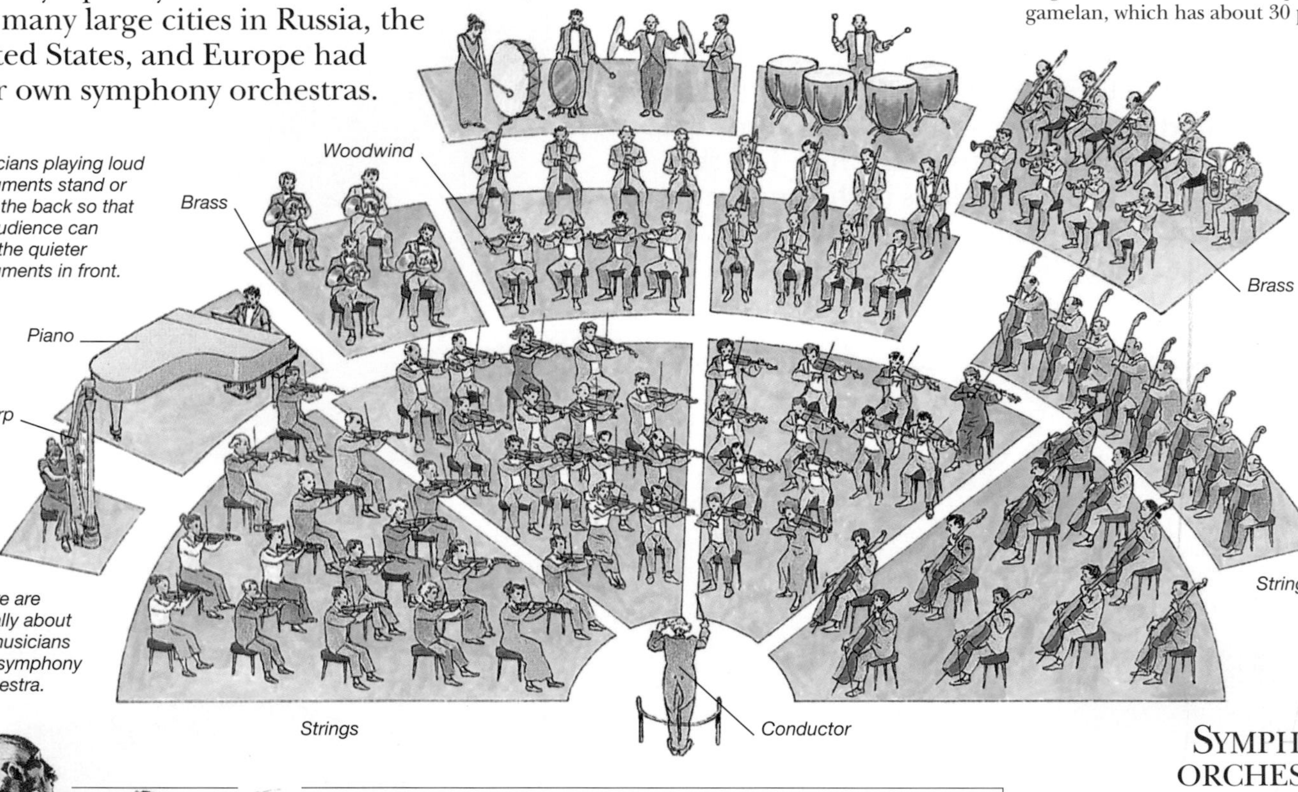

Percussion

Woodwind

Brass

Musicians playing loud instruments stand or sit at the back so that the audience can hear the quieter instruments in front.

Piano

Harp

Brass

Strings

There are usually about 90 musicians in a symphony orchestra.

Strings

Conductor

THE CONDUCTOR

The conductor uses hand motions or a baton – a small stick – to give the orchestra the tempo, or speed, of the music. Conductors don't just direct the orchestra like a police officer directing traffic; they interpret the composer's music, so that each performance is special. Arturo Toscanini (1867-1957), shown here, was an exciting conductor.

The pattern of movement of the conductor's baton indicates the rhythm of the music to the orchestra.

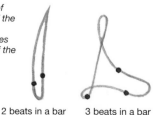

2 beats in a bar   3 beats in a bar   4 beats in a bar   5 beats in a bar

SYMPHONY ORCHESTRA

Great composers such as Wolfgang Amadeus Mozart (Austria) and Ludwig van Beethoven (Germany) wrote major pieces of orchestral music called symphonies. Symphony orchestras take their name from this kind of music, but they also play other kinds of classical music, film and television scores, and pop songs.

Find out more
COMPOSERS
MUSIC
MUSICAL INSTRUMENTS
OPERA AND SINGING

OSTRICHES AND EMUS

THERE ARE MANY KINDS of birds that cannot fly, including ostriches and emus, and most of these birds are large. Ostriches are the biggest of all living birds, at more than 8 ft (2.5 m) high. They live in the dry grassland areas of Africa, and their feathers are soft and fluffy because they are not needed for flying. Ostrich eggs are the biggest of any living bird. The egg shells are only ⅛ in (3 mm) thick but very hard. Ostriches and emus are speedy runners on land, and emus also swim well. The emu is a well-known pest to farmers in Australia, where it tramples on wheat fields. Other flightless birds include the secretive cassowary, which lives in the dense forests of Australasia, and the kiwi, which is found only in New Zealand. Kiwis are about 1 ft (30 cm) high, with tiny, useless wings. The rhea, a fast-running flightless bird, lives in the grassland areas of Brazil and Argentina in South America. Rheas gather in large flocks in winter.

BIGGEST EGG
An ostrich egg is 8 in (20 cm) long and 30 times heavier than a hen's egg. This makes ostrich eggs the largest bird's eggs in the world.

Male ostrich spreads out wings to defend chick against predator.

Female ostrich guards chicks.

Newly hatched ostrich young have speckled necks at first.

FASTEST BIRD ON LAND
The ostrich runs faster than any other bird and faster than most animals. It can run at 30 mph (50 km/h) for several minutes and may reach 45 mph (70 km/h) in short bursts.

OSTRICHES
Both ostriches guard the chicks, but the male usually looks after the eggs until they hatch. Within a month of hatching, the young ostrich chicks can run fast and feed themselves. Adult ostriches have strong, powerful legs and large, flexible feet for running quickly.

EMU
The Australian emu grows to 6 ft (2 m) tall, which makes it the second-largest living bird. Emus eat a varied diet of seeds, leaves, fruit, shoots, and insects. The female lays up to 15 green eggs in a shallow nest on the ground. The newly hatched young are striped and stay with their parents for the first 18 months.

CASSOWARY
Three different kinds of cassowary live in Australasia, wandering the dense, dark forests in search of fruit and seeds. The female common cassowary usually lays about five bright green eggs in a shallow nest lined with leaves. The male cassowary sits on the eggs to keep them warm and stays with the chicks after they hatch for up to one year.

RHEA
The male rhea makes a shallow nest called a scrape which can contain up to 60 eggs. This Darwin's rhea is about 3 ft (1 m) tall.

Find out more
AUSTRALIAN WILDLIFE
BIRDS
GRASSLAND WILDLIFE

OTTOMAN EMPIRE

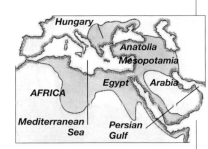

Ottoman Empire at its greatest extent

DURING THE LATE 13TH CENTURY, a group of nomadic Turkish tribes settled in Anatolia (modern Turkey). They were led by Osman, their first sultan, or ruler. He gave his name to the Ottoman Empire – one of the greatest empires in the world. By 1566, the empire had spread along the Mediterranean Sea across the Middle East to the Persian Gulf. The Ottomans owed their success to their military skill. Their armies included many Christian recruits organized into groups of highly trained foot soldiers called Janissaries. The empire grew wealthy on the trade it controlled throughout the Middle East. Art and architecture flourished within its borders. Discontent with Ottoman rule eventually weakened the empire, and it declined during the 19th century before it finally collapsed in 1918. The country of Turkey emerged out of its ruins.

SULEIMAN THE MAGNIFICENT
The greatest of all Ottoman sultans was Suleiman I (1495-1566), known as Suleiman the Magnificent. During his reign the Ottoman Empire reached the height of its power. A patron of the arts, Suleiman reformed the educational and legal systems.

Janissaries could be recognized by their elaborate headdresses.

Public letter writers wrote letters for people.

THE OTTOMANS
Although the Ottomans were Muslims, they allowed Christians and Jews to practice their own religions and tolerated the many different peoples who lived within their empire. The sultans lived in great luxury and wealth and encouraged the arts and learning. Ottoman women had to live in a separate section of the household called a harem.

OTTOMAN EMPIRE

1281-1324 Osman founds Ottoman Empire.

1333 Ottomans capture Gallipoli, Turkey, giving them a foothold in Europe.

1453 Ottomans capture city of Constantinople (now Istanbul), the capital of the Byzantine Empire; the city becomes the capital of the new empire.

1566 Ottoman Empire reaches its greatest extent.

1571 Christian navy destroys Turkish fleet at Lepanto.

1697-1878 Russia slowly expels the Turks from the lands around the Black Sea.

1878-1913 Turks expelled from most of their European possessions.

1914-18 Ottoman Empire fights on the side of Germany and Austria in World War I.

1918 Troops of several allied nations, including Britain and Greece, occupy the Ottoman Empire.

1922 Last sultan is overthrown. Turkey is declared a republic.

BATTLE OF LEPANTO
To stop the growth of Ottoman power, Pope Pius V formed a Christian league that included Spain, Venice, Genoa, and Naples. In 1571 the Christian forces defeated the Turks at the Battle of Lepanto, off the coast of Greece. The defeat was the first major setback to the Ottoman Empire and ended Turkish naval power in the Mediterranean Sea.

SICK MAN OF EUROPE
During the 19th century, the Ottoman Empire lost its grip on its European possessions and was in danger of falling apart. The empire became known as the "Sick Man of Europe."

A CONSULTATION ABOUT THE STATE OF TURKEY.

A 19th-century cartoon mocks the declining state of the Ottoman empire.

Find out more
BYZANTINE EMPIRE
ISLAM

OUTLAWS AND BANDITS

PEOPLE WHO LIVE OUTSIDE the law are called outlaws or bandits. They do not just break one or two laws: their whole way of life is illegal, or against the law. Some outlaws and bandits are criminals who hope to get rich by stealing. Many of the famous bandits of the Wild West lived like this. It was easy for them to avoid getting caught, because there were so few people to enforce the law. But other outlaws are "social bandits." They are outlaws because they try to change and improve society. Many countries have laws that benefit rich and powerful people and punish the poor and weak. These are the laws that social bandits break. Social bandits often escape capture for many years because many ordinary people support them. From their supporters the bandits can get food and shelter. There have been social bandits in most countries of the world at one time in their history. Some have become legendary figures, and people still tell stories of their daring deeds.

REWARDS

Rewards encouraged people to tell lawmen or police where outlaws were hiding. If there was a reward for the capture of an outlaw, he was said to have "a price on his head." Rewards were printed on posters such as the one above.

NED KELLY

Australian outlaw Ned Kelly (1855-80) was the son of a convict who had been sent to Tasmania as punishment for crimes in Ireland. He took up crime, and soon the British-led police were on his trail. Kelly and his gang became outlaws after they shot three policemen in 1878. Local people hid them, but the police trapped the gang in a hotel in 1880. Protected by homemade armor, Ned (left) tried to shoot his way out. The police caught him, and he was executed.

ROBIN HOOD

One of the most famous outlaws was Robin Hood. People believe he lived in England around 1300. He and his band of followers, or "merry men," hid in Sherwood Forest, close to Nottingham. They defended the peasants from the unjust rule of the landowners. Robin Hood robbed rich people so that he could give their money and possessions to the poor.

BELLE STARR

One of the handful of female outlaws was Belle Starr. She was the partner of several male outlaws and shared their lives of crime. In 1880, she and a Cherokee Native American named Sam Starr had a large ranch in Oklahoma. It became a hideout for outlaws. An unknown killer shot Belle Starr in 1889.

HIGHWAYMEN

In 18th-century England, bandits were called highwaymen. They stopped stagecoaches on lonely roads and robbed the wealthy travelers inside. The most famous of the highwaymen was Dick Turpin (1705-39). He robbed coaches on the busy roads to the northeast of London. He had a reputation for generosity and for giving away the valuables that he stole.

Find out more

AUSTRALIA, HISTORY OF
MYTHS AND LEGENDS
PIRATES

OWLS

Fringed edges on wing feathers help produce silent flight.

MOST OWLS HUNT BY NIGHT and are not often seen during the day. There are 133 different kinds, and more than 20 of these kinds are on the official list of threatened species. Many owls that live in tropical forests are rare and in danger of extinction because their homes are being destroyed. An owl is easily recognized by its big face and huge eyes. It has powerful feet and claws called talons for seizing prey, and a hooked bill for tearing flesh. An owl has a small body, big wings, and soft wing feathers, so it can swoop down silently on its prey. The snowy owl, from the Arctic and other northern regions, is about 2 ft (60 cm) long and hunts during the day. The elf owl of North America, which makes its nest hole in a cactus, is no bigger than a sparrow. Eagle owls, the largest owls, weigh about 9 lb (4 kg).

WISE BUT OMINOUS
The owl is known to be a wise bird because it has an intelligent appearance. In some cultures, its sighting is believed to be ominous (a sign of bad luck).

TAWNY OWL
The tawny owl lives in northern Asia and Europe and hunts all sorts of small mammals and birds. Its prey also includes worms, snails, and even fish.

BARN OWL
Throughout the world the barn owl is known as the farmer's friend because it catches rats and mice that live in barns and eat grain.

Tawny owl pellets also contain the remains of other birds, such as the starling skull and lower bill shown here.

This pellet has soft fur, hair, and feathers wrapped around the sharp bones and teeth inside.

Contents of owl pellet

Starling skull

Lower bill

Remains of three field mice

Skulls

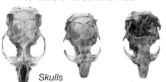

Leg bones

Hip bones

OWL PELLETS
Owls swallow their prey whole, but do not digest the bones, fur, feet, or beaks. Instead, the owl regurgitates, or coughs up, these remains in the form of pellets, which fall to the ground under the owl's roost, where it perches. Take a pellet apart, and you can tell what the owl has eaten recently.

SIGHT AND SOUND
Owls have good eyesight and hearing. Their eyes are at the front of the head, so they can see ahead with both eyes, unlike most birds, whose eyes are on each side of the head. Owl eyes cannot swivel in their sockets, but the bird has a very flexible neck, and can turn its head right around to see behind – as shown by this eagle owl.

Find out more
BIRDS
EAGLES
and other birds of prey
FLIGHT, ANIMAL
NORTH AMERICAN WILDLIFE

OXYGEN

WE CANNOT SEE, SMELL, or taste oxygen, yet without it, none of us could survive longer than a few minutes. It is fortunate, then, that oxygen is the most common substance on Earth. Oxygen is a gas. Mixed with other gases, it makes up about one-fifth of the air we breathe. Most of the oxygen in the world, though, does not float free as a gas. Instead, the oxygen is bound up in combination with other substances – in a solid or liquid form. This is because oxygen is chemically reactive: it readily combines with other substances, often giving off energy in the process. Burning is an example of oxygen at work. When a piece of timber burns, oxygen is combining with the wood and giving off heat. Oxygen is also found in water, combined with atoms of another gas, hydrogen. Oxygen can be extracted from water by passing an electric current through it. The electricity breaks the water into its parts – the gases oxygen and hydrogen – and oxygen bubbles off.

RESPIRATION
Our bodies need oxygen to release the energy consumed when we use our muscles. The oxygen we breathe in is used to "burn" the food we eat, producing energy. This process is called respiration. Blood carries the oxygen from the lungs, which extract it from the air, to the muscles where it is needed.

BURNING
Nothing can burn without oxygen. In outer space there is no air or oxygen, so it would be impossible to light a fire. The rocket motors used to launch spacecraft need oxygen to burn the rocket fuel and propel the craft upward. Spacecraft carry their own supply of pure oxygen, which mixes with the fuel in the rocket motor. When anything burns in pure oxygen, it produces a very hot flame. In welding machines a fuel gas is burned with pure oxygen, producing a flame hot enough to melt metals.

OXYGEN CYCLE
Breathing air or burning fuel removes oxygen from the atmosphere and gives off carbon dioxide. Plants do the reverse. During the day, they produce energy for growth by the process of photosynthesis. The green parts of the plant take in sunlight, water, and carbon dioxide to make new cells, and give off oxygen. Thus, oxygen continually passes into and out of the air. This is called the oxygen cycle.

People and animals breathe in oxygen.

Green plants absorb carbon dioxide breathed out by living creatures.

Mountain climbers, astronauts, and undersea divers carry a supply of oxygen to breathe. A special valve releases the oxygen at the correct pressure for breathing.

OXYGEN IN WATER
Sea water contains dissolved oxygen. Fish use this oxygen to breathe. Water flows over their gills, which extract the oxygen. Unlike other fish, some sharks can breathe only when moving in the water. To avoid suffocating, they must swim constantly, even when asleep.

Find out more
AIR
CHEMISTRY
FIRE
HUMAN BODY
PLANTS

PACIFIC OCEAN

ON A MAP OF THE PACIFIC OCEAN, the sunny, tropical Pacific islands look like tiny grains of sand scattered on the sea. The first adventurous settlers of these islands sailed from Southeast Asia. They spread gradually across the region, traveling over the vast expanses of ocean in their light wooden sailing boats. Today the islands are divided into three main groups: Micronesia to the north, Melanesia to the south, and Polynesia to the east. There are twelve independent countries in the Pacific, including Fiji, Tonga, and Nauru, one of the world's smallest nations. Europeans first arrived in the Pacific in the 16th century, and a number of islands maintain strong links with Europe. New Caledonia, for instance, is French. Many Pacific islanders lead lives that have barely changed for centuries; but there are a number of important modern industries, including large-scale fishing and mining, as well as tourism.

There are some 25,000 Pacific islands, but only a few thousand are inhabited. They stretch across the central part of the Pacific Ocean, straddling the equator and occupying an area larger than the whole of Asia. To the west and southwest lie Southeast Asia, Australia, and New Zealand; North and South America are to the east.

Wooden sailing boats called outriggers have a main hull and floats on either side.

ISLAND LIFE
Many Pacific islands are very small. They are the tops of submerged mountains. Coral reefs protect them from the Pacific waves. On the more remote islands, people live much as their ancestors did. Their simple houses have thatched roofs made of palm fronds. Families keep pigs and chickens and grow fruit and vegetables. They use traditional boats for fishing and for trade between the islands.

Those taking part in the spectacular traditional dances of Papua New Guinea wear costumes decorated with feathers and beads.

United States military bases cover virtually all of some Pacific Islands, mainly in Micronesia.

EASTER ISLAND
Tiny, remote Easter Island is one of the farthest east of the Pacific islands. A Dutch admiral gave the island its name when he landed there on Easter Day in 1722. More than 1,000 years ago the islanders' Polynesian ancestors carved mysterious stone statues, which still dot the dry, barren landscape.

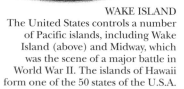

WAKE ISLAND
The United States controls a number of Pacific islands, including Wake Island (above) and Midway, which was the scene of a major battle in World War II. The islands of Hawaii form one of the 50 states of the U.S.A.

PAPUA NEW GUINEA
New Guinea, one of the world's largest islands, is part of Melanesia. Half of it belongs to Indonesia and is called Irian Jaya. The other half is a mountainous independent country called Papua New Guinea. Its thick tropical forests are the home of many remote tribes who have little contact with the outside world.

There are more than 600 of these huge heads on Easter Island, some over 65 ft (20 m) tall.

Find out more

OCEANS AND SEAS
WORLD WAR II

Volcano | Mountain | Ancient monument | Capital city | Large city/town | Large city and port

STATISTICS
Area: 305,106 sq miles (790,225 sq km)
Population: 7,820,900
Number of independent countries: 12
Languages: English, local languages and dialects
Religions: Protestant, Roman Catholic, Hindu
Highest point: Mount Wilhelm (Papua New Guinea) 14,793 ft (4,509 m)
Main occupations: Agriculture, fishing

NEW CALEDONIA
The Isle of Pines (above) is one of the smallest inhabited islands in the New Caledonia group. Like many of the Pacific Islands, New Caledonia is governed by a larger, more powerful country. France rules New Caledonia, and French aid provides one third of the country's income. Most of the rest comes from the export of nickel – the islands have 40 per-cent of the world's reserves of the metal.

 FIJI
Area: 7,054 sq miles (18,270 sq km)
Population: 839,000
Capital: Suva
Currency: Fiji dollar

 KIRIBATI
Area: 274 sq miles (710 sq km)
Population: 98,500
Capital: Bairiki
Currency: Australian dollar

 MARSHALL ISLANDS
Area: 70 sq miles (181 sq km)
Population: 56,400
Capital: Delap District
Currency: US dollar

 MICRONESIA
Area: 1,120 sq miles (2,900 sq km)
Population: 108,100
Capital: Palikir
Currency: US dollar

 NAURU
Area: 8.2 sq miles (21.2 sq km)
Population: 12,600
Government Center: Yaren
Currency: Australian dollar

 PAPUA NEW GUINEA
Area: 178,700 sq miles (462,840 sq km)
Population: 5,700,000
Capital: Port Moresby
Currency: Kina

 PALAU
Area: 192 sq miles (497 sq km)
Population: 19,700
Capital: Koror
Currency: US dollar

 SAMOA
Area: 1,027 sq miles (2,840 sq km)
Population: 178,000
Capital: Apia
Currency: Tala

 SOLOMON ISLANDS
Area: 111,583 sq miles (289,000 sq km)
Population: 477,000
Capital: Honiara
Currency: Solomon Islands dollar

 TONGA
Area: 290 sq miles (750 sq km)
Population: 108,100
Capital: Nuku'alofa
Currency: Tongan pa'anga

 TUVALU
Area: 10 sq miles (26 sq km)
Population: 11,300
Capital: Fongafale
Currency: Australian dollar

 VANUATU
Area: 4,706 sq miles (12,190 sq km)
Population: 212,000
Capital: Port-Villa
Currency: Vatu

DEPENDENCIES
Besides the 12 independent nations listed at the top of the page, there are many other island groups in the Pacific. Most of these islands depend on aid from a larger country, and some have very low populations. Pitcairn, for example, is a British colony and is the home of less than 100 people.

SCALE BAR
0   1000   2000   km
0   1000   2000   miles

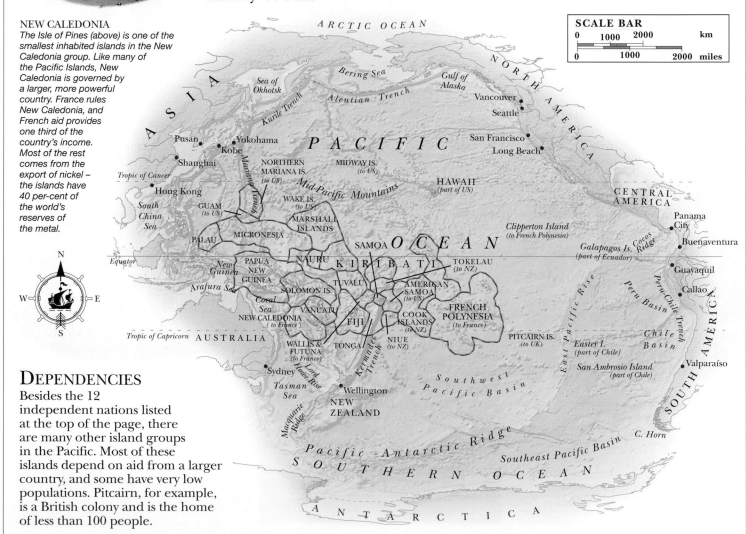

ARCTIC OCEAN

ASIA   NORTH AMERICA

Sea of Okhotsk   Bering Sea   Gulf of Alaska

Kurile Trench   Aleutian Trench

Pusan   Yokohama   Vancouver
Kobe   Seattle
Shanghai

PACIFIC

San Francisco
Long Beach

Tropic of Cancer

NORTHERN MARIANA IS. (to US)   MIDWAY IS. (to US)

Mid-Pacific Mountains   HAWAII (part of US)

Hong Kong

South China Sea

GUAM (to US)   WAKE IS. (to US)

CENTRAL AMERICA

PALAU   MICRONESIA   MARSHALL ISLANDS

Clipperton Island (to French Polynesia)

Panama City

SAMOA   OCEAN

Galapagos Is. (part of Ecuador)   Cocos Ridge   Buenaventura

Equator

New Guinea   PAPUA NEW GUINEA   NAURU   KIRIBATI   TOKELAU (to NZ)

Guayaquil

Arafura Sea   SOLOMON IS.   TUVALU   AMERICAN SAMOA (to US)

Callao

Coral Sea   VANUATU   FIJI   COOK ISLANDS (to NZ)   FRENCH POLYNESIA (to France)

NEW CALEDONIA (to France)

Peru Basin   Peru-Chile Trench

East Pacific Rise

Tropic of Capricorn   AUSTRALIA

WALLIS & FUTUNA (to France)   TONGA   NIUE (to NZ)   PITCAIRN IS. (to UK)

Easter I. (part of Chile)   Chile Basin

SOUTH AMERICA

Kermadec Trench

Sydney   Lord Howe Rise

San Ambrosio Island (part of Chile)

Valparaíso

Tasman Sea   Wellington

Southwest Pacific Basin

NEW ZEALAND

Macquarie Ridge

C. Horn

Pacific-Antarctic Ridge   Southeast Pacific Basin

SOUTHERN OCEAN

ANTARCTICA

N W E S

PAINTERS

ARTISTS USE PAINT in the same way that writers use words to convey ideas on paper. Painters capture the likeness of a face or a flower, but they can do much more than just paint a realistic image. Painters work skillfully with color, texture, and shape to create all kinds of eye-catching images of the world as they see it. Every culture throughout history has produced its own great painters, from Giotto in the 14th century to Picasso in the 20th century. There have been many different groups, or movements, in painting, such as classicism, cubism, and pop art. Painters change the way we see the world. Rembrandt's portrait paintings, for example, are powerful studies from real life, while Salvador Dali's strange surrealist (dreamlike) landscapes are drawn from his imagination. Painters use all kinds of paint to create a picture – thick blobs of oil paint daubed onto a canvas with a palette knife; delicate brushstrokes of water-color on a sheet of paper. Some painters dab paint on with sponges, rags, even their fingers; others flick paint onto a surface. Whatever the medium (materials) used, each great painter has his or her own distinctive style.

EARLY PAINTERS
The artists of Ancient Egypt decorated the walls of tombs with scenes of gods and goddesses and of hunting and feasting. The Minoan people of early Greece painted their houses and palaces with pictures of dancers, birds, and flowers. Roman artists painted gods and goddesses and scenes from classical mythology.

MEDIEVAL PAINTERS
Up until the 14th century, Western artists painted mostly Christian subjects – the life of Christ and the saints. Painters used rich colors and thin layers of gold to make these religious paintings. These early artists used different methods of painting people from later Western painters, and although the paintings may look flat to us, they are no less powerful. Artists worked on wood panels for altarpieces and painted directly on church walls.

People in medieval paintings sometimes look stiff and expressionless, like the figures in this 11th-century picture (left) of an emperor, a saint, and an angel.

The Sistine Chapel ceiling, painted by Michelangelo.

RENAISSANCE
One of the greatest periods in European painting was the Renaissance, which reached its height in Italy in the early part of the 16th century. During the Renaissance, painters developed more realistic styles of painting. They studied perspective and the human body, painted more realistic landscapes, and developed portrait painting.

MICHELANGELO
Michelangelo Buonarroti (1475-1564) is one of the best-known Italian Renaissance painters. Much of his work was for Pope Julius II, who commissioned him to paint the ceiling of the Sistine Chapel in the Vatican, in Rome, between 1508 and 1512.

Michelangelo had difficulty in reaching certain parts of the ceiling in the Sistine Chapel, so he built a scaffold and sometimes lay on his back to paint.

GIOTTO
The Italian artist Giotto (c.1266-1337) painted at the beginning of the Renaissance. He brought a new sense of naturalness to paintings. The painting shown above is called *The Flight into Egypt*. It shows Mary and Jesus on a donkey being led by Joseph.

REMBRANDT

Most people know the Dutch artist Rembrandt H. van Rijn (1606-69) only by his first name. He is well-known for his portraits that are full of expression. The painting shown here is one of many self-portraits.

ROMANTIC MOVEMENT

During the late 18th and early 19th centuries, painters such as the French artist Eugène Delacroix (1798-1863) began a new style of painting, which became known as the Romantic movement. The romantics used bright color and a free handling of paint to create their dramatic pictures. The English painter J.M.W. Turner (1775-1851) painted landscapes and seascapes flooded with light and color.

ASIAN PAINTERS

While European art was developing, Asian artists were evolving their own styles of painting. The Chinese observed nature accurately and painted exquisite pictures with simple brushstrokes in ink on silk and paper. Some Japanese artists, such as Hokusai (1760-1849), made beautiful prints.

This painting is by the modern Japanese painter Kaii Higashiyama (born 1918); it is called Flowery Glow.

PICASSO

Many people believe that the Spanish painter Pablo Picasso (1881-1973) was the most creative and influential artist of the 20th century. From a very young age, Picasso was extremely skillful at drawing and painting. His restless personality led him to paint in many different styles. One style was his "blue period" of painting, when he concentrated on blue as the main color for his pictures. In 1907, Picasso painted a picture called *Les Demoiselles D'Avignon*, which shocked many people – it was a painting of human figures represented by angular and distorted shapes. This led to a style of painting called cubism.

This is a detail from the painting by the French artist Fragonard (1732-1806) called The Swing.

The Poppy Field, *by Claude Monet*

This photograph shows Picasso with a painting of his children, Claude and Paloma. He is on his way to show this painting at an exhibition of his work.

IMPRESSIONISM

At an exhibition in Paris in 1874 a painting by the French artist Claude Monet caused an uproar. Art critics and the public were used to seeing realistic objects in pictures, but Monet and his fellow artists, known as impressionists, painted in dabs of color to create the effect of light and shade. Other great artists of the impressionist movement were Camille Pissarro, Pierre Auguste Renoir, Edgar Degas, Mary Cassatt, and Alfred Sisley.

MONET

Claude Monet (1840-1926) was the leader of the impressionists. He painted many pictures of the flowers in his garden at Giverny and in the French countryside, including the picture above right, called *The Poppy Field*. Seen close up, the picture consists of many brushstrokes of different colors, but from a distance the dabs of color come together to form a field of red flowers.

HOCKNEY

David Hockney (born 1937) is a well-known British painter. He is famous for his pictures of California, especially paintings of swimming pools like this one, called *A Bigger Splash*. Hockney works with many different materials, including photographs and color photocopies.

MODERN PAINTERS

Since the beginning of the 20th century, painters have experimented with different ways of creating pictures. Picasso and Georges Braque stuck fabric, sand, and newsprint onto canvases to make collages. Piet Mondrian painted in straight lines and right angles. Action painting was developed by the American artist Jackson Pollock, who splashed paint onto huge canvases on his studio floor.

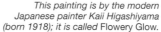

Find out more
DRAWING
LEONARDO DA VINCI
PAINTERS, US
PAINTING
RENAISSANCE
SCULPTURE

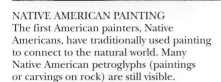

Ancient Native American petroglyphs in Utah

US PAINTERS

FROM NATIVE AMERICAN CAVE DRAWINGS to graffiti art, American painters have developed a uniquely American style. Portraits of heroes and battle scenes dominated 18th-century painting. In the 19th century, many painters went to Europe to study. Some of these painters returned home and drew on their experience to develop an American style, with American subjects. At the turn of the 20th century, realism was popular, as painters began to capture ordinary people and landscapes. During World War II, several prominent European painters moved to America, and their presence ignited the first American art movement to gain international attention: abstract expressionism. In the 1950s, Pop Art emerged, borrowing styles from comic books and advertising.

NATIVE AMERICAN PAINTING
The first American painters, Native Americans, have traditionally used painting to connect to the natural world. Many Native American petroglyphs (paintings or carvings on rock) are still visible.

COLONIAL PAINTING
Portraits were the most popular type of painting in the American colonies. Self-trained portrait painters called limners rode from town to town to paint their subjects. Among the most famous painters in the colonial years were John Singleton Copley – who painted President John Adams (left) – and Gilbert Stuart, remembered for his portraits of George Washington.

MARY CASSATT'S *THE BATH*
Born near Pittsburgh, Pennsylvania, Mary Cassatt (1845–1926) spent much of her life in France. She embraced the ideas of the French impressionist painters, using dabs of light and bright color to give the effect of what the eye sees at a glance. Many of her paintings show the daily lives of women, often with their children.

Mother About to Wash Her Sleepy Child (1880), by Mary Cassatt

Self Portrait (1902), by Thomas Eakins

AMERICAN PAINTERS ABROAD
Many American artists traveled to Europe, especially to Paris, in the 1800s. Some chose to remain there, but others brought European influences – especially realism in painting – back home. Thomas Eakins painted vivid and realistic portraits that shocked many people with their directness.

REGIONALISM
In the early 1920s, a group of American painters decided to break away from the influences of European art to focus on traditional American subjects. A movement called "regionalism" emerged. The most famous painting from this movement is Grant Wood's *American Gothic*, a portrait of an American farmer and his daughter.

American Gothic (1930), by Grant Wood

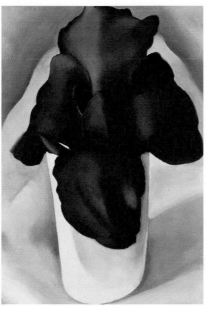

GEORGIA O'KEEFFE
One of America's most important artists, Georgia O'Keeffe (1887-1986) is famous for her precise paintings of natural objects, from rocks and bones to shells and clouds. Among the best known of her vibrant and colorful paintings are giant images of flowers, which she painted large enough to show exactly what she saw in each blossom. O'Keeffe's subjects were usually American, from the red hills near her ranch in New Mexico to a sun-bleached cattle skull in the desert. Her works played a large part in shaping the identity of American art.

Red Gladiola in a White Vase (1928), by Georgia O'Keeffe

NEW YORK CITY
During World War II, a number of important and influential European painters came to the United States as refugees. Many settled in New York City, which became the center of American painting.

Yellow, Gray, Black (1948), by Jackson Pollock

ABSTRACT EXPRESSIONISM
The Europeans who came to America helped found abstract expressionism, a movement that used bold colors and experimental styles to express strong emotions and unconscious impulses. For the first time, the United States became the center of the Western art world.

Woman Sitting (1943), by Willem de Kooning

WILLEM DE KOONING

One of the first important painters to emerge from the abstract expressionist movement was Willem de Kooning (1904-1997). De Kooning was born in Rotterdam, the Netherlands, in 1904, and emigrated to the United States in 1926. Unlike his contemporaries, who painted non-naturalistic images, de Kooning painted people. In his best-known works, a series of paintings of women, de Kooning used layer upon layer of thick paint and quick brushstrokes to convey a feeling of energy while distorting his figures amidst a whirl of color.

RECENT AMERICAN PAINTING
Modern American painters work in an enormous variety of styles, their subjects reflecting every aspect of contemporary American life. Keith Haring and Jean-Michel Basquiat brought the styles of the city – especially graffiti – to the canvas. Julian Schnabel and David Salle led a movement called neo-expressionism. These painters portrayed real objects in a nonrealistic style, using bold brushwork and vivid colors to make their works more personal and immediate.

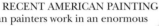

Arroz con Pollo (1981), by Jean-Michel Basquiat

POP ART
In the late 1950s, a new movement arose to challenge abstract expressionism. Pop Art (short for popular art) embraced popular culture as its subject matter, from hamburgers to gas stations, and celebrated the age of mass production. Pop artists such as Jim Dine, Roy Lichtenstein, and Andy Warhol used styles more often seen in comic strips and advertising. Warhol's *Campbell's Soup Cans* (above) is one of the best-known examples of Pop Art.

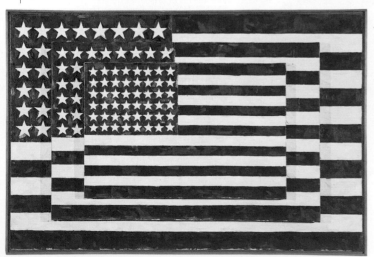

JASPER JOHNS'S *THREE FLAGS*

American artist Jasper Johns is famous for using common objects in paintings and sculptures to challenge people to think about the distinctions between the real world and art. Johns was born in Augusta, Georgia, but lived and worked in New York City. He painted simple, strong subjects such as flags, numbers, and targets, and sculpted with everyday objects such as cans and light bulbs. Johns also used collage, fastening objects to a canvas background to build an image. In his most famous work, *Three Flags* (1958), Johns sought to make the images seem almost like objects rather than a painting.

Three Flags (1958), by Jasper Johns

Find out more
PAINTING
SCULPTURE
UNITED STATES, HISTORY OF

PAINTING

SINCE PREHISTORIC PEOPLE first applied natural pigments to cave walls, artists have painted to express themselves. Paintings can be important historical documents, providing clues as to how people dressed at the time of the painting and what their customs and interests were. Training is not necessary in order to paint, but it can help in learning basic techniques. A painting can be done with oil paints, watercolors, or as a fresco – that is, painting onto wet plaster. The type of paint depends on what the powdered pigment or color is mixed with to allow it to be brushed onto the painting. Oil paints use a vegetable oil such as linseed or poppy oil. Before oil paints were developed in the 15th century, artists made tempera paintings in which the pigments were mixed with an emulsion such as egg yolk. Artists may paint onto almost any surface: from rock and wood to fabric, paper, metal, plastics – even skin. They may also choose any subject, such as a still life or something abstract like random shapes.

CAVE PAINTING
Eighteen thousand years ago, people used burned bones and wood, and different-colored soil mixed with water or animal fat, to paint scenes on cave walls. South African bushmen produced this cave painting. It shows men hunting an eland, a type of deer.

OIL PAINTING
Oil paint has the advantage of drying slowly. This gives the artist time to change things on the painting while the paint is still wet, and makes it easier to blend colors and tones or even scrape off the paint where it is not working successfully. Oil paint can be applied thickly or thinly. It is flexible enough to be built up in layers to produce a particular effect. The paint is applied to a canvas (a piece of fabric stretched onto a frame) with brushes, a painting knife, or fingers.

Palette

Thumb hole allows artist to hold palette with one hand while painting with the other.

Linseed oil is a popular binder for oil paint.

Turpentine for thinning paint

The best brushes for oil painting are made from hog's hair or sable. Some brushes are made of synthetic fibers.

Pigments for making oil paints may come from natural sources such as berries, bark, roots, and earth, or from petroleum and metals.

The artist staples the canvas to a wooden frame. This makes the canvas taut.

A coat of primer prevents the canvas from absorbing the paint; then an outline is done.

The artist applies oil paint in layers. When dry, the painting will be coated with varnish to protect it against dirt.

PREPARING FOR OIL PAINTING
Linen or cotton canvas is a popular surface or "support" for oil painting. Before beginning, the canvas must be specially prepared (left). Once it is ready, the painter can begin to apply layers of paint. Some artists draw outlines in charcoal or pencil on the canvas first; others put the paint straight on. Oil paint can be thinned down with turpentine to produce an effect much like a watercolor.

RESTORATION

Paintings lose their freshness over the years. Oil paints tend to turn yellow and crack, canvases may rot, and strong light and air pollution may damage pictures.

To clean and repair paintings, highly skilled picture restorers use both modern science and knowledge of great artists' techniques and the types of paint they used.

BODY PAINTING

For thousands of years, people have used red, yellow, and brown earth, chalk, and dyes made from plants and animals to paint designs on their bodies. Some designs are purely for decoration at special festivals; others have more significance. Many tribes painted their bodies with the markings of the animals they were about to hunt; they believed this gave them power over their prey. Indian brides traditionally paint beautiful designs on their hands with a dye made from the henna plant (above).

WATERCOLOR PAINTING

The paints used in watercolors are finely ground pigments bound with gum arabic, from the acacia tree. The paint is mixed with water, and the gum helps it stick to the paper. There are two types of watercolor painting; transparent, in which the white of the paper provides a clear background to the transparent colors, and opaque, in which thicker "gouache" paints are used to create opaque colors on the painting.

Good quality paper is the best surface on which to do a watercolor painting.

Poster paints

Artists use large sable brushes to apply watercolor to paper.

Acrylic paints – pigments bound with a synthetic resin – were developed in the 20th century. They are popular with painters because they dry quickly and can be applied to almost any surface.

FRESCO PAINTING

Fresco painting (meaning "fresh" in Italian) involves brushing pigments ground in water directly onto the plaster while it is still wet. This way the paint is absorbed deep into the plaster. The painter has to work very quickly within small areas. The technique reached its height during the Italian Renaissance; Michelangelo (1475-1564) took several years to paint a fresco showing scenes from the Bible on the ceiling of the Sistine Chapel in Rome. The Ancient Greeks were expert fresco painters.

This colorful dolphin fresco is in the queen's apartment of the Minoan palace of Knossos, in Crete.

Find out more

DRAWING
MINOANS
PAINTERS
RENAISSANCE
SCULPTURE

PAPER

TEAR A PIECE OF PAPER, and you will see tiny fibers along the tear. These are plant fibers, and a piece of paper contains millions of them stuck together. Paper may also contain other materials, such as a filler to make it stiff, resin to keep ink from soaking into the fibers, and dye to color the paper. Using different materials produces different kinds of paper, from stiff, heavy cardboard to light, fluffy tissues. The plant fibers in paper come mainly from trees. Millions of trees are cut down every year to provide us with paper, and new trees are planted in their place. Rags are also used to make some paper, and waste paper can be reused to make new paper. Recycled paper is paper made completely or partly from waste paper. Making paper in this way saves forests, uses much less energy, and reduces air and water pollution. Paper is named after papyrus, a reedlike plant that the Ancient Egyptians used as a writing material more than 5,000 years ago. The Chinese invented the paper that we use about 2,000 years ago. But wasps have been making paper for much longer. They chew up wood and plant fibers to make paper nests.

Wallpaper

Party decorations

DECORATION
Wallpaper gives a special look to a room. The pattern is printed on the surface of heavy paper or pressed paper. People hang paper decorations at parties and other festive occasions.

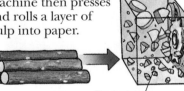

Cardboard packaging

Newspaper

Paper napkin

Tissues

Check

Teabag

Photograph

PAPER IN THE HOME
Paper is good for tasks such as cleaning because it can absorb liquids. Light paper soaks up liquid and is used to make tissues and paper towels.

INFORMATION
A huge amount of information is recorded on paper, either as printed words and pictures or as photographs. People also use paper for money, in the form of banknotes and checks.

Writing paper

Notepaper

PAPER MAKING
A paper mill is a large factory that turns trees into big rolls of paper. The trees are ground up and mixed with water to make wood pulp. A machine then presses and rolls a layer of pulp into paper.

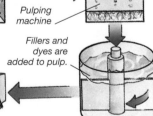

Waste paper is added to the pulping machine to make recycled paper.

Pulping machine

Trees are cut down and sawed into logs. The logs are then sent to paper mills.

The bark is removed and the logs are cut into tiny chips.

Fillers and dyes are added to pulp.

PAPER TYPES
There are many different types of paper. They range from the most delicate handmade papers to the toughest cardboard, and they have many uses. The color, strength, and texture of the paper can be changed by printing and dyeing, and by mixing it with materials such as wax or plastic.

Wrapping paper

Handmade paper

TREES FOR PAPER
A big tree has to fall to provide each person with a year's supply of paper. A new tree is planted in its place, usually at a special tree farm. It takes between 15 and 50 years for a freshly planted tree to grow large enough to be used for paper making.

PAPER-MAKING MACHINE
Wet wood pulp flows onto a belt with a mesh of tiny holes. Water is sucked out, and the wet paper passes through rollers and heated cylinders that press and dry it. The finished paper is wound onto a large roll.

Find out more
BOOKS
NEWSPAPERS
POLLUTION
PRINTING
TREES

ANCIENT
PERSIANS

MORE THAN 3,000 YEARS AGO, the present-day country of Iran was home to various tribes, including the Medes and the Persians. For many years, the Medes ruled the area, but in 549 B.C. Cyrus, the Persian king of a small state called Ashan, conquered the Medes and set out to create a vast kingdom. Within 30 years Persia had become the most powerful nation in the world, and the Persian Empire covered all of Mesopotamia, Anatolia (Turkey), the eastern Mediterranean, and what are now Pakistan and Afghanistan. For more than 200 years the Persian Empire was the greatest the world had ever seen. The Persians were skilled warriors, horse riders, and craftworkers. They were also highly organized. Under Darius I, also called Darius the Great, the empire was divided into provinces called satrapies. A network of roads linked the provinces and enabled people to trade easily. Darius introduced a postal system and a single currency to unify the empire. The empire flourished until the Greek leader Alexander the Great conquered Persia in 331 B.C.

CYRUS THE GREAT
Cyrus (ruled 549-529 B.C.) founded the Persian Empire. During his reign many different peoples, including Babylonians, Egyptians, Greeks, and Syrians, lived in the Persian Empire.

People bringing gifts to the royal palace

Reliefs show people arriving for a festival on New Year's Day

PERSEPOLIS
In about 520 B.C. Darius I began to build the city of Persepolis. Building continued in the reign of Xerxes I (486-465 B.C.). Persepolis was the site of many beautiful buildings, including the royal palace. The city was used only once a year at New Year, when the peoples of the empire brought tributes (gifts) to the king.

Remains of Persepolis include statues such as the carved head of this horse in the Central Palace.

Sardis
Nineveh
Babylon **Susa**
Jerusalem **Parsagadae**
Persepolis
Thebes

PERSIAN EMPIRE
At its height, the Persian Empire stretched from the borders of India to the Nile River in Egypt. The city of Susa was the administrative capital of the empire, Persepolis was the royal capital, and Parsagadae was the city where kings were crowned.

ZOROASTRIANISM
The Persian people followed the teachings of a prophet named Zoroaster, who lived from about 628 to 551 B.C. Zoroastrianism was the main religion in Persia until the country became Muslim in the 7th century A.D.

Zoroastrian priests carried a mace with a bull's head as a symbol of the priests' religious battle against evil.

PERSEPOLIS TODAY
When Alexander the Great invaded the Persian Empire, he burned Persepolis to the ground. But the ruins of the city, including the royal palace, can still be seen today in southern Iran.

ANCIENT PERSIANS

549 B.C. Cyrus the Great defeats the Medes peoples and forms the Persian Empire.

538 B.C. Cyrus conquers the Babylonian Empire.

529 B.C. Cyrus dies.

525 B.C. Persians conquer Egypt.

521-486 B.C. Reign of Darius the Great.

510 B.C. Persians invade southeast Europe and Central Asia.

500-449 B.C. Persian Wars between Persian Empire and Greek states, because Persian kings felt threatened by the democracy of Greece.

490 B.C. Greeks defeat Persians at the Battle of Marathon.

480 B.C. Greek navy defeats Persians at the Battle of Salamis.

334 B.C. Alexander the Great invades Persia.

331 B.C. Alexander defeats Persians at the Battle of Gaugamela. Persian Empire collapses.

Find out more
ALEXANDER THE GREAT
ASSYRIANS
BABYLONIANS
GREECE, ANCIENT
MIDDLE EAST

PAPER

TEAR A PIECE OF PAPER, and you will see tiny fibers along the tear. These are plant fibers, and a piece of paper contains millions of them stuck together. Paper may also contain other materials, such as a filler to make it stiff, resin to keep ink from soaking into the fibers, and dye to color the paper. Using different materials produces different kinds of paper, from stiff, heavy cardboard to light, fluffy tissues. The plant fibers in paper come mainly from trees. Millions of trees are cut down every year to provide us with paper, and new trees are planted in their place. Rags are also used to make some paper, and waste paper can be reused to make new paper. Recycled paper is paper made completely or partly from waste paper. Making paper in this way saves forests, uses much less energy, and reduces air and water pollution. Paper is named after papyrus, a reedlike plant that the Ancient Egyptians used as a writing material more than 5,000 years ago. The Chinese invented the paper that we use about 2,000 years ago. But wasps have been making paper for much longer. They chew up wood and plant fibers to make paper nests.

ORIGAMI
Folding a sheet of paper into a decorative shape is called origami. The art of origami is at least 300 years old and began in Japan.

Wallpaper

Party decorations

DECORATION
Wallpaper gives a special look to a room. The pattern is printed on the surface of heavy paper or pressed paper. People hang paper decorations at parties and other festive occasions.

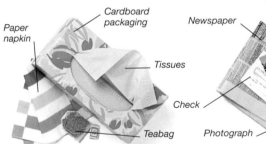

Cardboard packaging

Paper napkin

Tissues

Check

Teabag

Newspaper

Photograph

PAPER IN THE HOME
Paper is good for tasks such as cleaning because it can absorb liquids. Light paper soaks up liquid and is used to make tissues and paper towels.

INFORMATION
A huge amount of information is recorded on paper, either as printed words and pictures or as photographs. People also use paper for money, in the form of banknotes and checks.

Writing paper

Notepaper

Wrapping paper

Handmade paper

PAPER MAKING

A paper mill is a large factory that turns trees into big rolls of paper. The trees are ground up and mixed with water to make wood pulp. A machine then presses and rolls a layer of pulp into paper.

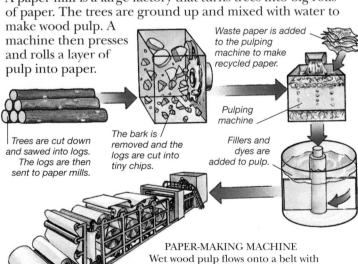

Waste paper is added to the pulping machine to make recycled paper.

Pulping machine

Fillers and dyes are added to pulp.

Trees are cut down and sawed into logs. The logs are then sent to paper mills.

The bark is removed and the logs are cut into tiny chips.

PAPER-MAKING MACHINE
Wet wood pulp flows onto a belt with a mesh of tiny holes. Water is sucked out, and the wet paper passes through rollers and heated cylinders that press and dry it. The finished paper is wound onto a large roll.

PAPER TYPES

There are many different types of paper. They range from the most delicate handmade papers to the toughest cardboard, and they have many uses. The color, strength, and texture of the paper can be changed by printing and dyeing, and by mixing it with materials such as wax or plastic.

TREES FOR PAPER
A big tree has to fall to provide each person with a year's supply of paper. A new tree is planted in its place, usually at a special tree farm. It takes between 15 and 50 years for a freshly planted tree to grow large enough to be used for paper making.

ANCIENT
PERSIANS

MORE THAN 3,000 YEARS AGO, the present-day country of Iran was home to various tribes, including the Medes and the Persians. For many years, the Medes ruled the area, but in 549 B.C. Cyrus, the Persian king of a small state called Ashan, conquered the Medes and set out to create a vast kingdom. Within 30 years Persia had become the most powerful nation in the world, and the Persian Empire covered all of Mesopotamia, Anatolia (Turkey), the eastern Mediterranean, and what are now Pakistan and Afghanistan. For more than 200 years the Persian Empire was the greatest the world had ever seen. The Persians were skilled warriors, horse riders, and craftworkers. They were also highly organized. Under Darius I, also called Darius the Great, the empire was divided into provinces called satrapies. A network of roads linked the provinces and enabled people to trade easily. Darius introduced a postal system and a single currency to unify the empire. The empire flourished until the Greek leader Alexander the Great conquered Persia in 331 B.C.

CYRUS THE GREAT
Cyrus (ruled 549-529 B.C.) founded the Persian Empire. During his reign many different peoples, including Babylonians, Egyptians, Greeks, and Syrians, lived in the Persian Empire.

People bringing gifts to the royal palace

Reliefs show people arriving for a festival on New Year's Day

PERSEPOLIS
In about 520 B.C. Darius I began to build the city of Persepolis. Building continued in the reign of Xerxes I (486-465 B.C.). Persepolis was the site of many beautiful buildings, including the royal palace. The city was used only once a year at New Year, when the peoples of the empire brought tributes (gifts) to the king.

Remains of Persepolis include statues such as the carved head of this horse in the Central Palace.

PERSIAN EMPIRE
At its height, the Persian Empire stretched from the borders of India to the Nile River in Egypt. The city of Susa was the administrative capital of the empire, Persepolis was the royal capital, and Parsagadae was the city where kings were crowned.

ZOROASTRIANISM
The Persian people followed the teachings of a prophet named Zoroaster, who lived from about 628 to 551 B.C. Zoroastrianism was the main religion in Persia until the country became Muslim in the 7th century A.D.

Zoroastrian priests carried a mace with a bull's head as a symbol of the priests' religious battle against evil.

PERSEPOLIS TODAY
When Alexander the Great invaded the Persian Empire, he burned Persepolis to the ground. But the ruins of the city, including the royal palace, can still be seen today in southern Iran.

ANCIENT PERSIANS

549 B.C. Cyrus the Great defeats the Medes peoples and forms the Persian Empire.

538 B.C. Cyrus conquers the Babylonian Empire.

529 B.C. Cyrus dies.

525 B.C. Persians conquer Egypt.

521-486 B.C. Reign of Darius the Great.

510 B.C. Persians invade southeast Europe and Central Asia.

500-449 B.C. Persian Wars between Persian Empire and Greek states, because Persian kings felt threatened by the democracy of Greece.

490 B.C. Greeks defeat Persians at the Battle of Marathon.

480 B.C. Greek navy defeats Persians at the Battle of Salamis.

334 B.C. Alexander the Great invades Persia.

331 B.C. Alexander defeats Persians at the Battle of Gaugamela. Persian Empire collapses.

Find out more
ALEXANDER THE GREAT
ASSYRIANS
BABYLONIANS
GREECE, ANCIENT
MIDDLE EAST

PETS

LIKE TRUSTED FRIENDS, pets give us comfort and affection. In return, pets need people to provide food and shelter and to care for their health. Pets are tame animals kept for companionship or because they are attractive to look at. Humans first tamed animals for their milk or meat 11,000 years ago, but people have kept pets only since about 2000 B.C. At that time the Ancient Egyptians tamed hyenas, cats, and even lions for company. Choosing the right pet is an important decision. Some pets, such as large dogs, need space to run around, so it is cruel to keep them in a small home. Cats thrive almost anywhere, but enjoy exploring outdoors. And many pets need very little attention or space – there's room in even the smallest home for a fish tank or a birdcage.

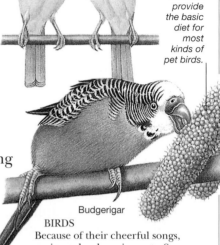

Canaries

Seeds and fruit provide the basic diet for most kinds of pet birds.

Budgerigar

CATS
Mammals make rewarding pets because they are affectionate and often become fond of their owners. Cats and dogs are the most common pets; there are more than 50 million pet cats in the United States alone.

KEEPING PETS
In their natural habitat, animals look after themselves. But few pets can hunt or exercise in a natural way. It is therefore important to understand a pet's requirements and give it what it needs to stay healthy. Exercise and a suitable diet are most important, but all pets also need a clean living area and the care of a vet when they get sick.

Hamsters exercise by running inside a wheel.

The hamster drinks from a drip feeder.

Hamsters keep their teeth sharp by gnawing, so their cages have to be made with sturdy metal bars.

Hamsters eat dried food such as seeds and nuts, as well as fresh vegetables.

BIRDS
Because of their cheerful songs, canaries make charming pets. Some cage birds, especially parrots and mynah birds, can be trained to imitate human speech. The world's most talkative bird was an African gray parrot that knew more than 800 words.

BREEDING PETS
All pets may produce young if adult males and females are put together. In a large aviary (above), birds will pair off and make nests, just as they do in the wild. For especially valuable pets, breeding pairs are carefully selected, since the best males and females usually produce the best young.

GUINEA PIGS
In warm weather guinea pigs can live in outdoor cages and feed on fresh grass. Some special breeds have long, glossy coats, which have to be kept well brushed. Guinea pigs are not actually pigs at all, but small rodents that came originally from South America.

Gerbils like to play in cardboard tubes, but they also tend to gnaw them.

Turtles like to swim, so they have to be kept in tanks containing pools of water.

If handled correctly, pythons make good pets.

TRAINING
Any pet that lives outside a cage has to be trained so that it does not soil the home. Without training, dogs can be especially destructive and even dangerous.

At dog shows, prizes are awarded to the best-trained dogs.

UNUSUAL PETS
Almost any animal could be a pet, but unusual pets require special care and some knowledge about how these animals live and behave in the wild.

Find out more
CATS
DOGS, WOLVES, AND FOXES
FARM ANIMALS
HORSES, ZEBRAS, AND ASSES
VETERINARIANS

PHOENICIANS

A TINY GROUP OF CITIES perched along the coast of the Mediterranean produced the most famous sailors and traders of the ancient world. These seafaring people were called the Phoenicians. The cities of Phoenicia were linked by the sea, and they traded in many goods, including purple dyes, glass, and ivory. From 1200 to 350 B.C. the Phoenicians controlled trade throughout the Mediterranean. They spread their trading links to many points around the coast. Their most famous trading post was Carthage on the north coast of Africa. During its history, Phoenicia was conquered by several foreign empires, including the Assyrians, Babylonians, and Persians. These foreign rulers usually allowed the Phoenicians to continue trading. But in 332 B.C. Alexander the Great conquered Phoenicia, and Greek people came to live there. The Greeks brought their own culture with them, and the Phoenician culture died out.

Phoenicians made purple dye from the liquid produced by crushing murex seashells.

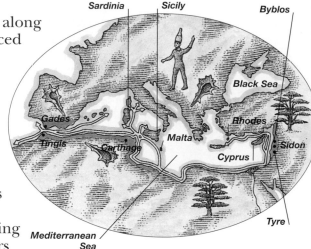

Sardinia · Sicily · Byblos · Black Sea · Rhodes · Gades · Tingis · Carthage · Malta · Cyprus · Sidon · Tyre

Mediterranean Sea

PHOENICIA
Phoenicia lay on the coast of the eastern Mediterranean roughly where Lebanon is today. The Phoenicians spread throughout the Mediterranean, to Carthage, Rhodes, Cyprus, Sicily, Malta, Sardinia, Gades (Cadiz), and Tingis (Tangier).

When arriving at a new place to trade, the Phoenicians would lay their goods out on the beach and let the local people come and look at what they had brought.

Sculptures show that Phoenician men wore distinctive conical hats.

Phoenicians traded in a vast array of goods from the Mediterranean, including metals, farm animals, wheat, cloth, jewelry, and gemstones.

Phoenician glassware, such as this glass jar, was a luxury in the ancient world.

PHOENICIAN SHIPS
The Phoenicians' ships were famous all over the Mediterranean, and were the main reason for the Phoenicians' success as traders. The ships had oarsmen, sails, and heavy keels, which enabled them to sail in any direction.

DYEING
The Phoenicians were the only people who knew how to produce a vivid purple dye from murex shells. The dye was considered to be exceptionally beautiful but it was also very expensive. Only high government officials, for example, could wear purple-dyed cloth in the Roman Empire.

PHOENICIAN GLASSWARE
Ancient Egyptians made glass many years before the Phoenicians did, but Egyptian glass was cloudy, while Phoenician glass was clear. The Phoenicians were able to make clear glass because their sand contained large amounts of quartz.

BYBLOS
The Phoenician port of Byblos was famous for its trade in papyrus – a kind of paper made in Egypt by pressing together strands of papyrus reeds. The Greeks called papyrus *biblos* after the port of Byblos. A number of our words concerned with books, such as Bible, and bibliography (a list of books), come from *biblos*.

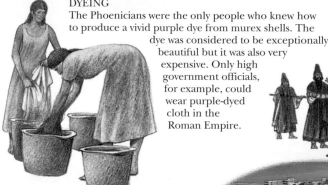

The papyrus reed grows in the warm, damp conditions of the Nile River in Egypt.

Find out more
ALEXANDER the great
ALPHABETS
ASSYRIANS
BABYLONIANS
GREECE, ANCIENT
PERSIANS, ANCIENT
SUMERIANS

PHOTOGRAPHY

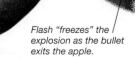

A 19th-century photographer tries to hold a baby's attention while he struggles to operate his bulky camera.

MORE THAN TWO HUNDRED million times a day, a camera shutter clicks somewhere in the world to take a photograph. There are family snapshots capturing happy memories, dramatic news pictures, advertising and fashion shots, pictures of the planet beamed back from satellites in space, and much more. The uses of photography are numerous, and new applications are being found all the time. The first photographs were made by coating sheets of polished metal with light-sensitive chemicals, but the images appeared in dull, silvery gray and could only be seen from certain angles. During the 19th century, new processes were invented for spreading the chemicals onto a glass plate or onto a film of cellulose (a kind of plastic). Eventually, photographs could be made in either black-and-white or full color. Film is still in use today, although it is quickly being replaced by digital photography. Digital cameras use a light-sensitive chip, instead of film, and store pictures as digital image files that can be transferred to a computer. There, they can be altered before being printed or sent anywhere in the world via the Internet.

HIGH-SPEED PHOTOGRAPHY

With the use of special cameras and lights, high-speed photography can reveal movement too fast for the eye to see. A brief burst of light from an electronic flash, lasting less than one millionth of a second, can capture the image of an object moving at hundreds of miles per hour.

Flash "freezes" the explosion as the bullet exits the apple.

HISTORY OF PHOTOGRAPHY

A Frenchman named Joseph Niépce took the first photograph in 1826. The exposure took eight hours to make, and the picture was fuzzy and dark. In 1837, another Frenchman, Louis Daguerre, discovered how to make sharp photographs in a few minutes. Just two years later, English scientist William Fox Talbot invented the process that is still used for developing film today. In the early days, cameras were bulky, and for each picture photographers had to carry a separate glass plate. Then, in 1888, American George Eastman invented the Kodak camera. It was small and light and came loaded with a roll of film rather than plates. Taking a picture became so easy that anyone could try it.

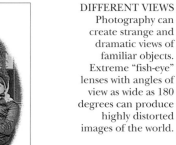

People in early portraits often look uncomfortable and stiff because they had to keep still for several minutes.

The Kodak Box Brownie was so simple that Eastman claimed even a child could use it.

DIFFERENT VIEWS

Photography can create strange and dramatic views of familiar objects. Extreme "fish-eye" lenses with angles of view as wide as 180 degrees can produce highly distorted images of the world.

A special macro lens is needed to focus at distances as close as this.

Circular fish-eye shot of the view from the top of the Great Pyramid of Khufu in Egypt

CLOSE-UP PHOTOGRAPHY

Macro, or close-up, photography magnifies tiny details barely visible to the naked eye, such as the beautiful gold-colored eye of a leaf frog (right).

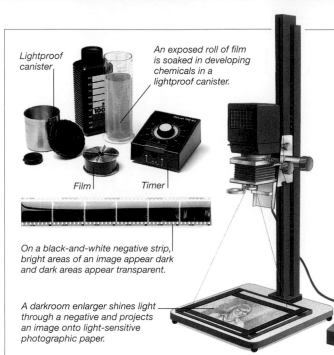

Lightproof canister

An exposed roll of film is soaked in developing chemicals in a lightproof canister.

Film *Timer*

On a black-and-white negative strip, bright areas of an image appear dark and dark areas appear transparent.

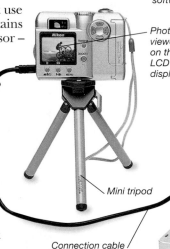

A darkroom enlarger shines light through a negative and projects an image onto light-sensitive photographic paper.

DEVELOPING AND PRINTING

When a picture is taken with a traditional camera, light enters the lens briefly and strikes the film. Each grain of light-sensitive silver on the film is subtly changed by the light that falls on it, and an invisible image is recorded. The film must be processed before the picture can be seen. It is immersed in a bath of chemicals called developer. This turns the exposed silver salts into silver metals. The developed film is then washed and "fixed" to create a negative or transparency that is no longer affected by light. In a darkroom the image is enlarged by projecting it onto light-sensitive paper, which in turn must be developed to make a print.

The exposed print is developed and fixed in the same way as film.

DIGITAL PHOTGRAPHY

A digital camera does not use film at all. Instead, it contains a light-sensitive image sensor – a chip made up of millions of tiny silicon photo diodes, each of which records the brightness and color of the light falling on it when the picture is taken. The picture information is then translated into digital data and stored on the camera's memory card. It can then be printed or downloaded to a computer.

Photo-management software

Photos can be viewed immediately on the camera's LCD (liquid crystal display) screen.

Mini tripod

Connection cable

Laptop computer

A digital image enlarged until it becomes "pixelated"

Film grain magnified until it becomes visible

DIGITAL AND FILM IN CLOSE-UP

Both digital and film images are made up of tiny blocks of color, so small that they are normally invisible to the naked eye. However, it is possible to see individual pixels when a digital photograph is enlarged on screen and to see separate grains when film or a photographic print is viewed under a microscope or magnifying glass.

CAMERA PHONES

Many new cell phones have built-in digital cameras, capable of taking photographs and recording short video clips. Both pictures and movies can be sent immediately to other cell phones or transferred wirelessly to TVs, computers, printers, and other digital devices. As image quality improves, many people may choose to use a single device to combine the function of phone, camera, video camera, and music player.

Find out more

CAMERAS
COLOR
LIGHT
MOVIES
TELEVISION AND VIDEO

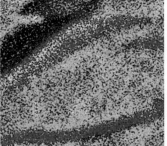

PHYSICS

THE SCIENCE OF PHYSICS used to be called natural philosophy, which means thinking about and investigating the natural world. Physicists seek to understand and explain the universe from the largest, most distant galaxy to the tiniest invisible particle. Great physicists have wrestled with fundamental questions such as what it is that holds us to the Earth, what time is, and what is inside an atom. Physicists work with theory and experiment. They conduct experiments and then think of a theory, or idea, that explains the results. Then they try new experiments to test their theory. Some theories have become so good at explaining nature that many people refer to them as the laws of physics. For example, one such law states that nothing can travel faster than the speed of light. The German-born physicist Albert Einstein (1879-1955) proposed this in 1905 as part of his revolutionary theory of relativity.

ASTROPHYSICS
Astronomers use physics to find out about the origins and interiors of the Sun and stars. This branch of physics is called astrophysics.

BRANCHES OF PHYSICS
Physics is the science of energy and matter (the materials of which everything is made). There are several branches of physics. They cover a range of subjects from atoms to space.

OPTICS AND THERMAL PHYSICS
Heat and light are important forms of energy: the Sun sends out light and heat that make life possible on Earth. The physics of light is called optics; the branch of physics concerned with heat is called thermal physics.

LANDMARKS IN PHYSICS

200s B.C. Greek scientist Archimedes explains floating and how levers work.

1687 English physicist Isaac Newton puts forward the laws of motion and gravity.

1900 German physicist Max Planck introduces quantum theory.

1905 German physicist Albert Einstein publishes his theory of relativity.

1938 German physicists Fritz Strassmann and Otto Hahn split the atom.

English physicist Stephen Hawking (born 1942) published theories about the nature of matter, black holes in space, and the origin of the universe. These have opened doors to new possibilities in physics.

STATICS
Statics is the branch of physics concerned with calculating and understanding forces that support buildings and bridges.

Satellites transmit radio waves for long-distance communication.

Laws of mechanics are put to use to design and run a car.

MECHANICS
The study of force and movement is a branch of physics known as mechanics.

Coal is burned to produce electricity.

ELECTRICITY
One of the most useful forms of energy is electricity. Physicists study the nature of electricity and find ways of using it in electrical appliances, microchips, and computers.

Accelerator speeds up atomic particles and forces them to collide.

ELECTROMAGNETISM
Physicists have discovered a group of mostly invisible rays called electromagnetic waves. Electromagnetism is the physics of the relationship between magnetism and electric currents.

KINETIC THEORY
Physicists use the idea of molecules to explain the way solids, liquids, and gases behave. This branch of physics is called kinetic theory.

MAGNETISM
Physicists study magnets and the forces that magnets produce. This includes the Earth's magnetism, which comes from the movements of the molten metal core at the center of the Earth.

Sound waves reflected from the ocean floor bring back information about deep-sea structures.

ACOUSTICS
The science of sound is called acoustics. Physicists can use sound to study the interior of the Earth and the oceans.

QUANTUM MECHANICS
Energy can only exist in tiny packets called quanta. This idea is very important in the study of atoms, and it has given rise to a branch of physics called quantum mechanics.

NUCLEAR PHYSICS
Physicists are constantly searching for a greater understanding of the particles that make up the nucleus (center) of an atom. This branch of physics is called nuclear physics.

Atomic particles crash into each other to release vast amounts of energy.

GEOPHYSICS
The interior of the Earth is hidden from us, but physicists have discovered that there is great heat and pressure beneath the Earth's crust, which sometimes erupts in volcanoes. Geophysics is the branch of physics concerned with the Earth.

Find out more
EINSTEIN, ALBERT
ELECTRICITY
FORCE AND MOTION
GRAVITY
HEAT
LIGHT
MAGNETISM
SCIENCE
SOUND

PILGRIMS

ON A BLUSTERY SEPTEMBER DAY in 1620, a small ship set sail from the port of Plymouth, England, bound for North America. The 102 settlers on board hoped that in the New World they could worship freely in their own way, which they had not been able to do in England. Because of their Puritan faith, and because they started one of the colonies that would later grow into the United States, the group became known as the Pilgrims. The Pilgrims landed in what is now Massachusetts and established a settlement they named Plymouth. The first winter was hard. The settlers had little food, and it was difficult to farm and fish. But with help from the local Native Americans, the settlement eventually prospered. The Pilgrims replaced their wooden homes with more secure dwellings and started trading furs with the Native Americans. More groups of Puritans came to join the original settlers; together they created one of the first successful European settlements in North America.

September 16, 1620
Mayflower sets sail from Plymouth.

November 19
Cape Cod is sighted.

Cape Cod Bay

November 21
Mayflower anchors in Provincetown harbor.

December 26
Plymouth colony founded, Massachusetts.

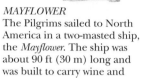

MAYFLOWER
The Pilgrims sailed to North America in a two-masted ship, the *Mayflower*. The ship was about 90 ft (30 m) long and was built to carry wine and other cargo.

EARLY SETTLEMENT

The first settlements in Plymouth were built of wood from the local forests. The chimneys were made of sticks held together with clay, and the roofs were waterproofed with bark.

Splitting logs to make planks

Food had to be cooked in the open.

Every member of the family had to work hard to build a house and plant crops for food.

GOVERNMENT
The early Plymouth settlers elected their own government, which met annually to make laws and levy taxes.

PURITANISM
The Puritan religion stressed hard work and obedience and disapproved of frivolity and idleness.

The Pilgrims held prayer meetings outside until they built churches.

PURITANS

The people known as the Puritans wished to purify the Church of England of its pomp and ritual. They dressed in simple clothes and tried to live in accordance with the Bible.

THANKSGIVING
In the fall of 1621, the Pilgrims celebrated their first successful harvest. They invited the local Native Americans to join them in a feast of thanksgiving. Thanksgiving, which became a national holiday in 1863, is celebrated in the United States on the fourth Thursday in November.

Find out more

EXPLORERS
FESTIVALS AND FEASTS
UNITED STATES OF AMERICA,
history of

PIRATES

IN TALES ABOUT PIRATES, shady figures row through the moonlight to bury treasure on tropical islands. The reality of a pirate's life, though, was very different from the storybook version. Most pirates were simply criminals who robbed ships at sea and often murdered the crews. Pirates first appeared when trading ships began to cross the Mediterranean about 4,000 years ago. They have flourished ever since in every ocean of the world, but were particularly active from 1500 to 1800. Some pirates, such as Blackbeard, cruised the Caribbean Sea, which was also called the Spanish Main. Others, such as Captain Kidd, attacked ships in the Indian Ocean. Sometimes countries at war encouraged piracy, but only against enemy shipping. They called the pirate ships privateers and gave them letters of marque – official licenses to plunder enemy ships. Until recently, pirates existed in the South China Sea. They robbed families fleeing by boat from Vietnam.

PIRATE SHIPS

Traditional pirate vessels were generally small, fast, and maneuverable. They floated high in the water so they could escape into shallow creeks and inlets if pursued. They were armed with as many cannons as possible. Some cannons were heavy guns that fired large metal balls; others were lighter swivel guns that fired lead shots.

TREASURE MAPS
Buried pirate treasure, marked with an X on a map, is largely the invention of adventure writers. Most of the time pirates attacked lightly armed merchant ships, stealing food and weapons.

ANNE BONNY
Anne Bonny was born in Ireland. She fell in love with the pirate "Calico Jack" Rackham and sailed with him. On a captured ship she met another female pirate, Mary Read. The women were arrested in 1720 but escaped the gallows, since they were both expecting babies.

BLACKBEARD
One of the most terrible pirates was Edward Teach. His nickname was Blackbeard, and his favorite drink was rum and gunpowder. In battle he carried six pistols and wore burning matches twisted into his hair. He died during a fight with a British warship in 1718.

DOUBLOONS
The pirate's currency was a Spanish gold dollar called the doubloon. Doubloons were also called *doblón de a ocho*, meaning pieces of eight, because each was worth eight Spanish gold escudos.

Find out more
OUTLAWS AND BANDITS

PLANETS

THE EARTH IS one of nine roughly spherical objects that move around our Sun. These objects are planets – vast balls of rock, metal, and gases that orbit a star. All planets travel in the same direction around the Sun, each revolving in an elliptical (oval) orbit. Through a telescope, the planets appear as disks of light moving across the night sky. They do not, however, produce light themselves, but reflect light from the Sun. Some planets, such as Earth and Venus, are surrounded by a layer of gas called an atmosphere. The largest planets, such as Jupiter and Saturn, are also surrounded by rings. The planets vary greatly in temperature: Mercury, closest to the Sun, is hotter than an oven by day; Pluto, at the edge of the solar system, is at night five times colder than a deep freeze. As far as we know, Earth is the only planet in our solar system that supports life. However, there are millions of stars similar to our Sun in the universe, many believed to have their own planets. It is possible that some of these also support life forms.

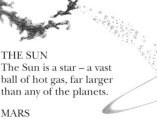

THE SUN
The Sun is a star – a vast ball of hot gas, far larger than any of the planets.

MARS
Mars is a small, dry planet with a red, rocky surface. It is cold – about -9°F (-23°C) – and has two polar caps of ice and frozen gas. Mars has two tiny moons named Phobos and Deimos.

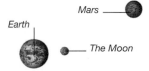

Mars

Earth

Venus

The Moon

MERCURY
Mercury is so close to the Sun that it has no atmosphere or oceans. It has a rocky surface that rises to a temperature of about 662°F (350°C).

VENUS
Thick clouds cover the whole surface of Venus. They trap the Sun's heat, making Venus the hottest planet in the solar system. The surface temperature of Venus is about 896°F (480°C).

EARTH
The Earth has an atmosphere of air and oceans filled with water. The Earth's average temperature is 72°F (22°C). A source of energy and liquid water are essential for life on the planet. If the Earth were hotter, the water would evaporate; if it were colder, the water would freeze.

JUPITER
Jupiter is the largest planet in the solar system. It has no solid surface as it is made up of a mixture of liquids and gases, with belts of swirling gas forming an atmosphere around it. It is a cold planet, surrounded by a ring of dust, and orbited by more than 60 moons.

ASTEROIDS
Thousands of tiny bodies called asteroids orbit the Sun, mainly traveling in a belt between Mars and Jupiter. Dating from the earliest days of the solar system, most asteroids are lumps of rock and metal just a few miles in diameter. Jupiter's gravitational pull can send asteroids into erratic orbits, causing them to collide with planets and other asteroids. Many objects made of ice and rock are also known to exist in the Kuiper Belt, an area in the solar system beyond the orbit of Neptune.

PLANET PICTURES
Space technology has shown us what the other planets in the solar system look like and what they are made of; it has also established that these other planets are unlikely to support life. The images shown right and at the foot of the next page were taken from a variety of spacecraft.

The heavily cratered surface of Mercury is revealed in this composite photograph taken by the space probe Mariner 10.

Photograph taken by the Pioneer-Venus probe shows thick yellowish clouds covering the surface of Venus.

Picture of the Earth taken by the Meteosat weather satellite. Colors have been enhanced using a computer.

Picture of Mars constructed from 100 images taken by the Viking 1 space probe.

SATURN'S RINGS

Jupiter, Saturn, Uranus, and Neptune are all surrounded by rings. Saturn's rings are the most spectacular, visible from the Earth through binoculars. They consist of millions of lumps of ice mixed with fragments of rock. Astronomers are not sure how the rings formed. They may have formed at the same time as the planet, or may represent the remains of a large, icy moon that broke apart.

NEPTUNE

Neptune (below) has a striking blue atmosphere made up of hydrogen, helium, and methane gases, surrounding a rocky core about as large as the Earth. Neptune has four rings and eight known moons.

PLUTO

Pluto (above) is the outermost and smallest planet, only one-fifth the size of the Earth. It is the coldest planet in the solar system, with a temperature of about -382°F (-230°C). Pluto has one moon which is almost half its size.

URANUS

Uranus (left) has a solid core of metal surrounded by ice and gases. Its blue-green atmosphere is made of gases, including methane, hydrogen, and helium. Uranus is extremely cold – about -353°F (-214°C). It has 11 rings and 27 moons.

SATURN

Saturn (left) is huge, almost as big as Jupiter. Dense storm clouds circle the planet, giving it a banded appearance. It has a solid core of rock and ice, surrounded by hydrogen in liquid and gas form. The planet spins so fast – the rotation takes only 10 hours – that its poles are noticeably flattened and its equator bulges outward. Saturn has at least 47 known moons.

VOYAGER SPACECRAFT

We have incredible pictures of the planets and their moons because space probes have flown to all of the planets except Pluto. *Voyager 2* was one of the most successful interplanetary spacecraft. It traveled for over a decade photographing the planets, and in 1990, made its way out of the solar system. *Voyager 2* made use of the gravity of the planets to give it an extra push on its long journey – a similar effect to stepping off a merry-go-round while it is moving.

SOLAR SYSTEM

The solar system consists of the Sun, planets, moons, asteroids, and comets. It formed about 4.5 billion years ago from a huge cloud of gas and dust. The Sun's force of gravity holds all the planets in their orbits. The planets are grouped in two bands. The inner band consists of Mercury, Venus, Earth, and Mars; in the outer band are Jupiter, Saturn, Uranus, Neptune, and Pluto.

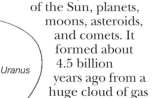

Artist's impression of Pluto, based on images viewed through the Hubble Space Telescope in 1994.

Voyager 1 picture of Jupiter showing the Great Red Spot which is thought to be a huge storm.

Image taken by Voyager 1 showing Saturn and its rings, which are thought to consist of a mixture of ice and rock.

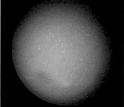

Voyager 2 image of Uranus. Its atmosphere looks blue because the methane gas it contains cuts out red light.

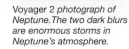

Voyager 2 photograph of Neptune. The two dark blurs are enormous storms in Neptune's atmosphere.

Find out more

ASTRONOMY
GRAVITY
MOON
SUN
UNIVERSE

PLANTS

LIFE ON EARTH could not exist without plants. Humans and animals need plants for food and oxygen. The cereal you eat for breakfast, the orange juice you drink, even the jeans you wear, are all derived from plants. Trees provide us with wood for fuel, furniture, and tools. In almost every country, flowers and vegetables are grown by the millions for food and pleasure. Scientists use plants to make drugs such as digitalis (from foxglove) and morphine (from poppies). Plants range from tiny mosses to gigantic coniferous trees so tall you cannot see their tops. What they all have in common is their unique ability to capture and use the Sun's light as an energy source. This process is called photosynthesis, and it powers all plant life and growth. About 400,000 plants are already known to us, from rare exotic flowers to common garden vegetables. Even more plants await discovery, especially in tropical regions. Today, however, more than 25,000 different trees, flowers, and other plants are in danger of extinction due to the destruction of their natural habitats.

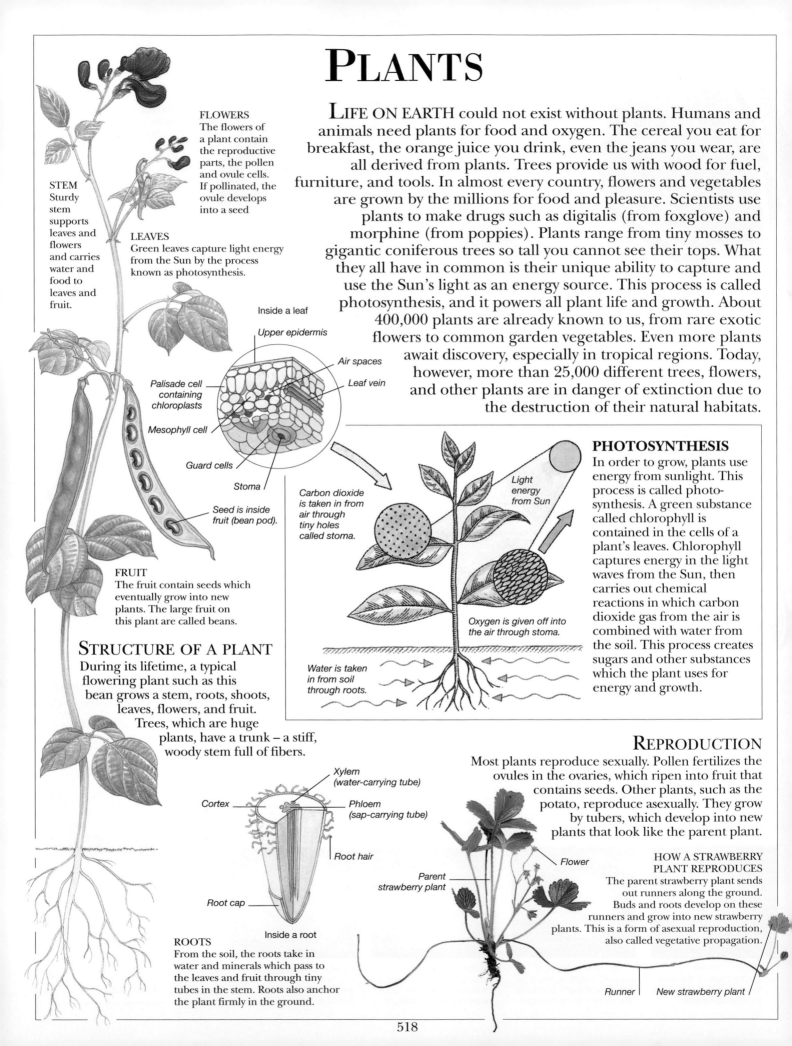

STEM
Sturdy stem supports leaves and flowers and carries water and food to leaves and fruit.

FLOWERS
The flowers of a plant contain the reproductive parts, the pollen and ovule cells. If pollinated, the ovule develops into a seed

LEAVES
Green leaves capture light energy from the Sun by the process known as photosynthesis.

Inside a leaf

Upper epidermis

Air spaces

Palisade cell containing chloroplasts

Leaf vein

Mesophyll cell

Guard cells

Stoma

Seed is inside fruit (bean pod).

FRUIT
The fruit contain seeds which eventually grow into new plants. The large fruit on this plant are called beans.

STRUCTURE OF A PLANT
During its lifetime, a typical flowering plant such as this bean grows a stem, roots, shoots, leaves, flowers, and fruit. Trees, which are huge plants, have a trunk – a stiff, woody stem full of fibers.

Carbon dioxide is taken in from air through tiny holes called stoma.

Light energy from Sun

Oxygen is given off into the air through stoma.

Water is taken in from soil through roots.

PHOTOSYNTHESIS
In order to grow, plants use energy from sunlight. This process is called photosynthesis. A green substance called chlorophyll is contained in the cells of a plant's leaves. Chlorophyll captures energy in the light waves from the Sun, then carries out chemical reactions in which carbon dioxide gas from the air is combined with water from the soil. This process creates sugars and other substances which the plant uses for energy and growth.

REPRODUCTION
Most plants reproduce sexually. Pollen fertilizes the ovules in the ovaries, which ripen into fruit that contains seeds. Other plants, such as the potato, reproduce asexually. They grow by tubers, which develop into new plants that look like the parent plant.

Xylem (water-carrying tube)

Cortex

Phloem (sap-carrying tube)

Root hair

Root cap

Inside a root

ROOTS
From the soil, the roots take in water and minerals which pass to the leaves and fruit through tiny tubes in the stem. Roots also anchor the plant firmly in the ground.

Flower

Parent strawberry plant

HOW A STRAWBERRY PLANT REPRODUCES
The parent strawberry plant sends out runners along the ground. Buds and roots develop on these runners and grow into new strawberry plants. This is a form of asexual reproduction, also called vegetative propagation.

Runner

New strawberry plant

MAIN GROUPS OF PLANTS

The plant kingdom is made up of many different groups. These groups are divided into flowering and non-flowering plants, as shown here.

Microscopic plants are so small that we can see them only through a microscope.

Lichen is now classified as a fungi. It has no true leaves, stems, or roots.

Ferns grow in all parts of the world. Some are as large as trees; others are tiny and look like moss.

Seaweed is an alga that grows in sea water and attaches itself to rocks.

Moss grows on logs and walls and in moist, shady woodland areas.

Liverworts are small non-flowering plants related to mosses.

Horsetails were among the earliest plants on Earth.

Club mosses are among the first plants to develop with true stems.

Coniferous trees include fir trees and pine trees. They are also called evergreen trees.

Weeds are unwanted flowering plants that include dandelions, nettles, and buttercups.

Fruit trees provide many kinds of fruit, including apples, lemons, and bananas. All are rich in vitamins.

Vegetables are edible flowering plants that are rich in vitamins and minerals. They include carrots, potatoes, spinach, tomatoes, and beans.

True flowering plants include roses, tulips, and other garden plants.

Bushes are woody plants that are smaller than trees. They usually have one main stem.

Herbs have scented leaves. They include basil and oregano.

Grasses include lawn grass and cereals such as wheat, rice, barley, and corn.

Deciduous trees are also called broadleaved trees. They lose their leaves each fall.

Shrubs are woody plants with more than one main branch growing from the ground.

WEEDS

A weed is simply a plant growing where it is troublesome to humans. Most weeds grow fast, come into flower quickly, then spread their seeds. Some weeds, such as the convolvulus shown above, have pale, delicate flowers; others are colorful, such as the dandelions and buttercups that grow on lawns.

CHOCOLATE

Inside every large fruit, or pod, of the tropical cacao tree are about 40 cacao beans. These beans are roasted, shelled, then ground into a paste. The cacao paste is mixed with sugar at a high temperature to make chocolate.

FOOD FROM PLANTS

We grow plants for food on farms and in gardens, too. Food plants include cereals such as rice, fruit such as oranges, and vegetables such as carrots. Spices such as cinnamon are parts of plants and are used for flavoring. Some plant parts cannot be eaten because they are bitter, sour, or poisonous. Potatoes are an important food crop, but we eat only the tuber that grows underground. The fruit and leaves of the potato plant, which grow above ground, are poisonous.

THE BIGGEST FLOWER

The giant rafflesia is a parasitic plant. It has no leaves and draws its food from the liana creepers it lives on. It has the world's largest flower, at 3 ft (1 m) across. Because of its smell, it is also called the stinking giant.

CARNIVOROUS PLANTS

Some plants obtain extra food from animals. One plant, commonly called the Venus's-flytrap, usually grows in swamps, where the soil is poor. Flesh-eating or carnivorous plants trap and digest insects and other small creatures.

Venus's-flytrap flower

The flytrap shuts in one fiftieth of a second, when trigger hairs at the base of each leaf are moved.

MISTLETOE

This plant "steals" its food and energy by growing and feeding on trees. It grows high up in the branches, and its roots grow into the bark and absorb the tree's nutrients.

When a small creature touches sensitive hairs on the leaves of the Venus's-flytrap, the leaves snap shut with one of the fastest movements in the plant world.

Find out more

FLOWERS AND HERBS
FRUITS AND SEEDS
GRASSES AND CEREALS
MOSSES,
liverworts, and ferns
SOIL
TREES

PLASTICS

MANY MATERIALS that we use are natural, such as cotton, wool, leather, wood, and metal. They come from plants or animals, or they are dug from the ground. Plastics can be used in place of natural materials, and they are used to make clothes, parts for cars, and many other products. Plastics are synthetic materials, which means that they are made from chemicals in factories. The chemicals come mainly from oil, but also from natural gas and coal. An important quality of plastics is that they are easy to shape. They can be used to make objects of all kinds, as well as fibers for textiles. Extra-strong glues, long-lasting paints, and lightweight materials that are stronger than metal – all of these products are made of plastics with special qualities. None can be made with natural materials.

BAKELITE
Bakelite was invented in 1909 by the American chemist Leo Baekeland. It was the first plastic to be made from synthetic chemicals.

PVC
Electrical wires have a coating of flexible PVC (polyvinyl chloride), which is also used to make inflatable toys.

POLYETHYLENE
Plastic bags are often made of polyethylene, a plastic that can be made into a tough, flexible film. When produced in thicker layers, polyethylene is also used to make bottles, bowls, and other household containers.

KINDS OF PLASTICS
There are thousands of different plastics. Some of the most common types are shown here.

Molecule of polyethylene

POLYMERS
Plastics are polymers, which are substances with molecules composed of long chains of atoms. This is why the names of plastics often begin with poly, which means "many." Long molecules give plastics their special qualities, such as flexibility and strength.

NYLON
Fibers of nylon, a strong but flexible plastic, are used to make ropes and hard-wearing fabrics. Solid nylon is used to make gearwheels and other hardware.

POLYSTYRENE
Packaging made from polystyrene is light and rigid. Tough plastics often contain polystyrene.

BEECH STARSHIP 1
In aircraft, composites can be used to replace many metal parts. This aircraft is made almost entirely of composites that are highly resistant to corrosion and cracking.

POLYCARBONATE
Goggles need to be clear and strong, two qualities of polycarbonate plastic. Other uses include car lights and crash helmets.

COMPOSITES
Strong fibers are put into tough plastics to create materials called composites, (right) which are very strong yet light and easily shaped. Thin fibers of glass, carbon, or Kevlar (a strong plastic) are used.

Carbon-fiber sheet
Layer of epoxy (plastic adhesive)
Honeycomb of tough plastic
Epoxy layer
Carbon-fiber sheet

Find out more
ATOMS AND MOLECULES
CHEMISTRY
COAL
MATERIALS
OIL
TEXTILES

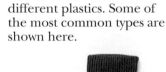

POETRY

THE VERY FIRST LITERATURE produced by any culture is usually poetry. Poetry is written in language that is strong and vivid enough to be memorable and to provoke a lasting, and often emotional, response from the reader. All poems are written in lines. Many poems rhyme, have a regular rhythm, and use figures of speech such as metaphor to make the language different to that used in everyday speech, but this is not always the case. These varying patterns and the way they are used allow poets to create different moods, from fast-moving and witty to sad and slow. The most important thing about a poem is that it should make a strong impression on the reader. Although we read poems today, much ancient poetry was passed on by oral (spoken) traditions.

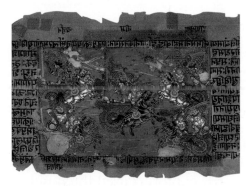

MAHABHARATA
The longest poem ever written is the Indian epic called the *Mahabharata*. It has more than 90,000 couplets (pairs of rhyming lines) and was written in ancient Sanskrit by various writers before the 4th century A.D. It tells many stories about the ancient Indian kingdom of Kurukshetra.

Stanza from *The Tiger* by William Blake

Stressed syllable   Unstressed syllable

Ti|ger! Ti|ger! burn|ing bright
 1   2   3   A

In the fo|rests of the night,
 1   2   3   A

What im|mor|tal hand or eye
 1   2   3   B

Could frame thy fear|ful sym|metry?
 1   2   3   4   B

Pairs of lines rhyme with each other, creating a pattern AABB

Lear also published funny sketches.

LIMERICKS
The limerick is a type of funny five-line poem made popular in the 19th century by British writer Edward Lear (1812-88). Limericks can be written on any subject, but always begin with a line like "There once was a person from…"

POETIC FORMS
Traditional poetry is written in verse lines. They contain repeating patterns of stressed (emphasized) and unstressed syllables (units of sound in a word), put together in different ways. These patterns of syllables are called "feet." There are different names for each kind of foot. The way the lines rhyme makes another set of patterns, called a rhyme scheme. Groups of rhyming lines are called stanzas and there may be several of them in a poem. Breaking down a poem into its separate parts is called scanning, or scansion.

—U   Trochee
—UU   Dactyl
U—   Iamb

AABB   Rhyme scheme
⌐   Foot
| Scansion break

PERFORMANCE POETRY
Poetry is written to be read aloud. Like medieval bards (singing poets), who sang their own lyrics, many modern poets prefer to perform their work in public in theaters, cafés, clubs, or wherever people gather to be entertained. Poets such as Jamaican-born writer Linton Kwesi Johnson (b. 1952), for example, act out the scenes and characters in their work, making poetry entertaining for people who may not have enjoyed reading verse before.

Performance poet Linton Kwesi Johnson often uses music in his work.

NURSERY RHYME
Children have been singing and reciting nursery rhymes such as "Little Bo Peep" for hundreds of years. Most of the verses have changed little, although there are variations in different regions and countries. No one knows who wrote these poems. Some of them seem to describe real events, but others may be political ideas or jokes about important people disguised as harmless children's rhymes.

Find out more
LITERATURE
LITERATURE, US
WRITERS AND POETS

POLAR EXPLORATION

THE COLDEST PLACES on Earth were the very last to be explored. At the North and South poles fierce, icy winds lash the surrounding masses of snow. The first European explorers to reach the poles risked their lives in the attempt, and some of them never returned. They used primitive equipment and simple transportation. Explorers traveled part of the way by ship, then went on foot or skis for the remaining distance, carrying their equipment on sledges pulled by husky dogs, ponies, or their own human effort. They faced terrible hazards. The low temperatures made frostbite common, and they had to carry with them everything they needed, including enough food for the long journey to the pole and back. These early explorers used the position of the sun to tell them when they had reached their goal, because there were no landmarks in the polar landscapes. Later, explorers had the advantage of more modern vehicles, but it was not until the middle of the 20th century that both polar regions had been fully explored.

ROBERT PEARY
Robert Peary (1856-1920) was the first person to reach the North Pole on April 6, 1909, together with one other American and four Inuits.

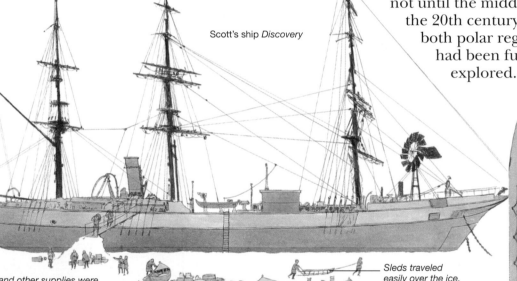

Scott's ship *Discovery*

Food and other supplies were stored in dumps on the ground, ready for recovery by the party returning from the pole.

Sleds traveled easily over the ice.

Scott's expedition took only a few dogs, and instead used ponies and manpower to haul sleds.

AMUNDSEN AND SCOTT

In 1912 the specially built wooden ship *Discovery* took an expedition led by British Captain Robert Scott (1868-1912) to within 900 miles (1,450 km) of the South Pole. When Scott's party reached the pole, they discovered that they were not the first. A Norwegian team led by Roald Amundsen (1872-1928) had arrived at the South Pole on December 14, 1911, well ahead of their British rivals. Scott's group died before they could complete their return journey.

MODERN RESEARCH
Today, explorers have been replaced by scientists who carry out research at the poles using more advanced equipment, but in the same harsh and unfriendly environment.

Early explorers' clothing

A heavy hood slowed heat loss from the head.

Fur mitten

Goggles prevented sunlight from dazzling the explorers.

NORTH POLE

982 Viking Eric the Red discovers Greenland.

1607 Henry Hudson tries to sail around northern Canada.

1827 Sir William Parry tries to reach the pole using dog sleds.

1893-96 Norwegian ship *Fram* freezes in pack ice and drifts close to the pole.

1909 Peary reaches pole.

1926 First flight to pole.

1959 US submarine *Skate* surfaces at pole.

SOUTH POLE

1820 First sighting of Antarctic continent.

1821 A Russian sails around Antarctica, and an American sets foot on it.

1911 Five expeditions race to the pole; Roald Amundsen wins.

1928 First airplanes used in Antarctica.

Find out more
ANTARCTICA
ARCTIC
EXPLORERS
GLACIERS AND ICE CAPS

POLAR WILDLIFE

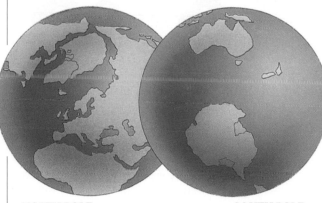

THE NORTH AND SOUTH POLES are the coldest places on Earth. But despite freezing temperatures, icy water, and biting winds, many different plants and animals live near the poles and are found nowhere else in the world. All survive because they have adapted to the harsh conditions. Plants in these regions are low-growing, to protect them from the cold wind, and they complete their life cycle during the few short weeks of summer. Polar animals, too, have adapted to the cold conditions; some have thick fur or feathers; others have a layer of fatty blubber to conserve body warmth. The biggest animals, the great whales, roam the waters of Antarctica, near the South Pole and the largest bear, the polar bear, lives in the Arctic, near the North Pole. Many other warm-blooded animals, including wolves, foxes, reindeer, hares, and lemmings, also live here. Polar animals are often white in color for camouflage on the ice. The cold seas are also teeming with life, particularly in summer. Around Antarctica, ocean currents bring up nutrients from the deep sea to feed the plankton, which in turn feeds animals such as krill.

NORTH POLE
In the central Arctic Ocean at the top of the globe, there are vast areas of drifting ice many feet thick.

SOUTH POLE
At the bottom of the globe, the continent of Antarctica is almost completely covered by a massive sheet of ice.

ARCTIC SKUA
The skua snatches food from other birds such as gulls and puffins. It pesters them in midair until they drop their catch of fish.

NARWHAL
The narwhal belongs to the whale family. It hunts in small groups among pack ice searching for cod, flatfish, shrimps, and squid. Narwhals have only two teeth. In the male, the left tooth usually develops into a tusk, which can measure up to 8 ft (2.5 m) long.

POLAR BEAR CUBS
Young polar bears are born in winter in a den made by their mother under the snow. The cubs stay in the den for four months, feeding on their mother's milk, then begin to learn how to hunt. The cubs leave their mother at about two years old.

BEARDED SEAL
Bearded seals live all around the Arctic region, mainly in shallow water. They eat shellfish on the seabed, as well as crabs and sea cucumbers. In the breeding season, male bearded seals make eerie noises under water. The female seals give birth to pups on ice floes in the spring.

HOODED SEAL
In summer, hooded seals migrate north to the waters around Greenland. They hunt deep-water fishes such as halibut and redfish, as well as squid. They spend the winter further south, off northeastern North America, resting on ice floes and rarely coming onto land.

The male hooded seal inflates the hood – a sac of loose skin on its nose – to scare off other males.

POLAR BEAR
The huge polar bear is covered in thick, water-repelling fur, except for its footpads and the tip of its nose. Polar bears have an excellent sense of smell for locating prey, and they can bound across the ice at great speed. An adult polar bear weighs about half a ton. It is so strong that a single blow of its paw can kill a person.

Claws are very sharp for gripping prey.

Polar bears eat seals, fish, birds, and small mammals. They also scavenge on the carcasses (dead bodies) of whales.

CONSERVATION

Today, polar bears and whales are protected from hunting by law. But many polar animals are still threatened by oil spills from ships and by overfishing. Fishing boats catch huge quantities of fish, which affects the numbers of animals that depend on fish for food.

KRILL

The shrimplike creatures shown left are called krill. They are the main food for baleen (whalebone) whales, such as the blue whale, which scoop up thousands of krill from the ocean every day.

PENGUINS

There are 17 different kinds of penguins; all live in the southern hemisphere. Penguins cannot fly, but they are expert swimmers and divers. They can speed along in the water after fish and squid using their flipper-shaped wings.

EMPEROR PENGUIN

The emperor penguin has a bright orange bib around its neck. To escape the leopard seal, it dives out of the water with great speed. It breeds in the coldest place on Earth – on Antarctic ice where the average temperature is -4°F (-20°C). After the female has laid an egg, the male penguin keeps it warm between his feet and belly for about 60 days. The newborn chicks stay warm by standing on their parents' feet.

ICE FISH

The blood of most fish freezes solid at about -32°F (-35°C), and the waters in the polar regions sometimes drop even lower. The ice fish, also called the crocodile fish, has special chemicals in its blood to stop it from freezing.

LEOPARD SEAL

The four main kinds of seals around Antarctica are the leopard, crabeater, Ross, and Weddell seals. The leopard seal measures up to 10 ft (3 m) in length. It patrols the pack ice and island coasts hunting for penguins and other seals, especially crabeater seals.

There is little life on the continent of Antarctica itself, apart from a few mosses, lichens, and tiny creatures such as mites.

TUNDRA

The lands on the edge of the Arctic Ocean are bleak and treeless. This region is called the tundra. The brief summer in the Arctic allows small plants such as sedges, cushion-shaped saxifrages, heathers, mosses, and lichens to grow. These plants provide food for many insects and the grazing caribou. Birds such as snow geese breed along the shores and migrate south in autumn.

MUSK OX

The musk ox is a type of goat. It is the only large mammal that can survive winter on the tundra. The musk ox's thickset body has dense underfur and a thick, shaggy outer coat of tough hairs. Musk oxen stand together in a herd for warmth and as protection against predators such as wolves.

SNOW GOOSE

About 100 kinds of birds migrate to the tundra to breed in spring. Snow geese arrive two weeks before there are any plants to eat, but they have a store of body fat which allows them to make a nest and lay eggs before they eat. Later they feed the chicks on the newly growing grasses.

Dwarf willows are among the world's smallest shrubs. They grow low and spread sideways to stay out of the icy winds.

ARCTIC SAXIFRAGE

The cushion shapes of tundra flowers such as saxifrage and crowberry help prevent the plants from freezing. These plants also provide shelter for the tiny creatures living inside them.

> ### Find out more
> ANTARCTICA
> ARCTIC
> BEARS AND PANDAS
> FISH
> SEA BIRDS
> SEALS AND SEA LIONS
> WHALES AND DOLPHINS

POLICE

ALL SOCIETIES HAVE RULES OR LAWS to protect the rights of their citizens. In a few communities the people themselves enforce the laws and identify and catch anyone who breaks them. But in most societies law enforcement is the job of the police. Police officers have many different duties, including chasing dangerous criminals, stopping motorists who drive too fast, and patrolling neighborhood streets. Some work in offices, carefully studying information for clues in order to solve a crime. The police arrest people suspected of committing a crime, then charge the suspects (accuse them of the crime) and hand them over to the courts for trial. The police must be careful to enforce only existing laws and not to arrest people for imagined crimes. In some countries, such as the United States, the police are civilians who are employed by the government. In other countries the police are similar to soldiers. In many nations the government uses the police to hold on to power and to stop political opposition.

FBI
The Federal Bureau of Investigation (FBI) was created in 1908. This picture shows FBI agents raiding an illegal alcohol factory run by gangsters during the Prohibition era (1919-33). Today the FBI investigates violations of federal law, such as kidnapping, bank robbery, spying, and organized crime.

Detectives produce a composite picture of the suspects they are seeking from descriptions provided by witnesses.

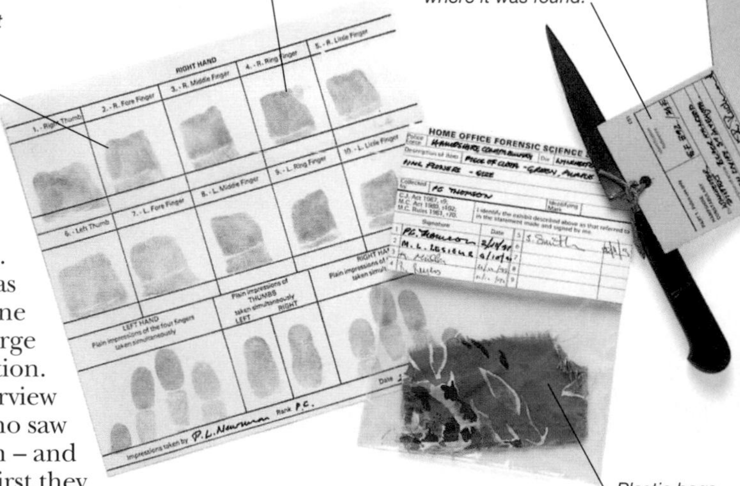

The pattern on the skin of every person's hands is unique. Detectives look for the fingerprints of the suspect at the scene of the crime.

Detectives carefully label evidence to show where it was found.

Police keep fingerprint records of every known criminal.

DETECTIVES
Police officers with special training in investigating crime are called detectives. When a crime has been committed, one detective takes charge of the investigation. Detectives interview witnesses – people who saw the crime happen – and search for evidence. First they look for evidence that will help track down the person who committed the crime. When they have arrested a suspect, detectives look for evidence that will prove their suspicions.

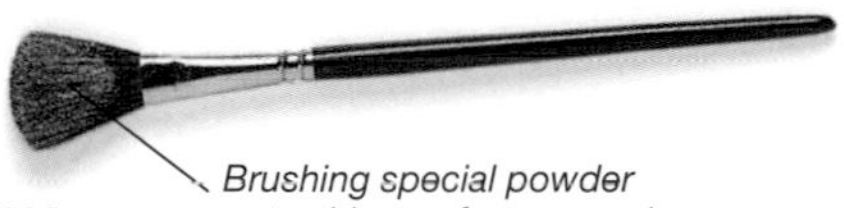

Brushing special powder onto shiny surfaces reveals fingerprints.

Plastic bags keep small pieces of evidence from the scene of the crime safe.

UNIFORMED POLICE
Detectives often wear ordinary clothes, but most police officers wear a uniform. The uniform enables members of the public to recognize the police officers. In some countries traffic police wear a completely different uniform from the criminal investigation police. A uniform must be practical, with pockets for a two-way radio, notebooks, handcuffs, a club, and other equipment. In some countries, such as the United States, the police are armed. In other countries, such as Britain, police do not usually carry guns.

Japan

Zimbabwe

United States

Thailand

RIOT POLICE
Sometimes large demonstrations or marches become violent. The demonstrators may loot stores or attack members of the public. Riot police move in to control such disturbances. They try to stop the violence by arresting the worst troublemakers and dispersing the crowd so that peace returns. Some riot police are specially trained personnel; others are regular officers equipped with special riot equipment including helmets, full-length shields to protect the body, and heavy clubs.

SQUAD CAR

The automobile was first used for police work in Akron, Ohio, in 1899. Today, many police officers travel their beats in specially equipped squad cars. Each has a two-way radio system linked with police headquarters. Most have onboard computers that connect with local and national crime data bureaus, giving officers almost instant access to lists of stolen goods and missing or wanted people. Other police support vehicles include paramedic units, mobile operations units, and aircraft, especially helicopters.

Women make up about 20 percent of the US police force.

POLICE ON PATROL

Patrol work is the major part of a police officer's job. Patrol officers, usually in teams of two, travel their assigned areas, or beats, on foot, by patrol car, or by motorcycle. In some cities officers ride bikes or horses. Their presence can help people feel safe and keep public order. As they watch over their beats, they use portable two-way radios to keep in touch with police headquarters. They receive assignments over their radios to investigate crimes or accidents.

CITY POLICE

Each city has a police force to enforce laws within city limits. A small town might have only one or two police officers, but a big city may employ thousands of officers in several precincts, or divisions. New York City established America's first permanent city police force in 1844. Today, it is one of the largest departments in the US, with 38,000 officers.

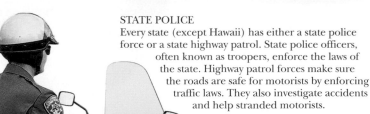

New York City police officers on duty

Sheriff's badge

COUNTY POLICE

Most US counties have a police force headed by a sheriff, who is elected by local voters. The county force is responsible for enforcing the law within county boundaries.

STATE POLICE

Every state (except Hawaii) has either a state police force or a state highway patrol. State police officers, often known as troopers, enforce the laws of the state. Highway patrol forces make sure the roads are safe for motorists by enforcing traffic laws. They also investigate accidents and help stranded motorists.

Customs police search the waters around Miami for boats carrying illegal goods.

SPECIAL UNITS

Large police forces have special units, trained with the skills for specific tasks. Bomb squads respond to bomb threats, searching sites where bombs may be planted, and try to stop any bombs from exploding. Hostage-negotiating teams try to persuade criminals to release their captives without harm. SWAT teams (SWAT stands for "special weapons and tactics") deal with heavily armed criminals. Search-and-rescue teams comb mountaintops, forests, and other remote areas to find missing people.

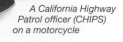

A California Highway Patrol officer (CHIPS) on a motorcycle

Find out more

GOVERNMENT AND POLITICS
LAW
OUTLAWS AND BANDITS

POLITICAL PARTIES

AN ESSENTIAL FEATURE OF DEMOCRATIC GOVERNMENT, political parties bring people with common political ideas together. The Constitution made no mention of political parties, but as the first American government took shape, several issues divided its politicians. A group known as the Federalists supported strong national government; the Anti-Federalists formed to oppose them. These groups developed into the first American political parties: the Federalists, led by Alexander Hamilton, and the Democratic-Republicans, led by Thomas Jefferson. Today, America has a two-party system, with most elected officials belonging to either the Democratic or the Republican party. Both parties are complex organizations, with offices at local, state, and national level.

Republicans campaign with their elephant mascot.

REPUBLICAN PARTY

Founded in 1854, the Republican party was established to oppose the spread of slavery and provide strong opposition to the powerful Democrats. The first successful Republican presidential candidate was Abraham Lincoln, elected in 1860. The party supported the rights of the people against big government, a policy that appealed to many groups, including farmers, merchants, and industrialists. In 1874, a political cartoonist used an elephant to represent the Republican vote; to this day, the elephant symbolizes the Republican party.

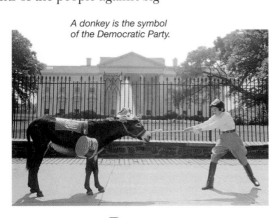

A donkey is the symbol of the Democratic Party.

"BOSS" TWEED

The power of politics has attracted many greedy people. Perhaps the most famous political "boss" was William Macy Tweed, who ran the New York City Democratic party headquarters in the mid-1800s. Tweed traded favors, offering jobs to immigrants and workers in exchange for their support, giving him enough votes to influence lawmakers.

DEMOCRATIC PARTY

The oldest existing political party in the United States, the Democratic party was once part of Jefferson's Democratic-Republicans. After the party split in the 1820s, Andrew Jackson led his new Democratic party to its first presidential victory in 1828. The party championed the common people and supported a strong federal government. During the Civil War, disagreements over slavery weakened the party, giving the Republicans power.

A 19th-century Prohibition poster illustrates the Temperance League's battle against alcoholism.

PARTY CONVENTIONS

Democrats and Republicans hold national conventions (left) every four years, in the same year as a presidential election. The purpose of the convention is to officially nominate candidates for president and vice president, and to adopt a party platform, a list of the party's goals and policies.

THIRD PARTIES

No third party has ever won the presidency. However, their ideas have often won such support that the two major parties have adopted them. Many third parties support a single issue, such as gun laws or Prohibition (of alcohol).

Find out more

CONGRESS
CONSTITUTION
GOVERNMENT AND POLITICS
PRESIDENCY

POLLUTION

OIL ON BEACHES, vehicle exhaust fumes, litter, and other waste products are called pollutants, because they pollute (dirty) our environment. Pollutants can affect our health and harm animals and plants. We pollute our surroundings with all kinds of chemical waste from factories and power stations. These substances are the unwanted results of modern living. Pollution itself is not new – a hundred years ago factories sent out great clouds of poisonous smoke. Today, there are many more factories and many more pollutants. Pollution has spread to the land, air, and water of every corner on Earth, even to Antarctica and Mount Everest. Scientists are worried that the gases released by factories and vehicles are even changing the atmosphere and causing the surface temperature of the planet to heat up. We can reduce pollution by recycling waste and using biodegradable materials that eventually break down in the soil.

ACCIDENTAL POLLUTION
Besides everyday pollution, there is also accidental pollution – for example, when a ship leaks oil and creates a huge oil slick in the ocean. This kind of pollution causes damage to the environment and kills millions of fish and seabirds, like the oil-covered birds shown above.

ACID RAIN
Vehicle exhausts produce fumes that contain nitrogen oxides. The coal we burn in power stations produces sulfur dioxide. When these two substances mix with water in the air, they turn into acids, then fall as acid rain. Acid rain damages trees, eats into buildings, and kills wildlife in rivers. Today, it is possible to reduce the amount of sulfur dioxide given off by power stations, but the process is expensive.

ATMOSPHERIC POLLUTION
Ozone is a kind of oxygen present in the atmosphere. It forms a protective layer that blocks out the Sun's ultraviolet radiation, which can cause skin cancer in humans. Chemicals called CFCs (chlorofluorocarbons) damage the ozone layer.

GLOBAL WARMING
Burning fossil fuels releases carbon gases into the atmosphere. They act like the panes of glass in a greenhouse, trapping the heat. Many scientists now believe that the Earth is becoming too warm. If the Earth becomes just a few degrees warmer, sea levels will rise, drowning low-lying coastal cities.

Many factories release pollutants as a by-product.

Farmers spray crops with fertilizers to help them grow, and pesticides to control pests and weeds, but these chemicals can harm the other kinds of wildlife that live and feed on the crops.

RECYCLING
If we save the glass, metal, plastics, and paper that we use every day, they can be recycled and used again. This helps preserve the Earth's natural resources. Recycling cuts down litter, reduces air and water pollution, and can save energy. Many towns have "bottle banks" to collect glass for recycling.

TRAFFIC POLLUTION
Truck, car, and bus exhausts belch out lead (which can damage the nervous system), carbon monoxide, carbon dioxide, and nitrogen oxides, which cause acid rain and the smog called photochemical smog. Some of these harmful substances are reduced by special catalytic converters attached to vehicle exhausts.

Ships leak oil into the sea, which is harmful to sea creatures.

Every day we drop litter on the ground – candy wrappers, paper bags, empty tin cans, and bottles. Litter is ugly, unhygienic, and a fire risk, and it can kill animals that eat it.

WASTE DUMPING
In many parts of the world people bury toxic (poisonous) chemicals and other dangerous waste products. These substances leak into the soil and water, killing wildlife. We treat the seas as waste dumps, and the North Sea is now seriously polluted. For the wildlife in the seas to survive, we must produce less harmful waste products.

HOLES IN THE OZONE LAYER
In the late 1970s, scientists detected "holes" in the ozone layer above the South and North poles. Probably caused by air pollutants, particularly CFCs and methane, the "holes" seemed to be growing larger. In 1987, more than 30 countries signed an agreement called the Montreal Protocol, which sharply reduced CFC production worldwide.

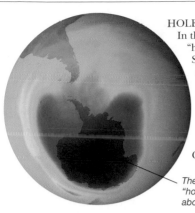

The dark patch is the "hole" in the ozone layer above the Antarctic.

An aerosol is a mixture of product and propellant.

The can is pressurized by the propellant gas.

HOUSEHOLD POLLUTION
Some of the polluting gases that were destroying the ozone layer came from household devices. The most damaging were chlorofluorocarbons (CFCs), used as propellants in aerosol cans and inside the cooling systems of refrigerators. Today, in the move to reduce pollution, less harmful gases have replaced CFCs.

CLEANING UP
Neutralizing chemicals can be used to clean up pollution. Spilled oil, for example, can be countered with detergents. But unfortunately these chemicals can do just as much damage as the original spill. Sometimes the only way to clean up is to physically remove the pollutant. Sadly the damage is often already done, although it may not be very obvious.

Where possible, mechanical scoops remove spilt oil sludge.

Special V-shaped paddles are used to push the oil sludge into heaps.

OIL BARRIER
Crude oil is a particularly harmful chemical pollutant. However, because oil floats on water, an oil slick created by a spillage from a wrecked tanker can be contained by barriers. The oil must then be dispersed or collected quickly because, if it is left, it will eventually thicken and sink. Also, oil barriers cannot withstand storms.

ENERGY SAVING
Much of the pollution that we produce is the result of burning fossil fuels in power plants and motor vehicles. Generators and engines can be made more efficient so that they use less fuel. Individuals too can save energy and reduce pollution by making use of energy-efficient light bulbs and other appliances in the home, and by using cars less.

Energy-saving lamps reduce pollution, but just switching off lights helps even more.

RAIN FORESTS
Since 1945, more than half of the world's rain forests have been destroyed. They are cut down for timber or burned to clear space for farmland. Burning produces carbon dioxide, contributing to global warming. Scientists are increasingly concerned about the impact of this on the environment.

Find out more
ATMOSPHERE
CLIMATES
CONSERVATION
and endangered species
ENERGY

PORTS AND WATERWAYS

SHIPS LOAD AND UNLOAD their cargoes at ports, or harbors – sheltered places on coasts or rivers with cranes and warehouses to handle ships, passengers, and goods. Road and rail connections link the ports with inland areas. The earliest ports were simply landing places at river mouths. Here ships were safe from storms, and workers on board could unload cargo into smaller boats for transport upriver. Building walls against the riverbanks created wharfs to make loading easier. In the 18th and 19th centuries, port authorities added docks – deep, artificial pools – leading off the rivers. Ships and boats use waterways to sail to inland towns or as shortcuts from one sea to another. Waterways can be natural rivers, or artificial rivers called canals. One of the world's largest waterway systems, based on the Mississippi River, links the Great Lakes with the Gulf of Mexico. It includes 15,000 miles (24,000 km) of waterways.

Navigation lights guide ships safely into the port.

Because oil burns easily, oil tankers use special terminals to unload their cargo.

Huge tanks at the terminal store the oil until it is needed.

Ships and boats unload at wharfs.

LOADING AND UNLOADING
Ships carry nearly two-thirds of all cargo in containers, but many items do not fit neatly inside them. Cranes lift these individual large pieces of cargo on and off the ships. Loose cargo such as grain is sucked up by huge pumps and carried ashore through pipes. Vehicles drive onto special ships known as "ro-ros": roll-on, roll-off ferries.

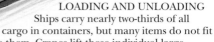

CONTAINERS
A special wheeled crane handles containers. It lifts them off the ship and can either stack them nearby or lower them onto the back of a truck. Cranes, ships, and trucks around the world have the same size fittings so that they can move containers easily between different countries.

DOCKS
Huge gates at the entrance to the docks maintain the water level inside. The warehouses and cranes of the old-style docks are disappearing today as more ships carry cargo in containers – large steel boxes of standard size that are easy to stack and move.

LOCKS
To raise or lower ships from one water level to another, canals and harbors have locks. If a ship is going to a lower water level, the lock fills with water and the ship sails in. Closing the upper gates and letting out the water gradually lowers the ship to the level of the water outside the lower gates.

SINGAPORE
At the center of the sea routes of southern Asia lies Singapore, one of the busiest ports in the world. Its large, modern docks handle goods from all over the world. Many large ships from Europe and the Americas unload their cargoes here into smaller vessels for distribution to nearby countries.

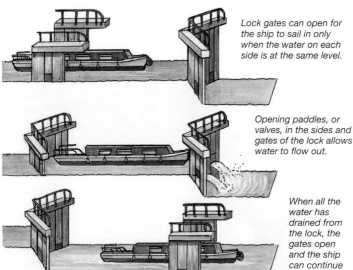

Lock gates can open for the ship to sail in only when the water on each side is at the same level.

Opening paddles, or valves, in the sides and gates of the lock allows water to flow out.

When all the water has drained from the lock, the gates open and the ship can continue on its way.

PANAMA CANAL
Ships traveling around the South American coast from the Caribbean Sea to the Pacific Ocean once had to sail nearly 6,000 miles (10,000 km) – until the United States built a huge canal through Panama in Central America where the Pacific and the Caribbean are just 51 miles (82 km) apart. The canal opened in 1914.

Find out more

NAVIGATION
SHIPS AND BOATS
TRADE AND INDUSTRY

PORTUGAL

PORTUGAL'S LONG ATLANTIC coast has shaped its destiny as a seafaring nation. It is a land with few natural resources, and its economy has traditionally been based on fishing and farming. The grapes that grow on the moist, fertile slopes of the Douro River produce fine wines and port, while olives, cork, and canned fish are also major exports. Today, Portugal is becoming more industrialized, and its textile industry is expanding. Although it has a good internal road network, its transportation links to its eastern neighbor, Spain, are poor, and most heavy goods are still moved by ship. Tourism, especially in the mild south coast, is increasingly important.

On the southwestern side of the Iberian Peninsula, which it shares with Spain, Portugal is the westernmost country in mainland Europe. It also includes the Azores and Madeira, two self-governing island groups in the Atlantic Ocean.

ALGARVE

The fertile coastal lowlands in the south of Portugal are densely inhabited. Inland, the mainly agricultural economy is based on grain, figs, olives, almonds, and grapes. Many fishing villages line the coast. In recent years, these quiet backwaters have been transformed by tourism (above). Some traditional villages have been completely swallowed up by tourist development. Tourists come for mild winters, fine scenery, and some of the best golf courses in Europe.

VINEYARDS

Vineyards blanket the terraced hills that line the valley of the Douro River (left). The grapes harvested here are used to make Portugal's distinctive wines and famous fortified wine, which is named "port" after Porto, a major town on the Douro Estuary. Grapes are transported down the river by barge to the towns of Porto and Villa Nova da Gaia, where the wine is blended and matured in casks and bottles and shipped all over the world. The island of Madeira is also famous for its wine, which is heated over a period of six months by a combination of hot water pipes and the rays of the sun. It is then fortified with brandy, which helps to give Madeira wine a richer flavor.

Port is a sweet wine, made by adding brandy to the fermenting grapes.

LISBON

Portugal's capital and main port lies on the banks of the Tagus River, 8 miles (13 km) from the coast. Baixa, the historic city center (below), lies on the north bank. In 1755, most of the city was destroyed by an earthquake and then completely rebuilt. Today, it is the bustling commercial heart of the city. Lisbon's manufacturing center, dominated by large cement and steel works, lies on the south bank.

CORK CULTIVATION

Portugal is the world's leading producer of cork, made from the outer bark of the cork oak tree. Trees are first stripped of cork at 15 to 20 years old, and then every 10 years thereafter. Cork is used to make stoppers for bottles and jars.

FESTIVALS

Portugal is mostly a Roman Catholic country; many villages hold an annual festival to mark a particular saint's day or religious holiday. Colorful parades march through the streets, accompanied by the Portuguese guitar (a type of mandolin), and the entire village comes together for a lavish meal, with music and dancing. Plaintive folk songs (*fados*) are famous throughout Portugal.

Find out more

EUROPE, HISTORY OF
PORTUGAL, HISTORY OF

| Volcano | Mountain | Ancient monument | Capital city | Large city/town | Small city/town |

STATISTICS
Area: 35,670 sq miles
(92,390 sq km)
Population: 10,100,000
Capital: Lisbon
Languages: Portuguese
Religions: Roman
Catholic, Protestant
Currency: Euro
Main occupations:
Finance, tourism,
manufacturing,
agriculture
Main exports: Clothes,
shoes, wine, tomatoes,
citrus fruits, cork,
sardines, tungsten,
copper, tin
Main imports: Oil

FARMING
On the whole, the land
in Portugal is fertile and well-
watered, although in the far south
it is very arid. A wide range of
crops are grown: wheat, rye, oats,
barley, olives, figs, grapes and
tomatoes. Goats and sheep are
found throughout Portugal, and
are well adapted to the arid south.
Most farms are small, family-
owned, and use very traditional
farming methods. In the Alentejo
region in the south (below), some
of the land is being successfully
farmed by village cooperatives.

FISHING
Fishing has always been important in
Portugal, and many fishing villages are
located along its long Atlantic coast.
Small fishing boats net large catches of
tuna, anchovies, sardines, oysters and
mackerel, which are then processed in
coastal factories. Portugal has become a
major exporter of canned sardines. The
national Portuguese dish is *bacalháo* – dried,
salted cod – which is caught by offshore
Portuguese fleets in the Atlantic.

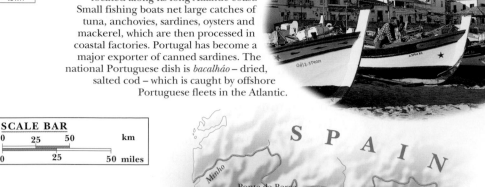

SCALE BAR
0 25 50 km
0 25 50 miles

CERAMICS
This glazed, ceramic
azulejos tile comes from
the Minho in the north.
These tiles, painted with
pictorial scenes, have
been used for centuries
to decorate walls.

HISTORY OF
PORTUGAL

PART OF THE IBERIAN peninsula, Portugal only became a separate country in the 1100s. When the Romans colonized the area, they called it Lusitania. The Moors took over the region in the 700s, and Portugal thrived under their rule. In the 1400s, Portuguese explorers set up a great empire in competition with Spain, which occupied Portugal in the 16th century. In 1910, Portugal became a republic. Ruled by a dictatorship for many years, Portugal has been a democracy since 1974.

AFONSO III
Portugal emerged as an independent country in the 11th century, but the Moors still occupied the southern region. In 1248, Afonso III became king, and finally drove the Moors out of Portugal.

REVOLT
In 1580, Philip II of Spain conquered Portugal. The Portuguese resented this, but were unable to rebel successfully until 1640, by which time Spain was greatly weakened by a war with France. John, Duke of Braganza, Portugal's greatest landowner, led the revolt against Spain. The Spaniards were driven out, and John was crowned John IV, first king of the House of Braganza, which ruled Portugal until the monarchy ended in 1910.

PORTUGUESE EMPIRE
In the 1400s, encouraged by Prince Henry the Navigator (son of John I, the King of Portugal), Portuguese navigators made long voyages of exploration around the world. In 1498, Vasco da Gama led four ships to Calicut in India, and two years later Pedro Álvares Cabral reached Brazil. Soon Portugal ruled a vast empire with lands in southern Asia, Africa, and Brazil.

Battle scene during the Portuguese revolt

PORTUGAL
201 B.C. Romans colonize Iberian peninsula.

700s Moors (Muslims from North Africa) occupy Portugal.

1100s Christians drive out Moors; Portugal becomes a separate country from Spain.

1419 Portuguese begin exploring overseas.

1494 Treaty of Tordesillas: Spain and Portugal divide the world.

1500 Portugal claims Brazil.

1580-1640 Spain rules Portugal.

1822 Portugal loses Brazil.

1910 Portugal becomes a republic.

1974 Military coup overthrows dictatorship.

1986 Portugal joins European Union.

ANTONIO DE SALAZAR
Portugal's prime minister from 1932, António de Oliviera Salazar ruled as a dictator until 1968, when he retired after a stroke. He was succeeded by Marcello Caetano. In 1974, a military coup overthrew the regime.

LISBON EARTHQUAKE
In 1755, a massive earthquake destroyed the low-lying part of Lisbon, Portugal's capital, killing more than 60,000 people. São Jorge Castle, once the home of Portuguese kings, survived because it was on a hill. The Marquis of Pombal, Portugal's prime minister (1756-77), had the city rebuilt.

Find out more
DEMOCRACY
EARTHQUAKES
EXPLORERS
SPAIN, HISTORY OF

POTTERY

HEATING CLAY DUG FROM THE GROUND transforms it from oozing wet mud to the strong, hard, waterproof material that we call pottery. Pottery has many uses because its properties are so different from those of clay. The potter (pot maker) can easily mold the soft clay into a wide variety of shapes, from flat plates for eating to deep jars for storage. Firing, or baking the pot, sets its shape forever. The potter's art is very old. The first potters worked in the Middle East 9,000 years ago. They made simple pressed pots and coiled pots as shown below left. And 3,500 years ago potters started to use small turntables, now called potter's wheels, to make their pots perfectly round. We know this because pottery does not decay in the ground as wood does. Archaeologists use pottery fragments to learn about the people who made the pots centuries ago.

PORCELAIN
By adding sand to clay, potters create a special kind of pottery called porcelain. The sand turns to glass in firing, making the porcelain almost translucent. The Chinese invented porcelain more than 1,200 years ago, but their art remained a secret until the 18th century.

PRESSED POTS
A potter can make many identical pots by pressing clay into a plaster mold.

MAKING POTS
There are three main stages in making pots: shaping the clay, firing, and glazing. Potters use many different methods of shaping clay. To make perfectly circular objects, they "throw" the pot from a lump of clay on a revolving wheel. As the wheel spins, the potter uses both hands to draw the lump of clay upward and form the sides of the vessel.

COILED POTS
Pots can be made without a wheel by coiling long, thin rolls of clay.

FIRING
Pots must dry out after shaping. Then the potter stacks them carefully in the kiln – a big oven. Gas or electricity heats the kiln to more than 1,100°F (600°C) to turn the dry, brittle clay into rigid pottery. To make pots, the potter must control the temperature of the firing and how long it lasts.

Different glazes fired at different temperatures produce a wide range of colors.

The potter measures the firing temperature with a special thermometer or by placing small ceramic cones in the kiln. The cone melts when the temperature is high enough to fire the pots.

Throwing (molding) pots on a wheel takes great skill.

Potters must keep their hands wet while they mold the clay.

The lump of clay must be centered on the wheel, or it will wobble out of control.

SLIP CASTING
Pouring liquid clay (slip) into the plaster mold of a pot coats the inside. When dry, the clay forms a perfect replica of the mold.

Dry pottery waiting to be fired.

Clay is stored in large bins, covered with plastic or wet cloth. This keeps the clay moist and easy to work.

GLAZING
After the first firing, pottery is porous – water can still seep through it. Glazing the pottery completely seals its surface with a very hard, glasslike coating. Glaze is a mixture of metal oxides and minerals in water. The potter dips the pot into the glaze or pours the glaze on. The glaze dries, then the pot goes back into the kiln for a second firing. This melts the glaze and makes it stick to the pot.

TRADITIONAL POTTERY
Potters in every culture have shaped and decorated their pots in unique ways. Many made useful pots such as bowls and cooking vessels. But craft potters as far apart as South America and Korea also made objects for decoration and enjoyment, including beads and musical instruments.

Glazing makes the pot more attractive and seals its surface.

Before glazing their pots, potters decorate them with slip, underglaze colors, or enamel.

___ *Find out more* ___
CHINA, HISTORY OF
GLASS AND CERAMICS
ROCKS AND MINERALS

PREHISTORIC LIFE

2 BILLION YEARS AGO
The earliest forms of life were bacteria and blue-green algae. The algae grew in rings or short columns called stromatolites, which are fossilized in rocks. Today, stromatolites still form in shallow tropical seas.

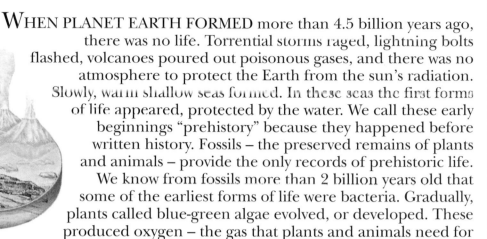

WHEN PLANET EARTH FORMED more than 4.5 billion years ago, there was no life. Torrential storms raged, lightning bolts flashed, volcanoes poured out poisonous gases, and there was no atmosphere to protect the Earth from the sun's radiation. Slowly, warm shallow seas formed. In these seas the first forms of life appeared, protected by the water. We call these early beginnings "prehistory" because they happened before written history. Fossils – the preserved remains of plants and animals – provide the only records of prehistoric life. We know from fossils more than 2 billion years old that some of the earliest forms of life were bacteria. Gradually, plants called blue-green algae evolved, or developed. These produced oxygen – the gas that plants and animals need for life. Oxygen was released into the air from the sea and formed a protective blanket of ozone in the atmosphere. The ozone screened out the sun's radiation, and living things began to invade the land and take to the air. Millions of kinds of animals and plants have existed since the first signs of life – some, such as insects, have thrived; others, such as the dinosaurs, have died out as the Earth's environment has changed.

Some of the earliest remains of the life on Earth are fossils called stromatolites.

600 MILLION YEARS AGO
Rare fossils of soft-bodied creatures show us that many different animals had evolved by this time. They included the first kinds of jellyfish, corals, sea pens, and worms.

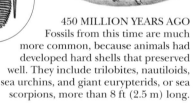

Sea pens existed 600 million years ago.

One of the first fishes, about 390 million years old

390 MILLION YEARS AGO
Fish were the first creatures with backbones. They evolved quickly into many different kinds. Gradually, they developed jaws and fins. The first small land plants, such as mosses, appeared on the swampy shores.

Trilobites were common 450 million years ago. They are ancient relatives of crabs.

450 MILLION YEARS AGO
Fossils from this time are much more common, because animals had developed hard shells that preserved well. They include trilobites, nautiloids, sea urchins, and giant eurypterids, or sea scorpions, more than 8 ft (2.5 m) long.

Cooksonia was one of the first land plants to appear on Earth.

HOW WE KNOW THE AGE OF FOSSILS

Stages		Million years ago (mya)
	Quaternary period	2 mya–today
	Tertiary period	65–2 mya
	Jurassic and Cretaceous periods	195–65
	Triassic period	230–195
	Carboniferous and Permian periods	345–230
	Devonian period	395–345
	Ordovician and Silurian periods	500–395
	Cambrian period	570–500
	Pre-cambrian period	4,000–570

Scientists called paleontologists find out how old a fossil is from the age of the rocks around it. This is called relative dating. They also measure the amounts of radioactive chemicals in the rocks and fossils to find out when they formed. This is called absolute dating.

Prehistoric time is divided into different stages, called eras, which are further divided into periods. Each of these stages lasted for many millions of years. If you dig deep down into the Earth's surface, you can find fossils of animals and plants that lived during the different periods.

350 MILLION YEARS AGO
As plants became established on land, they were soon followed by the first land animals, such as millipedes and insects. Woody trees that looked like conifers stood more than 100 ft (30 m) high. Sharks and many other fish swam in the seas.

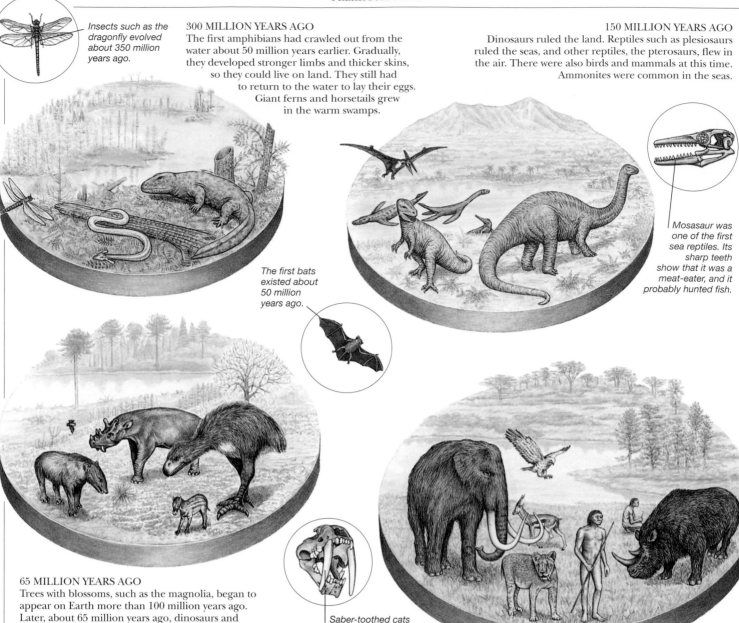

Insects such as the dragonfly evolved about 350 million years ago.

300 MILLION YEARS AGO
The first amphibians had crawled out from the water about 50 million years earlier. Gradually, they developed stronger limbs and thicker skins, so they could live on land. They still had to return to the water to lay their eggs. Giant ferns and horsetails grew in the warm swamps.

150 MILLION YEARS AGO
Dinosaurs ruled the land. Reptiles such as plesiosaurs ruled the seas, and other reptiles, the pterosaurs, flew in the air. There were also birds and mammals at this time. Ammonites were common in the seas.

Mosasaur was one of the first sea reptiles. Its sharp teeth show that it was a meat-eater, and it probably hunted fish.

The first bats existed about 50 million years ago.

65 MILLION YEARS AGO
Trees with blossoms, such as the magnolia, began to appear on Earth more than 100 million years ago. Later, about 65 million years ago, dinosaurs and many other living things became extinct (died out). During the next few million years different kinds of mammals and birds became more common.

Saber-toothed cats existed 19 to 2 million years ago. Their huge teeth enabled them to attack and kill large prey.

EXTINCTION
There is concern over the fact that many animals and plants are in danger of dying out, or becoming extinct. But ever since life began, animals and plants have died out, to be replaced by others. This process is part of nature. As the conditions on Earth change, some living things cannot adapt; they eventually become extinct. Scientists believe that 99 percent of all the different plants and animals that ever lived have died out naturally. In prehistoric times there were mass extinctions when hundreds of different things died out together. These extinctions were often due to dramatic changes in climate. About 225 million years ago, 90 percent of all the living things in the sea died out. Today, animals and plants are dying out more quickly because humans damage and destroy the areas where they live.

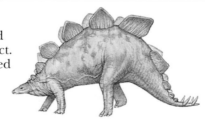

STEGOSAURUS
This dinosaur lived about 150 million years ago in North America. It became extinct about 140 million years ago.

NEANDERTHAL PEOPLE
These people lived from about 120,000–35,000 years ago. They were the immediate, and smaller, predecessors of *Homo sapiens* (modern humans). As humans evolved (developed), these people died out.

GREAT ICE AGE
About 2 million years ago, several ice ages gripped the Earth, with warmer stretches between. Humans evolved – probably in Africa – and spread around the world. In the north, they hunted woolly mammoths, woolly rhinos, and saber-toothed cats. About 18,000 years ago, ice sheets covered much of northern Europe, northern Britain, and North America.

Find out more
COAL
DINOSAURS
EVOLUTION
FOSSILS
PREHISTORIC PEOPLES

PREHISTORIC PEOPLES

COMPARED WITH the rest of life on Earth, human beings arrived quite recently, after the dinosaur age and the age of mammals. The whole story of human evolution is incomplete, because many parts of the fossil record have never been found. Humanlike mammals first emerged from the ape family about five million years ago in Central Africa. They came down from the trees and began to walk on two legs. Hominids, or early humans, were more apelike than human and lived in the open. Over millions of years they learned to walk upright and developed bigger brains. These large brains helped them to develop language and the ability to work together. Hominids lived in groups and shared work and food, wandering through the countryside gathering fruits, roots, nuts, berries, and seeds, and hunting animals. Standing upright left their hands free to make tools and weapons, shelters and fire. They lived in caves and in shelters made from branches and stones. These early humans spread slowly over the rest of the world and soon rose to dominate life on Earth.

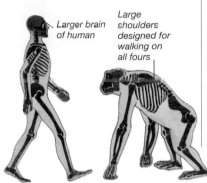

Larger brain of human

Large shoulders designed for walking on all fours

HUMAN OR APE?
Humans have smaller jaws and larger brains than apes. The human hand has a longer thumb; apes have longer fingers. The human pelvis and thigh allow upright motion, giving the spine an S-shaped curve. Human legs are longer than arms; apes have the reverse. Unlike apes, humans cannot use their big toes as extra thumbs; the foot has adapted to walking and can no longer grasp.

WISDOM TOOTH
Early people needed wisdom teeth in order to eat roots and berries. Today, we no longer need wisdom teeth, and many people do not even develop them.

Lucy's remains were found at Hadar.

Simple stone tool

Homo erectus made more advanced tools, such as this spear.

Sophisticated carving

Lucy gathered fruit to eat.

Fossil remains of the earliest hominids have all been found in East Africa.

Simple clothing

Sewn leather clothing

Rough woven cloth

Modern people wore shoes.

Homo habilis

Homo erectus

Neanderthal man

LUCY
In 1974, archaeologists discovered a complete fossil hominid skeleton in Ethiopia, northeastern Africa. She was nicknamed Lucy, after the Beatles' song *Lucy in the Sky with Diamonds*.

Lucy was 3 million years old. Although nearly human, she was probably not one of our direct ancestors.

When alive, Lucy was about the same height as a 10-year-old girl, and weighed 66 lb (30 kg).

FROM HOMINIDS TO HUMANS
About 2.5 million years ago hominids called *Homo habilis* (meaning "handy man") shaped crude stone tools and built rough shelters. Other, more advanced hominids, called *Homo erectus*, moved out of Africa into Europe and Asia. They lived in camps, made use of fire, and probably had a language. After the Ice Age, Neanderthals lived in Europe. Neanderthals looked much like people today, wore clothes, made flint tools and fire, and buried their dead. They vanished about 30,000 years ago and were replaced by "modern people," who invented farming about 9,000 years ago and began to settle down in communities. Shortly after, the first civilizations began.

MODERN PEOPLE
When humans learned to domesticate animals and grow crops, they stopped wandering and settled down on farms and later towns began to develop.

Find out more
ARCHAEOLOGY
BRONZE AGE
EVOLUTION
PREHISTORIC LIFE
STONE AGE

PRESIDENCY

THE PRESIDENCY OF THE UNITED STATES may be the most powerful office in the world. Its duties and responsibilities are immense – the president is head of the government, commander-in-chief of the armed forces, chief of state, leader of his or her political party, foreign policy director, legislative leader, and the voice of the American people. The president is elected every four years after a long, intense, and expensive campaign. Once elected, the new president swears an oath to faithfully execute the duties of the office, and preserve, protect, and defend the Constitution.

1600 PENNSYLVANIA AVENUE
The president lives and works in the White House in Washington, D.C.. This 132-room mansion was first occupied by President John Adams in 1800. The president's headquarters is the Oval Office, where the chief executive meets with government officials.

President John F. Kennedy's inauguration speech, 1961

Republican delegates cheer at the Republican convention in 1988.

ROAD TO THE WHITE HOUSE

Presidential elections take place every four years. Primary elections allow voters to choose between candidates. The major political parties then meet at conventions, to officially select their presidential and vice-presidential candidates. The chosen candidates campaign across the nation, giving speeches and trying to win the support of voters. People vote on the first Tuesday in November.

THE PEOPLE'S CHOICE

The Constitution provided for a president elected by the people, but the popular vote does not directly decide the winner. Instead, it determines how the delegates who represent each state will vote. These delegates, known as the electoral college, vote in December of an election year for the person that their state voted for in November. Each state has as many electoral votes as the total of its senators and representatives in Congress.

George Washington (left), the first President of the United States, sitting with the first US cabinet

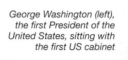

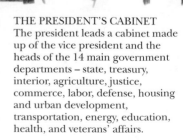

THE PRESIDENT'S CABINET
The president leads a cabinet made up of the vice president and the heads of the 14 main government departments – state, treasury, interior, agriculture, justice, commerce, labor, defense, housing and urban development, transportation, energy, education, health, and veterans' affairs.

FIRST FAMILIES

The president's family attracts a great deal of media attention. The president's wife is known as the first lady. In recent years, first ladies such as Laura Bush (right, with George W. Bush) have played an increasingly important role, both in public service and in shaping national and international policy. Although only one child has ever been born in the White House (to Grover Cleveland), many have made it their home – John Tyler's 15 children lived there during his term of office.

Find out more

CONSTITUTION
GOVERNMENT AND POLITICS
POLITICAL PARTIES

PRINTING

1 TYPESETTING
To set the type for a book, the words are typed into a computer. The computer sends signals to a machine containing a laser that prints the words onto a plastic, light-sensitive film, called the type film.

2 COLOR SEPARATION
All the colors and illustrations in a book are reproduced with just four colored inks; each is printed with a plate made from a separate film. To make the separate films (called color separations), all the pictures are laid on a spinning drum. A laser scans over the pictures four times – once for each separation.

Original picture containing all colors

Yellow color separation

Cyan color separation

Magenta color separation

Black color separation

3 PRINTING PRESS
The printing plates are made photographically, by shining light through the type and color films so that the details are recorded by the plate's light-sensitive coating. Each of the plates is treated with chemicals to bring out the print image, then fitted onto rollers in the printing press. There are four plates altogether, one for each of the colored inks. As the paper runs through the press, it passes over each of the four inked plates in turn. These plates add the four colors one by one. Separate rollers run over the plates and keep them wet with fresh ink. The paper emerges at the far end as printed pages in full color.

HAVE YOU EVER THOUGHT about how many times you look at print each day? Printed words and pictures have found their way into almost every part of our lives: on advertisements, road signs, food labels, clothes, newspapers, and, of course, in books such as this. Today, we take this information for granted, but before the invention of printing, all information had to be laboriously written by hand, and only a few people had access to education. The introduction of printing caused a revolution. Printing means that numerous identical copies of words and pictures can be made quickly and cheaply. Printing presses use a mirror image of the original to apply ink to paper, cardboard, and other materials. In the old days, printers used to set type (form words) in "hot" metal. They put pages together from metal blocks, each one of which printed either a single letter or a single line of text. Nowadays, entire complex pages like this one can be printed from sheets of transparent film or from digital text-and-image files created on a computer.

A design needs to be engraved in reverse (as a mirror image) to print the right way.

Adding yellow ink

Adding cyan ink

Adding magenta ink

Adding black ink

Page printed with yellow ink only.

THE HISTORY OF PRINTING
In A.D. 868, the Chinese were printing books using carved wooden blocks. In about 1450, Johannes Gutenberg of Germany developed movable type, in which separate pieces of type print each letter on a handpress (right). This process remained in use for 350 years until the invention of power-driven presses which allowed books to be printed more easily.

Gutenberg and his press

FOUR-COLOR PRINTING
All the colors you see on this page are made up of dots printed with just four different colored inks: yellow, cyan (green-blue), magenta (blue-red), and black. More colors are sometimes used for high-quality prints, but this costs more, since most printing presses are set up to print in four colors only.

Final printed page built up from yellow, cyan, magenta, and black inks.

After the paper is printed on one side, it is fed back through the press for printing on the other side.

Find out more
BOOKS
COLOR
NEWSPAPERS
PAPER

PUPPETS

THE PUPPET SHOW is one of the oldest forms of theater, and each age has produced new traditions. In Africa, China, and India, puppets were used in early times to dramatize legends and religious stories. In the 18th century, the Bunraku puppets of Japan acted out dramatic stories to the words of a narrator with the puppeteers in full view. Punch and Judy in England and Petrushka in Russia are puppets that grew out of the characters of Italian comedy of the 16th to 18th centuries. There are many different ways to work a puppet. It takes just one hand to work simple finger puppets, but some complicated Japanese puppets require three operators. Puppets sometimes comment on what is going on in the real world and can be quite mischievous. Modern puppeteers, such as the late Jim Henson, the creator of the Muppets, have replaced the strings and rods of traditional puppets with electronic mechanisms.

MARIONETTES
String puppets, or marionettes, require two hands and great skill. The operator controls the puppet by moving a wooden bar to which the strings are attached. Some strings are linked to synchronize movements; for example, raising one leg lowers the other.

FINGER PUPPETS
Making a finger puppet is simple – and operating one is just as easy. With a little practice, you can stage a whole puppet play using just the fingers of both hands.

Several operators are needed to control the body puppet.

The puppet's eyes can open and close.

So that the mouth can move, it is attached to the frame by hinges.

The person inside the puppet can hear directions from the operator.

A television set shows the operator what the viewer sees.

The puppet is moved by a cable link to the operator.

BODY PUPPETS
Life-size puppets are a real team effort. The person inside the suit maneuvers the limbs while other operators control the face. The puppet is made from foam rubber over a rigid frame, so it is very light and easy to move.

The television camera films only the puppet; Jim Henson (center) and the other operators below remain hidden.

SHADOW PUPPETS
In this ancient form of puppetry, the operator holds the puppet close to a screen. The light behind casts a shadow that the audience can see from the other side of the screen. Javanese puppets such as this one can be more than 3 ft (1 m) tall. The arms are moved by rods held from below. These puppets are traditionally made from buffalo hide and are brightly colored in golds, reds, and blues.

HAND PUPPETS
Glove puppets are very simple to operate. A hand inside makes the puppet move, with the index finger supporting and turning the head. The arms of these Muppets are moved by a combination of glove and rod techniques.

> ### *Find out more*
> THEATER

PUZZLES

CROSSWORD PUZZLES
Crosswords are word puzzles. You must solve two sets of numbered clues correctly to fill in the blanks that fit across and down the grid.

ANYTHING THAT CONFUSES THE BRAIN until a solution can be found may be called a puzzle. The human brain is good at solving puzzles. Some scientists believe that the human race developed so successfully because of people's curiosity and ability to understand and solve problems. Nowadays, survival does not depend so much on problem-solving, and most puzzles are made for amusement. They can take many forms—from verbal and visual puzzles, such as crosswords and jigsaw puzzles, to three-dimensional puzzles, such as mazes, Rubik's cubes, and virtual-reality games. Some puzzles, such as riddles or brainteasers, require a lot of thought to solve. When we read a crime novel or watch a suspense movie, we are also solving puzzles, following clues to find out who did it. Mysteries in the real world are also called puzzles. Most are eventually solved by science, but some, such as the puzzle of the Bermuda Triangle, have still to be explained.

JIGSAW PUZZLES

These puzzles are named after the jigsaw, the tool once used to make the puzzles by cutting out the pieces from sheets of wood. Most "jigsaw puzzles" today are punched out of cardboard using tools called cutting dies. Jigsaws may be simple or very difficult, have as few as four or as many as 10,000 pieces, and can be made to suit any age. Jigsaws are visual puzzles. Putting them together teaches patience and concentration.

A viewing device allows the game player to see a three-dimensional picture.

A virtual world as seen by the game player.

MAZES

The misleading pathways of maze puzzles test your sense of direction and ability to think logically while in a confusing situation. The aim is to reach the center of the maze, and then to try to make your way out again. In Ancient Egypt and Greece, mazes were built as prisons, but modern mazes are for fun.

COMPUTER GAMES
In many computer games, players follow puzzling quests or solve clues to move on to the next stage. Virtual-reality games challenge players to solve puzzles outside the real world.

BRAIN ACTIVITY
Most of us enjoy the challenge of a puzzle because of the way our brains work. Human intelligence makes us curious, so we become determined to find the solution to the puzzle. The stimulation of tackling and solving a puzzle makes our brains release chemicals called endorphins, which make us feel pleased or happy.

The midbrain is used to process language.

The cerebrum controls reasoning and judgement.

The medulla oblongata controls our metabolism.

The cerebellum controls our muscular reflexes.

Looking out into the Bermuda Triangle

BERMUDA TRIANGLE
An unusually high number of aircraft and ships have gone missing in a triangular area between Bermuda, Florida, and Puerto Rico in the Atlantic Ocean. The "Bermuda Triangle" was first described in 1964. The area is particularly busy and prone to dramatic weather changes, so ships and planes that disappeared could have crashed or been sunk. So far, noone has come up with a satisfactory explanation.

Find out more
ATLANTIC OCEAN
BRAIN AND NERVES
COMPUTERS
GAMES

RABBITS AND HARES

ONE FEMALE wild rabbit produces more than 20 young each year, making the common rabbit one of the most numerous mammals. Originally from Europe, rabbits are now found in every region except Antarctica. In many places they are serious pests to farmers because they eat crops, but in recent years a disease called myxomatosis has reduced their numbers. The common rabbit belongs to a large group of animals called lagomorphs. They include hares, cottontails, and a small, furry creature called the pika. Rabbits and hares are fast, agile runners. They can walk but usually hop at great speeds. Rabbits and hares have sensitive whiskers and sharp senses. They also have long rodentlike front teeth to gnaw grass, roots, and leaves. Rabbits and hares have an unusual method of double digestion. They eat food, digest some of it, expel soft droppings, and then eat these to obtain more nutrients. Finally they leave small, hard pellets on the ground. Rabbits build burrows; hares live in open country. Young hares are born covered in fur with their eyes open; newborn rabbits are bald at first, and their eyes are closed.

Small white tail is used as a danger signal to other rabbits.

Large ears swivel to find direction of a sound.

Whiskers help rabbit find its way in tunnels and at night.

Body is about 16 in (40 cm) long.

Eyes stick out for all-around vision.

COMMON RABBIT

Most common rabbits usually stay within 150 yards (140 m) of their warren. Although rabbits usually feed at twilight and at night, they sometimes come above ground by day. Rabbits nibble grasses and other plants, cropping them close to the ground. Each rabbit spends much time grooming its coat with its claws, tongue, and teeth to remove dirt and the fleas that may carry the disease called myxomatosis.

WARREN

The warren is a system of tunnels dug among tree roots or in a bank or sand dune. It is home to about 10 adult rabbits and their young. Other smaller burrows in the rabbits' territory are used in emergencies. A doe (female rabbit) often raises her kits (young) in a separate tunnel called a stop.

PIKA

The pika, found in Asia and North America, is much smaller than its relative, the rabbit. In summer it breaks off stems of grass, leaves them to dry in the sun, then piles the dried grass into tiny haystacks. The pika uses the dried grass as a food store during the winter months.

Long ears and excellent hearing

Large, round eyes give hare keen eyesight.

HARE

Hares are larger and longer than rabbits, with longer hind legs and ears. Male hares are called jacks, and females are called jills. The jill gives birth to two or three young, called leverets. While the mother is away feeding, the young crouch in a shallow scoop in the grass called a form. The young are well camouflaged – as long as they keep perfectly still.

European hare

White tail

Body measures more than 20 in (50 cm) in length.

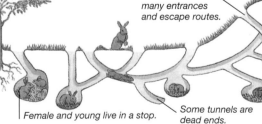

Rabbit warren has many entrances and escape routes.

Female and young live in a stop.

Some tunnels are dead ends.

Hare has long, slim front legs.

Long, powerful back legs

JACKRABBIT

Despite its name, the North American jackrabbit is actually a hare. Jackrabbits are speedy animals; some can run at more than 50 mph (80 km/h), outpacing many other creatures. In hot deserts jackrabbits lose excess heat through their huge ears. The black-tailed jackrabbit causes much damage by eating crops in the western part of North America.

Find out more

ANIMALS
CAMOUFLAGE, ANIMAL
MAMMALS
NESTS AND BURROWS
WEASELS, STOATS,
and martens

RADAR

FROM HUNDREDS OF MILES AWAY, a radar operator can track the movements of ships and aircraft even in dark or cloudy conditions. Radar finds objects by bouncing high-frequency radio waves off them and detecting the reflected waves. Radar is an extremely valuable tool. It helps aircraft find their way safely through crowded skies, warns weather forecasters of approaching storms, and reduces the risk of collisions at sea. Astronomers use radar to study the planets, while armies, air forces, and navies use radar for aiming missiles and locating opposing forces.

In the 1930s, a group of British scientists headed by Sir Robert Watson-Watt (1892-1973) developed an early radar system. During World War II (1939-45), this system gave early warning of bombing attacks, which allowed defending aircraft time to take to the air.

Radar in aircraft's nose detects bad weather.

When transponder detects radar pulses, it beams out its return pulse.

Plane reflects radar pulses back to antenna.

RADAR
The word *radar* stands for "radio detecting and ranging."

Secondary radar system picks up pulses from the aircraft's transponder.

Pulses from secondary radar scanner

Pulses from primary radar scanner

Radar antenna spins slowly to scan for aircraft in all directions.

RADAR SYSTEMS
There are two main types of radar systems: primary radar, which detects a radar "echo," and secondary radar, which detects a pulse transmitted by the target. Secondary radar is important for air traffic control. Airliners carry a transponder, a device that sends out a signal whenever a pulse from an air traffic control radar system strikes the plane. The transponder signal carries information such as the aircraft's identity, height, and speed.

HOW RADAR WORKS
A radar antenna sends out short bursts, or pulses, of radio waves. Between pulses the antenna listens for a return signal that has bounced off the target plane or ship. The direction in which the antenna is pointing gives the direction of the target. The delay between the transmitted pulse and the return pulse shows the distance of the target.

Ship's radar

Radar image of coastline

Yellow line indicates direction of ship's travel.

RADAR SCREEN
A radar screen inside a ship or aircraft displays a computer-generated map of the nearby land and sea. A central dot indicates the position of the ship or plane; other craft are represented by symbols on the screen.

MILITARY RADAR
Long-range ground-based radar scans the skies for intercontinental missiles; radar on high-altitude planes searches for low-flying aircraft approaching beneath the long-range beams. High-speed fighter aircraft have some of the most advanced radar systems. The radar scans the ground ahead so that the plane can fly rapidly just above the treetops and attack an enemy without warning.

Radio waves from speed trap

Radio waves bounce back off speeding car.

Radar scanner

SPEED TRAP
Police officers use radar to measure the speed of passing cars. A radar scanner sends out a beam of radio waves that bounce off an approaching car. The car's forward movement squeezes up the waves, so the reflected signal has a fractionally shorter wavelength than the original signal. The radar set measures the change in wavelength and calculates the car's speed.

The change in the wavelength of a signal caused by the movement of its source is called the Doppler effect.

Find out more
AIRCRAFT
AIRPORTS
MILITARY AIRCRAFT
NAVIGATION
RADIO

RADIO

EARLY RADIO WAS often called "the wireless" because radio uses invisible waves instead of wires to carry messages from one place to another. Today, radio waves are an important means of communicating sounds and pictures all over the world. Within the circuits of a radio transmitter, rapidly varying electric currents generate radio waves of different lengths that travel to a radio receiver. Radio waves are a type of electromagnetic (EM) wave, similar to light and x-rays. Like these waves, radio waves travel at the speed of light, 186,000 miles (300,000 km) per second, nearly one million times the speed of sound waves. Radio waves can travel through the air, solid materials, or even empty space, but are sent most efficiently by putting the transmitting antenna on high ground like a hill.

MORSE CODE
Early radio signals consisted of beeps, made by tapping a key. Operators tapped out a message using a series of short and long beeps called Morse code, invented by Samuel Morse (1791-1872) in 1837.

RADIO STUDIO
A microphone converts sound waves from the announcer's voice into electrical signals, which are then transmitted as radio waves.

Long waves (30-300 kHz) can travel about 600 miles (1,000 km). They are used for national broadcasts and to send information to ships.

A transmitter receives radio programs by cable from the studio. The transmitter antenna beams radio waves that spread out like ripples in water.

Communications satellites pick up and rebroadcast radio programs using super-high-frequency waves with frequencies of more than 3 million kHz.

Television programs are carried on UHF (ultra-high-frequency) radio waves (300,000-3,000,000 kHz).

Dish sends and receives radio waves

RADIO FREQUENCIES
Radio waves consist of rapidly oscillating (varying) electric and magnetic fields. The rate of oscillation is called the frequency of the wave, measured in hertz (Hz). One Hz equals one oscillation per second; one kilohertz (kHz) equals 1,000 hertz. Bands of certain frequencies are used to transmit different kinds of information.

VHF (very-high-frequency) radio waves (30,000-300,000 kHz) move in straight lines so they cannot travel over the horizon. Police, fire department, and citizens' band radios use VHF waves for short-range communications.

Many radio stations transmit programmes on the medium-wave band. These medium-frequency (300-3,000 kHz) channels are restricted to within a few hundred kilometres.

International radio stations and amateur radio enthusiasts use shortwave radio signals. Short waves (3,000-30,000 kHz) can travel great distances. They bounce around the world, reflected off the Earth's surface and a layer of the atmosphere called the ionosphere.

RADIO RECEIVER
When radio waves reach the antenna of a radio set, they produce tiny varying electric currents in the antenna. As the tuner knob is turned, an electronic circuit selects a single frequency from these currents corresponding to a particular radio channel. This signal is amplified (boosted) to drive the loudspeaker, which then converts the signal into sound waves.

PIONEERS OF RADIO
In 1864, Scottish physicist James Clerk Maxwell developed the theory of electromagnetic waves, which are the basis of radio. In 1888, Heinrich Hertz, a German physicist, discovered radio waves. Italian Guglielmo Marconi (1874-1937, right) created the first radio system in 1895, and in 1901 he transmitted radio signals across the Atlantic.

Find out more
ASTRONOMY
NAVIGATION
RADAR
TELEPHONES
TELEVISION AND VIDEO

RADIOACTIVITY

SOME ELEMENTS GLOW in the dark. We cannot always see the glow because our eyes are not sensitive to it, but it is still present. The glow is radiation, a form of energy, like the light and heat that we generate from electricity. Unlike heat and light, radiation is generated inside the substance itself, which is radioactive. Radioactive means producing radioactivity. A radioactive substance, such as uranium, is made up of big, unstable atoms. Some of the particles that form the atoms break away in a process called radioactivity. They are radiated as rays of alpha or beta particles, or as gamma waves. Eventually atoms reach a stable state, stop decaying, and the substance is no longer radioactive. This process can take millions of years.

MARIE CURIE
Polish-born Marie Curie (1867-1934), and husband, Pierre, won the 1903 Nobel physics prize for discovering radioactivity. She did not know it was harmful, and died from radiation poisoning.

Large alpha particle

Small beta particle

High-frequency gamma radiation wave

Alpha radiation

Beta radiation

Gamma radiation

GEIGER COUNTER
A geiger counter consists of a gas-filled tube and a meter. It can detect radioactivity.

TYPES OF RADIOACTIVITY
Radioactive substances give off three types of radiation: alpha, beta, and gamma. Alpha particles are larger than those of beta radiation, so cannot penetrate as far. Gamma radiation is a very high frequency wave and can pass through most materials. Only direct collisions with atoms can stop it. Shields to protect people from gamma radiation are made from dense material such as lead.

SOURCES OF RADIATION

The Sun emits a type of radiation that includes radiant heat, and all the colors of visible light. This radiation is called electromagnetic radiation.

Objects such as this aircraft reflect the Sun's electromagnetic radiation as light waves.

The explosion of a nuclear weapon produces both electromagnetic and radioactive radiation, with devastating effect.

In a nuclear power station, the heat produced by radioactivity is used to make steam and drive an electricity generator.

Television sets and computer monitors work by converting electrical energy into the visible electromagnetic radiation that we call light.

RADIOGRAPHY
Radioactive substances also produce x rays. These are like gamma rays, but with a longer wavelength. In 1895, German scientist Wilhelm Roentgen (1845-1923) discovered x rays could pass through the body, but dense tissue such as bone stopped them. This meant that broken bones and hard objects could be detected inside people, and photographed in the process known as radiography.

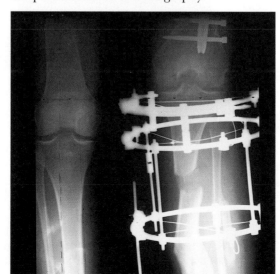

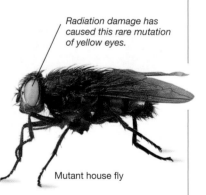

Radiation damage has caused this rare mutation of yellow eyes.

Mutant house fly

GENE MUTATION
Alpha and beta particles, x-rays, and gamma rays produced by radioactivity can damage living things, because they alter the DNA of genes. This can result in life-threatening diseases such as cancer. It can also lead to mutations, or changes, in the next generation.

Find out more
ATOMS AND MOLECULES
GENETICS
NUCLEAR ENERGY
X RAYS

RAIN AND SNOW

THE WATER THAT FALLS from the sky as rain or snow is taking part in a continuous cycle. It begins when the water on the Earth's surface evaporates, or dries out, and enters the air as invisible water vapor. Rising air carries the vapor into the sky. The air cools as it rises, and the water vapor turns into tiny water droplets. These droplets are so small that they float in the air, and a cloud forms. A rain cloud contains millions of water droplets that merge together to form larger drops. When these drops become too large and heavy to float, they fall to the ground as rain and the cycle starts all over again. If the air is very cold, the water in the cloud freezes and forms snowflakes or hailstones. However, rainfall and snowfall are not equally distributed all over the world. Deserts have hardly any rain; tropical regions can have so much rain that there are severe floods, while in the polar regions snow falls instead of rain.

LIFE-GIVING RAIN
Rain is vital to life on Earth. Plants need water to grow, providing food for us and other animals. Rain also fills the rivers and lakes that provide our water supply.

WATER CYCLE
Water enters the air from lakes, rivers, seas, and oceans through the process of evaporation. In addition, plants, animals, and people give out water vapor into the atmosphere. The vapor stays in the air for an average time of 10 days and then falls as rain or snow. It joins the sea, rivers, and underground water-courses, and the cycle begins once more.

Trees and other plants release water vapor into the air from their leaves.

Cloud begins to form from water vapor in the atmosphere.

Water joins rivers and streams and flows down to the sea.

Water droplets fall from a cloud especially over high ground where the air is cooler. The general name for rain, snow, sleet, hail, mist, and dew is precipitation.

Wind and the sun's heat cause water to evaporate from the oceans and other large areas of water.

Water seeps underground through a layer of porous rock and flows down to the sea.

RAINBOW
If the sun shines on a shower of rain, you may see a rainbow if you are looking toward the rain, and the sun is behind you. The raindrops in the shower reflect the sun's light back to you. As the sunlight passes through the raindrops, it splits up into a circular band of colors. You see the top part of this circle as a rainbow.

SNOW AND HAIL
In cold weather, the water in a cloud freezes and forms ice crystals. These crystals stick together and fall as snowflakes. The snow may melt slightly as it falls, producing sleet. In some clouds, strong air currents can toss frozen raindrops up and down. Each time they rise and fall, the frozen drops collect more ice crystals and water, and frozen layers build up like the skin around an onion. Eventually they become so heavy that they fall to the ground as hailstones.

ICE CRYSTAL
A microscope reveals that snowflakes are made of tiny six-sided ice crystals. No two crystals are exactly the same.

Find out more
COLOR
RIVERS
STORMS
WATER
WEATHER
WIND

REFERENCE BOOKS

WHEN PEOPLE NEED INFORMATION about a subject, they often use a reference book. Unlike works of fiction, reference books provide factual information on all sorts of subjects, from the meanings of individual words to facts about history, science, and the world around us. Reference books may include information on one subject only, or a variety of subjects. They may be general reference books, or specialized books such as dictionaries, atlases, and encyclopedias. Most reference books contain not only words, but also maps, illustrations, photographs, and diagrams, which make subjects easier to understand. Many also include cross-references that direct readers to pages in the book covering related topics, and an index at the back of the book, so readers can look up specific topics. Reference books need regular updating and revising.

EARLY DICTIONARIES
In Ancient Greece, dictionaries were used to provide explanations of difficult or obscure words. In 1755, the writer Samuel Johnson, published *A Dictionary of the English Language*. It was the standard dictionary of the English language for more than a century.

Reference books usually have hard covers to make them more resistant to wear and tear.

ENCYCLOPEDIA
An encyclopedia is a book containing information on people, places, things, and events, and may consist of one or more volumes. General encyclopedias, such as this book, cover a wide range of topics. Specialized encyclopedias focus on a particular area of study. A music encyclopedia, for example, covers only musical topics. The Ancient Greek philosopher Aristotle produced an encyclopedia c. 300 B.C.

HOW A DICTIONARY WORKS
A dictionary is an alphabetical list of words that gives the spelling, pronunciation, and meaning of each word. Every dictionary is designed to match the needs of its users. Dictionaries for young people, for instance, may include pictures. Specialized dictionaries contain only those words relevant to a particular subject, such as scientific or technical words.

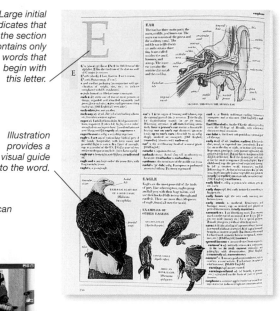

Large initial indicates that the section contains only words that begin with this letter.

Illustration provides a visual guide to the word.

ATLASES
An atlas is a collection of maps. Traditional atlases include maps that show physical features, such as rivers, mountains, and deserts, as well as towns, cities, and roads. Maps can also show population, and the distribution of resources and crops. Some atlases specialize in subjects such as astronomy.

World atlases group countries by continent or region.

Sound and moving images can be included with the text to achieve a more effective explanation of a topic.

ELECTRONIC FORMAT
Many reference books are now published as CD-ROM, or on the Internet. Electronic formats allow enormous amounts of information to be put on a single disc. Users of the Internet can access up-to-date facts with ease and convenience.

Find out more
BOOKS
EDUCATION
INFORMATION TECHNOLOGY
LITERATURE
MAPS

REFORMATION

ON OCTOBER 31, 1517, German monk Martin Luther pinned a list of 95 arguments, or complaints, on a church door in Wittenberg, Saxony. This sparked a movement known as the Reformation because its followers demanded the reform of the Roman Catholic Church, then the most powerful force in Europe. Many, like Luther, believed it was corrupt, and attacked its wealth and the sale of indulgences (pardons for sins). In 1521, Luther was expelled from the Church. Followers of Luther and other reformers became known as Protestants because they "protested" against what they felt were the errors of the Catholic Church. Protestantism spread throughout Europe. Then, in a movement called the Counter-Reformation, the Catholic Church began to reform itself. The Counter-Reformation led to religious persecution and bitter civil wars.

MARTIN LUTHER
Martin Luther (1483-1546) inspired the Reformation. He attacked the sale of indulgences and said that no amount of money paid to the clergy could pardon an individual for his sins. Only through faith could people be saved.

England
Germany
France
Spain
Italy

///Catholic and Protestant   ■ Protestant   □ Catholic

PROTESTANTISM
By 1560, Europe had two main religions – Roman Catholic and Protestant. Protestantism began in Germany. Many German rulers adopted the new religion so that they could break away from the control of the Pope and the Holy Roman Emperor (the "political" Catholic ruler).

War started after two Protestants were thrown out of a window in Prague.

Battle scene during Thirty Years' War

THIRTY YEARS' WAR
The Thirty Years' War lasted from 1618 to 1648. It began as a religious struggle between Catholics and Protestants in Germany. Then it grew into a war between the Hapsburg rulers of the Holy Roman Empire and the kings of France for possession of land. In 1648, by the Peace of Westphalia, the Protestants won the struggle.

COUNCIL OF TRENT
The Counter-Reformation began when Catholic leaders met at the Council of Trent in 1545. The council established the main principles of Catholicism and set up places for training priests and missionaries. During this time the Jesuits, an important teaching order founded in 1534, became popular.

INQUISITION
In 1231, the Pope set up the Inquisition – a special organization that searched out and punished heretics (those who did not conform to the Catholic faith). Inquisitors arrested, tortured, and executed alleged heretics and witches (above). During the Reformation, 300 years later, the Inquisition tried to crush the new Protestant churches, but failed.

Find out more

EUROPE
FRANCE, HISTORY OF
GERMANY, HISTORY OF
HAPSBURGS
UNITED KINGDOM, HISTORY OF

RELIGIONS

PEOPLE HAVE ALWAYS SEARCHED for answers to life's mysteries and unexpected events. This questioning may have led to the growth of religions, to give meaning to life and death. Most religious people believe in a god or several gods. Gods are thought of as supreme beings who created the world or who control what happens in it. Religions may be highly organized, and teach people how to live, with a set of beliefs and rituals to follow. There may be special places in which to worship, and a spiritual leader for guidance. Some religions believe there is a spirit or a god in every object, from animals to rocks. Many believe in a life after death. Other religions have less formal rules, and people follow beliefs in their own way. The world's six major organized religions are Christianity, Judaism, Islam, Hinduism, Buddhism, and Sikhism.

MOTHER GODDESSES
Pregnant female figures found at ancient holy sites were probably worshiped as a symbol of the making of new life.

RELIGION AND ART
Many people use art, architecture, and sculpture to convey their religious ideas, and to show the important icons of their religion. This Christian sculpture of the Virgin Mary holding Jesus shows her crowned as the Queen of Heaven.

GODS
Many religions worship either a single God, or several gods. There may be myths or stories associated with the god, which demonstrate an important lesson. Ganesha (right) is the Hindu god of wisdom. According to legend, his father accidentally cut off his head and in desperation replaced it with that of an elephant.

WORSHIP AND PRAYER
Each religion has its own system of worship and prayer. Worship shows reverence towards a god or deity, in a public ceremony or service. It often takes place in a special building, such as a mosque or church. Prayers can be spoken or thought during worship or in private, and are a thanksgiving or request to a god or holy object. The girl above prays during the Buddhist Festival of Hungry Ghosts in Singapore.

JERUSALEM
Jerusalem is sacred to three religions. Jews pray at the Wailing Wall, the ruins of a temple destroyed in A.D. 70. The Dome of the Rock mosque is holy to Muslims as the place where Prophet Muhammad rose to heaven. The Church of the Holy Sepulcher is built on the site of the crucifixion and burial of Jesus Christ.

DEATH AND HEAVEN
Many faiths believe that the human body is a temporary container for the soul. After death the soul may be reborn in another body or go to heaven as a reward for good deeds on earth. Most religions have special rituals or funerals to honor and remember the dead, such as the Day of the Dead in Mexico (above). Candles are lit to help dead relatives find their way to the land of the living.

SACRED TEXTS
Many religions have texts which teach and guide. Muslims read the Qur'an, Christianity is based on the Bible, Buddhists follow the Dharma, and the Talmud (above) is central to Judaism.

JUDAISM

The religion of the Jewish people, Judaism, began over 4,000 years ago. Jews worship one God. They believe that God has made the Jews His chosen people, and that they must live according to the laws He set out for them. The Jewish festival of Passover, held in spring, commemorates the time when the Jews escaped captivity in Egypt to return to Israel.

Plate with Passover meal

HINDUISM

The Hindu religion developed in India thousands of years ago. Hindus have many gods, but they are all part of one great power, called Brahman. Hindus believe that when we die, we are reborn as a person, animal, or plant. The better our deeds in one life, the better our rebirth. The Hindu festival of Diwali celebrates the victory of good over evil.

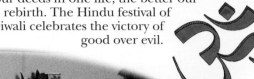

Candles are lit at the festival of Diwali.

Buddhist monks have few possessions and devote their lives to explaining the Buddha's teachings.

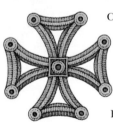

BUDDHISM

Followers of the great Indian teacher, the Buddha, are known as Buddhists. Like Hindus, they believe in rebirth after death. By trying to follow a lifestyle of correct behavior, meditation, and wisdom, they hope to break out of the cycle of death and rebirth to reach a state of purity known as enlightenment.

CHRISTIANITY

Christians believe that Jesus of Nazareth was the son of God. He lived in the Roman province of Palestine and was crucified. Christians believe that Jesus's life, death, and resurrection free believers from their state of sin. Easter, which celebrates the resurrection of Jesus, is the most important Christian festival. Eggs are given to symbolize the coming of new life.

Easter egg

ISLAM

Followers of Islam are called Muslims. Their faith was first revealed to the prophet Muhammad in the 7th century. Muslims believe in one God. They promise to pray five times a day, fast during the month of Ramadan, give alms to the poor, and make the pilgrimage to the holy city of Mecca at least once in their lives.

When they pray, Muslims face the direction of Mecca.

Sikh boy wearing turban

SIKHISM

The spiritual leader Guru Nanak founded Sikhism in northern India in the 16th century. Sikhs follow the ten Gurus who revealed the truth about God, and stress the importance of serving the community, as well as worship. Male (and some female) Sikhs wear the turban to show their faith and their membership of the Sikh community.

Find out more
BUDDHISM
CHRISTIANITY
HINDUISM
ISLAM
JUDAISM

RENAISSANCE

ITALY IN THE 15TH CENTURY was an exciting place. It was here that educated people began to develop new ideas about the world around them and rediscovered the arts and learning of Ancient Greece and Rome. For a period of about 200 years that became known as the Renaissance (rebirth) people made great advances in education, technology, and the arts. Helped by the invention of printing, the Renaissance gradually spread from Italy to the rest of Europe. Although the Renaissance mainly affected the wealthy, it had a huge impact on the way that everybody lived and perceived the world around them. The Renaissance produced great artists such as Michelangelo and Raphael. It also produced a new way of thinking called humanism, as scholars and thinkers such as Erasmus began to challenge the authority of the Roman Catholic Church. Humanism gave human beings more importance. It meant that artists such as Leonardo da Vinci began to produce realistic images instead of symbolic scenes. Scientists challenged old ideas about the nature of the universe, and conducted pioneering experiments.

COPERNICUS
By observing the movement of planets and stars, astronomers such as Nicolaus Copernicus (1473-1543) began to challenge ideas about the solar system which had been accepted since the time of the Ancient Greeks. Copernicus was first to suggest that the Earth revolves every 24 hours and that it travels around the Sun once a year. Many people did not accept his findings until many years later.

TECHNOLOGY
Renaissance scientists invented or developed new scientific instruments to help them in their work. The armillary sphere, a skeleton sphere with the Earth in the center, was used to measure the position of the stars. Galileo invented the useful proportional compass, which could be set at any angle.

Armillary sphere

Proportional compass

Galileo at work

GALILEO
Galileo Galilei (1564-1642) was an Italian astronomer and physicist. He disproved many of the Ancient Greek thinker Aristotle's theories, including the theory that heavy objects fall faster than light ones. He perfected a refracting telescope and observed that the Earth and all the planets of the solar system revolve around the Sun.

RENAISSANCE MUSIC
When the first music was printed in Italy in the late 15th century, new musical styles began to spread throughout Europe. Nonreligious music became more common, showing the influence of the humanist approach to life which characterized the Renaissance period. Music became more harmonious and melodic than before. William Byrd (1543-1623), left, was the first Englishman to have his music printed in England. He was a well known organist, first at Lincoln Cathedral, and then later at the Queen Elizabeth I Chapel Royal in London. He was also a composer, and developed the first madrigals (music for singing without any accompanying instruments).

ERASMUS

Desiderius Erasmus (1466-1536), a Dutch priest, wanted to reform the Roman Catholic Church. He criticized the superstitions of the clergy, and published studies of the Old and New Testaments, giving a better understanding of the Bible. A leading humanist, he questioned the authority of the Church – a shocking idea at the time.

BOTTICELLI

The paintings of Sandro Botticelli (1444-1510) show many of the features typical of Renaissance art: clear lines, even composition, and an emphasis on human activity. Renaissance artists painted realistic, mythological, and Biblical subjects. Most tried to make their paintings as realistic as possible by using perspective to give scenes an appearance of depth. Above is the Botticelli painting *Venus and Mars*.

MEDICIS

The Medicis were a great banking family who ruled Florence for more than 300 years. They became very powerful. Many of them, particularly Lorenzo "the Magnificent" (1449-92), encouraged artists such as Michelangelo, and helped them financially.

MICHELANGELO

Michelangelo (1475-1564) was a very skilled Italian artist and sculptor. His marble statue of David (left) is one of the finest examples of Renaissance sculpture. People admired the statue's youthful strength and beauty, which demonstrated the new realistic style of art.

Dome rises more than 400 ft (120 m) from the floor of the church.

Begun in 1505, the building took 150 years to complete.

ST. PETER'S

Situated in Vatican City, Rome, Italy, St. Peter's Church has a rich history. Ten different architects worked on its construction. Michelangelo designed the dome. The Italian architect Bernini (1598-1680) designed the inside of the church and the majestic piazza outside the church. St. Peter's houses many fabulous works of art, and marble and detailed mosaics decorate the walls.

SCULPTURE

Renaissance sculptors made great use of marble, copying the style of Ancient Roman statues. A new understanding of anatomy inspired sculptors to carve nude figures, with accurate depictions of muscles and joints. Some sculptors even dissected corpses to discover how the human body works.

ARCHITECTURE

Renaissance architecture was modeled on classical Roman building styles. Architects featured high domed roofs, vaulted ceilings, decorative columns, and rounded arches in their buildings. One of the most influential architects was Andrea Palladio (1508-80). The classical designs used by Palladio for his many villas and palaces were widely copied by later architects.

RENAISSANCE

1420-36 Architect Filippo Brunelleschi develops the system of perspective.

1430-35 Donatello's sculpture of David is the first large nude statue since the Roman Empire.

1480-85 Sandro Botticelli paints *The Birth of Venus*.

1497 Leonardo da Vinci paints *The Last Supper*.

1501 Petrucci publishes first printed music in Venice.

1501-4 Michelangelo sculpts *David*.

1502 Leonardo paints the *Mona Lisa*.

1505 Architect Donato Bramante begins the new St. Peter's in Rome. Completed in 1655.

1508 Artist Raphael begins to decorate the Pope's apartments in the Vatican.

1508-12 Michelangelo decorates the Sistine chapel.

1509 Erasmus writes *In Praise of Folly*, criticizing the Church.

c.1510 Renaissance art in Venice reaches its peak with artists such as Titian, Veronese, and Tintoretto.

1513 Death of Pope Julius II

1532 Niccolo Machiavelli's book *The Prince* is published, suggesting how a ruler should govern a state.

1543 Astronomer Copernicus claims that the Earth and the other planets move around the sun.

1552 Architect Palladio begins to build the Villa Rotunda in Venice.

1564 Death of Michelangelo

1593 Galileo develops the thermometer.

1608 Galileo develops the telescope.

Find out more
ARCHITECTURE
ITALY, HISTORY OF
LEONARDO DA VINCI
PAINTERS
SCULPTURE

REPRODUCTION

FOR LIFE TO CONTINUE on Earth, humans and other animals must produce young. The process of creating new life is called reproduction. Human beings reproduce in much the same way as other mammals. From birth, a woman has many tiny pinhead-sized ova (egg cells) in two glands inside the abdomen called ovaries. From puberty onward, one of these egg cells is released each month as part of the menstrual cycle. Throughout life, a man produces small tadpole-shaped cells called sperm in sex organs called the testes. During sexual intercourse, sperm cells leave the man's body and enter the woman's body, swimming towards her ovaries. If a sperm meets a ripe egg cell, the two join together. This is called fertilization. The egg cell can only be fertilized for about three days after ovulation. Fertilization makes the egg cell begin to develop in the woman's uterus. During the following nine months the tiny egg develops into a fully formed baby, ready to be born.

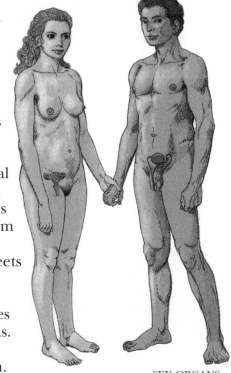

FETUS
A developing baby, or fetus, lives inside the uterus, cushioned from bumps, bright lights, and noise by a surrounding fluid called the amniotic fluid. However, the baby can hear the regular thump of the mother's heartbeat and the gurgling of food in her intestines.

SEX ORGANS
The main female sex organs, the ovaries, are inside the abdomen. The main male organs, the testes and penis, hang outside the abdomen. Other differences between males and females, such as the woman's breasts, are called secondary sexual characteristics.

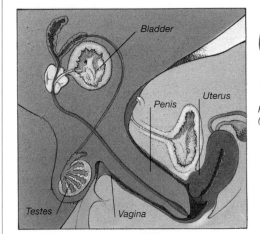

Bladder
Penis
Uterus
Testes
Vagina
Vagina

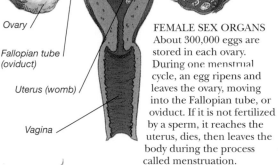

Ovary
Fallopian tube (oviduct)
Uterus (womb)
Vagina

FEMALE SEX ORGANS
About 300,000 eggs are stored in each ovary. During one menstrual cycle, an egg ripens and leaves the ovary, moving into the Fallopian tube, or oviduct. If it is not fertilized by a sperm, it reaches the uterus, dies, then leaves the body during the process called menstruation.

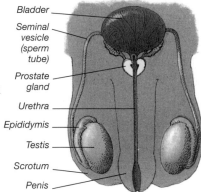

Bladder
Seminal vesicle (sperm tube)
Prostate gland
Urethra
Epididymis
Testis
Scrotum
Penis

MALE SEX ORGANS
Each testis makes more than 250 million sperm cells every day. The cells are stored in the testis itself and in a long, winding tube called the epididymis. If they are not released, they break down and are reabsorbed into the bloodstream.

SEXUAL INTERCOURSE
During sexual intercourse, the man's penis becomes stiff enough to insert into the woman's vagina, which also enlarges. After a while muscular contractions squeeze sperm cells from the man's testes out of the penis and into the vagina, in a fluid called semen. This process is called ejaculation. The sperm cells swim through the uterus, propelled by their tails, and travel along the Fallopian tube. Sometimes, one of these sperm cells reaches the egg cell and fertilizes it, resulting in pregnancy.

Sperm cells cluster around egg cell in Fallopian tube

Only one sperm penetrates egg to fertilize it.

Fertilized egg divides into two cells within 36 hours, four within 48 hours, then eight, and so on. Barrier around dividing cells keeps out other sperm cells.

FERTILIZATION
An egg cell begins to divide and develop into a baby only when it is joined by a sperm cell. After intercourse, hundreds of sperm cells may reach the egg, but only one breaks through the outer layer. Once this occurs, genetic material in the sperm – the instructions needed to make a new human – joins the genetic material inside the egg. The coming together of sperm and egg and their genes is called fertilization, or conception.

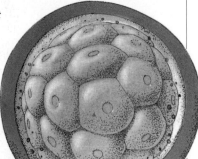

Embryo enters uterus about three days after fertilization as a solid ball of 16-32 cells.

PREGNANCY

About one week after fertilization, the ball of cells embeds itself in the blood-rich lining of the uterus where it absorbs nutrients. The cells continue to divide and change, forming the first body tissues such as blood vessels and nerves. Gradually the ball of cells folds and twists into the basic body shape of the baby. Meanwhile, other cells form the placenta, a saucer-shaped organ, in the lining of the uterus. The placenta is fed with blood from the mother, and oxygen and nutrients pass to the baby through the umbilical cord. This lifeline consists of three blood vessels; the largest vein carries nutrients and oxygen-rich blood to the baby, and the smaller ones carry waste and blood low in oxygen back to the placenta.

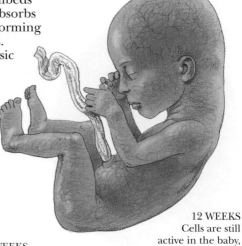

12 WEEKS
Cells are still active in the baby, dividing and growing and putting the finishing touches on the body, such as eyelids, fingernails, and toenails. The baby is about 5 in (13 cm) long. There are still 28 weeks to go before it is born.

8 WEEKS
The baby is about 1 in (25 mm) long, and all the major parts of the body have formed – even the fingers and toes. The developing baby is now called a fetus.

5 WEEKS
The developing baby is now about ½ in (10 mm) long. It has a recognizable head, back, and heart, and the beginnings of a mouth and eyes. The limbs are forming as small buds. At this stage, the developing baby is called an embryo.

PUBERTY

Babies and children have sex organs, but they are not able to release egg or sperm cells. At puberty, which generally starts when people are between 10 and 15 years old, chemicals called sex hormones are released into the bloodstream from hormonal glands. These sex hormones cause the sex organs to mature (become fully developed). Other changes occur at this time too, particularly a spurt in growth.

In a boy, the testes produce a sex hormone called testosterone. This makes hair grow on the face and body. It also makes the voice deeper, encourages muscle development, and sets off production of sperm.

In a girl, the ovaries produce progesterone and estrogen, which cause the breasts to develop and fatty tissue to form, giving the body a more rounded shape. From puberty onward, a woman's body also undergoes a monthly process called the menstrual cycle or period, as shown below. Changing levels of hormones thicken the uterus lining and enrich it with blood, which will nourish a fertilized egg if it implants.

BIRTH

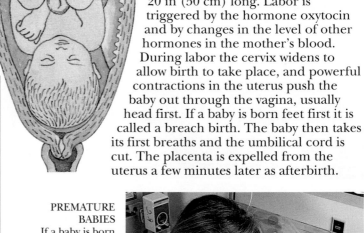

Birth is the process that ends pregnancy and carries a baby out of the uterus, usually after 38-42 weeks of pregnancy. When the baby has reached full term (left), it is about 20 in (50 cm) long. Labor is triggered by the hormone oxytocin and by changes in the level of other hormones in the mother's blood. During labor the cervix widens to allow birth to take place, and powerful contractions in the uterus push the baby out through the vagina, usually head first. If a baby is born feet first it is called a breach birth. The baby then takes its first breaths and the umbilical cord is cut. The placenta is expelled from the uterus a few minutes later as afterbirth.

PREMATURE BABIES
If a baby is born before the 37th week of pregnancy it is called premature and may have difficulty breathing. The baby is placed in an incubator and monitored very carefully until it is strong enough to breathe for itself.

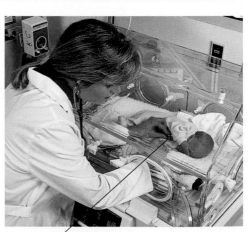

A doctor checks the heartbeat of a premature baby in its incubator.

1st week	2nd week	3rd week	4th week
Lining of uterus breaks down and passes out of the vagina as menstrual blood flow, called menstruation.	Lining starts to thicken again in preparation for next egg. Next egg begins to ripen in ovary.	Ripe egg is released from ovary. Egg can be fertilized for up to 36 hours in Fallopian tube.	Egg reaches uterus and implants if fertilized, or breaks down if not fertilized.

Find out more

ANIMALS
HUMAN BODY

REPTILES

SCALY-SKINNED ANIMALS such as alligators, turtles, and snakes are called reptiles. Some reptiles live in water and some on land; most are found in the warmer parts of the world. There are six main groups; lizards, snakes, worm lizards, turtles and tortoises, crocodiles and alligators, and the tuatara. Tortoises and turtles are the only reptiles with shells. Lizards make up the largest group, with about 4,300 different kinds, yet there is only one kind of tuatara. Reptiles are among the most ancient of all animals. The ancestors of today's reptiles were the dinosaurs. Dinosaurs roamed the Earth for about 150 million years, then suddenly died out 65 million years ago. Today, there are more than 8,000 kinds of reptiles, from the long reticulated python, measuring 33 ft (10 m), to the tiny dwarf gecko, only 1.3 in (33 mm) in length. Unlike warm-blooded (endothermic) mammals, reptiles are cold-blooded (ectothermic) – they need the warmth of the Sun to give them the energy to move.

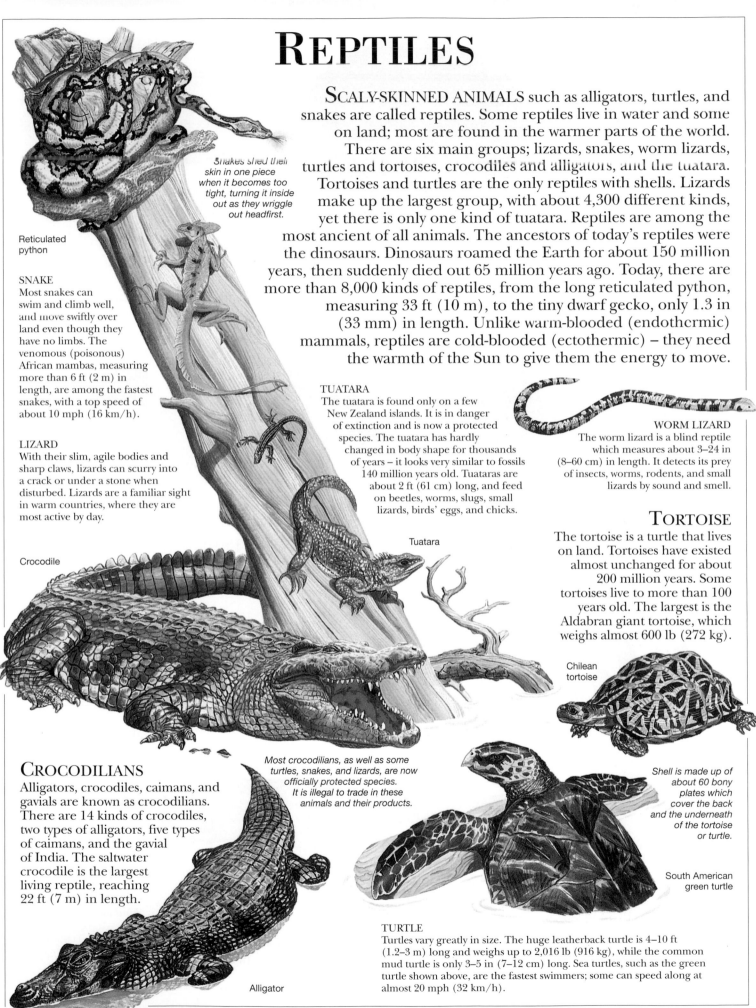

Snakes shed their skin in one piece when it becomes too tight, turning it inside out as they wriggle out headfirst.

Reticulated python

SNAKE
Most snakes can swim and climb well, and move swiftly over land even though they have no limbs. The venomous (poisonous) African mambas, measuring more than 6 ft (2 m) in length, are among the fastest snakes, with a top speed of about 10 mph (16 km/h).

LIZARD
With their slim, agile bodies and sharp claws, lizards can scurry into a crack or under a stone when disturbed. Lizards are a familiar sight in warm countries, where they are most active by day.

Crocodile

TUATARA
The tuatara is found only on a few New Zealand islands. It is in danger of extinction and is now a protected species. The tuatara has hardly changed in body shape for thousands of years – it looks very similar to fossils 140 million years old. Tuataras are about 2 ft (61 cm) long, and feed on beetles, worms, slugs, small lizards, birds' eggs, and chicks.

Tuatara

WORM LIZARD
The worm lizard is a blind reptile which measures about 3–24 in (8–60 cm) in length. It detects its prey of insects, worms, rodents, and small lizards by sound and smell.

TORTOISE
The tortoise is a turtle that lives on land. Tortoises have existed almost unchanged for about 200 million years. Some tortoises live to more than 100 years old. The largest is the Aldabran giant tortoise, which weighs almost 600 lb (272 kg).

Chilean tortoise

CROCODILIANS
Alligators, crocodiles, caimans, and gavials are known as crocodilians. There are 14 kinds of crocodiles, two types of alligators, five types of caimans, and the gavial of India. The saltwater crocodile is the largest living reptile, reaching 22 ft (7 m) in length.

Most crocodilians, as well as some turtles, snakes, and lizards, are now officially protected species. It is illegal to trade in these animals and their products.

Shell is made up of about 60 bony plates which cover the back and the underneath of the tortoise or turtle.

South American green turtle

TURTLE
Turtles vary greatly in size. The huge leatherback turtle is 4–10 ft (1.2–3 m) long and weighs up to 2,016 lb (916 kg), while the common mud turtle is only 3–5 in (7–12 cm) long. Sea turtles, such as the green turtle shown above, are the fastest swimmers; some can speed along at almost 20 mph (32 km/h).

Alligator

BREEDING

Most reptiles lay eggs, from which the young hatch. Snake and lizard eggs usually have a leathery, flexible shell. The eggs of crocodiles and tortoises are hard and rigid, and the temperature at which the eggs are incubated determines the sex of the hatchlings. The loggerhead turtle, shown here, digs a deep hole in the beach sand and lays its eggs under the cover of darkness. The eggs take several weeks to hatch and are at risk from foxes and monitor lizards, which dig them up and eat them. After hatching, the young turtles have to avoid sea birds and crabs as they scuttle down to the sea.

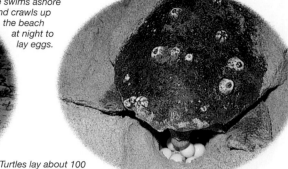

The female loggerhead turtle swims ashore and crawls up the beach at night to lay eggs.

Turtles lay about 100 eggs in the sand.

WALL GECKO
Wall geckos have tiny sticky pads on their toes, which enable them to run up smooth glass windows and upside-down across the ceiling.

BLUE-TONGUED SKINK
The reptiles tongue has several uses. Lizards and snakes use it to detect their surroundings. The tongue flicks out to pick up chemicals in the air and carries them back to Jacobson's organs, special sensory organs in the roof of the mouth. When in danger, the Australian blue-tongued skink opens its mouth wide, thrusts out its bright blue tongue, hisses, and puffs up its body to frighten away a predator.

SCALES
A reptile's scaly skin provides good protection against predators and stops the animal from drying out. The arrangement of the scales helps scientists identify species. Some reptiles, such as chameleons, have special cells in the skin. These cells make the colored pigments inside the skin expand or contract. This is how the chameleon changes its color, for camouflage.

Some geckos are smaller than the human palm.

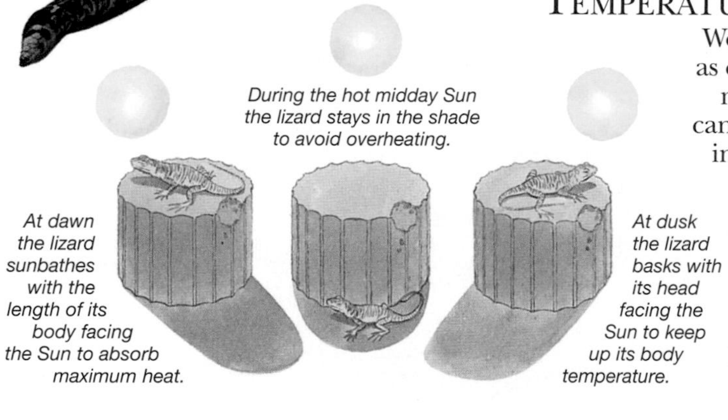

TEMPERATURE REGULATION
We often describe reptiles as cold-blooded, but this is not strictly true. Reptiles cannot generate body heat internally, in the way that mammals do, but they can control their body temperature by their behaviour. Reptiles bask in the Sun to absorb warmth, then hide in the shade when they become too hot.

During the hot midday Sun the lizard stays in the shade to avoid overheating.

At dawn the lizard sunbathes with the length of its body facing the Sun to absorb maximum heat.

At dusk the lizard basks with its head facing the Sun to keep up its body temperature.

LARGEST AND SMALLEST REPTILES
The saltwater crocodile is the largest reptile, although some snakes, such as the reticulated python, are longer, growing to 33 ft (10 m) in length. The largest lizard is the Komodo dragon, a type of monitor lizard. The smallest of all reptiles are some kinds of geckos, only about a half-inch long when fully grown.

COELOPHYSIS
The first reptiles appeared on Earth more than 300 million years ago and gradually took over from amphibians as the largest animals on land. Dinosaurs, such as the *Coelophysis* shown here, were early reptiles that evolved about 200–220 million years ago. *Coelophysis* was about the size of an adult human.

Coelophysis probably hunted lizard-like reptiles and other small animals of the time.

Find out more

ANIMALS
CROCODILES AND ALLIGATORS
DINOSAURS
LIZARDS
SNAKES

RHINOCEROSES
AND TAPIRS

THE FIRST RHINOCEROSES existed about 30 million years ago, and some evolved into the largest land mammals that ever lived. Today, few creatures are in such a desperate plight as the rhinoceros. Thousands have been killed for their horns, and all are on the official list of endangered species. Rhinoceroses are herbivores, or plant eaters. There are five different kinds – the white and black rhinoceroses of Africa, and the Indian, Javan, and Sumatran rhinoceroses of Asia. Rhinos usually live on their own, unless they are mothers with young calves. They are short-sighted animals, but have good hearing and an excellent sense of smell.

Tapirs are closely related to rhinoceroses. They are stout, piglike mammals that live mainly in forests. Tapirs are most active at night, when they feed on plants. They are good swimmers and spend much of their time in water. Tapirs are rare in many areas today, because of overhunting by humans.

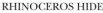

WHITE RHINOCEROS
With a weight of more than two tons, this is the second-largest animal on land (the elephant is largest). It is very shortsighted and sometimes charges at objects it does not recognize. It snips off grasses and other ground plants with its broad, blunt lips. White rhinoceroses are poached for their horns, which some people believe have medicinal properties.

BLACK RHINOCEROS
The black rhinoceros shown here is slightly smaller than the white rhinoceros. Black rhinos are found in central and southern Africa. They cannot focus clearly on things further than about 100 ft (30 m) away and sometimes charge at suspicious objects. Black rhinoceroses feed mainly at night on trees and bushes. They grasp the leaves and shoots with their long, hooked lips.

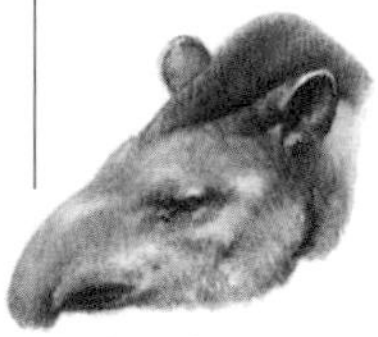

American tapir

Black rhinoceros

White square-lipped rhinoceros

FACES
Black rhinoceroses have long, hooked upper lips. The white rhinoceros has a square-shaped mouth. Tapirs have an elongated snout, which is used as a snorkel when the animal is in water.

RHINOCEROS HORN
Horn is made of hairlike fibers pressed together into a hard mass; there is no bone inside. The Indian rhinoceros (right) and the Java rhinoceros have only one horn; the other kinds of rhinoceros have two horns.

Tough, leathery hide

Movable ears and good hearing

Poor eyesight

Horn on nose

Very keen sense of smell

Hooked lip for grasping plant food

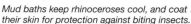

Mud baths keep rhinoceroses cool, and coat their skin for protection against biting insects.

RHINOCEROS HIDE
Rhinoceros skin, or hide, is extremely thick and tough. It hangs in flat sheets, with folds and creases around the legs and neck. It looks like a suit of armor on the Indian rhinoceros shown here. Only the Sumatran rhinoceros has hair on its body; all other rhinoceroses are bald.

MALAYAN TAPIR

Tapirs give birth to one young after a gestation (pregnancy) of 400 days. A newborn Malayan tapir has a spotted coat which gives good camouflage in the dappled forest undergrowth. At about six months, the spots and stripes fade and the tapir begins to look like its parents. An adult tapir has a large white patch on its black body, which helps to break up the animal's shape in dim light.

Find out more
AFRICAN WILDLIFE
ANIMALS
CONSERVATION AND
endangered species
MAMMALS

RIVERS

Rain feeds the river system.

WATER RUNS DOWN from high ground, cutting out a channel in the rock as it moves. This flowing water forms a river, which can be fed by a melting glacier, an overflowing lake, or a mountain spring. Rivers shape the landscape as they flow: the water sweeps away soil and eventually creates deep valleys in the land. One of the world's deepest valleys, cut by the Kali Gandak River through the Himalayas, is 3.4 miles (5.5 km) deep. Rivers also flow deep underground, slowly wearing away limestone rocks to form caves.

Rivers are important for transportation and as a source of water, which is why most big cities lie on rivers. The longest rivers are the Nile River in Africa, which is 4,145 miles (6,670 km) long, and the Amazon River in South America, which is 4,007 miles (6,448 km) long.

RIVER SYSTEM

Small rivers and streams feed a large river with water. A river system consists of the whole group of rivers and streams. A watershed, or high ridge, separates one river system from another. Streams flow in opposite directions on either side of a watershed.

RIVER VALLEY
The river carries along stones and mud, which grind against the riverbed and sides, deepening and widening the V-shaped valley.

OXBOW LAKE
The river cuts through the neck of a loop by wearing away the bank. Material is deposited at the ends of the loop, eventually forming a lake.

DELTA
The river sometimes fans out into separate streams as it reaches the sea. The streams dump mud which forms an area of flat land called a delta.

FLOOD PLAIN
Further down the river, the valley flattens out. This area, called the flood plain, is sometimes submerged during floods. The river runs through the plain in loops called meanders.

Some rivers do not form deltas, but flow into the sea through a single wide channel called an estuary.

TRIBUTARIES
The streams and rivers that flow into a big river are called its tributaries.

WATERFALL
The river plunges over a shelf of hard rock to form a waterfall.

GORGE
The waterfall slowly wears away the rock, cutting a deep gorge.

RAPIDS
Fast, swirling currents form where water flows down a steep slope. These parts of the river are called rapids.

Weathering on the valley sides breaks up soft rock and soil. This material falls into the river and is carried away by the current.

NIAGARA FALLS
The Niagara River plunges almost 180 ft (55 m) at Niagara Falls, which is situated on the border of the United States and Canada.

FLOODS
Rivers can overflow with heavy rain, or when water surges up from the sea. Flooding is severe in low-lying places, such as parts of Brazil in South America, which are often hit by tropical storms. Destruction of surrounding forests may be increasing the flow of water, making floods worse.

USES OF RIVERS
Great rivers that flow across whole countries carry boats that take goods from place to place. Some rivers have dams which build up huge stores of water in reservoirs. This water is used to supply towns and cities, irrigate crops, and generate electricity in hydroelectric power stations. Rivers are also a source of fish, but many rivers are now polluted by farms and factories.

RHINE RIVER
The Rhine River is an important trade route. Barges carry goods between towns in northern Europe.

Find out more
DAMS
GLACIERS AND ICECAPS
LAKE AND RIVER WILDLIFE
LAKES
RAIN AND SNOW
WATER

ROADS AND HIGHWAYS

THE UNITED STATES has more roads than any other country. They stretch almost 4 million miles (more than 6 million km). You would have to drive nonstop at 50 mph (80 km/h) for almost nine years to travel all of them. Great networks of roads and highways cover most countries. Major highways link cities, and minor roads crisscross cities and towns to reach neighborhoods and homes. Cars and buses speed along roads and highways carrying people from place to place. Trucks bring the goods that we buy in stores. In most countries, motorists drive on the righthand side of the road. In some countries, including Britain, India, Japan, and Australia, motorists drive on the left. Most large cities contain systems of one-way streets which help traffic to flow smoothly.

ANCIENT ROADS
The Ancient Romans were great road builders. They constructed a system of roads throughout their European empire about 2,000 years ago. These and many other old roads still exist, now surfaced for motor vehicles. Ancient roads were also trade routes. From as early as the 3rd century B.C., the Silk Road was used to bring silk from China across Asia to Europe.

Narrow roads twist through the countryside and over hills, often following old tracks and paths.

Flyovers allow vehicles to change roads without crossing other lines of traffic.

HIGHWAYS
Highways carry traffic nonstop between cities and around city centers. They are very wide, usually with three lanes in each direction, so they can carry large amounts of traffic. A central barrier separates the two sides of the road.

Bypass carries traffic around the edge of the city, avoiding the city center.

ROAD BUILDING
To build a major road that carries heavy traffic, bulldozers first clear and level the ground and build embankments or dig trenches if necessary. Drains are laid to carry rainwater away, and the road is then built in several layers. One or more layers of crushed stone are placed on the soil. The top layer can be made of concrete, or a "blacktop" of tar and stone chips. Steamrollers squash down each layer to make it firm.

Multistoried parking lots make the most use of valuable land space.

The sidewalk is for pedestrians.

Tarmac or concrete

Layers of crushed stone

Compressed soil

Traffic meets at crossroads, and the vehicles on one road yield to those on the other road.

Pedestrianized street in which vehicles are forbidden

Pedestrian crossing

Bicycle lane

TRAFFIC JAM
By 2025 there will be around one billion cars in the world. Already, vehicles contribute a lot to the pollution around us.

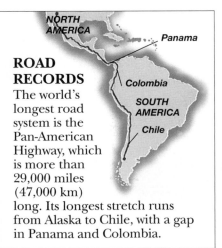

ROAD RECORDS
The world's longest road system is the Pan-American Highway, which is more than 29,000 miles (47,000 km) long. Its longest stretch runs from Alaska to Chile, with a gap in Panama and Colombia.

NORTH AMERICA

Panama

Colombia

SOUTH AMERICA

Chile

TRAFFIC CONTROL
Road signs, such as speed limits and warnings of hazards ahead, help make the traffic move more safely. Road markings keep traffic in lanes, and traffic signals keep vehicles from colliding at crossroads. Police officers monitor busy roads using video cameras, and computers control city traffic, operating groups of signals to speed traffic flow and prevent jams.

Find out more
BRIDGES
BUILDING
CITIES
ROMAN EMPIRE
TUNNELS

ROBOTS

WHEN PEOPLE THINK OF ROBOTS, they often imagine the metal monsters of science fiction movies. However, most robots at work today look nothing like this. A robot is simply a computer-controlled machine that carries out mechanical tasks. The Czech playwright Karel Capek invented the word *robot,* which comes from a Czech word meaning "forced labor." Indeed, robots do jobs that would be dangerous or boring for people to do. Many factories have robots that consist of a single arm that is fixed in one spot. The robot simply repeats a task that it has been instructed to perform, such as spray-painting car parts. Today, engineers are developing much more sophisticated robots. These robots can move around, and their electronic detectors enable them to sense their surroundings. They also have "intelligence," which means that they can respond to what they see and hear and make decisions for themselves. Intelligent robots are designed to act as guards and fire fighters, and may travel into space to study distant worlds.

SCIENCE FICTION ROBOTS
The robots of science fiction, such as C-3P0 from the film *Star Wars,* are often anthropoid (humanlike). In reality, anthropoid robots are rare. However, Japanese engineers have built experimental robots with two legs.

Held too tightly – loosen grip.

Brain sends nerve signals to muscles in the hand, adjusting the strength of the grip so the egg is neither dropped nor squashed.

Held too loosely – tighten grip.

Touch sensors in your hand detect how hard you are pressing on the egg.

FEEDBACK
When you pick up an egg, your senses begin sending signals to your brain. From this information, your brain automatically adjusts the movement of your hand and the pressure of your fingers. This adjustment is called feedback. Advanced robots control their actions by feedback from electronic detectors such as lasers, television cameras, and touch sensors.

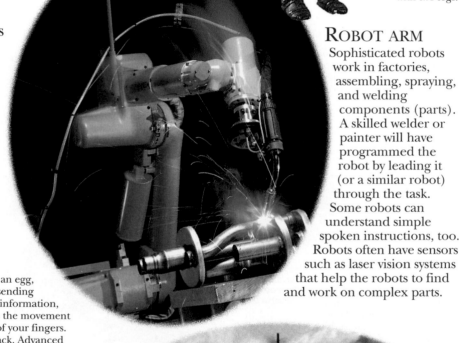

ROBOT ARM
Sophisticated robots work in factories, assembling, spraying, and welding components (parts). A skilled welder or painter will have programmed the robot by leading it (or a similar robot) through the task. Some robots can understand simple spoken instructions, too. Robots often have sensors such as laser vision systems that help the robots to find and work on complex parts.

SPACE ROBOT
In January 2004, two unmanned exploration rovers, *Spirit* (right) and *Opportunity,* touched down on Mars. They photographed the planet and analyzed samples of rock. Robot space probes such as these are designed to obey instructions from controllers on Earth, but decide for themselves how to carry out the orders.

Space probes need to be able to work independently because radio instructions could take minutes or even hours to travel from Earth.

REMOTE CONTROL
Mobile robots do dangerous jobs such as repairing and dismantling nuclear reactors and detonating concealed bombs. These robots are remotely controlled – a human operator controls the general actions of the robot from a safe distance, and onboard computers control detailed movements.

This bomb disposal robot runs on tracks so that it can climb into awkward places. It carries cameras to send back pictures to the operator, and a gun for detonating the bomb.

> ### Find out more
> COMPUTERS
> FACTORIES
> TECHNOLOGY

ROCK AND POP

A NEW TYPE OF MUSIC EMERGED IN THE US in the 1950s. First known as rock 'n' roll, it is now called rock music. It drew on many different musical styles including folk, gospel, blues, country and western, classical, and world music. The main thing that distinguished rock music from any previous music was that it was listened to, and often performed by, young people rebelling against the music and lifestyles of their parents. Pop music is a softer style of rock. Image is very important in the world of rock and pop, with fans identifying with particular groups or singers by copying their clothes and hairstyles, and rock and pop are listened to all over the world. Millions of people of all ages buy and play rock and pop music. It is a mass-market industry.

Bono and The Edge, members of Irish rock band U2.

Rock'n'roll dancing involves fast, energetic movements.

INSTRUMENTS
The first rock 'n' roll bands were formed in the 1950s, with Bill Haley and the Comets' hit "Rock Around the Clock" launching the new music style. The new bands featured electric guitars and drum kits, giving their music great volume and rhythm. Since then, the classic band lineup has consisted of a singer, lead guitarist, rhythm guitarist, bass guitarist, and drummer.

RHYTHM AND BLUES
In the 1940s, US blues musician Muddy Waters (1915-83), and others, took the haunting blues music of rural black America and played it fast and loud on electric guitars. This new music – rhythm and blues – influenced rock music.

Aretha Franklin

ELVIS PRESLEY
Singer Elvis Presley (1935-77) was the first international rock 'n' roll star. His good looks made him one of the first mass teen idols. Raised in Mississippi and Tennesse, he grew up listening to every kind of popular music, inspiring him to create a wild, energetic rock 'n' roll style that appealed to black and white audiences alike.

ROCK 'N' ROLL
Teenagers in the 1950s rebelled against the slow, romantic music that their parents liked. They wanted their own kind of music to listen to: loud, fast, rhythmic songs which they could, literally, rock 'n' roll to on a Saturday night.

THE BEATLES
Four young musicians from Liverpool, England – John Lennon, Paul McCartney, George Harrison, and Ringo Starr – first recorded together in 1962. By 1964 their group, the Beatles, was the biggest rock band in the world. They broke up in 1970, but their songs are still hugely popular today.

SOUL MUSIC
Written and performed by black musicians such as Marvin Gaye (1939-84) and Otis Redding (1941-67), soul music was a fusion of blues and gospel music. Many soul musicians, notably Aretha Franklin (b. 1942), began by singing gospel music in church. Franklin sings soul music with similar power and emotion.

REGGAE

Coming from the Caribbean island of Jamaica, reggae music is influenced by jazz, gospel, rhythm and blues, and soul. It is an infectious music combining catchy melodies with words of strength and hope. The most important reggae star, Bob Marley (1945-81), turned reggae into an international music style.

Bob Marley

Woodstock attracted over 400,000 people.

The festival was held on a farm.

Woodstock music festival

ROCK FESTIVALS

Rock festivals began in the 1960s in California, when thousands of people turned up to hear free, all-day concerts. The most famous festival ever took place at Woodstock, New York, in 1969, with performers such as Jimi Hendrix, Janis Joplin, and The Who. Today, most festivals are large, commercially organized events, where you can hear a wide range of rock and pop bands.

ROCK AND POP

1951 First rock 'n' roll records.

1954 Elvis Presley records *"That's All Right,"* his first single.

1955-58 Elvis has a run of 14 million-selling records, including *"Heartbreak Hotel."*

1962 Beatles record *"Love Me Do,"* their first single.

1964 Beatles have top five singles in US charts.

1965 Bob Dylan introduces electric guitar to folk music.

1967 Aretha Franklin makes her first soul records.

1969 Woodstock festival.

1975 Bob Marley becomes major international star with *"No Woman No Cry."*

1976 Punk music erupts.

1983 Madonna's first album.

1995 "Britpop" dominates the UK charts.

DANCE MUSIC

The first music written specially for dancing in clubs was 1970s disco music. In the 1980s, house music – a combination of rapid rhythms and electronic sounds – emerged. Today there are many types of electronic music, including house, breakbeat, and drum and bass.

DJ Norman "Fatboy Slim" Cook.

MADONNA

US singer Madonna (b. 1958) started out in the early 1980s, singing simple pop songs. She soon became one of the most successful recording artists of recent years, with huge-selling albums. Her fame is partly due to her ever-changing image.

OutKast is one of the most popular mainstream hip hop acts.

HIP HOP

Hip hop is a type of popular music, which began in the African American communities of New York in the 1970s and has become hugely successful around the world. It often features effects produced using turntables, samples from other records, and rhythmic vocals known as rap. OutKast, a duo from Atlanta, Georgia, USA, are one of the most successful hip hop acts ever, having sold more than 20 million albums worldwide.

Find out more
DANCE
MUSIC
MUSICAL INSTRUMENTS

ROCKETS AND MISSILES

THE INVENTION OF THE ROCKET ENGINE was a landmark in history.
Not only did it give humans a tool with which to explore space, but it also
produced the missile, a weapon of terrible destructive power. A rocket
engine is the most powerful of all engines. It has the power
to push a spacecraft along at more than 25,000 mph
(40,000 km/h), the speed necessary for it to break free
from Earth's gravity. In a rocket engine, fuel burns
to produce gases that rush out of the nozzle at the
back, thrusting the rocket forward. However,
unlike other engines, rockets do not need to
use oxygen from the air to burn their fuel.
Instead they carry their own supply of
oxygen, usually in the form of a liquid,
so that they can operate in space
where there is no air. There
is one major difference
between a missile and
a space rocket: missiles
carry an explosive
warhead instead
of a satellite or
human cargo.

A few seconds after takeoff,
booster fuel is expended.

Third stage fires for about
12 minutes, carrying its
satellite payload into orbit
about 200 miles (320 km)
above the Earth's surface.

Once first stage has
run out of fuel, it
falls away and
second stage takes
over, burning for
about two minutes.

First stage propels rocket for about three
minutes, by which time rocket is more
than 30 miles (50 km) above the Earth.

SPACE ROCKET
Most space rockets are
made up of several stages,
or segments, each with its
own rocket engines and
propellant, or fuel. By
detaching the stages
as they are used, the
rocket can reach higher
speeds because its weight is kept
to a minimum. There are two main
types of rocket propellant: solid
and liquid. Solid fuel burns
rapidly and cannot be controlled
once ignited. But rockets powered
by liquid propellant can be controlled by
opening and closing valves that adjust
the flow of fuel into the engine.

NUCLEAR MISSILES
Deadly nuclear warheads
and precise navigational
systems make nuclear
missiles the most
dangerous weapons
in the history of
warfare. A single
warhead has the
power to destroy
a large city and cause
millions of deaths.
Nuclear missiles can
be launched from
submarines, aircraft,
trucks, and hidden
underground launch sites.

ARIANE ROCKET

Vehicle equipment bay
contains satellite that
is being carried into orbit.

Guidance systems keep
rocket on the correct course.

Third stage with one
liquid-propellant rocket

Tank containing oxidizer, a
liquid that contains oxygen

Tank containing highly
inflammable liquid fuel

Pumps push fuel and
oxidizer to the nozzle,
where they burn and
produce a violent rush
of hot gases that push
the rocket upwards.

Second stage with one
liquid-propellant rocket

Two solid-propellant
and two liquid-
propellant strap-on
booster rockets give
space rocket an extra
push in the first part
of its flight.

First stage with four
liquid-propellant
rocket engines

TYPES OF MISSILES
Huge intercontinental
ballistic missiles
(ICBMs) blast up
into space and come
down on their targets
thousands of miles
away. However, not all
rocket-powered missiles
travel into space; many
have replaced guns for
short-range attacks
on tanks, ships, and
aircraft. Many of these
missiles home in
on their targets
automatically.

ICBM
armed
with
nuclear
warhead

Anti-aircraft
missile,
usually
launched
from a ship

Size of rockets
compared to a child
4 ft (1.2 m) tall

Radar-guided anti-ship missile.
It can be launched from the air,
from land, or from a warship.

Anti-tank missile,
guided to target
by remote control

DEVELOPMENT OF ROCKETS
In the 13th century, the Chinese used
a simple type of rocket powered by
gunpowder to scare enemy horses. Six
hundred years later, Englishman Sir William
Congreve developed a gunpowder rocket
that the English forces used during the
Napoleonic Wars. During World War II
(1941-45), German scientist Wernher
von Braun invented the first successful
long-range rocket, the V-2, the
forerunner of the ICBM.

Early
Chinese
rockets

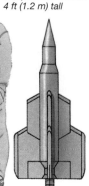

> ### *Find out more*
> MILITARY AIRCRAFT
> NAPOLEONIC WARS
> NUCLEAR AGE
> NUCLEAR ENERGY
> SPACE FLIGHT
> SUBMARINES
> WEAPONS
> WORLD WAR II

ROCKS AND MINERALS

WE LIVE ON THE SURFACE of a huge ball of rock, the Earth. The landscape everywhere is made up of rocks. Most are covered by soil, trees, or grass. Others, such as Uluru (Ayers Rock) in Australia, a massive lump of sandstone 1,142 ft (348 m) high, rise from the ground and are visible. The oldest rocks on Earth are about 3.8 billion years old. Other rocks are much more recent, and new rocks are forming all the time. All rocks contain substances called minerals. Marble consists mainly of calcite, for example, and granite contains the minerals mica, quartz, and feldspar.

Rocks form in different ways: from molten rock within the Earth, from the fossils of animals and plants, and by the action of heat and pressure on ancient rocks inside the Earth. But no rocks, however hard, last forever on the Earth's surface. They are slowly eroded, or worn away, by the action of wind, rain, and other weather conditions.

HOW ROCKS FORM
All rocks started out as clouds of dust in space. The dust particles came together and formed the rocks that make up the planets, moons, and meteorites. There are now three main kinds of rocks on the Earth's surface: igneous, sedimentary, and metamorphic rocks. Each kind of rock forms in a different way.

GIANT'S CAUSEWAY
The steps of this unusual rock formation in Northern Ireland are made of columns of basalt, rock which developed when lava from a volcano cooled and set. The rock cracked into columns as it cooled.

Mud and pebbles are buried and squashed together, producing a hard sedimentary rock called conglomerate.

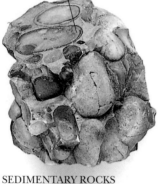

SEDIMENTARY ROCKS
Ice, wind, and running water wear away rocks into pebbles and small particles called sediment. Layers of sediment containing sand, clay, and animal skeletons are buried and squeezed so that they slowly change into hard rocks called sedimentary rocks.

Limestone contains the remains of shellfish. Chalk, another kind of limestone, is made of the skeletons of sea animals.

Clay forms shale, a sedimentary rock that crumbles easily. This rock is slate, the metamorphic rock which forms from shale.

Bubbles of gas trapped in the lava created holes in this piece of rock.

When lava from a volcano cools on the Earth's surface, it forms basalt.

IGNEOUS ROCKS
Deep underground the heat is so intense that some rock is molten (melted). When it cools, this molten rock, or magma, sets hard to produce an igneous rock. This may happen underground, or the magma may rise to the surface as lava and solidify.

Lava flows from a volcano and solidifies, forming basalt, an igneous rock.

Sedimentary rocks, such as conglomerate, form on the beach at the mouth of a river.

River carries sediment from the land to the sea.

Red-hot magma heats surrounding limestone, turning it into marble.

Hot magma solidifies, forming granite, an igneous rock.

Shale forms from clay at the river bed.

When magma slowly cools deep underground, it often forms granite, a hard rock which is used as a building material.

METAMORPHIC ROCKS
Heat and pressure deep underground bake and squeeze sedimentary and igneous rocks. The minerals within the rocks change, often becoming harder. In this way they form new rocks called metamorphic rocks. After millions of years, the top rocks are worn away and metamorphic rocks appear on the surface.

Heating and compressing limestone turns it into marble, a hard metamorphic rock.

MINERALS

An impressive rock collection will feature rocks that contain beautiful mineral crystals. Minerals are the different substances of which rocks are made. For example, limestone and marble contain the white mineral calcite. Minerals include precious stones, such as diamonds, and ores – minerals that contain metals such as iron and aluminum. Almost all metals are produced by mining and quarrying ores, and then treating the ores to extract their metals.

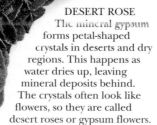

DESERT ROSE

The mineral gypsum forms petal-shaped crystals in deserts and dry regions. This happens as water dries up, leaving mineral deposits behind. The crystals often look like flowers, so they are called desert roses or gypsum flowers.

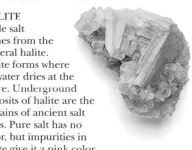

TURQUOISE

Jewelers cut beautiful gemstones and ornaments from turquoise, a blue-green mineral that often runs in a thin vein through other rocks.

HALITE

Table salt comes from the mineral halite. Halite forms where seawater dries at the shore. Underground deposits of halite are the remains of ancient salt lakes. Pure salt has no color, but impurities in halite give it a pink color.

SULFUR

Yellow crystals form when molten sulfur cools. Large underground deposits in places such as the United States provide sulfur for making rubber and chemicals.

GALENA

Glistening gray crystals of galena stick out from a piece of white limestone. Galena forms cubic crystals. It is the main ore in which lead is found, and it often appears as a vein in limestone. Lead is combined with sulfur in galena. Smelting the ore by heating it in a furnace removes the sulfur and leaves lead metal.

CRYSTALS

Minerals often form crystals – solids which grow in regular shapes with flat sides. Light sparkles from crystals because they are often transparent and have smooth, shiny surfaces. Each mineral forms crystals with particular shapes, such as columns and cubes. Crystals grow from molten minerals or minerals that are dissolved in liquids, such as water.

Hexagonal crystals form in six-sided columns.

Cubic crystals form in four-sided columns.

Some minerals, such as solecite, form needle-shaped crystals.

Crystals form in columns, such as in this piece of the mineral beryl.

QUARTZ

Quartz is one of the most common minerals. Electronic clocks and watches contain small cut pieces of quartz that control time-keeping with great accuracy.

USES OF ROCK

Rocks in one form or another surround us in towns, cities, and the countryside. Hard rocks such as granite, sandstone, and limestone provide good building materials for houses and walls, and roads contain fragments of crushed rock. Soft rocks have uses, too. Heating clay or shale with crushed limestone produces cement for making concrete and laying bricks. Bricks themselves are made by baking clay in molds.

The first tools were made of stone. Early people broke pieces of rocks and stone to make sharp cutting implements such as axes.

Sculptors work rocks, stones, and pure minerals to make statues and ornaments.

Find out more

ATOMS AND MOLECULES
CLOCKS AND WATCHES
COMETS AND METEORS
FOSSILS
GEMS AND JEWELRY
GEOLOGY
VOLCANOES

ROMAN EMPIRE

TWO THOUSAND YEARS AGO, a single government and way of life united most of western Europe, the Middle East, and the northern coast of Africa. The Roman Empire was based on good organization and centralized control. Towns in different countries were planned in exactly the same way. A network of stone-paved roads (parts of which remain today) connected every area to Rome. The reign of the first emperor, Augustus, began a long period of stability known as the Pax Romana, or Roman Peace, which lasted for about 200 years. Strong border defenses manned by the Roman army protected the empire, while a skilled civil service governed it. Trade flourished and the people were united. The empire reached the height of its power in about A.D. 200 and then began to decline slowly. It was divided into two parts in 284. In 476, barbarian tribes conquered the Western Empire (based in Rome). The Eastern Empire (based in Constantinople, now called Istanbul, Turkey) continued until 1453.

GRAFFITI
The Romans were fond of making fun of each other. This caricature was found on a wall in Pompeii. It is a mockery of a leading local citizen – probably a noble, judging from his laurel wreath.

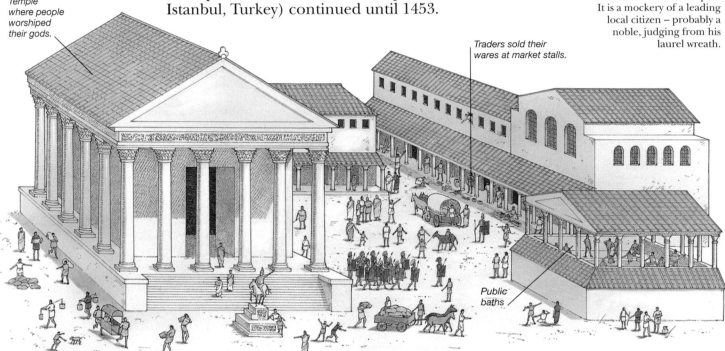

Temple where people worshiped their gods.

Traders sold their wares at market stalls.

Public baths

CITY LIFE

Roman cities were carefully planned with straight streets, running water, and sewers. The forum, or central market-place, was surrounded by stores, law courts, and the town hall. The rich, always Roman citizens, lived in fine villas; the poor lived in apartment-style buildings. There were many temples. Most of the hard work was done by slaves, who had none of the rights granted to citizens, such as access to the baths.

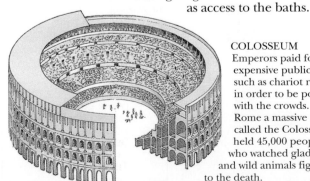

COLOSSEUM
Emperors paid for expensive public games, such as chariot racing, in order to be popular with the crowds. In Rome a massive theater called the Colosseum held 45,000 people, who watched gladiators and wild animals fight to the death.

ROMAN BATHS

The Romans loved bathing. They scraped off the dirt, rubbed oil into their skin, relaxed in steam rooms, swam in warm pools, and plunged into icy water.

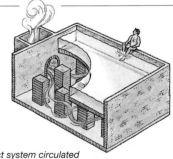

The hypocaust system circulated hot air under the floors and through the walls to heat houses and baths.

People rubbed oil, which they carried in oil flasks, on their bodies.

Bathers scraped the sweat and dirt off their bodies with strigils.

Commanding officers often wore crests on their helmets so that their men could recognize them in battle.

ROMAN ARMY

The power of the empire depended on the might of its professional armies, or legions. Soldiers belonging to a legion (about 5,000 men) were called legionaries. They were highly trained and well equipped with spears, shields, and short swords. They built roads and forts to defend their conquests. Upon retirement, veteran soldiers were often given land in colonies throughout the empire.

ROMAN EMPIRE

c.753 B.C. First settlement built.

509 B.C. Etruscans driven out of Rome. Republic established.

275 B.C. Italy conquered. Expansion overseas begins.

146 B.C. Destruction of Carthage gives Rome control of Spain and North Africa.

71 B.C. Slaves revolt, led by Spartacus.

52 B.C. Gaul (France) conquered by Julius Caesar.

44 B.C. Caesar assassinated.

27 B.C. Augustus becomes first emperor.

A.D. 43 Claudius conquers Britain.

A.D. 117 Empire reaches its greatest size.

A.D. 284 Empire splits into two halves.

A.D. 410 Visigoths sack Rome.

A.D. 476 Western part of the Empire falls.

THE ROMAN EMPIRE
At its height, the Roman Empire stretched from the Middle East to Britain. The inhabitants were of many different races and spoke many different languages.

HADRIAN'S WALL
The emperor Hadrian ordered a wall to be built across northern Britain to defend Roman lands from the fierce, unconquered tribes who lived in the mountains of Scotland. The wall, parts of which can still be seen today, was 75 miles (120 km) long, and studded with forts. The army built defensive ditches, fortress bases, and signal towers along it.

TECHNOLOGY AND CRAFTS

The Romans were highly skilled engineers and craftworkers. Their towns had water supplies and drains, and rich people lived in centrally heated houses. The houses often had detailed mosaics on the floors. Artisans worked with glass, metals, bone, and clay to make beautiful objects that have lasted to this day.

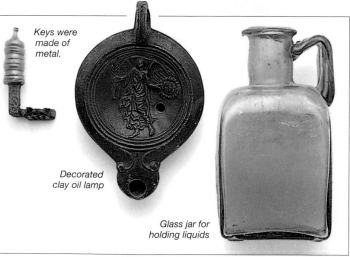

Keys were made of metal.

Decorated clay oil lamp

Glass jar for holding liquids

Find out more

ARMIES
BARBARIANS
BYZANTINE EMPIRE
CAESAR, JULIUS
ITALY, HISTORY OF

FRANKLIN DELANO
ROOSEVELT

IN 1932 THE UNITED STATES was at one of its lowest points in history. Thirteen million people – nearly one-third of the country's work force – were unemployed. Then a new president was elected with a mission to make Americans prosperous again. When Franklin Delano Roosevelt was disabled by polio in the summer of 1921, it appeared to be the end of a promising political career. But Roosevelt was a fighter and, helped by his wife, Eleanor, he regained the partial use of his legs. In 1928 he was elected governor of New York, then ran for president in 1932. He won a landslide victory, and for 13 years – the longest time any United States president has ever served – Roosevelt worked to overcome the effects of unemployment and poverty, telling Americans that "the only thing we have to fear is fear itself." He launched the New Deal – a series of social reforms and work programs. During World War II, Roosevelt proved to be an able war leader, and with his Soviet and British allies he did much to shape the postwar world.

NEW DEAL
During the Depression of the 1930s, Roosevelt promised a "New Deal." Federal programs provided jobs for the unemployed and tried to return the country to prosperity. New laws were passed that provided better conditions for workers and pensions for retired workers.

The New Deal as seen by a cartoonist of the time.

FIRESIDE CHATS
President Roosevelt was an expert communicator who used the then-new medium of the radio to explain his controversial policies to the nation. These informal "fireside chats" established firm links between the president and the American people.

ELEANOR ROOSEVELT
Throughout her life President Roosevelt's wife, Eleanor (1884-1962), was a tireless campaigner for human rights. After 1945 she represented her country in the United Nations.

YALTA CONFERENCE
In February 1945, President Roosevelt, Winston Churchill, the British prime minister (far left), and Joseph Stalin, Soviet premier (far right), met in the Soviet resort of Yalta to discuss the postwar world. Together they decided to set up the United Nations.

Find out more

DEPRESSION of the 1930s
UNITED NATIONS
UNITED STATES OF AMERICA, history of
WORLD WAR II

RUSSIAN FEDERATION

The Russian Federation stretches from eastern Europe in the west across the entire width of Asia to the Pacific Ocean in the east, and from the Arctic Circle in the north to Central Asia in the south.

THE LARGEST NATION in the world is the Russian Federation. Also called Russia, it consists of 20 autonomous (self-governing) republics and more than 50 other regions. It covers one-tenth of the earth's land area – one-third of Asia, and two-fifths of Europe. Russia has a very varied climate and a landscape that ranges from mountains in the south and east to vast lowlands and rivers in the north and west. The population is varied, too, although most of the 143 million people are of Russian origin and speak the Russian language. The Russian Federation came into being in 1991 after the break up of the Soviet Union, or USSR. After 1991, the Russian people experienced greater political freedom but also economic hardship as their country changed from a state-planned to a free-market economy. The Russian Federation has vast agricultural resources. It is also rich in minerals, and has considerable industry. Although many people in Russia are very poor, the country now has some of the world's richest billionaires.

MODERN RUSSIA
Large Russian cities look similar to cities elsewhere in the world, but the bright lights hide economic problems. Both luxury and essential goods are often in short supply. Lining up for food (above) is a daily occupation, and clothes and consumer goods are scarce and often of poor quality. Most homes are rented from the government, but housing is in limited supply, which means that overcrowding is common.

MOSCOW
The capital city of the Russian Federation is Moscow. It was founded during the 12th century. At the city's heart, on the banks of the Moscow River, lies the Kremlin. This is a walled fortress housing all the government buildings. Within these walls lies the impressive Red Square. The stunning St. Basil's Cathedral stands at the southern end of the square. It was built in the 16th century to celebrate a military victory.

Nevsky Prospect is St. Petersburg's busiest shopping street.

RUSSIAN ORTHODOX CHURCH
The chief religion in Russia is the Russian Orthodox Church. Under Communism, all religions were persecuted. In the late 1980s, freedom of worship returned to Russia, and today millions of people worship without fear (above). The Russian Federation also contains many Muslims, Jews, and Buddhists.

ST. PETERSBURG
The second-largest city in the Russian Federation, St. Petersburg has a population of 4.5 million. Before 1917, St. Petersburg (called Leningrad from 1924 to 1991) was the capital of Russia. It still contains many beautiful, historical buildings, such as the Hermitage Art Gallery, once the summer palace of the czars.

AGRICULTURE

Most agriculture in the Russian Federation takes place on the fertile Russian plain that stretches from the western border into Central Asia. Here, farmers produce wheat and other cereals, meat, dairy products, wool, and cotton. The Russian Federation is one of the world's biggest grain producers, but often fails to grow enough food to feed its own population and has to import grain.

Agriculture in the Russian Federation is mainly confined to the southern and western regions because of the cold climate in the northern margins.

RUBLES AND KOPECKS

The unit of Russian money is the ruble, which is divided into 100 kopecks. Following the break up of the Soviet Union in 1991, Russia moved from a state-planned to a free-market economy. This led to economic instability and fluctuating exchange rates. In recent times the currency has begun to stabilise.

RUSSIAN PEOPLE

Most people in the Russian Federation are Russian in origin, but there are at least 100 minority groups, including Tatars, Ukrainians, Bashkirs, and Chukchis. Some, such as the Yakut hunters, shown here in traditional clothing, are Turkish in origin; other groups are Asiatic. The population is not spread evenly through this vast nation. About 75 percent live west of the Ural Mountains; less than 25 percent live in Siberia and the far east of the country.

The Bolshoi Theater, home of the Bolshoi Ballet

The Yakut (left) are distributed across a large area centered on the Lena River. The economy of the more southerly Yakut is based on the husbandry of cattle and horses, while the Yakut farther north engage in hunting, fishing, and herding.

BOLSHOI BALLET

The world-famous Bolshoi Ballet dance company was founded in Moscow in 1773. It became famous touring the world with performances of Russian folk dances and classic ballets such as *Swan Lake*. Other Russian art forms did not enjoy the same freedom of expression under the old Soviet regime. Artists opposed to the Communist government worked in secret. For example, the novels of Aleksandr Solzhenitsyn (born 1918) were banned for many years. His most famous works, such as *The Gulag Archipelago*, were smuggled in from Europe or retyped by readers and circulated secretly.

Ленингра́д

RUSSIAN LANGUAGES

In the Russian Federation, more than 112 languages including Tatar, Ukrainian, and Russian are spoken. Russian is the primary language of the majority of people in Russia, and is also used as a second language in other former republics of the Soviet Union. Russian writers use the Cyrillic alphabet, part of which is shown here.

TECHNOLOGICAL ACHIEVEMENTS

As part of the Soviet Union, Russian science developed unevenly. Today, the Russian Federation leads the world in some medical techniques, particularly eye surgery (right), but lags far behind Western Europe and the United States in areas such as computers. In the field of space research, the Soviet Union led the world, launching the first satellite in 1957, and putting the first man in space, Yuri Gagarin, in 1961. More recently, the Russians have launched the first paying passengers into space.

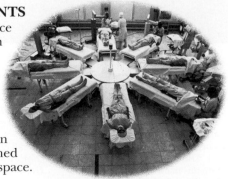

SIBERIA

The vast region of Siberia is in the northeast of the Russian Federation, and it stretches from the Ural Mountains in the west to the tip of Alaska in the east. Although Siberia occupies nearly 80 percent of the land area of the Russian Federation, it is thinly populated. Most Siberian people live close to the route of the Trans-Siberian Railway, which runs for 5,864 miles (9,438 km) between Moscow and Vladivostok. Much of northern Siberia lies inside the Arctic circle, and during the summer months the sun never sets, but simply dips close to the horizon at night.

VOLGA RIVER

Russia contains Europe's longest river, the Volga River. Flowing 2,194 miles (3,531 km) from the Valdai Hills to the Caspian Sea, it is the country's leading waterway, and of great economic importance. Large boats transport oil, wheat, timber, and machinery across the country. Canals link the river to the Baltic and White Seas. The river itself is a rich source of fish, particularly sturgeon. Sturgeon's roe (eggs) is pickled to make the delicacy called caviar.

LAKE BAIKAL

With an area of 12,150 sq miles (31,468 sq km), Lake Baikal is the largest freshwater lake in the world. It is also the world's deepest lake, reaching depths of 6,367 ft (1,940 m). In recent years, logging and chemical industries have polluted the water, prompting a major campaign to protect its fragile environment.

Lake Baikal is known as the "blue eye of Siberia", and contains more than 20 percent of the world's entire supply of fresh water.

TRANS-SIBERIAN RAILWAY

The Trans-Siberian Railway links European Russia with the Pacific coast across Siberia. It is the world's longest continuous rail line, starting at Moscow and ending 5,777 miles (9,297 km) away in the Pacific port of Vladivostok. Construction of the railway enabled Siberia's mineral wealth to be exploited, and large cities have developed along its route. The journey takes eight days, and crosses eight time zones. Only one passenger train runs each way daily, but freight trains run every five minutes, day and night.

Founded in 1893, where the Trans-Siberian Railway crosses the Ob' River, Novosibirsk, 1,978 miles (3,183 km) east of Moscow, has developed into an important commercial center.

FEMALE WORKFORCE

Many more Russian men than women died during World War II and in the labor camps set up by the Soviet leader Stalin. As a result, women had to go out to work, and many took up physical jobs traditionally done by men. In the Soviet period, good child care enabled women with children to go out to work. Today, more women in Russia hold jobs in science, technology, and engineering than in the rest of Europe, but very few reach the top jobs in these fields.

Female scientist working to detect pirate CDs.

Find out more

COLD WAR
COMMUNISM
RUSSIA, HISTORY OF
RUSSIAN REVOLUTION
SOVIET UNION, HISTORY OF

Volcano	Mountain	Ancient monument	Capital city	Large city/town	Small city/town

STATISTICS

Area: 6,592,812 sq miles (17,075,400 sq km)
Population: 143,000,000
Capital: Moscow
Languages: Russian
Religions: Russian Orthodox
Currency: Ruble
Main occupations: Engineering, research, agriculture
Main exports: Oil, natural gas, electricity, vodka
Main imports: Cars, machinery

SPACE PROGRAM

Russia's space program began with the launch of the Sputnik satellite in 1957. In 1965, the Russian cosmonaut Aleksei Leonov became the first person to walk in space. In 1969, the Russians lost the race with the US to land a spacecraft on the Moon. The world's most successful space station (permanent spacecraft in orbit round the Earth) was the Russian craft Mir, which orbited the Earth from 1986 to 2001. It was made up of modules that were added to the station at different dates. Astronauts stayed on board for lengthy periods of time, because supplies were delivered by visiting spacecraft.

RUSSIAN BOX
Lacquered boxes have been made in the Moscow region for the last four centuries. The papier-mâché boxes are decorated with miniature paintings of folk stories, rural scenes, dances, forests, and fairy tales, and are then lacquered.

CAVIAR
Caviar, an expensive delicacy, is made from the tiny black eggs of the beluga sturgeon, a type of fish that lives in the Black and Caspian Seas. Caviar is exported worldwide.

LADA
In 1965, the Soviet government signed a deal with the Italian car company Fiat to manufacture an economy car called the Lada in the Soviet Union. Today, Ladas, which are based on the Fiat, are exported to the West. Relatively few Russians own a car; but the demand for luxury western cars is growing.

HISTORY OF
RUSSIA

BEFORE THE NINTH CENTURY A.D., Russia consisted of scattered tribes from eastern Europe who farmed a barren landscape of marshes, forests, and steppes. In 882, the first Russian state was established at Kiev, an important trading center. But in the 1200s, huge Mongol armies destroyed much of Russia. The Russian princes survived the attack only by brutally taxing their own people on behalf of the Mongols. Their methods began a long-lasting system of cruel government in Russia. In the 15th century, after the Mongols had withdrawn, Moscow became the capital of Russia. Over the next 300 years, the czars (emperors) conquered new lands, and Russia became the largest country in the world. However, Russia was slow to modernize and remained backward compared with other nations. After 1900, Russia slowly began to emerge into modern life, but its newfound strength was wasted in wars. There was a huge contrast between the czar's wealth and the poverty of the people. In 1917, the Russian Revolution overthrew czarist rule. The Communists took power, and from 1917 to 1991, Russia was the largest republic in the Soviet Union. With the collapse of the Soviet Union in 1991, Russia became independent once more.

KIEV
In 882 a Viking named Oleg captured Kiev and made it the capital of Russia. After this, Russian princes, who recognized Kiev's importance as a trade route between the Baltic Sea and the Black Sea, ruled the city. In 988, Prince Vladimir I of Kiev became a Christian and made Russian Orthodoxy the state religion. In 1240, Kiev fell to the Mongols.

ST. BASIL'S CHURCH
In 1552, Ivan the Terrible built St. Basil's Church, Moscow. It was very ornate to show the great wealth and prosperity of Moscow. Legend has it that Ivan had the architects blinded to prevent them from designing anything as beautiful again.

MOSCOW
It was under Mongol control that Moscow (then called Muscovy) rose to power. The Mongols let Prince Ivan I (nicknamed "Moneybags") collect taxes for them. He kept some of the money and began to expand Russia's territory. He also made Moscow the religious center of Russia. Ivan III (the Great) enlarged Moscow's territory. He also drove out the Mongols, leaving Moscow the most powerful city in Russia.

The colorful decorations and onion-shaped domes on the outside of St. Basil's are typical of Russian Orthodox churches.

IVAN THE TERRIBLE
Under Czar Ivan IV (1530-84), Moscow gained more power. But Ivan was brutal and wicked, and earned the name Ivan the Terrible. He hated and feared the boyars (nobles) and had hundreds of them murdered. He even murdered his own son. His harsh rule brought poverty to millions and reduced the peasants to near slavery.

PETER THE GREAT
In 1682 Peter the Great became czar. During his reign he modernized the army, defeated Sweden, and gained control of the Baltic coast, giving Russia an outlet to the West. He built a new capital at St. Petersburg and improved industry and education. He traveled through Europe in disguise to learn about Western life and tried to modernize Russia by using Western methods. He cut off the beards of the Orthodox Russians as a symbol of all he intended to change.

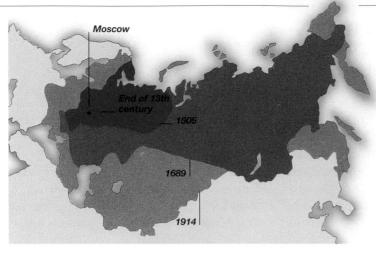

Moscow

End of 13th century

1505

1689

1914

RUSSIAN EXPANSION

From the 14th century, Russia grew in size as a result of conquests. Part of the reason for this expansion was the search for a port which was ice-free all year round. The pioneers who settled in the new areas, such as Poland, lived mostly on tiny farms, scratching out a miserable existence. Power lay in the hands of the czar and a few very rich nobles. Communication across such vast distances was difficult, so the czars had no idea of the problems and poverty of their people.

RUSSIA

882 Vikings establish first Russian state at Kiev.

988 Prince Vladimir I forces all Russians to accept the Russian Orthodox faith.

1237 Mongols invade Russia.

1480 Ivan III breaks Mongol control of Russia; brings other cities under Moscow's control.

1547 Ivan IV introduces serfdom, which forces the peasants to stay in one place and work for a landowner.

1604-13 "Time of Troubles": Russia suffers civil wars as rival groups struggle for power.

1613 Michael Romanov becomes czar. Romanovs rule Russia until 1917.

1703 Czar Peter the Great begins to build his new capital at St. Petersburg. Brings in experts to modernize industry.

1774 Peasants' revolt.

1812 French emperor Napoleon invades Russia. Most of his army dies in the freezing Russian winter.

1825 "Decembrist Uprising": Army officers demand an elected government.

1905 Japan defeats Russia in Russo-Japanese War. A workers' revolution forces Nicholas II to establish a parliament, called the Duma.

1914-17 Russia fights against Germany in World War I. Discontent pushes the people into revolution.

1917-91 Communists control Russia.

1991 Soviet Union collapses; Russia independent.

CATHERINE THE GREAT

During Catherine's reign (1762-96) Russia's territory expanded. Catherine created a glittering court which was much admired outside Russia. She gave more power to the nobles but did nothing for the peasants. They were used as slave labor in distant areas and suffered untold misery.

Russian peasants working on the land

Catherine the Great

FABERGÉ EGG

In 1884, Peter Fabergé became jeweler to the czars. He created magnificent pieces covered in gold, jewels, and colored enamel for the rich nobles of the Russian court. His most famous creations were the Easter eggs he made for czars Alexander III and Nicholas II.

ALEXANDER II

Czar Alexander II (1818-81) realized that Russia had to keep up with the West in order to succeed. He freed the peasants and helped them buy land. But they were disappointed with the quality of their land and the high taxes they had to pay. In 1881, a revolutionary group assassinated Alexander.

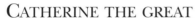

Find out more

COMMUNISM
NAPOLEONIC WARS
RUSSIAN FEDERATION
RUSSIAN REVOLUTION
SOVIET UNION, HISTORY OF

RUSSIAN REVOLUTION

IN 1917, THE PEOPLE OF RUSSIA staged a revolution that was to change the course of modern history. The Russian people were desperate for change. Russia was suffering serious losses against Germany in World War I. Food and fuel were scarce. Many people were starving. Czar Nicholas II, ruler of Russia, was blamed for much of this. In March 1917 (February in the old Russian calendar), a general strike broke out in Petrograd (today's St. Petersburg). The strike was in protest against the chaos caused by the war. Nicholas was forced to give up his throne, and a group of revolutionaries, called the Mensheviks, formed a provisional government. This government soon fell because it failed to end the war. In November, the Bolsheviks, a more extreme revolutionary group, seized power. They ended the war with Germany and, led by Vladimir Lenin, set up the world's first communist state. They declared the country a Soviet republic. This revolution was the first communist takeover of a government. It inspired more to follow.

1905 REVOLUTION
In 1905 unarmed workers marched on Nicholas II's Winter Palace in St. Petersburg. The czar's troops fired on the crowd. Nicholas set up an elected parliament, or Duma. But the Duma had no real power, so distrust of the czar grew.

OCTOBER REVOLUTION
What is known as the October Revolution broke out on November 7, 1917 (October 25 in the old Russian calendar used before the revolution). The cruiser *Aurora* fired blanks across the Neva River at the headquarters of the Menshevik government in the Winter Palace. The Bolsheviks also attacked other important buildings in Petrograd.

LENIN
Vladimir Lenin (1870-1924), founder of the Bolshevik party, believed in the ideas of the German writer Karl Marx. He lived mostly in exile from Russia, until the October Revolution. He was a powerful speaker whose simple slogan of "Peace, land, and bread" persuaded many Russians to support the Bolsheviks. He ruled Russia as dictator.

NICHOLAS II
Russia's last czar, Nicholas (1868-1918), was out of touch with his subjects. They blamed him for the Russian defeats in World War I (1914-18), where he commanded at the front. His sinister adviser, a monk named Rasputin, was widely hated and feared. After Nicholas gave up the throne, he and his family were arrested. The Bolsheviks shot them all the following year.

RUSSIAN REVOLUTION

1914 Russia joins World War I against Germany and Austria.

1916 One million Russian soldiers die after German offensive. Prices in Russia rise.

1917 March International Women's Day march in Petrograd turns into bread riot. The Mensheviks set up a provisional government. The Bolsheviks organize another government made up of committees called soviets.

July Lenin flees Russia.

October Lenin returns to Petrograd.

November 7 Armed workers seize buildings in Petrograd.

November 15 Bolsheviks control Petrograd.

Find out more

COMMUNISM
HUMAN RIGHTS
RUSSIA, HISTORY OF
SOVIET UNION, HISTORY OF
WORLD WAR I

SAILING AND BOATING

ONCE A VITAL MEANS of transportation, sailing is now a popular recreational sport. The smallest sailing boats are one-person crafts, but oceangoing racing yachts have a crew of 20 or more. Anyone can learn to sail a simple sailing boat. There is a rudder to point it in the right direction, and a keel or centerboard to stop it from slipping sideways. The skill of sailing lies in the positioning of the sail according to the direction of the wind. Rowing and canoeing do not rely on the wind. Rowing with one oar per person is called sculling. Canoeing is a popular way of touring rivers and lakes at a leisurely pace. "Whitewater" canoeing is far from leisurely. Canoeists have to paddle through fast-flowing rivers while avoiding hidden rocks.

AMERICA'S CUP
One of the world's most famous ocean sailing races is the America's Cup. Two yachts, which represent two different nations, race over a triangular course, and the nation that wins receives the cup as a prize. The trophy is named for the US yacht *America*, which won the cup in 1851. The New York Yacht Club kept the cup for 132 years by beating all challengers.

Pieces of colored plastic show the crew how the wind is blowing across the sail.

Aluminum mast is lighter and stronger than traditional wood.

Sails are made of artificial fiber such as Dacron.

The spinnaker pole supports the billowing spinnaker sail that the crew raises when the wind is behind the boat.

The mainsheet adjusts the position of the mainsail.

Windows enable the crew to see through the sail.

Ropes on sailing vessels are called sheets or lines.

The centerboard drops into a slot to keep the boat on course, but lifts out so the boat can sail in shallow water.

Tiller extension bar lets the helm turn the rudder while leaning out to balance the boat.

RACING SAILBOAT
Most races are for matched boats of the same class, or type. In this way, sailing skill and tactics determine the winner, rather than the boat's design. Even the simplest training sailboat can compete in races. Some racing sailboats require a crew of more than one.

Rudder steers the boat through the water.

Hull is made of glass-reinforced plastic, which is lightweight but very strong.

The crew member who controls the boat's direction is called the helm.

CANOEING
The kayak, an enclosed canoe, is used for touring or racing. It is propelled with a double-bladed paddle. Canoeists use a single-bladed paddle in open canoes. In Canada canoe racers use a similar paddle and race in a high kneeling position.

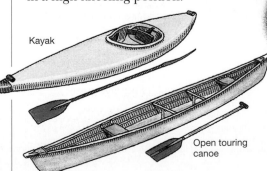

Kayak

Open touring canoe

SAFETY
Sailors must always take safety precautions such as wearing a life belt or a life jacket. A sailing boat should have a bucket for bailing out water and a paddle in case the wind drops to levels too insufficient to sail by.

THE UNIVERSITY BOAT RACE
Every year since 1829 crews from Oxford and Cambridge universities in England have held a now-famous rowing match. The two rowing boats race over a winding 4-mile (6.4-km) course on the Thames River in London.

Find out more
NAVIGATION
PORTS AND WATERWAYS
SHIPS AND BOATS

SATELLITES

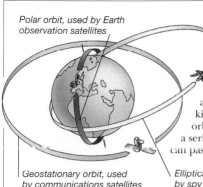

Polar orbit, used by Earth observation satellites

SATELLITE ORBITS
A communications satellite takes exactly 24 hours to orbit the Earth, so it appears to remain fixed over one spot. This kind of orbit is called geostationary. A polar orbit allows a satellite to see the whole Earth in a series of strips. In an elliptical orbit, a satellite can pass low over a selected part of the Earth.

Geostationary orbit, used by communications satellites

Elliptical orbit, used by spy satellites

Solar panels generate electricity from sunlight to power the satellite.

Radar altimeter provides data on wind speed, ocean currents, and tides.

WHEN AIRCRAFT and balloons first took to the skies, the people in them were amazed at their new view of the world. From hundreds of feet up they could see the layout of a large city, the shape of a coastline, or the patchwork of fields on a farm. Today, we have an even wider view. Satellites circle the Earth, not hundreds of feet, but hundreds of miles above the ground. From this great height, satellites provide a unique image of our planet. Some have cameras that take photographs of land and sea, giving information about the changing environment on Earth. Others plot weather patterns or peer out into space and send back data (information) about planets and stars. All of these are artificial satellites that have been launched into space from Earth. However, the word satellite actually means any object that moves around a planet while being held in orbit by the planet's gravity. There are countless natural satellites in the universe: the Earth has one, which is the Moon.

Infrared scanner measures water vapor in the atmosphere and the temperatures of seas and cloud tops.

Earth observation satellite ERS-2

Antenna for transmitting data back to Earth

ARTIFICIAL SATELLITES
There are many types of artificial satellite. Weather satellites observe rain, storms, and clouds, and measure land and sea temperatures. Communications satellites send radio and television signals from one part of the Earth to another. Spy satellites observe military targets from low altitudes and send back detailed pictures to ground stations. Earth observation satellites monitor vegetation, air and water pollution, population changes, and geological factors such as mineral deposits.

MAPPING THE EARTH
Resources satellites take pictures of the Earth's surface. The cameras have various filters so they can pick up infrared (heat) radiation and different colors of light. Vegetation, for instance, reflects infrared light strongly, showing up forests and woodlands. Computer-generated colors are used to pick out areas with different kinds of vegetation and minerals.

SPUTNIK 1
On October 4, 1957, the Soviet Union launched the world's first artificial satellite, *Sputnik 1*. It carried a radio transmitter that sent signals back to Earth until *Sputnik 1* burned up in the atmosphere 92 days later.

Satellite map image of San Francisco Bay, California. Clearly visible are two bridges: the Golden Gate Bridge on the left and the Bay Bridge on the right.

NATURAL SATELLITES
There are more than 150 known natural satellites, or moons, in the solar system. Most of these orbit (move around) the four giant outer planets: Jupiter, Saturn, Uranus, and Neptune. The largest moons are bigger than Pluto, the smallest planet; the smallest moons are only a few miles across and have irregular, potato-like shapes.

The planet Jupiter with two of its moons, Io (left) and Europa (right)

Find out more

ASTRONOMY
GEOLOGY
NAVIGATION
SPACE FLIGHT
TELEPHONES
TELEVISION AND VIDEO

SCANDINAVIA

AT THE FAR NORTH of Europe are the countries of Scandinavia, which have much in common, yet in some ways could not be more different. Their economies are closely linked, but each uses its own currency. They are all independent nations; but in times past, several of them have been bound together in a single union. Each country has its own language, yet strong cultural ties exist between the nations. Landscapes are different, however. Denmark is flat – the biggest hill is only 567 ft (173 m) high – and most of the country is very fertile; but both Norway and Iceland are mountainous, with little farmland. Sweden and Finland are dotted with lakes – more than 180,000 in Finland alone. Greenland is almost entirely covered in ice and snow. Politically, the different countries cooperate through the Nordic Council, which aims to strengthen ties between the nations. Denmark, Finland, and Sweden are members of the European Union, a trade alliance of European nations. Most Scandinavians enjoy a high standard of living and an active cultural life. Norway and Sweden award the annual Nobel Prizes for sciences, literature, and the promotion of peace.

Cross country skiing is a popular sport in many parts of Scandinavia.

Geographically, Scandinavia consists of the Norwegian/Swedish peninsula. But the name is also used widely to include Denmark and Finland. The Faeroe Islands, Iceland, and Greenland are often associated with Scandinavia.

The frozen north of Scandinavia, called Lappland, is the home of 40,000 Lapplanders. Many of them live by herding reindeer for their hides and meat.

FINLAND

Although Finland is part of Scandinavia, it is closely tied to the Russian Federation, and the two countries share a long frontier. Until 1917, Finland was a province of the old Russian empire. Today Finnish trade is still conducted with the Russian Federation. Forests cover two-thirds of Finland, and the paper industry dominates the economy. Shipbuilding and tourism are also important. Finland is one of the world's northernmost countries, and throughout the winter months only the southern coastline is free of ice.

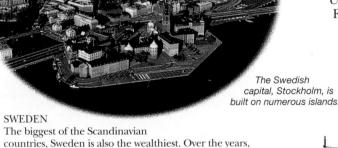

The Swedish capital, Stockholm, is built on numerous islands.

SWEDEN
The biggest of the Scandinavian countries, Sweden is also the wealthiest. Over the years, the Swedes have developed a taxation and social welfare system that has created a good standard of living for most people. As a result, few people in Sweden are either very rich or very poor. The population numbers about 8.9 million, most of whom live in the south and east of the country; the mountainous north lies within the Arctic Circle and is almost uninhabited.

NORWAY
Shipping, forestry, and fishing were the traditional Norwegian industries. In 1970, however, oil was discovered in the Norwegian sector of the North Sea, and the country's fortunes were transformed. Today, the 4.5 million Norwegians enjoy a high standard of living, low taxes, and almost no unemployment. But Norway has almost no natural resources apart from oil and timber. The wooded country is mountainous and indented with numerous inlets, or fjords, from the North Atlantic Ocean. These fjords make communications difficult between the cities in the south and the more sparsely populated regions in the north.

Deep-sea fishing is a major occupation throughout Scandinavia.

FISHING
The North Atlantic Ocean provides a rich marine harvest for Scandinavian fishermen. High-quality cod and mackerel are caught in the cold, nutrient-rich waters. Fish farming, especially in the fjords, is on the increase in Norway, the world's largest salmon producer.

NORTH SEA OIL

Discoveries of oil and natural gas beneath the North Sea began in 1959, when a seaward extension of a major natural gas field in the northeastern part of the Netherlands was identified. Within two decades, natural gas production sites were located along a 100-mile band stretching from the Netherlands to eastern England. Farther north, Norway's first offshore oilfield went into production in 1971. Today, Norway's economy largely depends on its abundant natural resources, and the country is Europe's largest oil producer. Norway is self-sufficient in natural gas and oil.

North Sea oil, produced on oil rigs such as the one pictured above, is exported globally. Norway is a world leader in the construction of drilling platforms.

FJORDS

During the ice age, glaciers carved steep-sided valleys in the rocks along Norway's coast. As the ice melted, the North Sea flowed in, creating fjords. Glaciers have cut hundreds of fjords into Scandinavia's Atlantic coastline. Fjords are usually deeper in their middle and upper reaches than at the seaward end. The water in these inlets is calmer than in the open sea.

SAUNAS

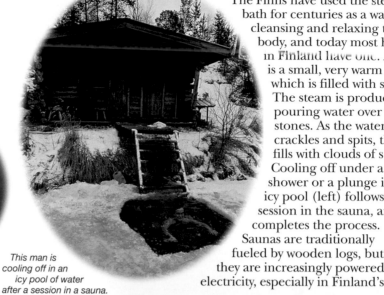

Finland is home to the sauna, which has become a national institution. The Finns have used the steam bath for centuries as a way of cleansing and relaxing the body, and today most houses in Finland have one. A sauna is a small, very warm room which is filled with steam. The steam is produced by pouring water over hot stones. As the water crackles and spits, the air fills with clouds of steam. Cooling off under a cold shower or a plunge in an icy pool (left) follows a session in the sauna, and completes the process. Saunas are traditionally fueled by wooden logs, but they are increasingly powered by electricity, especially in Finland's cities.

This man is cooling off in an icy pool of water after a session in a sauna.

COPENHAGEN

Copenhagen (right) is the capital of Denmark, and about one-quarter of all Danish people live in and around the city. Copenhagen is on the east coast of Zealand, the largest of 482 islands that make up about 30 percent of Denmark. The low-lying Jutland Peninsula to the west makes up the rest of the land area.

FARMING IN SWEDEN

The fertile soil in southern Sweden makes this area the most productive farming area in the country, with pig farming, dairy farming, and crops such as wheat, barley, and potatoes. Many Swedish farmers belong to agricultural cooperatives which process and distribute their crops.

The farming regions close to the Gulf of Bothnia is best known for dairy products.

The tranquil waters of a Norwegian fjord. Fjords often reach great depths. The great weight of the glaciers which formed them eroded the bottom of the valley far below sea level. The best farming land is found in the lowland areas around fjords.

Find out more

ANTARCTICA
ARCTIC
EUROPE
SCANDINAVIA, HISTORY OF

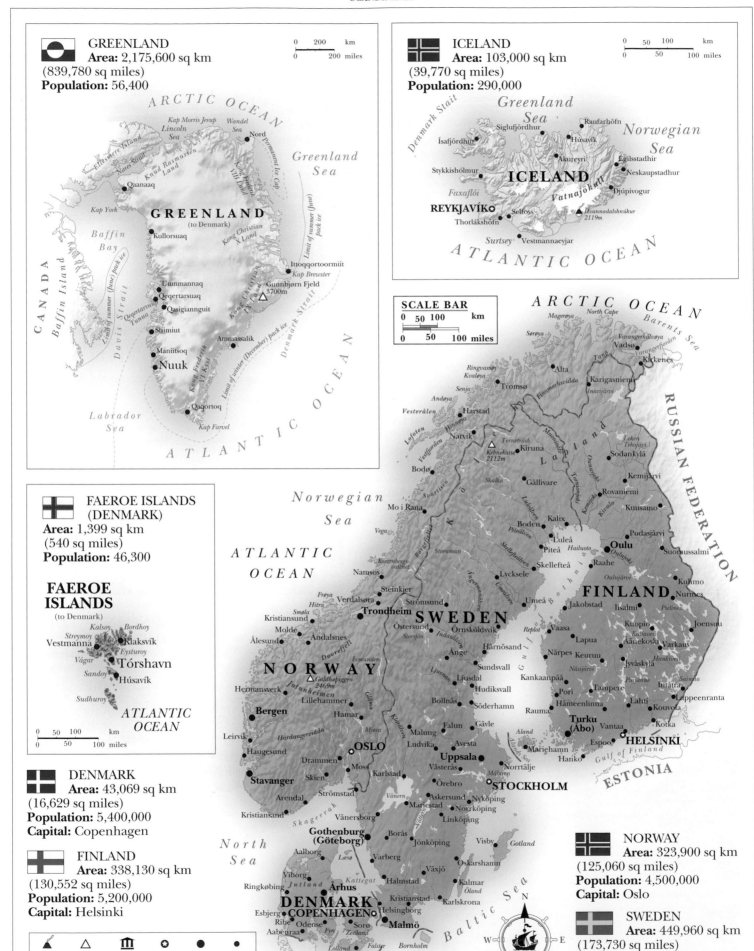

GREENLAND
Area: 2,175,600 sq km
(839,780 sq miles)
Population: 56,400

0 200 km
0 200 miles

ARCTIC OCEAN

Kap Morris Jesup
Lincoln Sea
Wandel Sea
Nord
Greenland Sea

Kap York
Ellesmere Island
Nares Strait
Knud Rasmussen Land
Kong Frederik VIII Land
Permanent Ice Cap
Limit of summer (June) pack ice

Qaanaaq
Baffin Bay
GREENLAND
(to Denmark)
Kong Christian IX Land
Limit of summer (June) pack ice

CANADA
Baffin Island
Kullorsuaq
Davis Strait
Uummannaq
Ittoqqortoormiit
Kap Brewster
Gunnbjørn Fjeld 3700m
Kong Christian IX Land
Qeqertarsuaq
Qasigiannguit
Qeqertarsuup Tunua
Sisimiut
Ammassalik
Denmark Strait
Maniitsoq
Nuuk

Labrador Sea
Qaqortoq
Kap Farvel
ATLANTIC OCEAN

ICELAND
Area: 103,000 sq km
(39,770 sq miles)
Population: 290,000

0 50 100 km
0 50 100 miles

Denmark Strait
Greenland Sea
Norwegian Sea
Siglufjördhur
Raufarhöfn
Ísafjördhur
Húsavík
Akureyri
Egilsstadhir
Stykkishólmur
Neskaupstadhur
ICELAND
Djúpivogur
Faxaflói
Vatnajökull
REYKJAVÍK
Selfoss
Hvannadalshnúkur 2119m
Thorlákshöfn
Surtsey
Vestmannaeyjar
ATLANTIC OCEAN

SCALE BAR
0 50 100 km
0 50 100 miles

ARCTIC OCEAN
Magerøya
North Cape
Barents Sea
Sørøya
Vardø
Varangerhalvøya
Vadsø
Varangerfjorden
Kirkenes
Alta
Ringvassøy
Kvaløya
Karigasniemi
Tromsø
Finnmarksvidda
Inarijärvi
Senja
Andøya
Harstad
Sodankylä
Vesterålen
Hinnøya
Narvik
Loken Tekojärvi
Lofoten
Kebnekaise 2112m
Kiruna
Kemijärvi
Bodø
Vestfjorden
Torneträsk
Lapland
Rovaniemi
Kuusamo
Gällivare
Skalka
Pudasjärvi

FAEROE ISLANDS
(DENMARK)
Area: 1,399 sq km
(540 sq miles)
Population: 46,300

FAEROE ISLANDS
(to Denmark)

Kalsoy
Bordhoy
Streymoy
Klaksvík
Vestmanna
Eysturoy
Tórshavn
Vágar
Húsavík
Sandoy
Suduroy
ATLANTIC OCEAN

0 50 100 km
0 50 100 miles

Mo i Rana
Kalix
Boden
Luleå
Oulu
Norwegian Sea
Vega
Piteå
Hailuoto
ATLANTIC OCEAN
Kvitberysvattnet
Storuman
Skellefteå
Raahe
Namsos
Lycksele
Umeå
Oulujärvi
Steinkjer
Verdalsøra
Strömsund
Umeå
Kuhmo
Frøya
Trondheim
SWEDEN
Örnsköldsvik
Nurmes
Hitra
Smøla
Östersund
Jakobstad
Iisalmi
Kristiansund
Storsjön
Härnösand
Vaasa
Pielinen
Molde
Andalsnes
Indalsälven
Ange
Replot
Joensuu
Ålesund
Dovrefjell
Sundsvall
Kuopio
Ljungan
Närpes
Kallavesi
Galdhøpiggen 2469m
Ljusdal
Kankanpää
Keuruu
Äänekoski
Varkaus
NORWAY
Jotunheimen
Hudiksvall
Pori
Näsijärvi
Jyväskylä
Haukivesi
Hermansverk
Lillehammer
Bollnäs
Söderhamn
Tampere
Päijänne
Inkeroinen
Hamar
Rauma
Hämeenlinna
Lahti
Lappeenranta
Bergen
Falun
Gävle
Leirvik
Klarälven
Malung
Avesta
Turku
Kouvola
Hardangervidda
(Åbo)
Vantaa
Kotka
Haugesund
OSLO
Ludvika
Mariehamn
Espoo
Drammen
Uppsala
HELSINKI
Moss
Västerås
Åland
Hanko
Gulf of Finland
Stavanger
Skien
Karlstad
Norrtälje
Arendal
Strömstad
Örebro
STOCKHOLM
Åland Sea
ESTONIA
Kristiansand
Askersund
Nyköping
Vänern
Mälaren
DENMARK
Area: 43,069 sq km
(16,629 sq miles)
Population: 5,400,000
Capital: Copenhagen
Vänersborg
Mariestad
Norrköping
Linköping
North Sea
Gothenburg
(Göteborg)
Borås
Jönköping
Visby
Gotland
NORWAY
Area: 323,900 sq km
(125,060 sq miles)
Population: 4,500,000
Capital: Oslo
Varberg
Växjö
Oskarshamn
Aalborg
Læsø
Halmstad
Kalmar
Öland
FINLAND
Area: 338,130 sq km
(130,552 sq miles)
Population: 5,200,000
Capital: Helsinki
Viborg
Jutland
Ringkøbing
Århus
Kattegat
Kristianstad
Karlskrona
SWEDEN
Area: 449,960 sq km
(173,730 sq miles)
Population: 8,900,000
Capital: Stockholm
Esbjerg
Helsingborg
Ribe
Odense
Fyn
Soro
Malmö
Baltic Sea
Aabenraa
Zealand
DENMARK
COPENHAGEN
Lolland
Falster
Nykøbing
Bornholm
W   E
GERMANY

Volcano Mountain Ancient monument Capital city Large city/town Small city/town

580

HISTORY OF
SCANDINAVIA

HISTORICALLY, the region called Scandinavia, in northern Europe, consisted of Norway, Sweden, and Denmark. Today, Finland and Iceland are also considered part of Scandinavia. All are independent countries, but their history has been intertwined since ancient times. Seafaring Vikings were among the earliest people to live in the region of Scandinavia, more than 1,000 years ago. During the 900s, the three separate nations of Denmark, Norway, and Sweden emerged for the first time. Over the next few centuries, the three countries were often united. During the 16th century, Sweden broke away to build its own empire and became a huge European power. This left Norway and Denmark closely linked. In 1814, Norway came under Swedish rule. But in 1905, Norway became an independent nation. Today, the Scandinavian nations are world leaders in environmental and health issues.

KING CANUTE
In 1014, Canute (c.995-1035) became king of Denmark. He invaded England in 1015 and conquered Norway in 1028. Canute ruled his huge empire with justice and fairness until his death.

MARGARET I
Margaret I (1353-1412) became queen of Denmark (1375), Norway (1380), and Sweden (1389). In 1397, she united the three countries in the Kalmar Union.

Thatched roof

Cowshed

Hollowed-out tree trunks were fixed with wheels and used as carts.

Storehouse

Livestock such as geese stayed close to the house.

Women cooked on the central hearth.

People slept in wooden beds with animal hide covers.

Chopped firewood

THOR
The Vikings worshiped many different gods. Thor was one of the most powerful. As ruler of the sky, he controlled the weather and was the god of thunder, lightning, rain, and storms. Vikings prayed to him for good harvests and good luck. He gave his name to Thor's day, or Thursday.

VIKING HOUSE
The Vikings built sturdy one-story houses with sloping roofs. The houses had timber frames, wooden or stone walls, and thatched roofs. The hearth was the central feature in the house. It provided heat, light, and a place to cook. Viking houses had no windows, so the one room was usually very smoky.

SWEDEN

In 1523, Sweden left the Kalmar Union and declared independence under King Gustavus I (1496-1560). Gustavus introduced many reforms to strengthen Sweden. He made Protestantism the state religion, built up an efficient army, and improved the country's economy. During the reign of Gustavus II, which lasted from 1611 to 1632, Sweden became a major European power. Gustavus increased Swedish territory, gaining most of Finland from Russia. He also built a strong navy.

EDVARD GRIEG
During the 19th century, Sweden ruled Norway. The Norwegian composer Edvard Grieg (1843-1907) supported independence. He became known as the Voice of Norway, because he wrote patriotic music based on old Norwegian folk songs. His most famous work is music for the playwright Ibsen's *Peer Gynt*.

GREAT NORTHERN WAR

Between 1563 and 1658, the Swedes fought wars with their neighbors that resulted in the Swedish domination of the Baltic Sea, an important waterway. For the next 40 years there was an uneasy peace in the region. Then, in 1700, Russia, Denmark, and Poland declared war to end Swedish power. The Great Northern War, as it was called, lasted for 21 years. The Swedes lost lands in the east to Russia.

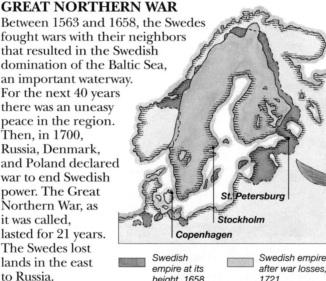

St. Petersburg

Stockholm

Copenhagen

Swedish empire at its height, 1658

Swedish empire after war losses, 1721

CHRISTIAN X
Germany invaded Norway and Denmark during World War II (1939-45). The Norwegian king, Haakon VII, went into exile in Britain, and Vidkun Quisling, a German supporter, took over. The word quisling is still used today to describe a traitor. In Denmark, King Christian X (left) led passive resistance to German rule. The Germans demanded that all Jews wear a yellow star, so Christian stated that he, too, would wear a star. The Danes then helped many Jews escape to neutral Sweden.

GRO BRUNDTLAND
In 1987, Norwegian Prime Minister Gro Brundtland published *Our Common Future: The Brundtland Report*, a major work that described environmental problems and their effects on the poor of the world. It also suggested solutions.

NOBEL PRIZE
Swedish chemist Alfred Nobel (1833-96) invented dynamite. He disliked its military uses, and left money in his will to fund prizes to promote peace and learning. Prizes – for physics, chemistry, medicine, literature, and peace – have been awarded since 1901.

___ *Find out more* ___

SCANDINAVIA
VIKINGS

SCHOOLS

Most people remember starting school. Schools vary depending on the local culture of a country, but most of us felt the same mixture of confusion and excitement on our first day at school. Many of us share other early school experiences, too. Schools all over the world aim to teach the basic skills that we need to live in society. For this reason most schoolchildren take classes in reading, writing, and arithmetic. In most Western countries, these early school years are known as primary or elementary school, because they are a preparation for later years of education. Reading skills, for example, are essential for everyone throughout their lives. In some other countries, though, school ends for many children at the age of 10, or even earlier. Schooling is expensive, and only the wealthier countries can afford to operate free schools for all children beyond the first four or five years. Even in those countries where primary education is free, many families need the extra money that younger children can earn; so millions of children work as well as – or instead of – attending school.

MEDIEVAL TEACHING
Discipline was strict and the school day was long for the 13th-century student. There was little reading and writing, and students learned mainly by listening to the teacher and asking questions. However, by the end of the 15th century, books of Latin grammar were a popular teaching aid.

Learning about other peoples, languages, and places helps us understand the world around us.

Most schoolchildren enjoy painting and sculpture; experience in school can lead to an appreciation of the great artists.

Playing a musical instrument demands good coordination and precise timing. Performing with other musicians means learning the skill of cooperation.

SCHOOLS IN THE 19TH CENTURY
In the last century free schooling for all became common in many European countries and in the United States. The school schedule was similar to that of today, but learning was not as exciting as it is now. For example, 19th-century teachers expected children to remember long lists of facts which they recited out loud in the classroom.

OPEN-AIR CLASSROOMS
In parts of Africa and India where money is too scarce to provide enough school buildings, many classes take place outdoors. In countries where the population is scattered, schools are far apart and children may walk several miles to learn. When the nearest school is very distant, as in Australia, a two-way radio brings the school to the pupil.

THE SOCIAL SIDE
School life includes learning to share, communicate, and get along with others. Members of a class must learn to work together and listen to other people's opinions and ideas. The school is also a place where young people learn how to make friends and cope with differences.

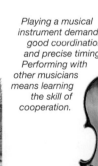

BRAILLE
Children with a mental or physical disability may find learning difficult. Special equipment helps them study. Braille books with raised letters enable the sight-impaired to read. Children with hearing loss learn sign language or lip reading.

Regular exercise not only improves physical health, but is also vital for mental wellbeing. Physical education teaches children about discipline and endurance, and encourages both teamwork and the ability to perform as an individual.

Both boys and girls study food technology – planning a meal, shopping to a budget, preparation, and presentation – as well as the essentials of a healthy and nutritious diet to prepare them for an independent adult life.

The ability to calculate and measure is essential in everyday life, as well as in many careers. Mathematical skills also improve logic and aid problem-solving in other scientific subjects.

HISTORY OF AMERICAN SCHOOLS

Colonists established the first schools in the early 1600s. Students of all grades learned together, usually in a single room. In frontier areas, one-room schoolhouses were the norm until the 1900s (above). Students were taught reading, writing, arithmetic, and religion. In the 1800s, the demand for public education grew. States collected taxes to pay for new schools, and boards of education set school policies.

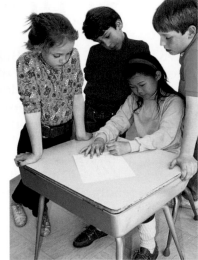

KINDS OF SCHOOLS

Most American children spend 12 years in school. At age five or six, many children enter kindergarten, to prepare them for formal education. Elementary schools have six to eight grades, and teach students basic subjects. Students attend junior high schools to ease the transition between elementary and secondary schools. High schools provide the final four to six years of a student's education. Classes are designed to prepare them for college, and also include vocational programs to teach job skills.

HOW SCHOOLS WORK

Public schools are controlled by each state, and financed by taxpayers. School districts run the schools, with most decision-making in the hands of a board of education. School boards hire teachers, set educational targets, and handle school budgets. They also choose principals, who direct the day-to-day running of a school.

SCHOOL BUS

In the late 19th century students traveled to school on horse-drawn wagons. However, by the 1930s, vehicles specially designed for student transportation were available. Today, more than 24 million students use school buses. The familiar yellow fleet is the largest mass transportation system in the country, traveling more than 4.5 billion miles a year.

A school principal distributes mail to children at a school in the Florida Keys.

GRADUATION

High school students celebrate the end of their compulsory school years with a commencement, or graduation, ceremony (right). Students wear a graduation cap and gown, a tradition that dates back to the 12th century, when the first European colleges were founded. Students who successfully complete their studies are awarded a document called a diploma.

Students sing a patriotic song at a Flag Day Observance ceremony.

EXTRACURRICULAR ACTIVITIES

Many schools sponsor a variety of activities outside the classroom. These extracurricular activities give students a chance to explore new interests and develop their social skills through participating in student government, representing their school in sports, or working in the local community.

Find out more

COLONIES
and colonial America
EDUCATION
UNITED STATES, HISTORY OF

SCIENCE

THERE ARE MANY FORMS OF SCIENCE, and together the sciences seek to understand the nature and behavior of the universe and everything in it. Science comes from the Latin word for "to know." Scientists find out what they want to know by practical methods. They observe, take measurements, make experiments, and write down the results. There are four main categories (types) of science: natural sciences, physical sciences, technological sciences, and social sciences. Natural sciences include the life sciences, such as biology and botany, and earth sciences, such as geology. Physical sciences include physics and chemistry. Technological science includes engineering, and uses information discovered by scientists to make or build things in the real world. Social sciences study people, and include anthropology and psychology. All the sciences depend on mathematics.

A glass rod in a beaker of water looks bent because light waves travel slower through water than through air.

PHYSICS
Physics is the study of matter and energy and how they work together. Because there are many different kinds of matter and forms of energy, there are many different branches of physics. Optics, for example, looks at the different way light waves can behave. For instance, they travel at different speeds through space, air, glass, or water.

SCIENTIFIC METHOD
Scientific method involves using observation and hypothesis (theory) to explain things, and then testing these theories with experiments. To be sure that their results are accurate, scientists always follow strict rules when making an experiment. A sample of the materials used in the experiment is set aside as a "control." If the result is unusual, the control materials can be tested to make sure that they have not been changed and so affected the result of the experiment.

A simple experiment to find out how much salt can be dissolved in water

A measured amount of salt is mixed in to a measured amount of water.

More salt is added to the water until the salt no longer dissolves, but sinks to the bottom of the jar. This is called the saturation point.

Water and salt act as a control for the study.

Bean shoot

Shoot grows up toward the sun.

LIFE SCIENCES
Any of the sciences that study living things is called a life science. Biology is the study of life of all kinds, botany is the study of plants, and zoology is the study of animals. Because animal and plant life depend on each other, scientists also study them together. Ecology is the study of the relationships between living things of all kinds and how they fit in with and affect their environments.

Roots absorb water and nutrients.

EARTH SCIENCES
Geography and geology are earth sciences. Earth scientists study the structure of our planet and the way it changes. The study of rocks and fossils can tell us a lot about the way the planet and its life have evolved. Since Earth is a living planet, the earth sciences are linked to the life sciences.

Geologists study rocks and crystals.

Chrysocolla

Cyanotrichite

SOCIAL SCIENCES
The sciences that study people are called social sciences. There are various kinds. Anthropology is the study of the life and culture of the whole of humanity. Sociology studies the way humans behave together in groups; it looks at how families work, how society is made up, what makes it change, and how the changes affect people. Psychology is also a social science, but it looks at how people behave as individuals.

Find out more

BIOLOGY
CHEMISTRY
EARTH
PHYSICS
ROCKS AND MINERALS

HISTORY OF
SCIENCE

SPACE TRAVEL, computers, and reliable medical care are just a few of the things that owe their existence to scientists and inventors. Scientists study the natural world, from distant galaxies to tiny atoms, and try to explain what they see. The work of a scientist is based on a cycle of experiment, observation, and theorization (making theories). For instance, in the 17th century, English scientist Isaac Newton experimented with sunlight passing through a prism. From the spectrum (bands of colors) that he observed, he suggested the theory that white light is a mixture of colors. Inventors are people who think of a new idea that can be put into practice. An invention may be the result of a scientific discovery, such as the laser, which Theodore Maiman (born 1927) built because of his knowledge of light and atoms. However, this is not always the case. Early people invented the lever before they knew how it worked. Whatever their chosen fields, scientists and inventors have one thing in common: they are people of rare insight who make discoveries new to the world.

ANCIENT TIMES

Early people first invented tools about 2 million years ago. About 10,000 years ago, people began to settle in communities and started farming and building. The first civilizations grew up in the Middle East, Africa, India, and China. There, people studied the sun and stars, built simple clocks, developed mathematics, and discovered how to make metals and pottery.

This stone blade was used about 200,000 years ago in Egypt.

The plow was invented in about 4000 B.C.

The wheel was invented in about 3500 B.C.

The pump was invented in the 2nd century B.C.

Hero of Greece built the first simple steam engine in the 1st century A.D.

GREEKS AND ROMANS

From about 600 B.C., the Greeks began to study their world. Great philosophers (thinkers) such as Pythagoras developed the "scientific method" – the principle of observation and experiment that is still the basis of science today. The Greeks studied mathematics and astronomy and invented simple machines. At around the same time, the Romans used Greek scientific ideas to help them build great structures.

ARCHIMEDES

Greek scientist Archimedes (287-212 B.C.) explained how levers and pulleys work and discovered how things float. This idea is said to have come to him while he was in his bath.

A balloon first carried people in 1783.

Archimedes's screw was a device for raising water.

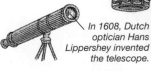

In 1608, Dutch optician Hans Lippershey invented the telescope.

ISAAC NEWTON

In 1666, Isaac Newton (1642-1727) proposed the daring idea that gravity is a universal force, keeping planets and moons in their orbits as well as causing things to fall to the ground. Newton (right) also put forward the famous laws of motion, and found that white light is composed of the colors in the rainbow.

LEONARDO DA VINCI

The great Italian artist and inventor Leonardo da Vinci (1452-1519) designed many machines, including a parachute and a helicopter. However, these machines were not built in his lifetime.

A.D. 1000-1600

During this period, Arabic civilizations made several discoveries, particularly about the nature of light. After about A.D. 1000, people in Europe began to use the scientific method of the Ancient Greeks. Polish astronomer Nicolaus Copernicus (1473-1543) suggested that the Earth orbits the sun, and Andreas Vesalius (1514-64), a Flemish doctor, made discoveries about human anatomy.

In 1438, Johannes Gutenberg of Germany (c.1398-1468) invented the modern printing process.

1600-1800

Italian scientist Galileo Galilei (1564-1642) made discoveries about force, gravity, and motion. Modern astronomy began in 1609 when German astronomer Johannes Kepler (1571-1630) discovered the laws of planetary motion and Galileo built a telescope to observe the heavens. During the 1700s, the first engines were built by inventors such as James Watt (1736-1819) of Scotland. Chemistry advanced as scientists discovered how everything is composed of chemical elements such as oxygen and hydrogen.

1800-1900

The invention of the battery by Italian Alessandro Volta (1745-1827) led to discoveries about electricity and magnetism by scientists such as Englishman Michael Faraday (1791-1867) and many electrical inventions such as electric light. Englishman John Dalton (1766-1844) and other scientists found out that everything is made of tiny atoms. Frenchman Louis Pasteur (1822-95) showed that bacteria cause disease, which led to better health care. Transportation advanced with the invention of locomotives, powered ships, and cars.

The telephone was invented by a Scottish-American, Alexander Graham Bell, in 1876.

In 1804, Englishman Richard Trevithick invented the steam locomotive.

THOMAS EDISON

Thomas Edison (1847-1931) was one of the world's most successful inventors. He made more than 1,000 inventions, including the record player (patented 1878) and a system for making motion pictures. Edison was also one of the inventors of the electric light bulb.

In 1895, Italian scientist Guglielmo Marconi invented radio transmission.

1900 TO THE PRESENT

Scientists delved into the atom, finding electrons and the nucleus, and then studied the nucleus itself. This led to the invention of nuclear power and to the science of electronics, which brought us television and the computer. Scientists also explored living cells and found new ways of fighting disease. Astronomers studied stars, planets, and distant galaxies. The invention of aircraft and space flight allowed people to travel into the air and out into space.

Le Petit Journal

WRIGHT BROTHERS
In 1903, Orville Wright (1871-1948) and his brother Wilbur (1867-1912) made the first powered airplane flight.

Several scientists developed television during the 1920s. The first public television service started in the 1930s.

Theodore Maiman and Charles Townes invented the first working laser in 1960.

WILLIAM SHOCKLEY
Computers, televisions, and other electronic devices depend on the transistor, invented in 1948 by a team of scientists headed by William Shockley (born 1910). Now millions of transistors can be packed into a tiny microchip.

Artificial satellites were first launched in 1957.

In 1946 a team of American scientists built the first fully electronic computer.

ALBERT EINSTEIN
In 1905 and 1915, the German scientist Albert Einstein (1879-1955) proposed his theories of relativity. They showed that light is the fastest thing in the universe, and that time would slow down, length would shorten, and mass would increase if you could travel at almost the speed of light. The sun's source of energy and nuclear power, and how black holes can exist in space are explained by his discoveries.

MAX PLANCK
In about 1900, German scientist Max Planck (1858-1947) published his quantum theory, which explained the nature of energy and led to many new ideas. For example, although we usually think of light as waves, quantum theory explains how light sometimes seems to behave as tiny particles called photons.

Find out more
BIOLOGY
CHEMISTRY
MEDICINE, HISTORY OF
PHYSICS
RENAISSANCE
SCIENCE
TECHNOLOGY

SCULPTURE

By CARVING SOLID STONE or pouring liquid metal, a sculptor can create art in three dimensions. Like paintings and drawings, the resulting sculpture is a vivid image from the artist's imagination. But unlike paintings, which are flat, sculpture is solid, so that you can often walk around it. Sometimes you can touch the sculpture and feel its texture. But it is the depth of sculpture that makes it so interesting. Looking at a sculpture from a different angle changes its appearance completely. For this reason, city planners often use sculpture to brighten up public parks and other outdoor places. Sculptures of people and animals are called statues. But modern sculptors also create abstract sculptures – works that do not represent any real thing but make the space they occupy more interesting, exciting, or restful.

BAS-RELIEF
Not all sculptures are freestanding. Some, called bas-reliefs, are like raised pictures made of wood, metal, or stone. The sculpted figures project a bit from the background, giving a more lifelike quality. Ancient civilizations often recorded great events in their history in bas-relief panels.

Woodcarvers hit their sharp chisels with a wooden mallet to remove large pieces of wood.

For finer work, they shave wood away by pushing the chisel with their hands.

Modeling clay is so soft that even lightweight tools can shape it.

Metal scrapers are useful for shaving the surface of set plaster.

WOOD SCULPTURE
African carvers are expert in wood sculpture. They cut, shave, and polish the wood to make gleaming statues of people and forest or grassland animals. In Europe, woodcarvers decorated the insides of many churches and cathedrals. English sculptor Grinling Gibbons (1648-1720) carved fruits and flowers from wood and decorated St. Paul's Cathedral, London.

SCULPTOR'S TOOLS
Because sculptors create their art from many different materials, they use a great variety of tools. Hard materials such as stone require powerful cuts from heavy chisels. But to make a sculpture that will be cast in bronze, scrapers and other small tools are all that is needed.

Heavy hammer helps chip stone into shape.

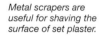

BRONZE CASTING
Most cast sculptures are made of bronze – an alloy, or mixture, of copper and tin. The sculptor creates the original work in a soft material such as clay or plaster. From this master, the sculptor can make an identical copy in wax. Covering the model in plaster and heating it melts away the wax and leaves a perfect mold. Filling the mold with the molten (liquid) metal creates the sculpture. Finally, the sculptor cuts off unwanted metal and sometimes polishes the finished work.

MODERN SCULPTURE
Artists sometimes use sculpture to express ideas about society. American artist Javacheff Christo (born 1935) wraps landscapes and buildings to make people think about the packaging that covers everything they buy.

By wrapping the Pont Neuf, Paris, Christo transformed this French landmark into a work of art.

STONE SCULPTURE
Sculptors work with many kinds of stone, but marble is popular because it does not fracture unpredictably when the sculptor strikes it. Before starting work, the sculptor generally makes a plaster maquette, or small model, of the sculpture. Chipping away with chisels and hammer, the sculptor shapes the stone roughly before making the final cuts. A final polish gives the stone a beautiful finish.

Find out more
METALS
PAINTERS
PAINTING
RENAISSANCE

SEABIRDS

Stormy petrel has tube-shaped nostrils on its bill.

ALL KINDS OF BIRDS live near the sea, gliding over the waves and feeding along the shore or diving for fish. Seabirds belong to a number of different bird groups, all of which live near the sea. Most have webbed feet for swimming, waterproof feathers, and sharp bills for gripping slippery fish. Seabirds include razorbills and guillemots, whose small wings act like flippers for swimming. Other seabirds, such as albatrosses and petrels, have long, slim wings for soaring high in the sky. Gulls and skuas are scavengers and take almost any food, from dead flesh to other seabirds' eggs and chicks. The great skua attacks birds in midflight, making them drop their food, which it then catches. Gannets and boobies dive for fish from 100 ft (30 m). Penguins cannot fly, but they swim expertly with their wings, chasing fish in the oceans south of the equator.

WANDERING ALBATROSS

There are 21 kinds of albatross, and most live south of the equator. Their wings are the longest of any bird, more than 10 ft (3 m) from tip to tip. They glide over the oceans for hours without flapping, picking fish from the water.

HERRING GULL

Noisy and aggressive, herring gulls live in Europe, North America, North Africa, and Asia. They trail after fishing boats for leftovers, visit rubbish dumps, and follow the farmer's plow to feed on worms, insects, and small mammals.

GANNET
A gannet collects grasses for its nest, then returns to the gannetry, its clifftop breeding colony. Sometimes more than 50,000 gannets nest in the same place.

Spear-shaped bill for piercing fish

Long, narrow albatross wings are a perfect shape for gliding on the wind.

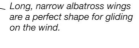
Atlantic puffin

BREEDING COLONIES

Most seabirds raise their young on cliffs and small islands. Their food is nearby, and the chicks are safe from predators on the steep ledges. The noise of a sea bird colony is deafening. Kittiwakes, cormorants, and guillemots are nesting together here, but each nest is well out of the way of all the other birds' stabbing bills.

Cormorants, kittiwakes, and guillemots share the same clifftop nesting place.

Guillemot egg has pointed tip.

PUFFIN
The Atlantic puffin can hold a dozen sand eels or small fish in its big, bright bill. When its bill is full, the puffin carries the food to its chick in the burrow.

A kittiwake's nest is made of pieces of seaweed and plant stuck together with droppings.

EGGS
Guillemots do not make nests. Their eggs are pointed at one end, so they spin in a circle if they roll, and do not fall off the cliff edge.

Find out more
BIRDS
FLIGHT, ANIMAL
MIGRATION, ANIMAL
SEASHORE WILDLIFE

SEALS AND SEA LIONS

WITH THEIR STREAMLINED BODIES, seals and sea lions are well equipped for life in the ocean. Despite their large size, they are speedy, energetic swimmers. A thick layer of blubber under the skin keeps them warm in cold waters, helped by their oily, glossy fur. Seals swim gracefully with alternate strokes of their back flippers. On land, however, they are clumsy without water to support their bodies, so they clamber over the shore by wriggling along on their bellies. Unlike seals, sea lions waddle along quickly on land. Sea lions also sit up on rocks, supported by their front flippers, and tuck their back flippers under their bodies. They use their front flippers like oars as they speed after fish in the sea. There are more than 30 kinds of seals and sea lions.

HARP SEAL
Newborn harp seals have white fur to camouflage them on the ice. After a few weeks their coats change to gray.

CALIFORNIA SEA LION
The best-known performing seals are California sea lions. Thousands of them live off the coast of California. They feed on squid, fish, and other small sea creatures.

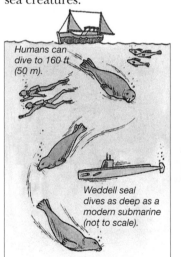

Humans can dive to 160 ft (50 m).

Weddell seal dives as deep as a modern submarine (not to scale).

COMMON SEAL
This seal is also known as the harbor seal, since it is often seen around harbors, ports, and even a short way up rivers. Fish is its main food, and it lives around the northern shores of the Atlantic and Pacific oceans.

WEDDELL SEAL
This seal can dive to 2,000 ft (600 m), holding its breath for almost an hour. Only a submarine can dive to the same depth.

BREEDING COLONIES
Seal colonies are very crowded places during the breeding season – in spring and early summer. All kinds of seals and sea lions come ashore to breed, and live together in their hundreds. The males, or bulls, battle for a territory, as these two huge elephant seal bulls (left) are doing. Once the bulls have established their territory, the pregnant females arrive. Each female gives birth to one pup and feeds it with her milk for several weeks. At 3 tons in weight, the adult elephant seal is the heaviest member of the seal family.

WALRUS
The icy Arctic Ocean is the home of the walrus, a close relative of the seal. Males can grow to more than 10 ft (3 m) in length; females are slightly smaller. These sea mammals paddle with their back flippers and steer with the front ones. Their tough skin is 1 in (2.5 cm) thick, covered with short, coarse hairs. Females give birth to one walrus calf every other year, and the calf may stay with its mother for the first two years. Walruses can live for up to 40 years.

WALRUS TEETH
Walruses have huge upper canine teeth, or tusks, that grow more than 20 in (50 cm) long. Tusks are a status symbol, and the male with the largest tusks usually becomes the leader of the herd. Walruses use their strong tusks for chopping holes in the ice and for hauling themselves out of the water and onto ice floes to rest.

> *Find out more*
> ANIMALS
> MAMMALS
> OCEAN WILDLIFE
> POLAR WILDLIFE

SEASHORE WILDLIFE

591

A SEASHORE IS FORMED wherever the land meets the sea, and can be a polar ice cliff or a tropical beach. The endless motion of the waves, and the tide going in and out, means the shore changes constantly with time. Each seashore has its own selection of plant and animal life, specially adapted to an environment governed by the rhythm of the tides. Inhabitants of the seashore must survive pounding waves, salty seawater, fresh rainwater, drying winds, and hot sunshine. Plants thrive along rocky coasts and in some muddy areas, providing food and shelter for creatures, but they cannot grow on shifting sand or pebbles. Here the inhabitants depend on the tide to bring new supplies of food, in the form of particles floating in the water. Successful seashore animal groups include mollusks and crustaceans, both of which are protected by hard casings.

SEASIDE DANGERS
Most of these baby turtles, hatching from eggs buried by their mother in the sand, will die. They are food for gulls, crabs, lizards and other hunters. Humans also steal the eggs. Conservation efforts are now being made to protect turtles.

Gulls hover over the sea looking for fish, while waders hunt around the shore.

Lace coral can survive harsh rubbing by the wave-washed sand grains. It provides a refuge for animals in its lacy folds.

Common starfish

Many seabirds patrol the coast, searching for food or scavenging on the dead bodies of cast-up sea creatures.

SANDY BEACHES
Waves roll and tumble the tiny grains of sand on the beach. Plants cannot get a firm hold on this type of shore, so they usually grow higher up. Although the sandy beach often looks deserted, dozens of creatures are just below the surface. Sand makes an ideal hiding place for burrowing creatures. Many filter food from the seawater when the tide is in or digest tiny edible particles in the sand.

WADING BIRDS
Waders probe into sand or mud with their long, narrow bills to find shellfish and worms. Large species with the longest bills, such as the curlew (above), reach down several inches for deeply buried items. Smaller waders, such as the black-bellied dunlin, take food from just below the surface.

GHOST CRAB
There are hundreds of kinds of shore crabs along the world's coastlines. They are the seashore's "cleaners;" they consume almost anything edible – living or dead. The ghost crab (above right) takes its name from its ghostly pale color.

RAZOR CLAM
So called because it looks like an old-fashioned cut-throat razor, the razor clam has a hinged shell. The mollusk inside digs quickly by pushing its strong, fleshy foot into the sand and then pulling the shell down.

The burrowing sea anemone's arms spread out to sting and catch small prey. Its stalk, up to 12 in (30 cm) long, is used to hold on to the sand.

SAND HOPPER
Sand hoppers are crustaceans which feed on rotting vegetation. They swarm over seaweed which has washed up on shore and, when in danger, leap away on their strong back legs, hence their name.

EGG CASES
Sharks and rays lay their eggs near the shore, anchored to seaweeds or rocks by clinging tendrils. When the young fishes hatch, the egg cases, known as "mermaid's purses," come free and are often washed up on the shore.

WEEVER FISH
The weever lies half buried in the sand, waiting to gobble up small fishes, crabs, and shrimps. It has poisonous spines on its fins, which give a nasty sting if the fish is stepped on.

SAND EEL
Many animals, from puffins to herrings, feed on the sand eel (right). In turn, the sand eel eats even smaller fishes, as well as worms and plankton. It is not a true eel, but an eel-shaped member of the perch group. It lives in shallow water.

SALT MARSHES

Salt marshes form at the back of the shore, where the tide floods flat areas of land near a river's mouth. Plants such as cordgrass, glasswort, eelgrass, sea club rush, and sea starwort are able to survive in the salt that builds up in the soil. Birds such as geese, gulls, and terns can feed on salt marshes all year round, especially in winter, when inland areas are frozen hard. Some birds use salt marshes as summer breeding grounds, some as stopovers while migrating.

Some large seaweeds are called kelps, such as sugar kelp and oarweed.

CLIFFS

Only a few very agile land animals, such as snakes, can reach precarious cliff ledges. So the ledges are safe nesting sites for a variety of birds, from gannets to gulls, razorbills, and cormorants. A few plants, like thrift ("sea pink"), also gain a foothold, provided they can withstand strong winds and salty spray.

Periwinkles seal themselves to the rock with mucus as the tide retreats, to keep from losing water and drying out.

SEAWEED

There are three main kinds of rocky-shore seaweeds, also known as algae: brown, red, and green. They do not have roots, stems, or leaves. Instead, most anchor themselves to the rocks by structures called holdfasts. The larger brown and red weeds have stemlike stipes, ending in leaflike blades known as laminae or fronds.

ROCKY SHORES

Rocks provide a firm surface for seaweed, and many creatures shelter among the fronds. But the weeds still face problems. Waves smash them against the hard stony surface, and they are regularly submerged by salt water, then left high and dry at low tide. Shellfish cling to the rocks, and a variety of fish and crabs adapt themselves to the ever-changing conditions, hiding from predators in holes and crevices.

WHELKS

These rocky-shore scavengers hunt for dead or dying animals. They are relatives of land snails and find prey by "smelling" the water, which they draw in through a periscope-like siphon.

ANEMONES

These jellyfish relatives use their tentacles to sting small fish, shrimps, and other creatures, and draw them into the mouth in the body cavity. When the tide goes out, the tentacles fold inward for protection.

Barnacle

CHITON

Chitons are also called "coat of mail shells" because they look like chainmail armor. Each chiton has an eight-part shell set into its broad, fleshy body. It can grip a rock very firmly. These mollusks feed on small algae from the rock surface.

MANTIS SHRIMP

The mantis shrimp, a crustacean, hides in a hole waiting for prey. When a fish or other victim approaches, the shrimp stuns it by a lightning blow from its club-shaped second "leg."

Branching holdfast provides shelter for small animals

Red seaweed

SEA STAR

The biscuit sea star feeds on shellfish, sea squirts, corals, sponges, and other animals. It glides along on dozens of tiny, sucker-tipped hydraulic tube feet located on its underside.

Find out more

CORALS, ANEMONES, and jellyfish
CRABS AND OTHER CRUSTACEANS
FISH
OCEAN WILDLIFE
SEABIRDS
SHELLS AND SHELLFISH
STARFISH AND SEA URCHINS

WILLIAM SHAKESPEARE

THE GREATEST PLAYWRIGHT of all time was probably the Englishman William Shakespeare. He was born in Stratford-upon-Avon, where he went to school, and later married. When he was in his 20s, he went to London to work as an actor and a playwright. His plays were very successful, and 37 of them survive. Some, such as *Hamlet*, are tragedies, serious plays that often end with the death of the hero. Others, such as *Twelfth Night*, are comedies, full of amusing characters who get into terrible difficulties that are eventually resolved. Shakespeare also wrote histories that are based on real-life events, such as *Henry IV*. Most of Shakespeare's plays are written in an unrhymed verse form called blank verse. They are famous worldwide for their use of language, fascinating characters, and wide appeal.

THE GRAMMAR SCHOOL
With its rows of wooden desks, the old grammar school still stands in Stratford. Shakespeare was probably educated here.

1564 Born, Stratford-upon-Avon, England.

1582 Marries Anne Hathaway.

1592 Writes his first plays in London.

1594-99 Produces early comedies, and many history plays.

1599 Globe Theater constructed.

1600-08 Writes many of his greatest tragedies.

1616 Dies in Stratford-upon-Avon.

Henry Wriothesley

POETRY
Shakespeare was a fine poet, and wrote a series of 14-line love poems called sonnets. They are addressed to two different people, "a dark lady" and Mr. W.H. Scholars believe that Mr. W.H. may have been Henry Wriothesley, the Third Earl of Southampton, who was Shakespeare's patron.

Male actors played female roles.

The audience stood around the stage.

KING'S MEN
In the 1590s, Shakespeare joined a troupe of actors called the Lord Chamberlain's Men, and became their resident writer. When James I came to the throne in 1603, they gained his support and became known as the King's Men. They had their own theater, the Globe, near the Thames River in London.

WAS IT BACON?
In the 19th century, some people thought that the learned writer Francis Bacon (1561-1626) had written Shakespeare's plays, because Shakespeare had not gone to college, but there is no real evidence that proves this.

English actress Maggie Smith in a performance of A Midsummer Night's Dream.

A MIDSUMMER NIGHT'S DREAM
One of Shakespeare's most popular plays, *A Midsummer Night's Dream*, is a comedy. The play has a huge cast of characters, including two young couples who fall in and out of love, a group of workmen, and the king and queen of the fairies, who create hilarious confusion with their magic.

Find out more
ELIZABETH I
LITERATURE
THEATER
WRITERS AND POETS

SHARKS AND RAYS

A PERFECT SHAPE FOR SPEED, an incredible sense of smell, and a mouth brimming with razor-sharp teeth make sharks the most fearsome fish in the sea. Sharks have existed for 350 million years, and their basic shape has hardly changed at all during this time. As adults, they have no predators and fear nothing in the ocean. The great white shark is the largest predatory fish, at more than 27 ft (9 m) in length and 2.7 tons in weight. Dozens of huge teeth line its jaws. The great white shark prowls the ocean, eating any kind of meat, alive or dead, and often swallows its prey in one gulp. Sharks have to keep moving in order to take in enough oxygen, and the great white travels more than 300 miles (500 km) in a day. Although most fish have bony skeletons, sharks and their relatives, the rays, have skeletons made of a substance called cartilage. Rays are flat-bodied, with a wide mouth on the underside and blunt teeth for crushing clams and other shellfish. Rays live close to the seabed and move gracefully by flapping their huge wings.

Good sense of smell for hunting

Long tail used for rounding up fish in the water

The thresher shark lashes the water with its tail to sweep fish into a group. Then, with its mouth open, the shark charges through, gobbling them up.

Excellent eyesight for spying prey

THRESHER SHARK
This shark measures 20 ft (6 m) in length. It lives mainly in the warm coastal waters of the Atlantic and Pacific oceans but sometimes strays north in summer.

FIN
A shark's dorsal (back) fin cuts the sea's surface as the shark circles before attacking. The dolphin's fin is more crescent-shaped.

Stingrays have a poison spine on the tail.

STINGRAY
There are about 100 kinds of stingrays – the biggest measures 12 ft (4 m) across.

Huge wings

Shark tooth

Sharks' teeth have a serrated edge so they can saw through flesh.

TEETH
Sharks have many rows of teeth. As they grow, the teeth move from inside the mouth to the outside edge, where they are used for tearing flesh. Eventually the teeth wear away or break off, only to be replaced by the teeth behind.

SKIN
Shark skin is covered with toothlike scales, and has a texture like sandpaper.

Dorsal fin

Dorsal fin

WHALE SHARK
The harmless whale shark cruises slowly through the tropical oceans, feeding by filtering tiny floating animals (plankton) from the water. It is a peaceful creature and is the biggest fish of any kind, at 50 ft (15 m) long.

A human can swim safely with the gentle whale shark, the biggest fish in the sea.

Upper lobe of caudal fin (tail)

Pectoral fin

Nostrils are excellent at detecting the smell of blood in the water.

SWIMMING MACHINE
The shark's swimming power comes from its tail. The larger upper lobe drives it down with each stroke and helps keep the body level; otherwise the creature's weight would tilt its head down. A shark cannot swivel its fins to stop quickly. It must veer to one side instead.

HAMMERHEAD
The eyes and nostrils of the hammerhead shark are on the two "lobes" of its head. Hammerheads prey on stingrays, unharmed by the poison in their spines.

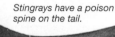

**Find out more**
ANIMAL SENSES
ANIMALS
FISH
OCEAN WILDLIFE

SHELLS AND SHELLFISH

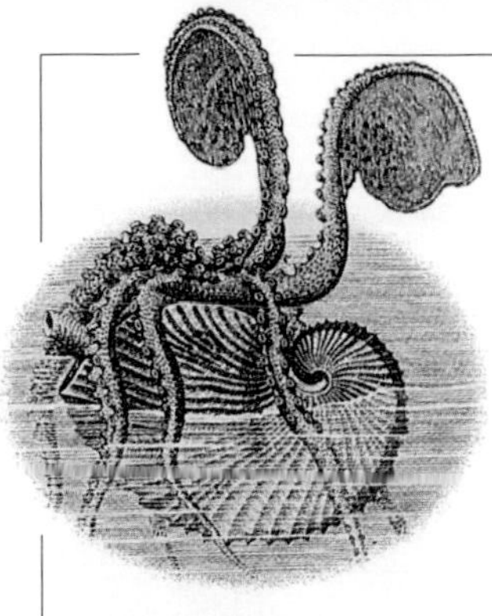

ALL THE WONDERFUL SHELLS you find on the seashore were once the homes of soft-bodied sea creatures. These creatures are commonly known as shellfish, although they are not fish at all, but mollusks, like slugs and snails. There are thousands of different kinds of shellfish living in the sea, including mussels, oysters, and clams. Many, such as the winkle, have small, delicate shells; others, such as the queen conch, have big, heavy shells. The shell itself is like a house, built by the shellfish. As it feeds, the shellfish extracts calcium carbonate from the water. This mineral is used by the shellfish to build up layers of shell, little by little. As the creature grows bigger, its shell grows bigger too. Some shellfish live in a single, coiled shell; others, known as bivalves, have a hinged shell with two sides that open and close for feeding.

ARGONAUT
The paper nautilus is a type of octopus that makes a thin shell to keep its eggs in. It is also known as the argonaut, after the sailors of Greek legend, because people believed they used its papery shell as a boat.

Tentacles
Head

INSIDE A SHELL
The pearly nautilus has a shell with many chambers. As it grows, the animal shuts off more chambers by building a "wall", and lives only in the last chamber.

NAUTILUS
This predator and scavenger hunts at night. It lives in the Indian and Pacific oceans, and has more than 30 tentacles for catching prey.

HOW SHELLS GROW
Shellfish hatch as larvae from eggs, then develop shells. Creatures with single coiled shells, such as this triton, grow by adding layers of shell-building material (calcium carbonate) to the open end. Hinged-shell creatures, such as cockles, add calcium carbonate to the rounded edges, in the form of coils called growth rings.

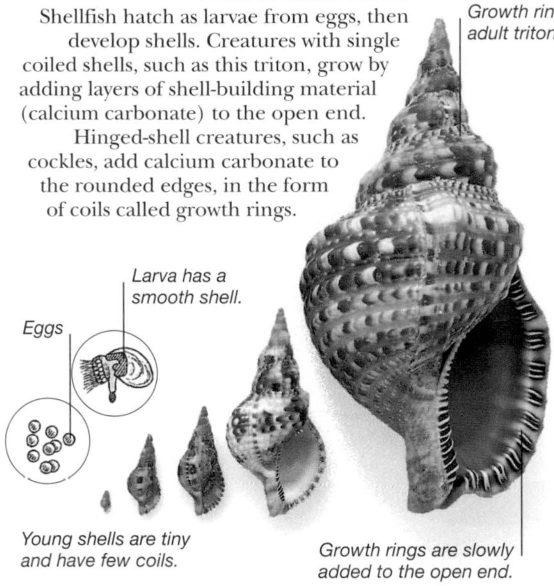

Growth rings on adult triton shell

Larva has a smooth shell.

Eggs

Young shells are tiny and have few coils.

Growth rings are slowly added to the open end.

HINGED SHELLS
The two sides of a hinged shell (bivalve) are held together by a tough ligament. Powerful muscles keep the valves closed for protection. The valves open slightly to allow the creature to breathe and feed.

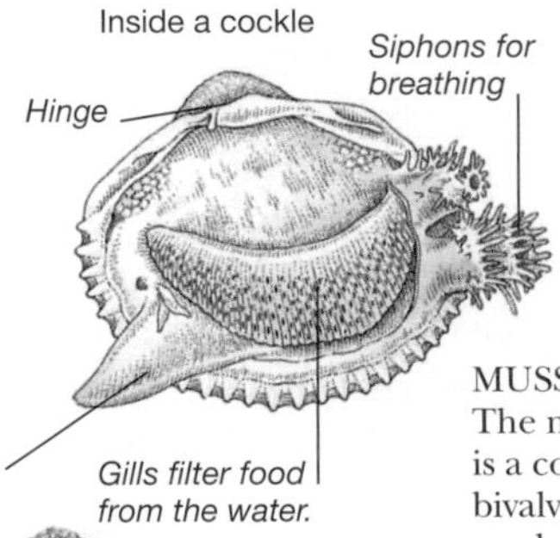

Inside a cockle

Hinge

Siphons for breathing

Foot

Gills filter food from the water.

MUSSEL
The mussel is a common bivalve on many seashores.

COCKLE SHELL
The ridged cockle buries itself in sand and feeds when the tide comes in.

SCALLOP
The scallop is able to swim by "flapping" its two valves. By snapping the two sides shut, it can shoot through the water to escape from a predator.

Inside a scallop

HOW A PEARL IS MADE
If a piece of grit gets lodged in an oyster's shell, the oyster covers it with mother-of-pearl (nacre), a substance lining its shell.

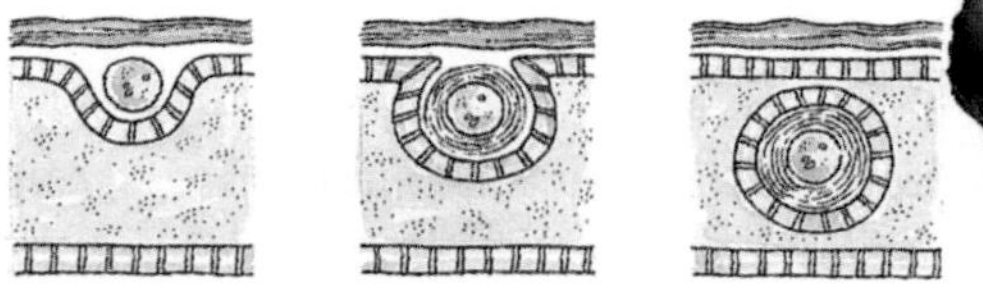

Tiny piece of grit irritates oyster.

Mother-of-pearl (nacre) forms over grit.

Pearl comes free, removing the irritation.

PEARL
We value oyster pearls highly because of their white, shiny appearance, but other kinds of shellfish make pearls too. The Caribbean conch makes pink pearls, and some shellfish make orange ones. The pearl shown here is a "blister pearl" on a black-lipped oyster shell.

Find out more
ANIMALS
ANIMAL SENSES
FOOD AND FOOD TECHNOLOGY
OCEAN WILDLIFE
SEASHORE WILDLIFE

SHIPS AND BOATS

Traditional craft such as this Chinese junk are still used in some parts of the world.

EVER SINCE OUR EARLIEST ancestors discovered that wood floats on water, ships and boats have played a major part in human history. The first boats helped people cross streams and rivers and carried hunters into shallow waters so they could go fishing. Better ways of building ships and boats began to develop when people left their homes to explore new territories. Since more than two-thirds of the Earth is covered by water, these early explorers had to go out to sea to discover new lands, and they needed vessels that could make long voyages. Ships and boats changed and improved over thousands of years as distant nations began to trade and opposing navies fought battles at sea. Today, there are thousands of different types of ships and boats. Ships are seagoing vessels; boats are generally smaller and travel on coastal or inland waters.

SHIPBUILDING
Modern ships are built of steel plates welded together. Ship builders make all the parts separately and finally assemble the ship in the shipyard. After months of sea trials to check its safety, the ship is ready for service.

The captain commands the ship from the bridge, which houses the steering wheel and navigation instruments such as compasses, radar equipment, and charts.

A crane (called a derrick), driven by steam or electricity, is used to load and unload cargo.

Weight of ship pushing downward

Upthrust from water pushing upward

HOW SHIPS FLOAT
Although metal is very heavy, a ship contains large spaces filled with air. The hull (main body) of a ship pushes water out of the way, and the water pushes back on the ship with a force called upthrust. The upthrust balances the weight of the ship and keeps it afloat.

Propeller

Rudder

RUDDER AND PROPELLER
A rotating propeller forces the ship through the water, and the rudder steers the ship. When the rudder twists, the weight of water thrusting against it turns the ship.

A powerful diesel engine drives one or more propellers at the stern (back) of the ship.

Cabins for crew to sleep in when not on duty

Main body of the ship is called the hull.

The front end of a ship is called the bow.

KINDS OF SHIPS
There are many kinds of ships. They range from passenger vessels to cargo ships that carry goods of all types to and from the world's ports.

Cargo is stored in a large compartment below the deck, called a hold. Large modern cargo vessels may have 12 or more holds. Ships that carry fresh food have refrigerated holds.

CARGO SHIP
Every year, cargo ships carry millions of tons of goods across the world's oceans. Some cargo ships, called container ships, carry huge loads piled up in large, steel boxes that stack together like building blocks. The largest ships of this kind carry more than 4,000 such containers.

FERRY
Ferries take people and goods across a stretch of water. Large ferries carry cars, trucks, and trains as well as people.

OIL TANKER
Oil is transported at sea in huge tankers. The engines and bridge are at the stern to give more storage space.

CRUISE LINER
Liners are large ships that carry passengers on scheduled routes. Most liners are like floating hotels and take tourists on lengthy cruises.

TRAWLER
Trawlers are engine-powered fishing boats that drag a net (the trawl) along the seabed in order to catch fish that swim near the bottom of the sea.

HISTORY OF SHIPS AND BOATS

The development of ships began more than 6,000 years ago with rafts and reed boats, and continues today with the introduction of nuclear-powered ships and boats made of light, strong plastics.

HIDE BOAT
About 6,000 years ago the Ancient Egyptians used boats made of a wicker framework covered with animal skins. In about 3200 B.C. the Egyptians invented sails.

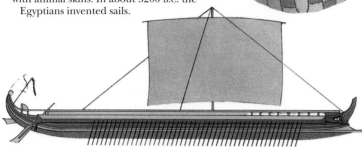

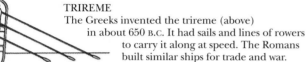

TRIREME
The Greeks invented the trireme (above) in about 650 B.C. It had sails and lines of rowers to carry it along at speed. The Romans built similar ships for trade and war.

Groups of rowers were positioned on two levels.

CLIPPER
Fast sailing ships called clippers (above) appeared during the 19th century, the height of the age of sailing. They carried many sails and had sleek lines to increase speed. Clippers were used mainly for trade.

STEAMSHIPS
Oceangoing steamships (below) took to the seas early in the 19th century. The earliest vessels had paddles connected to the engine and sails to gain extra speed in high winds. Ships with propellers entered service during the 1840s.

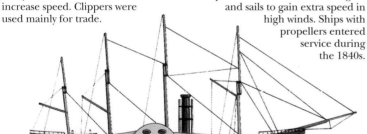

KINDS OF BOATS

Different boats have different uses. Many boats, such as yachts, are pleasure craft; tugs and fishing boats, however, are the workhorses of coastal waters.

POWERBOAT
Powerboats are small, fast boats driven by powerful gas or diesel engines. They are used either for pleasure or for racing.

TUGBOAT
Tugs tow larger vessels, guiding them through difficult or shallow waters at sea or on inland waterways such as canals.

HYDROFOIL
A boat's engine has to work hard to overcome the resistance of the water. Light, fast boats called hydrofoils avoid this problem because they rise up on skis at high speeds. With the hydrofoil traveling so rapidly, water behaves as if it were a solid, so the hydrofoil skims over the water surface just like an airplane wing in air.

Any force can be divided into two parts at right angles to each other. The part along the length of the boat drives the boat forward.

Air rushing past the sail produces a force that tends to move the boat at right angles to the wind.

Wind rushing past sail

Wind pushing on sail

HOW A BOAT SAILS
Modern sailing boats do not need the wind behind them to move – they can travel in almost any direction. In the same way that air rushing over the wings of an airplane produces an upward force called lift, wind moving past a sail produces a force at right angles to the sail. Adjusting the sail makes the boat move in different directions.

Centerboard prevents boat from drifting with the wind and stops the boat from capsizing.

With the wind behind the boat, the sail is stretched out across the boat.

Direction of wind

Direction of movement

A sailing boat cannot travel directly into the wind. Instead, it must follow a zigzag path. This is called tacking.

The boat heads into the wind with the sail drawn in as tightly as possible.

With the wind to the side of the boat, the sail is drawn in more tightly. The boat travels fastest with the wind in this position.

Direction of movement

YACHT
Yachts are pleasure boats. They have engines or sails. Racing yachts are built purely for speed and are made of strong, light materials.

Find out more
NAVIES
NAVIGATION
PORTS AND WATERWAYS
SAILING AND BOATING
SUBMARINES
WARSHIPS

SHOPS AND SHOPPING

IF YOU NEED TO BUY FOOD, or perhaps a book for school, there is probably a shop or a department store close to your home that sells just what you want. But shopping has not always been so easy. Shops started only with the introduction of money in Ancient China. In earlier times people used barter: in exchange for the goods they needed, they traded crops or objects they had made. The first shops sold just a few specialized products; the butcher sold meat, and the baker sold bread. In 1850 the first department store, a shop that sells many different items under one roof, opened in Paris. Self-service stores developed in the United States in the 1930s. They replaced the old methods of serving customers individually by selling prepackaged goods straight from the shelves. Modern supermarkets have parking lots and provide customers with carts so they can shop weekly instead of daily. Nowadays you do not even have to leave home to go shopping. You can shop by mail, by telephone, or through the Internet.

COWRIE SHELLS
People in the Pacific Islands, India, and parts of Africa once used cowrie shells as money.

MEDIEVAL SHOPPING
In the Middle Ages shoppers liked to test the goods and argue over the price. Traveling peddlers carried their goods from place to place, selling and trading.

MAIL ORDER
Shopping by mail has been possible for a hundred years. It was introduced for people who lived in remote areas a long way from any shops.

FRONTIER STORE
The frontier store supplied early American settlers with everything from food to tools. There was no packaging and little choice of goods. Supplies often ran out, and sometimes customers could not pay until they had sold their crops.

SHOPPING MALL
The modern shopping mall is a large, enclosed collection of shops. It is usually multistoried and air-conditioned and has benches and restaurants to make shopping a pleasant social experience.

BAR CODES
The packages of most modern products identify the contents both in words and with a code of black-and-white stripes. A laser scanner at the register reads the price and other information from this bar code. The register records the price, adds up the bill, and tells a central computer when to reorder the item.

MARKETS
Markets are found in all parts of the world. They were the earliest kind of shops where people could bring their surplus goods to exchange or sell. They developed at important trading places where roads crossed.

CASH REGISTERS
Cash registers were invented in Ohio in 1879. They recorded each sale and kept the money safe. Modern electronic registers add up the bill and print a receipt.

Find out more
ADVERTISING
MONEY
TRADE AND INDUSTRY

SIGNS AND SYMBOLS

THERE ARE SIGNS AND SYMBOLS all around us. A sign is an object that stands for something else or points to another object. Road signs are some of the most familiar examples. Signs are usually quite easy to understand and often use simplified pictures without any words. Symbols work in a similar way, but can be more complex, and we often have to know something about how they are used to understand them fully. A good example of a symbol is the sun, which is used in different ways in different parts of the world. The sun often stands for light and warmth, but, because it helps the crops to ripen, it can also be a symbol of growth and fertility.

The sun and the moon are symbols of male and female creative energy.

NATURAL SYMBOLS
Every culture uses symbols drawn from the world of nature. Plants and trees symbolize the cycle of life, from birth to death. Flowers can stand for beauty and love; herbs for the magical power of plants to heal the sick. Sun, moon, planets, and stars are often used as symbols of gods who can influence life on earth.

Sri Lankan mask of a snake demon, a symbol of both creation and destruction

UNIVERSAL SYMBOLS
Some symbols are so powerful that many different peoples use and understand them. Nearly everywhere, for example, the sun is a symbol of life. But some of these popular symbols change their meaning from place to place. Most peoples use the snake as a symbol, but the creature can stand for many things – life, power, lightning, cunning, or temptation.

COLOR SYMBOLS
The same colors can mean different things to different people. For example, in the Western world, white means purity and holiness, while in Asia it is often the color of mourning. Some color symbols, such as green for "go" and red for "danger," are the same almost everywhere.

Taurus the bull, Cancer the crab, and Pisces the fish are three of the sun signs used in Western astrology.

SYSTEMS OF SYMBOLS
Specialist subjects, from music to the sciences, have their own sets of symbols which work together in a system. Once you learn the symbols, you can use them like a language, to play a piece of music or work out a scientific formula. Astrology uses one of the most interesting of these systems, in which each sun sign has its own symbol.

Red can mean many things. A red car is a symbol of excitement and power; a priest's red robes symbolize the blood of the Christian martyrs, and a red rose represents the beauty of love.

ANIMAL SYMBOLS
The creatures we have hunted, our farm animals, and pets – animals have always played a key role in human life. Nearly every animal, from the strong lion and noble eagle to the mischievous monkey and peaceful dove, can therefore be used as a symbol. Birds, with their ability to fly, are often seen as messengers of the gods. Amphibians and fish are common symbols of life, because of the life-giving water in which they live.

Black cats are linked with night, witches, and both good and bad luck.

UNIVERSAL SIGNS

Many signs – for example, arrows that point the way – are so easy to understand that we forget they are signs at all. People everywhere can tell what they mean at a glance. Some signs, such as the Olympic emblem, the United Nations flag, and the red cross (Islamic countries use a red crescent instead), are so common that nearly everyone recognizes them.

PUBLIC INFORMATION

All sorts of standard signs are used to give information in public places. These signs are designed to be easy to understand without using words, to help travelers from abroad. Most are simplified pictures, like the symbol for wheelchair access or the male and female figures used to label public toilets, but sometimes letters are used, such as the "i", which indicates a tourist information point.

MYTHOLOGY

The world's mythologies are rich sources of symbols, some of which are still used. In most mythologies, there are many gods and goddesses, each standing for one aspect of life or nature. For example, Athena was the Ancient Greek goddess of warfare and learning; her symbol was an owl. Thor was the Norse god of thunder, and his symbol was a hammer.

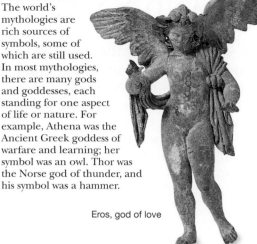

Eros, god of love

INSTRUCTION SIGNS

At work, on the road, and in the home, signs and symbols are useful ways of giving instructions. One international system of signs gives basic instructions about how to wash and care for different types of clothes and fabrics. The symbols indicate different washing temperatures and instructions for drying and ironing. A cross through a symbol means, "Do not do this."

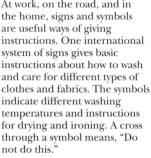

TRADEMARK

A symbol or name that identifies a company and its products can be registered as a trademark. Registering protects the trademark to prevent others from using it. One of the world's most famous trademarks, the "golden arches," belongs to McDonald's Restaurants. In 1955, one of the first McDonald's restaurants was designed with an arch either side of the building. Although they were not designed as an initial, when looked at from a certain angle the arches formed an "M", and so the golden arches became the symbol for the restaurant chain.

BRAILLE

This system of printing and writing for the blind uses patterns of raised dots to stand for the different letters and numbers. Blind people read Braille by moving their fingertips along the lines of dots. The system takes its name from the blind Frenchman Louis Braille (1809-52), who invented the system during the 19th century.

WRITTEN LANGUAGES

Any writing system is made up of a group of symbols, which can stand for whole words or parts of words. Early writing systems, such as Ancient Egyptian hieroglyphs, usually started as picture symbols standing for whole words or ideas. Some picture writing is quite recent, like the symbols shown here, which were created in Bamum, Cameroon, Africa, in the early 20th century.

| Thread | Child | House | Plate | No | To go | To give |

IDENTIFIERS

It is vital that people like nurses, soldiers, and police officers stand out in a crowd. Symbols such as uniforms and badges show instantly to which group the wearer belongs. If you look more closely at a uniform, you can find out more about the person in it: there are variations in uniforms to show different ranks and indicate particular jobs. Medals are awarded as signs of special acts of bravery or service.

US Congressional
Medal of Honor

TRAFFIC SIGNS

Road signs are agreed internationally, so most of them are the same the world over. Different shapes indicate different types of message. Triangular signs are used for warnings, such as signs warning of slippery roads or other hazards. Round signs are mostly for prohibitions, such as no entry or no cycling. Rectangular signs usually give directions and other information.

WARNING SIGNS

Triangular warning signs can be used for all sorts of hazards. Road users in the US are familiar with signs warning of cattle or deer on the road; in the Middle East, camel warnings are treated in the same way. A triangular sign with a yellow background is often used for warnings about environmental hazards such as dangerous chemicals, poisons, or radioactive material.

Find out more

ALPHABETS
DESIGN
MYTHS AND LEGENDS

SKELETONS

INSIDE THE HUMAN BODY, hundreds of bones link together like scaffolding to form the skeleton. Without a skeleton, the body would collapse. The skeleton holds the body rigid and gives shape to all the softer parts. It also protects the organs – the skull surrounds the brain, and the ribs act as a protective cage around the lungs and heart. The skeleton is also an anchor for the muscles, which move the different parts of the body. Bone is made of living cells surrounded by a framework of minerals, particularly calcium and phosphate, and a stringy, elastic substance called collagen. In a newborn baby, many of the bones are made of a soft, rubbery substance called cartilage. As a baby grows, the cartilage gradually turns into hard bone. Our wrists and ankles are among the last to become bone. In later life, bones gradually become more fragile and brittle, and break more easily.

INTERNAL SKELETONS

Humans and other mammals, fish, birds, and reptiles all have an inner skeleton, or endoskeleton, made up of many separate bones. The central part of the skeleton is the spine (vertebral column or backbone). The spinal joints can move only a little, but the spine as a whole is very flexible. Some creatures, such as worms, have no bones. Instead the pressure of fluid inside their bodies helps them keep their shape. They are said to have a hydrostatic skeleton.

Lizard has an internal skeleton, like other vertebrates.

JOINTS

Bones are linked together at joints. There are several types of joints, including fixed, hinge, and ball-and-socket joints. Fixed joints, such as those between the separate bones in the skull, cannot move. Hinge joints, such as those in the elbow, allow movement in one direction only. Ball-and-socket joints, such as the hip, allow the bones to swing in two directions and also to twist.

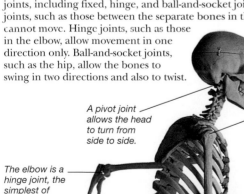

A pivot joint allows the head to turn from side to side.

The shoulder and the hip are both ball-and-socket joints and allow the greatest range of movement.

The elbow is a hinge joint, the simplest of joints, and moves mainly back and forth.

The wrist is formed by an ellipsoidal joint which can be flexed or extended and moved from side to side.

HUMAN SKELETON

There are 206 bones in the human skeleton, including 29 in the skull, 26 in the spine, 32 in each arm, 31 in each leg, and 25 in the chest. The largest bone is in the thigh, and the smallest ones are the ossicles, which are three tiny bones inside each ear.

Skull

Maxilla (upper jaw)

Mandible (lower jaw)

Cervical (neck) vertebrae

Clavicle (collarbone)

Scapula (shoulder blade)

Sternum (breastbone)

12 pairs of ribs

Humerus (upper-arm bone)

Lumbar (lower back) vertebrae

Ulna (forearm bone)

Radius (forearm bone)

Carpals (wrist bones)

Metacarpals (palm bones)

Phalanges (finger bones)

Hip joint

Pelvis (hipbone)

Femur (thighbone)

Patella (kneecap)

Tibia (shin bone)

Fibula (calf bone)

Tarsals (ankle bones)

Metatarsals (foot bones)

Phalanges (toe bones)

Soft, spongy bone inside

Hard, compact bone outside

Medullary cavity

Thin, tough outer layer called the periosteum

BONE

Living bone is tough and slightly flexible – only dead bone is white and brittle. Blood vessels pass through small holes in the bone's surface, and carry a steady supply of blood to the bone. Some bones contain a jellylike substance called bone marrow, which makes blood cells.

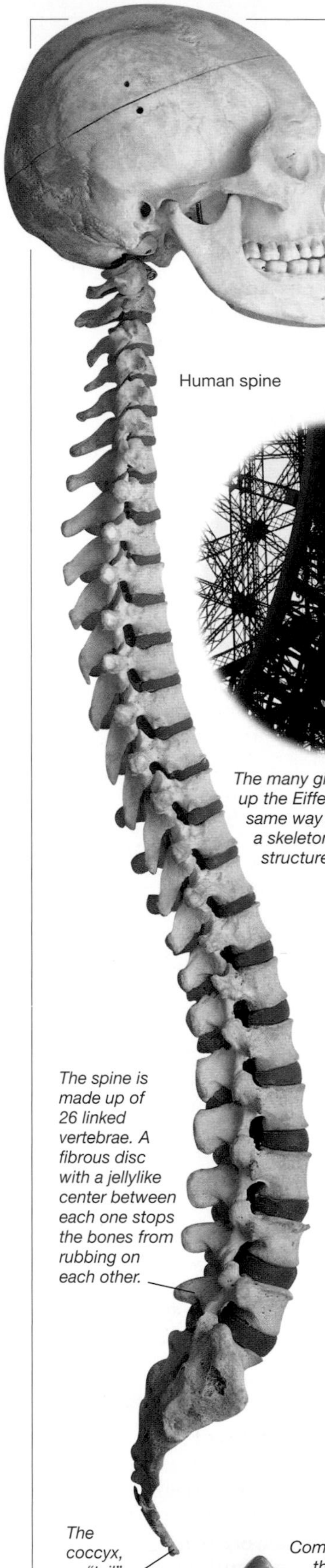

SPINE

The spine, or backbone, runs down the back of the body. It supports other parts of the skeleton, such as the skull, rib cage, and pelvis. Animals, known as vertebrates, which include humans, get their name from the flexible row of spine bones, called vertebrae, which protect the spinal chord. The spine can flex and bend because each vertebra can move slightly against the next one.

Human spine

The many girders that make up the Eiffel Tower act in the same way as the bones of a skeleton, keeping the structure's shape rigid.

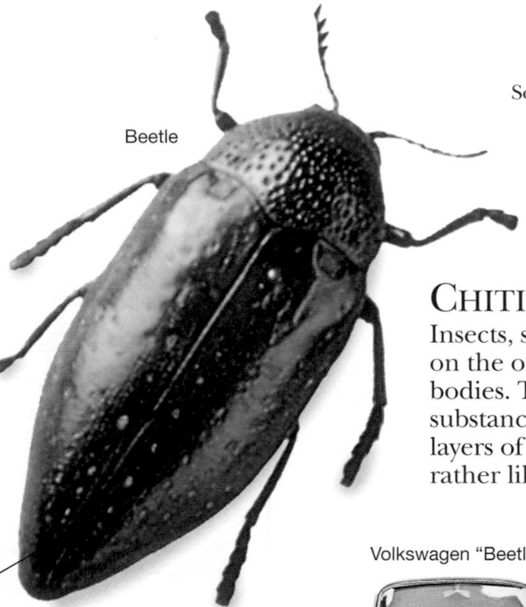

The spine is made up of 26 linked vertebrae. A fibrous disc with a jellylike center between each one stops the bones from rubbing on each other.

The coccyx, or "tail".

Earthworm

The body of an earthworm is filled with pressurized fluid.

The circular wall of a wading pool is held up by the water contained within it.

HYDROSTATIC SKELETON

Some skeletons are made from materials that are not rigid at all. Instead, they are divided into compartments that can be filled with fluid, and this hydrostatic pressure makes them rigid. Many of the microscopic cells which form plants and animals keep their shape in this way, and so do some artificial objects.

CHITIN

Insects, spiders, and scorpions have skeletons on the outside rather than the inside of their bodies. They are made of a tough plasticlike substance called chitin. This is built up from layers of fiber arranged in different directions, rather like plywood.

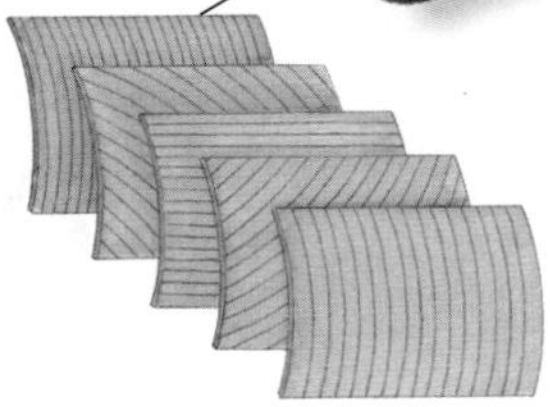

Beetle

Chitin

Volkswagen "Beetle"

Nicknamed "beetle" because of its shape, this car's bodywork is an exoskeleton

EXTERNAL SKELETON

Skeletons that grow on the outside the body of an animal or insect are called exoskeletons. Many objects made by people also have exoskeletons, rather than internal ones. Modern cars, for instance, are made like this. Flat sheet metal is molded into curved shapes to make a strong outer shell to protect the inside.

PNEUMOSTATIC SKELETON

Just as hydrostatic skeletons are inflated with fluids to make them rigid, some skeletons are inflated with gas or air. They are called pneumostatic skeletons. Gases are much lighter than fluids, so the skeleton can have thinner walls. It will also float on water, or even rise up into the air.

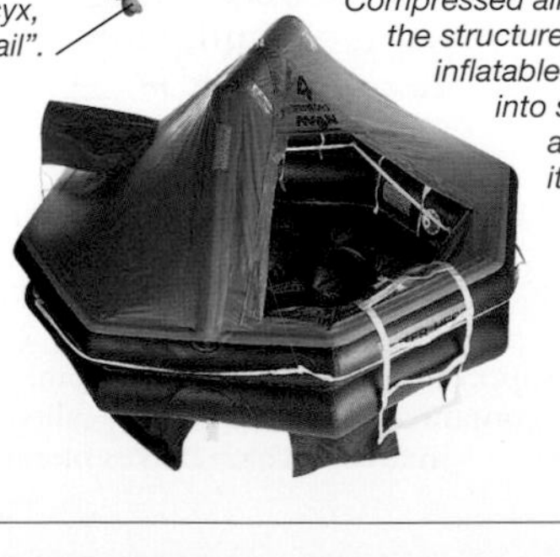

The Portuguese man-of-war floats on the surface of the ocean supported by a gas-filled bladder.

Compressed air pushes the structure of this inflatable life raft into shape, and holds it rigid.

Tentacles hang from the gas-filled bladder.

Find out more

ANIMALS
HUMAN BODY
MUSCLES AND MOVEMENT

SLAVERY

FIVE THOUSAND YEARS AGO, the Sumerians put their prisoners to work on farms as slaves. The workers had no rights and no pay, and their masters regarded them as property. In ancient Greece and Rome, slaves produced most of the goods and also worked as household servants. During the 16th century, European nations began to colonize the Americas, and imported thousands of Africans to work as slaves on their plantations and silver mines. Between 1500 and 1800, European ships took about 12 million slaves from their homes to the new colonies. By the 19th century, those against slavery set up movements in the United States and Britain to end it. Slavery was formally abolished, or ended, in the British Empire and the United States in the mid-1800s. Sadly, it continues today in many parts of the world, most often affecting children and immigrants.

ROMAN SLAVES
Most wealthy Roman citizens owned slaves. Some slaves lived as part of the family; others were treated very badly. Some earned manumission (a formal release from slavery) through loyalty to a master.

TRIANGLE OF TRADE
The British trade in slaves was known as the triangular trade. Ships sailed from British ports laden with goods such as guns and cloth. Traders exchanged these goods with African chiefs for slaves on the western coast of Africa. The slave ships then carried their cargo across the Atlantic to the Americas and the Caribbean. Here, slaves were in demand for plantation work, so the traders exchanged them for sugar, tobacco, rum, and molasses. The ships then returned to Britain carrying this cargo, which was sold at huge profits.

Ships sailed back to Europe with goods.

Britain

Ships departed from Britain carrying guns and cloth.

NORTH AMERICA

Tobacco

AFRICA

Slave coast

Ships carried slaves across the Atlantic.

SOUTH AMERICA

Rum, sugar, and molasses

Slave ship

SLAVE SHIPS
Slavers (slave traders) packed their ships with Africans to sail on what was known as the middle passage across the Atlantic. The slaves were chained and kept below deck for most of the voyage. Unclothed and underfed, thousands of Africans died on the Atlantic crossing.

SLAVE REBELLIONS
Many Africans fought against slavery. In 1791, one of the most famous rebellions began in the French colony of Haiti. A slave named Toussaint L'Ouverture led an army of slaves against the French soldiers in a rebellion that lasted 13 years. L'Ouverture was captured and died in prison in 1803. In 1804, Haiti gained independence and became the world's first black republic.

SLAVE MARKET
Once the slaves reached the West Indies or the southern states of America, they were auctioned at a slave market. Here, they were treated like animals. Families were sometimes separated, and people were sold singly to plantation owners. Slaves were put to work on cotton, sugar, and tobacco plantations. Many received cruel treatment. Severe whipping was a common punishment for slaves who tried to escape.

SLAVERY AND WEALTH

England dominated the slave trade, and some British cities became very rich as a result. Bristol and Liverpool, for instance, imported goods such as sugar and tobacco produced by slaves in the West Indies. Ships from both cities carried slaves from Africa to American plantations.

Ships in Bristol harbor

COTTON

African slave laborers were made to grow sugar in Brazil and the Caribbean. Later, tobacco was also grown. By the late 1700s there were huge cotton plantations in North America, and the British textile industry began to flourish, stimulating the Industrial Revolution. Cotton was made into cloth in Glasgow and Manchester.

AM I NOT A MAN & A BROTHER

GRANVILLE SHARP

In 1772, British clerk Granville Sharp defended a black immigrant named James Somerset in a legal case known as the Somerset Case. This established that slavery was not recognized in Britain, and a slave who stepped on British soil was automatically free. The ruling was seen as officially abolishing slavery in England.

OLAUDAH EQUIANO

Africans themselves played a part in the antislavery movement. One of the best-known African antislavery campaigners was Olaudah Equiano (1745-97). Born in Nigeria, he was captured with his sister when he was eleven, and taken to Britain as a servant. His autobiography was influential and is one of the earliest important works by an African written in English.

ABOLITIONISTS

On both sides of the Atlantic, Quakers, evangelical Christians, and liberal thinkers fought to abolish slavery. In Britain, Granville Sharp and William Wilberforce (1759-1833), founded the Anti-Slavery Society in 1787-88. Members campaigned for the abolition of slavery and the freeing of all slaves. As part of the campaign, pottery owner Josiah Wedgwood produced a special medal. In 1833, the Emancipation Act freed slaves in the British Empire.

ANTISLAVERY MOVEMENT

In 1840, a World Anti-Slavery Convention took place in London, with delegates from the United States. Women took an active part in the abolition movement, often linking their situation with that of slaves. American feminists Lucretia Mott (1793-1880) and Susan B. Anthony (1820-1906) were leading campaigners.

Find out more

AFRICA, HISTORY OF
CARIBBEAN, HISTORY OF
CIVIL WAR
INDUSTRIAL REVOLUTION
TUBMAN, HARRIET

SNAILS AND SLUGS

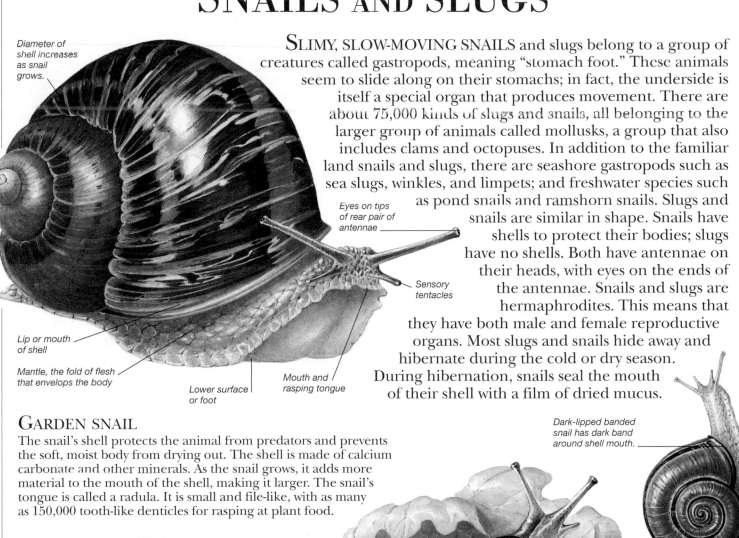

SLIMY, SLOW-MOVING SNAILS and slugs belong to a group of creatures called gastropods, meaning "stomach foot." These animals seem to slide along on their stomachs; in fact, the underside is itself a special organ that produces movement. There are about 75,000 kinds of slugs and snails, all belonging to the larger group of animals called mollusks, a group that also includes clams and octopuses. In addition to the familiar land snails and slugs, there are seashore gastropods such as sea slugs, winkles, and limpets; and freshwater species such as pond snails and ramshorn snails. Slugs and snails are similar in shape. Snails have shells to protect their bodies; slugs have no shells. Both have antennae on their heads, with eyes on the ends of the antennae. Snails and slugs are hermaphrodites. This means that they have both male and female reproductive organs. Most slugs and snails hide away and hibernate during the cold or dry season. During hibernation, snails seal the mouth of their shell with a film of dried mucus.

Diameter of shell increases as snail grows.

Eyes on tips of rear pair of antennae

Sensory tentacles

Lip or mouth of shell

Mantle, the fold of flesh that envelops the body

Lower surface or foot

Mouth and rasping tongue

Dark-lipped banded snail has dark band around shell mouth.

GARDEN SNAIL
The snail's shell protects the animal from predators and prevents the soft, moist body from drying out. The shell is made of calcium carbonate and other minerals. As the snail grows, it adds more material to the mouth of the shell, making it larger. The snail's tongue is called a radula. It is small and file-like, with as many as 150,000 tooth-like denticles for rasping at plant food.

YOUNG
After mating, the snail or slug lays eggs, either singly or in batches, in mucus. The young snails and slugs hatch from their eggs after about two to four weeks.

SLIME
Snails and slugs make several types of slime. As the slug crawls along, it lays down one kind of slime in patches. Another kind of slime is given off when the creature is attacked by a predator. A slug crawls by waves of muscle contractions passing along its foot.

SLUG
Slugs are unpopular with gardeners because some do serious damage to plants and vegetables. Most slugs have no shells; some have a very small shell embedded in the back. Slugs avoid drying out by living in damp places and emerging only at night or after rain.

SEA SLUG
There are many beautifully colored sea slugs in the shallow coastal waters of the world, particularly around coral reefs. Many have feathery or tufted gills for absorbing oxygen from the water. Sea slugs are predators, feeding mainly on sponges, barnacles, sea mats, and sea anemones.

TOPSHELL
The purple topshell snail lives close to the high-tide mark.

Find out more

OCEAN WILDLIFE
SEASHORE WILDLIFE
SHELLS AND SHELLFISH

SNAKES

LONG, LEGLESS, SCALY, and slithering, snakes are a very successful group of reptiles. They are found everywhere except the coldest regions, highest mountain peaks, and a few islands. Most snakes can swim and climb well. All snakes are hunters. Some, such as pythons and boa constrictors, squeeze and suffocate their prey to death; others, such as cobras, paralyze their victims with a poisonous bite. Fast-moving snakes such as sand snakes hunt down insects, small birds, and mammals. Blind snakes are burrowers that eat ants and termites. More than 400 kinds of snakes are venomous (poisonous), but only some can give a fatal bite to humans. Deadly poisonous snakes include cobras, boomslangs, and mambas.

FANGS
The pair of hollow teeth at the front of the upper jaw are called fangs. The fangs lie flat along the jaw and swing forward when the snake strikes. Muscles pump venom from glands down the fangs into the victim.

RATTLE
Rattlesnakes are so named because they shake the tip of the tail (the rattle) to scare off predators. The rattle consists of a row of hollow tail segments that make a noise when the snake shakes them.

Rattle at tip of tail

SNAKE CHARMING
This is an ancient entertainment in Africa and Asia. Snake charmers fascinate snakes with movements that make the snakes sway to the music.

Snake's long belly has large scales called ventral scutes, which overlap like tiles on a roof.

Emerald tree boa constricts or squeezes its prey.

RATTLESNAKE
At more than 7 ft (2 m) long, the eastern diamondback is the largest rattlesnake, and the most poisonous snake in North America. The rattlesnake feeds mainly on rats, rabbits, and birds. Unlike many other snakes, which lay eggs, the rattlesnake gives birth to about 10 live young in late summer.

MILK SNAKE
The non-venomous milk snake shown left is found all over North America, down to the north of South America. It looks similar to the poisonous coral snake, but the milk snake has yellow bands bordered by black, whereas the poisonous coral snake has black bands bordered by yellow. The milk snake hunts small mammals, birds, and other reptiles, including rattlesnakes. It coils around its prey and chokes it to death.

YOUNG SNAKES
Some snakes are described as viviparous, because they give birth to fully formed young. Others lay eggs in a burrow or under a log, leaving the young to hatch and fend for themselves. Certain kinds of pythons coil around the eggs and protect them until they hatch.

The sea snake's body follows S-shaped curves, pushing sideways and backward.

Young grass snake hatches from its egg head first and flicks its tongue to sense its surroundings.

CONSTRICTOR
Boas and pythons are called constrictors because they constrict or coil around their prey and suffocate it. There are 66 kinds of boas and pythons; they include some of the largest snakes on Earth. Anacondas are boas of the Amazon region in South America. These massive snakes reach more than 25 ft (8 m) in length and weigh 500 lbs (225 kg).

SEA SNAKE
There are 50 kinds of sea snakes – the yellow-bellied sea snake shown left is the most common. It measures up to 32 in (80 cm) in length, preys on fish, and gives birth to about five young at sea. Sea snakes spend their lives swimming in the warm waters of the Indian Ocean, around Southeast Asia and Australia, and in the western Pacific.

Find out more
ANIMALS
AUSTRALIAN WILDLIFE
DESERT WILDLIFE
FOREST WILDLIFE
REPTILES

SOCCER

THE MOST POPULAR TEAM SPORT IN THE WORLD, soccer is played across the globe. The roots of today's game lie in England, where the sport developed in the 1800s. Soccer is played on a rectangular field, with two nets called goals at either end. Two teams of 11 players compete to put a ball into the opposing team's goal, using only the feet, head, or body. One player on each team serves as the goalkeeper. This player must guard the goal and block shots to prevent the other team from scoring. A referee ensures that the rules of the game are followed. The team that scores the most goals during two 45-minute halves of play wins the game. One of the greatest players in soccer history, Brazil's Pele, called soccer "the beautiful game." Today, the beautiful game is one of the most popular participation sports for young Americans.

Goalkeeping gloves give a good grip on the ball and take the sting out of saving hard shots.

HISTORY OF SOCCER

Soccerlike games have been played for thousands of years, from China to ancient Rome. The birthplace of modern soccer is England, where a uniform set of rules was established at Trinity College, Cambridge, in 1848. The first professional soccer league, England's Football Association, was founded in 1863.

Shin guards

Goalkeeping gloves

Soccer shoe, with cleats (studs)

EQUIPMENT

Cleated shoes are the most important part of a soccer player's equipment. They enable the player to use both the inside and outside of the foot while passing and kicking the ball. Shin guards are usually worn inside knee-high socks, to protect the vulnerable shins from stray kicks. The ball itself is made of leather.

GOAL!

There are several ways to score a goal, including sliding in a low shot with the foot, volleying the ball through the air, and heading the ball. Some goals are set up with a sequence of precise passes, while others are the result of individual skill.

PLAYERS

There are 11 players on each team – one goalkeeper and ten outfield players. The outfield players include defenders, who try to stop the opposition from moving into goal-scoring positions, midfielders, who switch between offensive and defensive play, and forwards, who try to score goals. The ball may be kicked, headed, or dribbled (moved with the foot). Each team has a goalkeeper to defend its goal. The goalkeeper is the only player allowed to handle the ball.

Goal Penalty area   Halfway line

Goal area

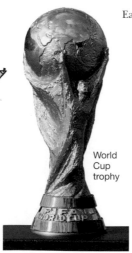

World Cup trophy

SOCCER FIELD

A soccer field is a rectangle, divided in two by the halfway line. The goals stand in the center at each end of the field. Each goal is 24 ft (7 m) wide and 8 ft (2.4 m) high. The large rectangle in front of the goal is known as the penalty area; the smaller rectangle is the goal area. Penalties (free shots) are awarded to players fouled by the defending team in the penalty area.

SOCCER COMPETITIONS

The most famous international soccer competition is the World Cup, held every four years. Over 100 national all-star teams compete to reach the final game, which attracts a worldwide television audience of a billion people.

Find out more

BALL GAMES
BASKETBALL
FOOTBALL
SPORTS

SOIL

IF YOU REACH DOWN and pick up a handful of soil, you will be holding one of the Earth's most basic and valuable resources. Soil teems with life. A plot of earth the size of a small garden may contain millions of insects and microorganisms, plus organic matter from dead or dying plants and animals. Soil provides the foundation for roots, a source of food for plants, and a home not only for burrowing animals, such as moles, but also for millions of spiders and centipedes. There are many different types of soil, from thick silt and loose sand to waterlogged mud and dry desert. Soil is formed from the wearing down of rocks and takes many years to develop. Each 1 sq in (6.5 sq cm) of soil, for instance, may take 100 to 2,000 years to form. The quality of soil varies from region to region. In hot countries such as Africa and Australia, where there is little rain, the soil is very dry. In temperate regions such as Europe and North America, much of the soil is rich and fertile. But soil can be destroyed in just a fraction of the time it takes to form. Overfarming the land, for example, has led to soil erosion in many parts of the world.

FERTILIZER
Farmers add fertilizers to poor soil. The fertilizer is rich in minerals that help the crops to grow.

TYPES OF SOIL
Soil may be black, brown, red, yellow, orange, or cream in color, depending on the minerals it contains. Rich, dark, peaty soil is ideal for garden plants.

Peaty soil

Clay soil

Chalky soil

Sandy soil

SOIL EROSION
In overfarmed areas, or where natural vegetation is removed, soil is no longer protected from rain or held in place by roots. Winds blow away the loose particles as dust, and rains wash them away as mud. The land becomes infertile and cannot support life. Today, soil erosion affects more than 198,000 sq miles (513,000 sq km) in the USA alone.

SOIL LAYERS
Soil is formed from several different layers that merge into each other. On top is a layer of humus, consisting of dead and rotting leaves. Underneath this layer is the topsoil where decayed plant and animal matter is broken down and recycled by insects, fungi, and bacteria. The subsoil layer, which contains less organic matter, lies below the topsoil and above a loose layer of partly weathered rock. A hard layer of solid bedrock lies below all the other layers.

HUMUS
Humus is the layer of decaying leaves and other plant material in the soil.

TOPSOIL
Topsoil is full of burrowing bugs, worms, and other creatures. It also gives anchorage to plants with shallow root systems.

Moles tunnel in the upper part of rich soil, where there are many worms to eat.

Beetle

Centipede

SUBSOIL
The subsoil layer is reached only by deep-rooted plants such as trees.

PARTLY WEATHERED ROCK ZONE
This layer of rocks has weathered and been crumbled into loose chunks and contains no organic matter.

Slug

Earthworm

Beetle

Snail

Caterpillar

Potato tuber

POTATO
All plants, including the potato, use the energy in sunlight, mineral nutrients in the soil, water, and carbon dioxide from the air to grow. The potato plant stores its food reserves in the potatoes that we eat.

Tree roots reach into subsoil layer.

COMPOST
Fungi, bacteria, worms, and insects thrive in a compost heap, helping the contents to decay and be recycled.

RECYCLING
All living things eventually rot away, back into the soil. The compost heap is a valuable recycler. In time, it turns domestic organic garbage such as apple peelings, banana skins, eggshells, and grass cuttings into humus, a food supply for the soil. In this way, valuable resources are recycled.

Find out more
FLOWERS AND HERBS
MUSHROOMS
toadstools, and other fungi
PLANTS
TREES

SONGBIRDS

MOST BIRDS MAKE SOME KIND OF SOUND. Some birds make loud, complicated warbles and whistles that are so pleasing to our ears that we call these birds songbirds. There are more than 5,000 kinds of songbird, also called perching birds because they perch in trees to sing. Many songbirds are small and dull-colored, and stay hidden in trees. In dark, shady woodlands, a loud, clear singing voice is more useful for communicating with others than brightly colored feathers. The male is usually the chief singer. He sings to show other birds where his territory is and to attract a female. Each kind of songbird has its own way of singing. Birdsongs vary from place to place, in the same way that humans pronounce words in different ways. Among the most outstanding singers are the robin chats of Africa, the warblers of Europe and Asia, and the babblers and bellbirds of Australasia.

DAWN CHORUS
As soon as the sun rises, birds finish their nightly rest and begin the day's activities. Many birds sing loudly at this time, and sing again at dusk. Each bird's song tells neighbors that it has survived the night and is still occupying its territory.

SONG THRUSH
This bird has a loud, cheerful, musical song. Its favorite singing perches include television aerials and high tree branches. Song thrushes eat snails, often breaking the shell open on a stone to extract the flesh.

NIGHTINGALE
Many people describe the nightingale's song as the most beautiful of all. It has inspired poets and musicians throughout the ages. The nightingale (right) sings both day and night, but its song is noticed most at night. It makes its nest in low, tangled bushes where its eggs are well hidden in the shadows cast by leaves and branches.

ROBIN REDBREAST
During the spring, when robins have paired off to build a nest and raise young, the male robin's sweet, sad song tells intruders to stay out of his territory. The robin's warning call, a sharp *tic-tic-tic*, warns other birds of a nearby cat or hawk.

BIRDSONG
There are several ways of describing a bird's song with words and symbols. Tape recordings help people learn how to identify birds by their particular songs.

SARDINIAN WARBLER
Loud, fast warbles

NIGHTINGALE
Smooth, liquid sounds

YELLOW WARBLER
In North and Central America, the yellow warbler is well known in parks and orchards. Its song often starts with three or four sweet *wheet* sounds and ends with a quick burst of high and low notes. Yellow warblers feed on caterpillars, moths, beetles, and spiders. They use their probing beaks to pick insects from leaves and bark.

Find out more
ANIMALS
BIRDS
FLIGHT, ANIMAL
MIGRATION, ANIMAL

SOUND

WE LIVE IN A NOISY WORLD. The roar of city traffic, the music from a piano, the bark of a dog, all come to our ears as sound waves traveling through the air. Sound is generated when a disturbance sets air moving – for example, when someone plucks a guitar string. We hear sounds when sound waves – tiny vibrations in the air – strike our eardrums. Sound waves need a substance to travel through. This substance may be a liquid, such as water; a solid, such as brick and stone; or a gas, such as air.

Sounds such as musical notes have a certain pitch. A high-pitched sound makes the air vibrate backward and forward more times each second than a low-pitched sound. The number of vibrations per second is called the frequency of the sound and is measured in hertz (cycles per second). Humans cannot hear sounds with frequencies above about 20,000 hertz or below about 30 hertz.

SPEED OF SOUND

Sound travels in air at a speed of about 760 mph (about 1,224 km/h). It travels more slowly when the temperature and pressure of the air are lower. In the thin, cold air 7 miles (11 km) up, the speed of sound is about 620 mph (1,000 km/h). In water, sound travels at 3,350 mph (about 5,400 km/h), much faster than in air.

LOUDNESS AND DECIBELS

The sound of a train is louder than the sound of a whisper because the train produces larger vibrations in the air. The loudness of sound also depends on how close you are to its source. Loudness is measured in decibels (dB). A jet airliner taking off is rated at about 120 dB; the rustling of leaves is about 33 dB.

ECHOES

If you shout in a large hall or near mountains, you can hear your voice echo back to you. An echo occurs when a sound bounces off a surface such as a cliff face and reaches you shortly after the direct sound. The clarity of speech and music in a room or concert hall depends on the way sounds echo inside it.

The distance from one region of highest pressure to the next is called the wavelength of the sound. The higher the pitch, or frequency, of the sound, the shorter the wavelength.

Region of high-pressure air

Region of low-pressure air

The noise of the boat's engine sends sound waves through the water.

SOUND WAVES

A sound wave consists of air molecules vibrating backward and forward. At each moment the molecules are crowded together in some places, producing regions of high pressure, and spaced out in others, producing regions of low pressure. Waves of alternately high pressure and low pressure move through the air, spreading out from the source of the sound. These sound waves carry the sound to your ears.

HARMONICS

In a musical note, secondary frequencies, called harmonics, are mixed with the main frequency. Harmonics are characteristic of different instruments, which is why a note played on a piano sounds different from the same note played on a violin. Harmonics bring life to the sound of musical instruments: an electronically produced sound of a single pure frequency sounds artificial and dull.

RESONANCE

An object such as a glass gives out a musical note when struck because it has its own natural frequency of vibration. If you sing a musical note of this frequency, the object vibrates at its natural frequency, pushed by the sound waves that hit it. This is called resonance. A very loud sound can make a glass resonate so strongly that it shatters.

Find out more
EARS
MUSIC
RADIO
SOUND RECORDING

SOUND RECORDING

TODAY WE CAN STORE SOUND and reproduce it at will. We can hear music whenever we wish, produce "talking books" for the blind, record sounds into miniature recorders, and much more. All recording systems store sounds by making an image, or copy, of the sound waves. This image may be in the form of magnetism on a tape, the spiral groove in a record, or the pits in a compact disk. In a recording studio, sound is recorded using many microphones, each producing a recording on one track. Traditionally, these tracks were stored on magnetic tape, but most studios now store tracks on a computer. The sound engineer can modify the music on each track separately to perfect the tone and loudness of any instrument or singer. The studio recording is the master version of the music, which factories then use to make thousands of copies on compact disks, minidisks, records, and cassette tapes.

RECORD PLAYER
The earliest recordings consisted of grooves cut into wax-coated cylinders. In 1887, German-American Emile Berliner first demonstrated the gramophone disk, or record. The gramophone above is the famous trademark of the record company His Master's Voice (HMV).

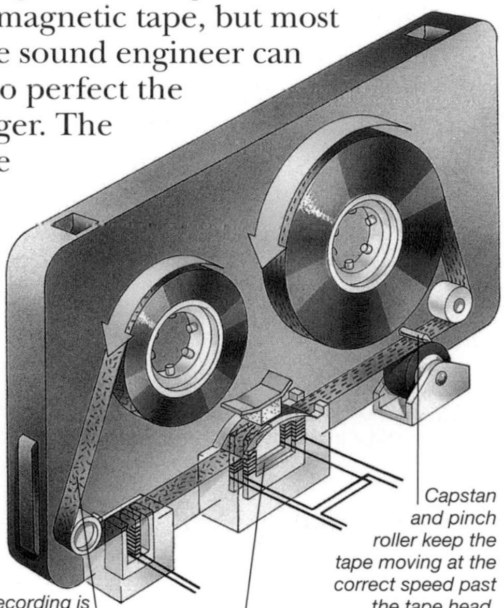

Protective grill prevents diaphragm from being damaged.

Fragile diaphragm made of plastic or thin metal foil

Whenever a coil moves within a magnetic field, a current is produced in the coil.

Permanent magnet produces magnetic field.

Coil of wire fixed to the diaphragm

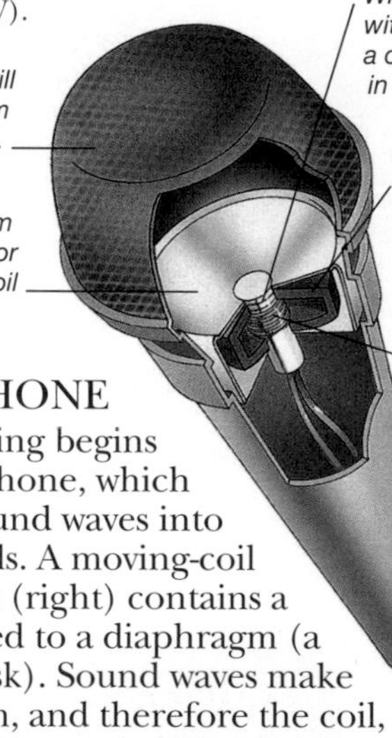

MICROPHONE
Every recording begins with a microphone, which converts sound waves into electrical signals. A moving-coil microphone (right) contains a wire coil attached to a diaphragm (a thin, flexible disk). Sound waves make the diaphragm, and therefore the coil, vibrate. The coil moves within the magnetic field of a small magnet; this movement generates an electric current in the coil. The current fluctuates in strength in the same way as the sound wave.

TAPE RECORDING
A cassette holds a spool of plastic tape coated with tiny metal grains. The grains are magnetic, and when sound is recorded onto the tape, the magnetism of the grains changes. The new magnetic pattern represents the sound.

Capstan and pinch roller keep the tape moving at the correct speed past the tape head.

During recording, the tape head arranges the magnetic pattern of the grains to record an image of the sound onto the tape.

Before a recording is made, the magnetic grains in the tape point in all directions.

Compact disks reproduce sounds of very high quality.

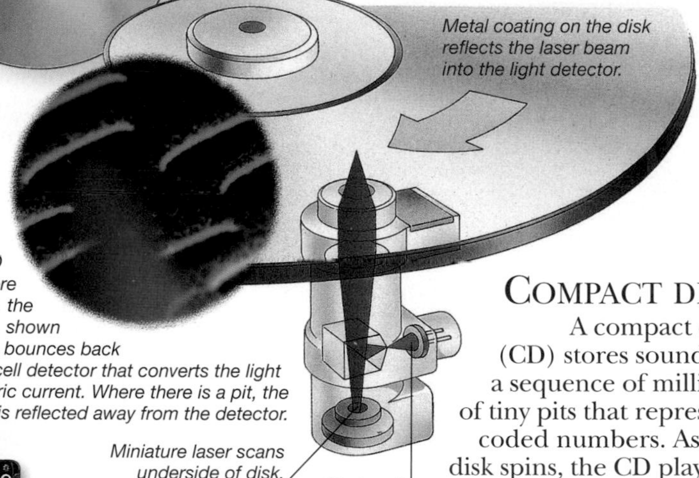

Metal coating on the disk reflects the laser beam into the light detector.

An amplifier boosts the signal from the CD player before it reaches the speaker.

Loudspeakers are usually fitted in a cabinet.

Electromagnet consists of a coil of wire.

Varying field in electromagnet moves cone to and from permanent magnet.

Cone vibrates, producing sound waves.

Permanent magnet

At a place on the CD where there is no pit, the laser beam, shown here in red, bounces back to a photocell detector that converts the light into electric current. Where there is a pit, the beam is reflected away from the detector.

Miniature laser scans underside of disk.

Photocell detector

COMPACT DISK
A compact disk (CD) stores sounds as a sequence of millions of tiny pits that represent coded numbers. As the disk spins, the CD player's laser beam reads the sequence of pits and sends a signal to the loudspeaker.

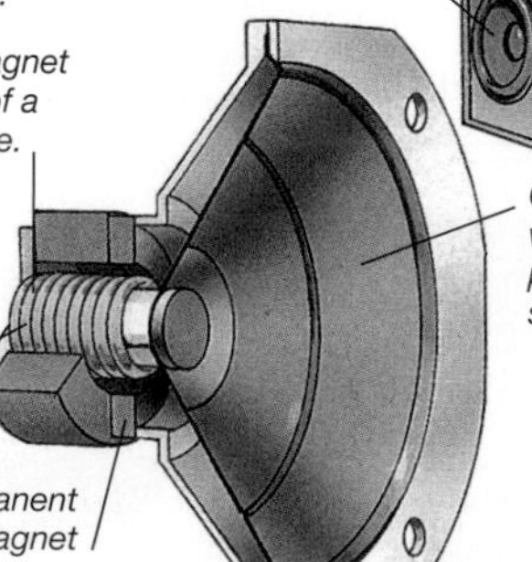

LOUDSPEAKER
A loudspeaker changes electrical signals into sound waves. Inside a loudspeaker, a varying electric current from a source such as a CD player or cassette deck powers an electromagnet, producing a varying magnetic field. This field makes a cone-shaped diaphragm vibrate, producing sound.

MINIDISK AND MP3
New types of data storage for sound recording are always being developed. A minidisk is a digital audio storage disk similar to a CD. However, the sound quality on a minidisk is less perfect than a CD because its small size means that data is heavily compressed. MP3 is a digital music file format that can be stored on a computer or a small portable player similar to a personal stereo. MP3 sound quality is crystal clear and near to perfect.

Find out more

BROADCASTING
LASERS
MUSIC
ROCK AND POP
SOUND

SOUTH AFRICA

AFRICA'S SOUTHERNMOST LAND, South Africa is immensely rich in natural resources and has a varied landscape and diverse animal species. In the 17th century, the Cape Town region was settled by Dutch colonists, who were soon followed by the British. From the 1830s, the Dutch (or Boers) began to penetrate the interior. Here, they clashed with the black majority, particularly the Zulus, a disciplined fighting force. In the 20th century, South Africa was dominated by the white minority. The black population was deprived of the vote until 1994, when South Africa held its first multiracial, democratic elections. South Africa's diverse economy is based on mining and agriculture. It is just beginning to exploit its tourist potential. Two independent countries, Lesotho and Swaziland, are marooned within South Africa, and economically dependent on their neighbor.

Situated at the southern tip of the African continent, South Africa is bordered by both the Atlantic and Indian oceans. Much of the country consists of a broad plateau, bordered in the northeast by the arid Namib and Kalahari Deserts, and in the south by mountains and a sandy, coastal plain.

CAPE TOWN
Cape Town, home to the South African parliament, is situated along the southwestern shores of Table Bay. The town is dominated by the distinctive shape of Table Mountain, which rises to 3,300 ft (1,005 m). Cape Town was the first place to be settled by Dutch colonists in the 17th century. It was strategically placed on the main shipping routes between Europe and Asia. Today, it is still a major port and commercial center.

THE DRAKENSBERG
The Drakensberg, or Dragon Mountains, are a large range in the southeast of South Africa. They form a steep escarpment, reaching the height of 11,424 ft (3,482 m), which rises out of South Africa's central plateau. Much of South Africa's interior is dominated by tableland. This is an area of dry, rolling grassland (*veld*), with scattered trees. In places it is more than 3,900 ft (1,200 m) above sea level. It is grazed by both sheep and cattle.

SERVING FOOD
Wooden vessels are used throughout the African continent. Bowls like this one from Lesotho are traditionally carved from a single block of wood.

TOWNSHIPS

Until 1994, the apartheid system enforced the separation of the black majority from the ruling, white minority. Many black people were forced to live in specially-built "townships," and still live there today. Soweto is a sprawling group of townships with a population of about two million. It is situated outside Johannesburg, where most of its inhabitants work, forcing them to travel long distances each day.

MINERALS
South Africa is the world's largest gold producer. It also exports large quantities of diamonds, manganese, chromium, and platinum.

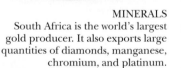

A FERTILE LAND
With its fertile soils and warm climate, South Africa is ideally situated for agriculture. The main crops grown for export are wheat, sugarcane, potatoes, peanuts, citrus fruits, and tobacco. Sheep and cattle graze the *veld*. European settlers brought vines to South Africa in the 17th century. The Cape province is a major wine-producing area, and South African wine is exported all over the world.

Find out more

AFRICA
AFRICA, HISTORY OF
AFRICAN WILDLIFE
ELEPHANTS
NATIONAL PARKS

🌋	△	🏛	✪	●	•
Volcano	Mountain	Ancient monument	Capital city	Large city/town	Small city/town

STATISTICS
Area: 471,443 sq miles
(1,221,040 sq km)
Population: 45,000,000
Capital: Pretoria
Languages: English,
Afrikaans, Zulu, Xhosa,
Ndebele, Setswana,
Siswati, North Sotho,
South Sotho,
Tsongo, Venda
Religions: Protestant,
Roman Catholic, Hindu,
Muslim
Currency: Rand
Main occupations:
Finance, manufacturing,
Main exports: Gold,
diamonds, manganese,
chrome ore, vanadium,
vermiciline, uranium,
platinum

SANGOMA
In the tribal communities of South Africa, a person known as a *sangoma* (healer) performs many functions. He or she treats illness, predicts the future, and communicates with the ancestors. Music and dance are central to these practices; music is used to summon spirits and accompany healing rituals.

A South African healer discusses the healing properties of his medicines with a patient.

SWAZILAND
The tiny kingdom of Swaziland is bordered on three sides by South Africa and by Mozambique to the east. Most of the country consists of high plateaus and mountains. The economy is dominated by agriculture, and sugarcane is the main export. Most of the people live in traditional clans, centered on scattered villages. Swaziland is ruled by a king; his mother, known as the "Great She-Elephant" is a powerful figure. South African tourists come to Swaziland for its game reserves and casinos.

South Africa has three capital cities; Pretoria, the principal city, is the administrative capital, Cape Town the legislative capital, and Bloemfontein is the judicial capital.

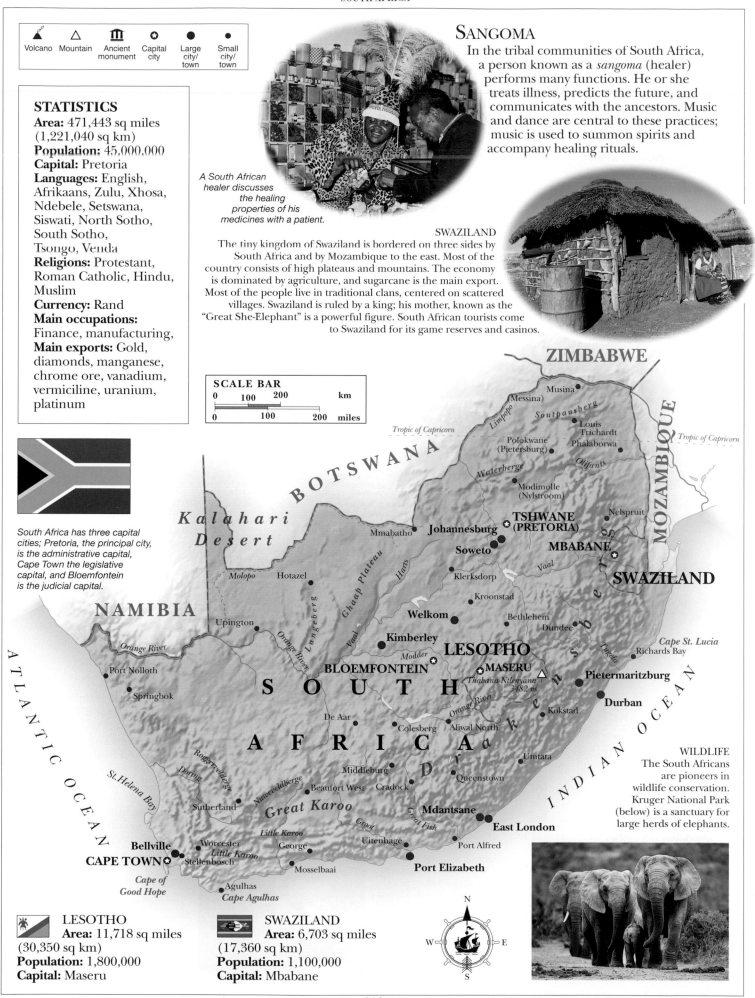

WILDLIFE
The South Africans are pioneers in wildlife conservation. Kruger National Park (below) is a sanctuary for large herds of elephants.

LESOTHO
Area: 11,718 sq miles
(30,350 sq km)
Population: 1,800,000
Capital: Maseru

SWAZILAND
Area: 6,703 sq miles
(17,360 sq km)
Population: 1,100,000
Capital: Mbabane

HISTORY OF
SOUTH AFRICA

WHEN THE FIRST EUROPEANS settled in South Africa in the 1600s, they found a rich, fertile country long inhabited by African civilizations. The Europeans set up supply ports for ships sailing to and from India and the Far East. They moved inland, bringing them into conflict with Zulus and other African kingdoms. In 1910, South Africa became independent, but its black population was denied political power for many years. Today South Africa is a multiracial country with a black president. All races are represented in government.

ZULUS

The original inhabitants of South Africa were the Bushmen, Khoikoi, Bantus, and Zulus, who settled in the country over many thousands of years. The Zulus were fierce and warlike, living in protected homesteads made of wood with grass-thatched roofs.

Oxen pulled covered wagons through rough country.

SOUTH AFRICA

1652 Dutch establish port of Cape Town.

1814 Britain gains Cape Province from Dutch.

1836-45 Great Trek.

1852 Boers set up Transvaal and (1854) Orange Free State.

1879 Zulu war.

1899-1902 Boer War, won by the British.

1910 South Africa becomes independent in British Empire.

1948 Nationalist Party introduces apartheid.

1960 67 Africans killed while protesting against apartheid, Sharpeville.

1994 First multiracial election.

THE GREAT TREK

The Dutch were the first Europeans to settle in South Africa, establishing Cape Town in 1652. The colony grew, but in 1814, the British took control. Relations between the Dutch farmers, known as Boers, and the British, were poor. Between 1836-45 more than 15,000 Boers trekked north, settling in Natal and the Transvaal.

Boers trekking north

APARTHEID

In 1948, the Nationalist Party won power, and introduced a policy of apartheid, or racial separation. Black and white South Africans were kept apart. Blacks were not allowed to vote in their own country, and were forced to live in poor areas called homelands.

MAJORITY RULE
The African National Congress (ANC) led opposition to apartheid, with support from people worldwide. In 1990, South African president, F. W. de Klerk, began to negotiate the end of apartheid with the ANC and released Nelson Mandela from prison. Apartheid was ended. In 1994, South Africa held its first-ever multiracial elections, won by the ANC.

BOER WAR

In 1886, gold was discovered in the Boer-ruled Transvaal. British miners flooded into the country. The Boers felt threatened by these *Uitlanders* (foreigners), and, in 1899, declared war on Britain. At first they won victories, but, in 1900, the British occupied Boer lands. The Boers continued fighting, but many died in British concentration camps. In 1902, peace was declared.

Find out more
AFRICA
AFRICA, HISTORY OF
MANDELA, NELSON
SOUTHERN AFRICA

SOUTH AMERICA

THREE VERY DIFFERENT TYPES of landscape dominate the triangular continent of South America. Along the western coast the towering Andes Mountains reach to more than 22,600 ft (6,900 m) in height. Dense rain forest covers the hot and humid northeastern area. Further south are great open plains of grass and scrub. There are also huge mineral deposits and rich farming lands. Despite this, some of the 12 nations which make up the continent are among the poorest in the world. Until about 170 years ago, Spain and Portugal ruled almost all of South America. Most people still speak Spanish or Portuguese. The population is made up of three groups: those descended from European settlers, Native Americans, and people of mixed ancestry. Many people are desperately poor and can barely afford to buy food. Large sections of the population are uneducated and cannot read or write. Many South American governments are insecure or unstable. Most have borrowed large sums of money from wealthier nations. The cost of repaying these debts makes it hard for the South American countries to develop industries which would take advantage of the natural resources.

South America lies south of the isthmus of Panama, between the Atlantic and Pacific oceans. It covers 6.9 million sq miles (17.8 million sq km).

USING THE LAND

Large herds of cattle roam the grasslands of the Pampas, supporting the meat-packing trade in Argentina, Uruguay, and Paraguay. Corn is grown as a staple crop across the continent. Coffee is grown as a cash crop in Brazil and Colombia, while coca plants grown in Bolivia, Peru, and Colombia provide most of the world's cocaine, an illegal drug.

Care of the Argentine cattle is the job of cowboys called gauchos.

ANDES MOUNTAINS
Stretching the entire length of the continent, the Andes mountain chain is 4,500 miles (47,250 km) long. As well as mineral deposits, the Andes have rich farming land in mountain valleys and on the Altiplano, a large plateau in Peru and Bolivia.

Roads crossing the Andes follow routes through the few low passes.

PERU
With a population of nearly 27 million, Peru is one of the larger South American countries. It includes a long stretch of the Andes and part of the rain forest. Many people live on mountain farms and are very poor. Others work on plantations growing coffee, sugar, and cotton for export. Oil has recently been discovered and is bringing some wealth to Peru.

Coffee is still picked by hand in parts of South America.

LAKE TITICACA
In the Andes Mountains on the border between Peru and Bolivia, Lake Titicaca is the highest large lake in the world. The lake's surface is 12,507 ft (3,812 m) above sea level. Some parts are 600 ft (180 m) deep. Although large ships operate on the lake, the local people still use reed to build their traditional fishing boats.

BOLIVIA

The mountain nation of Bolivia has no coastline. Its only links with the rest of the world are railroads and roads running through Peru and Chile. Although there are large deposits of oil, tin, and silver in the high Andes, the nation remains very poor. About 70 percent of the population are Aymara or Quechua Native Americans who grow just enough food in the mountains to feed themselves. Some farmers make extra money by growing the coca plant, which is processed to make the illegal drug cocaine.

A woman from Bolivia in traditional dress

SOCCER

Supported passionately, soccer is a favorite sport in most South American countries. Argentina, Brazil, and Uruguay have been very successful in international competitions. In 1930, Uruguay became the first country to host the World Cup. Uruguay also managed to win the tournament in the same year. World Cup victories in 1958, 1962, 1970, 1994, and 2002 mean that Brazil has won this fiercely contested event more times than any other country in the world.

Argentinian soccer fans parade the streets, demonstrating support for their national soccer team. Argentina won the Fédération Internationale de Football Association (FIFA) World Cup in 1978 and 1986.

The Native Americans of South American forests live in large huts shared by many families. They sleep in hammocks hung between the posts of the huts.

NATIVE AMERICANS

The first peoples of South America were Native Americans. In the lowlands, Native Americans lived in small villages and gathered food from the forest, but in the Andes they built great civilizations. The arrival of European explorers destroyed these great cultures, and today only a few remote tribes still live in the forest as their ancestors did. However, the destruction of the rain forest for farming and mining threatens to eliminate even these last traces of Native American society.

FALKLAND ISLANDS

Located in the Atlantic Ocean, the Falkland Islands were discovered by the English navigator John Davis, in his ship *Desire* in 1592. In 1690, the islands were named after Viscount Falkland, treasurer of the British navy. Islas Malvinas, the Argentinian name, comes from "Les Malouines," the name given to the islands by French sailors in the 1700s. The islands were occupied at various times by England, Spain, France, and Argentina.

Rockhopper, Magellanic, and Gento penguins are common on the Falkland Islands.

AMAZON

The longest river in South America is the Amazon, which rises in the Andes and flows 4,050 miles (6,516 km) to the Atlantic. For most of its length the river flows through a rain forest which covers 2.5 million sq miles (6.5 million sq km). In recent years much of the rain forest has been cut down to provide farmland. Although the destruction continues, it is now beginning to slow down.

Find out more
ARGENTINA
BRAZIL
COLOMBIA
INCAS
SOCCER

MINERALS IN CHILE

Copper is Chile's largest export. Chuquicamata (above) is the country's most productive copper mine. Metallic minerals are plentiful along the length of the Andes Mountains. They are formed over thousands of years by pressure and heat during mountain-building processes. The Atacama Desert in the northern third of the country stores copper, silver, gold, and abundant deposits of sodium nitrate.

* Countries covered on other pages.

ARGENTINA *
Area: 1,068,296 sq miles (2,766,890 sq km)
Population: 38,400,000
Capital: Buenos Aires

BOLIVIA
Area: 424,162 sq miles (1,098,580 sq km)
Population: 8,800,000
Capital: Sucre, La Paz
Languages: Spanish, Quechua, Aymará
Religions: Roman Catholic
Currency: Boliviano
Main occupations: Subsistence farming, mining, trading
Main exports: Gold, silver, zinc, lead, tin, oil, natural gas

BRAZIL *
Area: 3,286,472 sq miles (8,511,970 sq km)
Population: 179,000,000
Capital: Brasília

CHILE
Area: 292,258 sq miles (756,950 sq km)
Population: 15,800,000
Capital: Santiago
Languages: Spanish, Amerindian languages
Religions: Roman Catholic, non-religious
Currency: Chilean peso
Main occupations: Mining, agriculture
Main exports: Copper, fresh fruit, fishmeal, salmon, wine, lithium, molybdenum, gold

COLOMBIA *
Area: 439,733 sq miles (1,138,910 sq km)
Population: 44,200,000
Capital: Bogotá

ECUADOR
Area: 109,483 sq miles (283,560 sq km)
Population: 13,000,000
Capital: Quito
Languages: Spanish, Quechua, other Amerindian languages
Religions: Roman Catholic, Protestant, Jewish
Currency: Sucre
Main occupations: Oil production, agriculture, fishing
Main exports: Oil, bananas, fish

FRENCH GUIANA
Area: 32,252 sq miles (83,533 sq km)
Population: 186,900
Capital: Cayenne
Status: French department

GUYANA
Area: 83,000 sq miles (214,970 sq km)
Population: 765,000
Capital: Georgetown
Languages: English Creole, Hindi, Tamil, Amerindian languages, English
Religions: Christian, Hindu, Muslim
Currency: Guyana dollar
Main occupations: Subsistence farming, mining, forestry
Main exports: Gold, sugar, bauxite, diamond, timber, rice

PARAGUAY
Area: 157,046 sq miles (406,750 sq km)
Population: 5,900,000
Capital: Asunción
Languages: Guaraní, Spanish
Religions: Roman Catholic
Currency: Guaraní
Main occupations: Agriculture
Main exports: Energy, cotton, oilseeds, soya

PERU
Area: 496,223 sq miles (1,285,220 sq km)
Population: 27,200,000
Capital: Lima
Languages: Spanish, Quechua, Aymará
Religions: Roman Catholic
Currency: Nuevo sol
Main occupations: Subsistence farming, fishing, manufacturing
Main exports: Oil, fish, cotton, coffee, textiles, copper, lead, coca leaves, sugar

SURINAME
Area: 63,039 sq miles (163,270 sq km)
Population: 436,000
Capital: Paramaribo
Languages: Pidgin English (Taki-Taki), Dutch, Hindi, Javanese, Saramacca, Carib
Religions: Christian, Hindu, Muslim
Currency: Paramaribo
Main occupations: Agriculture, forestry, mining, fishing
Main exports: Bauxite, gold, oil, rice, bananas, citrus fruits, shrimp, aluminum

URUGUAY
Area: 67,494 sq miles (174,810 sq km)
Population: 3,400,000
Capital: Montevideo
Languages: Spanish
Religions: Roman Catholic, Protestant, Jewish, non-religious
Currency: Uruguayan peso
Main occupations: Agriculture, tourism, manufacturing
Main exports: Wool, meat, rice

INCA TERRACES
These terraces near Cuzco, Peru, were built by the Incas to enable cultivation of the hillside. They are still farmed by descendants of the Inca people today.

VENEZUELA
Area: 352,143 sq miles (912,050 sq km)
Population: 25,700,000
Capital: Caracas
Languages: Spanish, Amerindian languages
Religions: Roman Catholic, Protestant
Currency: Bolivar
Main occupations: Mining, agriculture, oil production
Main exports: Coal, bauxite, iron, gold, bitumen fuel, steel, aluminum, oil, coffee

At a height of 3,212 ft (979 m), the majestic Angel Falls in Venezuela (above), is the highest uninterrupted waterfall in the world. It was named after bush pilot Jimmy Angel.

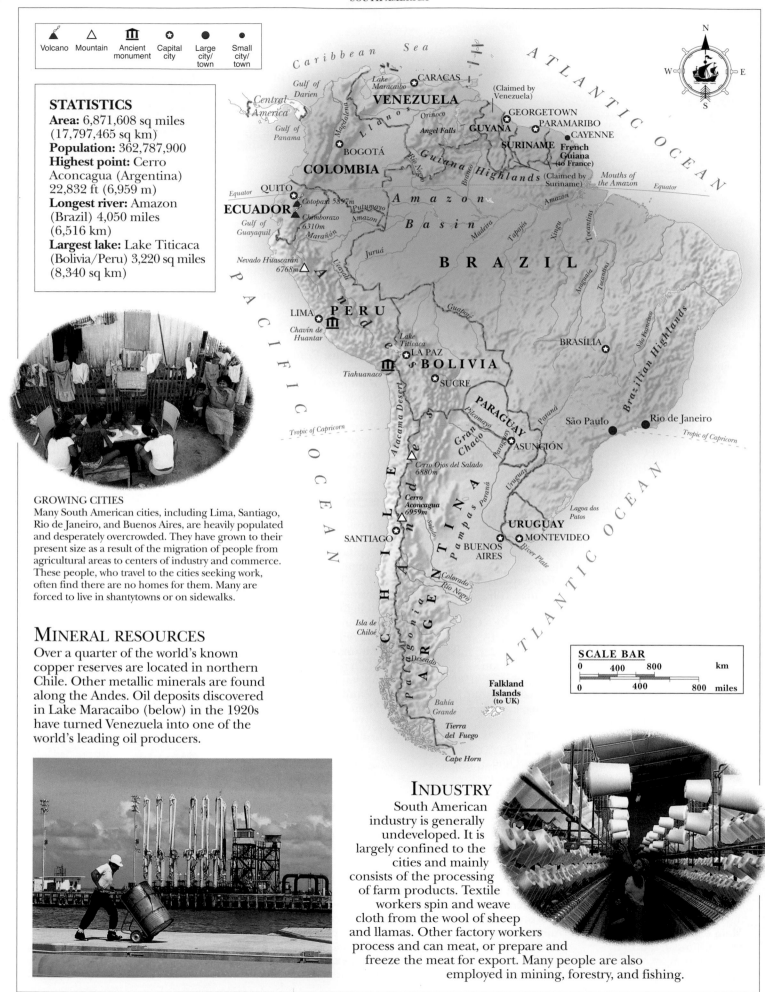

Volcano	Mountain	Ancient monument	Capital city	Large city/town	Small city/town

STATISTICS

Area: 6,871,608 sq miles (17,797,465 sq km)
Population: 362,787,900
Highest point: Cerro Aconcagua (Argentina) 22,832 ft (6,959 m)
Longest river: Amazon (Brazil) 4,050 miles (6,516 km)
Largest lake: Lake Titicaca (Bolivia/Peru) 3,220 sq miles (8,340 sq km)

GROWING CITIES

Many South American cities, including Lima, Santiago, Rio de Janeiro, and Buenos Aires, are heavily populated and desperately overcrowded. They have grown to their present size as a result of the migration of people from agricultural areas to centers of industry and commerce. These people, who travel to the cities seeking work, often find there are no homes for them. Many are forced to live in shantytowns or on sidewalks.

MINERAL RESOURCES

Over a quarter of the world's known copper reserves are located in northern Chile. Other metallic minerals are found along the Andes. Oil deposits discovered in Lake Maracaibo (below) in the 1920s have turned Venezuela into one of the world's leading oil producers.

INDUSTRY

South American industry is generally undeveloped. It is largely confined to the cities and mainly consists of the processing of farm products. Textile workers spin and weave cloth from the wool of sheep and llamas. Other factory workers process and can meat, or prepare and freeze the meat for export. Many people are also employed in mining, forestry, and fishing.

SCALE BAR

0	400	800	km
0	400	800	miles

HISTORY OF
SOUTH AMERICA

Attendants, uniformly dressed, carry the dead king on a bier.

Gold mask

Dead Chimu king is prepared for burial in a sitting position.

Chimu burial ceremony

CHIMU EMPIRE

The Chimu empire centered on the vast capital city of Chan Chan, in what is now northern Peru. The empire covered much of the Pacific coast of South America and reached the height of its power in the 15th century. In 1460, the Incas conquered the Chimu empire, and Chan Chan fell into ruin. The Chimu are remembered as a highly civilized society. The royal dead were buried with a wealth of funeral offerings.

SOUTH AMERICA

200 B.C.-A.D. 600 Nazca empire in Peru.

600 City-states of Tiahuanaco and Huari in Peru.

1000-1470 Chimu empire in Peru.

1200 Inca empire in Bolivia, Chile, Ecuador, and Peru.

1494 Treaty of Tordesillas divides New World between Spain and Portugal.

1499-1510 Amerigo Vespucci explores coast of South America; the continent is named after him.

1530 Portuguese colonize Brazil.

1532-33 Spanish led by Francisco Pizarro conquer Inca empire.

1545 Silver discovered in Peru.

1808-25 Liberation wars: Spanish and Portuguese colonies.

1822-89 Empire of Brazil

1879-84 Border wars between Peru, Chile, and Bolivia.

1932-35 War between Paraguay and Bolivia over disputed territory.

1946 Juan Perón becomes president of Argentina.

1967 Che Guevara killed in Bolivia.

FOR THOUSANDS OF YEARS, the continent of South America developed independently from the rest of the world. Great cultures rose and fell, among them the Nazcas, Chimus, and Incas, all of which developed highly advanced civilizations of great wealth and achievement. In 1532, the Spaniards invaded the Inca empire, and within a few years ruled over most of the continent. The Portuguese established control over Brazil. Soon Spanish and Portuguese became the main languages of South America, and for the next 300 years the affairs of South America were decided in Europe. The native peoples were almost wiped out by disease and ill-treatment. When Spain and Portugal became involved in the Napoleonic wars in Europe, the South Americans seized the chance to win their independence. Afterward, the new countries were ruled by European families who had settled in South America. Many more Europeans arrived during the 19th and early 20th centuries. The nations of South America have only recently begun to control their destinies.

Line of demarcation 1494

Portuguese territories

Spanish territories

TREATY OF TORDESILLAS
In the 1494 Treaty of Tordesillas, Spain and Portugal divided the nonEuropean world between them. They drew a rough line down the South American continent, giving Spain the lands to the west and Portugal the lands to the east of the line.

SPANISH DOMINATION
From 1532 to 1810, Spain controlled the whole of South America apart from Portuguese-owned Brazil. The vast Spanish Empire was divided into three viceroyalties – New Granada in the north, Peru in the center, and Rio de la Plata in the south. On the right is Santiago, the patron saint of Spanish soldiers.

NATIVE AMERICANS
The Native Americans were put to work as slaves in the silver mines. They were also forced to labor in the big plantations of sugar and other crops that were exported to Europe. Most Native Americans died of poor conditions, overwork, and European diseases they had no immunity against.

SIMÓN BOLÍVAR

In 1808, Spain was involved in a war with French emperor Napoleon Bonaparte; the South American colonies took this opportunity to declare their independence. Led by Simón Bolívar (1783-1830) and José de San Martín (1778-1850), the colonies fought against Spanish control; all gained their freedom by 1825. Bolívar hoped to unite all of South America, but many disliked his dictatorial approach. In 1822, Brazil declared its independence from Portugal, leaving only Guiana in the north under European control.

ROMAN CATHOLIC CHURCH

When the Spanish arrived in South America, they brought the Roman Catholic religion with them. Catholic priests tried to stamp out local religions and convert the Native Americans to their faith. In the end, the priests were forced to include parts of the old Native American religions in their services. In some places, the priests tried to protect the Native Americans against Spanish rulers who were cruel to them, but most priests upheld the Spanish colonial government. During the 20th century, the Roman Catholic Church took a more active role in supporting the poor against powerful landlords and corrupt governments.

Bolívar leads soldiers into battle

Pedro arrives in Recife (formerly Pernambuco), a prosperous town in the empire.

Stamp bearing a portrait of Pedro II

BRAZILIAN EMPIRE

From 1822 to 1889, Brazil was an empire. Under Emperor Pedro II (1825-1891) roads and railroads were built, and the coffee and rubber industries began to prosper. Thousands of immigrants poured into the country from Italy, Portugal, and Spain. In 1888, the African slaves who had been brought over to work the plantations were freed. This angered many landowners, since they had been using the slaves as cheap labor. The landowners withdrew their support from Pedro, and in 1889 the army took over the empire and a republic was declared.

ERNESTO "CHE" GUEVARA

One of the most popular heroes of the 20th century, Che Guevara (1928-1967) was born into a rich Argentinian family. Guevara was a doctor before choosing to spend his life supporting revolutions against oppressive South American governments. In 1959, he helped Fidel Castro overthrow the Cuban government. Guevara served under Castro until 1965. In late 1966 he went to Bolivia, where he based himself in the countryside among poor peasants. In 1967, he was killed by the Bolivian army. His death made him a hero for revolutionaries everywhere. In 1997, he was reburied in Cuba.

JUAN PERÓN

From 1946 to 1955, Argentina was ruled by President Juan Perón (1895-1974). Poor people living in the cities supported Perón and his wife, Eva. He introduced many reforms but did not allow anyone to oppose him. After the economy weakened in the early 1950s, and after Eva's death in 1952, Perón became much less popular. He was overthrown by the army in 1955. In 1973, he again held power but died the following year. His third wife, Isabel Martínez de Perón, succeeded him as president.

Find out more

CENTRAL AMERICA
CONQUISTADORS
INCAS
SOUTH AMERICA

SOUTHEAST ASIA

AT ITS SOUTHEAST CORNER, the continent of Asia extends far out into the sea, in two great peninsulas and a vast chain of islands. In this region, which is called Southeast Asia, over 543 million people live in 11 independent countries. The area has a rich and varied culture, and music and dancing are particularly important. Their performance is often governed by strict rituals and rules, some of them religious. There are several different religions in the area: most people on the mainland are Buddhist; Indonesia is chiefly Muslim; and Christianity is the religion of most people in the Philippines. For much of last century the lives of many Southeast Asian people were disrupted and destroyed by wars. The fighting made normal trade, agriculture, and industry impossible, and turned Laos and Cambodia into the two poorest nations on Earth. In Cambodia guerrilla warfare until recently claimed the lives of soldiers and civilians. Other Southeast Asian countries, particularly the island nations, have escaped the worst fighting. These countries are now more prosperous and peaceful.

Southeast Asia is the part of Asia to the south of China, and east of India. The mainland portion has an area of 640,000 sq miles (1.6 million sq km). The region continues to the south as a chain of islands which separate the Pacific and Indian oceans. The island of Sumatra is 1,070 miles (1,720 km) long; other islands are tiny.

Sap is extracted by tapping – cutting or shaving the bark with a sharp knife.

Plantation workers drain the sticky sap from the trees in the morning when the flow of sap is fastest.

THAILAND
There are 62.8 million people in Thailand, and the country is among the wealthiest in the region. Most people in the cities work in mining and industry; in the countryside most are farmers growing rice, sugar, and rubber trees. The country's rich heritage includes ritual temple dances and beautiful architecture.

Singapore City began as a small British trading station; today, giant skyscrapers dominate the skyline.

RUBBER
One of the most important products of Southeast Asia is rubber. The industry began about a century ago when British traders brought rubber trees to the region from Brazil. The sap of the trees is collected, then mixed with acid to form solid sheets of latex, which are hung out to dry.

SINGAPORE
The tiny island state of Singapore occupies just 239 sq miles (620 sq km) off the coast of Malaysia. The nation is highly industrialized and very rich. Most of Singapore's 4.4 million people earn their living from industries such as textiles and electronics.

The Borobudur Temple was built with about 2,000,000 cubic ft (56,600 cubic m) of gray volcanic stone.

JAVA
The country of Indonesia is made up of 13,677 islands. Java is the most populated island, with 127 million people. Many are farmers producing large quantities of rice. The capital city, Jakarta, is a center for the textile industry. The island has much unique wildlife, including species of tiger and rhinoceros found nowhere else.

BOROBUDUR TEMPLE
A massive Buddhist monument in Java, the Borodubur Temple was constructed between 778 and 850 A.D. From about 1000 B.C. it was buried under volcanic ash until its discovery by the English lieutenant governor Thomas Stamford Raffles in 1814. A team of Dutch archaeologists restored the site in 1907-11 and a second restoration was completed by 1983.

Protected by law, orangutans still face hunting and destruction of their rain forest habitat. Orangutan is the Malaysian for "person of the forest."

VIETNAM

Vietnam is a mountainous land which occupies the eastern part of the IndoChina peninsula in Southeast Asia. Its population, which is mainly rural, mostly lives in the lowland deltas of the Red and Mekong rivers. Three-quarters of its people work in agriculture. Rice takes up more land area than all other crops produced in Vietnam put together. Other crops include rubber, corn, sugar, bananas, coconuts, pepper, tea, tobacco, and sweet potatoes. Northern Vietnam is more industrialized than the agricultural south. It has mineral resources, which include coal, salt, tin, and iron. Farmers often work in salt farms (left) to supplement their earnings from agriculture.

ORANGUTAN

The orangutan is a large humanlike ape that is now restricted to lowland swamp forests in Borneo and a small part of Sumatra. Orangutans once lived in the jungles of mainland Southeast Asia as well, but numbers have been depleted by human hunters. With its short, thickset body, long arms, and short legs, the orangutan displays many physical similarities to gorillas and chimpanzees. However, a shaggy, reddish coat, and an even greater disproportion between arm and leg lengths, sets the orangutan apart from its related primates. The male orangutan may be about 4.5 ft (1.37 m) tall and weigh about 185 lbs (85 kg) when grown, while females usually weigh about 90 lbs (40 kg).

MYANMAR (BURMA)

Myanmar gained independence from British colonial control in 1948 and immediately adopted a policy of political and economic isolation. Once a rich nation, the country was subsequently reduced to one of the world's poorest despite its plentiful natural resources. The Irrawaddy river basin occupies most of the country and provides rich farming land. Myanmar has in recent years been ruled by a military government which has excluded all foreign influences. Over 89 percent of the population are Buddhists, but in the countryside many still worship the *nats* – ancient spirits of the forest and mountains. Devotees of Buddhism pray at temples such as the Shwedagon Pagoda (below) in Rangoon (Yangon).

DAO PEOPLE

With a population of 47,000, the Dao people are the eighth-largest ethnic group in Vietnam, where they inhabit all the northern bordering areas. The Dao can also be found in the neighboring countries of China, Laos, and Thailand. The origins of the first Dao groups in Vietnam are uncertain, but it appears that they emigrated from their native provinces of southern China in the 18th and 19th centuries.

ELEPHANT SCHOOL

Elephants in Thailand are trained to work for a living. They have proved themselves to be far more cost-efficient than modern tractors. They need little fuel and do not rust or need spare parts. Tractors last for about six years, an elephant lives for 30. In addition, elephants are less harmful to the environment. They move timber and take tourists for rides in the rain forest.

BRUNEI
Area: 2,228 sq miles (5,770 sq km)
Population: 358,000
Capital: Bandar Seri Begawan
Languages: Malay, English, Chinese
Religions: Muslim, Buddhist, Christian
Currency: Brunei dollar

 MYANMAR (BURMA)
Area: 261,200 sq miles (676,550 sq km)
Population: 49,500,000
Capital: Rangoon (Yangon)
Languages: Burmese, Karen, Shan, Chin, Kachin, Mon, Palaung, Wa
Religions: Buddhist, Christian, Muslim, Hindu
Currency: Kyat

 CAMBODIA
Area: 69,000 sq miles (181,040 sq km)
Population: 14,100,000
Capital: Phnom Penh
Languages: Khmer, French, Chinese, Vietnamese, Cham
Religions: Theravada Buddhist
Currency: Riel

 EAST TIMOR
Area: 5,794 sq miles (15,007 sq km)
Population: 778,000
Capital: Dili
Languages: Tetum, Bahasa Indonesia, Portuguese
Religions: Roman Catholic
Currency: US dollar

 INDONESIA
Area: 735,555 sq miles (1,904,570 sq km)
Population: 220,000,000
Capital: Jakarta
Languages: Javanese, Madurese, Sundanese, Bahasa Indonesia, Dutch
Religions: Muslim, Protestant, Roman Catholic, Hindu, Buddhist
Currency: Rupiah

 LAOS
Area: 81,428 sq miles (236,800 sq km)
Population: 5,700,000
Capital: Vientiane
Languages: Lao, Miao, Yao, Vietnamese, Chinese, French
Religions: Buddhist, Animist
Currency: New kip

 MALAYSIA
Area: 127,317 sq miles (329,750 sq km)
Population: 24,400,000
Capital: Kuala Lumpur
Languages: Malay, Chinese, Tamil
Religions: Muslim, Buddhist, Chinese faiths, Christian, traditional beliefs
Currency: Ringgit

 PHILIPPINES
Area: 115,831 sq miles (300,000 sq km)
Population: 80,000,000
Capital: Manila
Languages: Filipino, Cebuano, Hiligaynon, Samaran, Ilocano, Bikol, English
Religions: Roman Catholic, Protestant, Muslim, Buddhist
Currency: Philippine peso

SINGAPORE
Area: 239 sq miles (620 sq km)
Population: 4,300,000
Capital: Singapore City
Languages: Chinese, Malay, Tamil, English
Religions: Buddhist, Christian, Muslim
Currency: Singapore dollar

THAILAND
Area: 198,116 sq miles (513,120 sq km)
Population: 62,800,000
Capital: Bangkok
Languages: Thai, Chinese, Malay, Khmer, Mon, Karen, Miao
Religions: Theravada Buddhist, Muslim, Christian
Currency: Baht

VIETNAM
Area: 127,243 sq miles (329,560 sq km)
Population: 81,400,000
Capital: Hanoi
Languages: Vietnamese, Chinese, Thai, Khmer, Muong, Nung, Miao, Yao, Jarai
Religions: Buddhist, Christian, nonreligious
Currency: Dông

The magnificent, golden-domed Omar Ali Saifuddin mosque, Brunei

BRUNEI

Lying on the northwestern coast of the island of Borneo, Brunei is ruled by a sultan. Since gaining independence from Britain in 1984, the country has become increasingly ifluenced by Islam. Its interior is mostly rain forest and the nation's abundant oil and gas reserves have brought its citizens one of the highest standard of living in the world.

The bustling city of Yogyakarta lies at the foot of a volcano.

PHILIPPINES
Most of the islands in the Philippines are mountainous and forested. The Filipino people live in towns and villages on the narrow coastal plains, or on plateaus between the mountain ranges. The volcanic cone of Mount Mayon, 200 miles (320 km) southeast of Manila, is one of the most beautiful in the world. However, its beauty hides its dangerous character. The volcano is still active, and past eruptions have destroyed parts of the nearby city of Albay.

INDONESIA
Although more than 13,500 islands make up the Republic of Indonesia, only about 6,000 are inhabited. Most Indonesian people live in the countryside and work on farms. However, some cities are densely populated. For example, the city of Yogyakarta (left), on the southern coast of the heavily populated island of Java, has a population of about 600,000.

Find out more
ISLAM
SOUTHEAST ASIA, HISTORY OF
VIETNAM WAR

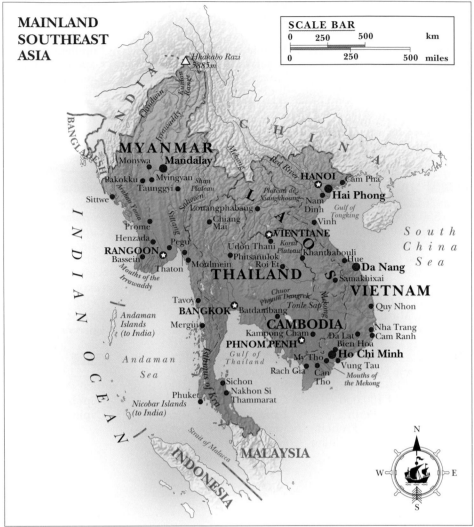

MAINLAND SOUTHEAST ASIA

Volcano ▲ **Mountain** △ **Ancient monument** 🏛 **Capital city** ✪ **Large city/town** ● **Small city/town** •

STATISTICS

Area: 1,728,157 sq miles (4,477,761 sq km)
Population: 543,336,000
No. of independent countries: 11
Religions: Buddhism, Islam, Taoism, Christianity, Hinduism
Largest city: Jakarta (Indonesia) 8,540,100
Highest point: Hkakabo Rasi (Myanmar) 19,309 ft (5,885 m)
Longest river: Mekong 2,600 miles (4,184 km)
Main occupation: Farming
Main exports: Sugar, fruits, timber, rice, rubber, tobacco, tin
Main imports: Machinery, iron and steel products, textiles, chemicals, fuels

POPULATION

The population on mainland Southeast Asia is concentrated in the river valleys, plateaus, or plains. The population of maritime Southeast Asia is unevenly distributed; Java is densely settled, while other islands are barely occupied.

SCALE BAR

MARITIME SOUTHEAST ASIA

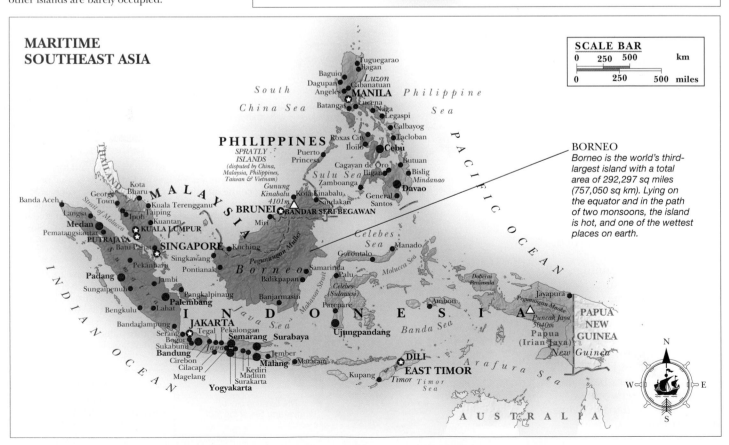

SCALE BAR

BORNEO

Borneo is the world's third-largest island with a total area of 292,297 sq miles (757,050 sq km). Lying on the equator and in the path of two monsoons, the island is hot, and one of the wettest places on earth.

HISTORY OF
SOUTHEAST ASIA

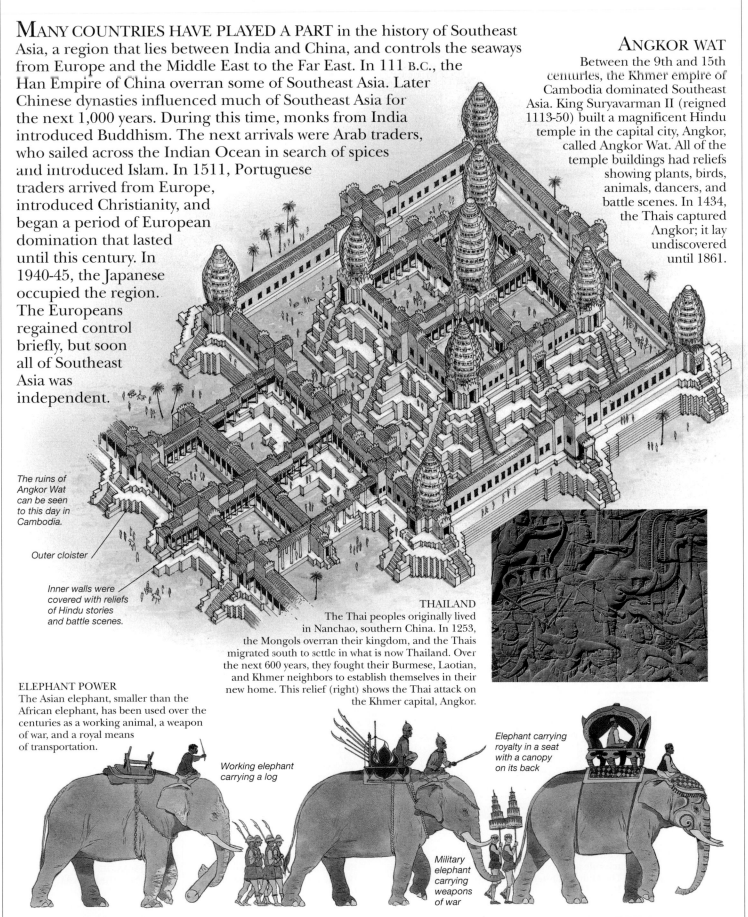

MANY COUNTRIES HAVE PLAYED A PART in the history of Southeast Asia, a region that lies between India and China, and controls the seaways from Europe and the Middle East to the Far East. In 111 B.C., the Han Empire of China overran some of Southeast Asia. Later Chinese dynasties influenced much of Southeast Asia for the next 1,000 years. During this time, monks from India introduced Buddhism. The next arrivals were Arab traders, who sailed across the Indian Ocean in search of spices and introduced Islam. In 1511, Portuguese traders arrived from Europe, introduced Christianity, and began a period of European domination that lasted until this century. In 1940-45, the Japanese occupied the region. The Europeans regained control briefly, but soon all of Southeast Asia was independent.

ANGKOR WAT
Between the 9th and 15th centuries, the Khmer empire of Cambodia dominated Southeast Asia. King Suryavarman II (reigned 1113-50) built a magnificent Hindu temple in the capital city, Angkor, called Angkor Wat. All of the temple buildings had reliefs showing plants, birds, animals, dancers, and battle scenes. In 1434, the Thais captured Angkor; it lay undiscovered until 1861.

The ruins of Angkor Wat can be seen to this day in Cambodia.

Outer cloister

Inner walls were covered with reliefs of Hindu stories and battle scenes.

THAILAND
The Thai peoples originally lived in Nanchao, southern China. In 1253, the Mongols overran their kingdom, and the Thais migrated south to settle in what is now Thailand. Over the next 600 years, they fought their Burmese, Laotian, and Khmer neighbors to establish themselves in their new home. This relief (right) shows the Thai attack on the Khmer capital, Angkor.

ELEPHANT POWER
The Asian elephant, smaller than the African elephant, has been used over the centuries as a working animal, a weapon of war, and a royal means of transportation.

Working elephant carrying a log

Elephant carrying royalty in a seat with a canopy on its back

Military elephant carrying weapons of war

SPICE TRADE

During the 15th century, European explorers who arrived in the islands of Southeast Asia were delighted to find a wide variety of spices, such as nutmeg, pepper, and cloves. Spices were in great demand for cooking but were very expensive in Europe. As a result, first the Portuguese and the Spanish, then the Dutch and the British, fought for control of the profitable spice trade.

Rich Dutch merchants landed on Asian shores to trade with the local people.

SINGAPORE

In 1824, Britain took control of the island of Singapore because it had an important harbor. But in 1942, during World War II (1939-45) Japanese troops took over the island, forcing the British to surrender (left). Several years later, Britain reoccupied the country. In 1965, Singapore became an independent nation.

SOUTHEAST ASIA

111 B.C. Chinese invade Vietnam; dominate northern area.

A.D. 0-500 Buddhism spreads throughout Southeast Asia.

802 Khmers establish empire in Cambodia and Laos.

1113-1150 Construction of Angkor Wat temple.

1300s Arab traders introduce Islam to Indonesia.

1434 Thais capture Angkor Wat and overrun Khmer empire.

1564 Spanish conquer Philippines.

1700 British East India Company establishes a trading base in Borneo.

1766-69 Chinese invade Burma.

1786 British East India Company establishes a base in Malaya.

1799 Dutch take over all of Indonesia.

1800s Thailand is only country in region independent of Europe.

1819 Singapore founded by British merchant Sir Stamford Raffles. Becomes richest port in region.

1824-1886 British take control of Burma.

1859-1893 French take control of Vietnam, Cambodia, and Laos.

1896 Britain establishes control over Malaya.

1940-1945 Japanese occupy Southeast Asia during World War II.

1946-54 French fight to maintain control of their empire in Southeast Asia.

1948 Burma independent.

1949 Indonesia independent.

1953 Cambodia and Laos win independence from France.

1956 Civil war begins in Vietnam.

1957 Malaya independent.

1967 Formation of ASEAN (Association of Southeast Asian Nations).

1965-73 US fully involved in Vietnam War.

1975 Vietnam War ends, North Vietnamese take control.

1997 Hong Kong returned to Chinese rule.

INDONESIA

On August 11, 1945, Sukarno (1901-70) declared Indonesia's independence from Dutch rule and became president of the Republic of Indonesia. The Dutch transferred sovereignty four years later. By the end of the 1950s, Malaysia, Laos, Vietnam, Cambodia, and Burma had all become independent.

CORAZON AQUINO

From 1986 to 1992, Corazon Aquino was the president of the Philippines. She entered politics when her husband, Benigno, a popular political leader, was assassinated by the dictator, Ferdinand Marcos, who ruled the Philippines for 20 years. Marcos attempted to prevent Corazon from winning the country's general election. But the people rose up against him, and he was forced to flee the country.

Find out more

JAPAN, HISTORY OF
SOUTHEAST ASIA
VIETNAM WAR

CENTRAL
SOUTHEAST EUROPE

Lying to the south of the Alps, the west of the region is mountainous with deep wooded valleys. The rocky coast of the Adriatic Sea lies to the southeast of the region. To the east lie the flat plains of the Danube, which drains into the Black Sea, and rolling steppelands.

THE NOBLE DANUBE RIVER cuts central Southeast Europe in half, providing fertile farmland along its lower course, in the heart of the region. This area of flatland, called the Danubian Plain, is surrounded by mighty mountain systems including the Carpathians to the north, and the Balkans and Rhodope mountains in the south. Following World War II, the countries of central Southeast Europe were governed for more than 50 years by strict Communist regimes, until the collapse of the Soviet Union in the early 1990s. Serbia was once part of federal Yugoslavia. The collapse of the federation led to civil war in 1991, after which five separate states emerged. Kosovo, an area in southern Serbia inhabited by Muslim Albanian Kosovans, became an autonomous region after a war in 1999.

BULGARIAN TOBACCO
Bulgaria has fertile soils and a mild climate, and a wide range of crops is grown there, including cereals, sunflower seeds, grapes, and tomatoes. High-quality red wine, made from grapes grown on the Danubian plain, is exported. In the south of the country, Turkish-style tobacco is grown; it is processed in factories around the town of Plovdiv. Here, women can be seen stringing the harvested tobacco leaves together. They are then left to cure in the heat of the sun before being graded by size and color.

A Romanian gypsy makes a living by selling berries

RURAL MOLDOVA
Once a part of Romania, Moldova became a Soviet state in 1940. In 1991, with the breakup of the Soviet Union, Moldova became independent. This small country is dominated by fertile rolling steppes. Most of the population works in agriculture. Warm summers and even rainfall provide ideal conditions for growing vegetables, fruits, and grapes, and Moldova is internationally famous for its wines. Although the Soviets mechanized state-owned farms, there are now many small-scale farmers, who cultivate their land using traditional methods.

GYPSIES
Romania has the largest gypsy (or Romany) population in Europe. Gypsies, who have a distinct language and culture, are thought to have originated in India and moved to Europe via the Middle East. Traditionally, they wandered from place to place, selling goods, repairing metal utensils, and dealing in horses and livestock. They have suffered many centuries of persecution from the countries in which they settled, where some people found it difficult to understand their different customs and ways of life.

TRANSYLVANIA
The Romanian region of Transylvania is a high plateau, surrounded by the Carpathian Mountains. To the east and south the mountains form an impassable barrier. The region, a place of rugged scenery and dramatic castles, has had a colorful history, passing from Hungarian to Ottoman Turkish to Hapsburg (Austrian) rule. Among its tyrannical rulers was the 15th-century prince, Vlad the Impaler, notorious for his cruelty. When the author Bram Stoker wrote *Dracula* in 1897, he borrowed from Slavic and Hungarian legends. His blood-sucking vampire is based on Vlad the Impaler.

ROSES
Vast fields of roses are grown in Bulgaria. Petals are picked at dawn to produce attar, the essential oil of roses.

> ### *Find out more*
> COMMUNISM
> DANCE
> EUROPE
> FLOWERS AND HERBS
> TOURISM AND TRAVEL

Volcano ▲ **Mountain** 🏛 **Ancient monument** ✪ **Capital city** ● **Large city/town** ∙ **Small city/town**

BULGARIA
Area: 42,683 sq miles (110,550 sq km)
Population: 7,900,000
Capital: Sofia
Currency: Lev

MACEDONIA
Area: 9,929 sq miles (25,715 sq km)
Population: 2,020,000
Capital: Skopje
Currency: Macedonian denar

MOLDOVA
Area: 9,929 sq miles (25,715 sq km)
Population: 4,300,000
Capital: Chişinău
Currency: Moldovan leu

ROMANIA
Area: 88,934 sq miles (230,340 sq km)
Population: 22,300,000
Capital: Bucharest
Currency: Leu

SERBIA AND MONTENEGRO
Area: 39,449 sq miles (102,173 sq km)
Population: 10,500,000
Capital: Belgrade
Currency: Dinar

THE IRON GATES
The Danube, Europe's second-longest river, flows from Germany to the Black Sea. On the Romanian-Serbian border the river is forced through a narrow gorge – the Iron Gates. A power station has been built here, which uses the water's energy to make electricity.

CARPATHIAN MOUNTAINS
The Carpathians are a major mountain system that extend 830 miles (1,500 km) along the northern and eastern side of the Danubian plain. They link the Alps with the Balkans.

SCALE BAR
0   75   150   km
0   75   150 miles

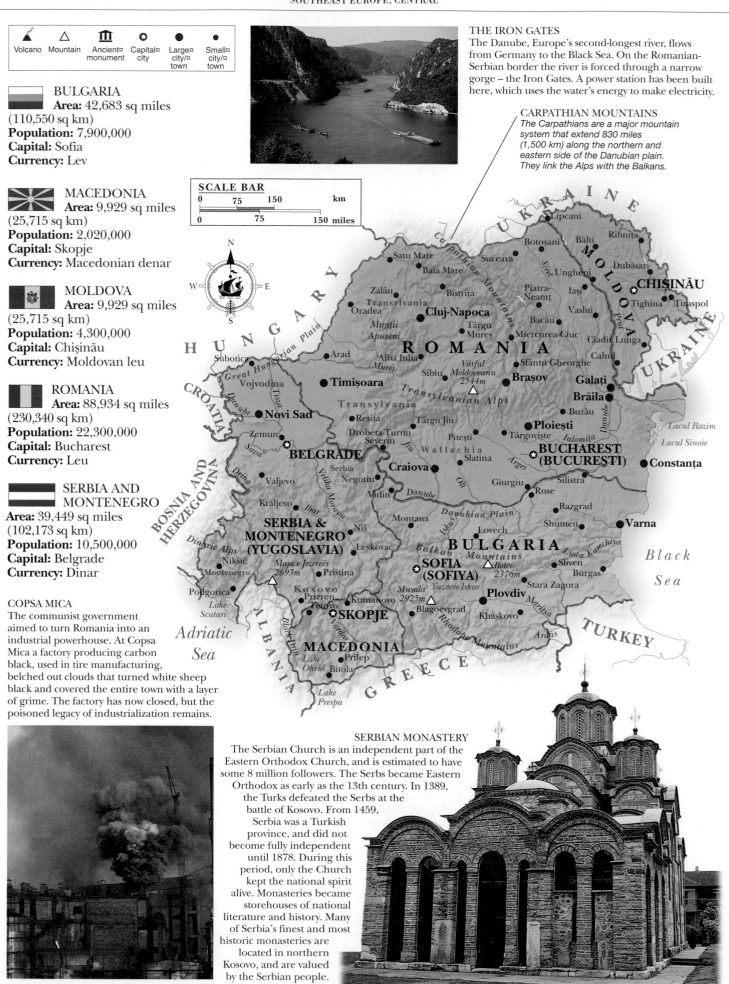

COPSA MICA
The communist government aimed to turn Romania into an industrial powerhouse. At Copsa Mica a factory producing carbon black, used in tire manufacturing, belched out clouds that turned white sheep black and covered the entire town with a layer of grime. The factory has now closed, but the poisoned legacy of industrialization remains.

SERBIAN MONASTERY
The Serbian Church is an independent part of the Eastern Orthodox Church, and is estimated to have some 8 million followers. The Serbs became Eastern Orthodox as early as the 13th century. In 1389, the Turks defeated the Serbs at the battle of Kosovo. From 1459, Serbia was a Turkish province, and did not become fully independent until 1878. During this period, only the Church kept the national spirit alive. Monasteries became storehouses of national literature and history. Many of Serbia's finest and most historic monasteries are located in northern Kosovo, and are valued by the Serbian people.

628

MEDITERRANEAN
SOUTHEAST EUROPE

THE LANDSCAPE of Mediterranean Southeast Europe is composed of rugged mountains, rocky coasts, and isolated valleys. The region has experienced many centuries of conflict and invasions from both Europe and Asia. Croatia, Bosnia and Herzegovenia, and Albania were once part of the Turkish Ottoman Empire. Slovenia was annexed by the Habsburg and Austria-Hungarian Empires, and the cultural influences of these two dynasties remains. After World War II, most of Southeast Europe became part of the Communist bloc. In 1990, Slovenia elected a noncommunist government which led to civil strife and the final breakup of the Yugoslavian Federation. Slovenia joined the European Union in 2004 and Croatia is a candidate for future EU membership.

Mediterranean Southeast Europe is largely mountainous. Ranges including the Dinaric Alps run from the north to the south, parallel to the western coast. The western shores of the region are washed by the Adriatic Sea, an arm of the Mediterranean Sea.

Slovenian dancers wear leather trousers and dirndl skirts

SARAJEVO

The capital of Bosnia and Herzegovina, which straddles the Miljacka river, has a strongly Muslim character, with mosques, wooden houses, and an ancient Turkish marketplace. In 1992, when Bosnia declared independence from Yugoslavia, Sarajevo became the focus of a civil war. Thousands of Muslims were driven from the countryside by the fighting and fled to Sarajevo. The city suffered terrible damage in 1993, when it was surrounded by Serb forces and bombarded.

SLOVENIAN TOURISM

Slovenia is an increasingly popular tourist destination, especially for people from the German-speaking countries. More than 3 million tourists visit each year to see the Adriatic coastal resorts, historic spa towns, and the mountains, where they can enjoy skiing, hiking, boating, and fishing. Lake Bled (above), at the foot of the Julian Alps is a popular resort, famous for bathing in summer and as a winter sports center.

SLOVENIAN DANCERS
Slovenia shares a long history with its northern neighbor, Austria. Culturally, Slovenia has more in common with its Alpine neighbors, Switzerland and Austria, than the countries to the south. Cultural traditions are kept alive through music and dance. National costumes are distinctly Alpine.

ZAGREB
The Croatian capital is a major commercial center. Vegetables and fruits produced by local farmers are sold in markets in the town's squares. Much of the city dates to the 19th century, although there are some medieval buildings dating from the 13th century. Zagreb is Croatia's main industrial center, specializing in manufacturing, textiles, and chemicals.

DUBROVNIK

The most picturesque city on the Adriatic coast, Dubrovnik has a history which dates back 1,000 years. With its steep and twisting narrow streets, ancient city walls, and historic fortifications, Dubrovnik was once one of Croatia's main tourist attractions. In 1991, this beautiful city came under fire as a result of Croatia's independence struggle. The tourist industry has now recovered from the effects of civil war.

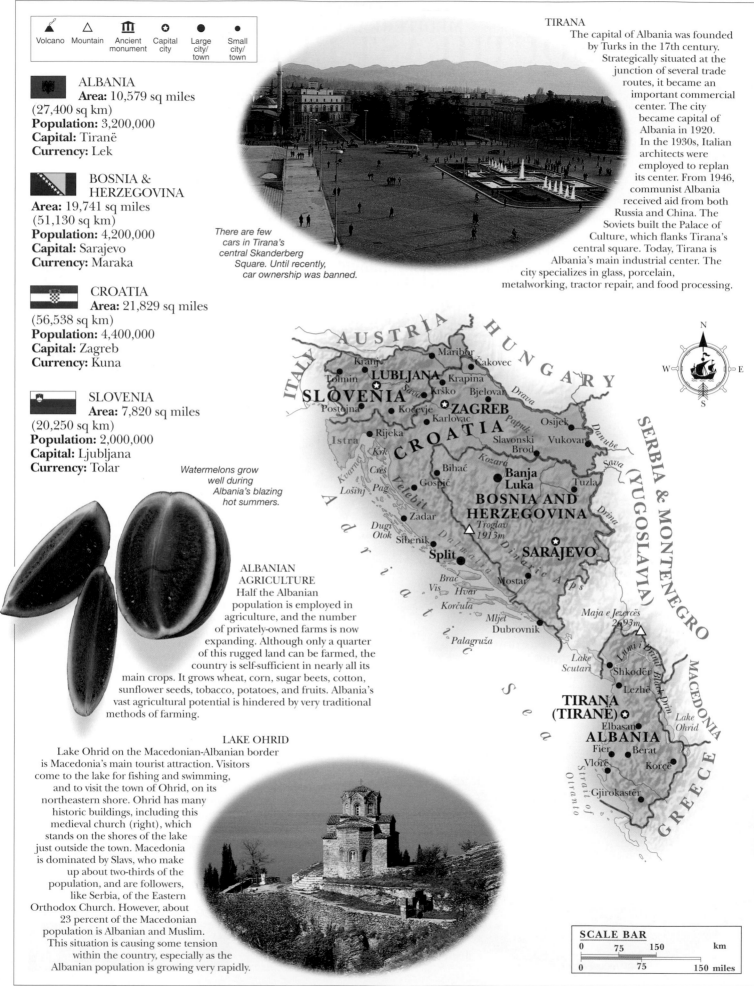

Volcano	Mountain	Ancient monument	Capital city	Large city/town	Small city/town

ALBANIA
Area: 10,579 sq miles (27,400 sq km)
Population: 3,200,000
Capital: Tiranë
Currency: Lek

BOSNIA & HERZEGOVINA
Area: 19,741 sq miles (51,130 sq km)
Population: 4,200,000
Capital: Sarajevo
Currency: Maraka

CROATIA
Area: 21,829 sq miles (56,538 sq km)
Population: 4,400,000
Capital: Zagreb
Currency: Kuna

SLOVENIA
Area: 7,820 sq miles (20,250 sq km)
Population: 2,000,000
Capital: Ljubljana
Currency: Tolar

Watermelons grow well during Albania's blazing hot summers.

TIRANA
The capital of Albania was founded by Turks in the 17th century. Strategically situated at the junction of several trade routes, it became an important commercial center. The city became capital of Albania in 1920. In the 1930s, Italian architects were employed to replan its center. From 1946, communist Albania received aid from both Russia and China. The Soviets built the Palace of Culture, which flanks Tirana's central square. Today, Tirana is Albania's main industrial center. The city specializes in glass, porcelain, metalworking, tractor repair, and food processing.

There are few cars in Tirana's central Skanderberg Square. Until recently, car ownership was banned.

ALBANIAN AGRICULTURE
Half the Albanian population is employed in agriculture, and the number of privately-owned farms is now expanding. Although only a quarter of this rugged land can be farmed, the country is self-sufficient in nearly all its main crops. It grows wheat, corn, sugar beets, cotton, sunflower seeds, tobacco, potatoes, and fruits. Albania's vast agricultural potential is hindered by very traditional methods of farming.

LAKE OHRID
Lake Ohrid on the Macedonian-Albanian border is Macedonia's main tourist attraction. Visitors come to the lake for fishing and swimming, and to visit the town of Ohrid, on its northeastern shore. Ohrid has many historic buildings, including this medieval church (right), which stands on the shores of the lake just outside the town. Macedonia is dominated by Slavs, who make up about two-thirds of the population, and are followers, like Serbia, of the Eastern Orthodox Church. However, about 23 percent of the Macedonian population is Albanian and Muslim. This situation is causing some tension within the country, especially as the Albanian population is growing very rapidly.

SCALE BAR

| 0 | 75 | 150 | km |

| 0 | 75 | 150 miles |

SOUTHERN AFRICA

THE COUNTRIES OF SOUTHERN AFRICA are dominated by dry savannah and woodland, with humid subtropical forests in the north and, to the center and west, the Kalahari and Namib Deserts. Traditionally, agriculture has been the mainstay of these countries' economies, but rich mineral deposits, in particular diamonds, uranium, copper, and iron, are being discovered and exploited, especially in Namibia, Zambia, and Botswana. Economically, the region is dominated by South Africa, with its well-developed mining industries and large cities. Zimbabwe has reserves of coal, gold, and nickel, but the country's economy has been brought close to collapse by drought and misgovernment. Both Angola and Mozambique, former Portuguese colonies, have been devastated by civil wars since independence and are only now beginning to rebuild their shattered economies.

Bordered on the west by the Atlantic Ocean and on the east by the Indian Ocean, much of southern Africa lies within the tropics. The landscape includes the Namib and Kalahari Deserts. Madagascar, the fourth-largest island in the world, lies to the east.

DESERT NOMADS
The nomadic San of the Kalahari in Botswana live by gathering fruits and vegetables and hunting springbok and wildebeest.

URANIUM WEALTH

The largest open-pit uranium mine in the world is located at Rössing in the Namib Desert. The mine was opened in 1976 by a group of British, South African, French, and Canadian companies. As well as being the world's largest uranium producer, Namibia also has extensive reserves of tin, lead, zinc, copper, silver, and tungsten, and produces 30 percent of the world's diamond output.

GOLD CITY

Founded in 1886, Johannesburg was the center of South Africa's gold-mining industry for nearly a century, and remains the country's chief industrial, commercial, manufacturing, and financial center. Greater Johannesburg is one of Africa's largest cities, the heart of an expanding highway system and the South African rail network.

VICTORIA FALLS

Located on the Zambezi River, on the border between Zimbabwe and Zambia, the Victoria Falls are 5,500 ft (1,700 m) at their widest point, and fall to a maximum depth of 354 ft (108 m) in the chasm below. The huge volume of plummeting water creates a mighty roar, known to locals as "the smoke that thunders," which can be heard 25 miles (40 km) away. From the chasm, the river carves a narrow gorge before plunging into a deep pool known as the Boiling Pot.

NAMIB DESERT
The Namib Desert extends up to 100 miles (160 km) inland along the coast of southwest Africa. Sand dunes can reach heights of 800 ft (240 m). Moisture from coastal fogs supports some vegetation.

Find out more
AFRICA
AFRICA, HISTORY OF
AFRICAN WILDLIFE
SOUTH AFRICA

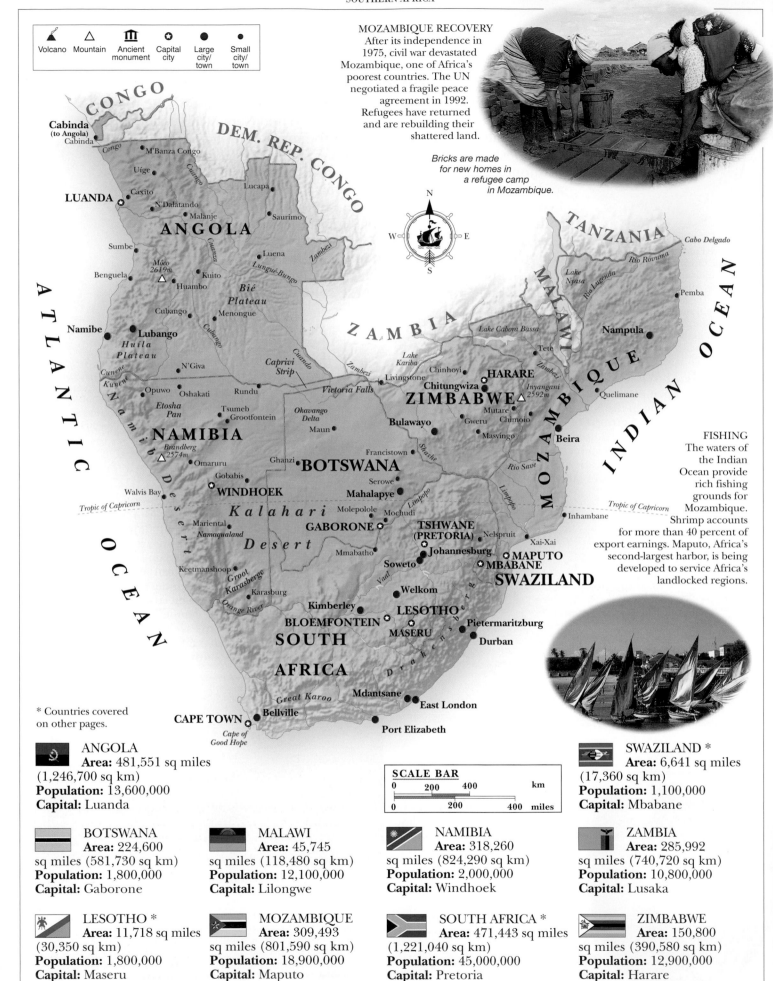

Legend:
- Volcano
- Mountain
- Ancient monument
- Capital city
- Large city/town
- Small city/town

MOZAMBIQUE RECOVERY
After its independence in 1975, civil war devastated Mozambique, one of Africa's poorest countries. The UN negotiated a fragile peace agreement in 1992. Refugees have returned and are rebuilding their shattered land.

Bricks are made for new homes in a refugee camp in Mozambique.

FISHING
The waters of the Indian Ocean provide rich fishing grounds for Mozambique. Shrimp accounts for more than 40 percent of export earnings. Maputo, Africa's second-largest harbor, is being developed to service Africa's landlocked regions.

CONGO
DEM. REP. CONGO
TANZANIA
ATLANTIC OCEAN
INDIAN OCEAN

Cabinda (to Angola)
Cabinda
M'Banza Congo
Uíge
Caxito
LUANDA
N'Dalatando
Malanje
Lucapa
Saurimo
ANGOLA
Sumbe
Môco 2619m
Benguela
Kuito
Huambo
Menongue
Bié Plateau
Luena
Lungué-Bungo
Cuango
Cuanza
Namibe
Lubango
Huíla Plateau
Cubango
N'Giva
Cuando
Capricci Strip
Cunene
Kunene
Opuwo
Oshakati
Rundu
Etosha Pan
Tsumeb
Grootfontein
NAMIBIA
Brandberg 2574m
Omaruru
Gobabis
Ghanzi
Walvis Bay
WINDHOEK
Namaqualand
Mariental
Kalahari Desert
GABORONE
Mmabatho
Keetmanshoop
Groot Karasberge
Karasburg
Orange River
Kimberley
BLOEMFONTEIN
SOUTH AFRICA
Great Karoo
CAPE TOWN
Bellville
Cape of Good Hope
Port Elizabeth
Mdantsane
East London

ZAMBIA
Lake Cabora Bassa
Tete
Zambezi
Lake Kariba
Chinhoyi
Livingstone
Victoria Falls
Zambezi
HARARE
Chitungwiza
ZIMBABWE
Inyangani 2592m
Mutare
Bulawayo
Gweru
Chimoio
Masvingo
Beira
Francistown
Shashe
BOTSWANA
Serowe
Maun
Okavango Delta
Mahalapye
Limpopo
Molepolole
Mochudi
TSHWANE (PRETORIA)
Nelspruit
Xai-Xai
Johannesburg
Soweto
MAPUTO
MBABANE
SWAZILAND
Vaal
Welkom
LESOTHO
Pietermaritzburg
MASERU
Durban
Drakensberg

MALAWI
Lake Nyasa
Rio Lugenda
Rio Rovuma
Cabo Delgado
Pemba
Nampula
Quelimane
MOZAMBIQUE
Rio Save
Inhambane

Tropic of Capricorn

SCALE BAR
0 200 400 km
0 200 400 miles

* Countries covered on other pages.

ANGOLA
Area: 481,551 sq miles (1,246,700 sq km)
Population: 13,600,000
Capital: Luanda

BOTSWANA
Area: 224,600 sq miles (581,730 sq km)
Population: 1,800,000
Capital: Gaborone

MALAWI
Area: 45,745 sq miles (118,480 sq km)
Population: 12,100,000
Capital: Lilongwe

NAMIBIA
Area: 318,260 sq miles (824,290 sq km)
Population: 2,000,000
Capital: Windhoek

ZAMBIA
Area: 285,992 sq miles (740,720 sq km)
Population: 10,800,000
Capital: Lusaka

LESOTHO *
Area: 11,718 sq miles (30,350 sq km)
Population: 1,800,000
Capital: Maseru

MOZAMBIQUE
Area: 309,493 sq miles (801,590 sq km)
Population: 18,900,000
Capital: Maputo

SOUTH AFRICA *
Area: 471,443 sq miles (1,221,040 sq km)
Population: 45,000,000
Capital: Pretoria

ZIMBABWE
Area: 150,800 sq miles (390,580 sq km)
Population: 12,900,000
Capital: Harare

SWAZILAND *
Area: 6,641 sq miles (17,360 sq km)
Population: 1,100,000
Capital: Mbabane

HISTORY OF THE
SOVIET UNION

IN 1922, A NEW NATION came into being. The Union of Soviet Socialist Republics, or the Soviet Union, was the new name for Communist Russia, led by Vladimir Lenin (1870-1924). The years following the 1917 Revolution were difficult. Civil war between Communists and anti-Communists had torn Russia apart. More than 20 million people had died. When Lenin died, Joseph Stalin took over as dictator. In a reign of terror, he eliminated all opposition to his rule. He started to transform the Soviet Union into a modern industrial state. The huge industrial effort made the Soviet Union strong. It survived German invasion in 1941, although World War II (1939-1945) cost the nation many lives. After 1945 the Soviet Union became a superpower, but it still had difficulty providing enough goods for its people. In 1985, Mikhail Gorbachev came to power. He introduced reforms and began a policy of openness with the West. In 1991, the Communist Party was declared illegal, and the Soviet Union broke up.

INDUSTRIALIZATION
Stalin introduced a series of Five-Year Plans to increase production of coal, steel, and power. The plans were successful for the country, but workers had little reward for their efforts and many were used as slave labor.

Posters showing muscular workers encouraged people to work hard.

This shows how collective farms were organized under Stalin. The collective included a school where children were educated, a factory, and a hospital. The collective had to send fixed deliveries of crops to the State.

School, hospital, and factory

Workers' homes

Private plots for fruit, vegetables, and poultry

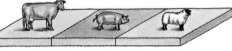
Grazing land for pigs, sheep, and cattle

Land for growing crops

JOSEPH STALIN
Born in poverty in Georgia, southwestern Russia, Joseph Stalin (1879-1953) was a follower of Lenin. After Lenin's death, Stalin seized power and destroyed his opponents. He formed a secret police force to arrest, torture, and execute millions of suspected enemies. These ruthless "purges" enabled Stalin to remain unchallenged as Soviet leader until his death.

COLLECTIVE FARM
Stalin wanted to get rid of all the old-fashioned peasant farms and increase productivity. He reorganized the land into *kolkhozy* (giant collective farms) controlled by the government. The government took the land and livestock of millions of *kulaks* (richer peasants). Those who protested were sent to work in prison camps. Most of the collective farms' products were exported, or sent to the government to feed the city workers.

ALEXANDRA KOLLONTAI
Communism was supposed to introduce equality into Soviet society. However, while women worked alongside men in heavy industry, they were not allowed to hold real power. But a woman named Alexandra Kollontai (1872-1952) did become a member of Stalin's government. She made many important speeches and wrote several articles about peace and women's rights.

WORLD WAR II

In 1941, German armies invaded the Soviet Union and reached the gates of Moscow, the capital. The Soviets resisted heroically. Stalingrad and Leningrad survived long and bitter sieges. New factories in the east began to produce advanced weapons, such as the T-34 tank, in large numbers. In 1943, Soviet armored forces, led by Marshal Zhukov, fought and won the largest tank battle ever. But the Soviets paid a high price for victory. They suffered more military casualties than any other country in the war. More than 20 million people died.

SOVIET UNION

1917 Russian Revolution

1922 Soviet Union formed.

1924 Lenin dies and is replaced by Stalin.

1941-45 More than 20 million Soviets die in World War II.

1955 Warsaw Pact, an alliance of Communist states, created.

1962 Soviet Union builds missile bases on Cuba. US Navy blockades island. Soviet Union removes missiles.

1980 Soviet invasion of Afghanistan.

1988 Soviet troops withdraw from Afghanistan.

1991 Soviet Union breaks up as Lithuania, Latvia, and other republics declare their independence.

CHERNOBYL

In 1986, there was a major disaster at Chernobyl, near Kiev. A nuclear power plant exploded, killing at least 30 people and injuring hundreds more. Radioactive dust and smoke blew all over Europe and exposed thousands of people to contamination. Instead of keeping this disaster secret, the Soviets followed their new policy of *glasnost*, or openness, and warned the rest of the world of the danger.

SPACE RACE

On October 4, 1957, the whole world listened in amazement to a strange beeping sound that came from space. The Soviet Union had launched the first satellite, called *Sputnik 1*, into orbit around Earth. It was followed four years later by Yuri Gagarin (left), the first human in space.

COLLAPSE OF COMMUNISM

After his appointment in 1985, Soviet premier Mikhail Gorbachev introduced policies of *glasnost* (openness) and *perestroika* (economic reform) to improve the poor state of the Soviet economy. People under Soviet control began to demand more freedom. The Communist Party ceased to be the only political party. In Rumania, the Communist dictator, Nicolae Ceausescu, was overthrown and executed in 1989. In the Soviet Union, anti-Communist demonstrations took place. People destroyed statues of Lenin and other Communist leaders. In Moscow, the statue of Felix Dzerzhinsky, head of the hated KGB, or security police, was toppled.

GORBACHEV AND YELTSIN

Throughout the late 1980s, Soviet people suffered from terrible economic hardship. Many thought that the changes brought about by Gorbachev's policy of *perestroika* were too slow. Mikhail Gorbachev (right) resigned in 1991. Boris Yeltsin (left) became the leader of the new Russian Federation. The Soviet Union broke up as the republics formed their own governments. Boris Yeltsin resigned in December 1999.

Find out more

CAUCASUS REPUBLICS
COLD WAR
COMMUNISM
RUSSIA, HISTORY OF
RUSSIAN REVOLUTION
WORLD WAR II

SPACE FLIGHT

SPACE SHUTTLE

A space shuttle is an aircraft that can make repeated flights into space. Since the *Columbia* disaster in 2003, when a shuttle broke up on re-entry to the Earth's atmosphere, the shuttle program has been restricted for safety reasons. A new type of spacecraft is currently being developed to replace the shuttle.

Smaller engines guide the shuttle into orbit.

A large fuel tank feeds the main engines. It breaks away at a height of 70 miles (110 km), just eight minutes after launch.

The booster rockets break away at a height of about 29 miles (47 km). They are recovered from the ocean and used again.

A spacecraft must reach a speed of about 17,500 mph (28,000 km/h) in order to get into orbit. If it attains a speed of about 25,000 mph (40,000 km/h), it can break free from the Earth's gravity and travel out into space. This speed is called the Earth's escape velocity.

ONLY A FEW DECADES ago, stories about space flight were found only in science fiction books. Today, spacecraft blast off regularly from the Earth, placing artificial satellites in orbit around the planet and carrying space probes and astronauts into space. Space flight became a reality because of two inventions: the rocket engine, which is the only engine that can work in the vacuum of space; and the computer, which is needed to guide a spacecraft on its mission. Spacecraft have been used to do many jobs in space including launching satellites that map the Earth and provide communication links between countries. However, the most exciting part of space flight is the exploration of space itself. Spacecraft have carried astronauts to the Moon. Although this dramatic journey took three days, it covered only a tiny speck of the universe. The real space explorers are *Voyager, Pioneer,* and other unmanned craft that travel many years through the solar system and beyond, photographing planets, moons, and other objects on their way.

SPACE ROCKET

Spacecraft are carried into space by launch vehicles, or rockets. The launch rocket consists of several parts called stages, each with its own rocket engine. Each stage breaks away as it uses up its fuel, eventually leaving only the spacecraft to fly in space. Returning to the Earth, spacecraft use a small engine to slow them down until they fall out of orbit.

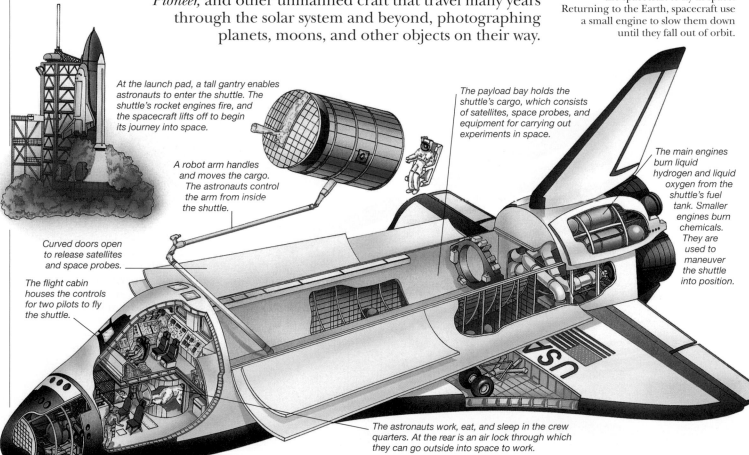

At the launch pad, a tall gantry enables astronauts to enter the shuttle. The shuttle's rocket engines fire, and the spacecraft lifts off to begin its journey into space.

The payload bay holds the shuttle's cargo, which consists of satellites, space probes, and equipment for carrying out experiments in space.

A robot arm handles and moves the cargo. The astronauts control the arm from inside the shuttle.

The main engines burn liquid hydrogen and liquid oxygen from the shuttle's fuel tank. Smaller engines burn chemicals. They are used to maneuver the shuttle into position.

Curved doors open to release satellites and space probes.

The flight cabin houses the controls for two pilots to fly the shuttle.

The astronauts work, eat, and sleep in the crew quarters. At the rear is an air lock through which they can go outside into space to work.

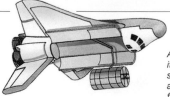

Once in orbit, the shuttle may release satellites and space probes, or retrieve damaged satellites for repair.

At the end of its mission, the shuttle turns around and fires its engines to slow it down.

Once the shuttle is traveling slowly enough, it leaves its orbit and begins to descend toward Earth.

When the shuttle enters the Earth's atmosphere, friction of the air makes the heat-proof underside of the shuttle glow red-hot.

The shuttle glides down toward a runway, just like an ordinary aircraft.

The shuttle lands on the runway and rolls to a halt. After months of intensive checking, it is ready to fly again.

FIRSTS IN SPACE

1957 The first artificial satellite, *Sputnik 1* (Soviet Union), goes into orbit around the Earth.

1959 *Luna 3* (Soviet Union), the first successful space probe, flies past the Moon and sends back the first picture of the Moon's far side.

1961 Russian Yuri Gagarin becomes the first person to fly in space, making one orbit of the Earth.

1962 *Mariner 2* (US), the first successful planetary space probe, flies past Venus.

1969 Neil Armstrong (US) becomes the first person to walk on the Moon.

1971 The first space station, *Salyut 1* (Soviet Union), goes into orbit.

1981 US space shuttle *Columbia* makes its first test flight into space.

1986 European space probe *Giotto* sends back close-up pictures of the nucleus (centre) of Halley's Comet.

1995 *Discovery* (US) is the first shuttle mission to be flown by a female pilot, Eileen Collins.

2001 Businessman Dennis Tito becomes the first space tourist, aboard the Russian craft *Soyuz*.

SPACE PROBES

Space probes leave the Earth and travel out into space. They are equipped with cameras and all kinds of sensors that collect information about space and the planets, which is beamed back to Earth by radio.

Radio antenna to communicate with Earth

Instruments for studying Jupiter's surface

Atmospheric entry probe

GALILEO
In 1995, the *Galileo* spacecraft entered orbit around Jupiter. It discovered that Jupiter's largest moon Ganymede has magnetism within the strong magnetism of Jupiter, a phenomenon not known anywhere else in the solar system.

A parachute lowered the entry probe into Jupiter's atmosphere.

The spacecraft released a probe containing instruments that measured conditions in Jupiter's atmosphere. They worked for only 75 minutes because Jupiter's gravity crushed the probe like an egg when it got close to the planet's surface.

Heat shield

INSIDE THE ISS
While on board the International Space Station (ISS), astronauts conduct experiments and repair equipment under weightless conditions. The space station is still currently under construction, due to be completed in 2010.

SPACE STATION

People can make the longest space flights on board space stations – large spacecraft that spend several years in orbit around the Earth. Smaller spacecraft carry teams of astronauts to the space station, where they will live and work for weeks or months at a time. Supplies and relief crews come aboard in spacecraft that dock, or link up, with the space station.

Solar panels rotate to point at the Sun

Thermal control panels regulate temperature

Pressurized modules provide living quarters and laboratories

Spacecraft dock at ports in positions like this one

Radiators turn edge-on to the Sun to lose excess heat

International Space Station

Remote sensing instruments look down on Earth

Find out more
ASTRONAUTS
COMETS AND METEORS
GRAVITY
MOON
PLANETS
ROCKETS AND MISSILES
SATELLITES

SPAIN

SPAIN SHARES THE IBERIAN PENINSULA with Portugal. It is the fourth-largest country in Europe, and both its landscape and its people are varied. The center of Spain is a hot, dry plateau with snowy mountain ranges to the north and south. The southern region of Spain contains Europe's only desert. The Spanish are divided into regional groups, each with its own language and culture. About 16 percent are Catalan; Galicians make up seven percent, and just two percent are Basques. Most of the rest are Castilian Spanish. The country was torn apart by a vicious civil war from 1936-39, and right-wing dictators ruled Spain for much of the 20th century. However, in the mid-1970s the country formed a democratic government. This change allowed Spain to join the European Community – now known as the European Union (EU) – in 1986, and to benefit from the higher standard of living in the rest of Europe. Once reliant on farming and fishing for its income, Spain has experienced economic growth since joining the EU. The economy is now dominated by tourism.

Spain is situated on the Iberian Peninsula in the southwest corner of Europe. France and the Bay of Biscay are to the north, the Mediterranean Sea to the east, the Strait of Gibraltar and Africa are to the south, and Portugal is to the west.

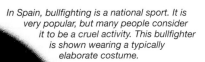

In many parts of Spain and Portugal, the donkey cart is still a common form of transportation.

FLAMENCO

Flamenco music and dance were developed by gypsies in Andalucia, in southern Spain. Flamenco songs deal with the entire range of human emotion, from despair to ecstasy. Dancers dress in traditional costume and are usually accompanied by guitars and their own handheld percussion instrument called castanets. The men's steps are intricate, with toe and heel clicking; women's dancing depends on the grace of the hands and body, rather than on footwork.

TOURISM

More than 60 million tourists visit Spain each year. Tourism employs 10 percent of the workforce and is a major source of income. Tourists come to enjoy the sun, as the climate is mild in the winter and hot in the summer. The country boasts fine beaches, and its old towns are full of interesting buildings and fine works of art.

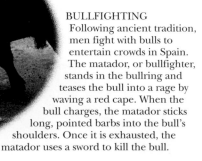

In Spain, bullfighting is a national sport. It is very popular, but many people consider it to be a cruel activity. This bullfighter is shown wearing a typically elaborate costume.

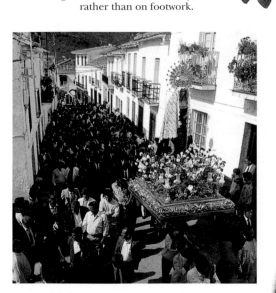

RELIGION

The Roman Catholic Church plays an important part in the lives of most Spanish people. Nearly everybody is a member of the church and attends Mass on Sundays. The priest is an influential member of the community, and the church is a center of local activities.

BULLFIGHTING

Following ancient tradition, men fight with bulls to entertain crowds in Spain. The matador, or bullfighter, stands in the bullring and teases the bull into a rage by waving a red cape. When the bull charges, the matador sticks long, pointed barbs into the bull's shoulders. Once it is exhausted, the matador uses a sword to kill the bull.

Old-fashioned horse drawn carriages carry tourists around a number of Spanish cities. These carriages (left) are pictured in the Plaza de España, Seville.

KING JUAN CARLOS

The Spanish Civil War of 1936-39 resulted in a dictatorship by General Franco. In 1975, Franco died and was succeeded by King Juan Carlos, grandson of the last Spanish king. Under his rule, Spain became a multiparty democracy, and attained membership in the EU.

Juan Carlos and Princess Sophia of Greece (right) were married in Athens on May 14, 1962.

SEVILLE

Seville is a major port as well as an important industrial, cultural, and tourist center. With the discovery of the New World, Seville entered its greatest period of prosperity, being the chief port of trade with the new colonies until 1718 when it was superseded by Cádiz. The city is the capital of bullfighting in Spain and a center of the Andalusian gypsies, famed for their songs and dances.

Salt-cured ham (above), Spanish omelette – a tasty dish of potato and onion (left) – and mussels in an onion and garlic sauce (below)

The splendid gardens and architecture of the Moorish palace in Granada

GRANADA

North African Muslims, known as the Moors, once ruled most of Spain. The town of Granada was the capital of their kingdom, and the Alhambra fortress overlooking the town enclosed a magnificent Moorish palace that remains to this day. The palace and its gardens (left) gradually fell into ruin after the Moors were defeated in 1492, but they have since been restored to their former glory.

REGIONAL FOOD

Spain boasts a variety of regional dishes, the most famous of which are paella and tapas. Paella is a classic dish from the Valencia region, where rice is grown. It consists of a variety of meat, fish, fresh vegetables, and saffron-flavored rice. Tapas, sometimes known as pinchos, are small snacks that originated in Andalusia in the 19th century to accompany wine. Stemming from a bartenders' practice of covering a glass with a saucer or tapa (cover) to keep out flies, the custom progressed to food being placed on a platter to accompany a drink. Tapas range from cold meats or cheeses to elaborately prepared hot dishes of seafood, meat, or vegetables. A tapa is a single serving, while a *ración* serves two or three.

SPANISH GUITAR

The guitar originated in Spain in the 16th century. It plays a central role in flamenco, traditionally accompanying the singer. The flamenco guitar developed from the modern classical guitar, and evolved in Spain in the 19th century. Flamenco guitars have a lighter, shallower construction and a thickened plate below the soundhole, used to tap rhythms. Today, flamenco guitarists often perform solo.

The climax of Pamplona's (left) annual fiesta, Los Sanfermines, is when bulls stampede through the city.

FIESTAS

More than 3,000 fiestas take place each year in Spain. On any day of the year there is a fiesta happening somewhere – usually more than one. Fiestas are a means for a village, town, or city to honor either its patron saint, the Virgin Mary, or the changing seasons. Fiestas can take the form of processions, bull-running (above), fireworks, reenacted battles, ancestral rites, or a mass pilgrimage to a rural shrine. Whatever the pretext, a fiesta is a chance for everybody to take a break from everyday life and let off steam, with celebrations going on around the clock.

The classical guitar is Spain's national instrument.

PAINTING

Many great artists lived and worked in Spain. Diego Velasquez (1599-1660) was famous for his pictures of the Spanish royal family. Several modern painters, including Pablo Picasso (1881-1973) and Salvador Dalí (1904-89), were born in Spain.

Velasquez included himself as the painter in his picture The Maids of Honor.

INDUSTRY

Farming and fishing were once the basis of the Spanish economy. The country has now developed additional industries including textiles, metals, shipbuilding, auto production, and tourism. Iron, coal, and other minerals are mined in the Cordillera Cantabrica in the north of Spain. In the 1980s, many foreign-owned electronics and high-tech industries began to locate in the country. Major agricultural products include cereals, olives, grapes for wine, and citrus fruits, especially oranges from around Seville.

In the coastal towns of Spain many people work in fishing or in the related industries of boatbuilding and netmaking.

BARCELONA

The city of Barcelona lies on the Mediterranean coast of eastern Spain. It is the second-largest city in the country (Madrid is the largest) and is a bustling port of almost two million people. Barcelona is the capital of the province of Catalonia. It lies at the heart of a large industrial area and was the site of the 1992 Olympic Games. Its people speak Catalan, a language that sounds similar to Spanish but has many differences. The city is renowned for its beautiful architecture and many historic buildings.

The Cathedral of Sagrada Familia in Barcelona was designed by Antonio Gaudí and begun in 1882. It is still not finished today.

GIBRALTAR

Spain claims that Gibraltar, at its southern tip, is Spanish. However, since 1713 this rocky outcrop has been a British colony. Gibraltar is just 2.5 sq miles (6.5 sq km) in area. Most of the 28,000 inhabitants work in tourism.

The Rock of Gibraltar towers over the entrance to the Mediterranean Sea.

OLIVES

The deep fertile soils and warm climate of southern and eastern Spain are ideal for olive cultivation. The country is one of the world's leading olive producers. Most of the crop is made into olive oil.

Find out more

EUROPE, HISTORY OF
EUROPEAN UNION
PORTUGAL, HISTORY OF
SPAIN, HISTORY OF

SPAIN

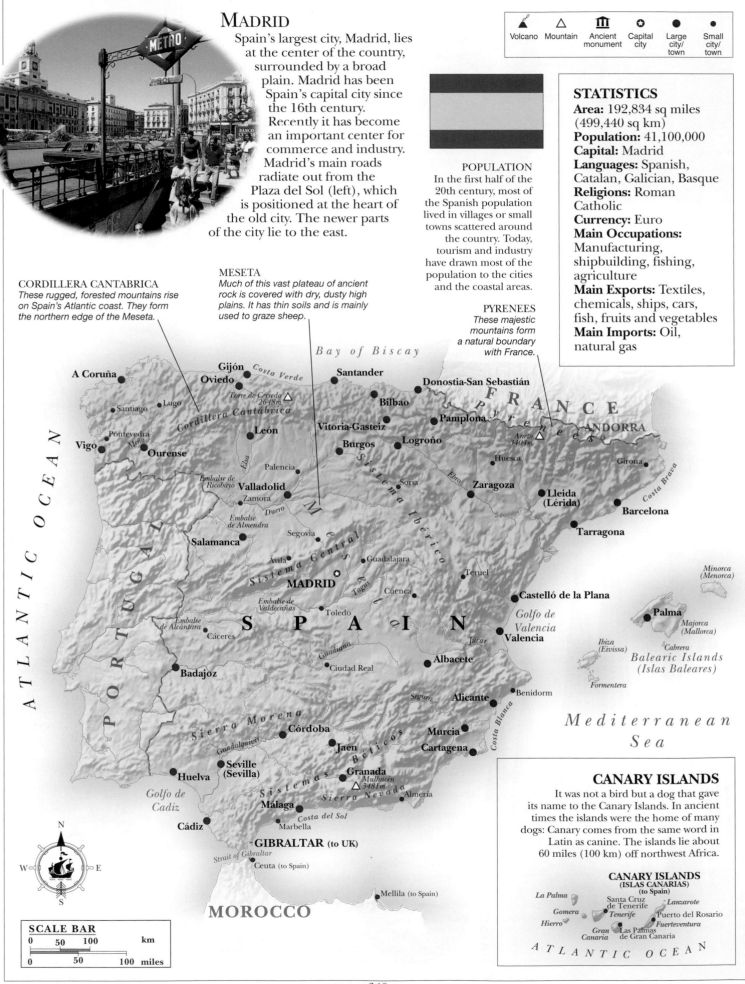

MADRID

Spain's largest city, Madrid, lies at the center of the country, surrounded by a broad plain. Madrid has been Spain's capital city since the 16th century. Recently it has become an important center for commerce and industry. Madrid's main roads radiate out from the Plaza del Sol (left), which is positioned at the heart of the old city. The newer parts of the city lie to the east.

POPULATION
In the first half of the 20th century, most of the Spanish population lived in villages or small towns scattered around the country. Today, tourism and industry have drawn most of the population to the cities and the coastal areas.

STATISTICS
Area: 192,834 sq miles (499,440 sq km)
Population: 41,100,000
Capital: Madrid
Languages: Spanish, Catalan, Galician, Basque
Religions: Roman Catholic
Currency: Euro
Main Occupations: Manufacturing, shipbuilding, fishing, agriculture
Main Exports: Textiles, chemicals, ships, cars, fish, fruits and vegetables
Main Imports: Oil, natural gas

CORDILLERA CANTABRICA
These rugged, forested mountains rise on Spain's Atlantic coast. They form the northern edge of the Meseta.

MESETA
Much of this vast plateau of ancient rock is covered with dry, dusty high plains. It has thin soils and is mainly used to graze sheep.

PYRENEES
These majestic mountains form a natural boundary with France.

CANARY ISLANDS
It was not a bird but a dog that gave its name to the Canary Islands. In ancient times the islands were the home of many dogs: Canary comes from the same word in Latin as canine. The islands lie about 60 miles (100 km) off northwest Africa.

640

HISTORY OF
SPAIN

BY 1550, SPAIN had become one of the greatest powers in Europe. It had explored other lands and set up a huge empire with colonies in Africa, the Americas, the Caribbean, and Asia. Its early story is one of visiting conquerors. First of all came Celts from the north. From about 1000 B.C., the Phoenicians, then the Carthaginians and Greeks, built trading colonies on the peninsula. The Romans, and then the Visigoths, a Germanic tribe, occupied the whole land. In A.D. 711 Muslim Moors from North Africa invaded Spain and Portugal. By the end of the 15th century Spain, together with Portugal, had driven out the Moors, but rivalry between the two countries developed when they competed in building up their empires overseas. In 1580, Spain invaded Portugal and held it for 60 years. After this, the Portuguese became determined to remain independent of Spanish rule. Spain fought against Portugal during the Napoleonic Wars with the French. More recently, Spain was ruled by a dictator until his death in 1975. Now it has a democratic government.

HISPANIA
In 201 B.C. the Romans conquered Spain. The Romans named the region Hispania and introduced Latin as the official language. They also built huge aqueducts (such as the one in Segovia, Spain, above), which carried water to cities. Several of Rome's greatest emperors, including Hadrian and Trajan, were born in Hispania.

ALHAMBRA
Begun in 1248, the Alhambra palace in Granada was the last stronghold of the Moors in Spain. The outer wall is made of red bricks, which gave the palace its name (*alhambra* is the Arabic word for red). It also has 13 towers. The Alhambra contains the finest examples of Moorish art in Europe.

SPANISH CONQUESTS
During the European age of discovery in the late 1400s, Spain, on the edge of the Atlantic, was in an ideal spot to send out explorers to the Americas. By the middle of the 16th century it had colonized the area from Mexico to Peru.

EL CID
During the Moorish occupation, the people of Castile in northern Spain emerged as champions of Christianity. Rodrigo Díaz de Vivar (1040-99) was a nobleman and soldier who heroically fought the Christian cause under King Sancho II of Castile. But when Sancho's brother Alfonso became king, he banished Rodrigo. Rodrigo quickly gathered a small army and fought the Moors. In 1094, he captured the city of Valencia from the Moors. He was given the title El Cid (from the Arabic word *sidi*, meaning "lord") and is one of Spain's national heroes. He died immensely wealthy, ruler of his own kingdom.

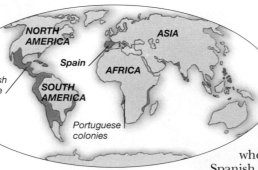

The Spanish empire, 1588

SPANISH EMPIRE
In the Treaty of Tordesillas the Pope divided the non-European world between Spain and Portugal, to avoid wars between them. In 1588, when Portugal was under Spanish rule, the Spanish Empire was at the height of its power.

Elaborately designed and inscribed with its history, this sword was surrendered by the French governor of a Spanish fortress during the Peninsular War.

PENINSULAR WAR

In 1807, Spain agreed to support French Emperor Napoleon I in a war with Portugal. French troops defeated Portugal but occupied major Spanish cities in the process. In 1808, Napoleon overthrew the Spanish monarch and had his brother Joseph Bonaparte proclaimed king of Spain. The Spanish people rose in revolt and finally, by 1814, drove out the French. Spain calls it the Spanish War of Independence.

The policy of Philip II was to establish an absolute monarchy.

PHILIP II

King Philip II (1527-98) ruled Spain at the height of its power. Under him, Spanish art, writing, and fashions led Europe. He united Spain with Portugal and conquered the Philippines. He was involved in many wars; during a war against the English, the Spanish Armada (fleet) was destroyed. Poverty spread throughout Spain because of these wars, and after Philip died, Spanish power began to fail.

BASQUES

The Basque people have lived in the Pyrenees (mountains between France and Spain) for thousands of years. They have their own language, called Euskera. In the 1960s, the Spanish Basques demanded a separate, independent Basque state. Some Basques formed terrorist groups to fight against the Spanish government. The Basques now have their own parliament and some control over their government.

SPANISH CIVIL WAR

In February 1936, a left-wing (radical) Republican government was elected in Spain. Most of the Spanish army (right-wing and conservative) rebelled and tried to overthrow the government. Led by General Franco, the army fought bitterly with the Republicans for nearly three years. Mussolini sent Italian troops, and Hitler sent German troops to help the right-wing cause. Thousands of Spaniards died in this bloody civil war. In 1939, the Republican armies collapsed, and Franco emerged as dictator of Spain.

FRANCO

General Francisco Franco (1892-1975) had a successful army career before he became dictator of Spain. He kept Spain out of World War II (1939-45). After the war there was rapid economic growth, and the standard of living improved. But many people were unhappy with Franco's restrictions on personal freedom. Many Spaniards were arrested and executed by Franco's police for protesting and demanding more freedom.

SPAIN

800-200 B.C. Phoenicians, Carthaginians, and Greeks set up trading colonies along the coast of Spain.

201 B.C. Roman control begins.

711 A.D. Visigoths invade. Muslim Moors from North Africa conquer Spain.

1094 El Cid captures Valencia.

1385 Spaniards attempt invasion of Portugal but are defeated.

1494 Treaty of Tordesillas between Spain and Portugal carves out their empires.

1580 Philip II of Spain invades Portugal and unites the two countries.

1588 English navy defeats the Spanish Armada.

1640 Spain loses Portugal and all the Portuguese colonies. Decline of the Spanish empire begins.

1807 Peninsular War begins.

1898 Spanish war with United States over Cuba leads to the end of the Spanish empire.

1931 King Alfonso XIII of Spain flees the country. Spain becomes a republic.

1936-39 Spanish Civil War.

1939 General Franco becomes dictator of Spain.

1975 General Franco dies. Spain becomes a democracy.

1986 Spain joins the European Community (EC).

1992 Summer Olympic games held in Barcelona.

Find out more

COLUMBUS, CHRISTOPHER
HAPSBURGS
SOUTH AMERICA, HISTORY OF
SPAIN

SPIDERS AND SCORPIONS

FEW ANIMALS ARE MORE FEARED but less understood than spiders and scorpions. We often call these scurrying little creatures insects, but they really belong to the group of animals called arachnids, along with ticks and mites. Insects have six legs; spiders and other arachnids have eight legs. There are about 40,000 kinds of spiders and 1,400 kinds of scorpions. All are carnivores (meat-eaters). Scorpions hunt down their prey and kill it with their pincers. If the prey is big, or struggles, the scorpion uses the sting in its tail. Many spiders capture insects by spinning a silken web. The silk of some webs is stronger than steel wire of the same thickness. Not all spiders spin webs, however; some catch their prey by dropping a net of silk onto it. A few spiders, such as the trap-door spider, rush out at their victim from a burrow. Some scorpions and several spiders are dangerous to humans, including the Australian funnel web spider and the Durango scorpion of Mexico.

WEB
Spiders make webs with a special silken thread from glands at the rear end of the body. Tubes called spinnerets squeeze out the thread like toothpaste. The silk hardens as the spider's legs pull it out.

GARDEN SPIDER

Thousands of spiders live in our houses and gardens, feeding on flies, gnats, and moths. The common garden spider spins a beautiful, complicated web called an orb web, often between the stems of plants. Some spiders lie in wait for their prey in the center of the web; others hide nearby. Many orb-web spiders spin a new web almost every day.

The female black widow has a deadly bite.

SPIDERLINGS
Young spiders are called spiderlings. They hatch from eggs inside a silken cocoon and feed on stores of yolk in their bodies. After a few days, weeks, or months, depending on the weather, they cut their way out of the cocoon and begin to hunt for food.

BLACK WIDOW
The female black widow spider is so named because it sometimes kills its mate. This spider is also one of the few spiders that can kill humans. The female black widow shown here is standing near its eggs, which are wrapped in a silken egg sac or cocoon.

TARANTULA
True tarantulas are shy spiders that live mainly in burrows. False tarantulas, such as the big spider shown here, include various large, hairy hunting spiders from North and South America. They are also called bird or monkey spiders. Their bite is painful to humans, but it is less poisonous than the bite of smaller spiders such as the black widow.

FOOD
Spiders eat animal prey. Their most common victims are insects, worms, sow bugs, and other spiders. The spider's venom subdues or paralyzes the prey while the spider wraps it up in a silk bag to eat later.

YOUNG SCORPIONS
Scorpions are born fully formed. At first the female scorpion carries the young on its back, where they are well protected from predators. After the young have molted (shed their skin) for the first time, they leave their mother to fend for themselves.

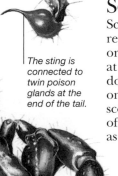

Mother carries the young on her back.

Imperial scorpion

The sting is connected to twin poison glands at the end of the tail.

SCORPION

Scorpions live mainly in warm regions, lurking beneath rocks or in cracks or burrows. Most feed at night, ambushing or hunting down their prey. They feed mainly on insects and spiders. The scorpion uses the sting at the end of the tail in self-defense, as well as to subdue its prey.

Scorpion's large pincers are called pedipalps. They seize, crush, and tear the prey, then pass it to the jaws.

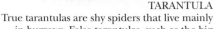

Find out more

ANIMALS
AUSTRALIAN WILDLIFE
DESERT WILDLIFE

SPIES AND ESPIONAGE

MATA HARI
The most notorious spy of World War I was a dancer who worked in Paris using the stage name Mata Hari. She was born in the Netherlands as Gertrude Margarete Zelle in 1876. Mata Hari was probably a double agent: she spied on the Germans for their enemies the French, but she also gave French secrets to the Germans. She was arrested by the French and executed in 1917.

Charmed by Mata Hari's beauty, military men gave her secret information.

Undercover spies may seek low-paying work such as cleaning in offices where they know secrets are filed.

NATIONS AT WAR try hard to discover what their enemy will do next, so that they can mount a more secure defense or an effective attack. Secretly trying to discover the plans of an enemy or competitor is called spying, or espionage. The people who do it are called spies, and they have a difficult job. They often pretend to be working for one side while collecting information for the other. Their work is also dangerous: spies caught in wartime are executed.

Spying is an ancient trade, but it reached a peak during World War II (1939-45) and in the years that followed. Though the United States and the former Soviet Union were not at war, each feared attack from the other. So both sides used espionage to estimate the strength of the opponent's forces. Today, much spying is not military but industrial. By copying a competitor's plans, a manufacturer can make a similar product without the cost of research.

SECRET AGENTS
Spies may use false identities to hide their activities. They seem to lead regular lives but are secretly collecting information. These spies are called agents or secret agents. They may bribe people to steal secrets. Or they use blackmail: they find out damaging facts about someone who has access to secrets, then threaten to reveal these facts unless the victim becomes a spy.

Tiny bugs transmit signals that a spy can pick up a city block away.

Night-vision binoculars help spies see long distances in darkness.

Phone capsule transmitters broadcast telephone calls and are difficult to detect.

Even a cigarette pack is big enough to hide a tiny tape recorder.

Cameras hidden in watches enable spies to take photographs secretly.

Bug detectors disguised as pens give warning that a spy has hidden a bug in the room.

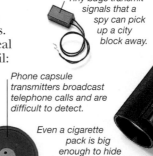

CODES
When spies send messages, they encode them – write them in code – to hide the meaning. The spy changes each letter for a different one, so that only someone else who knows the code can read the words. On this code disc, the letters of the message are marked in blue, and their coded form is in green. For example, C becomes X. HELP I AM TRAPPED would be SVOK R ZN GIZKKVW in code. This code is easy to break, or understand. But computer-generated codes are almost impossible to break.

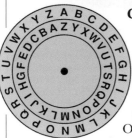

SPY EQUIPMENT
Spies need special equipment so that they can watch and listen to people and send messages secretly. To hear private conversations, spies hide "bugs" – tiny microphones and radio transmitters – in their subjects' homes or offices. The spy tunes in a radio receiver to hear the signals transmitted by the bug. A spy can use a camera with a powerful magnifying lens to take embarrassing photographs with which to blackmail. Hacking into a computer to discover top-secret files of government and big business is a growing trend.

SPY SATELLITES
In 1961, the United States launched the first spy satellite. It had cameras pointed at the ground to photograph troop movements. Today, there are many spy satellites, and they are much more sophisticated. They can monitor radio signals and distinguish individual vehicles on the ground. Spying from space has greatly reduced the need for conventional spies.

Find out more
LAW
POLICE
SATELLITES
WORLD WAR II

SPORTS

EVERYONE WHO takes part in a sport does so for his or her own individual reasons. Early-morning joggers feel good by keeping fit and trying to beat a personal-best time. Backpackers enjoy the fresh air and like to learn outdoor survival skills. And in a sports competition, no experience can match the sensation of winning. Sports are games and activities that involve physical ability or skill. Competitive sports have fixed rules and are organized so that everyone has an equal opportunity to succeed. Many of today's sports developed from activities that were necessary for survival, such as archery, running, and wrestling. Some sports, such as basketball and volleyball, are modern inventions. And as the equipment improves, the rules change to ensure that no competitor has an advantage. Sponsorship and television are now major influences on sports. Leading players become millionaires, and most popular events have huge international audiences.

Many ancient sports are still played today but some, such as foot-wrestling, have long been forgotten.

Officials make sure each game lasts the same time.

EQUIPMENT AND UNIFORMS
Uniforms are important in team sports. They help players and spectators quickly recognize fellow team members and tell them apart from the opposing side. Underneath the basic shirt and shorts or jersey and trousers, players wear protective gear, especially in games such as football and hockey. Shoes are designed to suit the playing surface – rubber-soled for a basketball court, for example, and cleated (spiked) for grass. Other equipment includes a standard ball and, for some sports, bats or rackets.

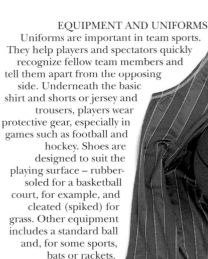

FIELD
The rules of every team sport include standard sizes for the field or court, its markings, and other features such as goal posts. There may be more than one standard if the game is played by both adults and young people. For example, the dimensions of the free-throw lane and the backboard are different for high school, college, and professional basketball. The rules of some sports, such as baseball and soccer, give the largest and smallest sizes allowed for the playing area.

TEAM SPORTS
In a team sport such as basketball, everybody must cooperate, or work together, in order to win. The stars in a team sport are usually the attacking players who score points or kick for a goal. However, if every player tried to be a star, there would be no one to play a defensive role and prevent the opposing team from scoring. So every player on the team has a special job, and each plays an equal part in a successful game.

Basketball hand signals

Personal foul

One free throw

Time out

RULES
Each team sport has its own rules so that everyone taking part knows how to play the game. Referees, umpires, or other judges stand at the edge of the playing area and make sure that the players obey the rules. In some sports, they use a loud whistle to stop and start play. They also signal with their hands or with flags to let the players know their decisions.

The ring of the basket stands 10 ft (3 m) above the floor.

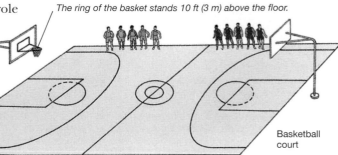

Basketball court

COMPETITION

In individual competition, contestants compete alone. Some try to beat a record; some measure their performance against other contestants. Players compete "one-on-one" in sports such as fencing, judo, and tennis. Several contestants compete together in racing sports such as horse racing or the 100-meter dash. In some sports, such as alpine skiing and archery, contestants compete separately to record the best timing or scores. In other sports, such as diving or gymnastics, judges decide the scores.

Skis enable the wearer to slide swiftly over snow.

GYMNASTICS

In classic gymnastics, contestants perform exercises on the floor and on pieces of apparatus. These include a padded stand called a horse, wooden rings hanging from straps, and arrangements of bars. Men and women do different exercises, and each is excluded from certain events. For instance, only men compete on rings, and only women use the balance beam.

Men's rings

Men's pommel horse

Women's balance beam

Women's uneven parallel bars

Men's horse vault

Men's parallel bars

Women's floor exercises

COMBAT SPORTS

Modern combat sports originated in the fighting sports of Ancient Greece, although people wrestled for sport 15,000 years earlier. Various styles of unarmed combat evolved – boxing and wrestling in the West and jujitsu in the East. The martial arts, such as judo, karate, aikido, and tae kwon do, come from jujitsu.

Archery target

TARGET SPORTS

Firing at targets began with archery, or bow-and-arrow practice, about 500 years ago. In modern archery, competitors shoot a series of arrows at a target from a range of distances. They score ten points for arrows that hit the centre, or bull, and get lower scores the closer the arrow is to the edge of the target. Another target sport is shooting, in which competitors fire rifles or pistols at targets.

WHEEL SPORTS

Competitions on wheels include everything from roller-skating to Grand Prix automobile racing. Physical skill and fitness are most important in unpowered wheel sports such as skateboarding, cycling, and bicycle motocross.

AIR SPORTS

Flying, gliding, and skydiving provide some of the greatest thrills in sports. Pilots race airplanes and, in aerobatics, perform maneuvers. Glider, balloon, and hang glider pilots use warm air currents to move around without power. Skydiving parachutists "free fall" for thousands of feet, linking hands in formation before opening their parachutes to land safely.

ANIMAL SPORTS

Greyhounds, pigeons, camels, and sled dogs compete in races, but horse racing is the best-known animal sport. Horse racing takes place over jumps as well as on flat ground. In harness racing, the horse pulls its driver around a track in a two-wheeled "sulky," like the chariot of ancient times. Other horse sports include show jumping, eventing, dressage, and polo.

In parasailing, a tow vehicle lifts the participant into the air with the aid of a special parachute.

Find out more

ATHLETICS
BALL GAMES
FOOTBALL
GAMES
GYMNASTICS
OLYMPIC GAMES

STAMPS AND POSTAL SERVICES

MILLIONS OF LETTERS pass through the postal system each day.
Even those mailed to you from the other side of the world reach your
home within only a few days. To accomplish this, the postal system relies
on a network of sorting offices. Every letter passes through several sorting
processes at different offices. If you mail a letter to a friend far away, workers
from the post office first collect your letter from the mailbox. Then they take
it back to the sorting office and put it into a sack along with others destined
for the same county or urban area. Vans, trains, or
airplanes rush the sack to the correct destination,
where more postal workers empty out the sack and
sort the letters once more – this time by town, or by
city district. Again, the post travels onward to the local
sorting office, then on to a neighborhood office. There,
postal workers sort the letters by street and by house
before delivering them on foot
or by van.

HILLTOP BEACONS
Fires carried messages
long before there was a
regular postal service.
During the 16th century
a chain of hilltop fires warned
the British of the danger of a Spanish invasion. Watchers
on each hilltop lit their beacon when they saw a flame on
the horizon. The signal traveled from beacon to
beacon faster than a messenger
could ride on horseback.

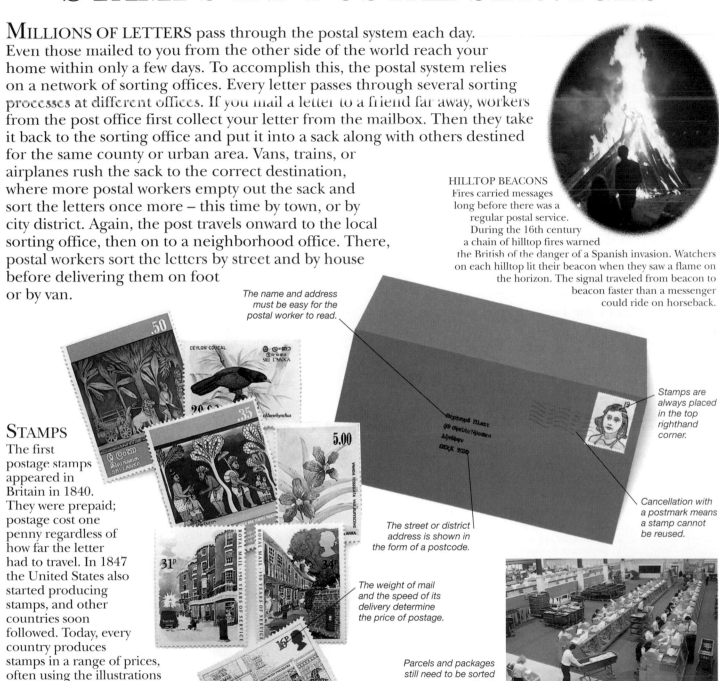

The name and address
must be easy for the
postal worker to read.

STAMPS
The first
postage stamps
appeared in
Britain in 1840.
They were prepaid;
postage cost one
penny regardless of
how far the letter
had to travel. In 1847
the United States also
started producing
stamps, and other
countries soon
followed. Today, every
country produces
stamps in a range of prices,
often using the illustrations
to commemorate national
events and famous citizens.

Stamps are
always placed
in the top
righthand
corner.

Cancellation with
a postmark means
a stamp cannot
be reused.

The street or district
address is shown in
the form of a postcode.

The weight of mail
and the speed of its
delivery determine
the price of postage.

Parcels and packages
still need to be sorted
by hand.

SORTING SYSTEM
The use of machines has made the
task of sorting mail much quicker
and easier. Machines read and
postmark the stamps so they cannot
be used again. A keyboard operator
translates the postal codes into a
series of phosphor dots that can be
sorted automatically. A modern
sorting system can deal with
350,000 letters per hour.

PONY EXPRESS
In 1860, the "Pony Express" in the United States
introduced a fast postal service between Missouri
and California. Stagecoach post took six weeks,
but the relays of riders employed by the Pony
Express cut this to eight days, with each rider
covering up to 75 miles (120 km) a day.
There were 80 riders. One of them was
14-year-old William Cody, later famous
as the showman "Buffalo Bill." The
service was short-lived and was soon
replaced by the telegraph.

Find out more
TRADE AND INDUSTRY
TRANSPORTATION, HISTORY OF

STARFISH AND SEA URCHINS

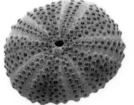

THE SEABED PROVIDES HOMES for many spiny-skinned creatures including starfish, sea urchins, and brittle stars. Starfish range in size from 3 in (8 cm) to 3 ft (1 m) across, and have a central body from which five arms radiate outward. The sea urchin looks like a starfish whose arms have curled upward and joined at the top to make a ball shape.

Sea urchins have a hard outer skeleton covered with long spines. Starfish usually have short spines, like little bumps on the skin. Sea urchins graze on tiny animals and plants from rocks and the seabed, and starfish feed on corals and shellfish. Both animals move using tubes inside the body that pump water in and out of hundreds of "tube feet." These tube feet lengthen and bend under the pressure of the water, propeling the creature along. Each tube foot has a sucker on the end. Using these suckers, a sea urchin can move up a vertical rock, and a starfish can prize open a shellfish and eat the flesh inside.

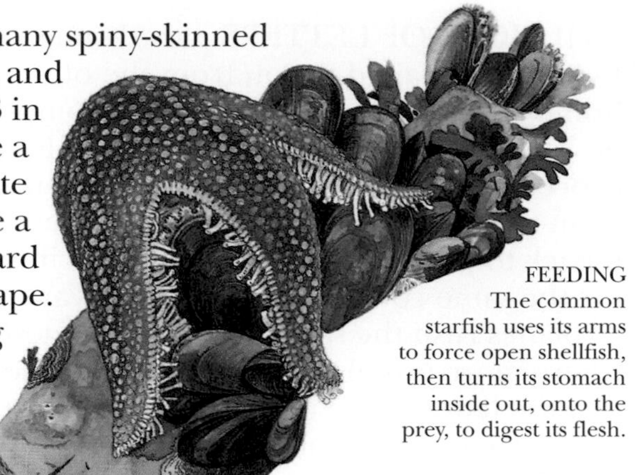

A sea urchin's shell is also known as a test. This one has lost all its spines.

FEEDING
The common starfish uses its arms to force open shellfish, then turns its stomach inside out, onto the prey, to digest its flesh.

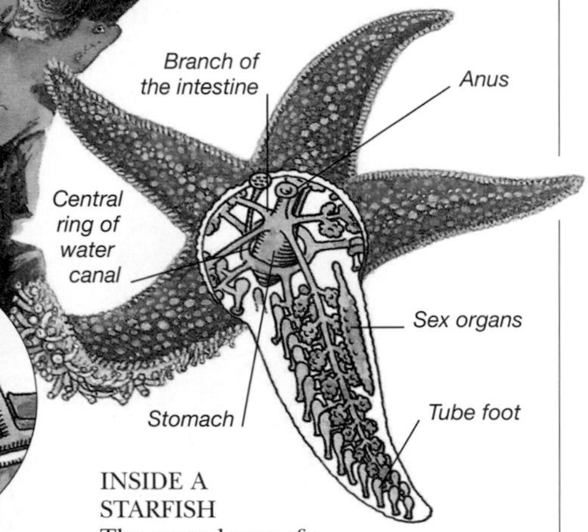

Branch of the intestine

Anus

Central ring of water canal

Sex organs

Stomach

Tube foot

INSIDE A STARFISH
The central part of a starfish contains a stomach, with the mouth below and the anus above. Branches of the nerves, stomach, and water canals go into each arm.

A sea urchin's mouth is a complex five-sided set of jaws.

Main spine

Pedicellariae

Sucker tube foot

SEA POTATO
Sea urchins such as sea potatoes burrow in sand with their flattened spines. Their tube feet are shaped at the tips for passing food to the mouth. An extra long tube foot reaches the surface of the sand like a periscope, so that the sea urchin can breathe. There is another tube foot for passing out waste products.

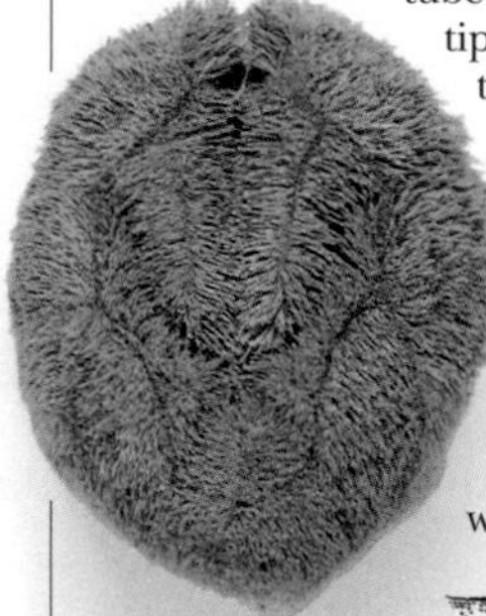

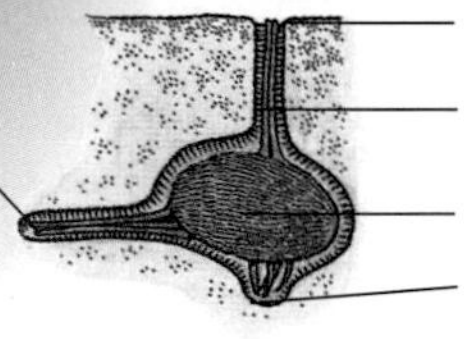

Waste-matter tube foot

Sand surface

Breathing tube foot

Sea potato

Tube feet burrow in sand.

SEA URCHIN
A sea urchin has long spines for defense, and between them wave the tube feet with suckers on the end. Some tube feet bear tiny pincers for clinging on to prey. These are called pedicellariae. In some urchins the pedicellariae are surrounded by venom sacs that are full of poison.

GROWING NEW ARMS
Most starfish can grow new body parts, particularly arms, if the old ones are broken or bitten off. This means they can leave an arm behind to escape from a predator. A new arm grows within a few weeks.

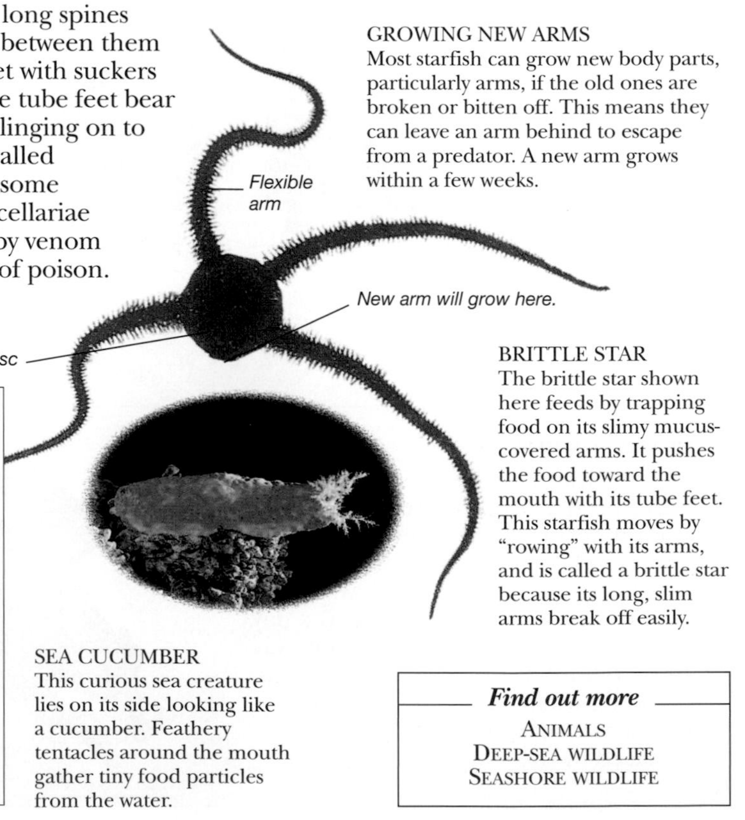

Flexible arm

New arm will grow here.

Central disc

BRITTLE STAR
The brittle star shown here feeds by trapping food on its slimy mucus-covered arms. It pushes the food toward the mouth with its tube feet. This starfish moves by "rowing" with its arms, and is called a brittle star because its long, slim arms break off easily.

CROWN-OF-THORNS STARFISH
These large, prickly starfish eat living coral, and they have severely damaged many coral reefs, including Australia's Great Barrier Reef. Covered with razor-sharp poisonous spines, crown-of-thorns starfish attack coral reefs from Kenya to Tahiti.

The crown-of-thorns has more than a dozen arms covered with poisonous spines.

SEA CUCUMBER
This curious sea creature lies on its side looking like a cucumber. Feathery tentacles around the mouth gather tiny food particles from the water.

Find out more
ANIMALS
DEEP-SEA WILDLIFE
SEASHORE WILDLIFE

STARS

IF YOU LOOK UP AT THE SKY on a clear night, it is possible to see about 3,000 of the billions of stars in our galaxy. Although they appear as tiny dots, they are, like our closest star the Sun, huge, hot balls of gas, deep in space. Some stars are gigantic – if placed in the center of our solar system, they would stretch beyond the Earth's orbit. Others are far smaller, about the size of our planet, and give off only faint light. Stars are unimaginably distant; so distant, in fact, that light from our nearest star (apart from the Sun) takes more than four years to reach us.

Ancient skywatchers noticed that stars seem to form patterns in the sky. They imagined that the shapes represented pictures called constellations. These constellations, such as the Great Bear, are still useful for learning the positions of the stars. Astronomers identify the brightest individual stars according to their constellation and with Greek letters such as alpha, beta, and gamma (which stand for A, B, and C). For example, the second brightest star in the constellation of Centaurus (the Centaur) is called Beta Centauri.

BLACK HOLE
The remains of a very massive star may collapse into a tiny volume, forming a black hole. The gravitational pull of a black hole is so strong that matter and radiation, such as

NEUTRON STAR
A supernova may leave a neutron star – a spinning ball with a mass greater than the Sun's, yet only about 10 miles (16 km) across. As a neutron star spins, it sends out a powerful beam of radiation.

SUPERNOVA
When a massive star dies, it collapses in less than one second. This is followed by a colossal explosion called a supernova. The explosion produces other substances which scatter through space in an expanding gas cloud.

RED SUPERGIANT
Some dying stars grow into huge, cool stars called red supergiants, which can be up to 1,000 times the diameter of the Sun. A red supergiant contains many substances formed by nuclear reactions.

A group of growing stars in a cluster.

The gas and dust in a miniglobule pack closer together, and it spins faster and gets hotter. The miniglobule has become a protostar (a young star).

Death of a massive star

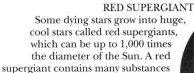

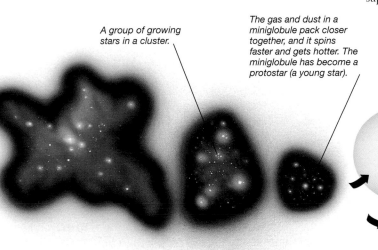

Temperature at center of red supergiant is about 18 billion°F (10 billion°C).

STAR STARTS TO SHINE
When the center of the protostar reaches about 18 million°F (10 million°C), nuclear reactions begin which slowly change hydrogen into helium. The protostar begins to shine, and has become a true star.

The planetary nebula survives only for a few thousand years.

White dwarf

NEBULA
Stars are born from great clouds of dust particles and hydrogen gas, called nebulae. The word nebula (plural nebulae) comes from the Latin for "mist."

BIRTH OF A STAR
Gravity pulls parts of a nebula into blobs called globules. These get smaller and spin faster, finally breaking up into a few hundred "mini-globules." Each of these will eventually become a star.

Death of a star about the size of the Sun

RED GIANT
As a sunlike star runs low in hydrogen, it swells into a cooler, larger star called a red giant. This will happen to our own Sun in about 5,000 million years.

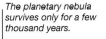

LIFE AND DEATH OF A STAR
Throughout the universe, new stars form and old stars die. The birthplaces of stars are clouds of gas and dust scattered through space. Stars the size of the Sun shine for about 10 billion years. The most massive stars (which contain 100 times as much matter as the Sun) shine very brightly, but live for a shorter time – only about 10 million years.

PLANETARY NEBULA
At the end of its life, a red giant blows off its outer layers of gas. These make a glowing shell called a planetary nebula, which eventually disperses. At the center is a white dwarf, a tiny hot star that is the burned out core of the red giant. It will outlast the nebula by billions of years

TWINKLING STARLIGHT

Nuclear reactions inside a star heat the star up from the center, causing it to emit light and heat from its surface. A star appears to flicker or twinkle because its light passes through the Earth's atmosphere, which is a constantly shifting blanket of gases. Seen from a travelling spacecraft, stars shine steadily because there is no surrounding atmosphere to disturb the path of the light.

CONSTELLATIONS

Modern astronomers group stars into 88 constellations. Each has a Latin name, such as Ursa Major (the Great Bear) or Corona Australis (the Southern Crown). The "sun signs" of astrology have the same names as the 12 constellations of the zodiac – the band of sky along which the Sun and planets appear to pass during the course of a year.

When the constellation of Orion (above) is in the night sky, it can be seen from anywhere on Earth.

WHITE DWARF

At the end of its life, a sunlike star shrinks to about the size of the Earth, forming a white dwarf. A white dwarf is intensely hot, but because it is so small it is very faint.

BLACK DWARF

After perhaps thousands of millions of years, a white dwarf will cool to become a dark, cold, black dwarf. However, no black dwarf has ever been observed because there may not yet have been enough time since the creation of our galaxy for one to appear.

VARIABLE STARS

Many stars, called variable stars, appear to vary in brightness. Some stars constantly swell and shrink, becoming alternately fainter and brighter. Other variables are really two stars that circle each other and block off each other's light from time to time.

Double stars circle around each other. When one star is in front of the other, the brightness dims. When both stars can be seen, the brightness increases.

Some variable stars are produced by exploding stars. The explosion makes the star appear much brighter than usual for a period that can last from a few days to a few years.

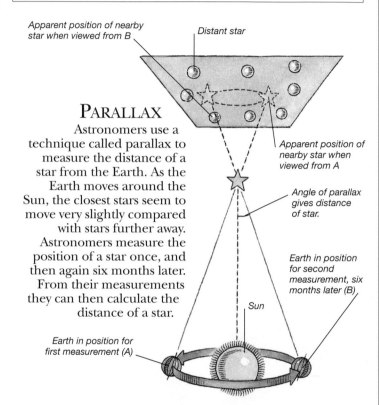

Apparent position of nearby star when viewed from B

Distant star

Apparent position of nearby star when viewed from A

Angle of parallax gives distance of star.

Earth in position for second measurement, six months later (B)

Sun

Earth in position for first measurement (A)

PARALLAX

Astronomers use a technique called parallax to measure the distance of a star from the Earth. As the Earth moves around the Sun, the closest stars seem to move very slightly compared with stars further away. Astronomers measure the position of a star once, and then again six months later. From their measurements they can then calculate the distance of a star.

STAR QUALITIES

The color of a star's light corresponds to the surface temperature of the star: red stars are the coolest, blue stars are the hottest. A star's brightness (the amount of energy it gives out) is linked to its mass (the amount of material it contains): heavier stars are brighter than lighter stars. Astronomers can use the color and brightness of the light emitted from a star to help calculate its size and distance from the Earth.

Neutron stars (pulsars) are the smallest stars. They have about the same mass as the Sun, but are only about 10 miles (16 km) in diameter.

White dwarfs are small stars at the end of their life; some are smaller than the Earth.

Yellow dwarfs, or medium-sized stars, are about the same size as the Sun.

Giants have diameters between 100 and 1,000 times larger than that of the Sun.

Supergiants are the largest stars, with diameters up to 1,000 times that of the Sun.

Find out more

ASTRONOMY
BLACK HOLES
GRAVITY
NAVIGATION
PLANETS
SUN
TELESCOPES
UNIVERSE

STATISTICS

THE WORD STATISTICS has two meanings. First, statistics are actual data, or facts, that are given as numbers – for instance, how many children there are in a class, how often it rains every year, or how much money is raised through taxes. Secondly, statistics is the way in which statisticians (people who work with statistics) analyze or interpret numerical data in order to understand and use it. For instance, by analyzing data such as annual rainfall, statisticians can work out averages and percentages, and forecast how much rain may fall in the future, which could be useful for farmers, or people planning vacations. Statistics is a science, and a branch of mathematics. Governments, industry, and planners of all kinds use statistics.

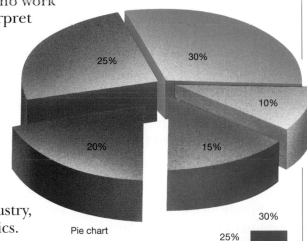

Pie chart

COLLECTING DATA
Before statistics can be analyzed, data must be collected. If statistics are about people, the data can be collected through interviews or by asking people to fill in questionnaires (written questions). People being questioned may belong to a particular group or may be chosen at random. They may answer in words or by checking a box, but all answers must be converted into numerical data.

CENSUS
One way of gathering statistical information about people is to hold a census. A census is an official survey or examination of a country's population carried out by its government. A census counts the number of people in the country, as well as asking about people's age, income, and gender. The first modern census was in the US in 1790.

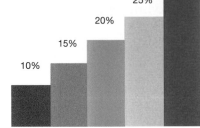

Bar chart

PIE AND BAR CHARTS
Statistical information can be shown as tables of data, but these can be difficult to read. An easier way is to show the information on a pie chart or a bar chart. Pie charts look like pies with slices cut out. Bar charts show information as columns, or bars, of different heights.

Some 19th-century schoolchildren were shown how to fill in a census form, because their parents could not read.

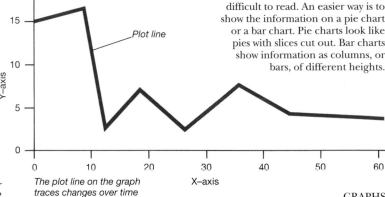

Plot line

The plot line on the graph traces changes over time

Y-axis

X-axis

The child in the center represents the average height for this set of five children.

GRAPHS
Like charts, graphs show statistical data in a way that is easy to understand. The vertical line, called the Y-axis, is marked to show one kind of information—for example, numbers of things, people, or events. The horizontal line, or X-axis, is marked to show a different kind of information—for example, periods of time. The plot line shows at a glance what is happening.

AVERAGES
An average is a quantity that is typical of a certain group or set. It is not a guess; it is calculated mathematically by adding all the figures together and then dividing the total by the number of figures in the set. The average height of five people, for example, can be found by adding their heights together and then dividing the total by five.

Find out more

MATHEMATICS
NUMBERS
SCIENCE

STATUE OF LIBERTY

ON A BRONZE PLAQUE inside the base of the Statue of Liberty are the words of a poem written by Emma Lazarus in 1883. Part of it reads: "Give me your tired, your poor,/ Your huddled masses yearning to breathe free./ The wretched refuse of your teeming shore./ Send these, the homeless, tempest-tost to me./ I lift my lamp beside the golden door!" The "masses" were the people fleeing poverty and oppression in Europe; the "golden door," the opportunity to start a new life in the United States. The French historian Edouard de Laboulaye planned the statue in 1865 to symbolize liberty and to commemorate the friendship of France with the United States. It was designed by Frédéric Auguste Bartholdi and built by Alexandre Gustave Eiffel, whose famous Eiffel Tower dominates the skyline of Paris.

STATUE OF LIBERTY

Supported by four steel columns with a framework of iron, the copper-covered Statue of Liberty represents a woman dressed in a long classical robe, standing 151 ft (46 m) high. The head measures 10 ft by 17 ft (3 m by 5 m) the right arm holding the torch is 42 ft (13 m) long. The torch at the top of the statue is 305 ft (93 m) above the water.

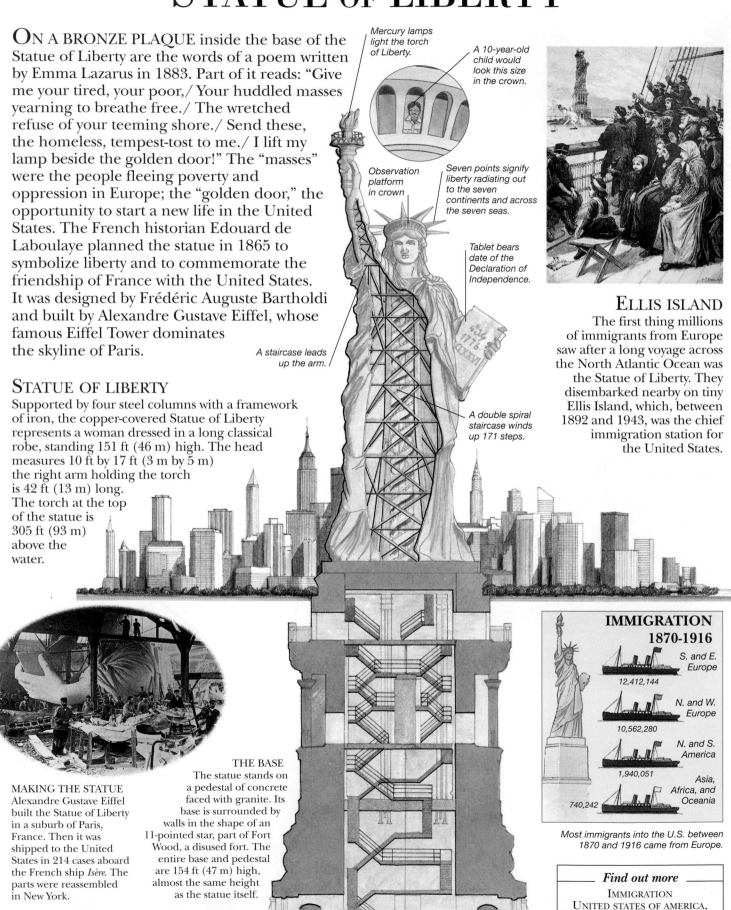

Mercury lamps light the torch of Liberty.

A 10-year-old child would look this size in the crown.

Observation platform in crown

Seven points signify liberty radiating out to the seven continents and across the seven seas.

Tablet bears date of the Declaration of Independence.

A staircase leads up the arm.

A double spiral staircase winds up 171 steps.

ELLIS ISLAND

The first thing millions of immigrants from Europe saw after a long voyage across the North Atlantic Ocean was the Statue of Liberty. They disembarked nearby on tiny Ellis Island, which, between 1892 and 1943, was the chief immigration station for the United States.

MAKING THE STATUE

Alexandre Gustave Eiffel built the Statue of Liberty in a suburb of Paris, France. Then it was shipped to the United States in 214 cases aboard the French ship *Isère*. The parts were reassembled in New York.

THE BASE

The statue stands on a pedestal of concrete faced with granite. Its base is surrounded by walls in the shape of an 11-pointed star, part of Fort Wood, a disused fort. The entire base and pedestal are 154 ft (47 m) high, almost the same height as the statue itself.

Visitors enter here and take an elevator to the base of the statue.

IMMIGRATION 1870-1916

S. and E. Europe
12,412,144

N. and W. Europe
10,562,280

N. and S. America
1,940,051

Asia, Africa, and Oceania
740,242

Most immigrants into the U.S. between 1870 and 1916 came from Europe.

Find out more
IMMIGRATION
UNITED STATES OF AMERICA, history of

STOCK EXCHANGE

A STOCK EXCHANGE IS A MARKET where stocks are bought and sold. The public is not allowed into a stock exchange. Buying and selling is done by special traders called brokers. If ordinary people want to buy or sell shares, they usually have to pay brokers to do it for them.

A share or stock is a certificate to show that you have invested – paid for a part-ownership – in a company. Most companies sell shares to bring in money so they can expand their business. People buy shares because they can make money by waiting until the shares go up in value and then selling them. Sometimes this only takes a few hours. The first exchange in Europe was founded in 1531 in Antwerp, Belgium. In the US, the New York Stock Exchange was set up in 1792 on Wall Street, where brokers originally met under a buttonwood tree. Today, the world's most important stock exchanges are in Tokyo, Hong Kong, London, and New York.

COFFEEHOUSE EXCHANGE
In 1760, Jonathan's Coffeehouse was the first home of what would become the modern London stock exchange. Brokers met there to buy and sell shares. In 1773, it changed its name to the Stock Exchange. The London Stock Exchange is now one of the biggest in the world.

WALL STREET CRASH
In 1929, shares in many American companies fell in price all at once. This was known as the Wall Street Crash. Companies closed, and millions lost their jobs.

SHARE TRADING

In a traditional stock exchange, traders worked in areas called "pits." Each pit dealt in shares in a particular type of company. Brokers outside the pits sent messages to those inside to buy or sell shares on instructions from their customers. Today, many exchanges buy and sell by telephone and on the Internet.

Traders on the New York Stock Exchange buy and sell for their customers.

INDICATORS AND INDEXES
Inside a stock exchange, huge electronic boards called indicators show the prices of shares. To see how the market is doing at a glance, the share prices are added up and an average, called an index, is worked out. The index is given in points, not money. It can go up and down daily. Falling markets are called "bear" markets; rising markets are known as "bull" markets.

Oranges for juice

Coffee beans

CHECKING INVESTMENTS
Information technology has made it quicker and easier for everybody to buy shares. Some people are given stock in the company they work for as part of their earnings. Anybody can find out how their stocks are doing by looking at the lists of share prices published daily in financial newspapers or on the Internet.

FUTURES
A future is a contract to buy a quantity in something for an agreed price at a set time in the future. For example, you buy "futures" in next year's harvest of coffee beans or oranges. If the price goes higher than the one you agreed, you make money because you still pay the agreed price; but if it goes lower, you lose money.

Find out more
ASIA, HISTORY OF
MONEY
SHOPS AND SHOPPING
TRADE AND INDUSTRY

STONE AGE

MORE THAN TWO MILLION YEARS AGO, stone was the most valuable raw material known to people. They made stone tools and weapons, usually from flint. These early people were called hominids, and were more apelike than modern humans. They gradually learned to make specialized implements, such as knife blades. Stone Age people moved constantly, looking for hunting areas and setting up camps in small groups. A few groups lived in caves during the coldest seasons. They gathered fruits, berries, and roots, and hunted wild animals. By the start of the Mesolithic Age (Middle Stone Age; 10,000 years ago) many types of larger animals had died out. Mesolithic people, who were "modern people" (*Homo sapiens*) like us, used new stone-edged tools to fish and hunt deer and wild pigs. About 5,000 years ago some Neolithic (New Stone) Age people learned how to domesticate animals and grow crops. They settled on farms.

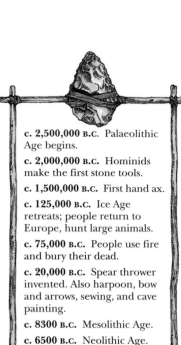

c. 2,500,000 B.C. Palaeolithic Age begins.

c. 2,000,000 B.C. Hominids make the first stone tools.

c. 1,500,000 B.C. First hand ax.

c. 125,000 B.C. Ice Age retreats; people return to Europe, hunt large animals.

c. 75,000 B.C. People use fire and bury their dead.

c. 20,000 B.C. Spear thrower invented. Also harpoon, bow and arrows, sewing, and cave painting.

c. 8300 B.C. Mesolithic Age.

c. 6500 B.C. Neolithic Age.

c. 3000 B.C. Metal tools and weapons replace stone.

MAMMOTH HUNT

From about 50,000 years ago, "modern people" hunted wild animals. By cooperating in groups and using their superior brainpower, they could kill creatures much larger than themselves. They sometimes slaughtered large numbers of deer and similar creatures by driving whole herds over cliffs. Elephant-like woolly mammoths were popular game; they are now extinct.

Mammoth has been lured into a pit trap covered in branches.

Hunters killed prey with sharp stone weapons.

Woman cooks a hare on a spit over the fire.

Dwelling places made from animal hides and mammoth bones kept out the cold wind.

Stretching hide to make clothing.

Man is using a bone hammer to chip away at a flint core.

MAKING FLINT TOOLS AND WEAPONS

1 The first flint implements were crude. People used the sharp edge of a broken rock as a cutting tool.

2 Later tools were much better. The toolmaker prepared a flint core by skillful chipping.

3 Hitting the core with a bone hammer made flakes, each one a special tool.

HAND AX
The hand ax was the first deliberately shaped tool made by humans. It was gripped at the rounded end and used to cut meat or dig roots. Popular for over a million years, it was used longer than any other tool.

This flint hand ax was found in a desert area near Thebes, Egypt.

Find out more
ARCHAEOLOGY
IRON AGE
EVOLUTION
PREHISTORIC PEOPLES

STORMS

TORNADOES

The most violent storms are tornadoes, or whirlwinds. A twisting column of rising air forms beneath a thunder cloud, sometimes producing winds of 250 mph (400 km/h). The air pressure at the center is very low, which can cause buildings to explode. A waterspout is a tornado over water, formed when water is sucked up into the funnel of air. Dust devils are tornadoes that have sucked up sand over the desert.

Severe storms build up as moist air, heated by warm land or sea, rises. Storm clouds develop as the rising air cools and rain forms. Air rushes in to replace the rising air, and strong winds begin to blow.

The rising air spirals up the column, sucking up dirt and objects as heavy as trucks from the ground.

The base of the tornado is fairly narrow – about 1 mile (1.5 km) across.

ABOUT 2,000 thunderstorms are raging throughout the world at this very moment, and lightning has struck about 500 times since you started reading this page. Storms have enormous power: the energy in a hurricane could illuminate more light bulbs than there are in the United States. A storm is basically a very strong wind. Severe storms such as thunderstorms, hurricanes, and tornadoes all contain their own strong wind system and blow along as a whole. Certain areas, such as the region around the Gulf of Mexico, are hit regularly by severe storms because of the local conditions. Storms can cause great damage because of the force of the wind and the devastating power of the rain, snow, sand, or dust that they carry along. One of the most destructive forces of a hurricane is a storm surge. The level of the sea rises because of a rapid drop in air pressure at the center of the storm. This rise combines with the effect of the wind on the sea to create a huge wall of water that causes terrible damage if it hits the coast.

DESTRUCTION AND DEVASTATION

Winds of 200 mph (320 km/h) leave a trail of destruction (below) when the hurricane strikes the shore. The strongest winds are in a belt around the calm eye.

THUNDER AND LIGHTNING

Thunder clouds often form on hot, humid days. Strong air currents in the cloud cause raindrops and hailstones to collide, producing electric charges. Lightning flashes in giant sparks between the charges, and often leaps to the ground. A burst of heat from the flash makes the air nearby expand violently and produces a clap of thunder.

Negative charges in the bottom of the cloud attract positive charges in the ground. Eventually, a huge spark of lightning leaps from the cloud to the highest point on the ground.

Buildings are protected by lightning rods – strips of metal on the roof that attract the lightning and lead the electricity safely to the ground.

HURRICANES

When warm, moist air spirals upward above tropical oceans, it forms a hurricane – a violent storm that is also called a typhoon or a cyclone. The spin of the Earth causes the storm winds to circle around a calm center called the eye. The eye usually moves along at about 15 mph (25 km/h). It can measure as much as 500 miles (800 km) across.

Find out more
CLIMATES
RAIN AND SNOW
TORNADOES AND HURRICANES
WEATHER
WIND

SUBMARINES

THE GREAT POWER of a submarine lies in its ability to remain hidden. It can travel unseen beneath the waves, carrying its deadly cargo of missiles and torpedoes, and remain underwater for months at a time. However, the submarine had humble beginnings; legend states that during the siege of Tyre (Lebanon) in 332 B.C., Alexander the Great attacked the inhabitants from a submerged glass barrel. Aided by the invention of the electric motor for underwater propulsion and the torpedo for attacking ships, modern submarines developed into powerful weapons during the two world wars of the 20th century. Today's submarines are powered either by a combination of diesel and electric motors or by nuclear-powered engines. There are two main types: patrol submarines, which aim to seek and destroy ships and other submarines, and missile-carrying submarines. Small submarines called submersibles are used mainly for non-military purposes, such as marine research.

NUCLEAR SUBMARINE

The most powerful of all weapons is the nuclear missile-carrying submarine. Its nuclear-powered engines allow it to hide underwater almost indefinitely without coming up for air, and it carries sufficient nuclear missiles to destroy several large cities.

Propeller drives the submarine through the water.

Diesel-electric engines are specially designed to make as little noise as possible.

Periscope and communication antennas

The conning tower stands clear of the water when the submarine is on the surface.

Torpedoes ready for firing

Small movable wings called hydroplanes control the submarine's direction.

Tubes for launching torpedoes

HUNTER-KILLER SUBMARINE

A diesel engine powers this hunter-killer submarine when it travels on the surface, and an electric motor when it is underwater. Buoyancy tanks fill with water to submerge the submarine; to surface again, compressed air pushes the water out of the tanks.

Crew's living quarters are usually cramped. Some submarines carry a crew of more than 150.

Control room, from where the captain commands the submarine

Anti-submarine helicopter trails active sonar system in the water.

SONAR

Helicopters, ships, and hunter-killer submarines are equipped with sonar (sound navigation and ranging) for detecting submarines. Passive sonar consists of microphones that pick up the sound of the submarine's engines. Active sonar sends out ultrasonic sound pulses that are too high-pitched to be heard but bounce off a hidden submarine and produce a distinctive echo.

Hunter-killer submarine uses active sonar to detect enemy submarine.

The missile-carrying submarine will dive to escape its attackers.

Submarine captain sees helicopter through periscope.

TORPEDOES

Torpedoes are packed with explosives and have their own motors to propel them to their targets. They are launched by compressed air from tubes in the nose and rear of the submarine.

PERISCOPE

With a periscope, the captain can see what is on the surface while the submarine is submerged. A periscope is a hollow tube that extends from the conning tower. It contains an angled mirror at either end and a system of lenses that form an image of the object on the surface.

Find out more
NAVIES
ROCKETS AND MISSILES
SHIPS AND BOATS
UNDERWATER EXPLORATION
WARSHIPS

SUMERIANS

THE WORLD'S FIRST CITIES were built on the banks of the Tigris and Euphrates rivers in what is now Iraq. About 5,000 years ago, the people of Sumer, the area of southern Iraq where the two rivers flow together, began to build what would become great, bustling cities. They made bricks from the riverside mud to build houses and massive temples. The Sumerians also developed one of the world's earliest writing systems, by making marks in soft tablets of clay, which they left in the sun to harden. Their earliest cities, such as Ur and Uruk, became famous all over the Middle East as Sumerian merchants traveled abroad trading food grown in the fertile local fields. The Sumerians flourished until about 2000 B.C., when desert tribes invaded.

MESOPOTAMIA
The land between the Tigris and Euphrates rivers is known as Mesopotamia. The home of the Sumerians was in southern Mesopotamia and Ur was one of their greatest cities.

GILGAMESH
The Sumerians created the earliest written story that has survived to modern times. Written on clay tablets, the story tells of Gilgamesh, King of Uruk and the son of a goddess and a man. Gilgamesh begins as a cruel king, but be becomes a hero when he kills two fearsome monsters. Later, Gilgamesh visits the underworld to try to search for immortal life.

Cuneiform script consisted of wedge-shaped marks made with a reed writing-stylus.

ZIGGURAT
At the center of each Sumerian city was a stepped tower called a ziggurat, topped by a temple. By building their ziggurats high, the Sumerians believed that they were reaching up to the heavens, so that each temple could become a home for one of Sumer's many gods and goddesses. Only priests were allowed to worship in the temples.

SUMER
The land between the two rivers was fertile but dry. Farmers dug canals to bring water to their fields, and found that this meant they could produce huge harvests – there was usually enough to sell. The Sumerians found other useful resources near the rivers. They used reeds for boat-building and simple houses, and clay for making bricks and pottery.

Mud-brick ziggurat towered over the city.

Palm trees provided dates and wood.

Sumerians traveled along the rivers in boats made from local reeds. Fishermen used similar boats.

Reed beds grew on the banks of the river

Farmers scattered seeds by hand.

Oxen pulled wooden plows.

Brickmakers poured soft mud into a mold.

Reed huts were common in southern Mesopotamia.

Neatly-trimmed beard typical of Mesopotamian fashion.

SARGON
Originally the servant of a king of Kish, in Akkad, north of Sumer, Sargon rose to become Akkad's ruler. In around 2350 B.C., he conquered Sumer, Mesopotamia, and the eastern territory of Elam. He made Mesopotamia into a united country for the first time. Sargon was a powerful king who protected merchants and built up flourishing trade.

Bricks were left to bake dry in the hot sun.

Workers dug up clay to make bricks.

Find out more
ALPHABET
BRONZE AGE
WHEELS

SUN

THE NIGHT SKY is full of stars, so distant that they are mere points of light. The Sun is one of these stars, but we are closer to it than to any other star. Along with the other planets of the solar system, the Earth moves around the Sun, trapped in orbit by the force of gravity. The Sun is a ball of glowing gases, roughly three-quarters hydrogen and one-quarter helium, along with traces of other elements. Within its hot, dense core, hydrogen particles crash together. This produces nuclear reactions that release enormous amounts of energy, keeping the core of the Sun very hot. The energy travels outwards and leaves the Sun's surface mainly as light, and infrared and ultraviolet radiation. The Sun sustains nearly all life on Earth with its light and heat. Energy sources that humans use to provide power originate from the Sun. For example, coal is the remains of ancient plants, which trapped the Sun's energy.

STORY OF THE SUN
The Sun formed just under 5,000 million years ago from a cloud of hydrogen and helium, and dust that contracted (shrank) under its own gravity. The contraction heated the cloud until nuclear reactions began, converting hydrogen into helium. At this point the Sun began to shine steadily. It is believed that the Sun will continue to shine for another 5 billion years before it runs out of hydrogen fuel and begins to die.

SOLAR FLARES
Huge explosions on the Sun's surface, called solar flares, fire streams of electrically charged particles into space.

CORONA AND SOLAR WIND
A thin pearl-white atmosphere of gases called the corona extends for millions of miles around the Sun. A blast of electrically charged particles, called the solar wind, blows out from the corona at a rate of millions of tons each second. The Earth is protected from these particles by its magnetic field, but they can damage spacecraft and satellites. Coronal Mass Ejections are sudden blasts of great clouds from the corona. These are thought to cause auroras – colored lights in the sky above the Earth's poles – and magnetic storms.

Energy travels outward in the form of heat and electromagnetic waves such as infrared, light, and radio waves.

Relatively cool and dark areas, called sunspots, form on the surface of the Sun. Sunspots develop in places where the Sun's magnetic field becomes particularly strong.

Great streamers of glowing hydrogen gas, called prominences, frequently soar up from the Sun. Prominences are often about more than 37,000 miles (60,000 km) long.

Light from the Sun takes about eight minutes to reach the Earth.

Core extends to about 110,800 miles (175,000 km) from the Sun's center.

The hot, glowing surface of the Sun is called the photosphere (sphere of light). It is about 250 miles (400 km) deep.

A glowing red layer of hydrogen gas called the chromosphere (sphere of color) lies above the photosphere. The chromosphere is a few thousand miles deep.

Warning: Never look at the Sun, either directly or through dark glasses. The intense light could seriously damage your eyesight.

The Sun's diameter is 109 times that of the Earth. More than 1,300,000 globes the size of the Earth could fit into the Sun.

SOLAR ENERGY
Electronic devices called solar cells convert sunlight into electricity. Solar cells power satellites and produce electricity in experimental houses and cars. In 2003, the solar-powered *Nuna II* car (below) drove across Australia at an average speed of 60 mph (96.8 km/h).

Umbra is the center of the Moon's shadow, where the Sun is completely hidden.

Penumbra is the outer part of the Moon's shadow, where part of the Sun can be seen.

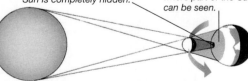

SOLAR ECLIPSES
When the Moon passes between the Earth and the Sun, the Sun is hidden. This is called a solar eclipse. A total solar eclipse occurs at places on the Earth where the Sun appears to be completely hidden (although prominences, chromosphere, and corona can be seen). Elsewhere the eclipse is partial, and parts of the Sun can be seen.

SUN FACTS
Earth–Sun distance	92,9 million miles (149,6 million km)
Diameter at equator	864,950 miles (1,392,000 km)
Time to rotate once	25,4 days
Temperature at surface	10,000°F (5,500°C)
Temperature at center	27,000,000°F (15,000,000°C)

Find out more
ASTRONOMY
ENERGY
STARS

SUPREME COURT

Thurgood Marshall leaves the Supreme Court with his wife.

THE HIGHEST COURT in the United States, the Supreme Court is the ultimate court of appeal. Established in 1789, the court's basic duty is to interpret and rule on the laws laid down in the Constitution. The court consists of nine members – a Chief Justice and eight Associate Justices. They have the power of judicial review, to determine if state or federal laws conflict with how the court interprets the Constitution. However, most of the 6,500 cases the court hears each year are on appeal from lower courts. In its landmark cases, the court has made decisions that have shaped American law and the American way of life.

Chief Justice Warren Burger reads the oath

John O'Connor holds the Bible

Sandra Day O'Connor is sworn in as a Supreme Court justice

SUPREME COURT JUSTICES

The members of the Supreme Court are appointed by the President, with the approval of the Senate. The justices may serve for life. In 1967, Thurgood Marshall became the first African American to be appointed to the court. In 1981, Sandra Day O'Connor became the first female Supreme Court justice.

THE COURT DECIDES

Some 6,500 cases come before the court each year. After written and oral arguments, the justices discuss the case together and vote. A majority vote decides the outcome of the case. If the Chief Justice votes with the majority, he or she selects a justice to write the opinion of the court. A justice who disagrees may write a dissenting opinion.

COURT TRADITIONS

Supreme Court justices follow many long-standing traditions. Since 1800, the justices have worn black robes. Quill pens are placed on their tables each day, and at the beginning of each session, each justice always shakes hands with the other eight.

Supreme Court justices first wore traditional black robes in the early 19th century.

LANDMARK CASES

1803 Marbury v. Madison Gave the court the power to determine an act of Congress unconstitutional.

1857 Dred Scott v. John Sanford Blacks, even those freed from slavery, could not become citizens.

1954 Brown v. Board of Education Declared that segregation of whites and nonwhites was unequal and therefore a violation of the Constitution.

1961 Mapp v. Ohio No conviction from evidence gained by entering a house without a search warrant.

1962 Engel v. Vitale Prayer not compulsory in public schools.

1966 Miranda v. Arizona Criminal suspects must be informed of their rights.

1973 Roe v. Wade Right Right to abortion in the first trimester of pregnancy.

African-American schoolchildren defy segregation in the aftermath of the Brown versus Board of Education case.

CIVIL RIGHTS AND THE COURT

Many of the court's landmark cases deal with civil rights. In 1951, eight-year-old Linda Brown was turned away from a whites-only school in Topeka, Kansas; she was the wrong color. In 1954, the court ruled in "Brown versus Board of Education of Topeka" that school segregation was a violation of the 14th Amendment.

Find out more

CIVIL RIGHTS
CONSTITUTION
LAW

SWIMMING

FROM CROWDS ON A BEACH TO BATHERS by a pool, most people enjoy swimming. It is one of the most popular sports for people of all ages. Swimming – using your arms and legs to move through water – exercises every part of the body, encouraging health and fitness. It is also an important international sport. Competitive swimmers need to be very strong and fit. They train for hours, swimming huge distances every week. For swimmers such as these, an Olympic gold medal is the ultimate goal. But almost anyone can learn to swim, whether using a fast-moving crawl, slower breaststroke, or even a doggy paddle. Learning to swim well is an important safety measure, and it can save lives.

CAPTAIN WEBB
On August 25, 1875, Captain Matthew Webb became the first person to swim across the English Channel. It took him 22 hours to cross between England and France. Long-distance swimming needs stamina. Swimmers cover themselves with grease for insulation against the cold water.

FUN AND SAFETY
Swimming is fun, whether on vacation at the beach, or at the local pool or water park. But knowing how to swim properly also makes other water sports such as canoeing, boating, surfing, and waterskiing much safer.

Snorkel and mask

Dive weights

Goggles

Flippers

SWIMMING STROKES
There are four main strokes, or methods of swimming: freestyle, or crawl, backstroke, butterfly, and breaststroke. Crawl is the fastest. Swimmers kick up and down, bringing their arms forward out of the water. For backstroke, swimmers lie on their backs. Butterfly involves using arms and legs together, pulling the body forward. In breaststroke, swimmers pull their hands sidewise, and kick like a frog.

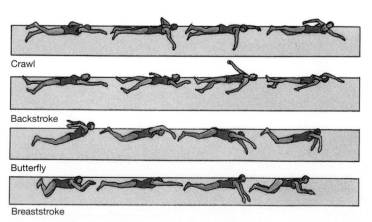
Crawl

Backstroke

Butterfly

Breaststroke

MAKING A TURN
Swimmers save time by doing somersault, or tumble, turns when they finish a length. Just before the end of the pool the swimmer takes a breath, swivels underwater and pushes off from the wall with their feet. A good turn can mean the difference between winning and losing.

EQUIPMENT
Using a mask and snorkel, a swimmer can see and breathe underwater; the top of the snorkel sticks above the surface of the water. Goggles protect the eyes and allow swimmers to see what is going on without their eyes stinging. Flippers are like the fins of fish, and make swimming easier. Diving weights make it easy to stay underwater.

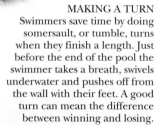

___ *Find out more* ___
HEALTH AND FITNESS
SPORTS
WATER SPORTS

SWITZERLAND

Switzerland is a landlocked country at the heart of Europe. The Alps create a major barrier to the south. To the north, the Jura Mountains form its border with France. Lake Geneva, on the French border, is formed by the Rhône River.

LIECHTENSTEIN
Area: 62 sq miles (160 sq km)
Population: 33,100
Capital: Vaduz
Languages: German, Alemannish dialect, Italian
Religions: Roman Catholic, Protestant
Currency: Swiss franc

SWITZERLAND
Area: 15,940 sq miles (41,290 sq km)
Population: 7,200,000
Capital: Bern
Languages: German, Swiss-German, French, Italian, Romansch
Religions: Roman Catholic, Protestant, Muslim, nonreligious
Currency: Swiss franc

A LAND OF HIGH MOUNTAINS and isolated valleys, the 26 provinces (cantons) of Switzerland have been a united confederation since 1291. With access to the north via the Rhine River and control of the alpine passes to the south, Switzerland has dominated Europe's north-south trade routes for many centuries. The country lacks natural resources, but has become a wealthy financial, banking, and commercial center, with a worldwide reputation for precision engineering, especially watchmaking. Although mountains cover nearly three-quarters of the land, dairy farming is very important, and the Swiss export a wide range of cheeses and milk chocolate. Liechtenstein, a tiny mountainous country on Switzerland's eastern border, is also an important financial and manufacturing center.

ALPINE PASTURES
Most alpine villages are clustered at the base of mountain slopes and in valley plains. These locations provide fertile soil, adequate water, and temperate weather. Vines can even be grown on south-facing slopes. Swiss dairy farmers keep their cattle in the valleys during the winter. In summer they are taken up to lush, green alpine meadows to graze.

WINTER SPORTS
Over 100 million visitors a year come to the Swiss Alps to enjoy climbing, hiking, and winter sports. Alpine skiing has been included in the Olympic Games since 1936. Mountain resorts with chair lifts, ski runs, and ski instructors cater to winter visitors. But tourism is having a dangerous impact. Trees are cleared to make way for ski runs, and without these natural barriers, there is a much greater risk of avalanches.

LAKE GENEVA
Picturesque villages line the shores of Europe's largest Alpine lake, especially to the north, where the soil is fertile. Geneva, at the southwest of the lake, is a major banking and insurance center. Many international organizations, such as the Red Cross, are based in the city.

SCALE BAR
0   50 km
0   30 miles

Volcano | Mountain | Ancient monument | Capital city | Large city/town | Small city/town

Find out more
EUROPE, HISTORY OF
MOUNTAINS
MOUNTAIN WILDLIFE
TUNNELS

TANKS

MILLIONS OF YEARS AGO, nature equipped animals such as turtles with a shell of armor to protect them from enemies. Early in the 20th century, armies adopted the same idea in battle. The result was the tank – a steel monster that lumbered over the battlefields of World War I (1914-18), destroying enemy defenses and machine-gun positions. Tanks have now developed into sophisticated weapons that combine fire power, protection, and mobility. Each tank is fitted with a powerful gun which is guided by computers and a laser rangefinder to ensure pinpoint accuracy. Hardened-steel armor, which may be up to 4.3 in (11 cm) thick, protects the crew. Tanks can maneuver their way over terrain that would stop any other vehicle, including water, and some light tanks can travel at speeds of more than 50 mph (80 km/h).

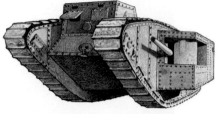

THE EARLY TANK
In 1916, the British Mark I became the first tank to be used in battle. Its strange shape allowed it to cross the wide trenches, mud, and barbed wire of the battlefield. Over the next 30 years, tanks evolved into advanced fighting machines. Recent developments are concerned with improving weaponry, speed, and the armor of tanks.

MAIN BATTLE TANK
The German-built *Leopard 2* battle tank is one of the most powerful tanks in the world. It can travel at 45 mph (72 km/h) despite its weight of 54 tons (55 tonnes), which is equivalent to more than 30 small family cars. It is armed with a main gun and two machine guns and carries a crew of four.

Machine gun is used to defend tank against aircraft.

Main gun is guided by laser sight and computers.

Smoke dischargers produce huge cloud of smoke to hide the tank if it is under attack.

Commander's cupola with periscopes that give all-around vision.

Turret allows main gun to move and be aimed in any direction.

Gun loader operates main gun and radio communications.

Periscope allows driver to see out from inside the hull of the tank.

Ammunition store with shells for main gun

CATERPILLAR TRACKS
Tanks run on caterpillar tracks, which are endless belts running over several wheels. To turn the tank, the driver makes the tracks on either side of the tank run at different speeds.

SELF-PROPELLED GUN
Because mobile artillery weapons are mounted on a tanklike vehicle, they can move rapidly into new positions.

ARMORED CAR
Armored cars are perfect for reconnaissance (scouting) missions and patrols because they are small and fast.

M1 Abrams

120mm cannon fires rocket-shaped projectiles to penetrate enemy tanks and explode.

PERSONNEL CARRIER
Soldiers travel into battle inside an armored personnel carrier. It transports them on water and on land, propelled by its caterpillar tracks.

US ABRAMS
The M1 Abrams took 10 years to develop and was used by the US Army during the 1980s and 1990s. It has a more comfortable cabin and stronger armor than older tanks. It uses lasers to calculate the distance to a target. During the Gulf War in 1991 it destroyed more than 2,000 enemy tanks without any US losses.

Find out more
ARMIES
GUNS
WEAPONS
WORLD WAR I
WORLD WAR II

TECHNOLOGY

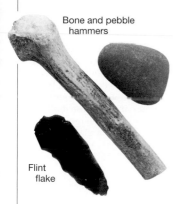

Bone and pebble hammers

Flint flake

EARLY TECHNOLOGY
Humans living during the Stone Age developed a variety of tools for everyday purposes. They used rounded pebbles and bones as hammers to form cutting tools from a strong stone called flint. Flint was chipped and flaked to produce a sharp cutting edge like a blade.

THE INVENTION OF STONE TOOLS more than two million years ago marked the beginning of technology. For the first time in history, people found that cutting or chopping was easier to do with tools than with bare hands. Technology is the way in which people use the ideas of science to build machinery and make tasks easier. Although technology began in prehistoric times, it advanced rapidly during and after the Industrial Revolution, beginning in the 18th century. Since that time technology has dramatically changed our world. It has given us fast, safe transport, materials such as plastics, increased worldwide communications, and many useful daily appliances. Perhaps the greatest benefits of technology are in modern medicine, which has improved our health and lengthened our lives. Advances in technology have been mainly beneficial to humans and our lifestyle. However, increased technology has a negative side, too – it has produced weapons with the power to cause death and destruction. Technology and development have caused many environmental problems such as ozone depletion, and is often dependent on nonrenewable resources, such as oil, which has a limited life. Governments and other organizations are now trying to use new technology to find solutions to these problems.

COMPUTERS

The development of computers has been one of the most important recent advances in technology. The invention of the microchip (right) changed the emphasis of producing goods from mechanical to electronic. This meant that many tasks which had previously been done manually were now automated. Computers perform many different tasks and are used in banking, architecture, manufacturing, and a range of other businesses. Computers also aid new technology, because they can help develop new machines.

Threshing machines help farmers separate the heads from the stalks of rice plants. Previously, this job had to be done by hand.

Microchips lie at the heart of a computer. These tiny devices store and process huge amounts of information at high speed.

SMALL-SCALE TECHNOLOGY

People in poorer countries cannot afford to buy the technological goods that are common in richer parts of the world such as North America and Europe. Their primary concern is feeding and housing their families, and they tend to use smaller, simpler machines, such as windmills that drive pumps for irrigation.

Synthetic clothing materials are lightweight, machine-washable, and allow ease of movement.

The cyclist's helmet is made from plastic and polystyrene. It has an aerodynamic shape to increase the speed of the cyclist.

Disabled members of the community can participate in more activities because of advanced technology, such as this specially designed tricycle.

Wheel technology, developed in 3500 B.C, revolutionized machines and modes of transportation.

LIFESTYLE
In the western world, technology has generally made daily life easier. Washing machines, cars, and cash machines all make daily tasks more convenient, providing more time for leisure, hobbies, and sports. People also now have the time and means to travel to other countries to experience different cultures and environments.

MEDICAL TECHNOLOGY

Inventions such as x-ray machines and brain scanners help doctors to detect and treat illness. Doctors can transplant organs, implant tiny electronic pacemakers to keep a heart beating, and repair damaged tissue with plastic surgery. Medical technology, such as glasses, contact lenses, or hearing aids, also helps to improve the daily lives of many people affected by impaired vision or hearing. Prosthetic (artificial) limbs are also being improved and now allow their users more movement and flexibility.

Laser surgery can correct many eye defects without needing to cut the eye.

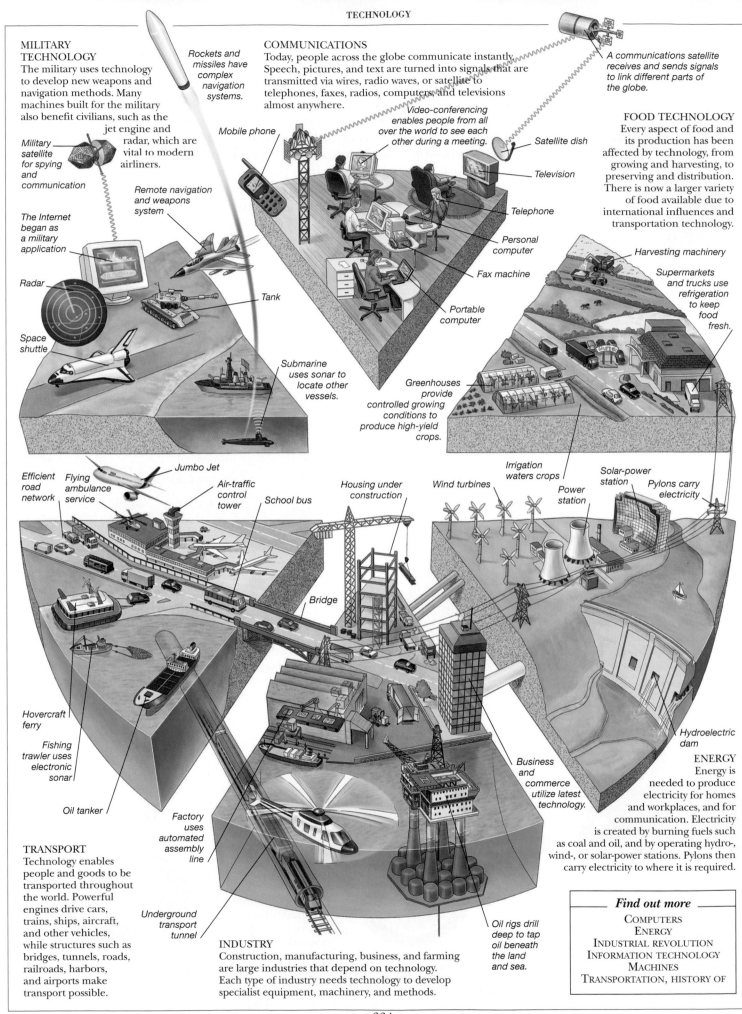

MILITARY TECHNOLOGY

The military uses technology to develop new weapons and navigation methods. Many machines built for the military also benefit civilians, such as the jet engine and radar, which are vital to modern airliners.

Rockets and missiles have complex navigation systems.

Military satellite for spying and communication

The Internet began as a military application

Remote navigation and weapons system

Radar

Space shuttle

Tank

COMMUNICATIONS

Today, people across the globe communicate instantly. Speech, pictures, and text are turned into signals that are transmitted via wires, radio waves, or satellite to telephones, faxes, radios, computers, and televisions almost anywhere.

Mobile phone

Video-conferencing enables people from all over the world to see each other during a meeting.

A communications satellite receives and sends signals to link different parts of the globe.

Satellite dish

Television

Telephone

Personal computer

Fax machine

Portable computer

Submarine uses sonar to locate other vessels.

FOOD TECHNOLOGY

Every aspect of food and its production has been affected by technology, from growing and harvesting, to preserving and distribution. There is now a larger variety of food available due to international influences and transportation technology.

Harvesting machinery

Supermarkets and trucks use refrigeration to keep food fresh.

Greenhouses provide controlled growing conditions to produce high-yield crops.

Irrigation waters crops

Wind turbines

Solar-power station

Power station

Pylons carry electricity

Efficient road network

Flying ambulance service

Jumbo Jet

Air-traffic control tower

School bus

Housing under construction

Bridge

Hovercraft ferry

Fishing trawler uses electronic sonar

Oil tanker

Factory uses automated assembly line

Underground transport tunnel

Business and commerce utilize latest technology.

Hydroelectric dam

TRANSPORT

Technology enables people and goods to be transported throughout the world. Powerful engines drive cars, trains, ships, aircraft, and other vehicles, while structures such as bridges, tunnels, roads, railroads, harbors, and airports make transport possible.

INDUSTRY

Construction, manufacturing, business, and farming are large industries that depend on technology. Each type of industry needs technology to develop specialist equipment, machinery, and methods.

Oil rigs drill deep to tap oil beneath the land and sea.

ENERGY

Energy is needed to produce electricity for homes and workplaces, and for communication. Electricity is created by burning fuels such as coal and oil, and by operating hydro-, wind-, or solar-power stations. Pylons then carry electricity to where it is required.

Find out more

COMPUTERS
ENERGY
INDUSTRIAL REVOLUTION
INFORMATION TECHNOLOGY
MACHINES
TRANSPORTATION, HISTORY OF

TEETH

EVERY TIME WE EAT we use our teeth – to bite, chew, crunch, and grind food. Teeth enable us to break up food properly so that our bodies can digest it and turn it into energy. A tooth has three main parts – the crown of the tooth, which shows above the gum; the neck, which shows at gum level; and the root, which is hidden in the jawbone. The root of the tooth is fixed securely in the jaw by a substance called cementum. A tooth has three layers – creamy white enamel on the outside (the hardest substance in the body); a layer of dentine beneath; and the pulp cavity in the center. The pulp contains many nerves, which connect to the jawbone. There are four main kinds of teeth; each kind is shaped for a different job. Chisel-like incisors at the front of the mouth cut and slice food; longer, pointed canines tear and rip food; and flat, broad premolars and molars crush and grind it. During our lives, we have two sets of teeth – milk teeth as children, and a second set of teeth as adults.

HEALTHY TEETH
It is important to take care of your teeth to keep them healthy. Teeth should be cleaned with a toothbrush and toothpaste after every meal. Dental floss should be used regularly. Sugary foods are damaging to teeth and cause tooth decay.

Enamel
Pulp cavity
Dentine
Gum
Blood vessels
Root
Jawbone
Cementum
Nerve

Cross section of a molar

STRUCTURE OF A TOOTH
Teeth have one, two (like this molar), three, or occasionally four roots, which anchor them securely in the jawbone and withstand the pressure of biting and chewing. Blood vessels which carry nutrients and oxygen, and nerves which transmit sensation, pass out through tiny holes in the base of each root.

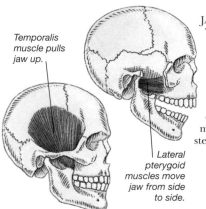

Temporalis muscle pulls jaw up.

JAWS
The upper jaw is fixed to the skull and does not move. Powerful muscles in the cheeks and the side of the head pull the lower jaw up toward the upper jaw, so that the teeth come together with great pressure for biting. Other muscles pull the lower jaw sideways, so that we can chew with both up-down and side-to-side movements. Teeth are an important first step in the process of digesting food.

Lateral pterygoid muscles move jaw from side to side.

DENTISTS
Dentists use x-rays (right) to see the roots of teeth and to identify any cavities. In the past, dentists extracted decaying teeth, but now only the affected parts are removed and the hole is filled with hard artificial materials. The white areas on this x-ray are fillings and two crowns on posts.

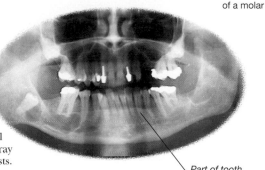

Part of tooth shows below the gum line.

MILK TEETH AND ADULT TEETH
Children have 20 milk teeth which gradually fall out and are replaced by a second set of permanent adult teeth. Adults have 32 teeth in total. Each jaw has 4 incisors, 2 canines, 4 premolars, and 6 molars (2 of which are wisdom teeth). Wisdom teeth grow when a person is about 20, although some never push through the gum.

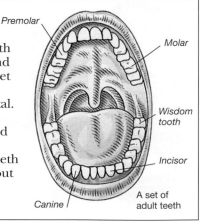

Premolar
Molar
Wisdom tooth
Incisor
Canine
A set of adult teeth

TUSKS
Animals use their teeth for more than just eating food. Large teeth help defend an animal against its enemies, or when fighting rivals during the mating season. The tusks of the warthog shown here are huge canine teeth – like the tusks of an elephant. Tusks are used to frighten off predators and, sometimes, to dig up food.

___ *Find out more* ___
FOOD AND DIGESTION
HUMAN BODY
SKELETONS

TELEPHONES

Earpiece

A loudspeaker, called the receiver, contains a thin metal disk that vibrates, converting electric signals into sound waves.

Silicon chip

Electronic circuits generate signals corresponding to each button as it is pressed. They also amplify (boost) incoming electric signals and send them to the receiver.

WITH THE PUSH of a few buttons on the telephone, it is possible to talk to someone nearly anywhere else in the world. By making instant communication possible, the telephone has done more to "shrink" the world than almost any other invention. A telephone signal can take several forms on its journey. Beneath the city streets it travels in the form of electric currents in cables, or as light waves in thin glass fibers. Telephone signals also travel as radio waves when they beam down to other countries via satellites, or when they carry messages to and from cell phones. Many electronic devices "talk" to each other by sending signals via telephone links. Computers exchange information and programs with one another, and fax machines use telephone lines to send copies of pictures and text to other fax machines across the world within seconds.

TELEPHONE HANDSET
A small direct (one-way) electric current flows in the wires connected to a telephone handset. Signals representing sounds such as callers' voices, computer data, and fax messages consist of rapid variations in the strength of this current.

Microphone

Sound waves of the user's voice strike a microphone called the transmitter, creating an electrical signal that is sent down the telephone cable.

The electric cable connects to the telephone network, allowing access all over the world.

Communication satellites orbit the Earth at such a height and speed that they remain stationary over the same part of the globe all the time. They receive telephone signals from one country on Earth, boost the signals, then beam them back down to another country.

TELEPHONE NETWORK
Computer-controlled telephone exchanges make the connections needed to link two telephones. When a person dials a telephone number, automatic switches at the local exchange link the telephone lines directly. International calls travel along undersea cables or, in the form of radio waves, by way of satellites.

Words and pictures printed by a fax machine have jagged edges because they are made up of thousands of dots.

Fiber-optic cables use light waves to carry thousands of phone calls at one time.

FAX
A facsimile, or fax, machine scans a picture or a written page, measuring its brightness at thousands of individual points. The machine then sends signals along the telephone wire, each representing the brightness at one point. A printer inside the receiving fax machine prints a dot wherever the original picture is dark, making a copy.

ALEXANDER GRAHAM BELL
The inventor of the telephone was a Scottish-American teacher named Alexander Graham Bell (1847-1922). In 1875, Bell was experimenting with early telegraph systems. For this he used vibrating steel strips called reeds. He found that when a reed at one end of the line vibrated, a reed at the other end gave out a sound. In 1876, Bell patented the world's first practical telephone.

PORTABLE PHONES
A cordless telephone has a built-in radio transmitter and receiver. It communicates with a unit connected to a telephone line in a home. Cell phones (left) work with the aid of powerful relay stations such as cellular exchanges. Cell phones are becoming increasingly versatile. Many now also function as cameras and can connect to the Internet.

Find out more

INTERNET
RADIO
SATELLITES
TECHNOLOGY

TELESCOPES

FROM FAR AWAY, a person looks like a tiny dot. But with a telescope, you can see a clear, bright image that reveals all of the details of that person's face. Large modern telescopes make it possible to see incredibly distant objects. The Hale telescope on Mount Palomar, California, can detect objects in space called quasars, which are about 20,000 million billion miles (30,000 million billion km) from the Earth. Less powerful telescopes are important too: they are valuable tools for mapmakers, sailors, and bird-watchers. Telescopes have helped scientists make some of the greatest discoveries about the universe. In 1609, the Italian scientist Galileo first turned a telescope to the skies. His observations led him to suggest that the Earth moved around the Sun and was not the center of the universe, as people believed at that time. Since then astronomers have used telescopes to probe into the farthest reaches of our solar system and beyond, discovering new stars and planets.

OPERA GLASSES

Opera glasses are the simplest kind of binoculars. They consist of two small telescopes placed side by side.

Eyepiece lenses are adjustable to match the strength of each eye.

Prisms "fold up" the light inside the binoculars, which magnifies objects as much as a long telescope.

A prism is a triangular-shaped piece of glass.

BINOCULARS

Binoculars are more complex than opera glasses. They contain a system of lenses and prisms that makes them powerful yet small in size.

When the Hale telescope was first built, the observer sat inside the telescope itself to view the stars. Today, there is an electronic detector placed there instead.

Doors of observatory slide open to give telescope a view of the stars.

Light enters the front of the telescope.

REFLECTING TELESCOPE

Most astronomers use reflecting telescopes, which are the best telescopes for picking up the faint light from distant stars. A large curved mirror catches the light and concentrates it to form an image. A smaller mirror then carries the image to a lens called the eyepiece. A camera or electronic light detector is often fitted to the eyepiece of astronomical telescopes.

Concave mirror is curved inward to focus the light. This mirror is called the objective mirror because it forms an image of a distant object.

The mountings allow the telescope to turn in order to follow the stars as the Earth moves.

RADIO TELESCOPES

Stars and other objects in space give out invisible radio waves as well as light. Astronomers study the universe with radio telescopes, which are large dish-shaped antennas that pick up radio waves from space. Radio astronomy has led to the discovery of dying stars and distant galaxies that would not have been seen from their light alone.

The eyepiece lens focuses the image into the observer's eye.

The objective lens is a convex lens that concentrates the light to form an image.

The middle lens turns the image the right way up.

The mirror is made as large as possible to collect the maximum amount of light and distinguish fine details. The objective mirror on the Hale telescope (above) is 16.6 ft (5.8 m) wide and weighs 20 tons.

REFRACTING TELESCOPE

A large lens at the front of a refracting telescope refracts, or bends, the light to form an image of a distant object. The eyepiece lens is at the back. Some refractors have a third lens in the middle. Without this lens, the telescope would produce an upside-down image.

Find out more

ASTRONOMY
LIGHT
MICROSCOPES
SCIENCE, HISTORY OF

TELEVISION AND VIDEO

SINCE ITS INVENTION early in the 20th century, television has become one of the world's most important sources of opinion, information, and entertainment. Television gives us the best seats in the theater, at a rock concert, or at the Olympic Games. It also beams us pictures of war and disaster, the conquering of space, and other world events as they happen. Television programs are actually electronic signals sent out as radio waves by way of satellites and underground cables. A television set converts the signals into sound and pictures. People can watch pre-recorded films and record broadcast programs to play at a later time using a videocassette recorder (VCR), optical discs (DVDs), or a digital video recorder (DVR). Lightweight video cameras can also be used to make home movies. Closed-circuit (nonbroadcast) television cameras are used to guard stores and offices, monitor traffic conditions, and survey crowds in public places.

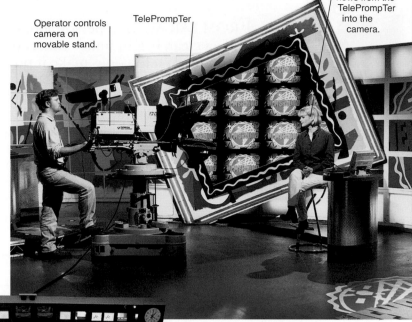

Operator controls camera on movable stand.

TelePrompTer

Host reads the news from the TelePrompTer into the camera.

TELEVISION STUDIO

Within the space of a few hours, a studio might be used for a game show, a play, a variety show, and a panel discussion, so studio sets have to be changed very rapidly. Presenters and people working behind the cameras receive instructions from the control room via headphones. Most programs are recorded, sometimes months before they are broadcast.

CONTROL ROOM

The director and vision mixer sit in the control room (shown above) in front of a bank of screens showing pictures from several sources, such as from cameras at various angles in the studio and at outside broadcast locations, from videotape machines, and from satellites. Other screens show still photographs, captions, and titles. The vision mixer is instructed by the director which image to broadcast on screen and for how long. Sound is also mixed in at the same time. The producer has overall control of the final program.

TELEPROMPTER

The presenter reads the script from a TelePrompTer. The words are displayed on a monitor screen and reflected in a two-way mirror in front of the camera lens. An operator on the studio floor controls the speed at which the words move.

OUTSIDE BROADCAST

Outside broadcast teams use portable cameras when mobility is important, as in a news report, and large, fixed cameras for events such as football games. The pictures are recorded on videotape or beamed back to the studio via a mobile dish antenna.

Sound is recorded through a sound boom.

Sections of video are cut, edited, and reordered.

The editor watches the original recordings and puts together the final program.

EDITING SUITE

When a program is not broadcast live, an editor gathers all the video recorded from each camera and selects the best sections and edits them together in the right order. This is done in an editing suite (left) with specialized equipment. Editing allows filming to be done out of sequence, and from many different angles. Smooth editing can be crucial to the flow and final cut of the program.

TELEVISION RECEIVER

A television receiver (or TV set) picks up signals broadcast by television stations and converts them to moving pictures using a picture tube. Images appear to move because 25-30 pictures appear each second. Beams of electrons (tiny charged particles from atoms) sweep across the inside surface of a color screen, hitting dots of chemicals called phosphors. The electrons cause the dots to glow red, green, or blue, depending on the phosphor, and combine to reproduce every color in the picture.

The picture tube is made of thick glass. The air inside it has been removed to allow movement of electrons.

Shadow mask pinholes ensure each electron beam falls on phosphor dots of the correct color.

Internal parts of a television set

Three electron guns fire electrons onto the screen.

A coil produces a magnetic field that deflects the electron beams, sweeping them rapidly across, and up and down, the screen.

Glass screen front

TELEVISION TRANSMISSION

Television signals can reach a viewer by several routes. Usually, transmitters broadcast television signals directly to homes as ultrahigh frequency (UHF) radio waves. Alternatively, the signals are sent up to a satellite, which transmits them over a larger region. Individual homes receive the satellite broadcast via dish antennas (right). In other cases, a ground station picks up the signals and sends them out along cables.

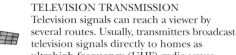

Satellite television sends signals from the TV station to homes via a satellite.

Television station

House aerial picks up UHF signals.

Cable television

Cable feeds the signal into the house to the receiver.

The horn collects concentrated incoming waves

Zoom lens

Camcorder

NEW TECHNOLOGIES

Today's widescreen TV sets increasingly have flat plasma screens or liquid crystal displays instead of bulky picture tubes. Videocassette tapes are being replaced by optical discs (DVDs), which are like high-density music CDs, and by digital video recorders (DVRs), which work in the same way as computer hard disc drives. Movies and TV shows can now be downloaded from the Internet, too. Digital broadcasting uses binary code to carry TV signals with better quality sound and pictures. And with interactive television, viewers can select what to watch and when from a wide range of options.

Hand-held television

Flatscreen television

Digital video recorder

INVENTION

In 1926, Scottish engineer John Logie Baird (1888-1946) gave the first public demonstration of television. At about the same time, the Russian American engineer Vladimir Zworykin (1889-1982) invented the electronic camera tube, which was more sophisticated than Baird's system and is the basis of today's television sets. In 1956 the U.S. company Ampex first produced videotape; videocassette recorders appeared in 1969, produced by Sony of Japan.

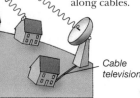

VIDEO CAMERAS

Today's video cameras or "camcorders" are tiny in comparison with the giant studio cameras used in the early days of TV. They fit easily in the palm of one hand. Most are now digital and record high-quality video sequences – including stereo sound as well – in the form of binary code stored on magnetic tape, optical DVD discs, memory cards, or a hard disc drive built into the camera.

Find out more

CAMERAS
ELECTRONICS
INFORMATION TECHNOLOGY
RADIO
SOUND RECORDING

TEXTILES

SPINNING, WEAVING, AND KNITTING turn a mass of short fibers into something much more useful: a textile. We are surrounded by decorative textiles; most clothing is made from them. Textiles keep us warm because they trap air within their mesh of threads. The air acts as an insulator, preventing body heat from escaping. But textiles do much more than keep out the cold. Tightly woven artificial fibers are flexible but tough, so they are ideal for making knapsacks, sails, and parachutes. The loose-weave loops of natural fibers in a towel have a great thirst for water, drying us quickly after a bath. Some special textiles are as strong as armor; Kevlar fabric, for instance, can stop a bullet.

Textiles date back to the taming and breeding of animals about 12,000 years ago. The people of Mesopotamia (now Iraq) rolled sheep wool into a loose yarn for weaving clothes. Plant fibers such as cotton came later, and synthetic fibers have been available only since the invention of nylon in 1938.

SPINNING WHEEL
Spinning thread by twisting fibers between the fingers is hard work. The pedal-powered spinning wheel made the process quicker and easier.

Wool thread

Fibers of wool

SOURCES OF TEXTILES
Natural fibers for textiles come from cotton bolls, flax (for linen), fleece (for wool), and silk cocoons. Synthetic fibers, such as nylon, are made of chemicals that are mostly produced from crude oil.

Cotton boll

Crude oil

Fleece

SPINNING
Natural fibers in a boll or fleece are tangled together. Spinning machines separate the fibers. They then twist natural or synthetic fibers together so the fibers firmly grip each other and form a strong thread.

SYNTHETIC FIBERS
Squeezing a liquid called a polymer through tiny holes makes synthetic fibers. The polymer sets as it emerges.

WEAVING AND KNITTING
Looms are machines that crisscross long threads to make woven textiles. Knitting by hand requires just a pair of needles, but a machine does the job more quickly. Pressing unspun fibers together produces a thick textile called felt that is often used for hats.

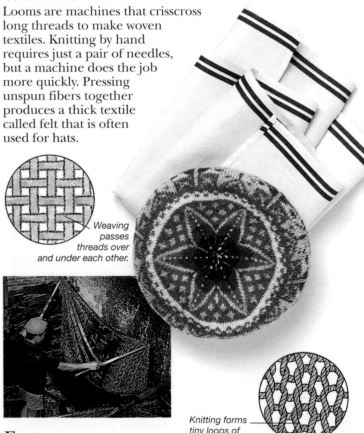

Weaving passes threads over and under each other.

Knitting forms tiny loops of thread that interlock.

FINISHING TEXTILES
Many textiles are printed with beautiful patterns. Batik (above) uses wax or other materials to make a pattern by restricting where the dye penetrates the fabric. Special treatments make textiles fluffy or waterproof, or stop them from shrinking or wrinkling.

CARPET MAKING
A carpet loom weaves strong threads of wool, cotton, or synthetic fibers onto a mesh backing to make a carpet. The threads may also be knotted together or formed into loops. Cutting the loops turns the tufts of fibers into a carpet pile.

Find out more
BUTTERFLIES AND MOTHS
CLOTHES
INDUSTRIAL REVOLUTION
PLASTICS

THEATER

AT THE HEART OF ALL THEATER lies the excitement of watching a live performance. Bringing a play to life involves many people. The words of the dramatist, or playwright, the ideas of the director, and the actors' skill combine to make an audience believe that what is happening on the stage – the drama – is real. Early theater grew out of religious festivals held in Greece in honor of the god Dionysus, and included singing and dancing as well as acting. The different forms of theater that emerged in India, China, and Japan also had religious origins. In medieval Europe people watched "miracle plays," which were based on religious stories. Later, dramatists began to write about all aspects of life, and companies of actors performed their plays in permanent theaters. Theater changes to suit the demands of each new age for fantasy, spectacle, or serious drama.

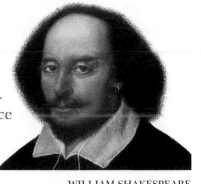

WILLIAM SHAKESPEARE
This most famous of all playwrights was born in Stratford-upon-Avon, England, but moved to London as a young man. He wrote more than 37 plays, including tragedies such as *Hamlet*, comedies such as *As You Like It*, and history plays such as *Henry V*. He died in 1616 at the age of 52.

The theater's curved shape amplified sounds for the audience.

This theater was built 2,500 years ago and could seat 5,000 people.

The walls were about 30 ft (9 m) high with tiny windows.

There was little scenery, and actors entered through doors at the back.

People could pay more to sit in galleries which protected them from the rain.

OPEN-AIR THEATER
Ancient Greek theater made use of landscapes like this one at Delphi. Actors wore exaggerated masks so that characters could be recognized from afar.

GREEK THEATER
The audience sat in a semicircle of steplike seats. There was a circular orchestra – a space for dancing and singing – and a low stage for actors.

ROMAN THEATER
Based on Greek theaters, the Roman theater was usually open to the sky and enclosed on three sides. A permanent wooden roof sheltered the raised stage.

THE OPEN STAGE
Some modern theaters have an open stage without a curtain. The actors can address the audience more directly, as if holding a conversation.

THEATER-IN-THE-ROUND
Here the audience surrounds the cast on all four sides, bringing everyone close together. The actors enter through aisles between the seats.

The yard audience stood very close to the actors on stage.

GLOBE PLAYHOUSE
Shakespeare was an actor and a writer at this famous theater on the south bank of the Thames River in London. There was room for more than 2,000 people in the round wooden building. The audience stood in the open yard or sat in the enclosed gallery to watch a performance. In 1995, the Globe was rebuilt at a nearby site in London.

BROADWAY MUSICALS
Many shows combine acting and music. Some of these performances are called opera, but the more popular type are known as musicals. The theaters in New York's Broadway area have hosted many famous musicals over the years. A successful musical such as *Cats* (right) may run for many years, playing to full houses every night.

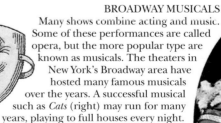

DRAMA AND DRAMATISTS
Playwrights adapt drama to suit what they want to say. Watching the downfall of characters in a tragedy helps us to understand more about life. Comedy makes us laugh, but some dramatists, such as George Bernard Shaw, used it to say serious things about society. Modern dramatists, such as Samuel Beckett and Bertolt Brecht, have experimented with words and characters to push the boundaries of drama even further.

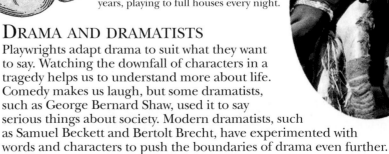

THE PICTURE FRAME
Clever use of scenery and a sloping stage helps to change the audience's view through the proscenium arch (the frame of the stage) and makes the stage look deeper.

PROFILE-SPOT
Stagehands control this light from the rear of the upper circle. They use the strong beam to pick out and follow an actor in a pool of brilliant light.

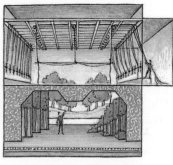

UP IN THE FLIES
High above the stage there is "fly" space in which scenery and equipment hang. A system of pulleys makes it possible to lower scenery.

Lowering the curtain, or tabs, hides the stage while stagehands change scenery.

The flameproof safety curtain seals off the stage from the auditorium if fire breaks out.

Some of the actors share a dressing room where they put on makeup and change into costume.

Fly ropes raise and lower the lights as they are needed.

Loudspeaker announcements warn the actors to get ready to make their entrance.

Actors who play the lead roles may have a dressing room to themselves.

The wardrobe department makes the costumes and stores them until needed.

Scenery and props wait in the wings for rapid scene changes.

By raising or angling the stage slightly the designer can change the audience's view.

Musicians may sit in an orchestra pit below the front of the stage.

The elevator can lift an actor or prop onto the stage in a split second.

Most traditional theaters have a "picture frame" stage – the play takes place under a proscenium arch.

The busy carpentry department builds the sets. Props, such as furniture, are stored here when not in use.

Actors enter and leave the theater by the stage door.

From the lighting control board or console, the operator can dim or brighten any light in the theater. A lighting change can alter the mood of a play in seconds.

SOUND EFFECTS
Sound effects must happen at exactly the right moment. If an actor falls down before the sound of a gunshot, the whole scene is ruined. The sound operator listens and watches carefully for each cue.

Find out more
BALLET
LITERATURE
MUSIC
OPERA AND SINGING
SHAKESPEARE, WILLIAM

TIME

In reality, the Earth is 400 times farther away from the Sun than it is from the Moon.

Earth Moon Sun

HOUR FOLLOWS HOUR as time passes. Time always flows steadily in the same direction. Behind us in time lies the past, which we know. Ahead lies the future, which we cannot know. We cannot change time, but we can measure it. People first measured time in days and nights, which they could easily see and count. They also measured time in months, by watching the phases of the Moon, and in years, by watching the cycle of the seasons. Today, we have clocks and watches that can measure time in fractions of a second.

In 1905, German physicist Albert Einstein proposed the scientific theory of relativity. This says that time is not constant, but that it would pass more slowly if you could travel very fast (near the speed of light), or in strong fields of gravity. Scientists believe that time may even come to a stop in black holes deep in space.

HOURGLASS
Sand draining through an hourglass shows the passing of time. It takes one hour for the sand to run from the top to the bottom bulb.

UNITS OF TIME
One full day and night is the time in which the Earth spins once. This is divided into 24 hours: each hour contains 60 minutes, and each minute contains 60 seconds. The Babylonians fixed these units about 5,000 years ago, using 24 and 60 because they divide easily by 2, 3, and 4.

The Earth spins counterclockwise.

7 a.m. in New York City

9 a.m. in Rio de Janeiro, Brazil

The International Date Line is at 180 degrees longitude.

3 p.m. in Moscow, Russian Federation

12 noon in London, England

2 p.m. in Cairo, Egypt

The prime meridian is at 0 degrees longitude.

YEARS AND MONTHS
A year is based on the time the Earth takes to go once around the Sun, which is 365.26 days. Months vary from 28 to 31 days. They were originally based on the time the Moon takes to go around the Earth, which is 27.3 days.

INTERNATIONAL DATE LINE
The western side of the International Date Line is one day ahead of the eastern side. When you cross the line, the date changes.

TIME ZONES
The world is divided into 24 regions, called time zones, each with a different time of day. This was done to avoid having several time differences within one area, and to ensure that all countries have noon during the middle of the day.

UNIVERSAL TIME
The time at the prime meridian is used as a standard time known as Universal Time (UT) or Greenwich Mean Time (GMT).

DAYS AND NIGHTS
The Sun lights up one half of the Earth, where it is day. The other half, away from the Sun, is dark, and there it is night. Days and nights come and go because the Earth spins once every 24 hours. But the day and night may last different lengths of time because the Earth is tilted at an angle to the Sun.

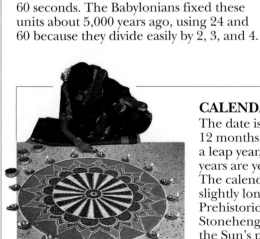

The Hindu calendar is based on lunar months. Diwali, the Festival of Lights, marks the start of the new year, which falls in October or November.

CALENDARS
The date is fixed by the calendar, which contains 12 months with a total of 365 days. Every fourth year is a leap year, which has one extra day, February 29. Leap years are years that divide by four, such as 2008 and 2012. The calendar contains leap years because the Earth takes slightly longer than 365 days to go once around the Sun. Prehistoric peoples may have used monuments such as Stonehenge, in southern England (below), to measure the Sun's position and find the exact length of the year.

Twice a year the Sun is directly overhead at 12 noon.

Find out more

CLOCKS AND WATCHES
EARTH
EINSTEIN, ALBERT
PHYSICS
SCIENCE
STARS
UNIVERSE

TORNADOES AND HURRICANES

TWO OF THE EARTH'S MIGHTIEST and most devastating storms are tornadoes and hurricanes. A tornado's killer winds can reach 300 miles (400 km) an hour – strong enough to lift cars, mobile homes, and people into the sky. With speeds of up to 200 miles (320 km) an hour, a hurricane's winds can uproot trees and lift roofs off buildings. Tornadoes and hurricanes develop from and are fed by warm, moist air. Both bring driving winds, heavy rain, hail, and low air pressure that can devastate a region. However, several characteristics separate the two kinds of storms. Tornadoes form on land, while hurricanes develop over oceans. A tornado twists in a funnel-shaped column, while a hurricane swirls around a calm center called the eye. A tornado strikes quickly and with little warning, while a hurricane is much larger and can rage for days.

A TWISTER STRIKES

Tornadoes, also known as twisters, are born from severe thunderstorms. Moist, warm air rises until it meets a higher layer of cooler air. Storm clouds grow as the trapped air cools and rain forms. Air rushing in to replace the rising air creates strong winds that spiral upward, whipping dust and debris into a huge, black cloud. The deadly spiral of air cuts its path across the land. The United States, particularly the Midwest, is hit by over 1,000 tornadoes a year – more than any other country.

BIRTH OF A HURRICANE

Hurricanes develop from warm, moist air over tropical oceans. The air flows into low-pressure areas, where it rises and cools to form clouds. More warm air is drawn upward, creating winds; the spin of the Earth causes the storm winds to circle around a low-pressure area at the center of the storm called the eye. Most of these storms die out and never reach land, but in a typical year six hurricanes hit the Gulf of Mexico and the Atlantic coast states during "hurricane season," from summer to early fall.

A tornado has cut a devastating path through this town in Kentucky.

TAKING A TOLL
The awesome power of tornado and hurricane winds can bring sudden and widespread destruction. Many recent storms have damaged property, crops, and land estimated at billions of dollars. The effect on storm survivors is impossible to measure.

TRACKING A STORM
Meteorologists (weather scientists) gather information from weather balloons, satellites, and radar to predict and track storms. Specially equipped planes, known as hurricane hunters, fly directly into the eye of hurricanes to measure wind speeds, temperatures, and humidity. Computer programs assess the data to help predict the path of the hurricane.

STORM SURGE
The most dangerous part of a hurricane is its storm surge – a huge mass of water that piles up under the storm. As the bulging dome of water reaches shallow waters near the shore, the surge slows down before rising to drown the coastline, swallowing boats and houses and flooding the land. In 1900, a hurricane in Galveston, Texas, created a surge that killed 6,000 people – the worst natural disaster in American history.

<table>
<tr><td>Find out more</td></tr>
<tr><td>STORMS
WATER
WEATHER
WIND</td></tr>
</table>

TOURISM AND TRAVEL

IT USED TO BE VERY UNUSUAL for people to travel far from their homes. It took weeks to make trips that today take hours in a car, and months or years to reach destinations that are now a few hours' flight away. Religious pilgrimages were one of the few reasons why people made journeys. In the 17th and 18th centuries, only the rich could afford to travel. With the arrival of trains in the 19th century, and buses in the 20th century, journeys became cheaper, and tourism – travel for pleasure – began. Today, inexpensive air travel has made trips abroad available to many people. A huge industry has grown up to serve the tourist trade, which is now an important part of the world's economy.

Cockle shell

PILGRIMS
Since ancient times, people all over the world have made pilgrimages – journeys to holy places – to pray for help and spiritual guidance. In medieval Europe, pilgrims who travelled to the shrine of St. James at Santiago de Compostela in Spain brought back a cockle shell to show that they had made the journey.

GRAND TOUR
A trip around Europe became fashionable among the British aristocracy in the 18th century, when it was considered a desirable way to complete a young person's education. The travelers would spend weeks, or possibly months, in cities such as Rome and Vienna, often staying with relatives or friends. Only the very rich could afford to do a Grand Tour.

PACKAGE VACATIONS
Travel agencies and vacation companies put together flights, hotels, and meals to create all-inclusive vacation packages for tourists. Spain, Greece, and other places that have hot weather and sandy beaches have built lots of hotels for tourists from colder countries. Package vacations are a huge business that provides millions of jobs.

Snowboards are a challenging way to enjoy the ski slopes.

COOK'S TOURS
The first person to make a successful business from organizing excursions and travel groups was Thomas Cook (1808-92) in the late 1800s. He brought vacations to the middle classes by making them affordable, and created the modern tourism industry. The travel agency named after him is part of a worldwide business.

Eiffel Tower, Paris tourist attraction

DAYTRIPPING
The development of railroads and buses made travel quicker as well as cheaper. Day trips were now possible for ordinary people. The souvenir industry grew up, making small ornaments and items for day-trippers to take back to their friends and family as gifts, or to remind them of the places they had visited.

OUTDOOR VACATIONS
Some people want to be lazy on vacations, while others prefer to be active. Many tourists choose to go on adventure vacations, which focus on sports such as scuba diving and windsurfing. Skiing is also very popular and has become a big business. In recent years, many young people have decided to go backpacking – traveling to less-visited places, away from the tourist crowds.

Find out more
SPORTS
TRANSPORTATION, HISTORY OF
WATER SPORTS

TOYS

ALTHOUGH THE MAIN purpose of a toy is fun or amusement, toys have other functions, too. Some toys prepare children for the activities of adult life. For example, hobbyhorses helped children learn about horseback riding long before they were old enough to sit in the saddle. Similarly, today's toy cars can teach driving skills. In the Middle Ages, toys such as tops and rattles were popular, but in later centuries only rich families could afford the elaborate toys that became fashionable. In strict families the only toys allowed on Sunday were those associated with the Bible, such as a model of Noah's Ark. Today, there are more toys than ever before. Children have a vast choice of mass-produced playthings, but there is still a demand for simple homemade toys like those that amused Ancient Egyptian children.

HOOPS
With a little imagination, everyday objects can become toys. A stick becomes a hobbyhorse, an old box a doll's bed. For centuries, children of many lands have used wooden wheels or rings from barrels as hoops. They can be rolled along, thrown in the air, or whirled around the body.

ANCIENT TOYS
Baked clay horses found in Egypt were made almost 2,500 years ago. Archaeologists in Rhodes, Greece, have discovered other animal toys that are even older. These ancient toys give us an idea of how children played long ago.

DOLLS
Dolls were among the first toys. They have been made from rags, wax, wood, and paper. During the last century dolls were beautifully dressed and had fragile china heads. Modern dolls are much sturdier and some are able to walk, talk, and eat.

The ball is a universal toy and is found in every society.

Blocks can be used for games of counting, balancing, and building.

ELECTRONIC TOYS
Battery-powered games test a player's mental agility and speed of reflexes. The computer brains inside are tiny, so even complex games are small enough to fit in a pocket.

TOY CARS
Both children and adults enjoy and collect model cars. Some toy cars can be operated by remote control.

TEDDY BEARS
On a hunting trip in 1902, President Theodore "Teddy" Roosevelt refused to kill a bear cub. Soon after this was reported in the newspapers, a shopkeeper began to sell cuddly toys called "teddy bears." In Europe, a German company called Steiff made similar bears with movable arms and legs. This favorite toy now comes in all colors and sizes, but the basic shape remains the same.

CONSTRUCTION TOYS
Construction toys such as Lego® really challenge building skills and imagination. Sections of various sizes fit together to create model forts, castles, and spacecraft.

Find out more
GAMES
PUPPETS
PUZZLES

TRACK AND FIELD SPORTS

TRACK AND FIELD SPORTS have produced some of the greatest athletic achievements over the years. These are the feats of strength and discipline, and are performed on specialized tracks or fields. Track sports include sprinting, middle-distance running, relay racing, and hurdles, which involves leaping over low gates while running. They may take place on a track, a road, or a cross-country route. Field events are held in special arenas and include the high jump, the long jump, and several throwing events. All athletic events require stamina, speed, power, and determination. In the shortest sprinting events, competitors may reach speeds of 22 mph (36 km/h). Many people do not compete but pursue athletics purely for their fitness and health benefits.

MARATHON
Men and women of very mixed abilities take part in marathon races, run over a distance of 26 miles, 385 yards (42.2 km). Marathons usually follow a route around the closed streets of a city such as New York.

RUNNING EVENTS
Races take place around the track in a counter-clockwise direction. Runners in races up to 437 yds (400 m) must stay in lanes.

JUMPING EVENTS
These include triple jumps and the pole vault, for men only, and the long and high jumps, for both men and women. Competitors in the long and triple jumps land in sandpits; in the high jump and pole vault, they land on soft foam beds.

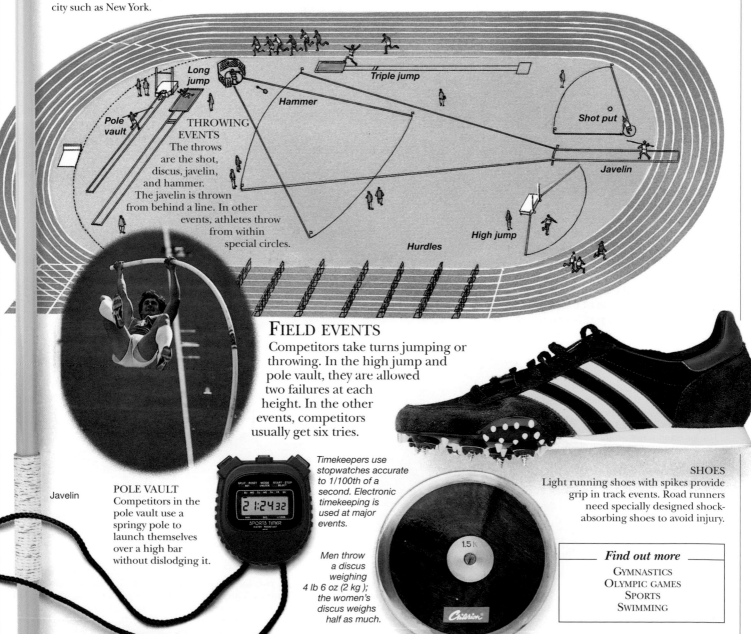

Long jump

Triple jump

Hammer

Shot put

Pole vault

THROWING EVENTS
The throws are the shot, discus, javelin, and hammer. The javelin is thrown from behind a line. In other events, athletes throw from within special circles.

Javelin

High jump

Hurdles

FIELD EVENTS
Competitors take turns jumping or throwing. In the high jump and pole vault, they are allowed two failures at each height. In the other events, competitors usually get six tries.

Javelin

POLE VAULT
Competitors in the pole vault use a springy pole to launch themselves over a high bar without dislodging it.

Timekeepers use stopwatches accurate to 1/100th of a second. Electronic timekeeping is used at major events.

21:24:32

Men throw a discus weighing 4 lb 6 oz (2 kg); the women's discus weighs half as much.

1.5 K

SHOES
Light running shoes with spikes provide grip in track events. Road runners need specially designed shock-absorbing shoes to avoid injury.

Find out more
GYMNASTICS
OLYMPIC GAMES
SPORTS
SWIMMING

TRADE AND INDUSTRY

WITHOUT TRADE AND INDUSTRY, people would have to create everything they needed to live. If you wanted a loaf of bread you would have to grow wheat, grind the wheat to make flour, mix the dough, and bake it in an oven. You would also need to build the mill and make the oven! Industry organizes the production of bread, so that just a few farmers, millers, and bakers can make bread for everyone. Similarly, industry supplies us with most other essential and luxury goods, from fresh water to cars. Trade is the process of buying and selling. Trade gets the products from the people who make them to the people who need them. And through trade, manufacturers can buy the raw materials they need to supply their factories and keep production going. Together, the trade and industry of a nation are sometimes called the economy.

SILK ROAD
Trade between different regions and peoples goes back to ancient times. The Silk Road was one of the earliest and most famous trade routes. Traders led horses and camels along this route between 300 B.C. and A.D. 1600, carrying silk from China to Europe.

INTERNATIONAL TRADE
Goods move around the world by sea, land, and air. This international trade takes materials such as oil from the countries that have a surplus to those that have no or insufficient oil deposits. International trade is also necessary because goods do not always fetch a high price in the country where they are made. For example, many clothes are made by hand in countries where wages are low. But the clothes are sold in another country where people are richer and can pay a high price. Money earned this way helps less rich countries pay for their imports.

India exports cotton textiles to Europe.

India exports tea to the Russian Federation.

India imports cars from Japan.

India imports oil from the Middle East.

India exports rice to Australia.

Imports

Exports

IMPORTS AND EXPORTS
Goods that are traded internationally are called imports and exports. Goods that one country sells to another are called exports; imports are goods that a country buys from another. In most nations, private businesses control imports and exports. But in others, the government imposes strict controls on what can be bought and sold.

TRADE AGREEMENTS
Some countries sign trade agreements in order to control trade between them. The agreement may simply fix the price at which the two countries buy and sell certain goods, such as tea and wheat. The European Union (EU) has a complicated network of trade agreements that allows free exchange of goods between member countries. The EU also restricts trade with countries that are not members of the Union. This helps encourage industry within the Union.

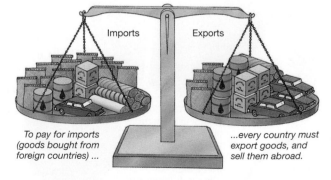

Imports

Exports

To pay for imports (goods bought from foreign countries) ...

...every country must export goods, and sell them abroad.

BALANCE OF PAYMENTS
Each country pays for imports with the money it earns by selling goods to other countries. This balance between imports and exports is called the balance of trade, or the balance of payments. Countries that do not export enough must borrow money from abroad to pay for imports.

FACTORIES

Some industry takes place in people's homes, but workers in factories make most of the products that we buy. In a factory each person has a small task in the manufacturing process. He or she may operate a large machine or assemble something by hand. No one person makes an entire product. This process of mass production makes manufacturing cheaper and quicker. Most factories are owned by large companies; a few factories are owned by governments or by the people who work in them.

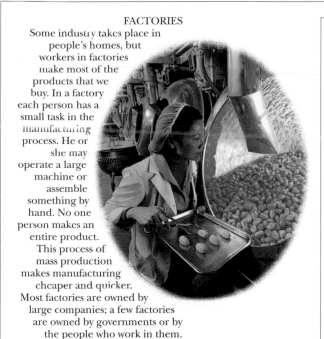

SUPPLY AND DEMAND

Companies set up factories to produce goods that they think people will want. They sell the goods at a price that allows the company to make a profit. As long as there is a demand for the goods, the factory will continue to supply them. When fewer people buy the goods that the factory makes, prices drop to try to attract buyers, and workers in the factory may lose their jobs.

A factory starts by making a small number of umbrellas.

Shops put a few umbrellas on sale at a high price.

Many people need umbrellas and buy them, increasing demand.

The factory employs more people to make more umbrellas.

When everyone has an umbrella, demand for umbrellas falls.

Prices drop, and the factory needs fewer umbrella workers.

The restaurant industry provides the service of cooking and serving food.

SERVICE INDUSTRIES

Not all industries make objects for sale. Some industries provide a service in return for money. A garage, for instance, might charge a fee to adjust a car so that it runs more efficiently. People pay for this service rather than do the work themselves.

Final assembly of the car may take place in Spain.

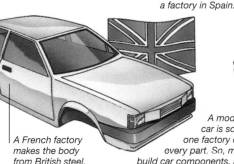

The engine comes from a factory in Spain.

A French factory makes the body from British steel.

A modern car is so complex that one factory cannot make every part. So, many factories build car components, and an assembly plant puts the vehicle together.

The transmission is made in Germany.

TRADE UNIONS

During the 19th century, workers began to form trade unions. The job of a trade union is to obtain better pay and conditions for its members. If the union is not successful, its members may go on strike – stop work – until their demands are met.

Trade Unions in 19th century America and Europe had to struggle for many decades against inhumanly long hours of work. The 8-hour working day was finally achieved in the late 1930s.

MANUFACTURING

The basic form of industry is manufacturing. This means working on materials to manufacture, or make, a finished product. Almost everything we use is the product of manufacturing, and most manufacturing takes place in large factories. However, craftworkers manufacture goods alone or in small groups. Some goods go through many stages of manufacturing. For example, workers making cars assemble manufactured components or parts which, in turn, have been made in many other factories, often in other countries.

Find out more

ADVERTISING
DEPRESSION OF THE 1930S
FACTORIES
INDUSTRIAL REVOLUTION
MONEY
SHOPS AND SHOPPING

TRAINS

WHEN THE FIRST RAILROADS were built more than 150 years ago, many people said they were the most wonderful of all inventions. Others said the snorting, smoking steam engines were like ugly metal monsters. Trains and railroads certainly changed our world. Not only did embankments and cuttings alter the landscape, but also, for the first time, people and goods could be carried long distances in vast quantities – and at speeds undreamed of. Railroads also allowed cities to grow more than ever before. Today, large networks of railroads stretch through many countries. If the tracks of the world's main rail routes were laid end to end, they would circle the Earth more than 116 times. Trains are an efficient method of transportation. They use less fuel and produce less pollution than cars and trucks because they carry large cargoes in a single journey. Because of the damage road vehicles do to our environment, many people believe that trains are the best form of transportation for the future.

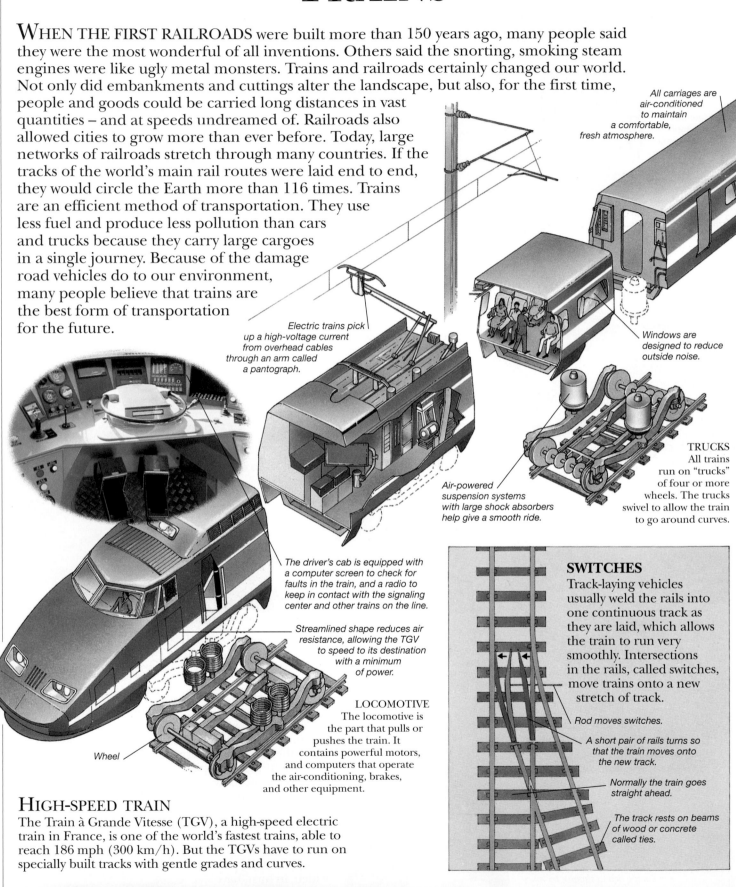

All carriages are air-conditioned to maintain a comfortable, fresh atmosphere.

Electric trains pick up a high-voltage current from overhead cables through an arm called a pantograph.

Windows are designed to reduce outside noise.

Air-powered suspension systems with large shock absorbers help give a smooth ride.

TRUCKS
All trains run on "trucks" of four or more wheels. The trucks swivel to allow the train to go around curves.

The driver's cab is equipped with a computer screen to check for faults in the train, and a radio to keep in contact with the signaling center and other trains on the line.

Streamlined shape reduces air resistance, allowing the TGV to speed to its destination with a minimum of power.

LOCOMOTIVE
The locomotive is the part that pulls or pushes the train. It contains powerful motors, and computers that operate the air-conditioning, brakes, and other equipment.

Wheel

SWITCHES
Track-laying vehicles usually weld the rails into one continuous track as they are laid, which allows the train to run very smoothly. Intersections in the rails, called switches, move trains onto a new stretch of track.

Rod moves switches.

A short pair of rails turns so that the train moves onto the new track.

Normally the train goes straight ahead.

The track rests on beams of wood or concrete called ties.

HIGH-SPEED TRAIN
The Train à Grande Vitesse (TGV), a high-speed electric train in France, is one of the world's fastest trains, able to reach 186 mph (300 km/h). But the TGVs have to run on specially built tracks with gentle grades and curves.

RICHARD TREVITHICK

In 1804, a steam locomotive (right) built by Englishman Richard Trevithick ran on rails for the first time. Trevithick thought that steam power had a future, and bet that his steam engine could haul 9 tons of iron 9.5 miles (15 km) along a mine railroad in Wales. Trevithick won his bet; the engine carried not only the iron but also 70 cheering coal miners who climbed aboard.

The Rocket, built by English engineer George Stephenson in 1829, was a new design that heralded the age of the passenger train.

A front truck was introduced on early American locomotives to give a smoother ride around curves.

During the mid-1800s, England's railroad system developed into a large network.

Engines could reach 126 mph (200 km/h) by the 1930s – the peak of the steam age.

Steam locomotives of the 1930s were very sophisticated compared to the first engines.

UNDERGROUND TRAINS

In crowded cities, underground trains are the quickest way to travel. The first underground system was opened in London in 1863. Now many cities have their own network. The Metro in Paris is one of the most efficient underground systems in the world.

STEAM RAILWAYS

Railroads date back 4,000 years to the Babylonians, who pushed carts along grooves. But the age of railroads really began in the early 1800s when steam engines first ran on rails. In 1825, the first passenger line opened in England; 30 years later, vast railroad systems stretched across Europe and North America. By the 1890s, steam engines could reach speeds of more than 100 mph (160 km/h).

SIGNALS AND SAFETY

Trackside signals tell the driver how fast to go and when to stop. In the past, signals were mechanical arms worked by levers in the signal box. Today they are usually sets of colored lights controlled by computers that monitor the position of every train.

MAGLEVS AND MONORAILS

One day we may be whisked along silently at speeds of 300 mph (480 km/h) on trains that glide a small distance above special tracks, held up by magnetic force – which is why they are called Maglevs (for magnetic levitation). Some countries, such as Japan, already have Maglev lines. Other new designs include monorail trains, which are electric trains that run on, or are suspended from, a single rail.

TRANSCONTINENTAL RAILROAD

The building of the 1,800 mile (2,900 km) transcontinental railroad linking the East and West coasts of the US allowed people to travel from New York to San Francisco in just eight days; it had previously taken three months. The railroad was completed in 1869, when tracks built by the Central Pacific and Union Pacific companies met at Promontory Summit, Utah. At the ceremony, a golden spike was driven into the ground to link the two tracks.

Find out more

BUSES
ENGINES
TOURISM AND TRAVEL
TRANSPORTATION, HISTORY OF

HISTORY OF
TRANSPORTATION

WE LIVE IN AN AGE when people can fly across the Atlantic Ocean in less than three hours. Straight roads link city to city across the world. Yet 7,000 years ago, the only way that people could get from one place to another was by walking. In around 5,000 B.C. people began to use donkeys and oxen as pack animals, instead of carrying their goods on their backs or heads. Then, 1,500 years later, the first wheeled vehicles developed in Mesopotamia. From around A.D. 1500, deep-sea sailing ships developed rapidly as Europeans began to make great ocean voyages to explore the rest of the world. During the 1700s, steam power marked another milestone in transportation. Steam engines were soon moving ships and trains faster than anyone had imagined. During the next century the first cars took to the road and the first flying machines took to the air.

STAGECOACH
So called because they stopped at stages on a route to change horses, stagecoaches were the most popular type of public land transport during the 17th and 18th centuries. Coaching inns sprung up along popular stagecoach routes.

Railroads began to appear in the United States in the 1820s. Trains could carry more freight and people than any other kind of transport.

LAND TRAVEL

Land travel is the most common kind of transportation. It all began with walking. Two thousand years ago the Romans built a network of superb roads over which people traveled by foot or by horse-drawn cart. It was only in the 1800s that steam power took the place of horse power. Steam locomotives provided cheap long-distance travel for ordinary people. In the early years of this century, engine-powered cars, trucks, and buses were developed.

CARS
Cars are now the most popular form of private transport. They were invented toward the end of the 19th century.

JUNK
One of the world's strongest sailing ships, the junk has been used in Asia for thousands of years. Mainly a trading vessel, it has large, highly efficient sails made of linen or matting.

BARGE
A barge is a sturdy boat that transports cargo, such as coal, from place to place along canals and rivers.

SEA TRAVEL

Floating logs led to the first watercraft, the simple raft. In around 3500 B.C. the Sumerians and the Egyptians made fishing boats out of reeds from the riverbank. They also built watertight wooden ships with oars and a sail, for seagoing voyages. In the 19th century, steel replaced wood, and steam engines gradually took over from sails. Today's engine-powered ships can carry huge loads of cargo at speeds never reached under sail.

Ocean liners (below) are used as floating hotels. They take passengers on cruises and call at different resorts along the way.

AIR TRAVEL

In 1783, the Frenchmen Pilâtre de Rozier and the Marquis d'Arlandes made the first human flight in a hot-air balloon. Then, in 1903, to everyone's amazement, brothers Orville and Wilbur Wright built and flew the first powered plane near Kitty Hawk, North Carolina. Aircraft developed rapidly in the two world wars that followed. In 1918, the U.S. Post Office began the first airmail service. Today, it is hard to imagine a world without aircraft.

FLY THERE BY

BALLOONS

Long before airplanes were invented, people flew in balloons – bags filled with hot air or a lighter-than-air gas. In 1783, the Montgolfier brothers of France built the first balloon to lift humans into the air. Balloons were used by the French emperor Napoleon as flying lookout posts, and later, balloons were used during the Civil War and World War I. Today, ballooning is a popular sport.

In the early days of flying, airline companies used colorful posters to encourage people to fly with them.

AIRPLANES

Today, millions of people depend on airplanes for both business and pleasure. But the golden age of airplane development occurred only 80 years ago, when daring pilots took great risks in testing airplanes and flying long distances. Jet-powered passenger airplanes appeared in the 1950s. A supersonic airliner, *Concorde*, was in service from 1976 to 2003. At 1,550 mph (2,500 km/h), it traveled faster than the speed of sound.

The Apollo II spacecraft

SPACE TRAVEL

Not content with the sky, humans wanted to explore space and distant planets as well. In 1957, the Soviets fired the first satellite, *Sputnik*, into orbit (a path around the Earth). In 1968, the United States sent the first manned craft around the Moon. Then, in 1969, astronaut Neil Armstrong became the first person to walk on the Moon.

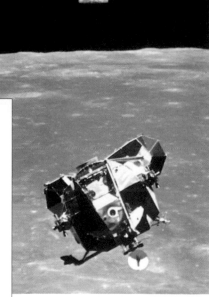

POLLUTION-FREE TRANSPORTATION

Many of today's forms of powered transportation pollute the environment because their engines send out dangerous gases. Cars, in particular, upset the natural balance of the atmosphere. Lead-free gasoline helps reduce the amount of poison that cars release into the air. The transportation systems that cause the least pollution are those using natural power, such as wind. On land, people can help preserve our planet by walking, bicycling, or using animals to pull wheeled vehicles. At sea, large loads can be moved in sailing ships powered only by the wind.

In-line skating

Skateboarding

Walking

Bicycling

Find out more

AIRCRAFT
BALLOONS AND AIRSHIPS
CARS
SHIPS AND BOATS
TRAINS

TREES

WITHOUT PLANTS such as trees there could be no life on Earth. Trees take in carbon dioxide from the air and give off oxygen by the process of photosynthesis, thus maintaining the balance of the atmosphere. Tree roots stabilize the soil so it is not washed away by the rain, and their leaves give off vast amounts of water vapor, which affects the balance of the world's weather. Forests cover about 15 million sq miles (39 million sq km) of the planet's surface. Trees vary greatly in size, from huge redwoods to dwarf snow willows, only a few inches high. They supply food for millions of creatures, and produce wood to make buildings, furniture – even the pages of this book.

Giant sequoia trees are the largest living things – more than 270 ft (84 m) high, and 2,000 tons in weight; an elephant weighs about 5 tons.

Leaves

English oak tree in spring and fall

Buds

Oak bark

Acorns are the fruits of the oak tree; they develop from the pollinated female flowers during the fall.

The roots of a deciduous tree may reach out sideways to the same distance as the tree's height.

CONIFEROUS TREES

Pines, firs, cedars, and redwoods are called coniferous trees, or conifers, because they grow their seeds in hard, woody cones. The long, narrow leaves, called needles, stay on the tree all winter. These trees are also called evergreens, because they stay green all year.

CONES
Each tree has its own type of cone, which develops from the fertilized female flowers.

Larch cone

Scots pine needles grow in pairs.

Pine cone

Arolla pine needles

Conifer roots usually spread out sideways.

Sitka spruce cone turns brown as it ripens.

NEEDLES
Every conifer has distinctively shaped needles that grow in a certain pattern. Sitka spruce needles are long and sharp.

Needle

Sitka spruce is an evergreen coniferous tree often seen in forest plantations.

BROAD-LEAVED TREES

Oaks, beeches, willows, and many other trees are called broad-leaved because their leaves are broad and flat, unlike the sharp needles on coniferous trees. Some broad-leaved trees are also called deciduous, because their leaves die and drop off in the fall.

LEAVES
Broad-leaved trees can be recognized by the shape of their leaves and the pattern in which the leaves grow on the twigs. In winter, you can identify a bare tree by its bark, buds, and overall shape.

Leaves of the holly tree are spiky.

Japanese maple leaves have deep notches.

The gingko tree has fan-shaped leaves.

Rowan or mountain ash trees have compound leaves.

Sweet chestnut leaves have a jagged edge.

GROWTH

All trees grow from small seeds inside their fruit. Each seed contains a food store and a tiny embryo tree. The seed begins to grow when the temperature and moisture of the soil are suitable. A young tree is called a sapling.

Shoot grows from between seed leaves.

First true leaves develop and seed case falls away.

Seed case splits.

Beech seed (or beechnut) is contained in hard seed case.

Root begins to emerge.

Root and stem of seedling grow longer.

New leaves develop each spring.

SEASONAL GROWTH

In temperate regions, where there are definite seasons each year, trees grow during spring and summer. Growth occurs mainly at the ends of the tree, the tips of the branches, and the roots. The twigs lengthen, and flowers and leaves appear from the buds. Root tips grow longer and push their way through the soil. The roots and branches thicken, as does the tree trunk, so that the tree's girth, or waistband, also increases in size.

Twig tips grow.

Trunk and branches thicken.

Roots become fatter.

Root tips lengthen.

TREE TRUNK

During spring and early summer, when growth is rapid, tree trunks thicken. Large thin-walled cells form light-colored wood. Slower growth during the rest of the year produces thick-walled cells that make darker-colored wood. One light-colored ring plus one dark ring indicates one year's growth. Some tropical trees grow all year round; they have faint rings or none at all.

A.D. 1800 Washington, D.C., becomes U.S. capital.

A.D. 1400 Joan of Arc burned at the stake.

A.D. 800 Charlemagne crowned emperor.

Native Americans used the smooth bark of birch trees to make canoes.

Coconut palm tree

INSIDE A TREE

Bark cambium (growing area) of young tree

Counting the rings on a section of trunk can tell us the age of a tree. This is a section of a very old giant sequoia tree.

Young bark is smooth.

Bark grows from the inside and pushes the older bark outward.

Old bark cracks and flakes.

BARK

The tree's bark is its skin. It shields the living wood within, stops it from drying out, and protects it from extreme cold and heat. Bark prevents damage from molds, but some animals, such as deer and beavers, eat the bark, and a few wood-boring beetles can tunnel through. A tree with no leaves can be identified by the color and texture of its bark.

The rough bark of the cork tree is stripped off every eight to 10 years; it is used to make bottle stoppers and floor tiles.

PALM TREES

The 2,700 kinds of palm tree are found in warm Mediterranean and tropical regions. These tall, straight trees provide many products, including palm oils, dates, and coconuts from the coconut palm.

Native Americans carved whole tree trunks to create totem poles.

WOOD

Each year we use thousands of tons of wood in building, as fuel for cooking and heating, and to make tools, furniture, and paper. As the world's population grows, vast areas of forests are cut down in ever-increasing numbers, particularly in South America, where much of the tropical rain forest has been destroyed.

Whole tree trunks are used to make telephone poles.

In the past, loggers had to float logs to the sawmill.

The outer husk of the coconut is used to make coconut matting (above). Coconuts are a valuable source of milk, edible fats, and animal food.

Find out more

FOREST WILDLIFE
FRUITS AND SEEDS
PLANTS
SOIL

TRUCKS

FROM THE SMALLEST VAN to the largest juggernaut that towers over all other traffic, trucks play a vital role in our lives. They are powerful, rugged vehicles designed to carry goods of all kinds. They transport food to stores, raw materials to factories, fuel to power stations, and much more. In many countries, trucks now carry all but the bulkiest goods. Trains can carry larger loads, but they are restricted to railroad networks. A truck can pick up and deliver goods from door to door. It can be specially built to carry nearly any kind of load – big or small, heavy or light, liquid or solid, and a truck can reach remote places far from the nearest railroad. For the icy settlements of Finland, the desert towns of the Middle East, and many starving people in countries such as Ethiopia, trucks are an essential lifeline.

ROUGH-ROAD TRUCKS
Trucks are often the only way to get goods in and out of rugged mountain regions. But to survive the rough tracks, the trucks have to be tough and reliable. They also need big wheels to give plenty of ground clearance.

The air deflector, a specially shaped metal flap, helps air flow smoothly over the tractor and trailer and cuts down on fuel consumption.

Long-distance truck drivers spend many hours on the road, so the cab is made as comfortable as possible. Many cabs contain a bed for overnight stops.

The turbocharged diesel engine is very powerful, because it must pull heavy loads. Some trucks have up to 20 forward and 10 reverse gears, allowing them to cope with all kinds of road conditions.

Cab tips forward to make the engine easier to work on.

Triple wheels spread the load over a bigger road area.

Trailer pivots on a special joint. When necessary, hydraulic rams lift the trailer for disconnection.

ARTICULATED TRUCKS
Most large, modern trucks are articulated, or jointed. The load is pulled along on a separate trailer behind a tractor unit containing the engine and the driver's cab. Because an articulated truck bends, it is much more maneuverable than a rigid one. Articulated trucks have different kinds of trailers that are built to carry a wide range of loads, such as food, wood, oil, and animals.

SPECIAL VEHICLES
There are several kinds of trucks that are designed for special purposes. Many carry particularly large or heavy loads, such as this quarry truck (below), or the huge trailer that carries the space shuttle to its launch pad.

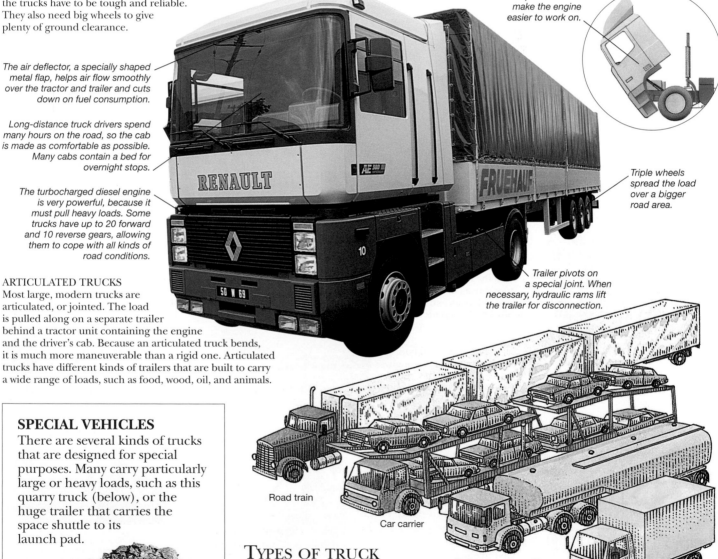

Road train

Car carrier

Tanker   Van

TYPES OF TRUCK
The world's roads rumble under the wheels of all kinds of trucks. Road trains thunder over the Australian plains hauling two, or even three, trailers to keep costs low. Car carriers have trailers, too, to take up to 18 cars. Tankers carry gasoline, wine, milk, and even flour. Most common are vans, which are able to carry many small loads.

Find out more
BUSES
CARS
TRANSPORTATION, HISTORY OF

HARRIET
TUBMAN

c. 1820 Born into slavery.

1849 Escapes from slavery via the Underground Railroad.

1850 Fugitive Slave Act makes it a crime to help runaway slaves. Tubman makes her first trip as a "conductor."

1850-61 Leads over 300 people to freedom.

1857 Leads her parents to freedom in Auburn, New York.

1861-65 Serves as nurse, scout, and spy for the Union Army.

1913 Dies.

BLACK AMERICANS OWE MUCH to the bravery and determination of Harriet Tubman. Between 1850 and 1861, she led more than 300 black American slaves to freedom on what was known as the "Underground Railroad." Her courageous work earned her the nickname "General Moses," after the Biblical figure Moses who led the Jews out of slavery in Egypt. Tubman was born into slavery and like many other slaves experienced brutal treatment at the hands of her white masters. In 1849, she escaped from a Maryland plantation and made her way to Philadelphia. She vowed to go back and rescue other slaves, and a year later, she returned to Maryland to help members of her family escape. In all, she made 19 journeys back to the South, risking capture, and possible death. During the Civil War (1861-65), she worked for the Union Army in South Carolina. After slavery was abolished, she continued to fight for black rights, setting up schools for black children, and a home for elderly black Americans.

VALUABLE GANG OF YOUNG NEGROES
By JOS. A. BEARD.

Will be sold at Auction,
ON WEDNESDAY, 25TH INST.
At 12 o'clock, at Banks' Arcade,
17 Valuable Young Negroes
Men and Women, Field Hands.
Sold for no fault; with the best city guarantees.
Sale Positive and without reserve!
TERMS CASH.
New Orleans, March 24, 1840.

SLAVES FOR SALE
Slaves had no rights. They were bought and sold as property. By law, they were not allowed to own anything, assemble in groups of more than five, or even learn to read and write.

UNDERGROUND RAILROAD

The "Underground Railroad" was not really a railroad, but an elaborate network of escape routes that was described using railway terms. Runaway slaves, known as "freight" or "passengers," were helped to flee secretly at night. Guides called "conductors" led them from one "station," or stopping place, to the next. The escape routes stretched all the way from the states of the South to the North and Canada. During the day, helpers hid fugitives in barns and haylofts. Thousands of anti-slavery campaigners – both black and white, and many of them women – risked their lives to operate the "railroad."

CANADA
Ogdensburg
Montpelier
Kingston
L. Ontario
Toronto
Oswego
Rochester
Buffalo
Syracuse
Albany
L. Erie
Boston
Jamestown
Elmira
Erie
New Haven
UNITED STATES
Appalachian Mountains
New York
Philadelphia
Atlantic Ocean

Map of Underground Railroad escape routes

STOPPING PLACE
Every 10–20 miles (15–30 km) along the route was a "station," or safe house, where the "passengers" could rest or hide in safety. This sign (right) commemorates a "station" of 1821.

The GOODWIN SISTER'S HOUSE
ELIZABETH & ABIGAIL
UNDERGROUND RAILWAY
1821

Harriet Tubman (far left) with a group of freed slaves

GENERAL MOSES

Harriet Tubman was a brave woman who believed that God gave her courage and strength. She was so successful a "conductor" that angry plantation owners offered a $40,000 reward for her capture. She traveled during winter, meeting runaway slaves about 10 miles (15 km) from their plantations and then leading them to safety. She escaped capture more than once, and never lost a slave on her escape missions.

$150 REWARD

RANAWAY from the subscriber, on the night of the 2d instant, a negro man, who calls himself Henry May, about 22 years old, 5 feet 6 or 8 inches high, ordinary color, rather chunky built, bushy head, and has it divided mostly on one side, and keeps it very nicely combed; has been raised in the house, and is a first rate dining-room servant, and was in a tavern in Louisville for 18 months. I expect he is now in Louisville trying to make his escape to a free state, [in all probability to Cincinnati, Ohio.] I hope to any try to get employment on a steamboat. He is a good cook, and is handy in any capacity as a house servant. Had on when he left a dark cassinett coat, and dark striped cassinett pantaloons, new rather had other clothing. I will give $50 reward if taken in Louisville, 100 dollars if taken one hundred miles from Louisville in this State, and 150 dollars if taken out of this State, and delivered to me, or secured in any jail so that I can get him again. WILLIAM BURK.
Bardstown, Ky., September 3d, 1838.

RUNAWAY SLAVES
The Northern states had banned slavery by the early 1800s, but it remained legal in the South until 1865. Laws passed in 1793 and 1850 made it a crime to help runaway slaves.

Find out more

CIVIL RIGHTS
CIVIL WAR
KING, JR., MARTIN LUTHER
SLAVERY
UNITED STATES, HISTORY OF

TUNNELS

A CITY HIDES MANY of its most important structures from view; some we never see at all. Among these are tunnels, and a city may be honeycombed with them. Beneath the streets run tunnels carrying trains, pedestrians, motor vehicles, sewage, water supplies from reservoirs, and even small rivers. These kinds of tunnels serve cities and towns. Other tunnels allow trains and motor vehicles to pass through hills and mountains and under rivers and seas. Canals, which must be level, sometimes have tunnels to take boats under hills. Mine systems have the deepest tunnels of all. People dug tunnels in ancient times, hacking out the rock with picks. On the island of Samos in Greece, a tunnel dug in about 525 B.C. can still be seen. It is 3,400 ft (1 km) long. The tunnel was started from both ends, and the teams of diggers met in the middle of the mountain. In medieval times, many palaces and forts had tunnels to serve as escape routes in case of seige.

RECORD TUNNELS
The St. Gotthard Road Tunnel in Switzerland (above) is one of the world's longest road tunnels. It is 10 miles (16 km) long. The longest rail tunnel is the Seikan Rail Tunnel in Japan. It has a length of 33.5 miles (54 km). At 105 miles (169 km), a water supply tunnel in New York State is the longest of all.

KINDS OF TUNNELS

Many city tunnels are "cut-and-cover" tunnels. Machines excavate a deep trench; a cover is then placed over it. Other tunnels are bored through rock or soil, and may go much deeper. Still others, designed for use under rivers, are made in sections on land and joined together on the riverbed.

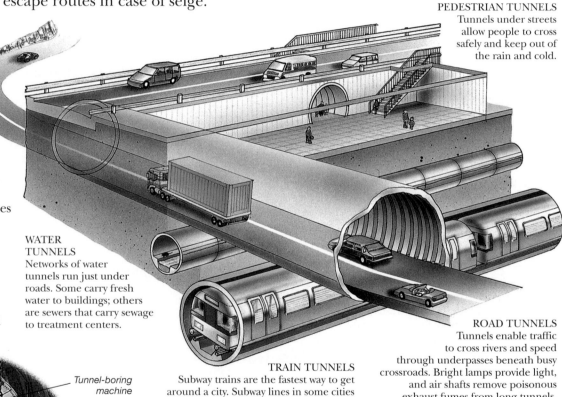

PEDESTRIAN TUNNELS
Tunnels under streets allow people to cross safely and keep out of the rain and cold.

WATER TUNNELS
Networks of water tunnels run just under roads. Some carry fresh water to buildings; others are sewers that carry sewage to treatment centers.

Tunnel-boring machine

ROAD TUNNELS
Tunnels enable traffic to cross rivers and speed through underpasses beneath busy crossroads. Bright lamps provide light, and air shafts remove poisonous exhaust fumes from long tunnels.

TRAIN TUNNELS
Subway trains are the fastest way to get around a city. Subway lines in some cities travel under streets just below the roadway. In other cities train tunnels are very deep.

English coast

Sea level

150 ft (50 m)

French coast

300 ft (100 m)

BORING A TUNNEL

Huge tunneling machines, often guided by lasers and computers, bore tunnels through rock and soil. At the front of the machine is a round cutting head that digs out the rock or soil. Sections of tunnel lining are fitted behind the cutting head. The lining supports the roof, floor, and sides of the tunnel.

CHANNEL TUNNEL
In 1994 a rail tunnel was opened under the English Channel linking Britain and France. It is 31 miles (50 km) long, out of which 23 miles (38 km) are under the sea. It has three tubes, one each to travel in the two directions and the third for emergencies and maintenance work. Special trains have been designed to carry cars through the tunnel.

Find out more
CITIES
COAL
TRAINS
WATER

TURKEY

TURKEY LIES IN BOTH ASIA AND EUROPE.
Today it is on the verge of becoming part of
modern Europe, yet retains many elements of its
Asian history. Western Turkey was an important
part of both the Greek and Roman worlds. The
invasion of Turkish nomads (Ottomans) from
the east in the 15th century brought the Islamic
religion and the nomadic culture of Central Asia.
Turkey became a republic in 1923, and rapidly
entered the 20th century. Islam is no longer the
state religion, although it is widely practiced. A
wide range of manufacturing and textile industries
have strengthened Turkey's growing economic
links with Europe. With its warm climate
and fertile soils, Turkey is able to
produce all its own food – even
in the arid southeast, huge
dams on the Euphrates River
are used to water the land.
The west and south coasts
are visited by increasing
numbers of tourists.

Turkey lies at the western edge of
Asia, and extends into the southeastern tip of Europe. It is bounded
on three sides by the Black,
Mediterranean, and Aegean seas.

MARKET PRODUCE
Street markets are an important
part of every Turkish town. Stalls
sell a variety of products, from
olives, spices, and vegetables to
clothing and household goods.
This woman is wearing traditional
Turkish clothes – loose, baggy
trousers and a printed headscarf –
which are still widely worn,
especially in the countryside.

ISTANBUL
Turkey's largest city and seaport straddles the continents of
Europe and Asia, which are separated by
the Bosporus Strait. Founded by
Greeks in the 8th century B.C.,
later to become capital of
the Eastern Roman
Empire, Istanbul fell to
the Ottoman Turks in
1453. The Ottomans
beautified the capital
with mosques and
built the sumptuous
Topkapi Palace, the
home of the sultan and
his many wives. Today,
Istanbul is a sprawling,
bustling city with a population
of more than 6 million.

*Bodrum's
St. Peter's
castle (right) is a
fine example of
Crusader architecture.*

TURKISH TOURISM
Turkey's warm climate, beautiful
coastline, and rich history attract many
tourists from northern Europe. Most
tourists travel to the Aegean and
Mediterranean coasts, where
picturesque harbors such as Bodrum
(above) are accessible to beautiful
beaches. There are some worries that
the fast pace of development is spoiling
the landscape.

*The Library of Celsus at Ephesus
was built in the 2nd century A.D.
for a Roman consul.*

ANKARA
Ankara became capital of
the new Turkish republic in 1923
– a break with the Ottoman past.
Ankara's history dates back to
the 2nd millennium B.C. It was an
important Ottoman cultural and
commercial center, located on
the main trade routes. Today,
the modern city center is the
headquarters of the government.

CLASSICAL RUINS
The Aegean coast was colonized by Greeks by
the 7th century B.C., and western Turkey was an
important part of the Greek and subsequently
the Roman worlds. Many well-preserved
classical cities attract both archaeologists and
tourists to Turkey. Ephesus was the home of the
Temple of Artemis, one of the seven Wonders
of the ancient world.

Find out more
ASIA, HISTORY OF
GREECE, ANCIENT
OTTOMAN EMPIRE
ROMAN EMPIRE
WONDERS
of the ancient world

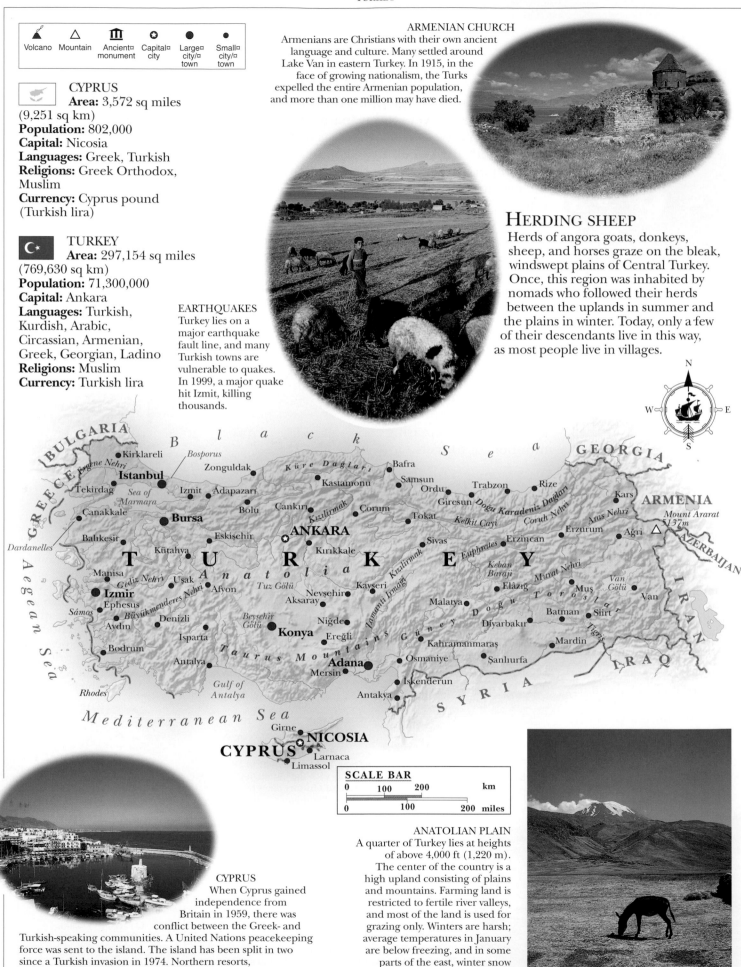

Legend
Volcano | Mountain | Ancient monument | Capital city | Large city/town | Small city/town

CYPRUS
Area: 3,572 sq miles (9,251 sq km)
Population: 802,000
Capital: Nicosia
Languages: Greek, Turkish
Religions: Greek Orthodox, Muslim
Currency: Cyprus pound (Turkish lira)

TURKEY
Area: 297,154 sq miles (769,630 sq km)
Population: 71,300,000
Capital: Ankara
Languages: Turkish, Kurdish, Arabic, Circassian, Armenian, Greek, Georgian, Ladino
Religions: Muslim
Currency: Turkish lira

ARMENIAN CHURCH
Armenians are Christians with their own ancient language and culture. Many settled around Lake Van in eastern Turkey. In 1915, in the face of growing nationalism, the Turks expelled the entire Armenian population, and more than one million may have died.

EARTHQUAKES
Turkey lies on a major earthquake fault line, and many Turkish towns are vulnerable to quakes. In 1999, a major quake hit Izmit, killing thousands.

HERDING SHEEP
Herds of angora goats, donkeys, sheep, and horses graze on the bleak, windswept plains of Central Turkey. Once, this region was inhabited by nomads who followed their herds between the uplands in summer and the plains in winter. Today, only a few of their descendants live in this way, as most people live in villages.

SCALE BAR
| 0 | 100 | 200 | km |
| 0 | 100 | 200 | miles |

CYPRUS
When Cyprus gained independence from Britain in 1959, there was conflict between the Greek- and Turkish-speaking communities. A United Nations peacekeeping force was sent to the island. The island has been split in two since a Turkish invasion in 1974. Northern resorts, such as Girne (above), attract increasing numbers of tourists.

ANATOLIAN PLAIN
A quarter of Turkey lies at heights of above 4,000 ft (1,220 m). The center of the country is a high upland consisting of plains and mountains. Farming land is restricted to fertile river valleys, and most of the land is used for grazing only. Winters are harsh; average temperatures in January are below freezing, and in some parts of the east, winter snow cover lasts for up to four months.

UKRAINE

Volcano	Mountain	Ancient monument	Capital city	Large city/town	Small city/town

The Carpathian Mountains form Ukraine's western border. To the south lies the Black Sea. The Crimean peninsula extends into the Black Sea, forming the Sea of Azov to the east. Ukraine's flat steppes are bisected by the Dnieper river, which drains into the Black Sea.

INDUSTRIAL HEARTLAND
Eastern Ukraine, with its rich reserves of iron, coal, gas, and oil, is a major center of industry. Ukraine is one of the world's top steel producers, and large iron and steel works dominate the landscape. Ukraine also manufactures mining and transportation equipment, cars, locomotives, ships, and turbines.

UKRAINE HAS BEEN an independent republic since 1991, when the Soviet Union collapsed. The country is dominated by rolling flat grasslands, rich in fertile soils, and is crossed by major rivers such as the Dnieper, Donets, and Bug. The year-round warm climate and sandy beaches of the Crimean peninsula attract many tourists, especially from Russia and Germany. With its fertile land and mild climate, Ukraine is a major cereals producer, once called the "breadbasket" of the Soviet Union. In the east, the basin of the Donets river is rich in deposits of coal, iron ore, manganese, zinc, and mercury. It is the center of a major industrial heartland. During the Soviet era, Ukraine was a major weapons producer; efforts are now being made to convert weapons factories for the manufacture of consumer goods. In 1986, a radiation leak at Chornobyl', one of Ukraine's nuclear power stations, caused panic in Europe. Much of the land around the plant is still contaminated and towns stand desolate and empty.

STATISTICS

Area: 223,090 sq miles (603,700 sq km)
Population: 47,700,000
Capital: Kiev
Languages: Ukrainian, Russian, Tatar
Religions: Ukrainian Orthodox, Roman Catholic, Protestant, Jewish
Currency: Hryvna
Main occupations: Agriculture, mining
Main exports: Coal, titanium, iron ore, manganese ore, steel
Main imports: Oil, natural gas

KIEV
Kiev is one of Eastern Europe's oldest towns. It is believed to have existed as a commercial center in the early 5th century.

KIEV

The capital of Ukraine lies on the Dnieper river, 591 miles (952 km) from the river's mouth on the Black Sea. Kiev was founded in the 8th century as the capital of the state of Kievan Rus. The focus of the city is the ancient Upper Town, where historic buildings still survive despite the damage done during World War II. The Church of Saint Sophia (left), founded in the 11th century, is a famous landmark of the Eastern Orthodox faith.

Find out more
EUROPE
EUROPE, HISTORY OF
IRON AND STEEL
NUCLEAR ENERGY
SOVIET UNION, HISTORY OF

UNDERWATER EXPLORATION

BENEATH THE WAVES lies another world waiting to be discovered. Divers go down to explore the edges of this underwater world. Only a few feet below the surface they can find fascinating sea creatures, beautifully colored coral reefs, and strange rock formations. On the seabed lie wrecks of ships which may have sunk thousands of years ago. They contain pots, coins, and other objects which show how people lived in ancient times. Divers also work in the sea. They service underwater structures, such as oil rigs, and study life on the seabed. But diving can be dangerous, and divers must follow strict safety rules.

The dark depths of the ocean lie beyond divers. Only submersibles, which are small submarines, can reach the ocean floor. There they have discovered previously unknown creatures and have studied undersea mountains and trenches that reveal the structure of the Earth.

DIVING BELL
Early underwater explorers used diving bells – air-filled chambers that were lowered to the seabed.

SNORKELING
By wearing a face mask and breathing through a tube called a snorkel, a swimmer can look down into the water and make short dives.

SCUBA DIVING
Self-contained underwater breathing apparatus (scuba for short) enables divers to swim underwater for an hour or so. The safe maximum depth for scuba diving is 160 ft (50 m).

REACHING THE DEPTHS

People can dive simply by holding their breath and swimming down into the water. But such dives are short-lived and shallow. In order to dive deeper, divers carry air cylinders or receive air pumped through tubes from the surface. Divers using special equipment can reach a maximum depth of approximately 1,600 ft (500 m). Underwater vessels take people on the deepest dives.

SUBMERSIBLES
Teams of people dive to the ocean floor in submersibles, which sometimes go as deep as 20,000 ft (6,000 m). The submersible dives from, and returns to, a mother ship on the surface.

Float contains gas which keeps bathyscaphe weightless in the water.

UNDER-WATER ROBOTS
Robot submersibles are small and maneuverable. They collect samples and send television pictures to the surface.

Mechanical arms take samples and grip tools.

The steel cabin holds two crew members. Its spherical shape helps it withstand the enormous water pressure.

BATHYSCAPHES
Special deep-diving vessels called bathyscaphes can dive to the deepest seabed. In 1960 the bathyscaphe *Trieste* dived almost 7 miles (11 km) to reach the very deepest part of the ocean, the Marianas Trench in the Pacific Ocean. The descent took nearly five hours.

EXPLORING THE *TITANIC*
In 1986, the US submersible *Alvin* explored the wreck of the great ocean liner *Titanic*. The crew used a robot submersible, called *Jason Junior* (left), to inspect the hull and look inside the ship. The *Titanic*, which was thought to be unsinkable, struck an iceberg on its maiden voyage in 1912. It sank more than 2 miles (3.2 km) to the floor of the North Atlantic Ocean.

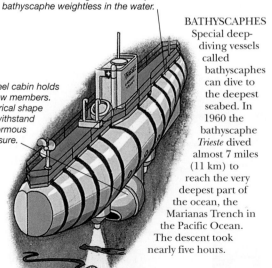

SCUBA EQUIPMENT

A diver needs several pieces of equipment to survive underwater. An aqualung provides air, and a wet suit keeps the diver warm. A buoyancy jacket may also be necessary, since divers tend to sink in the water as they dive deeper. The diver maintains a constant depth by blowing air into or expelling air from the jacket.

A computer indicates the amount of air in the cylinder, the depth of the water, the duration of the dive, and the safe speed at which the diver should return to the surface.

Face mask made of rubber and toughened glass

Snorkel for use in emergencies

Mouthpiece for inflating buoyancy jacket in emergency

Mouthpiece and demand valve

AQUALUNG

The diver breathes from an aqualung, which consists of an air cylinder, a pressure-reducing valve, and a tube that leads air to the mouthpiece. The cylinder contains air at high pressure. The diver can only breathe in air at the same pressure as the surrounding water. The demand valve on the mouthpiece automatically controls the air pressure so the diver can breathe in and out easily.

Air from the aqualung inflates the buoyancy jacket. The emergency cylinder can be used if the main one fails, or the diver can blow into the mouthpiece.

Emergency air cylinder

Main air cylinder

Compass for navigating underwater

JACQUES COUSTEAU
Two Frenchmen, Jacques Cousteau (above) and Emile Gagnan, invented the aqualung in 1943. Later, Cousteau became a famous underwater explorer.

ATMOSPHERIC DIVING SUIT
Divers can reach greater depths, make longer dives, and avoid the dangers of the bends by using an atmospheric diving suit. This suit encloses the diver's body, and has its own air supply so the diver can breathe normally.

Buoyancy tank

Thrusters propel suit.

Hand-operated manipulators

Diaphragm moves in and out as diver inhales and exhales.

Lever opens and closes air inlet valve.

Tube from air cylinder

Air outlet valve opens when diver breathes out.

Air inlet valve

Weights on the belt cancel out the buoyancy of the diving suit and help the diver sink. The belt can be released in an emergency.

A film of water trapped between the rubber wet suit and the diver's body prevents heat from escaping and keeps the diver warm in cold water.

Knife

DANGERS OF DIVING
Air contains nitrogen gas. Increasing pressure forces nitrogen into a scuba diver's blood as he or she dives deeper. Too much nitrogen is harmful, so the diver must not dive too deep or stay underwater too long. The diver must return slowly from a deep dive, or the nitrogen forms bubbles in the blood. This condition, called the bends, is very painful and can cause permanent injury.

Scuba divers wear large fins, or flippers, to propel themselves through the water.

The spherical cabin can be released from the Alvin to carry the crew back to the surface in an emergency.

UNDERWATER ARCHAEOLOGY

Ancient vessels often carried pottery containers called amphorae that were used to store wine or oil.

Divers are able to uncover the wrecks of old ships just as archaeologists on land dig up the remains of old buildings. They carefully recover objects from the shipwrecks, some of which contain treasure. A few ships have been raised to the surface and preserved.

Batteries power motors.

Thrusters for maneuvering in the water

Thrusters for propulsion

Ballast tanks to adjust buoyancy of submersible

Batteries power the motors.

Spherical cabin resists the pressure of the surrounding water.

Porthole

Television camera

Twin-lens stereo camera

Manipulator arm

Equipment tray

THE *ALVIN* SUBMERSIBLE
Since it began service in 1964, *Alvin* has made more than 2,000 dives deep into the world's oceans. The submersible mainly undertakes scientific research. Three people – one pilot and two scientists – make dives of six to ten hours to a maximum depth of 13,000 ft (4,000 m).

Find out more
DEEP-SEA WILDLIFE
OCEANS AND SEAS
SUBMARINES

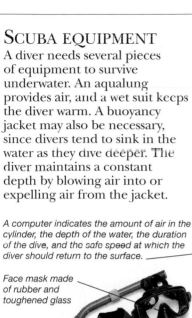

UNITED KINGDOM

THE UNITED KINGDOM of Great Britain and Northern Ireland was formed under the Act of Union of 1801. It is made up of England, Wales, and Scotland, which together form the island of Great Britain, and the province of Northern Ireland. In the late 1990s, the British government devolved (decentralized) power to regional governments by creating new parliaments in Northern Ireland, Scotland, and Wales. The English countryside is famed for its gently sloping hills and rich farmland. Wales and Scotland are mostly wild and mountainous. Much of Northern Ireland is low-lying and marshy. In Wales and parts of Scotland, many of the people speak a language of their own. Britain is a multicultural country, for the English, Scots, Welsh, and Irish are all separate peoples. Also, in the last 100 years refugees and immigrants from Europe, Africa, Asia, and the Caribbean have settled in Britain, bringing with them their own languages and religions. Britain once controlled a vast empire that stretched around the world. In recent years its economy has declined, but the discovery of oil in the North Sea has helped to make the country self-sufficient in energy.

The United Kingdom is just off the northwest coast of Europe. To its east lies the North Sea. The Atlantic Ocean washes its northern and western coasts. The English Channel separates the country from mainland Europe.

Distinctive red double-decker buses and black taxis ferry Londoners around their city.

LONDON

When the Roman armies invaded Britain almost 2,000 years ago, they built a fortified town called Londinium to safeguard the crossing over the Thames River. By 1100, the city of London had grown in size to become the capital of the entire country. Today, London is a huge city of almost 7 million people and is the political, financial, and cultural center of Britain. Tourists come from all over the world to admire the historic buildings, particularly the Tower of London (left), an 11th-century fortress.

Cricket began in Britain and is the country's national sport. Many villages have their own teams.

CITY OF LONDON

The ancient heart of London is called the City. London is one of the world's leading financial centers, and most of the nation's banks and businesses have their headquarters here. The modern building shown on the left is the Lloyd's Building, where the world's shipping is registered and insured.

ENGLAND

The biggest and most populated part of the United Kingdom is England. Many people live in large towns and cities such as London, Birmingham, and Manchester. Parts of southeast and northern England are very crowded. The English countryside is varied, with rolling farmland in the south and east and hilly moors in the north and west. England is dotted with picturesque villages where old houses and shops are often grouped around a village green.

The rose is the national flower of England.

Thousands of colorful flowers are used to decorate floats for Jersey's "Battle of the Flowers" festival.

JERSEY AND GUERNSEY

The Channel Islands of Jersey and Guernsey are closer to France than they are to Britain. The French coast is just 15 miles (24 km) away from Jersey, the largest island. Close to Jersey and Guernsey are some smaller islands that are also part of the Channel Islands group. All of the islands have a mild climate, so one of the principal occupations is the growing of vegetables. The warm weather and ample sunshine also attract vacationers who swell the islands' usual population of 156,000 in the summer months.

NORTHERN ENGLAND

The north of England has traditionally been the most heavily industrialized part of the United Kingdom. During the Industrial Revolution of the 19th century, factories and mills made goods for export to a British empire that covered half the world. Today the industrial cities of the north remain, but many of the factories stand empty because manufacturing is more profitable in other parts of the world. Northern England is also famous for its natural beauty; in the northwest is a rugged, mountainous region called the Lake District. Here, deep lakes separate steep hills which rise to a height of more than 3,200 ft (975 m). The Lake District attracts many visitors and tourists.

"Mad Sunday" motorcyclist on the Isle of Man

ISLE OF MAN

The Isle of Man is part of the United Kingdom but enjoys a certain amount of independence. The Manx people, as islanders are called, have their own government, the Tynwald, which makes many decisions about how the island is run. There is also a Manx language, though it is now used only for formal ceremonies. For a long period in its history, the Isle of Man was independent; between 1405 and 1765 the island was a kingdom separate from England.

FISHING INDUSTRY

The waters of the northeast Atlantic are among the world's richest fishing grounds. However, EU regulations, designed to reduce catches and conserve fish stocks, are causing widespread discontent among fishermen.

The United Kingdom has many fishing ports, like this one in Scotland.

PEOPLE

The United Kingdom is densely populated, with most of the people living in urban areas, particularly in the southeast of England. Almost 12 percent of the total population of the country lives in London. The southeast is also the most prosperous area. Other parts of the country are less crowded. For example, the Highlands in Scotland have fewer inhabitants today than 200 years ago.

SHETLAND AND ORKNEY

To the northeast of Scotland, two groups of islands form Britain's northernmost outposts. Orkney and Shetland comprise about 170 islands in all, but only the larger islands are inhabited. The landscape is bleak and there are few trees. The land is too poor to make farming profitable, and the traditional local industry is fishing. The islands are also famous for their handknitted woolen clothes: Fair Isle has given its name to a distinctive knitting pattern.

A Welsh village has the longest place name in the United Kingdom.

LLANFAIRPWLLGWYNGYLLGOGERYCHWYRN-DROBWLLLLANTYSILIOGOGOGOCH

WALES

Farming, forestry, and tourism are the most important occupations in the rural regions of Wales. Farms tend to be small and average 16 acres (40 hectares) in size. Farmers in the upland regions keep cattle and sheep. Wales was once one of the main coal-producing areas in the world. There were 630 collieries in the region in 1913. However, the coal industry declined in the years after World War I. By 1990, a mere seven collieries remained open.

PUBLIC HOUSES

Public houses, more usually called pubs, developed from inns which offered travelers food, drink, and shelter. The pub played a part in British culture, too. In the *Canterbury Tales* by Geoffrey Chaucer (1340-1400), pilgrims on their way to Canterbury in southeast England rest at pubs and tell each other tales. Many of the plays of William Shakespeare (1564-1616) were performed in the yards of London pubs. Today the pub is a social center where adults meet to discuss the events of the day. Pubs often entertain their customers with music or poetry, and many British rock bands began their careers playing in a pub.

The leek is the Welsh National emblem.

By custom, the first son of the British king or queen becomes Prince of Wales, and wears a gold crown.

EISTEDDFOD

Every year a festival of poetry, music, and drama celebrates and promotes the Welsh language. This National Eisteddfod began in the 7th century. Today, colorful choirs and orchestras compete for awards at the event.

SCOTTISH TOURISM

Tourism is an important source of income for Scotland. People are lured to the region by its beautifully wild Highland scenery. Scotland is steeped in history and visitors often take the opportunity to visit its many ancient castles. For centuries, Scotland was dominated by struggles between rival families, known as clans. Today, one of the most popular tourist souvenirs is tartan – textiles woven in the colors of the clans.

Most of Scotland consists of high mountains and remote glens or valleys.

The Scottish emblem is the thistle.

The Irish shamrock emblem.

NORTHERN IRELAND

Prior to the the 1960s, the economy of Northern Ireland was based on manufacturing, engineering, shipbuilding, and textiles. Heavy industry was concentrated in Belfast where shipbuilding (above) was the largest employer. However, civil disorder after 1968 had a detrimental effect on the economy, and, as across the UK as a whole, the manufacturing industry has been in decline.

Find out more

EUROPE, HISTORY OF
NORTHERN IRELAND
UNITED KINGDOM, HISTORY OF

STATISTICS
Area: 94,550 sq miles
(244,880 sq km)
Population: 59,800,000
Capital: London
Languages: English,
Welsh, Scottish Gaelic,
Irish Gaelic
Religions: Anglican,
Roman Catholic,
Presbyterian, Muslim,
Methodist
Currency: Pound
sterling
Main occupations:
Finance, engineering,
oil and gas production,
manufacturing,
agriculture
Main exports: Oil,
natural gas, chemicals,
electronics, cars,
aircraft
Main imports:
Machinery, fruits and
vegetables, metals, raw
materials

ENGLAND
Area: 50,356
sq miles (130,423 sq km)
Population: 50,093,800
Capital: London

SCOTLAND
Area: 30,167 sq miles
(78,133 sq km)
Population: 5,078,400
Capital: Edinburgh

WALES
Area: 8,017 sq miles
(20,766 sq km)
Population: 2,952,500
Capital: Cardiff

NORTHERN
IRELAND (no official flag)
Area: 5,674 sq miles
(14,695 sq km)
Population: 1,700,000
Capital: Belfast

Legend:
Volcano | Mountain | Ancient monument | Capital city | Large city/town | Small city/town

SCALE BAR
0 50 100 km
0 50 100 miles

SHETLAND ISLANDS

CHANNEL ISLANDS

ENGLISH CHANNEL
*British people call the narrow
stretch of sea that separates
their country from France the
English Channel, but the
French call it La Manche,
which means "The Sleeve."*

NORTH SEA OIL
The discovery of oil under the North
Sea greatly benefited the British
economy from the 1980s. Construction
and operation of the oil drilling
platforms provided many jobs, and
money from oil sales allowed the
British government to cut taxes.

HISTORY OF THE
UNITED KINGDOM

IN 1801, THE UNITED KINGDOM came into being with the Act of Union. Before that there had been four separate nations: England, Wales, Scotland, and Ireland. However, England had begun taking over the government of Wales in the 1000s, Ireland in the 1100s, and had shared a joint monarchy with Scotland since 1603. The United Kingdom is a small country, but by 1850 it had become the richest and most powerful nation in the world, controlling the largest empire in history. Even today, the British Commonwealth of Nations includes more than 40 independent countries that were once British colonies. The United Kingdom has often been forced to fight long and bitter wars, but has survived and prospered because of its island position and its strong navy. The British system of laws and government by Parliament has become a model which many other nations have copied.

PALEOLITHIC SETTLERS
A quarter of a million years ago, during mild conditions between two Ice Ages, people began to settle in Britain. They walked across the bridge of land which joined Britain to Europe at the time.

BATTLE OF HASTINGS

In 1066, a battle changed the course of English history. A Norman army led by William the Conqueror defeated an English king, Harold of Wessex, at Hastings, in southern England. William's descendants have ruled the country ever since. As king, he built castles in his new kingdom and gave land to powerful barons. They in turn give land to local lords for agreeing to fight for them. Peasants farmed the land of the local lord, and paid rent in produce and money. This system was called feudalism.

HENRY VIII
A truly multitalented king, Henry VIII was an expert at many things, from jousting and archery to lute-playing and languages. His impact on England was tremendous. In 1541, he forced the Irish Parliament to recognize him as king of Ireland. He also broke from the Roman Catholic Church, in order to divorce his wife, and became head of a new Church of England. Henry was an absolute ruler who executed anyone who displeased him, including two of his six wives.

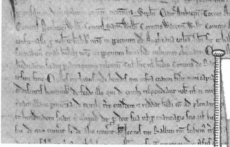

MAGNA CARTA
The Magna Carta (Great Charter) of 1215 was an agreement between the king and the nobles of England. The charter promised that the king would not abuse his royal power to tax the nobles. This important moment in English history was the start of the belief that even kings must obey certain laws of the land.

UNITED KINGDOM

A.D. 43 Ancient Romans, under Claudius, invade Britain and make it part of their empire.

400 Romans leave Britain.

c. 500 Christian missionaries arrive in Britain and preach Christianity to the people.

UNION FLAG
The flag of the United Kingdom is made up from the red crosses of St. George of England and St. Patrick of Ireland, plus the white St. Andrew's cross of Scotland, on a blue background. Wales has its own flag.

c. 870 Viking conquest of Britain begins.

1066 Normans invade Britain.

1215 Magna Carta agreement between the king and the nobles of England.

1282 Edward I, king of England, conquers Wales.

1485 Battle of Bosworth. Henry VII becomes the first Tudor king.

1534 Parliament declares Henry VIII head of the Church of England.

1588 English navy defeats the Spanish Armada (fleet) sent by Philip II, king of Spain.

CHARLES II

The Parliamentary army defeated and executed King Charles I during the English Civil War (1642-51). For nine years Oliver Cromwell (1599-1658), a member of Parliament, and his army ruled the country as a republic. In 1660, Charles' son returned from travels abroad (above) and claimed the throne as King Charles II. The nation, weary of the republic, welcomed him.

ADMIRAL NELSON

The most famous and daring commander of the British Royal Navy was Admiral Horatio Nelson (1758-1805), who defeated the Spanish and French at the Battle of Trafalgar. Before the battle he said "England expects every man to do his duty." Nelson was fatally wounded in the battle.

CHARTISTS

During the 19th century, British people fought for the right to vote. Groups such as the Chartists (1837-48) organized demonstrations demanding a fairer system with representation for all, a secret voting system, and regular elections. Above is a Chartist riot being crushed by the police.

IMMIGRATION

The United Kingdom has become a multiracial and multicultural society, with immigration mainly from Commonwealth countries in the Caribbean, and from many of the Asian nations. This picture, taken in the 1960s, shows new arrivals from Jamaica receiving meals at a hostel set up to provide support for immigrants.

NEW LABOUR

When the Labour Party achieved a landslide victory over the Conservatives in 1997, Tony Blair (left) became prime minister of the United Kingdom. Under Blair's leadership, the Party moved to the political center, re-christening themselves "New Labour." Blair won two more elections, in 2001 and 2005, despite widespread criticism of his decision to take part in the invasion of Iraq.

WELFARE STATE

In 1945, following the end of World War II, a Labour government came into power and introduced a welfare state. This put a number of private businesses under public control. It also provided welfare for people "from the cradle to the grave," including free medical treatment under the National Health Service.

UNITED KINGDOM

1642-51 Civil War between the King and Parliament.

1660 Charles II becomes King of England.

1707 Act of Union unites England, Wales, and Scotland.

1801 Ireland united with Great Britain.

1900 Britain is the strongest, richest country in the world.

1914-18 Britain fights in World War I.

1931 Commonwealth of Nations is established.

1939-45 Britain fights in World War II.

1945 Welfare state introduced.

1973 Britain becomes a member of the European Union (EU).

1997 Scotland votes in favor of its own parliament.

Find out more

CIVIL WAR, ENGLISH
ELIZABETH I
INDUSTRIAL REVOLUTION
IRELAND, HISTORY OF
NORMANS
UNITED KINGDOM
VICTORIANS

UNITED NATIONS

IN 1945, AT THE END of World War II, the nations that opposed Germany, Italy, and Japan decided that such a war must never be repeated. They set up the United Nations, with the aim of preventing future conflicts, and drew up the United Nations Charter. The United Nations (UN) met for the first time in San Francisco in 1945. Today, 185 nations belong to the UN. The UN consists of six main organs: the General Assembly, the Security Council, the Secretariat, the Economic and Social Council, the Trusteeship Council, and the International Court of Justice. Each is concerned with world peace and social justice. The UN also has agencies that deal with global issues such as health. Each member nation of the UN has a seat in the General Assembly; 15 nations sit on the Security Council. The UN is not without problems. Its members often disagree, and it suffers financial difficulties.

LEAGUE OF NATIONS
In 1919, the victors of World War I founded the League of Nations to keep peace. But in 1935 the League failed to prevent Italy from invading Ethiopia. In 1946, the League's functions were transferred to the UN. Haile Selassie, emperor of Ethiopia, is seen addressing the League, above.

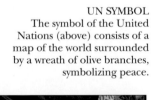

UN SYMBOL
The symbol of the United Nations (above) consists of a map of the world surrounded by a wreath of olive branches, symbolizing peace.

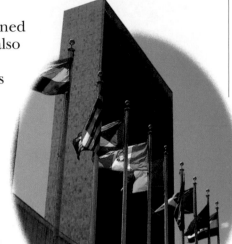

UNITED NATIONS
The headquarters of the UN in New York City is where the General Assembly and Security Council meet, as well as many of the specialist agencies of the organization. Politicians from every member nation come to New York to address the UN, and many international disputes and conflicts are settled here.

SECURITY COUNCIL
The aim of the Security Council is to maintain peace in the world. It investigates any event that might lead to fighting. The council has five permanent members – Britain, the United States, the Russian Federation, France, and China – and 10 members elected for two years each.

UNICEF
The United Nations Children's Fund (UNICEF) is one of the most successful agencies of the UN. UNICEF was originally founded to help child victims of World War II. The fund now provides education, health care, and medical help for children across the world, particularly in areas devastated by war or famine. Much of its work takes place in the poorer countries of Africa and Asia.

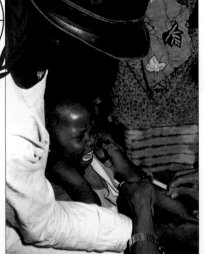

Children in underdeveloped countries are immunized against disease, thanks to UNICEF.

PEACEKEEPING
The UN is sometimes called on to send a peacekeeping force to a country in order to prevent war. In 1989, a UN force was sent to Namibia, southern Africa, to supervise the elections that led to Namibia's independence. More recently, UN forces were sent to Ethopia, in eastern Africa, to uphold a peace agreement with neighboring Eritrea.

> ### *Find out more*
> ARMIES
> GOVERNMENTS AND POLITICS
> WORLD WAR I
> WORLD WAR II

UNITED STATES OF AMERICA

ON THE FLAG OF the United States, 50 identical stars represent the country's 50 states. But the states themselves could not be more different. If the stars showed their land areas, the largest, for Alaska, would be nearly 500 times bigger than the star for the smallest state, Rhode Island. If the stars showed population, Alaska's star would be the smallest, and the star for California, which has the most people, would be 60 times larger. The states vary in other ways, too. The Rocky Mountains in the western states reach more than 14,400 ft (4,400 m) in height, but flat plains extend for a thousand miles across the country's center. At Barrow, Alaska, the northernmost town, the average temperature is just 9°F (-13°C), yet in Arizona temperatures have reached 134°F (57°C). Since 1945, the US has played a leading role in world affairs. The nation is the most powerful in the Western world. American finance, culture, and politics have spread outward from the United States. Products made in the United States are available in every country. Decisions made by American politicians affect the lives of people everywhere.

The United States covers much of the continent of North America. It reaches from the Atlantic to the Pacific oceans and from the Mexican border to Canada. The nation covers a total of 3.68 million sq miles (9.37 million sq km).

NASA

The United States is a world leader in technology, particularly in space research. The National Aeronautics and Space Administration (NASA) spends billions of dollars every year on satellites and spacecraft. In 1969, Neil Armstrong, commander of NASA's *Apollo 11*, became the first man to walk on the moon. One of NASA's recent successes is the Space Shuttle, a reusable spacecraft.

Technicians monitor data in a NASA Space Shuttle control center.

STATE AND FEDERAL GOVERNMENT

The United States is a democracy and has a written constitution which sets out how government works. State governments, which meet in the state capital, have the authority to make laws affecting their own residents. The states were once nearly self-governing, but today the federal, or national, government has more power. It makes decisions on foreign policy and can pass laws which affect the entire country.

NEW YORK CITY

At the mouth of the Hudson River on the east coast of the United States is New York City, the country's biggest city. It is also one of the oldest. New York was founded in the 1620s and is now home to about 8 million people. The city is the financial heart of the nation and houses the offices of many large companies, plus hundreds of theaters, museums, and parks. Skyscrapers more than 1,000 ft (300 m) tall dominate the city centre, Manhattan.

Manhattan, the center of New York City, is an island between the Hudson and East rivers.

HAWAII AND ALASKA

Hawaii, a group of tropical islands in the Pacific Ocean, became the fiftieth US state in 1959. The islands produce pineapples, sugar, and coffee. Polynesians first settled Hawaii in the 700s, and many native Polynesians still live here. Alaska lies outside the United States, too, separated from the other states by Canada.

The Sugar Train *on the Hawaiian island of Maui*

CALIFORNIA

In 1848 gold was discovered in California, and many people rushed to the region to prospect for it. California is still the state with the most inhabitants. Nearly 36 million people live there. Most of the state has a mild, sunny climate and produces vast amounts of fruit. Many towns in California have become resorts. Modern industries have started up in California; Northern California's Silicon Valley, for example, is a center for the computer business.

Cable cars still carry passengers up some of the 43 hills on which the city of San Francisco in California is built.

AMERICAN PEOPLE

Native Americans, the original Americans, now make up only a small part of the total population of 295 million. Most Americans are the descendants of settlers from overseas and speak English. They live in the same neighborhoods and mingle in everyday life. Their cultures have also mingled, producing a new form of English different from that spoken in Britain. Many Americans also maintain the language, culture, and traditions of the countries they or their ancestors came from originally.

The Grand Canyon is a favorite tourist attraction. Many people ride to the bottom on mules.

BASEBALL
Baseball is the USA's top sport, and was first played between two organized teams in 1846.

HOLLYWOOD
Hollywood, in Los Angeles, was founded in 1887 as a community for Christians. Today, it is the center of America's film industry. Many movie studios are based here, and actors, actresses, and other celebrities live and work nearby. The area is a favorite tourist attraction. Visitors come to spot the stars and to take photos of the Hollywood sign (right) in the Hollywood Hills.

BLUES
During the 17th, 18th, and 19th centuries hundreds of thousands of Africans were brought to America as slaves. Slavery was outlawed in 1865, and since then black writers, artists, and musicians have made their mark on American culture. The popular music known as blues originated among slaves in the southern states.

Famous blues singer B.B. King (born 1925) has played his guitar, named Lucille, in concerts all over the world.

GRAND CANYON
There are many natural wonders in the United States; one of the most impressive is the Grand Canyon in Arizona. The Colorado River took thousands of years to cut the canyon by natural erosion through solid rock. It is 18 miles (29 km) wide in places and more than 6,000 ft (1,800 m) deep.

Find out more

GOVERNMENT AND POLITICS
KING JR., MARTIN LUTHER
NATIVE AMERICANS
ROOSEVELT, FRANKLIN

SEAT OF GOVERNMENT

 DISTRICT OF COLUMBIA
Area: 61 sq miles (159 sq km)
Population: 553,500
Capital: Washington, D.C.

STATES, with date of admission to Union

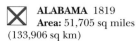

 ALABAMA 1819
Area: 51,705 sq miles (133,906 sq km)
Population: 4,530,200
Capital: Montgomery

 ALASKA 1959
Area: 591,000 sq miles (1,530,572 sq km)
Population: 655,400
Capital: Juneau

 ARIZONA 1912
Area: 114,000 sq miles (295,237 sq km)
Population: 5,743,800
Capital: Phoenix

 ARKANSAS 1836
Area: 53,187 sq miles (137,744 sq km)
Population: 2,752,600
Capital: Little Rock

 CALIFORNIA 1850
Area: 158,706 sq miles (411,017 sq km)
Population: 35,893,800
Capital: Sacramento

 COLORADO 1876
Area: 104,091 sq miles (269,575 sq km)
Population: 4,601,400
Capital: Denver

 CONNECTICUT 1788
Area: 5,018 sq miles (12,996 sq km)
Population: 3,503,600
Capital: Hartford

 DELAWARE 1787
Area: 2,045 sq miles (5,296 sq km)
Population: 830,400
Capital: Dover

 FLORIDA 1845
Area: 58,664 sq miles (151,928 sq km)
Population: 17,397,200
Capital: Tallahassee

 GEORGIA 1788
Area: 58,910 sq miles (152,565 sq km)
Population: 8,829,400
Capital: Atlanta

HAWAII 1959
Area: 6,471 sq miles (16,759 sq km)
Population: 1,262,800
Capital: Honolulu

 IDAHO 1890
Area: 83,564 sq miles (216,414 sq km)
Population: 1,393,300
Capital: Boise

 ILLINOIS 1818
Area: 56,345 sq miles (145,922 sq km)
Population: 12,713,600
Capital: Springfield

 INDIANA 1816
Area: 36,185 sq miles (93,712 sq km)
Population: 6,237,600
Capital: Indianapolis

 IOWA 1846
Area: 56,275 sq miles (145,740 sq km)
Population: 2,954,500
Capital: Des Moines

 KANSAS 1861
Area: 82,277 sq miles (213,081 sq km)
Population: 2,735,500
Capital: Topeka

 KENTUCKY 1792
Area: 40,410 sq miles (104,654 sq km)
Population: 4,145,900
Capital: Frankfort

 LOUISIANA 1812
Area: 47,752 sq miles (123,678 sq km)
Population: 4,515,800
Capital: Baton Rouge

 MAINE 1820
Area: 33,265 sq miles (86,150 sq km)
Population: 1,317,300
Capital: Augusta

 MARYLAND 1788
Area: 10,460 sq miles (27,089 sq km)
Population: 5,558,100
Capital: Annapolis

 MASSACHUSETTS 1788
Area: 8,284 sq miles (21,454 sq km)
Population: 6,416,500
Capital: Boston

 MICHIGAN 1837
Area: 58,527 sq miles (151,573 sq km)
Population: 10,112,600
Capital: Lansing

MINNESOTA 1858
Area: 84,402 sq miles (218,584 sq km)
Population: 5,101,000
Capital: St. Paul

 MISSISSIPPI 1817
Area: 47,689 sq miles (123,505 sq km)
Population: 2,903,000
Capital: Jackson

 MISSOURI 1821
Area: 69,697 sq miles (180,501 sq km)
Population: 5,754,600
Capital: Jefferson City

 MONTANA 1889
Area: 147,046 sq miles (380,820 sq km)
Population: 926,900
Capital: Helena

 NEBRASKA 1867
Area: 77,355 sq miles (200,334 sq km)
Population: 1,747,200
Capital: Lincoln

 NEVADA 1864
Area: 110,561 sq miles (286,331 sq km)
Population: 2,334,800
Capital: Carson City

 NEW HAMPSHIRE 1788
Area: 9,279 sq miles (24,031 sq km)
Population: 1,299,500
Capital: Concord

 NEW JERSEY 1787
Area: 7,787 sq miles (20,167 sq km)
Population: 8,698,900
Capital: Trenton

 NEW MEXICO 1912
Area: 121,593 sq miles (314,902 sq km)
Population: 1,903,300
Capital: Santa Fe

 NEW YORK 1788
Area: 49,108 sq miles (127,180 sq km)
Population: 19,227,100
Capital: Albany

 NORTH CAROLINA 1789
Area: 52,669 sq miles (136,402 sq km)
Population: 8,541,200
Capital: Raleigh

NORTH DAKOTA 1889
Area: 70,702 sq miles (183,104 sq km)
Population: 634,400
Capital: Bismarck

OHIO 1803
Area: 41,330 sq miles (107,036 sq km)
Population: 11,459,000
Capital: Columbus

OKLAHOMA 1907
Area: 69,919 sq miles (181,076 sq km)
Population: 3,523,600
Capital: Oklahoma City

OREGON 1859
Area: 97,073 sq miles (251,400 sq km)
Population: 3,594,600
Capital: Salem

 PENNSYLVANIA 1787
Area: 45,308 sq miles (117,339 sq km)
Population: 12,406,300
Capital: Harrisburg

 RHODE ISLAND 1790
Area: 1,212 sq miles (3,139 sq km)
Population: 1,080,600
Capital: Providence

 SOUTH CAROLINA 1788
Area: 31,113 sq miles (80,576 sq km)
Population: 4,198,100
Capital: Columbia

 SOUTH DAKOTA 1889
Area: 77,116 sq miles (199,715 sq km)
Population: 770,900
Capital: Pierre

 TENNESSEE 1796
Area: 42,144 sq miles (109,145 sq km)
Population: 5,901,000
Capital: Nashville

 TEXAS 1845
Area: 266,807 sq miles (690,977 sq km)
Population: 22,490,000
Capital: Austin

 UTAH 1896
Area: 84,899 sq miles (219,871 sq km)
Population: 2,389,000
Capital: Salt Lake City

 VERMONT 1791
Area: 9,614 sq miles (24,898 sq km)
Population: 621,400
Capital: Montpelier

 VIRGINIA 1788
Area: 40,767 sq miles (105,578 sq km)
Population: 7,459,800
Capital: Richmond

 WASHINGTON 1889
Area: 68,139 sq miles (176,466 sq km)
Population: 6,203,800
Capital: Olympia

WEST VIRGINIA 1863
Area: 24,232 sq miles (62,756 sq km)
Population: 1,815,400
Capital: Charleston

WISCONSIN 1848
Area: 56,153 sq miles (145,425 sq km)
Population: 5,509,000
Capital: Madison

 WYOMING 1890
Area: 97,809 sq miles (253,306 sq km)
Population: 506,500
Capital: Cheyenne

| Volcano | Mountain | Ancient monument | Capital city | Large city/ town | Small city/ town |

STATISTICS

Area: 3,681,760 sq miles (9,372,610 sq km)
Population: 295,734,000
Capital: Washington, D.C.
Languages: English, Spanish, Italian, German, French, Polish, Chinese, Tagalog, Greek
Religions: Protestant, Roman Catholic, Jewish, non-religious
Currency: US dollar
Main occupations: Research, manufacturing, agriculture
Main exports: Energy, raw materials, food, electronics, cars, coal
Main imports: Oil

MIDWEST

The United States is the world's largest exporter of wheat and produces nearly half of the corn on Earth. This enormous quantity of food is grown on the open plains which cover the Midwest between the Mississippi River and the Rockies. Grain farming is highly mechanized, with giant machines operating in fields hundreds of acres in size. The United States also produces one-quarter of the world's oranges, one-seventh of the world's nuts, and half of the world's soybeans.

The seemingly endless wheat fields of the Midwest

INDUSTRY

Most of the industries in the United States are the largest and most profitable of their type in the world. America has abundant mineral deposits, raw materials, and energy sources. The most economically important industries in the US include car manufacturing, food processing, textile and clothing manufacture, and the computer industry. "Silicon Valley" in California is a world center for microelectronics. New York City is the nation's financial capital while Washington State has an important aerospace industry.

ALASKA

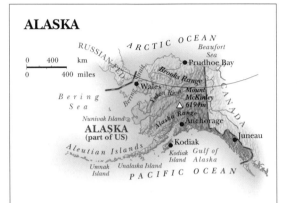

BORDER
The border between Canada and the US is the world's longest land border between any two countries.

SCALE BAR

HAWAII
Hawaii is the only state that is not on the North American mainland. The eight main islands of the group are some 2,100 miles (3,380 km) southwest of San Francisco. Although most of the population lives on the island of Oahu, Hawaii itself is the biggest island.

DISTRICT OF COLUMBIA
When members of Congress passed laws in 1790 and 1791 to create the national capital, they wanted to avoid rivalry between northern and southern states. So when the site for the capital city was chosen, the region was created as a special district, called the District of Columbia (D.C.). However, D.C. is not a state, and although the people who live there take part in Congressional elections, their delegate in the House of Representatives cannot vote.

HISTORY OF THE
UNITED STATES

TODAY, THE UNITED STATES OF AMERICA is the most powerful nation on Earth. Yet, just 230 years ago, the United States was a new and vulnerable nation. It occupied a narrow strip of land on the Atlantic coast of North America and had a population of only about four million people. Beyond its borders lay vast areas of unclaimed land. Throughout the 19th century, American settlers pushed the frontier westward across that land, fighting the Native Americans for control. At the same time, millions of immigrants from Europe were arriving on the East Coast. By 1900, the nation's farms and factories were producing more than any other country. That wealth and power led to its involvement in international affairs and drew it into two world wars. But the country continued to prosper. Since 1945 the system of individual enterprise that inspired the founders of the United States has made its people among the world's richest. American business, influence, and culture have spread to every other nation in the world.

FOUNDING FATHERS

The United States originally consisted of 13 states, each with its own customs and history. In 1787 George Washington and other leaders, sometimes called the Founding Fathers, drew up the United States Constitution, a document that established a strong central government. The Constitution, which also safeguards the rights of the states and those of their people, has been in force since 1789.

STARS AND STRIPES

The first official flag was made in 1777 and had one stripe and one star for each of the original 13 states of the Union. After 1818, a new star was added to the flag each time a state joined the Union. Today there are 50 stars.

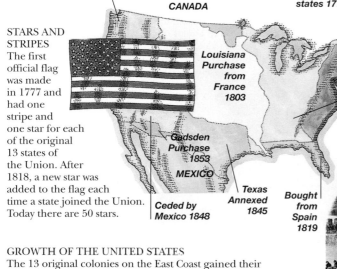

Oregon 1846

CANADA

13 original states 1776

Louisiana Purchase from France 1803

Acquired in 1783

Gadsden Purchase 1853

MEXICO

Texas Annexed 1845

Bought from Spain 1819

Ceded by Mexico 1848

GROWTH OF THE UNITED STATES

The 13 original colonies on the East Coast gained their independence from Britain in 1783, and acquired all the land as far west as the Mississippi River. In 1803 the vast area of Louisiana was bought from France, and by 1848 the United States had reached the Pacific Ocean.

FALL OF THE SOUTH

The Civil War ended in 1865, leaving the South in ruinous poverty. The hatred and bitterness caused by the war lasted for many years as the federal government took temporary control of the defeated southern states.

SPREAD OF THE RAILROAD

In 1860 there were more than 30,000 miles (48,000 km) of track in the eastern United States, but almost none had been built west of the Mississippi River. On May 10, 1869, the first transcontinental railroad was completed, and the two coasts of America were joined for the first time. A ceremony was held at Promontory Point in Utah to mark the occasion. The growth of the railroad network helped unify the country.

IMMIGRATION

During the 19th century many Europeans crossed the Atlantic in search of new freedoms and opportunities. The United States welcomed Irish people escaping famine, eastern European Jews fleeing persecution, and countless others. By 1890, half a million immigrants were arriving each year in the United States. As a result, the country became a mixture of many different cultures and religions.

INDUSTRY

The United States offered an endless supply of raw materials to 19th-century industrialists, who soon took advantage of these resources. Manufacturers such as Ransom Olds pioneered mass production of cars and many other goods. In the Olds Motor Works, cars moved along a production line, with workers at intervals each performing a single task. This technique made assembly faster, and Henry Ford and other manufacturers quickly adopted it.

Immigrants arriving in the United States were examined at a reception center on Ellis Island in New York Harbor.

JOHN F. KENNEDY

In 1960, John F. Kennedy (1917-63) became the youngest man ever elected president. In 1961, Kennedy approved the invasion of Communist Cuba by US-backed Cuban exiles. The invasion, at the Bay of Pigs, was a disaster, and Kennedy was severely criticized. In 1962 the Soviets stationed nuclear missiles on the island. For one week, nuclear war seemed unavoidable, but Kennedy persuaded the Soviet Union to remove the missiles and averted the war. Kennedy's presidency ended tragically on November 22, 1963, when he was assassinated during a visit to Dallas, Texas, after serving for exactly 1,000 days in office.

CHICAGO DAILY NEWS

PRESIDENT IS KILLED

Texas Sniper Escapes; Johnson Sworn In

Story Begins on Next Page

THE UNITED STATES AT WAR

Until the United States entered World War I in 1917, its armed forces had rarely fought overseas. After the war ended the United States tried once again to stay out of conflicts abroad. But in 1941 the Japanese attacked Pearl Harbor naval base in Hawaii, bringing the U.S. into World War II. Since 1945, the U.S. has fought in several overseas wars, notably in Korea (1950-53) and Vietnam (1961-73).

The Iwo Jima monument in Arlington National Cemetery is a memorial to Americans who died in World War II. It shows Marines raising the flag on Iwo Jima Island in the Pacific.

EQUAL OPPORTUNITIES

Since 1789, the US Constitution has guaranteed basic civil rights. In reality, many minority groups are only now starting to achieve equality. The photograph above shows David Dinkins, New York City's first black mayor.

UNITED STATES

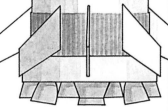

1783 The 13 colonies win their freedom from Britain.

1787 Constitution is drafted.

1789 George Washington becomes the first president.

1790-1800 A new capital, Washington, D.C., is built on the Potomac River.

1803 Louisiana Purchase doubles size of the country.

1845 Texas joins the Union.

1848 US defeats Mexico and acquires California and other territories.

1861-65 Civil War ends slavery

1869 First transcontinental railroad is completed.

1917-1918 US fights in World War I.

1929 Economic depression.

1941 United States enters World War II.

1963 President Kennedy assassinated.

1969 Neil Armstrong walks on the moon.

1991 US leads United Nations forces against Iraq in the Gulf War.

2001 Islamic terrorists destroy the World Trade Center.

2003 US invades Iraq.

Find out more

AMERICAN REVOLUTION
CIVIL WAR
IMMIGRATION
KENNEDY, JOHN F.
NUCLEAR AGE
PILGRIMS
UNITED STATES OF AMERICA
WASHINGTON, GEORGE

UNIVERSE

THE VAST EXPANSE OF SPACE that we call the universe contains everything there is. It includes the Sun, the planets, the Milky Way galaxy, and all other galaxies, too. The universe is continually growing, and each part is gradually moving farther away from every other part. We know about the universe by using powerful telescopes to study light, radio waves, X rays, and other radiations that reach Earth from space. Light travels nearly 6 billion miles (9.5 billion km) in a year. We call this distance a light-year. The light from a distant star that you can see through a telescope may have traveled thousands of light-years to reach us. Most scientists believe that the universe was created by a massive explosive event that happened billions of years ago. This idea is called the Big Bang theory. Many scientists now believe that visible matter makes up only 7% of the universe and that the rest is dark matter and dark energy.

Milky Way has a halo of stars and gas.

MILKY WAY
The Sun is just one of 100 billion stars in the large spiral galaxy we call the Milky Way. Like most other spiral galaxies, the Milky Way has curved arms of stars radiating from a globe-shaped center. The Milky Way is 100,000 light-years across, and the Sun is 30,000 light-years from its center.

GALAXIES
Galaxies, which contain gas, dust, and billions of stars, belong to one of three main groups – elliptical, irregular, or spiral. Most galaxies are elliptical, ranging from sphere shapes to egg shapes. A few galaxies are irregular. Others, such as the Milky Way, are spirals. The universe consists of billions of galaxies of all types.

Pieces of paper represent clusters of galaxies.

GALAXY CLUSTERS
Most galaxies belong to groups called clusters, which may contain thousands of galaxies of all types. These clusters form "walls" with great voids in between, so that the universe is like a foam.

In this image the galaxies are yellow and red, and the blue haloes around them represent dark matter.

Balloon expands in the same way that the universe is expanding.

THE EXPANDING UNIVERSE
You can get an idea of how the universe is expanding by imagining several small pieces of paper glued onto a balloon. Each piece represents a cluster of galaxies. As you blow up the balloon, all the paper pieces move farther away from each other. In the same way, galaxy clusters are moving farther away from each other. The farther a cluster is, the faster it travels away from us.

THE INVISIBLE UNIVERSE
When scientists estimate the mass of a galaxy cluster, the figure usually turns out to be much more than the mass of the visible galaxies alone. The extra, invisible matter is called dark matter, and no one knows what it is. Dark matter and ordinary matter together account for only 30% of the universe. Scientists call the remaining 70% dark energy. Dark energy is like a force that acts against gravity and pushes the galaxies apart. It is causing the expansion of the universe to speed up.

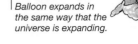

Galaxy is 100 million light-years away. Light left this galaxy when the dinosaurs lived on Earth.

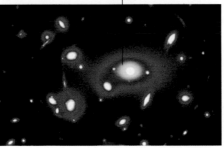

Dinosaurs lived on Earth 65–215 million years ago.

LOOKING BACK IN TIME
If you look through a telescope you can see galaxies millions of light-years away. You are not seeing them as they are now, but as they were long ago, when their light first set out on its journey – so in a sense, you are looking into the past.

Find out more
BIG BANG
BLACK HOLES
COMETS AND METEORS
EARTH
LIGHT
MOON
PLANETS
STARS
SUN
TELESCOPES

VETERINARIANS

UNLIKE HUMANS, ANIMALS cannot explain where the pain is when they are ill. This makes healing sick animals particularly difficult. This healing is the job of the veterinarian. Veterinarians are doctors who study the care and healing of animals. Originally, they treated horses and farm animals. Today, veterinarians look after household pets, too. They carry out regular health checks on farm animals and help with delivering lambs and calves. Some veterinarians treat zoo animals, and some are animal dentists. If an animal is very sick or in great pain, a veterinarian may have to put it down (kill it painlessly) to relieve its suffering. The first veterinary schools opened in Europe in the 18th century. Today, veterinarians study for five years or more to learn the skills they need.

Vets often use the same instruments as doctors, such as stethoscopes.

FARRIERS
Before there were vets, farriers (blacksmiths) treated horses and other farm animals, such as cattle, using traditional folk remedies.

VETERINARIAN'S OFFICE
Many different animals go to the veterinarian's office for treatment. To avoid fights and prevent the spread of infection, dogs must be kept on a leash and cats should stay in pet carriers. The veterinarian examines the animal and asks the owner what the signs of the illness are. The veterinarian may need to give medicine or injections, take X rays, or operate.

People wait with their pets in the waiting room.

Inoculating chickens prevents one diseased bird from infecting the whole flock.

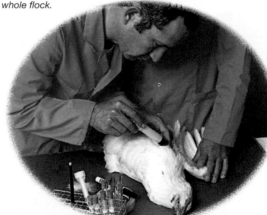

VETERINARY RESEARCH
Constant research is necessary to learn more about animal health. Research veterinarians look for cures to the diseases that make animals sick. They also try to control animal diseases that humans can catch, such as rabies.

Vets sometimes have to use helicopters to locate and treat animals that roam over wide areas.

FARM ANIMALS
Veterinarians are essential for modern farming. Today's farm animals are bred to produce meat or eggs as efficiently as possible, but they need special care because breeding may reduce their resistance to disease. Veterinarians help the farmer keep livestock healthy.

CONSERVATION
Some veterinarians are involved in wildlife conservation and treating wild animals. Large or ferocious animals, such as giraffes and lions, may have to be given a calming drug before the veterinarian can handle them. The drug eventually wears off, and does not harm the animal.

Find out more
CONSERVATION
and endangered species
FARMING
PETS

VICTORIANS

UNDER THE RULE OF QUEEN VICTORIA, the British people enjoyed a long period of prosperity. Profits gained from the Empire overseas, as well as from industrial improvements at home, allowed a large, educated middle-class to develop. Great advances were made in the arts and sciences. In the cities, department stores were opened for the convenience of those with cash to spend. Domestic servants were employed in many homes, although vast numbers of people remained poor and lived in slums. Public transport, police forces, clean water supplies, and sewage treatment were introduced to ease conditions in the new towns. Like Victoria, middle-class people set high moral standards, and devised programmes to "improve" the lives of the poor. The Victorians thought themselves the most advanced society in the world.

QUEEN VICTORIA
Victoria (1819-1901) is best remembered dressed all in black and in mourning for her husband Albert, who died in 1861. Queen Victoria had great dignity and was highly respected by her subjects.

CRYSTAL PALACE
In 1851, a new building was erected in Hyde Park, London, to house the Great Exhibition. It was made entirely of glass and cast iron. Joseph Paxton designed it so it could be moved later and rebuilt in south London.

VICTORIAN STYLE
Victorians loved elaborate decoration. Almost all Victorian objects, from lampposts to teaspoons were covered in carvings, patterns, and other ornamentation. Large houses and public buildings, such as St. Pancras station, London (right), were built in the style of ancient castles, cathedrals, and palaces.

St. Pancras station

THE GREAT EXHIBITION
In 1851, Prince Albert organized the first international exhibition in Britain. More than 6 million people visited the Crystal Palace (above) to celebrate the industrial age. The 14,000 exhibits included a 24-ton lump of coal, a railway engine, the Koh-i-noor diamond from India, and a stuffed elephant.

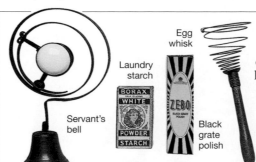

Egg whisk

Laundry starch

BORAX WHITE POWDER STARCH

ZEBO BLACK GRATE POLISH

Black grate polish

Servant's bell

DOMESTIC LIFE
Servants were a feature of every upper- and middle-class household. Maids worked long hours for little or no pay, sometimes only for board and lodging. In 1871, more than $1/3$ of British women aged 12-20 were "in service".

VICTORIANS

1837 Victoria becomes queen.

1842 Mines Act prevents women and children from working underground in mines.

1851 Great Exhibition held in London.

1863 First underground railway (the Metropolitan Line) opens, London.

1864 Factory Act bans children under eight years old from factory work.

1881 First electric street lighting is installed.

1884 Married Women's Property Act gives married women legal ownership of their property.

1891 Primary education in state schools becomes free.

1901 Queen Victoria dies.

MUSIC HALLS

Working people went to music halls (vaudeville theaters) for cheap entertainment. Audiences could eat and drink while enjoying melodramas, acrobats, comedians, and singers. Sentimental songs were especially popular.

Acrobats performed exciting feats on stage in music halls.

The Martini-Henry rifle appeared around 1871. It had a range of 300 yards (275 m).

EMPIRE BUILDING

During Victoria's reign, there were dozens of small-scale wars as the various European nations carved out empires in Africa and Asia. The people who already lived in these places stood little chance against trained troops equipped with rifles and automatic guns.

The Gatling gun fired bullets at a rate of 1,000 rounds per minute.

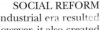

SOCIAL REFORM

In Victorian times, a new industrial era resulted in a wealthy middle class. However, it also created a vast working class who often suffered terrible living and working conditions. Some boys worked as chimney sweeps in wealthy homes (above). Their plight was publicized by Charles Kingsley's *Water Babies*, and reformers such as Lord Shaftesbury campaigned for new labor laws.

IRONCLAD BATTLESHIPS

Britain kept a huge navy to protect and control an empire which spanned the world. Fast gunboats and powerful battleships – with armor-plated wooden hulls for protection – sailed to areas where there was conflict, defending British political and commercial interests wherever these were threatened.

HMS Warrior

Find out more

INDUSTRIAL REVOLUTION
TRANSPORTATION, HISTORY OF
UNITED KINGDOM, HISTORY OF

VIETNAM WAR

BETWEEN 1956 AND 1975 Vietnam was the scene of one of the most destructive wars in modern history. In 1954, Vietnam defeated French colonial forces and was divided into two countries – a Communist North and a non-Communist South Vietnam. The Viet Cong (Vietnamese Communists) rebelled against the South Vietnamese government and, helped by North Vietnam under Ho Chi Minh, fought to reunite the country. This brought in the United States, which believed that if Vietnam fell to the Communists, nearby countries would fall too. During the 1960s the United States poured troops and money into Vietnam, but found itself in an undeclared war it could not win. Despite intensive bombing and the latest military technology, the Viet Cong were better equipped and trained for jungle warfare. Casualties in Vietnam were appalling, and strong opposition to the war developed in the United States. A cease-fire was negotiated, and in 1973 all American troops were withdrawn. Two years later North Vietnam captured Saigon, capital of South Vietnam, and Vietnam was united as a Communist country.

VIETNAM
Vietnam is in Southeast Asia. The war was fought in the jungles of South Vietnam and in the skies above North Vietnam. Viet Cong fighters received supplies from the North along the Ho Chi Minh trail. At the end of the war, the country was reunited with its capital at Hanoi. Saigon, the southern capital, was renamed Ho Chi Minh City.

TROOPS
The first American military personnel arrived in Vietnam during 1961 to advise the South Vietnamese government. By 1969 there were about 550,000 American troops in Vietnam.

DESTRUCTION
The lengthy fighting had a terrible effect on the people of Vietnam. Their fields were destroyed, their forests stripped of leaves, and their houses blown up, leaving them refugees. Thousands were killed, injured, or maimed.

COSTS
It is unlikely that the exact cost of the Vietnam war will ever be known, but in terms of lives lost, money spent, and bombs dropped, it was enormous. Both sides suffered huge casualties and emerged with seriously damaged economies.

The United States spent $150 billion on the war; there are no figures for what North Vietnam spent.

Four times as many bombs were dropped by the American Air Force on Vietnam than were dropped by British and American bombers on Germany during the whole of World War II.

More than one million South Vietnamese and between 500,000 and one million North Vietnamese died in the war; over 58,000 American service people lost their lives.

The US Air Force bombed the jungle with chemicals to strip the leaves off the trees. Much of Vietnam is still deforested today.

Find out more

SOUTHEAST ASIA, HISTORY OF
UNITED STATES, HISTORY OF

VIKINGS

BETWEEN THE 8TH AND 12TH CENTURIES A.D., fierce warriors called Vikings terrorized the people of Europe, looking for loot. They came from Norway, Sweden, and Denmark, where the weather was cold and the soil was poor. At first they made lightning raids on coastal villages and isolated farms. They stole horses and food, captured prisoners for slaves, and robbed churches of their gold and silver. Later they conquered and settled in parts of England, France, Germany, Italy, and Russia. The Vikings were the finest shipbuilders of the time, and their swift, light boats could travel far from their homelands. They settled in Iceland and Greenland and were the first Europeans to reach North America. Although they are chiefly remembered for their conquests, most Nordic people lived peacefully in small settlements and worked as farmers, merchants, and craftworkers.

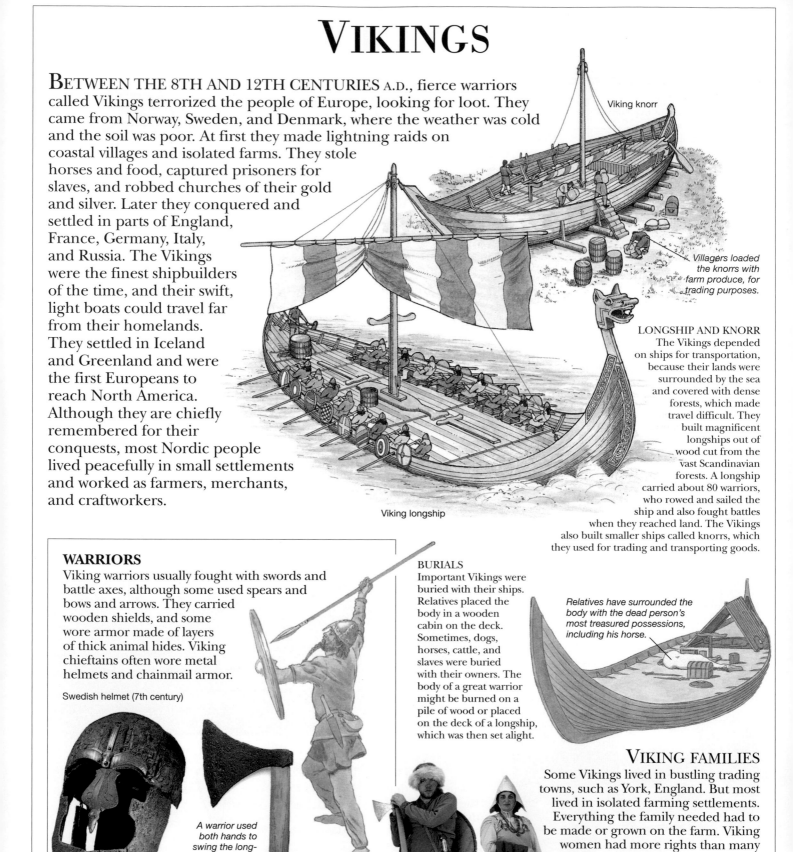

Viking knorr

Villagers loaded the knorrs with farm produce, for trading purposes.

Viking longship

LONGSHIP AND KNORR
The Vikings depended on ships for transportation, because their lands were surrounded by the sea and covered with dense forests, which made travel difficult. They built magnificent longships out of wood cut from the vast Scandinavian forests. A longship carried about 80 warriors, who rowed and sailed the ship and also fought battles when they reached land. The Vikings also built smaller ships called knorrs, which they used for trading and transporting goods.

WARRIORS
Viking warriors usually fought with swords and battle axes, although some used spears and bows and arrows. They carried wooden shields, and some wore armor made of layers of thick animal hides. Viking chieftains often wore metal helmets and chainmail armor.

Swedish helmet (7th century)

A warrior used both hands to swing the long-handled battle ax at an enemy.

The sword was a Viking's most important weapon.

BURIALS
Important Vikings were buried with their ships. Relatives placed the body in a wooden cabin on the deck. Sometimes, dogs, horses, cattle, and slaves were buried with their owners. The body of a great warrior might be burned on a pile of wood or placed on the deck of a longship, which was then set alight.

Relatives have surrounded the body with the dead person's most treasured possessions, including his horse.

VIKING FAMILIES
Some Vikings lived in bustling trading towns, such as York, England. But most lived in isolated farming settlements. Everything the family needed had to be made or grown on the farm. Viking women had more rights than many other European women of the time. For instance, they were allowed to get divorced if they wished.

Find out more
NORMANS
SCANDINAVIA, HISTORY OF

VOLCANOES

LIVING IN THE SHADOW of a volcano can be a source of constant fear. An active volcano can erupt with little warning: smoke and hot ash billow from the crater at the volcano's summit, and red-hot lava flows down the slopes, setting fire to everything in its path. Volcanoes are caused by the movement of vast slabs of rock, called plates, in the Earth's surface. When the plates collide or spread apart, molten rock from deep underground is forced to the surface, at or near the place where the plates meet. There are about 850 active volcanoes in the world. Most lie in a belt called the Ring of Fire, which surrounds the Pacific Ocean. Volcanoes also occur in the ocean, where they form underwater mountains, or islands such as Hawaii.

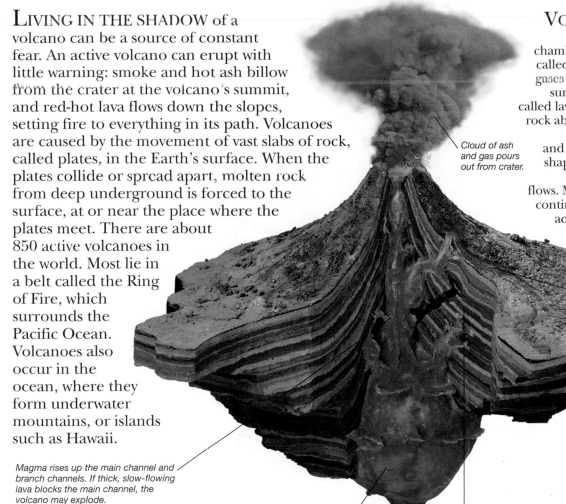

Cloud of ash and gas pours out from crater.

Magma rises up the main channel and branch channels. If thick, slow-flowing lava blocks the main channel, the volcano may explode.

Magma chamber forms deep underground.

Volcano builds up with layers of ash and solidified lava.

Red-hot lava flows down side of volcano.

Earth's crust is formed of layers of different kinds of rock. Close to the center of the Earth, the intense heat melts the rock.

VOLCANIC ERUPTIONS

A volcano lies over a deep chamber of red-hot, molten rock, called magma. Pressure from hot gases forces the magma up to the surface. The molten rock, now called lava, melts a hole through the rock above and flows out. Layers of lava and volcanic ash cool and solidify, building up a cone-shaped mountain with a central channel through which lava flows. Most volcanoes do not erupt continuously. Between eruptions, active volcanoes are said to be dormant. Extinct volcanoes are those that are no longer active.

MAGMA
A volcano's shape depends on the magma it produces. Thick magma produces a steep cone; runny magma results in a flattened, shieldlike volcano. Some volcano cones are made only of ash.

LAVA
Molten rock which has escaped to the Earth's surface is called lava. A bubbling lake of molten rock fills the crater of the volcano, and fountains of fiery lava leap high into the air. Glowing streams of lava pour out of the crater and flow down the sides of the volcano like rivers of fire. The lava has a temperature of about 2,000°F (1,100°C), which is hot enough to melt steel.

PUMICE
Lava containing bubbles of gas hardens to form a rock called pumice, which is peppered with tiny holes. The holes make pumice very light; it is the only rock that can float in water.

POMPEII
In A.D. 79, Mount Vesuvius in Italy erupted, burying the Roman city of Pompeii and its inhabitants in a deep layer of hot ash. Archaeologists have now uncovered Pompeii, much of which is well preserved. The bodies of victims left hollows in the ash; the plaster cast below is made from such a hollow and shows the last moments of one victim. Vesuvius last erupted in 1944. It could erupt again at any time. One of the greatest of all volcanic disasters occurred when the island of Krakatoa, Indonesia, exploded in 1883.

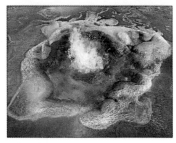

GEYSERS
A jet of boiling water which suddenly shoots up from the ground is called a geyser. Hot rock deep below the surface heats water in an underground chamber so that it boils. Steam forces the water out in a jet. When the chamber refills and heats up, the geyser blows again.

Find out more
CONTINENTS
EARTHQUAKES
GEOLOGY
MOUNTAINS
ROCKS AND MINERALS

WARSHIPS

IN A MODERN NAVY, there are several different types of warships, each designed to carry out a special function. The largest warship is the aircraft carrier, which is like a floating runway more than 1,000 ft (300 m) long that acts as a base for up to 100 aircraft. Battleships are heavily armored warships equipped with powerful guns that can fire shells over distances of about 20 miles (30 km). Other warships include destroyers for protecting fleets of ships; frigates, which are usually armed with missiles; mine-sweepers for clearing mines; and small coastal-protection vessels. The role of the warship has changed with the invention of nuclear arms. One of its most important functions is the ability to locate and attack missile-carrying submarines. Thus, warships increasingly rely on advanced electronic equipment to detect their targets, and are armed with an array of guided missiles and guns.

FRIGATE

A frigate is a light, fast, medium-sized warship, that is particularly useful for escorting other ships. Frigates carry equipment for seeking submarines, anti-ship missiles for defense against other warships, and an array of anti-aircraft weapons.

Cross-section of British-built Type 22 frigate

Radar for detecting enemy aircraft

Anti-aircraft missiles

Main living quarters for crew of about 250

Captain commands the ship from the bridge.

Ship's helicopter, used for reconnaissance (scouting), transport, rescue work, and anti-submarine warfare

Anti-aircraft missiles with a range of about 3 miles (5 km)

Hull made of aluminum, which is lighter than steel and makes the frigate faster and more maneuverable

Twin gas-turbine engines capable of producing a top speed of 35 mph (55 km/h) with a range of about 5,200 miles (8,300 km)

Control room, from where all weapons are fired and guided

The first modern battleship was the British Navy Dreadnought, which was introduced in 1906. The Dreadnought was armed with heavy guns and protected by thick steel armor.

Anti-ship missiles, for use against enemy warships up to 20 miles (32 km) away

HISTORY OF WARSHIPS

The first true warships were the galleys of Ancient Greece and Rome, which used oars and sails for propulsion. Major leaps forward came with the invention of the cannon, steam power, and the use of steel in shipbuilding. During World War I (1914-18) and World War II (1941-45), warships developed into huge, heavily armed battleships, the forerunners of today's warship.

The heavily armed galleon was developed by the Spanish in the early 15th century and used in their voyages of conquest in the Americas and Asia.

During the 9th century, Viking warriors used longships to travel from their homelands in Scandinavia to conquer countries of northern Europe.

The trireme, or Roman galley, of 200 B.C. had three banks of oars. The pointed beak at the prow (front) of the ship allowed it to ram enemy vessels.

MODERN WARSHIPS

Many warships now carry missiles as well as guns. Warships have various types of missile. Some are used as a defense against aircraft. Other types of missile can attack enemy warships, which may be so distant that they are visible only on a radar screen.

Find out more
NAVIES
ROCKETS AND MISSILES
SUBMARINES
WEAPONS
WORLD WAR I
WORLD WAR II

GEORGE
WASHINGTON

1732 Born in Westmoreland, Virginia.

1759-74 Member of the Virginia legislature.

1775-81 Leads Continental forces in the Revolution.

1787 Helps draft the Constitution of the United States of America.

1789 Chosen as first president of the United States.

1793 Elected to second term as president.

1797 Retires as president.

1799 Dies at Mount Vernon.

"THE FATHER OF HIS COUNTRY" was a nickname that George Washington earned many times over. First, he led the American forces to victory against the British in the American Revolution, then he served the American people again as the first president of the United States. As a military leader, he was capable and strong-willed. Even when the British seemed set to win the war, Washington did not give up hope and continued to encourage the American troops. As president, he was an energetic leader who used his great prestige to unite the new nation. Yet, despite his many personal strengths, Washington was an unlikely figure to lead a revolution. He was born into a wealthy family and trained as a surveyor before serving in the local militia. He could have had a brilliant military career, but at the age of 27 he returned to farming in Virginia. He did the same at the end of the Revolution, and only went back to national politics in 1787 because he felt the country needed his help once more.

VICTORY AT TRENTON
On Christmas night, 1776, George Washington led his troops across the icy Delaware River and attacked the British in Trenton, New Jersey, before they had time to prepare themselves for battle. The surprise attack did much to increase American morale at the start of the Revolution.

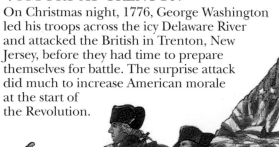
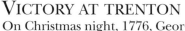

Troops had to break the ice in order to make their way across the river.

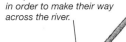

CONTINENTAL CONGRESS
In 1774, the 13 British colonies in North America set up a Continental Congress to protest against unfair British rule. George Washington was one of the delegates from Virginia. Although the Congress favored reaching an agreement with Britain, fighting broke out between the two sides in 1775. The Congress raised an army under Washington and on July 4, 1776, issued the Declaration of Independence. Peace was declared in 1781 and the Congress became the national government of the newly formed United States of America. In 1789 it was abolished and a new government structure was established.

MOUNT VERNON
Built in 1743, Mount Vernon was the home of George Washington for more than 50 years. The wooden house overlooks the Potomac River near Alexandria, Virginia, and is now a museum dedicated to Washington.

Find out more

AMERICAN REVOLUTION
CONSTITUTION
UNITED STATES, HISTORY OF

WATER

WE ARE SURROUNDED by water. More than 70 percent of the Earth's surface is covered by vast oceans and seas. In addition, 10 percent of the land – an area the size of South America – is covered by water in the form of ice. However, little new water is ever made on Earth. The rain that falls from the sky has fallen billions of times before, and will fall billions of times again. It runs down the land to the sea, evaporates (changes into vapor) into the clouds, and falls again as rain in an endless cycle. Water has a huge effect on our planet and its inhabitants. All plants and animals need water to survive; life itself began in the Earth's prehistoric seas. Seas and rivers shape the land over thousands of years, cutting cliffs and canyons; icy glaciers dig out huge valleys. Water is also essential to people in homes and factories and on farms.

The force of surface tension holds water molecules together so that they form small, roughly spherical drops.

SURFACE TENSION

The surface of water seems to be like an elastic skin. You can see this if you watch tiny insects, such as water striders, walking on water – their feet make hollows in the surface of the water, but the insects do not sink. This "skin" effect is called surface tension. It is caused by the attraction of water molecules to each other. Surface tension has another important effect: it causes water to form drops.

Molecules at the surface have other molecules pulling on them only from below. This means there is a force pulling on this top layer of molecules, keeping them under tension like a stretched elastic band.

In the body of the liquid, each water molecule is surrounded by others, so the forces on them balance out.

WATER FOR LIFE

All plants and animals, including humans, are made largely of water and depend on water for life. For instance, more than two thirds of the human body is water. To replace water lost by urinating, sweating, and breathing, we must drink water every day to stay healthy. No one can survive more than four days without water.

ICE

Water freezes when the temperature drops below 32°F (0°C). Water expands, or takes up more space, as it freezes. Water pipes sometimes burst in very cold winters as the water inside freezes and expands.

STATES OF WATER

Pure water is a compound of two common elements, hydrogen and oxygen. In each water molecule there are two hydrogen atoms and one oxygen atom; scientists represent this by writing H_2O. Water is usually in a liquid state, but it can also be a solid or a gas. If left standing, water slowly evaporates and turns into water vapor, an invisible gas. When water is cooled down enough, it freezes solid and turns to ice.

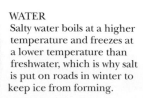

WATER

Salty water boils at a higher temperature and freezes at a lower temperature than freshwater, which is why salt is put on roads in winter to keep ice from forming.

WATER VAPOR

Water boils at 212°F (100°C). At this temperature it evaporates so rapidly that water vapor forms bubbles in the liquid. Water vapor is invisible; visible clouds of steam are not water vapor but tiny droplets of water formed when the hot vapor hits cold air.

Water falls as rain and is collected in lakes and reservoirs.

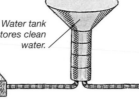

Water is cleaned in a treatment plant.

Water tank stores clean water.

Once the water is treated, it is pumped up into a high tank, ready to be used.

With the water high above the ground, the faucet can be turned on so the water runs out.

WATER TREATMENT
Water in a reservoir is usually not fit to drink. It must pass through a treatment center which removes germs and other harmful substances. Chlorine gas is often dissolved into the water to kill bacteria and viruses. In addition, the water is stored in huge basins so that pieces of dirt sink to the bottom; filters made of stones and sand remove any remaining particles.

Water can provide an unlimited supply of power, unlike underground resources such as coal and gas.

HYDROELECTRIC POWER
People have used water as a source of power for more than 2,000 years. Today, water is used to produce electricity in hydroelectric (water-driven) power stations. Hydroelectric power stations are often built inside dams. Water from a huge lake behind the dam flows down pipes. The moving water spins turbines which drive generators and produce electricity. Hydroelectric power produces electricity without causing pollution or using scarce resources.

SOLUTIONS
Pure water is rarely found in nature because water dissolves other substances to form mixtures called solutions. For example, seawater is salty because there are many minerals dissolved in it. Water solutions are vital to life; blood plasma, for instance, is a water solution.

Sugar dissolves in water, making a sweet-tasting sugar solution.

The sugar disappears when it is completely dissolved.

If three identical holes are drilled in the side of a water-filled container, water spurts out much farther from the lowest hole because of the weight of the water above.

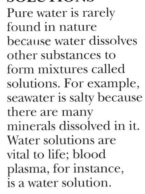

WATER PRESSURE
Water rushes out of a faucet because it is under pressure; that is, it is pushed from behind. Pressure is produced by pumps that force water along using pistons or blades like those on a ship's propeller. Water pressure is also created by the sheer weight of water above. The deeper the water, the greater the pressure. If you dive into a pool, you can feel the water pressure pushing on your eardrums.

POLLUTION AND DROUGHT
In many places, such as East Africa, there is insufficient rain and constant drought. Plants cannot grow, and people and animals must fight a constant battle for survival. Fresh, clean water can also be difficult to obtain even in places with lots of rain. This is because waste from cities and factories pollutes the water, making it unsafe to drink.

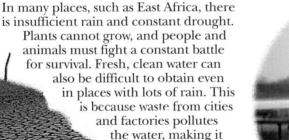

Fire fighters connect their hoses to fire engines which contain powerful pumps. The pumps increase the pressure so that the water can reach flames high up in buildings.

Underground water supplies exist below the surface of the Earth. After a drought, these supplies dry out; it may take years for them to be refilled.

Find out more
ELECTRICITY
HEAT
LAKES
OCEANS AND SEAS
RAIN AND SNOW
RIVERS

WATER SPORTS

SPLASHING AROUND IN WATER – whether swimming, diving, surfing, or just floating on your back – is one of the most enjoyable ways of relaxing and keeping in shape. Water sports are fun for people of all ages: even babies can learn to swim. And for the elderly or people with disabilities, swimming provides a gentle yet vigorous way to exercise. Swimming became popular for fitness and recreation with ancient peoples in Egypt, Greece, and then Rome. Swimming races began in the 19th century and were included in the first Olympics, in 1896. Like swimming, surfing and water-skiing take place on the surface of the water. Scuba divers, however, dive deep below the waves. They can stay underwater for an hour or more by breathing air from cylinders on their backs. Snorkelers swim to a depth of about 30 ft (9 m) with just a face mask, flippers, and a snorkel, or breathing tube.

Diver twists in midair.

Straightening out as he descends

The body should enter the water straight, with legs, arms, and hands extended.

There are three types of competitive water-skiing: slalom, jumping, and trick-skiing.

WATER POLO

In water polo, seven players on each side try to throw the ball into their opponents' goal. The playing area measures 98 ft by 66 ft (30 m by 20 m). Only the goalkeeper may hold the ball with both hands.

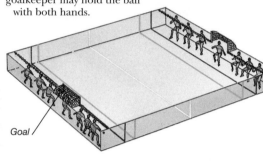

Goal

WATER-SKIING
A fast powerboat tows waterskiers along at the end of a rope. Skiers can cross from side to side behind the boat, and can jump through the air by skiing up a ramp in the water.

DIVING
In diving competitions, judges award points for technique as each competitor performs a series of dives. More difficult dives win higher points. Divers leap from a platform at 33 ft (10 m) above the water, and from a springboard at 10 ft (3 m).

Sail by which the board is steered

WHITEWATER RAFTING

Rowing in turbulent waters (or rapids) is a dangerous and thrilling sport because it takes extraordinary skill and agility to go over the water without tipping over. It has taken its name from the white foam that tips the waves of fast-flowing water. Whitewater rafts have to be light in order to stay afloat and navigate between rocks and sharp turns in the river, and are therefore made of inflated rubber.

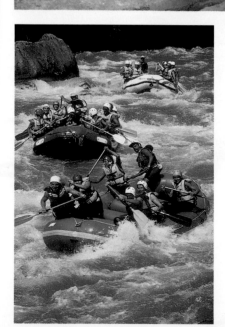

Surfer balances the craft.

WINDSURFING
Windsurfing, or sailboarding, began as a leisure activity in the 1960s and became a competitive Olympic event in 1984. The windsurfer balances the craft by holding on to a boom fixed around the sail. A daggerboard, or fin, on the underside of the board keeps the board upright in the water. There are several kinds of competition in the sport. These include racing around buoys, slalom races, and performing tricks of balance and dexterity.

Board on which surfer stands

Find out more
SAILING AND BOATING
SPORTS
SWIMMING
UNDERWATER EXPLORATION

WEAPONS

PREHISTORIC HUNTERS LEARNED that they could kill their prey more quickly and safely with a stone knife than with their bare hands. This crude weapon later became refined into the dagger and the sword. Both are members of a group of weapons we now call sidearms. However, an even less dangerous way to hunt was to use missile weapons. By throwing rocks or spears, early hunters could disable wild beasts and human enemies alike from a distance. Simple changes to a missile weapon made it much more effective: with slingshots or bows and arrows, hunters could hit smaller, more distant targets. Since these early times, better technology has greatly increased the range and accuracy of weapons. Seven centuries ago the invention of gunpowder made possible much more powerful weapons. Gunpowder launched bullets and cannonballs much faster than an arrow could fly. Muskets and cannons were thus more deadly than bows, and quickly came to dominate the battlefield. Modern developments have increased both power and range still farther. Today, nuclear weapons can destroy, in seconds, a whole city on the other side of the world.

Spears could be thrown or used for stabbing.

Boomerangs return to the thrower if they miss their target.

Even simple bows can shoot arrows great distances.

Some fighting axes were made to be thrown.

The weighted ropes of the bolas wrap around an animal's legs and trip it up.

Powerful crossbows were even more deadly and accurate than simple bows.

Medieval dagger made about 1400

SWORDS

Armed with swords, warriors could inflict injuries at a greater distance than with daggers or knives. The earliest swords were made in about 1500 B.C., when bronzeworking first developed. Later swords were made of iron and steel. Many different types evolved. Some were for thrusting, others for cutting. Today, pistols have replaced swords in close combat, but the sword still has a role to play. It is used as a symbol of power in military ceremonies, in courts of law, and in governments.

SAMURAI DAGGER
Very high-quality steel was used for Samurai weapons such as this dagger. It took craftworkers many hours to produce them.

RAPIER
Around 1580, a new type of sword, called the rapier, was invented. It was long and thin and was used for thrusting.

BRONZE AGE SWORD
Shaping the sword so that it was wider near the end of the blade made it more effective as a slashing weapon. The handle of this Bronze Age sword would have been wrapped in leather.

SAMURAI WARRIORS

Swordfighting and archery were the two most important skills of the Samurai warriors of Japan. These warriors first appeared in the 12th century as private armies of landowners. They became very powerful, and the shogun, head of all the Samurai warlords, controlled Japan for the next seven centuries.

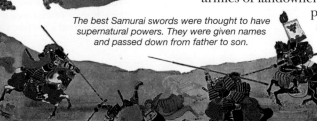

The best Samurai swords were thought to have supernatural powers. They were given names and passed down from father to son.

ARROWS

A well-made arrow must be perfectly straight and have the right weight and flexibility. The tip shape depends on the arrow's use.

Broad arrowhead for hunting

Narrow arrowhead for piercing armor

BOWS AND ARROWS

Before the invention of gunpowder the most powerful missile weapon was the bow and arrow. The springy wood of the bow stored the archer's energy as he gradually drew the string; letting go of the string released the energy and propelled the arrow farther and more accurately than it could be thrown by hand. Cave paintings created more than 10,000 years ago show hunters using simple bows.

How archers grip string and arrow

CROSSBOW

The crossbow was a short, very powerful bow mounted on a wooden "stock." Some crossbows were so strong that the archer needed a winch to draw the string. A catch held the string back while the archer loaded a short arrow, called a bolt, and took aim. Pulling a trigger fired the weapon.

Native American arrows from about 1800

SHORT AND LONG BOWS

Early bows were very short. Native Americans used bows that were about 3.5 ft (1 m) long. The powerful English longbow of the 14th to 16th centuries was as long as the archer was tall.

CANNONS

The cannon is a large or heavy gun usually mounted on wheels. Lighting the charge of gunpowder at the closed end of a cannon caused a mighty explosion. The strong tube of the cannon directed the explosion forward, hurling the stone or iron ball 1 mile (1.5 km) or more. Later, explosive shells replaced the simple ball.

Wadding holds ball and charge in place.

Fuse for lighting charge

Cannonballs ready for loading

Damp rags put out sparks.

Cannonball

Explosive charge

Rammer forces charge into barrel.

Screw removes unburned powder.

MODERN WEAPONS

The grenade is a small explosive bomb which is set on a time fuse and thrown at the enemy. Modern soldiers are also armed with machine guns, which fire many bullets in rapid succession without the need for reloading. More sophisticated and powerful weapons used today include nuclear missiles, rockets, and explosive mines.

Percussion cap

Grenade is safe until this ring is pulled.

Explosive charge

Throwing the grenade releases this lever.

As the lever rises, it frees a hammer.

The hammer strikes a percussion cap.

The cap lights a short fuse.

The grenade explodes after a few seconds when the fuse burns down to the charge.

Cast-iron body

THE NUCLEAR DETERRENT

A single nuclear weapon can kill the population of an entire city, and a nuclear war might destroy all life on Earth. Some politicians call these weapons the nuclear deterrent. They believe that the terrible results of nuclear war discourage or deter a nation from launching a nuclear attack.

Nuclear weapons create an extremely powerful blast, searing heat, and lethal nuclear radiation.

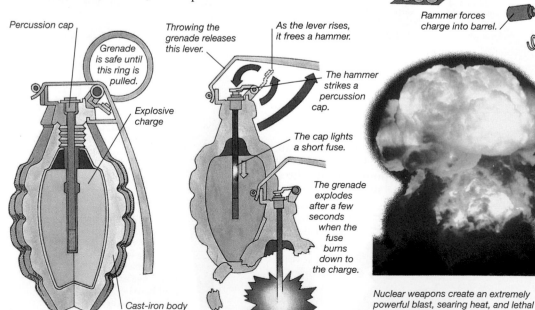

Find out more

ARMIES
ARMOR
GUNS
NUCLEAR AGE
ROCKETS AND MISSILES

WEASELS,
STOATS, AND MARTENS

WITH THEIR SHARP TEETH and agile bodies, weasels, stoats, and martens are excellent hunters. These fierce, lean predators are speedy and muscular, ideally suited to chasing prey into tight spaces. Their eyesight and hearing are good, and they have a keen sense of smell to pick up the scent of their victim. Their teeth are pointed for gripping their prey. Weasels, stoats, and martens can leap and twist their bodies with great ease as they chase after mice, rabbits, and birds. Of the three animals, the weasel is the smallest – the smallest weasel, measuring only 8 in (20 cm) in length, can kill rabbits, which are much larger than itself. The stoat, also called the ermine, resembles the weasel in shape. Martens also look like weasels; they have thick brown fur with a yellowish patch on the chest. Weasels, stoats, and martens all belong to the family of animals called mustelids. This family includes polecats (or ferrets), mink, skunks, badgers, otters, and wolverines. Most of them raise their young in burrows. After a few weeks, the young leave the burrow to pounce and tumble in mock play, practicing for their lives as hunters.

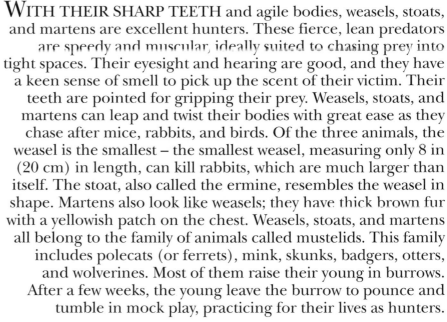

MARTEN
Although it hunts mainly on the ground, the pine marten is a skillful climber. It is so nimble in the treetops that it can easily catch a squirrel. Pine martens hunt beetles, mice, birds' eggs and chicks, and also eat berries.

STOAT
During the spring and summer months, stoats are brown like weasels. In winter, however, their coats change color to white, and this coat is known as ermine. In the coldest parts of northern Europe, North America, and Asia the stoat's white fur provides good camouflage as the animal hunts rabbits, lemmings, and mice in the snow. Like other members of the weasel family, stoats steal birds' eggs and raid chicken coops in search of eggs.

MINK
With their partly webbed feet and supple bodies measuring 16 to 20 in (40 to 50 cm) in length, mink are expert swimmers and divers. They live on the banks of rivers and lakes, where they feed on water birds, water voles, and fish. Many mink have been killed for their beautiful fur, and in some areas they are bred for this purpose.

Mink

POLECAT
The polecat is also called the ferret. There are three kinds – the European polecat, the steppe polecat, and the black-footed ferret from North America. Black-footed ferrets are on the official list of endangered species. They are threatened because their main source of food – the prairie dog – has been greatly reduced in numbers.

Markings on face enable ferrets to recognize one another.

Lithe, muscular body

Sharp claws for digging and for catching prey

Black-footed ferret

COMMON WEASEL
With its long, thin body and short legs, the European common weasel can dart into a rabbit burrow or rat tunnel to grab its prey. Weasels are so long and slender and flexible that they can easily perform a U-turn in a rabbit burrow. Weasels are fierce hunters, ripping a mouse or vole apart within seconds in a flurry of teeth and claws.

The weasel sniffs around a tunnel entrance in search of prey such as young rabbits.

Common weasel

When it finds a victim such as a rabbit, the weasel gives it a fatal bite to the back of the neck.

Find out more
ANIMALS
BADGERS AND SKUNKS
CONSERVATION
and endangered species
MAMMALS
RABBITS AND HARES

WEATHER

WEATHER DESCRIBES CONDITIONS, such as rain, wind, and sunshine, that occur during a short period of time in a particular place; climate is the overall pattern of weather in a region. From one moment to the next the weather can change. A warm, sunny day can be overtaken by a violent storm. Dark clouds form, high winds blow, and rain lashes the ground, yet it may be only a few minutes before the sunny weather returns. However, in some parts of the world, such as the tropics, the weather barely changes for months at a time. There it is always hot, and heavy rains fall.

Meteorologists are scientists who measure and forecast the weather. They do this by studying clouds, winds, and the temperature and pressure of the Earth's atmosphere. But despite the use of satellites, computers, and other technology in weather forecasting, weather remains a force of nature that is hard to predict.

The air over the Sahara Desert is so stable and dry that rain seldom falls.

Clouds hang over the hot and rainy tropics of Central Africa.

Swirls of cloud mark patterns of winds.

Snow and ice cover the cold Antarctic continent.

WORLD WEATHER
The Sun is the driving force for the world's weather. The heat of the Sun's rays produces wind and evaporates water from the seas, which later forms clouds and rain. The direct heat above the equator makes the weather hot, while the poles, which get less of the Sun's heat, are cold and cloudy.

A scale of hours on the recorder shows at what times the Sun was shining.

SUNSHINE RECORDER
The more direct sunshine a region receives, the warmer it becomes. An instrument called a sunshine recorder measures daily hours of sunshine. The glass ball works like a powerful lens, focusing the Sun's rays, which leave a line of burn marks on a piece of cardboard.

MEASURING THE WEATHER
Several thousand weather stations on land, ships, and aircraft measure weather conditions around the world. The stations contain instruments that record temperature, rainfall, the speed and direction of wind, air pressure, and humidity (the amount of water vapor in the air). Balloons called radiosondes carry instruments to take measurements high in the air. Weather satellites in space send back pictures of the clouds.

The wind spins the cups, and the wind speed is shown on a dial.

Rain pours through a funnel into a container. After every 24 hours the collected water is poured into a measuring cylinder that gives a reading of the day's total rainfall.

Barograph gives a permanent record of air pressure on a chart.

ANEMOMETER
The Sun's heat produces winds – moving currents of air that flow over the Earth's surface. Meteorologists use anemometers to measure wind speed, which shows the rate of approaching weather.

RAIN GAUGE
Droplets of water and tiny ice crystals group together to form clouds, and water falls from the skies as rain and snow. Meteorologists measure rainfall, which is the depth of water that would occur if the rain did not drain away.

BAROGRAPH
A barograph measures air pressure. This is important in weather forecasting because high pressure often brings settled weather; low pressure brings wind and rain.

CLOUDS

Low-lying clouds at the top of a hill cause the air to become cold, foggy, and damp. This is because the clouds contain many tiny droplets of water. Clouds form in air that is rising. The air contains invisible water vapor. As the air ascends, it becomes cooler. Colder air cannot hold so much vapor, and some vapor turns to tiny droplets or freezes to ice crystals, forming a cloud. Slow-rising air produces sheets of cloud. Air that is ascending quickly forms clumps of cloud.

CLOUD FORMATION

There are three main kinds of clouds, that form at different heights in the air. Feathery cirrus clouds float highest of all. Midway to low are fluffy cumulus clouds. Sheets of stratus clouds often lie low in the sky; gray stratus bears rain. Cumulonimbus cloud, a type of cumulus cloud, towers in the sky and often brings thunderstorms.

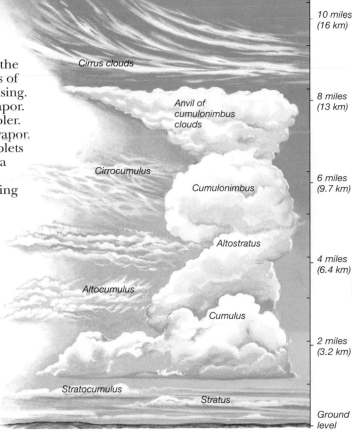

Cirrus clouds

Anvil of cumulonimbus clouds

Cirrocumulus

Cumulonimbus

Altostratus

Altocumulus

Cumulus

Stratocumulus

Stratus

10 miles (16 km)

8 miles (13 km)

6 miles (9.7 km)

4 miles (6.4 km)

2 miles (3.2 km)

Ground level

CIRRUS CLOUDS

Cirrus clouds form high in the sky so they contain only ice crystals. Cirrocumulus (above) and cirrostratus also form at high altitudes.

CUMULUS CLOUDS

Separate masses of cloud are called cumulus clouds. Altocumulus is medium-high patchy cloud, and low stratocumulus contains low, dense clumps of cloud.

AIR MASSES AND FRONTS

Huge bodies of air, called air masses, form over land and sea. Air masses containing warm, cold, moist, or dry air bring different kinds of weather as they are carried by the wind. A front is where two air masses meet. The weather changes when a front arrives.

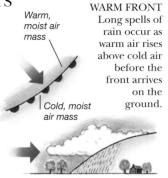

Warm, moist air mass

Cold, moist air mass

WARM FRONT

Long spells of rain occur as warm air rises above cold air before the front arrives on the ground.

COLD FRONT

Cold air moves in under warm air, bringing heavy rain followed by showers.

Cold air mass

Warm air mass

OCCLUDED FRONT

A cold front overtakes a warm front, lifting warm air above it. Rain also falls along an occluded front.

Cold air mass

Warm air mass

Cold air mass

WEATHER FORECASTING

The weather centers in different countries receive measurements of weather conditions from satellites and observers around the world. They use this data to forecast the weather that lies ahead. Supercomputers do the many difficult calculations involved and draw charts of the weather to come. Forecasters use the charts to predict the weather for the next few days, producing weather reports for television, newspapers, shipping, and aircraft.

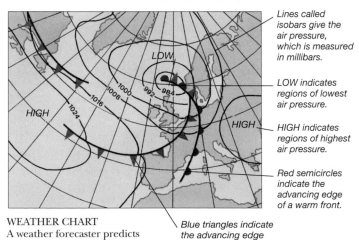

LOW

HIGH

HIGH

1000
1008
1016
1024
992
984

Lines called isobars give the air pressure, which is measured in millibars.

LOW indicates regions of lowest air pressure.

HIGH indicates regions of highest air pressure.

Red semicircles indicate the advancing edge of a warm front.

Blue triangles indicate the advancing edge of a cold front.

HIGHS AND LOWS

The pressure of the air varies from time to time and from place to place. Regions of low pressure are called cyclones or lows. The air rises and cools, bringing clouds and rain. An anticyclone, or high, is a region of high pressure. The air descends and warms, bringing clear, dry weather. Winds circle around highs and lows, as can be seen in this satellite picture of a cyclonic storm.

WEATHER CHART

A weather forecaster predicts the day's weather using a chart showing air pressure and fronts over a large region. Lines called isobars connect regions with the same atmospheric pressure. Tight loops of isobars of decreasing pressure show a low, where it is windy and possibly rainy. Isobars of rising pressure indicate a high, which gives settled weather.

Find out more
ATMOSPHERE
CLIMATES
EARTH
RAIN AND SNOW
STORMS
WIND

WEIGHTS AND MEASURES

HOW FAR AWAY is the moon? How deep are the oceans? How tall are you? How hot is it on Mars? It is possible to measure all of these things and many more. Every day we need to make measurements. In cooking, for example, a recipe requires the correct weight of each ingredient, and once mixed, the ingredients have to be cooked at a certain temperature. We make measurements using measuring instruments. For example, a thermometer measures temperature, a ruler measures distance, and a clock measures time. All measurements are based on a system of units. Time, for example, is measured in units of minutes and seconds; length is measured in feet or meters. Precise measurements are very important in science and medicine. Scientists have extremely accurate measuring instruments to determine everything from the tiny distance between atoms in a piece of metal, to the temperature of a distant planet, such as Neptune.

Scale pan carries fixed weights in units of ounces or grams.

WEIGHT
Weighing scales measure how heavy things are. They compare the weight of an object in one pan with a known weight that sits in the other pan.

VOLUME
Volume measures the amount of space that an object or liquid takes up. A measuring jug measures the volume of a liquid. By reading the level of the liquid against a scale of units, you can find the volume of the liquid in the jug.

Thermometers measure temperature.

LENGTH AND AREA
Tape measures and rulers indicate length. They can also be used to calculate area, which indicates, for example, the amount of land a football field takes up or the amount of material needed to make a coat.

We can also measure things that we cannot see. This digital meter measures the strength of an electric current in amperes (A).

UNITS OF MEASUREMENT
When you measure something, such as height, you compare the quantity you are measuring to a fixed unit such as a foot or a meter. Scientists have set these units with great precision, so that if you measure your height with two different rulers, you will get the same answer. The meter, for example, is defined (set) by the distance traveled by light in a specific time. This gives a very precise measure of length.

TIME
Time is measured in hours, minutes, and seconds. A digital stopwatch can measure the time of a race to the nearest hundredth of a second.

METRIC SYSTEM
A system of measurement defines fixed units for quantities such as weight and time. Most countries use the metric system, which was developed in France about 200 years ago. Then the meter was fixed as the 10-millionth part of the distance between the North Pole and the equator. The meter is now fixed using the speed of light.

IMPERIAL SYSTEM
Units of the imperial system include inches and feet for length, pints and gallons for volume, and pounds and tons for weight. The imperial system is used mainly in the U.S.

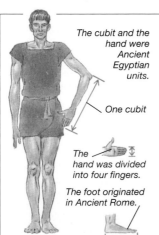

The cubit and the hand were Ancient Egyptian units.

One cubit

The hand was divided into four fingers.

The foot originated in Ancient Rome.

BODY MEASUREMENTS
The earliest systems of units were based on parts of the human body, such as the hands or feet. Both the Ancient Egyptians (about 3000 B.C.) and the Romans (from about 800 B.C.) used units of this kind. However, body measurements present a problem. They always give different answers because they depend on the size of the person making the measurement.

Many imperial units were first used in Ancient Rome. The mile was 1,000 paces, each pace being two steps. The word mile comes from the word for 1,000 in Latin.

Find out more
CLOCKS AND WATCHES
EGYPT, ANCIENT
MATHEMATICS
ROMAN EMPIRE

WEST AFRICA

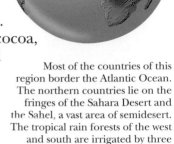

THE VARIED CLIMATES, landscapes, and resources of the countries of West Africa have attracted both traders and colonizers. Arabs operated trading caravans across the Sahara Desert, while the Europeans sought both West African slaves and gold. Today, most of the countries in this region are desperately poor, their problems made worse by corrupt governments, debt, and occasional civil wars. The vast majority of people live by farming. Coffee, cocoa, and oil palms are all cultivated in the humid tropical lowlands of the west and south, while cattle, sheep, and goats are herded by the nomads of the Sahel. Vast reserves of oil have been found in the Niger Delta and off Ivory Coast, and there is mineral wealth in both Mauritania and Sierra Leone, but these resources are still not having an impact on most peoples' daily lives.

Most of the countries of this region border the Atlantic Ocean. The northern countries lie on the fringes of the Sahara Desert and the Sahel, a vast area of semidesert. The tropical rain forests of the west and south are irrigated by three major rivers – the Niger, Volta, and Senegal.

PLANTAINS
Plantains are members of the banana family. They are cooked and mashed to make a staple food in many parts of tropical West Africa.

FISHING IN MAURITANIA
Two-thirds of Mauritania is covered by the Sahara Desert. Only one percent of the land, the area drained by the Senegal River, can be cultivated. However, Mauritania has some of the richest fishing grounds in the world. Many other nations fish there. Catches are sold through the state fishing company, and fishing provides over half of Mauritania's export earnings.

A Mauritanian fisherman uses a pole to carry his nets to the water's edge. Local fishing is small-scale and traditional.

SAHARA DESERT
The Sahara is spreading south, turning much of Mauritania, Mali, and Niger into desert. In Mauritania, 75 percent of grazing land has been lost in the past 25 years. Drought, cutting down trees for fuel, and overgrazing are all contributing to this process. When soil has no roots to cling to, the wind blows it away. Windbreaks of trees and shrubs are being planted in order to halt the desert's advance.

ISLAM
Many of the countries of West Africa are Islamic. The religion was spread by Arab traders, who controlled the great caravan trading routes across the Sahara from the 8th century. The rulers of the West African kingdoms adopted Islam from the 13th century. The Grand Mosque at Djenne, in Mali, is the largest mud-brick building in the world. It dates to the 14th century, but requires constant rebuilding.

The streets of Senegal's capital, Dakar, are lined with market stalls and street sellers. This busy, expanding port has a population of more than one million.

FARMING
Throughout West Africa, most people live by small-scale farming. In Senegal, the main crops that are grown for export include peanuts, cotton, and sugarcane. Rice, millet, and sorghum are staple foods. Many farmers travel regularly into local towns, or even Dakar, the capital city, to sell their excess produce. Most farmers rely on the flooding of the Senegal River to water their land. The damming of the river is disrupting this natural cycle.

The main dye used in this cloth is indigo, a blue color produced by pulping the leaves of the indigo vine.

The Wodaabe are nomadic cattle herders, who only come into towns for trading and festivals.

WODAABE PEOPLE

The nomadic Wodaabe people graze their herds along the Nigerian-Niger borderlands. Every year they hold a beauty contest in which the men compete for wives. Under the careful scrutiny of the women, they parade themselves in makeup which emphasizes their eyes and teeth.

NIGERIAN TEXTILES
The Yoruba and Hausa are the main ethnic groups in Nigeria. The Hausa are found in the north of the country, the traditionally city-dwelling Yoruba in the southwest. Both groups produce patterned textiles, hand-dyed using natural plant extracts.

DOWNTOWN LAGOS

Lagos is Nigeria's largest city, chief port, and until 1991, the country's capital. It developed as a major Portuguese slave center until it fell under British control in 1861. The city sprawls across the islands and sandbars of Lagos Lagoon, linked by a series of bridges. Most of the population is concentrated on Lagos Island. The southwest of the island, with its striking high-rise skyline, is the commercial, financial, and educational center of the city. Lagos is Nigeria's transportation hub; it is served by a major international airport, and is also the country's main outlet for exports. Lagos suffers from growing slums, traffic congestion, and overcrowding. Pollution is also a major problem.

BAMBUKU HEAD
In many parts of West Africa, traditional beliefs are still very much alive. Ancestors are worshiped, or called upon to cure sickness and help people in difficulties. Spirits are worshiped at rituals and ceremonies. In eastern Nigeria, the fierce expression on this Bambuku head is used to frighten away evil spirits. It is left in a small shelter at the entrance to the village.

NIGERIAN OIL

Since the 1970s, Nigeria has become dependent on its vast oil reserves in the Niger Delta. It is the tenth-largest producer in the world, and oil accounts for 90 percent of its exports. The Nigerian government has become over-dependent on oil; the country was once a major exporter of tropical fruits, but agriculture has declined. When world oil prices fell in the 1980s, Nigeria was forced to rely on financial assistance from the World Bank. There are also growing concerns about the pollution problems caused by the oil industry in the Niger Delta. Protesters have attacked Shell, one of the main companies operating in Nigeria.

The use of modern
equipment (left) in the
logging industry in
Ivory Coast is speeding
up the process
of deforestation.

LOGGING IN IVORY COAST

The tropical rain forests in the moist, humid
interior of Ivory Coast have suffered considerable
damage. Many trees have been cut down in order
to grow more profitable cocoa trees which thrive
in the tropical conditions. Cocoa beans are
transported to factories along the coast where
they are made into cocoa butter, an ingredient in
chocolates and some cosmetics. Exports are sent
through the port of Abidjan, once the capital
and now West Africa's main port.

AFRICAN GOLD
The gold of West Africa is found
underground, or as a fine dust
obtained by sifting soil in shallow
riverbeds. In the 19th century,
African gold produced great wealth
for European traders. In Asante,
Ghana, goldsmiths were a
privileged class. They created this
magnificent head, taken as loot
by the British in 1874.

The yield of
cocoa trees
(right) is very low.
An average fully-
grown tree bears
only 20 cocoa pods.

COCOA BEANS
Cocoa beans were first discovered by the
Aztec peoples of Mexico. They used the
seeds to make a drink called *chocolatl*, which
was exported to Europe by Spanish and
Portuguese colonists, where it became an
instant success. West Africa now produces over
half the world's supply of cocoa beans. Seeds are
sun-dried, fermented, roasted, and ground to make
cocoa butter.

TOURISM IN GAMBIA
Gambia is a narrow country,
clinging to the banks of the
Gambia River, and almost
entirely surrounded by
Senegal. Most people live
off the land, but increasing
numbers are moving to the
coast. Here, sandy beaches and
mild winters are attracting many
visitors from northern Europe.
Tourism is Gambia's fastest-growing industry.

Liberian refugees, who
have been driven away
from their homes by the
civil war, are forced to
live in makeshift shelters
(left) where they rely on
foreign aid for food
and medicine.

LIBERIAN REFUGEES

Liberia has never been colonized, making
it the oldest independent republic in Africa.
It was founded by Americans in the 1820s as
a refuge for Africans who had been freed
from slavery. The name Liberia means
"freed land." Descendants of the American
slaves mixed uneasily with the majority native
population. For many years, Liberia was a
devastated war zone, the result of violent
conflict between the country's ethnic groups,
which include the Kpelle, Bassa, and Kru
peoples. Homeless victims of the fighting
were forced to live in vast refugee camps,
where disease and food shortages were
common. In 2003, UN peacekeepers
entered the country, and the armed groups
have now largely been disbanded.

LAKE VOLTA
One of the largest artificial lakes in
the world, Lake Volta was formed by
the building of the Askosombo Dam
on Ghana's Volta River in 1965.
Some 78,000 people, living in 740
villages, were resettled when the dam
was built. The lake is a major fishing
ground, and also supplies water for
farmers. The hydroelectric dam
generates most of Ghana's power.

> ### Find out more
> AFRICA
> AFRICA, HISTORY OF
> AFRICAN WILDLIFE
> DESERTS
> VOLCANOES

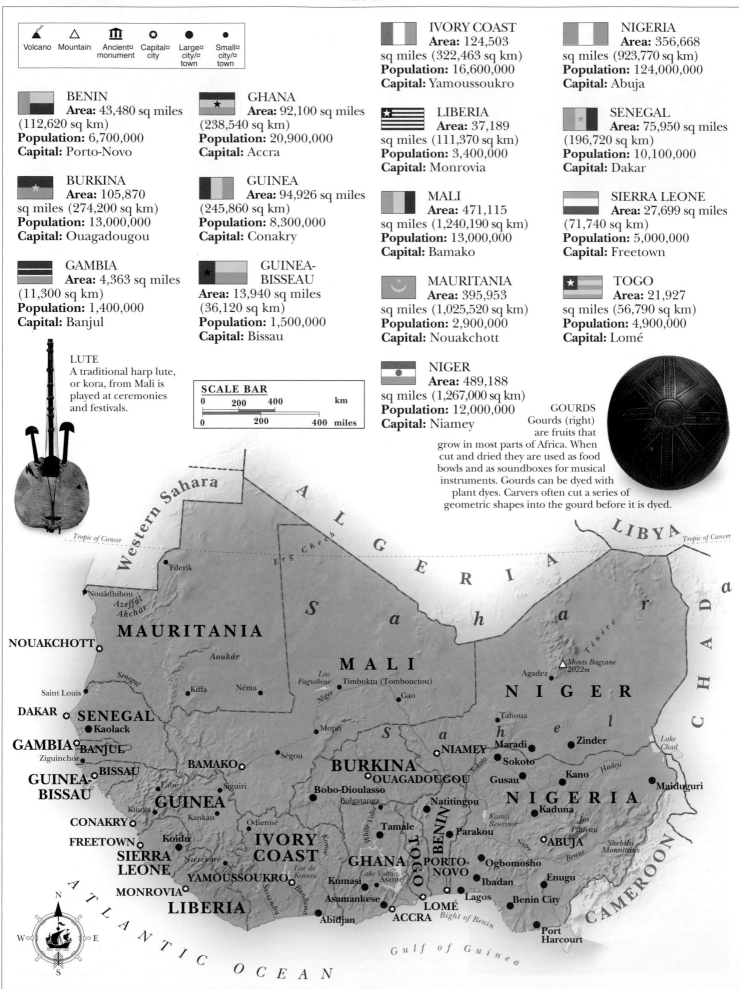

| Volcano | Mountain | Ancient monument | Capital city | Large city/ town | Small city/ town |

IVORY COAST
Area: 124,503 sq miles (322,463 sq km)
Population: 16,600,000
Capital: Yamoussoukro

NIGERIA
Area: 356,668 sq miles (923,770 sq km)
Population: 124,000,000
Capital: Abuja

BENIN
Area: 43,480 sq miles (112,620 sq km)
Population: 6,700,000
Capital: Porto-Novo

GHANA
Area: 92,100 sq miles (238,540 sq km)
Population: 20,900,000
Capital: Accra

LIBERIA
Area: 37,189 sq miles (111,370 sq km)
Population: 3,400,000
Capital: Monrovia

SENEGAL
Area: 75,950 sq miles (196,720 sq km)
Population: 10,100,000
Capital: Dakar

BURKINA
Area: 105,870 sq miles (274,200 sq km)
Population: 13,000,000
Capital: Ouagadougou

GUINEA
Area: 94,926 sq miles (245,860 sq km)
Population: 8,300,000
Capital: Conakry

MALI
Area: 471,115 sq miles (1,240,190 sq km)
Population: 13,000,000
Capital: Bamako

SIERRA LEONE
Area: 27,699 sq miles (71,740 sq km)
Population: 5,000,000
Capital: Freetown

GAMBIA
Area: 4,363 sq miles (11,300 sq km)
Population: 1,400,000
Capital: Banjul

GUINEA-BISSAU
Area: 13,940 sq miles (36,120 sq km)
Population: 1,500,000
Capital: Bissau

MAURITANIA
Area: 395,953 sq miles (1,025,520 sq km)
Population: 2,900,000
Capital: Nouakchott

TOGO
Area: 21,927 sq miles (56,790 sq km)
Population: 4,900,000
Capital: Lomé

LUTE
A traditional harp lute, or kora, from Mali is played at ceremonies and festivals.

NIGER
Area: 489,188 sq miles (1,267,000 sq km)
Population: 12,000,000
Capital: Niamey

SCALE BAR
0   200   400   km
0   200   400   miles

GOURDS
Gourds (right) are fruits that grow in most parts of Africa. When cut and dried they are used as food bowls and as soundboxes for musical instruments. Gourds can be dyed with plant dyes. Carvers often cut a series of geometric shapes into the gourd before it is dyed.

WESTERN EXPANSION

JUST ONE HUNDRED YEARS AGO, much of the western region of the United States was a wild and lawless place. Far from government control in Washington, the settlers in the West made their own law. The discovery of gold and silver made people rich overnight, providing temptation for outlaws. Gunfights were common, and life in the new towns was often violent. Native Americans, the original inhabitants of the area, resented the settlers and fought many wars to protect their lands. By 1869 the railroad had crossed the continent, and by 1890 many Native Americans had been forced to live on reservations; the frontier had all but disappeared.

NATIVE AMERICANS
Land-hungry settlers claimed the frontier as their own. Their attempts to drive out the Native Americans, who had lived on the land for centuries, led to years of bitter fighting.

There were no trees or rocks to use as building materials on the Great Plains. So the first settlers built their houses from dirt that they shaped into bricks. These "soddies" could last 10 years, but were dirty and damp.

FRONTIER LIFE
Life on the frontier was harsh and lonely for the settlers, many of whom lived far from any town. The whole family had to work long hours on the land to produce enough food to eat, and settlers found it difficult to obtain supplies.

Pan for separating gold from rubble; gold dust stuck to the greasy bottom of the pan.

THE GOLD RUSH
In January 1848, the first gold fields were discovered in California. At first, only local people prospected (searched) for gold, but in 1849 a huge rush of prospectors came to make their fortunes. In 1849 alone, the population of California rose from 20,000 to more than 100,000 people.

FRONTIER TOWNS
As the West was settled, new towns were built next to railroads or at river crossings. These towns often consisted of no more than a few dirt roads lined with small buildings with false fronts, to make them look grander. Most towns had a bank, a lawyer's office, a general store, and a blacksmith. There were also saloons and dancehalls where the locals and visiting cowboys and miners could enjoy themselves. The new towns were often rough and violent because settlers tried to protect their families and their property by using guns. Sheriffs kept the peace as best they could. However, they were often powerless to prevent gunfights.

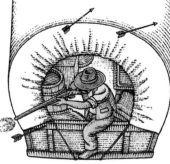

THE WILD WEST

1836 Siege of the Alamo leads Texas to break away from Mexico and join the United States in 1845.

1842 Thousands of settlers begin to travel west along the Oregon Trail to live in the new territories.

1845-48 United States gains California, Nevada, and parts of Utah, New Mexico, and Arizona following a war with Mexico.

1847 Mormon settlers establish Salt Lake City, Utah.

1848 Gold is discovered in California.

1849 Gold rush brings many prospectors to California.

1858 First regular stagecoach service between East and West coasts.

1861-65 Civil War splits nation over issue of slavery.

1861-90 Frequent wars between the Native Americans and settlers in the Midwest.

1862 Homestead Act offers settlers 65 hectares (160 acres) of virtually free land on the Great Plains; it leads to the population and cultivation of the Midwest.

Find out more

COLONIES
and Colonial America
NATIVE AMERICANS
UNITED STATES OF AMERICA,
history of

WHALES AND DOLPHINS

TEN MILLION YEARS before humans first lived on Earth, whales were swimming in the oceans. Whales are among the most intelligent of all creatures. They are also the largest living animals, and among the most gentle and graceful. Whales, dolphins, and porpoises make up a fascinating group of mammals. They are warm-blooded, but unlike seals, they have no fur; a thick layer of fatty blubber under the skin keeps them warm. The whale group is divided into those with teeth (toothed whales) and those without teeth (baleen whales). There are dozens of different toothed whales, including the friendly bottle-nosed dolphin and the ferocious killer whale, which eats almost anything in the sea. Toothless or baleen whales include the humpback and blue whales, which feed by sieving small sea creatures, such as krill, into their mouths. Since all whales and dolphins breathe air, they must swim to the surface of the water regularly. Whales and dolphins swim by moving their tails up and down; fish move their tails from side to side. Whales have suffered greatly from hunting by humans, and 21 kinds are on the official lists of endangered species. Today, whaling is not allowed, in the hope that the population of whales will increase.

THE SOCIABLE DOLPHIN
One of the most playful creatures in the world is the dolphin. This sociable animal lives in "schools" of up to 1,000. They race through the waves, and sometimes can be seen scooting along in front of boats.

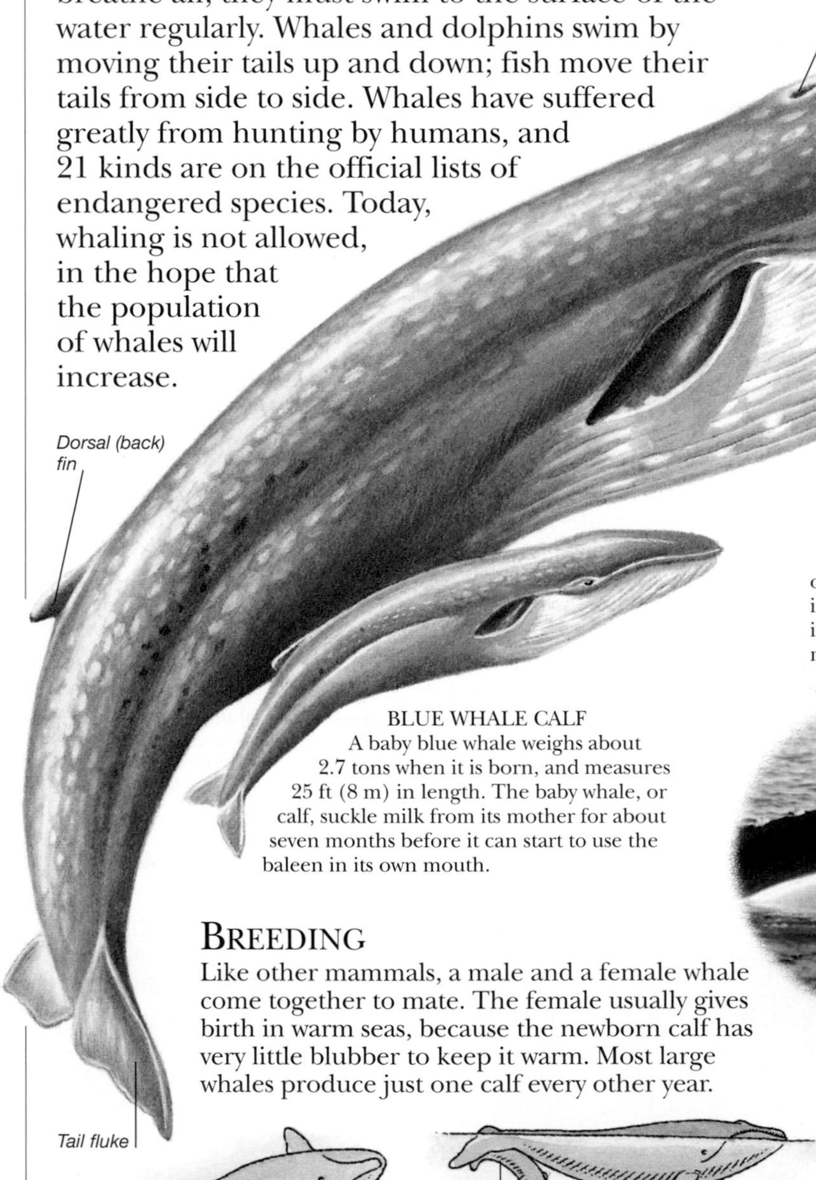

Baleen plates for feeding

Blowhole (nostrils)

BLUE WHALE
The blue whale is the largest animal alive today, and it roams all oceans. Blue whales can live to 80 years of age. The skin on the blue whale's throat has many grooves, and expands hugely as the whale feeds.

Throat pleats

PORPOISE
There are six different kinds of porpoise. Common, or harbor, porpoises such as the one shown here are often seen in shallow water close to harbors and beaches.

Dorsal (back) fin

BOTTLE-NOSED DOLPHIN
Of all the animals on Earth, the delightful, highly intelligent bottle-nosed dolphin is one of the friendliest and most gentle toward humans.

BLUE WHALE CALF
A baby blue whale weighs about 2.7 tons when it is born, and measures 25 ft (8 m) in length. The baby whale, or calf, suckle milk from its mother for about seven months before it can start to use the baleen in its own mouth.

TEETH AND BALEEN
Toothed whales, such as the bottle-nosed dolphin shown above, have dozens of sharp teeth for gripping fish and other slippery prey. Baleen whales, such as the right whale shown left, have comb-like baleen plates, also known as whalebone, for sieving krill from the sea.

BREEDING
Like other mammals, a male and a female whale come together to mate. The female usually gives birth in warm seas, because the newborn calf has very little blubber to keep it warm. Most large whales produce just one calf every other year.

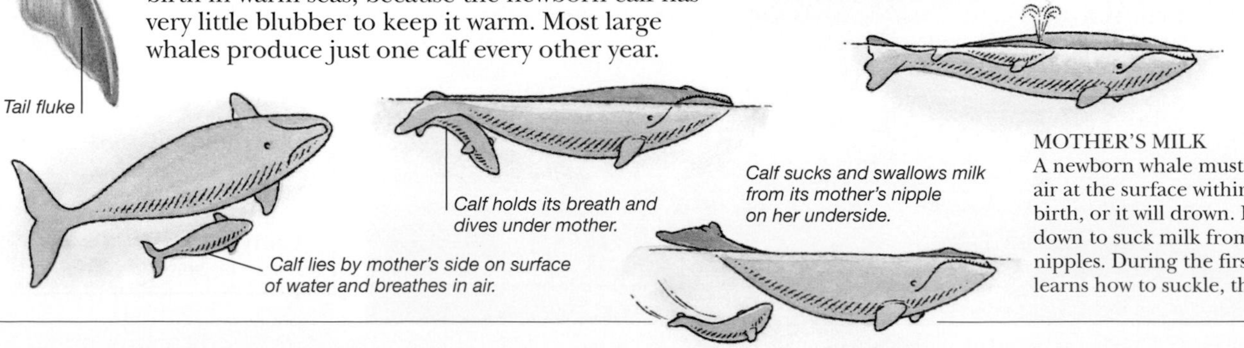

Tail fluke

Calf returns to surface, breathes out and rests.

Calf holds its breath and dives under mother.

Calf sucks and swallows milk from its mother's nipple on her underside.

Calf lies by mother's side on surface of water and breathes in air.

MOTHER'S MILK
A newborn whale must learn to breathe air at the surface within a few minutes of birth, or it will drown. It must also dive down to suck milk from its mother's nipples. During the first few days the calf learns how to suckle, then surface for air.

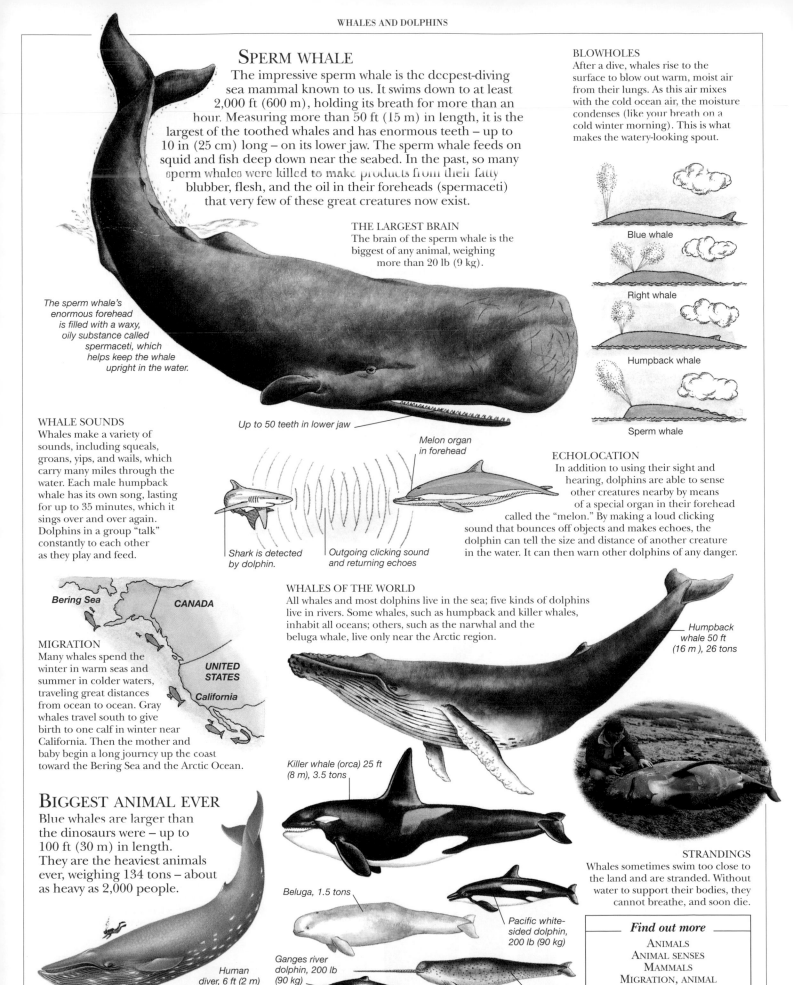

SPERM WHALE

The impressive sperm whale is the deepest-diving sea mammal known to us. It swims down to at least 2,000 ft (600 m), holding its breath for more than an hour. Measuring more than 50 ft (15 m) in length, it is the largest of the toothed whales and has enormous teeth – up to 10 in (25 cm) long – on its lower jaw. The sperm whale feeds on squid and fish deep down near the seabed. In the past, so many sperm whales were killed to make products from their fatty blubber, flesh, and the oil in their foreheads (spermaceti) that very few of these great creatures now exist.

The sperm whale's enormous forehead is filled with a waxy, oily substance called spermaceti, which helps keep the whale upright in the water.

THE LARGEST BRAIN
The brain of the sperm whale is the biggest of any animal, weighing more than 20 lb (9 kg).

Up to 50 teeth in lower jaw

BLOWHOLES
After a dive, whales rise to the surface to blow out warm, moist air from their lungs. As this air mixes with the cold ocean air, the moisture condenses (like your breath on a cold winter morning). This is what makes the watery-looking spout.

Blue whale

Right whale

Humpback whale

Sperm whale

WHALE SOUNDS
Whales make a variety of sounds, including squeals, groans, yips, and wails, which carry many miles through the water. Each male humpback whale has its own song, lasting for up to 35 minutes, which it sings over and over again. Dolphins in a group "talk" constantly to each other as they play and feed.

Melon organ in forehead

ECHOLOCATION
In addition to using their sight and hearing, dolphins are able to sense other creatures nearby by means of a special organ in their forehead called the "melon." By making a loud clicking sound that bounces off objects and makes echoes, the dolphin can tell the size and distance of another creature in the water. It can then warn other dolphins of any danger.

Shark is detected by dolphin.

Outgoing clicking sound and returning echoes

Bering Sea

CANADA

MIGRATION
Many whales spend the winter in warm seas and summer in colder waters, traveling great distances from ocean to ocean. Gray whales travel south to give birth to one calf in winter near California. Then the mother and baby begin a long journey up the coast toward the Bering Sea and the Arctic Ocean.

UNITED STATES

California

WHALES OF THE WORLD
All whales and most dolphins live in the sea; five kinds of dolphins live in rivers. Some whales, such as humpback and killer whales, inhabit all oceans; others, such as the narwhal and the beluga whale, live only near the Arctic region.

Humpback whale 50 ft (16 m), 26 tons

BIGGEST ANIMAL EVER
Blue whales are larger than the dinosaurs were – up to 100 ft (30 m) in length. They are the heaviest animals ever, weighing 134 tons – about as heavy as 2,000 people.

Killer whale (orca) 25 ft (8 m), 3.5 tons

Beluga, 1.5 tons

Ganges river dolphin, 200 lb (90 kg)

Human diver, 6 ft (2 m) in length. Blue whale 100 ft (30 m) in length.

Pacific white-sided dolphin, 200 lb (90 kg)

Narwhal, 1.5 tons

STRANDINGS
Whales sometimes swim too close to the land and are stranded. Without water to support their bodies, they cannot breathe, and soon die.

Find out more
ANIMALS
ANIMAL SENSES
MAMMALS
MIGRATION, ANIMAL
OCEAN WILDLIFE

WHEELS

SOMETIMES THE SIMPLEST INVENTIONS are the most important. Although no one is sure exactly who invented the first wheel, the earliest records go back to about 5,500 years ago. The wheel has made possible a whole range of machines, from photocopiers to jet engines, that we take for granted today. Wheels have a unique characteristic – they are circular, without corners, enabling them to roll or spin evenly. This allows almost all forms of land transportation – bicycles, cars, trains, and trams – to roll smoothly along roads, rails, and rough ground. In addition, the circular motion of a wheel means that it can transmit power continuously from an engine. Many more inventions are based on wheels. The crane, for example, relies on pulleys (grooved wheels around which a rope is passed), which reduce the effort needed to lift heavy weights; gears multiply or reduce the speed and force of a wheel and are essential in countless other machines.

AXLE AND BEARINGS
A wheel spins on a shaft called an axle. Wheels often have ball bearings – several small steel balls that run between the axle and the wheel, allowing it to turn smoothly. Without bearings, the great weight of a Ferris wheel (above) would squeeze the wheel against the axle and prevent it from turning.

Before wheels were invented, people had to push or drag heavy loads over the ground. Perhaps watching a smooth rock roll down a hill gave people the idea of using wheels for transport.

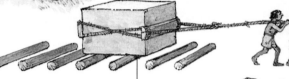

About 4,500 years ago, the Ancient Egyptians built great triangular pyramids as tombs and temples. Gangs of workers dragged huge blocks of stone with the aid of log-rollers.

The first vehicle wheels used for carts were solid wood. They were made of two or three planks of wood fixed together and cut into a circle. They first appeared in about 3200 B.C.

INVENTING THE WHEEL
The first recorded use of a wheel dates back to around 3500 B.C. This was the potter's wheel, a simple turntable used in southwest Asia by Mesopotamian pottery workers to make smooth, round clay pots. About 300 years later, the Mesopotamians fitted wheels to a cart, and the age of wheeled transportation began.

GYROSCOPES
A gyroscope is a rotating wheel mounted on a frame. When the wheel spins, its momentum makes it balance like a spinning top. Once a gyroscope is spinning, it always tries to point in the same direction. Aircraft, ships, and missiles use gyroscopes to navigate, or direct themselves, to their destinations.

Wheels with spokes developed in about 2000 B.C. Spoked wheels are lighter and faster than solid wheels and were fitted to war chariots.

The gear wheels are connected by teeth that interlock (fit exactly) into each other. Their mutual positions decide how the force changes.

Bibendum, the famous symbol of the French tire company Michelin

Wheels held together by wire spokes appeared in about 1800. They are very light and strong, and were first used for cars, bicycles, and early airplanes. In the 1950s, metal wheels replaced wire wheels on cars.

TIRES
Car and bicycle wheels have rubber tires filled with air. They give a comfortable ride and all, except those of racing cars, have a tread (a pattern of ridges) to help them grip the road. Scottish engineer Robert W. Thomson invented the first air-filled tire in 1845.

GEARS
Sets of interlocking toothed wheels are called gears. Gears transfer movement in machines and change the speed and force of wheels. For example, a large gear wheel makes a small gear wheel rotate faster, but the faster moving wheel produces less force. Gears can also change the direction of the motion.

Find out more

BICYCLES AND MOTORCYCLES
CARS
TRANSPORTATION, HISTORY OF

WIND

AS A GENTLE BREEZE or a powerful hurricane, wind blows constantly around the world. Winds are belts of moving air that flow from one area to another, driven by the Sun's heat. Warm air is lighter than cold air, so warm air rises as it is heated by the Sun, and cold air flows in to take its place. This sets up a circular current of air which produces winds. Light, warm air exerts less pressure on the Earth than cold air, creating an area of low pressure toward which cold air flows. Similarly, cold air sinks and produces an area of high pressure from which air flows outward. The greater the difference in pressure between two areas, the stronger the winds. Weather forecasters use the Beaufort scale to measure the speed of wind. It runs from 0 to 12: for example, force 2 is a light breeze; force 12 is a hurricane. The size and shape of areas of land and water affect local winds, which are often given special names, such as the chinook in North America and the sirocco in Italy.

WIND DIRECTION
A wind is often named according to the direction from which it is coming. For example, a wind which comes from the west is called a westerly. Windsocks (above) and vanes are used to show wind direction.

At the equator, the Sun's heat warms the air. In this area, the air rises, causing a belt of calm air called the doldrums.

Horse latitudes

Path of air

Doldrums

When the air has risen very high, it cools and sinks back to the Earth in the horse latitudes.

Doldrums

Path of air

Horse latitudes

Polar easterlies

Westerlies

The westerlies are warm winds which blow away from the horse latitudes in the direction of the poles.

Horse latitudes

NE trade winds

The trade winds flow from the horse latitudes toward the equator.

Equator

In between the westerlies and the trade winds is an area of calm called the horse latitudes. The name may refer to the many horses that died on ships that were becalmed in this region.

SE trade winds

Horse latitudes

Westerlies

The polar easterlies are cold winds which blow away from the poles.

WORLD WINDS
Besides local and seasonal winds, there are certain winds that always blow. These are called prevailing winds. There are three main belts of prevailing winds on each side of the equator. They are called the trade winds, the westerlies, and the polar easterlies. The direction they blow in is affected by the spin of the Earth. They are angled toward the left in the southern hemisphere and toward the right in the northern hemisphere.

WIND TURBINES
The earliest ships used wind power to carry them across the sea. Wind also powers machines. Windmills were used in Iran as long ago as the 7th century for raising water from rivers, and later for grinding corn. Today huge windmills, or wind turbines, can produce electricity; a large wind turbine can supply enough electricity for a small town. Wind turbines cause no pollution but they are large and noisy and take up huge areas of land.

A wind farm in the United States uses 300 wind turbines to produce electricity.

MONSOONS
Seasonal winds that blow in a particular direction are called monsoons. For example, during the summer in southern Asia, the wind blows from the Indian Ocean toward the land, bringing heavy rains. In winter, the wind blows in the opposite direction, from the Himalayas toward the ocean.

Find out more
CLIMATES
ENERGY
STORMS
WEATHER

WOMEN'S RIGHTS

UP TO TWO HUNDRED YEARS AGO women had few rights. They were not allowed to vote, and in some societies were considered the property of their fathers or husbands. By the mid-19th century, women were demanding equality with men. They wanted suffrage – the right to vote in elections – and an equal chance to work and be educated. They demanded the right to have their own possessions, to divorce their husbands, and to keep their children after divorce. The fight for women's rights was also called feminism, and involved many dedicated women. The first organized demand for the vote occurred in the United States in 1848. By the 1920s, women had won some battles, particularly for the vote and greater education. In the 1960s, women renewed their call for equal rights. This new protest was named the women's liberation movement. It led to new laws in many countries to stop discrimination against women.

WORKING WOMEN
In the United States about 43 percent of workers are women. But relatively few hold important positions, and most earn less than men doing the same jobs.

WOMEN'S RIGHTS

1792 Mary Wollstonecraft of Britain published *A Vindication of the Rights of Woman.*

1848 First women's rights conference, Seneca Falls, New York, calls for voting rights for women.

1893 New Zealand is first country to grant voting rights to women.

1917 Jeannette Rankin of Montana is the first woman elected to Congress.

1920 19th amendment grants women over 30 a vote.

1923 Alice Paul introduces the first equal rights amendment to Congress.

1960 Sirimavo Bandaranaike of Sri Lanka becomes world's first woman prime minister.

1963 Federal Equal Pay Act outlaws paying women less than men for the same job.

1966 National Organization for Women (NOW) founded.

1979 UN passes Convention on the Elimination of All Forms of Discrimination Against Women.

EMILY DAVISON
In 1913 British suffragette Emily Davison leaped under a racehorse owned by King Edward VII and died. Her protest drew attention to the Votes for Women campaign.

SUSAN B. ANTHONY
One of the leaders of the suffrage movement in the United States, Susan B. Anthony (1820-1906) helped launch *Revolution*, the first feminist newspaper.

SUFFRAGETTES

In 1905, a newspaper used the word *suffragette* to insult women who were fighting for the vote. However, the suffragettes were delighted with the name, which has been used ever since. Many suffragettes broke the law and went to prison for their beliefs. Women who used peaceful means to obtain the vote were called suffragists.

FORCE–FEEDING
In 1909, suffragettes in prison refused to eat. Jailers fed them by pouring liquid food down tubes forced through the women's noses into their stomachs. It was painful and seriously injured some women. Force-feeding ended in 1913.

Suffragettes publicized their campaign by chaining themselves to the railings of famous buildings.

ON HER THEIR LIVES DEPEND

WOMEN MUNITION WORKERS

Enrol at once

WOMEN AT WAR
During World War I (1914-18), women in Britain worked to keep factories going while the men fought. They proved that women were just as capable as men. In 1918, British women over 30 got voting rights. Two years later, all American women also gained the vote.

WOMEN'S LIBERATION FRONT

WOMEN'S LIBERATION MOVEMENT
During the late 1960s and 1970s, the women's liberation movement fought for further improvements in women's rights. Women everywhere demonstrated for equal pay, better health care, and an end to pornography and violence against women.

SENECA FALLS

The first national women's rights convention was held at Seneca Falls, New York, in July 1848. Its organizers included Lucretia Mott and Elizabeth Cady Stanton (right), two abolitionists who were leaders of the growing women's movement. Delegates at the meeting demanded equal rights and opportunities for women, including the right to vote. Seneca Falls is now the site of the Women's Rights National Historical Park.

Elizabeth Cady Stanton and Women's Rights

NOW FOR WOMEN

Founded in 1966 to fight for women's equality issues, the National Organization for Women (NOW) became the strongest women's rights group in the country. One of its founders and its first president was author Betty Friedan (right), whose groundbreaking 1963 book, *The Feminine Mystique*, helped launch the women's liberation movement. NOW has campaigned on many women's issues, including sex discrimination in the workplace and the Equal Rights Amendment. Today, NOW has more than 600 chapters in 50 states.

Geraldine Ferraro was the first female vice-presidential candidate in America.

EQUAL RIGHTS AMENDMENT

Originally written by suffragette Alice Paul in 1923, the Equal Rights Amendment (ERA) was passed by Congress in 1972, and sent to each state for approval. This amendment to the Constitution declared, "Equality of rights under the law shall not be denied or abridged by the United States or by any State on account of sex." Over the next few decades, women campaigned for its introduction. However, when the deadline for ratification came in 1982, only 35 of the necessary 38 states supported the amendment, and the ERA failed.

A VOICE FOR ALL WOMEN

Although the women's liberation movement sought to unite all women, some nonwhite women did not feel part of a movement led mostly by whites. Shirley Chisholm (left), the first African-American woman elected to Congress, founded one of many women's rights organizations that encouraged women from minorities to vote.

WOMEN IN POLITICS

Winning the right to vote was an important victory in the quest for equality between the sexes. Since that time, women have been able to influence the decision-making process by becoming candidates for political office. In recent years, record numbers of women have been elected to government posts at the local, state, and national levels. Women have also been chosen for important federal jobs, such as Supreme Court justice, attorney general, surgeon general, and ambassador to the United Nations.

Find out more

ABOLITIONIST MOVEMENT
CIVIL RIGHTS
HUMAN RIGHTS

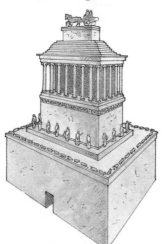

WONDERS
OF THE ANCIENT WORLD

TWO THOUSAND YEARS AGO, Ancient Greek and Roman tourists visited the world's great landmarks just as we do today. Ancient "travel agents" compiled lists of amazing things that travelers should see. These "wonders" were outstanding examples of human artistic or engineering achievement. The seven most commonly listed monuments to human endeavor are called the Seven Wonders of the Ancient World. They all had qualities that made them stand out from the rest. Some were the most beautiful statues, others the largest structures of the day. Of the seven wonders, only one, the Great Pyramids, can still be seen today. The Hanging Gardens, the Temple of Artemis, the Statue of Zeus, the Mausoleum, the Colossus, and the Lighthouse at Pharos have all vanished or are in ruins.

PYRAMIDS
Three pyramids were built at Giza, Egypt, in about 2600 B.C. as tombs for three Egyptian kings. The largest, made from more than two million huge blocks of limestone, stands 482 ft (147 m) high.

MAUSOLEUM
The Mausoleum at Halicarnassus (in modern Turkey) was a huge marble tomb built for Mausolus, a rich governor. It stood 135 ft (41 m) high, with a base supporting 36 columns, under a stepped pyramid. An earthquake destroyed most of the mausoleum.

LIGHTHOUSE
The Greek architect Sostratos designed the world's first lighthouse. It was built around 304 B.C. on the island of Pharos, Alexandria, Egypt. It stood about 440 ft (134 m) high. A fire burned at the top to mark the harbor entrance.

HANGING GARDENS
In 605 B.C. Nebuchadnezzar II, king of Babylon, built the Hanging Gardens in his kingdom. He planted many exotic plants on a brick terrace 75 ft (23 m) above the ground. Machines worked by slaves watered the plants.

COLOSSUS
The bronze statue of the sun god Helios towered 120 ft (37 m) over the harbor entrance on the island of Rhodes in the Aegean Sea. Built in 292 B.C., it was about the same size as the Statue of Liberty.

TEMPLE OF ARTEMIS
This, the largest temple of its day, was dedicated to Artemis, goddess of the moon and hunting. Built almost entirely of marble by the Greeks at Ephesus (in modern Turkey), it burned down in 356 B.C., leaving only a few broken statues.

ZEUS
The great Statue of Zeus, king of the Greek gods, stood 40 ft (12 m) high at Olympia, Greece. Phidias, a famous Greek sculptor, created the statue in about 435 B.C. The god's robes and ornaments were made of gold, and the skin was of ivory.

LOCATION OF THE WONDERS
The map shows the location of the Seven Wonders of the Ancient World. Travelers visited many of them by ship. Most of the wonders were destroyed by earthquakes or fire, but some remains can still be seen in the British Museum in London, England.

Find out more
ALEXANDER THE GREAT
BABYLONIANS
EGYPT, ANCIENT

WORLD WAR I

BETWEEN 1914 AND 1918, a terrible war engulfed Europe. The war was called the First World War, or the Great War, because it affected almost every country in the world. It began because of the rivalry between several powerful European countries. Fighting started when the empire of Austria and Hungary declared war on Serbia. Soon, other countries joined the war. They formed two main groups: the Allies, composed of Britain, France, Italy, Russia, and the United States, versus the Central Powers – Germany, Austria-Hungary, and Turkey. In the beginning everyone thought the war would be short and glorious. Young men rushed to join the armies and navies. But it soon became clear that none of the opposing armies was strong enough to win a clear victory. Thousands of troops died, fighting to gain just a few hundred feet of the battlefield. In the end, the war, which some called the "war to end all wars," had achieved nothing. Within a few years a worse war broke out in Europe.

ARCHDUKE FERDINAND
On June 28, 1914, a Serbian terrorist shot Franz Ferdinand, heir to the throne of Austria and Hungary. Germany encouraged Austria to retaliate, or fight back, by declaring war on Serbia. A month after the assassination, World War I had begun.

Allied countries are green, Central Powers are pink, and neutral countries are shown in beige.

COUNTRIES AT WAR
The war involved nearly 30 countries – more countries than any previous war. There was fighting in the Middle East, Africa, and the Pacific. However, most of the war was fought in Europe. The western front in northern France was a line of trenches that stretched from Switzerland to the English Channel. Soldiers on the eastern front fought in what is now Poland. Fighting took place on land, at sea, and in the air.

Norway
Denmark
Sweden
Russia
English Channel
Great Britain
Netherlands
Poland
Germany
Belgium
Austria-Hungary
France
Italy
Spain
Romania
Serbia
Bulgaria
Montenegro

RED BARON
World War I was the first war in which airplanes were used for fighting. Germany's Manfred von Richthofen (the Red Baron) became one of the first air aces.

YPRES
The Belgian city of Ypres was a battleground several times during World War I. It was here that the Germans first used poison gas on the western front. By 1918 the town was devastated (left).

TRENCH WARFARE
The armies advanced as far they could, then dug trenches for shelter. Life in the trenches was miserable. Soldiers were often up to their knees in mud. Lice and rats added to their discomfort. When soldiers left the trenches to advance further, the enemy killed them by the millions with machine guns. Each side also had artillery – guns that fired huge shells – which killed many more and churned up the battlefield into a sea of mud.

U-BOATS
German submarines called underwater boats, or U-boats, sank many cargo ships in the Atlantic, causing food shortages in Britain.

LUSITANIA
On May 7, 1915, a German U-boat torpedoed the British passenger liner *Lusitania*. More than 100 American passengers drowned, some of whom were very rich and famous. This angered many Americans and turned them against Germany. The sinking helped to bring the United States into the war on the Allied side.

WORLD WAR I
June 1914 Assassination of Archduke Franz Ferdinand

July 1914 Austria-Hungary declares war on Serbia.

August 1914 Germany declares war on Russia and France and invades Belgium. Britain declares war on Germany and Austria-Hungary.

May 1915 Italy joins Allies.

July 1916 Allies use tanks for the first time in France.

April 1917 United States enters the war.

March 1918 Russia signs treaty with Germany. Germany's final huge attack fails.

September 1918 Allies begin their final attack.

November 1918 Germany signs armistice, ending the war.

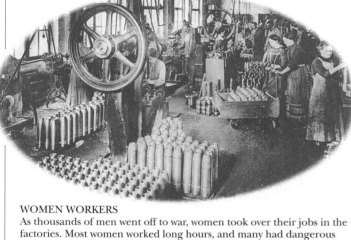

WOMEN WORKERS
As thousands of men went off to war, women took over their jobs in the factories. Most women worked long hours, and many had dangerous jobs, such as making ammunition. Their efforts disproved the old idea that women were inferior to men, and eventually led to women gaining the right to vote. But when the troops returned after the war, there was massive unemployment, and women lost their jobs.

PROPAGANDA
Wartime posters and newspapers aimed to persuade people that the enemy was evil and that war must go on. The message of this propaganda, or government-controlled news, was that everyone should help by fighting, working, raising money, and making sacrifices. The poster (left) shows a frightening image of Germany with its hands on Europe.

COMMUNICATION
People at home had little idea of the real conditions of the war. Officers read mail from soldiers and censored, or cut out, information that told the true story. Troops returning home were often too sickened by life in the trenches to explain what it was really like or to tell how many soldiers had been killed or wounded.

GERMANS
Until 1918, it looked as if Germany and her allies might win. But they were outnumbered, and when the British navy blocked the ports and cut off supplies of food and vital war materials, the German people rioted. They demanded food and peace, and the Kaiser – the German emperor – gave up his throne. Germany then made a peace treaty called the Treaty of Versailles with the Allied forces. The Germans lost much land and took the blame for starting the war.

DEATH TOLL
Germany and Russia each lost nearly two million soldiers in the war. Britain lost nearly one million. In all, 10 million died.

Find out more

DEPRESSION OF THE 1930S
WOMEN'S RIGHTS
WORLD WAR II

WORLD WAR II

IN 1939, GERMAN TANKS and bombers attacked Poland, and the bloodiest war in history began. Like World War I, World War II was a global war and was fought on the ground, in the air, and at sea. The war was a result of the rise to power of the German National Socialist or Nazi party, led by Adolf Hitler. The Nazis wanted to wipe out the memory of defeat in World War I. Within a year, German armies, with help from Italy, had occupied much of Europe. Only Britain opposed them. In 1941, Hitler invaded the Soviet Union. But the Soviet people fought hard and millions died. In the Pacific, the Japanese formed an alliance, called the Axis, with Germany and Italy. Japanese warplanes bombed the American naval base at Pearl Harbor, in Hawaii. This brought the United States into the war, and they joined the Soviet Union and Britain to form the Allies. By June 1945, Allied forces had defeated the Nazis in Europe; Japan surrendered in August. When the war ended, 45 million people had died and much of Europe was in ruins. Two new "superpowers" – the Soviet Union and the United States – began to dominate world politics.

HITLER
In 1933, Adolf Hitler came to power in Germany as leader of the Nazi party. The Nazis were fascists: they were against Communism and believed in strong national government. The Nazis ruthlessly crushed anyone who opposed them. They enslaved and murdered Jews, gypsies, and other minorities, whom they blamed for all of Germany's problems, from defeat in World War I to unemployment and inflation.

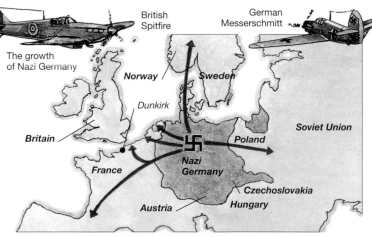

British Spitfire

German Messerschmitt

The growth of Nazi Germany

Norway · Sweden · Dunkirk · Britain · France · Nazi Germany · Poland · Soviet Union · Austria · Czechoslovakia · Hungary

INVASION
In 1938, Hitler took control of Austria and parts of Czechoslovakia. Britain and France did not oppose him, and he went on to invade Poland. Britain and France then declared war on Germany. German troops smashed into France in 1940, sweeping aside the armies of Britain and France. Fleets of fishing boats and pleasure steamers from the southern coast of England helped the Royal Navy to rescue the retreating Allied soldiers from the beaches at Dunkirk, on the coast of France.

BLITZ
Between August and October 1940, the British Royal Air Force fought the Luftwaffe – the German air force – in the Battle of Britain, and finally won. Without control of the skies, Hitler could not invade Britain. His bombers began to bomb British cities during the night. This "blitzkrieg" or blitz, killed 40,000 people, mostly civilians.

EVACUATIONS
During the bombing of major cities, such as London, thousands of British children were evacuated to country towns and villages where they were much safer.

MIDWAY

Japan conquered many Pacific islands and invaded mainland Asia. But the United States fleet defeated the Japanese on June 3–6, 1942, at the Battle of Midway. The battle turned the Pacific war in favor of the Allies.

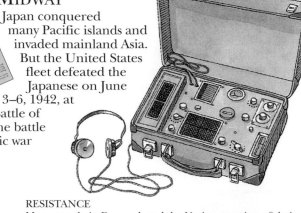

RESISTANCE

Many people in Europe hated the Nazi occupation of their countries. So they formed secret resistance movements to spy on and fight the enemy. They used hidden radios (above) to work behind the battle lines. Resistance workers risked torture and death if they were discovered.

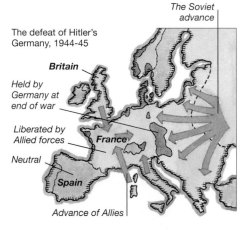

The defeat of Hitler's Germany, 1944–45

Britain

Held by Germany at end of war

Liberated by Allied forces

France

Neutral

Spain

The Soviet advance

Advance of Allies

PEACE IN EUROPE

By the spring of 1945, the Allies had recaptured most of occupied Europe and began to cross the Rhine River into Germany. In the east, the Soviet army swept toward Berlin, Germany's capital. Crushed between these two powerful forces, the German armies surrendered. Hitler committed suicide, and the biggest and most expensive war in human history ended.

D-DAY

In June 1944, Allied troops invaded occupied Europe in the greatest seaborne landing ever mounted. Invasion day was code-named D-day. The D stood for deliverance. After a bitter struggle, and aided by resistance fighters, the Allied forces broke through, and the German soldiers retreated or were taken as prisoners.

CONCENTRATION CAMP

After Germany surrendered, Allied troops discovered horrifying concentration (prison) camps throughout Europe, where the Nazis had imprisoned up to 26 million people they considered "undesirable," including millions of Jews. The prisoners were starved and tortured, and many were eventually gassed to death.

VE DAY

On May 8, 1945, the Allies celebrated VE (Victory in Europe) Day. However, there were still another three months of bitter fighting in the Pacific. In August 1945, US planes dropped two atom bombs on Japan, destroying the cities of Hiroshima and Nagasaki. This was done to force Japan to surrender quickly and so save Allied lives that would be lost if the Allies invaded Japan. Within a few weeks the Japanese surrendered and the war ended.

WORLD WAR II

September 1, 1939 Germany invades Poland. Britain and France declare war on Germany two days later.

April 1940 Germany invades Denmark and Norway.

May 1940 Germany invades Belgium, the Netherlands, and France.

June 1940 Germans enter Paris, and France signs an armistice (peace agreement) with Germany.

April 1941 Germany invades Greece and Yugoslavia.

June 1941 Germany invades the Soviet Union.

September 1941 Siege of Leningrad (Soviet Union) begins; lasts over two and a half years.

December 7, 1941 Japanese planes attack Pearl Harbor. The United States, Britain, and Canada declare war on Japan.

February 1942 Japanese capture many Pacific islands.

August 1942 German attack on Stalingrad (Soviet Union) begins.

November 1942 Under General Montgomery the British defeat Germany, led by Rommel, at El Alamein, Egypt. Allied troops land in French North Africa to fight Germany and Italy.

January 1943 German armies besieged in Stalingrad surrender.

May 1943 German armies in North Africa surrender to the Allies.

July 1943 Allies invade Sicily.

September 1943 Allied forces land in Italy. Italy surrenders.

June 1944 Allied forces land in Normandy, north-west France, in the D-day invasion.

May 1945 German forces surrender; war in Europe ends.

August 1945 Allies drop atomic bombs on Japan.

September 2, 1945 Japan signs an unconditional surrender, ending World War II.

Find out more

CHURCHILL, SIR WINSTON
HOLOCAUST
NUCLEAR AGE
ROOSEVELT, FRANKLIN DELANO
WORLD WAR I

WORMS

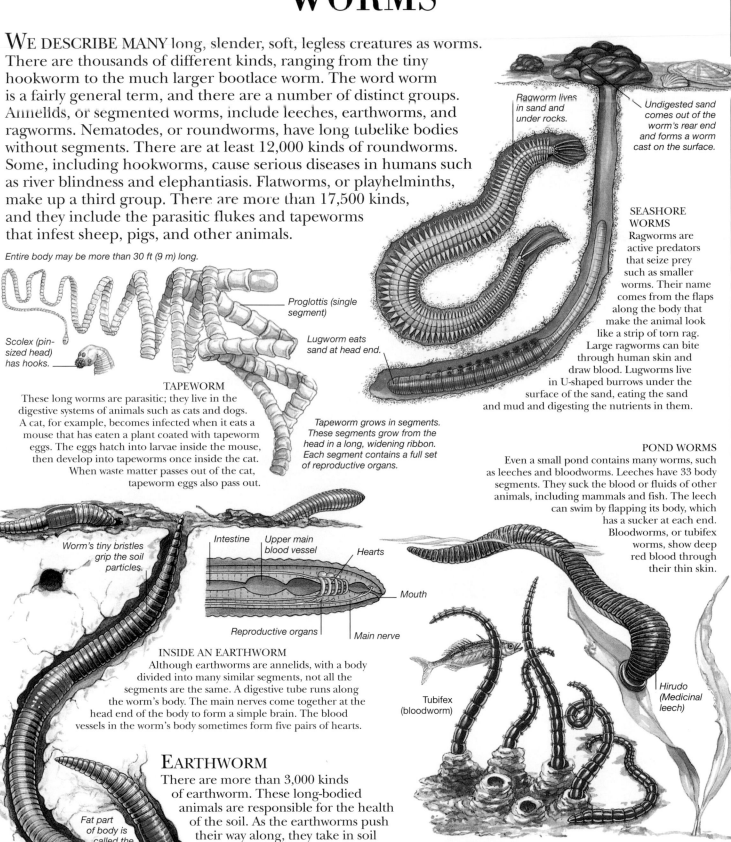

WE DESCRIBE MANY long, slender, soft, legless creatures as worms. There are thousands of different kinds, ranging from the tiny hookworm to the much larger bootlace worm. The word worm is a fairly general term, and there are a number of distinct groups. Annelids, or segmented worms, include leeches, earthworms, and ragworms. Nematodes, or roundworms, have long tubelike bodies without segments. There are at least 12,000 kinds of roundworms. Some, including hookworms, cause serious diseases in humans such as river blindness and elephantiasis. Flatworms, or playhelminths, make up a third group. There are more than 17,500 kinds, and they include the parasitic flukes and tapeworms that infest sheep, pigs, and other animals.

Entire body may be more than 30 ft (9 m) long.

Scolex (pin-sized head) has hooks.

Proglottis (single segment)

Lugworm eats sand at head end.

TAPEWORM

These long worms are parasitic; they live in the digestive systems of animals such as cats and dogs. A cat, for example, becomes infected when it eats a mouse that has eaten a plant coated with tapeworm eggs. The eggs hatch into larvae inside the mouse, then develop into tapeworms once inside the cat. When waste matter passes out of the cat, tapeworm eggs also pass out.

Tapeworm grows in segments. These segments grow from the head in a long, widening ribbon. Each segment contains a full set of reproductive organs.

Ragworm lives in sand and under rocks.

Undigested sand comes out of the worm's rear end and forms a worm cast on the surface.

SEASHORE WORMS

Ragworms are active predators that seize prey such as smaller worms. Their name comes from the flaps along the body that make the animal look like a strip of torn rag. Large ragworms can bite through human skin and draw blood. Lugworms live in U-shaped burrows under the surface of the sand, eating the sand and mud and digesting the nutrients in them.

POND WORMS

Even a small pond contains many worms, such as leeches and bloodworms. Leeches have 33 body segments. They suck the blood or fluids of other animals, including mammals and fish. The leech can swim by flapping its body, which has a sucker at each end. Bloodworms, or tubifex worms, show deep red blood through their thin skin.

Worm's tiny bristles grip the soil particles.

Intestine *Upper main blood vessel* *Hearts*

Mouth

Reproductive organs *Main nerve*

INSIDE AN EARTHWORM

Although earthworms are annelids, with a body divided into many similar segments, not all the segments are the same. A digestive tube runs along the worm's body. The main nerves come together at the head end of the body to form a simple brain. The blood vessels in the worm's body sometimes form five pairs of hearts.

Tubifex (bloodworm)

Hirudo (Medicinal leech)

EARTHWORM

There are more than 3,000 kinds of earthworm. These long-bodied animals are responsible for the health of the soil. As the earthworms push their way along, they take in soil at the head end, digesting nutrients in the soil particles. The undigested remains that come out at the rear end form a worm cast. By burrowing in the earth, worms mix the soil layers, and their burrows allow air and water to soak downward, generally increasing the fertility of the soil.

Fat part of body is called the saddle.

BLOODWORM TAILS

Pond-dwelling bloodworms, or tubifex worms, wave their rear ends in the water to gather oxygen. Their heads are buried in the mud, taking in nutrients.

Find out more

ANIMALS
MEDICINE, HISTORY OF
SOIL

WRITERS AND POETS

A READER'S IMAGINATION can be excited by the way in which writers and poets use words. Writers create fantasy worlds for readers to explore. Historical novelists and science fiction writers transport us back to the past or into the distant future. Others writers, such as journalists, write in a way that creates a lifelike picture of real events they have experienced. And poets arrange words into patterns or rhymes that bring pleasure just by their sound or their shape on the page. A writer is anyone who expresses facts, ideas, thoughts, or opinions in words. Most writers hope or expect that their work will be published – printed in books or magazines and read by thousands of people. But some writers, including diarists such as the Englishman Samuel Pepys (1633-1703), write for their own pleasure. They do not always expect their work to be published. Poets are people who write in verse, or poetry. Poets make sure the lines of their poems form a regular pattern, so that, unlike prose, or ordinary writing, the poem has a rhythmic sound.

HOMER
One of the world's first writers was the Ancient Greek poet Homer, who lived about 2,700 years ago. He wrote long epic verses called *The Iliad* and *The Odyssey*. In *The Odyssey* the beautiful singing of the bird-like sirens lured sailors to the island where the sirens lived.

WRITING
Even a short novel has more than 50,000 words, so writing can be hard work. To make it easier, most writers organize their work carefully. Writing methods are quite individual. Although many authors use word processors, pen and paper are still popular writer's tools. American Raymond Chandler (1888-1959), who wrote detective novels, had a favorite way of writing throughout his working life.

Like any author, Chandler would have used maps to check his hero's movements around Los Angeles, the setting for many of his novels.

Chandler typed the first draft, or version, of his books on yellow paper. He used half-size sheets because he made changes by retyping, not by changing words with a pen. Retyping a whole sheet would have taken longer.

Books such as J.S. Hatcher's Textbook of Pistols gave Chandler the accurate information he needed to make his stories seem lifelike and real.

Chandler's secretary typed a clean version of the finished draft on white paper.

ANNE FRANK
During World War II, the German Nazi government persecuted millions of European Jews. To escape, Anne Frank (born 1929) and her Jewish family hid in a secret attic in a Netherlands office. The diary that Anne wrote while in hiding was later published. It is a deeply moving and tragic account of her ordeal. Anne died in a prison camp in 1945.

MANUSCRIPT
A writer's original typed or handwritten version of a work is called a manuscript. The publisher writes instructions to the printer on the manuscript, and may also make changes and revisions to improve the writing. For example, F. Scott Fitzgerald (1896-1940) was bad at spelling, and his publisher corrected these errors.

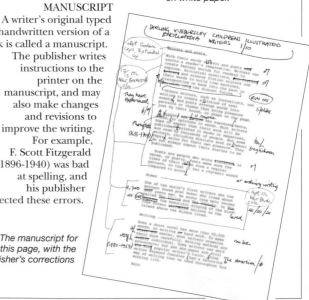

The manuscript for this page, with the publisher's corrections

CHAUCER

Geoffrey Chaucer (c.1340-1400) was an English government official. He wrote poems in English at a time when most English writers were writing in French and Latin. Chaucer began his most famous work, the *Canterbury Tales*, in about 1386. It is a collection of stories told by pilgrims traveling from London to Canterbury. The stories tell us much about 14th-century life and are often very amusing.

HARRIET BEECHER STOWE

Uncle Tom's Cabin is a powerful antislavery novel written by Harriet Beecher Stowe (1811-96) in 1852. It became extremely popular all over the world, even in the southern states of America, where owning a copy was illegal at the time.

DICKENS

Some of the greatest novels in the English language are the work of Charles Dickens (1812-70). He wrote colorful and exciting novels, such as *Oliver Twist*, *Nicholas Nickleby*, and *David Copperfield*, which also drew attention to the poverty and social injustices of 19th-century England.

LONGFELLOW

During his lifetime, Henry Wadsworth Longfellow (1807-82) was the most popular poet in the United States. His *Song of Hiawatha*, which was published in 1855, sold more than one million copies while Longfellow was still alive. The poem tells the story of a Native American tribe before America was colonized by Europeans. Longfellow wrote on many subjects and in many styles, but he is best remembered for his romantic "picture poems" about American life.

NEIL SIMON

Playwright Neil Simon was born in New York City on July 4, 1927. He has written more than 25 plays and musicals, many of which have been made into films. Most of his plays deal with aspects of ordinary American life. However, the writer's insight and sense of humor ensure that his plays appeal to people of all nationalities.

The Goodbye Girl, *one of Neil Simon's best-loved films, is set in New York.*

LITERARY FILE

c. 2300 B.C. Ancient Egyptian writers create the world's first literature, the *Book of the Dead*.

c. 600 B.C. Greek poet Sappho writes early lyric poetry (poetry with music).

c. 500 B.C. Greek poet Aeschylus (525-456 B.C.) writes the earliest dramas.

c. A.D. 100 Greek writer Plutarch (A.D. 46-120) writes *The Parallel Lives*, the first biography.

1420 Zeami Motokiyo (1363-1443), the greatest writer of Japanese Noh dramas, writes *Shikadosho* (Book of the Way of the Highest Flower).

1740-42 Englishman Samuel Richardson (1689-1761) writes one of the first English novels, *Pamela, or, Virtue Rewarded*.

1765 Horace Walpole (1717-97), an Englishman, writes a ghost story, *The Castle of Otranto*.

1819-20 American Washington Irving (1783-1859) publishes one of the first books of short stories, which includes *The Legend of Sleepy Hollow* and *Rip Van Winkle*.

1841 American writer Edgar Allan Poe (1809-49) publishes *The Murders in the Rue Morgue*, the first detective story.

1847 English novelist Charlotte Brontë writes *Jane Eyre* under the false name Currer Bell, because it is still unacceptable for "respectable" women to write fiction.

1864 Jules Verne (1828-1905), a Frenchman, writes the first science fiction story, *Journey to the Center of the Earth*.

1956 The performance of *Waiting for Godot* by Irish-French dramatist Samuel Beckett (1906-89) opens the way for modern drama.

1993 American novelist Toni Morrison (born 1931), author of *Song of Solomon* and *Beloved*, becomes the first black American to win the Nobel Prize for Literature.

Find out more

BOOKS
LITERATURE
POETRY
SLAVERY

X RAYS

To THE EARLY pioneers of medicine, the thought of looking through the body of a living person would probably have seemed like magic. But today it is routine for doctors and dentists to take pictures of their patients' bones and teeth with an X-ray camera. X rays are invisible waves, like light or radio waves. They can travel through soft materials just as light passes through glass. For example, X rays can travel through flesh and skin. But hard materials such as bone and metal stop X rays, so bone and metal show up as a shadow on an X-ray picture. X rays have many uses: scientists use them to probe into the molecular structure of materials such as plastics, and engineers make X-ray scans of aircraft to find cracks that could cause mechanical failure. In addition, the sun, stars, and other objects in space produce X rays naturally.

WILHELM ROENTGEN
The German scientist Wilhelm Roentgen (1845-1923) discovered X rays in 1895. Roentgen did not understand what these rays were, so he named them X rays.

Scanner is lined with lead to prevent X rays from escaping.

Array of photodiodes – electronic detectors that produce electrical signals when X rays hit them.

Conveyor belt carries suitcases into the scanner.

A metal object such as a pistol does not allow X rays to pass through it, so the pistol shows up on screen.

Computer receives electrical signals from the photodiodes and converts them into an image of the case.

X-ray tube produces X rays.

Monitor screen displays contents of case to security guards.

X-RAY TUBE
Like a light bulb, an X-ray tube is filled with an inert (non-reacting) gas, but produces X rays instead of light.

A strong electric current heats a wire. The energy from the electric current knocks some electrons out of the atoms in the wire.

As the electrons crash into the target, atoms of the metal produce the X-ray beam.

A powerful electric field pulls electrons at high speed toward the metal target.

BAGGAGE SCANNER
Airports have X-ray scanners (left) to check baggage for weapons and other dangerous objects. An X-ray tube produces a beam of X rays, and a conveyor belt carries each suitcase into the path of the beam. Electronic detectors pick up the X rays once they have passed through the case. A computer uses signals from the detectors to build up a picture of the contents of the case.

MEDICAL X RAYS
Doctors and dentists use X-ray machines to look inside their patients' bodies without using surgery. The machine makes an X-ray picture on a piece of photographic film. The photograph is a negative, and bones show up in white. Large doses of X rays are harmful, so X-ray examinations must be carefully controlled as a precaution.

X RAYS IN SPACE
Satellites containing X-ray telescopes orbit the Earth. The telescopes detect X rays coming from the sun and stars, and from objects such as black holes. The satellites send X-ray pictures back to Earth. Astronomers use these pictures to discover and understand more of the universe.

Find out more
AIRPORTS
ATOMS AND MOLECULES
DOCTORS
MEDICINE, HISTORY OF
STARS

ZOOS

PEOPLE BEGAN TO KEEP animals in zoological gardens, or zoos, more than 3,000 years ago, when rulers in China established a huge zoo, called the Gardens of Intelligence. Today, most cities have a zoo, wildlife park, or aquarium, which provide a chance to observe and study hundreds of different animals. However, many people do not agree on the value of zoos. Zoo supporters say that zoos give people the opportunity to be close to animals, which they would never otherwise experience; zoos help us appreciate the wonder of the natural world; and zoo staff carry out scientific research and important conservation work, such as breeding rare species. Zoo critics believe that it is wrong to keep animals in captivity; the creatures behave unnaturally, and in poorly run zoos they suffer because of stress, unsuitable food, dirty conditions, and disease.

EARLY ZOOS
In early zoos, animals such as elephants were taught to perform for the visitors, as shown in this picture. Animals are no longer trained to perform for the public. The purpose of a zoo is to enable people to see how wild animals behave in their natural surroundings. The ideal solution is to save wild areas, with their animals and plants, and allow people to visit these, but this is not always possible.

This huge birdcage is called an aviary.

Tons of animal food are delivered to the zoo each week from all over the world, including eucalyptus leaves from Australia for the koalas.

Storehouse, where food is stored. Zoo trucks take food from here to the animals.

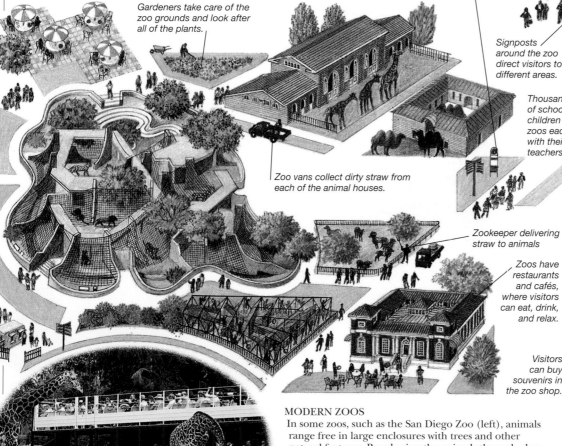

Gardeners take care of the zoo grounds and look after all of the plants.

Display boards and guide books full of information provide education.

Signposts around the zoo direct visitors to different areas.

Thousands of school-children visit zoos each year with their teachers.

Zoo vans collect dirty straw from each of the animal houses.

Zookeeper delivering straw to animals

Zoos have restaurants and cafés, where visitors can eat, drink, and relax.

Visitors can buy souvenirs in the zoo shop.

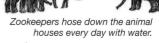

Zookeepers hose down the animal houses every day with water.

HOW ZOOS ARE RUN
A zoo employs zookeepers to look after the animals, zoologists (scientists who study animals), veterinarians, accountants, architects, cooks, gardeners, builders, and many other people. The zoo manager must keep all of these people organized because there are many jobs to do, such as ordering the correct food for each animal and running the souvenir shop and the restaurants. Visitors have to pay an entrance fee toward the upkeep of the zoo, but most zoos also need government funds.

MODERN ZOOS
In some zoos, such as the San Diego Zoo (left), animals range free in large enclosures with trees and other natural features. People view the animals through glass panels rather than iron bars. You can even see the animals from an open-topped bus. In most countries, inspectors can arrive unannounced to check the welfare of the creatures. A few zoos still treat their captives badly, and organizations such as Zoo Check work toward ensuring better conditions in zoos.

Find out more
ANIMALS
CONSERVATION
and endangered species

FACT FINDER

This section is a reference source to support the subjects in the main entry pages. The Fact Finder provides an in-depth, at-a-glance guide to history, geography, nature, science, and the world around us. Topics are arranged using tables and charts that provide quick and clear access to information.

B.C.	7000	6000	5000	4000	3000	2000
AFRICA	c. 7000 Fishing starts in the Sahara, North Africa		c. 5000 Farming begins in Egypt	c. 3200 The earliest hieroglyphic script, Egypt	c. 2650 Pyramid building begins in Egypt	
AMERICAS	c. 7000 Earliest crops grown in Mexico		c. 5000 Corn first cultivated in Mexico	c. 3500 Llama first used as pack animal, Peru		c. 1100 Olmec culture, San Loren:
ASIA	c. 7000 Farming begins in western Asia		c. 5000 Stone Age settlements appear in China	c. 3100 Bronze casting starts in the Middle East	c. 2300 Sumer civilization reaches its height	c. 2000 Sumerian rule ends
EUROPE	c. 6500 Cereal farming begins in Southeast Europe	c. 6000 Copper and gold metalworking starts	c. 4500 Vinca copper culture begins in Yugoslavia		c. 3000 Bronze Age begins in Crete	c. 2000 Minoan civilization, Crete
OCEANIA	Oceania remains in Stone Age until A.D. 1770.					

AFRICA

EARLIEST PEOPLES — 1,500,000 B.C. – 2500 B.C.

1,500,000 B.C.
Our direct ancestors, *Homo erectus*, inhabit Africa and move outward to Middle East and the rest of the world.

c. 7000 B.C.
People begin to herd cattle in the Sahara.

c. 3000 B.C.
Egyptians develop hieroglyphic writing.

c. 2600 B.C.
Construction of the Great Pyramid at Giza, Egypt.

GREAT CIVILIZATIONS — 2500 B.C. – A.D. 1400

c. 1503 B.C.
Hatshepshut, woman pharaoh (ruler) of Egypt, begins her reign.

900 B.C.
Kingdom of Meroë established. Towns, temples, and pyramids are built, all showing influence of Egypt.

814 B.C.
Phoenicians found the city of Carthage in North Africa. Phoenician industries include dyeing, metal-working, glass-working, pottery, and carving.

c. 671 B.C.
Assyrians conquer Egypt. They are great builders, and decorate their palaces with big stone reliefs.

500 B.C.
Nok culture begins in Nigeria. People produce terra-cotta sculptures.

332 B.C.
Alexander the Great conquers Egypt.

c. 290 B.C.
World's greatest library founded in Alexandria, Egypt.

EUROPEAN IMPACT AND THE SLAVE TRADE — 1400 – 1900

100 B.C.
Camel arrives in the Sahara from Arabia.

A.D. 100
Civilization of Aksum begins in Ethiopia. It trades at sea and exports ivory.

A.D. 641
Islamic Arabs occupy Egypt; they begin a conquest of North Africa.

A.D. 971
The world's first university is founded in Cairo, Egypt.

c. 1300
West African kingdom of Benin excels in casting realistic figures in bronze.

1430
Great Zimbabwe is built and trades gold to Muslims on the East African coast.

1488
The Portuguese navigator Bartholomeu Diaz rounds the Cape of Good Hope.

1510
The first African slaves are shipped to the Caribbean.

1652
Boers – Dutch settlers – set up a colony in Cape of Good Hope.

1787
The British establish a colony in Sierra Leone, West Africa.

1795
The British acquire the Cape of Good Hope from Dutch.

1822
United States sets up Liberia, West Africa, as a home for freed slaves.

1835-37
Boers trek north from the Cape to escape British rule.

1899-1902
Boer War is fought between the Boers and the British. Treaty makes Boer republics British colonies.

INDEPENDENCE AND THE MODERN WORLD — 1900 – 2000

1910
Union of South Africa is created.

1914-1918
World War I: German colonies in Africa conquered by British and French.

1935
Italy conquers Ethiopia; leads to end of League of Nations.

1949
Apartheid (separation of races) begins in South Africa.

1954
Gamal Abdel Nasser becomes premier of Egypt.

1957
Ghana becomes independent; it is the first African state to gain independence.

1962
Algeria wins independence from France.

1963
Organization of African Unity (OAU) is founded.

1964
ANC leader Nelson Mandela is jailed for life.

1965
Rhodesia declares independence from Britain.

1967-70
Civil war fought in Nigeria.

1975
Moroccans begin occupation of the Spanish Sahara.

1980
Rhodesia becomes independent and is renamed Zimbabwe.

1984
Ten-year drought leads to appalling famine in Ethiopia, Sudan, and Chad.

1989
Namibia, the last colony in Africa, becomes independent from South Africa.

1993
Eritrea becomes independent.

1994
Nelson Mandela, released in 1990, becomes president of South Africa.

1000	500	A.D. 100	400	500	600	800

. 700 Ironworking begins n Africa	c. 400 Copper smelting begins in Mauritania	238 Revolt in Africa begins against Roman rule	c. 400 Use of iron spreads through eastern Africa	c. 500 Rise of the Ghanaian Empire, West Africa		
. 600 Oaxaca culture grows stronger, Mexico	c. 200 Beginning of early Mayan period	c. 100 Moche civilization begins on Peruvian coast		c. 500 Thule people move into Alaska	c. 600 Height of Mayan civilization	
57-529 Reign of Cyrus the Great, Persia	c. 250 Arsaces I founds the Parthian kingdom, Persia	c. 224 Parthian rule ends in Persian Empire	c. 400 Gupta Empire stretches across India	c. 500 The figure zero is introduced in India	634 Arab Empire begins	
. 1000 Early Iron Age begins in Italy	431 Great Peloponnesian War	116-117 Roman Empire is at its greatest extent		527-565 Reign of Justinian, Byzantine emperor	787 Vikings make their first raids on the coasts of Britain	c. 800 First castles built
	c. 500 Aboriginal culture develops	c. 300 Beginning of early eastern Polynesian culture		c. 500 Polynesians navigate eastwards	c. 700 First Polynesians settle in the Cook Islands	

AMERICAS

EARLIEST PEOPLES (40,000 – 2000 B.C.)

c. 40,000 B.C.
The first peoples arrive in the Americas from Siberia across the Bering Strait.

c. 15,000 B.C.
Cave art produced in what is now Brazil.

c. 6500 B.C.
Farming begins in the Peruvian Andes, South America.

c. 3200 B.C.
Pottery begins to be made in Ecuador, and Colombia, South America.

EMPIRES AND CIVILIZATIONS (2000 B.C. – A.D. 1450)

2000 B.C.
The Mayan culture begins in Central America. Farmers begin to settle in villages.

c. 1150 B.C.
Olmec people in Mexico, North America, develop a picture-writing and number system that spreads through continent.

c. 300 B.C.
Mayan culture develops. Large political and religious centres are built, such as Palenque.

C. A.D. 300
Hopewell Indians build burial mounds and trade in North America.

C. A.D. 700
People weave tapestries in Peru, South America. Cotton and wool tapestry, above, shows jaguars.

C. A.D. 900
Toltecs conquer the Mayans and create an empire in Central America.

C. A.D. 1000
Vikings from Europe arrive in North America.

EUROPEAN CONQUEST AND TRADE (1450 – 1750)

1492
Italian explorer Christopher Columbus reaches the Caribbean and claims islands for Spain; other Europeans follow with horses and guns, seeking treasure.

1494
Treaty of Tordesillas divides the Americas between Spain and Portugal.

1499
Amerigo Vespucci explores the Amazon, South America; gives his name to the American continent.

c. 1510
First African slaves are taken to the Caribbean.

1519
Hernando Cortés, a Spanish Conquistador, conquers Mexico; the Aztec Empire, under emperor Montezuma, ends.

1620
Mayflower ship arrives in New England, North America, carrying Puritan refugees from Britain (the Pilgrims).

1636
The first university in the future US, Harvard College, is founded.

THE NEW NATIONS (1750 – 1900)

1783
Birth of Simón Bolívar, liberator of South America.

1776
America issues Declaration of Independence.

1787
Dollar currency is introduced into America.

1791
Slave revolt in Haiti, led by Toussaint L'Ouverture against the French.

1803
Louisiana Purchase: US buys land from France, doubling the size of the country.

1861-65
American Civil War.

1849
Gold rush begins in California.

1852
Elisha Otis invents the elevator.

1861-65
Civil War fought in United States. Slaves are freed.

1867
Canada becomes independent.

1869
Railroad crosses United States from coast to coast.

1876
Battle of the Little Bighorn between Indians and white troops.

1877
Thomas Edison invents the phonograph.

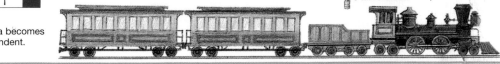

1895
King C. Gillette invents the safety razor, with a convenient disposable blade.

THE MODERN WORLD (1900 – 2000)

1903
Wright brothers make first powered flight.

1908
Henry Ford produces Model T Ford car.

1913
Hollywood becomes center of film industry.

1917
United States enters World War I, following rupture in diplomatic relations with Germany.

1920
Boom years: jazz age follows World War I (1914-18).

1929
The Wall Street crash: the US Stock Exchange collapses; start of Depression of 1930s.

1941
United States enters World War II.

1945
United Nations begins, San Francisco.

1958
Silicon chip developed by Texas Instruments Co.

1959
Ernesto "Che" Guevara helps Fidel Castro overthrow Cuban government.

1969
Apollo 11 takes US astronauts to the Moon. Neil Armstrong is the first man to walk on the Moon.

1987
Intermediate-Range Nuclear Forces (INF) Treaty signed with Soviet Union.

1991
Gulf War.

2001
Islamic terrorists destroy the Twin Towers of the World Trade Center in New York City.

A.D.	900	950	1000	1050	1100	1150
AFRICA		969 Cairo is built and becomes capital of Egypt	c. 1000 Kingdoms of Takrur and Gao flourish in West Africa		c. 1100 Ghana Empire in West Africa declines	1173 Muslim warrio Saladin, is Sultan of
AMERICAS	c. 900 Mayan power in northern Mexico starts to fade		c. 1000 Farmers in Peru grow corn and potatoes		c. 1100 Rise of Incas, farmers led by warrior chiefs, in Peru	c. 1150 End of Hop culture in North Am
ASIA	906-906 Tang Dynasty, China collapses after years of war	969 China is reunified under the Song Dynasty	c. 1000 Chinese perfect the art of making gunpowder	c. 1090 Mechanical clock, driven by water, built in China	1099 Crusaders capture Jerusalem, Palestine	
EUROPE	911 Rollo, a Viking chief, settles in Normandy, France	962 Otto the Great is crowned Holy Roman Emperor	c. 986 Viking Eric the Red sets up colony in Greenland	1066 Normans conquer England, Battle of Hastings	1132-35. The first Gothic church is built in Paris	1171-72 Henry II in Ireland, becoming i
OCEANIA	c. 900 First settlers reach South Island, New Zealand		c. 1000 Maori people settle in New Zealand		c. 1100 Organized societies form in Hawaiian Islands	c. 1150 Maoris settl river areas of New Z

ASIA

800,000 B.C. – 1500 B.C. EARLIEST CIVILIZATIONS

800,000 B.C. First humans arrive in Asia from Africa.

c. 9000 B.C. Palestinian sheep are the world's first domesticated animals identified so far.

c. 8350 B.C. Jericho, the world's first known walled city, is founded. It consists of mud brick houses behind a strong wall.

c. 3500 B.C. The Sumerians invent the wheel.

c. 3250 B.C. The Sumerians develop picture writing and build the world's first cities. They also grow barley, bake bread, and make beer. Sumerian picture writing was called cuneiform, and was scratched onto clay tablets.

c. 2698 B.C. Legendary Chinese emperor Shen Nung writes Chinese "Canon of Herbs" with over 252 plant descriptions.

c. 2500 B.C. Indus Valley civilization, based on agriculture, in India.

c. 1750 B.C. Hammurabi establishes the Babylonian Empire.

1500 B.C. – A.D. 1500 EMPIRES AND RELIGIONS

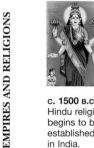

c. 1500 B.C. Hindu religion begins to be established in India.

c. 1200 B.C. Beginning of Judaism, Palestine.

650s B.C. World's first coins are produced in the Near East.

c. 600 B.C. Chinese philosopher Lao-tzu develops philosophy of Taoism.

c. 563 B.C. Birth of Siddhartha Gautama, the Buddha, founder of Buddhism, India.

551 B.C. Birth of Confucius, founder of a philosophical system in China.

200s B.C. Great Wall of China is built to keep out invaders.

C. A.D. 30 Jesus Christ is executed; Christianity is born in Judea.

C. A.D. 100 Paper is invented in China.

A.D. 606 First examinations for entry to public offices in China.

A.D. 632 Death of Muhammad, the Prophet. Spread of Islamic religion, led by caliphs (successors).

A.D. 868 World's first printed book, Diamond Sutra, in China

C. A.D. 1000 The Chinese perfect their invention of gunpowder.

A.D. 1206 Mongols begin conquest of Asia.

1259 Kublai Khan becomes Mongol ruler of China; sets up Yuan dynasty, which lasts 1279-1368.

1290 Ottomans (Turkish Muslims) rise to power.

1333 China suffers drought, famine, floods, and plague. Five million people die.

1421 Peking (now Beijing) becomes capital of China.

1453 Ottomans capture Constantinople, ending the Byzantine Empire.

1498 Portuguese navigator Vasco da Gama reaches India, via Africa.

1500 – 1900 TRADE AND CONQUEST

1556 Akbar the Great, the greatest of the Mogul rulers, comes to power, India.

1600 English East India trading company is founded.

1639 Japan closed to foreigners.

1648 Taj Mahal is built in India by emperor Shah Jahan as a tomb for his favorite wife, Mumtaz Mahal.

1649 Russians conquer Siberia and reach the Pacific Ocean.

1857 Outbreak of Indian Mutiny against British rule. Put down by British a year later.

1900 – 2000 THE MODERN WORLD

1911 China becomes a republic.

1918 Ottoman Empire collapses.

1920 Mahatma Gandhi begins campaign for Indian independence.

1921 Mao Zedong and Li Ta-chao found the Chinese Communist Party in Beijing.

1926 Hirohito becomes the emperor of Japan.

1934 Communists in China, led by Mao Zedong, begin Long March through the mountains of China to Yenan, where they set up government.

1941 Japanese attack US fleet at Pearl Harbor, Hawaii.

1945 World's first atomic bombs are dropped on Japan.

1947 India and Pakistan independent.

1947 Partition of Palestine into Arab and Jewish states leading to fighting between Arabs and Jews in Palestine.

1948 Jewish state of Israel founded.

1966 Mao Zedong starts Cultural Revolution in China.

1967 Six-Day War between Arabs and Israelis.

1980-1989 War between Iran and Iraq.

1989 Pro-democracy movement in Beijing is crushed by military force.

Mao Zedong

1990-1991 Gulf War. Iraq invades Kuwait. UN intervenes.

2003 US and British forces invade Iraq.

2004 Tsunami around Indian Ocean kills 300,000 people.

1200	1250	1300	1350	1400	1450	1500

1200-30 King of Ethiopia as churches cut from rock	c. 1250 Kanem kingdom breaks up into rival factions	1348 Egypt devastated by plague, called the Black Death		c.1400 Gold trade thrives in Kingdom of Great Zimbabwe	c. 1450 Songhai Empire reaches its greatest height	
. 1200 Incas in Peru center round settlement of Cuzco	c. 1250 Chimu people expand their empire in Peru	c. 1300 Incas expand their empire in the central Andes		c. 1400 Inca Empire flourishes in South America		1519 Conquistadors destroy Aztec and Inca Empires
206 Ghengis Khan founds Mongol Empire	c. 1254 Explorer, Marco Polo, born in Venice	c. 1300 Osman founds Ottoman Dynasty in Turkey	1368 Mongols are driven out of China		c. 1450 Portuguese set up trading posts in Indian Ocean – Christianity spreads in Asia	
215 English King John seals Magna Carta	1282-84 Edward I of England conquers Wales	1337 Start of 100 Years' War between England and France	1370 Chaucer writes his first book, *Book of the Duchess*	c. 1400 Renaissance of art and learning begins		
	c. 1250 Valley irrigation schemes in Hawaiian islands	c. 1300 Huge stone statues are built on Easter Island	c. 1350 Maoris flourish in North Island, New Zealand		c. 1450 Advanced societies develop in Polynesian islands	

EUROPE

EARLY PEOPLES AND THE ANCIENT WORLD

1,000,000 B.C. – A.D. 450

1,000,000 B.C.
First humans arrive in Europe.

6500 B.C.
People begin farming in Greece and the Balkans.

c. 1900 B.C.
Civilization of Mycenae develops in Greece. The Mycenaeans build splendid, rich palaces.

c. 1500 B.C.
Linear B script, used to write an early version of the Greek language, develops in Crete.

c. 1250 B.C.
Trojan War between Greeks of Mycenae and the Trojans. According to legend, after a 10-year siege the Greeks entered Troy hidden inside a huge wooden horse, and destroyed the city.

c. 753 B.C.
Rome founded by the legendary brothers Romulus and Remus.

776 B.C.
First Olympic Games held in Greece.

750 B.C.
Homer composes the *Iliad*, an epic poem describing the Trojan War.

c. 500 B.C
Celts occupy much of Europe.

146 B.C.
Romans conquer Greece.

RELIGION AND THE MIDDLE AGES

A.D. 450 – 1450

44 B.C.
Julius Caesar is assassinated.

A.D. 391
Christianity becomes the official religion of the Roman Empire.

A.D. 500
Barbarian tribes overrun much of western Europe.

793
Vikings raid northern Europe.

1096
First Crusade leaves England for Palestine.

c. 1150
One of the first European universities is founded in Paris.

1290
Reading glasses are invented in Italy.

1348
Bubonic plague, called the Black Death, kills one-third of the population of Europe.

1454
The German Johann Gutenberg publishes the Gutenberg Bible, the first printed book in Europe. It was printed with movable copper type.

EXPLORATION AND SCIENCE

1450 – 1780

1453
Ottoman Turks capture Constantinople; end of Byzantine Empire.

1516
Hapsburg Empire expands under Charles V of Spain.

1517
German Martin Luther pins a list of complaints about Roman Catholic Church practices on a church door in Wittenberg; Reformation begins.

1519-1521
Portuguese Ferdinand Magellan leads the first voyage around the world.

REVOLUTION AND THE MODERN WORLD

1760 – 2000

1531
Polish astronomer Copernicus suggests that Earth revolves around the Sun.

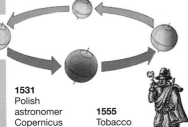

1555
Tobacco taken to Europe from the Americas.

1603
Union of Scotland and England.

1628
William Harvey, English doctor, discovers circulation of blood.

1665
English scientist Isaac Newton discovers laws of gravity.

1682
Peter the Great becomes czar of Russia.

1683
Ottoman Turks fail in their siege of Vienna.

1690
William III of England defeats the exiled Catholic James II and his Irish supporters at the Battle of the Boyne, Ireland.

1710
Russia conquers Swedish provinces in the Baltic.

1789
French Revolution breaks out.

1805
British Admiral Nelson defeats French in the sea battle of Trafalgar.

1825
First passenger railroad, Britain

1840
First postage stamp, the Penny Black, is issued in Britain.

1846
Potato famine in Ireland.

1848
Karl Marx and Friedrich Engels write *Communist Manifesto*.

1859
Charles Darwin publishes theory of evolution.

1876
Alexander Graham Bell invents telephone.

1895
Italian Guglielmo Marconi invents the radio.

1902
Polish scientist Marie Curie and her French husband, Pierre, discover radium, a chemical element to treat cancer.

1914
World War I begins.

1917
Russian Revolution breaks out.

1922
The Irish Free State is formed.

1930s
Economic depression in Europe.

1939
German scientists discover that energy can be released by splitting uranium atoms into two.

1939
World War II begins.

1949
North Atlantic Treaty Organization (NATO) formed.

1957
European Union is formed.

1957
Soviets launch first space satellite.

1961
Berlin Wall built.

1990
East and West Germany unite.

1991
Soviet Union collapses.

1992
Civil war breaks out in Bosnia.

1999
NATO forces attack Serbia in defence of Kosovan Muslims.

2002
Euro introduced.

A.D.	1550	1600	1650	1700	1725	1750
AFRICA	c. 1500 Songhai Empire expands in West Africa	c. 1600 Ivory trade expands in Kalonga kingdom	1652 Dutch found Cape Town in South Africa		c. 1740 The Lunda create prosperous new kingdom	1755 The first outbr of smallpox, Cape To
AMERICAS		c. 1608 Quebec in Canada founded by France		c. 1700 North American colonies begin to prosper	1727 First discovery of diamonds in Brazil	1776 US Declaration Independence, July 4
ASIA		c. 1619 Dutch control spice trade in Indonesian islands	c. 1620 Japan restricts contact with rest of world	1709 Death of shogun Tsunayoshi of Japan	1722-35 Siberian-Mongolian border defined	
EUROPE	1558-1603 Reign of Elizabeth I of England	1618-48 30 Years War involves all Europe but Britain	1652-54 First Dutch war with England	1707 Act of Union unites England and Scotland		1789 Outbreak of French Revolution
OCEANIA		1642-44 Abel Tasman founds Tasmania	c. 1680 Civil war starts on Easter Island	c. 1700 First contact between Tahitians and Europeans		1768-71 Captain Coo first voyage to Pacifi

OCEANIA

50,000 B.C. – A.D. 1600 FIRST SETTLERS

c. 40,000 B.C.
Aboriginal people arrive in Australia from Southeast Asia.

c. 2000 B.C.
People arrive in New Guinea.

c. 1300 B.C.
People reach Fiji, Tonga.

c. A.D. 300
People reach Polynesia.

c. A.D. 950
Polynesians, later known as Maori people, settle in New Zealand and the Pacific islands.

1600 – 1850 CONQUEST AND COLONIZATION

1606
Dutch navigator Willem Jansz visits Australia.

1642
Dutch navigator Abel Tasman sails around Australia to New Zealand.

1770
English navigator Captain Cook claims Australia for Britain. He discovers species of animals and plants not yet heard of in Europe.

1788
First British convicts are transported from British prisons to Botany Bay, site of the first European settlement, Australia.

1826
English settlers and Aboriginals fight in the "Black War" in Tasmania.

1840
In the Treaty of Waitangi, Maori chiefs in New Zealand give sovereignty over New Zealand to Britain. New Zealand becomes British colony.

1851
Gold rush, Victoria, Australia. Settlers arrive from Europe.

1850 – 2000 THE MODERN WORLD

1860
Burke and Wills are the first people to cross Australia from coast to coast. Both die of starvation on the journey back in 1861.

1893
New Zealand women gain the vote.

1901
Australia gains independence from Britain; Commonwealth of Australia is proclaimed.

1907
New Zealand gains independence from Britain.

1927
Canberra becomes the capital city of Australia.

1941-42
Japan invades the Pacific islands.

1945
Assisted passages to Australia for Europeans. Two million people emigrate.

1950s
Nuclear testing carried out in the Pacific islands.

1951
ANZUS defense treaty between Australia, New Zealand, and the United States.

1985
South Pacific Forum treaty – Pacific is a nuclear-free zone.

1993
Australia passes Native Title Bill to confirm the Aboriginal right to claim back land.

PRESIDENTS OF THE UNITED STATES

GEORGE WASHINGTON (1732-1799) Term of office: 1789-1797

JOHN ADAMS (1735-1826) Term of office: 1797-1801

THOMAS JEFFERSON (1743-1826) Term of office: 1801-1809

JAMES MADISON (1751-1836) Term of office: 1809-1817

JAMES MONROE (1758-1831) Term of office: 1817-1825

JOHN QUINCY ADAMS (1767-1848) Term of office: 1825-1829

ANDREW JACKSON (1767-1845) Term of office: 1829-1837

MARTIN VAN BUREN (1782-1862) Term of office: 1837-1841

W.H. HARRISON (1773-1841) Term of office: Mar.-Apr. 1841

JOHN TYLER (1790-1862) Term of office: 1841-1845

JAMES K. POLK (1795-1849) Term of office: 1845-1849

ZACHARY TAYLOR (1784-1850) Term of office: 1849-1850

MILLARD FILLMORE (1800-1874) Term of office: 1850-1853

FRANKLIN PIERCE (1804-1869) Term of office: 1853-1857

JAMES BUCHANAN (1791-1868) Term of office: 1857-1861

ABRAHAM LINCOLN (1809-1865) Term of office: 1861-1865

ANDREW JOHNSON (1808-1875) Term of office: 1865-1869

ULYSSES S. GRANT (1822-1885) Term of office: 1869-1877

RUTHERFORD B. HAYES (1822-1893) Term of office: 1877-1881

JAMES A. GARFIELD (1831-1881) Term of office: Mar.-Sept. 1881

CHESTER A. ARTHUR (1830-1886) Term of office: 1881-1885

GROVER CLEVELAND (1837-1908) Term of office: 1885-1889

BENJAMIN HARRISON (1833-1901) Term of office: 1889-1893

GROVER CLEVELAND (1837-1908) Term of office: 1893-1897

WILLIAM MCKINLEY (1843-1901) Term of office: 1897-1901

THEODORE ROOSEVELT (1858-1919) Term of office: 1901-1909

WILLIAM H. TAFT (1857-1930) Term of office: 1909-1913

WOODROW WILSON (1856-1924) Term of office: 1913-1921

WARREN G. HARDING (1865-1923) Term of office: 1921-1923

CALVIN COOLIDGE (1872-1933) Term of office: 1923-1929

HERBERT HOOVER (1874-1964) Term of office: 1929-1933

FRANKLIN D. ROOSEVELT (1882-1945) Term of office: 1933-1945

HARRY S. TRUMAN (1884-1972) Term of office: 1945-1953

DWIGHT EISENHOWER (1890-1969) Term of office: 1953-1961

JOHN F. KENNEDY (1917-1963) Term of office: 1961-1963

LYNDON B. JOHNSON (1908-1973) Term of office: 1963-1969

RICHARD NIXON (1913-1994) Term of office: 1969-1974

GERALD R. FORD (BORN 1913) Term of office: 1974-1977

JIMMY CARTER (BORN 1924) Term of office: 1977-1981

RONALD REAGAN (1911-2004) Term of office: 1981-1989

GEORGE BUSH (BORN 1924) Term of office: 1989-1993

BILL CLINTON (BORN 1946) Term of office: 1993 to 2001

GEORGE W. BUSH (BORN 1946) Term of office: 2001 to date

1800	1825	1850	1900	1925	1950	1990

	1825 Egyptians found the city of Khartoum in Sudan	1897 Slavery banned in Zanzibar	1902 End of second Boer War in South Africa	1930 White women given vote in South Africa	1958-60 Independence for Zaire, Nigeria, Somalia	
1801 Thomas Jefferson becomes third US president	1849 California Gold Rush begins	1861-65 Civil War between southern and northern states		1929 US Stock Exchange crashes	1963 US president John F. Kennedy assassinated	
1819 Stamford Raffles founds Singapore		1851 Thailand is open to foreign trade	1905 Japan becomes world power after defeat of Russia		1965-73 Vietnam War	
1804 Napoleon becomes Emperor of the French	1837 Victoria becomes Queen, United Kingdom		1914-18 World War I	1939-1945 World War II	1961 Berlin Wall divides East and West Germany	
1810 Kamehameha I becomes king of Hawaii	1840 British and Maoris sign Treaty of Waitangi	1860-70 Second Maoris War in New Zealand	1907 New Zealand becomes a dominion	1927 Canberra becomes federal capital of Australia	1970 Tonga and Fiji gain independence from Britain	

KINGS AND QUEENS OF GREAT BRITAIN

RULERS OF ENGLAND

Saxon line	REIGNED		REIGNED
EGBERT	827-839	HENRY I	1100-1135
ETHELWULF	839-858	STEPHEN	1135-1154
ETHELBALD	858-860	**House of Plantagenet**	
ETHELBERT	860-865	HENRY II	1154-1189
ETHELRED I	865-871	RICHARD I	1189-1199
ALFRED THE GREAT	871-899	JOHN	1199-1216
EDWARD THE ELDER	899-924	HENRY III	1216-1272
ATHELSTAN	924-939	EDWARD I	1272-1307
EDMUND	939-946	EDWARD II	1307-1327
EDRED	946-955	EDWARD III	1327-1377
EDWY	955-959	RICHARD II	1377-1399
EDGAR	959-975	**House of Lancaster**	
EDWARD THE MARTYR	975-978	HENRY IV	1399-1413
ETHELRED		HENRY V	1413-1422
THE UNREADY	978-1016	HENRY VI	1422-1461
EDMUND IRONSIDE	1016	(also)	1470-1471
Danish line		**House of York**	
CANUTE (CNUT)	1016-1035	EDWARD IV	1461-1470
HAROLD I HAREFOOT	1035-1040	(also)	1471-1483
HARDECANUTE	1040-1042	EDWARD V	1483
Saxon line		RICHARD III	1483-1485
EDWARD THE CONFESSOR	1042-1066	**House of Tudor**	
HAROLD II		HENRY VII	1485-1509
(GODWINSON)	1066	HENRY VIII	1509-1547
House of Normandy		EDWARD VI	1547-1553
WILLIAM I (THE		MARY I	1553-1558
CONQUEROR)	1066-1087	ELIZABETH I	1558-1603
WILLIAM II	1087-1100		

MONARCHS OF SCOTLAND

MALCOLM II	1005-1034	JOHN DE BALIOL	1292-1296
DUNCAN I	1034-1040	ROBERT I (BRUCE)	1306-1329
MACBETH	1040-1057	DAVID II	1329-1371
MALCOLM III	1057-1093	**House of Stuart**	
DONALD BANE	1093-1094	ROBERT II	1371-1390
DUNCAN II	1094	ROBERT III	1390-1406
DONALD BANE	1094-1097	JAMES I	1406-1437
EDGAR	1097-1107	JAMES II	1437-1460
ALEXANDER I	1107-1124	JAMES III	1460-1488
DAVID I	1124-1153	JAMES IV	1488-1513
MALCOLM IV	1153-1165	JAMES V	1513-1542
WILLIAM THE LION	1165-1214	MARY	1542-1567
ALEXANDER II	1214-1249	JAMES VI	
ALEXANDER III	1249-1286	(became James I of England)	1567-1625
MARGARET OF			
NORWAY	1286-1290		

MONARCHS OF GREAT BRITAIN

House of Stuart			
JAMES I	1603-1625	GEORGE III	1760-1820
CHARLES I	1625-1649	GEORGE IV	1820-1830
Commonwealth	1649-1660	WILLIAM IV	1830-1837
CHARLES II	1660-1685	VICTORIA	1837-1901
JAMES II	1685-1688	**House of Saxe-Coburg-Gotha**	
WILLIAM III	1689-1702	EDWARD VII	1901-1910
MARY II	1689-1694	**House of Windsor**	
ANNE	1702-1714	GEORGE V	1910-1936
House of Hanover		EDWARD VIII	1936
GEORGE I	1714-1727	GEORGE VI	1936-1952
GEORGE II	1727-1760	ELIZABETH II	1952 to date

PRIME MINISTERS OF GREAT BRITAIN

Sir Robert Walpole

William Pitt

Sir Winston S. Churchill

Benjamin Disraeli

William E. Gladstone

PRIME MINISTER	TERM OF OFFICE	PRIME MINISTER	TERM OF OFFICE
SIR ROBERT WALPOLE	1721-1742	BENJAMIN DISRAELI	1868
EARL OF WILMINGTON	1742-1743	WILLIAM E. GLADSTONE	1868-1874
HENRY PELHAM	1743-1754	BENJAMIN DISRAELI	1874-1880
DUKE OF NEWCASTLE	1754-1756	WILLIAM E. GLADSTONE	1880-1885
DUKE OF DEVONSHIRE	1756-1757	MARQUESS OF	
DUKE OF NEWCASTLE	1757-1762	SALISBURY	1885-1886
EARLE OF BUTE	1762-1763	WILLIAM E. GLADSTONE	1886
GEORGE GRENVILLE	1763-1765	MARQUESS OF	
MARQUESS OF		SALISBURY	1886-1892
ROCKINGHAM	1765-1766	WILLIAM E. GLADSTONE	1892-1894
WILLIAM PITT		EARL OF ROSEBERY	1894-1895
(EARL OF CHATHAM)	1766-1767	MARQUESS OF	
DUKE OF GRAFTON	1767-1770	SALISBURY	1895-1902
LORD NORTH	1770-1782	ARTHUR J. BALFOUR	1902-1905
MARQUESS OF		SIR HENRY CAMPBELL-	
ROCKINGHAM	1782	BANNERMAN	1905-1908
EARL OF SHELBORNE	1782-1783	HERBERT HENRY	
DUKE OF PORTLAND	1783	ASQUITH	1908-1915
WILLIAM PITT (THE		HERBERT HENRY	
YOUNGER)	1783-1801	ASQUITH	1915-1916
HENRY ADDINGTON	1801-1804	DAVID LLOYD GEORGE	1916-1922
WILLIAM PITT	1804-1806	ANDREW BONAR LAW	1922-1923
BARON GRENVILLE	1806-1807	STANLEY BALDWIN	1923-1924
DUKE OF PORTLAND	1807-1809	J. RAMSAY MACDONALD	1924
SPENCER PERCEVAL	1809-1812	STANLEY BALDWIN	1924-1929
EARL OF LIVERPOOL	1812-1827	J. RAMSAY MACDONALD	1929-1931
GEORGE CANNING	1827	J. RAMSAY MACDONALD	1931-1935
VISCOUNT GODERICH	1827-1828	STANLEY BALDWIN	1935-1937
DUKE OF WELLINGTON	1828-1830	NEVILLE CHAMBERLAIN	1937-1940
EARL GREY	1830-1834	WINSTON S. CHURCHILL	1940-1945
VISCOUNT MELBOURNE	1834	CLEMENT R. ATTLEE	1945-1951
DUKE OF WELLINGTON	1834	SIR WINSTON S.	
SIR ROBERT PEEL	1834-1835	CHURCHILL	1951-1955
VISCOUNT MELBOURNE	1835-1841	SIR ANTHONY EDEN	1955-1957
SIR ROBERT PEEL	1841-1846	HAROLD MACMILLAN	1957-1963
LORD JOHN RUSSELL	1846-1852	SIR ALEC	
EARL OF DERBY	1852	DOUGLAS-HOME	1963-1964
EARL OF ABERDEEN	1852-1855	HAROLD WILSON	1964-1970
VISCOUNT PALMERSTON	1855-1858	EDWARD HEATH	1970-1974
EARL OF DERBY	1858-1859	HAROLD WILSON	1974-1976
VISCOUNT PALMERSTON	1859-1865	JAMES CALLAGHAN	1976-1979
EARL RUSSELL	1865-1866	MARGARET THATCHER	1979-1990
EARL OF DERBY	1866-1868	JOHN MAJOR	1990-1997
		TONY BLAIR	1997 to date

THE WORLD

SINCE TIME BEGAN, world population has risen and fallen as health and food supplies have changed. The number of people alive at any one time rose when there was plenty of food, and fell when famine or disease struck. Until about 800 A.D., the population of the world stayed below 200 million. But since then it has risen dramatically. The rise was greatest in the 20th century; by the year 2020, experts predict that there will be more than 8.5 billion people on Earth. The population graph below charts the world's rising population since 1500, and includes a forecast.

1. SLOVENIA
2. CROATIA
3. BOSNIA & HERZEGOVINA
4. SERBIA & MONTENEGRO
5. MACEDONIA
6. ALBANIA
7. BELGIUM
8. LUXEMBOURG
9. LIECHTENSTEIN
10. SWITZERLAND
11. MOLDOVA
12. ANDORRA
13. MONACO
14. SAN MARINO
15. VATICAN CITY
16. NETHERLANDS
17. HUNGARY

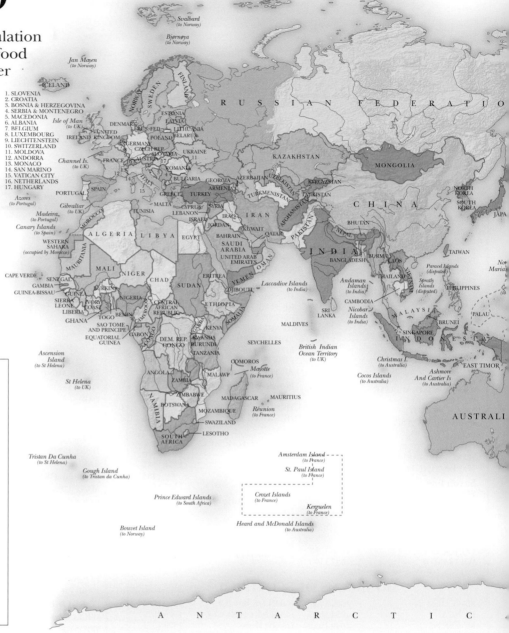

BIGGEST CITY AGGLOMERATIONS

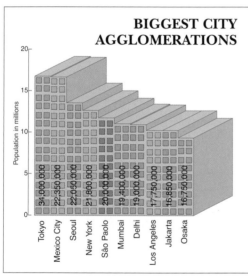

Population in millions

City	Population
Tokyo	34,000,000
Mexico City	22,350,000
Seoul	22,050,000
New York	21,800,000
São Paolo	20,000,000
Mumbai	19,400,000
Delhi	19,000,000
Los Angeles	17,750,000
Jakarta	16,850,000
Osaka	16,750,000

HEALTH CARE

How many patients must each doctor care for?

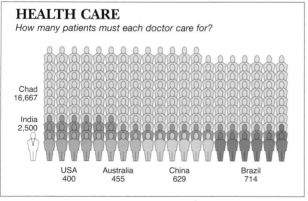

Chad 16,667
India 2,500

USA 400
Australia 455
China 629
Brazil 714

CALORIES

How many calories are available as a percentage of need?

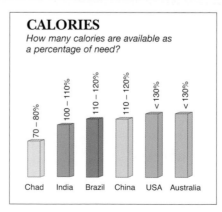

Chad	India	Brazil	China	USA	Australia
70 – 80%	100 – 110%	110 – 120%	110 – 120%	<130%	<130%

WATER

How many cubic meters of water are available per person?

(NOTE: 1 cubic meter = 1.307 cubic yards)

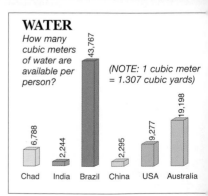

Chad	India	Brazil	China	USA	Australia
6,788	2,244	43,767	2,295	9,277	19,198

WORLD POPULATION GROWTH SINCE 1500

One figure represents 500 million people

1500   1600   1700

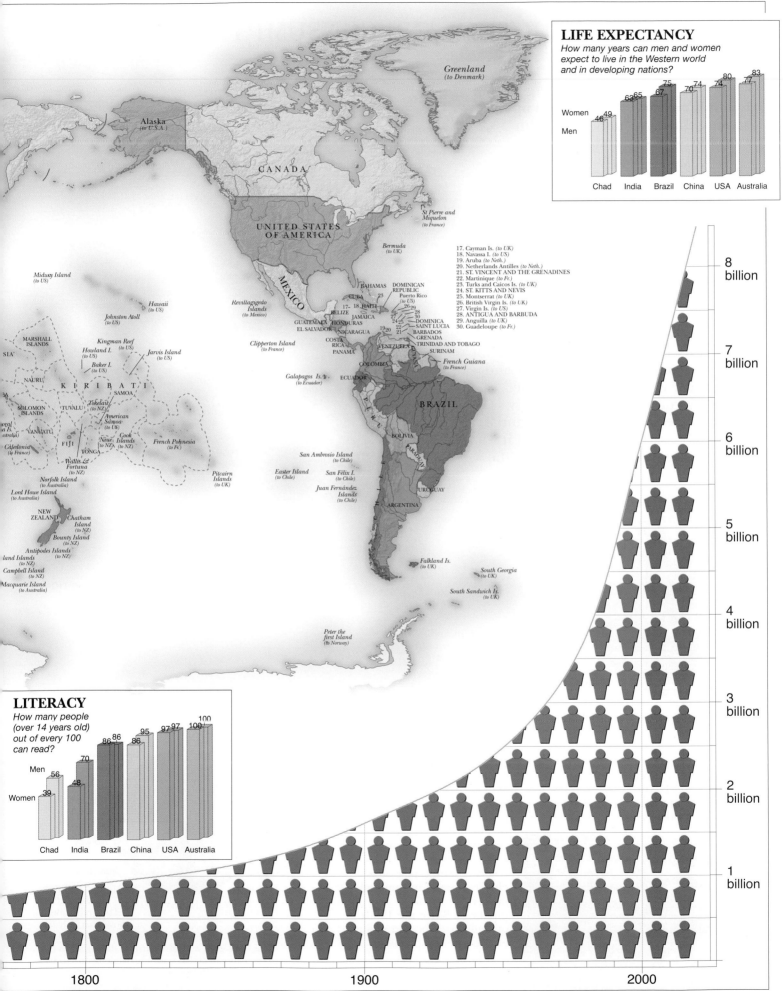

LIFE EXPECTANCY

How many years can men and women expect to live in the Western world and in developing nations?

Women
Men

	Chad	India	Brazil	China	USA	Australia
Men	46	63	67	70	74	77
Women	49	65	75	74	80	83

17. Cayman Is. *(to UK)*
18. Navassa I. *(to US)*
19. Aruba *(to Neth.)*
20. Netherlands Antilles *(to Neth.)*
21. ST. VINCENT AND THE GRENADINES
22. Martinique *(to Fr.)*
23. Turks and Caicos Is. *(to UK)*
24. ST. KITTS AND NEVIS
25. Montserrat *(to UK)*
26. British Virgin Is. *(to UK)*
27. Virgin Is. *(to US)*
28. ANTIGUA AND BARBUDA
29. Anguilla *(to UK)*
30. Guadeloupe *(to Fr.)*

8 billion
7 billion
6 billion
5 billion
4 billion
3 billion
2 billion
1 billion

LITERACY

How many people (over 14 years old) out of every 100 can read?

Men
Women

	Chad	India	Brazil	China	USA	Australia
Women	39	48	86	86	97	100
Men	56	70	86	95	97	100

1800   1900   2000

ENERGY PRODUCTION AND CONSUMPTION

Fossil fuels – oil, coal, and gas – still supply most of the world's energy, but they are rapidly being used up. Most of the fossil fuels come from countries in the Middle East. Although each year new reserves of oil and natural gas are found, no one knows how long these reserves will last. Because people in the developed countries have so many cars and electrical appliances, they use far more energy than people in the less-developed countries. The US alone uses 25 percent of the world's energy, but has only 5 percent of its population. Nuclear power is being used in increasing amounts, but there are concerns about its safety and the nuclear waste it produces. The use of alternative sources of energy, such as wave power, solar power, and wind power, is also increasing, but it still only supplies a tiny fraction of the energy the world needs.

GEYSER POWER
Iceland gets 17 percent of its electricity from geothermal power.

WIND POWER
Denmark now leads the world in the use of offshore wind farms

1. SLOVENIA
2. CROATIA
3. BOSNIA & HERZEGOVINA
4. SERBIA & MONTENEGRO
5. MACEDONIA
6. ALBANIA
7. BELGIUM
8. LUXEMBOURG
9. LIECHTENSTEIN
10. SWITZERLAND
11. MOLDOVA
12. ANDORRA
13. MONACO
14. SAN MARINO
15. VATICAN CITY
16. NETHERLANDS
17. HUNGARY

ENERGY CONSUMPTION
(Kilograms of coal equivalent per person a year)

- more than 10,000
- 5000 – 10,000
- 1000 – 5000
- 100 – 1000
- less than 100
- no data

WOOD POWER
In the villages of Africa, Brazil, and India, the burning of wood is the main source of energy. As forests are cut down, firewood becomes increasingly hard to find. Collecting wood is traditionally women's work. Where wood is scarce, women can spend up to four hours a day searching for it and carrying it long distances back to their villages.

OIL
Modern industrial economies greatly depend on oil to drive their machines and factories. To feed the global appetite for oil, almost 9.9 million tons of oil are produced each day. Saudi Arabia is the world's largest oil producer; the US is the largest consumer. Countries that produce more oil than they need export it to countries that have no oil reserves. The crude oil is either shipped in huge oil tankers, or through pipelines. Since the 1960s, oil spills have been a major environmental problem, polluting the oceans and destroying wildlife.

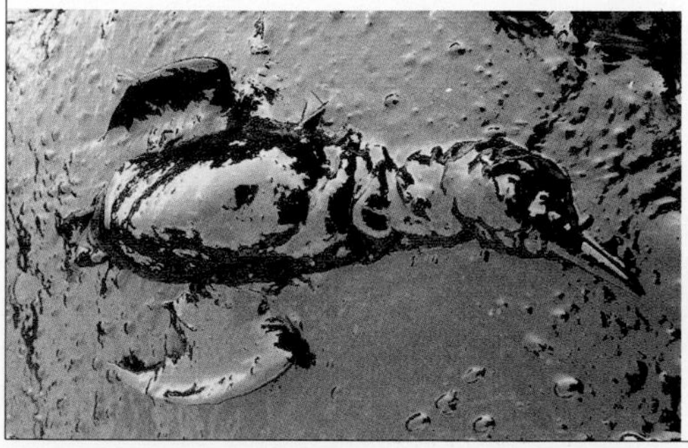

WORLD EXPORTERS OF ENERGY

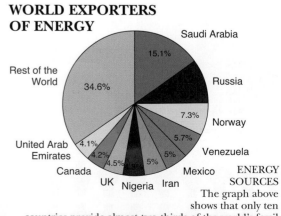

- Saudi Arabia 15.1%
- Russia 7.3%
- Norway 5.7%
- Venezuela 5%
- Mexico 5%
- Iran 4.5%
- Nigeria 4.2%
- UK 4.1%
- Canada
- United Arab Emirates
- Rest of the World 34.6%

ENERGY SOURCES
The graph above shows that only ten countries provide almost two thirds of the world's fossil fuels – oil, coal, and gas. Burning these fuels is the major cause of global warming, while hydroelectric power is a cheap and renewable energy source.

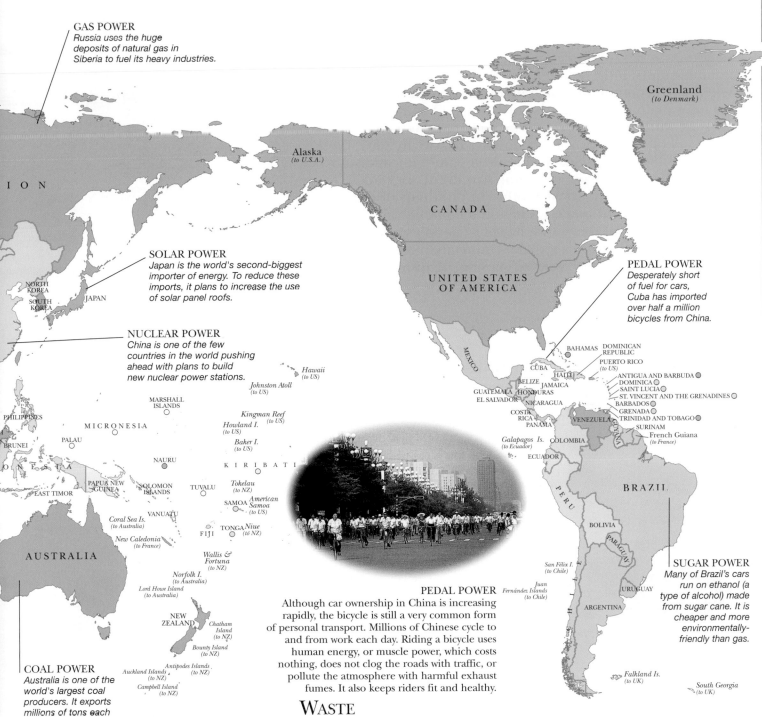

GAS POWER
Russia uses the huge deposits of natural gas in Siberia to fuel its heavy industries.

SOLAR POWER
Japan is the world's second-biggest importer of energy. To reduce these imports, it plans to increase the use of solar panel roofs.

NUCLEAR POWER
China is one of the few countries in the world pushing ahead with plans to build new nuclear power stations.

PEDAL POWER
Desperately short of fuel for cars, Cuba has imported over half a million bicycles from China.

SUGAR POWER
Many of Brazil's cars run on ethanol (a type of alcohol) made from sugar cane. It is cheaper and more environmentally-friendly than gas.

COAL POWER
Australia is one of the world's largest coal producers. It exports millions of tons each year, much of it to Japan.

PEDAL POWER
Although car ownership in China is increasing rapidly, the bicycle is still a very common form of personal transport. Millions of Chinese cycle to and from work each day. Riding a bicycle uses human energy, or muscle power, which costs nothing, does not clog the roads with traffic, or pollute the atmosphere with harmful exhaust fumes. It also keeps riders fit and healthy.

WASTE

The richer and more developed a country is, the more waste it produces. Every day people in the US dump tons of paper, newspapers, disposable daipers, aluminum cans, clothing, and car tires. Getting rid of these mountains of waste is a major world problem. Recycling trash helps; of the 551,000 tons (520,000 tonnes) of waste produced by the US every day, 20 percent is recycled. Germany has the best record for recycling waste. In some cities in the less-developed world, the poor make a living by picking through garbage dumps and selling what they find to recycling centers.

USED CARS
Every day, hundreds of thousands of vehicles roll off the world's production lines. By the year 2025, there will be an estimated one billion cars on the world's roads. The US and Japan manufacture more cars each year than any other country in the world. But every day in the US some 35,000 tons of used cars are put on the scrap-heap. The exhaust from cars pollutes the air. In many of the world's major cities, the very act of breathing is a health hazard.

Find out more
COAL
ENERGY
GAS
NUCLEAR ENERGY
OIL
POLLUTION
TRADE AND INDUSTRY

GLOBAL COMMUNICATIONS

Today, dozens of satellites circle the globe, providing communications links between all points on Earth. If you have a telephone, a computer, and a modem, you can receive and send information, log on to the Internet, and communicate across the world. The Internet is growing so fast that every three years the number of users doubles in size. In 2005, there were 900 million users. Special low-orbit communications satellites will soon provide reception worldwide for mobile phone users, all talking to each other in hundreds of different languages. Americans make 1.3 billion telephone calls every day. In some parts of the world, however, people cannot afford a telephone, or it takes years to get connected. In rural areas television images can be received via satellite dishes. In the last 20 years, the number of television sets in the world has nearly tripled to one billion.

Key:
1. SLOVENIA
2. CROATIA
3. BOSNIA & HERZEGOVINA
4. YUGOSLAVIA
5. MACEDONIA
6. ALBANIA
7. BELGIUM
8. LUXEMBOURG
9. LIECHTENSTEIN
10. SWITZERLAND
11. MOLDOVA
12. ANDORRA
13. MONACO
14. SAN MARINO
15. VATICAN CITY
16. NETHERLANDS
17. HUNGARY

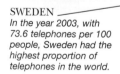

CELL PHONES

Every day, around two billion cell phones are in use across the world. With your phone in your pocket, you can leave home and still be able to telephone someone almost anywhere on the planet. You can make a phone call from a bus or call home from abroad. Using the high-resolution screen available on some phones, it is now possible to send and receive emails and faxes, play a computer game, or access the Internet. It will soon be possible to watch television programs on your cell phone.

SWEDEN
In the year 2003, with 73.6 telephones per 100 people, Sweden had the highest proportion of telephones in the world.

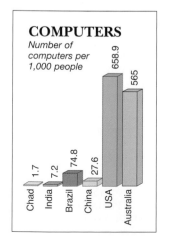

COMPUTERS
Number of computers per 1,000 people

Country	Number
Chad	1.7
India	7.2
Brazil	74.8
China	27.6
USA	658.9
Australia	565

AFRICA
By the year 2010, 21,749 miles (35,000 km) of cable will provide telephone links for 41 countries in Africa.

PHONE CONNECTION
(Mainline telephones per 100 people)

- more than 70
- 51–70
- 31–50
- 11–30
- less than 11
- no data

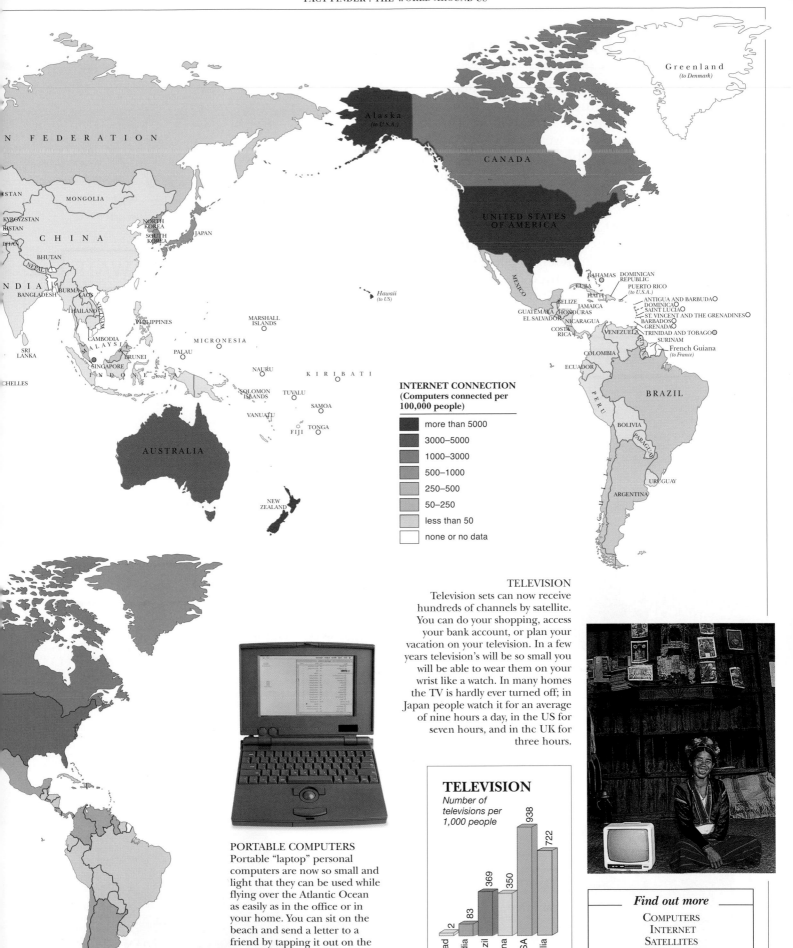

Greenland
(to Denmark)

Alaska
(to U.S.A.)

CANADA

UNITED STATES
OF AMERICA

N FEDERATION

MONGOLIA

KYRGYZSTAN

CHINA

NORTH
KOREA

SOUTH
KOREA

JAPAN

BHUTAN

NEPAL

INDIA

BANGLADESH

BURMA

LAOS

THAILAND

CAMBODIA

SRI
LANKA

MALAYSIA

BRUNEI

SINGAPORE

INDONESIA

CHELLES

PHILIPPINES

PALAU

MICRONESIA

MARSHALL
ISLANDS

Hawaii
(to US)

NAURU

KIRIBATI

SOLOMON
ISLANDS

TUVALU

SAMOA

VANUATU

TONGA

FIJI

AUSTRALIA

NEW
ZEALAND

MEXICO

BELIZE
GUATEMALA
EL SALVADOR

HONDURAS
NICARAGUA

COSTA
RICA

CUBA

BAHAMAS

HAITI

JAMAICA

DOMINICAN
REPUBLIC

PUERTO RICO
(to U.S.A.)

ANTIGUA AND BARBUDA
DOMINICA
SAINT LUCIA
ST. VINCENT AND THE GRENADINES
BARBADOS
GRENADA
TRINIDAD AND TOBAGO

VENEZUELA

SURINAM

French Guiana
(to France)

COLOMBIA

ECUADOR

PERU

BOLIVIA

PARAGUAY

BRAZIL

URUGUAY

ARGENTINA

INTERNET CONNECTION
(Computers connected per 100,000 people)

- more than 5000
- 3000–5000
- 1000–3000
- 500–1000
- 250–500
- 50–250
- less than 50
- none or no data

TELEVISION

Television sets can now receive hundreds of channels by satellite. You can do your shopping, access your bank account, or plan your vacation on your television. In a few years television's will be so small you will be able to wear them on your wrist like a watch. In many homes the TV is hardly ever turned off; in Japan people watch it for an average of nine hours a day, in the US for seven hours, and in thc UK for three hours.

PORTABLE COMPUTERS

Portable "laptop" personal computers are now so small and light that they can be used while flying over the Atlantic Ocean as easily as in the office or in your home. You can sit on the beach and send a letter to a friend by tapping it out on the keyboard, or you can send a voice message by talking into the computer's microphone.

TELEVISION
Number of televisions per 1,000 people

Chad	India	Brazil	China	USA	Australia
2	83	369	350	938	722

Find out more

COMPUTERS
INTERNET
SATELLITES
TELEPHONES
TELEVISION AND VIDEO

UNITED STATES REGION BY REGION

FROM SEA TO SHINING SEA, the United States stretches across the North American continent from the Atlantic Ocean in the east, to the Pacific coastline in the west. This vast nation also includes Alaska, in the frozen northwestern corner of North America, and Hawaii, a chain of sunswept islands far off in the middle of the Pacific Ocean. Its regions are as varied as its people, from the vast prairies of the Midwest to the densely-populated cities of the Middle Atlantic states, the magnificent peaks of the Rocky Mountains to the painted deserts of the Southwest, and the historical towns of New England to the bayous of the Southern states.

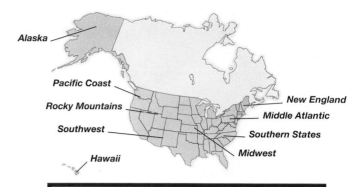

PACIFIC COAST

States
California, Oregon, Washington

Cities
Sacramento, Los Angeles, San Diego, San Jose, and San Francisco (California); Salem and Portland (Oregon); Seattle, Olympia, and Spokane (Washington)

Rivers and lakes
Crater Lake (Oregon); Columbia River

Mountains
Mt Whitney (California); Mt Rainier (Washington)

Historic places
Yosemite (California); Grand Coulee Dam (Washington)

Amazing facts
The largest concentration of automobiles in the world is in Los Angeles County, while Oregon produces more lumber than any other state in the US.

ALASKA AND HAWAII

Cities
Juneau, Anchorage, and Fairbanks (Alaska); Honolulu (Hawaii)

Mountains
Mt Denali/Mt McKinley (Alaska); Mauna Loa volcano (Hawaii)

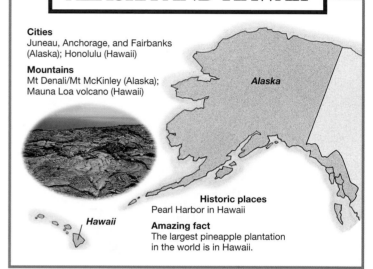

Historic places
Pearl Harbor in Hawaii

Amazing fact
The largest pineapple plantation in the world is in Hawaii.

SOUTHWEST

States
Arizona, New Mexico, Oklahoma, Texas

Cities
Phoenix and Tucson (Arizona); Santa Fe and Albuquerque (New Mexico); Oklahoma City and Tulsa (Oklahoma); Austin, Houston, Dallas, and San Antonio (Texas)

Monument Valley, Utah

Rivers
Rio Grande; Red River

Historic places
Grand Canyon (Arizona); the Alamo, San Antonio (Texas).

Amazing fact
Texas was once a completely independent nation. It won its independence from Mexico in 1836, and did not become a member of the United States until 1845.

ROCKY MOUNTAINS

States
Colorado, Idaho, Montana, Nevada, Utah, Wyoming

Cities
Denver and Colorado Springs (Colorado); Boise (Idaho); Helena, Billings, and Great Falls (Montana); Carson City, Las Vegas, and Reno (Nevada); Salt Lake City and Provo (Utah); Cheyenne and Casper (Wyoming)

Mountains
Rocky Mountains

Rivers
Colorado River; Snake River

Lakes
Great Salt Lake (Utah)

Covered wagon

Historic places
Yellowstone National Park (Wyoming); Little Bighorn (Montana); Hoover Dam (Nevada/Arizona border)

Amazing fact
The largest copper mine in the US, in Bingham, Utah, has operated since 1865 – the last year of the Civil War.

TERRITORIES

Several islands in the Carribbean Sea and the Pacific Ocean are held in possession by the United States. More than 3 million people live in these territories, most of them in Puerto Rico. The majority of these territories govern themselves. Some territories, including Puerto Rico, Guam, American Samoa, and the US Virgin Islands, have a voice in the United States Congress, sending representatives to vote in congressional committees.

Territories

Caribbean:
Puerto Rico
US Virgin Islands

Pacific:
Guam
American Samoa
Midway Islands
Northern Mariana Islands
Wake Island

Wake Island (left) is situated far out in the Pacific Ocean, more than 3,500 miles (5,500 km) from the US mainland.

MIDDLE ATLANTIC

States
New Jersey, New York, Pennsylvania

Cities
Trenton and Newark (New Jersey); New York City, Buffalo, and Albany (New York); Harrisburg, Philadelphia, and Pittsburgh (Pennsylvania)

Mountains
Appalachian Mountains

Historic places
Flatiron Building, Empire State Building, Statue of Liberty and Ellis Island (New York City); Liberty Bell in Philadelphia (Pennsylvania)

Statue of Liberty, New York

New York

Pennsylvania

New Jersey

Amazing facts
New Jersey is the most densely populated state in the nation. On average, there are 1,031 people per sq mile (2,675 per sq km). The first commercial oil well in America was drilled in Titusville, Pennsylvania, in 1859.

NEW ENGLAND

States
Connecticut, Maine, Massachusetts, New Hampshire, Rhode Island, Vermont

Cities
Hartford and Bridgeport (Connecticut); Augusta and Portland (Maine); Boston (Massachusetts); Concord and Manchester (New Hampshire); Montpelier and Burlington (Vermont)

Mountains
White Mountains

Historic places
Plymouth Rock, Bunker Hill (both Massachusetts)

Amazing fact
Four-fifths of Maine is covered by forest.

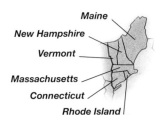

Maine

New Hampshire

Vermont

Massachusetts

Connecticut

Rhode Island

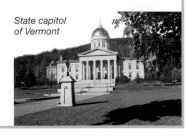

State capitol of Vermont

MIDWEST

States
Illinois, Indiana, Iowa, Kansas, Michigan, Minnesota, Missouri, Nebraska, North Dakota, Ohio, South Dakota, Wisconsin

Cities
Springfield and Chicago (Illinois); Indianapolis (Indiana); Des Moines and Cedar Rapids (Iowa); Topeka and Wichita (Kansas); Detroit and Grand Rapids (Michigan); St Paul and Minneapolis (Minnesota); Kansas City and St Louis (Missouri); Lincoln and Omaha (Nebraska); Bismarck and Fargo (North Dakota); Cleveland, Columbus, and Cincinnati (Ohio); Pierre and Sioux Falls (South Dakota); Milwaukee (Wisconsin)

Minnesota

North Dakota

South Dakota

Wisconsin

Michigan

Nebraska

Iowa

Ohio

Kansas

Indiana

Missouri

Illinois

Rivers
Ohio River; Platte River; Missouri River

Historic places
Henry Ford Museum, Dearborn, near Detroit; Gateway Arch, St Louis; Mount Rushmore near Rapid City (South Dakota)

Amazing facts
Huge glaciers carved out the Great Lakes. Together, they form the greatest area of fresh water on Earth. Combined, the Great Lakes would cover the whole of both New York state and Pennsylvania.

SOUTHERN STATES

States
Alabama, Arkansas, Delaware, Florida, Georgia, Kentucky, Louisiana, Maryland, Mississippi, North Carolina, South Carolina, Tennessee, Virginia, West Virginia

Cities
Birmingham and Montgomery (Alabama); Little Rock (Arkansas); Wilmington and Dover (Delaware); Tallahassee, Jacksonville, and Miami (Florida); Atlanta and Columbus (Georgia); Frankfort and Lexington (Kentucky); Baton Rouge and New Orleans (Louisiana); Annapolis and Baltimore (Maryland); Jackson, Biloxi, and Greenville (Mississippi); Raleigh and Charlotte (North Carolina); Columbia and Charleston (South Carolina); Nashville and Memphis (Tennessee); Richmond, Virginia Beach, and Norfolk (Virginia); Charleston and Huntington (West Virginia)

Delaware

Maryland

West Virginia

Virginia

Kentucky

North Carolina

Tennessee

South Carolina

Arkansas

Georgia

Mississippi

Louisiana

Florida

Alabama

Rivers
Mississippi River; Tennessee River; Arkansas River

Mountains
Appalachian Mountains

Historic places
Kennedy Space Center (Florida); St Augustine (Florida); Mammoth Cave (Kentucky); Great Smoky Mountains National Park (North Carolina); Kitty Hawk (North Carolina); Fort Sumter, South Carolina (first battle of Civil War); Jamestown, Virginia (first permanent English settlement); Harpers Ferry, West Virginia (John Brown's raid); Washington, DC

George Washington's home, Mount Vernon, Virginia

UNITED STATES BY NUMBERS

HOME TO MORE THAN 275 million people, the United States of America is the third most populated country in the world, and the fourth largest country in area. Just 500 years ago, the land that became the United States was mostly dense forests and wide open prairies, settled by groups of native peoples. Today, the US is one of the most productive and developed nations in the world; its people represent a vast melting pot of cultures, religions, and races from all over the globe.

LAND

Area of land
3,536,278 sq miles (9,158,960 sq km)

Area of water
251,041 sq miles (650,196 sq km)

Total area
3,787,319 sq miles (9,809,156 sq km)

Rural area
97.5 percent

Urban area
2.5 percent

Highest point
Mt Denali (Mt McKinley), Alaska, 20,320 ft (6,194 m)

Lowest point
Death Valley, California, 282 ft (86 m) below sea level

Northernmost point
Point Barrow, Alaska

Southernmost point
Ka Lae, Hawaii

Easternmost point
West Quoddy Head, Maine

Westernmost point
Attu Island, Alaska

Geographic center
Butte County, South Dakota

Coastline
12,383 miles (19,929 km)

Deepest lake
Crater Lake, Oregon, 1,932 ft (589 m)

Largest canyon
Grand Canyon, 1 mile (1.6 km) deep and 278 miles (440 km) wide

Largest lake
Superior, 31,820 sq miles (82,414 sq km)

Longest river
Missouri River, 2,540 miles (4,090 km)

Largest island
Hawaii, 4,038 sq miles (10,458 sq km)

Tallest waterfall
Upper Yosemite Falls, California, 1,430 ft (436 m)

Largest volcano
Mauna Loa, Hawaii, 13,677 ft (4,169 km) above sea level

Grand Canyon

PLACES

Largest city
New York City, 8 million people

Cities of more than 1 million people
Los Angeles, Chicago, Houston, Philadelphia, Phoenix, San Diego, San Antonio, Dallas, Detroit

Largest metropolitan area
New York-Newark, 17 million people

Smallest state
Rhode Island, 1,231 sq miles (3,188 sq km)

Largest state
Alaska, 615,230 sq miles (1,593,445 sq km)

Tallest structure
TV tower, Blanchard, North Dakota, 2,063 ft (629 m)

Tallest building
Sears Tower, Chicago, Illinois, 1,450 ft (441 m)

Longest bridge
Verrazano-Narrows Bridge, New York, 4,260 ft (1,278)

Highest dam
Oroville, Feather, California, 770 ft (235 m)

New York City skyline

PEOPLE

Population at 1990 Census
249,632,692

Estimated 2005 population
295,734,134

Density
76 persons per sq mile (29 persons per sq km)

Distribution
75 percent urban, 25 percent rural

Ethnic groups
70 percent white, 12 percent African American, 9 percent Hispanic American, 3 percent Asian American, 1 percent Native American, 5 percent other

Sex
51 percent female, 49 percent male

TRANSPORT

Airports
19,300

Largest airport
Denver International Airport

Busiest airport
Chicago O'Hare

Railroad system
150,000 miles (240,000 km)

Railroad stations
500

Cars
75 per 100 people

Roads and highways
3,900,000 miles (6,200,000 km)

Busiest ports
New Orleans, New York City, Houston

Waterway system
25,425 miles (41,009 km) of inland channels

Longest waterway
St Lawrence Seaway 181 miles (293 km)

Oil pipelines
171,120 miles (276,000 km)

Heliports
122

Natural gas pipelines
205,220 miles (331,000 km)

SYMBOLS

The original flag of the United States had 13 stars, one for each of the first 13 states.

Flag, adopted June 14, 1777
The flag of the United States has 50 stars, one for each state, and 13 stripes, representing the first 13 states, giving it the nickname the "stars and the stripes." The first US flag was commissioned in 1777 but was not in use until 1783, after the American Revolution. In 1818, Congress directed that a new star be added for each new state that joined the Union. The last stars, for Alaska and Hawaii, were added in 1959 and 1960 respectively.

The Star-Spangled Banner, adopted March 3, 1931
The lyrics of the American national anthem were written in 1814 by Francis Scott Key. He was inspired while he watched a tattered United States flag flying over Fort McHenry, Maryland, as British ships shelled it during the War of 1812.

Bald eagle, adopted June 20, 1782
The majestic bald eagle is a symbol of the United States. Statesman Benjamin Franklin (1706–90) proposed that the wild turkey be designated the official bird, but he was outvoted. As a national emblem, the bald eagle is a protected species in the United States. Bald eagles can be found in Maine and Alaska.

In God We Trust, adopted July 30, 1956
This motto originally appeared on coins during the Civil War (1861–65), a time of increased religious sentiment. It disappeared and reappeared on American currency until July 11, 1955, when Congress ordered that it be placed on all paper money and coins. On July 30, 1956, President Dwight D. Eisenhower declared it the national motto of the United States.

COMMUNICATIONS

Telephones
182 million

Cellular phone users
158 million

Radios
575 million

Computers
200 million

Online at home
Internet access for 105 million

Daily newspapers
1,500

Weekly newspapers
8,000

Radio stations
13,000

Televisions
219 million

Television stations
1,550

Cable television systems
1,400

Cable television
67 percent of homes

EDUCATION

Literacy
95.5 percent of population

Elementary schools
76,000

High schools
23,000

Combined schools
11,000

Colleges and universities
3,500

Public school students
46 million from age 12

Private schools
5 million

Spending
5.1 percent of gross national product spent on public education

Public libraries
9,137

Computers at school
Used by 69 percent of students

Internet use
99 percent of schools have Internet access

COAST TO COAST

American settlers heading west in their wagons in the 1840s and 1850s took about six hazardous months to cross the United States. Today, the return journey can be done in air-conditioned comfort and safety in less than five hours by jumbo jet.

At 608 mph (978 k/ph), a jumbo jet can cover the distance from San Francisco to New York in four hours and 38 minutes.

At 4,534 mph (7,297 k/ph), the X-15A-2 rocket plane could cover the distance from San Francisco to New York in less than 38 minutes.

At 3.7 mph (6 k/ph), it would take 31 days and nine hours to walk 2,807 miles (4,517 km), the distance between San Francisco and New York.

At 45 mph (72 k/ph), it would take a 1923 Model T Ford two days and 15 hours to travel 2,807 miles (4,517 km).

At 21 mph (34 k/ph), a stagecoach would take five days and 13 hours to travel 2,807 miles (4,517 km).

At 103 mph (165 k/ph), the Empire State Express could travel the distance from San Francisco to New York in less than 28 hours.

OLYMPIC GAMES

The categories for the Games are reviewed frequently. Some of the most popular events are listed below.

Archery
Athletics
Badminton
Baseball

Field hockey
Judo
Pentathlon
Rowing

Basketball
Boxing
Canoeing
Cycling

Shooting
Swimming
Tennis
Volleyball

Equestrian sports
Soccer
Gymnastics

Water polo
Weightlifting
Wrestling
Yachting

SUMMER GAMES HISTORY

SITE	YEAR
Athens	1896
Paris	1900
St. Louis	1904
London	1908
Stockholm	1912
Antwerp	1920
Paris	1924
Amsterdam	1928
Los Angeles	1932
Berlin	1936
London	1948
Helsinki	1952
Melbourne	1956
Rome	1960
Tokyo	1964
Mexico City	1968
Munich	1972
Montreal	1976
Moscow	1980
Los Angeles	1984
Seoul	1988
Barcelona	1992
Atlanta	1996
Sydney	2000
Athens	2004
Beijing	2008

INTERNATIONAL ORGANIZATIONS

Listed below are some of the major international organizations that work towards cooperation between their member countries. The subjects that each are concerned with range from financial matters and trade, to peace, education, and crime.

INTERPOL
International Criminal Police Organization
Est. 1994
182 member states
www.interpol.com

IMF
International Monetary Fund
Est. 1945
184 member states
www.imf.org

UNESCO
United Nations Educational, Scientific, and Cultural Organization
Est. 1945
191 member states
www.unesco.org

ILO
International Labor Organization
Est. 1919
www.ilo.org

WTO
World Trade Organization
Est. 1995
148 member states
www.wto.org

COMPOSERS

The list below gives the birth and death dates of some major composers, and the country in which they were born, together with one of their most famous works.

Vivaldi, Antonio
1675-1741 Italy
The Four Seasons

Bach, Johann Sebastian
1685-1750 Germany
St. Matthew Passion

Bach

Handel, George F.
1685-1759 Germany
Messiah

Haydn, Franz Joseph
1732-1809 Austria
The Creation

Mozart, Wolfgang
1756-91 Austria
The Magic Flute

Beethoven, Ludwig van
1770-1827 Germany
Symphony No. 9 "Choral"

Chopin, Frédéric
1810-49 Poland
Piano Études

Verdi, Giuseppe
1813-1901 Italy
La Traviata

Brahms, Johannes
1833-97 Germany
Hungarian Dances

Tchaikovsky, Peter I.
1840-93 Russia
The Nutcracker

Puccini, Giacomo
1858-1924 Italy
Madame Butterfly

Mahler, Gustav
1860-1911 Czech Republic
Resurrection Symphony

Debussy, Claude
1862-1918 France
La Mer

Strauss, Richard
1864-1949 Germany
Der Rosenkavalier

Rachmaninov, Sergei
1873-1943 Russia
Piano Concerto No. 3

Ravel, Maurice
1875-1937 France
Bolero

Stravinsky, Igor
1882-1971 Russia
The Rite of Spring

Prokofiev, Sergei
1891-1953 Russia
Love for Three Oranges

Gershwin, George
1898-1937 US
Rhapsody in Blue

Copland, Aaron
1900-90 US
Appalachian Spring

Bernstein, Leonard
1918-90 US
West Side Story

Many composers use the piano as a tool to help them write music.

ARTISTS

The list of artists below gives their birth and death dates, the country in which they were born, and one of their most famous works.

Da Vinci, Leonardo
1452-1519 Italy
Mona Lisa

Dürer, Albrecht
1471-1528 Germany
The Great Piece of Turf

Michelangelo
1475-1564 Italy
David

Raphael
1483-1520 Italy
Sistine Madonna

Rubens, Peter Paul
1577-1640 Belgium
Self-Portrait

Rembrandt van Rijn
1606-69 Holland
The Night Watch

Goya, Francisco
1746-1828 Spain
The Gypsies

Hokusai
1760-1849 Japan
The Wave

Degas, Edgar
1834-1917 France
Dancers on a Stage

Cézanne, Paul
1839-1906 France
The Card Players

Rodin, Auguste
1840-1917 France
The Burghers of Calais

Monet, Claude
1840-1926 France
Water Lilies

Renoir, Pierre-Auguste
1841-1919 France
Le Jugement de Paris

Cassatt, Mary
1845-1926 US
Morning Toilette

Gauguin, Paul
1848-1903 France
The Yellow Christ

Van Gogh, Vincent
1853-90 Holland
Sunflowers

Toulouse-Lautrec
1864-1901 France
At the Moulin Rouge

Matisse, Henri
1869-1954 France
The Dance

Picasso, Pablo
1881-1973 Spain
Guernica

O'Keeffe, Georgia
1887-1986 US
Pelvis Series

Rothko, Mark
1903-70 Russia
Yellow Band

Dalí, Salvador
1904-89 Spain
Persistence of Memory

Kahlo, Frida
1907-54 Mexico
The Wounded Deer

Pollock, Jackson
1912-56 US
Full Fathom Five

Warhol, Andy
1928-87 US
Campbell's Soup Cans

Riley, Bridget
1931- UK
Colour Moves

Hockney, David
1937- UK
A Bigger Splash

Picasso

WRITERS

The list of adults' and children's writers below gives the birth and death dates of each, the country in which they were born, and the title of one of their most famous works.

Chaucer, Geoffrey
1040-1400 England
The Canterbury Tales

Cervantes, Miguel de
1547-1616 Spain
Don Quixote

Shakespeare, William
1564-1616 England
Romeo and Juliet

Swift, Jonathan
1667-1745 UK
Gulliver's Travels

Voltaire
1694-1778 France
Candide

Wordsworth, William
1770-1850 UK
The Daffodils

Austen, Jane
1775-1817 UK
Pride and Prejudice

Austen

Byron, Lord
1788-1824 UK
Don Juan

Poe, Edgar Allan
1809-49 USA
The Raven

Dickens, Charles
1812-70 UK
Oliver Twist

Dostoevsky, Fyodor
1821-81 Russia
Crime and Punishment

Ibsen, Henrik
1828-1906 Norway
Hedda Gabler

Dickinson, Emily
1830-86 USA
Letters of Emily Dickinson

Stevenson, Robert Louis
1850-94 Scotland
Treasure Island

Chekhov, Anton
1860-1904 Russia
The Cherry Orchard

Colette
1873-1954 France
Chéri

Frost, Robert
1874-1963 USA
The Road Not Taken

Joyce, James
1882-1941 Ireland
Ulysses

Lawrence, D.H.
1885-1930 UK
The Rainbow

Eliot, T.S.
1888-1965 UK
The Wasteland

Faulkner, William
1897-1962 USA
Absalom, Absalom!

Hemingway, Ernest
1899-1961 USA
For Whom the Bell Tolls

Morrison, Toni
1931- USA
Beloved

Plath, Sylvia
1932-63 USA
The Bell Jar

Lovelace, Earl
1935- Trinidad
The Dragon Can't Dance

Allende, Isabel
1942- Chile
The House of Spirits

Walker, Alice
1944- USA
The Color Purple

Walker

Seth, Vikram
1952- India
A Suitable Boy

Okri, Ben
1959- Nigeria
The Famished Road

CHILDREN'S WRITERS

Andersen, Hans Christian
1805-75 Denmark
The Snow Queen

Carroll, Lewis
1832-98 UK
Alice in Wonderland

Twain, Mark
1835-1910 US
The Adventures of Tom Sawyer

Baum, L. Frank
1856-1919 US
The Wonderful Wizard of Oz

White, E.B.
1899-1985 US
Charlotte's Web

Kipling, Rudyard
1865-1936 UK
The Jungle Book

Potter, Beatrix
1866-1943 UK
The Tale of Peter Rabbit

Seuss, Dr.
1904-91 US
The Cat in the Hat

Dahl, Roald
1916-90 UK
Willy Wonka and the Chocolate Factory

Rowling, J.K.
1965- UK
Harry Potter

The Cat in the Hat

CLASSIFYING LIVING THINGS

SCIENTISTS CLASSIFY living things (organisms) into groups called kingdoms. This chart shows the five main kingdoms and typical organisms that belong to each one. Within a kingdom, organisms are divided into groups called phyla (singular, phylum). Scientists divide phyla into subphyla, and again into classes. Classes are divided into orders, then into suborders. Orders and their suborders are divided into families, then into genera (singular, genus), and finally into species.

MONERANS

The moneran kingdom includes simple organisms such as bacteria, which live in the air, on land, and in water. There are at least 4,000 species of monerans.

PROTOCTISTS

The protoctist kingdom includes simple organisms such as amoebas, which live mainly in water. There are about 50,000 species of protoctists.

Bacteria
About 2,000 species

Blue-green algae
About 2,000 species

Amoebas
10,000 species

Diatoms
2,000 species

Euglenas
10,000 species

Slime molds
5,000 species

Green algae
6,000 species

Red algae
4,000 species

Brown algae
2,000 species

ANIMALS

The animal kingdom includes organisms which are able to move around, and survive by eating other animals or plants. There may be more than 10 million species in the animal kingdom.

Sponges
5,000 species

Coelenterates
9,400 species

Bryozoans
4,000 species

Small phyla
5,500 species

Flatworms
10,000 species

Nematode worms
12,000 species

True worms
12,000 species

Arthropods
More than 1 million species

Mollusks
40,000 species

Echinoderms
6,000 species

Corals

Hydras

Jellyfish

Sea anemones

Ctenophores (comb jellies)

Velvet worms

Ribbon worms
Lamp shells

Flukes

Free-living flatworms

Tapeworms

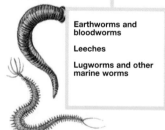
Earthworms and bloodworms

Leeches

Lugworms and other marine worms

Chitons

Clams and other bivalves

Snails and slugs
Tooth shells

Octopuses, cuttlefish, and squid

Brittle stars

Sea urchins

Sea cucumbers

Starfish

Sea lilies and feather stars

Cockroaches

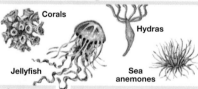
Earwigs

Flies, mosquitoes, and gnats

Lice

Fleas

Stoneflies

Ants, bees, and wasps

Termites

Thrips

Scorpionflies

Weevils and beetles

Silverfish and bristletails

Dragonflies and damselflies

Bugs

Lacewings and antlions

Stick and leaf insects

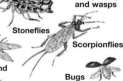
Grasshoppers, crickets, and locusts

Mantises

Butterflies and moths

Millipedes
7,000 species

Centipedes
1,700 species

Insects
More than 1 million species

Crustaceans
40,000 species

Arachnids
70,000 species

Barnacles
Crabs and prawns
Fish lice
Sand hoppers
Water fleas
Woodlice

Spiders
Scorpions
Daddy-longlegs
Mites and ticks
King crabs

FUNGI

The fungi kingdom includes mushrooms, toadstools, and molds, which are neither plants nor animals. There are more than 100,000 species of fungi.

PLANTS

The plant kingdom contains living organisms which can produce their own food using sunlight. Unlike animals, plants cannot move around freely. There are at least 400,000 species in the plant kingdom.

HOW TO USE THE CHART
These colors are a guide to the main plant and animal groupings. You can see at a glance which groups each organism belongs to.

Kingdom		Class
Phylum		Subclass
Subphylum		Order

Zygomycetes
765 species

True fungi
About 100,000 species

Mosses and liverworts
25,000 species

Ferns
12,000 species

Club mosses
400 species

Horsetails
35 species

Conifers
500 species

Flowering plants
at least 300,000 species

MONOCOTYLEDONS
A group of 55,000 species with a single pair of seed leaves (cotyledons) when they germinate.

Irises
Grasses and cereals
Orchids

DICOTYLEDONS
A group of 250,000 species, these plants have two pairs of cotyledons when they germinate, providing food for the embryo plant.

Buttercups
Nettles
Daisies
Primroses
Roses
Teas
Poppies
Legumes
Cabbages
Cacti
Oaks
Myrtles and gums
Elms
Lilacs
Heathers
Maples
Parsleys and carrots
Willows

Chordates
44,000 species

Jawless fish
60 species

Sharks and rays
700 species

Bony fish
21,000 species

Reptiles
6,600 species

Birds
8,800 species

Perching birds (order includes more than half of all kinds of birds, such as crows and thrushes)

Albatrosses and petrels

Cranes and coots

Cuckoos and roadrunners

Ducks, geese, and swans

Eagles, hawks, and vultures

Gulls, terns, and waders

Herons, storks, and flamingos

Kingfishers, bee-eaters, and hornbills

Nightjars, swifts, and hummingbirds

Ostriches, emus, and kiwis

Owls

Parrots, woodpeckers, and toucans

Pelicans, gannets, and cormorants

Penguins

Pheasants, turkeys, and jungle fowl

Pigeons, doves, and sand grouse

Mammals
4,070 species

Marsupial mammals

Placental mammals

Monotreme mammals

Elephants

Aardvarks

Lemurs, monkeys, apes, and humans

Tree shrews

Anteaters, armadillos, and other toothless mammals

Cats, dogs, and other carnivores

Squirrels, mice, and other rodents

Bats and flying foxes

Camels, horses, and other hoofed mammals

Rabbits, hares, and pikas

Seals, sea lions, and walruses

Hedgehogs and other insectivores

Whales, dolphins, and porpoises

Sea cows and dugongs

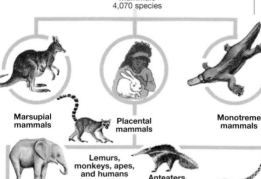

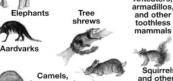

owfins, garfish
ristlemouths, viperfish, dragonfish
arps, catfish, characins, hatchetfish
oelacanth, birchir, lungfish
od, anglers, clingfish
lephant fish, featherbacks
els, tarpons
errings, anchovies
anternfish, lancetfish
erch, barracudas, sea horses,
wordfish
ike, salmon, trout
ilversides, ricefish, flying fish
turgeons, paddlefish

Amphibians
3,100 species

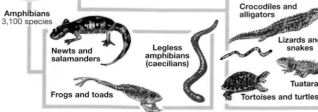
Newts and salamanders

Legless amphibians (caecilians)

Frogs and toads

Crocodiles and alligators

Lizards and snakes

Tuatara

Tortoises and turtles

WILDLIFE FACTS

Here are dozens of useful facts about all kinds of plants and animals.

PLANT AND ANIMAL LIFESPANS

The chart below shows you how long wild plants and animals live. The ages given are the maximum average lifespans.

HOW TO USE THE CHART
The colors in this key indicate nine main groups to which each plant or animal belongs.

SEVERAL HOURS	SEVERAL DAYS	SEVERAL WEEKS	SEVERAL MONTHS	1-5 YEARS	5-15 YEARS	15-30 YEARS	30-45 YEARS	45-60 YEARS	60-80 YEARS	80-10 YEAR
Some bacteria 20 minutes	Morning glory flower 1 day	Footprint carp 8 months		Common poppy 1 year	Common starfish 6 years	Jewel beetle 35 years		Blue whale 45 years	Alligator 61 years	Acti se anem 80 y
Mayfly (adult) 12 hours	Fruit fly 2 weeks	Common housefly 3 weeks		Monarch butterfly 1-2 years	Pitcher plant 20 years	Fruit bat 25 years	Canary 34 years	Orangutan 50 years	Blue macaw 64 years	Euro e 80 y
Some kinds of fungi 18 hours	Fairy ring mushroom 5 days	Skipper butterfly 3 weeks	Common field speedwell 6 months	Wild parsnip 2 years	Red fox 8 years	Badger 15 years	Brown bear 40 years	Green turtle 50 years	Andean condor 70 years	La stur 81 y
	Water flea 7 days	Shepherd's purse 6 weeks	Bedbug 6 months	Common shrew 3 years	Badger 15 years Goldfish 30 years	Queen ant 15 years	Common boa 40 years	Royal albatross 53 years	Elephant 75 years	Kil wha 90 y
		Black widow spider 3-9 months				Komodo dragon 30 years				

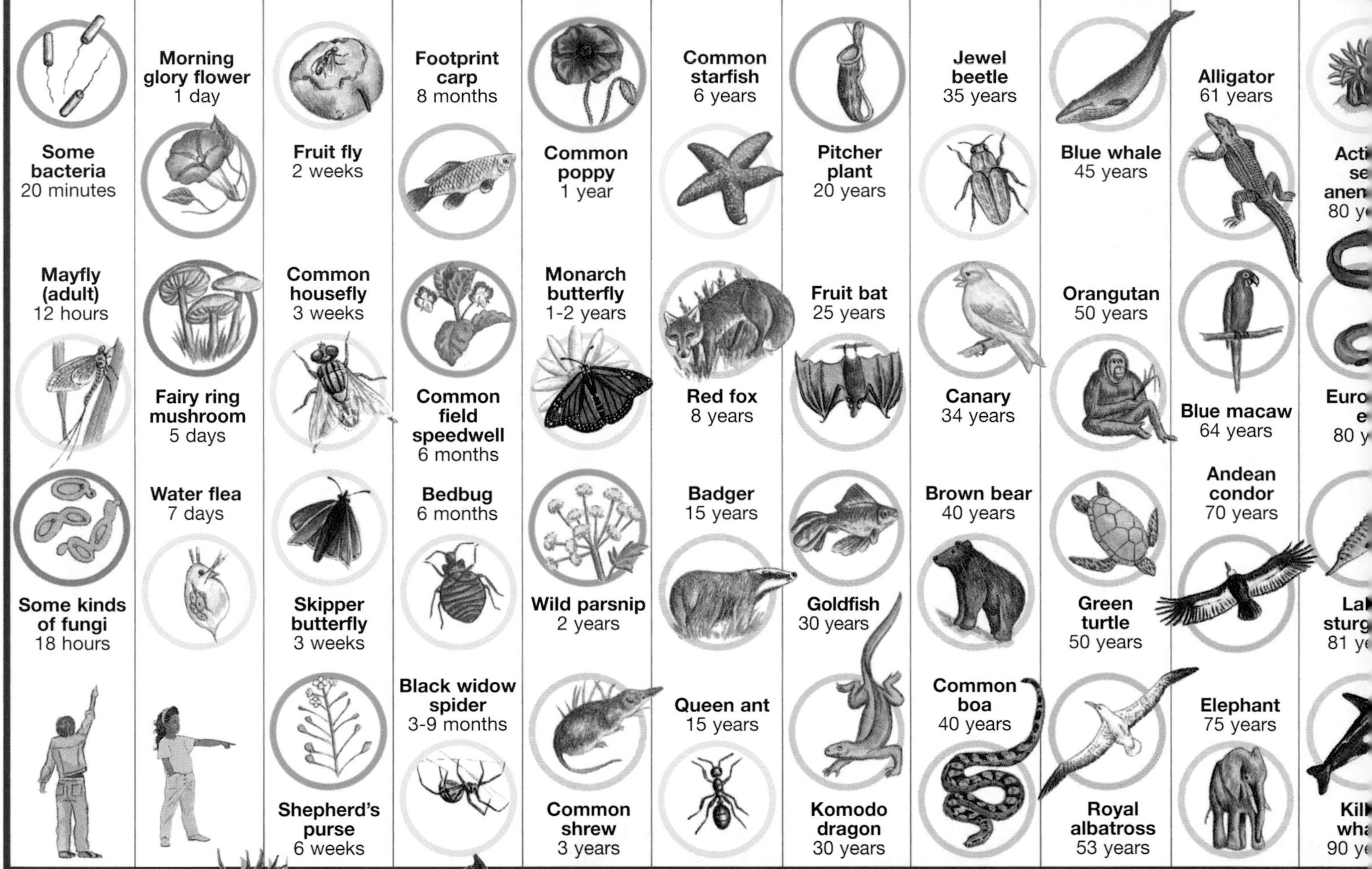

Reindeer
Reindeer (caribou) walk hundreds of miles each year in search of fresh pasture.

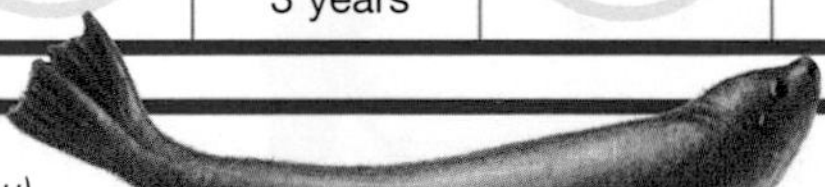

Locust
Swarms of desert locusts migrate more than 2,000 miles (3,000 km) in less than 2 months.

Fur seal
The Northern fur seal makes a journey of 2,000 miles (3,000 km) and back again each year.

European swallow
This swallow flies about 7,000 miles (11,000 km) from Northern Europe to South Africa and back again each year.

MIGRATION FACTS

Many animals migrate great distances once, and often twice, a year to find fresh pasture, a place to breed, or to escape harsh winters. Here are some animals that migrate – by land, sea, or air.

ANIMAL SPEEDS

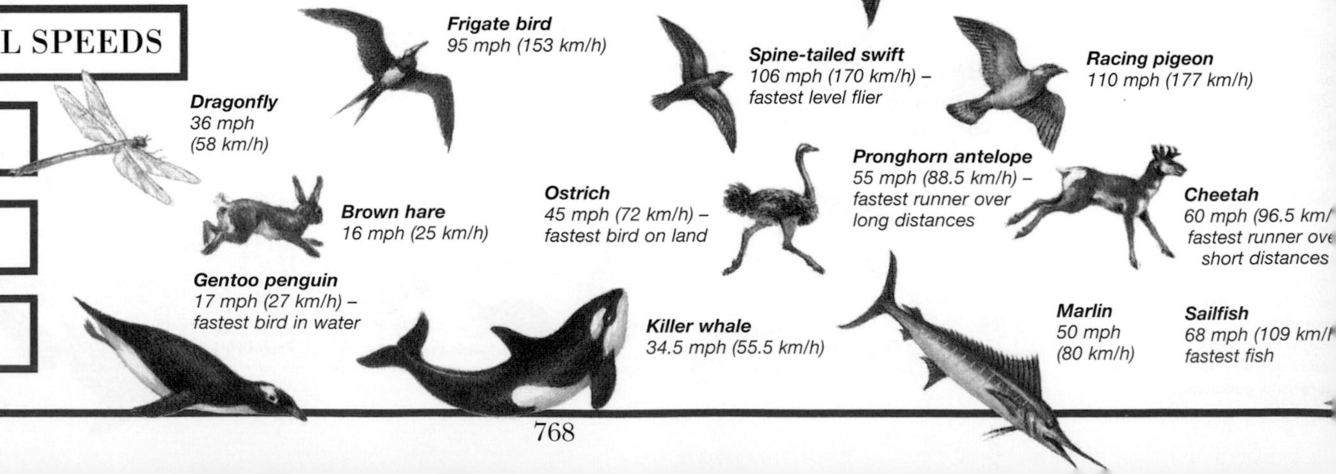

AIR

LAND

SEA

Dragonfly 36 mph (58 km/h)

Frigate bird 95 mph (153 km/h)

Spine-tailed swift 106 mph (170 km/h) – fastest level flier

Racing pigeon 110 mph (177 km/h)

Brown hare 16 mph (25 km/h)

Ostrich 45 mph (72 km/h) – fastest bird on land

Pronghorn antelope 55 mph (88.5 km/h) – fastest runner over long distances

Cheetah 60 mph (96.5 km/ fastest runner ove short distances

Gentoo penguin 17 mph (27 km/h) – fastest bird in water

Killer whale 34.5 mph (55.5 km/h)

Marlin 50 mph (80 km/h)

Sailfish 68 mph (109 km/ fastest fish

MAMMALS	FISH	FUNGI
BIRDS	ARTHROPODS	PLANTS
REPTILES, AMPHIBIANS	OTHER INVERTEBRATES	SIMPLE ORGANISMS

PLANT AND ANIMAL RECORDS
This chart gives you information about plant and animal sizes. It is divided into groups, such as mammals, fish, and birds.

HOW TO USE THE CHART
The colors in this key indicate the different habitats of each of the plants and animals on this page.

LAND
AIR
WATER

100-1,000 YEARS

Tuatara
101 years

Tortoise
120 years

European beech
300 years

Ponderosa pine
700 years

OVER 1,000 YEARS

English oak
1,500 years

Yew
3,500 years

Giant sequoia
6,000 years

Creosote bush
11,000 years

Arctic tern
The greatest migrator. It flies 22,000 miles (36,000 km) twice a year.

Peregrine falcon
226 mph (362 km/h) – fastest bird in a dive

| MAIN GROUP | BIGGEST | | SMALLEST | | LONGEST | TALLEST | MOST POISONOUS |

MAMMALS including pouched mammals, monotreme, and placental mammals

African elephant
10 ft 6 in (3.2 m) high; weighs 5.1 tons (5.2 tonnes).

Blue whale
100 ft (30 m) long; weighs 118 tons (120 tonnes).

Pygmy shrew
This shrew is 1.6 in (40 mm) long and weighs 0.05 oz (1.5 g).

Bumblebee bat
6 in (15 cm) long; weighs 0.05 oz (1.5 g).

Finback whale
The longest mammal after the blue whale is 85 ft (25 m) long.

Giraffe
The giraffe is 17 ft (5.2 m) high and weighs 1.2 tons (1.2 tonnes).

Some moles and shrews can give a bite that contains poisonous saliva (spit).

BIRDS including flying and nonflying birds

Kori bustard
The biggest flying bird, weighing 40 lb (18 kg).

Ostrich
The ostrich is the biggest of all birds, weighing 280 lb (130 kg).

Bee hummingbird
2.2 in (57 mm) long; weighs 0.06 oz (1.6 g).

Hummingbirds use so much energy that they eat half their weight in food every day.

Phoenix red jungle fowl
This bird has tail feathers 33 ft (10 m) long.

The ostrich is the tallest bird on Earth, measuring 8 ft (2.4 m) in height.

The only poisonous birds are the Hooded Pitohui and the Ifrita, both from Papua, New Guinea.

REPTILES such as snakes

AMPHIBIANS such as frogs and newts

Chinese giant salamander
Biggest amphibian, 6 ft (1.8 m) long; weighs 0.89 tons (0.91 tonnes).

Saltwater crocodile
Biggest reptile, 18 ft (5 m) long; weighs 0.98 tons (1 tonne).

Gecko
Some geckos are only 0.7 in (1.8 cm) long.

Cuban arrow-poison frog
0.5 in (1 cm) long.

Reticulated python
33 ft (10 m) long.

Giant tortoise
This tortoise is 4 ft (1.2 m) high.

Black-headed sea snake
The black-headed sea snake is the most poisonous of all reptiles.

FISH including bony fish, jawless fish, and cartilaginous fish

Whale shark
This is 60 ft (18 m) long and weighs 39 tons (40 tonnes).

Dwarf pygmy gobi
This is 0.8 in (2.03 cm) long and weighs 0.00018 oz (5 mg).

Some of the smallest fish eggs are those of the ling, which lays millions during its lifetime.

Oarfish
46 ft (14 m) long.

Ocean sunfish
14 ft (4.3 m) high; 10 ft (3 m) long; weighs 2.1 tons (2.2 tonnes).

Stonefish horrida
A stonefish that has spines to inject its victim with venom.

ARTHRO-PODS such as spiders, insects, centipedes, and crabs

Goliath beetle
The heaviest insect, weighing 3.5 oz (100 g), is 4.3 in (110 mm) long.

Japanese spider crab
The biggest crustacean, 11 ft (3.5 m) across.

Fairy fly
The fairy fly is the smallest insect, only 0.0008 in (0.02 mm) long when adult.

Alonella water flea
The smallest crustacean is only 0.0098 in (0.25 mm) long.

Giant stick insect
Biggest insect, 15 in (38 cm) long.

Sydney funnel-web spider
This spider has a deadly poisonous bite.

INVERTE-BRATES (animals without a backbone) such as mollusks

Giant squid
The biggest mollusk, this squid is 57 ft (17.4 m) long.

African giant snail
The largest land mollusk, weighing 2 lb (907 g).

Amoebas
These are too small to be seen with the naked eye.

African giant earthworm
The longest segmented worm is 22 ft (6.7 m) long.

Arctic giant jellyfish
The longest coelenterate, with 120 ft (36 m) tentacles.

Australian sea wasp
This sea wasp has the most painful sting of all animals.

FUNGI such as mushrooms, toadstools, molds, and yeasts

Bracket fungus
This fungus can be several feet across.

American giant puffball
A large fungus, this generally measures 76 in (194 cm) across.

All fungi produce microscopic spores. Bracket fungi release 30 million a day.

WARNING! DO NOT TOUCH WILD FUNGI. MANY ARE EXTREMELY POISONOUS.

Fungi roots (mycelia) Can stretch for hundreds of yards underground.

Some fungi, such as the bootlace fungi, grow inside trees, to the very top.

Death cup
The death cup is the most poisonous of all the fungi.

PLANTS, such as trees, flowering plants, and grasses

Giant sequoia tree
Tree is 274.9 ft (83.8 m) high and weighs 1,970 tons (2,000 tonnes).

Rafflesia
This is the largest of all flowering plants.

Dwarf snow willow
A few inches long, this is the smallest land plant.

Lemna aquatic duckweed
Only 1/42 in (0.6 mm) long.

Pacific giant kelp seaweed
The longest seaweed, measuring 200 ft (60 m).

Douglas fir
The tallest tree on Earth, the Douglas fir grows up to 415 ft (126.5 m) high.

Deadly nightshade
This is one of the most poisonous of all plants.

THREATS TO WILDLIFE

The main threat to wildlife is loss of habitat, with pollution another damaging factor. Some animals are also hunted, or must compete with people for food. Rare plants are removed from the wild by collectors.

These two maps show areas of the world covered by rain forests 100 years ago and today. You can see how the forests are being destroyed.

North America

Asia

Africa

South America

Australia

Rain forests 100 years ago

North America

Asia

Africa

South America

Australia

Rain forests today

POLLUTION PYRAMID
This picture and the key (right) show how a small amount of chemical pesticide sprayed onto plants becomes concentrated in the bodies of the animals that feed on each other up the food chain.

Eagle (carnivore) eats fox cubs.

Foxes (carnivores) eat voles.

Voles (herbivores) feed on plants containing chemicals.

Farmer sprays chemical pesticide onto each plant in a field.

Concentrated level of pesticide in the body of each animal

Eagle

Fox

Vole

Plant

POLLUTION
Traffic fumes, oil slicks, acid rain, litter, and chemicals threaten the lives of plants and animals. When we spray crops with chemicals, a residue is left on the plant. If an animal feeds on these crops, the chemical enters its body. As each creature is eaten by another, certain amounts of the chemical work their way up the food chain. This is called a pollution pyramid. Many animals die as a result of chemical crop spraying.

ATMOSPHERIC WASTE (ACID RAIN)

Woodland plants

Forest trees

Fish

Beavers

DUMPING WASTE AT SEA

Seals

Fish

Penguins

PESTICIDES (CHEMICAL SPRAYS)

Butterflies

Ladybirds

HABITAT LOSS
Only 100 years ago, large areas of the world were covered by forests, where millions of species of plants and animals lived. Today forests are much smaller due to people burning the forests and cutting down the trees for farmland and housing. All sorts of unusual animals and plants now have nowhere to live. Today many species are rare, and scientists believe that huge numbers are already extinct.

RAIN FOREST DESTRUCTION (DEFORESTATION)

Woolly spider monkeys

Orchids

Tree frogs

Toucans

Indris

Monkey-eating eagles

OTHER HABITAT LOSS (GRASSLAND)

Pampas deer

White-throated wallabies

Pygmy hogs

COMPETING WITH HUMANS
All kinds of sea creatures, including seals and dolphins, are at risk from humans because they feed on the fish that humans want. Many dolphins die each year because they become caught up in fishing nets. Other sea creatures die because they cannot get enough food.

Dolphins

Seals

Porpoises

RATE OF EXTINCTION
Many species of animals have died out since the Earth formed. This is often due to habitat loss, and the exploitation of animals for profit. In recent years, many more species have become extinct and, if this continues at the current rate, 50,000 species will die out each year. This graph shows some of the animals which have become extinct in the past few hundred years. It also shows those that are in danger of extinction today.

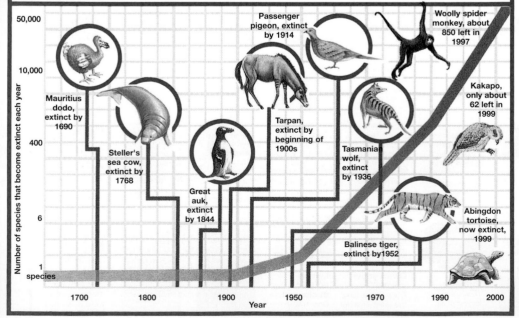

Number of species that become extinct each year

50,000

10,000

400

6

1 species

Mauritius dodo, extinct by 1690

Steller's sea cow, extinct by 1768

Great auk, extinct by 1844

Passenger pigeon, extinct by 1914

Tarpan, extinct by beginning of 1900s

Tasmanian wolf, extinct by 1936

Balinese tiger, extinct by1952

Woolly spider monkey, about 850 left in 1997

Kakapo, only about 62 left in 1999

Abingdon tortoise, now extinct, 1999

1700   1800   1900   1950   1970   1990   2000
Year

HUNTING AND COLLECTING
Many plants and animals are on the verge of extinction because people have hunted them for centuries for fur, horns, meat, and skin. Today it is illegal to hunt many species of animals, including big cats, rhinoceroses, and whales. It is also illegal to dig up plants from the wild in many areas.

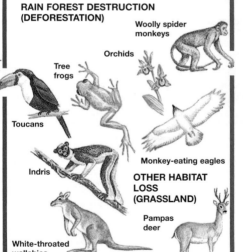

Butterflies

Polar bears

Green turtles

Rhinoceroses

CONSERVATION ACTION

There arc many organizations around the world concerned with the protection of wildlife, working to stop the trade in animal products – and to save animals and plants from extinction. Some of the best-known international organizations and their contact details are listed below.

WORLD WILDLIFE ORGANIZATIONS

WORLD SOCIETY FOR THE PROTECTION OF ANIMALS (WSPA USA)
34 Deloss Street
Framingham, MA 01702
1-508-879-8350
www.wspa-usa.org

Seeks to relieve the suffering of all animal life throughout the world

WORLD WIDE FUND FOR NATURE (WWF US)
1250 24th Street, NW
P.O. Box 97180
Washington, DC 20037-1124
1-800-CALL-WWF
www.wwfus.org

Protects all kinds of wildlife

FRIENDS OF THE EARTH US
1717 Massachusetts Avenue, NW, 600
Washington, DC 20036-2002
1-877-843-8687
www.foe.org

Committed to the preservation and sensible use of the environment

INTERNATIONAL FUND FOR ANIMAL WELFARE (IFAW US)
411 Main Street
P.O. Box 193
Yarmouth Port, MA 02675
1-508-744-2000
www.ifaw.org

Aims to ensure the kind treatment of all animals

GREENPEACE USA
702 H Street, NW
Washington, DC 20001
1-202-462-1177
www.greenpeaceusa.org

Works as a pressure group against damage to the natural world

In many parts of the world wildlife parks and reserves help endangered animals and plants survive in their natural habitats. This chart lists some of the parks and wildlife reserves around the world. The information tells you how large these wildlife areas are, when they were set up, and the animals and plants they seek to protect.

NATIONAL WILDLIFE PARKS AND RESERVES

SALONGA RESERVE, DEM. REP. CONGO, AFRICA

Forest habitat
14,115 sq miles
(36,417 sq km)
The biggest wildlife reserve in Africa
.
African elephants, pygmy chimps

GREENLAND NATIONAL PARK, SCANDINAVIA

Tundra habitat
270,271 sq miles
(700,000 sq km)
The world's largest park

Polar bears, seals, walruses

FIORDLAND NATIONAL PARK, NEW ZEALAND

Mountain and island habitat
3,950 sq miles
(10,232 sq km)

Sea birds, seals

EVERGLADES NATIONAL PARK, FLORIDA

Swamp habitat
2,185 sq miles
(5,661sq km)

Alligators, West Indian manatee

KUSHIRO PARK, HOKKAIDO, JAPAN

Wetland marsh habitat
77 sq miles
(200 sq km)

Japanese red-crowned crane

GREEK NATIONAL MARINE PARK, GREECE

Island habitat

Mediterranean monk seal

GALAPAGOS ISLANDS, SOUTH AMERICA

Island habitat
2,668 sq miles
(6,912 sq km)

Giant tortoise, finches, marine iguana

WOOD BUFFALO NATIONAL PARK, CANADA

Forest habitat
17,335 sq miles
(44,900 sq km)

Buffalo, lynx, reindeer

YELLOWSTONE PARK, NORTH AMERICA

Mountain habitat
3,467 sq miles
(8,945 sq km)

Bighorn sheep, moose

SNOWDONIA NATIONAL PARK, WALES, UK

Mountain habitat
845 sq miles
(2,188 sq km)

Mountain plants, kite, merlin, peregrine falcon

GREAT BARRIER REEF, CAIRNS SECTION, AUSTRALIA

Sea habitat
13,899 sq miles
(36,000 sq km)

Corals, jellyfish, and other sea creatures

IGUAZU NATIONAL PARK, ARGENTINA, SOUTH AMERICA

Forest and riverbank habitat
189 sq miles
(492 sq km)

Caiman, jaguar

TAI NATIONAL PARK, IVORY COAST, AFRICA

Moist forest habitat
1,274 sq miles
(3,300 sq km)

Many rare trees

ULURU NATIONAL PARK, AUSTRALIA

Desert habitat
51,671 sq miles
(132,490 sq km)

Desert plants, thorny devil

ROYAL CHIAWAN SANCTUARY, NEPAL, ASIA

Forest habitat
359 sq miles
(932 sq km)

Rhinoceros, tigers

PYRENEES OCCIDENTALES PARK, FRANCE

Mountain habitat
176 sq miles
(457 sq km)

Bears, chamois

STAR MAPS

ABOUT 6,000 STARS are visible from Earth without using a telescope – roughly 3,000 in the northern sky and 3,000 in the southern sky. Constellations, or groups of stars, are visible depending on the season, the time of night, and which hemisphere you are in. Clarity is also affected by city lights, which light up the sky and make stars harder to see. These star maps show the main stars visible from the Northern and Southern Hemispheres.

Milky Way

NORTHERN HEMISPHERE

The size of the stars on the maps represents their brightness as seen from Earth. The larger the dot, the brighter the star.

Ursa Minor, also called the Little Bear

Pisces · Cetus · Pegasus · Aries · Delphinus · Andromeda · Triangulum · Taurus · Perseus · Cygnus · Sagitta · Cassiopeia · Aquila · Orion · Cepheus · Auriga · Monoceros · Lyra · Polaris (North Star) · Ursa Minor · Gemini · Ophiuchus · Hercules · Draco · Corona Borealis · Canis Minor · Ursa Major · Cancer · Serpens Caput · Boötes · Canes Venatici · Leo Minor · Hydra · Leo · Virgo

As the Earth spins on its axis, so the stars appear to move across the sky. This means you will need to rotate these star maps so that they match up with the night sky.

LUNAR PROBES

LUNA 1 (USSR)
Launched January 2, 1959. First probe to successfully fly past the Moon.

LUNA 3 (USSR)
Launched October 4, 1959. Took first photographs of the far side of the Moon.

RANGER 7 (US)
Launched July 28, 1964. Took first close-up photographs of the lunar surface.

Ranger 7

APOLLO 11 (US)
Launched July 16, 1969. First spacecraft to carry people to the Moon. On July 20, 1969, Neil Armstrong and Edwin Aldrin landed on the Moon.

Apollo 11 lunar module

SMART-1 (EUROPE)
Launched September 27 2003. Used new technology in the form of solar-powered ion thrusters.

SOLAR PROBES

YOHKOH (JAPAN)
Launched August 30, 1991. Studied x-rays from the Sun.

ULYSSES (US)
Launched December 2, 1995. Monitors changes on the Sun and solar radiation.

THE SOLAR SYSTEM

Planet	Diameter at equator		Average Distance from Sun (millions of)		Mass	Volume	Surface temperature	
	miles	km	miles	km	(Earth = 1)	(Earth = 1)	°C	°F
Mercury	3,033	4,879	36.0	57.9	0.055	0.056	+350	+662
Venus	7,523	12,104	67.2	108.2	0.86	0.82	+480	+896
Earth	7,928	12,756	93	149.6	1	1	+22	+72
Mars	4,222	6,794	141.5	227.9	0.107	0.15	-23	-9
Jupiter	142,884	88,784	483.3	778.3	318	1,319	-150	-238
Saturn	74,914	120,536	886.1	1,427	95	744	-180	-292
Uranus	31,770	51,118	1,783	2,871	15	67	-214	-353
Neptune	31,410	50,538	2,793	4,497	17	57	-220	-364
Pluto	1,519	2,360	3,666	5,914	0.002	0.01	-230	-382

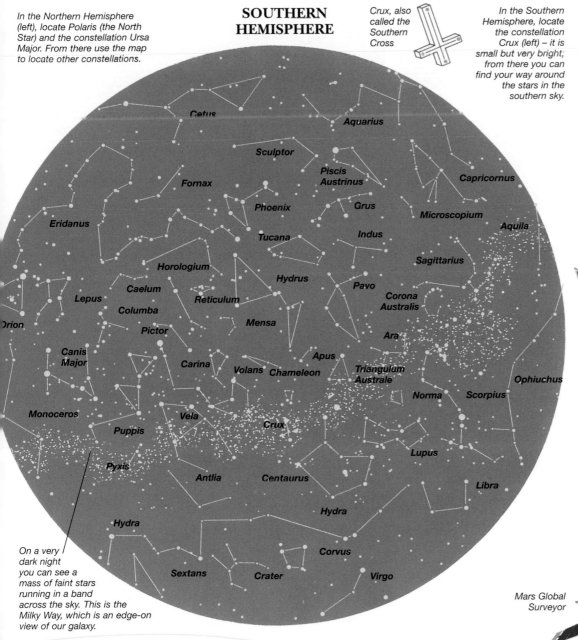

In the Northern Hemisphere (left), locate Polaris (the North Star) and the constellation Ursa Major. From there use the map to locate other constellations.

SOUTHERN HEMISPHERE

Crux, also called the Southern Cross

In the Southern Hemisphere, locate the constellation Crux (left) – it is small but very bright; from there you can find your way around the stars in the southern sky.

Constellations labeled on the star map: Cetus, Aquarius, Sculptor, Piscis Austrinus, Fornax, Capricornus, Phoenix, Grus, Microscopium, Eridanus, Tucana, Indus, Aquila, Horologium, Hydrus, Sagittarius, Caelum, Reticulum, Pavo, Corona Australis, Lepus, Columba, Mensa, Pictor, Ara, Canis Major, Carina, Apus, Triangulum Australe, Orion, Volans, Chameleon, Ophiuchus, Norma, Scorpius, Monoceros, Vela, Crux, Puppis, Lupus, Pyxis, Antlia, Centaurus, Libra, Hydra, Corvus, Hydra, Sextans, Crater, Virgo

On a very dark night you can see a mass of faint stars running in a band across the sky. This is the Milky Way, which is an edge-on view of our galaxy.

PLANETARY PROBES

These are some of the most important space probes launched to date.

VOYAGER (US)
Two probes, *Voyager 1* and *2*, were launched in 1977. Between them they explored much of the solar system, including Jupiter, Saturn, Uranus, and Neptune.

Voyager 1

MAGELLAN (US)
Launched May 4, 1989. Collected information about Venus's gravity field and used radar to map the surface of the planet.

Magellan

GALILEO (US)
Launched October 18, 1989. Probe launched from the space shuttle *Atlantis*, which entered Jupiter's atmosphere on December 7, 1995. First probe to measure the atmosphere of the solar system's large planet.

NEAR SHOEMAKER (US)
Launched February 17, 1996. The first spacecraft to orbit an asteroid, it studied 433 Eros, a near Earth asteroid.

Near Shoemaker

Mars Global Surveyor

MARS GLOBAL SURVEYOR (US)
Launched November 7, 1996. Orbited Mars and sent back pictures and data.

CASSINI (US)
Launched October 6, 1997. Mission to learn about Saturn and its moon Titan.

MARS EXPLORATION ROVERS (US)
Launched June 10 and July 7, 2003. Two unmanned rovers, Spirit and Opportunity, landed on different sides of Mars in 2004. They carried out scientific experiments on rocks found there and transmitted the information back to Earth.

DEEP IMPACT (US)
Launched January 12, 2005. Mission to learn about comet Tempel 1. Released first probe to impact on a comet's nucleus.

Surface gravity (Earth = 1)	Time taken to orbit Sun	Time taken to spin once on axis	Orbital velocity per second		Number of moons
			miles	km	
0.38	87.97 days	58.65 days	29.7	47.9	0
0.9	224.7 days	243.16 days	21.8	35	0
1	365.26 days	23 hr 56 min 4 sec	18.5	29.8	1
0.38	779.9 days	24 hr 37 min 23 sec	15	24.1	2
2.64	11.86 years	9 hr 50 min 30 sec	8.1	13.1	63
1.16	29.46 years	10 hr 39 min	6	9.6	47
0.93	84.01 years	17 hr 14 min	4.2	6.8	27
1.2	164.8 years	16 hr 3 min	3.4	5.4	13
0.05	247.7 years	6 days 9 hr	2.9	4.7	1

WORLD'S GREATEST OCEANS AND SEAS

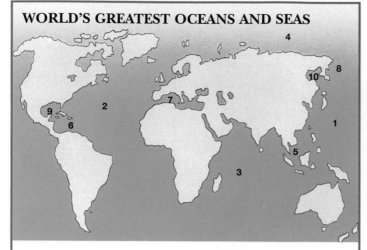

1 Pacific Ocean
*64,185,629 sq miles
(166,240,000 sq km)*
2 Atlantic Ocean
*33,421,006 sq miles
(86,560,000 sq km)*
3 Indian Ocean
*28,351,484 sq miles
(73,430,000 sq km)*
4 Arctic Ocean
*5,108,132 sq miles
(13,230,000 sq km)*

5 South China Sea
1,148,499 sq miles (2,974,600 sq km)
6 Caribbean Sea
1,062,939 sq miles (2,753,000 sq km)
7 Mediterranean Sea
969,116 sq miles (2,510,000 sq km)
8 Bering Sea
872,977 sq miles (2,261,000 sq km)
9 Gulf of Mexico
595,749 sq miles (1,542,985 sq km)
10 Sea of Okhotsk
589,788 sq miles (1,527,570 sq km)

WORLD'S GREATEST DESERTS

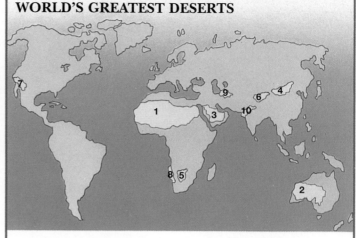

1 Sahara Desert (North Africa)
3,500,000 sq miles (9,000,000 sq km)
2 Australian Desert
1,470,000 sq miles (3,800,000 sq km)
3 Arabian Desert (Southwest Asia)
502,000 sq miles (1,300,000 sq km)
4 Gobi Desert (Central Asia)
401,500 sq miles (1,040,000 sq km)
5 Kalahari Desert (Southern Africa)
201,000 sq miles (520,000 sq km)

6 Takla Makan Desert (West China)
125,000 sq miles (327,000 sq km)
7 Sonoran Makan Desert (US/Mexico)
120,000 sq miles (310,000 sq km)
8 Namib Desert (Southwest Africa)
120,000 sq miles (310,000 sq km)
9 Kara Kum (Turkmenistan)
105,000 sq miles (270,000 sq km)
10 Thar Desert (India and Pakistan)
100,000 sq miles (260,000 sq km)

WORLD'S LARGEST ISLANDS

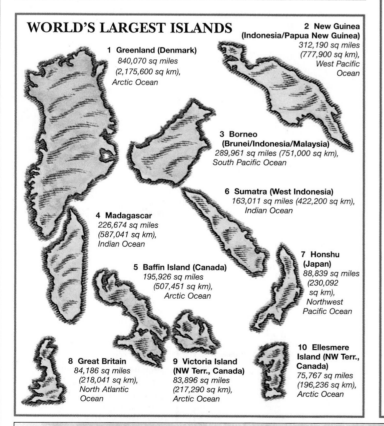

1 Greenland (Denmark)
*840,070 sq miles
(2,175,600 sq km),
Arctic Ocean*

**2 New Guinea
(Indonesia/Papua New Guinea)**
*312,190 sq miles
(777,900 sq km),
West Pacific
Ocean*

**3 Borneo
(Brunei/Indonesia/Malaysia)**
*289,961 sq miles (751,000 sq km),
South Pacific Ocean*

6 Sumatra (West Indonesia)
*163,011 sq miles (422,200 sq km),
Indian Ocean*

4 Madagascar
*226,674 sq miles
(587,041 sq km),
Indian Ocean*

**7 Honshu
(Japan)**
*88,839 sq miles
(230,092
sq km),
Northwest
Pacific Ocean*

5 Baffin Island (Canada)
*195,926 sq miles
(507,451 sq km),
Arctic Ocean*

8 Great Britain
*84,186 sq miles
(218,041 sq km),
North Atlantic
Ocean*

**9 Victoria Island
(NW Terr., Canada)**
*83,896 sq miles
(217,290 sq km),
Arctic Ocean*

**10 Ellesmere
Island (NW Terr.,
Canada)**
*75,767 sq miles
(196,236 sq km),
Arctic Ocean*

WEATHER RECORDS

Greatest Snowfall
102 ft (31.1 m), Paradise, Mt. Rainier, Washington State, US, 19 February 1971 to 18 February 1972

Greatest Rainfall
In a 24-hour period 6.1 ft (1.9 m), Cilaos, Réunion, Indian Ocean, 15-16 March 1952

Driest Place / Longest Drought
Annual average of nil in the Atacama Desert, near Calama, Chile. 400 years of drought also in Atacama Desert, 1571-1971

Highest Surface Wind Speed
231 mph (371 km/h), Mt. Washington (6,288 ft/1,916 m), New Hampshire, US, 12 April 1934

Maximum Sunshine
97% (more than 4,300 hours), Eastern Sahara Desert, North Africa

Minimum Sunshine
Nil, for average winter stretches of 182 days, North Pole

Highest Shade Temperature
136.4°F (58°C), al'Azizyah, Libya (367 ft/111 m), 13 Sept 1922

Hottest Place
Annual average of 94°F (34.4°C), Dallol, Ethiopia, 1960-66

Coldest Place
Average of -70°F (-56.6°C), Plateau Station, Antarctica

Most Rainy Days
Annual average of 350 days, Mt. Waialeale 5,148 ft (1,569 m), Kauai, Hawaii

Windiest Place
Gales can reach 200 mph (320 km/h), Commonwealth Bay, George V Coast, Antarctica

WORLD'S MAJOR MOUNTAINS

*All of the world's highest mountains lie
in the Himalayas, South Asia.*

10 Annapurna I	9 Nanga Parbat	8 Cho Oyu	7 Manaslu I	6 Dhaulagiri I	5 Makalu I	4 Lhotse	3 Kanchenjunga	2 K2 (Dapsang)	1 Mount Everest
8,078 m (26,504 ft)	8,126 m (26,660 ft)	8,153 m (26,750 ft)	8,156 m (26,760 ft)	8,172 m (26,810 ft)	8,470 m (27,790 ft)	8,501 m (27,890 ft)	8,598 m (28,208 ft)	8,611 m (28,250 ft)	8,846 m (29,022 ft)

EARTHQUAKES

There are two different scales for measuring earthquakes: the Richter scale and the Modified Mercalli scale.

RICHTER SCALE

The Richter scale measures the strength of an earthquake at its source. It is a logarithmic scale, which means that each time the magnitude increases by one unit, the ground moves 10 times more and the earthquake releases about 30 times as much energy. The scale below gives an indication of the probable effects of earthquakes of particular magnitudes.

Magnitude	Probable effects
1	Detectable only by instruments.
2-2.5	Can just be felt by people.
4-5	May cause slight damage.
6	Fairly destructive.
7	A major earthquake.
8-9	A very destructive earthquake.

MODIFIED MERCALLI SCALE

The Modified Mercalli scale measures how much an earthquake shakes the ground at a particular place. This is called the felt intensity. The scale below gives a list of descriptions of earthquake effects.

Intensity	Probable effects
1	Not felt by people.
2	May be felt by some people on upper floors.
3	Detected indoors. Hanging objects may swing.
4	Hanging objects swing. Doors and windows rattle.
5	Felt outdoors by most people. Small objects moved or disturbed.
6	Felt by everyone. Furniture moves. Trees and bushes shake.
7	Difficult for people to stand. Buildings damaged, loose bricks fall.
8	Major damage to buildings. Branches of trees break.
9	General panic. Large cracks form in the ground. Some buildings collapse.
10	Large landslides occur. Many buildings are destroyed.
11	Major ground disturbances. Railway lines buckle.
12	Damage is almost total. Large objects thrown into the air.

BEAUFORT SCALE OF WIND SPEED

Force	Description	Average Speed mph	Average Speed km/h
0	Calm	Less than 1	Less than 1
1	Light air	1-3	1-5
2	Light breeze	4-7	6-11
3	Gentle breeze	8-12	12-19
4	Moderate breeze	13-18	20-29
5	Fresh breeze	19-24	30-39
6	Strong breeze	25-31	40-50
7	Moderate gale	32-38	51-61
8	Fresh gale	39-46	62-74
9	Strong gale	47-54	75-87
10	Whole gale	55-63	88-101
11	Storm	64-73	102-117
12	Hurricane	Above 74	Above 119

TALLEST STRUCTURES

Towers (including those supported by guy ropes)

		Feet	Meters	Built
1	KTHI-TV Tower, North Dakota, US	2,064	629	1963
2	CN Tower, Toronto, Canada	1,815	553	1975

Habitable Buildings

		Feet	Meters	Built
1	Taipei 101, Taipei, Taiwan	1,671	509	2003
2	Petronas Towers, Kuala Lumpur, Malaysia	1,482	452	1997
3	Sears Towers, Chicago, Illinois, US	1,454	443	1974
4	Jin Mao Tower, Shanghai, China	1,380	421	1998
5	Two International Finance Center, Hong Kong	1,362	415	2003
6	CITIC Plaza, Guangzhou	1,283	391	1997
7	Shun Hing Square, Shenzhen	1,260	384	1996
8	Empire State Building, New York City, US	1,250	381	1931
9	Central Plaza, Hong Kong	1,227	374	1992
10	Bank of China Tower, Hong Kong	1,205	367	1990

The Petronas Towers in Malaysia are one of the world's tallest habitable buildings.

LONGEST BRIDGES

The figures given below show the top ten longest bridges in the world. The measurements relate to the length of the central span of each bridge. All the bridges listed are suspension bridges.

1 Akashi-Kaikyo
5,839 ft (1,780 m), Honshu-Shikoku, Japan, completed 1997
2 Great Belt East
5,328 ft (1,624 m), Denmark, completed 1998
3 Humber Estuary
4,626 ft (1,410 m), Humber, UK, completed 1980
4 Jiangyin
4,544 ft (1,385 m), China, completed 1999
5 Tsing Ma
4,518 ft (1,377 m), Hong Kong, completed 1997
6 Verrazano-Narrows
4,260 ft (1,298 m), New York City, US, completed 1964
7 Golden Gate
4,200 ft (1,280 m), San Francisco, US, completed 1937
8 Höga Kusten
3,937 ft (1,200 m), Sweden, completed 1997
9 Mackinac Straits
3,800 ft (1,158 m), Michigan, US, completed 1957
10 Minami Bisan-Seto
3,608 ft (1,100 m), Japan, completed 1988

LONGEST RAIL SYSTEMS

The list below provides the measurements of the ten longest rail systems in the world, and where they are.

1 US
149,129 miles (240,000 km)
2 Russia
95,691 miles (154,000 km)
3 Canada
43,605 miles (70,176 km)
4 India
38,812 miles (62,462 km)
5 China
36,287 miles (58,399 km)
6 Germany
27,319 miles (43,966 km)
7 Australia
23,962 miles (38,563 km)
8 Argentina
23,556 miles (37,910 km)
9 France
21,059 miles (33,891 km)
10 Brazil
17,037 miles (27,418 km)

The total length of all world rail systems is estimated to be 746,476 miles (1,201,337 km).

Many geographical statistics are approximate because of factors such as seasonal changes and the method of measurement.

AREA AND VOLUME

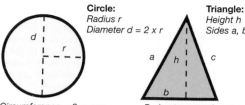

Circle:
Radius r
Diameter d = 2 x r

Circumference = 2 x π x r
Area = π x r² (π = 3.1416)

Triangle:
Height h
Sides a, b, c

Perimeter = a + b + c
Area = ¹/₂ x b x h

Rectangle:
Sides a, b

Perimeter = 2 x (a + b)
Area = a x b

Cylinder:
Height h
Radius r

Surface area = 2 x π x r x h (excluding ends)
Volume = π x r² x h

Cone:
Height h
Radius r
Side l

Surface area = π x r x l (exclud...
Volume = ¹/₃ x π x r² x l

UNITS OF MEASUREMENT

METRIC UNIT	EQUIVALENT	IMPERIAL UNIT	EQUIVALENT
Length		**Length**	
1 centimeter (cm)	10 millimeters (mm)	1 foot (ft)	12 inches (in)
1 meter (m)	100 centimeters (cm)	1 yard (yd)	3 feet
1 kilometer (km)	1,000 meters	1 mile	1,760 yards
Mass		**Mass**	
1 kilogram (kg)	1,000 grams (g)	1 pound (lb)	16 ounces (oz)
1 tonne (t)	1,000 kilograms	1 ton	2,240 pounds
Area		**Area**	
1 square centimeter (cm²)	100 square millimeters (mm²)	1 square foot (ft²)	144 square inches (in²)
1 square meter (m²)	10,000 square centimeters	1 square yard (yd²)	9 square feet
1 hectare	10,000 square meters	1 acre	4,840 square yards
1 square kilometer (km²)	1 million square meters	1 square mile	640 acres
Volume			
1 cubic centimeter (cc)	1 millilitre (ml)	1 pint	34.68 cubic inches (in³)
1 litre (l)	1,000 millilitres	1 quart	2 pints
1 cubic meter (m³)	1,000 litres	1 gallon	4 quarts

METRIC-IMPERIAL CONVERSIONS
Metric units into imperial units

To convert	into	multiply by
Length		
Centimeters	inches	0.39
Meters	feet	3.28
Kilometers	miles	0.62
Area		
Square cm	square inches	0.16
Square meters	square feet	10.76
Hectares	acres	2.47
Square km	square miles	0.39
Volume		
Cubic cm	cubic inches	0.061
Litres	pints	1.76
Litres	gallons	0.22
Mass		
Grams	ounces	0.04
Kilograms	pounds	2.21
Tonnes	tons	0.98

BINARY SYSTEM

The binary number system is used in computers to represent numbers and letters. The binary system uses only two symbols – 0 and 1 – which represent "On" and "Off" in computer circuits.

Decimal	Binary
1	1
2	10
3	11
4	100
5	101
6	110
7	111
8	1000
9	1001
10	1010
11	1011
12	1100

MATHEMATICAL SYMBOLS

+	plus
−	minus
±	plus or minus
x	multiplication (times)
÷	divided by
=	equal to
≠	not equal to
≈	approximately equal to
>	greater than
<	less than
≥	greater than or equal to
≤	less than or equal to
%	per cent
√	square root
π	pi (3.1416)
°	degree
'	minute, foot
"	second, inch

PERIODIC TABLE

The periodic table classifies chemical elements in order of atomic number (the number of protons in each atom of the element). The elements are arranged in horizontal rows, called periods, and vertical columns, called groups. In this way, elements with similar chemical properties (such as the alkali metals) lie in the same vertical group.

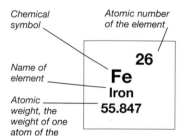

Chemical symbol
Atomic number of the element
Name of element
Atomic weight, the weight of one atom of the element compared to an atom of the element carbon. When the figure is in parentheses, refers to the most stable isotope.

26
Fe
Iron
55.847

H 1 Hydrogen 1.008								
Li 3 Lithium 6.941	**Be** 4 Beryllium 9.012							
Na 11 Sodium 22.990	**Mg** 12 Magnesium 24.305							
K 19 Potassium 39.098	**Ca** 20 Calcium 40.08	**Sc** 21 Scandium 44.956	**Ti** 22 Titanium 47.90	**V** 23 Vanadium 50.941	**Cr** 24 Chromium 51.996	**Mn** 25 Manganese 54.938	**Fe** 26 Iron 55.847	**Co** 2 Cobalt 58.933
Rb 37 Rubidium 85.468	**Sr** 38 Strontium 87.62	**Y** 39 Yttrium 88.906	**Zr** 40 Zirconium 91.22	**Nb** 41 Niobium 92.906	**Mo** 42 Molybdenum 95.94	**Tc** 43 Technetium (97)	**Ru** 44 Ruthenium 101.07	**Rh** 4 Rhodium 102.906
Cs 55 Caesium 132.910	**Ba** 56 Barium 137.34		**Hf** 72 Hafnium 178.49	**Ta** 73 Tantalum 180.948	**W** 74 Tungsten 183.85	**Re** 75 Rhenium 186.207	**Os** 76 Osmium 190.2	**Ir** 7 Iridium 192.22
Fr 87 Francium (223)	**Ra** 88 Radium 226.025		**Unq** 104 Unnilquadium (260)	**Unp** 105 Unnilpentium (262)	**Unh** 106 Unnilhexium (263)	**Uns** 107 Unnilseptium (262)	**Uno** 108 Unniloctium (265)	**Une** 10 Unnilennium (266)

La 57 Lanthanum 138.906	**Ce** 58 Cerium 140.12	**Pr** 59 Praseodymium 140.908	**Nd** 60 Neodymium 144.24	**Pm** 61 Promethium (145)	**Sm** 62 Samarium 150.4	**Eu** 63 Europium 151.96	**Gd** 6 Gadolinium 157.25
Ac 89 Actinium (227)	**Th** 90 Thorium 232.038	**Pa** 91 Protactinium 231.036	**U** 92 Uranium 238.029	**Np** 93 Neptunium 237.048	**Pu** 94 Plutonium (244)	**Am** 95 Americium (243)	**Cm** 9 Curium (247)

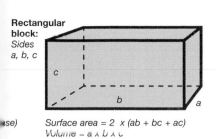

Rectangular block:
Sides a, b, c

(se) Surface area = 2 x (ab + bc + ac)
Volume = a x b x c

mperial units into metric units

To convert	into	multiply by
Length		
nches	centimeters	2.54
Feet	meters	0.30
Miles	kilometers	1.61
Area		
Square inches	square cm	6.45
Square feet	square meters	0.09
Acres	hectares	0.41
Square miles	square km	2.59
Volume		
Cubic inches	cubic cm	16.39
Pints	litres	0.57
Gallons	litres	4.55
Mass		
Ounces	grams	28.35
Pounds	kilograms	0.45
Tons	tonnes	1.02

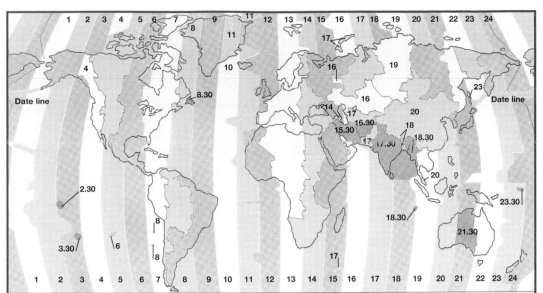

TIME ZONES

As Earth spins, the Sun appears to rise and set. However, while the Sun is rising at one place on the globe, it is setting at another. For instance, when it is 5 A.M. in New York, it is 8 P.M. in Australia. To take account of this, the Earth is divided into a series of time zones, starting from the Date line. Clocks are set to a different time in each zone, calculated to ensure that in every part of the world, the time is about 12 noon during the middle of the day, and midnight during the middle of the night.

Alkali metals	Alkaline earth metals
Transition metals	Other metals
Nonmetals	Noble gases
Lanthanide series	Actinide series

2 He Helium 4.003

			5 B Boron 10.81	**6 C** Carbon 12.011	**7 N** Nitrogen 14.007	**8 O** Oxygen 15.999	**9 F** Fluorine 18.998	**10 Ne** Neon 20.179
			13 Al Aluminium 26.982	**14 Si** Silicon 28.086	**15 P** Phosphorus 30.974	**16 S** Sulphur 32.06	**17 Cl** Chlorine 35.453	**18 Ar** Argon 39.948
28 Ni Nickel 58.70	**29 Cu** Copper 63.546	**30 Zn** Zinc 65.38	**31 Ga** Gallium 69.72	**32 Ge** Germanium 72.59	**33 As** Arsenic 74.922	**34 Se** Selenium 78.96	**35 Br** Bromine 79.904	**36 Kr** Krypton 83.80
46 Pd Palladium 106.4	**47 Ag** Silver 107.868	**48 Cd** Cadmium 112.40	**49 In** Indium 114.82	**50 Sn** Tin 118.69	**51 Sb** Antimony 121.75	**52 Te** Tellurium 127.60	**53 I** Iodine 126.905	**54 Xe** Xenon 131.30
78 Pt Platinum 195.09	**79 Au** Gold 196.967	**80 Hg** Mercury 200.59	**81 Tl** Thallium 204.37	**82 Pb** Lead 207.2	**83 Bi** Bismuth 208.98	**84 Po** Polonium (209)	**85 At** Astatine (210)	**86 Rn** Radon (222)

New elements are sometimes discovered, but it takes time for them to be officially recognized and named.

65 Tb Terbium 158.925	**66 Dy** Dysprosium 162.50	**67 Ho** Holmium 164.930	**68 Er** Erbium 167.26	**69 Tm** Thulium 168.934	**70 Yb** Ytterbium 173.04	**71 Lu** Lutetium 174.97
97 Bk Berkelium (247)	**98 Cf** Californium (251)	**99 Es** Einsteinium (254)	**100 Fm** Fermium (257)	**101 Md** Mendelevium (258)	**102 No** Nobelium (255)	**103 Lr** Lawrencium (260)

TEMPERATURE SCALES

To convert from Celsius to Fahrenheit:
$$°F = °C \times 9/5 + 32$$
To convert from Fahrenheit to Celsius:
$$°C = (°F - 32) \times 5/9$$

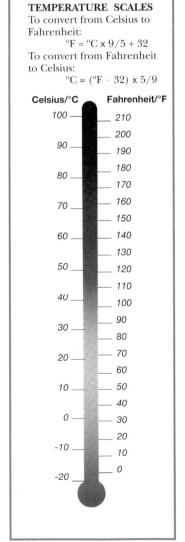

INDEX

Page numbers in **bold** type have most information in them. Numbers in *italics* refer to pages in the Fact Finder.

A

Aachen cathedral 139
abacus 420
abolitionist movement **12**, 604, 735
aboriginal Australians **13**, 63, 64, 67-68
Abraham 374
absolute zero 317
abstract expressionism 504
Abu Dhabi 435
acceleration 268
accent (on letters) 29
accidents
   first aid 255
   hospitals 328
accretion discs 95
acid rain 528
acorns 282, 684
acoustics 513
Acre 185
Act of Union (1707) 699
actors 671, 672
acupuncture 143, 422
Adams, John 189, 538
addax 197
Adelaide 480
administrative law 388
adult education 222
advertising **14**
aerial photography 40, 438
aeroplanes *see* aircraft
Aeschylus 743
aestivation 319
Afghanistan 51, 137, 138
AFL-CIO 382
Afonso III, King of Portugal 533
Africa **15-18**
   communications *758*
   deserts 195
   history of **19-20**, *748*
   slave trade 19, 603
   wildlife 22, 216, **304-305**
   see also Benin; Central Africa; East Africa; North Africa; South Africa; Southern Africa; West Africa
African-Americans **21**, 153, 400, 659, *762*
   and the American Civil War 154
African elephants 229
African National Congress (ANC) 20, 415, 614
African violets 175
African wild cat 127
agriculture *see* farming
AIDS 203
aikido 646
air **23**
   atmosphere 61
   clouds 723
   for divers 693
   oxygen 498, 535
   wind 733
air forces **26**
air pressure 23
air resistance 23
air traffic control 27
aircraft **24-25**
   fuselages 427, 438, 520

history of 683
   jet engines 233
   military 26, 161, **438**
   navigation 467
   radar 24, 26, 438, 543
   see also gliders; helicopters
aircraft carriers 466, 714
aircrew 26
airports 27, 744, *762*
airships **77**
Akashi-Kaikyo bridge 102, *775*
Alans 79
Alaric 79
Alaska 476, 479, 701, 702, 704, *760, 762*
albatrosses 589
Albert, Prince Consort 709, 710
Alcatraz 463
Alcázar (Segovia) 126
alchemy 140
Alcock, John 25
Aldrin, Edwin 446
Alexander the Great **28**
   conquests 73, 224, 508
   spreads Greek culture 308
   submarine 656
Alexander II, Czar 574
Alexandria 28, 152, 736
alfalfa 65
Alfonso XIII, King of Spain 642
algae 433, 535
Algarve 531
algebra 420
Algeria 277, 475
Algiers 474
Alhambra palace (Granada) 641
alimentary canal 200
Allah 359
alligators 175, **183**, 555
alloys 427
alphabets **29**, 570
Alps 448, 661
aluminum 427
alveolus (lungs) 408
Alvin submersible 693
Amazon River 100, 558, 616
Amazonian Indians 100
amber 227
ambulances 255
ameba 433
American Antislavery Society 12
American Civil War 80, **154-155**, 394, 705, 714
American Federation of Labor 382
American Red Cross **80**
   see also Red Cross
American Revolutionary War **30-31**, 715
Americans, Native *see* Native Americans
America's Cup 576
Amerindians *see* Native Americans
ammonites 271
Amnesty International 332
Ampex company 669
amphibians 280, 536, *767*
amphisbaenid *see* worm lizards
Amritsar 339
Amsterdam 404

Amundsen, Roald 522
anacondas 606
anarchism 299
Anatolia 495, 690
anatomy 390
ancestor worship 726
Ancient Egypt **223-224**
   Alexandrian library 28
   art 501
   boats 597
   books 96
   cats 128
   hieroglyphics 29
   pyramids 223, 732, 736
   scribes 221
   Tutankhamun's tomb 40
   units of measurement 724
   see also Alexander the Great
Ancient Greece 241, **308-309**
   Alexander the Great 28
   alphabet 29
   architecture 41
   art 501
   boats 597
   clothes 159
   democracy 193
   education 221
   gods and goddesses 460
   medicine 423
   Olympic Games 491
   scientists 290, 586
   theaters 671
   tunnels 688
   warships 714
   wonders of the ancient world 689, **736**
Ancient Rome *see* Roman Empire
Andersen, Hans Christian 398
Andes Mountains 45, 448, 615
anemometers 722
anemones, sea 180, 592
anesthetics 208
angelfish 488
Angkor Wat 625
anglerfish 190
Angles 426
angles (geometry) 290
animal symbols 599
animals **32-35**
   camouflage 109, **114**, 244
   classification *766-767*
   conservation 175-176, *770*
   in deserts 196-197
   ecology and food webs 218-219
   evolution 243-244
   extinction 536
   farm animals **249-250**, 251
   flight in **261-262**
   in forests 269-270
   fossils 271, 564
   grassland 304-305
   hearing 211
   hibernation 319, 440
   horns 192, 557
   lake and river 383-384
   lifespans *768-769*
   lungs and breathing 408
   marsh and swamp 418
   migration 437, *768-769*
   mountain 448-449
   nests and burrows 468
   pets 509
   polar 523
   records *768-769*
   reptiles 555-556
   senses **34-35**
   skeletons 601
   teeth 665
   vets 708

zoology 91
   see also mammals; wildlife; zoos
animated movies 124
annelids 741
anole lizards 402
Antarctic Ocean 485
Antarctica **36-37**
   climate 156
   exploration of 179, **522**
   ice 37, 297
   map 37
   wildlife **523-524**
anteaters 304, 413
antelopes **192**, 197, 305
antennae (insects) 350
anthers 263
Anthony, Susan B. 734
anthracite 160
Anti-Federalists 527
anti-slavery movement *see* abolitionist movement
antibiotics 208, 455
antique furniture 283
antiseptics 424
antlers 192
ants **38**, 304, 432
anus 200
Apache Indians 464
apartheid 20, 332, 415, 612, 614
apartment buildings 329
Apennine Mountains 361, 363
apes **444-445**, 537
aphids 349
Apollo spacecraft 446, 683, 701
Apollo (sun god) 460
Appaloosa horses 327
apples 281
Aqua-Lung 693
aqueducts 102, 241, 276, 641
Aquino, Benigno 626
Aquino, Corazon 626
Arab-Israeli wars 435
Arabia 359
Arabian Desert 195
Arabian Peninsula **434-435**
Arabic numbers 484
Arabs
   in Asia 49, 625
   Middle East 434-435
arachnids 643
Aral Sea 137
Arawak peoples 166
Archaeopteryx 261
archeology **39-40**
   underwater 693
archer fish 418
archery 719, 720
   medieval 125
   Mongols 443
   as sport 646
Archimedes 513, 586
Archimedes' screw 409
architecture **41-42**, 390
   Caribbean 119
   European 236
   houses 329
   Norman 473
   Renaissance 552
Arctic **43-44**
   exploration 179, **522**
   ice 297
   Siberia 49
   tundra 524
   wildlife **523-524**
   see also Inuits
Arctic fox 114
Arctic hare 114
Arctic Ocean 43, 44, 485

Arctic tern 44, 261, 437
Ardagh chalice 356
area and volume *776-777*
Argentina **45-46**, 616, 617, *771*
argonauts 595
Ariane rocket 563
Aristarchus 58, 213
Aristophanes 309
Aristotle 28, 91, 221
arithmetic 420
   see also statistics
Arizona 167, 701
Arkwright, Richard 345
Arlington National Cemetery 706
Armada, Spanish 230, 642, 698
armadillos 197, 304, 414
Armenia 51, 129, 690
armies **47**
   of Alexander the Great 28
   Roman 111, 567
   tanks 662
armillary spheres 551
armor **48**, 378
armored cars 662
Armstrong, Neil 56, 446, 636
aromatherapy 422
arrows 719, 720
art
   aboriginal 13
   European 237
   galleries 454
   Greek 309
   Inuit 352
   Renaissance 552
   see also drawing; painting; sculpture
Artemis, Temple of 689, 736
arteries 315
arthropods 132, *766, 769*
Arthur, King 379
artillery weapons 310, 662
artists 390, **501-504**, *765*
Aryans 340
Asclepius 423
Ashurbanipal II, King of Assyria 55
Asia **49-52**, 178
   deserts 195
   history of **53-54**, *750*
   Mongol Empire 443
   wildlife 304-305, 622
   see also Central Asia; Southeast Asia
Asian elephants 229
Asoka, Emperor 340
asses 326, 327
Assyrians **55**
asteroids 516
Astley, Philip 151
astrology 599
astronauts **56**, 498, 635-636
astronomical clocks 157
astronomy **57-58**
   comets and meteors 167
   radio waves 544
   Renaissance 551
   see also Moon; planets; stars; Sun; telescopes
astrophysics 513
Aswan High Dam 186
Atacama Desert 195
Atahualpa 174
Athena 460
Athens 41, 307, 308, 460
athletics **677**
Atlantic Ocean **59-60**, 178, 485
atlas moths 270
Atlas Mountains 448, 475
atlases 417, 547
atmosphere **61**, 212

D · E

K·L·M

U·V·W

GAZETTEER

A

Abu Dhabi United Arab Emirates **436**
Abuja Nigeria **728**
Acapulco Mexico **429**
Accra Ghana **727**
Addis Ababa Ethiopia **217**
Adelaide Australia **66**
Aden Yemen **436**
Adriatic Sea *sea* Mediterranean Sea **363**
Aegean Sea *sea* Mediterranean Sea **307**
Afghanistan *country* C Asia **138**
Africa *continent* **18**
Alabama *state* USA **704**
Alaska *state* USA **704**
Albania *country* SE Europe **630**
Alberta *province* Canada **117**
Alexandria Egypt **475**
Algeria *country* N Africa **475**
Algiers Algeria **475**
Alicante Spain **640**
Alice Springs Australia **66**
Alps *mountains* C Europe **239**
Amazon *river* Brazil/Peru **101**
Amazon Basin *basin* South America **101**
American Samoa *dependency* Pacific Ocean **500**
Amman Jordan **436**
Amsterdam Netherlands **405**
Andes *mountains* S America **618**
Andorra *country* SW Europe **275**
Andorra la Vella Andorra **275**
Angola *country* SW Africa **632**
Anguilla *dependency* West Indies **120**
Ankara Turkey **690**
Antananarivo Madagascar **343**
Antarctica *continent* Antarctica **37**
Antigua and Barbuda *country* West Indies **120**
Antwerp Belgium **405**
Appennines *mountains* Italy/San Marino **363**
Arabian Peninsula *peninsula* SW Asia **436**
Arabian Sea *sea* Indian Ocean **52**
Arctic Ocean *ocean* **44**
Argentina *country* S South America **46**
Arizona *state* USA **704**
Arkansas *state* USA **704**
Armenia *country* SW Asia **129**
Aruba *dependency* West Indies **120**
Ascension Island *dependency* Atlantic Ocean **60**
Ashgabat Turkmenistan **138**
Ashmore and Cartier Islands *dependency* Indian Ocean **343**
Asia *Continent* **52**
Asmara Eritrea **217**
Astana Kazakhstan **52**
Asunción Paraguay **618**
Atacama Desert *desert* Chile **618**
Athens Greece **307**
Atlantic Ocean *Ocean* **60**

Atlas Mountains *mountains* N Africa **475**
Auckland New Zealand **471**
Australia *country* Oceania **66**
Australian Capital Territory *territory* Australia **66**
Austria *country* W Europe **71**
Ayers Rock *see* Uluru
Azerbaijan *country* SE Asia **129**

B

Baffin Bay *bay* Atlantic Ocean **117**
Baghdad Iraq **436**
Bahamas *country* West Indies **120**
Bahrain *country* SW Asia **436**
Baku Azerbaijan **129**
Balearic Islands *islands* Spain **640**
Baltic Sea *sea* Atlantic Ocean **239**
Bamako Mali **728**
Bandar Seri Begawan Brunei **624**
Bangalore India **339**
Bangkok Thailand **624**
Bangladesh *country* S Asia **339**
Bangui Central African Republic **134**
Banjul Gambia **728**
Barbados *country* West Indies **120**
Barcelona Spain **640**
Basel Switzerland **661**
Basseterre Saint Kitts and Nevis **120**
Bavarian Alps *mountains* Austria/Germany **71**
Beijing China **144**
Beirut Lebanon **436**
Belarus *country* E Europe **78**
Belfast UK **697**
Belgium *country* NW Europe **405**
Belgrade Serbia and Montenegro **628**
Belize *country* Central America **136**
Belmopan Belize **136**
Belo Horizonte Brazil **101**
Ben Nevis *mountain* UK **697**
Bengal, Bay of *bay* Indian Ocean **339**
Benin *country* W Africa **728**
Bering Strait *strait* Russian Federation/USA **704**
Berlin Germany **294**
Bermuda *dependency* Atlantic Ocean **60**
Bern Switzerland **661**
Berner Alpen *mountains* Switzerland **661**
Bethlehem West Bank **360**
Bhutan *country* S Asia **339**
Birmingham UK **697**
Biscay, Bay of *bay* Atlantic Ocean **640**
Bishkek Kyrgyzstan **138**
Bissau Guinea-Bissau **728**
Black Forest *physical region* Germany **294**
Black Sea *sea* Atlantic Ocean **239**
Blackpool UK **697**

Blanc, Mont *mountain* France/Italy **363**
Bloemfontein South Africa **613**
Bogotá Colombia **163**
Bohemian Forest *mountains* C Europe **294**
Bolivia *country* W South America **618**
Bombay *see* Mumbai
Bonn Germany **294**
Bordeaux France **275**
Borneo *island* SE Asia **624**
Bosnia and Herzegovina *country* SE Europe **630**
Boston USA **704**
Botswana *country* S Africa **632**
Bouvet Island *dependency* Atlantic Ocean **60**
Brahmaputra *river* S Asia **144**
Brasília Brazil **101**
Bratislava Slovakia **239**
Brazil *country* C South America **101**
Brazzaville Congo **134**
Bridgetown Barbados **120**
Brisbane Australia **68**
Bristol Channel *inlet* UK **697**
British Columbia *province* Canada **117**
British Indian Ocean Territory *dependency* Indian Ocean **343**
British Virgin Islands *dependency* West Indies **120**
Bruges Belgium **405**
Brunei *country* SE Asia **624**
Brussels Belgium **405**
Bucharest Romania **628**
Budapest Hungary **239**
Buenos Aires Argentina **46**
Bujumbura Burundi **217**
Bulgaria *country* SE Europe **628**
Burkina *country* W Africa **728**
Burma *see* Myanmar
Burundi *country* C Africa **217**

C

Cabinda *province* Angola **134**
Cádiz Spain **640**
Cairo Egypt **475**
Calais France **275**
Calcutta *see* Kolkata
Calgary Canada **117**
California *state* USA **704**
California, Gulf of *gulf* Pacific Ocean **429**
Cambodia *country* SE Asia **624**
Cameroon *country* W Africa **134**
Canada *country* N North America **117**
Canary Islands *islands* Spain **640**
Canberra Australia **66**
Cape Town South Africa **613**
Cape Verde *country* Atlantic Ocean **60**
Caracas Venezuela **618**
Cardiff UK **697**
Cardigan Bay *bay* Atlantic Ocean **697**
Caribbean Sea *sea* Atlantic Ocean **479**

Cartagena Colombia **163**
Casablanca Morocco **475**
Castries Saint Lucia **120**
Cayenne French Guiana **618**
Cayman Islands *dependency* West Indies **120**
Central African Republic *country* C Africa **134**
Central America *geopolitical region* **136**
Chad *country* C Africa **134**
Channel Islands *islands* W Europe **697**
Chennai India **339**
Chicago USA **704**
Chile *country* SW South America **618**
China *country* E Asia **144**
Chisinau Moldova **691**
Christchurch New Zealand **471**
Christmas Island *dependency* Indian Ocean **343**
Cocos Islands *dependency* Indian Ocean **343**
Cologne Germany **294**
Colombia *country* N South America **163**
Colombo Sri Lanka **339**
Colorado *state* USA **704**
Comoros *country* Indian Ocean **343**
Conakry Guinea **728**
Congo *country* C Africa **134**
Congo Basin *basin* C Africa **134**
Congo, Democratic Republic of *country* C Africa **134**
Connecticut *state* USA **704**
Cook Islands *dependency* Pacific Ocean **500**
Copenhagen Denmark **580**
Corfu *island* Greece **307**
Cork Ireland **355**
Corsica *island* France **275**
Costa Rica *country* Central America **136**
Crete *island* Greece **307**
Crimea *peninsula* Ukraine **691**
Croatia *country* SE Europe **630**
Cuba *country* West Indies **120**
Cyprus *country* Mediterranean Sea **52**
Czech Republic *country* C Europe **239**

D

Dakar Senegal **728**
Dallas USA **704**
Damascus Syria **436**
Danube *river* C Europe **294, 628**
Darwin Australia **66**
Dead Sea *salt lake* Israel/Jordan **360**
Delaware *state* USA **704**
Delhi India **339**
Denmark *country* N Europe **580**
Detroit USA **704**
Dhaka Bangladesh **339**
Dijon France **275**
Dili East Timor **624**
Dingle Bay *bay* Atlantic Ocean **355**

Djibouti *country* E Africa **217**
Djibouti Djibouti **217**
Dodecanese *islands* Greece **307**
Dodoma Tanzania **217**
Doha Qatar **436**
Dominica *country* West Indies **120**
Dominican Republic *country* West Indies **120**
Donegal Bay *bay* Atlantic Ocean **355**
Dordogne *river* France **275**
Douro *river* Portugal/Spain **532**
Dubai United Arab Emirates **436**
Dublin Ireland **355**
Durban South Africa **613**
Dushanbe Tajikistan **138**
Düsseldorf Germany **294**

E

East Timor *country* SE Asia **624**
Ecuador *country* NW South America **618**
Edinburgh UK **697**
Egypt *country* NE Africa **475**
Eiger *mountain* Switzerland **661**
El Salvador *country* Central America **136**
Elburz Mountains *mountains* Iran **353**
England *national region* UK **697**
English Channel *channel* France/United Kingdom **239**
Equatorial Guinea *country* C Africa **134**
Erie, Lake *lake* Canada/USA **704**
Eritrea *country* E Africa **217**
Estonia *country* NE Europe **78**
Ethiopia *country* E Africa **217**
Etna, Monte *volcano* Italy **363**
Euphrates *river* SW Asia **690**
Europe *Continent* **239**
Everest, Mount *mountain* China/Nepal **339**

F

Faeroe Islands *dependency* NW Europe **580**
Falkland Islands *dependency* Atlantic Ocean **46**
Fiji *country* Pacific Ocean **500**
Finland *country* N Europe **580**
Florence Italy **363**
Florida *state* USA **704**
Florida Keys *islands* USA **704**
France *country* W Europe **275**
Frankfurt am Main Germany **294**
Freetown Sierra Leone **728**
French Guiana *dependency* N South America **618**
French Polynesia *dependency* Pacific Ocean **500**

G

Gabon *country* C Africa **134**
Gaborone Botswana **632**
Galilee, Sea of *lake* Israel **360**
Galway Bay *bay* Atlantic
  Ocean **355**
Gambia *country* W Africa **728**
Ganges *river* S Asia **339**
Garda, Lago di *lake* Italy **363**
Garonne *river* France **275**
Gaza Strip *disputed region*
  Gaza Strip **360**
Geneva Switzerland **661**
Geneva, Lake *lake*
  France/Switzerland **661**
Genoa Italy **363**
Georgetown Guyana **618**
Georgia *country* SW Asia **129**
Georgia *state* USA **704**
Germany *country* N Europe
  294
Ghana *country* W Africa **728**
Gibraltar *dependency* **640**
Glasgow UK **697**
Gothenburg Sweden **580**
Grampian Mountains
  mountains UK **697**
Gran Chaco *lowland plain*
  South America **46**
Grand Canyon *canyon* USA
  704
Great Barrier Reef *reef*
  Australia **66**
Great Bear Lake *lake* Canada
  117
Great Lakes *lakes*
  Canada/USA **704**
Great Plains *plains*
  Canada/USA **117**
Great Rift Valley *depression*
  Asia/Africa **217**
Great Slave Lake *lake* Canada
  117
Great Wall of China *Ancient
  monument* China **144**
Greater Antilles *islands* West
  Indies **120**
Greece *country* SE Europe
  307
Greenland *dependency* NE
  North America **580**
Grenada *country* West Indies
  120
Grenoble France **275**
Guadeloupe *dependency* West
  Indies **120**
Guam *dependency* Pacific
  Ocean **500**
Guatemala *country* Central
  America **136**
Guatemala City Guatemala
  136
Guernsey *island* Channel
  Islands **697**
Guinea *country* W Africa **728**
Guinea-Bissau *country* W
  Africa **728**
Guyana *country* N South
  America **618**

H

Haifa Israel **360**
Haiti *country* West Indies **120**
Halifax Canada **117**
Hamburg Germany **294**
Hamilton New Zealand **471**
Hanoi Vietnam **624**

Hanover Germany **294**
Harare Zimbabwe **632**
Havana Cuba **120**
Hawaii *state* USA **500, 704**
Hebrides *islands* **697**
Hebron Israel **360**
Helsinki Finland **580**
Himalayas *mountains* S Asia
  339
Hindu Kush *mountains*
  Afghanistan/Pakistan **138**
Hiroshima Japan **368**
Hô Chi Minh Vietnam **624**
Hobart Australia **66**
Hokkaido *island* Japan **368**
Honduras *country* Central
  America **136**
Hong Kong *former UK
  dependency* China **144**
Honshu *island* Japan **368**
Houston USA **704**
Hudson Bay *bay* Atlantic
  Ocean **117**
Hungary *country* C Europe **239**

I · J

Ibiza *island* Spain **640**
Iceland *country* NW Europe
  580
Idaho *state* USA **704**
Illinois *state* USA **704**
India *country* S Asia **339**
Indian Ocean *ocean* **343**
Indiana *state* USA **704**
Indianapolis USA **704**
Indonesia *country* SE Asia **624**
Indus *river* S Asia **339**
Innsbruck Austria **71**
Iowa *state* USA **704**
Iran *country* SW Asia **353**
Iranian Plateau *plateau* Iran
  353
Iraq *country* SW Asia **436**
Ireland *country* NW Europe
  355
Irian Jaya *province* Indonesia
  624
Irish Sea *sea* Atlantic Ocean
  355
Islamabad Pakistan **339**
Isle of Man *dependency* NW
  Europe **697**
Israel *country* SW Asia **360**
Istanbul Turkey **690**
Italy *country* S Europe **363**
Ivory Coast *country* W Africa
  728
Jakarta Indonesia **624**
Jamaica *country* West Indies
  120
Japan *country* E Asia **368**
Java *island* Indonesia **624**
Jersey *island* Channel Islands
  697
Jerusalem Israel **360**
Johannesburg South Africa
  613
Jordan *country* SW Asia **436**
Jutland *peninsula* Denmark **580**

K · L

K2 *mountain* China/Pakistan
  339
Kabul Afghanistan **138**
Kalahari Desert *desert* S Africa
  632

Kamchatka *peninsula* Russian
  Federation **572**
Kampala Uganda **217**
Kansas *state* USA **704**
Kathmandu Nepal **339**
Kazakhstan *country* C Asia **52**
Kentucky *state* USA **704**
Kenya *country* E Africa **217**
Khartoum Sudan **217**
Khyber Pass *pass*
  Afghanistan/Pakistan **339**
Kiev Ukraine **691**
Kigali Rwanda **217**
Kilimanjaro *volcano* Tanzania
  217
Killarney Ireland **355**
Kingston Jamaica **120**
Kingstown Saint Vincent and
  the Grenadines **120**
Kinshasa Congo, Dem. Rep.
  of **134**
Kiribati *country* Pacific Ocean
  500
Kisangani Congo, Dem. Rep.
  of **134**
Kobe Japan **368**
Kolkata India **339**
Kosovo *Cultural region* Serbia
  and Montenegro **628**
Kuala Lumpur Malaysia **624**
Kuwait *country* SW Asia **436**
Kuwait City Kuwait **436**
Kyoto Japan **368**
Kyrgyzstan *country* C Asia **138**
Kyushu *island* Japan **368**
La Paz Bolivia **618**
Laâyoune Western Sahara
  475
Lahore Pakistan **339**
Land's End *headland* UK **697**
Laos *country* SE Asia **624**
Latvia *country* NE Europe **78**
Lausanne Switzerland **661**
Le Havre France **275**
Lebanon *country* SW Asia
  436
Leeds UK **697**
Leeward Islands *islands* West
  Indies **120**
Lesbos *island* Greece **307**
Lesotho *country* S Africa **613**
Lesser Antilles *islands* West
  Indies **120**
Liberia *country* W Africa **728**
Libreville Gabon **134**
Libya *country* N Africa **475**
Libyan Desert *desert* N Africa
  18
Liechtenstein *country* C
  Europe **239**
Liffey *river* Ireland **355**
Lille France **275**
Lilongwe Malawi **18**
Lima Peru **618**
Limoges France **275**
Lisbon Portugal **532**
Lithuania *country* NE Europe
  78
Liverpool UK **697**
Ljubljana Slovenia **630**
Llanos *physical region*
  Colombia/Venezuela **618**
Loire *river* France **275**
Lomé Togo **728**
London UK **697**
Los Angeles USA **704**
Louisiana *state* USA **704**
Luanda Angola **632**
Lusaka Zambia **18**
Luxembourg *country* NW
  Europe **405**
Luxembourg Luxembourg
  405
Lyon France **275**

M

Maastricht Netherlands **405**
Macedonia *country* SE Europe
  628
Madagascar *country* Indian
  Ocean **343**
Madras *see* Chennai
Madrid Spain **640**
Maine *state* USA **704**
Majorca *island* Spain **640**
Malabo Equatorial Guinea **134**
Málaga Spain **640**
Malawi *country* S Africa **18**
Malaysia *country* SE Asia **624**
Maldives *country* Indian
  Ocean **343**
Male Maldives **343**
Mali *country* W Africa **728**
Malta *country* S Europe **363**
Managua Nicaragua **136**
Manama Bahrain **436**
Manchester UK **697**
Manila Philippines **624**
Manitoba *province* Canada **117**
Maputo Mozambique **632**
Marrakech Morocco **475**
Marseille France **275**
Marshall Islands *country*
  Pacific Ocean **500**
Martinique *dependency* West
  Indies **120**
Maryland *state* USA **704**
Maseru Lesotho **613**
Massachusetts *state* USA **704**
Massif Central *plateau* France
  275
Matterhorn *mountain*
  Italy/Switzerland **661**
Mauritania *country* W Africa
  728
Mauritius *country* Indian
  Ocean **343**
Mayotte *dependency* Indian
  Ocean **343**
Mbabane Swaziland **613**
Mecca Saudi Arabia **436**
Mediterranean Sea *sea*
  Atlantic Ocean **239**
Mekong *river* SE Asia **144**
Melbourne Australia **66**
Memphis USA **704**
Mexico *country* Central
  America **429**
Mexico City Mexico **429**
Mexico, Gulf of *gulf* Atlantic
  Ocean **479**
Michigan *state* USA **704**
Micronesia *country* Pacific
  Ocean **500**
Midway Islands *dependency*
  Pacific Ocean **500**
Milan Italy **363**
Minnesota *state* USA **704**
Minorca *island* Spain **640**
Minsk Belarus **78**
Mississippi *state* USA **704**
Mississippi River *river* USA
  704
Missouri *state* USA **704**
Mogadishu Somalia **217**
Moldova *country* SE Europe
  691
Mombasa Kenya **217**
Monaco *country* W Europe **275**
Mongolia *country* E Asia **52**
Monrovia Liberia **728**
Montana *state* USA **704**
Montevideo Uruguay **618**
Montréal Canada **117**
Montserrat *dependency* West
  Indies **120**

Morocco *country* N Africa **475**
Moroni Comoros **343**
Moscow Russian Federation
  572
Mozambique *country* S Africa
  632
Mumbai India **339**
Munich Germany **294**
Muscat Oman **436**
Myanmar *country* SE Asia **624**

N

Nagasaki Japan **368**
Nairobi Kenya **217**
Namib Desert *desert* Namibia
  632
Namibia *country* S Africa **632**
Naples Italy **363**
Nassau Bahamas **120**
Nauru *country* Pacific Ocean
  500
Navassa Island *dependency*
  West Indies **120**
Nazareth Israel **360**
Ndjamena Chad **134**
Nebraska *state* USA **704**
Negev *desert* Israel **360**
Nepal *country* S Asia **339**
Netherlands *country* NW
  Europe **405**
Nevada *state* USA **704**
New Brunswick *province*
  Canada **117**
New Caledonia *dependency*
  Pacific Ocean **500**
New Delhi India **339**
New Hampshire *state* USA **704**
New Jersey *state* USA **704**
New Mexico *state* USA **704**
New Orleans USA **704**
New South Wales *state*
  Australia **66**
New York USA **704**
New York *state* USA **704**
New Zealand *country* Oceania
  471
Newcastle upon Tyne UK **697**
Newfoundland *province*
  Canada **117**
Niagara Falls *waterfall*
  Canada/USA **117, 704**
Niamey Niger **728**
Nicaragua *country* Central
  America **136**
Nice France **275**
Nicosia Cyprus **52**
Niger *country* W Africa **728**
Niger *river* W Africa **728**
Nigeria *country* W Africa **728**
Nile *river* N Africa **18**
Niue *dependency* Pacific Ocean
  500
North America *Continent* **479**
North Carolina *state* USA **704**
North Dakota *state* USA **704**
North European Plain *plain* N
  Europe **239**
North Geomagnetic Pole *pole*
  44
North Island *island* New
  Zealand **471**
North Korea *country* E Asia **380**
North Pole *pole* **44**
North Sea *sea* Atlantic Ocean
  239
Northern Ireland *political
  division* UK **697**
Northern Mariana Islands
  dependency Pacific Ocean
  500

ACKNOWLEDGMENTS

Contributors Simon Adams, Neil Ardley, Norman Barrett, Gerard Cheshire, Judy Clark, Chris Cooper, Margaret Crowther, John Farndon, Will Fowler, Adrian Gilbert, Barbara Gilgallon, Peter Lafferty, Margaret Lincoln, Caroline Lucas, Antony Mason, Rupert Matthews, Dan McCausland, Steve Parker, Steve Peak, Theodore Rowland-Entwistle, Sue Seddon, Marilyn Tolhurst, Marcus Weeks, Philip Wilkinson, Frances Williams, Tim Wood, Elizabeth Wyse
Additional editorial assistance Sam Atkinson, Jane Birdsell, Lynn Bresler, Azza Brown, Liza Bruml, Caroline Chapman, Claire Gillard, Carl Gombrich, Samantha Gray, Sudhanshu Gupta, Prita Maitra, Caroline Murrell, Pallavi Narain, Connie Novis, Louise Pritchard, Ranjana Saklani, Jill Somerscales, Gary Werner
Additional design assistance Sukanto Bhattacharjya, Tina Borg, Duncan Brown, Darren Holt, Shuka Jain, Ruth Jones, Sabyasachi Kundu, Clare Watson, Simon Yeomans
Illustration Coordinator Ted Kinsey
Picture Research Maureen Cowdroy, Julia Harris-Voss, Diane LeGrand, Samantha Nunn, Deborah Pownall, Louise Thomas, Bridget Tily, Emma Wood
Cartographers Pam Alford, Tony Chambers, Ed Merritt, Rob Stokes, Peter Winfield
DTP Harish Aggarwal, Georgia Bryer, Siu Chan, Nomazwe Madonko, Pankaj Sharma, Claudia Shill
Photography Stephen Oliver
Index Hilary Bird, Sylvia Potter
Gazetteer Sylvia Potter
Additional production Chris Avgherinos

ADVISORS AND CONSULTANTS

Chemistry and Physics
Ian M. Kennedy BSc
Jeff Odell BSc, MSc, PhD
David Glover

Culture and Society
Iris Barry
Margaret Cowan
John Denny B.Mus.Hons
Dr. Peter Drewett BSc, PhD, FSA, MIFA
Dr. Jamal, Islamic Cultural Centre
Miles Smith-Morris
Dr. Kimberly Springer
Brian Williams BA
The Buddhist Society

Earth Resources
April Arden Dip.M
Hedda Bird BSc
Conservation Papers Ltd.
Peter Nolan, British Gas Plc
Stephen Webster BSc, M. Phil
Earth Conservation Data Centre

Earth Sciences
Erica Brissenden
Alan Heward PhD
Keith Lye BA, FRGS
Rodney Miskin MIPR, MAIE
Shell UK Ltd.
Christine Woodward
The Geological Museum, London
Meteorological Office

Engineering
Karen Barratt
Jim Lloyd, Otis Plc
Alban Wincott
Mark Woodward MSc, DICC.Eng

History
Reg Grant
Dr. Anne Millard BA, Dip Ed, PhD
Ray Smith
The Indian High Commission
Campaign for Nuclear Disarmament

Medicine and the Human Body
Dr. Sue Davidson
Dr. T. Kramer MB, BS, MRCS, LRCP
Dr. Frances Williams MB, BChir, MRCP

Music
Simon Wales BA, MBA,
London Symphony Orchestra

Natural History
Kim Bryan
Wendy Ladd and the staff of the Natural History Museum
London Zoo

Space Science
NASA
Neil MacIntyre MA, PhD, FRGS
Dr. Jacqueline Mitton
John Randall BSc, PGCE
Christian Ripley BSc, MSc
Carole Stott BA, FRAS

Sport
Brian Aldred
David Barber
Lance Cone
John Jelley BA
International Olympic Committee

Technology
Alan Buckingham
Jeremy Hazzard BISC
Paul Macarthy BSc, MSc
Cosson Electronics Ltd.
Robert Stone BSc, MSc,
C. Psychol, AFBsF, M.ErgS,
Advanced Robotic Research Ltd.
Stuart Wickes B. Eng

Transportation
Doug Lloyd, Westland Helicopters
John Pimlott BA, PhD
Tony Robinson
Wing Commander Spilsbury, RAF
M. J. Whitty GI Sore.E

In addition, Dorling Kindersley would like to thank the following people and organizations for their assistance in the production of this book:

Liz Abrahams, BBC; Alan Baker; All England Tennis Club; Alvis Ltd.; Amateur Swimming Assoc.; Apple UK Ltd.; Ariane Space Ltd.; David Atwill, Hampshire Constabulary; Pamela Barron; Beech Aircraft Corp; Beaufort Air Sea Equipment; Bike UK Ltd.; BMW; Boeing Aircraft Corporation; BP Ltd.; British Amateur Athletics Assoc.; British Amateur Gymnastics Assoc.; British Antarctic Survey; British Canoe Union; British Coal Ltd.; British Forging Industry Assoc.; British Foundry Assoc.; British Gas Ltd.; British Museum; British Paper and Board Federation; British Parachuting Assoc.; British Post Office; British Ski Federation; British Steel; British Sub-Aqua Club; British Telecom International Ltd.; Paul Bush; Michelle Byam; Karen Caftledine, Courtauld Fibres; Martin Christopher, VAG Group; Citroen; CNHMS; Colourscan, Singapore; "Coca-Cola" and "Coke" are registered trade marks which identify the same products of The Coca-Cola Company; Commander Richard Compton-Hall; Lyn Constable-Maxwell; Cottrell & Co Ltd.; Geoffrey Court; Sarah Crouch, Black & Decker Ltd.; F. Darton and Co. Ltd.; Department of Energy, Energy Conservation Support Unit; Adrian Dixon; DRG Paper Ltd.; Patrick Duffy, IBA Museum; Earth Observation Data Centre; Electronic Arts; Embassy of Japan, Transport Department; Esso Plc; Eurotunnel Ltd.; Ford UK Ltd.; Sub Officer Jack Goble, London Fire Brigade; Julia Golding; Brian Gordon; Paul Greenwood, Pentax Cameras Ltd.; Patrick and Betty Gunzi; Hamleys, Regent Street, London; Helmets Ltd.; Jim Henson Productions Ltd.; Alan Heward, Shell UK Ltd.; cartoon frames taken from "Spider in the Bath", reproduced by permission from HIBBERT RALPH ENTERTAINMENT © and SILVEYJEX PARTNERSHIP ©; Hoover Ltd.; Horniman Museum; House of Vanheems Ltd.; IAL security products; ICI Ltd.; Ilford Ltd.; Imperial War Museum; Institute of Metals; Institution of Civil Engineers; Janes Publications Ltd.; Nina Kara; Jonathan Kettle, Haymarket Publishing; Julia Kisch, Thorn EMI Ltd.; Kite Shop, London; Sarah Kramer; Krauss-Maffei GMBH; Lambda Photometrics Ltd.; Sandy Law; Richard Lawson Ltd.; Leica GmbH; Leyland Daf Ltd.; London Transport Museum; London Weather Centre; The Lord Mayor of Westminster's New Year Parade; Lyndon-Dykes of London; Joan MacDonnell, Sovereign Oil and Gas Ltd.; Neil MacIntyre; Marconi Electronic Devices Ltd., Lincoln; Paul McCarthy, Cosser Electronics Ltd.; McDonnell Douglas Aircraft Corporation; Philip Mead; Mercedes; The Meteorological Office, London; Ruth Milner, Comark Ltd.; A. Mondadori Editore, Verona; Mysteries New Age Centre, London; National Army Museum; National Grid Company Ltd.; National Physical Laboratory; National Remote Sensing Centre, Farnborough; Nautilus Ltd.; Newcastle Hindu Temple; Helene Oakley; Olympus Ltd.; The Ordinance Survey; Osel Ltd.; Otis PLC; Gary Palmer, Marantz Ltd.; Personal Protection Products; Pilkington Glass Ltd.; Pioneer Ltd.; Philips Ltd.; Porter Nash Medical; Powell Cotton Museum; John Reedman Associates; Renaissance Musée du Louvre; Robertson Research Ltd.; Tony Robinson; Rockware Glass Ltd.; Rod Argent Music; Rolls Royce Ltd.; Liz Rosney; Royal Aircraft Establishment; Royal Astronomical Society, London; Royal Military Academy, Sandhurst; SNCF; Andrew Saphir; Malcolm Saunders, Simon Gloucester Saro Ltd.; Seagate Ltd.; Sedgewick Museum; Shell UK Ltd.; Skyship International Ltd.; Dennis Slay, Wessex Consultants Ltd.; Amanda Smith, Zanussi Ltd.; Ross Smith, Winchcombe Folk Police Museum; Sony Ltd.; Rachael Spaulding, McDonald's Restaurant Ltd.; Stanfords Map Shop, London; Steelcasting Research and Trade Assoc.; Stollmont Theatres Ltd.; Swatch Watches Ltd.; Tallahassee Car Museum; Texaco Ltd.; The Theatre Museum, Covent Garden, London; Toyota; Trafalgar House, Building and Civil Engineering; Trevor Hyde; Wastewatch; Jim Webb; Westland Helicopters Ltd.; Westminster Cathedral; Malcolm Willingale, V Ships, Monaco; Wiggins Teape Ltd.; Howard Wong, Covent Garden Records, London; Woods Hole Oceanographic Institute; Yarrow Shipbuilders Ltd.; The YHA Shop, London.

PICTURE SOURCES

The publisher would like to thank the following for their kind permission to reproduce their photographs:

Abbreviations: a = above, b = below, c = centre, f = far, l = left, r = right, t = top.

A

Action Plus: Glyn Kirk 715bl; Richard Francis 88tl, 311bl.
Airship Industries: 79crb.
AKG London: 324bc, 550bl; Michael Teller 324c.
Alamy Images: Keith Dannemiller 442bl; Image Etc Ltd 317tr; Tom Tracy Photography 204br.
Album: 451t.
Allsport: Mike Powell 322tc, 322bc, 607br.
Bryan and Cherry Alexander Photography: 414bc.
Max Alexander: Alvis Ltd: 560br.
Allsport: 101cl; Ben Bradford 119cl; Howard Boylan 696cl; Shaun Botterill 467bl.
Amtrak: 232br.
Ancient Art and Architecture Collection: 27cl, 346tl, 390tl, 390bc; N. P .Stevens 232tr; Ronald Sheridan 308cla, 346bl, 356tl, 372crb, 439tr, 439bc, 506bl, 551ca, 657tl.
Animal Photography: Sally Anne Thompson 508bl.
Animals Unlimited: Patty Cutts 508cr.
Ardea London Ltd: 180tr; Francies Gohier 178bc.
The Art Archive: 137bc, 239cl, 239bl, 373cr, 416bl, 462tr, 462crb; bib Arts Decoratifs Paris 675c; Chateau Malmaison 240cla; 31tr, 388tl, 399cr, 504tl.
Ashmolean Museum, Oxford: 27tr, 238bc.
Catherine Ashmore: 77c.
Associated Press Ap: 238cr, 376crb, 626cl, 634crb.
Australian Tourist Commission: 65bl.
National Archaeological Museum: 104cl.
Neil Audley: 59bl.
Australian Overseas Information Services, London: 12bc, 70bl.
Axiom: Chris Bradley 474c; Chris Caldicott 474cl, 475tr, 549br.

B

Barnaby's Picture Library: 673bl.
N. S. Barrett: 268tr.
Beech Aircraft Corporation: 521clb, 521bc.
Belkin.com: 172fcrb. **Walter Bibikow:** 559bl.
Bite Communications Ltd.: 351cl, 351c.
The Boeing Company: 22ca, 24c.
D.C. Brandt, Joyce and Partners: 42cb, 43clb.
Bridgeman Art Library, London / New York: portrait of *Catherine, Mulatte of the Bradeo* A. Durer 1491 87br; *Greeks under siege* by Eugene Delacroix 169tl, 232tr, 253cla; *King James I of England* by Paul Van Somer, 403br, 406tr; portrait, William Morris, photo by Hollyer 1914 502bc; *Henry Wrothesley, 3rd Earl Southampton* 593cl; Sir Francis Bacon bust by Roubillac 593cr, 604tr, 745tr; Archivo de la Catedral Oviedo Altonso III c. 838-910 533tl; Ashmolean Museum Oxford Chinese Stirrup 6th-7th century bronze 325tr; Bibliotheque Nationale, Paris 501c; Bristol City Museum Art Gallery, *Bristol Harbour 1825*, Nicholas Pocock 604tl; British Museum 28cb, Benin sword 87bc; British Museum London clay tablet 7th century B.C.; Nineveh Epic of Gilgamesh 657tl; British Museum, London 64cb, 295tl, 423cl, 501tl; Cairo Museum/Giraudon 41clb; Chateau de Versailles 365c; Chester Beatty Library and Gallery of Art 369bc; Christies, London 18bl, 535tr, 574bl, 719bl; City of Bristol Museum Art Gallery 372tl; Department of the Environment 754cra; Eton College, Windsor 423cr; Fabbir 111cb; Forbes Magazine Collection 461crb; Galleria dell Accademia Firenze 551bl; Hertford Cathedral 417tl; Lauros Girandon Musée de la Ville de Paris, Carvaralet 407tr; Leeds Museum and Gallery *Kirkstall Abbey* by George Alexander; Liberty and Co. London 1972, Bauhaus fabric by Collier and Campbell for Liberty 198br; Louvre, Paris 277tc, 308bc, 548bc; Mallett & Sons Antiquities, London 283cl; *Mozart and his sister Maria-Anna*, ivory by Eusebius Johann Alphen, Mozart Museum, Salzburg, Austria, 73c; Musée Conde,

Chantilly 276bc; Musée d'Orsay, Paris © DACS 502cr; Musée des Beaux Arts, Tourcoing, Giraudon 208br; National Army Museum, London 341tc; National Maritime Museum, Greenwich 466tr; National Portrait Gallery 232tl; New Zealand High Commission, London 468cl; Oriental Museum, Durham University 521tl; Prado, Madrid 462tl, 638tr, 642cl; private collection, chariot Qin dynasty 145tr; Sherlock Holmes 403br, 705cr; Queensland Art Gallery, Brisbane 12tl; Roy Miles Gallery, London 364bc; Royal Albert Memorial Museum, Olaudah Equiano portrait 1820's 604bc; Sante Maria delle Grazie, Milano 372bl; *Self-portrait with Gloves*, Albrecht Durer, 1469 (panel), Prado, Madrid, Spain 293tr; *Snow White and the Seven Dwarves*, c.1942 (block print), English School, Stapleton Collection, UK, 293b; Staaliche Museen zu Berlin 131bc; T.U.C. London 345cb; Tate Gallery, London 75bc; Victoria and Albert Museum, London 340bl; Wilberforce House Museum, Hull, *The Kneeling Slave,* 18th-century painting, 604cl; William Morris Gallery, Walthamstow 378br; Christies Images, London/ARS, NY and DACS, London 2020 Yellow Grey Black 504cla; City of Bristol Museum and Art Gallery, *T. Jefferson* by Sharples 371tl; Historical Society of Pennsylvania, *Fourth of July Celebration* by Krimmel 192br; Los Angeles County Museum of Art, *Mother about to wash her sleepy child*, Mary Cassatt 503cr; Louvre, Paris, *T. Jefferson* by David d'Angers 371c; Musée Franco Americaine, Bleran Court, Chantry, France, *Portrait of Thomas Jefferson* by Healey 192tr; National Academy of Design, New York, Thomas Eatus self-portrait 1932 503cl; private collection, Phillis Wheatley 181bl, 323cl; *Drafting of declaration of Independence* 371cr, 527br; private collection/ADAGP, Paris and DACS, London 2020, Jean Michel Basquiat, *Arraz con Pollo* 504c; private collection/Jasper Johns/VAGA, New York/ DACS, London 2020 *Three Flags* by Jasper Johns 1988 504bl; private collection/© licensed by the Andy Warhol Foundation for the Visual Arts, Inc./DACS, London 2020, trademarks licensed by Campbell Soup company all rights reserved 504cra; private collection/ARS, NY and DACS, London 2020, *Red Gladiola in a White Vase* 503b; private collection /Willem di Kooning, ARS, NY and DACS, London 2020, *Woman sitting* 504tr; Science Museum, Model of the *Mayflower* 166cr.
Paul Brierly: 611bl.
British Library, London: 93cra, 93crb, 95tl, 104bl, 428bl, 428bc, 439bl, 472clb.
British Museum, London: 74cl, 104br, 290tr, 421bc, 763cb; Museum of Mankind 421tl.
British Airways Archive Museum Collection: 317cra, 683tr.
British Steel: 358cl, 358crb.
British Tourist Authority: 694bl.

C

Camera Press: 90br, 103cb. **Casio:** 669tr.
Jean-Loup Charmet: 166br.
Coca-Cola Company: 13tr, 13cr.
Bruce Coleman Ltd.: 97orb, 135cr, 141cr, 143ll, 180bl, 180br, 184cl, 208cl, 210bl, 211tl, 238clb, 274cl, 282bc, 324tr, 358clb, 379cl, 457cr, 468cl, 480cra, 499bc, 499bcr, 519crb, 583c, 588tl, 589tc, 589crb, 589bl, 590cra, 598bl, 648br, 670bc, 671cl, 685br, 702bl, 706bc, 721cl; Jack Dermid 592tl; A.J. Deane 336br; Alain Compost 265tl, 493tr, 540bl, 670crb; Bernol Thies 592cla; Bob and Clara Calhoun 83clb; Brian and Cherry Alexander 578tr; Brian Coates 92bl, 181bl, 499bcl; C.B. Frith 203tl, 325tr, 493bc; C.B. & D.W. Frith 105c; Charles Henneghien 156bv, 385tr, 637bl; Charlie Ott 542cl; Chris Hollerbeck 285bl, 702tl; Colin Moyneux 372tc; David C. Houston 338bl; David Davies 558bc; David Hughes 591tl; Dieter and Mary Plage 733crb, 457cl; Douglas Pike 15cl; Dr. Echart Pott 394bc, 528bl; Dr. Frieder Sanct 433c; E. Breeze-Jones 497tl; Eric Crichton 263cb; Erwin and Peggy Bauer 254bl; Fitz Prenzel 63bl; Frans Lanting 465crb; Fransisco Erize 590bc; Fritz Penzel 238clb, 492tr; G.D. Plage 324cl, 396cl, 209tl, 325c; G. Zienter 112crb; Gene A. Ahrens 701tl; Gerald Cubitt 50bc, 176cr, 253clb, 298tl, 320bc, 342c, 413bl, 505tl; H. Rivarola 85cl, 86cl; Hans Reinhardt 127tr, 238bl; 413cb; Hans Richard 232tr; Herbert Kranawetter 276cl; Inigo Everson 525tc,

525cr; Jane Burton 36bc, 228bc, 305cl, 430bc, 455crb, 557tl; Jaroslav Poncar 717cla; Jeff Foott 36c, 590cb; Jeff Simon 385clb; Jen and Des Bartlett 395tr; Joe Van Wormer 525bl; John Markhom 93clb; John Shaw 212c, 216cl, 437clb, 546br; John Topham 274tr; John Wallis 493bl; Jonathan T. Wright 369cl, 485tl, 597tr; Joseph Van Werner 493br; Keith Gunner 450cl; Kim Taylor 132bl, 228bc, 253cl, 455cra, 600cl, 700tl; L.O. Marigo 228br, 253ca, 325br, 534bc; Lee Lyon 76cr; Leonard Lee Rue III 481clb, 665br; Liz Marigo 283cb; M. Timothy O' Keefe 556tr; Marquez 418tl; Michael Fogden 195tr, 511br; Michael Freeman 148br, 320clb, 459bc; Michael Klinec 157tr, 160bl; Michel Viard 455tl; N.A.S.A. 211cr, 228tl, 446bl; Neville Fox-Davies 447clb; Norbert Rosig 238tr; Norbert Schwertz 713crb; Norman Myers 14br, 445bl, 528tr; Norman Owen Tomalin 35tr, 60tl, 444crb, 558cra, 700cra; Norman Plyers 396tr; R. Campbell 271crb; R.I.M. Campbell 41ca, 41cl; Robert Perron 511cr; Rod Williams 109bc, 445cl; Ron Cartnell 395br; Stephen J. Krasemann 84tr, 481tl; Udo Hirsch 335cl; Vatican Museums and Galleries, Rome 501clb; Walter Lankinen 385cl, 319cb, 319bl, 63bc; Werner Stoy 211c, 713clb.
Collections: Bill Wells 484bc; Brian Keen 696cr; Brian Shuel 354cr, 355bl, 386tc; Gena Davies 715cla; Geoff Howard 386crb; John Miller 386bl; Richard Davies 228c; Sandra Lousada 696br; Yuri Lewinski 32cr.
Collection Viollet: 373tl.
Colorific!: Eric Sampers 454bl; Joe McNally/Wheeler Pics 298cra; Roger de la Harpe 631tr; D. Halstead /Contact 300tl; Lisa Rudy Hoke/Black Star 389cl; R. Crandall 300tr.
Columbia Pictures: 187bl.
Thomas Cook Archive: 675bl.
Corbis UK Ltd.: Archivo Iconografico S.A. 691bl; Dean Conger 137b, 571b, 691cl; Earl and Nasima Kowall 138br; John Noble 44b; Lawrence Manning 531crb; Michael St. Maur Sheil 405bc; Nik Wheeler 639br; Stephanie Maze 579tc; 21c, 21cr, 21b, 151tl, 151cr, 152tl, 166bl, 192bl, 375tr, 375cl, 526tr, 526cl, 538cl, 584tl, 659tl, 659cl, 762br; © AFP 400bl; © Sunday Felsenthal, *American Gothic* by G. Wood 503cr; © The Purcell Team 323tl; AFP 538b; Bettmann Archive 334tl, 399tl, 31cl, 176bl, 278br, 301tl, 301tr, 301cr, 321tr, 333tr, 333cr, 333b, 381br, 400tl, 400tr, 503c, 527cl, 527cr, 527bl, 583br, 659tl, 659bl, 12tl, 12cl, 12cr, 12b, 21cbl, 82tl, 150bl, 166tc, 228tr, 265tl, 322tl, 371br, 375tl, 375br, 381cr, 389tr, 399cl, 399c, 399bl, 399br, 399b, 735tl, 735cr; Bob Krist 334tr; Dan Lament 321tl; Dave G. Hauser 333tl; David H. Wells 300cl; Flip Shulke 21tl; Francis G Mayer 12c, 181br; Genevieve Naylor 228c; Jacques M. Chenet 735cl; James L. Amos 463br; Josef Scaylea 333cl; Joseph John, Chromo John Inc. 265cl, 301br , 334brr; Kevin Fleming 192tl; Lee Snider 278bc; Leif Skoogfors 381cl; Nathan Benn 375cr; Nick Wheeler 265cr; Philip Gould 538cr; Richard T. Nowitz 176cl, 323tr; Robert Maas 300cr; Roger Ressneyer 400br; Sandy Felsenthal 334cl; Seattle Post Intelligencer Collection 527tl; Shelley Gazin 735tr; Ted Spiegel 584cl; Ted Streshinksy 735b; Underwood and Underwood 181cra; Brooks Kraft 538bc; Reuters 389tl; Frederic Larson/San Francisco Chronicle 214clb; Walt Disney Pictures/Pixar Animation/Bureau L.A. Collections 124br; Ariel Skelley 351crb; Tom Wagner 348tl.
H.M. Customs and Excise: 25bl.

D

James Davis Travel Photography: 61cr, 404cl, 531b, 689bl, 690br.
Duncan Brown: 569tr, 569c, 569br.
Douglas Dickens: 625cr.
C.M. Dixon: 340tl.
DK Images: NASA 636bl; Lindsey Stock 172crb.
Dominic Photography: Zoe Dominic 593bl.
Zoe Dominic: 492c, 492br.
Courtesy of **Dyson:** 198bc.

E

Earth Satellite Corporation: 417crb.
Empics Ltd.: 265cr, 491tr; 265cr; Andy Heading

718cl, 718bl; Tony Marshall 265tl.
The English Heritage Photo Library: Down House 188bl; Jonathan Bailey, Down House 188tl.
T. Malcolm English: 318bc.
Environmental Images: 253bc; Toby Adamson 288bl.
European Space Agency: 59cra, 531cra.
European Parliament Photo Library: 238cl, 238bl.
Mary Evans Picture Library: 19tl, 19tr, 23br, 25crb, 40tr, 41bc, 64tr, 64bl, 70tl, 70cl, 77cr, 79tl, 79cl, 82tl, 88tr, 102cr, 110clb, 118crb, 121cl, 124cr, 131tl, 145bl, 146clb, 149c, 150tr, 157tl, 157cl, 174cr, 174bl, 174br, 185cr, 185bl, 185bl, 187tl, 188bc, 193tr, 193cl, 204tr, 207tr, 208cl, 212bv, 228bl, 228tl, 228tc, 232bl, 238cb, 238tr, 238cb, 238bl, 253tl, 253ce, 253cla, 253tr, 253clb, 253tl, 259tr, 266tl, 276br, 277cla, 279tl, 288tc, 289bl, 295br, 298tl, 298tc, 298ca, 299tl, 299br, 309clb, 310tl, 312bl, 324tl, 325tl, 345tl, 345clb, 345bl, 356cb, 365tl, 365tc, 370cl, 372bc, 373bc, 386tl, 394cl, 403tl, 407tc, 407cl, 420bl, 423bl, 423br, 424cb, 424bc, 432clb, 439crb, 439bc, 460clb, 460bl, 461bl, 464tr, 467cra, 489tl, 491c, 493bl, 495bc, 496clb, 511tr, 511clb, 519cr, 519cr, 521cra, 525tl, 533bl, 539bc, 544tr, 544bc, 546tr, 547tr, 550br, 573bl, 574c, 574bc, 575tr, 575clb, 581tl, 581tr, 582cl, 582bl, 583cl, 586ca, 586bc, 587tl, 587ca, 598c, 598bc, 600cra, 603clb, 604cr, 604bl, 611tc, 620cl, 642crb, 642t, 645tl, 653tl, 666bc, 667tl, 670tl, 671tr, 673tl, 674tl, 678tr, 679bl, 681cr, 681cr, 685cr, 685bc, 692tr, 706tl, 708tl, 709tl, 709cl, 710cr, 715br, 720tr, 734c, 738tl, 738tc, 738cla, 739ca, 742tl, 743tc, 743ca, 743cl, 743cb, 744tr; Bruce Castle Museum 496bl; Explorer 170cla, 170cl, 279cl; Illustrazione 240tr; ILN 651cl; 607tl .
Eye Ubiquitous: David Cumming 404tl; David Foreman 690bl; Helen A. Lisher 696tl; Mike Southern 61tl; P. Maurice 690tc; Tim Durham 531cb.

F
Family Life Picture Library: Angela Hampton 347c, 351br.
FLPA–Images of Nature: David Headley 674tl; Mark Newman 463cl, 589cl, 655clb; Dick Jones 132bc; Roger Wilmshurst 45ctr; W.S. Clark 478tl.
Michael and Patricia Fogden: 264cr.
Werner Forman Archive: 56tr, 460bc, 566tr, 712bl; British Museum 56clb; Metropolitan Museum of Art, New York 283tr; Mr. and Mrs. C.D. Wertheim 370cr.
Ford Motor Company Ltd: 21cl, 253cl.
Format Photographers: Jacky Chapman 121tr.
Fortean Picture Library: Allen Kennedy 239tl.
French Railways: 680cl.
John Frost Historical Newspapers: 740tl.

G
General Motors Corporation: 658bl.
Geoscience Features: 130bc, 214bl, 289tr, 508crb.
German National Tourist Office: 292b.
Getty Images: 562bl; AFP 435bc; 2005 Dave M. Benett 562c; Iconica 512br; Leslie E. Kossoff/AFP 301cb; Hadi Mizban-Pool 389bl; Photographer's Choice 477br; Stone 116cr, 511cr; Stone/Loren Santow 222bl; Taxi 516br.
Photographie Giraudon: 428ca, 462bc; Lauros 461cl.
Google: 351bl.
Greenpeace Inc.: 172tl.

H
Sonia Halliday Photographs: 110bc, 239cr, 274b, 379cra, 495tl; James Wellard 253tc; R.H.C. Birch 308tr.
Hampshire County Constabulary: 525cra.
David Hamilton: 694cl.
Robert Harding Picture Library: 14tl, 15br, 17tr, 37bc, 46cr, 46bc, 59cr, 117tc, 136tc, 142tl, 142cr, 145cb, 145cb, 145bc, 145bc, 163cl, 273cl, 273b, 353bl, 353br, 362bl, 369tl, 434cr, 467br, 467t, 474br, 475br, 476tr, 588tr, 588clb, 612cr, 617tr, 623cl, 726cl, 727cl; Adam Woolfit 628bc, 629tr; C. Bowman 478cr; David Hughes 238bc; F.J. Jackson 44cl; Frans Lanting 142c; Fraser Hall 612bc; G.P. Corrigan 43tl; G. Renner 38tc; G. Boutin 474bl; G.M. Wilkins 613tc; G.R. Richardson 291bl; Gavin Hellier 73br, 612ct; Goldstrand 628cr; J.K.Thorne 470bl; James Strachan 137tr; Jeff Greenberg 80cl; Jeremy Lightfoot 307c; J.H.C. Wilson 338cl; Julia Thorne 532bl; Michael Jenner 367br, 436b;

Mitsuaki Iwago 38tr; Paul van Riel 363br; Phil Robinson 627br; R. Ashworth 353tl; R. Cundy 478ct; Rob Cousins 117cr; Robert Cundy 612clb; Robert Francis 67cl; Robert Frerck/Odyssey 478cl; Roy Rainford 476bl; T. van Gouberen 405tc; T. Waltham 479tr; Thierry Borridon 272bl; Victor Engelbert 727cr; Weisbecker 337cr.
Henson Association Inc.: 540cr, 540cb.
Frames taken from "Spider in the Bath" reproduced by permission from **Ralph Entertainment** © and **Silveryjex Partnership:** 124t.
Hewlett Packard: 172br.
Kaii Higashiyama: 502tr.
The Historical Society of Pennsylvania: 715bl.
© **Michael Holford:** 75tl, 75clb, 137c, 149crb, 340br, 508cb, 510cr, 515br; British Library 166cr; British Museum 456tr.
Holt Studios International: Duncan Smith 253bl; Richard Anthony 663cr.
Houses and Interiors: Nick Huggins 199clb.
Hulton Getty: 27tl, 55tr, 70cb, 89tl, 94tr, 104tl, 104tr, 150tl, 150bl, 163br, 168bc, 194bc, 228tl, 228tr, 238bl, 238tr, 238 tl, 238cr, 253bc, 290tl, 322br, 324tr, 341cl, 341c, 356clb, 365cl, 370cb, 381bl, 382tl, 382c, 382cr, 394tl, 522tl, 545tr, 568tl, 587crb, 587bl, 614cb, 626clb, 634cl, 660tl, 734bc, 737clb, 739bl, 740c, 740clb, 740cb, 742bl; A.C. Bettmann Archive 42cl, 514bc; Bettmann/UPI 102crb; Ernst Haas 228c; Keystone 121br, 382bl; Keystone, Max Schneider, Zurich 614clb; MPI Archives 151c, 163tl, 388bl, 653tr.
Kobal Collection: 20th Century Fox 400cl
Jacqui Hurst: Robert Aberman 435br.
Hutchison Library: 46cl, 54tl, 54br, 55br, 98cl, 99tr, 99ctl, 133cr, 146bc, 163bl, 168bl, 338c, 342cl, 343tr, 360br, 506bc, 608c, 615cl, 616tr, 617tl, 725cl, 727bl; Anna Tully 204bl; Bernard Green 608tl; Bernard Regent 133bl, 133bc, 510bc, 727ctl; Carlos Freste 336bc; Christina Dodwell 342cl; Christine Pemberton 55tl; Crispin Hughes 215bl, 629tc, 725cr, 727ctr; Eric Lawrie 616tl; Felix Greene 13br, 55c, 416cr; H.R. Dorig 423tl, 619crb; Jeremy Horner 54crb, 142cl; John Downman 479br; John G. Egan 629cr; Juliet Highey 337tl; Kerstin Rodseps 734tl; Leslie Woodhead 726tl; Mary Jeliffe 134tr, 474tr; Maurice Harvey 571clb; Melanie Friend 627cl, 629b; N. Durrell McKenna 144tr; Nick Haslam 80tr, 80bl, 571cr, 628tr; Nigel Sitwell 99cr; P. Moszynski 207cr; P.E. Parker 708br; R. Ian Lloyd 380bc; Richard Howe 98br; Robert Aberman 689br; Robert Francis 54cra; Sarah Erinngton 17c, 134bc, 141br, 203bc, 215tl, 253bl, 253tl, 632br, 726br; Timothy Beddow 215c; Titus Moser 138tr; Trevor Page 129bl, 137cl; V. Ivleva 137cr; Vanessa S. Boeye 54bl.

I
I.A.L. Security Products: 744cr. **I.C.I.:** 670cb.
Illustrated London News Picture Library: 341bl, 682br.
Image Bank: 51tr, 53br, 67tl, 67br, 74crb, 78cr, 114c, 115c, 115bc, 119tr, 119tl, 119bl, 119br, 136br, 143cr, 143bl, 160cl, 174tr, 186bl, 266tl, 275bc, 285bc, 298bc, 324bc, 360tl, 360bl, 367bl, 435cl, 443bc, 453tl, 500cr, 576bc, 615cl, 615b, 618cl, 618br, 621bc, 641tl, 645tl, 655bl, 656tl, 665tl, 679tl, 681tr, 682bc, 718cl, 718br; Alan Beeker 682ca; Alex Hamilton 410bc; Andrea Pistolesi 564tl; Anne der Vaeren 149tl; Anthony A. Broccaccio 255cl; Ben Rose 511c; Bernard van Berg 275tr; Brett Frooner 259bc; Brian McNeely 692cla; Colin Molyneux 316tl; 268bl; David Hiser 385ca; David Martin 410tr; David W. Hamilton 126tc, 702tr; Don Klumpp 434b, 436tr; Dr. J. Gebhardt 259cb; Eric L. Wheeler 112cb; Erik Leigh 467crb; Francis Hildago 335bc; Francisco Ontanon 638bl; Frank Roiter 75crb; Fulvio Roiter 306bc; G.A. Wilton 201tr; G. Gundberg 579br; G. Rontmeester 697bc; Gary Gladstone 679tl; Georgina Bowater 292t; Gianalberto Cigolini 148tl; Giulliano Colliva 115bl; Guido Alberto Rossi 718cl, 637bc, 114cr, 361cl, 638br; Hank Delespinesse 645cl; Harold Sand 428cr, 704tr; Isy-Schwart 253cl; J. Bronsseau 106crb; J. Bryson 113bl; Jean Pierre Pienchat 546bl; Joe Azzara 732cr; John P. Keely 718br; Joseph B. Brignolo 435tr, 530crb, 686bl; Kay Charmost 228c; Kaz Mori 211cl; Kodansha Images 596tr; Lou Jones 610cr; Luis Castaneda 238bl; M. Melford 427bc; Marc Solomon 266br; Marvin E. Newman 578cl; Michael Melford 544cla; Michael Salas 69tr; Milan Skarya 25crb; P. and G. Bower 126tr; Paul Kleuenz 621cr; Peter Thomann 160cl; Robert Holland 498crb; Robert Phillips 530bl; Ronald R. Johnson 366tl, 637cr; Sah Zarember 674cl; Stan Drexter 149bl; Steve Dunwell 440bl; Steve Niedorf 204br, 422ca;

Stockphotos 412cr; Thomas R. Rampy 85crb; Toyotumi Mori 367c; Trevor Wood 696tl; Ulli Seer 509tl.
Imperial War Museum: 48tl, 104cla, 734clb, 738c.
Innes Photo Library: Ivor Innes 102cl, 102clb; John Blackburn 102bl.
Intercity: 232crb.

J · K
Lou Janitz: 609tl.
JET Joint Undertaking: 483tl.
Katz Pictures: Resnick 653c.
Royal Borough of Kensington and Chelsea Public Library: 228cl.
Barnabas Kindersley: 367tl, 367clb, 367crt; 141bl.
David King Collection: 168tr.
Kobal Collection: 65br, 338tl, 457bc, 560tr, 743bl.
Courtesy of **Kodak:** 512tr.

L
Lada: 572bl.
Leitz: 291br.
Link Picture Library: 415cb; Greg English 415br; Orde Eliason 415cl, 415bl; Philip Schelder 614bc.
London Features International: 459crb.
Lotus Cars Ltd.: 298cb.
Lupe Cunha: 313cl, 324clb, 422ce.
Ann Lyons: 647tr.

M
Magnum: Alex Webb 526br; Bruce Davidson 150cl, 150cr; Cornell Capa 375tl; Elliott Erwitt 150tl; Peter Marlow 163cr. 634bc.
Mander and Mitchenson: 151cl, 151cr, 151cb.
Mansell/Time Inc.: 169br.
Mansell Collection: 40bc, 70cr, 111cl, 581bl, 737tl.
Marshall Cavendish: Osel Group 693cr.
McDonald's Restaurants Ltd.: 600c.
Mercedes Benz: 122clb.
The Metropolitan Museum of Art: Rogers Fund 1934 373clb.
Michelin: 732clb.

N
N.A.S.A.: 56cl, 63cr, 167c, 446cb, 498bl, 531c, 560bl, 636cr, 683cl, 683br, 722tl, 723bl; Don Dixon 707clb; Finlay Holiday Films 298cr; N.A.S.A. 94c.
National Gallery, London: 502tl, 551tl.
National Trust Photographic Library: Martin Trelawny 715c.
National Maritime Museum, London: 179tl, 239bc, 466tl, 495bl; James Stevenson 142br, 290clb.
The Natural History Museum, London: 39tl, 271cr.
Network Photographers Ltd.: 135br, 525crb; Gideon Mendel 415tl, 415cr; Goldwater 48bc; Jenny Matthews 228bl; Louise Gubb 415tc.
Peter Newark's Pictures: 30cl, 30bl, 30br, 31tl, 31c, 31cr, 151bl, 161cl, 161br, 166cl, 181tl, 181cl, 192bc, 278c, 382br, 389cla; American Pictures 278tl, 278bl, 463tr; Western Americana Pictures 176br; 29cl, 29cr, 150cr, 159c, 194c, 194br, 394tr, 464crb, 464bc, 465tl, 465cl, 496br, 515bc, 603bc, 619br, 647bc, 652tr.
N.H.P.A.: 47cl, 68tr, 99bc, 616br, 617br; Anthony Bannister 132tl; Bill Wood 556tc; Brian and Cherry Alexander 44tr, 44c, 476cl; Daryl Balfour 217tr; J.H. Carmichael 487cra; Jerry Sauvanet 270tl; John Shaw 478b; Manfred Danegger 451bl; Martin Harvey 622br; Phillipa Scot 402cla; Roger Tidney 197tl; Stephen Dalton 82c; Stephen Krasemann 216t; Willima S. Pakon 418c.
Nobel Foundation: 582crb. **Nokia:** 172cb, 666br.
Novosti: 569br, 573tl, 575bl, 633tr, 633crb, 633bc; Vladimir Vyatkin 571bl.

O
Olympic Co-ordination Authority: 491tr.
Open University: 228bc.
Ordnance Survey © Crown Copyright: 417c.
Christine Osborne: 12cl, 50bl, 422tl, 588cr, 686tl.
OSF/photolibrary.com: 70crb.

Oxford Scientific Films: 605bc, 606bc, 616bl; Animals Animals, M. Austerman 557bl; Fran Allen 324cr, 325cr; B.G. Murray/J.R. Garth Scenes 546c; David Fox 209cl; Edward Panker 20tr; Fritz Penzel 72bc; G.I. Bernard 260bc, 545crb; J.A.L. Cooke 39bc, 303cr, 350tl, 605clb; John Paling 36clb; Kathie Atkinson 71tr, 413tl; Kim Westerskov 191tc; Lawrence Gould 257cl; Michael Fogden 72cl; Pam and Willy Kemp 228tl; Raymond Blythe 86tl; Ronald Toms 733bl; Stan Osolinksi 183c; Sue Trainer 287bc. Courtesy of **Otis' Elevators:** 238bc.

P · Q

Palace of Versailles: 403cra. **Panasonic:** 113cl.
Panos Pictures: 46bl, 725br; Alain le Garsmeur 759cr; Alfredo Cadeno 99bl; B. Klass 339b; Caroline Penn 618bl, 761br; Chris Stowers 628c; Dermot Tatlow 549bc; Dominic Harcourt-Webster 215cr; Fred Hoogervorst 758bl; Giacomo Pirozzi 613 ctr; 15tr, 133tr, 133cl; Gregory Wrona 129tl; Heidi Bradner 628bl; Howard Davies 629tl; Jean-Leo Dugast 622tc; Jeremy Hartley 725br; John Miles 99cl; Liba Taylor 216bl; Maya Kardum 158cl; N. Durrell Mc Kenna 631c; Neil Cooper 632tr; Pietro Cenini 215br; Trgve Bolstad 631cl.
PA News Photo Library: 299bl.
Performing Arts Library: Henrietta Butter 400cr.
Philips Scientific: 432bc, 432cb.
Pickthall Picture Library: Barry Pickthall 576tl.
Pictor International: 299cr, 307cl, 307cr, 361cr, 362tr, 404tr, 404b, 477br, 531tr, 531cr, 579bl, 627tr, 627c, 628tl, 639tl, 694tr.
Picture Mate: 113cr.
Planet Earth Pictures: 45bl, 594bl, 613br, 693tr, 693bl, 745bl; Adam Jones 476cr, 477cl; Anup Shah 216br, 622tl; Brian and Cherry Alexander 44cr; Christin Petron 41cr; David Phillips 447bc; Doug Perrine 477tl; Gary Bell 68c; John Downer 631bl; Jonathan Scott 216cr, 708bl; Joyce Photographics 37cr; Mary Clay 477cr; Paul Cooper 259crb; Peter David 190tr, 190bcl; Peter Lillie 631br; Tom Walker 337bl, 476br; Warren Williams 483ca; William Smithey 191c.
Richard Platt: 79bc, 232bc, 411crb, 417cl.
Popperfoto: 19cl, 19c, 55cb, 103bc, 146crb, 148bl, 150cl, 150br, 240tc, 240cl, 240cb, 277bl, 277bc, 298cl, 303bc, 376bl, 450tr, 485bl, 491br, 502clb, 533bc, 568bl, 568br, 587c, 620cb, 620bl, 644t, 700tl, 711cl, 711cr; David Crosling, Dmitri Messinis 240cb; Dylan Martinez, /Reuters: Michael Stephens 228bc; Jim Bourg 389tl; Larry Downing 150br; Colin Bradley 321br; Dr. Jim McFadden 674cl; Gary Hershan 176cl.
Post Office Picture Library: 647cb.
Powerstock Photolibrary/Zefa: 103tl, 253crb, 324tl, 374bl, 454cr, 519tr, 598cr, 679cr, 762bl; 454bc; D.H. Teuffen 40tl; Geoff Kalt 610tr; Hales 673bc; Ingo Seiff 122tl; R.G. Everts 145br; S. Palmer 744bl; Scholz 145cr; T. Schneider 137tl; Transglobe 407bc.
Public Record Office Picture Library: 473cb.
© **QA Photos Ltd.:** Eurotunnel 688bl.

R

Redferns: Charlyn Zlotnik 561bl; David Redfern 562tl; Des Willie 561tl; Elliot Landy 562tr; Glenn A. Baker Archives 561cb; Kieran Doherty 562c; Michael Ochs 561crb, 562bl; Patrick Ford 562cr; S and G 561br; Simon Ritter 561tc; Steve Grillett 457tl.
Reuters: 658bl.
Rex Features: 51tl, 61br, 103bc, 159cl, 238tla, 238tlb, 294t, 313cl, 416tl, 468bc, 475bl, 521bc; David Pratt 138bl; Fotex 579tl; LXL 561tl; J. Sutton-Hibbert 288c; Sipa 121bc, 758bl; Steve Wood 639tr; Times 653cl; Wheeler 238tl.
Ann Ronan Picture Library: 167bc, 253c, 425tl; 176c, 538tl, 674tr, 674cr, 674b; Erik Penzich 323cr; Joely Abraityte 323bl; Robert Trippett 389cr, 389bl; SIPA Press 163tr, 176cr; /W Luski 163cl.
Cliff Rosney: 702bc. **Rover Group:** 238cr.
The Royal Collection (© 2019 Her Majesty Queen Elizabeth II): 169tr, 390crb.
The Royal Mint, Crown Copyright: 440tl.

S

Scala: 501br, 586crb; Museo Nazionale Athenai 104cb.
Science and Society Picture Library: 454cl; Science

Museum 103c, 103bl.
Science Photo Library: 517br, 648bl, 667bl, 681bl; Alan Hart-Davies 316br; Alexander Isiaras 483clb, 663br; Alta Greenberg 701cr; Astrida Hans Frieder Michler 663c; Chris Bjornberg 203bl; Chris Butler 517br; CNRI 200bc, 203cl, 203cr; David Parker 543cl; David Parker 600 Group 560c; David Parker/Max Planck Institut for Aeronomie 167c; David Wintraub 479tl; Dr. Fred Espenak 650tl, 420cl; Dr. Gerald Schatten 313br; Dr. Jeremy Burgess 433tl, 433bl; Dr. T.E. Thompson 204c; Earth Satellite Corporation 477cl, 577ca; Eric Grave 432c; EW Space Agency 510bcl, Frank Espanak 59cra, Hubert Raguet 780cl, Ian Boddy 313r; I.B.M. 432br; Jane Stevenson 553tl; Jim Stevenson 111tl; John Bavosi 200bl; John Mead 759bl; John Sanford 167bl, 446tl; Johns Hopkins University Physics Laboratory 773cr; Julian Baum 773crb; Ken Briggs 238bl; Lawrence Migoale 203bl; M.I. Walker 433cl; Michael Dohrn 21cb, 284tr; N.A.S.A. 59cl, 387br, 516bl, 516bc, 517bc, 517 bl, 517bcl, 517bcr, 529tl, 572tr, 744bc; N.I.B.S.C. 315bl; N.R.A.O. 59b; Pasieka 203bc; Philippe Plailly 422cb; Philippe Reilly 387bl; Professor Harold Edgerton 511cra; Professor R. Gehz 59ca; R.E. Litchfield 433bc; Royal Greenwich Observatory 157bc; Simon Fraser 156tr, 522bl; Smithsonite Institution 59tc; St. Mary's Hospital Medical School 424c; Takeshi Takahara 681bl; Tim Malyon 387tr; Tom McHugh 325bl; U.S. Navy 720bc; U.S. Geological Survey 516br; W. Crouch & R. Ellis/NASA 707crb; William Curtsinger 37tr; Yves Bauken 348cb.
National Museums Of Scotland: Mayan bowl 421crb.
Shakespeare Globe Trust: 593tr.
Shell UK: 489bc.
Ronald Sheridan: 473t.
Silkeborg Museum: 41tl.
SKR Photos: LFI 456bl.
Sky TV: 669crb.
Sony United Kingdom Limited: 669br.
South American Pictures: 620cra; Tony Morrison 74bc.
Spectrum Colour Library: 186br; E. Hughes 695cl.
Frank Spooner Pictures: 15cr, 17bl, 118bl, 273tr, 366bc, 678bl; Bartholomew Liaison 193cr; Blanche 482bc; Chip Hines 193bc, 298bc; Eric Bouver 19bc; Eric Bouvet/Gamma 626cb; G. Nel Figaro 472cl; Gamma 142tr, 356bc, 380tl, 435bl, 563cr; Gamma/V. Shone 214tr; Jacques Graf 513crb; John Chiason 49br; K. Kristen 482ca; Kahu Karita 370bl; L. Novovitch-Liaison 706bc; Manaud/Figaro 582cb; Nickelsberg/Gamma 310bl; Novosti/Gamma 634ca; Pierre Perin/Gamma 642bl.
Sporting Pictures (UK) Ltd.: 88cr, 268cr, 274tl, 361bl, 491cl, 498tl, 588bc, 646cl.
Still Pictures: 529c; Edward Parker 529clb; Harmut Schwartzbach 253bl; Mark Edwards 529br.
The Stock Market: 374cb; Zefa 554br.
Tony Stone Images: 62tr, 96tr, 98bl, 101br, 238br, 342br, 348cla, 348cl, 348bl, 406bl, 470bc, 622bl, 679cl; Bob Thompson 478tr; Demetrio Carrasco 549cra; Donald Nausbaum 101tc; Donovan Reese 103cr; Doug Armand 293tl; Gary Yeowell 689tl; Glen Allison 476c; Hugh Sitton 362bc, 689c; James Balog 661c; John Beatty 45tl, 61cl; John Callahan 343cr; John Lamb 272br; Jon Gray 679cl; Manfred Mehlig 73bl, 661bl; Martin Puddy 342tr; Nigel Hillier 689cr; Nigel Snowdon 67tr; Peter Cade 660tr; Ragnar Sigurdsson 61bc; Randy Wells 477tc; Robert Everts 627bl; Rohan 405bl; Seigfried Layda 293c; Shaun Egan 362tl; Stephen Studd 661tr; Stuart Westmoreland 65cr; Tom Parker 695bc; Tom Walker 45tc; Bob Thomas 607b; David Young-Wolff 388cl; Michael Frye 503tl.
Superstock Ltd.: 675cr.
Survival Anglia Photo Library: 176cl, 176c; Jeff Foott 176crb.
Syndication International: 652bl.

T

Tass News Agency: 299clb, 636cl.
Ron and Valerie Taylor: 489clb.
Telegraph Colour Library: 543cr, 585cl; Bavania/Bild Agentur 653crb; Jason Childs 65cl; 228bl, 763cr; David Noton 300b, 761cr; F.P.G. © F. McKinney 300tc; P. Grindley 301cl; Walter Bibikow 301bl.
Thames and Hudson Ltd.: *The Complete Architecture Works* 152bc.
Louise Thomas: 622cr.

Topham Picturepoint: 376cl, 482tl, 482cl, 644b, 668bl, 669bl, 699cb, 739tl; Image Works, Lee Snider 454tr.
Toy Brokers Ltd.: 602tl.
Toyota (GB) PLC: 232bl.
Art Directors and TRIP: 228br; H. Rogers 584cr; J. Rettie 526bl; Jeff Greenberg 238tr, 238c, 584tr; Jerry Dennis 463bl; M. Jenkin 463tl, 526tl; M. Lee 463cr; Roberta Bromley Elter 152cl; S. Grant 334cr, 334bl, 388cla, 388cr, 584bl, 584br; T. Bognar 760tr; T. Freeman 321cl, 321cr, 321bl; B. Vikander 690tr; G. Spenceley 629cl.

U · V

Unicef: 700bc.
United Nations: 700cl.
Reproduced by permission of **United Feature Syndicate Inc.:** 124cl.
University Of Manchester: Barri Jones, Department of Archaeology 41tr.
V and A Picture Library: 145br, 146tl, 198crb.
La Vie Du Rail: 681.
View Pictures: Dennis Gilbert 324br.
Virginia Museum of Fine Arts: gift of Col. and Mrs. Edgar W. Garbisch 705tr.

W · X · Y

National Museum Of Wales: 695cra.
The Wallace Collection: 502c.
John Walmsley Photo Library: 90tr, 549ca, 715bc.
John Watney: 354c.
Wilberforce House, Hull City Museums: 21cb; Tina Chambers 21cb.
Reg Wilson: 77cl, 170, 492tr.
Winchester City Council: 27crb.
Windsor Castle Royal Library (by permission of HM The Queen): 206br.
Harland and Wolf: 695cr.
Alexander Wolf/Herge Verlag: 124bc.
Woods Hole Oceangraphic Instititution: 692bl.
Xinhua News Agency: 635tl.
Jerry Young: 261bl.

Z

Zefa Picture Library: 48cl, 53bl, 67bl, 108bl, 114cl, 120c, 130tl, 136cr, 143bc, 145br, 238bc, 277tl, 292cr, 292bl, 312bc, 355t, 359bc, 361tr, 362r, 429cr, 429bl, 470cl, 486cl, 549bc, 571tl, 623cr, 639cl, 641cra, 655c, 679cr, 695tl, 696bl, 708cb, 714cr, 715br, 716c, 717crb; Abril 558c; B. Croxford 435cr; B. Keppelmeyer 273cr; Colin Kaket 339tr; Damm 276tl, 435bl, 623bc; Dr. David Conker 93bl; Dr. R. Lorenz 506tl; Fritz 472bc; G. Hunter 114bl; Groebel 569cr; H. Grathwohl 429tr; Heilman 253tl, 253bc; Helbig 83tr; J. Zittenzieher 339tr; K. Goebel 238tl, 293cr, 434cl; K. Keith 639tl; K. Scholz 15tl, 439crb; Kim Heebig 195crb; Klaus Hackenburg 688tl; Knight and Hunt Photo 195bc; Kohler 292cl; Leidmann 338tr; Messershmidt 152tr; O. Langrand 299bc; Orion Press 105tr; Praedel 579cr; R.G. Everts 299crb; Scholz 145cr; Starfoto 337cl; UWS 396cr; W. Benser 337c; W. Deuter 259cr; W.F. Davidson 149tl; W. Mole 456br; W.F. Davidson 713bc; Werner H. Muller 148cr.

All other images © Dorling Kindersley
For further information see: www.dkimages.com

Additional thanks to: Max Alexander; Peter Anderson; Tony Barton Collection; Geoff Brightling; Jane Burton; Peter Chadwick; Joe Cornish; Andy Crawford; Geoff Dann; Tom Dobbie, Philip Dowell; Niel Fletcher; Bob Gathany; Frank Greenaway; Steve Gorton; Alan Hill; Chas Howson; Colin Keates; Barnabas Kindersley; Dave King; Bob Langrish; Liz McAulay; Andrew McRobb; Ray Moller; Tracey Morgan; Stephen Oliver; Susannah Price; Rob Reichenfeld; Tim Ridley; Kim Sayer; Karl Shone; Steve Shott; Clive Streeter; Harry Taylor; Kim Taylor; Wallace Collection; Matthew Ward; Francesca Yorke, Jerry Young.

Every effort has been made to trace the copyright holders and we apologise in advance for any unintentional omissions. We would be pleased to insert the appropriate acknowledgments in any subsequent edition of the publication.

ILLUSTRATION CREDITS

Abbreviations: a = above, b = below, c = center, l = left, r = right, t = top.

A

Graham Allen: 444
David Ashby: 26bl; 122cl, tl, tr; 310t; 345; 461cl; 539; 603cr; 634tl; 686b; 705; 706r; 749
Graham Austen/Garden Studios: 192tl, bl

B

Stephen Biesty: 24; 25; 122cr; 125; 126; 318t; 656c; 662; 667; 672c; 672tl; 714; 749
Rick Blakely/Studio Art and Illustration: 226cl; 317; 387; 409c; 432; 446; 466c; 543t; 563c; 577tl; 596c; 597t, c; 611; 635; 636b, l; 679; 744; 772bl; 773r
Peter Bull Art Studio: 106 tl, cr, bl; 113tr; 233bc; 297c; 290tr; 347c, bc; 483cl, cr; 544bl; 693br; 723
Christopher Butzer: 390c

C

Julia Cobbold: 130; 377b; 448c; 528; 558; 694br; 695tr
Stephen Conlin: 27c; 41t; 42c; 149; 152; 199bc; 277c; 433cr; 441; 552c; 701b
John Crawford-Fraser: 187cr; 460cr; 492; 540cr

D

William Donahue: 110c; 364; 439; 566c, bl; 625t; 680; 712t; 736
Richard Draper: 58
Keith Duran/Linden Artists: 507bl

E

Angelika Elsebach: 32t, c; 33c; 38; 83; 87; 206cr; 244; 249; 250; 269 except tl; 270; 281cl, br; 282; 302bl; 350; 396tl, c, b; 414; 418; 589; 605; 609; 643; 684tl; 721; 730c
Angelika Elsebach/David Moore: 684tr, bl
Gill Elsebury: 196; 197; 280; 303; 468; 606

G

L.R. Galante: 28cl; 55cr; 246bc; 312cl; 332c, cr; 333c; 403cr
Tony Gibbons: 596b; 597b

H

Nick Hall: 212; 213c; 535; 536; 664
Nicholas Hewetson: 13cr; 15c, bl; 23t; 26cr; 27bc; 39c, bc; 47r; 49r; 51; 56t, b; 72t; 73cl; 105; 115tr, bl, cr; 119cr; 119tl; 135tr; 141cl, tr; 159b; 168cl; 170; 179c, br; 193bl; 202cr; 204cl; 221; 223; 224b, tl; 253; 255; 272cr; 274c; 284t; 292; 295c; 299tr; 306bl; 308c; 309cl; 312tl, cl; 314; 316b; 320; 335; 336c; 352 tl, bl; 354br; 366b; 369; 370; 372tr; 373; 374; 377tl, cl; 392bl; 397; 403br; 411bl; 416tr; 424tl; 430cr; 431b;

443; 451tl; 457tr; 458; 466b; 471tl, cr; 472tl; 473cl, cr; 491; 495cl, br; 496; 498; 522c, cr; 525; 534; 537tr, b; 542br; 551c; 556cl; 560cl; 565b; 568cr; 570; 574c; 576cr; 577tl, br; 581; 610bc; 615cl; 616; 619; 620; 621cl; 625b; 626r; 637cl; 642tl; 644cl; 646; 652c; 699tl; 702; 707cr, bl; 708cl; 709; 712bl; 720tl, tr; 722; 724bl, br; 734tr
Trevor Hill: 310b
Adam Hook/ Linden Artists: 55cr; 188c; 464c; 613cl

J

Kevin Jones Associates: 483

K

Aziz Khan: 28cr; 54l; 82br; 88tr, bl; 121bl; 164tl; 166tr; 174cr; 177bl; 185cl; 188bl; 211c; 240cr, br; 242br; 246cr; 278tl; 288br; 322cl; 323c; 324bl; 347tr; 371bl; 381cr, tl; 403cr; 404br; 419tr; 461cr; 514tl; 533br; 549bc; 561cl; 603c; 613tr; 650cr; 657tr; 659br; 760tr
Steven Kirk: 202tl; 555; 556tl, b

L

Jason Lewis: 89; 145; 160; 233tl; 283; 318r; 329; 464tc
Richard Lewis: 26cl; 167; 213c; 231; 268; 316c; 513; 544; 560bl; 577tr; 610tc, bl; 655t; 658; 678; 751cl
Ruth Lindsay: 69; 70; 86; 108; 112; 128; 205cr; 263tl; 264; 304; 305; 319; 327; 349; 401br; 402; 430l; 449 except cl; 509; 731bl; 748
Chen Ling: 748; 749; 750; 751
Mick Loates/Linden Artists: 34; 35b; 74b; 84; 85r; 175; 176; 184t; 190; 191; 209bl, br; 218; 243; 383; 384; 395; 489; 516; 517; 590t; 771

M

Janos Marffy: 466cr
Coral Mula: 480; 654tl, bl

P

Brian Poole: 85b
Warren Poppiti: 521c

Q

Sebastian Quigley/Linden Artists: 183; 186t, bl; 298bl; 427; 448b; 520cr; 688c; 768b

R

Eric Robson/Garden Studios: 22c, bl; 557; 591; 592
Jackie Rose: 378l, b; 378r, b
Clifford Rosney: 750cl
Simon Roulstone: 90c, bl, bc; 95tl, cl; 125c; 157c, cr; 171c; 225cl; 232tl; 233cl; 235cl, cr, tr; 289c; 316cr; 352tr; 359c; 467bl; 539c; 544c; 559c; 663

S

Sergio: 98; 211; 247; 315; 332cl, bl; 408; 453; 553; 554
Rodney Shackell: 28c; 41b; 43b; 55br; 91cl; 140; 228; 246c (insets); 258cl; 259r; 284bl; 295bl; 302c; 308b; 336bl; 309bc; 352tr; 409tc; 410br; 501; 502; 505b; 506tl; 510tr; 549; 586; 587tc; 603tl; 649tr; 694bl; 695ct, cb, cr; 753tc
Eric Shields: 378c
Rob Shone: 23bl, cr; 36bl; 147; 148; 155; 178br; 195c; 265cr; 276tr; 277r; 286br; 385; 392r, cl; 393; 460r; 498; 537tl, cr; 546; 564c; 564cr; 566t, cl; 655br; 670; 693; 711; 719; 720
Francesco Spadoni: 185tl, bc, br; 443cl; 514tc, cr, bl
Francesco Spadoni/Lorenzo Cecchi: 166cl, tr, bl, br
Clive Spong/Linden Artists: 285; 598tl; 692
Mark Stacey: 111cr; 139cr; 153cl; 162bl; 174cl; 385cl; 394cr; 419c; 593c

T

Eric Thomas: 19cr; 20br; 30; 67; 68bl; 79c; 92bl, br; 94; 118tr, cl, bc; 122tc; 131; 199tc; 230bl; 234cl; 236cl; 238; 279; 291c; 340; 341tr; 354tr, cl; 356c; 357; 359; 366b; 404c; 425r; 426; 440tl, cr; 455; 458; 462tr, cl; 510c; 515; 548tl, cl; 573; 575; 626t; 637tr; 641cl; 654c; 671bl; 681tl, cl; 698cr; 710; 715c; 737br; 738bl; 745; 748; 749; 750; 751; 751c, cr; 752tl

V

François Vincent: 636tr

W

Richard Ward/Precision: 19tr; 20tl; 56c; 61t; 62t; 68tl; 69tl; 73tr; 77c; 79cr; 110tl; 142br; 156; 161c; 165; 168cr; 178t, bl; 190cr; 195bl; 214c, cr, b; 219; 245t; 260bl; 269tl; 272tl; 289; 306cr; 341br; 372cl; 396b (maps); 409br; 410tl, bl; 412bl; 416c; 417bc; 437; 438; 449cl; 464bl; 465bl; 481tl; 482; 485; 486; 508bcl, bl; 523tl; 543b; 574tl; 652br; 656b; 673; 686cr; 707t, c; 716tc; 732br; 733; 752cr, bc; 770tl, bl, tr; 772t, br; 773l; 774t; 775r; 777
Craig Warwick/Linden Artists: 490
Phil Weare: 518l; 608bl; 741
David Webb/Linden Artists: 35t; 92bc; 132; 180; 181c; 209c; 229; 256bl, tl; 260tc, tr, bc, br; 261bl; 440c, b; 413br; 480; 481b; 483; 487; 523b; 525; 542tr, bl; 731t, bc; 768t; 770br
Ann Winterbotham: 114br; 210br; 256r; 447c; 494tr; 594; 648tr
Gerald Wood: 55bl; 76c; 107; 251; 254; 260cr; 328; 450; 451br; 508tlc; 530; 645br; 668bc; 677; 682; 683tl, cr; 688b; 718; 732c; 739
John Woodcock: 15cr; 29cb; 61c; 77b; 93tl, c; 182; 184br; 203; 208b; 209t, cr; 210tr; 226c; 257bl; 296; 309r; 312tr, br; 326; 344b; 356br; 365r; 412tl, c, cr; 422l; 424br; 433cr; 462bl; 473bc; 494tl, cl; 495tr; 518cr; 552c; 566br; 574r; 576bl; 577bl; 582cr; 587r; 590bl; 595cl, bl; 633; 634tr; 642; 645bl; 648cl; 650cr; 671cl; 671bc; 685; 698b; 699b; 700; 717; 730b; 731cl, tr, c; 737c, cr; 738tr, br; 740; 743; 769; 770 (insets); 774t; 775t, l
Dan Wright: 127; 260c; 445; 767br; 770bl

JACKET CREDITS

Abbreviations: FC = front cover, BC = back cover, a = above, b = below, c = center, l = left, r = right, t = top.

Pekka Parviainen/Science Photo Library: FC al
Corbis © Renee Lynn/Corbis: FC br
Corbis © Bettmann/Corbis: FC cl
ESA, NASA, and P. Anders (Göttingen University Galaxy Evolution Group, Germany): BC cl